Exploring

Environmental
Science for AP®

ABOUT THE COVER PHOTO

Experiencing and Learning from Nature

Environmental scientists have identified our increasing isolation from nature as one of the major causes of the environmental problems we face. More than half of the world's people live in urban areas, many of which do not have enough parks and recreational areas to make it easy for people to experience nature. Many children and young adults spend most of their free time indoors playing video games, watching TV, and using smart phones, computers, and other electronic devices.

Research indicates that children and adults can gain many benefits by playing and exploring outdoors—hiking, jogging, snorkeling, fishing, gardening, bird watching, or any number of other pursuits. Such activities can foster better health, reduce stress, improve mental abilities, and stimulate imagination and creativity.

Experiencing nature can also provide a sense of wonder and connection to earth's life-support system, which keeps us alive and supports our economies. Without an understanding of our complete dependence on nature for food, shelter, clean air, clean water, and many other natural resources and services, we are more likely to continue behaving in ways that contribute to the degradation of our life-support system.

In the face of threats to the environment and to our own health and well-being, experiencing and learning from and about nature could help us live more sustainably with energizing joy and hope instead of with immobilizing fear. We want to present a positive vision of our environmental future based on realistic optimism, and we hope this book will inspire you to become involved in this change in the way we view and treat our only planet. Earth care is also self-care.

Exploring
Environmental
Science for AP®

G. Tyler Miller

Scott E. Spoolman

CENGAGE

Australia • Brazil • Mexico • Singapore • United Kingdom • United States

Exploring Environmental Science for AP®
G. Tyler Miller, Scott E. Spoolman

Product Director: Dawn Giovanniello

Product Manager: Maureen McLaughlin

Senior Content Developer: Philip Lanza

Content Developer: Julie Allen

Product Assistant: Emma Collins

Product Marketing Manager: Mark Hoffman

Senior Content Project Manager:
   Andrea Wagner

Manufacturing Planner: Karen Hunt

IP Analyst: Christine Myaskovsky

IP Project Manager: Kathryn Kucharek

Production Service: SPi Global

Compositor: SPi Global

Art Directors: Michael Cook, Andrei Pasternak

Text Designer: Jeanne Calabrese

Cover Designer: Michael Cook

Cover Image: Westend61/Getty Images

For product information and technology assistance, contact us at
Cengage Customer & Sales Support, 1-888-915-3276
or SchoolCustomerService@cengage.com.

To locate your sales consultant, go to **NGL.Cengage.com/RepFinder.**

For permission to use material from this text or product,
submit all requests online at **www.cengage.com/permissions.**

Library of Congress Control Number: 2017957035

Student Edition:
ISBN: 978-1-3379803-8

Cengage
20 Channel Center Street
Boston, MA 02210
USA

Cengage is a leading provider of customized learning solutions with employees residing in nearly 40 different countries and sales in more than 125 countries around the world. Find your local representative at **www.cengage.com.**

Cengage products are represented in Canada by Nelson Education, Ltd.

To learn more about Cengage platforms and services, visit **www.cengage.com.**

To find online supplements and other instructional support, please visit **login.cengage.com.**

AP® and Advanced Placement® are trademarks registered by the College Board, which is not affiliated with, and does not endorse, this product.

Printed in the United States of America
Print Number: 01   Print Year: 2017

Brief Contents

Contents

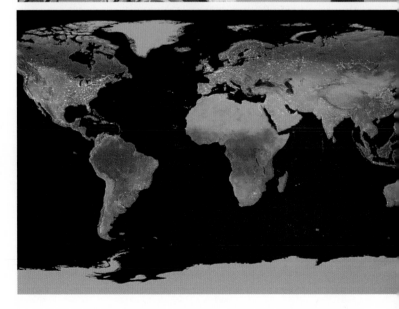

Preface

This is the first edition of a text designed for Advanced Placement® Environmental Science (APES) courses. We wrote this book to help AP® teachers and students achieve three important goals: *first,* to understand the basics of environmental science; *second,* to use this scientific foundation to understand the environmental problems that we face and to evaluate possible solutions to them; and *third,* to become inspired to make a difference in how we treat the earth on which our lives and economies depend, and thus in how we treat ourselves and our descendants. In dedicating yourself to this experience, the work you do in AP® Environmental Science can reveal the significance, beauty and nuance of the natural world. This course invites you to find your own understanding of the complex world we live in. The ideas you will encounter can be life-changing.

For this new edition, we are delighted in our partnership with *National Geographic Learning.* One result has been the inclusion of many stunning and informative photographs, numerous maps, and several stories of National Geographic Explorers—people who are making a positive difference in the world. With these tools, we are able to tell of the good news from various fields of environmental science, hoping to inspire young people to commit themselves to making our world a more sustainable place to live for their own and future generations.

Features of *Exploring Environmental Science for AP®*

This book was designed not only to facilitate your success on the AP® Environmental Science Exam, but also to help you become scientifically literate and to think critically about environmental issues. *Exploring Environmental Science for AP®* is closely aligned with the AP® Course description and focuses on the "big picture" – the interrelationships found in environmental science. There are several important features in each chapter that are meant to help you acquire a strong foundation in environmental science and be successful on the AP® exam.

- **Order of Chapters.** Understanding first how nature functions *without* human interference is essential to understanding the impact of humans on the natural world. With this idea in mind, there is a purpose to the sequence of chapters. The book is divided into five units that begin in Unit 1 with an introduction to environmental science and a review of science fundamentals. The chapters of Unit 2 investigate the natural world without the influence of humans and concentrates on ecology, evolution, and population biology.

Resources utilized by humans are the focus of Unit 3, followed by an investigation into nonrenewable and renewable energy in Unit 4. The book culminates with Unit 5 as it looks at various environmental topics such as pollution and climate change.

- **AP® Course Themes.** The College Board describes the AP® Environmental Science course through a set of six theme that provide a foundation for the structure of the course. Those themes are:

  1. Science is a process.
  2. Energy conversions underlie all ecological processes.
  3. The earth itself is one interconnected system.
  4. Humans alter natural systems.
  5. Environmental problems have a cultural and social context.
  6. Human survival depends on developing practices that will achieve sustainable systems.

The high-level organization of chapters in this book follows this sequence of themes.

- **Checkpoint for Understanding.** At the end of each section within the chapters you will find several "checkpoint" questions designed to help you become an active reader (see below, as well as pp. 23, 98, and 186).

CHECKPOINT FOR UNDERSTANDING 6.2

1. Explain why most aquatic life is found in coastal areas. Why is most commercial fishing done in the continental shelf region rather than out in the open ocean?

2. Describe how intertidal organisms adapt to the stressful conditions of the intertidal zone.

3. Explain the importance of upwellings.

They can help you practice reading with the purpose of comprehending and constructing knowledge, rather than simply skimming the pages and going through the motions of reading. You may find that it will save you the time of re-reading the material later. By anticipating the questions at the end of each section, you will train yourself to critically engage with the text and look for important relationships and relevance. Checkpoint questions ask you to summarize the important concepts in the chapter and to apply your understanding. This is an important skill necessary in critical analysis and helps you to be in control of your reading comprehension.

Checkpoint questions also give you continuous practice responding to verb prompts such as *identify, explain, describe,* and *discuss* that are the foundation of free-response questions on the AP® exam. You will find the answers to the checkpoint questions at the end of each chapter. Formulate your own answers first, then use the answer keys to check your accuracy and improve your approach to visualizing systems and processes, and expressing your ideas in clear and complete prose.

■ ***Critical Concepts in Sustainability.*** The overarching theme of this book is sustainability. In each chapter you will find at least one feature box emphasizing a critical concept important to AP® Environmental Science (see below, as well as pp. 142, 268, and 345).

CRITICAL CONCEPTS IN SUSTAINABILITY

Oxygen Sag Curves

Flowing rivers and streams can recover rapidly from moderate inputs of biodegradable, oxygen-demanding pollution through a combination of dilution and biodegradation. A flowing river or stream can also dilute heated water released from a power plant. However, this natural recovery process does not work when a stream becomes overloaded with biodegradable pollutants, or when drought, damming, or water diversion reduces its flow (Concept 17.2A). Also, this process does not eliminate slowly degradable or nondegradable pollutants such as heavy metals.

In a flowing stream, the breakdown of biodegradable wastes by bacteria depletes dissolved oxygen and creates an oxygen sag curve (Figure 17.C). This reduces or eliminates populations of organisms with high oxygen requirements until the stream is cleansed of oxygen-demanding wastes.

In this graph the blue line indicates dissolved oxygen in ppm, and the red line indicates biochemical oxygen demand (BOD). Recall that BOD is the amount of dissolved oxygen needed (i.e., demanded) by aerobic biological organisms to break down organic material present in a given water sample.

Upstream of the effluent pipe dissolved oxygen is 8 ppm, a level that allows intolerant species such as trout and mayflies to thrive. BOD is low because there is little organic waste that requires degradation by aerobic bacteria and, subsequently, depletion of oxygen in the water at that point in the stream.

At the point where waste enters the stream (identified as the decomposition zone), aerobic bacteria begin consuming the waste, using up oxygen in the process. There is a shift in the type of organisms that can inhabit the stream as oxygen levels drop. The septic zone is characterized by a lack of oxygen, and anaerobic bacteria take over decomposition of waste. Only the most tolerant species, such as blood worms and leeches, can survive in these conditions.

Once the waste is consumed and the flowing stream moves and dilutes it, oxygen levels start to recover. Notice that the recovery zone is similar to the decomposition zone in that the amount of dissolved oxygen is similar as are the species that inhabit that zone of the stream. Once the stream has been cleansed of biodegradable waste, the stream is fully recovered and intolerant species are able to thrive.

FRQ Application
Question: Refer to the graph in Figure 17.C. **Explain** the relationship between the lines depicting dissolved oxygen content and biological oxygen demand. **Describe** how the scale on the horizontal axis of this graph would change if the amount of effluent emitted from the pipe were doubled.

Possible Response: As biodegradable waste is emitted into a body of water, aerobic bacteria break it down. As a result, the more active the bacteria, the more oxygen consumed from the water. The graph shows oxygen levels declining as waste is being consumed by the aerobic bacteria. Biological oxygen demand is the amount of oxygen required by bacteria to consume waste. The relationship between the two lines is inverse. If there is little waste in the water, there is no demand by the bacteria and oxygen levels stay relatively high. If there is an abundance of waste in the water, then the demand for oxygen increases, and oxygen levels drop.

The scale on the horizontal axis shows stream recovery over distance. If more waste was emitted into the stream, the areas shown on the graph would be farther apart and it would take longer for the stream to recover at a distance farther from the origin.

FIGURE 17.C Natural capital: A stream can dilute and decay degradable, oxygen-demanding wastes and also dilute heated water. This figure shows the oxygen sag curve (blue) and the curve of oxygen demand (red).

These presentations highlight the importance of each concept, how it relates to the idea of sustainability, and how it might appear as a topic on the AP® exam. Each Critical Concept explanation concludes with an FRQ Application question and possible response(s). Acceptable responses can vary widely; many times there are several acceptable ways to answer a free-response question. This feature can also help you to become an active

reader. As you read the content of this book, formulate your own questions and anticipate how you might be asked about topics on the AP® exam.

■ ***Math Connection.*** Demonstrating your understanding of science by problem-solving using math is an important skill necessary for your success on the AP® exam. Each chapter in this book includes a Math Connection that demonstrates a critical math skill you will need to master (see below, as well as pp. 44, 51, and 82).

MATH CONNECTION

Parts per Million and Parts per Billion

Because the dose of a toxin can be a very small amount, scientists use parts per million (ppm) and parts per billion (ppb) to measure the concentration of a chemical in a solution.

Parts per million means a ratio of one part or unit of a solute for every 1 million units of a solvent. One part per billion is one part of solute per 1 billion parts solvent. Figure 16.B shows the concentration of PCBs in organisms that are biomagnified in the tissues of organisms in a lake food chain. What is the difference between parts per million and parts per billion? Since there is 1,000 million in 1 billion, to express parts per billion as parts per million, it is necessary to divide by 1000.

For example, if PCB concentration in phytoplankton is measured to be 2.5 parts per billion, what is the concentration in parts per million?

$$2.5 \text{ ppb PCBs} / 1,000 = 0.0025 \text{ parts per million PCBs}$$

| Water 0.000002 ppm | Phytoplankton 0.0025 ppm | Zooplankton 0.123 ppm | Rainbow smelt 1.04 ppm | Lake trout 4.83 ppm | Herring gull 124 ppm | Herring gull eggs 124 ppm |

FIGURE 16.B Biological magnification of polychlorinated biphenyls (PCBs) in an aquatic food chain in the Great Lakes.

FRQ Application
Lake Ontario has a volume of 1639 km³. The PCB concentration in Lake Ontario water is 0.000002 ppm. Using the facts that, for water, 1ppm = 1mg/L and 1mL = 1cm³, how many metric tons of PCBs are there in Lake Ontario? You may round to the nearest metric ton.

1ppm = 1mg/L, so there are 0.000002 mg/L PCBs in Lake Ontario

1 mL = 1 cm³, so 1 L = 1000 cm³ = 0.001 m³

The volume of Lake Ontario in liters is

$$1639 \text{ km}^3 \times \frac{(1000 \text{ m})^3}{1 \text{ km}^3} \times \frac{1 \text{ L}}{0.001 \text{ m}^3} = 1.639 \times 10^{15} \text{ L of water in Lake Ontario}$$

The total amount of PCBs in Lake Ontario is

$$1.639 \times 10^{15} \text{ L} \times \frac{0.000002 \text{ mg PCB}}{\text{L}} \times \frac{1 \text{ g}}{1000 \text{ mg}} = 3.278 \times 10^7 \text{ g PCBs}$$

$$3.278 \times 10^7 \text{ g PCBs} \times \frac{1 \text{ kg}}{1000 \text{ g}} \times \frac{1 \text{ metric ton}}{1000 \text{ kg}} = 33 \text{ metric tons of PCBs in Lake Ontario}$$

You should be able to calculate percent change, use dimensional analysis, convert metrically, interpret and construct graphs, and calculate cost benefit analyses, all without the use of a calculator. It is important to practice doing math throughout the course, since you will be required to do calculations on both the multiple-choice and FRQ portions of the AP® exam.

■ ***AP® Review Questions.*** At the end of each chapter you will find 20 AP®-style multiple-choice questions and one practice free-response question (FRQs begin with Chapter 3). These questions were carefully written in the AP® exam style. Use these questions to prepare for your chapter assessment. Each Unit also concludes with AP® Review Questions. Unit 1 has a set of 30 multiple-choice items. Units 2-5 include multiple-choice items and two practice FRQs. The more you practice applying your knowledge, the more prepared you will be at exam time.

It takes skill to answer multiple-choice questions correctly. To help you develop your test-taking skills, throughout these practice sets you will find examples of each type of multiple-choice question you can expect to encounter on the AP® exam. Writing quality FRQs also requires skill and preparation. Using the practice FRQs in this book will help you develop your approach to each of the three types of FRQ questions—data-set, document-based, and synthesis and evaluation.

- **AP® Practice Exam.** A complete AP® Practice Exam appears at the end of the book. Section I includes 100 multiple-choice questions, and Section II presents four free-response items—one data-set question, one document-based question, and two synthesis and evaluation questions. You might want to use the Practice Exam as a diagnostic test in the late winter or early spring when you begin more intensive exam preparation. It can help point you to areas where you need to focus. When you take the Practice Exam, be sure to emulate a real testing situation as closely as possible. Find a quiet place to work, and be sure to time yourself accurately on each section.

Sustainability Is the Integrating Theme of This Book

We view environmental problems and possible solutions to them through the lens of *sustainability*—the integrating theme of this book. For those people concerned about the environment, sustainablity is a watchword for the 21st century. We believe that most people can live comfortable and fulfilling lives, and that societies will be more stable and prosperous when sustainability becomes one of the chief measures by which personal choices and public policies are made.

Six **principles of sustainability** play a major role in carrying out this book's sustainability theme. These principles are introduced in Chapter 1. They are depicted in Figure 1.2 (p. 6), in Figure 1.6 (p. 9), and on the inside back cover of the book and are used throughout the book, with each reference marked in the margin by (see pp. 5 and 6).

We use the following five major subthemes to integrate material throughout this book.

- **Natural capital.** Sustainability depends on the natural resources and ecosystem services that support all life and economies. See Figures 1.3, p. 7, and 6.4, p. 156.

- **Natural capital degradation.** We describe how human activities can degrade natural capital. See Figures 8.4, p. 209, and 12.12, p. 349.

- **Solutions.** We present existing and proposed solutions to environmental problems in a balanced manner and challenge students to use critical thinking to evaluate them. See Figures 10.11, p. 276, and 12.28, p. 364.

- **Trade-offs.** The search for solutions involves trade-offs, because any solution requires weighing advantages against disadvantages. Our Trade-offs diagrams present the benefits and drawbacks of various environmental technologies and solutions to environmental problems. See Figures 12.21, p. 357; 13.8, p. 387; and 15.9, p. 466.

- **Individuals Matter.** Throughout the book, Individuals Matter boxes and some of the Case Studies describe what various scientists and concerned citizens (including several National Geographic Explorers) have done to help us work toward sustainability (see pp. 10, 164, and 648). Also, a number of *What Can You Do?* diagrams describe how readers can deal with the environmental problems we face (see Figures 9.12, p. 246; 12.31, p. 366; and 13.26, p. 404). Especially important ways in which individuals can live more lightly on the earth are summarized in Postscript Figure 1 (p. 675).

Other Important Features of This Textbook

- **Up-to-Date Coverage.** Topics and issues in the field of environmental science change rapidly. Current topics you will see covered in this text include biomimicry, fracking, ocean acidification, and developments in battery technology. Discussions also point to recent events such as the Flint, Michigan drinking water crisis, the Dakota Access Pipeline controversy, and the spillway failure on the Oroville Dam in California.

- **Concept-Centered Approach.** To help students focus on the main ideas, we built each major chapter section around a key question and one to three key concepts, which state the section's most important take-away messages. In each chapter, all key questions are listed at the front of the chapter (see p. 3), and each chapter section begins with its key question and concepts (see pp. 5 and 10). Also, the concept applications are highlighted and referenced throughout each chapter.

- **Science-Based.** Chapters 2 through 8 cover scientific principles important to the course and discuss how scientists work (see Brief Contents, p. v). Important environmental science topics are explored in depth in

Science Focus boxes distributed among the chapters throughout the book (see pp. 39 and 248) and integrated throughout the book in various Case Studies (see pp. 100 and 161) and in numerous figures.

- **Global Coverage.** This book also provides a global perspective, first on the ecological level, revealing how all the world's life is connected and sustained within the biosphere, and second, through the use of information and images from around the world. This includes dozens of maps throughout the chapters and in Supplement 5 at the end of the book.

- **Core Case Studies.** Each chapter opens with a Core Case Study (see pp. 4, 236, and 338), which is applied throughout the chapter. These applications are indicated by the notation (Core Case Study) wherever they occur (see pp. 8 and 13). Each chapter ends with a summary of KEY IDEAS and a Core Case Study Checkpoint question to focus on the important concepts from the chapter (see pp. 25 and 110).

- **Case Studies.** In addition to the 20 Core Case Studies, more than 40 additional Case Studies (see pp. 171, 194, and 274) appear throughout the book (and are listed in the Detailed Contents, pp. vi–xv). Each Case Study provides an in-depth look at specific environmental problems and their possible solutions.

- **Critical Thinking.** The Learning Skills section (p. xxii) describes critical thinking skills, and specific critical thinking exercises are used throughout the book in several ways:

  - In all *Core Case Studies* (see pp. 66 and 120).
  - In all *Science Focus* boxes (see pp. 195 and 285).
  - In dozens of *Thinking About* prompts that ask students to analyze material immediately after it is presented (see pp. 135 and 170).
  - In dozens of *Connections* boxes that stimulate critical thinking by exploring often surprising connections related to environmental problems (see pp. 72 and 182).
  - In the captions of many of the book's figures (see Figures 6.14, p. 165 and 9.7, p. 243).
  - In end-of-chapter questions (see pp. 116 and 176).

- **Data Analysis.** A data or ecological footprint analysis exercise appears at the end of each chapter, and data analysis questions are also integrated into the captions of many figures that include data graphs (see Figures 1.9, p. 15 and 7.17, p. 193).

- **Visual Learning.** With a design heavily influenced by material from National Geographic Learning and more than 300 photographs, many of them from the archives of National Geographic, this is the most visually interesting environmental science textbook available (see Figure 1.5, p. 8; Chapter 6 opening photo, pp. 152–153; and Figure 9.4, p. 240). Add in the more than 130 diagrams, each designed to present complex ideas in understandable ways relating to the real world (see Figures 7.12, p. 188, and 11.21, p. 325), and you also have one of the most visually informative textbooks available.

- **In-Text Study Aids.** Each chapter begins with a list of *Key Questions* showing how the chapter is organized (see p. 3). Wherever a new *key term* is introduced and defined, it appears in boldface type and all such terms are summarized in an end-of-chapter glossary (see pp. 25–26) and a complete glossary at the end of the book. In most chapters, *Thinking About* exercises reinforce learning by asking students to think critically about environmental issues and solutions immediately after they are discussed in the text (see pp. 135 and 363). The captions of many figures contain similar critical thinking questions (see Figure 6.5, p. 157 and Figure 8.2, p. 207). In their reading, students also encounter *Connections* boxes describing links between human activities and environmental consequences, environmental and social issues, and environmental issues and solutions (see pp. 76 and 354). *Learning from Nature* boxes give quick summaries of how we can benefit by understanding nature's ingenuity (see pp. 69 and 291). *Eco-numbers* highlight important statistics (see pp. 14, 93, and 208). The text of each chapter concludes with three *Key Ideas*, summarizing and reinforcing the major messages from each chapter, and a *Core Case Study Checkpoint* that asks students to reflect on the Core Case Study introduced at the beginning of the chapter (see pp. 25 and 144). These concluding features help students understand and tie together the main messages of the chapter and the over-arching themes of sustainability.

Supplements for Teachers

- **Teacher's Edition** (ISBN: 978-1-337-70607-0). The Teacher's Edition of this text is designed to guide the AP® teacher in planning units efficiently while including course essentials. Within the teacher notes for each chapter, the *AP® Big Picture* provides an overview of chapter goals from the perspective of the AP® course outline. A *Pacing Guide* suggests the sequence of regular class periods needed to cover all of the material, and points to supporting materials in the Teacher's Resource Guide including practice problem sets, labs and projects, classroom activities, and chapter review worksheets.

Teaching tips for each section include *Discussion Prompts* and *Tapping Prior Knowledge* meant to help students find relevance and initiate classroom debate and discussion. *Illustrate a Concept, Quick Demonstrations,* and *Interpreting Graphs and Data* use visuals to help students understand scientific concepts. There are also suggestions for presenting anticipatory ideas prior to a lab, and *In Your Community* offers ideas for field trips and guest speakers. Finally, each chapter's notes culminate with a review designed to tie together all of the big ideas and map the relationships essential to understanding environmental science.

- **Teacher's Resource Guide** (ISBN: 978-1-337-70569-1). This teacher supplement is designed to correlate to the pacing guide for each chapter in the Teacher's Edition. Each chapter module provides a practice problem set for that chapter, hands-on classroom activities, essential labs or projects, and a chapter wrap-up worksheet. As the AP® Exam does not allow the use of calculators during the test, the practice problem sets focus on strengthening math skills and strategies. Activities are designed to help students understand concepts through simulation and to investigate relationships between concepts. Labs and projects provide authentic experiences for students in field skills, data collection, and critical analysis. Chapter wrap-up worksheets pull together the major concepts to create the big picture for that chapter.

- **AP® MindTap.** MindTap is a new approach to highly personalized online learning. Beyond an eBook, homework solution, digital supplement, or premium website, MindTap is a digital learning platform that works alongside your school's Learning Management System (LMS) to deliver course curriculum across the range of electronic devices in your life. MindTap is built on an "app" model allowing enhanced digital collaboration and delivery of engaging content across a spectrum of Cengage and non-Cengage resources. Visit the Instructor's Companion Site for tips on maximizing your MindTap course.

- **Companion Site.** This collection of book-specific lecture and class tools is available online via www.cengage.com/login. Access and download PowerPoint presentations, image and video libraries, additional support materials, a digital version of the Teacher's Resource Guide, test banks, and more.

- **Cognero Test Bank.** Available to adopters. This online test bank includes basic assessment items per chapter, as well as additional AP®-specific multiple-choice and free-response items. Cengage Learning Testing Powered by Cognero is a flexible, online system that allows you to:
  - author, edit, and manage test bank content from multiple Cengage Learning solutions;
  - create multiple test versions in an instant; and
  - deliver tests from your LMS, your classroom, or wherever you want.

Supplements for Students

You have a large variety of digital and other supplemental materials available to you to help you take your learning experience beyond this textbook:

- **AP® MindTap.** MindTap provides you with the tools you need to better manage your limited time—you can complete assignments whenever and wherever you are ready, with course material specially customized for you by your teacher in one proven, easy-to-use interface. MindTap includes an online homework solution that helps you learn and understand key concepts through focused assignments, exceptional text-art integration, and immediate feedback. MindTap also includes a digital version of *Fast Track to a 5: Preparing for the AP® Environmental Science Exam*, so you have online course tools and AP® test prep materials all in one place. With these resources and an array of tools and apps—from note taking to flashcards—you'll get a true understanding of course concepts, helping you to achieve better grades and setting the groundwork for your future courses.

- **VitalSource® eBook.** VitalSource® Bookshelf® gives students access to an online, downloadable, and mobile eBook. Students can download the eBook to any mobile device or access it online in any browser.

- **Global Environment Watch.** Integrated within MindTap and updated several times a day, the Global Environment Watch is a focused portal into GREENR—the Global Reference on the Environment, Energy, and Natural Resources—an ideal one-stop site for classroom discussion and research projects. This resource center keeps courses up-to-date with the most current news on the environment. Users get access to information from trusted academic journals, news outlets, and magazines, as well as statistics, an interactive world map, videos, primary sources, case studies, podcasts, and much more.

- **Fast Track to a 5: Preparing for the AP® Environmental Science Exam** *Workbook* (ISBN: 978-1-337-70574-5). This AP® test preparation manual provides valuable test-taking strategies, review topics based on the College Board AP® course outline, and full-length diagnostic and practice exams. Keyed to this text, it helps students efficiently and effectively prepare for the AP® exam.

Help Us Improve This Book and Its Supplements

Researching and writing a book that covers and connects the numerous major concepts from the wide variety of environmental science disciplines is a challenging and exciting task. Almost every day, we learn about some new connection in nature. However, in a book this complex, there are bound to be some errors—some typographical mistakes that slip through and some statements that you might question, based on your knowledge and research. We invite you to contact us to correct any errors you find, point out any bias you see, and suggest ways to improve this book and its supplements. Please e-mail your suggestions to Tyler Miller at mtg89@hotmail.com or Scott Spoolman at sspoolman@gmail.com.

Now start your journey into this fascinating and important study of how the earth's life-support system works and how we can leave our planet in a condition at least as good as what we now enjoy. Have fun.

Very Special Thanks to Jeanne Kaidy, AP® Contributor

In creating this new title for AP® teachers and students, we have been very fortunate to team up with Jeanne Kaidy as our AP® Contributor. She currently teaches biology and AP® Environmental Science at McQuaid Jesuit in Rochester NY, and has taught environmental science as an adjunct at Monroe Community College, also in Rochester. Jeanne's collaboration proved invaluable for both her deep content knowledge and her expertise in Advanced Placement® instruction. She has taught APES since 1999, and became an exam reader in 2003. Jeanne has served as a College Board Consultant since 2006, and has also served as a Consultant Coach and Mentor. She earned her B.S. in Biology from SUNY Brockport, and an M.S. in science education from Nazareth College. She has worked for several years as a mentor for the New Teacher Center, working one-on-one with new science teachers around the country, and has conducted research in her biology classroom for the National Science Foundation. Jeanne received the Presidential Award for Excellence in Math and Science Teaching in 2009, and served as a review panelist, critiquing nominee's applications and recommending finalists for the award in 2015 and 2016.

Acknowledgments

It takes a village to produce a textbook, and the members of the talented production team, listed on the copyright page, have made vital contributions. Our special thanks go to Product Director Dawn M. Giovanniello, Product Manager Maureen A. McLaughlin, Senior Content Developer Philip Lanza, Content Developer Julie Allen, Senior Content Project Manager Andrea Wagner, Product Assistant Emma Collins, Director of Marketing Jeremy Walts, and Product Marketing Manager Mark Hoffman.

G. Tyler Miller

Scott E. Spoolman

AP® Reviewers

Additional special thanks go to the following individuals, all experienced AP® Environmental Science professionals, for their review work and significant content contributions to this text and its supplements: Mary Beth Bauer, Our Lady of the Hills Regional Catholic High School, Kerrville, TX; Andrew Milbauer, Poudre High School, Fort Collins, CO; and Richard Woods, Oceanside High School, Oceanside, NY.

Finally, we wish to thank the following AP® teachers who have also provided reviewer input for this new book: Holly Anderson, Coppell High School, Coppell, TX; Susan Berrend, Alma Heights Christian School, Pacifica, CA; Brian Cherniak, Cascade High School, Everett School District, Everett, WA; Amy Fassler, Marshfield High School, Marshfield, WI; Brian Kaestner, Saint Mary's Hall, San Antonio, TX; Catherine McCloskey, Weddington High School, Matthews, NC; Jim Morrill, The Hotchkiss School, Lakeville, CT; Katherine Nall, Basha High School, Chandler, AZ; P.J. Shlachtman, Miami Palmetto Senior High School, Pinecrest, FL; Ben Smith, Palos Verdes Peninsula High School, Rolling Hills Estates, CA; Anne Soos, The Hun School of Princeton, Princeton, NJ; Rachel B. Trim, Flowery Branch High School, Flowery Branch, GA; and Matthew D. Wells, Cypress Lakes High School, Houston, TX.

Learning Skills

Study nature, love nature, stay close to nature. It will never fail you.

Frank Lloyd Wright

Why Is It Important to Study Environmental Science?

Welcome to **environmental science**—an *interdisciplinary* study of how the earth works, how we interact with the earth, and how we can deal with the environmental problems we face. Because environmental issues affect every part of your life, the concepts, information, and issues discussed in this book and the course you are taking will be useful to you now and throughout your life.

Understandably, we are biased, but *we strongly believe that environmental science is the single most important course that you could take.* What could be more important than learning about the earth's life-support system, how our choices and activities affect it, and how we can reduce our growing environmental impact? Evidence indicates strongly that we will have to learn to live more sustainably by reducing our degradation of the planet's life-support system. We hope this book will inspire you to become involved in this change in the way we view and treat the earth, which sustains us, our economies, and all other living things.

You Can Maximize Your Study and Learning Skills

Making the most of your ability to learn might involve improving your study and learning skills. Here are some suggestions for doing so:

Make daily to-do lists. Put items in order of importance, focus on the most important tasks, and assign a time to work on these items. Shift your schedule as needed to accomplish the most important items.

Set up a study routine in a distraction-free environment. Study in a quiet, well-lit space. Take breaks every hour or so. During each break, take several deep breaths and move around; this will help you to stay more alert and focused.

Avoid procrastination. Do not fall behind on your reading and other assignments. Set aside a particular time for studying each day and make it a part of your daily routine.

Make hills out of mountains. It is psychologically difficult to read an entire book, read a chapter in a book, write

a paper, or cram to study for a test. Instead, break these large tasks (mountains) down into a series of small tasks (hills). Each day, read a few pages of a book or chapter, write a few paragraphs of a paper, and review what you have studied and learned.

Ask and answer questions as you read. For example, "What is the main point of a particular subsection or paragraph?" "How does it relate to the key question and key concepts addressed in each major chapter section?"

Focus on key terms. Use the glossary in your textbook to look up the meaning of terms or words you do not understand. This book shows all key terms in **bold** type and lesser, but still important, terms in *italicized* type. The *Chapter Review* questions at the end of each chapter also include the chapter's key terms in bold. A Flashcard app for testing your mastery of key terms for each chapter is available in MindTap, or you can make your own.

Interact with what you read. You could highlight key sentences and paragraphs and make notes in the margins. You might also mark important pages that you want to return to.

Review to reinforce learning. Before each class session, review the material you learned in the previous session and read the assigned material.

Become a good note taker. Learn to write down the main points and key information from any class session using your own shorthand system. Review, fill in, and organize your notes as soon as possible after each class.

Check what you have learned. At the end of each chapter, you will find review questions that cover all of the key material in each chapter section. We suggest that you try to answer each of these questions after studying each chapter section.

Write out answers to questions to focus and reinforce learning. Write down your answers to the critical thinking questions found in the *Thinking About* boxes throughout the chapters, in many figure captions, and at the end of each chapter. These questions are designed to inspire you to think critically about key ideas and connect them to other ideas and to your own life. Also, write down your answers to all chapter-ending review questions. The website for each chapter has an additional detailed list of review questions for that chapter. Save your answers for review and test preparation.

Use the buddy system. Study with a friend or become a member of a study group to compare notes, review material, and prepare for tests. Explaining something to someone else is a great way to focus your thoughts and reinforce your learning. Attend any review sessions offered by your teacher.

Become a good test taker. Avoid cramming. Eat well and get plenty of sleep before a test. Arrive on time or early. Calm yourself and increase your oxygen intake by taking several deep breaths. (Do this also about every 10–15 minutes while taking the test.) Look over the test and answer the questions you know well first. Then work on the harder ones. Use the process of elimination to narrow down the choices for multiple-choice questions. For essay questions, organize your thoughts before you start writing. If you have no idea what a question means, make an educated guess. You might earn some partial credit and avoid getting a zero.

Take time to enjoy life. Every day, take time to laugh and enjoy nature, beauty, and friendship.

You Can Improve Your Critical Thinking Skills

Critical thinking involves developing skills to analyze information and ideas, judge their validity, and make decisions. Critical thinking helps you to distinguish between facts and opinions, evaluate evidence and arguments, and take and defend informed positions on issues. It also helps you to integrate information and see relationships and to apply your knowledge to dealing with new and different problems, as well as to your own lifestyle choices. Here are some basic skills for learning how to think more critically.

Question everything and everybody. Be skeptical, as any good scientist is. Do not believe everything you hear and read, including the content of this textbook, without evaluating the information you receive. Seek other sources and opinions.

Identify and evaluate your personal biases and beliefs. Each of us has biases and beliefs taught to us by our parents, teachers, friends, role models, and our own experience. What are your basic beliefs, values, and biases? Where did they come from? What assumptions are they based on? How sure are you that your beliefs, values, and assumptions are right and why? According to the American psychologist and philosopher William James, "A great many people think they are thinking when they are merely rearranging their prejudices."

Be open-minded and flexible. Be open to considering different points of view. Suspend judgment until you gather more evidence, and be willing to change your mind. Recognize that there may be a number of useful and acceptable solutions to a problem, and that very few issues are either black or white. Understand that there are trade-offs involved in dealing with any environmental issue, as you will learn in reading this book.

Be humble about what you know. Some people are so confident in what they know that they stop thinking and questioning. To paraphrase American writer Mark Twain, "It's what we know is true, but just ain't so, that hurts us."

Find out how the information related to an issue was obtained. Are the statements you heard or read based on firsthand knowledge and research or on hearsay? Are unnamed sources used? Is the information based on reproducible and widely accepted scientific studies or on preliminary scientific results that may be valid but need further testing? Is the information based on a few isolated stories or experiences or on carefully controlled studies that have been reviewed by experts in the field involved? Is it based on unsubstantiated and dubious scientific information or beliefs?

Question the evidence and conclusions presented. What are the conclusions or claims based on the information you're considering? What evidence is presented to support them? Does the evidence support them? Is there a need to gather more evidence to test the conclusions? Are there other, more reasonable conclusions?

Try to uncover differences in basic beliefs and assumptions. On the surface, most arguments or disagreements involve differences of opinion about the validity or meaning of certain facts or conclusions. Scratch a little deeper and you will find that many disagreements are based on different (and often hidden) basic assumptions concerning how we look at and interpret the world around us. Uncovering these basic differences can allow the parties involved to understand each other's viewpoints and to agree to disagree about their basic assumptions, beliefs, or principles.

Try to identify and assess any motives on the part of those presenting evidence and drawing conclusions. What is their expertise in this area? Do they have any unstated assumptions, beliefs, biases, or values? Do they have a personal agenda? Can they benefit financially or politically from acceptance of their evidence and conclusions? Would investigators with different basic assumptions or beliefs take the same data and come to different conclusions?

Expect and tolerate uncertainty. Recognize that scientists cannot establish absolute proof or certainty about anything. However, the reliable results of science have a high degree of certainty.

Check the arguments you hear and read for logical fallacies and debating tricks. Here are six of many examples of such debating tricks: *First*, attack the presenter of an argument rather than the argument itself. *Second*, appeal to emotion rather than facts and logic. *Third*, claim that if one piece of evidence or one conclusion is false, then all other related pieces of evidence and conclusions are false. *Fourth*, say that a conclusion is false because it has not been scientifically proven. (Scientists never prove anything absolutely, but they can establish high degrees of certainty.) *Fifth*, inject irrelevant or misleading information to divert attention from important points. *Sixth*, present only either/or alternatives when there may be a number of options.

Do not believe everything you read on the Internet. The Internet is a wonderful and easily accessible source of information that includes alternative explanations and opinions on almost any subject or issue—much of it not available in the mainstream media and scholarly articles. Blogs of all sorts have become a major source of information, even more important than standard news media for some people. However, because the Internet is so open, anyone can post anything they want to some blogs and other websites with no editorial control or review by experts. As a result, evaluating information on the Internet is one of the best ways to put into practice the principles of critical thinking discussed here. Use and enjoy the Internet, but think critically and proceed with caution.

Develop principles or rules for evaluating evidence. Develop a written list of principles to serve as guidelines for evaluating evidence and claims. Continually evaluate and modify this list on the basis of your experience.

Become a seeker of wisdom, not a vessel of information. Many people believe that the main goal of their education is to learn as much as they can by gathering more and more information. We believe that the primary goal is to learn how to sift through mountains of facts and ideas to find the few nuggets of wisdom that are especially useful for understanding the world and for making decisions. This book is full of facts and numbers, but they are useful only to the extent that they lead to an understanding of key ideas, scientific laws, theories, concepts, and connections. The major goals of the study of environmental science are to find out how nature works and sustains itself (*environmental wisdom*) and to use *principles of environmental wisdom* to help make human societies and economies more sustainable, more just, and more beneficial and enjoyable for all. As writer Sandra Carey observed, "Never mistake knowledge for wisdom. One helps you make a living; the other helps you make a life."

To help you practice critical thinking, we have supplied questions throughout this book, found within each chapter in brief boxes labeled *Thinking About*, in the captions of many figures, at the end of each Science Focus box, and at the end of each chapter. There are no right or wrong answers to many of these questions. A good way to improve your critical thinking skills is to compare your answers with those of your classmates and to discuss how you arrived at your answers.

Know Your Own Learning Style

People have different ways of learning and it can be helpful to know your own learning style. *Visual learners* learn best by reading and viewing illustrations and diagrams. *Auditory learners* learn best by listening and discussing. They might benefit from reading aloud while studying and using a tape recorder in lectures for study and review. *Logical learners* learn best by using concepts and logic to uncover and understand a subject rather than relying mostly on memory.

This book and its supporting website materials contain plenty of tools for all types of learners. Visual learners can benefit from using the Flashcard app in MindTap to memorize key terms and ideas. This is a highly visual book with many carefully selected photographs and diagrams designed to illustrate important ideas, concepts, and processes. Auditory learners can make use of our ReaderSpeak app in MindTap, which can read the chapter aloud at different speeds and in different voices. For logical learners, the book is organized by key concepts that are revisited throughout any chapter and related carefully to other concepts, major principles, and case studies and other examples. We urge you to become aware of your own learning style and make the most of these various tools.

This Book Presents a Positive, Realistic Environmental Vision of the Future

Our goal is to present a positive vision of our environmental future based on realistic optimism. To do so, we strive not only to present the facts about environmental issues, but also to give a balanced presentation of different viewpoints. We consider the advantages and disadvantages of various technologies and proposed solutions to environmental problems. We argue that environmental solutions usually require *trade-offs* among opposing parties, and that the best solutions are *win-win* solutions. Such solutions are achieved when people with different viewpoints work together to come up with a solution that both sides can live with. And we present the good news as well as the bad news about efforts to deal with environmental problems.

One cannot study a subject as important and complex as environmental science without forming conclusions, opinions, and beliefs. However, we argue that any such results should be based on the use of critical thinking to evaluate conflicting positions and to understand the trade-offs involved in most environmental solutions. To that end, we emphasize critical thinking throughout this textbook, and we encourage you to develop a practice of applying critical thinking to everything you read and hear, both in school and throughout your life.

AP® Topics Correlation

This table correlates the Topic Outline from the Environmental Science AP® Course Description to the sections of this text.

AP® Course Topics	Correlation to *Exploring Environmental Science for AP®*
I. EARTH SYSTEMS AND RESOURCES	
A. Earth Science Concepts	
Geologic time scale	Section 11.1
Plate tectonics	Section 11.6
Earthquakes	Section 11.6
Volcanism	Section 11.6
Seasons	Section 5.2
Solar intensity and latitude	Section 5.2
B. The Atmosphere	
Composition	Section 19.1
Structure	Section 19.1
Weather and climate	Sections 5.1, 5.2
Atmospheric circulation and the Coriolis effect	Section 5.2
Atmosphere-ocean interactions	Section 5.1
ENSO	Section 5.1
C. Global Water Resources and Use	
Freshwater/saltwater	Sections 6.1, 6.2, 6.4
Ocean circulation	Section 5.2
Agricultural, industrial, and domestic use	Sections 12.3, 13.3-13.5, 17.4
Surface and groundwater issues	Sections 13.1, 13.2, 13.4, 17.2, 17.3
Global problems	Sections 13.1, 13.3, 13.5, 17.1, 17.2, 17.4
Conservation	Sections 12.3, 13.5
D. Soil and Soil Dynamics	
Rock cycle	Section 11.1
Formation	Section 11.2
Composition	Sections 3.2, 11.2
Physical and chemical properties	Section 11.2
Main soil types	Section 11.2
Erosion and other soil problems	Section 12.3
Soil conservation	Section 12.5
II. THE LIVING WORLD	
A. Ecosystem Structure	
Biological populations and communities	Sections 3.2, 6.1, 6.2, 6.4, 7.2
Ecological niches	Section 4.3
Interactions among species	Sections 4.3, 7.1
Keystone species	Section 4.3
Species diversity and edge effects	Section 4.2
Major terrestrial and aquatic biomes	Sections 5.3, 6.2, 6.4
B. Energy Flow	
Photosynthesis and cellular respiration	Section 3.2
Food webs and trophic levels	Section 3.3
Ecological pyramids	Section 3.3

AP® Course Topics	Correlation to *Exploring Environmental Science for AP®*
C. Ecosystem Diversity	
Biodiversity	Sections 1.1, 4.2, 6.2, 20.2
Natural selection	Section 4.4
Evolution	Section 4.4
Ecosystem services	Sections 1.1, 9.1-9.3
D. Natural Ecosystem Change	
Climate shifts	Sections 4.5, 20.1-20.4
Species movement	Sections 4.5, 6.2, 6.5, 9.1
Ecological succession	Section 7.2
E. Natural Biogeochemical Cycles	
Carbon, nitrogen, phosphorus, sulfur, water	Section 3.4
Conservation of matter	Section 2.2

III. POPULATION

AP® Course Topics	Correlation
A. Population Biology Concepts	
Population ecology	Section 7.3
Carrying capacity	Section 7.3
Reproductive strategies	Section 7.3
Survivorship	Section 7.3
B. Human Population	
Human population dynamics:	
historical population sizes	Section 8.1
distribution	Section 7.3
fertility rates	Section 8.2
growth rates and doubling times	Sections 1.3, 7.3, 8.2
demographic transition	Section 8.4
age-structure diagrams	Section 8.3
Population size:	
strategies for sustainability	Section 8.3
case studies	Section 8.4
national policies	Section 8.4
Impacts of population growth:	
hunger	Section 12.1
disease	Section 16.2
economic effects	Sections 8.1, 8.3
resource use	Section 8.1
habitat destruction	Sections 8.1, 9.3

IV. LAND AND WATER USE

AP® Course Topics	Correlation
A. Agriculture	
Feeding a growing population:	
human nutritional requirements	Section 12.1
types of agriculture	Section 12.2
Green Revolution	Section 12.2
genetic engineering and crop production	Section 12.2

AP® Course Topics	Correlation to *Exploring Environmental Science for AP®*
deforestation	Section 10.1
irrigation	Sections 12.3, 13.2, 13.5
sustainable agriculture	Sections 12.4–12.6
Controlling pests:	
types of pesticides	Section 12.4
costs and benefits of pesticide use	Section 12.4
integrated pest management	Section 12.4
relevant laws	Section 12.4
B. Forestry	
Tree plantations	Section 10.1
Old-growth forests	Section 10.1
Forest fires	Section 10.1
Forest management	Section 10.1
National forests	Sections 10.3, 10.4
C. Rangelands	
Overgrazing	Section 10.2
Deforestation	Section 10.1
Desertification	Section 10.1
Rangeland management	Section 10.2
Federal rangelands	Section 10.2
D. Other Land Use	
Urban land development:	
planned development	Section 10.5
suburban sprawl	Section 10.5
urbanization	Section 10.5
Transportation infrastructure:	
federal highway system	Section 10.5
canals and channels	Section 13.4
roadless areas	Section 10.4
ecosystem impacts	Section 10.4
Public and federal lands:	
management	Section 10.1
wilderness areas	Section 10.4
national parks	Section 10.4
wildlife refuges	Section 10.4
forests	Sections 10.1, 10.4
wetlands	Sections 6.2, 10.3
Land conservation options:	
preservation	Section 10.4
remediation	Sections 10.2-10.4
mitigation	Sections 10.3, 10.4
restoration	Section 10.3
Sustainable land-use strategies	Sections 10.2-10.4
E. Mining	
Mineral formation	Section 11.1
Extraction	Section 11.4

AP® Course Topics	Correlation to *Exploring Environmental Science for AP®*
Global reserves	Section 11.3
Relevant laws and treaties	Section 11.4
F. Fishing	
Fishing techniques	Section 12.2
Overfishing	Section 12.3
Aquaculture	Section 12.3
Relevant laws and treaties	Section 12.3
G. Global Economics	
Globalization	Section 1.4
World Bank	Section 16.1
Tragedy of the Commons	Section 1.1
Relevant laws and treaties	Sections 9.3, 9.4, 19.7, 20.3

V. ENERGY RESOURCES AND CONSUMPTION

A. Energy Concepts	
Energy forms	Section 2.3
Power	Section 2.3
Units	Supplement 1
Conservation	Section 15.2
Laws of Thermodynamics	Section 2.2
B. Energy Consumption	
History:	
Industrial Revolution	Section 1.3
exponential growth	Section 1.3
energy crisis	Section 14.2
Present global energy use	Section 14.1
Future energy needs	Sections 15.1, 15.9
C. Fossil Fuel Resources and Use	
Formation of coal, oil, and natural gas	Sections 14.2-14.4
Extraction/purification methods	Sections 14.2-14.4
World reserves and global demand	Section 14.2
Synfuels	Section 14.4
Environmental advantages/disadvantages of sources	Sections 14.2-14.4
D. Nuclear Energy	
Nuclear fission process	Section 14.5
Nuclear fuel	Section 14.5
Electricity production	Section 14.5
Nuclear reactor types	Section 14.5
Environmental advantages/disadvantages	Section 14.5
Safety issues	Section 14.5
Radiation and human health	Section 14.5
Radioactive wastes	Section 14.5
Nuclear fusion	Section 14.5
E. Hydroelectric Power	
Dams	Sections 13.3, 15.7
Flood control	Sections 13.3, 13.6

AP® Course Topics	Correlation to *Exploring Environmental Science for AP®*
Salmon	Section 13.3
Silting	Section 13.3
Other impacts	Sections 13.3, 15.7
F. Energy Conservation	
Energy efficiency	Section 15.1
CAFE standards	Section 15.2
Hybrid electric vehicles	Section 15.2
Mass transit	Section 10.5
G. Renewable Energy	
Solar energy	Section 15.3
Solar electricity	Section 15.3
Hydrogen fuel cells	Section 15.8
Biomass	Section 15.6
Wind energy	Section 15.4
Small-scale hydroelectric	Section 15.7
Ocean waves and tidal energy	Section 15.7
Geothermal	Section 15.5
Environmental advantages/disadvantages	Sections 15.2-15.8

VI. POLLUTION

A. Pollution Types

Air pollution:

sources—primary and secondary	Section 19.2
major air pollutants	Section 19.2
measurement units	Section 19.2
smog	Section 19.2
acid deposition—causes and effects	Section 19.3
heat islands and temperature inversions	Sections 10.5, 19.2
indoor air pollution	Section 19.4
remediation and reduction strategies	Section 19.5
clean Air Act and other relevant laws	Section 19.5

Noise pollution:

sources	Section 10.5
effects	Section 10.5
control measures	Section 10.5

Water pollution:

types	Section 17.1
sources, causes, and effects	Section 17.1
cultural eutrophication	Sections 6.4, 17.2
groundwater pollution	Section 17.3
maintaining water quality; water purification	Section 17.3, 17.5
sewage treatment/septic systems	Section 17.5
clean Water Act and other relevant laws	Section 17.5

AP® Course Topics	Correlation to *Exploring Environmental Science for AP®*
Solid waste:	
types	Section 18.1
disposal	Sections 18.2, 18.4
reduction	Sections 18.3, 18.6
B. Impacts on the Environment and Human Health	
Hazards to human health:	
environmental risk analysis	Section 16.5
acute and chronic effects	Sections 16.2-16.4
dose-response relationships	Section 16.4
air pollutants	Sections 19.2, 19.4
smoking and other risks	Sections 16.1, 16.5
Hazardous chemicals in the environment:	
types of hazardous waste	Sections 18.1, 18.5
treatment/disposal of hazardous waste	Section 18.5
cleanup of contaminated sites	Section 18.5
biomagnification	Section 9.3
relevant laws	Section 18.5
C. Economic Impacts	
Cost-benefit analysis	Section 15.2
Externalities	Section 11.5
Marginal costs	Section 14.4
Sustainability	Sections 1.1-1.6, 3.1, 9.1-9.4, 10.1-10.5, 11.4, 11.5, 12.4, 12.5, 13.2, 13.5, 14.1-14.5, 15.1-15.9, 18.1-18.6, 20.3
VII. GLOBAL CHANGE	
A. Stratospheric Ozone	
Formation of stratospheric ozone	Section 19.1
Ultraviolet radiation	Section 19.1
Causes of ozone depletion	Section 19.7
Effects of ozone depletion	Section 19.7
Strategies for reducing ozone depletion	Section 19.7
Relevant laws and treaties	Section 19.7
B. Global Warming	
Greenhouse gases and the greenhouse effect	Sections 3.1, 20.1
Impacts and consequences of global warming	Section 20.2
Reducing climate change	Section 20.3
Relevant laws and treaties	Section 20.3
C. Loss of Biodiversity	
Habitat loss; overuse; pollution; introduced species	Sections 9.1, 9.3
Endangered and extinct species	Section 9.1
Maintenance through conservation	Section 9.4
Relevant laws and treaties	Section 9.4

Taking on the challenge and rigor of an Advanced Placement® course can be an enriching experience in your academic career. Whether you are taking this AP® course at your school or you are working independently, the stage is set for an immeasurable intellectual experience. As the school year progresses, you will gain a deeper understanding of the scientific processes, concepts, and methodologies required to understand the mechanisms that drive our natural world. Environmental science is an interdisciplinary study by which you will acquire the ability to identify and analyze both natural and anthropogenic environmental problems. By the end of this course, you will also be able to assess the relative risks associated with these environmental problems as well as suggest more sustainable solutions and alternatives to the current conventional behaviors that cause environmental stress and degradation. This course will provide an exhilarating and awakening experience for you through the study and understanding of today's global environmental problems and their solutions.

But sometime in January, when the examination begins to loom on a very real horizon, the prospect of working your way up to and through the AP® exam can seem downright intimidating. At times, the amount of material you must master to be successful may feel overwhelming. If you are nervous about preparing for and taking the exam, just know that you are not the only one, and the feeling is completely normal. Believe it or not, attitude and confidence *do* help. The best way to deal with an AP® exam is to master it, and not let it master you. If you can think of the exam as your opportunity to show off how much environmental science you know, you have a leg up!

Setting Up a Review Schedule

First and foremost, it is essential to maintain the motivation and a positive attitude to guide your preparation. If you manage your time effectively, you will meet this one major challenge—mastery of a large amount of material in a short period of time. Develop a review schedule to help direct your study time so that you spread out your review over the course of at least several weeks to a month or more prior to the exam. Do not rely on just a few short days of cramming. Sticking to your review schedule and allowing enough practice time prior to the exam will help you master the course material and will also give you an invaluable amount of confidence on the day of the exam.

What's in *Exploring Environmental Science for AP®* That Will Help Your Preparation

The best way to ensure mastery of the content for this exam is to keep up with your reading, homework, and laboratory assignments each week of the school year. Even if you have not been able to master each content area during the year, there are several elements in this text that will help you assemble a strong collective knowledge of the course material during your review and exam preparation time.

- Review the *Checkpoint for Understanding* questions and answers that appear throughout each chapter. These will help you highlight and focus in on key ideas, and gain practice answering FRQ-style questions.

- Review the *Critical Concepts in Sustainability* features throughout the book. Each one contains a sample FRQ question and possible responses, showing the significance of these topics within the AP® Environmental Science framework, and how they might be addressed on the exam.

- Work through the *Math Connection* features in each chapter. Be sure you understand the various kinds of data set questions that can appear on the exam, and that you are comfortable performing dimensional analysis and basic arithmetic and algebraic calculations. Remember that calculators are not allowed on the exam, and you must show all of your work in the answer booklet.

- Pay attention to the many opportunities for *Critical Thinking* throughout each chapter and in end-of-chapter questions. All of the critical thinking features of this text will help you learn to analyze information, evaluate evidence, and formulate ideas that you can express and defend.

- Complete the multiple-choice AP® review questions at the end of each chapter and unit. They are a good representation of the types of multiple choice questions you will see on the exam.

- Carefully work through the free-response AP® review questions that appear in Chapters 3-20 and in the Unit Review sets. These will provide valuable practice formulating and writing out responses to data-set, document-based, and synthesis and evaluation questions.

- Take the AP® Practice Exam at the end of the book to get a sense of your overall preparedness for the exam. Find a quiet place to work and set aside an appropriate amount of time so you can treat it like a real testing situation. Use your results on the practice test to identify topic areas for further review.

Before the Examination

First and foremost, you need to make sure you are registered to take the AP® exam. Most schools take care of this detail and handle the fees for their students, but you should check with your teacher or AP® coordinator to make sure your paperwork has been submitted to the College Board. This typically takes place in March. If you have a documented disability and will need testing accommodations on the exam, you should ensure that it has been reported by your AP® coordinator to the College Board. If you are studying independently, call AP® Services at the College Board for the name of the local coordinator, who will help you through the registration process. You should also check your calendar for conflicts and speak to your school's AP® coordinator about making arrangements to take an alternate AP® exam on a later date, if necessary. The College Board will allow students scheduled with more than one AP® exam at the same time on the same day to take an alternate exam on a later date. Other acceptable circumstances that warrant an alternate exam include conflicts with International Baccalaureate or state-mandated exams and religious holidays. Conflicts with athletic or academic contests and even family vacations are also acceptable; however, there is an additional charge for taking an alternate exam for those reasons.

Just like with any test, the night before the exam you should get plenty of sleep so that you have enough energy to stay focused during the entire three hours of testing. This is not the time to stay up studying all night. Instead, focus on briefly reviewing broad concepts such as common solutions to major environmental problems or frequently used vocabulary terms. The night before the test is a good time to get together everything you will need the next morning for the exam.

What will you need on the morning of the exam? First you need to eat a good breakfast so that you have plenty of energy for the test—being tired can cause you to give up too easily on a question and cost you points on the exam. You need a sharpened No. 2 pencil to answer the multiple-choice section. Also, you need a blue or black ink pen for your essays on the free-response portion of the exam. If possible, take two or three pencils and pens so that you have plenty of back-ups on hand if one fails to work properly. It is also a good idea to take a simple watch for tracking your time (one without Internet connectivity—no smartwatches) in case the testing room does not have a clock. It will be important to be aware of the time on both your multiple-choice section and the free-response to allow you to utilize your time effectively. Make sure you take with you anything that has been requested by your AP® coordinator—such as your Social Security number, photo ID, or registration ticket. Remember that calculators are NOT allowed on the AP® Environmental Science exam. Cell phones and other personal electronics are also not permitted in the exam rooms. Check with your teacher if you have questions about what items are and are not allowed.

Finally, it is important that you are completely comfortable while taking the exam. Wear clothes and shoes that are comfortable. Some students also like to bring a jacket or sweatshirt in case the testing room is too cold and becomes uncomfortable. It is also a good idea to bring a snack to eat during the break. You will have a short break between the multiple-choice portion, which is 90 minutes long, and the free-response portion, which is also 90 minutes long. Three hours of testing is a long time, and you don't want to be hungry going into the essay section of your test.

The AP® Environmental Science examination consists of two sections: Section I has 100 multiple-choice questions; Section II has 4 free-response questions. You will have 90 minutes for each section. There will be a short break between the two sections of the exam. You must write an essay for each of the four questions. You should monitor the time during both sections of the exam and move nimbly through both sections so that you do not get bogged down on one multiple-choice question or on one essay.

Strategies for the Multiple-Choice Section

Here are some important rules of thumb to help you work your way through the multiple-choice questions:

- **Terminology.** Each question has a stem that may be in the form of a question or statement and five options that are the possible answers to the question. Exactly one of the five options is correct.

- **There is one correct answer; however...** Sometimes, the "correct" answer is "the best" among the options given. In that case, more than one answer may actually be correct, but one is the best option.

- **Manage the time.** With 90 minutes to answer 100 questions, you have less than one minute to answer each question. Check your pace; try to answer 25 questions every 20 minutes. This will leave 10 minutes at the end of the exam to look back over your answers.

- **Use the "3 times through" method.** This is another approach to time management, and it is helpful in that, historically, the final questions on the exam are often easier than those in the middle portion of the test. Go through the multiple choice questions the first time, answering only those questions that are "easy" for you to answer. Go through the multiple-choice portion a second time answering those that are moderate in difficulty. Go through the test one final time answering those questions that are most difficult, guessing if necessary.

- **Cover the options.** Try reading the stem with the options covered. Answer in your mind, and then select the option that is closest to your answer.

- **Read the entire question carefully and completely.** The item writers may have intentionally included attractor options—choices that initially appear to be "obvious" or "correct," but are not—for students who are rushing through the exam.

- **Write in your multiple-choice booklet.** As you eliminate options, cross them out by drawing a line through them. On questions with a negative stem or Roman numerals (see question types below) label true and false statements with a T or an F next to the options as you work through the question. If you skip an extremely difficult or long question, circle it and return to it after you have answered all of the easy questions. If it helps you to do so, underline key words in a question that help you to focus on what is important in the question. Use the test booklet as scratch paper for any questions that require calculations. Calculator use is not permitted on the AP® Environmental Science exam.

- **Fill in your answer document carefully.** If you must erase, do so completely. Bring a white plastic eraser to use on your answer document. Your exam will be scored by a machine, and any stray marks may be read as answers. When you skip questions, don't forget to skip the corresponding lines on your answer sheet, or you will waste time erasing and moving answers later.

- **Answer every question.** Points are no longer deducted for incorrect answers on AP® exams, so you should mark an answer for every question.

- **Guessing advice.** If you must guess, make a random selection from the options that you did not eliminate. Avoid picking an option that you do not know is correct, if it only "sounds right" to you. Picking options that sound right could lead you into a trap set by the item writer for a student who, like you, knows a little bit, but not quite enough about the question to select the one best answer. If you must make a guess, do so by making an unbiased random selection from the options that remain after you have eliminated those you are certain are wrong.

Types of Multiple-Choice Questions

There are several different types of multiple-choice questions on the AP® Environmental Science exam.

Options-First Questions

The multiple-choice section of the AP® Environmental Science exam usually begins with about 15-20 options-first questions. These questions require you to use the same set of options for a series of questions. You may use the same option as the answer for one question, for more than one of the questions, or some options may not be used at all. A good way to think about this type of question is as a series of questions that all happen to have the same set of options. If you think about them in that way, you will never wonder if an option can be correct more than once, or if you will use all of the options. For example:

(A) Mercury

(B) Carbon monoxide

(C) Lead

(D) Ozone

(E) Sulfur dioxide

1. A secondary air pollutant that is formed in photochemical smog

2. A contaminant of coal that accumulates in the tissues of some species of fish

3. Reacts in air to form acids that can fall to the ground as acid rain

ANSWERS:

1–D. Ozone is the only secondary pollutant among the five options.

2–A. Mercury is a contaminant in coal that vaporizes when the coal is burned. After falling back to earth, the mercury is washed into aquatic ecosystems where it may be assimilated in the tissues of fish.

3–E. Sulfur dioxide reacts with other substances in the air to form acids that can fall to the ground as acid rain.

Traditional Questions

Nearly all of the multiple-choice questions will be traditional multiple-choice questions. These questions will be straightforward questions with five options and one correct

or best answer. These questions simply require you to read the question and select the most correct answer. For example:

1. Which of the following is an asphyxiant produced during incomplete combustion reactions?

(A) Mercury

(B) Carbon monoxide

(C) Lead

(D) Ozone

(E) Sulfur dioxide

ANSWER: B. Carbon monoxide is produced during incomplete combustion, and it is an asphyxiant.

Negative-Stem Questions

You should expect to encounter few of this type of question, but be prepared for them. They may be the hardest questions on the exam. If the answer is not immediately obvious to you, you may want to circle this type of question and return to it later. In negative-stem questions, all of the options are correct except for one. These questions usually begin with a statement like, "All of the following are correct EXCEPT…" or "Which of the following is NOT…" In either case, there will be four options that are in the correct context, and one that is not—that one is the correct answer. One way to approach these questions is as a series of true/false statements. There is only one false statement, and that is the correct answer. It will help you to keep track of which options are true and false if you mark them with a T or an F as you read. For example:

1. Which of the following is NOT one of the criteria air pollutants monitored by the U.S. EPA?

(A) Mercury

(B) Carbon monoxide

(C) Lead

(D) Ozone

(E) Sulfur dioxide

ANSWER: A. Mercury is not one of the criteria air pollutants monitored by the U.S. EPA. The criteria air pollutants are carbon monoxide, lead, ozone, sulfur dioxide, nitrogen oxides, and particulate matter. If you marked the options with a T or F, answer A should be the only option that is marked differently from the other four.

Roman Numeral Questions

You should also expect to encounter relatively few Roman numeral questions. These questions are not as difficult as the negative-stem questions because you are looking for correct answers. In Roman numeral questions, there are usually three or four answers labeled with Roman numerals. One or more of the answers could be correct. You are then provided with a series of options from which you select the correct Roman numeral or set of Roman numerals. The option with the Roman numerals followed by the correct answers is correct. For example:

1. Which of the following are toxic heavy metals?

   I. Mercury

  II. Carbon monoxide

 III. Lead

  (A) I only

  (B) II only

  (C) III only

  (D) I and II only

  (E) I and III only

ANSWER: E. Mercury and lead are toxic heavy metals, and carbon monoxide is not a toxic heavy metal, which makes "I and III only" the correct answer.

Least and Most Likely Questions

This type of question may have two or more options that are correct, but only one that is the least or most likely. When answering these questions, don't answer until you have read through all of the options, and if more than one is correct, rank the likeliness of each correct option by placing a number next to the option.

1. If released or formed in the atmosphere, which of the following will least likely result in long-term environmental damage to an ecosystem?

  (A) Mercury

  (B) Carbon monoxide

  (C) Lead

  (D) Ozone

  (E) Sulfur dioxide

ANSWER: B. Carbon monoxide is not persistent, nor does it bioaccumulate. Unlike ozone or sulfur dioxide, carbon monoxide does not produce long-term ecological damage.

Data Interpretation and Analysis Questions

In this type of question, there is a data set, graph, or chart for you to review and interpret. These questions may require that you do some calculations to determine the answer. Often there is more than one question that makes use of the data set, graph, or chart. You should do all scratch work in the test booklet. Calculators are not permitted on the AP® Environmental Science exam.

U.S. Airborne Lead Air Quality 1980–2005

Year	Lead Concentration ($\mu g/m^3$)
1980	1.25
1985	0.67
1990	0.29
1995	0.11
2000	0.09
2005	0.09

1. The percent change in the airborne lead concentration between 1980 and 2000 was closest to which of the following?

  (A) 10%

  (B) 17%

  (C) 81%

  (D) 87%

  (E) 93%

ANSWER: E. To determine the percent change, take the difference between the two values, divide that difference by the original value, and multiply by 100. In this case $1.25 - 0.09 = 1.16$ divided by 1.25 equals 0.928 multiplied by 100 equals 92.8%, which is closest to 93%. You should be prepared to do arithmetic like this on your AP® Environmental Science exam. Remember, no calculators are allowed, so practice your math.

2. Which of the following best explains the trend in the data of U.S. airborne lead concentrations?

  (A) The inclusion of lead in the EPA's list of Criteria Air Pollutants

  (B) The phase-out of the use of lead-based paints

  (C) The widespread use of catalytic converters

  (D) The elimination of lead additives in gasoline

  (E) The use of wet scrubbers on coal-fired power plants

ANSWER: D. The plummet in airborne lead concentrations during the 1980s and 1990s is due to the phase-out of the use of tetraethyl lead as an additive in gasoline. Note that more than one of the options are reasonable reasons why lead emissions were reduced; this question illustrates the second bullet in the strategies above: "**There is one correct answer; however...** Sometimes, the 'correct' answer is 'the best' among the options given."

Conversion Questions

In this type of question, you are given data, and you are asked to set up a unit conversion. Your answer options will suggest a variety of ways to do the conversion; your job will be to choose the most correct way to solve the problem. The method used is often termed *dimensional analysis* in chemistry; it is a method that involves setting up the problem in such a way that all units through the conversion process will cancel out until you reach the answer expressed in the desired units.

1. When 1 gallon of gas is burned (mass of 13.9 kg), the reaction of the gasoline with the oxygen in the air results in the production of 20 lb of carbon dioxide. If a person drives 30 miles per day in a car that has an efficiency of 25 miles per gallon, how many pounds of carbon dioxide is produced in a week?

   (A) (13.9 kg) (30 mi/day) (20 lb CO_2) (25 mi/gal)

   (B) (20 lb CO_2/gal) (30 mi/day) (7 day/week) (25 mi/gal)

   (C) (20 lb CO_2/gal) (30 mi/day) (25 mi/gal) (13.9 kg)

   (D) (20 lb CO_2/gal) (30 mi/day) (7 day/week) (1 gal/25 mi)

   (E) (13.9 lb CO_2/gal) (30 mi/day) (7 day/week) (25 mi/gal)

ANSWER: D. If you analyze choice D, gallons, miles, and days can all be canceled out (eliminated) in the algebraic simplification, leaving a final unit of pounds per week. The datum 13.9 kg is extraneous.

Free-Response Questions

The free-response (FRQ) portion of the AP® Environmental Science exam is 90 minutes long. During this time you must answer four questions. This allows you approximately 22 minutes for each essay. It is very important that you watch your time on each essay and not to get wrapped up in just one. Remember that these essays account for 40% of your exam score, and therefore, each essay is worth 10% of your overall grade.

While individual free-response questions may have several subparts, keep in mind that the total of all parts is worth 10 points. Typically, each subpart of a free-response question will be worth 2–4 points, depending on the complexity and number of parts of the question. It is possible for the points available to total more than 10, but the maximum score for any free-response question is 10. Different parts of a free-response question often are not of equal difficulty, but usually one or two parts will be simpler than others. Answer the easiest part of the question first, and do not omit an entire question just because some parts seem difficult. Partial credit is always available on such questions, but only if an answer is given and you can demonstrate some knowledge about the question being asked.

Each question in the free-response section will be broken down into separate parts such as: (a), (b), and (c). Even individual parts to a question can be broken down further. For example:

(a) Calculate the following by using statistics given in the table.

   (i) How many gallons of water did the family use in one month?

   (ii) What is the annual cost of electricity for operating their dishwasher?

Types of Free-Response Questions
Data-Set Question

You will have at least one question that is a data-set question, often referred to as the math question, and it will be based upon a graph, diagram, table/chart, or statistics given in the introductory paragraph. Approximately 50% of your points on this type of question will be earned by doing arithmetical calculations. Even though this type is considered the math question, these questions typically have one to two parts you can earn points on that do not deal directly with any calculations or graphing. Instead, they focus on the environmental issue or concept to which the question refers. So, if you don't feel you can do the math part of the question, **don't give up!** Read the remaining parts of the FRQ and answer the portions that are conceptual and not mathematical. Remember to always **show your work** (only in the pink answer booklet) for any calculation and give the appropriate units with each number written. **Include your units in the work you show, otherwise you may not receive credit.** Make sure you circle your answer so that the individual reading your response knows what you intend to be the final answer.

REMINDER: Calculators are not permitted on the AP® Environmental Science exam, so you will need to be comfortable using basic arithmetic and algebra such as multiplying, dividing, scientific notation, and percentages.

Document-Based Question (DBQ)

You will have one question that is prompted with some type of document that will pertain to the questions being asked. It is important to remember these prompts are primarily used to introduce the questions. Although you may need to use some numbers or information provided in the document to help answer a question, do not expect to pull all of your answers directly from the passage given. A common mistake that students make is to simply repeat information given in the document as their answer. At the same time, it is not uncommon to be able to answer one part of the DBQ directly from the given document. As mentioned, the purpose of the document is to introduce the question or questions. Students are expected to demonstrate comprehension by adding information learned from readings or class.

Synthesis and Evaluation Questions

There are two synthesis and evaluation questions on the free-response section of the AP® Environmental Science exam. It may be easier to understand what a synthesis and evaluation question is by understanding what it is not. That is, if you determine that a question is not a math question, and it is not a document-based question, then it is a synthesis and evaluation question. A question of this type will require you to write an essay in which you demonstrate your knowledge about one of the numerous topics of study in the AP® Environmental Science course.

Often these questions incorporate information from a variety of topics within environmental science. Additionally, these questions often include a part asking you to identify and describe the legislation that applies to that particular topic. Your ability to earn points in these essays will be determined by your knowledge of the subject matter. In rare cases, you may be required to perform a simple calculation in a synthesis and evaluation question; however, the calculation will likely be worth only one or two points.

These questions will usually have a small paragraph to introduce a topic and then four to five questions or prompts pertaining to that topic. As with all free-response questions you will be asked to identify, describe, explain, discuss, etc. Be sure to identify these verbs used to ask the question and follow the free-response tips discussed later

on pages xxxvii–xxxix when writing your essay. Synthesis and evaluation questions may look like the following:

1. The harvesting of wood for fuelwood, and charcoal made from fuelwood, is increasing at an alarming rate. This is causing the deforestation of many areas, particularly in developing countries. Many of these countries are now cutting down trees at a rate 10–20% faster than they are being replanted.

    (a) **Identify** TWO uses of fuelwood in developing countries.

    (b) **Describe** how deforestation impacts the global carbon cycle.

    (c) **Identify** and **describe** one environmental problem and one economic benefit that result from clear-cutting forests.

    (d) **Discuss** TWO sustainable forestry practices that could be implemented in these countries.

    (e) **Write an argument** in support of the practice of sustainably harvesting fuelwood.

Vocabulary Used in Free-Response Questions

You can earn a maximum of 10 points on each of the four free-response questions. You should pay close attention to the word choice used in each part of the FRQ. Keying in on what type of verb is being used in the question can help you maximize both your time and points on your essay section.

Identify or List

This term is asking you to give a specific object, advantage, disadvantage, cause, solution, etc. It is important to always write in prose **on every question**. Even if it may seem like you can answer this type of question in one word or with a simple list or chart, don't take short-cuts. You must write the answer in a complete sentence to get any credit. A complete sentence for this exam requires a subject and a predicate, that is, a noun and a verb.

For example, the question above states, "Identify two uses of fuelwood in developing countries." The answer can be as short as, "Two uses of fuelwood in developing countries are for home heating and cooking." However, you would earn no points for simply writing "heating and cooking."

Describe or Explain

These terms are asking you to further illustrate your answer by using details beyond just identifying an object or a solution. Often you will see these terms used with the exact number of solutions or objects you are to describe. A good description will usually take more than one sentence. A good description can also be made better by supporting it with an example when possible.

For example, the question may state, "Describe TWO benefits of using fuelwood." A good response to this prompt is, "Two benefits of using fuelwood are the ability for people to heat their homes and to cook their food without the need of fossil fuels. Unlike our conventional fuel sources, if managed sustainably, fuelwood can be a renewable resource."

As another example, consider the earlier question that stated, "Describe how deforestation impacts the global carbon cycle." A good response to this prompt is, "Deforestation removes trees that function as carbon reservoirs by absorbing carbon dioxide during photosynthesis. This will increase carbon dioxide levels in the atmosphere."

Note: It is also possible to have a combination of two verb choices in one question. They may ask you to either "Identify and describe…" or "Identify and explain…". You should simply follow the rules of both verbs as given in the examples here.

Discuss

When asked to discuss, you need to really *elaborate* on your answer to the question. Often, you will receive 2-3 points for this type of question; therefore, it is important to write additional detail and go beyond a simple description or explanation in your answer. A good discussion will usually take several sentences or an entire paragraph. Discussions almost always include a supporting example.

Questions asking to discuss a benefit, advantage, or disadvantage usually specify, for example, "ecological benefit," "environmental benefit," or "economic benefit." Many students miss points when they don't know the differences among these types of responses. Environmental and ecological benefits, advantages, and disadvantages may not make any mention of the benefit or advantage to humans.

For example, the question might ask, "Discuss an environmental benefit to using fuelwood over current conventional fossil fuels." A good response to this prompt is, "An environmental benefit of using fuelwood over fossil fuels is the reduction in sulfur dioxide emissions associated with coal-burning practices. By decreasing sulfur dioxide emissions, we also reduce acid deposition problems that cause tissue damage to trees in terrestrial ecosystems and cause fish kills due to lowered pH in aquatic systems."

Remember, your discussion questions require you not only to identify and define concepts but to further elaborate on the issue at hand.

As another example, consider the earlier question that stated, "Discuss TWO sustainable forestry practices that could be implemented in these countries." A good response to this prompt is, "One sustainable forestry practice is the use of tree plantations, which can grow fast-growing tree species and be managed so that the rate of tree harvesting is equal to the rate of replenishment. This will reduce the need to cut native forests. A second practice is selective cutting, which will remove some, but not all, of the trees from forests. Trees can then be replanted in the areas from which they were removed and the forest allowed to recover before being cut again. This will minimize the area of tree cover being lost in native forests."

Write an Argument

An argument is a series of statements all in support of a stated position on an issue. This is the only time that students may be rewarded for writing a lengthy list. An argument is the most *extensive* and detailed response that you could be called upon to write and it will likely be at least one paragraph in length.

For example, an earlier question above stated, "Write an argument in support of the practice of sustainably harvesting fuelwood." A good response to this prompt is, "Harvesting fuelwood sustainably avoids using practices like clear-cutting forests. Clear-cutting causes soil erosion and runoff into waterways causing sedimentation, which decreases primary productivity, increases fish kills due to suffocation, and results in poor water quality for people who depend on the waterways for their domestic water use. Furthermore, when the rate of tree harvesting exceeds the rate of replanting, tracts of forest that function as carbon dioxide reservoirs are no longer available, which will increase carbon dioxide levels in the atmosphere and further global climate change."

Free-Response Tips

Following are several best practices to help you develop your skills in writing FRQ responses and to use your time most effectively on this portion of the AP® Environmental Science exam.

■ **Pre-read all four questions.** Contemplate the questions and decide on what order to answer them. Students are typically most successful if they begin by answering their strongest question first and end with what they perceived to be their weakest question. If you answer the questions out of order, be sure to number your responses correctly in your answer book.

- **Be time-conscious.** You only have approximately 22 minutes per essay. If you work on the essays you feel most comfortable with first, it can increase the amount of time you have for the ones you don't know as well. Do not get bogged down early working on a question that is harder for you.

- **Pay attention to key words.** As you read each question, pay attention to the verb types being used such as *identify*, *describe*, *explain*, and *discuss*. Also, look for linking words that serve as directives, such as *and* and *or*. Take a few minutes to circle key terms in the question, jot down a few notes in the margins, and organize your answer in your mind before you begin.

- **Read the question carefully.** Read the entire question before answering. There may be information in the question that will help in constructing your response. Don't assume that all parts of the question stem from part (a) or some previous part of the question. Many times, different parts of the question ask about related topics. You may be prompted to describe an environmental problem in one part of a question, an economic problem in another, and an environmental benefit in a third. You may even be asked to evaluate the economic and ecological advantages and disadvantages of some action all in one segment of a free-response question. This is actually four questions in one.

- **Other key words.** You should know the difference between ecological and economic impacts, and between physical, biological, and chemical tests and effects. Underline or circle the key terms like "environmental" and "economic," and be certain to provide an appropriate response. Note: A good rule of thumb is to read "environmental" as "ecological" and to write about how the topic being addressed in the question affects the abundance, diversity, or distribution of life. Environmental and ecologic benefits are those that benefit the natural environment in some way. Economic benefits must benefit humans, generally by creating jobs, increasing revenue, or lowering cost.

- **Write in prose.** Always answer in complete sentences. Make sure you are writing clearly and large enough for the exam reader to read your answer easily. Outline forms or bulleted lists are not acceptable and will not be graded. Make sure once you are done answering that you actually answered **all** the parts to the question and followed the key word prompts such as *identify*, *describe*, *explain*, and *discuss*.

- **Use examples appropriately.** Shy away from using examples or solutions that are uniquely your own ideas. Examples, however, may be specific to your local region or experience as long as they are accurate. Among the AP® exam readers there are designated members who check the validity of all non-typical examples. If an example cannot be verified, it will not earn you any credit. If you remember a more commonly known example of a concept, it is probably in your best interest to use that one. Remember, answers on the rubric for the free-response section must be able to be applied to every single student across the country and around the world who takes this exam. Avoid fabricating information as well. It is a waste of time and will not earn any points.

- **Make appropriate connections.** When asked to make a *connection*, for example, "For each positive effect in part (a), describe…" then your response must make a *connection* to the component identified in the previous part of the FRQ. If you describe another component that you did not mentioned in the previous part, you will not receive credit, even if your description is correct.

- **Be specific.** When asked to *describe* an effect or impact, for example, be specific and detailed in your answer. Avoid generalizations and phrases such as "pollutes," "has an adverse effect," "causes environmental problems," or "has a negative impact." Use specific terminology such as "SO_2 emissions cause acid precipitation" rather than "air pollution has an adverse effect on the environment."

- **Explain fully.** When asked to *explain*, for example, the effect of a particular impact, be sure to explain fully, including all the steps involved. For instance, when explaining the impact of agricultural runoff, you might say that "nutrients enter the water and cause an algal bloom, cutting off light and reducing photosynthesis. This results in lower levels of dissolved O_2 in the water, causing death to organisms, which further robs the water of oxygen due to decomposition and causes a shift in the food web."

- **Follow through with your thoughts or examples.** Define or explain any key terms you use. Many students fail to get points because they didn't finish their thoughts. An easy way to accomplish this is to define any key terms you use in the essay and provide examples to illustrate what you mean. A simple technique to ensure that you elaborate fully is "DDEE": *define, describe, elaborate,* and give an *example*. If you do this for the questions that ask you to do more than "identify," you should have sufficient elaboration to earn all available points on that segment. Students can even earn elaboration points when they demonstrate knowledge beyond the scope of the question.

- ***Do not write long lists as your answer!*** If the question says "Identify TWO," then identify ONLY TWO items. The graders are instructed to grade only the first two items even if a student writes a longer list. Thus, if two items are requested, and a student lists six items of which the first two are incorrect, no points will be given even if the last four of the six answers were correct. Always give your best answer first in a list.

- ***Do not use clichés.*** Avoid answers like "there is no 'away' in pollution" or "not in my backyard." Instead, you should scientifically explain your answer to get the points for the question.

- ***Be concise, but not too concise.*** Do not tell the reader everything you know related to a topic with the hope that some part will be the right response. Make sure you are only answering what is asked for so you do not waste valuable time that could be used on other essays. That being said, you need to provide sufficient detail to demonstrate your understanding about the particular question. Students often err on the side of brevity.

- ***Answer the question that you were asked.*** Do not reformulate the question into one for which you happen to know the answer. Sometimes, in an effort to fill space, students will launch into a dissertation that is not relevant to the question that was asked. Don't waste valuable time writing about all the things you know on another topic that is not related to the question.

- ***Strike out to save time.*** If you make a mistake, don't waste valuable time and lose your momentum on a question by attempting to completely obliterate or erase your work; cross or strike out your original answer with a single line or an "X" and keep moving forward.

- ***Label your answers.*** Be sure there is no doubt where your answer is. All questions have very specific parts such as (a), (b), (c), and (i), (ii), (iii). This will also help you ensure that you have finished answering the question and can move on or come back as needed.

- ***Do not restate the question.*** Restating the question in your answer is a waste of time. You also do not need to have any introduction or conclusion parts to your essay. Remember—you cannot win over your reader. The exam reader is simply looking for correct statements that demonstrate your knowledge of the concept.

- ***A picture is worth 1,000 words—only if they ask for it.*** Draw a picture or diagram **only** if it is specifically asked for in the question.

- ***Neatness counts.*** Messy or illegible writing is very difficult to grade. You do not want to make it hard for your exam reader to award you points on your essay. It is **always best** if the reader can easily find and read your answers for each essay question. If they cannot decipher your handwriting, then awarding points is more difficult. Practice your handwriting regularly. If you aren't used to writing for extended periods of time, your hand can get tired, and the handwriting deteriorates. It shows in test booklets as the last written FRQ responses become illegible. Also, practice writing in pen; the free-response questions require answers be written in pen, not pencil.

- ***Math-based free-response questions.*** When asked to do calculations, **show your work**. You normally need to show your work and **label units** to receive credit on math questions. Also, if you have no idea how to do the calculations portion of the free response, **keep reading!** A math-based free-response question almost always contains a part in the question that you could answer without the calculations being done. Make sure all of your work and answers are in your pink answer booklet!

- ***Practice your math!*** Every AP® Environmental Science student should be comfortable working with metric prefixes, decimals, percentages, fractions, algebra, exponents, and scientific notation.

- ***Graphing data.*** If you are asked to construct a graph of specific data, you must make sure that (1) the independent variable is on the *x*-axis and the dependent variable is on the *y*-axis, (2) both axes are labeled with a name and units of measurement, (3) both axes are numbered in consistent increments, (4) you use the correct type of graph for the data, and (5) you plot your data as accurately as possible. A rule of thumb is to use a bar graph to illustrate data that contain words and numbers and a line graph to illustrate data that consists of one set of measurements that depends on another set of measurements.

About the Authors

G. TYLER MILLER

G. Tyler Miller has written 62 textbooks for introductory courses in environmental science, basic ecology, energy, and environmental chemistry. Since 1975, Miller's books have been the most widely used textbooks for environmental science in the United States and throughout the world. They have been used by almost 3 million students and have been translated into eight languages.

Miller has a professional background in chemistry, physics, and ecology. He has a PhD from the University of Virginia and has received two honorary doctoral degrees for his contributions to environmental education. He taught college for 20 years, developed one of the nation's first environmental studies programs, and developed an innovative interdisciplinary undergraduate science program before deciding to write environmental science textbooks full time in 1975. Currently, he is the president of Earth Education and Research, devoted to improving environmental education.

He describes his hopes for the future as follows:

If I had to pick a time to be alive, it would be the next 75 years. Why? First, there is overwhelming scientific evidence that we are in the process of seriously degrading our own life-support system. In other words, we are living unsustainably. Second, within your lifetime we have the opportunity to learn how to live more sustainably by working with the rest of nature, as described in this book.

I am fortunate to have three smart, talented, and wonderful sons—Greg, David, and Bill. I am especially privileged to have Kathleen as my wife, best friend, and research associate. It is inspiring to have a brilliant, beautiful (inside and out), and strong woman who cares deeply about nature as a lifemate. She is my hero. I dedicate this book to her and to the earth.

SCOTT E. SPOOLMAN

Scott Spoolman is a writer with more than 30 years of experience in educational publishing. He has worked with Tyler Miller since 2003 as coauthor of *Living in the Environment, Environmental Science,* and *Sustaining the Earth.* With Norman Myers, he coauthored *Environmental Issues and Solutions: A Modular Approach.*

Spoolman holds a master's degree in science journalism from the University of Minnesota. He has authored numerous articles in the fields of science, environmental engineering, politics, and business. He worked as an acquisitions editor on a series of college forestry textbooks. He has also worked as a consulting editor in the development of over 70 college and high school textbooks in fields of the natural and social sciences.

In his free time, he enjoys exploring the forests and waters of his native Wisconsin along with his family—his wife, environmental educator Gail Martinelli, and his son Will and daughter Katie.

Spoolman has the following to say about his collaboration with Tyler Miller.

I am honored to be working with Tyler Miller as a coauthor to continue the Miller tradition of thorough, clear, and engaging writing about the vast and complex field of environmental science. I share Tyler Miller's passion for ensuring that these textbooks and their multimedia supplements will be valuable tools for students and instructors. To that end, we strive to introduce this interdisciplinary field in ways that will be informative and sobering, but also tantalizing and motivational.

If the flip side of any problem is indeed an opportunity, then this truly is one of the most exciting times in history for students to start an environmental career. Environmental problems are numerous, serious, and daunting, but their possible solutions generate exciting new career opportunities. We place high priorities on inspiring students with these possibilities, challenging them to maintain a scientific focus, pointing them toward rewarding and fulfilling careers, and in doing so, working to help sustain life on the earth.

My Environmental Journey—*G. Tyler Miller*

My environmental journey began in 1966 when I heard a lecture on population and pollution problems by Dean Cowie, a biophysicist with the U.S. Geological Survey. It changed my life. I told him that if even half of what he said was valid, I would feel ethically obligated to spend the rest of my career teaching and writing to help students learn about the basics of environmental science. After spending 6 months studying the environmental literature, I concluded that he had greatly underestimated the seriousness of these problems.

I developed an undergraduate environmental studies program and in 1971 published my first introductory environmental science book, an interdisciplinary study of the connections between energy laws (thermodynamics), chemistry, and ecology. In 1975 I published the first edition of *Living in the Environment*. Since then, I have completed multiple editions of this textbook, and of three others derived from it, along with other books.

Beginning in 1985, I spent 10 years in the deep woods living in an adapted school bus that I used as an environmental science laboratory and writing environmental science textbooks. I evaluated the use of passive solar energy design to heat the structure; buried earth tubes to bring in air cooled by the earth (geothermal cooling) at a cost of about $1 per summer; set up active and passive systems to provide hot water; installed an energy-efficient instant hot water heater powered by liquefied petroleum gas (LPG); installed energy-efficient windows and appliances and a composting (waterless) toilet; employed biological pest control; composted food wastes; used natural planting (no grass or lawnmowers); gardened organically; and experimented with a host of other potential solutions to major environmental problems that we face.

I also used this time to learn and think about how nature works by studying the plants and animals around me. My experience from living in nature is reflected in much of the material in this book. It also helped me to develop the six simple **principles of sustainability** that serve as the integrating theme for this textbook and to apply these principles to living my life more sustainably.

I came out of the woods in 1995 to learn about how to live more sustainably in an urban setting where most people live. Since then, I have lived in two urban villages, one in a small town and one within a large metropolitan area.

Since 1970, my goal has been to use a car as little as possible. Since I work at home, I have a "low-pollute commute" from my bedroom to a chair and a laptop computer. I usually take one airplane trip a year to visit my sister and my publisher.

As you will learn in this book, life involves a series of environmental trade-offs. Like most people, I still have a large environmental impact, but I continue to struggle to reduce it. I hope you will join me in striving to live more sustainably and sharing what you learn with others. It is not always easy, but it sure is fun.

Cengage Learning's Commitment to Sustainable Practices

We the authors of this textbook and Cengage Learning, the publisher, are committed to making the publishing process as sustainable as possible. This involves four basic strategies:

- *Using sustainably produced paper.* The book publishing industry is committed to increasing the use of recycled fibers, and Cengage Learning is always looking for ways to increase this content. Cengage Learning works with paper suppliers to maximize the use of paper that contains only wood fibers that are certified as sustainably produced, from the growing and cutting of trees all the way through paper production.

- *Reducing resources used per book.* The publisher has an ongoing program to reduce the amount of wood pulp, virgin fibers, and other materials that go into each sheet of paper used. New, specially designed printing presses also reduce the amount of scrap paper produced per book.

- *Recycling.* Printers recycle the scrap paper that is produced as part of the printing process. Cengage Learning also recycles waste cardboard from shipping cartons, along with other materials used in the publishing process.

- *Process improvements.* In years past, publishing has involved using a great deal of paper and ink for the writing and editing of manuscripts, copyediting, reviewing page proofs, and creating illustrations. Almost all of these materials are now saved through the use of electronic files. Very little paper and ink were used in the preparation of this textbook.

The Environment and Sustainability

No civilization has survived the ongoing destruction of its natural support system. Nor will ours.

LESTER R. BROWN

Key Questions

1.1 What are some key principles of sustainability?

1.2 How are our ecological footprints affecting the earth?

1.3 Why do we have environmental problems?

1.4 What is the role of economics?

1.5 What is the role of government?

1.6 What is an environmentally sustainable society?

Forests such as this one in California's Sequoia National Park help to sustain all life and economies.

Robert Harding World Imagery/Alamy

3

The Tragedy of the Commons

Sustainability is the capacity of the earth's natural systems that support life and human social systems to survive or adapt to changing environmental conditions indefinitely. Sustainability is the big idea and the integrating theme of this book.

Some of the resources we use are renewable and can be used on a sustainable basis repeatedly. Examples are the air in atmosphere and the fishes of the sea.

We are alive because natural processes purify the earth's air as long as we do not add pollutants to the air faster than the earth's natural processes can dilute or remove them. Populations of commercially valuable fish species such as Atlantic cod are renewable and sustainable as long as we do not remove them faster than the remaining fish can reproduce and replenish the population.

Both of these renewable resources are not owned by anyone and can be used by almost anyone. Air pollution and depletion of Atlantic cod can occur when each user of these open-access renewable resources reasons, "The little bit of pollution that I add to the air or the number of Atlantic cod that I catch in my fishing boat is not enough to matter, and anyway, they are renewable resources."

When the level of use is small, this logic works. Eventually, however, the cumulative effect of large numbers of people trying to exploit a readily available renewable resource can degrade it and eventually exhaust or ruin it. Then no one benefits and everyone loses. Biologist Garrett Hardin called such degradation of open-access renewable resources *the tragedy of the commons*.

For centuries, commercial fishing boats have been removing Atlantic cod from the fishing grounds off the coast of Newfoundland. However, in the 1960s and 1970s advances in commercial fishing technology greatly increased catches of the cod. By the 1990s, populations of Atlantic cod were so low that the Grand Banks fishing industry collapsed (Figure 1.1). This put at least 35,000 fishers and fish processors out of work in more than 500 coastal communities. Since then, Atlantic cod populations have remained low, and some scientists doubt that the fishery will ever recover.

The air, water, topsoil, and living species that make up the earth's life-support system are open-access renewable resources that are subject to the tragedy of the commons. As the human population grows and uses more of the earth's resources, there is growing concern that we can degrade the planet's life-support system for us and other species. This would be the ultimate tragedy of the commons.

In this book, you will learn how the earth's life-support system works, how we affecting this system, and how we can avoid the ultimate tragedy of the commons by learning how to live more sustainably on the planet that is our only home. ●

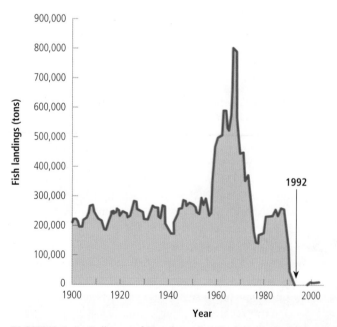

FIGURE 1.1 Collapse of Newfoundland's Atlantic cod fishery. ***Data analysis:*** By roughly what percentage did the catch of Atlantic cod drop between the peak catch in 1960 and 1970? (Compiled by the authors using data from Millennium Ecosystem Assessment.)

WHAT ARE SOME KEY PRINCIPLES OF SUSTAINABILITY?

CONCEPT 1.1A Life on the earth has been sustained for billions of years by solar energy, biodiversity, and chemical cycling.

CONCEPT 1.1B Our lives and economies depend on energy from the sun and on natural resources and ecosystem services (*natural capital*) provided by the earth.

CONCEPT 1.1C We could live more sustainably by following six principles of sustainability.

Environmental Science is a Study of Connections in Nature

The **environment** is everything around you. It includes all the living things (such as plants and animals) and the nonliving things (such as air, water, and sunlight) with which you interact. You are part of nature and live in the environment. Despite humankind's many scientific and technological advances, our lives depend on sunlight and on the earth for clean air and water, food, shelter, energy, fertile soil, a livable climate, and other components of the planet's *life-support system*.

Environmental science is a study of connections in nature. It is an interdisciplinary study of **(1)** how the earth (nature) works and has survived and thrived, **(2)** how humans interact with the environment, and **(3)** how we can live more sustainably. It strives to answer several questions: What environmental problems do we face? How serious are they? How do they interact? What are their causes? How has nature solved such problems? How can we use our understanding of nature to solve such problems? To answer such questions, environmental science integrates information and ideas from fields such as biology, chemistry, geology, engineering, geography, economics, political science, and ethics.

A key component of environmental science is **ecology**, the branch of biology that focuses on how living organisms interact with the living and nonliving parts of their environment. Each of the earth's organisms belongs to a **species**, or a group of organisms having a unique set of characteristics that set it apart from other groups.

A major focus of ecology is the study of ecosystems. An **ecosystem** is a set of organisms within a defined area of land or volume of water that interact with one another and with their environment of nonliving matter and energy. For example, a forest ecosystem consists of plants (especially trees; see chapter-opening photo), animals, and other organisms that decompose organic materials. These organisms interact with one another, with solar energy, and with the chemicals in the forest's air, water, and soil. These ecological interactions take place in the **biosphere**—the parts of the earth's air, water, and soil where life is found.

Environmental science and ecology should not be confused with **environmentalism** or **environmental activism**, which is a social movement dedicated to protecting the earth's life and its resources. Environmentalism is practiced more in the realms of politics and ethics than in science. However, the findings of environmental scientists can sometimes provide evidence to back the claims and activities of environmentalists.

Learning from the Earth: Three Scientific Principles of Sustainability

The earth is the best example that we have of a sustainable system. Life on the earth has existed for around 3.8 billion years. During this time, the planet has experienced several catastrophic environmental changes. They include gigantic meteorite impacts, ice ages lasting millions of years, long warming periods that melted land-based ice and raised sea levels by hundreds of feet, and five mass extinctions—each wiping out more 60% to 95% of the world's species. Despite these dramatic environmental changes, an astonishing variety of life has survived.

Our study of the history of life on the earth indicates that three scientific factors play key roles in the long-term sustainability of the earth's life, as summarized below and in Figure 1.2 (**Concept 1.1A**). Understanding these three **scientific principles of sustainability**, or major *lessons from nature*, can help us move toward a more sustainable future.

- **Dependence on solar energy**: The sun's energy warms the planet and provides energy that plants use to produce **nutrients**, the chemicals that plants and animals need to survive.

- **Biodiversity**: The variety of genes, species, ecosystems, and ecosystem processes are referred to as **biodiversity** (short for *biological diversity*). Interactions among species provide vital ecosystem services and keep any population from growing too large. Biodiversity also provides ways for species to adapt to changing environmental conditions and replace species wiped out by catastrophic environmental changes with new species.

- **Chemical cycling**: The circulation of chemicals or nutrients needed to sustain life from the environment (mostly from soil and water) through various organisms and back to the environment is called **chemical cycling**, or **nutrient cycling**. The earth receives a continuous supply of energy from the sun, but it receives no new supplies of life-supporting chemicals. Through billions of years of interactions with their

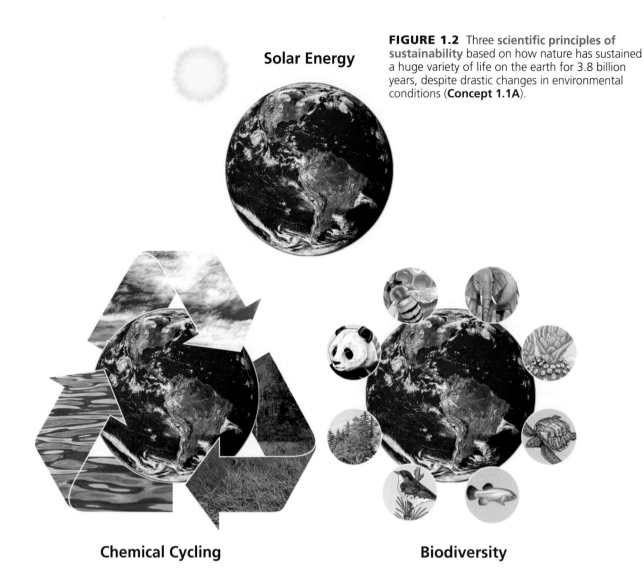

Solar Energy

Chemical Cycling

Biodiversity

FIGURE 1.2 Three **scientific principles of sustainability** based on how nature has sustained a huge variety of life on the earth for 3.8 billion years, despite drastic changes in environmental conditions (**Concept 1.1A**).

living and nonliving environment, organisms have developed ways to continually recycle the chemicals they need to survive. This means that the wastes and decayed bodies of organisms become nutrients or raw materials for other organisms. In nature,

waste = useful resources.

Key Components of Sustainability

Sustainability, the integrating theme of this book, has several key components that we use as subthemes. One is **natural capital**—the natural resources and ecosystem services that keep humans and other species alive and that support human economies (Figure 1.3).

Natural resources are materials and energy provided by nature that are essential or useful to humans. They fall into three categories: *inexhaustible resources, renewable resources,* and *nonrenewable (exhaustible) resources* (Figure 1.4). Solar energy is viewed as an **inexhaustible**

or **perpetual resource** because it is expected to last for at least 5 billion years until the death of the star we call the sun. A **renewable resource** is any resource that can be replenished by natural processes within hours to decades, as long as people do not use the resource faster than natural processes can replace it. Examples include forests, grasslands, fertile topsoil, fishes, clean air, and fresh water. The highest rate at which people can use a renewable resource indefinitely without reducing its available supply is called its **sustainable yield**.

Nonrenewable or **exhaustible resources** exist in a fixed amount, or *stock*, in the earth's crust. They take millions to billions of years to form through geological processes. On the much shorter human time scale, we can use these resources faster than nature can replace them. Examples of nonrenewable resources include fossil fuel energy resources (such as oil, coal, and natural gas), metallic mineral resources (such as copper and aluminum), and nonmetallic mineral resources (such as salt and

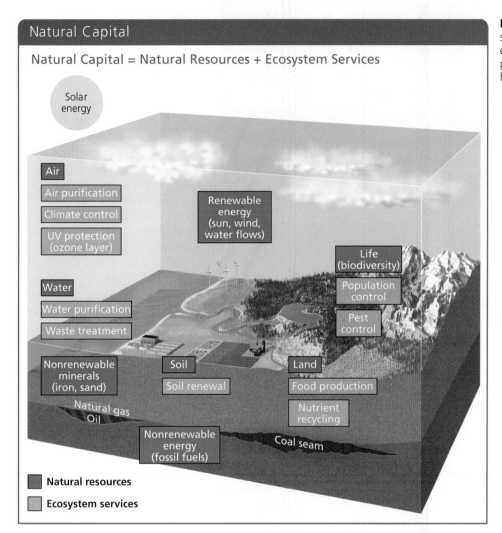

Natural Capital

Natural Capital = Natural Resources + Ecosystem Services

Solar energy

Air
- Air purification
- Climate control
- UV protection (ozone layer)

Renewable energy (sun, wind, water flows)

Life (biodiversity)
- Population control
- Pest control

Water
- Water purification
- Waste treatment

Nonrenewable minerals (iron, sand)

Soil
- Soil renewal

Land
- Food production
- Nutrient recycling

Natural gas
Oil

Nonrenewable energy (fossil fuels)

Coal seam

■ Natural resources
□ Ecosystem services

FIGURE 1.3 Natural capital consists of natural resources (blue) and ecosystem services (orange) that support and sustain the earth's life and human economies (**Concept 1.1B**).

Inexhaustible
Solar energy
Wind energy
Geothermal energy

Renewable
Trees
Topsoil
Freshwater

Nonrenewable (Exhaustible)
Fossil fuels (oil, natural gas, coal)
Iron and copper

FIGURE 1.4 We depend on a combination of inexhaustible, renewable, and exhaustible (nonrenewable) natural resources.

A vital ecosystem service is **nutrient cycling**, which is a **scientific principle of sustainability**. For example, without nutrient cycling in topsoil there would be no land plants, and no humans or other land animals. This would also disrupt the ecosystem services that purify air and water.

A second component of sustainability—and another subtheme of this text—is that human activities can *degrade natural capital*. We do this by using renewable resources faster than nature can restore them, for example, by depleting fisheries faster than the fish can reproduce or by overloading the earth's normally renewable air, water, and soil with pollution and wastes. These are both examples of the tragedy of the commons (**Core Case Study**). People in many parts of the world are replacing forests with crop plantations (Figure 1.5) that require large inputs of energy, water, fertilizer, and pesticides. We also add pollutants to the air and dump chemicals and wastes into rivers, lakes, and oceans faster than they can be cleansed through natural processes. Many of the plastics and other synthetic materials people use poison wildlife and disrupt nutrient cycles because they cannot be broken down and used as nutrients by other organisms.

FIGURE 1.5 Small remaining area of once diverse Amazon rainforest surrounded by vast soybean fields in the Brazilian state of Mato Grosso.

John Lee/Aurora Photos

sand). As we deplete nonrenewable resources, sometimes we can find substitutes.

Ecosystem services are natural services provided by healthy ecosystems that support life and human economies at no monetary cost to us (Figure 1.3). For example, forests help purify air and water, reduce soil erosion, regulate climate, and recycle nutrients. Thus, our lives and economies are sustained by energy from the sun and by natural resources and ecosystem services (natural capital) provided by the earth (**Concept 1.1B**).

This leads us to a third component of sustainability: creating *solutions* to the environmental problems we face. For example, a solution to the loss of forests (see chapter-opening photo) is to stop burning or cutting down mature forests. This cannot be done unless governments and citizens are aware of the ecosystem services forests provide and citizens pressure governments to pass laws to protect mature forests. Overfishing might be reduced by instituting fishing quotas or by issuing permits limiting the number of fish that can be taken by commercial fishing fleets so that fisheries have a chance to recover.

Conflicts can arise when environmental protection has a negative economic effect on groups of people or certain industries. Dealing with such conflicts often involves both sides making compromises or *trade-offs*. For example, a timber company might be persuaded to plant and harvest trees in an area that it had already cleared or degraded instead of clearing an undisturbed mature forest area. In return, the government may subsidize (pay part of the cost) of planting the new trees.

Each of us can play an important role in learning how to live more sustainably. Thus, *individuals matter*—another sustainability subtheme of this book.

Three Additional Principles of Sustainability

Economics, politics, and ethics can provide us with three additional **principles of sustainability** (Figure 1.6):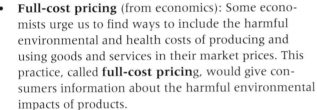

- **Full-cost pricing** (from economics): Some economists urge us to find ways to include the harmful environmental and health costs of producing and using goods and services in their market prices. This practice, called **full-cost pricing**, would give consumers information about the harmful environmental impacts of products.

- **Win-win solutions** (from political science): Political scientists often look for *win-win solutions* to environmental problems based on cooperation and compromise that will benefit the largest number of people as well as the environment.

- **Responsibility to future generations** (from ethics): Ethics is a branch of philosophy devoted to studying ideas about what is right or wrong. According to environmental ethicists, we should leave the planet's life-support systems in a condition that is as good as or better than it is now as our responsibility to future generations.

These six **principles of sustainability** (see inside back cover) can serve as guidelines to help us move toward a future that is more sustainable ecologically, economically, and socially.

Countries Differ in Their Resource Use and Environmental Impact

The United Nations (UN) classifies the world's countries (See Supplement 5, Figure 1, pp. S8-S9 for a map of the world's countries and Supplement 5, Figure 4, pp. S14 for a map of U.S. states) as economically more developed or less developed, based primarily on their average income per person (See Supplement 5, Figure 5, p. S15 for a map of counties based on their gross national incomes). **More-developed countries**—industrialized nations with high average incomes per person—include the United States, Japan, Canada, Australia, Germany, and most other European countries. These countries, with 17% of the world's population use about 70% of the earth's natural resources. The United States, with only 4.3% of the world's population, uses about 30% of the world's resources.

All other nations are classified as **less-developed countries**, most of them in Africa, Asia, and Latin America. Some are *middle-income, moderately developed countries* such as China, India, Brazil, Thailand, and Mexico. Others are *low-income, least-developed countries* including Nigeria, Bangladesh, Congo, and Haiti. The less-developed countries, with 83% of the world's population, use about 30% of the world's natural resources.

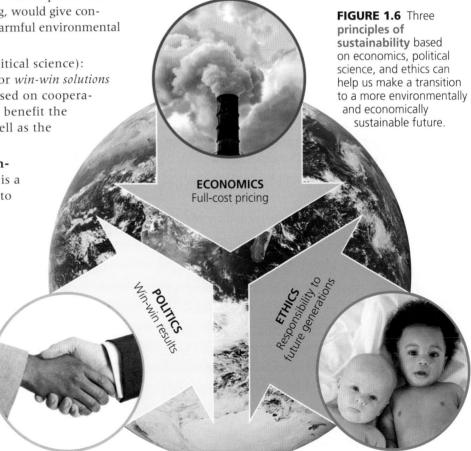

FIGURE 1.6 Three **principles of sustainability** based on economics, political science, and ethics can help us make a transition to a more environmentally and economically sustainable future.

ECONOMICS
Full-cost pricing

POLITICS
Win-win results

ETHICS
Responsibility to future generations

Janine Benyus: Learning from the Earth About Living More Sustainability

ecowatch.com

Biologist Janine Benyus has had a lifelong interest in learning how nature works and how to live more sustainably. In 1997, she coined the term **biomimicry**—the scientific effort to understand, mimic, and catalog the ingenious ways in which nature has sustained life on the earth for 3.8 billion years. She realized that 99% of the species that have lived on the earth became extinct because they could not adapt to changing environmental conditions. She views the surviving species as examples of *natural genius* that we can learn from.

Benyus says that when we need to solve a problem or design a product, we should ask: Has nature done this and how did it do it? We should also think about what nature does not do as a clue to what we should not do, she argues. For example, nature does not produce waste materials or chemicals that cannot be broken down and recycled.

Benyus has set up the nonprofit Biomimicry Institute that has developed a curriculum for K-12 and university students and has a two-year program to train biomimicry professionals. She has also established a network called Biomimicry 3.8, named for the 3.8 billion years during which organisms have developed their genius for surviving. It is a network of scientists, engineers, architects, and designers who share examples of successful biomimicry through an online database called AskNature.org.

Since 1997, Benyus and others working in the field of biomimicry have identified several principles that have sustained life on the earth for billions of years. They have found that life:

- Runs on sunlight, not fossil fuels
- Does not waste energy
- Uses only what it needs
- Adapts to changing environmental conditions
- Depends on biodiversity for population control and adaptation
- Creates no waste because the matter outputs of one organism are resources for other organisms
- Does not pollute its own environment
- Does not produce chemicals that cannot be recycled by the earth's chemical cycles.

By learning from nature and using such principles, innovative scientists, engineers, and business people are creating life-friendly goods and services and profitable businesses that could enrich and sustain life far into the future.

CHECKPOINT FOR UNDERSTANDING 1.1

1. Explain why chemical (nutrient) cycling is essential for maintaining life on earth.

2. Explain why biodiversity is important to ecosystem sustainability.

3. Discuss how our economy is related to ecosystem services.

4. Give an example of each type of resource: inexhaustible (perpetual), renewable, and nonrenewable. Under what circumstances might a renewable resource become nonrenewable?

5. Identify several human or social factors that can enhance sustainability.

1.2 HOW ARE OUR ECOLOGICAL FOOTPRINTS AFFECTING THE EARTH?

CONCEPT 1.2A Humans dominate the earth with the power to sustain, add to, or degrade the natural capital that supports all life and human economies.

CONCEPT 1.2B As our ecological footprints grow, we deplete and degrade more of the earth's natural capital that sustains us and our economies.

Good News: Many People Have a Better Quality of Life

As the world's dominant animal, we have an awesome power to degrade or sustain the life-support system for our own and other species. We decide whether forests are preserved or cut down and engineer the flows of rivers. Our activities affect the temperature of the atmosphere and the temperature and the acidity of the ocean. We also contribute to the extinction of species. At the same time, our creativity, economic growth, scientific research, grassroots political pressure by citizens, and regulatory laws have improved the quality of life for many of the earth's people, especially in the United States and in most other more-developed countries.

We have developed an astounding array of useful materials and products. We have learned how to use wood, fossil fuels, the sun, wind, flowing water, the nuclei of certain atoms, and the earth's heat (geothermal energy) to supply us with enormous amounts of energy. We have created artificial environments in the form of buildings and cities. We have invented computers to extend our brains, robots to do work for us, and electronic networks to enable instantaneous global communication.

Globally, lifespans are increasing, infant mortality is decreasing, education is on the rise, some diseases are being conquered, and the population growth rate has slowed. While one out of seven people live in extreme poverty, we have witnessed the greatest reduction in poverty in human history. The food supply is generally more abundant and safer, air and water are getting cleaner in many parts of the world, and exposure to toxic chemicals is more avoidable. We have protected some endangered species and ecosystems and restored some grasslands and wetlands, and forests are growing back in some areas that we cleared.

Scientific research and technological advances financed by affluence helped achieve these improvements in life and environmental quality. Education also spurred many citizens who insist that businesses and governments work toward improving environmental quality. We are a globally connected species with growing access to information and technologies that could help us to shift to a more sustainable path.

Bad News: We Are Living Unsustainably

According to a large body of scientific evidence, we are living unsustainably. We waste, deplete, and degrade much of the earth's life-sustaining natural capital—a process known as **environmental degradation**, or **natural capital degradation** (Figure 1.7).

Research reveals that human activities directly affect about 83% of the earth's land surface (excluding Antarctica) (Figure 1.8). This land is used for things such as growing crops, grazing livestock, harvesting timber, mining, burying wastes, towns and cities (urban land), and recreation such as hiking and skiing.

In parts of the world, we are destroying forests and grasslands, withdrawing water from some rivers and underground aquifers faster than nature replenishes them, and harvesting many fish species faster than they can be renewed. We also litter the land and oceans with wastes faster than they can be recycled by the earth's natural chemical cycles. In addition, we add pollutants to the air (including some that are altering the earth's climate), soil, underground aquifers, rivers, lakes, and oceans.

In many parts of the world, renewable forests are shrinking (Figure 1.5), deserts are expanding, and topsoil is eroding. The lower atmosphere is warming, floating ice and many glaciers are melting at unexpected rates, sea levels are rising, and ocean acidity is increasing. There are more intense floods, droughts, severe weather, and forest fires in many areas. In a number of regions, rivers are running dry, harvests of many species of fish are dropping sharply (Figure 1.1), and 20% of the world's species-rich coral reefs are gone and others are threatened. Species are becoming extinct at least 100 times faster than in prehuman times. In

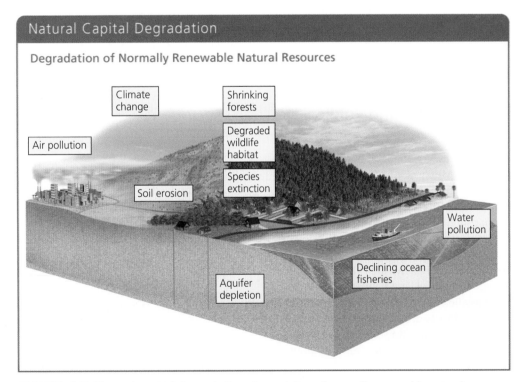

FIGURE 1.7 Natural capital degradation: Degradation of normally renewable natural resources and natural services (Figure 1.3), mostly from population growth and increased resource use per person.

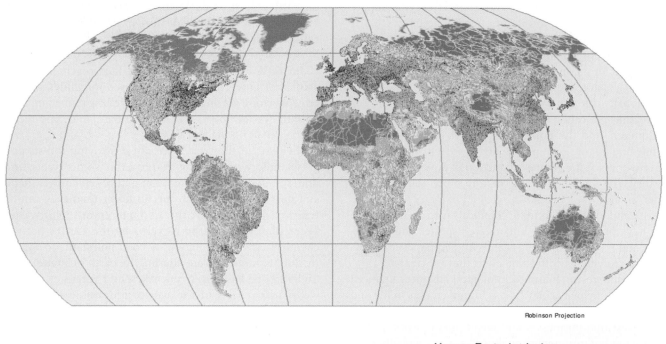

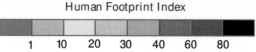

Human Footprint Index

| 1 | 10 | 20 | 30 | 40 | 60 | 80 |

Robinson Projection

Publish Date: 03/07/08

FIGURE 1.8 Natural capital use and degradation: The human ecological footprint has an impact on about 83% of the earth's total land surface. The Human Foot Index indicates the percentage of human influence throughout the earth on a scale of 1 (low impact) to 100 (high impact). See Supplement 5, Figure 6, p. S16 for a map of the ecological footprints for North America.

addition, extinction rates are projected to increase at least another 100-fold during this century, creating a sixth mass extinction caused by human activities.

Human Land Use: Private and Public Land

Humans use, and in some cases, degrade about 83% of the earth's land (Figure 1.8). Much of this land use benefits humans. However, land use by humans can also have harmful environmental effects. Examples are forest loss, overgrazing of grassland, soil erosion, runoff of fertilizers and pesticides from cropland, oil spills from oil wells, large pits created by mining, removal of mountaintops to extract coal, and loss of wildlife habitat. Indeed, the biggest threat to the earth's biodiversity of species is loss and fragmentation of land habitats.

Lands are often classified according to their use as private and public. **Private lands** are owned by individuals or business. Owners use them for purposes such growing crops, grazing livestock, harvesting timber, mining, housing, and other buildings.

Public lands are typically owned jointly by the citizens of a country but are managed by the government. In the United States, the federal government owns and

manages about 28% of the country's land. This includes 47% of the land in the western United States and 61% of the land in Alaska.

Federal public lands in the United States include the:

- *National Park System* managed by the National Park Service (NPS]

- *Nation Forest System* managed by the US Forest Service (USFS)

- Land managed by the Bureau of Land Management (BLM)

- *National Wildlife Refuges* managed by the US Fish and Wildlife Service

- *National Wilderness Preservation System* consisting of designated areas in the above systems and managed by the government agencies in charge of those systems. These protected lands are open only for recreational activities such hiking, fishing, camping, sport fishing, and nonmotorized boating.

The use and harmful environmental effects of private and public land is discussed in 14 of the 20 chapters in this book. In other words, land use is a major theme that runs throughout most of this book.

Our Growing Ecological Footprints

Using renewable resources benefits us but can result in natural capital degradation (Figure 1.7), pollution, and wastes. This harmful environmental impact is called an **ecological footprint**—the amount of biologically productive land and water needed to supply a population in an area with renewable resources and to absorb and recycle the wastes and pollution such resource use produces (see Figure 1.8 and Supplement 5, Figure 6, p. S16).

This measure of sustainability evaluates the ability or **biocapacity** of the earth's productive ecosystems to regenerate the renewable resources used by a population, city, region, country, or the world in a given year. The **per capita ecological footprint** is the average ecological footprint of an individual in a given country or area.

The World Wide Fund for Nature (WWF) and the Global Footprint Network estimate that we would need 1.5 planet earths to sustain the world's 2012 rate of renewable resource use far into the future. In other words, the world's total ecological footprint in 2012 was 50% higher than the planet's estimated long-term biocapacity and has increased since 2012. This overdraft of the earth's natural resources and ecosystem services is being passed on to future generations.

1.5 Number of earths needed to sustain the world's 2012 rate of renewable resource use indefinitely

IPAT Is Another Environmental Impact Model

In the early 1970s, scientists Paul Ehrlich and John Holdren developed a simple environmental impact model. This IPAT model shows that the environmental impact **(I)** of human activities is the product three factors: *population size* **(P)**, *affluence* **(A)** or resource consumption per person, and the beneficial and harmful environmental effects of *technologies* **(T)**. The following equation summarizes this IPAT model:

Impact **(I)** = Population **(P)** × Affluence **(A)** × Technology **(T)**

While the ecological footprint model emphasizes the use of renewable resources, the IPAT model includes the environmental impact of using both renewable and nonrenewable resources.

The T factor can be harmful or beneficial. Some forms of technology such as polluting factories, gas-guzzling motor vehicles, and coal-burning power plants increase our harmful environmental impact by raising the T factor. For example, new fishing technology for harvesting large quantities of fish led to the collapse of the Atlantic cod fishery (Figure 1.1)—an example of the tragedy of the commons in action (**Core Case Study**).

Other technologies reduce our harmful environmental impact by decreasing the T factor. Examples are pollution control and prevention technologies, fuel-efficient cars, and wind turbines and solar cells that generate electricity with a low environmental impact.

In a less-developed country such as India, population size is a more important factor than resource use per person in determining the country's environmental impact. In a highly developed country such as the United States with a much smaller population, resource use per person and the ability to develop environmentally beneficial technologies play key roles in the country's environmental impact.

Cultural Changes Can Increase or Shrink Our Ecological Footprints

Until about 10,000 to 12,000 years ago, we were mostly *hunter–gatherers* who obtained food by hunting wild animals or scavenging their remains, and gathering wild plants. Our hunter–gatherer ancestors lived in small groups, consumed few resources, had few possessions, and moved as needed to find enough food to survive.

Since then, three major cultural changes have occurred. *First* was the *agricultural revolution*, which began around 10,000 years ago when humans learned how to grow and breed plants and animals for food, clothing, and other purposes and began living in villages instead of frequently moving to find food. They had a more reliable source of food, lived longer, and produced more children who survived to adulthood.

Second was the *industrial–medical revolution*, beginning about 300 years ago when people invented machines for the large-scale production of goods in factories. Many people moved from rural villages to cities to work in the factories. This shift involved learning how to get energy from fossil fuels (such as coal and oil) and how to grow large quantities of food in an efficient manner. It also included medical advances that allowed a growing number of people to have longer and healthier lives. *Third*, about 50 years ago the *information–globalization revolution* began when we developed new technologies for gaining rapid access to all kinds of information and resources on a global scale.

Each of these three cultural changes gave us more energy and new technologies with which to alter and control more of the planet's resources to meet our basic needs and increasing wants. They also allowed expansion of the human population, mostly because of larger food supplies and longer lifespans. In addition, these cultural changes resulted in greater resource use, pollution, and environmental degradation and allowed us to dominate the planet and expand our ecological footprints (Figure 1.8).

On the other hand, some technological leaps have enabled us to shrink our ecological footprints by reducing our use of energy and matter resources and our production of wastes and pollution.

Many environmental scientists and other analysts see such developments as evidence of an emerging fourth major cultural change: a **sustainability revolution**, in which we could learn to live more sustainably during this century. This involves not degrading or depleting the natural capital that supports all life and our economies and restoring natural capital (Figure 1.3) that we have degraded. Making this shift involves learning how nature has sustained life for over 3.8 billion years and using these lessons from nature to shrink our ecological footprints and grow our beneficial environmental impacts.

GOOD NEWS

CHECKPOINT FOR UNDERSTANDING 1.2

1. Sustainability can be exercised in the harvesting of many different natural resources. Describe how commercial fishing might harvest fish sustainably.

2. The ecological footprints of some countries exceed their biocapacity, while other countries have ecological reserves. Discuss why the United States is an ecological debtor country.

1.3 WHY DO WE HAVE ENVIRONMENTAL PROBLEMS?

CONCEPT 1.3A Basic causes of environmental problems are population growth, wasteful and unsustainable resource use, poverty, avoidance of full-cost pricing, increasing isolation from nature, and different environmental worldviews.

CONCEPT 1.3B Our environmental worldviews play a key role in determining whether we live unsustainably or more sustainably.

Basic Causes of Environmental Problems

To deal with the environmental problems we face we must understand their causes. According to a significant number of environmental and social scientists, the major causes of today's environmental problems are:

- population growth
- wasteful and unsustainable resource use
- poverty
- omission of the harmful environmental and health costs in market prices
- increasing isolation from nature
- competing environmental worldviews

Human Population Growth

Exponential growth occurs when a quantity increases at a fixed percentage per unit of time, such as 0.5% or 2% per year. Exponential growth starts slowly but after a few doublings it grows to enormous numbers because each doubling is twice the total of all earlier growth. When we plot the data for an exponentially growing quantity, we get a curve that looks like the letter J.

For an example of the awesome power of exponential growth, consider a simple form of bacterial reproduction in which one bacterium splits into two every 20 minutes. Starting with one bacterium, after 20 minutes, there would be two; after an hour, there would be eight; ten hours later, there would be more than 1,000, and after just 36 hours (assuming that nothing interfered with their reproduction), there would be enough bacteria to form a layer 0.3 meters (1 foot) deep over the entire earth's surface.

The human population has grown exponentially (Figure 1.9) to the current population of 7.5 billion people. In 2016, the rate of growth was 1.20%. Although this rate of growth seems small, it added 89.8 million people to the world's huge base of 7.5 billion people. By 2050, the world's population could reach 9.9 billion—an addition of 2.4 billion people. The human population is still growing rapidly but its annual rate of growth has generally dropped since the 1960s.

No one knows how many people the earth can support indefinitely. However, our large and expanding ecological footprints and the resulting widespread natural capital degradation are disturbing warning signs.

Some analysts call for us to reduce environmental degradation by slowing population growth and level it off at around 8 billion by 2050 instead of 9.9 billion. We examine ways to do this in Chapter 8.

Affluence and Unsustainable Resource Use

The lifestyles of the world's expanding population of consumers are built on growing affluence, or resource consumption per person, as more people earn higher incomes. As total resource consumption and average resource consumption per person increase, so does environmental degradation, wastes, and pollution from the increase in environmental footprints.

The effects can be dramatic. The WWF and the Global Footprint Network estimate that the United States, with only 4.3% of the world's population, is responsible for about 23% of the global environmental footprint. The average American consumes about 30 times the amount of resources that the average Indian consumes and 100 times the amount consumed by the average person in the world's poorest countries. The WWF has projected that we would need five planet earths if everyone used renewable resources at the same rate as the average American did in 2012. The earlier number of earths involved the world's average per capita use of renewable resources. This one assumes that everyone if the world has the same use of renewable resources as the average American had in 2012"

5 Number of earths needed to sustain the world's population at US average per capita resources consumption rates in 2012

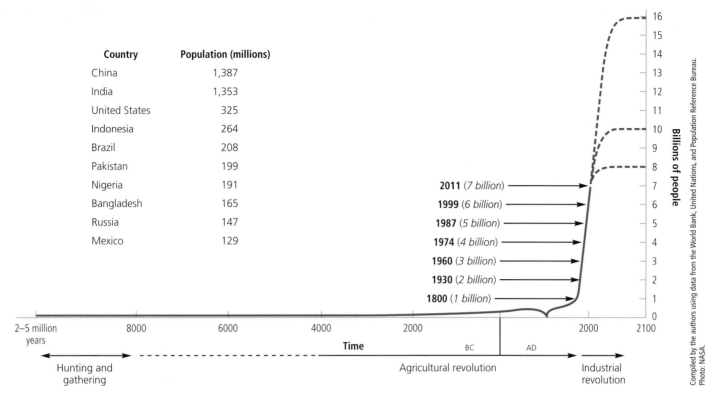

Country	Population (millions)
China	1,387
India	1,353
United States	325
Indonesia	264
Brazil	208
Pakistan	199
Nigeria	191
Bangladesh	165
Russia	147
Mexico	129

2011 (7 billion)
1999 (6 billion)
1987 (5 billion)
1974 (4 billion)
1960 (3 billion)
1930 (2 billion)
1800 (1 billion)

Billions of people

2–5 million years   8000   6000   4000   2000   2000   2100

Time   BC   AD

Hunting and gathering   Agricultural revolution   Industrial revolution

Compiled by the authors using data from the World Bank, United Nations, and Population Reference Bureau. Photo: NASA.

FIGURE 1.9 *Exponential growth*: The J-shaped curve represents past exponential world population growth, with projections to 2100 showing possible population stabilization as the J-shaped curve of growth changes to an S-shaped curve. The world's ten most populous countries in 2016 are shown to the left. ***Data Analysis:*** By what percentage did the world's population increase between 1960 and 2016? (This figure is not to scale.)

On the other hand, affluence can allow for widespread and better education that can lead people to become more concerned about environmental quality. Affluence also makes more money available for developing technologies to reduce pollution, environmental degradation, and resource waste along with ways to increase our beneficial environmental impacts.

Poverty Can Have Harmful Environmental and Health Effects

Poverty is a condition in which people lack enough money to fulfill their basic needs for food, water, shelter, health care, and education. *Bad News*: According to the World Bank, about one of every three people, or 2.6 billion people, struggled to live on less than $3.10 a day in 2015. In addition, 1 billion people living in in *extreme poverty* struggled to live on the equivalent of less than $1.90 a day—less than what many people spend for a bottle of water or a cup of coffee. Could you do this?

The daily lives of the world's poorest people center on getting enough food, water, and cooking and heating fuel to survive. Typically, these individuals are too desperate for short-term survival to worry about long-term environmental quality or sustainability. Thus, they may be forced to degrade forests, topsoil, and grasslands, and deplete fisheries and wildlife populations to stay alive.

Poverty does not always lead to environmental degradation. Some of the poor increase their beneficial environmental impact by planting and nurturing trees and conserving the soil that they depend on as a part of their long-term survival strategy.

CONSIDER THIS . . .

CONNECTIONS Poverty and Population Growth

To many poor people, having more children is a matter of survival. Their children help them gather firewood, haul water, and tend crops and livestock. The children also help take care of their aging parents, most of whom do not have social security, health care, and retirement funds. This daily struggle for survival is largely why populations in some of the poorest countries continue to grow at high rates.

Environmental degradation can have severe health effects on the poor. One problem is life-threatening *malnutrition*, a lack of protein and other nutrients needed for good health (Figure 1.10). Another effect is illness caused by limited access to adequate sanitation facilities and clean drinking water. As a result, about one of every nine of the world's people get water for drinking, washing, and cooking from sources polluted by human and animal feces.

The World Health Organization (WHO) estimates that these factors—mostly related to poverty—cause premature

Exponential Growth and Doubling Time: The Rule of 70

One important characteristic of a population is change in population size. Scientists analyze fluctuating populations in order to understand the relationship between a population and its environment. When environmental conditions are favorable, a population can grow very rapidly.

Doubling time is the amount of time it takes for a population to double in size. When a population grows at its maximum rate, it demonstrates **exponential growth**.

FRQ Application

Changes to population size are the result of the number of births minus the number of deaths within a population per year. This is called the **percent annual natural increase**. Imagine that within a population of humans, there were 28 births per 1000 people (called the crude birth rate) and 17 deaths per 1000 people (called the crude death rate).

The percent annual natural increase for this population would be calculated as:

$$\frac{28 \text{ births} - 10 \text{ deaths}}{1000} \times 100 = 1.8\%$$

The **doubling time** of this population or of any exponentially growing quantity can be calculated by using the **rule of 70**.

$$\text{Doubling time in years} = \frac{70}{\text{percent annual natural increase}}$$

Using what we calculated for the above population, doubling time for this population would be:

$$\text{Doubling time in years} = \frac{70}{1.8} = 39 \text{ years}$$

The world's population is growing at about 1.2% per year. At this rate how long would it take to double the number of humans on earth?

$$\text{Doubling time in years} = \frac{70}{1.2} = 58 \text{ years}$$

death for about 7 million children under age of 5 each year. Some hopeful news is that this number of annual deaths is down from about 10 million in 1990. Even so, every day an average of at least 19,000 young children die prematurely from these causes. This is equivalent to *95 fully loaded 200-passenger airliners crashing every day with no survivors*. The news media rarely cover this ongoing human tragedy.

Ways to reduce to reduce poverty include:

- Reducing malnutrition and infectious diseases that kill millions of people
- Providing universal primary school education for all children and for the world's nearly 800 million illiterate adults
- Reducing population growth, by elevating the social and economic status of women, reducing poverty, and providing access to family planning
- Making small, low-interest loans (microloans) to poor people who want to increase their income (Figure 1.11)

CONSIDER THIS . . .

THINKING ABOUT The Poor, the Affluent, and Environmental Harm

Some see the rapid population growth in less-developed countries as the primary cause of our environmental problems. Others say that the high rate of resource use per person in more-developed countries is a more important factor. Which factor do you think is more important? Why?

Prices of Goods and Services Rarely Include Their Harmful Environmental and Health Costs

Another basic cause of environmental problems has to do with how the marketplace prices goods and services. Companies providing goods for consumers generally are not required to pay for most of the harmful environmental and health costs of supplying such goods. For example, timber companies pay the cost of clear-cutting forests but do not pay for the resulting environmental degradation and loss of wildlife habitat.

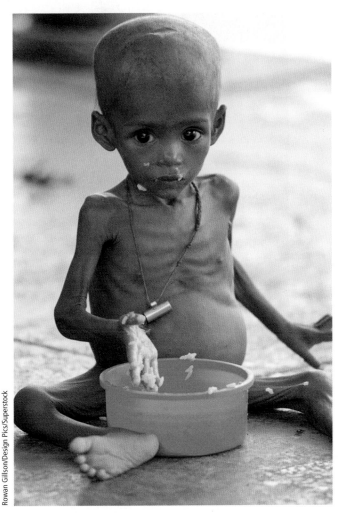

Rowan Gillson/Design Pics/Superstock

FIGURE 1.10 One of every three children younger than age 5 in less-developed countries, such as this starving child in Bangladesh, suffers from severe malnutrition caused by a lack of calories and protein.

©National Renewable Energy Laboratory

FIGURE 1.11 A microloan helped these women in a rural village in India to buy a small solar-cell panel (installed on the roof behind them) that provides electricity to help them make a living, thus applying the solar energy **principle of sustainability**.

CONSIDER THIS . . .

THINKING ABOUT Real Gasoline Prices
Suppose the price of gasoline included its harmful environment and health effects and costs $14 a gallon. How would this affect your decision on what type of car to buy or whether to go without a car and instead make greater use of walking, bicycling, and mass transit?

The primary goal of a company is to maximize profits for its owners or stockholders, so it is not inclined to add these costs to its prices voluntarily. Because the prices of goods and services do not include most of their harmful environmental and health costs, consumers have no effective way to know the harm caused by what they buy. This lack of information is a major reason for why we are degrading key components of our life-support system (Figure 1.7).

For example, producing and using gasoline results in air pollution and other problems that damage the environment and people's health. Scientists and economists have estimated that the price of gasoline to US consumers would rise by $3.18 per liter ($12 per gallon) if the estimated short- and long-term harmful environmental and health costs were included in its pump price. Thus, when gas costs $2 per gallon, US consumers are really paying about $14 per gallon. Consumers pay these hidden environmental and health costs, but not at the gas pump.

Isolation from Nature

Today, more than half of the world's people and three out of four people in more-developed countries live in urban areas. This shift from rural to urban living is continuing at a rapid pace. Urban environments and the increasing use of cell phones, computers, and other electronic devices are isolating people, especially children, from the natural world. Some argue that this has led to a phenomenon known as *nature deficit disorder*.

Children and adults can gain many benefits from outdoor activities. Research indicates that experiencing nature (see the chapter opening photo) can lead to better health, reduced stress, improved mental abilities, and increased imagination and creativity. It also can provide a sense of wonder and connection to the earth's life-support system that keeps us alive and supports our economies.

Differing Environmental Worldviews

One of the reasons why environmental problems persist is that people differ over the nature and seriousness of the world's environmental problems as well as how to solve them. These conflicts arise mostly because of differing environmental worldviews.

Your **environmental worldview** is the assumptions and beliefs that you have about how the natural world works and how you think you should interact with the environment. Your environmental worldview is determined partly by your **environmental ethics**—what you believe about what is right and what is wrong in your behavior toward the environment. For example, here are some important *ethical questions* relating to the environment:

- Why should we care about the environment?
- Are we the most important species on the planet or are we just another one of the earth's millions of forms of life?
- Do we have an obligation to see that our activities do not cause the extinction of other species? If so, should we try to protect all species or only some? How do we decide which to protect?
- Do we have an ethical obligation to pass the natural world on to future generations in a condition that is as good as or better than what we inherited?
- Should every person be entitled to equal protection from environmental hazards regardless of race, gender, age, national origin, income, social class, or any other factor?
- Should we seek to live more sustainably, and if so, how?

CONSIDER THIS . . .

THINKING ABOUT Our Responsibilities

How would you answer each of the questions above? Compare your answers with those of your classmates. Record your answers and, at the end of this course, return to these questions to see if your answers have changed.

Aldo Leopold (Figure 1.12)—wildlife manager, professor, writer, and conservationist—laid the groundwork for the field of environmental ethics through his writings, especially his 1949 book *A Sand County Almanac*. He argued that the role of the human species should be to protect nature, not conquer it.

People with different environmental worldviews can study the same data, be logically consistent in their analysis of those data, and arrive at quite different answers to such questions. This happens because they begin with different assumptions and values.

Revisiting the Tragedy of the Commons

The collapse of the Atlantic cod fishing industry in Newfoundland, Canada (**Core Case Study**) illustrates one of the causes of environmental problems. A growing population increases the consumption of fish, which puts pressure on the fishing industry to harvest increasingly larger fish catches. Rising affluence leads to increased resource use per person, which

FIGURE 1.12 Aldo Leopold (1887–1948) became a leading conservationist and his book, *A Sand County Almanac*, is considered an environmental classic that helped to inspire the modern conservation and environmental movements.

also promotes larger fish harvests. The resulting increase in industrialized commercial fishing can deplete populations of cod and other fish that some of the poor catch and eat in order to survive. The market prices of Atlantic cod and other fish do not include the harmful environmental and health effects of the industrialized fishing industry that uses large amounts of energy to catch and process fish, which adds pollutants to the air and water. Driving the Atlantic cod to commercial extinction also disrupts the aquatic ecosystem where it is found and affects other species that feed on the cod.

Because people are increasingly isolated from nature, they do not understand how the earth's life-support systems works and how it keeps them alive and supports the economies that provide them with goods and services, including Atlantic cod and other fish. Thus, there is little political pressure to regulate fishing industry catches to prevent the overfishing of commercially valuable fish species.

The predominant planetary management environmental worldview (Figure 1.A) is that we are in charge of nature and that nature exists primarily to meet our needs and wants. With this view, there is little pressure to develop regulations that could prevent the collapse of the Atlantic cod and other commercial fisheries by establishing sustainable harvest levels for each species.

One way to deal with the difficult problem of the tragedy of the commons is to use a shared or open-access renewable resource at a rate well below its estimated sustainable yield. Many coastal fishing communities have developed allotment and enforcement systems for controlling fish catches in which each fisher gets a share of the total allowable catch. This cooperative approach has sustained fisheries and fishing jobs in many communities for thousands of years. However, the rise of international

Environmental Worldviews

How do humans see themselves in relation to nature? The role of humans and how individuals believe the world works define a person's **environmental world view**. This view is also influenced by a person's **environmental ethics**—what one believes about what is right and what is wrong in our behavior toward the environment. Because of differing assumptions and values that individuals hold, there can be serious disagreement on environmental problems and possible solutions.

Most environmental worldviews are human-centered. They include **(1)** *planetary management* with humans managing nature mostly for their own benefit, **(2)** *stewardship* with humans managing nature for their benefit and for the rest of nature, **(3)** *environmental wisdom* based on learning how nature has sustained life for 3.8 billion years and integrating these lessons from nature into our actions (Figure 1.A).

FRQ Application

Question: Declining salmon fisheries are often the result of overfishing, pollution, and water-diversion projects that deprive fish populations of suitable habitat. This means less food for consumers and a loss of commercial fishing jobs. **Identify** each worldview position and discuss how each worldview would act to manage this problem.

Possible Response: (1) The Planetary Management worldview considers humans to be apart from and in charge of nature. People holding this viewpoint believe that whatever problems we may encounter, human ingenuity will ultimately solve them. Because we are the managers of the planet's resources, the solution to this problem might be to genetically engineer strains of salmon that grow more rapidly than wild strains, and to raise genetically modified salmon in energy-intensive fish farms.

(2) The Stewardship worldview believes that humans control nature, but have the duty to be responsible managers of nature and the resources it provides. A solution to this problem would be to protect salmon fisheries from pollution and diversion of river water and to establish fishing quotas so that salmon populations can recover each season.

(3) The Environmental Wisdom worldview relies on understanding how nature sustains itself and uses that knowledge to live more sustainably. Those who hold this view would recognize that salmon not only feed humans, but other predator species as well. Fishing would be kept at a minimum so that all species that depend on this resource could survive. Humans would not destroy salmon habitat. Edible parts of the salmon would be used for food and the remaining parts for fertilizer or feeding other animals.

Environmental Worldviews

Planetary Management
- We are apart from the rest of nature and can manage nature to meet our increasing needs and wants.
- Because of our ingenuity and technology, we will not run out of resources.
- The potential for economic growth is essentially unlimited.
- Our success depends on how well we manage the earth's life-support systems mostly for our benefit.

Stewardship
- We have an ethical responsibility to be caring managers, or stewards, of the earth.
- We will probably not run out of resources, but they should not be wasted.
- We should encourage environmentally beneficial forms of economic growth and discourage environmentally harmful forms.
- Our success depends on how well we manage the earth's life-support systems for our benefit and for the rest of nature.

Environmental Wisdom
- We are a part of and totally dependent on nature, and nature exists for all species.
- Resources are limited and should not be wasted.
- We should encourage earth-sustaining forms of economic growth and discourage earth-degrading forms.
- Our success depends on learning how nature sustains itself and integrating such lessons from nature into the ways we think and act.

FIGURE 1.A Comparison of Three Major Environmental Worldviews

industrialized fishing fleets has reduced the effectiveness of this approach. Today, some coastal fishing communities and the government work together to manage fisheries to prevent overfishing.

Another approach is to convert open-access renewable resources to private ownership. The reasoning is that if you own something, you are more likely to protect your investment. However, history shows that this does not necessarily happen. In addition, this approach is not possible for open-access resources such as the atmosphere, ocean fisheries, and our global life-support system, which cannot be divided up and sold as private property.

CHECKPOINT FOR UNDERSTANDING1.3

1. Explain why increasing population growth is an underlying factor for many environmental problems.

2. Describe the role of humans in the planetary management worldview. Explain how this compares to the role of humans in the stewardship and environmental wisdom worldviews.

1.4 WHAT IS THE ROLE OF ECONOMICS?

CONCEPT 1.4

CONCEPT 1.4A Ecological economists and most sustainability experts regard human economic systems as subsystems of the biosphere.

CONCEPT 1.4B We can use resources more sustainably by including the harmful environmental and health costs of producing goods and services in their market prices *(full-cost pricing)*, by subsidizing environmentally beneficial goods and services, taxing pollution and waste instead of wages and profits, and using environmental indicators.

Economic Systems Depend on Natural Capital

Economics is the social science that deals with the production, distribution, and consumption of goods and services to satisfy people's needs and wants. Most economic systems use three types of *capital*, or resources, to produce goods and services. **Natural capital** (Figure 1.3) includes resources and ecosystem services produced by the earth's natural processes that support all life and all economies. **Human capital** includes the physical and mental talents of the people who provide labor, organizational and management skills, and innovation. **Manufactured capital** includes the machinery, materials, and factories that people create using natural resources.

Economic growth is an increase in the capacity of a nation, state, city, or company to provide goods and services to people. Today, a typical industrialized country depends on a linear **high-throughput economy**, which attempts to boost economic growth by increasing the flow of matter and energy resources through the economic system to produce more goods and services (Figure 1.13). Such an economy produces valuable goods and services. However, it also converts large quantities of high-quality matter and energy resources into waste, pollution, and low-quality heat, which tend to flow into planetary *sinks* (air, water, soil, and organisms).

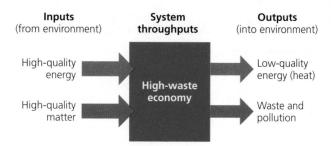

FIGURE 1.13 The *high-throughput economies* of most of the world's more-developed countries rely on continually increasing the flow of energy and matter resources to promote economic growth. *Critical Thinking:* What are three ways in which you regularly add to this throughput of matter and energy through your daily activities?

Ecological economists have a **biosphere-based model** for an economy. They view human economic systems as subsystems of the biosphere that depend heavily on the earth's irreplaceable natural resources and ecosystem services (Figure 1.14). (**Concept 1.4A**)

According to environmental economists and environmental scientists, the best long-term and more sustainable solution to our environmental and resource problems is to shift away from a linear, high-throughput (high-waste) economy based on ever-increasing matter and energy flow (Figure 1.13). The goal would be to shift to a more sustainable circular, **low-throughput (low-waste) economy** (Figure 1.15) over the next several decades.

A low-throughput economy works with nature by **(1)** reusing and recycling most nonrenewable matter resources; **(2)** using renewable resources no faster than natural processes can replenish them; **(3)** reducing resource waste by using matter and energy resources more efficiently; **(4)** reducing environmentally harmful forms of consumption; and **(5)** promoting pollution prevention and waste reduction.

Using Economic Tools to Deal with Environmental Problems

According to environmental economists, we could live more sustainably and increase our beneficial environmental impact by including the harmful environmental and health costs of the goods and services into market prices and placing a monetary value on the natural capital that supports all economies. This practice is called **full-cost pricing**, and is one of the six **principles of sustainability**. (**Concept 4.A**)

Another problem can arise when governments (taxpayers) give companies **subsidies** such as tax breaks and payments to assist them with using resources to run their businesses. This helps to create jobs and stimulate economies.

However, some subsidies can encourage the depletion and degradation of natural capital. Examples include

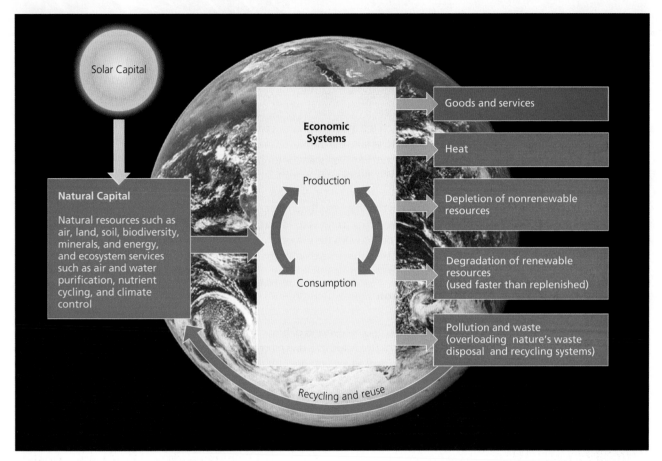

FIGURE 1.14 *Ecological economists* see all human economies as subsystems of the biosphere that depend on natural resources and ecosystem services provided by the sun and the earth. **Critical Thinking**: Can you think of any human activities that do not depend on natural capital? Explain.

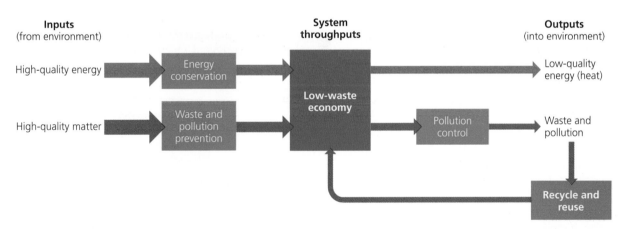

FIGURE 1.15 **Solutions**: Learning and applying lessons from nature can help us design and manage more sustainable *low-throughput economies* (Figure 1.13). **Critical Thinking**: Would you favor this type of economy over the traditional high-throughput economy? Explain.

depletion subsidies and tax breaks for extracting minerals and fossil fuels, cutting timber on public lands, and irrigating with low-cost water.

Environmental scientists and economists call for phasing out environmentally harmful subsidies and tax breaks and phasing in environmentally beneficial subsidies and tax breaks. **(Concept 4.A)** More subsidies and tax breaks would

go to businesses involved in pollution prevention, waste prevention, sustainable forestry and agriculture, conservation of water supplies, energy efficiency improvements, renewable energy use, and measures to slow projected climate change.

A number of economists call for taxing pollution and wastes that people want less of instead of taxing wages and profits that people want more of. **(Concept 4.A)**

The Economics of Supply and Demand

Economics is a social science that deals with the production, distribution, and consumption of goods and services to satisfy people's needs and wants. In a truly *free-market* economic system, all economic decisions are governed solely by the competitive interactions of *supply* and *demand*.

In Figure 1.B, *supply* is represented by the blue line (commonly called a *curve*) showing how much a producer of any good or service, in

this case oil, is willing to supply. When supply is low and demand is high, the price of the good goes up. When there is more than an ample supply of a good on the market, demand represented by the red line falls, and the market price falls as well. The price of oil can shift due to increased production, flooding the market with oil and lowering the price, or it can shift due to lowered production that limits the amount of oil on the market, driving prices up. *Market price equilibrium* occurs when the supplier's price matches what consumers are willing to pay for some quantity and a sale is made.

FRQ Application

Question: The success of recycling aluminum depends on the economic demand of businesses that use collected cans as a raw material for producing new aluminum cans. Consider the economic laws of supply and demand as they apply to the business of producing aluminum cans. **Discuss** ONE economic benefit of using aluminum cans to produce new cans and ONE economic impediment to using collected cans to produce new aluminum cans. In your discussion, include

how the market for recycled cans impacts the success of an aluminum recycling program.

Possible Response: When there is an abundance of aluminum cans available to producers, the price of the cans as a source of raw material for new cans is low because the demand is less. It is an economic benefit to producers to use cans rather than virgin aluminum, ultimately resulting in recycling the cans rather than disposing of them as waste material in a landfill. When used aluminum cans are in short supply, this raw material is in greater demand and the price increases, making it an economic drawback to use collected cans and more likely that producers would switch to using virgin aluminum ore for producing new cans. Maintaining a balance of supply and demand on the market so that the price of collected cans is attractive to can companies while the suppliers of those cans make a reasonable profit ensures a steady supply of raw material for can producers and also ensures that cans will be recycled rather than disposed of in landfills.

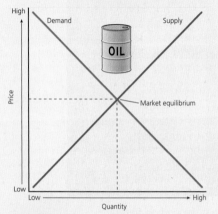

FIGURE 1.B Supply and demand curves.

CONSIDER THIS . . .

THINKING ABOUT Subsidies

Do you favor phasing out environmentally harmful government subsidies and tax breaks and phasing in environmentally beneficial ones? Explain.

A more environmentally sustainable economic and political system would *lower* taxes on labor, income, and wealth, and *raise* taxes on environmental activities that produce pollution, wastes, and environmental degradation. Figure 1.16 lists key advantages and disadvantages of using green taxes.

Economic growth is usually measured by the percentage of change per year in a country's **gross domestic product (GDP)**: the annual market value of all goods and services produced by all firms and organizations, foreign and domestic, operating within a country. A country's economic growth per person is measured by changes in the **per capita GDP**: the GDP divided by the country's total population at midyear.

GDP and per capita GDP indicators provide a standardized, useful method for measuring and comparing the economic outputs of nations. However, the GDP was

Trade-Offs

Environmental Taxes and Fees

Advantages		Disadvantages
Help bring about full-cost pricing		Low-income groups are penalized unless safety nets are provided
Encourage businesses to develop environmentally beneficial technologies and goods		Hard to determine optimal level for taxes and fees
Easily administered by existing tax agencies		If set too low, wealthy polluters can absorb taxes as costs

FIGURE 1.16 Trade-offs Using green taxes to help reduce pollution and resource waste has advantages and disadvantages. *Critical Thinking*: Which single advantage and which single disadvantage do you think are the most important? Why?

deliberately designed to measure such outputs without taking into account their beneficial or harmful environmental and health impacts. Environmental and ecological economists and environmental scientists call for the development and widespread use of new indicators—called *environmental indicators*—to help monitor environmental quality and human well-being. (**Concept 4.A**)

1.5 WHAT IS THE ROLE OF GOVERNMENT?

CONCEPT 1.5 Governments play a role in dealing with environmental problems by developing environmental policies that establish and enforce environmental laws, regulations, and programs and by providing environmental security.

Environmental Laws and Regulations

Governments play a key role in dealing with environmental problems. They do this by developing **environmental policy**. It consists of environmental laws, regulations, and programs that are designed, implemented, and enforced by one or more government agencies. (**Concept 1.5**)

During the 1950s and 1960s, the United States experienced severe pollution and environmental degradation as its economy grew rapidly without pollution control laws and regulations. This changed in the late 1960s and 1970s when massive protests by millions of US citizens led Congress to pass a number of major environmental laws (Figure 1.17) and establish government regulatory agencies to develop environmental regulations and implement them. These agencies include the *Environmental Protection Agency (EPA)*, the *Department of Energy (DOE)*, the *US Fish and Wildlife Service* (*USFWS*), *National Marine Fisheries Service* (*NMFS*), and the *Occupational Safety and Health Administration*) (*OSHA*). Implementing these laws has provided millions of jobs and profits from many new technologies for reducing pollution and environmental degradation.

Since 1980, a well-organized and well-funded movement has mounted a strong campaign to weaken the country's environmental laws (often by reducing EPA funding for implementing them) laws), repeal existing US environmental laws and regulations, and do away with the EPA. Since 2000, these efforts have intensified. Despite such intensive and prolonged efforts US environmental laws, have been effective, especially in controlling some forms of pollution and in protecting wild species from extinction. Implementing these laws has also provided millions of jobs and profits from many new technologies for reducing pollution and environmental degradation.

Global Environmental Security

Governments are legitimately concerned with *military security* and *economic security*. However, ecologists and many economists point out that all economies are supported by the earth's natural capital (Figure 1.3). They call for governments to increase their efforts for providing environmental security (**Concept 1.5**) and recognizing that environmental, economic, and national security are interrelated.

According to environmental scientist Norman Myers: "If a nation's environmental foundations are degraded or depleted, its economy may well decline, its social fabric deteriorate, and its political structure become destabilized as growing numbers of people seek to sustain themselves from declining resource stocks. Thus, national security is no longer about fighting forces and weaponry alone. It relates increasingly to watersheds, croplands, forests, genetic resources, climate, and other factors that, taken together, are as crucial to a nation's security as are military factors."

A number of international environmental organizations help shape global environmental policy and improve environmental security and sustainability. Perhaps the most influential is the United Nations, which houses a large family of organizations including the UN Environment Programme (UNEP), the World Health Organization (WHO), the UN Development Programme (UNDP), the World Bank, and the UN Food and Agriculture Organization (FAO).

1.6 WHAT IS AN ENVIRONMENTALLY SUSTAINABLE SOCIETY?

CONCEPT 1.6 Living sustainably means living on the earth's natural income without depleting or degrading the natural capital that supplies it.

Protecting Natural Capital and Living on Its Income

An **environmentally sustainable society** protects natural capital and lives on its income. Such a society would

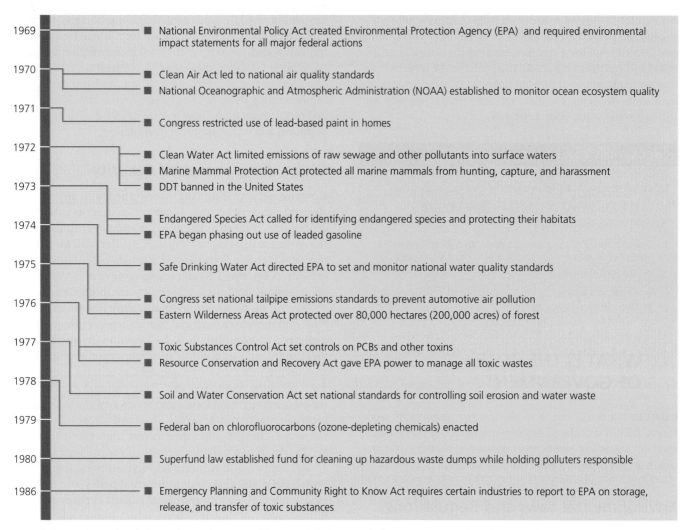

1969	■ National Environmental Policy Act created Environmental Protection Agency (EPA) and required environmental impact statements for all major federal actions
1970	■ Clean Air Act led to national air quality standards
	■ National Oceanographic and Atmospheric Administration (NOAA) established to monitor ocean ecosystem quality
1971	■ Congress restricted use of lead-based paint in homes
1972	■ Clean Water Act limited emissions of raw sewage and other pollutants into surface waters
	■ Marine Mammal Protection Act protected all marine mammals from hunting, capture, and harassment
1973	■ DDT banned in the United States
1974	■ Endangered Species Act called for identifying endangered species and protecting their habitats
	■ EPA began phasing out use of leaded gasoline
1975	■ Safe Drinking Water Act directed EPA to set and monitor national water quality standards
1976	■ Congress set national tailpipe emissions standards to prevent automotive air pollution
	■ Eastern Wilderness Areas Act protected over 80,000 hectares (200,000 acres) of forest
1977	■ Toxic Substances Control Act set controls on PCBs and other toxins
	■ Resource Conservation and Recovery Act gave EPA power to manage all toxic wastes
1978	■ Soil and Water Conservation Act set national standards for controlling soil erosion and water waste
1979	■ Federal ban on chlorofluorocarbons (ozone-depleting chemicals) enacted
1980	■ Superfund law established fund for cleaning up hazardous waste dumps while holding polluters responsible
1986	■ Emergency Planning and Community Right to Know Act requires certain industries to report to EPA on storage, release, and transfer of toxic substances

FIGURE 1.17 Some of the major environmental laws and their amended versions enacted in the United States since 1969. Very few new environmental laws have been passed since 1986, although some existing laws have been amended.

meet the current and future basic resource needs of its people. This would be done in a just and equitable manner without compromising the ability of future generations to meet their basic resource needs. This is in keeping with the **ethical principle of sustainability**.

Imagine that you win $1 million in a lottery. Suppose you invest this money (your capital) and earn 10% interest per year. If you live on just the interest income made by your capital, you will have a sustainable annual income of $100,000. You can spend $100,000 each year indefinitely and not deplete your capital. However, if you consistently spend more than your income, you will deplete your capital. Even if you spend just $10,000 more per year while still allowing the interest to accumulate, your money will be gone within 18 years.

The lesson here is an old one: *Protect your capital and live on the income it provides.* Deplete or waste your capital and you will move from a sustainable to an unsustainable lifestyle.

The same lesson applies to our use of the earth's natural capital (Figure 1.3). This natural capital is a global trust fund of natural resources and ecosystem services available to people

now and in the future and to the earth's other species. *Living sustainably* means living on **natural income**, which is the renewable resources such as plants, animals, soil, clean air, and clean water, provided by the earth's natural capital. By preserving and replenishing the earth's natural capital that supplies this income, we can reduce our environmental footprints and expand our beneficial environmental impact (**Concept 1.6**).

We Can Live More Sustainably

Living more sustainability means learning to live within limits imposed on all life by the earth and the unbreakable scientific laws that govern our use of matter and energy (discussed in the next chapter). Doing this requires:

- Learning from nature (Science Focus 1.1)
- Protecting natural capital
- Not wasting resources (there is no waste in nature)
- Recycling and reusing nonrenewable resources
- Using renewable resources no faster than nature can replenish them

- Incorporating the harmful health and environmental impacts of producing and using goods and services in their market prices
- Preventing future ecological damage and repairing past damage
- Cooperating with one another to find win-win solutions to the environmental problems we face
- Accepting the ethical responsibility to pass the earth that sustains us on to future generations in a condition as good as or better than what we inherited

Environmental problems are so complex and widespread that it may seem hopeless, but that is not true. There is plenty of reason to hope and to act. For instance, consider these two pieces of good news from the social sciences. *First*, research suggests that it takes only 5% to 10% of the population of a community, a country, or the world to bring about major social and environmental change. *Second*, this research also shows that such change can occur much faster than most people believe.

Anthropologist Margaret Mead summarized the potential for social change: "Never doubt that a small group of thoughtful, committed citizens can change the world. Indeed, it is the only thing that ever has." Engaged citizens in communities and schools around the world are proving Mead right.

One of our goals in writing this book has been to provide a realistic vision of how we can live more sustainably. We base this vision not on immobilizing fear, gloom, and doom, but on education about how the earth sustains life and on energizing and realistic hope.

CHECKPOINT FOR UNDERSTANDING 1.6

1. Explain how ethics and sustainability are related.

KEY IDEAS

- We can ensure a more sustainable future by relying more on energy from the sun and other renewable energy sources, protecting biodiversity through the preservation of natural capital, and avoiding the disruption of the earth's vital chemical cycles.
- A major goal for achieving a more sustainable future is full-cost pricing—the inclusion of harmful environmental and health costs in the market prices of goods and services.
- We will benefit ourselves and future generations if we commit ourselves to finding win-win solutions to environmental problems and to leaving the planet's life-support system in a condition as good as or better than what we now enjoy.

Core Case Study Checkpoint

Explain why the collapse of cod fisheries off the coast of Newfoundland is an example of the tragedy of the commons. Why is living sustainability important to the survival of humans and other organisms?

Chapter 1 Glossary

biocapacity: The ability of a productive ecosystem to regenerate renewable resources.

biodiversity: Variety of different species (*species diversity*), genetic variability among individuals within each species (*genetic diversity*), variety of ecosystems (*ecological diversity*), and functions such as energy flow and matter cycling needed for the survival of species and biological communities.

biosphere: The parts of the earth's air, water, and soil where life is found.

ecological footprint: Amount of biologically productive land and water needed to supply a population with the renewable resources it uses and to absorb or dispose of the pollution and wastes from such resource use.

ecology: Biological science that studies relationships between living organisms and their environment.

ecosystem: One or more communities of different species interacting with one another and with the chemical and physical factors making up their nonliving environment.

ecosystem services: Natural services or natural capital that support life on earth and are essential to the quality of human life and the functioning of the world's economies.

environment: All external conditions, factors, matter, and energy, living and nonliving, that affect any living organism or other specified system.

environmental degradation: Depletion or destruction of a potentially renewable resource.

environmental ethics: Human beliefs about what is right or wrong with how we treat the environment.

environmentalism: Social movement dedicated to protecting the earth's life-support systems for us and other species.

environmental science: Interdisciplinary study that uses information and ideas from the physical sciences (such as biology, chemistry, and geology) with those from the social sciences (such as economics, politics, and ethics) to learn how nature works, how we interact with the environment, and how we can help to deal with environmental problems.

environmental worldview: Set of assumptions and beliefs about how people think the world works, what they think their role in the world should be, and what they believe is right and wrong environmental behavior.

exponential growth: Growth in which some quantity, such as population size or economic output, increases at a constant rate per unit of time.

inexhaustible (perpetual) resource: Essentially inexhaustible resource such as solar energy because it is renewed continuously.

less-developed country: Country that has low-to-moderate industrialization and low-to-moderate per capita GDP.

more-developed country: Country that is highly industrialized and has a high per capita GDP.

natural capital: Natural resources and natural services that keep us and other species alive and support our economies.

natural resources: Materials such as air, water, and soil and energy in nature that are essential or useful to humans.

nonrenewable resource: Resource that exists in a fixed amount (stock) in the earth's crust and has the potential for renewal by geological, physical, and chemical processes taking place over hundreds of millions to billions of years.

nutrient: Any chemical an organism must take in to live, grow, or reproduce.

nutrient cycling: The circulation of chemicals necessary for life, from the environment through organisms and back to the environment.

per capita: Average per person.

poverty: Inability of people to meet their basic needs for food, clothing, and shelter.

private lands: Lands owned by individuals and businesses.

public lands: Lands typically owned jointly by the citizens of a country, but managed by the government.

renewable resource: Resource that can be replenished rapidly (hours to several decades) through natural processes as long as it is not used up faster than it is replaced.

species: Groups of similar organisms. For sexually reproducing organisms, they are a set of individuals that can mate and produce fertile offspring. Every organism is a member of a certain species.

subsidy: Payment intended to help a business grow and thrive; typically provided by a government in the form of a grant or tax break.

sustainability: Ability of the earth's various systems, including human cultural systems and economies, to survive and adapt to changing environmental conditions indefinitely.

sustainable yield: Highest rate at which a potentially renewable resource can be used indefinitely without reducing available supply.

Chapter Review

Core Case Study

1. (a) What is **sustainability**? (b) What is the tragedy of the commons? (c) Describe how the collapse of the Atlantic cod fishery illustrates this tragedy.

Section 1.1

2. (a) What are the three key concepts for this section? (b) Define **environment**. Distinguish among **environmental science**, **ecology**, and **environmentalism**. (c) What is a **species**? What is an **ecosystem**? What is the **biosphere**? (d) What are three **scientific principles of sustainability** derived from how the natural world works? (e) Define **solar energy**, **biodiversity**, and **chemical cycling** (or **nutrient cycling**) and explain why they are important to the earth's life.

3. (a) Define **natural capital** and **natural resources**. (b) Distinguish between an **inexhaustible resource** and a **renewable resource** and give an example of each. (c) What is the **sustainable yield** of a renewable resource? Define and give an example of a **nonrenewable** or **exhaustible resource**. (d) Define and give two examples of **ecosystem services**. (e) Give three examples of how we are degrading natural capital. (f) Explain how finding solutions to environmental problems involves making trade-offs. (g) Explain why individuals matter in dealing with the environmental problems we face. (h) What are three economic, political, and ethical **principles of sustainability**? (i) What is **full-cost pricing** and why is it important? (j) Describe the role of Janine Benyus in promoting the important and growing field of biomimicry and list eight principles of biomimicry. (k) Distinguish between **more-developed countries** and **less-developed countries** and give one example each of a high-income, middle-income, and low-income country.

Section 1.2

4. (a) What is the key concept for this section? (b) How have humans improved the quality of life for many people? (c) How are humans living unsustainably? Define and give three examples of **environmental degradation (natural capital degradation)**. About what percentage of the earth's land surfaces have been affected by human activities? (d) Define and give an example of **private lands**. Define **public lands** and give five examples of US public lands. (e) What is an **ecological footprint**? What is **biocapacity**? What is a **per capita ecological footprint**? (f) Use the ecological footprint concept to explain how we are living unsustainably. How many earths are needed to sustain the world's 2012 rate of renewable resource use indefinitely? (g) What is the IPAT model for estimating our environmental impact? (h) Explain how three major cultural changes taking place over the last 10,000 years have increased our overall environmental impact. (i) What would a **sustainability revolution** involve?

Section 1.3

5. (a) What are the two key concepts for this section? (b) Identify six basic causes of the environmental problems that we face. (c) What is **exponential growth**? What is the rule of 70? (d) What is the current size of the human population? How many people were added to the human population in 2016? How big is the world's population projected to be in 2050? (e) What percentage of the world's ecological footprint is the United States responsible for? How do Americans, Indians, and the average people in the poorest countries compare in terms of average resource consumption per person? How many earths will be needed to sustain the world's population if everyone used resources at the same average per capita rate of Americans in 2012? (f) Summarize the harmful and beneficial environmental effects of affluence.

6. (a) What is **poverty** and what are three of its harmful environmental and health effects? About what percentage of the world's people struggle to live on less than $3.10 a day? About what percentage have to live on less than $1.90 a day? (b) How are poverty and population growth connected? (c) List three major health problems faced by many of the poor. (d) List four ways to reduce poverty. (e) Explain how excluding the harmful environmental and health costs of production from the prices of goods and services affects the environmental problems we face.

7. (a) Explain how a lack of knowledge about nature and the importance of natural capital, along with our increasing isolation from nature, can intensify the environmental problems we face. What is *nature deficit disorder*? (b) What is an **environmental worldview**? What is **environmental ethics**? (c) Compare the *planetary management, stewardship,* and *environmental wisdom* worldviews (see Figure 1.A). What are two ways to deal with the tragedy of the commons involved in overfishing ocean species?

Section 1.4

8. (a) What are the two key concepts for this section? (b) What is **economics**? What three types of capital do most economic systems use? What is **economic growth**? What is the role of supply and demand in an economy? (c) Describe the model for a **high-throughput economy**. Describe the model for a **biosphere-based economy**. What is a **low-throughput (low-waste) economy**? (d) What is **full-cost pricing**? (e) What are government **subsidies**? What are the advantages and disadvantages of government subsidies? (f) Describe the proposed shift from environmentally harmful subsidies to environmentally beneficial government subsidies. (g) Describe the proposed shift from taxing wages and profits to taxing pollution and wastes and three requirements for making such a shift. (h) What are the advantages and disadvantages of green taxes? (i) Define **gross domestic product (GDP)** and **per capital GDP** and the inability of these economic indicators to evaluate the beneficial or harmful environmental impacts of an economy.

Section 1.5

9. (a) What is **environmental policy**? What are the four stages in the typical *policy lifecycle*? (b) Describe the role of massive citizen protest in the 1960s and 1970s that resulted in a number of environmental laws, regulatory agencies, and regulations in the United States. (c) Name three environmental laws and list the major accomplishments of US environmental laws. (d) Name two federal environmental regulatory agencies. (e) What are the goals of the US antienvironmental movement that has been in existence since the 1980s? (f) Why should we have *global environmental security*?

Section 1.6

10. (a) What is an **environmentally sustainable society**? What is the **natural income** and how is it related to living sustainably? (b) List 9 principles for living more sustainably. (c) What are two pieces of good news about making the transition to a more sustainable society? (d) What are this chapter's three key ideas?

Note: Key terms are in bold type. Knowing the meanings of these terms will help you in the course you are taking.

1. The population of Oceanside is currently growing at a rate of 1.75% per year. Approximately how many years will it take for its population to double?
   (A) 0.5 year
   (B) 20 years
   (C) 30 years
   (D) 40 years
   (E) 70 years

2. Countries such as China increasingly have populations that are attaining a middle-class status. This has led to all of the following EXCEPT
   (A) increased harmful effects of resource consumption
   (B) more people purchasing cell phones, cars, and appliances
   (C) a decrease in environmental impact as residents become increasingly aware of the effects of pollution
   (D) two-thirds of the world's most polluted cities being in China
   (E) less arable land available for farming

3. An ecological footprint is defined as
   (A) the impact an individual may have on a given area of land
   (B) the amount of biologically productive land and water needed to sustain an individual within a population
   (C) the carrying capacity of the earth for a given population
   (D) the amount of land and water that has been converted to nonproductive use within a given geographical region
   (E) the increase in biocapacity for an ecosystem to remain sustainable

Questions 4–6 refer to the graphs below.

4. India's per capita ecological footprint is approximately
   (A) 1/10 of China's ecological footprint
   (B) 1/5 of China's ecological footprint
   (C) 1/2 of China's ecological footprint
   (D) twice China's ecological footprint
   (E) equal to China's ecological footprint

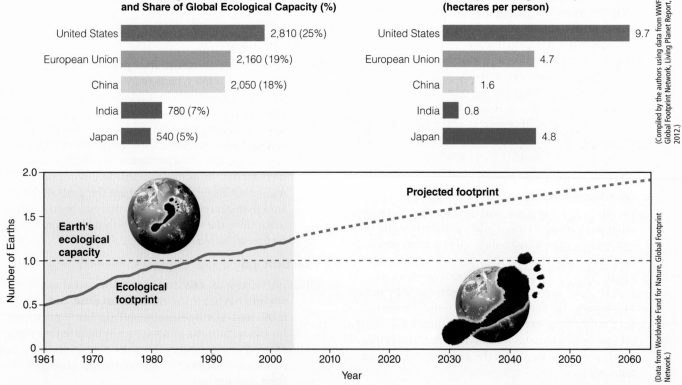

Total Ecological Footprint (million hectares) and Share of Global Ecological Capacity (%)

United States — 2,810 (25%)
European Union — 2,160 (19%)
China — 2,050 (18%)
India — 780 (7%)
Japan — 540 (5%)

Per Capita Ecological Footprint (hectares per person)

United States — 9.7
European Union — 4.7
China — 1.6
India — 0.8
Japan — 4.8

(Compiled by the authors using data from WWF Global Footprint Network, Living Planet Report, 2012.)

Number of Earths — Earth's ecological capacity — Ecological footprint — Projected footprint

Year: 1961, 1970, 1980, 1990, 2000, 2010, 2020, 2030, 2040, 2050, 2060

(Data from Worldwide Fund for Nature, Global Footprint Network.)

5. In the year 2000, what was the earth's ecological footprint?
   (A) 1.2 earths
   (B) 0.5 earth
   (C) 2.0 earths
   (D) 1.5 earths
   (E) 1 earth

6. All of the following ways would help reduce the projected ecological footprint EXCEPT
   (A) using shared resources at rates well below their estimated sustainable yields
   (B) converting open-access resources to private ownership
   (C) reducing the amount of land used for commercial forestry
   (D) recycling nonrenewable metallic resources
   (E) continuing reliance on the current fossil fuel–based, automobile-centered economy

7. Which of the following are considered to be causes of key environmental problems?
   I. Population growth
   II. Unsustainable resource use
   III. Poverty within a population
   (A) I only
   (B) II only
   (C) III only
   (D) I and II only
   (E) I, II, and III

8. Plants and trees can be cut down and replanted. These resources are therefore considered to be
   (A) renewable resources
   (B) nonrenewable resources
   (C) perpetual
   (D) exhaustible resources
   (E) sustainable

9. Which of the following is a primary factor used by the United Nations in classifying a country as developed or developing?
   (A) Gain in population
   (B) Resource use
   (C) Distribution of wealth in the population
   (D) Degree of industrialization
   (E) Annual birth rate

Questions 10–12 refer to the graph below.

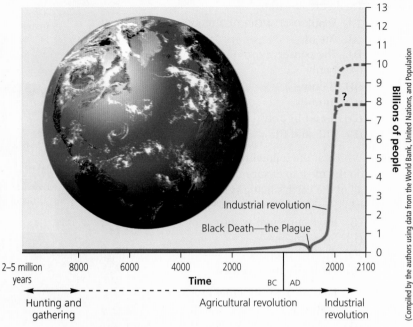

(Compiled by the authors using data from the World Bank, United Nations, and Population Reference Bureau.)

10. In what year did the human population reach 6 billion?
    (A) 8000 BC   (D) 1000 AD
    (B) 4000 BC   (E) 2000 AD
    (C) 2000 BC

11. The solid line on the graph illustrates which type of growth?
    (A) Exponential   (D) Parabolic
    (B) Linear   (E) Inverse
    (C) Logistic

12. Both dotted lines assume that population will
    (A) increase at a linear rate
    (B) decrease
    (C) increase exponentially
    (D) stabilize
    (E) collapse

13. The environmental impact of a population on a given area depends on
    I. Population size
    II. Combined environmental effects of technologies
    III. Affluence-level or consumption patterns within the population
    (A) I only
    (B) II only
    (C) I and II only
    (D) I and III only
    (E) I, II, and III

Question 14 refers to the figure at the right.

14. The figure illustrates
    I. The conservation of energy
    II. A cycle
    III. The conservation of matter
    (A) I only
    (B) II only
    (C) III only
    (D) II and III only
    (E) I, II, and III

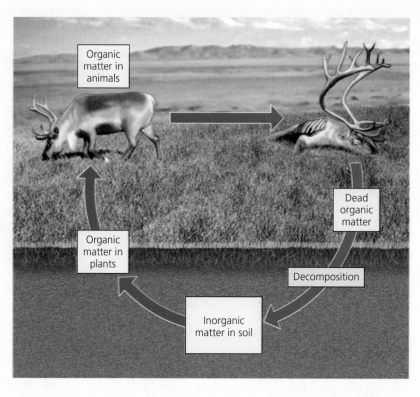

15. Which of the following perspectives will do the most to ensure the sustainability of all of the earth's living systems?
    (A) Ecocentric
    (B) Environmental wisdom
    (C) Stewardship
    (D) Anthropocentric
    (E) Planetary management

16. Solutions to environmental problems are not always easy. This is because
    (A) there is only one correct answer to environmental problems
    (B) it means that people will suffer
    (C) once a solution is suggested, it can never be changed
    (D) laws must always be written to solve the environmental problem
    (E) any solution has both advantages and disadvantages

17. Which of the below is an example of the tragedy of the commons?
    (A) Treaties allowing for the limited taking of whales for research purposes
    (B) Offshore clam beds in public areas depleted below replenishment levels by overfishing
    (C) Individuals catching their legal limit of fish on a daily basis
    (D) Shrimp boats accidentally catching turtles in their nets
    (E) A large storm smothering a large oyster bed with a new sand bar

18. Based on the *full-cost pricing* principle, the real cost of a car can be estimated to be about
    (A) the price the consumer paid the dealer
    (B) the price the consumer paid the dealer plus the cost of disposal at the end
    (C) the price the consumer paid the dealer plus the operation and maintenance costs
    (D) the price the consumer paid the dealer, plus the operations and maintenance costs, plus the cost of disposal at the end
    (E) the price the consumer paid the dealer, plus the cost of disposal at the end, plus the cost of the clean-up of all pollution attributable to the car, before, during, and after manufacture

19. All of the following are strategies suggested to reduce global poverty EXCEPT
    (A) increase the number of health care facilities and health care workers in developing countries
    (B) provide universal primary school education for all children
    (C) displace the governments of developing countries and replace them with democracies
    (D) reduce population growth
    (E) Make small low-interest loans to poor people to help them increase their income

20. Environmental ethics can best be defined as
    (A) using the environment wisely
    (B) maintaining environmental sustainability
    (C) examining the moral basis and extent of our environmental responsibility
    (D) educating people on the economic benefits of recycling
    (E) studying the interrelationships of living and non-living factors in ecosystems

Critical Thinking

1. What two things do you think could be done to deal with the tragedy of the commons?

2. What do you think are the three most environmentally unsustainable components of your lifestyle? List two ways in which you could apply each of the six **principles of sustainability** (Figures 1.2 and 1.6) to making your lifestyle more environmentally sustainable.

3. For each of the following actions, state one or more of the three **scientific principles of sustainability** that are involved: (a) recycling aluminum cans; (b) using a rake instead of a leaf blower; (c) walking or bicycling to class instead of driving; (d) taking your own reusable bags to a store to carry your purchases home; and (e) volunteering to help restore a prairie or other degraded ecosystem.

4. Explain why you agree or disagree with the following propositions:
   a. Stabilizing population is not desirable because, without more consumers, economic growth would stop.
   b. The world will never run out of resources because we can use technology to find substitutes and to help us reduce resource waste.
   c. We can shrink our ecological footprints while creating beneficial environmental impacts.

5. When you read that at least 19,000 children of ages 5 and younger die each day (13 per minute) from preventable malnutrition and infectious disease, what is your response? How would you deal with this problem?

6. Explain why you agree or disagree with each of the following statements: (a) humans are superior to other forms of life; (b) humans are in charge of the earth; (c) the value of other forms of life depends only on whether they are useful to humans; (d) all forms of life have a right to exist; (e) all economic growth is good; (f) nature has an almost unlimited storehouse of resources for human use; (g) technology can solve our environmental problems; (h) I don't have any obligation to future generations; and (i) I don't have any obligation to other forms of life.

7. What are the basic beliefs of your environmental worldview? Record your answer. At the end of this course, return to your answer to see if your environmental worldview has changed. Are the beliefs included in your environmental worldview consistent with the answers you gave to Question 6 above? Are your actions that affect the environment consistent with your environmental worldview? Explain.

8. Congratulations! You are in charge of the world. List the three most important components of your (a) plan to shift to a more environmentally sustainable economy and (b) national environmental policy.

Ecological Footprint Analysis

If the *ecological footprint per person* of a country or the world is larger than its *biological capacity per person* to replenish its renewable resources and absorb the resulting waste products and pollution, the country or the world is said to have an *ecological deficit*. If the reverse is true, the country or the world has an *ecological credit* or *reserve*. Use the data to the right to calculate the ecological deficit or credit for the countries listed. (As an example, this value has been calculated and filled in for World.)

1. Which three countries have the largest ecological deficits? For each of these countries, why do you think it has a deficit?

2. Rank the countries with ecological credits in order from highest to lowest credit. For each country, why do you think it has an ecological credit?

3. Rank all of the countries in order from the largest to the smallest per capita ecological footprint.

Place	Per Capita Ecological Footprint (hectares per person)	Per Capita Biological Capacity (hectares per person)	Ecological Credit (+) or Deficit (–) (hectares per person)
World	2.6	1.8	–0.8
United States	6.8	3.8	
Canada	7.0	13	
Mexico	2.4	1.3	
Brazil	2.5	9	
South Africa	2.5	1.2	
United Arab Emigrates	8.0	0.7	
Israel	4.6	0.3	
Germany	4.3	1.9	
Russian Federation	4.4	6.6	

Place	Per Capita Ecological Footprint (hectares per person)	Per Capita Biological Capacity (hectares per person)	Ecological Credit (+) or Deficit (–) (hectares per person)
India	0.9	0.4	
China	0.5	0.8	
Australia	7.5	15	
Bangladesh	0.65	0.35	
Denmark	4.0	4.0	
Japan	3.7	0.7	
United Kingdom	4.0	1.1	

Compiled by the authors using data from World Wide Fund for Nature Living Planet Report 2014.

Answers to Checkpoints for Understanding

Section 1.1

1. Nutrient cycling, driven by the energy of the sun, circulates chemicals needed for life through living organisms and back to the environment.

2. Species diversity keeps populations in check and ensures that there are species able to adapt to changing environmental conditions should there be a catastrophic event.

3. Ecosystem services provide clean water, clean air, pollination of crops, etc., all critical to providing natural resources needed for our survival and by our economy.

4. An example of a perpetual resource would be solar energy. An example of a renewable resource would be topsoil, timber, and fish. A nonrenewable resource would be coal, oil, and natural gas. A renewable resource might become nonrenewable when overharvesting occurs and the resource cannot regenerate within a reasonable timespan.

5. The human factors include, economics, ethics, and politics.

Section 1.2

1. Fishing until reaching an established quota that allows the fish population to rebound each season is a method of sustainable fishing.

2. The United States is an ecological debtor nation because it over-consumes and degrades natural resources without allowing them to regenerate, while importing resources from other countries.

Section 1.3

1. As population grows, demand for finite resources like water, energy, and food increase. Pollution and environmental degradation also increase as more people produce waste and overharvest resources.

2. In the planetary management worldview, humans control nature to benefit the human species. In the stewardship worldview, humans manage natural resources for human benefit but also recognize an ethical responsibility to preserve nature. In the environmental wisdom worldview, humans learn how nature sustains itself and use such lessons to achieve environmental sustainability.

Section 1.4

1. Economics requires natural capital, human capital, and manufactured capital. Natural capital is the natural resources and ecosystem services that nature supplies. Without preservation and sustainable use of natural capital, the human economy will collapse.

2. A high-throughput economy produces valuable goods and services, but at the cost of high energy use and high production of waste and pollution. A low-throughput economy is more sustainable in that it reuses and recycles resources, utilizes renewable energy, is more efficient, and reduces waste and prevents pollution.

3. Full-cost pricing involves including the harmful environmental and health costs of producing and using goods and services in their market prices. The full-cost pricing model is more realistic because it accounts for the economic, health, and

environmental impacts from each step of the product life cycle, and places an actual monetary value on the natural capital that we consume and degrade.

4. A subsidy is a tax break or government payment of tax-payer dollars that a company receives that helps them use resources more cheaply in order to create jobs or compete more effectively, and helps increase the company's profits. Subsidies can be used as an incentive for companies to produce goods and use resources more sustainably.

Section 1.5

1. Without laws and policies, natural capital (resources and ecosystem services) would be degraded or destroyed. Our economy depends on natural capital and without it, the economy would ultimately collapse.

Section 1.6

1. Living sustainably ensures that future generations will live on a planet that in as good a condition or better than what we have now.

Core Case Study

The tragedy of the commons is the degradation of potentially renewable resources to which people have free and unmanaged access. An example is the depletion of Atlantic cod by commercial fishing boats. When technology allowed fishing fleets to overharvest cod populations, it led to the collapse of the fishery and the loss of jobs for people who depended on the fishery for their livelihood. It is important to live sustainably because destroying or degrading a common or shared resource is a serious threat to many of the natural resources and ecosystem services that support all life and human economies.

Science, Matter, Energy, and Systems

> Science is built up of facts, as a house is built of stones; but an accumulation of facts is no more a science than a heap of stones is a house.
>
> HENRI POINCARÉ

Researchers measuring a 3,200-year-old giant sequoia in California's Sequoia National Park.

Michael Nichols/National Geographic Creative

Key Questions

2.1 What do scientists do?

2.2 What is matter and what happens when it undergoes change?

2.3 What is energy and what happens when it undergoes change?

2.4 What are systems and how do they respond to change?

How Do Scientists Learn about Nature? Experimenting with a Forest

Suppose a logging company plans to cut down all of the trees on the land behind your house. You are concerned and want to know about the possible harmful environmental effects of this action.

One way to learn about such effects is to conduct a *controlled experiment*, just as environmental scientists do. They begin by identifying key *variables*, such as water loss and soil nutrient content that might change after the trees are cut down. Then they set up two groups. One is the *experimental group*, in which a chosen variable is changed in a known way. The other is the *control group*, in which the chosen variable is not changed. They then compared the results from the two groups.

Botanist F. Herbert Bormann, forest ecologist Gene Likens, and colleagues carried out such a controlled experiment. Their goal was to compare the loss of water and soil nutrients from an area of uncut forest (the *control site*) with one

that had been stripped of its trees (the *experimental site*).

The scientists built V-shaped concrete dams across the creeks at the bottoms of each forest in the Hubbard Brook Experimental Forest in New Hampshire (Figure 2.1). The dams were designed so that all surface water leaving each forested valley had to flow across a dam, where they could measure its volume and dissolved nutrient content.

First, the researchers measured the amounts of water and dissolved soil nutrients flowing from an undisturbed forested area in one of the valleys (the control site) (Figure 2.1, left). These measurements showed that the undisturbed mature forest was efficient at storing water and retaining chemical nutrients in its soils.

Next, they set up an experimental forest area in a nearby valley (Figure 2.1, right). They cut down all the trees and shrubs in that valley, left them where they fell, and sprayed the area with herbicides

to prevent regrowth of vegetation. Then, for 3 years, they compared the outflow of water and nutrients in this experimental site with data from the control site.

The scientists found that, without plants to help absorb and retain water, the amount of water flowing out of the deforested valley increased 30–40%. This excess water ran over the ground rapidly, eroded soil, and removed dissolved nutrients from the topsoil. Overall, the loss of key soil nutrients from the experimental forest was six to eight times that in the nearby uncut control forest.

In this chapter, you will learn more about how scientists study nature and about the matter and energy that make up the world within and around us. ●

CRITICAL THINKING

List two ecosystem services that are found in an intact forest.

FIGURE 2.1 This controlled field experiment measured the loss of water and soil nutrients from a forest due to deforestation. The forested valley (left) was the control site; the cutover valley (right) was the experimental site.

2.1 WHAT DO SCIENTISTS DO?

CONCEPT 2.1 Scientists collect data and develop hypotheses, theories, and laws about how nature works.

Scientists Collect Evidence to Learn How Nature Works

Science is a field of study focused on discovering how nature works and using that knowledge to describe what is likely to happen in nature. Science is based on the assumption that events in the natural world follow orderly cause-and-effect patterns. These patterns can be understood through *observations* (by use of our senses and with instruments that expand our senses), *measurements*, and *experimentation*. Figure 2.2 summarizes the **scientific method**, a research process in which scientists identify a problem for study, gather relevant data, propose a hypothesis that explains the data, gather data to test the hypothesis, and modify the hypothesis as needed. Within this process, scientists use many different methods to learn more about how nature works.

There is nothing mysterious about the scientific process. You use it all the time in making decisions. As the famous physicist Albert Einstein put it, "The whole of science is nothing more than a refinement of everyday thinking."

In this chapter's **Core Case Study**, Bormann and Likens used the scientific method to see how clearing forested land can affect its ability to store water and retain soil nutrients. They designed an experiment to collect **data**, or information, to answer their question. From the data collected, they proposed a **scientific hypothesis**—a testable explanation of their data. Bormann and Likens came up with the following hypothesis to explain their data: land cleared of vegetation and exposed to rain and melting snow retains less water and loses soil nutrients. They tested this hypothesis twice. The first set of data measured the amount of soil nutrient nitrogen in the runoff. Later they repeated their controlled experiment to determine the amount of the soil nutrient phosphorus in the runoff. Both experiments confirmed their hypothesis.

The experimenters wrote scientific articles describing their research and submitted them to a scientific journal for publication. Before publishing the articles, the journal editor had them evaluated by other scientists in their fields (their peers in the scientific community). A larger body of experts in the field then evaluated the published articles. These reviews and further research by other scientists supported their results and hypothesis.

Another way to study nature is to develop a **model**, or an approximate physical or mathematical simulation of a system. Scientists use models to study complex systems such as the earth's climate and the forest studied by Bormann and Likens. Data from the research carried out

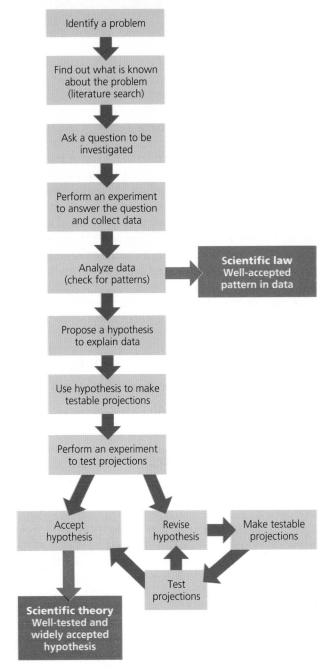

FIGURE 2.2 Scientific method: The general process that scientists use for discovering and testing ideas about how the natural world works.

by Bormann and Likens and from other scientists' research were fed into such models, which also supported the results of their research.

A well-tested and widely accepted scientific hypothesis or a group of related hypotheses is called a **scientific theory**, which is one of the most important and certain results of science. The research conducted by Bormann and Likens and other scientists led to the scientific theory that trees and other plants hold soil in place and retain water and nutrients needed to support the plants.

Jane Goodall: Chimpanzee Researcher and Protector

Jane Goodall is a scientist who studies animal behavior. She has a PhD from England's Cambridge University and is a National Geographic Explorer-in-Residence Emeritus. At age 26, she began a 50-year career of studying chimpanzee social and family life in the Gombe Stream Game Reserve in Tanzania, Africa.

One of her major scientific discoveries was that chimpanzees make and use tools. She watched chimpanzees modifying twigs or blades of grass and then poking them into termite mounds. When the termites latched on to these primitive tools, the chimpanzees pulled them out and ate the termites. Goodall and several other scientists have also observed that chimpanzees, including captive chimpanzees, can learn simple sign language, do simple arithmetic, play computer games, develop relationships, and worry about and protect one another.

In 1977 she established the Jane Goodall Institute, an organization that works to preserve great ape populations and their habitats. In 1991 Goodall started *Roots & Shoots*, an environmental education program for youth with chapters in more than 130 countries. She has received many awards and prizes for her scientific contributions and conservation efforts. She has written 27 books for adults and children and has been involved with more than a dozen films about the lives and importance of chimpanzees.

Goodall spends nearly 300 days a year traveling and educating people throughout the world about chimpanzees and the need to protect the environment. She says, "I can't slow down. . . . If we're not raising new generations to be better stewards of the environment, what's the point?"

JENS SCHLUETER/AFP/Getty Images

Scientists Are Curious and Skeptical and Demand Evidence

Good scientists are curious about how nature works (Individuals Matter 2.1). Scientists tend to be highly skeptical about new data and hypotheses. They say, "Show me your evidence. Explain the reasoning behind the scientific ideas or hypotheses that you propose to explain your data."

An important part of the scientific process is **peer review**. This involves scientists publishing details of the methods they used, the results of their experiments, and the reasoning behind their hypotheses for other scientists working in the same field (their *peers*) to evaluate. Scientific knowledge advances in this self-correcting way, with scientists questioning and confirming the data and hypotheses of their peers. Sometimes new data and analysis can lead to revised hypotheses (Science Focus 2.1).

Critical Thinking and Creativity Are Important in Science

Scientists use logical reasoning and critical thinking skills (see p. xxviii) to learn about nature. Thinking critically involves three steps:

1. Be skeptical about everything you read or hear.
2. Evaluate evidence and hypotheses using inputs and opinions from a variety of reliable sources.
3. Identify and evaluate your personal assumptions, biases, and beliefs and distinguish between facts and opinions before coming to a conclusion.

Logic and critical thinking are important tools in science, but imagination, creativity, and intuition are also vital. According to Albert Einstein, "There is no completely logical way to a new scientific idea."

Scientific Theories and Laws: The Most Important and Certain Results of Science

We should never take a scientific theory lightly. It has been tested widely, is supported by extensive evidence, and is accepted as being a useful explanation of some phenomenon by most scientists in a particular field or related fields of study. So when you hear someone say, "Oh, that's just a theory," you will know that he or she does not have a clear understanding of what a scientific theory is and how it is an important result of science.

Another important and reliable outcome of science is a **scientific law**, or **law of nature**—a well-tested and widely accepted description of what we find always happening in the same way in nature. An example is the *law of gravity*. After making many thousands of observations and measurements of objects falling from different heights, scientists developed the following scientific law: all objects fall to the earth's surface at predictable speeds. Scientific laws cannot be broken.

Science Can Be Reliable, Unreliable, and Tentative

Reliable science consists of data, hypotheses, models, theories, and laws that are accepted by most of the scientists who are considered experts in the field under study.

Revisions in a Popular Scientific Hypothesis

For years, the story of Easter Island has been used in textbooks as an example of how humans can seriously degrade their own life-support system and as a warning about what we are doing to our life-support system.

What happened on this small island in the South Pacific is a story about environmental degradation and the collapse of an ancient civilization of Polynesians living there. Over the years, many researchers have studied the island and its remains, including hundreds of huge statues (Figure 2.A).

Some scientists drilled cores of sediment from lakebeds and studied grains of pollen from palm trees and other plants in sediment layers to reconstruct the history of plant life on the island. Based on these data, they hypothesized that as their population grew, the Polynesians began living unsustainably by using the island's palm forest trees faster than they could be renewed.

By studying charcoal remains in the island's layers of soil, scientists hypothesized that when the forests were depleted, there was no firewood for cooking or keeping warm and no wood for building large canoes used to catch fish, shellfish, and other forms of seafood. They also hypothesized that, with the forest cover gone, soils eroded, crop yields plummeted, famine struck, the population dwindled, violence broke out, and the civilization collapsed.

In 2001 anthropologist Terry L. Hunt and archeologist Carl Lippo carried out new research to test the older hypotheses about what happened on Easter Island. They used radiocarbon data and other analyses to propose some new hypotheses. *First*, their research indicated that the Polynesians arrived on the island about 800 years ago, not 2,900 years ago, as had been thought. *Second*, their population size probably never exceeded 3,000, contrary to the earlier estimate of up to 15,000.

Third, the Polynesians did use the island's trees and other vegetation in an unsustainable manner, and visitors reported that by 1722, most of the island's trees were gone. However, one question not answered by the earlier hypothesis was, why did the trees never grow back? Based on new evidence Hunt and Lippo hypothesized that rats, which either came along with the original settlers as stowaways or were brought along as a source of protein for the long voyage, played a key role in the island's permanent deforestation. Over the years, the rats multiplied rapidly into the millions and devoured the seeds that would have regenerated large areas of the forests. According to this new hypothesis, the rats played a key role in the fall of the civilization on Easter Island.

Fourth, the collapse of the island's civilization was not due to famine and warfare. Instead, it likely resulted from epidemics when European visitors unintentionally exposed the islanders to infectious diseases to which they had no immunity. This was followed by invaders who raided the island and took away some islanders as slaves. Later Europeans took over the land, used the remaining islanders for slave labor, and introduced sheep that devastated the island's remaining vegetation.

Hunt and Lippo's research and hypotheses indicate that the Easter Island tragedy may not be as clear an example of the islanders bringing about their own ecological collapse as was once thought. This story is an excellent example of how science works. The gathering of new scientific data and the reevaluation of older data led to revised hypotheses that challenged some of the earlier thinking about the decline of civilization on Easter Island. Scientists are gathering new evidence to test these two versions of what happened on Easter Island. This could lead to some new hypotheses.

FIGURE 2.A These and several hundred other statues were created by an ancient civilization of Polynesians on Easter Island. Some of them are as tall as a five-story building and weigh as much as 89 metric tons (98 tons).

CRITICAL THINKING

Does the new doubt about the original Easter Island hypothesis mean that we should not be concerned about using resources unsustainably on the island in space that we call Earth? Explain.

Scientific results and hypotheses that are presented as reliable without having undergone peer review, or are discarded as a result of peer review or additional research, are considered to be **unreliable science**.

Preliminary scientific results without adequate testing and peer review are viewed as **tentative science**. Some of these results and hypotheses will be validated and classified as reliable. Others may be discredited and classified as unreliable. This is how scientific knowledge advances.

Science Has Limitations

Environmental science and science in general have several limitations. *First*, scientists cannot prove anything absolutely because there is always some degree of uncertainty in measurements, observations, models, and the resulting hypotheses and theories. Instead, scientists try to establish that a particular scientific theory has a very high *probability* or *certainty* (typically 90–95%) of being useful for understanding some aspect of the natural world.

Scientists do not use the word *proof* in the same way as many nonscientists use it, because it can falsely imply "absolute proof." For example, most scientists would not say: "Science has proven that cigarette smoking causes lung cancer." Instead, they might say: "Overwhelming evidence from thousands of studies indicates that people who smoke regularly for many years have a greatly increased chance of developing lung cancer."

CONSIDER THIS . . .

THINKING ABOUT Scientific Proof
Does the fact that science can never prove anything absolutely mean that its results are not valid or useful? Explain.

A *second* limitation of science is that scientists are human and not always free of bias about their own results and hypotheses. However, the high standards for evidence and peer review uncover or greatly reduce personal bias and falsified results.

A *third* limitation is that many systems in the natural world involve a huge number of variables with complex interactions. This makes it too difficult, costly, and time consuming to test one variable at a time in controlled experiments such as the one described in this chapter's **Core Case Study**. To deal with this, scientists develop *mathematical models* that can take into account the interactions of many variables and run the models on high-speed computers. In addition, science and engineering projects can fail and teach us lessons (see Science Focus 2.1).

A *fourth limitation* of science involves the use of statistical tools. For example, there is no way to measure accurately the number of metric tons of soil eroded annually worldwide. Instead, scientists use statistical sampling and mathematical methods to estimate such numbers.

Despite these limitations, science is the most useful way that we have of learning about how nature works and projecting how it might behave in the future.

CHECKPOINT FOR UNDERSTANDING 2.1

1. Explain why peer review is important to science.

2. Explain the difference between a scientific law and a scientific theory.

3. Discuss whether or not tentative science can eventually lead to reliable science.

2.2 WHAT IS MATTER AND WHAT HAPPENS WHEN IT UNDERGOES CHANGE?

CONCEPT 2.2A Matter consists of elements and compounds, which in turn are made up of atoms, ions, or molecules.

CONCEPT 2.2B Whenever matter undergoes a physical or chemical change, no atoms are created or destroyed (the law of conservation of matter).

Matter Consists of Elements and Compounds

Matter is anything that has mass and takes up space. It can exist in three *physical states*—solid, liquid, and gas—and two *chemical forms*—elements and compounds.

FIGURE 2.3 Mercury (left) and gold (right) are chemical elements. Each has a unique set of properties and cannot be broken down into simpler substances.

TABLE 2.1 Chemical Elements Used in This Book			
Element	Symbol	Element	Symbol
arsenic	As	lead	Pb
bromine	Br	lithium	Li
calcium	Ca	mercury	Hg
carbon	C	nitrogen	N
copper	Cu	phosphorus	P
chlorine	Cl	sodium	Na
fluorine	F	sulfur	S
gold	Au	uranium	U

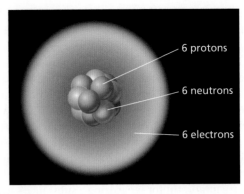

FIGURE 2.4 Simplified model of a carbon-12 atom. It consists of a nucleus containing six protons, each with a positive electrical charge, and six neutrons with no electrical charge. Six negatively charged electrons are found outside its nucleus.

An **element** such as gold or mercury (Figure 2.3) is a type of matter with a unique set of properties and that cannot be broken down into simpler substances by chemical means. Chemists refer to each element with a unique symbol such as C for carbon and Au for gold. They have arranged the known elements based on their chemical behavior in a chart known as the **periodic table of elements** (see Supplement 3, p. S6). The periodic table contains 118 elements, not all of which occur naturally. Table 2.1 lists the elements and their symbols that you need to know to understand the material in this book.

Most matter consists of **compounds**, combinations of two or more different elements held together in fixed proportions. For example, water is a compound (H_2O) containing the elements hydrogen and oxygen, and sodium chloride (NaCl) contains the elements sodium and chlorine.

Elements and Compounds Are Made of Atoms, Molecules, and Ions

The basic building block of matter is an **atom**—the smallest unit of matter into which an element can be divided and still have its distinctive chemical properties. The idea that all elements are made up of atoms is called the **atomic theory** and is the most widely accepted scientific theory in chemistry.

Atoms are incredibly small. For example, more than 3 million hydrogen atoms could sit side by side on the period at the end of this sentence. If you could view atoms with a supermicroscope, you would find that each different type of atom contains a certain number of three types of *subatomic particles*: **neutrons**, with no electrical charge; **protons**, each with a positive electrical charge (+); and **electrons**, each with a negative electrical charge (−).

Each atom has an extremely small center called the **nucleus**, which contains one or more protons and, in most cases, one or more neutrons. Outside of the nucleus, we find one or more electrons in rapid motion (Figure 2.4).

Each element has a unique **atomic number** equal to the number of protons in the nucleus of its atom. Carbon (C), with 6 protons in its nucleus, has an atomic number of 6, whereas uranium (U), a much larger atom, has 92 protons in its nucleus and thus an atomic number of 92.

Because electrons have so little mass compared to protons and neutrons, most of an atom's mass is concentrated in its nucleus. The mass of an atom is described by its **mass number**, the total number of neutrons and protons in its nucleus. For example, a carbon atom with 6 protons and 6 neutrons in its nucleus (Figure 2.4) has a mass number of 12 (6 + 6 = 12) and a uranium atom with 92 protons and 143 neutrons in its nucleus has a mass number of 235 (92 + 143 = 235).

Each atom of a particular element has the same number of protons in its nucleus. However, the nuclei of atoms of a particular element can vary in the number of neutrons they contain, and, therefore, in their mass numbers. The forms of an element having the same atomic number but different mass numbers are called **isotopes** of that element. Scientists identify isotopes by attaching their mass numbers to the name or symbol of the element. For example, the three most common isotopes of carbon are carbon-12 (with six protons and six neutrons, Figure 2.4), carbon-13 (with six protons and seven neutrons), and carbon-14 (with six protons and eight neutrons). Carbon-12 makes up about 98.9% of all naturally occurring carbon.

A second building block of matter is a **molecule**, a combination of two or more atoms of the same or different elements held together by *chemical bonds*. Molecules are the basic building blocks of many compounds. Examples are water, hydrogen gas, and methane (the main component of natural gas).

A third building block of some types of matter is an **ion**. It is an atom or a group of atoms with one or more net positive (+) or negative (−) electrical charges from losing or gaining negatively charged electrons. Chemists use a superscript after the symbol of an ion to indicate the number of positive or negative electrical charges, as shown in Table 2.2. The hydrogen ion (H^+) and sodium ion (Na^+) are examples of positive ions. Examples of negative ions are the hydroxide ion (OH^-) and chloride ion (Cl^-). Another example of a negative ion is the nitrate ion (NO_3^-), a nutrient essential for plant growth. In this chapter's **Core Case Study**, Bormann and Likens measured the loss of nitrate ions (Figure 2.5) from the deforested area (Figure 2.1, p. 36) in their controlled experiment.

Ions are important for measuring a substance's **acidity**, a measure of the comparative amounts of hydrogen ions (H^+) and hydroxide ions (OH^-) in a particular volume of a water solution. Scientists use **pH** as a measure of acidity. Pure water (not tap water or rainwater) has an equal number of H^+ and OH^- ions. It is called a *neutral solution* and has a pH of 7. An *acidic solution* has more hydrogen ions than hydroxide ions and has a pH less than 7. A *basic*

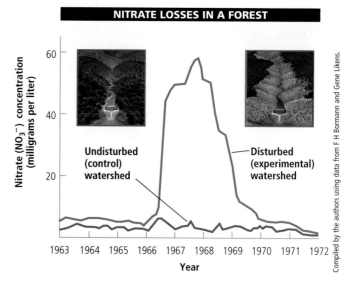

NITRATE LOSSES IN A FOREST

Undisturbed (control) watershed

Disturbed (experimental) watershed

FIGURE 2.5 Loss of nitrate ions (NO_3^-) from a deforested watershed in the Hubbard Brook Experimental Forest (**Core Case Study**, Figure 2.1, p. 36). ***Data analysis:*** By what percent did the nitrate concentration increase between 1965 and the peak concentration between 1967 and 1968?

solution has more hydroxide ions than hydrogen ions and has a pH greater than 7.

Each single unit change on the pH scale represents a tenfold increase or decrease in the concentration of hydrogen ions in a liter of solution. Scientists refer to such a scale as a *logarithmic scale*. For example, an acidic solution with a pH of 3 is 10 times more acidic than a solution with a pH of 4. Figure 2.6 shows the approximate pH of solutions for various common substances.

Chemists use a **chemical formula** to show the number of each type of atom or ion in a compound. The formula contains the symbol for each element present and uses subscripts to show the number of atoms or ions of each element in the compound's basic structural unit. Examples of compounds and their formulas encountered in this book are sodium chloride (NaCl) and water (H_2O, read as "H-two-O"). Sodium chloride is an *ionic compound* that is held together in a three-dimensional array by the attraction between oppositely charged sodium ions (Na^+) and chloride ions (Cl^-) (Figure 2.7). These and other key compounds used in this book are listed in Table 2.3.

Sodium chloride and many other ionic compounds tend to dissolve in water and break apart into their individual ions (Na^+ and Cl^-).

Other compounds called *covalent compounds* are made up of uncharged atoms. An example is water (H_2O). The bonds between the hydrogen and oxygen atoms in water molecules are called *covalent bonds* and form when the atoms in the molecule share one or more pairs of their electrons. Figure 2.8 shows the chemical formulas and shapes of molecules that are the building blocks for several common covalent compounds.

TABLE 2.2 Chemical Ions Used in This Book

Positive Ion	Symbol	Components
hydrogen ion	H^+	One hydrogen atom, one positive charge
sodium ion	Na^+	One sodium atom, one positive charge
calcium ion	Ca^{2+}	One calcium atom, two positive charges
aluminum ion	Al^{3+}	One aluminum atom, three positive charges
ammonium ion	NH_4^+	One nitrogen atom, four hydrogen atoms, one positive charge

Negative Ion	Symbol	Components
chloride ion	Cl^-	One chlorine atom, one negative charge
hydroxide ion	OH^-	One oxygen atom, one hydrogen atom, one negative charge
nitrate ion	NO_3^-	One nitrogen atom, three oxygen atoms, one negative charge
carbonate ion	CO_3^{2-}	One carbon atom, three oxygen atoms, two negative charges
sulfate ion	SO_4^{2-}	One sulfur atom, four oxygen atoms, two negative charges
phosphate ion	PO_4^{3-}	One phosphorus atom, four oxygen atoms, three negative charges

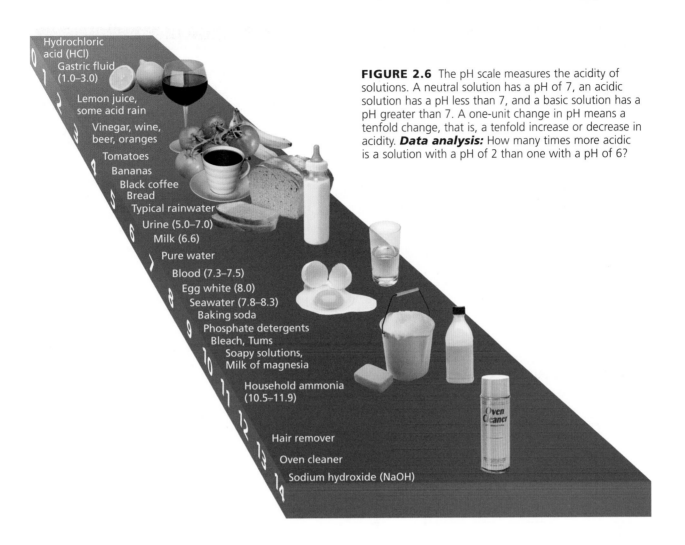

FIGURE 2.6 The pH scale measures the acidity of solutions. A neutral solution has a pH of 7, an acidic solution has a pH less than 7, and a basic solution has a pH greater than 7. A one-unit change in pH means a tenfold change, that is, a tenfold increase or decrease in acidity. ***Data analysis:*** How many times more acidic is a solution with a pH of 2 than one with a pH of 6?

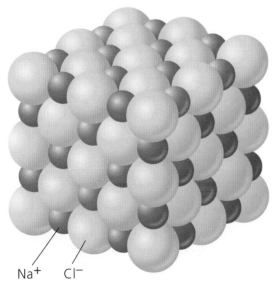

FIGURE 2.7 A solid crystal of an ionic compound such as sodium chloride (NaCl) consists of a three-dimensional array of oppositely charged ions held together by the strong forces of attraction between oppositely charged ions.

TABLE 2.3 Compounds Used in This Book

Compound	Formula	Compound	Formula
sodium chloride	NaCl	methane	CH_4
sodium hydroxide	NaOH	glucose	$C_6H_{12}O_6$
carbon monoxide	CO	water	H_2O
carbon dioxide	CO_2	hydrogen sulfide	H_2S
nitric oxide	NO	sulfur dioxide	SO_2
nitrogen dioxide	NO_2	sulfuric acid	H_2SO_4
nitrous oxide	N_2O	ammonia	NH_3
nitric acid	HNO_3	calcium carbonate	$CaCO_3$

Constructing a Line Graph

A graph is a diagram showing a relationship between two variables. Graphs are very useful in math and science as well as other disciplines such as economics, history, and the social sciences because they help to visualize data, relationships, and trends (see Supplement 2, pages S3–S5). A properly constructed graph has several important components. These include the following:

Independent variable: This variable, plotted on the *x*-axis, is intentionally changed to observe the effect on the dependent variable. Examples of independent variables are concentration of a solution, time, and distance.

Dependent variable: The variable, plotted on the *y*-axis, which changes as a function of the independent variable. Examples of dependent variables are rate of growth, temperature, and volume.

Title: Every graph should have a title that explicitly states the dependent variable as a function of the independent variable (**y** vs. **x**).

Axes: The **x-axis** is the horizontal axis, the **y-axis** is the vertical axis. The independent variable is always placed on the *x*-axis, and the dependent variable on the *y*-axis. It is necessary to include axis labels that designate clearly what is being plotted on each axis and specify the units being used.

Scale: The divisions, or increments, on each axis of a graph should be part of an easily identifiable scale (steps of 1, 2, 5, 10, or some multiple of one of these). To determine the value of a horizontal or vertical square on the graph paper, divide the range of the data by the number of squares available and round to the nearest common number.

FRQ Application

In this experiment 10 mL of catalase, an enzyme, was combined with 10 mL of hydrogen peroxide. This produced oxygen gas which was collected in a graduated cylinder. Because the experimenter determines how much time will elapse and that data will be collected every 5 seconds, the independent variable is time. The dependent variable is the cumulative mL of oxygen gas collected, a function of the time increments. Construct a line graph using the data in the table below. Figure 2.C shows how this data might be plotted and labeled in a line graph.

Time (seconds)	O_2 produced (mL)
0	0
5	16
10	24
15	28
20	32
25	36
30	38
35	40
40	40
45	40
50	40

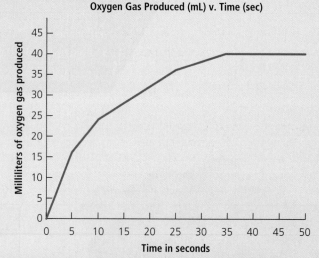

FIGURE 2.C This line graph shows milliliters of oxygen gas produced (dependent variable on the *y*-axis) plotted against time (independent variable on the *x*-axis).

A smooth curve can be fit to the plotted points that illustrates the relationship between the two variables. The shape of the graph shows that the reaction proceeds quickly in the beginning (a large change in the dependent variable in a short time) and then slows down over the measured time period.

Organic Compounds Are the Chemicals of Life

Plastics, table sugar, vitamins, aspirin, penicillin, and most of the chemicals in your body are called **organic compounds**, which contain at least two carbon atoms combined with atoms of one or more other elements. The exception is methane (CH_4), with only one carbon atom.

The millions of known organic (carbon-based) compounds include *hydrocarbons*—compounds of carbon and hydrogen atoms—such as methane (CH_4), the main component of natural gas. *Simple carbohydrates (simple sugars)* are organic compounds that contain carbon, hydrogen, and oxygen atoms. An example is glucose ($C_6H_{12}O_6$), which most plants and animals break down in their cells to obtain energy.

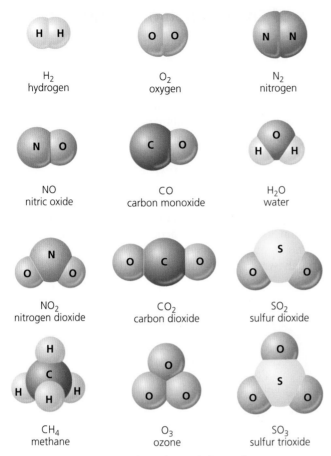

FIGURE 2.8 Chemical formulas and shapes for some covalent compound molecules.

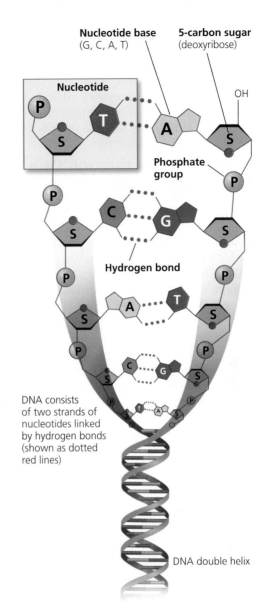

DNA consists of two strands of nucleotides linked by hydrogen bonds (shown as dotted red lines)

FIGURE 2.9 Portion of a DNA molecule, which is composed of spiral (helical) strands of nucleotides. Each nucleotide contains three units: phosphate (P), a sugar (S), which is deoxyribose), and one of four different nucleotide bases represented by the letters A, G, C, and T.

Larger and more complex organic compounds, called polymers or *macromolecules*, form when a large number of simple organic molecules (*monomers*) are linked together by chemical bonds, somewhat like rail cars linked in a freight train. Four types of macromolecules—*complex carbohydrates, proteins, nucleic acids,* and *lipids*—are the molecular building blocks of life.

Complex carbohydrates consist of two or more monomers of *simple sugars* (such as glucose, $C_6H_{12}O_6$) linked together. One example is the starches that plants use to store energy and to provide energy for animals that feed on plants. Another is cellulose, the earth's most abundant organic compound, which is found in the cell walls of bark, leaves, stems, and roots.

Proteins are large polymer molecules formed by linking together long chains of monomers called *amino acids*. Living organisms use about 20 different amino acid molecules to build a variety of proteins. Some proteins store energy. Others are components of the immune system and chemical messengers, or *hormones*, that turn various bodily functions of animals on or off. In animals, proteins are also components of hair, skin, muscle, and tendons. In addition, some proteins act as *enzymes* that catalyze or speed up certain chemical reactions.

Nucleic acids are large polymer molecules made by linking large numbers of monomers called *nucleotides*. Each nucleotide consists of a *phosphate group*, a *sugar molecule*, and one of four different *nucleotide bases* (represented by A, G, C, and T, the first letter in each of their names). Two nucleic acids—DNA (**d**eoxyribo**n**ucleic **a**cid) and RNA (**r**ibo**n**ucleic **a**cid)—help build proteins and carry hereditary information used to pass traits from parent to offspring. Bonds called *hydrogen bonds* between parts of the nucleotides in DNA hold two DNA strands together like a spiral staircase, forming a double helix (Figure 2.9).

The different molecules of DNA in the millions of species found on the earth are like a vast and diverse genetic library. Each species is a unique book in that library. If the

DNA coiled in your body were unwound, it would stretch about 960 million kilometers (600 million miles)—more than six times the distance between the sun and the earth.

Lipids, a fourth building block of life, are a chemically diverse group of large organic compounds that do not dissolve in water. Examples are *fats* and *oils* for storing energy, *waxes* for structure, and *steroids* for producing hormones.

Matter Comes to Life through Cells, Genes, and Chromosomes

All organisms are composed of one or more **cells**—the fundamental structural and functional units of life. The idea that all living things are composed of cells is called the **cell theory**. It is the most widely accepted scientific theory in biology.

DNA molecules are made up of sequences of nucleotides called **genes**. Each of these segments of DNA contains instructions, or codes, called *genetic information*. The coded information in each segment of DNA is a **trait** that passes from parents to offspring during reproduction in an animal or plant.

Thousands of genes make up a single **chromosome**, a double helix DNA molecule wrapped around one or more proteins. Genetic information coded in your chromosomal DNA is what makes you different from an oak leaf, a mosquito, and your parents. Figure 2.10 shows the relationships of genetic material to cells.

Matter Can Change

When matter undergoes a **physical change**, there is no change in its chemical composition. A piece of aluminum foil cut into small pieces is still aluminum foil. When solid water (ice) melts and when liquid water boils, the resulting liquid water and water vapor remain as H_2O molecules.

When a **chemical change**, or **chemical reaction**, takes place, there is a change in the chemical composition of the substances involved. Chemists use a *chemical equation* to show how chemicals are rearranged in a chemical reaction. For example, coal is made up almost entirely of the element carbon (C). When coal is burned completely in a power plant, the solid carbon in the coal combines with oxygen gas (O_2) from the atmosphere to form the gaseous compound carbon dioxide (CO_2). Chemists use the following shorthand chemical equation to represent this chemical reaction:

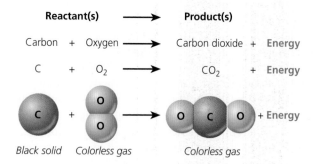

Reactant(s)   ⟶   Product(s)

Carbon + Oxygen ⟶ Carbon dioxide + **Energy**

C + O_2 ⟶ CO_2 + **Energy**

C + O·O ⟶ O·C·O + **Energy**

Black solid   *Colorless gas*   *Colorless gas*

Law of Conservation of Matter

We can change elements and compounds from one physical or chemical form to another. We cannot, however, create or destroy any of the atoms involved in the physical or chemical change. All we can do is to rearrange atoms, ions, or molecules into different spatial patterns (physical changes) or chemical combinations (chemical changes). This finding, based on many thousands of measurements, describes an unbreakable scientific law known as the **law of conservation of matter**: Whenever matter undergoes a physical or chemical change, no atoms are created or destroyed (**Concept 2.2B**).

Chemists obey this scientific law by balancing the equation for a chemical reaction to account for the fact that no atoms are created or destroyed. Passing electricity through water (H_2O) can break it down into hydrogen

A human body contains trillions of cells, each with an identical set of genes.

Each human cell (except for red blood cells) contains a nucleus.

Each cell nucleus has an identical set of chromosomes, which are found in pairs.

A specific pair of chromosomes contains one chromosome from each parent.

Each chromosome contains a long DNA molecule in the form of a coiled double helix.

Genes are segments of DNA on chromosomes that contain instructions to make proteins—the building blocks of life.

FIGURE 2.10 The relationships among cells, nuclei, chromosomes, DNA, and genes.

(H_2) and oxygen (O_2), as represented by the following equation:

$$H_2O \rightarrow H_2 + O_2$$

2 H atoms   2 H atoms   2 O atoms

1 O atom

This equation is unbalanced because one atom of oxygen is on the left side of the equation but two oxygen atoms are on the right side. We cannot change the subscripts of any of the formulas to balance this equation because that would change the arrangements of the atoms, leading to different substances. Instead, we must use different numbers of the molecules involved to balance the equation. For example, we could use two water molecules:

$$2 H_2O \rightarrow H_2 + O_2$$

4 H atoms   2 H atoms   2 O atoms

2 O atoms

This equation is still unbalanced. Although the numbers of oxygen atoms on both sides of the equation are now equal, the numbers of hydrogen atoms are not. We can correct this problem by recognizing that the reaction must produce two hydrogen molecules:

$$2 H_2O \rightarrow 2 H_2 + O_2$$

4 H atoms   4 H atoms   2 O atoms

2 O atoms

Now the equation is balanced, and the law of conservation of matter has been observed.

CHECKPOINT FOR UNDERSTANDING 2.2

1. Explain the relationship between elements and compounds.

2. Identify the force that holds ionic compounds together.

3. Explain how the law of conservation of matter would apply to trees burned in a forest fire.

2.3 WHAT IS ENERGY AND WHAT HAPPENS WHEN IT UNDERGOES CHANGE?

CONCEPT 2.3A Whenever energy is converted from one form to another in a physical or chemical change, no energy is created or destroyed (first law of thermodynamics).

CONCEPT 2.3B Whenever energy is converted from one form to another in a physical or chemical change, we end up with lower-quality or less-usable energy than we started with (second law of thermodynamics).

Energy Comes in Many Forms

Suppose you find this book on the floor and you pick it up and put it on your desktop. In doing this, you have to do *work*, or use a certain amount of muscular force to move the book from one place to another. In scientific terms, work is done when any object is moved a certain distance (work = force × distance). When you touch a hot object such as a stove, *heat* (or thermal energy) flows from the stove to your finger. Both of these examples involve **energy**: the ability to do work. Energy quantities are typically expressed in measurement units such as joules, kilojoules (1,000 joules), calories, and kilocalories (1,000 calories). (See Supplement 1, p. S1.)

There are two major types of energy: *moving energy* (called kinetic energy) and *stored energy* (called potential energy). Matter in motion has **kinetic energy**. Examples are flowing water, a car speeding down the highway, electricity (electrons flowing through a wire or other conducting material), and wind (a mass of moving air that we can use to produce electricity, as shown in Figure 2.11).

FIGURE 2.11 Kinetic energy, created by the gaseous molecules in a mass of moving air, turns the blades of these wind turbines. The turbines then convert this kinetic energy to electrical energy, which is another form of kinetic energy.

Electric power is the rate at which electric energy is transferred through a wire or other conducting material. It is commonly expressed in units of watts or megawatts (1 million watts) per hour.

In another form of kinetic energy called **electromagnetic radiation**, energy travels from one place to another in the form of *waves* formed from changes in electrical and magnetic fields. There are many different forms of electromagnetic radiation (Figure 2.12). Each form has a different *wavelength*—the distance between successive peaks or troughs in the wave—and *energy content*. Those with short wavelengths have more energy than do those with longer wavelengths. Visible light makes up most of the spectrum of electromagnetic radiation emitted by the sun.

Another form of kinetic energy is **heat**, or **thermal energy**, the total kinetic energy of all moving atoms, ions, or molecules in an object, a body of water, or a volume of gas such as the atmosphere. If the atoms, ions, or molecules in a sample of matter move faster, the matter will become warmer. When two objects at different temperatures make contact with each another, heat flows from the warmer object to the cooler object. You learned this the first time you touched a hot stove.

Heat is transferred from one place to another by three methods—radiation, conduction, and convection. **Radiation** is the transfer of heat energy through space by electromagnetic radiation in the form of infrared radiation (Figure 2.12). This is how heat from the sun reaches the earth and how heat from a fireplace is transferred to the surrounding air. **Conduction** is the transfer of heat from one solid substance to another cooler one when they are in physical contact. It occurs when you touch a hot object or when an electric stove burner heats a pan. **Convection** is the transfer of heat energy within liquids or gases when warmer areas of the liquid or gas rise to cooler areas and cooler liquid or gas takes its place. As a result, heat circulates through the air or liquid such as water being heated in a pan.

The other major type of energy is **potential energy**, which is stored and potentially available for use. Examples of this type of energy include a rock held in your hand, the water in a reservoir behind a dam, the chemical energy stored in the carbon atoms of coal or in the molecules of the food you eat, and **nuclear energy** stored in the strong forces that hold the particles (protons and neutrons) in the nuclei of atoms together.

You can change potential energy to kinetic energy. If you hold this book in your hand, it has potential energy. If you drop it on your foot, the book's potential energy changes to kinetic energy during its fall. When a car engine burns gasoline, the potential energy stored in the chemical bonds of the gasoline molecules changes into kinetic energy that propels the car, and into heat that flows into the environment. When water in a reservoir flows through channels in a dam (Figure 2.13), its potential energy becomes kinetic energy used to spin turbines in the dam to produce electricity—yet another form of kinetic energy.

Energy Is Renewable or Nonrenewable

Scientists divide energy resources into two major categories: renewable energy and nonrenewable energy. **Renewable energy** is energy gained from resources that are replenished by natural processes in a relatively short time. Examples are solar energy, wind, moving water, firewood from trees, and heat that comes from the earth's interior (geothermal energy).

Nonrenewable energy is energy from resources that can be depleted and are not replenished by natural processes within a human time scale. Examples are energy produced by the burning of oil, coal, and natural gas, and nuclear energy released when the nuclei of atoms of uranium fuel are split apart.

About 99% of the energy that keeps us warm and supports the plants that we and other organisms eat comes from the sun. This is the basis of the solar energy **principle of sustainability** (see Figure 1.2, p. 6). Without inexhaustible solar energy, the earth would be frozen and life as we know it would not exist.

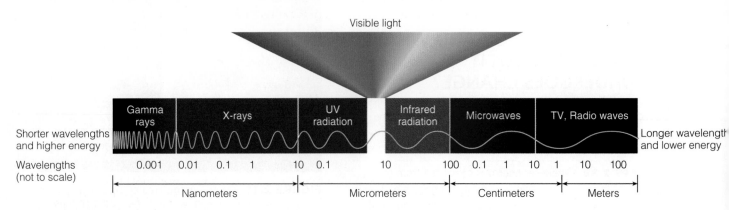

FIGURE 2.12 The *electromagnetic spectrum* consists of a range of electromagnetic waves, which differ in wavelength (the distance between successive peaks or troughs) and energy content.

FIGURE 2.13 The water stored in this reservoir behind a dam has potential energy, which becomes kinetic energy when the water flows through channels built into the dam where it spins a turbine and produces electricity—another form of kinetic energy.

Songquan Deng/Shutterstock.com

Commercial energy—energy that is sold in the marketplace—makes up the remaining 1% of the energy we use to supplement the earth's direct input of solar energy. About 90% of the commercial energy used in the world and 90% of that used in the United States comes from the burning of nonrenewable *fossil fuels*—oil, coal, and natural gas. They are called fossil fuels because they were formed over hundreds of thousands to millions of years as layers of the decaying remains of ancient plants and animals were exposed to intense heat and pressure within the earth's crust.

90 Percentage of the commercial energy used in the world and in the United States provided by fossil fuels.

Energy Varies in Its Quality

Some types of energy are more useful than others. **Energy quality** is a measure of the capacity of energy to do useful work. **High-quality energy** is concentrated energy that has a high capacity to do useful work. Examples are high-temperature heat, concentrated sunlight, high-speed wind, and the energy released when we burn wood, gasoline, natural gas, or coal.

By contrast, **low-quality energy** is so dispersed that it has little capacity to do useful work. The enormous number of moving molecules in the atmosphere or in an ocean together has such low-quality energy, and such a low temperature, that we cannot use them to move things or to heat things to high temperatures.

Energy Changes Obey Two Scientific Laws

After observing and measuring energy being changed from one form to another in millions of physical and chemical changes, scientists summarized their results in the **first law of thermodynamics**, also known as the **law of conservation of energy**. According to this scientific law, whenever energy is converted from one form to another in a physical or chemical change, no energy is created or destroyed (**Concept 2.3A**).

No matter how hard we try or how clever we are, we cannot get more energy out of a physical or chemical change than we put in. This law is one of nature's basic rules that we cannot violate.

Because energy cannot be created or destroyed, only converted from one form to another, you may be think we will never run out of energy. Think again. If you fill a car's tank with gasoline and drive around all day or run your cell phone battery down, something has been lost. What is it? The answer is *energy quality*, the amount of energy available for performing useful work.

Thousands of experiments have shown that whenever energy is converted from one form to another in a physical or chemical change, we end up with lower-quality or less-usable energy than we started with (**Concept 2.3B**). This is observation is known as the **second law of thermodynamics**. The low-quality energy usually takes the form of heat that flows into the environment. The random motion of air or water molecules further disperses this heat, decreasing its temperature to the point where its energy quality is too low to do much useful work.

In other words, *when energy is changed from one form to another, it always goes from a more useful to a less useful form.* This is another scientific law that cannot be violated. This means we cannot recycle or reuse high-quality energy to perform useful work. Once the high-quality energy in a serving of food, a tank of gasoline, or a chunk of coal is released, it is degraded to low-quality heat and dispersed into the environment.

Energy efficiency is a measure of how much work results from each unit of energy that is put into a system. Suppose you turn on a lamp with an incandescent bulb powered by electricity produced by a coal-burning power plant. This electricity is transported by a power line to your house and then through house wires to the light bulb. Because of the second law of thermodynamics, some of the original energy produced by burning the coal is lost as waste heat to the environment in each step of this process. The amount of heat lost in each step depends on the energy efficiency of the technologies used. As a result of these losses, only 5% of the chemical energy in the coal ends up producing the light from the bulb.

Thus, 95% of the money spent for the amount of light in this example was wasted. Some of this energy and money waste was the automatic result of the second law of thermodynamics. The rest was lost mostly because of low energy efficiency of the power plant (35%) and the light bulb (5%). A key to reducing this waste of energy and money is to improve the energy efficiency of the power plant and light bulb or replace them with newer, more energy-efficient technologies. We are still using the energy-wasting power plants but we are shifting from inefficient incandescent light bulbs to much more efficient light-emitting diode (LED) light bulbs.

Scientists estimate that about 84% of the energy used in the United States is either unavoidably wasted because of the second law of thermodynamics (41%) or unnecessarily wasted (43%). Thus, thermodynamics teaches us an important lesson: the cheapest and quickest way to get more energy and cut energy bills is to stop wasting almost half the energy we use. One way to reduce the unnecessary waste of energy and money is to improve the *energy efficiency* of the power plants, automobile engines, and devices powered by electricity such as lights, refrigerators, and air conditioners. This will save money and sharply reduce air pollution, including emissions of climate-changing carbon dioxide.

43 Percentage of the commercial energy used in the United States that is unnecessarily wasted

CHECKPOINT FOR UNDERSTANDING 2.3

1. A dam used to produce electricity possesses both energy of position and energy of motion. Explain where in this system you would find potential energy and where you would find kinetic energy.

2. Explain why it is difficult to harness and use the vast amount of heat energy in the ocean.

3. Explain, in terms of the second law of thermodynamics, why an LED lightbulb is more efficient than an incandescent bulb.

2.4 WHAT ARE SYSTEMS AND HOW DO THEY RESPOND TO CHANGE?

CONCEPT 2.4 Systems have inputs, flows, and outputs of matter and energy, and feedback can affect their behavior.

Systems and Feedback Loops

A **system** is any set of components that function and interact in some regular way. Examples are a cell, the human body, a forest, an economy, a car, a TV set, and the earth.

Most systems have three key components: **inputs** of matter, energy, and information from the environment; **flows** or **throughputs** of matter, energy, and information within the system; and **outputs** of matter, energy, and information to the environment (Figure 2.14) (**Concept 2.4**). Three different models of economic systems are shown in Figure 1.13 (p. 20), Figure 1.14 (p. 21), and Figure 1.15 (p. 21). A system can become unsustainable if the throughputs of matter and energy resources exceed the ability of the system's environment to provide the required resource inputs and to absorb or dilute the system's outputs of matter and energy (mostly heat).

Using Dimensional Analysis

Dimensional analysis is a problem-solving strategy that utilizes the relationship between quantities using their fundamental units of measure. For example, when calculating the decimal part of an hour when given time in minutes, the equation can be set up using the equivalent of 1 hour = 60 minutes.

$$38 \text{ minutes} \times \frac{1 \text{ hour}}{60 \text{ minutes}} = 0.63 \text{ hours}$$

The equation must be written so that units cancel, meaning that there should be *minutes above* the division bar and *minutes below*. When minutes cancel, the remaining unit indicates that the result is expressed in hours.

FRQ Application

A **watt** is a measurement of **power** that expresses the rate at which a device uses electricity. For example, a 60-watt lightbulb draws a constant 60 watts of electricity while it is turned on.

Electricity is measured in kilowatt hours. One kWh represents the amount of energy needed by a **1000**-watt device to operate for one hour. Leaving a 100-watt lightbulb on for 10 hours consumes 1 kilowatt (kWh) of energy (100 watts × 10 = 1000 watts = 1 kilowatt).

Coal-burning powerplants generate a constant output of electricity. Calculate the amount of power in kilowatt hours produced from burning one ton of coal. Use the following conversion factors:

> 1 ton = 2000 lbs.
>
> 12,500 British thermal units (BTU) produced per pound of coal
>
> 1 kWh = 3412 BTU

$$1 \text{ ton coal} \times \frac{2000 \text{ lbs.}}{1 \text{ ton}} \times \frac{12,500 \text{ BTU}}{1 \text{ lb.}} \times \frac{1 \text{ kWh}}{3412 \text{ BTU}} = 7327 \text{ kWh electricity}$$

When multiplying across the numerator (1 × 2,000 × 12,500 × 1) and dividing that number by the denominator (1 × 1 × 3412), units of tons, lbs., and BTU cancel out, leaving the total number of kWh as the result.

When people ask you for feedback they are usually seeking your response to something they said or did. They might feed your response back into their mental process to help them decide whether and how to change what they are saying or doing. Most systems are affected by **feedback**, any process that increases (positive feedback) or decreases (negative feedback) a change to a system (**Concept 2.4**). Such a process, called a **feedback loop**, occurs when an output of matter, energy, or information is fed back into the system as an input and changes the system. A **positive feedback loop** causes

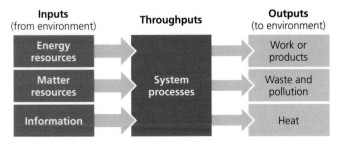

FIGURE 2.14 Simplified model of a system.

a system to change further in the same direction. An example is what happened when researchers removed the vegetation from a valley in the Hubbard Brook Experimental Forest (Figure 2.15) (**Core Case Study**).

When a natural system becomes locked into a positive feedback loop, it can reach an **ecological tipping point**. Beyond this point, the system can change so drastically that it suffers from severe degradation or collapse. Reaching and exceeding a tipping point is somewhat like stretching a rubber band. We can get away with stretching it to several times its original length. At some point, however, we reach an irreversible tipping point where the rubber band breaks. Similarly, if you lean back on the two rear legs of a chair, at some point the chair will tip back and you will land on the floor. Many types of ecological tipping points will be discussed throughout this book.

A **negative**, or **corrective**, **feedback loop** causes a system to change in the opposite direction. A simple example is a thermostat, a device that controls how often and how long a heating or cooling system runs (Figure 2.16). When the furnace in a house turns on and begins heating the house, we can set the thermostat to turn the furnace off

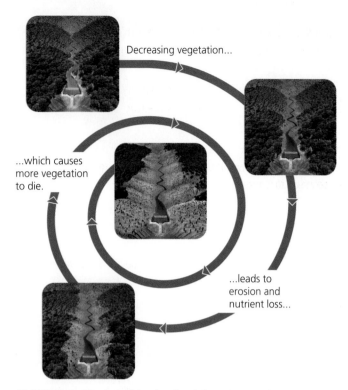

Decreasing vegetation...

...which causes
more vegetation
to die.

...leads to
erosion and
nutrient loss...

FIGURE 2.15 A *positive feedback loop*. Decreasing vegetation in a valley causes increasing erosion and nutrient losses that in turn cause more vegetation to die, resulting in more erosion and nutrient losses.

when the temperature in the house reaches the set number. The house then stops getting warmer and starts to cool.

Another example of a negative feedback loop is the recycling of aluminum. An aluminum can is an output of mining and manufacturing systems that requires large inputs of energy and matter and that produces pollution and solid waste. When we recycle, the output (the used can) becomes a new input that reduces the need for mining aluminum and manufacturing the can. This reduces the energy and matter inputs and the harmful environmental effects. Such a negative feedback loop is an application of the chemical cycling **principle of sustainability**.

Most systems in nature use negative feedback to enhance their long-term stability. For example, when we get too cold our brains send signals for us to shiver to produce more body heat. When we get too hot our brains cause us to sweat, which cools us as the moisture evaporates from our skin.

CHECKPOINT FOR UNDERSTANDING 2.4

1. During childbirth, as the uterus contracts, a hormone called oxytocin is released. Oxytocin speeds up and intensifies contractions. The more the uterus contracts, the more oxytocin is produced. Explain why this is an example of a positive feedback loop.

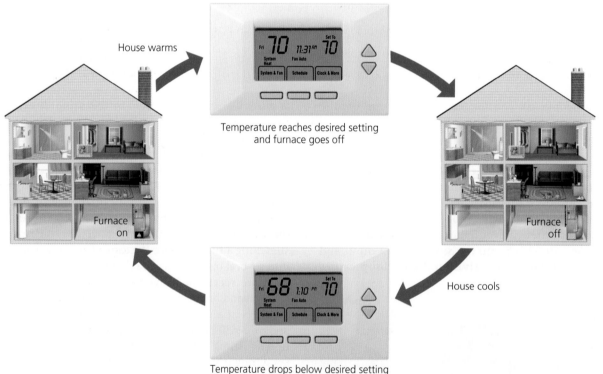

House warms

Temperature reaches desired setting
and furnace goes off

Furnace
on

Furnace
off

House cools

Temperature drops below desired setting
and furnace goes on

FIGURE 2.16 A *negative feedback loop*. When a house being heated by a furnace gets to a certain temperature, its thermostat is set to turn off the furnace, and the house begins to cool instead of continuing to get warmer. When the house temperature drops below the set point, this information is fed back to turn the furnace on until the desired temperature is reached again.

- According to the *law of conservation of matter*, no atoms are created or destroyed whenever matter undergoes a physical or chemical change. Thus, we cannot do away with matter; we can only change it from one physical state or chemical form to another.

- According to the *first law of thermodynamics*, or the *law of conservation of energy*, whenever energy is converted from one form to another in a physical or chemical change, no energy is created or destroyed. This means that in causing such changes, we cannot get more energy out than we put in.

- According to the *second law of thermodynamics*, whenever energy is converted from one form to another in a physical or chemical change, we always end up with a lower-quality or less-usable form of energy than we started with. This means that we cannot recycle or reuse high-quality energy.

Core Case Study Checkpoint

Describe how scientists used controlled experiments to investigate the ecological importance of forests.

Chapter 2 Glossary

acidity: comparative amounts of hydrogen ions (H⁺) and hydroxide ions (OH⁻) contained in a particular volume of a solution when a substance is dissolved in water. An acid solution has more hydrogen ions than hydroxide ions and a basic solution has more hydroxide ions than hydrogen ions.

atom: minute unit made of sub-atomic particles that is the basic building block of all chemical elements and thus all matter; the smallest unit of an element that can exist and still have the unique characteristics of that element.

atomic number: number of protons in the nucleus of an atom.

atomic theory: idea that all elements are made up of atoms; the most widely accepted scientific theory in chemistry.

cell: smallest living unit of an organism.

cell theory: the idea that all living things are comprised of cells.

chemical change: interaction between chemicals in which the chemical composition of the elements or compounds involved changes.

chemical formula: shorthand way to show the number of atoms (or ions) in the basic structural unit of a compound.

chemical reaction: interaction of chemicals in which the composition of the elements or compounds involved changes.

chromosome: a grouping of genes and associated proteins in plant and animal cells that carry certain types of genetic information.

complex carbohydrates: molecules consisting of carbon, hydrogen, and oxygen that provide energy to living organisms. Sugar, starch, and cellulose are examples.

compound: combination of atoms, or oppositely charged ions, of two or more elements held together by attractive forces called chemical bonds.

conduction: the process by which heat or electricity is directly transmitted through a substance when there is a difference of temperature or of electrical potential between adjoining regions.

convection: the transfer of heat via the movement in a gas or liquid in which the warmer parts move up and the colder parts move down.

data: factual information collected by scientists.

ecological tipping point: point at which an environmental problem reaches a threshold level, which causes an often irreversible shift in the behavior of a natural system.

electric power: rate at which electric energy is transferred by an electric circuit.

electromagnetic radiation: form of kinetic energy traveling as electromagnetic waves.

electron: tiny particle moving around outside the nucleus of an atom. Each electron has one unit of negative charge and almost no mass.

element: chemical, such as hydrogen (H), iron (Fe), etc., whose distinctly different atoms serve as the basic building blocks of all matter. Two or more elements combine to form compounds that make up most of the world's matter.

energy: capacity to do work by performing mechanical, physical, chemical, or electrical tasks or to cause heat transfer between two objects at different temperatures.

energy efficiency: percentage of the total energy input that does useful work and is not converted into low-quality, generally useless heat in an energy conversion system or process.

energy quality: ability of a form of energy to do useful work.

feedback: any process that increases (positive feedback) or decreases (negative feedback) a change to a system.

feedback loop: occurs when an output of matter, energy, or information is fed back into the system as an input and leads to changes in that system.

first law of thermodynamics: whenever energy is converted from one form to another in a physical or chemical change, no energy is created or destroyed, but energy can be converted from one form to another.

genes: coded units of information about specific traits that are passed from parents to offspring during reproduction. They consist of segments of DNA molecules found in chromosomes.

heat (thermal energy): total kinetic energy of all randomly moving atoms, ions, or molecules within a given substance, excluding the overall motion of the whole object.

high-quality energy: energy that is concentrated and has great ability to perform useful work.

input: matter, energy, or information entering a system.

ion: atom or group of atoms with one or more positive (+) or negative (−) electrical charges.

isotope: two or more forms of a chemical element that have the same number of protons but different mass numbers because they have different numbers of neutrons in their nuclei.

kinetic energy: energy that matter has because of its mass and speed, or velocity.

law of conservation of matter: in any physical or chemical change, no atoms are created or destroyed.

lipids: energy storing organic molecule such as fats, oils, and waxes.

low-quality energy: energy that is dispersed and has little ability to do useful work.

mass number: sum of the number of neutrons (n) and the number of protons (p) in the nucleus of an atom. It gives the approximate mass of that atom.

matter: anything that has mass (the amount of material in an object) and takes up space. On the earth, where gravity is present, we weigh an object to determine its mass.

model: approximate representation or simulation of a system being studied.

molecule: combination of two or more atoms of the same chemical element (such as O_2) or different chemical elements (such as H_2O) held together by chemical bonds.

negative (corrective) feedback loop: feedback loop that causes a system to change in the opposite direction.

neutron: elementary particle in the nuclei of all atoms (except hydrogen-1). It has a relative mass of 1 and no electric charge.

nonrenewable energy: resource that exists in a fixed amount in the earth's crust and has the potential for renewal by geological, physical, and chemical processes taking place over hundreds of millions to billions of years.

nuclear energy: energy released when atomic nuclei undergo a nuclear reaction such as the spontaneous emission of radioactivity, nuclear fission, or nuclear fusion.

nucleic acids: informational molecules such as DNA or RNA in a double-helix shape consisting of complementary nucleotides in a specific sequence.

nucleus: extremely tiny center of an atom, making up most of the atom's mass. It contains one or more positively charged protons and one or more neutrons with no electrical charge (except for hydrogen-1 atom, which has one proton and no neutrons in its nucleus).

output: matter, energy, or information leaving a system.

peer review: process of scientists reporting details of the methods and models they used, the results of their experiments, and the reasoning behind their hypotheses for other scientists working in the same field (their peers) to examine and criticize.

periodic table of elements: the organization of all known chemical elements according to atomic number, chemical properties, and electron configurations.

pH: numeric value that indicates the relative acidity or alkalinity of a substance on a scale of 0 to 14, with the neutral point at 7. Acidic solutions have a pH less than 7 and basic solutions have a pH greater than 7.

physical change: process that alters one or more physical properties of an element or a compound without changing its chemical composition.

positive feedback loop: feedback loop that causes a system to change further in the same direction.

potential energy: energy stored in an object because of its position or the position of its parts.

proteins: structural molecules consisting of a specific sequence of amino acids that serve as components of body tissue and as enzymes.

proton: positively charged particle in the nuclei of all atoms. Each proton has a relative mass of 1 and a single positive charge.

radiation: fast-moving particles or waves of energy.

reliable science: concepts and ideas that are widely accepted by experts in a particular field of science.

renewable energy: energy that comes from resources that are replaced by natural processes continually or in a relatively short time.

science: attempts to discover order in nature and use that knowledge to make predictions about what it likely to happen in nature.

scientific hypothesis: a tentative explanation of a scientific law or certain scientific observations.

scientific law: description of what scientists find happening in nature repeatedly in the same way, without known exception.

scientific method: the ways scientists gather data and formulate and test scientific hypotheses, models, theories, and laws.

scientific theory: a well-tested and widely accepted scientific hypothesis.

second law of thermodynamics: whenever energy is converted from one form to another in a physical or chemical change, we end up with lower-quality or less usable energy to do useful work. Some of the initial energy input is always degraded to lower-quality, more dispersed, less useful, usually

low-temperature heat that flows into the environment.

tentative science: preliminary scientific data, hypotheses, and models that have not been widely tested and accepted.

throughput: rate of flow of matter, energy, or information through a system.

trait: characteristic passed on from parents to offspring during preproduction in an animal or plant.

unreliable science: scientific results or hypotheses presented as reliable science without having undergone the rigors of the peer review process.

Chapter Review

Core Case Study

1. Describe the controlled scientific experiment carried out in the Hubbard Brook Experimental Forest.

Section 2.1

2. (a) What is the key concept for this section? (b) What is **science**? List the steps involved in a scientific process. (c) What are **data**? (d) Distinguish between a **scientific hypothesis** and a **scientific theory**. (e) What is **peer review** and why is it important? (f) What is a **model**? (g) Summarize scientist Jane Goodall's achievements. (h) Summarize the scientific lessons learned from research on the fall of the ancient civilization on Easter Island.

3. (a) Explain why scientific theories and laws are the most important and most certain results of science and why people often use the term *theory* incorrectly. (b) What is a **scientific law (law of nature)**? Explain why we cannot break such laws. Distinguish among **reliable science**, **unreliable science**, and **tentative science**. (c) What are four limitations of science?

Section 2.2

4. (a) What are the two key concepts for this section? (b) What is **matter**? Distinguish between an **element** and a **compound** and give an example of each. (c) What is the **periodic table of elements**? (d) Define **atom**, **molecule**, and **ion** and give an example of each. (e) What is the **atomic theory**? (f) Distinguish among **protons**, **neutrons**, and **electrons**. What is the **nucleus** of an atom? (g) Distinguish between the **atomic number** and the **mass number** of an element. What are **isotopes**? (h) What is **acidity**? What is **pH**? (i) Define **chemical formula** and give two examples.

5. (a) Define and give two examples of an **organic compound**. (b) What are three types of organic polymers that are important to life? (c) What is a **cell**? What is the **cell theory**? (d) Define **gene**, **trait**, and **chromosome**.

6. (a) Define and distinguish between a **physical change** and a **chemical change (chemical reaction)** in matter and give an example of each. (b) What is the **law of conservation of matter**?

Section 2.3

7. (a) What are the two key concepts for this section? (b) What is **energy**? Define and distinguish between **kinetic energy** and **potential energy** and give an example of each. (c) What is electric power? Define and give two examples of **electromagnetic radiation**. (d) What is **heat (thermal energy)**? Explain how heat is transferred from one place to another by radiation, conduction, and convection. (e) Distinguish between renewable energy and nonrenewable energy and give two examples of each. (f) What percentage of the commercial energy used in the world and what percentage used in the United States is provided by fossil fuels?

8. (a) What is **energy quality**? Distinguish between **high-quality energy** and **low-quality energy** and give an example of each. (b) What is the **first law of thermodynamics (law of conservation of energy)** and why is it important? (c) What is the **second law of thermodynamics** and why is it important? Explain why the second law means that we can never recycle or reuse high-quality energy. (d) What is **energy efficiency**? What percentage of the commercial energy used in the United States is unnecessarily wasted? Why is it important to reduce this waste and how can we do this?

Section 2.4

9. (a) What is the key concept for this section?
(b) Define and give an example of a **system**. Distinguish among the **inputs**, **flows (throughputs)**, and **outputs** of a system. (c) What is **feedback**? What is a **feedback loop**? Distinguish between a **positive** **feedback loop** and a **negative (corrective) feedback loop** in a system, and give an example of each. (d) What is an **ecological tipping point**?

10. What are this chapter's *three key ideas*?

_____

Note: Key terms are in bold type.

AP® Review Questions

1. The smallest unit of matter into which an element can be divided and still have the characteristic chemical properties of the element is called a (an)
   (A) atom
   (B) element
   (C) electron
   (D) molecule
   (E) cell

2. Matter is anything that
   (A) has mass and volume
   (B) gives off energy
   (C) is a solid at room temperature
   (D) cannot be chemically changed
   (E) has a definitive shape

3. Scientific theories must meet the following criteria:
   I. Be widely tested
   II. Be educated guesses which show mathematical relationships
   III. Be supported by extensive evidence
   (A) I only
   (B) II only
   (C) I and II only
   (D) I and III only
   (E) I, II, and III

4. Which of the following is an example of a chemical reaction?
   (A) Combustion of gasoline
   (B) Sugar dissolving in water
   (C) Sweat evaporating from your skin
   (D) Melting butter
   (E) Boiling water

5. The basic structural and functional units of life are called
   (A) organelles
   (B) bacteria
   (C) eukaryotes
   (D) cells
   (E) molecules

Question 6 refers to the graph below.

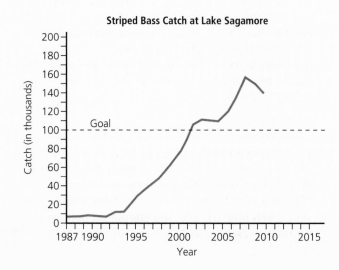

Striped Bass Catch at Lake Sagamore

6. What is the percent change in striped bass catch at Lake Sagamore from 1994–1999?
   (A) 20%
   (B) 50%
   (C) 100%
   (D) 200%
   (E) 500%

7. Which of the following scientific predictions due to global warming represents negative feedback?

    I. Increased global temperature causes an increase in the evaporation of water. Water vapor, a greenhouse gas, increases in the atmosphere.

    II. Increased carbon dioxide in the atmosphere increases global temperature. A resulting increase in algae increases the absorption of carbon dioxide needed for photosynthesis.

    III. Increased global temperature causes an increase in the evaporation of water. This increases cloud cover, blocking the sun's energy.

    (A) I only
    (B) II only
    (C) III only
    (D) II and III only
    (E) I, II, and III

8. Which of the following is an example of a high-quality energy source?

    (A) Atmospheric oxygen gas that humans need to survive
    (B) Recycled components of discarded computers and other electronic devices
    (C) Gasoline used to power automobiles
    (D) Heat released from boiling water
    (E) Iron molecules retrieved from the world's oceans

9. Which of the following is NOT an example of a macromolecule essential to life?

    (A) Glucose (monosaccharide) formed by photosynthesis
    (B) Keratin (protein) used in structural support
    (C) Triglyceride used in cells to store energy
    (D) DNA used by cells to carry the genetic code
    (E) Starch used by most plants to store energy

10. A large boulder rolling down a hill is an example of

    (A) potential energy
    (B) radioactive energy
    (C) kinetic energy
    (D) heat energy
    (E) chemical energy

11. The energy you use to walk from point A to point B is a result of several energy transformations from one form to another beginning with energy from the sun. The net result of these transformations is

    (A) a loss of useable energy
    (B) a loss of electrons
    (C) a decrease in heat energy
    (D) an increase in useable energy
    (E) a decrease in entropy

12. The warming of the oceans causing less carbon dioxide to be soluble in them, and at the same time leaving more carbon dioxide in the atmosphere causing an increased warming of the atmosphere, is an example of a

    (A) model of a system showing a paradigm shift
    (B) negative feedback system
    (C) positive feedback system
    (D) scientific principle of sustainability
    (E) natural law

13. A scientist made the following statement in 2008:

The striped bass Young of the Year (YOY) index for 2008, an annual measurement of the number of juvenile striped bass taken in the Maryland portion of the Chesapeake Bay, is one of the lowest recorded since data was recorded beginning in 1990. The 2008 YOY index for striped bass was 3.2 while the long-term average is 11.7.

(Kennebec Journal Morning Sentinel; "Chesapeake striped bass population down for '08" 10/29/2008; http://morningsentinel .mainetoday.com/sports/stories/227216717.html)

This statement is an example of

    (A) possible human bias introduced into scientific studies
    (B) scientists trying to prove their results
    (C) a limitation of science in that actual populations cannot be known
    (D) a scientific statement that points to the issue of decreasing striped bass populations
    (E) an example of how a scientific theory can become a law over time

14. Which of the organic molecules below is incorrectly paired with its function?

    (A) Starch–complex carbohydrate for energy storage
    (B) Proteins–components of human immune systems
    (C) Lipids–build muscle mass in humans
    (D) Nucleic Acids–facilitate the passing of traits from generation to generation
    (E) Glucose–enable animals to obtain energy

15. The installation of ice booms on the Niagara River may well have changed the erosion pattern along the river. The irreversible loss of an island from over 100 acres in size to less than 3 acres is an example of

    (A) a negative feedback loop
    (B) the principle of sustainability
    (C) a paradigm shift
    (D) the irreversible nature of human change
    (E) a tipping point

Questions 16–19 refer to the description of an experiment below.

Ecologists designed an experiment with lake nutrients, phosphates, and nitrates. A lake in Canada (known in the experiment as Lake 226) was divided into two equal-sized sections by a vinyl curtain. Each sub-basin of the lake was then fertilized, one with nitrates and carbon and the other with phosphates, nitrates, and carbon. The amount of phytoplankton in the lake was then measured in each side, with the side of the lake with phosphates added showing a greater rate of phytoplankton growth.

16. Frequently, studies in nature are difficult to set up and may lack some aspects of more traditional laboratory based experiments. What element of this experiment could be considered to be lacking?
    (A) An independent variable
    (B) Constants
    (C) A control
    (D) Repeated trials
    (E) A dependent variable

17. Which of the following is the independent variable in this experiment?
    (A) The location of the lakes
    (B) The two lakes separated by a vinyl curtain
    (C) The amount of phytoplankton growth
    (D) The depth of the lakes
    (E) The phosphate added to one side of the lake

18. Which of the following is the dependent variable in this experiment?
    (A) The amount of nitrates added
    (B) The amount of carbon added
    (C) The amount of phosphates added
    (D) The amount of phytoplankton growth
    (E) The size of each division of the lake

19. Which of the following would be a valid hypothesis for this experiment?
    (A) The amount of phytoplankton growth will vary with the depth of the lake.
    (B) If more phosphate is added to one side of the lake, then there will be more phytoplankton growth on that side.
    (C) If one side of the lake receives more sunlight, then that side will have more phytoplankton growth.
    (D) Phytoplankton grows faster with more nutrients added.
    (E) If scientists change the amount of nutrients, then the growth of phytoplankton will change.

20. Silver Lake has been a depository for industrial acids for many years. The bar graph below shows the change in the lake's acidity from 2015 to 2017.

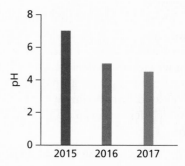

Approximately how many more times acidic is the water in 2016 compared to 2015?
    (A)   0.1
    (B)   2
    (C)   10
    (D)   100
    (E)   1000

Critical Thinking

1. What ecological lesson can we learn from the controlled experiment on the clearing of forests described in the **Core Case Study** that opened this chapter?

2. Suppose you observe that all of the fish in a pond have disappeared. How might you use the scientific process described in the **Core Case Study** and in Figure 2.2 to determine the cause of this fish kill?

3. Respond to the following statements:
    a. Scientists have not absolutely proven that anyone has ever died from smoking cigarettes.
    b. The *natural greenhouse effect*—the warming effect of certain gases such as water vapor and carbon dioxide in the lower atmosphere—is not a reliable idea because it is just a scientific theory.

4. A tree grows and increases its mass. Explain why this is not a violation of the law of conservation of matter.

5. How do the first and second laws of thermodynamics affect our use of energy resources such as fossil fuels, solar energy, and wind energy?

6. Suppose someone wants you to invest money in an automobile engine, claiming that it will produce more energy than is found in the fuel used to run it. What would be your response? Explain.

7. Use the second law of thermodynamics to explain why we can use oil only once as a fuel, or in other words, why we cannot recycle or reuse its high-quality energy.

8. For one day, (a) you have the power to revoke the law of conservation of matter, and (b) you have the power to violate the first law of thermodynamics. For each of these scenarios, list three ways in which you would use your new power. Explain your choices.

Data Analysis

Consider the graph to the right that compares the losses of calcium from the experimental and control sites in the Hubbard Brook Experimental Forest (**Core Case Study**). Note that this figure is very similar to Figure 2.5, which compares loss of nitrates from the two sites. After studying this graph, answer these questions.

1. In what year did the loss of calcium from the experimental site begin a sharp increase? In what year did it peak? In what year did it level off?

2. In what year were the calcium losses from the two sites closest together? In the span of time between 1963 and 1972, did they ever get that close again?

3. Does this graph support the hypothesis that cutting the trees from a forested area causes the area to lose nutrients more quickly than leaving the trees in place? Explain.

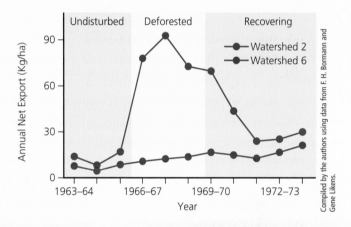

Answers to Checkpoints for Understanding

Section 2.1

1. Peer review is important because it validates methods of investigation, catches errors, and makes science self-correcting through the process of questioning and confirming data and hypotheses.
2. A scientific law is a predictable outcome of what happens in nature under a set of stated circumstances. A scientific theory is a broad base of knowledge that explains a particular phenomenon based on observations, hypotheses, and scientific laws.
3. Tentative science can become reliable science through replication of experiments, peer review, and additional testing.

Section 2.2

1. Elements are the simplest chemical substances and cannot be broken down further. Compounds are the combination of elements in a particular fixed proportion.
2. Ions are charged particles (either positively charged by losing an electron or negatively charged by gaining an electron). Ionic compounds are held together by the attraction of positive to negative ions.
3. The law of conservation of matter states that in any physical or chemical change no atoms are created or destroyed. When trees burn in a forest fire, the carbon atoms, for example, are not destroyed, but combine with O_2 during combustion to become CO_2.

Section 2.3

1. The potential energy is the water stored behind the dam. The kinetic energy is the water flowing through the interior of the dam and spinning the turbine to produce electricity.
2. The heat in the ocean is low-quality energy because it is dispersed and is at a low temperature.
3. An incandescent bulb is less efficient because more energy is lost as heat, and less electricity is converted to light energy. An LED bulb is more efficient because more electricity is converted to light energy and less is lost as waste heat.

Section 2.4

1. The definition of a positive feedback loop is one in which inputs are fed into the system causing a change in the same direction. In this case, the more oxytocin produced, the more the contractions increase, which in turn produces more oxytocin.

Core Case Study

Scientists compared the loss of water and soil nutrients from an area of intact forest (the control group) to an area of forest that was cut down (the experimental group). The data they collected was used to develop the widely accepted scientific theory that trees and plants hold soil in place and retain water and nutrients needed to support plants.

1. Which of the following are examples of sustainable practices?
   I. Implementing a mandatory recycling program
   II. Installing a new fleet of diesel buses
   III. Installing solar panels to reduce reliance on nonrenewable resources
   (A) I only
   (B) II only
   (C) III only
   (D) I and III only
   (E) I, II, and III

2. Which of the following best describes world population growth?
   (A) World population has been increasing at a constant rate.
   (B) World population is split evenly between developed and developing countries.
   (C) World population has been growing exponentially.
   (D) World population has been rising dramatically since 1963.
   (E) World population has been growing linearly.

3. A natural resource that can be used repeatedly and sustainably is a
   (A) metal ore
   (B) recyclable resource
   (C) mineral resource
   (D) renewable resource
   (E) limited resource

4. ALL of the following are true of nonrenewable resources EXCEPT
   (A) nonrenewable resources exist in a fixed quantity and are exhaustible
   (B) nonrenewable resources are formed on a geologic timescale of millions to billions of years
   (C) nonrenewable resources can be used on a sustainable yield basis to ensure they will always be available
   (D) nonrenewable resources include metallic minerals, such as aluminum, that can be recycled
   (E) many of the energy sources we currently rely on, such as coal, are nonrenewable

5. The tragedy of the commons refers to the overuse of
   (A) open-access resources
   (B) government subsidies
   (C) privately owned resources
   (D) venture capital
   (E) corporate revenue

6. Which of the following best describes environmental degradation?
   (A) The breakdown and movement of soil at the earth's surface
   (B) A process by which toxic materials can be broken down in natural systems
   (C) When we deplete, destroy, or waste the earth's natural capital
   (D) A type of environmental ethic in which human needs and intelligence allow us to use resources as we wish
   (E) A system of measurement used by environmental scientists to rate the health of a specific ecosystem

7. All of the following are true with respect to pollutants EXCEPT
   (A) they disrupt life-support systems for living organisms
   (B) they can damage property
   (C) they create nuisances within an environment
   (D) they contribute to the balance within an ecosystem
   (E) they can be hazardous to human health

8. A pollution prevention strategy would include
   (A) governments spending more money on cleanup initiatives
   (B) using incineration to reduce the volume of solid waste and transforming the pollution to a smaller air pollution problem
   (C) land being set aside for the burial of pollutants to allow the environment to naturally remediate existing pollutants
   (D) replacing old polluting systems with new technology which does not result in problematic waste
   (E) creating efficient waste collection and management systems in communities

9. If you wanted to determine whether a resource was being used in a sustainable way, which of the following data would you analyze?
   (A) The difference between the demand for the resource and the availability of the resource
   (B) The total amount of the resource available
   (C) The rate at which the resource was being recycled
   (D) The difference between the rate of resource consumption and the rate at which the resource is replenished
   (E) The change in population size since that resource was introduced

10. Which of the following represents nutrient cycling?
   I. The circulation of chemicals necessary for life through the living and nonliving systems of the environment
   II. One of the natural services of our ecosystems
   III. It is illustrated by the process of decaying matter returning nutrients to the soil to be taken up again by plants
   (A) I only
   (B) II only
   (C) III only
   (D) I and II only
   (E) I, II, and III

11. According the World Health Organization (WHO), poverty often results in premature death due to all of the following reasons EXCEPT
   (A) malnutrition
   (B) limited access to adequate sanitation
   (C) severe respiratory disease from indoor air pollution
   (D) available clean drinking water
   (E) lack of access to health care

12. Affluence can result in a safer, often more environmentally managed society in all ways EXCEPT
   (A) clean drinking water
   (B) abundant and safe food supply
   (C) increased resource use
   (D) reduction in life-threatening disease
   (E) education which spurs new technology, research, and environmental awareness

13. Given the following data on population size and land area, which of the countries has the highest population density?

Country	Population (in millions)	Land Area (in millions of hectares)
A	12	4
B	100	0.5
C	33	5.5
D	10	30
E	10	10

   (A) Country A
   (B) Country B
   (C) Country C
   (D) Country D
   (E) Country E

14. Which graph represents exponential growth?

(A)
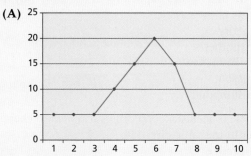

(B)
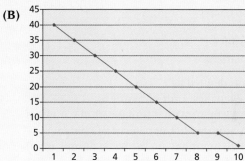

(C)
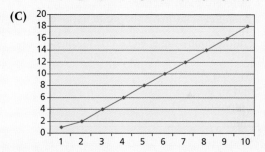

(D)
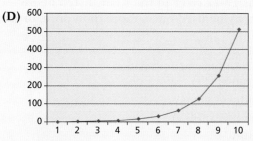

(E)
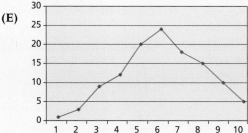

15. A well-tested and widely accepted description of what we find always happening in the same way in nature is known as a(n)
    (A) theory
    (B) hypothesis
    (C) scientific law
    (D) reason
    (E) assumption

16. This type of feedback loop causes a system to change further in the same direction.
    (A) Negative
    (B) Corrective
    (C) Nominal
    (D) Positive
    (E) Polarized

17. An ion is defined as
    (A) the smallest unit of matter
    (B) an element with a unique atomic number
    (C) an atom with a net electrical charge
    (D) an element having the same atomic number but a different mass number
    (E) a positively charged subatomic particle

18. Which of the following is NOT a physical state of matter?
    (A) Gas
    (B) Solid
    (C) Compound
    (D) Liquid
    (E) Vapor

Questions 19–22 refer to the items listed below. Choices may be used once, more than once, or not at all.
    (A) Heat
    (B) Electromagnetic radiation
    (C) Potential energy
    (D) Kinetic energy
    (E) Nuclear energy

19. Electricity

20. Starch molecules

21. Kinetic energy of moving atoms, ions, or molecules in an object

22. Waves of energy emitted from the sun

23. Which term describes the ability to do work and transfer heat?
    (A) Effort
    (B) Energy
    (C) Electromagnetic radiation
    (D) Nuclear fusion
    (E) Chemical reaction

24. The measure of how much useful work is accomplished by a particular input of energy into a system is known as
    (A) energy efficiency
    (B) sustainability
    (C) energy conservation
    (D) energy quality
    (E) energy law

25. While testing two pond sites, students found the water went from pH 7 at Site A to pH 6 at Site B. What can the students conclude?
    I. The water at Site A has more hydrogen ions ($H+$).
    II. The water at Site B is 10 times more acidic than the water at Site A.
    III. The water at Site A has fewer hydroxide ions ($OH-$).
    (A) I only
    (B) II only
    (C) III only
    (D) I and II only
    (E) I, II, and III

26. Which of the following is an example of an element?
    (A) Carbon dioxide
    (B) Mercury
    (C) Radiation
    (D) Salt
    (E) Glucose

27. Organic molecules
    (A) are particles that carry a positive or negative charge
    (B) contain both carbon and hydrogen
    (C) have a neutral pH
    (D) contain hydrogen and oxygen
    (E) transmit genetic information

28. All of the following are ecosystem services EXCEPT
    (A) climate regulation
    (B) pollination
    (C) nutrient cycling
    (D) movement of sediment by water and wind
    (E) purification of water

29. In science, the explanation of a phenomenon is
    (A) a hypothesis
    (B) an observation
    (C) a control in an experiment
    (D) a scientific theory
    (E) a scientific law

30. Which of the following are basic causes of environmental degradation?
    I.   Poverty
    II. Population growth
    III. Increased consumption of goods
    (A) I only
    (B) II only
    (C) I and II only
    (D) II and III only
    (E) I, II, and III

Ecosystems: What Are They and How Do They Work?

First Law of Ecology: Everything is connected to everything else.
BARRY COMMONER

Marine scientist measuring new growth on a table coral.

Brian J. Skerry/National Geographic Creative

Key Questions

3.1 How does the earth's life-support system work?

3.2 What are the major components of an ecosystem?

3.3 What happens to energy in an ecosystem?

3.4 What happens to matter in an ecosystem?

3.5 How do scientists study ecosystems?

Tropical Rain Forests Are Disappearing

Tropical rain forests are found near the earth's equator and contain an amazing variety of life. These lush forests are warm year round and have high humidity because it rains almost daily. Rain forests cover only 2% of the earth's land but contain up to half of the world's known terrestrial plant and animal species. These properties make rain forests natural laboratories in which to study *ecosystems*—communities of organisms that interact with one another and with the physical environment of matter and energy in which they live.

To date, at least half of the earth's rain forests have been destroyed or degraded by humans cutting down trees, growing crops, grazing cattle, and building settlements (Figure 3.1). The destruction and degradation of these centers of biodiversity is increasing. Ecologists warn that without protection, most of these forests will be gone or severely degraded by the end of this century.

Why should we care that tropical rain forests are disappearing? Scientists give three reasons. *First*, clearing these forests reduces the earth's vital biodiversity by destroying the habitats for many of the earth's species. *Second*, destroying these forests contributes to atmospheric warming and speeds up climate change, which you will learn about in Chapter 20. How does this occur? Eliminating large areas of trees faster than they can grow back decreases the ability of the forests to remove some of the human-generated emissions of carbon dioxide (CO_2), a gas that contributes to atmospheric warming and climate change.

Third, large-scale loss of tropical rain forests can change regional weather and climate patterns. Sometimes such changes can prevent the regrowth of rain forests in cleared or degraded areas. When this *ecological tipping point* is reached, tropical rain forests in such areas become less diverse tropical grasslands.

In this chapter, you will learn how tropical rain forests and other ecosystems work, how human activities are affecting them, and how we can help sustain them. ●

CRITICAL THINKING

How does the concept of Tragedy of the Commons apply to tropical deforestation?

FIGURE 3.1 Natural capital degradation: Satellite image of the loss of tropical rain forest, cleared for farming, cattle grazing, and settlements, near the Bolivian city of Santa Cruz between June 1975 (left) and May 2003 (right). This is the latest available view of the area, but forest degradation has continued since 2003.

HOW DOES THE EARTH'S LIFE-SUPPORT SYSTEM WORK?

CONCEPT 3.1A The four major components of the earth's life-support system are the atmosphere (air), the hydrosphere (water), the geosphere (rock, soil, and sediment), and the biosphere (living things).

CONCEPT 3.1B Life is sustained by the flow of energy from the sun through the biosphere, the cycling of nutrients within the biosphere, and gravity.

Earth's Life-Support System Has Four Major Components

The earth's life-support system consists of four main systems (Figure 3.2) that interact with one another. They are the atmosphere (air), the hydrosphere (water), the geosphere (rock, soil, and sediment), and the biosphere (living things) (**Concept 3.1A**).

The **atmosphere** is a spherical mass of air surrounding the earth's surface. Its innermost layer, the **troposphere**, extends about 17 kilometers (11 miles) above sea level at the equator and about 7 kilometers (4 miles) above the earth's North and South Poles. The troposphere contains

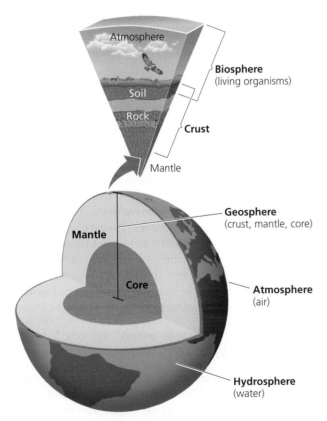

FIGURE 3.2 Natural capital: The earth consists of a land sphere (*geosphere*), an air sphere (*atmosphere*), a water sphere (*hydrosphere*), and a life sphere (*biosphere*) (**Concept 3.1A**).

the air we breathe. It is 78% nitrogen (N_2) and 21% oxygen (O_2). The remaining 1% of air is mostly water vapor, carbon dioxide, and methane.

The next layer of the atmosphere is the **stratosphere**. It reaches 17 to 50 kilometers (11–31 miles) above the earth's surface. The layer of the stratosphere closest to the earth's surface contains enough ozone (O_3) gas to filter out about 95% of the sun's harmful *ultraviolet (UV) radiation*. This global sunscreen allows life to exist on the surface of the planet.

The **hydrosphere** includes all of the water on or near the earth's surface. It is found as *water vapor* in the atmosphere, as *liquid water* on the surface and underground, and as *ice*—polar ice, icebergs, glaciers, and ice in frozen soil-layers called *permafrost*. Salty oceans that cover about 71% of the earth's surface contain 97% of the planet's water and support almost half of the world's species. About 2.5% of the earth's water is freshwater and three-fourths of that is ice.

The **geosphere** contains the earth's rocks, minerals, and soil. It consists of an intensely hot *core*, a thick *mantle* of very hot rock, and a thin outer *crust* of rock and soil. The crust's upper portion contains soil chemicals or nutrients that organisms need to live, grow, and reproduce. It also contains nonrenewable *fossil fuels*—coal, oil, and natural gas—and minerals that we extract and use.

The **biosphere** consists of the parts of the atmosphere, hydrosphere, and geosphere where life is found. If you compare the earth with an apple, the biosphere would be as thick as the apple's skin.

Three Factors Sustain the Earth's Life

Life on the earth depends on three interconnected factors (**Concept 3.1B**):

1. **One-way flow of high-quality energy from the sun.** The sun's energy supports plant growth, which provides energy for plants and animals, in keeping with the solar energy **principle of sustainability**. As solar energy interacts with carbon dioxide (CO_2), water vapor, and several other gases in the troposphere, it warms the troposphere—a process known as the **greenhouse effect** (Figure 3.3). Without this natural process, the earth would be too cold to support most of the forms of life we find here today.

2. *Cycling of nutrients* through parts of the biosphere. **Nutrients** are chemicals that organisms need to survive. Because the earth does not get significant inputs of matter from space, its fixed supply of nutrients must be recycled to support life. This is in keeping with the chemical cycling **principle of sustainability**.

3. *Gravity* allows the planet to hold on to its atmosphere and enables the movement and cycling of chemicals through air, water, soil, and organisms.

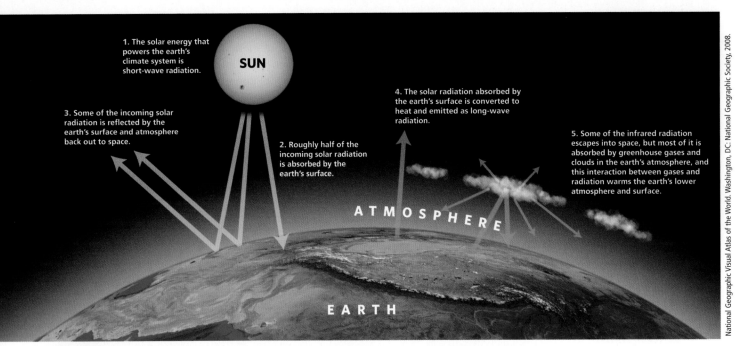

National Geographic Visual Atlas of the World. Washington, DC: National Geographic Society, 2008.

FIGURE 3.3 *Greenhouse Earth*. High-quality solar energy flows from the sun to the earth. It is degraded to lower-quality energy (mostly heat) as it interacts with the earth's air, water, soil, and life forms, and eventually returns to space. Certain gases in the earth's atmosphere retain enough of the sun's incoming energy as heat to warm the planet in what is known as the *greenhouse effect*.

CHECKPOINT FOR UNDERSTANDING 3.1

1. Define the natural greenhouse effect. Explain how it affects the current life found on the earth.

2. Explain how gravity plays a significant role in sustaining life on earth.

3.2 WHAT ARE THE MAJOR COMPONENTS OF AN ECOSYSTEM?

CONCEPT 3.2A Some organisms produce the nutrients they need, others get the nutrients they need by consuming other organisms, and some recycle nutrients back to producers by decomposing the wastes and remains of other organisms.

CONCEPT 3.2B Soil is a renewable resource that provides nutrients that support terrestrial plants and helps purify water and control the earth's climate.

Ecosystems Have Several Important Components

Scientists classify matter into levels of organization ranging from atoms to galaxies. Ecologists study five levels of matter—the *biosphere, ecosystems, communities, populations,* and *organisms*—which are shown and defined in Figure 3.4.

The biosphere and its ecosystems are made up of living (*biotic*) and nonliving (*abiotic*) components (Figure 3.5). Nonliving components include water, air, nutrients, rocks, heat, and solar energy. Living components include plants, animals, and microbes.

Ecologists assign each organism in an ecosystem to a *feeding level*, or **trophic level**, based on its source of nutrients. Organisms are classified as *producers* and *consumers*. **Producers** (also called **autotrophs**) are organisms, such as green plants, that make the nutrients they need from compounds and energy obtained from their environment (**Concept 3.2A**). In the process known as **photosynthesis**, plants capture solar energy that falls on their leaves. They use it to combine carbon dioxide and water and form carbohydrates such as glucose ($C_6H_{12}O_6$), to store chemical energy that plants need and emit oxygen (O_2) gas into the atmosphere. This oxygen keeps us and most other animal species alive. The following chemical reaction summarizes the overall process:

$$\text{carbon dioxide} + \text{water} + \textbf{solar energy} \rightarrow \text{glucose} + \text{oxygen}$$
$$6\,CO_2 + 6\,H_2O + \textbf{solar energy} \rightarrow C_6H_{12}O_6 + 6\,O_2$$

About 2.8 billion years ago, producer organisms called *cyanobacteria,* most of them floating on the surface of the ocean, started carrying out photosynthesis, which added oxygen to the atmosphere. After several hundred million years, oxygen levels reached about 21%—high enough to keep oxygen-breathing animals alive.

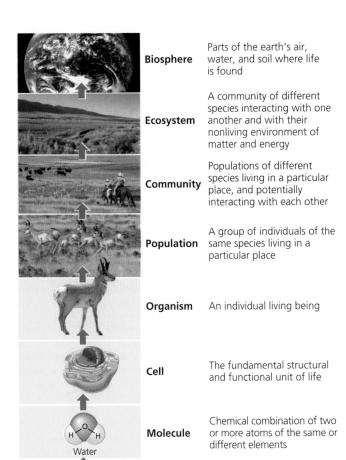

Biosphere	Parts of the earth's air, water, and soil where life is found
Ecosystem	A community of different species interacting with one another and with their nonliving environment of matter and energy
Community	Populations of different species living in a particular place, and potentially interacting with each other
Population	A group of individuals of the same species living in a particular place
Organism	An individual living being
Cell	The fundamental structural and functional unit of life
Molecule	Chemical combination of two or more atoms of the same or different elements
Atom	Smallest unit of a chemical element that exhibits its chemical properties

FIGURE 3.4 Ecology focuses on the top five of these levels of the organization of matter in nature.

Today, most producers on land are trees and other green plants. In freshwater and ocean ecosystems, algae and aquatic plants growing near shorelines are the major producers. In the open water of the oceans, floating and drifting microscopic organisms known as *phytoplankton* are the dominant producers.

Some producer bacteria live in dark and extremely hot water around fissures on the ocean floor. Their source of energy is heat from the earth's interior, or *geothermal energy*. They are an exception to the solar energy principle of sustainability.

The other organisms in an ecosystem are **consumers** (also called **heterotrophs**) that cannot produce the nutrients they need (**Concept 3.2A**). They get their nutrients by

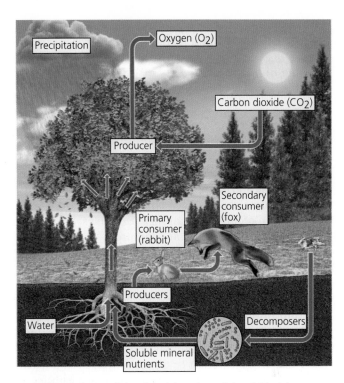

FIGURE 3.5 Key living (biotic) and nonliving (abiotic) components of an ecosystem in a field.

FIGURE 3.6 This lioness (a carnivore) is feeding on a freshly killed zebra (an herbivore) in Kenya, Africa.

feeding on other organisms (producers or other consumers) or on their wastes and remains.

There are several types of consumers. **Primary consumers**, or **herbivores** (plant eaters), are animals that eat mostly green plants. Examples are caterpillars, giraffes, and zooplankton (tiny sea animals that feed on phytoplankton). **Carnivores** (meat eaters) are animals that feed on the flesh of other animals. Some carnivores, including spiders, lions (Figure 3.6), and most small fishes, are **secondary consumers** that feed on the flesh of herbivores. Other carnivores such as tigers, hawks, and killer whales (orcas) are **tertiary** (or higher-level) **consumers** that feed on the flesh of herbivores and other carnivores. Some of these relationships are shown in Figure 3.5. **Omnivores** such as pigs, rats, and humans eat both plants and animals.

THINKING ABOUT What You Eat

When you ate your most recent meal, were you an herbivore, a carnivore, or an omnivore?

Decomposers are consumers that get nourishment by releasing nutrients from the wastes or remains of plants and animals. These nutrients return to the soil, water, and air for reuse by producers (**Concept 3.2A**). Most decomposers are bacteria and fungi. Other consumers, called **detritus feeders**, or **detritivores**, feed on the wastes or dead bodies (detritus) of other organisms. Examples are earthworms, soil insects, hyenas, and vultures.

Detritivores and decomposers can transform a fallen tree trunk into simple inorganic molecules that plants can absorb as nutrients (Figure 3.7). In natural ecosystems, the wastes and dead bodies of organisms are resources for other organisms in keeping with the chemical cycling **principle of sustainability**. Without decomposers and detritivores, many of which are microscopic organisms (Science Focus 3.1), the planet's land surfaces would be buried in plant and animal wastes, dead animal bodies, and garbage.

Producers, consumers, and decomposers use the chemical energy stored in glucose and other organic compounds to fuel their life processes. In most cells, this energy is released by **aerobic respiration**, which uses oxygen to convert glucose (or other organic nutrient molecules) back into carbon dioxide and water. The overall chemical reaction for the aerobic respiration is shown in the following equation:

$$glucose + oxygen \rightarrow carbon\ dioxide + water + \textbf{energy}$$
$$C_6H_{12}O_6 + 6\ O_2 \rightarrow 6\ CO_2 + 6\ H_2O + \textbf{energy}$$

To summarize, ecosystems and the biosphere are sustained by the *one-way energy flow* from the sun and the *nutrient cycling* of key materials—in keeping with two of the **scientific principles of sustainability** (Figure 3.8).

Soil Is the Foundation of Life on Land

Terrestrial life depends on soil, one of the most important components of the earth's natural capital. The minerals that make up your muscles, bones, and most other parts of your body come almost entirely from soil. Soil also supplies most of the nutrients needed for plant growth and purifies water. Through aerobic respiration, organisms living in soil remove some of the carbon dioxide in the atmosphere and store it as organic carbon compounds, thereby helping to control the earth's climate.

Soil is much more than the dirt that we wash off our hands and clothes. **Soil** is a complex mixture of rock pieces and particles, mineral nutrients, decaying organic matter, water, air, and living organisms that support plant life, which supports animal life (**Concept 3.2B**). Life on land depends on roughly 15 centimeters (6 inches) of topsoil—the earth's living skin.

Soil is a renewable resource but it is renewed very slowly and becomes a nonrenewable resource if we deplete it faster than nature can replenish it. The formation of just 2.5 centimeters (1 inch) of topsoil can take hundreds to

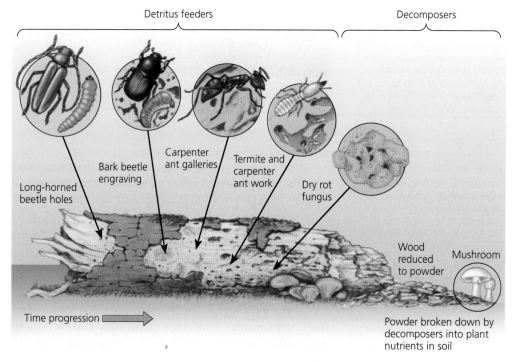

Detritus feeders

Decomposers

Long-horned beetle holes

Bark beetle engraving

Carpenter ant galleries

Termite and carpenter ant work

Dry rot fungus

Wood reduced to powder

Mushroom

Time progression

Powder broken down by decomposers into plant nutrients in soil

FIGURE 3.7 Various detritivores and decomposers (mostly fungi and bacteria) can "feed on" or digest parts of a log and eventually convert its complex organic chemicals into simpler inorganic nutrients that can be taken up by producers.

Many of the World's Most Important Organisms Are Invisible to Us

They are everywhere. Trillions can be found inside your body, on your skin, in a handful of soil, and in a cup of ocean water. They are *microbes*, or *microorganisms*, catchall terms for many thousands of species of bacteria, protozoa, fungi, and floating phytoplankton. Though most of them are too small to be seen with the naked eye, they are the biological rulers of the earth and play key roles in the earth's life-support system and in our bodies.

Microbes do not get the respect they deserve. Most of us view them primarily as threats to our health in the form of infectious bacteria or fungi that cause athlete's foot and other skin diseases, and protozoa that cause diseases such as malaria. But these harmful microbes are in the minority.

Researchers have identified more than 10,000 species of bacteria, fungi, and other microbes that live in or on our bodies. Many of them provide us with vital services. Bacteria in our intestinal tracts help break down the food we eat, and microbes in our noses help prevent harmful bacteria from reaching our lungs. Bacteria and fungi in the soil decompose organic wastes into nutrients that can be taken up by plants that are then eaten by humans and other plant eaters. Without these tiny creatures, we would go hungry and be up to our necks in waste matter.

Some microorganisms, particularly phytoplankton in the ocean, provide much of the planet's oxygen. They also help regulate the atmosphere's average temperature by removing some of the

carbon dioxide produced when we burn coal, natural gas, and gasoline from the atmosphere.

Some microorganisms assist us in controlling plant diseases and populations of insect species that attack our food crops. By relying more on these microbes for pest control, we could reduce the use of potentially harmful chemical pesticides. In other words, microbes are a vital part of the earth's natural capital.

CRITICAL THINKING

What are two advantages that microbes have over humans for thriving in the world?

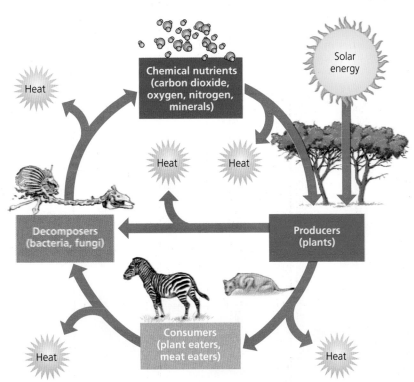

FIGURE 3.8 Natural capital: The main components of an ecosystem are energy, chemicals, and organisms. Nutrient cycling and the flow of energy—first from the sun, then through organisms, and finally into the environment as low-quality heat—link these components.

thousands of years. Removing plant cover from soil exposes its topsoil to erosion by water and wind. This explains why protecting and renewing topsoil is a key to sustainability. You will learn more about soil in Chapter 11 and more about soil erosion and soil conservation in Chapter 12.

CHECKPOINT FOR UNDERSTANDING 3.2

1. The earth's life-support system is comprised of biotic and abiotic components. What are the abiotic components? What are the biotic components?

2. Plants are the link between the sun and primary consumers. Explain why plants are critical to sustaining all other organisms.

3. Identify several reasons why microbes are critical to continued life on earth.

3.3 WHAT HAPPENS TO ENERGY IN AN ECOSYSTEM?

CONCEPT 3.3 As energy flows through ecosystems in food chains and food webs, there is a decrease in the high-quality chemical energy available to organisms at each successive feeding level.

Energy Flows through Ecosystems in Food Chains and Food Webs

Chemical energy, stored as nutrients in the bodies and wastes of organisms, flows through ecosystems from one trophic (feeding) level to another. A sequence of organisms with each one serving as a source of nutrients or energy for the next level of organisms is called a **food chain** (Figure 3.9).

Every use and transfer of energy by organisms from one feeding level to another involves a loss of some high-quality energy to the environment as low-quality energy in the form of heat, in accordance with the second law of thermodynamics. A graphic display of the energy loss at each trophic level is called a **pyramid of energy flow**. Figure 3.10 illustrates this energy loss for a food chain, assuming a 90% energy loss for each level of the chain.

The large loss in chemical energy between successive trophic levels explains why food chains and webs rarely have more than four or five trophic levels.

CONSIDER THIS . . .

CONNECTIONS Energy Flow and Feeding People

Energy flow pyramids explain why the earth could support more people if they all ate at a low trophic level by consuming grains, vegetables, and fruits directly rather than passing such crops through another trophic level and eating herbivores such as cattle, pigs, sheep, and chickens. About two-thirds of the world's people survive primarily by eating wheat, rice, and corn at the first trophic level, mostly because they cannot afford to eat much meat.

Ecologists can estimate the *number of organisms* feeding at each trophic level. Here is a hypothetical example: 100,000 blades of grass (producer) might support 30 rabbits (herbivore), which might support 1 fox (carnivore). Ecologists also measure **biomass**—the total mass of

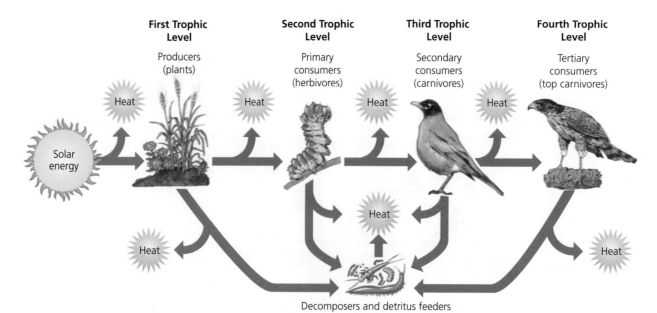

FIGURE 3.9 In a food chain, chemical energy in nutrients flows through various trophic levels. *Critical thinking:* Think about what you ate for breakfast. At what level or levels on a food chain were you eating?

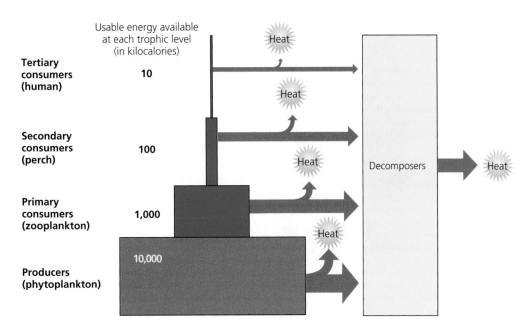

FIGURE 3.10 Generalized *pyramid of energy flow* showing the decrease in usable chemical energy available at each succeeding trophic level in a food chain or food web. This model assumes that with each transfer from one trophic level to another, there is a 90% loss of usable energy to the environment in the form of low-quality heat. (Calories and joules are used to measure energy. 1 kilocalorie = 1,000 calories = 4,184 joules.) **Critical thinking:** Why is a vegetarian diet more energy efficient than a meat-based diet?

organisms in each trophic level—as illustrated by this hypothetical example: 1,000 kilograms (2,200 pounds) of producers might provide 100 kilograms (220 pounds) of food for herbivores, which might provide 10 kilograms (22 pounds) of food for carnivores, which might supply a top carnivore with 1 kilogram (2.2 pounds) of food.

In natural ecosystems, most consumers feed on more than one type of organism, and most organisms are eaten or decomposed by more than one type of consumer. Because of this, organisms in most ecosystems form a complex network of interconnected food chains called a **food web**. Food chains and food webs show how producers, consumers, and decomposers are connected to one another as energy flows through trophic levels in an ecosystem. Figure 3.11 shows an aquatic food web and Figure 3.12 shows a terrestrial food web.

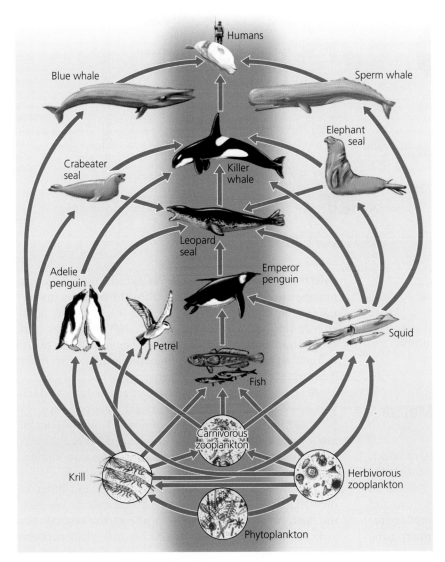

FIGURE 3.11 A greatly simplified aquatic food web found in the southern hemisphere. The shaded middle area shows a simple food chain that is part of these complex interacting feeding relationships. Many more participants in the web, including an array of decomposer and detritus feeder organisms, are not shown here.

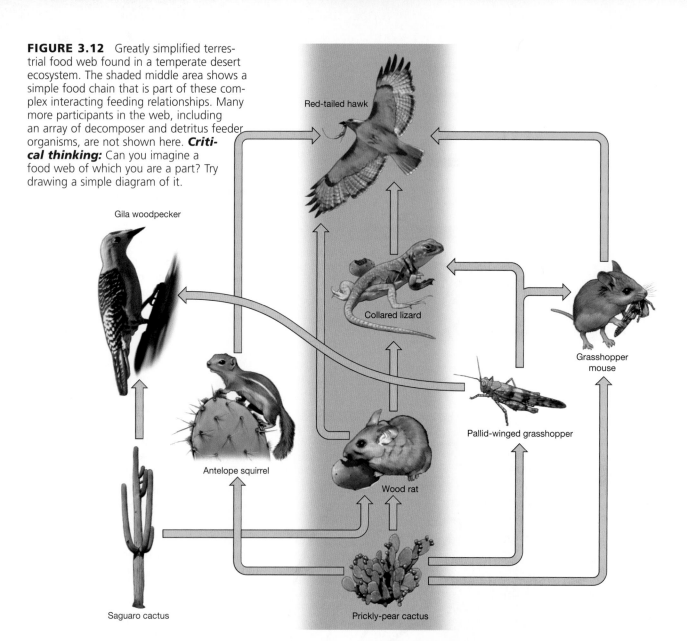

FIGURE 3.12 Greatly simplified terrestrial food web found in a temperate desert ecosystem. The shaded middle area shows a simple food chain that is part of these complex interacting feeding relationships. Many more participants in the web, including an array of decomposer and detritus feeder organisms, are not shown here. **Critical thinking:** Can you imagine a food web of which you are a part? Try drawing a simple diagram of it.

Red-tailed hawk

Gila woodpecker

Collared lizard

Grasshopper mouse

Antelope squirrel

Pallid-winged grasshopper

Wood rat

Saguaro cactus

Prickly-pear cactus

Some Ecosystems Produce Plant Matter Faster Than Others Do

Gross primary productivity (GPP) is the *rate* at which an ecosystem's producers (such as plants and phytoplankton) convert solar energy into chemical energy stored in compounds found in their tissues. To stay alive, grow, and reproduce, producers must use some of their stored chemical energy for their own respiration. **Net primary pro-**ductivity **(NPP)** is the *rate* at which producers use photosynthesis to produce and store chemical energy *minus* the *rate* at which they use some of this stored chemical energy through aerobic respiration. NPP measures how fast producers can make the chemical energy that is stored in their tissues and that is potentially available to other organisms (consumers) in an ecosystem.

Gross primary productivity is similar to the *rate* at which you make money, or the number of dollars you earn per year. *Net primary productivity* is similar to the amount of money earned per year that you can spend after subtracting your expenses such as the costs of transportation, clothes, food, and supplies.

Terrestrial ecosystems and aquatic life zones differ in their NPP as illustrated in Figure 3.13. Despite its low NPP, the open ocean produces more of the earth's biomass per year than any other ecosystem or life zone. This happens

What happens to energy in a food chain?

Ecological efficiency is the percentage of energy transferred from one trophic level to the next in an ecosystem. Energy transfer can differ slightly from level to level, but on average the percentage of energy transferred is approximately 10 percent, as shown in Figure 3.10. Ecologists refer to this as the **ten percent rule**.

If only 10 percent of the energy is transferred from trophic level to trophic level, where does the rest of the energy go? Most of it ends up as low-quality heat in the environment because of the second law of thermodynamics. According to this law, when high-quality energy is transferred by chemical reactions in the cells of organisms from one trophic level to another, roughly 90% of it is degraded to lower quality energy that flows into the environment as heat (see Figure 3.10).

While most of the energy at each trophic level will be converted into waste heat that results from metabolism, some energy will be contained in detritus or metabolic waste (indigestible biomass, feces, dead organisms that were not food for other organisms) that can be used as an energy source for decomposers and detritus feeders. As these detritivores consume the detritus, they too will generate waste heat through their own metabolism and within their own food chain (see Figure 3.9).

FRQ Application

Question: Consider a simple grassland food chain:

grass ➡ mouse ➡ snake ➡ hawk

Explain why many hectares of grass are required to support a single hawk. Include in your discussion how the second law of thermodynamics applies.

Possible Response: Many hectares of grass are required to support a single hawk because when high-quality chemical energy is transferred from one trophic level in a food chain to another roughly 90% of this energy is degraded to low-quality energy that is lost as heat to the environment, as required by the second law of thermodynamics.

because oceans cover 71% of the earth's surface and contain huge numbers of phytoplankton and other producers.

Tropical rain forests have a high net primary productivity because they have a large number and variety of producer trees and other plants. When these forests are cleared (**Core Case Study**) or burned to make way for crops or for grazing cattle, they suffer a sharp drop in net primary productivity. They also lose much of their diverse array of plant and animal species.

Only the plant matter represented by NPP is available as nutrients for consumers. Thus, *the planet's NPP ultimately*

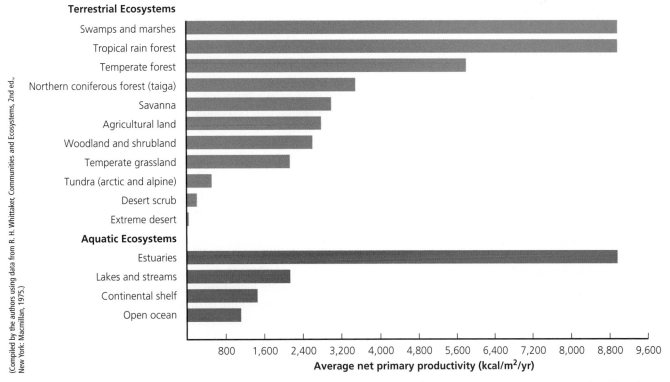

FIGURE 3.13 Estimated annual average *net primary productivity* in major life zones and ecosystems expressed as kilocalories of energy produced per square meter per year (kcal/m²/yr). **Question:** What are the three most productive and the three least productive systems?

limits the number of consumers (including humans) that can survive on the earth. This is an important lesson from nature.

CHECKPOINT FOR UNDERSTANDING 3.3

1. Explain why there are rarely more than four levels in a trophic pyramid.

3.4 WHAT HAPPENS TO MATTER IN AN ECOSYSTEM?

CONCEPT 3.4 Matter, in the form of nutrients, cycles within and among ecosystems and the biosphere, and human activities are altering these chemical cycles.

Nutrients Cycle Within and Among Ecosystems

The elements and compounds that make up nutrients move continually through air, water, soil, rock, and living organisms within ecosystems, in cycles called **nutrient cycles**, or *biogeochemical cycles* (life-earth-chemical cycles). They represent the chemical cycling **principle of sustainability** in action. These cycles are driven directly or indirectly by incoming solar energy and by the earth's gravity and include the hydrologic (water), carbon, nitrogen, and phosphorus cycles. Human activities are altering these important components of the earth's natural capital (see Figure 1.3, p. 7) (**Concept 3.4**).

CONSIDER THIS . . .

CONNECTIONS Nutrient Cycles and Life
Nutrient cycles connect past, present, and future forms of life. Some of the carbon atoms in your skin may once have been part of an oak leaf, a dinosaur's skin, or a layer of limestone rock. Your grandmother, George Washington, or a hunter–gatherer who lived 25,000 years ago may have inhaled some of the nitrogen (N_2) molecules you just inhaled.

The Water Cycle Sustains All Life

Water (H_2O) is an amazing substance that is necessary for life on the earth. The **hydrologic cycle**, also called the **water cycle**, collects, purifies, and distributes the earth's fixed supply of water, as shown in Figure 3.14.

The sun powers the water cycle. Incoming solar energy causes *evaporation*—the conversion of some of the liquid water in the earth's oceans, lakes, rivers, soil, and plants to vapor. This water vapor rises into the atmosphere, where it condenses into droplets. Gravity then draws the water back to the earth's surface as *precipitation* (rain, snow, sleet, and dew).

Most precipitation falling on terrestrial ecosystems becomes **surface runoff**. This water flows into streams,

rivers, lakes, wetlands, and oceans, from which it can evaporate to repeat the cycle. Some precipitation seeps into the upper layers of soils and is used by plants, and some evaporates from the soils back into the atmosphere. Some precipitation also sinks through soil into underground layers of rock, sand, and gravel called **aquifers**. This water stored underground is called **groundwater**. Some precipitation is converted to ice that is stored in *glaciers*.

Because water is good at dissolving many different compounds, it can easily be polluted. However, natural processes in the water cycle can purify water—an important and free ecosystem service.

Only about 0.024% of the earth's huge water supply is available to humans and other species as liquid freshwater in accessible groundwater deposits and in lakes, rivers, and streams. The rest of the planet's water is too salty, is too deep underground to extract at affordable prices, or is stored as ice.

Humans alter the water cycle in three major ways (see the red arrows and boxes in Figure 3.14). *First*, sometimes we withdraw freshwater from rivers, lakes, and aquifers at rates faster than natural processes can replace it. As a result, some aquifers are being depleted and some rivers no longer flow to the ocean.

0.024
Percentage of the earth's freshwater supply that is available to humans and other species

Second, we clear vegetation from land for agriculture, mining, road building, and other activities, and cover much of the land with buildings, concrete, and asphalt. This increases water runoff and reduces infiltration that would normally recharge groundwater supplies.

Third, we drain and fill wetlands for farming and urban development. Left undisturbed, wetlands provide the ecosystem service of flood control. They act like sponges to absorb and hold overflows of water from drenching rains or rapidly melting snow.

Carbon Cycles among Living and Nonliving Things

Carbon is the basic building block of the carbohydrates, fats, proteins, DNA, and other organic compounds required for life. Various compounds of carbon circulate through the biosphere, the atmosphere, and parts of the hydrosphere, in the **carbon cycle** shown in Figure 3.15.

A key component of the carbon cycle is carbon dioxide (CO_2) gas. It makes up about 0.040% of the volume of the earth's troposphere. Carbon dioxide (along with water vapor in the water cycle) affects the temperature of the atmosphere through the greenhouse effect (Figure 3.3) and thus plays a major role in determining the earth's

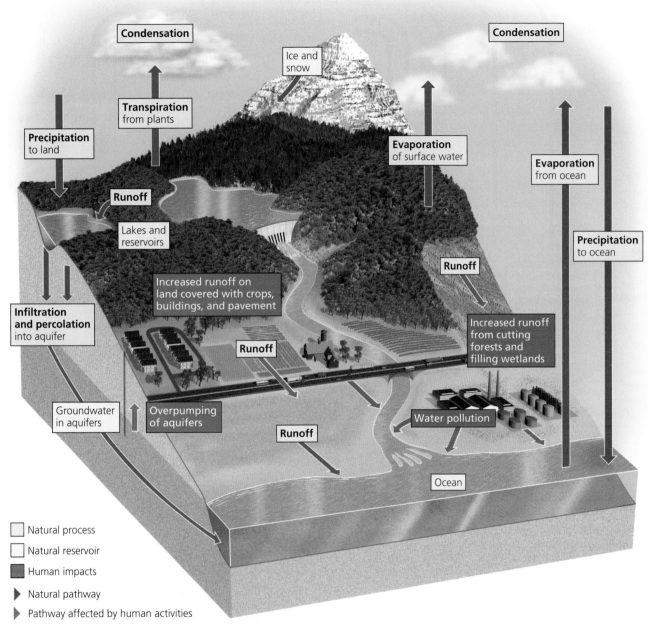

FIGURE 3.14 Natural capital: Simplified model of the *water cycle*, or *hydrologic cycle*, in which water circulates in various physical forms within the biosphere. The red arrows and boxes identify major effects of human activities on this cycle. ***Critical thinking:*** What are three ways in which your lifestyle directly or indirectly affects the hydrologic cycle?

climate. If the carbon cycle removes too much CO_2 from the atmosphere, the atmosphere will cool, and if it generates too much CO_2, the atmosphere will get warmer. Thus, even slight changes in this cycle caused by natural or human factors can affect the earth's climate, which helps determine the types of life that can exist in various places.

Carbon is cycled through the biosphere by a combination of *photosynthesis* by producers that removes CO_2 from the air and water, and *aerobic respiration* by producers, consumers, and decomposers that adds CO_2 in the atmosphere.

Typically, CO_2 remains in the atmosphere for 100 years or more. Some of the CO_2 in the atmosphere dissolves in the ocean. In the ocean, decomposers release carbon that is stored as insoluble carbonate minerals and rocks in bottom sediment for long periods. Marine sediments are the earth's largest store of carbon, mostly as carbonates.

Over millions of years, some of the carbon in deeply buried deposits of dead plant matter and algae have been converted into carbon-containing *fossil fuels* such as coal, oil, and natural gas (Figure 3.15). In a few hundred years,

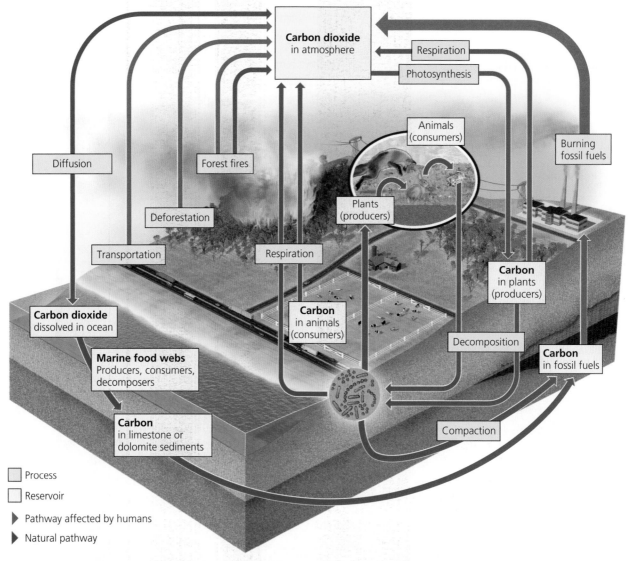

Diffusion

Forest fires

Carbon dioxide
in atmosphere

Respiration

Photosynthesis

Animals
(consumers)

Burning
fossil fuels

Deforestation

Plants
(producers)

Transportation

Respiration

Carbon
in plants
(producers)

Carbon dioxide
dissolved in ocean

Carbon
in animals
(consumers)

Marine food webs
Producers, consumers,
decomposers

Decomposition

Carbon
in fossil fuels

Carbon
in limestone or
dolomite sediments

Compaction

☐ Process

☐ Reservoir

▶ Pathway affected by humans

▶ Natural pathway

FIGURE 3.15 Natural capital: Simplified model showing the circulation of various chemical forms of carbon in the global *carbon cycle*. Red arrows show major harmful impacts of human activities shown by the red arrows. (Yellow box sizes do not show relative reservoir sizes.) ***Critical thinking:*** What are three ways in which you directly or indirectly affect the carbon cycle?

we have extracted and burned huge quantities of fossil fuels that took millions of years to form. This has added large quantities of CO_2 to the atmosphere and altered the carbon cycle (see red arrows in Figure 3.15). In effect, we have been adding CO_2 to the atmosphere faster than the carbon cycle can remove it.

As a result, levels of CO_2 in the atmosphere have been rising sharply since about 1960. There is considerable scientific evidence that this disruption of the carbon cycle is helping to warm the atmosphere and change the earth's climate. Another way in which we alter the cycle is by clearing carbon-absorbing vegetation from forests, especially tropical forests, faster than they can grow back (**Core Case Study**). This reduces the ability of the carbon cycle to remove excess CO_2 from the atmosphere and contributes to climate change, which we discuss in Chapter 20.

Nitrogen Cycle: Bacteria in Action

Nitrogen is a critical nutrient for all forms of life. Nitrogen gas (N_2) makes up 78% of the volume of the atmosphere, but N_2 cannot be used as a nutrient by plants. It becomes a plant nutrient only as a component of nitrogen-containing ammonia (NH_3), ammonium ions (NH_4^+), and nitrate ions (NO_3^-).

These chemical forms of nitrogen are created in the **nitrogen cycle** (Figure 3.16) by lightning, which converts N_2 to NH_3, and by specialized bacteria in topsoil. Other bacteria in topsoil and in the bottom sediments of aquatic systems convert NH_3 to NH_4^+ and nitrate ions (NO_3^-) that are taken up by the roots of plants. The plants then use these forms of nitrogen to produce various proteins, nucleic acids, and vitamins. Animals that eat plants consume these nitrogen-containing compounds, as do detritus feeders and

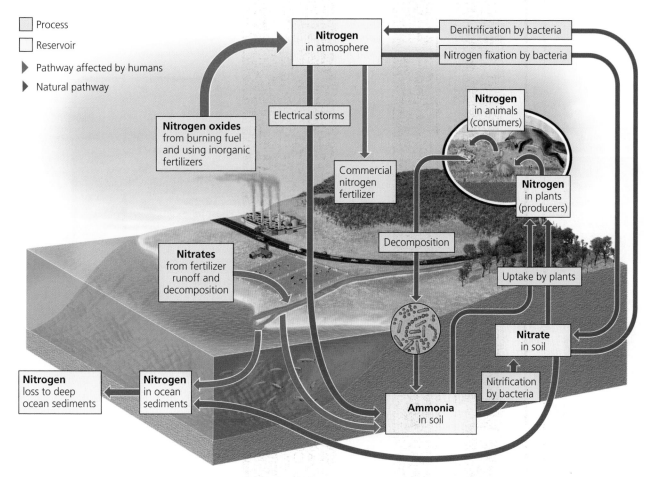

Nitrogen in atmosphere

Denitrification by bacteria

Nitrogen fixation by bacteria

Electrical storms

Nitrogen oxides from burning fuel and using inorganic fertilizers

Nitrogen in animals (consumers)

Commercial nitrogen fertilizer

Nitrogen in plants (producers)

Decomposition

Nitrates from fertilizer runoff and decomposition

Uptake by plants

Nitrate in soil

Nitrogen loss to deep ocean sediments

Nitrogen in ocean sediments

Nitrification by bacteria

Ammonia in soil

FIGURE 3.16 Natural capital: Simplified model showing the circulation of various chemical forms of nitrogen in the *nitrogen cycle*, with major harmful human impacts shown by the red arrows. (Yellow box sizes do not show relative reservoir sizes.) ***Critical thinking:*** What are two ways in which the carbon cycle and the nitrogen cycle are linked?

decomposers. Bacteria in waterlogged soil and bottom sediments of lakes, oceans, swamps, and bogs convert nitrogen compounds into nitrogen gas (N_2). The gas is released to the atmosphere to begin the nitrogen cycle again.

Humans intervene in the nitrogen cycle in several ways (see red arrows in Figure 3.16). When we burn gasoline and other fuels, the resulting high temperatures convert some of the N_2 and O_2 in air to nitric oxide (NO). In the atmosphere, NO can be converted to nitrogen dioxide gas (NO_2) and nitric acid vapor (HNO_3), which can return to the earth's surface as damaging *acid deposition*, commonly called *acid rain*. Acid rain damages buildings, statues, and forests.

We remove large amounts of N_2 from the atmosphere and combine it with H_2 to make ammonia ($N_2 + 3H_2 \rightarrow 2NH_3$) and ammonium ions ($NH_4^+$) used in fertilizers. We add nitrous oxide (N_2O) to the atmosphere through the action of anaerobic bacteria on nitrogen-containing fertilizer or organic animal manure applied to the soil. This greenhouse gas can warm the atmosphere and take part in reactions that deplete stratospheric ozone, which keeps most of the sun's harmful ultraviolet radiation from reaching the earth's surface.

We alter the nitrogen cycle in aquatic ecosystems by adding excess nitrates (NO_3^-) to these systems. The nitrates contaminate bodies of water through agricultural runoff of fertilizers, animal manure, and discharges from municipal sewage treatment systems. This plant nutrient can cause excessive growth of algae that disrupt aquatic systems. Human nitrogen inputs into the environment have risen sharply and are projected to continue rising.

Phosphorus Cycles through Water, Rock, and Food Webs

Phosphorus is another nutrient that supports life. The cyclic movement of phosphorus (P) through water, the earth's crust, and living organisms is called the **phosphorus cycle** (Figure 3.17). The major reservoir for phosphorus in this cycle is phosphate rocks that contain phosphate ions (PO_4^{3-}), which are an important plant nutrient. Phosphorus does not cycle through the atmosphere because few of its compounds exist as a gas. Phosphorus cycles more slowly than water, carbon, and nitrogen.

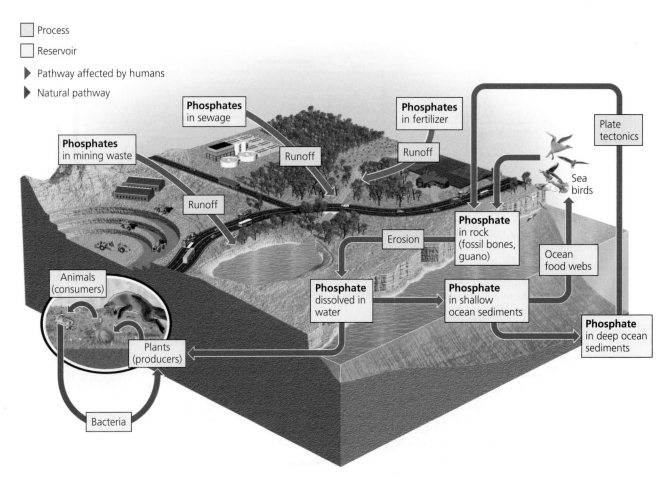

Process

Reservoir

▶ Pathway affected by humans

▶ Natural pathway

Phosphates in sewage

Phosphates in fertilizer

Plate tectonics

Phosphates in mining waste

Runoff

Runoff

Sea birds

Runoff

Erosion

Phosphate in rock (fossil bones, guano)

Ocean food webs

Animals (consumers)

Phosphate dissolved in water

Phosphate in shallow ocean sediments

Phosphate in deep ocean sediments

Plants (producers)

Bacteria

FIGURE 3.17 Natural capital: Simplified model showing the circulation of various chemical forms of phosphorus (mostly phosphates) in the *phosphorus cycle*, with major harmful human impacts shown by the red arrows. (Yellow box sizes do not show relative reservoir sizes.) *Critical thinking:* What are two ways in which the phosphorus cycle and the nitrogen cycle are linked? What are two ways in which the phosphorus cycle and the carbon cycle are linked?

As water runs over exposed rocks, it slowly erodes away inorganic compounds that contain phosphate ions. Water carries these ions into the soil, where they are absorbed by the roots of plants and by other producers. Phosphate compounds are then transferred by food webs from producers to consumers and eventually to detritus feeders and decomposers.

When phosphate and other phosphorus compounds wash into the ocean, they are deposited as marine sediment and can remain trapped for millions of years. Over time, geological processes can uplift and expose these seafloor deposits, from which phosphate can be eroded and freed up to reenter the phosphorus cycle.

Most soils contain little phosphate, which often limits plant growth on land unless phosphorus (as phosphate salts mined from the earth) is applied to the soil as a fertilizer. Lack of phosphorus also limits the growth of producer populations in many freshwater streams and lakes. This is because phosphate salts are only slightly soluble in water and do not release many phosphate ions to producers in aquatic systems.

Human activities, including the removal of large amounts of phosphate from the earth to make fertilizer, disrupt the phosphorus cycle (see red arrows in Figure 3.17). By clearing tropical forests (**Core Case Study**), we reduce phosphate levels in tropical soils. Eroded topsoil and fertilizer washed from fertilized crop fields, lawns, and golf courses carry large quantities of phosphate ions into streams, lakes, and oceans. There they stimulate the growth of producers such as algae and various aquatic plants, which can upset chemical cycling and other processes in bodies of water. According to a number of scientific studies, we are disrupting the phosphorus cycle because our inputs of phosphorus into the environment (primarily for use as fertilizer) have exceeded the planet's environmental limit for phosphorus.

CONSIDER THIS . . .

LEARNING FROM NATURE

Scientists study the water, carbon, nitrogen, and phosphorus cycles to help us learn how to recycle the wastes we create.

Planetary Boundaries

For most of the past 10,000–12,000 years, humans have been living in an era called the *Holocene*. During this era, we have enjoyed a favorable climate and other environmental conditions. This general stability allowed the human population to grow, develop agriculture, and take over a large share of the earth's land and other resources (see Figure 1.8, p. 12).

Most geologists contend that we are still living in the Holocene era, but some scientists disagree. According to them, when the Industrial Revolution began (around 1750) we entered an era called the *Anthropocene*, an era dominated by humans. In this new era, our ecological footprints have expanded significantly and are changing and stressing the earth's life-support system, especially since 1950.

In 2015 an international team of 18 leading researchers in their fields published a paper estimating how close we are to exceeding nine major *planetary boundaries*, or *ecological tipping points*, because of human activities. They warn that exceeding them could change how the planet operates and could trigger abrupt and long-lasting or irreversible environmental changes. This could seriously degrade the earth's life-support system and our economies.

The researchers estimated that we have exceeded four of these planetary boundaries. They are **(1)** *disruption of the nitrogen and phosphorus cycles*, mostly from greatly increased use of fertilizers to produce food; **(2)** *biodiversity loss* from replacing biologically diverse forests and grasslands with simplified fields of single crops; **(3)** *land system change* from agriculture and urban development; and **(4)** *climate change* from disrupting the carbon cycle, mostly by overloading the atmosphere with carbon dioxide produced by the burning of fossil fuels.

There is an urgent need for more research to fill in the missing data on these planetary boundaries.

CRITICAL THINKING

Which two of these boundaries do you think are the most important?

CHECKPOINT FOR UNDERSTANDING 3.4

1. Identify several ways that human activities are altering the hydrologic cycle.

2. Identify several harmful human activities that are altering the carbon cycle.

3. Discuss the role that bacteria play in the nitrogen cycle.

4. Identify several harmful human activities that are altering the phosphorus cycle.

3.5 HOW DO SCIENTISTS STUDY ECOSYSTEMS?

CONCEPT 3.5 Scientists use field research, laboratory research, and mathematical and other models to learn about ecosystems and how much stress they can take.

Some Scientists Study Nature Directly

Scientists use field research, laboratory research, and mathematical and other models to learn about ecosystems (**Concept 3.5**). *Field research*, sometimes called "muddy-boots biology," involves going into forests (see Chapter 2 opening photo, pp. 34–35), oceans (see opening photo this chapter), and other natural settings to study the structure of ecosystems and to learn what happens in them. Most of what we know about ecosystems has come from such research.

Scientists use a variety of methods to study tropical forests (**Core Case Study**). Some build tall construction cranes to reach the canopies. This, along with climbing trees and installing rope walkways between treetops, helps them identify and observe the diversity of species living or feeding in these treetop habitats.

Ecologists carry out controlled experiments by isolating and changing a variable in part of an area and comparing the results with nearby unchanged areas. You learned about a classic example of this in the Core Case Study of Chapter 2 (p. 36).

Scientists also use aircraft and satellites equipped with sophisticated cameras and other *remote sensing* devices to scan and collect data on the earth's surface. They use *geographic information system (GIS)* software to capture, store, analyze, and display this information. For example, GIS software can convert digital satellite images into global, regional, and local maps. These maps show variations in vegetation, gross primary productivity, soil erosion, deforestation, air pollution emissions, water usage, drought, flooding, pest outbreaks, and other variables.

Some researchers attach tiny radio transmitters to animals and use global positioning systems (GPSs) to track where and how far animals go. This technology is important for studying endangered species. Scientists also study nature by using cell phone cameras and mounting time-lapse cameras or video cameras on stationary objects or small drones.

Percent Change and Percent Difference

Percent change is calculated by finding the difference between two values being compared. The difference is divided by the original number and then multiplied by 100. If the result is a negative number, we have a percentage decrease. **Percent difference** is used when comparing two values or measurements. It is the *positive* difference between the values, divided by the average of the two values, multiplied by 100.

FRQ Application

In a laboratory Petri dish with an area of 58 cm², a population of *E. coli* bacteria colonies is estimated at 2320 colonies. How many colonies are there per cm²?

$$\frac{2320 \text{ colonies}}{58 \text{ cm}^2} = 40 \text{ colonies} / \text{cm}^2$$

After incubating the Petri dish for 12 hours, the *E. coli* increase to 3016 colonies. How many colonies are there per cm²?

$$\frac{3016 \text{ colonies}}{58 \text{ cm}^2} = 52 \text{ colonies} / \text{cm}^2$$

What is the **percent change** in colonies of *E. coli*?

$$\frac{(52 \text{ colonies} - 40 \text{ colonies})}{40 \text{ colonies}} \times 100 = \frac{12 \text{ colonies}}{40 \text{ colonies}} \times 100 = 30\% \text{ increase in } E. coli \text{ colonies}$$

What is the **percent difference** in colonies of *E. coli*?

$$\frac{(52 \text{ colonies} - 40 \text{ colonies})}{(52 \text{ colonies} + 40 \text{ colonies}) \div 2} \times 100 = \frac{12 \text{ colonies}}{46 \text{ colonies}} \times 100 = 26.1\% \text{ difference in } E. coli \text{ colonies}$$

Ecologists Do Laboratory Research and Use Models

Ecologists supplement their field research by conducting *laboratory research*. In laboratories, scientists create, set up, and observe models of ecosystems and populations. They create such simplified systems in containers such as culture tubes, bottles, aquariums, and greenhouses, and in indoor and outdoor chambers. In these structures, they control temperature, light, CO_2, humidity, and other variables.

These systems make it easier for scientists to carry out controlled experiments. Laboratory experiments are often faster and less costly than similar experiments in the field. However, scientists must consider how well their scientific observations and measurements in simplified, controlled systems in laboratory conditions reflect what takes place under the more complex and often-changing conditions found in nature.

Since the late 1960s, ecologists have developed mathematical models that simulate ecosystems, and they run the models on high-speed supercomputers. The models help them understand large and complex systems, such as lakes, oceans, forests, and the earth's climate, that cannot be adequately studied and modeled in field or laboratory research.

Ecologists call for greatly increased research on the condition of the world's ecosystems to see how they are changing. This will help them develop strategies for preventing or slowing their degradation. It will also help us to avoid going beyond ecological tipping points. Exceeding such boundaries could cause severe degradation and even the collapse of some ecosystems (Science Focus 3.2).

CHECKPOINT FOR UNDERSTANDING 3.5

1. Identify advantages and disadvantages of the use of field research versus laboratory research to understand how ecosystems work.

- Life is sustained by the flow of energy from the sun through the biosphere, the cycling of nutrients within the biosphere, and gravity.

- Some organisms produce the nutrients they need, others survive by consuming other organisms, and still others live on the wastes and remains of organisms while recycling nutrients that are used again by producer organisms.

- Human activities are altering the flow of energy through food chains and food webs and the cycling of nutrients within ecosystems and the biosphere.

Core Case Study Checkpoint

Identify three reasons for protecting large areas of tropical rain forest.

Chapter 3 Glossary

aerobic respiration: complex process that occurs in the cells of most living organisms, in which nutrient organic molecules such as glucose ($C_6H_{12}O_6$) combine with oxygen (O_2) to produce carbon dioxide (CO_2), water (H_2O), and energy.

aquifer: porous, water-saturated layers of sand, gravel, or bedrock that can yield an economically significant amount of water.

atmosphere: whole mass of air surrounding earth.

biomass: organic matter produced by plants and other photosynthetic producers; total dry weight of all living organisms that can be supported at each trophic level in a food chain or web.

biosphere: zone of the earth where life is found in the atmosphere, hydrosphere, and lithosphere.

carbon cycle: cyclic movement of carbon in different chemical forms from the environment to organisms and then back to the environment.

consumer (heterotroph): organism that cannot synthesize the organic nutrients it needs and gets its organic nutrients by feeding on the tissues of producers or other consumers.

decomposer: organism that digests parts of dead organisms and cast-off fragments and wastes of living organisms by breaking down the complex organic molecules in those materials into simpler water soluble inorganic compounds that are returned to the soil and water for use as nutrients by producers.

detritivore: consumer organism that feeds on detritus, parts of dead organisms, and cast-off fragments and wastes of living organisms.

food chain: series of organisms in which one eats or decomposes the preceding one. The sequence of organisms in an ecosystem through which energy is transferred.

food web: complex network of many interconnected food chains and feeding relationships.

geosphere: the earth's immensely hot core, thick mantle comprised mostly of rock and a thin outer crust that contains most of the earth's rock, soil, and sediment.

greenhouse effect: natural effect that releases heat into the atmosphere near the earth's surface. Water vapor, carbon dioxide, ozone, and other gases in the lower atmosphere (troposphere) absorb some of the infrared radiation radiated by the earth's surface and release it as longer-wavelength radiation (heat) into the troposphere.

gross primary productivity: rate at which an ecosystem's producers capture and store a given amount of chemical energy as biomass in a given length of time.

groundwater: water that sinks into the soil and is stored in slowly flowing and slowly renewed underground reservoirs called aquifers; underground water in the zone of saturation, below the water table.

hydrologic cycle: biogeochemical cycle that collects, purifies, and distributes the earth's fixed supply of water from the environment to living organisms and then back to the environment.

hydrosphere: the earth's liquid water (lakes, rivers, ponds, ocean, underground water), frozen water (icecaps, glaciers, permafrost), and gaseous water (water vapor in the atmosphere).

net primary productivity: rate at which all the plants in an ecosystem produce net useful chemical energy; equal to the difference between the rate at which the plants in an ecosystem produce useful chemical energy (gross primary productivity) and the rate at which they use some of that energy through cellular respiration.

nitrogen cycle: cyclic movement of nitrogen in different chemical forms from the environment to organisms and then back to the environment.

nutrient: any chemical an organism must take in to live, grow, or reproduce.

nutrient cycle (biogeochemical cycle): natural process that recycles nutrients in various chemical forms from the nonliving environment to living organisms and then back to the nonliving environment.

omnivore: animal that can use both plants and animals as food sources.

phosphorus cycle: cyclic movement of phosphorus in different chemical forms from the environment to organisms and then back to the environment.

photosynthesis: complex process in the cells of green plants that captures light energy and converts it to chemical bond energy.

primary consumer (herbivore): organism that feeds on some or all parts of plants or on other producers.

producer (autotroph): organism that uses solar energy (green plants) or chemical energy (some bacteria) to manufacture the organic compounds it needs as nutrients from simple inorganic compounds obtained from the environment.

pyramid of energy flow (trophic pyramid): diagram representing the flow of energy through each trophic level in a food chain or food web. With each energy transfer, only a small part (typically 10%) of the usable energy entering one trophic level is transferred to the organisms at the next trophic level.

secondary consumer (carnivore): organism that feeds only on primary consumers.

soil: complex mixture of inorganic minerals (clay, silt, pebbles, and sand), decaying organic matter, water, air, and living organisms.

stratosphere: second layer of the atmosphere, containing the ozone layer, which filters out most of the sun's harmful UV-light rays.

surface runoff: water flowing off the land into bodies of surface water.

tertiary consumer: animal that feeds on animal-eating animals.

trophic level: all organisms that are the same number of energy transfers away from the original source of energy (sun) that enters an ecosystem.

troposphere: innermost layer of the atmosphere.

Chapter Review

Core Case Study

1. What are three harmful effects of the clearing and degradation of tropical rain forests?

Section 3.1

2. (a) What are the two key concepts for this section? (b) Define and distinguish among the **atmosphere, troposphere, stratosphere, hydrosphere, geosphere,** and **biosphere**. (c) What three interconnected factors sustain life on the earth? (d) Describe the flow of energy to and from the earth. (e) What is the **greenhouse effect** and why is it important?

Section 3.2

3. (a) What are the two key concepts for this section? (b) Define **ecology**. Define **organism, population, community,** and **ecosystem**, and give an example

of each. (c) Distinguish between the living and non-living components in ecosystems and give two examples of each.

4. (a) What is a **trophic level**? Distinguish among **producers (autotrophs), consumers (heterotrophs), decomposers,** and **detritus feeders (detritivores)**, and give an example of each. (b) Summarize the process of **photosynthesis** and explain how it provides us with food and the oxygen in the air that we breathe. (c) Distinguish among **primary consumers (herbivores), carnivores, secondary consumers, tertiary consumers,** and **omnivores**, and give an example of each.

5. (a) Explain the importance of microbes. (b) What is **aerobic respiration**? (c) What two processes sustain ecosystems and the biosphere and how are they linked?

6. What is **soil**?

Section 3.3

7. (a) What is the key concept for this section? (b) Define and distinguish between a **food chain** and a **food web**. Explain what happens to energy as it flows through food chains and food webs. (c) What is a **pyramid of energy flow**? (d) Distinguish between **gross primary productivity (GPP)** and **net primary productivity (NPP)**, and explain their importance. (e) What are the two most productive land ecosystems and the two most productive aquatic ecosystems?

Section 3.4

8. (a) What is the key concept for this section? (b) What happens to matter in an ecosystem? (c) What is a **nutrient cycle**? Explain how nutrient cycles connect past, present, and future life. (d) Describe the **hydrologic cycle**, or **water cycle**. What three major processes are involved in the water cycle? (e) What is **surface runoff**? Define **groundwater**. What is an **aquifer**? (f) What percentage of the earth's water supply is available to humans and other species as liquid freshwater? (g) List three ways that humans are altering the water cycle. (h) Explain how clearing a rain forest can affect local weather and climate.

9. (a) Describe the **carbon, nitrogen,** and **phosphorus cycles**, and explain how human activities are affecting each cycle.

Section 3.5

10. (a) What is the key concept for this section? (b) List three ways in which scientists study ecosystems. Explain why we need much more basic data about the condition of the world's ecosystems. (c) Distinguish between the Holocene era and the proposed Anthropocene era. (d) What is a planetary boundary (ecological tipping point) and why are such boundaries important? List four boundaries that we may have exceeded. (e) What are this chapter's three key ideas?

_____

Note: Key terms are in bold type.

AP® Review Questions

1. A tipping point in the disappearance of the tropical rain forests would be
   (A) the change in regional weather patterns after clearing the forests that prevents their return
   (B) the clearing of rain forests for agricultural lands that adds carbon dioxide to the atmosphere
   (C) the loss of trees, causing less carbon dioxide to be absorbed from the atmosphere
   (D) the loss of habitat for endangered species as rain forests are cleared
   (E) the clearing of land for a new road to be built through the rain forest

2. The best example of a population is
   (A) a group of cats known as Felis concolor living and interbreeding in one area at the same time
   (B) a community of different species interacting with one another and their nonliving environment
   (C) groups of different species living in a specific place and potentially interacting with each other
   (D) the movement of nitrogen from a terrestrial system into the atmosphere
   (E) rabbits who are preyed upon by bobcats

3. Life on earth depends on three interconnected factors. Which of the following are involved in sustaining life on earth?
   I. Flow of high-quality energy
   II. Cycling of matter or nutrients
   III. Gravity
   (A) I only
   (B) II only
   (C) I and II only
   (D) I and III only
   (E) I, II, and III

4. All species interacting with one another and their nonliving environment is called a(n)
   (A) habitat
   (B) population
   (C) community
   (D) ecosystem
   (E) biosphere

5. Which is NOT an important ecological role of insects?
   (A) Pollinating almond and fruit trees in California so farmers do not have to do it
   (B) Eating insect pests that may irritate or harm other insects
   (C) Providing a nutritious food source for other insects and for animals such as bats and frogs
   (D) Fertilizing the soil with nutrients from their waste material and decomposition
   (E) Transmitting tropical disease to humans who visit locations between the Tropic of Cancer and the Tropic of Capricorn

Questions 6–9 refer to the following compounds. Choices may be used once, more than once, or not at all.
   (A) Nitrogen gas (N_2)
   (B) Oxygen gas (O_2)
   (C) Water (H_2O)
   (D) Phosphate (PO_4^{3-})
   (E) Methane (CH_4)

6. A greenhouse gas produced by raising cattle

7. Can be stored in marine sediment for long periods of time

8. A greenhouse gas emitted into the atmosphere through transpiration or evaporation

9. A limiting factor for most plant growth in lakes and terrestrial systems

10. The natural greenhouse effect
    (A) shortens the wavelengths of incoming light energy
    (B) recycles energy from the sun
    (C) converts infrared energy into light energy
    (D) defies the laws of thermodynamics
    (E) heats gases in the troposphere that warm the planet

11. Solar energy flowing to the earth does all of the following EXCEPT
    (A) warm the atmosphere
    (B) evaporate water
    (C) generate winds
    (D) promote cellular respiration
    (E) support plant growth

12. Which of the following is a correctly diagrammed food chain?
    (A) Algae → filter-feeding clam → octopus → shark
    (B) Hawk → snake → mouse → grass
    (C) Scavenging vulture → oak tree → squirrel → fungi
    (D) Apple tree → worm → salmon → mayfly
    (E) Crocodile → antelope → lion → vulture

13. Consider the food chain below.

Food chain

Maize	**Locust**	**Lizard**	**Snake**
Producer	Primary consumer	Secondary consumer	Tertiary consumer

Using the 10% rule, how many calories of corn will be needed to support a snake that consumes 200 calories of lizard biomass per feeding?
   (A)   20 calories
   (B)   200 calories
   (C)   2,000 calories
   (D)   20,000 calories
   (E) 200,000 calories

Source: http://igbiologyy.blogspot.com/2014/03/107-food-chains-food-web.html

Questions 14–15 refer to the terms listed below. Choices may be used once, more than once, or not at all.
   (A) Detritivores
   (B) Heterotrophs
   (C) Autotrophs
   (D) Producers
   (E) Omnivores

14. A type of consumer, these organisms feed on the waste or dead bodies of other organisms.

15. These organisms can feed at more than one trophic level.

16. Which of the following ecosystems has the highest net primary productivity?
    (A) Grassland
    (B) Tundra
    (C) Temperate deciduous forest
    (D) Agricultural land
    (E) Estuaries

17. The rate at which producers in an ecosystem convert solar energy into chemical energy is called
    (A) energy flow
    (B) gross primary productivity
    (C) ecological efficiency
    (D) biological diversity
    (E) range of tolerance

18. Generalized pyramid energy flow has only a 10% efficiency, while 90% of the energy is lost to the environment as heat. This phenomenon is explained by
    (A) the law of limiting factors
    (B) the law of conservation of matter
    (C) the food web corollary
    (D) the greenhouse effect
    (E) the second law of thermodynamics

19. Which of the below is NOT a human intervention in the nitrogen cycle?
    (A) Large amounts of nitric oxide (NO) are released into the atmosphere by smokestacks, which can cause acid rain
    (B) Nitrous oxide (N_2O) is added to the atmosphere through the action of bacteria on livestock waste
    (C) Large amounts of nitrogen are released into the atmosphere as forests are cleared
    (D) Large amounts of nitrates are added to the Chesapeake Bay, causing a eutrophic dead zone
    (E) Specialized bacteria convert ammonia into nitrate and then into nitrogen gas, reducing nitrogen available to plants

20. All of the following are true of the phosphorus cycle EXCEPT
    (A) it is found in rock as fossil bones and guano
    (B) it is a fast-moving atmospheric cycle
    (C) it is a limiting factor for many plants
    (D) it can be deposited as marine sediment and not be released for millions of years
    (E) it is returned to the soil as fertilizer and can cause algal blooms

AP® Free-Response Practice

1. Primary productivity is the *rate* at which an ecosystem's producers (usually plants) convert solar energy into chemical energy in the form of biomass found in their tissues. Net primary productivity is the *rate* at which producers use photosynthesis to produce and store chemical energy *minus* the rate at which they use some of this stored chemical energy through aerobic respiration. What is left as biomass in the plants is energy available to the next trophic level.

   (a) Using the graph below, answer the following questions:
       (i) **Calculate** the percent difference in net productivity between a temperate forest ecosystem and a temperate grassland ecosystem.
       (ii) **Identify** TWO abiotic factors that influence the productivity of ecosystems. **Explain** how these two factors influence the productivity of both temperate grassland and temperate forest ecosystems.

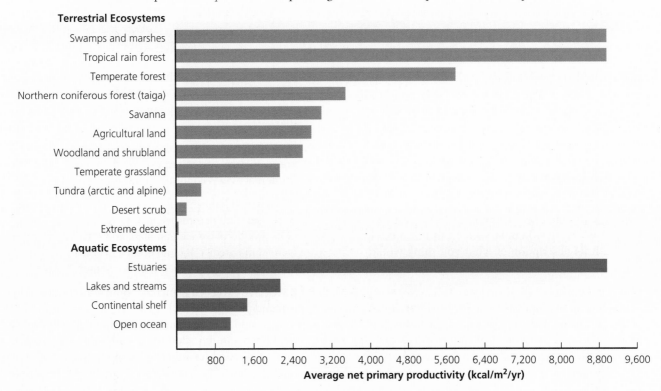

(b) Consider the following organisms found in a temperate grassland ecosystem:

Buffalo grass   Snake   Grasshopper   Frog

  (i) Label the trophic pyramid with the four organisms, placing them in the correct positon according to their energy relationships.

  (ii) Calculate how much usable energy is available to the frog in this trophic pyramid, considering that 90% of the energy is lost at each energy exchange. Assume net productivity of 2,400 kcal/m²/year.

  (iii) One of the above organisms can occupy both the secondary consumer and tertiary consumer levels. **Identify** that organism and **explain** how this could happen.

(c) Trophic pyramids with five levels are rarely found in nature.

  (i) Assume a hawk was positioned at the fifth level as a quaternary consumer. **Calculate** how much usable energy is available to the hawk, based on the above values for productivity.

  (ii) Explain why trophic pyramids of five levels rarely occur.

(d) Decomposers are critical to functioning ecosystems. **Identify** TWO ecosystem services that microbes provide.

Critical Thinking

1. How would you explain the importance of tropical rain forests (**Core Case Study**) to people who think that such forests have no connection to their lives?

2. Explain **(a)** why the flow of energy through the biosphere depends on the cycling of nutrients, and **(b)** why the cycling of nutrients depends on gravity.

3. Explain why microbes are important. What are two ways in which they benefit your health or lifestyle? Write a brief description of what you think would happen to you if microbes were eliminated from the earth.

4. Make a list of the foods you ate for lunch or dinner today. Trace each type of food back to a particular producer species. Describe the sequence of feeding levels that led to your feeding.

5. Use the second law of thermodynamics (see Chapter 2, p. 50) to explain why many poor people in less-developed countries live on a mostly vegetarian diet.

6. How might your life and the lives of any children or grandchildren you might eventually have be affected if human activities continue to intensify the water cycle?

7. What would happen to an ecosystem if **(a)** all of its decomposers and detritus feeders were eliminated, **(b)** all of its producers were eliminated, and **(c)** all of its insects were eliminated? Could an ecosystem exist with producers and decomposers but no consumers? Explain.

8. If we have exceeded planetary boundaries for the nitrogen and phosphorus cycles, biodiversity loss, land change, and climate change by disrupting the carbon cycle, how might this affect **(a)** you, **(b)** any children you might have, and **(c)** any grandchildren you might have?

Data Analysis

Recall that net primary productivity (NPP) is *the rate* at which producers can make the chemical energy that is stored in their tissues and that is potentially available to other organisms (consumers) in an ecosystem. In Figure 3.13, it is expressed as units of energy (kilocalories, or kcal) produced in a given area (square meters, or m^2) per year. Look again at Figure 3.13 and consider the differences in NPP among various ecosystems. Then answer the following questions:

1. What is the approximate NPP of a tropical rain forest in $kcal/m^2/yr$? Which terrestrial ecosystem produces about one-third of that rate? Which aquatic ecosystem has about the same NPP as a tropical rain forest?

2. Why do you think deserts and grasslands have dramatically lower NPP than swamps and marshes?

3. About how many times higher is NPP in estuaries than it is in lakes and streams? Why do you think this is so?

Answers to Checkpoints for Understanding

Section 3.1

1. The greenhouse effect is a natural process in which certain gases in the atmosphere (such as CO_2) absorb some of the sun's energy flowing from the earth back into space and release it as heat into the lower atmosphere. Without this natural warming effect, the earth would be so cold that most of its current forms of life (probably including humans) would become extinct.

2. Gravity allows the earth to hold on to its atmosphere and cycle the chemicals necessary to sustain life through air, water, soil, and organisms.

Section 3.2

1. The abiotic (nonliving) components of the atmosphere include N_2, O_2, water vapor, and other elements; the abiotic component of the hydrosphere is water; and the abiotic components of the geosphere are rocks, soil, and minerals. Other abiotic components can be the effects of physical characteristics such as temperature and light. The biotic (living) components are the plants, animals, and microbes found in the atmosphere, hydrosphere, and geosphere.

2. Plants (producers) convert the light energy of the sun to chemical bond energy in organic compounds produced by photosynthesis. These compounds serve as food (nutrients) for the plants. This energy is then passed on to animals that eat plants (primary consumer herbivores), animals that eat other animals (secondary and tertiary consumer omnivores and carnivores), and decomposers. Detritivores and decomposers cycle back nutrients to producers.

3. Bacteria in the gut help to break down food, and bacteria in our noses block out harmful bacteria from reaching the lungs. Bacteria purify water, decompose organic waste and make nutrients available to producers, and produce oxygen.

Section 3.3

1. There are rarely more than four levels (primary producer, primary consumer, secondary consumer, tertiary consumer) in a trophic pyramid because typically 90% of the available energy is lost when energy is transferred from one trophic level to another. The number of producers necessary to support an additional level would be so great that it limits the number of trophic levels in an energy pyramid.

Section 3.4

1. Withdrawing freshwater from rivers, lakes, and aquifers faster than natural process can replace it; increased water runoff and water pollution from land covered with crops, buildings, and pavement; and increased water runoff and water pollution from cutting forests and filling wetlands.

2. Adding excess carbon dioxide to the atmosphere by burning fossil fuels, clearing carbon-absorbing vegetation from forests and grasslands, and human caused forest fires.

3. Bacteria fix nitrogen into a form that can be utilized by plants, convert ammonia to nitrate, the preferred form that plants can assimilate, and convert nitrate back into gaseous N_2.

4. Removing large amounts of phosphate from the earth to make fertilizer; reducing phosphate levels in tropical soils by clearing tropical forests; runoff of phosphate fertilizer from land into streams, lakes, and oceans; and discharge of phosphates by sewage treatment plants which can upset chemical cycling and other processes in these bodies of water.

Section 3.5

1. Field research can take a long time but takes place in a natural and more complex ecological system. Laboratory research takes less time, is less expensive, and can isolate one particular variable while controlling all other constants. However, simplified laboratory experiments under controlled conditions may not reflect what takes place under the more complex and often changing conditions in nature.

Core Case Study

Large areas of tropical rain forest need to be protected because they serve as centers for terrestrial biodiversity, their loss contributes to atmospheric warming and climate change as a result of the loss of large areas of vegetation that remove carbon dioxide from the atmosphere. In addition, removing large areas of tropical forest can sometimes change regional weather patterns, which can prevent the regrowth of rain forest in cleared or degraded areas.

Biodiversity and Evolution

Nothing in biology makes sense except in the light of evolution.
THEODOSIUS DOBZHANSKY

Key Questions

4.1 What are the major types of life on the earth?

4.2 What is biodiversity and why is it important?

4.3 What roles do species play in ecosystems?

4.4 How does the earth's life change over time?

4.5 What factors affect biodiversity?

Why Are Amphibians Vanishing?

Amphibians—frogs, toads, and salamanders—were among the first vertebrates (animals with backbones) to leave the earth's waters and live on land. Amphibians have adjusted to and survived environmental changes more effectively than many other species, but their world is changing rapidly.

An amphibian lives part of its life in water and part on land. Human activities such as the use of pesticides and other chemicals can pollute the land and water habitats of amphibians. Many of the more than 7,500 known amphibian species have problems adapting to these changes.

Since 1980, populations of hundreds of amphibian species have declined or vanished (Figure 4.1). According to the International Union for Conservation of Nature (IUCN), about 33% of known amphibian species face *extinction*. A 2015 study by biodiversity expert Peter Crane found that 200 frog species have gone extinct since the 1970s, and frogs are going extinct 10,000 times faster than their historical rates.

No single cause can account for the decline of many amphibian species, but scientists have identified a number of factors that affect amphibians at various points in their life cycles. For example, frog eggs lack shells to protect the embryos they contain from water pollutants, and adult frogs ingest the insecticides present in many of the insects they eat. We explore these and other factors later in this chapter.

Why should we care if some amphibian species become extinct? Scientists give three reasons. *First*, amphibians are sensitive *bio-logical indicators* of changes in environmental conditions. These changes include habitat loss, air and water pollution, ultraviolet (UV) radiation from the sun, and climate change. The growing threats for an increasing number of amphibian species indicate that environmental conditions for amphibians and many other species are deteriorating in many parts of the world.

Second, adult amphibians play important roles in biological communities. Adult amphibians eat more insects (including mosquitoes) than many species of birds eat. In some habitats, the extinction of certain amphibian species could lead to population declines or extinction of animals that eat amphibians or their larvae, such as aquatic insects, reptiles, birds, fish, mammals, and other amphibians.

Third, amphibians play a role in human health. A number of pharmaceutical products come from compounds found in secretions from the skin of certain amphibians. Many of these compounds have been isolated and used as painkillers and antibiotics and in treatments for burns and heart disease. If amphibians vanish, these potential medical benefits vanish with them.

The threat to amphibians is part of a greater threat to the earth's biodiversity. In this chapter, we will learn about biodiversity, how it arose on the earth, why it is important, and how it is threatened. We will also consider possible solutions to these threats.●

FIGURE 4.1 Specimens of some of the nearly 200 amphibian species that have gone extinct since the 1970s.

Joel Sartore/National Geographic Creative

CRITICAL THINKING

If frog species go extinct, what might be the impact on humans?

4.1 WHAT ARE THE MAJOR TYPES OF LIFE ON EARTH?

CONCEPT 4.1 The earth's 7 million to 100 million species vary greatly in their characteristics and ecological roles.

Earth's Organisms Are Many and Varied

Every organism is composed of one or more cells. Based on their cell structure, organisms can be classified as *eukaryotic* or *prokaryotic*. All organisms except bacteria are **eukaryotic**. Their cells are encased in a membrane and have a distinct *nucleus* (a membrane-bounded structure containing genetic material in the form of DNA—see Figure 2.9, p. 45) and several other internal parts enclosed by membranes (Figure 4.2, right). Bacterial cells are **prokaryotic**, enclosed by a membrane but containing no distinct nucleus or other internal parts enclosed by membranes (Figure 4.2, left).

Eukaryotic cells are the building blocks of tissues and organ systems that make up the individual organisms that populate a species. A **species** is a group of living organisms with characteristics that distinguish it from other groups of organisms. In sexually reproducing organisms, individuals must be able to mate with similar individuals and produce fertile offspring in order to be classified as a species.

Estimates of the number of species range from 7 million to 100 million, with a best guess of 7–10 million species (**Concept 4.1**). Biologists have identified about 2 million species.

Almost half of the world's identified species are insects, and there may be 10–30 million insect species on the planet. We classify many insect species as *pests* because they compete with us for food, spread human diseases such as malaria, bite or sting us, and invade our lawns, gardens, and houses. Some people fear insects and many think the only good bug is a dead bug. They fail to recognize the vital roles insects play in sustaining the earth's life.

For example, *pollination* is a vital ecosystem service that allows flowering plants to reproduce. When pollen grains are transferred from the flower of one plant to a receptive part of the flower of another plant of the same species, reproduction occurs. Many flowering species depend on bees and other insects to pollinate their flowers (chapter-opening photo and Figure 4.3, left). In addition, insects that eat other insects—such as the praying mantis (Figure 4.3, right)—help to control the populations of at least half the species of insects that we call pests. This free pest control service is another vital ecosystem service. In addition, insects make up an increasingly large part of the human food supply in some parts of the world.

CHECKPOINT FOR UNDERSTANDING 4.1

1. Insects make up about half of all known species. Identify several important functions that they provide for humans.

---

2 million
The number of species that scientists have identified out of the world's estimated 7 million to 100 million species

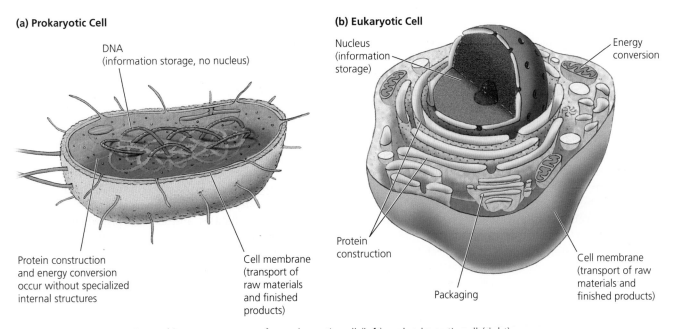

(a) Prokaryotic Cell

DNA (information storage, no nucleus)

Protein construction and energy conversion occur without specialized internal structures

Cell membrane (transport of raw materials and finished products)

(b) Eukaryotic Cell

Nucleus (information storage)

Energy conversion

Protein construction

Packaging

Cell membrane (transport of raw materials and finished products)

FIGURE 4.2 Comparison of key components of a prokaryotic cell (left) and eukaryotic cell (right).

 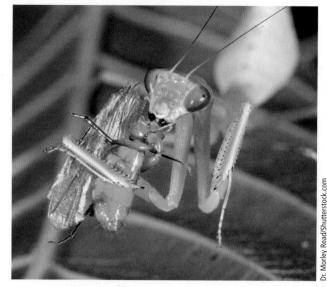

FIGURE 4.3 *Importance of insects:* Bees (left) and numerous other insects pollinate flowering plants that serve as food for many plant eaters, including humans. This praying mantis, which is eating a moth (right), and many other insect species help to control the populations of most of the insect species we classify as pests.

4.2 WHAT IS BIODIVERSITY AND WHY IS IT IMPORTANT?

CONCEPT 4.2 The biodiversity found in genes, species, ecosystems, and ecosystem processes is vital to sustaining the earth's life.

Biodiversity Is the Variety of Life

Biodiversity, or **biological diversity**, is the variety of life on the earth. It has four components, as shown in Figure 4.4.

One component of biodiversity is **species diversity**, the number and abundance of the different kinds of species living in an ecosystem. Species diversity has two components, one being **species richness**, the number of different species in ecosystem. The other is **species evenness**, a measure of the comparative abundance of all species in an ecosystem (see Math Connection: Measuring Biodiversity).

For example, a species-rich ecosystem has a large number of different species. However, this tells us nothing about how many members of each species are present. If it has many of one or more species and just a few of others, its species evenness is low. If it has roughly equal numbers of each species, its species evenness is high. For example, if an ecosystem has only three species, its species richness is low. However, if there are roughly equal numbers of each of the three species, it species evenness is high. Species-rich ecosystems such as rain forests tend to have high species evenness. Ecosystems with low species richness, such as tree farms, tend to have low species evenness.

The species diversity of ecosystems varies with their geographical location. For most terrestrial plants and animals, species diversity (primarily species richness) is highest in the tropics and declines as we move from the equator toward the poles. The most species-rich environments are tropical rain forests, large tropical lakes, coral reefs, and the ocean-bottom zone.

The second component of biodiversity is **genetic diversity**, which is the variety of genes found in a population or in a species (Figure 4.5). Genes contain genetic information that give rise to specific traits, or characteristics, that are passed on to offspring through reproduction. Species have a better chance of surviving and adapting to environmental changes if their populations have greater genetic diversity.

The third component of biodiversity, **ecosystem diversity**, refers to the earth's diversity of biological communities such as deserts, grasslands, forests, mountains, oceans, lakes, rivers, and wetlands. Biologists classify terrestrial (land) ecosystems into **biomes**—large regions such as forests, deserts, and grasslands characterized by distinct climates and certain prominent species (especially vegetation). Biomes differ in their *community structure* based on the types, relative sizes, and stratification of their plant species (Figure 4.6). Figure 4.7 shows the major biomes across the midsection of the United States. We discuss biomes in detail in Chapter 5.

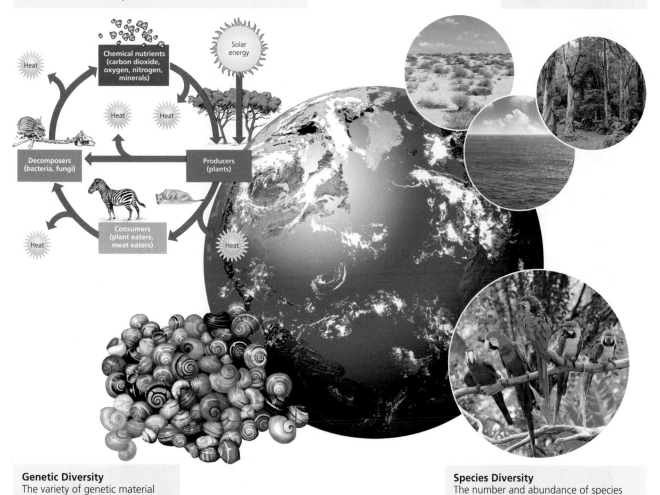

Functional Diversity
The biological and chemical processes such as energy flow and matter recycling needed for the survival of species, communities, and ecosystems.

Ecological Diversity
The variety of terrestrial and aquatic ecosystems found in an area or on the earth.

Solar energy

Chemical nutrients (carbon dioxide, oxygen, nitrogen, minerals)

Heat

Heat

Heat

Decomposers (bacteria, fungi)

Producers (plants)

Consumers (plant eaters, meat eaters)

Heat

Heat

Genetic Diversity
The variety of genetic material within a species or a population.

Species Diversity
The number and abundance of species present in different ecosystems.

FIGURE 4.4 Natural capital: The major components of the earth's *biodiversity*—one of the planet's most important renewable resources and a key component of its natural capital (see Figure 1.3, p. 7).

Right side, top left: Laborant/Shutterstock.com; right side, top right: leungchopan/Shutterstock.com; right side, top center: Elenamiv/Shutterstock.com; bottom right: Juriah Mosin/Shutterstock.com.

FIGURE 4.5 *Genetic diversity* in this population of a Caribbean snail species is reflected in the variations in shell color and banding patterns. Genetic diversity can also include other variations such as slight differences in chemical makeup, sensitivity to various chemicals, and behavior.

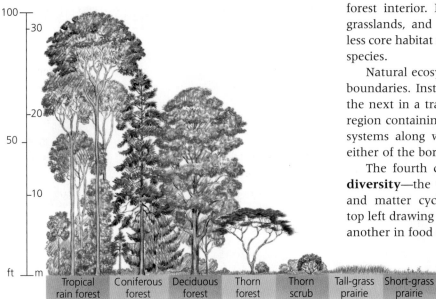

FIGURE 4.6 *Community structure:* Generalized types, relative sizes, and stratification of plant species in communities or ecosystems in major terrestrial biomes.

forest interior. Humans have fragmented many forests, grasslands, and other biomes into isolated patches with less core habitat and more edge habitat that supports fewer species.

Natural ecosystems within biomes rarely have distinct boundaries. Instead, one ecosystem tends to merge with the next in a transitional zone called an **ecotone**. It is a region containing a mixture of species from adjacent ecosystems along with some migrant species not found in either of the bordering ecosystems.

The fourth component of biodiversity is **functional diversity**—the variety of processes such as energy flow and matter cycling that occur within ecosystems (see top left drawing in Figure 4.4) as species interact with one another in food chains and food webs. This component of biodiversity includes the variety of ecological roles organisms play in their biological communities and the impacts these roles have on their overall ecosystems.

Large areas of forest and other biomes tend to have a *core habitat* and *edge habitats* with different environmental conditions and species, called **edge effect**. For example, a forest edge is usually more open, bright, and windy and has greater variations in temperature and humidity than a

A more biologically diverse ecosystem with a greater variety of producers can produce more plant biomass, which in turn can support a greater variety of consumer species. Biologically diverse ecosystems also tend to be more stable because they are more likely to include species with traits that enable them to adapt to changes in the environment, such as disease or drought.

FIGURE 4.7 The variety of biomes found across the midsection of the United States.

First: Zack Frank/Shutterstock.com; second: Robert Crum/Shutterstock.com; third: Joe Belanger/Shutterstock.com; fourth: Protasov AN/Shutterstock.com; fifth: Maya Kruchankova/Shutterstock.com; sixth: Marc von Hacht/Shutterstock.com

Measuring Biodiversity

Biodiversity is a biological indicator of ecosystem health. A highly diverse ecosystem provides a large variety of ecosystem services. Characteristics of biodiversity are *species richness*, the total number of different species in an ecosystem, and *species evenness*, the number of individuals of each species.

Simpson's Diversity Index measures both species richness and species evenness. As both of these factors increase, so does overall diversity. Ecologists use this biological measure as a way to objectively quantify ecosystem diversity. When humans understand the diversity of an ecosystem, it makes it easier to utilize its resources sustainably. The Convention on Biological Diversity, an international treaty committed to conserving and sustaining biodiversity around the world, reports that:

"At least 40 percent of the world's economy and 80 percent of the needs of the poor are derived from biological resources. In addition, the richer the diversity of life, the greater the opportunity for medical discoveries, economic development, and adaptive responses to such new challenges as climate change."

FRQ Application

To calculate Simpson's Diversity Index, scientists randomly sample organisms in an ecosystem, recording each species found and the number of individuals of each species. The index value is given by:

$$D = 1 - \frac{\Sigma n(n - 1)}{N(N - 1)}$$

D = diversity index
N = total number of individuals (of all species) in the sample
n = number of individuals of each species in the sample

When calculated, D takes on a value between 0 and 1, where 0 = no diversity and 1 = infinite diversity.

Consider the following data table indicating a total of 11 possible species of bottom dwelling (benthic) invertebrates found in a local freshwater pond and the number of individuals found in each species. Because there were zero Dobson flies found, the species richness is 10 different species.

Benthic Invertebrates	Number of Organisms in Each Group (n)	$n(n - 1)$
Mayflies	1	$1(1 - 1) = 0$
Stoneflies	3	$3(3 - 1) = 6$
Caddisflies	5	$5(5 - 1) = 20$
Dobson flies	0	$0(0 - 0) = 0$
Midges	6	$6(6 - 1) = 30$
Craneflies	1	$1(1 - 1) = 0$
Dragonflies	3	$3(3 - 1) = 6$
Scuds	6	$6(6 - 1) = 30$
Pouch snails	6	$6(6 - 1) = 30$
Tubifex worms	8	$8(8 - 1) = 56$
Leeches	5	$5(5 - 1) = 20$
TOTAL	**$N = 44$**	**$\Sigma n(n - 1) = 198$**

The symbol Σ (Greek sigma) means "sum of." Therefore, the total in the column "$n(n - 1)$" is the sum of all the calculations in that column. By plugging the total for "N" and the total for "$n(n - 1)$" into the formula, a number less than one will result:

$$D = 1 - \left(\frac{198}{44(43)}\right)$$

where 198 is the value for $\Sigma n(n - 1)$ and $N(N - 1)$ is equal to $44(44 - 1)$. Simplifying,

$$D = 1 - \left(\frac{198}{1892}\right) = 1 - 0.1047$$

$$D = 0.8953$$

Since this value of D is close to one, there is a high diversity of bottom dwelling (benthic) invertebrates in the freshwater pond.

Jim Harrison

Edward O. Wilson: Champion of Biodiversity

As a boy growing up in the southeastern United States, Edward O. Wilson became interested in insects at age 9. He has said, "Every kid has a bug period. I never grew out of mine."

Before entering college, Wilson decided he would specialize in the study of ants. He became one of the world's experts on ants and then steadily widened his focus, eventually to include the entire biosphere. One of Wilson's landmark works is *The Diversity of Life*, published in 1992. In that book, he presented the principles and practical issues of biodiversity more completely than anyone had to that point. Today, he is recognized as one of the world's leading experts on biodiversity. He is now deeply involved in writing and lecturing about the need for global conservation efforts and is working on Harvard University's *Encyclopedia of Life*, a database of information on the world's known species.

Wilson has won more than 100 national and international awards and has written 32 books, two of which won the Pulitzer Prize for General Nonfiction. In 2013 he received the National Geographic Society's highest award, the Hubbard Medal. About the importance of biodiversity, he writes: "How can we save Earth's life forms from extinction if we don't even know what most of them are? . . . I like to call Earth a little known planet."

We should care about and avoid degrading the earth's biodiversity because it is vital to sustaining the natural capital (see Figure 1.3, p. 7) that keeps us alive and supports our economies. We use biodiversity as a source of food, medicine, building materials, and fuel. Biodiversity also provides natural ecosystem services such as air and water purification, renewal of topsoil, decomposition of wastes, and pollination. In addition, the earth's variety of genetic information, species, and ecosystems provide raw materials for the evolution of new species and ecosystem services, as they respond to changing environmental conditions. Biodiversity is the earth's ecological insurance policy.

According to ocean researcher Sylvia Earle, "The bottom line answer to the question about why biodiversity matters is fairly simple. The rest of the living world can get along without us but we can't get along without them." We owe much of what we know about biodiversity to researchers such as Earle and biologist Edward O. Wilson (Individuals Matter 4.1).

1. Functional diversity, ecosystem diversity, species diversity, and genetic diversity are all essential for sustaining life on earth. Explain the role of each of these types of diversity.

2. Discuss why biodiversity is critical to the survival of humans.

4.3 WHAT ROLES DO SPECIES PLAY IN ECOSYSTEMS?

CONCEPT 4.3A Each species plays a specific ecological role called its *niche*.

CONCEPT 4.3B Any given species may play one or more of four important roles—native, nonnative, indicator, or keystone—in a particular ecosystem.

Each Species Plays a Role

Each species plays a role within the ecosystem it inhabits (**Concept 4.3A**). Ecologists describe this role as its **ecological niche**. It is a species' way of life in its ecosystem and includes everything that affects its survival and reproduction, such as how much water and sunlight it needs, how much space it requires, what it feeds on, what feeds on it, how and when it reproduces, and the temperatures and other conditions it can tolerate. The niche of a species differs from its **habitat**—the place, or type of ecosystem, in which a species lives and obtains what it needs to survive.

Ecologists use the niches of species to classify them as *generalists* or *specialists*. **Generalist species**, such as raccoons, have broad niches (Figure 4.8, right curve). They can live in many different places, eat a variety of foods, and often tolerate a wide range of environmental conditions. Other generalist species include flies, cockroaches, rats, coyotes, white-tailed deer, and humans.

In contrast, **specialist species**, such as the giant panda, occupy narrow niches (Figure 4.8, left curve). They may be able to live in only one type of habitat, eat only one or a few types of food, or tolerate a narrow range of environmental conditions. For example, different specialist species of shorebirds feed on crustaceans, insects, or other organisms found on sandy beaches and their adjoining coastal wetlands (Figure 4.9).

Because of their narrow niches, specialists are more prone to extinction when environmental conditions change. For example, China's *giant panda* is vulnerable to extinction because of a combination of habitat loss, low birth rate, and its specialized diet consisting mostly of bamboo.

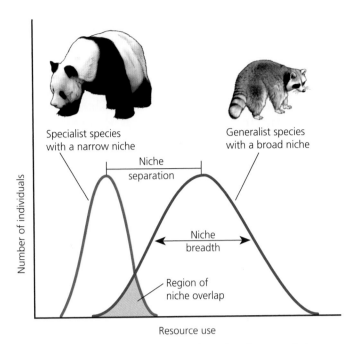

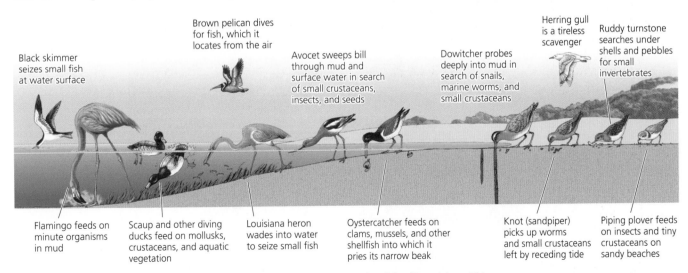

FIGURE 4.8 Specialist species such as the giant panda have a narrow niche (left curve) and generalist species such as the raccoon have a broad niche (right curve).

Is it better to be a generalist or a specialist? It depends. When environmental conditions undergo little change, as in a tropical rain forest, specialists have an advantage because they have fewer competitors. Under rapidly changing environmental conditions, the more adaptable generalist usually is better off.

There Are Four Major Ecosystem Roles for Species

Niches can be classified further in terms of specific roles that certain species play within ecosystems. Ecologists describe these roles as *native, nonnative, indicator,* and *keystone.* Any given species may play one or more of these roles in a particular ecosystem (**Concept 4.3B**).

Native species normally live and thrive in a particular ecosystem. Other species that migrate into or that are deliberately or accidentally introduced into an ecosystem are called **nonnative species**. They are also referred to as *invasive, alien,* and *exotic species.*

People often think of nonnative species as threatening. In fact, most nonnative species, including certain food crops, trees, flowers, chickens, cattle, fish, and dogs, have certainly benefitted people. However, some nonnative species compete with and reduce an ecosystem's native species, causing unintended and unexpected consequences.

For example, in 1957 Brazil imported wild African honeybees to help increase honey production. The opposite occurred. The more aggressive African bees displaced some of Brazil's native honeybee populations, which led to a reduced honey supply. African honeybees have since spread across South and Central America and into the southern United States. They have killed thousands of domesticated animals and an estimated 1,000 people in the Western Hemisphere, many of them allergic to bee stings.

Nonnative species can spread rapidly, if they find a new location with favorable conditions. In their new niches, some of these species may not face the predators and diseases they faced in their native niches. Sometimes they may out-compete some native species in their new locations. We examine this environmental threat in more detail in Chapter 9.

Indicator Species Can Sound the Alarm

Species that provide early warnings of changes in environmental conditions in an ecosystem are called **indicator species**. They are like biological smoke alarms. In this chapter's **Core Case Study**, you learned that some amphibians are classified as indicator species.

FIGURE 4.9 Various bird species in a coastal wetland occupy specialized feeding niches. This specialization reduces competition and allows for sharing of limited resources.

Scientists have been working hard to identify some of the possible causes of the declines in amphibian populations (Science Focus 4.1).

Birds are also excellent biological indicators. They are found almost everywhere and are affected quickly by environmental changes such as the loss or fragmentation of their habitats and the introduction of chemical pesticides.

Keystone Species Play Critical Roles

A keystone is the wedge-shaped stone placed at the top of a stone archway. Remove this stone and the arch collapses. In some communities and ecosystems, ecologists hypothesize that certain species play a similar role. A **keystone species** has a large effect on the types and abundance of other species in an ecosystem. Without the keystone species, the ecosystem would be dramatically different or might cease to exist.

Keystone species play several critical roles in helping to sustain ecosystems. One is the *pollination* of flowering plant species by butterflies, honeybees (Figure 4.3, left), hummingbirds, bats, and other species. In addition, top predator keystone species feed on and help to regulate the populations of other species. Examples are wolves, leopards, lions, some shark species, and the American alligator (see the following Case Study).

The loss of a keystone species in an ecosystem can lead to population crashes and extinctions of other species that depend on them for certain ecosystem services. This is why it so important for scientists to identify keystone species and work to protect them.

The American Alligator—A Keystone Species That Almost Went Extinct

The American alligator (Figure 4.10) is a keystone species in subtropical wetland ecosystems in the southeastern United States. These alligators play several important ecological roles. They dig deep depressions known as gator holes. During dry periods, these depressions hold freshwater and serve as refuges for aquatic life. The depressions supply freshwater and food for fishes, insects, snakes, turtles, birds, and other animals. The large nesting mounds alligators build provide nesting and feeding sites for some herons and egrets. Red-bellied turtles lay their eggs in old gator nests.

When alligators excavate holes and build nesting mounds, they help keep vegetation from invading shorelines and open water. Without this ecosystem service, freshwater ponds and coastal wetlands fill in with shrubs and trees, and dozens of species can disappear from these ecosystems, due to such changes. The alligators also help ensure the presence of game fish such as bass and bream by eating large numbers of gar, a predatory fish that hunts these species.

FIGURE 4.10
Keystone species: The American alligator plays an important ecological role in its marsh and swamp habitats in the southeastern United States by helping support many other species.

Martha Marks/Shutterstock.com

Causes of Amphibian Declines

Scientists who study reptiles and amphibians have identified natural and human-related factors that can cause the decline and disappearance of these indicator species.

One natural threat is *parasites* such as flatworms that feed on certain amphibian eggs. Research indicates that this has caused birth defects such as missing limbs or extra limbs in some amphibians.

Another natural threat comes from *viral and fungal diseases*. For example, the chytrid fungus infects a frog's skin and causes it to thicken. This reduces the frog's ability to take in water through its skin and leads to death from dehydration. Such diseases can spread easily, because adults of many amphibian species congregate in large numbers to breed.

Habitat loss and fragmentation is another major threat to amphibians. It is mostly a human-caused problem resulting from the clearing of forests and the draining and filling of freshwater wetlands for farming and urban development.

Another human-related problem is *higher levels of UV radiation* from the sun. Ozone (O_3) that forms in the stratosphere protects the earth's life from harmful UV radiation emitted by the sun. During the past few decades, ozone-depleting chemicals released into the troposphere by human activities have drifted into the stratosphere and have destroyed some the stratosphere's protective ozone. The resulting increase in UV radiation can kill embryos of amphibians in shallow ponds as well as adult amphibians basking in the sun for warmth. International action has been taken to reduce the threat of stratospheric ozone depletion, but it will take about 50 years for ozone levels to recover to those in 1960.

Pollution from human activities also threatens amphibians. Frogs and other species are exposed to pesticides in ponds and in the bodies of insects that they eat. This can make them more vulnerable to bacterial, viral, and fungal diseases and to some parasites.

Climate change is also a concern. Amphibians are sensitive to even slight changes in temperature and moisture. Warmer temperatures may lead amphibians to breed too early. Extended dry periods also lead to a decline in amphibian populations by drying up breeding pools that frogs and other amphibians depend on for reproduction and survival through their early stages of life (Figure 4.A).

Overhunting is another human-related threat, especially in areas of Asia and Europe, where frogs are hunted for their leg meat. Another threat is the invasion of amphibian habitats by *nonnative predators and competitors*, such as

FIGURE 4.A This golden toad lived in Costa Rica's high-altitude Monteverde Cloud Forest Reserve. The species became extinct in 1989, apparently because its habitat dried up.

certain fish species. Some of this immigration is natural, but humans accidentally or deliberately transport many species to amphibian habitats.

According to most amphibian experts, a combination of these factors, which vary from place to place, is responsible for most of the decline and extinctions of amphibian species.

CRITICAL THINKING

Of the factors listed above, which three do you think could be most effectively controlled by human efforts?

In the 1930s, hunters began killing American alligators for their exotic meat and their soft belly skin. People used the skin to make expensive shoes, belts, and purses. Other people hunted alligators for sport or out of dislike for the large reptile. By the 1960s, hunters and poachers had wiped out 90% of the alligators in the state of Louisiana, and the alligator population in the Florida Everglades was near extinction.

In 1967 the U.S. government placed the American alligator on the endangered species list. By 1977, because it was protected, its populations had made a strong comeback and the alligator was removed from the endangered species list. Today, there are more than a million alligators in Florida, and the state allows property owners to kill alligators that stray onto their land.

To conservation biologists, the comeback of the American alligator is an important success story in wildlife conservation. Recently, however, large and rapidly reproducing Burmese and African pythons released deliberately or accidently by humans have invaded the Florida Everglades. These nonnative invaders feed on young alligators, and could threaten the long-term survival of this keystone species in the Everglades.

CHECKPOINT FOR UNDERSTANDING 4.3

1. Identify several reasons why the American alligator is considered a keystone species in its ecological niche.

2. Native, nonnative, invasive, and indicator species are also roles that a species can fill. Identify all roles that apply to the American alligator.

4.4 HOW DOES THE EARTH'S LIFE CHANGE OVER TIME?

CONCEPT 4.4A The scientific theory of evolution through natural selection explains how life on the earth changes over time due to changes in the genes of populations.

CONCEPT 4.4B Populations evolve when genes mutate and give some individuals genetic traits that enhance their abilities to survive and to produce offspring with these traits (natural selection).

Evolution Explains How Organisms Change Over Time

How did the earth end up with such an amazing diversity of species? The scientific answer is **biological evolution** (or simply **evolution**)—the process by which the earth's life forms change genetically over time. These changes occur in the genes of populations of organisms from generation to generation (**Concept 4.4A**). According to this scientific theory, species have evolved from earlier, ancestral species through **natural selection**. Through this process, individuals with certain genetic traits are more likely to survive and reproduce under a specific set of environmental conditions. These individuals then pass these traits on to their offspring (**Concept 4.4B**).

A large body of scientific evidence supports this idea. As a result, *biological evolution through natural selection* has become a widely accepted scientific theory. It explains how the earth's life has changed over the past 3.8 billion years and why we have today's diversity of species.

Most of what we know about the history of life on the earth comes from **fossils**—the remains or traces of past organisms. Fossils include mineralized or petrified replicas of skeletons, bones, teeth, shells, leaves, and seeds, or impressions of such items found in rocks (Figure 4.11). Scientists have discovered fossil evidence in successive layers of sedimentary rock such as limestone and sandstone. They have also studied evidence of ancient life contained in ice core samples drilled from glacial ice at the earth's poles and on mountaintops.

This total body of evidence is called the *fossil record*. This record is uneven and incomplete because many past forms of life left no fossils and some fossils have decomposed. Scientists estimate that the fossils found so far represent probably only 1% of all species that have ever lived. There are still many unanswered scientific questions about the details of evolution by natural selection, and research continues in this area.

Evolution Depends on Genetic Variability and Natural Selection

The idea that organisms change over time and are descended from a single common ancestor has been discussed since the time of the early Greek philosophers. No one had

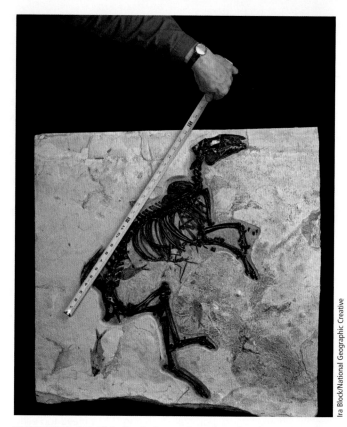

FIGURE 4.11 This fossil shows the mineralized remains of an early ancestor of the present-day horse. It roamed the earth more than 35 million years ago. Notice that you can also see fish skeletons on this fossil.

Ira Block/National Geographic Creative

developed an explanation of how this happened until 1858 when naturalists Charles Darwin (1809–1882) and Alfred Russel Wallace (1823–1913) independently proposed the concept of natural selection as a mechanism for biological evolution. Darwin gathered evidence for this idea and published it in his 1859 book, *On the Origin of Species by Means of Natural Selection*.

Biological evolution by natural selection involves changes in a population's genetic makeup through successive generations (**Concept 4.4A**). Populations—not individuals—evolve by becoming genetically different.

The first step in this process is the development of **genetic variability**: a variety in the genetic makeup of individuals in a population. This occurs primarily through **mutations**, which are changes in the coded genetic instructions in the DNA in a gene. During an organism's lifetime, the DNA in its cells is copied each time one of its cells divides and whenever it reproduces. In a lifetime, this happens millions of times and results in various mutations.

Most mutations result from random changes in the DNA's coded genetic instructions that occur in only a tiny fraction of these millions of divisions. Some mutations also occur from exposure to external agents such as radioactivity, ultraviolet radiation from the sun, and certain natural and human-made chemicals called *mutagens*.

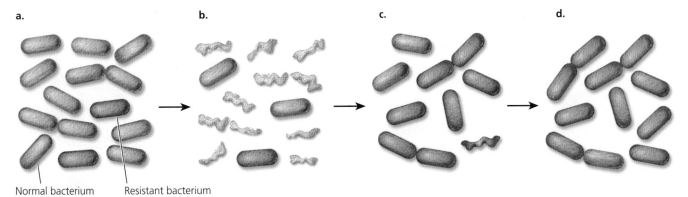

a.　　　　b.　　　　c.　　　　d.

Normal bacterium　　　Resistant bacterium

FIGURE 4.12 *Evolution by natural selection:* **(a)** A population of bacteria is exposed to an antibiotic, which **(b)** kills most individuals except those possessing a trait that makes them resistant to the drug; **(c)** the resistant bacteria multiply and eventually **(d)** replace all or most of the nonresistant bacteria.

Mutations can occur in any cell, but only those that take place in the genes of reproductive cells are passed on to offspring. Sometimes a mutation can result in a new genetic trait, called a *heritable trait*, which can be passed from one generation to the next. In this way, populations develop genetic differences among their individuals. Some mutations are harmful to offspring and some are beneficial.

The next step in biological evolution is *natural selection*, which explains how populations evolve in response to changes in environmental conditions by changing their genetic makeup. Through natural selection, environmental conditions favor increased survival and reproduction of certain individuals in a population. These favored individuals possess heritable traits that give them an advantage over other individuals in the population. Such a trait is called an **adaptation**, or **adaptive trait**. An adaptive trait improves the ability of an individual organism to survive and to reproduce at a higher rate than other individuals in a population can under prevailing environmental conditions.

An example of natural selection at work is *genetic resistance*. It occurs when one or more organisms in a population have genes that can tolerate a chemical (such as a pesticide or antibiotic) that is designed to kill them. The resistant individuals survive and reproduce more rapidly than the members of the population that do not have such genetic traits. Genetic resistance can develop quickly in populations of organisms such as bacteria and insects that produce large numbers of offspring. For example, some disease-causing bacteria have developed genetic resistance to widely used antibacterial drugs, or *antibiotics* (Figure 4.12).

Our own species is an example of evolution by natural selection. If we compressed the earth's 4.6 billion years of geological and biological history into a 24-hour day, the human species arrived about a tenth of 1 second before midnight. In that short time, and especially during the last 100 years, we have dominated most of the earth's land and aquatic systems with a growing ecological footprint (see Figure 1.8, p. 12). Evolutionary biologists attribute our ability to dominate the planet to three major adaptations:

- *Strong opposable thumbs* that allowed humans to grip and use tools better than the few other animals that have thumbs

- *The ability to walk upright*, which gave humans agility and freed up their hands for many uses

- *A complex brain*, which allowed humans to develop many skills, including the ability to talk, read, and write in order to transmit complex ideas

To summarize the process of biological evolution by natural selection: Genes mutate, individuals are selected, and populations that are better adapted to survive and reproduce under existing environmental conditions evolve (**Concept 4.4B**).

Evolutionary biologists study patterns of evolution by examining the similarities and differences among species based on their physical and genetic characteristics. They use this information to develop branching **evolutionary tree**, or **phylogenetic tree**, diagrams that depict the hypothetical evolution of various species from common ancestors. They use fossil, DNA, and other evidence to hypothesize the evolutionary pathways and connections among species. Figure 4.13 is a phylogenetic tree diagram tracing the hypothesized development of the earth's six kingdoms of life over 3.8 billion years.

On an evolutionary timescale, as new species arise, they have new genetic traits that can enhance their survival as long as environmental conditions do not change dramatically. The older species from which they originated and the new species evolve and branch out along different lines or lineages of species that can be recorded in phylogenetic tree diagrams (Figure 4.13).

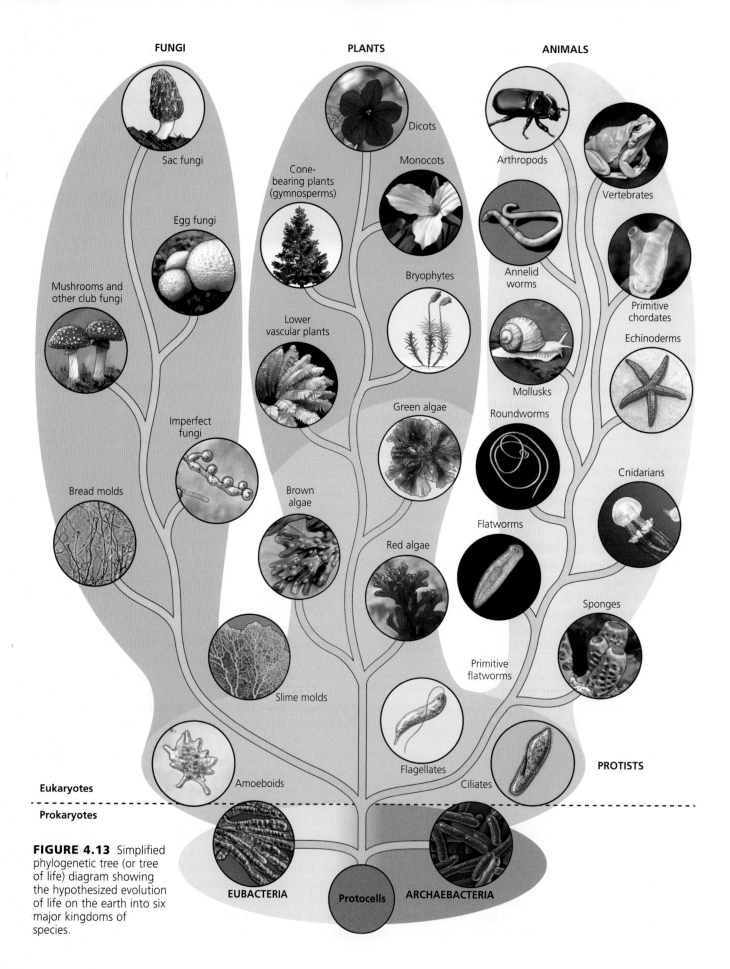

FUNGI

Sac fungi

Egg fungi

Mushrooms and other club fungi

Imperfect fungi

Bread molds

PLANTS

Dicots

Monocots

Cone-bearing plants (gymnosperms)

Bryophytes

Lower vascular plants

Green algae

Brown algae

Red algae

ANIMALS

Arthropods

Vertebrates

Annelid worms

Primitive chordates

Echinoderms

Mollusks

Roundworms

Cnidarians

Flatworms

Sponges

Primitive flatworms

Slime molds

Flagellates

Ciliates

PROTISTS

Amoeboids

Eukaryotes

Prokaryotes

EUBACTERIA

Protocells

ARCHAEBACTERIA

FIGURE 4.13 Simplified phylogenetic tree (or tree of life) diagram showing the hypothesized evolution of life on the earth into six major kingdoms of species.

Limits to Adaptation through Natural Selection

In the not-too-distant future, will adaptations to new environmental conditions through natural selection protect us from harm? Will adaptations allow the skin of our descendants to become more resistant to the harmful effects of UV radiation, enable our lungs to cope with air pollutants, and improve the ability of our livers to detoxify pollutants in our bodies?

Scientists in this field say *not likely* because of two limitations on adaptation through natural selection. *First*, a change in environmental conditions leads to adaptation only for genetic traits already present in a population's gene pool, or if they arise from mutations—which occur randomly.

Second, even if a beneficial heritable trait is present in a population, the population's ability to adapt may be limited by its reproductive capacity. Populations of genetically diverse species that reproduce quickly can often adapt to a change in environmental conditions in a short time (days to years). Examples are dandelions, mosquitoes, rats, bacteria, and cockroaches. By contrast, species that cannot produce large numbers of offspring rapidly—such as elephants, tigers, sharks, and humans—take thousands or even millions of years to adapt through natural selection.

Myths about Evolution through Natural Selection

There are a number of misconceptions about biological evolution through natural selection. Here are five common myths:

- *Survival of the fittest means survival of the strongest.* To biologists, *fitness* is a measure of reproductive success, not strength. Thus, the fittest individuals are those that leave the most descendants, not those that are physically the strongest.

- *Evolution explains the origin of life.* It does not. However, it does explain how species have evolved after life came into being around 3.8 billion years ago.

- *Humans evolved from apes or monkeys.* Fossil and other evidence shows that humans, apes, and monkeys evolved along different paths from a common ancestor that lived 5 million to 8 million years ago.

- *Evolution by natural selection is part of a grand plan in nature in which species are to become more perfectly adapted.* There is no evidence of such a plan. Instead, evidence indicates that the forces of natural selection and random mutations can push evolution along any number of paths.

- *Evolution by natural selection is not important because it is just a theory.* This reveals a misunderstanding of what a scientific theory is. A scientific hypothesis becomes a scientific theory only after thorough testing and evaluation by the experts in a field. Numerous polls show that evolution by natural selection is widely accepted by over 95% of biologists because it is the best scientific explanation for the earth's biodiversity and how populations of different species have adapted to changes in the earth's environmental conditions over billions of years.

CHECKPOINT FOR UNDERSTANDING 4.4

1. The theory of evolution states that there must be variation within a population for evolution to take place. Identify the source of variation. Explain why organisms like bacteria and dandelions adapt more quickly than organisms like tigers and humans.

2. A farmer sprays his fields to control hornworms each season. The hornworms seem to have been eliminated. After a few seasons, the hornworms return and the farmer sprays again, but the pesticide is ineffective. Explain, in terms of evolution by natural selection, why the pesticide no longer works.

4.5 WHAT FACTORS AFFECT BIODIVERSITY?

CONCEPT 4.5A As environmental conditions change, the balance between the formation of new species and the extinction of existing species determines the earth's biodiversity.

CONCEPT 4.5B Human activities are decreasing biodiversity by causing the extinction of many species and by destroying or degrading habitats needed for the development of new species through natural selection.

How Do New Species Arise?

Under certain circumstances, natural selection can lead to an entirely new species. In this process, called **speciation**, one species evolves into two or more different species. For sexually reproducing organisms, a new species forms when a separated population of a species evolves to the point where its members can no longer interbreed and produce fertile offspring with members of another population of its species that did not change or that evolved differently.

Speciation, especially among sexually reproducing species, happens in two phases: first geographic isolation, and then reproductive isolation. **Geographic isolation** occurs when different groups of the same population of a species become physically isolated from one another for a long time. Part of a population may migrate in search of food and then begin living as a separate population in an area with different environmental conditions. Winds and flowing water may carry a few individuals far away where they establish a new population. A flooding stream, a new road, a hurricane, an earthquake, or a volcanic eruption, as well as long-term geological processes (Science Focus 4.2), can

Geological Processes Affect Biodiversity

The earth's surface has changed dramatically over its long history. Scientists discovered that huge flows of molten rock within the earth's interior have broken its surface into a number of gigantic solid plates, called *tectonic plates*. For hundreds of millions of years, these plates have drifted slowly on the planet's mantle (Figure 4.B).

Rock and fossil evidence indicates that 200–250 million years ago, all of the earth's present-day continents were connected in a supercontinent called Pangaea (Figure 4.B, left). About 175 million years ago, Pangaea began splitting apart as the earth's tectonic plates moved. Eventually tectonic

movement resulted in the present-day locations of the continents (Figure 4.B, right).

The drifting of tectonic plates has had two important effects on the evolution and distribution of life on the earth. *First*, the locations of continents and oceanic basins have greatly influenced the earth's climate, which plays a key role in where plants and animals can live. *Second*, the breakup, movement, and joining of continents has allowed species to move and adapt to new environments. This led to the formation of large number of new species through speciation.

Sometimes tectonic plates that are grinding along next to one another shift quickly. Such sudden movement of tectonic plates can cause *earthquakes*. This can affect biological evolution by causing fissures in the earth's crust that, on rare occasions, can separate and isolate populations of species. Over long periods, this can lead to the formation of new species as each isolated population changes genetically in response to new environmental conditions.

Volcanic eruptions that occur along the boundaries of tectonic plates can also affect extinction and speciation by destroying habitats and reducing, isolating, or wiping out populations of species. We discuss these geological processes in detail in Chapter 11.

225 million years ago

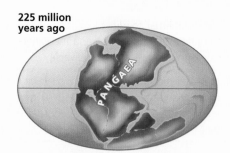

Present

FIGURE 4.B Over millions of years, the earth's continents have moved very slowly on several gigantic tectonic plates. **Critical thinking:** How might an area of land splitting apart cause the extinction of a species?

CRITICAL THINKING

The earth's tectonic plates, including the one you are riding on, typically move at about the rate at which your fingernails grow. If they stopped moving, how might this affect the future biodiversity of the planet?

---

also separate populations. Human activities, such as the creation of large reservoirs behind dams and the clearing of forests, can also create physical barriers for certain species. The separated populations can develop quite different genetic characteristics because they are no longer exchanging genes.

In **reproductive isolation**, mutation and change by natural selection operate independently in the gene pools of geographically isolated populations. If this process continues long enough, members of isolated populations of sexually reproducing species can become different in genetic makeup. Then they cannot produce live, fertile offspring if they are rejoined with their earlier population and attempt to interbreed. When that is the case, speciation has occurred and one species has become two (Figure 4.14).

Artificial Selection, Genetic Engineering, and Synthetic Biology

Scientists use **artificial selection** to change the genetic characteristics of populations with similar genes. First, they select one or more desirable genetic traits that already exist in the population of a plant or animal such as a type of wheat, dog, or fruit. Then they use *selective breeding*, or *crossbreeding*, to control which members of a population have the opportunity to reproduce to increase the numbers of individuals in a population with the desired traits (Figure 4.15).

Artificial selection is limited to crossbreeding between genetic varieties of the same species or between species that are genetically similar to one another, and is not a form of speciation. Most of the grains, fruits, and vegetables we eat are produced by artificial selection. Artificial

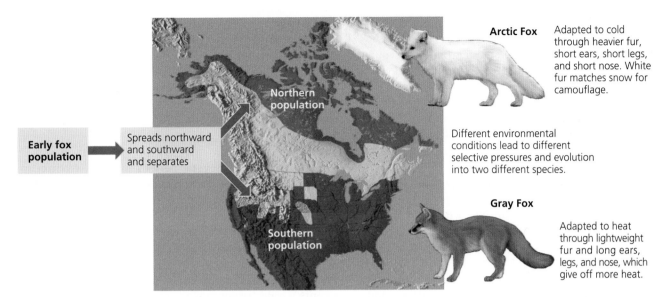

FIGURE 4.14 *Geographic isolation* can lead to reproductive isolation, divergence of gene pools, and speciation.

selection has also given us food crops with higher yields, cows that give more milk, trees that grow faster, and many different varieties of dogs and cats. However, traditional crossbreeding is a slow process.

Scientists have learned how to speed this process of change by manipulating genes to get desirable genetic traits or eliminate undesirable ones in a plant or animal. They do this by transferring segments of DNA with the desired trait from one species to another through a process called **genetic engineering**. In this process, also known as *gene splicing*, scientists alter an organism's genetic material by adding, deleting, or changing segments of its DNA to produce desirable traits or to eliminate undesirable ones. Scientists have used genetic engineering to develop modified crop plants, new drugs, pest-resistant plants, and animals that grow rapidly.

There are five steps in this process:

1. Identify a gene with the desired trait in the DNA found in the nucleus of a cell from the donor organism.

2. Extract a small circular DNA molecule, called a *plasmid*, from a bacterial cell.

3. Insert the desired gene from step 1 into the plasmid to form a *recombinant DNA plasmid*.

4. Insert the recombinant DNA plasmid into a cell of another bacterium, which rapidly divides and reproduces large numbers of bacterial cells with the desired DNA trait.

5. Transfer the genetically modified bacterial cells to a plant or animal that is to be genetically modified.

The result is a **genetically modified organism (GMO)** with its genetic information modified in a way not found in natural organisms. Genetic engineering enables scientists to transfer genes between different species that would not interbreed in nature. For example, scientists can put genes from a cold-water fish species into a tomato plant to give it properties that help it resist

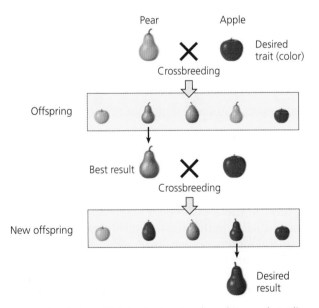

FIGURE 4.15 Artificial selection involves the crossbreeding of species that are close to one another genetically. In this example, similar fruits are being crossbred to yield a pear with a certain color.

cold weather. Recently, scientists have learned how to treat certain genetic diseases by altering or replacing the genes that cause them. Genetic engineering has revolutionized agriculture and medicine. However, it is a controversial technology, as we discuss in Chapter 12.

A new and rapidly growing form of genetic engineering is **synthetic biology**. It enables scientists to make new sequences of DNA and use such genetic information to design and create artificial cells, tissues, body parts, and organisms not found in nature.

Proponents of this new technology want to use it to create bacteria that can use sunlight to produce clean-burning hydrogen gas, which can be used to fuel motor vehicles. They also view it as a way to create new vaccines to prevent diseases and drugs to combat parasitic diseases such as malaria. Synthetic biology might also be used to create bacteria and algae that would break down spilled oil, industrial wastes, toxic heavy metals, pesticides, and radioactive waste in contaminated soil and water. Scientists are a long way from achieving such goals but the potential is there.

The problem is that like any technology, synthetic biology can be used for good or bad. For example, it could also be used to create biological weapons such as deadly bacteria that spread new diseases, to destroy existing oil deposits, or to interfere with the chemical cycles that keep us alive. This is why many scientists call for increased monitoring and regulation of this new technology to help control its use.

Extinction Eliminates Species

Another factor affecting the number and types of species on the earth is **extinction**. Extinction occurs when an entire species ceases to exist. When environmental conditions change dramatically, a population of a species faces three possible futures: (1) *adapt* to the new conditions through natural selection, (2) *migrate* (if possible) to another area with more favorable conditions, or (3) *become extinct*.

Species found in only one area, called **endemic species**, are especially vulnerable to extinction. They exist on islands and in other isolated areas. For example, many species in tropical rain forests have highly specialized roles and are vulnerable to extinction. These organisms are unlikely to be able to migrate or adapt to rapidly changing environmental conditions. Many of these endangered species are amphibians (**Core Case Study**).

Fossils and other scientific evidence indicate that all species eventually become extinct. In fact, the evidence indicates that 99.9% of all species that have existed on the earth have gone extinct. Throughout most of the earth's long history, species have disappeared at a low rate, called the **background extinction rate**. Based on the fossil record and analysis of ice cores, biologists estimate that the average annual background extinction rate has been about 0.0001% of all species per year, which amounts to 1 species lost for every million species on the earth per year. At this rate, if there were 10 million species on the earth, about 10 of them, on average, would go extinct every year.

Evidence indicates that life on the earth has been sharply reduced by several periods of **mass extinction** during which there is a significant rise in extinction rates, well above the background rate. In such a catastrophic, widespread, and often global event, large groups of species (30–90% of all species) are wiped out (See Supplement 4, p. S7). The causes of such extinctions are unknown, but possible events include gigantic volcanic eruptions and collisions with giant meteors and asteroids. Such events would trigger drastic environmental changes on a global scale, including massive release of debris into the atmosphere that would block sunlight for an extended period. This would kill off most plant species and the consumers that depend on them for food. Fossil and geological evidence indicates that there have been five mass extinctions (at intervals of 20–60 million years) during the past 500 million years (Figure 4.16).

A mass extinction provides an opportunity for the evolution of new species that can fill unoccupied ecological niches or newly created ones. Scientific evidence indicates that each past mass extinction has been followed by an increase in species diversity. This happens over several million years as new species rise to occupy new habitats or to exploit newly available resources (shown by the wedges in Figure 4.16) following each mass extinction.

As environmental conditions change, the degree of balance between speciation and extinction determines the earth's biodiversity (**Concept 4.5A**). The existence of millions of species today means that speciation, on average, has kept ahead of extinction. However, evidence indicates that the global extinction rate is rising dramatically, as we discuss more fully in Chapter 9. Many scientists see this is as evidence that we are experiencing the beginning of a new sixth mass extinction (Figure 4.16).

There is also considerable evidence that much of the current rise in the extinction rate and the resulting loss of biodiversity are primarily due to human activities (**Concept 4.5B**). As our ecological footprint spreads over the planet (see Figure 1.8, p. 12), so does extinction. Research indicates that the largest cause of the rising rate of species extinctions is the loss, fragmentation, and degradation of habitats. We examine this issue further in Chapter 9.

Adapt, Migrate, or Go Extinct

In a rapidly changing environment, it can be difficult for many species to survive changing conditions. Essentially, when the environment changes abruptly, organisms have three options: **adapt, migrate, or go extinct**. Environmental factors that impact species and lead to extinction include habitat loss, competition with invasive species, pollution, population growth, climate change, and overexploitation.

An example of this scenario is the polar bear. Because of climate change and the significant loss of sea ice, polar bears are less able to find seals they hunt for food (Figure 4.C). Polar bears spend much of their time in the ocean and when sea ice has melted, must swim farther to reach sheets of floating ice in order to find a place to rest, sometimes swimming for days and ultimately drowning.

The fact that polar bears reproduce slowly but are losing habitat quickly makes it very difficult for the species to evolve and develop adaptive traits. Polar bears may try to migrate to solid land in an attempt to find food or they may attempt to hunt different prey as a way to adapt. Those bears who have a behavioral adaptation that allows them to survive could potentially pass those genes onto their offspring, changing the gene pool for polar bears in future generations. However, the climate where they live is changing rapidly and it will take them a long time to develop adaptive traits.

FRQ Application

Question: The Florida panther is a top predator currently under pressure of extinction. These predatory cats can be found in the swamps and forests of Florida. Males of the species require an extensive territory in order to find mates. As of 2017, biologists reported that there were 120 to 230 Florida panthers left in the wild. **Explain** why this carnivore may have a particularly difficult time increasing its numbers in the wild.

Possible Response: Because the habitat of the panther has changed dramatically due to human encroachment, Florida panthers have the option of either migrating or adapting to new environmental conditions. To adapt, the panthers would have to be able to find appropriate food in a shrinking habitat as well as locate a suitable mate in order to reproduce. This would take a very long time. If they are unable to adapt, they would be forced to migrate. Because humans have constructed highways, housing developments, and other barriers to the movement of panthers, they could be unsuccessful in finding new habitat.

FIGURE 4.C On floating ice in the Arctic sea, this polar bear has killed a bearded seal, one of its major sources of food. *Critical thinking:* Do you think it matters that the polar bear may become extinct in the wild during this century primarily because of human activities? Explain.

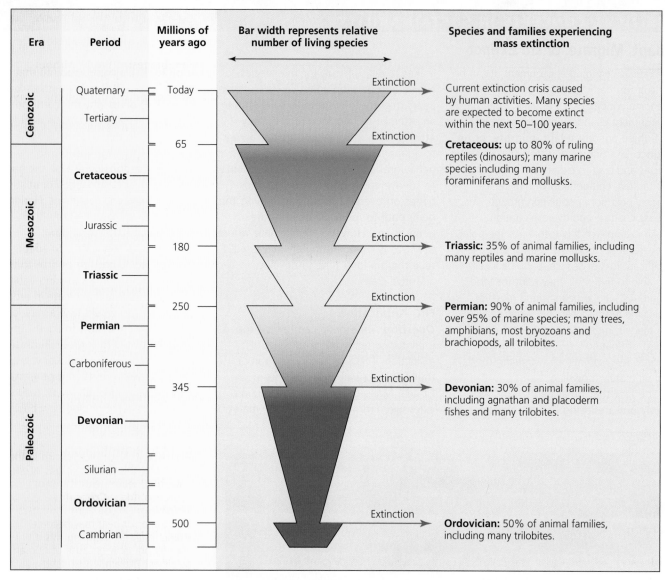

Era	Period	Millions of years ago	Bar width represents relative number of living species	Species and families experiencing mass extinction

Cenozoic
- Quaternary — Today — Extinction → Current extinction crisis caused by human activities. Many species are expected to become extinct within the next 50–100 years.
- Tertiary

65 — Extinction → **Cretaceous:** up to 80% of ruling reptiles (dinosaurs); many marine species including many foraminiferans and mollusks.

Mesozoic
- Cretaceous
- Jurassic

180 — Extinction → **Triassic:** 35% of animal families, including many reptiles and marine mollusks.

- Triassic

250 — Extinction → **Permian:** 90% of animal families, including over 95% of marine species; many trees, amphibians, most bryozoans and brachiopods, all trilobites.

Paleozoic
- Permian
- Carboniferous

345 — Extinction → **Devonian:** 30% of animal families, including agnathan and placoderm fishes and many trilobites.

- Devonian
- Silurian
- Ordovician

Extinction → **Ordovician:** 50% of animal families, including many trilobites.

500

- Cambrian

FIGURE 4.16 Scientific evidence indicates that the earth has experienced five mass extinctions over the past 500 million years and that human activities have probably initiated a new sixth mass extinction.

CHECKPOINT FOR UNDERSTANDING 4.5

1. In a rapidly changing environment, populations have only three options. Identify those options.

2. There have been several mass extinctions in the history of the earth. Explain why the sixth mass extinction that a number of scientists say we are experiencing now is different from those in the past.

Core Case Study Checkpoint

Identify three reasons for protecting amphibian species from extinction.

KEY IDEAS

- Each species plays a specific ecological role, called its *niche*, in the ecosystems where it is found.

- As environmental conditions change, the genes in some individuals mutate and give those individuals genetic traits that enhance their abilities to survive and to produce offspring with these traits.

- The degree of balance between speciation and extinction in response to changing environmental conditions determines the earth's biodiversity, which helps to sustain the earth's life and our economies.

Chapter 4 Glossary

adaptation: any genetically controlled structural, physiological, or behavioral characteristic that helps an organism survive and reproduce under a given set of environmental conditions.

artificial selection: process by which humans select one or more desirable genetic traits in the population of a plant or animal species and then use selective breeding to produce populations containing many individuals with the desired traits.

background extinction rate: normal extinction of various species as a result of changes in environmental conditions.

biodiversity: variety of different species (*species diversity*), genetic variability among individuals within each species (*genetic diversity*), variety of ecosystems (*ecological diversity*), and functions such as energy flow and matter cycling needed for the survival of species and biological communities (*functional diversity*).

biome: terrestrial regions inhabited by certain types of life, especially vegetation.

ecological diversity: the variety of forests, deserts, grasslands, oceans, streams, lakes, and other biological communities interacting with one another and with their nonliving environment.

ecological niche: total way of life or role of a species in an ecosystem. It includes all physical, chemical, and biological conditions that a species needs to live and reproduce in an ecosystem.

ecotone: transition area between two biomes.

edge effect: the changes in population or community structures that occur at the boundary of two habitats.

endemic species: species that is found in only one area. Such species are especially vulnerable to extinction.

eukaryotic cell: cell that is surrounded by a membrane and has a distinct nucleus.

evolution: change in the genetic makeup of a population of a species in successive generations. If continued long enough, it can lead to the formation of a new species. Note that populations, not individuals, evolve.

extinction: complete disappearance of species from the earth. It happens when a species cannot adapt and successfully reproduce under new environmental conditions or when a species evolves into one or more new species.

fossils: skeletons, bones, shells, body parts, leaves, seeds, or impressions of such items that provide recognizable evidence of organisms that lived long ago.

functional diversity: biological and chemical processes of functions such as energy flow and matter cycling needed for the survival of species and biological communities.

generalist species: species with a broad ecological niche. They can live in many different places, eat a variety of foods, and tolerate a wide range of environmental conditions.

genetic diversity: variability in the genetic makeup among individuals within a single species.

genetic engineering: insertion of an alien gene into an organism to give it a new genetic trait.

genetic variability: diversity in the genetic makeup among individuals within a single species.

geographic isolation: physical separation of populations of the same species into different areas for long periods of time.

habitat: place or type of place where an organism or population of organisms live.

indicator species: species whose decline serves as an early warning that a community or ecosystem is being degraded.

invertebrates: animals without backbones.

keystone species: species that play important roles in helping to sustain many other species in an ecosystem.

mass extinction: a catastrophic, widespread, often global event in which major groups of species are become extinct over a short time compared with the normal (background) extinction rates.

native species: species that normally live and thrive in a particular ecosystem.

natural selection: process by which a particular beneficial gene (or set of genes) is reproduced in succeeding generations more than other genes. The result of natural selection is a population that contains a greater proportion of organisms better adapted to certain environmental conditions.

nonnative species: species that migrate into an ecosystem or are deliberately or accidentally introduced into an ecosystem by humans.

phylogenetic tree: branching diagram showing the inferred relationships among various biological species based on similarities and differences in their physical or genetic characteristics and arising from a common ancestor.

prokaryotic cell: cell containing no distinct nucleus or organelles.

reproductive isolation: situation where different populations of sexually reproducing species have been geographically isolated for such a long time that their genetic makeup has changed and they can no longer produce live, fertile, offspring.

specialist species: species with a narrow ecological niche. They may be able to live in only one type of habitat, tolerate only a narrow range of climatic and other environmental conditions, or use only one type or limited types of food.

speciation: formation of two species from one species when different populations of a sexually reproducing species have been separated and exposed to different environmental conditions so long that their genetic makeup has changed; usually takes thousands of years.

species: group of similar organisms and for sexually reproducing organisms a set of individuals that can mate and produce fertile offspring.

species diversity: number of different species (species richness) combined with the relative abundance of individuals within each of those species (species evenness) in a given area.

species evenness: degree to which comparative numbers of individuals of each of the species present in a community are similar.

species richness: variety of species, measured by the number of different species contained in a community.

synthetic biology: Producing new sequences of DNA and using such human produced genetic information to design and create artificial cells, tissues, body parts, and organisms not found in nature.

vertebrates: animals with backbones.

Chapter Review

Core Case Study

1. Describe the threats to many of the world's amphibian species and explain why we should avoid hastening the extinction of amphibian species through our activities.

Section 4.1

2. (a) What is the key concept for this section? (b) Distinguish between **eukaryotic** and **prokaryotic** organisms in terms of their cell structures.

3. (a) What is a **species**? About how many species exist on the earth? How many of these species have we identified? (b) Why are insects such important species?

Section 4.2

4. (a) What is the key concept for this section? (b) Define **biodiversity (biological diversity)** and list and describe its four major components. Why is biodiversity important? (c) What is **species diversity**? Distinguish between **species richness** and **species evenness**. (d) What is **genetic diversity**? What is **ecosystem diversity**? (e) Define and give three examples of **biomes**. What are **edge effects**? What is an **ecotone**? What is **functional diversity**? (f) Summarize the scientific contributions of Edward O. Wilson.

Section 4.3

5. (a) What are the two key concepts for this section? (b) Define and distinguish between **ecological niche** and a **habitat**. (c) Distinguish between **generalist species** and **specialist species** and give an example of each.

6. (a) Define and distinguish among **native**, **nonnative**, **indicator**, and **keystone species** and give an example of each. (b) List six factors that threaten many species of frogs and other amphibians with extinction. (c) Describe the role of the American alligator as a keystone species.

Section 4.4

7. (a) What are the two key concepts for this section? (b) Define **biological evolution (evolution)** and **natural selection** and explain how they are related. What is the scientific theory of biological evolution through natural selection? (c) What are **fossils** and how do scientists use them to understand evolution? (d) What is a **mutation** and what role do mutations play in evolution through natural selection? What is **genetic variability**? What is an **adaptation**, or **adaptive trait**? (e) Explain how harmful bacteria can become genetically resistant to antibiotics. (f) What three genetic adaptations have helped humans to become such a dominant species? (g) What is an **evolutionary tree** or **phylogenetic tree**? How does it help describe evolution? (h) What are two limitations on evolution through natural selection? What are five common myths about evolution through natural selection?

Section 4.5

8. (a) What are the two key concepts for this section? (b) Define **speciation**. Distinguish between **geographic isolation** and **reproductive isolation** and explain how they can lead to the formation of a new species. (c) Explain how geological processes can affect biodiversity. (d) Define and distinguish between **artificial selection** and **genetic engineering**, give

an example of each, and explain how they differ from evolution by natural selection. (e) What is a **genetically modified organism (GMO)**? (f) What is **synthetic biology** and what are its pros and cons.

9. (a) What is **extinction**? What is an **endemic species** and why are such species vulnerable to extinction? (b) Define and distinguish between the **background extinction rate** and a **mass extinction**. (c) How many mass extinctions has the earth experienced? What is one of the leading causes of the rising rate of extinction?

10. What are this chapter's *three key ideas*?

_____

Note: Key terms are in bold type.

AP® Review Questions

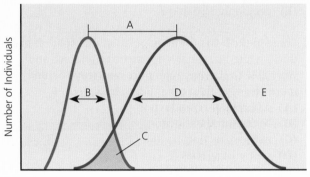

Resource Use

Questions 1–3 refer to the diagram above.

1. Which part of the diagram depicts the resource use that would be in competition if a new species moves into an area and is in direct competition with another species?
   (A) A
   (B) B
   (C) C
   (D) D
   (E) E

2. The niche of the black bear, an omnivore, would be best represented as
   (A) A
   (B) B
   (C) C
   (D) D
   (E) E

3. The area under the curve depicted by letter B would be best described as
   (A) the productivity of a producer, such as grass
   (B) the productivity of a tropical rain forest
   (C) the niche of a specialist, such as the panda bear, which eats only bamboo
   (D) the competition between a producer and a consumer
   (E) how far the niche of two species of animals are separated from each other

4. Which of the following is the best summary of evolution?
   (A) It is the need for organisms to evolve a more perfect form
   (B) It ensures that the strongest organisms will survive to reproduce
   (C) It is the change in the genetic makeup of successive generations of a species
   (D) The grand plan of nature determines how organisms will evolve
   (E) Organisms have desires for particular traits and so evolve them

5. A current example of evolution by natural selection is
   (A) skeletal remains in the fossil record
   (B) genetic resistance of some strains of bacteria to antibiotics
   (C) human opposable thumbs
   (D) plate tectonics
   (E) climate change

6. Which kind of diversity allows organisms on earth to adapt to and survive many changing environmental conditions?
   (A) Genetic diversity
   (B) Species diversity
   (C) Ecosystem diversity
   (D) Functional diversity
   (E) Community biodiversity

7. Keystone species, such as alligators in the southeast U.S., have an important role and effect on their environment through
   (A) having large numbers to regulate the producers
   (B) shaping the ecosystem in ways that benefit other species
   (C) feeding on large numbers of game fish such as bass and bream
   (D) controlling bacterial levels, preventing the infection of other species
   (E) eliminating all potential predators in the ecosystem

(A) Indicator species
(B) Keystone species
(C) Invasive species
(D) Native species
(E) Specialist species

8. As pollution levels in streams rise, many aquatic insects, such as the mayfly, quickly disappear. For this reason, many aquatic insects are studied intensively.

9. The beaver transforms its environment from streams to ponds and swamps, allowing a diverse collection of organisms to thrive that would not normally be able to survive.

10. Dutch elm disease has devastated native populations of American elm trees.

11. The *Chitymomma* is an agave that regionally helps or is used to define the Chihuahuan Desert of northern Mexico and the southwestern United States.

12. Protists are best described as
   (A) prokaryotes, such as cyanobacteria, consisting of single cells with no nucleus
   (B) single-celled bacteria, such as thermophiles, that live in extreme conditions, such as oxygen-free sediment in swamps, water with very high salinity, or heat, such as hydrothermal vents
   (C) eukaryotes, mostly single-celled organisms with a nucleus, such as diatoms and protozoans, some of which cause diseases in humans
   (D) usually multicelled; many are decomposers such as molds and mildews
   (E) multicelled organisms such as mosses and ferns, which can be annuals or perennials

13. Species richness is defined as
   (A) the abundance of individuals within a species
   (B) the number of different species within a community
   (C) the amount of food types a species consumes
   (D) the number of niches a species occupies
   (E) the diversity of species within a community

14. Which habitat has the greatest species richness?
   (A) Tropical rainforest
   (B) Temperate forest
   (C) Short-grass prairie
   (D) Savannah
   (E) Boreal forest

Questions 15 and 16 refer to the following passage.

Evidence has led scientists to believe that the polar bear is a relatively new species closely related to the brown bear. As some bears wandered in search of food, a population of brown bears was split off from the rest of the bears by glaciers.

15. This process is an example of
   (A) differential reproduction
   (B) survival of the fittest
   (C) mutation
   (D) background extinction
   (E) geographic isolation

16. Some of the bears in the population that split off had thick, white fur, suitable for arctic conditions, and were able to survive, reproduce, and leave behind more offspring than other bears, leading to
   (A) differential reproduction
   (B) background extinction
   (C) mass extinction
   (D) specialist species
   (E) reproductive isolation

17. The invasive cane toad shows a population growth rate of 7% per year. How many years will it take for this invasive population to grow from 4 million cane toads to 16 million cane toads?
   (A) 7 years
   (B) 10 years
   (C) 14 years
   (D) 20 years
   (E) 30 years

18. Which of the following are mechanisms of speciation?
   I. Reproductive isolation
   II. Mutation
   III. Natural selection
   (A) I only
   (B) II only
   (C) I and II only
   (D) II and III only
   (E) I, II, and III

19. The best example of an endemic species is
  (A) the golden toad, extinct since 1989, which lived in the Monteverde Cloud Forest Reserve
  (B) amphibians that live in ponds in agricultural areas
  (C) reindeer that live north of the Arctic Circle
  (D) humans that live in the Andes Mountains of South America
  (E) the gray wolf, which is locally extinct in the American Northeast

20. Which of the following is true regarding evolution?
  (A) Humans evolved from apes.
  (B) The purpose of evolution is the perfection of a species.
  (C) Individuals in a population do not evolve.
  (D) Survival of the fittest means that only the strongest individuals survive.
  (E) Evolution explains how life began on earth.

AP® Free-Response Practice

1. Read the following article and answer the questions that follow.

> Amphibians, such as frogs, are extremely sensitive to environmental changes. Frogs live much of their lives in water and have permeable skin that must be kept moist, thereby exposing them to pollutants in their aquatic habitat. Their eggs have no shells, which allows toxins to enter readily and UV light to pass through, causing mutations in offspring.
>
> *Chytrid* is a fungus, usually found in water, which affects frog species by causing a thickening of the infected amphibian's skin, preventing the animal from breathing properly. The infection can eventually lead to cardiac arrest, although some frog species are better able to cope with it than others.
>
> The African clawed frog (*Xenopus laevis*) seems unaffected by the fungus. Scientists speculate that some frog species, such as the golden toad of Montverde *(Incilius periglenes)* in Costa Rica, have gone extinct due to the disease. Other frog species, such as the mountain yellow-legged frog (*Rana muscosa*) in California, are endangered due to that species' lack of resistance to the disease. Even though the disease is devastating, it is possible that scientists may be able to save the mountain yellow-legged frog from extinction.

(a) Even though *chytrid* has caused some frog species to go extinct, disease is usually not a driving factor in extinction. The mountain yellow-legged frog population has dwindled but there is still a small population surviving. **Explain** why, even if this frog population is exposed, that some may survive.

(b) The golden toad of Montverde, now extinct, was an endemic species. **Explain** why an endemic species is more vulnerable to extinction.

(c) Frogs are considered an indicator species. **Explain** the role of frogs as a biological indicator.

(d) Biodiversity is used by scientists to assess the health of an ecosystem and is considered to be an "insurance policy" against ecological collapse.

   (i) **Identify** a biome with high biodiversity and **explain** why it is likely to recover from a chaotic event.

   (ii) **Identify** TWO human activities that reduce biodiversity.

Critical Thinking

1. What might happen to humans and a number of other species if most or all amphibian species (**Core Case Study**) were to go extinct?

2. How might a reduction in species diversity affect the other three components of biodiversity?

3. Is the human species a keystone species? Explain. If humans become extinct, what are three species that might also become extinct and what are three species whose populations might grow?

4. Why should we care about saving amphibians from extinction caused by human activities?

5. How would you respond to someone who tells you:
   a. We should not believe in biological evolution because it is "just a theory."
   b. We should not worry about air pollution because natural selection will enable humans to develop lungs that can detoxify pollutants.

6. How would you respond to someone who says that because extinction is a natural process, we should not worry about the loss of biodiversity when species become extinct largely because of our activities?

7. How do speciation and extinction determine the number of species on the earth?

8. List three aspects of your lifestyle that could be contributing to some of the losses of the earth's biodiversity. For each of these, what are some ways to avoid making this contribution?

9. Congratulations! You are in charge of the future evolution of life on the earth. What are the three most important things that you would do? Explain.

Data Analysis

The following table is a sample of a very large body of data reported by J. P. Collins, M. L. Crump, and T. E. Lovejoy III in their book *Extinction in Our Times—Global Amphibian Decline*. It compares various areas of the world in terms of the number of amphibian species found and the number of amphibian species that were endemic, or unique to each area. Scientists like to know these percentages because endemic species tend to be more vulnerable to extinction than do nonendemic species. Study the table and then answer the following questions.

1. Fill in the fourth column by calculating the percentage of amphibian species that are endemic to each area. (Percentage endemic = number of species divided by number of endemic species.)

2. Which two areas have the highest numbers of endemic species? Name the two areas with the highest percentages of endemic species.

3. Which two areas have the lowest numbers of endemic species? Which two areas have the lowest percentages of endemic species?

4. Which two areas have the highest percentages of nonendemic species?

Area	Number of Species	Number of Endemic Species	Percentage Endemic
Pacific/Cascades/Sierra Nevada Mountains of North America	52	43	
Southern Appalachian Mountains of the United States	101	37	
Southern Coastal Plain of the United States	68	27	
Southern Sierra Madre of Mexico	118	74	
Highlands of Western Central America	126	70	
Highlands of Costa Rica and Western Panama	133	68	
Tropical Southern Andes Mountains of Bolivia and Peru	132	101	
Upper Amazon Basin of Southern Peru	102	22	

Answers to Checkpoints for Understanding

Section 4.1

1. Insects pollinate plants we use for food, prey on other insect pests and help control their populations, and serve as food in some human cultures.

Section 4.2

1. Functional diversity is the variety of chemical and biological functions that cycle matter and move energy through ecosystems. Ecosystem diversity is the variety of aquatic and terrestrial ecosystems that provide habitat for the vast number of species that inhabit the earth. Species diversity is the number and abundance of different species in an ecosystem, and genetic diversity is the genetic variability within a population.

2. Biodiversity provides food, medicine, building materials, and fuel. It also is key to maintaining ecosystem services such as cleaning water and air, topsoil renewal, and a source of genetic material for evolution of species in case of abrupt change in the environment.

Section 4.3

1. The American alligator is a keystone species because of the many roles it plays in its ecosystem. Nesting mounds created by the alligators are used by birds to provide nesting materials and feeding sites, and red belly turtles lay their eggs in the depressions. They keep vegetation in check by digging these holes, and they keep the gar population under control by feeding on these fish, allowing other species to thrive.

2. Alligators are keystone species because of the many functions they fulfill that benefit other organisms in the ecosystems where they live. They are native species to the everglades ecosystem and thrive there. They are also indicator species because if they disappear, it will affect the populations and perhaps the existence of other species that depend on them for their survival.

Section 4.4

1. The source of variation is mutation, usually during the course of DNA replication. Organisms that reproduce very quickly, like bacteria, can adapt more readily to changes in the environment because variability happens faster. Top predators and other individuals who have only a few offspring and take years to reach maturity take far longer to adapt.

2. The hornworms have developed resistance to the pesticide. Because of genetic variability within the population, there are some individuals who are resistant to the pesticide. Those individuals, though few, are able to reproduce and pass their genes for resistance onto their offspring. Eventually most of the population has the resistance so that the pesticide no longer works.

Section 4.5

1. Populations may migrate, adapt, or go extinct.

2. The current mass extinction that many scientists say we are experiencing is due to human impact on the environment, most notably from the impact of habitat loss caused by an expanding human ecological footprint. Evidence also indicates that this is taking place much faster than past mass extinctions.

Core Case Study

Amphibian species should be protected from extinction because they are sensitive biological indicators of changes in environmental conditions, they play important ecological roles such as eating insects, and the skins of some species have chemicals that have been used as antibiotics, painkillers, and treatments for burns and heart disease.

Climate and Terrestrial Biodiversity

> When we try to pick out anything by itself, we find it hitched to everything else in the universe.
>
> JOHN MUIR

Key Questions

5.1 What factors influence weather?

5.2 What factors influence climate?

5.3 How does climate affect the nature and location of biomes?

Giraffes on tropical grassland (savanna) in Africa.

Oleg Znamensky/Shutterstock.com

African Savanna

The earth has a great diversity of species and *habitats*, or places where these species can live. Some species live in *terrestrial*, or land, habitats such as grasslands (see chapter-opening photo), forests, and deserts. These three major types of terrestrial ecosystems are called *biomes*. They represent one of the four components of biodiversity (Figure 4.4, p. 95), which is the basis for one of the three **scientific principles of sustainability**.

Why do grasslands grow on some areas of the earth's land while forests and deserts form in other areas? The answer lies largely in differences in *climate*, the average short-term weather conditions in a given region over at least three decades to thousands of years. Differences in climate result mostly from long-term differences in weather, based primarily on average annual precipitation and temperature. These differences lead to three major types of climate—*tropical* (areas near the equator, receiving the most intense sunlight), *polar* (areas near the earth's poles, receiving the least intense sunlight), and *temperate* (areas between the tropical and polar regions).

Throughout these regions, we find different types of ecosystems, vegetation, and animals adapted to the various climate conditions. For example, in tropical areas, we find a type of grassland called a *savanna*. This biome typically contains scattered trees and usually has warm temperatures year-round with alternating dry and wet seasons. Savannas in East Africa are home to *grazing* (primarily grass-eating) and *browsing* (twig- and leaf-nibbling) hoofed animals. They include wildebeests, gazelles, antelopes, zebras, elephants (Figure 5.1), and giraffes (chapter-opening photo), as well as their predators such as lions, hyenas, and humans.

Archeological evidence indicates that our species emerged from African savannas. Early humans lived largely in trees but eventually came down to the ground and learned to walk upright. This freed them to use their hands for using tools such as clubs and spears. Much later, they developed bows and arrows and other weapons that enhanced their abilities to hunt animals for food and clothing made from animal hides.

After the last ice age, about 10,000 years ago, the earth's climate warmed and humans began their transition from hunter-gatherers to farmers growing food on the savanna and on other grasslands. Later, they cleared patches of forest to expand farmland and created villages and eventually towns and cities.

Today, vast areas of African savanna have been plowed up and converted to cropland or used for grazing livestock. Towns are also expanding there, and this trend will continue as the human population in Africa—the continent with the world's fastest population growth—increases. As a result, populations of elephants, lions, and other animals that roamed the savannas for millions of years have dwindled. Many of these animals face extinction in the next few decades because of the loss of their habitats and because people kill them for food and their valuable parts such as the ivory tusks of elephants.

In this chapter, we distinguish between weather and climate and examine the role that climate plays in the location and formation of the major terrestrial ecosystems, called biomes. We also begin the study of human impacts on these important ecosystems. ●

CRITICAL THINKING

Why is it important to know the difference between weather and climate?

FIGURE 5.1 Elephants on a tropical African savanna.

WHAT FACTORS INFLUENCE
WEATHER?

CONCEPT 5.1 Key factors that influence weather are moving masses of warm and cold air, changes in atmospheric pressure, and occasional shifts in major winds.

Weather Is Affected by Moving Masses of Warm or Cold Air

Weather is the set of physical conditions of the lower atmosphere, including temperature, precipitation, humidity, wind speed, cloud cover, and other factors, in a given area over a period of hours to days. The most important factors in the weather in any area are atmospheric temperature and precipitation.

Meteorologists use equipment mounted on weather balloons, aircraft, ships, and satellites, as well as radar and stationary sensors, to obtain data on weather variables. They feed these data into computer models to draw weather maps for various parts of the world. Other computer models project upcoming weather conditions based on probabilities that air masses, winds, and other factors will change in certain ways.

Much of the weather we experience results from interactions between the leading edges of moving masses of warm air and cold air (**Concept 5.1**). Weather changes when one air mass replaces or meets another. The most dramatic changes in weather occur along a **front,** the boundary between two air masses with different temperatures and densities.

A **warm front** is the boundary between an advancing warm air mass and the cooler one it is replacing (Figure 5.2, left). Because warm air is less dense (weighs less per unit of volume) than cool air, an advancing warm air mass rises up over a mass of cool air. As the warm air rises, its moisture begins condensing into droplets, forming layers of clouds at different altitudes. Gradually, the clouds thicken, descend to a lower altitude, and often release their moisture as rainfall.

A **cold front** (Figure 5.2, right) is the leading edge of an advancing mass of cold air. Because cold air is denser than warm air, an advancing cold front stays close to the ground and wedges beneath less dense warmer air. It pushes this warm, moist air up, which produces rapidly moving, towering clouds called *thunderheads*. As it passes through, it can cause high surface winds and thunderstorms, followed by cooler temperatures and a clear sky.

Weather Is Affected by Changes in Atmospheric Pressure and Wind Patterns

Atmospheric pressure results from molecules of gases in the atmosphere (mostly nitrogen and oxygen) zipping around at very high speeds and bouncing off everything they encounter. Atmospheric pressure is greater near the earth's surface because the molecules in the atmosphere are squeezed together under the weight of the air above them.

An air mass with high pressure, called a *high,* contains cool, dense air that descends slowly toward the earth's surface and becomes warmer. Because of this warming, water molecules in the air do not form droplets—a process called *condensation*. Thus clouds, which are made of droplets, usually do not form in the presence of a high. Fair weather with clear skies follows as long as this high remains over the area.

A low-pressure air mass, called a *low,* contains low-density, warm air at its center. This air rises, expands, and cools. When its temperature drops below a certain level, called the *dew point*, moisture in the air condenses and forms clouds. The condensation process usually requires that the air contain suspended tiny particles of dust, smoke, sea salts, or volcanic ash, called *condensation nuclei*, around which water droplets can form. If the droplets in the clouds

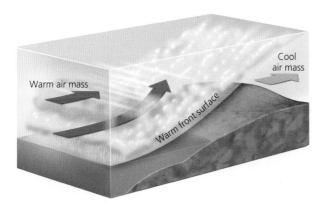
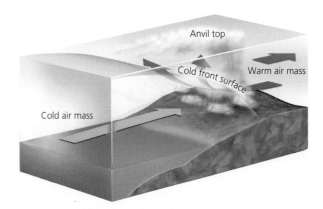

FIGURE 5.2 *Weather fronts:* A warm front (left) occurs when a moving mass of warm air meets and rises up over a mass of denser cool air. A cold front (right) forms when a moving mass of cold air wedges beneath a mass of less dense warm air.

coalesce into larger drops or snowflakes heavy enough to fall from the sky, precipitation occurs. Thus, a low tends to produce cloudy and sometimes stormy weather.

Movement of these air masses is influenced strongly by *jet streams*—powerful winds that circle the globe near the top of the troposphere. They are like fast-flowing rivers of air moving west to east, one in each hemisphere somewhere above and below the equator. They form because of the temperature difference between the equator and the poles, which causes air to move. As the air moves away from the equator, north and south, it is deflected by the earth's rotation and flows generally west to east. The greater the temperature difference, the faster the flow of these winds. Jet streams can influence weather by moving moist air masses from one area to another (**Concept 5.1**). We examine these air flow patterns in more depth later in this chapter.

Every few years, normal wind patterns in the Pacific Ocean (Figure 5.3, left) are disrupted and this affects weather around much of the globe. This change in wind patterns is called the *El Niño–Southern Oscillation*, or *ENSO* (Figure 5.3, right).

In an ENSO, often called simply *El Niño*, winds that usually blow more-or-less constantly from east to west weaken or reverse direction. This allows the warmer waters of the western Pacific to move toward the coast of South America. A horizontal zone of gradual temperature change called the *thermocline*, separating warm and cold waters, sinks in the eastern Pacific. These changes result in drier weather in some areas and wetter weather in other areas. A strong ENSO can alter weather conditions over at least two-thirds of the globe (Figure 5.4)—especially on the coasts of the Pacific and Indian Oceans.

An ENSO is a 1- to 2-year natural weather event. Although it is not a climate event, it can raise the earth's average temperature by as much as 0.25°C (0.45°F) for a year or two. As a result, it can affect the climate by temporarily increasing the earth's average temperature. ENSOs can be extreme in their effects. One such *super ENSO* occurred in 1997 and 1998. This 2-year period of extreme weather, including severe storms, flooding, and temperature extremes, caused $4.5 billion in damages and 23,000 deaths.

La Niña, the reverse of El Niño, cools some coastal surface waters. This natural weather event also occurs every few years and it typically leads to more Atlantic Ocean hurricanes, colder winters in Canada and the northeastern United States, and warmer and drier winters in the southeastern and southwestern United States. It also usually leads to wetter winters in the Pacific Northwest, torrential rains in Southeast Asia, and sometimes more wildfires in Florida. Scientists do not know the exact causes of these weather events or when they are likely to occur, but they do know how to detect and monitor them.

Tornadoes and Tropical Cyclones Are Violent Weather Extremes

Sometimes we experience *weather extremes*. Two examples are violent storms called *tornadoes* (which form over land) and *tropical cyclones* (which form over warm ocean water and sometimes pass over coastal land areas).

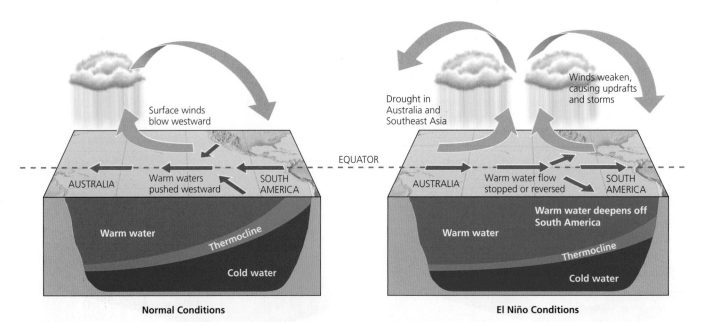

FIGURE 5.3 El Niño: Normal trade winds blowing east to west cause shore upwellings of cold, nutrient-rich bottom water in the tropical Pacific Ocean near the coast of Peru (left). A zone of gradual temperature change called the thermocline separates the warm and cold water. Every few years, a shift in trade winds known as the El Niño–Southern Oscillation (ENSO) disrupts this pattern (right) for 1 to 2 years.

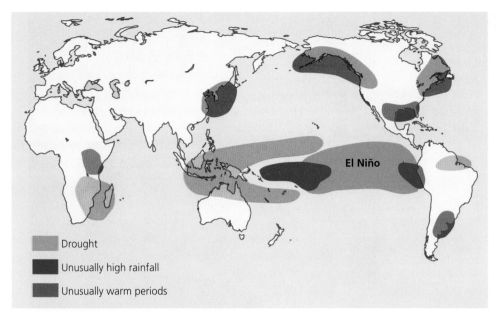

FIGURE 5.4 Typical global weather effects of an El Niño–Southern Oscillation. **Question:** How might an ENSO affect the weather where you live or go to school?

(Compiled by the authors using data from United Nations Food and Agriculture Organization and U.S. Weather Service.)

El Niño

Drought

Unusually high rainfall

Unusually warm periods

Tornadoes, or *twisters*, are swirling, funnel-shaped clouds that form over land. They can destroy houses and cause other serious damage in areas where they touch down. The United States is the world's most tornado-prone country, followed by Australia.

Tornadoes in the plains of the Midwestern United States often occur when a large, dry, cold front moving southward from Canada runs into a large mass of warm humid air moving northward from the Gulf of Mexico. As the large warm front moves rapidly over the denser cold-air mass, it rises swiftly and forms strong vertical convection currents that suck air upward (Figure 5.5). Scientists hypothesize that the interaction of the cooler air nearer the ground and the rapidly rising warmer air above causes a spinning, vertically rising air mass, or *vortex*. Most tornadoes in the American Midwest occur in the spring and summer when cold fronts from the north penetrate deeply into the Great Plains and the Midwest.

FIGURE 5.5 Formation of a tornado, or twister. The most active tornado season in the United States is usually March through August.

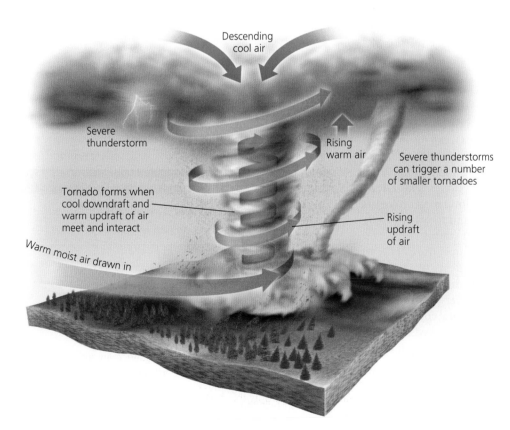

Descending cool air

Severe thunderstorm

Rising warm air

Severe thunderstorms can trigger a number of smaller tornadoes

Tornado forms when cool downdraft and warm updraft of air meet and interact

Rising updraft of air

Warm moist air drawn in

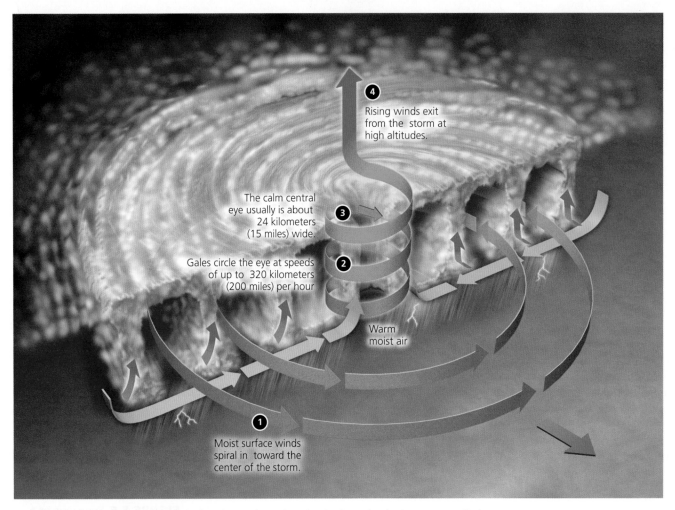

FIGURE 5.6 Formation of a tropical cyclone. Those forming in the Atlantic Ocean are called *hurricanes*. Those forming in the Pacific Ocean are called *typhoons*.

④ Rising winds exit from the storm at high altitudes.

③ The calm central eye usually is about 24 kilometers (15 miles) wide.

② Gales circle the eye at speeds of up to 320 kilometers (200 miles) per hour

Warm moist air

① Moist surface winds spiral in toward the center of the storm.

Tropical cyclones (Figure 5.6) are spawned by the formation of low-pressure cells of air over warm tropical seas. *Hurricanes* are tropical cyclones that form in the Atlantic Ocean. Those forming in the Pacific Ocean usually are called *typhoons*. Hurricanes and typhoons kill and injure people, damage property, and hinder food production. Unlike tornadoes, however, tropical cyclones take a long time to form and gain strength. This allows meteorologists to track their paths and wind speeds, and to warn people in areas likely to be hit by these violent storms.

For a tropical cyclone to form, the temperature of ocean water has to be at least 27°C (80°F) to a depth of 46 meters (150 feet). Areas of low pressure over these warm ocean waters draw in air from surrounding higher-pressure areas. The earth's rotation makes these winds spiral counterclockwise in the northern hemisphere and clockwise in the southern hemisphere. Moist air, warmed by the heat of the ocean, rises in a vortex through the center of the storm until it becomes a tropical cyclone (Figure 5.6).

The intensities of tropical cyclones are rated in different categories, based on their sustained wind speeds. The longer a tropical cyclone stays over warm waters, the stronger it gets. Significant hurricane-force winds can extend 64–161 kilometers (40–100 miles) from the center, or eye, of a tropical cyclone.

CHECKPOINT FOR UNDERSTANDING 5.1

1. Explain how tornadoes form.

2. Explain how cyclones or hurricanes form.

5.2 WHAT FACTORS INFLUENCE CLIMATE?

CONCEPT 5.2 Key factors that influence an area's climate are incoming solar energy, the earth's rotation, global patterns of air and water movement, gases in the atmosphere, and the earth's surface features.

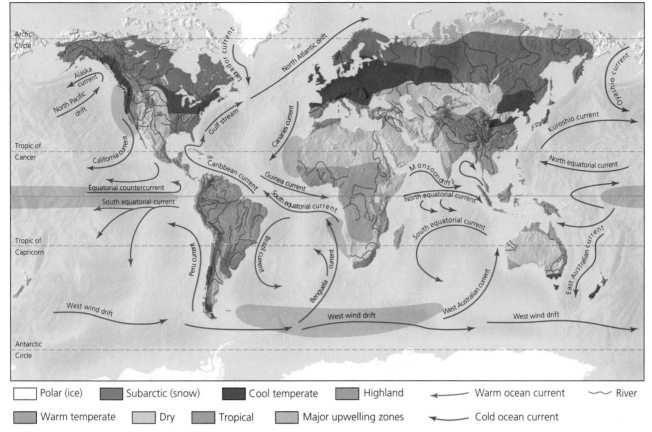

☐ Polar (ice)	◼ Subarctic (snow)	◼ Cool temperate	◼ Highland	← Warm ocean current		∼ River
◼ Warm temperate	☐ Dry	◼ Tropical	◼ Major upwelling zones	← Cold ocean current		

FIGURE 5.7 Natural capital: This generalized map of the earth's current climate zones also shows the major ocean currents and upwelling areas (where currents bring nutrients from the ocean bottom to the surface). **Question:** Based on this map, what is the general type of climate where you live?

Several Factors Affect Regional Climates

It is important to understand the difference between weather and climate. Weather is the set of short-term atmospheric conditions over hours to days to years, whereas **climate** is the general pattern of atmospheric conditions in a given area over periods ranging from at least three decades to thousands of years. Weather often fluctuates daily, from one season to another, and from one year to the next. However, climate tends to change slowly because it is the average of long-term atmospheric conditions over at last 30 years.

Climate varies among the earth's different regions primarily because of global air circulation and **ocean currents,** or mass movements of ocean water. Global winds and ocean currents distribute heat and precipitation unevenly between the tropics and other parts of the world. Scientists have described the various regions of the earth according to their climates (Figure 5.7).

Several major factors help determine regional climates. The first is the *cyclical movement of air driven by solar energy*. It is a form of **convection,** the movement of matter (such as gas or water) caused when the warmer and less dense part of a body of such matter rises while the cooler, denser part of the fluid sinks due to gravity. In the atmosphere, convection oc-

curs when the sun warms the air and causes some of it to rise, while cooler air sinks in a cyclical pattern called a **convection cell.**

For example, the air over an ocean is heated when the sun evaporates water. This transfers moisture and heat from the ocean to the atmosphere, especially near the hot equator. This warm, moist air rises, then cools and releases heat and moisture as precipitation (Figure 5.8, right side and top, center). Then the cooler, denser, and drier air sinks, warms up, and absorbs moisture as it flows across the earth's surface (Figure 5.8, left side and bottom) to begin the cycle again.

A second major climatic factor is the *uneven heating of the earth's surface by the sun*. Air is heated much more at the equator, where the sun's rays strike directly, than at the poles, where sunlight strikes at an angle and spreads out over a much greater area (Figure 5.9, left). Thus, solar heating varies with **latitude**—the location between the equator and one of the poles. Latitudes are designated by degrees (X°) north or south. The equator is at 0°, the poles are at 90° north and 90° south, and areas between range from 0° to 90°.

The input of solar energy in a given area, called **insolation**, varies with latitude. This partly explains why tropical regions are hot, polar regions are cold, and temperate regions generally alternate between warm and cool

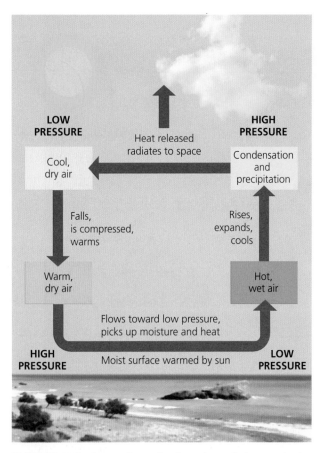

FIGURE 5.8 *Convection cells* play a key role in transferring energy (heat) and moisture through the atmosphere from place to place on the planet.

temperatures (Figure 5.9, right). The amount of solar radiation reaching the earth typically varies about every 11 years because of changes in solar magnetic activity that can warm or cool the planet.

A third major factor is the *tilt of the earth's axis and resulting seasonal changes*. The earth's axis—an imaginary line connecting the north and south poles—is tilted with respect to the sun's rays. As a result, regions north and south of the equator are tipped toward or away from the sun at different times, as the earth makes its annual revolution around the sun (Figure 5.10). This means most areas of the world experience widely varying amounts of solar energy, and thus very different seasons, throughout the year. This in turn leads to seasonal changes in temperature and precipitation in most areas of the globe, and over three or more decades these changes help determine regional climates.

A fourth major climatic factor is the *rotation of the earth on its axis*. As the earth rotates to the east (to the right, looking at Figure 5.9), the equator spins faster than the regions to its north and south. This means that air masses moving to the north or south from the equator are deflected to the east, because they are also moving east faster than the land below them. This deflection of an object's path due to the rotation of the earth is known as the **Coriolis effect**.

Some of this high, moving mass of warm air cools as it flows northeast or southeast from the equator. It becomes more dense and heavier and sinks toward the earth's surface at about 30° north and 30° south (Figure 5.9, left). Because

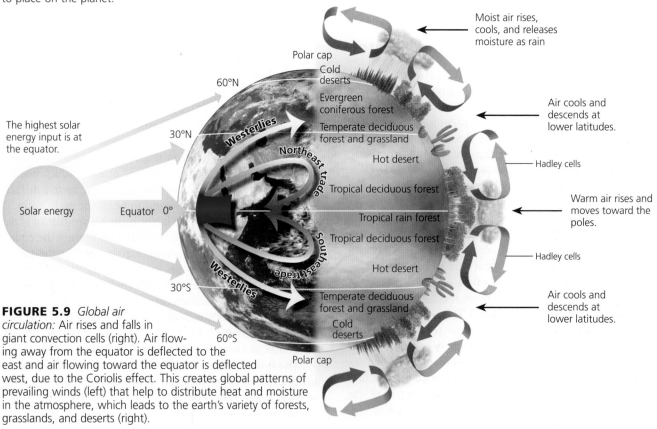

FIGURE 5.9 *Global air circulation:* Air rises and falls in giant convection cells (right). Air flowing away from the equator is deflected to the east and air flowing toward the equator is deflected west, due to the Coriolis effect. This creates global patterns of prevailing winds (left) that help to distribute heat and moisture in the atmosphere, which leads to the earth's variety of forests, grasslands, and deserts (right).

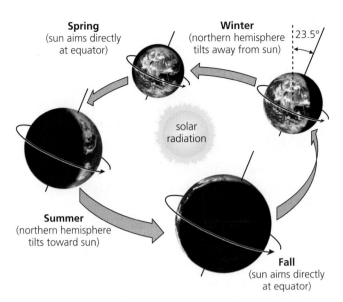

Spring (sun aims directly at equator)

Winter (northern hemisphere tilts away from sun)

23.5°

solar radiation

Summer (northern hemisphere tilts toward sun)

Fall (sun aims directly at equator)

FIGURE 5.10 The earth's axis is tilted about 23.5° with respect to the plane of the earth's path around the sun. The resulting variations in solar energy reaching the northern and southern hemispheres throughout a year result in seasons. **Critical thinking:** How might your life be different if the earth's axis was not tilted?

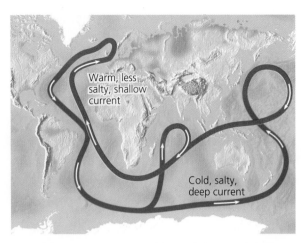

Warm, less salty, shallow current

Cold, salty, deep current

FIGURE 5.11 A connected loop of deep and shallow ocean currents transports warm and cool water to various parts of the earth.

it is part of a convection cell (Figure 5.8), it starts flowing back toward the equator in what is known as a *Hadley cell*. Because of the Coriolis effect, this air moving toward the equator curls in a westerly direction. In the northern hemisphere, it thus flows southwest from northeast. In the southern hemisphere, it flows northwest from southeast.

These winds are known as the *northeast trade winds* (north of the equator) and the *southeast trade winds* (south of the equator). They were named long ago when sailing ships used them to move goods in trade between the continents. They are examples of *prevailing winds*—major surface winds that blow almost continuously.

The warm air that does not descend in the Hadley cells at 30° north and 30° south continues moving toward the poles and curving to the east due to the Coriolis effect. These prevailing winds that blow generally from the west in temperate regions of the globe are known as *westerlies* (Figure 5.9, left).

This complex movement of air results in six huge regions between the equator and the poles in which warm air rises and cools, then falls and heats up again in great rolling patterns (Figure 5.9, right). The two nearest the equator are the Hadley cells. These convection cells and the resulting prevailing winds distribute heat and moisture over the earth's surface, thus helping to determine regional climates (**Concept 5.2**).

A fifth major factor determining regional climates is *ocean currents* (Figure 5.7). They help to redistribute heat from the sun, thereby influencing climate and vegetation, especially near coastal areas. This solar heat, along with differences in water density (mass per unit volume), creates warm and cold ocean currents. They are driven by prevailing winds and the earth's rotation (the Coriolis effect), and continental coastlines change their directions. As a result, between the continents, the currents flow in roughly circular patterns, called **gyres,** which move clockwise in the northern hemisphere and counterclockwise in the southern hemisphere.

Other long-term factors affecting the earth's climate are **(1)** slight changes in the shape of the Earth's orbit around the sun from mostly round to more elliptical over a 100,000 year cycle, **(2)** slight changes in the tilt of Earth's axis over a 41,000-year cycle, and **(3)** slight changes in Earth's wobbly orbit around the sun over a 20,000-year cycle. These three long-term factors are known as the *Milankovitch cycles*.

Water also moves vertically in the oceans as denser water sinks while less dense water rises. This creates a connected loop of deep and shallow ocean currents (which are separate from those shown in Figure 5.7). This loop acts somewhat like a giant conveyer belt that moves heat from the surface to the deep sea and transfers warm and cold water between the tropics and the poles (Figure 5.11).

Greenhouse Gases Warm the Lower Atmosphere

As energy flows from the sun to the earth, some of it is reflected by the earth's surface back into the atmosphere. Molecules of certain gases in the atmosphere, including water vapor (H_2O), carbon dioxide (CO_2), methane (CH_4), and nitrous oxide (N_2O), absorb some of this solar energy and release a portion of it as infrared radiation (heat) that warms the lower atmosphere and the earth's surface. These gases, called **greenhouse gases,** play a role in determining the lower atmosphere's average temperatures and thus the earth's climates.

The earth's surface absorbs much of the solar energy that strikes it and transforms it into longer-wavelength infrared radiation, which then rises into the lower

Prevailing winds pick up moisture from an ocean.

On the windward side of a mountain range, air rises, cools, and releases moisture.

On the leeward side of the mountain range, air descends, warms, and releases little moisture, causing rain shadow effect.

FIGURE 5.12 The *rain shadow effect* is a reduction of rainfall and loss of moisture from the landscape on the leeward side of a mountain. Warm, moist air in onshore winds loses most of its moisture as rain and snow that fall on the windward slopes of a mountain range. This leads to semiarid and arid conditions on the leeward side of the mountain range and on the land beyond.

atmosphere. Some of this heat escapes into space, but some is absorbed by molecules of greenhouse gases and emitted into the lower atmosphere as even longer-wavelength infrared radiation (see Figure 2.12, p. 48). Some of this released energy radiates into space, and some adds to the warming of the lower atmosphere and the earth's surface. Together, these processes result in a natural warming of the troposphere, called the **greenhouse effect** (see Figure 3.3, p. 68). Without this natural warming effect, the earth would be a very cold and mostly lifeless planet.

Human activities such as the production and burning of fossil fuels, clearing of forests, and growing of crops release large quantities of the greenhouse gases carbon dioxide, methane, and nitrous oxide into the atmosphere. According to a considerable body of scientific evidence, we are emitting greenhouse gases into the atmosphere faster than they can be removed by the earth's carbon and nitrogen cycles (see Figures 3.15, p. 78, and 3.16, p. 79).

Climate research and climate models indicate that these emissions have played an important role in warming the earth for almost 50 years and thus are helping to change its climate. In other words, human activities are enhancing the earth's natural greenhouse effect. If the earth's average atmospheric temperature continues to rise as projected, this will alter temperature and precipitation patterns, raise average sea levels, and shift areas where we can grow crops and where many types of plants and animals (including humans) can live. We discuss this issue more fully in Chapter 20.

The Earth's Surface Features Affect Local Climates

Various topographic features of the earth's surface can create local climatic conditions that differ from the general climate in some regions. For example, mountains interrupt

the flow of prevailing surface winds and the movement of storms. When moist air from an ocean blows inland and reaches a mountain range, it is forced upward. As the air rises, it cools, expands, and loses most of its moisture as rain and snow that fall on the windward slope of the mountain.

As shown in Figure 5.12, when the drier air mass passes over the mountaintops, it flows down the leeward slopes (facing away from the wind) and warms up. This warmer air can hold more moisture, but it typically does not release much of it. This tends to dry out plants and soil below. This process is called the **rain shadow effect.** Over many decades, it results in *semiarid* or *arid* conditions on the leeward side of a high mountain range. Sometimes this effect leads to the formation of deserts such as Death Valley, a part of the Mojave Desert, which lies within the U.S. states of California, Nevada, Utah, and Arizona.

Cities also create distinct microclimates based on their weather averaged over three decades or more. Bricks, concrete, asphalt, and other building materials absorb and hold heat, and buildings block wind. Motor vehicles and the heating and cooling systems of buildings release large quantities of heat and pollutants. As a result, cities on average tend to have more haze and smog, higher temperatures, and lower wind speeds than the surrounding countryside. These factors make cities *heat islands*.

CHECKPOINT FOR UNDERSTANDING 5.2

1. Identify the four factors that determine regional climates around the world.

2. Explain how a rain shadow desert forms.

Acres to Hectares

It is important in science to be able to convert between English and metric units, and also to move easily through the metric system. Rather than writing out all the zeroes in very large or very small numbers, it is often easier to express them using exponential notation and to calculate values by simply adding and subtracting exponents.

FRQ Application

To explore the relationship between acres and metric acres, or hectares, begin by using exponents to make conversions between given areas.

Conversion Factors:

1 km^2 = 1,000,000 m^2, which is a square with sides 1000 m long, or 10^3 meters long.

1 hectare (ha) = 10,000 m^2, which is a square with sides 100 meters long, or 10^2 meters long.

1 ha = 2.477 acres

1 acre = 43,560 ft^2

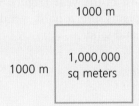

1 square kilometer = 1000 m × 1000 m = 1,000,000 square meters   OR 10^3 m × 10^3 m = 10^6 m^2

How many hectares in a square kilometer?

$$10^6 \ m^2 \times \frac{1 \ ha}{10^4 \ m^2} = 10^2 \ ha, \text{ or } 100 \text{ hectares}$$

Notice how the rules of multiplying and dividing with exponents have been illustrated in the calculations above. The area of a square kilometer is $10^3 \times 10^3$ square meters = 10^{3+3} m^2, or 10^6 m^2. The area of a hectare is $10^2 \times 10^2$ square meters = 10^{2+2} m^2, or 10^4 m^2. The number of hectares is given by 10^6 m^2 ÷ 10^4 m^2 = 10^{6-4}, or 10^2 hectares.

A hectare (ha) is a metric acre. Using dimensional analysis, calculate how many hectares there are in 62,500 square feet.

$$62,500 \ ft^2 \times \frac{1 \ acre}{43,560 \ ft^2} \times \frac{1 \ ha}{2.47 \ acres} = \frac{62,500 \ ha}{107,593.2} = 0.581 \ ha$$

By dividing 62,500 by (43,560 × 2.47), the result is 0.581 ha. Note in the dimensional analysis how the ft^2 and acre units cancel.

5.3 HOW DOES CLIMATE AFFECT THE NATURE AND LOCATION OF BIOMES?

CONCEPT 5.3 Desert, grassland, and forest biomes can be tropical, temperate, or cold depending on their climate and location.

Climate Helps to Determine Where Terrestrial Organisms Can Live

Differences in climate (Figure 5.7) help to explain why one area of the earth's land surface is a desert, another a grassland, and another a forest. Different climates based on long-term average annual precipitation and temperatures, global air circulation patterns, and ocean currents, lead to the formation of tropical (hot), temperate (moderate), and polar (cold) deserts, grasslands, and forests, as summarized in Figure 5.13 (**Concept 5.3**).

Figure 5.14 shows how scientists have divided the world into **biomes**—large terrestrial regions, each characterized by a certain type of climate and dominant forms of plant life. The variety of biomes and aquatic systems is one of the four components of the earth's biodiversity (see Figure 4.4, p. 95)—a vital part of the earth's natural capital. Figure 4.7 (p. 96) shows how major biomes along the midsection of the United States are related to different climates.

On maps such as the one in Figure 5.14, biomes are shown with sharp boundaries, and each biome is covered with one general type of vegetation. See Supplement 5, Figure 2, p. S10 for a map showing the vegetation features of different parts of the earth. In reality, biomes are not uniform. They consist of a variety of areas, each with somewhat different biological communities but with similarities typical of the biome. These areas occur because of the irregular distribution of the resources needed by plants and animals and because human activities have removed or altered the natural vegetation in many areas.

There are also differences in vegetation along the transition zone or ecotone between any two different ecosystems or biomes.

Three Types of Deserts

In a *desert*, annual precipitation is low and often scattered unevenly throughout the year. During the day, the baking sun warms the ground and evaporates water from plant leaves and from the soil. At night, most of the heat stored in the ground radiates quickly into the atmosphere. This explains why in a desert, you might roast during the day but shiver at night.

A combination of low rainfall and varying average temperatures over many decades creates a variety of desert types—tropical, temperate, and cold (Figures 5.13 and 5.14 and **Concept 5.3**). Tropical deserts (Figure 5.15, top photo) such as the Sahara and the Namib of Africa are hot and dry most of the year (Figure 5.15, top graph). They have few plants and a hard, windblown surface strewn with rocks and sand.

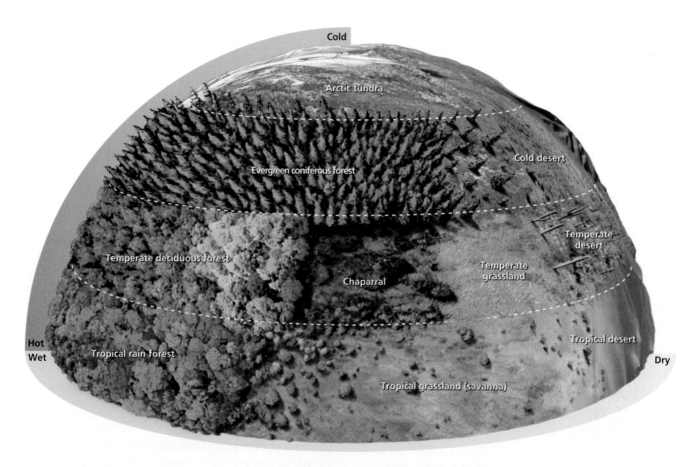

FIGURE 5.13 Natural capital: Average precipitation and average temperature, acting together as limiting factors over a long time, help to determine the type of desert, grassland, or forest in any particular area, and thus the types of plants, animals, and decomposers found in that area (assuming it has not been disturbed by human activities).

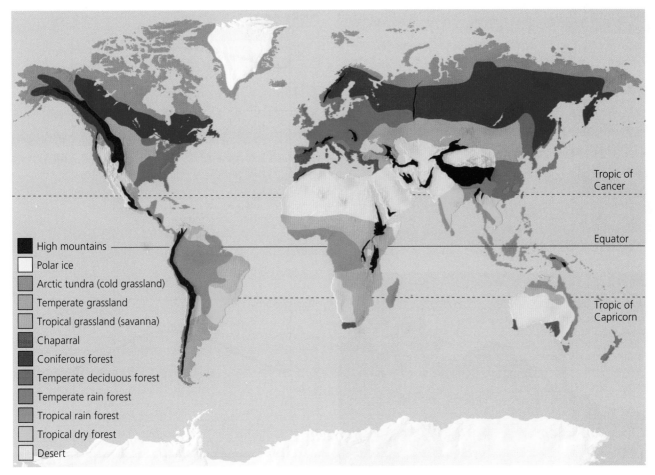

High mountains
Polar ice
Arctic tundra (cold grassland)
Temperate grassland
Tropical grassland (savanna)
Chaparral
Coniferous forest
Temperate deciduous forest
Temperate rain forest
Tropical rain forest
Tropical dry forest
Desert

Tropic of Cancer

Equator

Tropic of Capricorn

FIGURE 5.14 Natural capital: The earth's major *biomes* result primarily from differences in climate.

In *temperate deserts* (Figure 5.15, center photo), daytime temperatures are high in summer and low in winter and there is more precipitation than in tropical deserts (Figure 5.15, center graph). The sparse vegetation consists mostly of widely dispersed, drought-resistant shrubs and cacti or other succulents adapted to the dry conditions and temperature variations.

In *cold deserts* such as the Gobi Desert in Mongolia, vegetation is sparse (Figure 5.15, bottom photo). Winters are cold, summers are warm or hot, and precipitation is low (Figure 5.15, bottom graph). In all types of deserts, plants and animals have evolved adaptations that help them to stay cool and to get enough water to survive (Science Focus 5.1).

Desert ecosystems are vulnerable to disruption because they have slow plant growth, low species diversity, slow nutrient cycling, low bacterial activity in their soils, and very little water. It can take decades to centuries for their soils to recover from disturbances such as off-road vehicle traffic, which can also destroy the habitats for a variety of animal species that live underground.

The lack of vegetation, especially in tropical and polar deserts, also makes them vulnerable to heavy wind erosion from sandstorms.

Three Types of Grasslands

Grasslands occur primarily in the interiors of continents in areas that are too moist for deserts to form and too dry for forests to grow (Figures 5.13 and 5.14). Grasslands persist because of a combination of seasonal drought, grazing by large herbivores, and occasional fires—all of which keep shrubs and trees from growing in large numbers. The three main types of grassland—tropical, temperate, and cold (arctic tundra)—result from long-term combinations of low average precipitation and varying average temperatures (Figure 5.16) (**Concept 5.3**).

One major type of *tropical grassland* is *savanna* (**Core Case Study** and Science Focus 5.2). It contains widely scattered clumps of trees and usually has warm temperatures year-round with alternating dry and wet seasons (Figure 5.16, top graph). Herds of grazing and browsing

Tropical desert

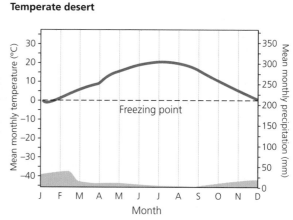

Temperate desert

Cold desert

FIGURE 5.15 These climate graphs track the typical variations in annual temperature (red) and precipitation (blue) in tropical (savanna), temperate, and cold deserts. Top photo: a *tropical desert* in Morocco. Center photo: a *temperate desert* in southeastern California, with saguaro cactus, a prominent species in this ecosystem. Bottom photo: a *cold desert*, Mongolia's Gobi Desert. **Data analysis:** Which month of the year has the highest temperature and which month has the lowest rainfall for each of the three types of deserts?

Staying Alive in the Desert

Adaptations for survival in the desert have two themes: *beat the heat* and *every drop of water counts*.

Desert plants have evolved a number of strategies based on such adaptations. During long hot and dry spells, plants such as mesquite and creosote drop their leaves to survive in a dormant state. *Succulent* (fleshy) *plants* such as the saguaro ("sah-WAH-ro") cactus (Figure 5.A and Figure 5.15, middle photo) have no leaves that can lose water to the atmosphere through *transpiration*. They also store water and synthesize food in their expandable, fleshy tissue and they reduce water loss by opening their pores only at night to take up carbon dioxide (CO_2). The spines of these and many other desert plants guard them from being eaten by herbivores seeking the precious water they hold.

Some desert plants use deep roots to tap into groundwater. Others such as prickly pear and saguaro cacti use widely spread shallow roots to collect water after brief showers and store it in their spongy tissues.

Some desert plants conserve water by having wax-coated leaves that reduce water loss. Others such as annual wildflowers and grasses store much of their biomass in seeds that remain inactive, sometimes for years, until they receive enough water to germinate. Shortly after a rain, these seeds germinate, grow, and carpet some deserts with dazzling arrays of colorful flowers (Figure 5.A) that last for up to a few weeks.

Most desert animals are small. Some beat the heat by hiding in cool burrows or rocky crevices by day and coming out at night or in the early morning. Others become dormant during periods of extreme heat or drought. Some larger animals such as camels can drink massive quantities of water when it is available and store it in their fat for use as needed. In addition, the camel's thick fur helps it keep cool because the air spaces in the fur insulate the camel's skin against the outside heat. In addition, camels do not sweat, which reduces their water loss through evaporation. Kangaroo rats never drink water. They get the water they need by breaking down fats in seeds that they consume.

Insects and reptiles such as rattlesnakes have thick outer coverings to minimize water loss through evaporation, and their wastes are dry feces and a dried concentrate of urine. Many spiders and

Anton Foltin/Shutterstock.com

FIGURE 5.A After a brief rain, these wildflowers bloomed in this temperate desert in Picacho Peak State Park in the U.S. state of Arizona.

insects get their water from dew or from the food they eat.

CRITICAL THINKING

What are three steps you would take to survive in the open desert if you had to?

---

animals migrate across the savanna to find water and food in response to seasonal and year-to-year variations in rainfall (Figure 5.16, blue areas in top graph) and food availability. Savanna plants, like those in deserts, are adapted to survive drought and extreme heat. Many have deep roots that tap into groundwater.

In a *temperate grassland*, winters can be bitterly cold, summers are hot and dry, and annual precipitation is sparse and falls unevenly throughout the year (Figure 5.16, center graph). Because the aboveground parts of most of the grasses die and decompose each year, organic matter accumulates to produce deep, fertile topsoil. This topsoil is held in place by a thick network of the grasses' intertwined roots unless the topsoil is plowed up, which exposes it to high winds found in these biomes. This biome's grasses are adapted to droughts and to fires that burn the plant parts above the ground but do not harm the roots, from which new grass can grow.

CONSIDER THIS . . .

CONNECTIONS Savanna Grassland Niches and Feeding Habits

As an example of differing niches, some large herbivores have evolved specialized eating habits that minimize competition among species for the vegetation found on the savanna (**Core Case Study**). For example, giraffes eat leaves and shoots from the tops of trees, elephants eat leaves and branches farther down, wildebeests prefer short grasses, and zebras graze on longer grasses and stems.

Tropical grassland (savanna)

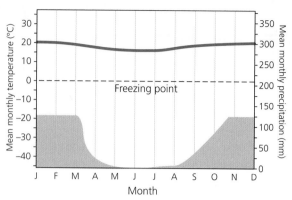

Temperate grassland (prairie)

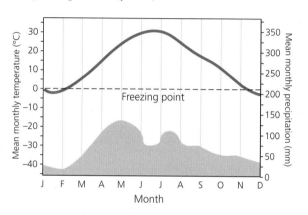

Cold grassland (arctic tundra)

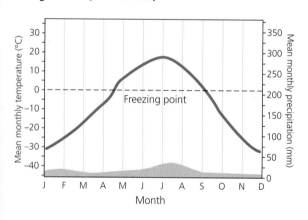

FIGURE 5.16 These climate graphs track the typical variations in annual temperature (red) and precipitation (blue) in tropical, temperate, and cold (arctic tundra) grasslands. Top photo: *savanna (tropical grassland)* in Kenya, Africa, with zebras grazing (**Core Case Study**). Center photo: *prairie (temperate grassland)* in the U.S. state of Illinois. Bottom photo: *arctic tundra (cold grassland)* in Iceland in fall. **Data analysis:** Which month of the year has the highest temperature and which month has the lowest rainfall for each of the three types of grassland?

FIGURE 5.17 Natural capital degradation: This intensively cultivated cropland is an example of the replacement of biologically diverse temperate grasslands (such as in the center photo of Figure 5.16) with a monoculture crop.

In the midwestern and western areas of the United States, we find two types of temperate grasslands depending primarily on average rainfall: *short-grass prairies* (Figure 5.16, center photo) and the *tallgrass prairies* (which get more rain). In all prairies, winds blow almost continuously and evaporation is rapid, often leading to fires in the summer and fall. This combination of winds and fires helps to maintain such grasslands by hindering tree growth. Many of the world's natural temperate grasslands have been converted to farmland, because their fertile soils are useful for growing crops (Figure 5.17) and grazing cattle.

Cold grasslands, or *arctic tundra*, lie south of the arctic polar ice cap (Figures 5.13 and 5.14). During most of the year, these treeless plains are bitterly cold (Figure 5.16, bottom graph), swept by frigid winds, and covered with ice and snow. Winters are long with few hours of daylight, and the scant precipitation falls primarily as snow.

CONSIDER THIS . . .

THINKING ABOUT Prairies

Some people say the widespread destruction and degradation of prairies is justified because they believe that these grasslands are being underutilized and should be put to use for humans. To others, the belief that prairies are not useful in their natural state reflects our lack of understanding of how nature works and of our separation from the rest of nature. Which view do you support? Why?

Under the snow, this biome is carpeted with a thick, spongy mat of low-growing plants, primarily grasses, mosses, lichens, and dwarf shrubs. Trees and tall plants cannot survive in the cold and windy tundra because they would lose too much of their heat. Most of the annual growth of the tundra's plants occurs during the short 7- to 8-week summer, when there is daylight almost around the clock.

Revisiting the Savanna: Elephants as a Keystone Species

As in all biomes, the African savanna (**Core Case Study**) has food webs, which define its character and keep it functioning (Figure 5.B). Like many food webs, savanna food webs often include one or more keystone species that play a major role in maintaining the structure and functioning of the ecosystem.

Ecologists view elephants as a keystone species in the African savanna. They eat woody shrubs and young trees. This helps keep the savanna from being overgrown by these woody plants and prevents the grasses, which form the foundation of the food web (Figure 5.B), from dying out. If they were to die out, antelopes, zebras, and other grass-eaters would leave the savanna in search of food and with them would go the carnivores such as lions and hyenas that feast on these grass-eaters. Elephants also dig for water during drought periods, creating or enlarging waterholes that are used

Pearl Media/Shutterstock.com

Steve O Taylor(GHF)/Nature Picture Library

FIGURE 5.C One reason African elephants are being threatened with extinction is their financially valuable ivory tusks.

by other animals. Without African elephants, savanna food webs would collapse and the savanna would become shrubland.

Conservation scientists classify the African elephant as *vulnerable* to extinction. In 1979 there were an estimated 1.3 million wild African elephants. Today, an estimated 400,000 remain in the wild. This sharp decline is due mostly to the illegal killing of elephants for their valuable ivory tusks (Figure 5.C, left). Since 1990 there has been an international ban on the sale of ivory, and in some areas elephants are protected as threatened or endangered species; however, the illegal killing of elephants for their valuable ivory continues (Figure 5.C, right).

Another major threat to elephants is the loss and fragmentation of their habitats as human populations have expanded and taken over more land. Elephants are eating or trampling the crops of settlers who have moved into elephant habitat areas, and this has caused the killing of some elephants by farmers. If the multiple threats are not curtailed, elephants may disappear from the savanna within your lifetime.

CRITICAL THINKING

Do you think African governments would be justified in setting aside large areas of elephant habitat and prohibiting development there? Explain your reasoning. What are other alternatives for preserving African elephants on the savanna?

Tertiary

Lion

Secondary

Vulture

Hyena

Cheetah

Primary

Elephant

Zeebra

Gazelle

Producers
(grass, trees, shrubs)

FIGURE 5.B A greatly simplified savanna food web.

One outcome of the extreme cold is the formation of **permafrost,** underground soil in which captured water stays frozen for more than 2 consecutive years. During the brief summer, the permafrost layer keeps melted snow and ice from draining into the ground. Thus, shallow lakes, marshes, bogs, ponds, and other seasonal wetlands form when snow and frozen surface soil melt. Hordes of mosquitoes, black flies, and other insects thrive in these shallow surface pools. They serve as food for large colonies of migratory birds (especially waterfowl) that migrate from the south to nest and breed in the tundra's summer bogs and ponds.

Animals in this biome survive the intense winter cold through adaptations such as thick coats of fur (arctic wolf, arctic fox, and musk oxen) or feathers (snowy owl) and living underground (arctic lemming). In the summer, caribou (often called reindeer) and other types of deer migrate to the tundra to graze on its vegetation.

Tundra is vulnerable to disruption. Because of the short growing season, tundra soil and vegetation recover very slowly from damage or disturbance. Human activities in the arctic tundra—primarily on and around oil and natural gas drilling sites, pipelines, mines, and military bases—leave scars that persist for centuries.

Another type of tundra, called *alpine tundra,* occurs above the limit of tree growth but below the permanent snow line on high mountains. The vegetation is similar to that found in arctic tundra, but it receives more sunlight than arctic vegetation gets. During the brief summer, alpine tundra can be covered with an array of beautiful wildflowers.

Chaparral—a Dry Temperate Biome

In many coastal regions that border on deserts, we find a biome known as *temperate shrubland* or *chaparral* (Spanish for *thicket*). Because it is close to the sea, it has a slightly longer winter rainy season than the bordering desert has and experiences fogs during the spring and fall seasons. Chaparral is found along coastal areas of southern California, the Mediterranean Sea, central Chile, southern Australia, and southwestern South Africa.

This biome consists mostly of dense growths of low-growing evergreen shrubs and occasional small trees with leathery leaves (Figure 5.18). Its animal species include mule deer, chipmunks, jackrabbits, lizards, and a variety of birds. The soil is thin and not very fertile. During the long, hot, and dry summers, chaparral vegetation dries out. In the late summer and fall, fires started by lightning or human activities spread swiftly.

Research reveals that chaparral is adapted to and maintained by occasional fires. Many of the shrubs store food reserves in their fire-resistant roots and have seeds that sprout only after a hot fire. With the first rain, annual grasses and wildflowers spring up and use nutrients released by the fire. New shrubs grow quickly and crowd out the grasses.

People like living in this biome because of its moderate, sunny climate. As a result, humans have moved in and modified this biome so much that little natural chaparral exists. The downside is that people living in chaparral assume the high risk of frequent fires, which are often followed by flooding during winter rainy seasons. When heavy rains come, torrents of water pour off the unprotected burned hillsides to flood lowland areas, often causing mudslides.

Three Types of Forests

Forests are lands that are dominated by trees. The three main types of forest—*tropical, temperate,* and *cold* (northern coniferous, or boreal)—result from combinations of varying precipitation levels and temperatures averaged over three decades or longer (**Concept 5.3**) (Figures 5.13 and 5.14).

Tropical rain forests (Figure 5.19, top photo) are found near the equator (Figure 5.14), where hot, moisture-laden air rises and dumps its moisture. These lush forests have year-round, warm temperatures, high humidity, and almost daily heavy rainfall (Figure 5.19, top graph). This warm and wet climate is ideal for a wide variety of plants and animals.

Tropical rain forests are dominated by *broadleaf evergreen plants,* which keep most

Minden Pictures/Superstock

FIGURE 5.18 Lowland chaparral in the Rio Grande River Valley, New Mexico (USA).

Tropical rain forest

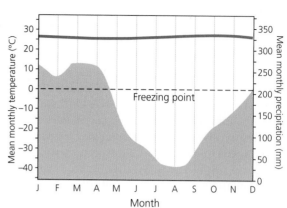

Temperate deciduous forest

Northern coniferous forest (boreal forest, taiga)

FIGURE 5.19 These climate graphs track the typical variations in annual temperature (red) and precipitation (blue) in tropical, temperate, and cold (northern coniferous, or boreal) forests. Top photo: the closed canopy of a *tropical rain forest* in Costa Rica. Middle photo: a *temperate deciduous forest near Hamburg, Germany,* in autumn. Bottom photo: a *northern coniferous forest* in Canada. ***Data analysis:*** Which month of the year has the highest temperature and which month has the lowest rainfall for each of the three types of forest?

of their leaves year-round. The tops of the trees form a dense *canopy* (Figure 5.19, top photo) that blocks most light from reaching the forest floor. Many of the relatively few plants that live at the ground level have enormous leaves to capture what little sunlight filters down to them.

Some trees are draped with vines (called *lianas*) that grow to the treetops to gain access to sunlight. In the canopy, the vines grow from one tree to another, providing walkways for many species living there. When a large tree is cut down, its network of lianas can pull down other trees.

Tropical rain forests have a high net primary productivity (see Figure 3.13, p. 75). They are teeming with life and possess incredible biological diversity. Although tropical rain forests cover only about 2% of the earth's land surface, ecologists estimate that they contain at least 50% of the known terrestrial plant and animal species. A single tree in these forests may support several thousand different insect species. Plants from tropical rain forests are a source of a variety of chemicals, many of which have been used as blueprints for making most of the world's prescription drugs.

Rain forest species occupy a variety of specialized niches in distinct layers, which contribute to their high species diversity. Vegetation layers are structured, for the most part, according to the plants' needs for sunlight, as shown in Figure 5.20. Much of the animal life, particularly insects, bats, and birds, lives in the sunny canopy layer, with its abundant shelter and supplies of leaves, flowers, and fruits.

Dropped leaves, fallen trees, and dead animals decompose quickly in tropical rain forests because of the warm, moist conditions and the hordes of decomposers. About 90% of the nutrients released by this rapid decomposition are quickly taken up and stored by trees, vines, and other plants. Nutrients that are not taken up are soon leached from the thin topsoil by the frequent rainfall and little plant litter builds up on the ground. The resulting lack of fertile soil helps explain why rain forests are not

FIGURE 5.20 Specialized plant and animal niches are *stratified*, or arranged roughly in layers, in a tropical rain forest. Filling such specialized niches enables many species to avoid or minimize competition for resources and results in the coexistence of a great variety of species.

good places to clear and grow crops or graze cattle on a sustainable basis.

At least half of the world's tropical rain forests have been destroyed or disturbed by human activities such as farming, and the pace of this destruction and degradation is increasing (see Chapter 3 Core Case Study, p. 66). Ecologists warn that without strong protective measures, most of these forests, along with their rich species biodiversity and highly valuable ecosystem services, could be gone by the end of this century.

The second major type of forest is the *temperate forest*, the most common of which is the *temperate deciduous forest* (Figure 5.19, middle photo). Such forests typically have warm summers, cold winters, and abundant precipitation—rain in summer and snow in winter months (Figure 5.19, middle graph). They are dominated by a few species of *broadleaf deciduous trees* such as oak, hickory, maple, aspen, and birch. Animal species living in these forests include predators such as wolves, foxes, and wildcats. They feed on herbivores such as white-tailed deer, squirrels, rabbits, and mice. Warblers, robins, and other bird species live in these forests during the spring and summer, mating and raising their young.

In these forests, most of the trees' leaves, after developing their vibrant colors in the fall (Figure 5.19, middle photo), drop off the trees. This allows the trees to survive the cold winters by becoming dormant. Each spring, the trees sprout new leaves and spend their summers growing and producing until the cold weather returns.

Because they have cooler temperatures and fewer decomposers than tropical forests have, temperate forests also have a slower rate of decomposition. As a result, they accumulate a thick layer of slowly decaying leaf litter, which becomes a storehouse of soil nutrients. On a global basis, temperate forests have been degraded by various human activities, especially logging and urban expansion, more than any other terrestrial biome.

Another type of temperate forest, the *coastal coniferous forests* or *temperate rain forests* (Figure 5.21), are found in scattered coastal temperate areas with ample rainfall and moisture from dense ocean fogs. These forests contain thick stands of large cone-bearing, or *coniferous*, trees that keep most of their leaves (or needles) year-round. Most of these species have small, needle-shaped, wax-coated leaves that can withstand the intense cold and drought of winter. Examples are Sitka spruce, Douglas fir, giant sequoia (see Chapter 2 opening photo, pp. 34–35), and redwoods that once dominated undisturbed areas of these biomes along the coast of North America, from Canada to Northern California in the United States.

In this biome, the ocean moderates the temperature so winters are mild and summers are cool. The trees in these moist forests depend on frequent rains and moisture from summer fogs. Most of the trees are evergreen because the abundance of water means that they have no need to shed their leaves. Tree trunks and the ground are frequently covered with mosses and ferns in this cool and moist environment. As in tropical rain forests, little light reaches the forest floor.

Many of the redwood, Douglas fir, and western cedar forests have been cleared for their valuable timber and there is constant pressure to cut what remains. This threatens species such as the spotted owl and marbled murrelet that depend on these ecosystems. Clear-cutting also loads streams in these ecosystems with eroded sediment and threatens species such as salmon that depend on clear streams for laying their eggs.

The third major forest type is the *cold*, or *northern coniferous forests* (Figure 5.19, bottom photo), also called *boreal forests* or *taigas* ("TIE-guhs"). They are found south of

FIGURE 5.21 Temperate rain forest in Olympic National Park in the U.S. state of Washington.

CrackerClips Stock Media/Shutterstock.com

arctic tundra in northern regions across North America, Asia, and Europe (Figure 5.14) and above certain altitudes in the Sierra Nevada and Rocky Mountain ranges of the United States. In the subarctic, cold, and moist climate of the northernmost boreal forests, winters are long and extremely cold, with winter sunlight available only 6 to 8 hours per day. Summers are short, with cool to warm temperatures (Figure 5.19, bottom graph), and the sun shines as long as 19 hours a day during midsummer.

Most boreal forests are dominated by a few species of *coniferous evergreen trees* or *conifers* such as spruce, fir, cedar, hemlock, and pine. Plant diversity is low because few species can survive the winters when soil moisture is frozen.

Beneath the stands of trees in these forests is a deep layer of partially decomposed conifer needles. Decomposition is slow because of low temperatures, the waxy coating on the needles, and high soil acidity. The decomposing conifer needles make the thin, nutrient-poor topsoil acidic, which prevents most other plants (except certain shrubs) from growing on the forest floor.

Year-round wildlife in this biome includes bears, wolves, moose, lynx, and many burrowing rodent species. Caribou spend winter in the taiga and summer in the arctic tundra (Figure 5.16, bottom). During the brief summer, warblers and other insect-eating birds feed on flies, mosquitoes, and caterpillars.

Mountains Play Important Ecological Roles

Some of the world's most spectacular environments are high on *mountains* (Figure 5.22), steep or high-elevation lands that cover about one-fourth of the earth's land surface.

Mountains are places where dramatic changes take place over very short distances. In fact, climate and vegetation vary according to *elevation*, or height above sea level,

just as they do with latitude (Figure 5.23). If you climb a tall mountain, from its base to its summit, you can observe changes in plant life similar to those you would encounter in traveling from a temperate region to the earth's northern polar region.

About 1.2 billion people (16% of the world's population) live in mountain ranges or in their foothills, and 4 billion people (54% of the world's population) depend on mountain systems for all or some of their water. Because of the steep slopes, mountain soils are easily eroded when the vegetation holding them in place is removed by natural disturbances such as landslides and avalanches, or by human activities such as timber cutting and agriculture. Many mountains are *islands of biodiversity* surrounded by a sea of lower-elevation landscapes transformed by human activities.

Mountains play an important ecological role. They contain a large portion of the world's forests, which are habitats for much of the planet's terrestrial biodiversity. They often are habitats for *endemic species*—those that are found nowhere else on earth. They also serve as sanctuaries for animals that are capable of migrating to higher altitudes and surviving in such environments. Every year, more of these animals are driven from lowland areas to mountain habitats by human activities and by the warming climate.

CONSIDER THIS . . .

CONNECTIONS Mountains and Climate

Mountains help regulate the earth's climate. Many mountaintops are covered with glacial ice and snow that reflect some solar radiation back into space, which helps to cool the earth. However, many mountain glaciers are melting, primarily because the atmosphere has warmed over recent decades. Whereas glaciers reflect solar energy, the darker rocks exposed by melting glaciers absorb that energy. This helps to warm the atmosphere above them, which melts more ice and warms the atmosphere more—in an escalating positive feedback loop.

FIGURE 5.22 Mountains, such as these surrounding a lake, provide vital ecosystem services.

Pichugin Dmitry/Shutterstock.com

Valuation of Natural Capital

The monetary value of **natural capital**, the natural resources and ecological services that keep us alive and support our economies, has been estimated by ecological economist Robert Costanza and his colleagues. For example, they estimate that the value of all the ecosystem services provided by the earth's forests is worth at least $15.6 trillion a year. This is many times greater than the estimated value of their economic services, showing why intact forests are far more valuable than the price of the timber they would yield.

Underpricing the value of natural resources is the basic problem in unsustainable practices of resource harvesting. The estimated economic value of ecosystem services provided by forests, oceans, and other ecosystems are not included in the market prices of timber, fish, and other goods we get from them. Until this underpricing is corrected, unsustainable use of forests, oceans, the atmosphere, and many of nature's other irreplaceable forms of natural capital will continue.

FRQ Application

Question: Colony collapse disorder (CCD) is a phenomenon that causes worker bees to disappear from the hive leaving only the queen and nurse bees to tend to the larvae. Scientists believe colony collapse may be due to the combination of overuse of pesticides and attack from parasites. Bee colonies provide important ecosystem services. **Identify** and **discuss** ONE ecological impact that results from the loss of honeybees, and ONE economic impact that results from CCD.

Possible Response: One ecological impact that results from the loss of honey bees is reduced pollination of flowering plants. If plants are not pollinated, no fruits or seeds may form, reducing the amount of food available to animals or humans that feed on them. One economic impact that results from the loss of honeybees is the decline of commercial crops, for example, tomatoes or apples, which require pollination. This drives the price of food higher for consumers, and declining yields result in loss of revenue for farmers and agricultural workers.

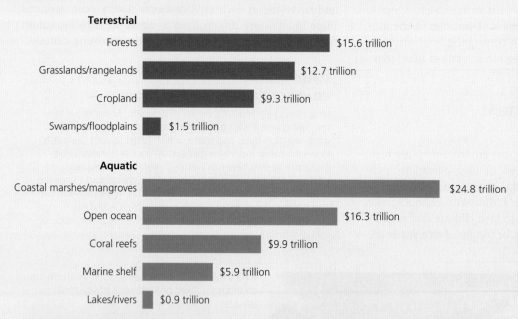

Ecosystem Services

Ecosystem services are important benefits or functions that nature provides for us and other species. Some of the most important services include the following:

- Pollination
- Clean water
- Seed dispersal
- Soil fertility
- Decomposition of organic waste
- Pest control
- Flood control
- Climate regulation
- Cycling of nutrients

FIGURE 5.D Natural capital: Estimated monetary value of ecosystem services provided each year by the world's major terrestrial and aquatic ecosystems.

(Compiled by the authors using data from Robert Costanza et al., "Changes in the Value of Ecosystem Services," *Global Environmental Change*, Elsevier, 2014.)

Mountains play a critical role in the hydrologic cycle (see Figure 3.14, p. 77) by serving as major storehouses of water. During winter, precipitation is stored as ice and snow. In the warmer weather of spring and summer, much of this snow and ice melts, releasing water to streams for use by wildlife and by humans for drinking and for irrigating crops. As the earth's atmosphere has warmed in recent decades, some mountaintop snow packs and glaciers have been melting earlier in the spring each year. This is leading to lower food production in certain areas, because much of the water needed throughout the summer to irrigate crops is released too early in the season and too quickly. Despite the ecological, economic, and cultural importance of mountain ecosystems, governments and many environmental organizations have not focused on protecting these areas.

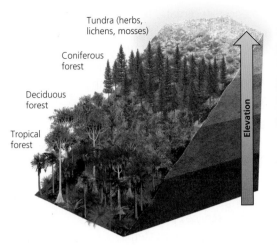

Tundra (herbs, lichens, mosses)

Coniferous forest

Deciduous forest

Tropical forest

Elevation

Latitude (south to north)

Tropical Forest | Deciduous Forest | Coniferous Forest | Tundra (herbs, lichens, mosses) | Polar ice and snow

FIGURE 5.23 Climate and vegetation represented by different biomes change with elevation as well as with latitude.

Humans Have Disturbed Much of the Earth's Land

About 60% of the world's major terrestrial ecosystems are being degraded or used unsustainably, as the human ecological footprint gets bigger and spreads across the globe (see Figure 1.8, p. 12), according to the 2005 Millennium Ecosystem Assessment and later updates of such research. Figure 5.24 summarizes the most harmful human impacts on the world's deserts, grasslands, forests, and mountains.

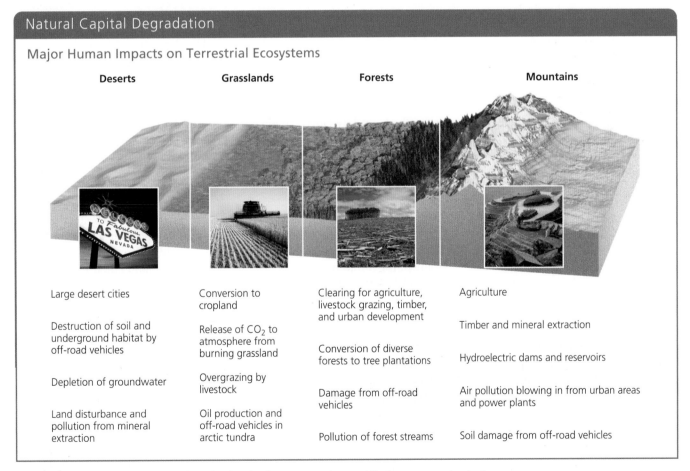

Natural Capital Degradation

Major Human Impacts on Terrestrial Ecosystems

Deserts | **Grasslands** | **Forests** | **Mountains**

Large desert cities

Destruction of soil and underground habitat by off-road vehicles

Depletion of groundwater

Land disturbance and pollution from mineral extraction

Conversion to cropland

Release of CO_2 to atmosphere from burning grassland

Overgrazing by livestock

Oil production and off-road vehicles in arctic tundra

Clearing for agriculture, livestock grazing, timber, and urban development

Conversion of diverse forests to tree plantations

Damage from off-road vehicles

Pollution of forest streams

Agriculture

Timber and mineral extraction

Hydroelectric dams and reservoirs

Air pollution blowing in from urban areas and power plants

Soil damage from off-road vehicles

FIGURE 5.24 Human activities have had major impacts on the world's deserts, grasslands, forests, and mountains, as summarized here. *Critical thinking:* For each of these biomes, which two of the impacts listed do you think are the most harmful? Explain.

How long can we keep eating away at these terrestrial forms of natural capital without threatening our economies and the long-term survival of our own and many other species? No one knows. But there are increasing signs that we need to come to grips with this vital issue.

Many environmental scientists call for a global effort to better understand the nature and state of the world's major terrestrial ecosystems and biomes and to use such scientific data to protect the world's remaining wild areas from harmful forms of development. In addition, they call for us to restore many of the land areas that have been degraded, especially in areas that are rich in biodiversity.

CHECKPOINT FOR UNDERSTANDING 5.3

1. Explain how it is possible to have both tropical desert and cold desert.

2. Explain why tundra or cold grassland is important to migrating flocks of birds.

3. Discuss why tropical forest trees don't drop their leaves like those of a temperate deciduous forest.

Core Case Study Checkpoint

Describe how the African savanna, a tropical grassland, is being threatened by human activities.

Chapter 5 Glossary

atmospheric pressure: force or mass per unit area of air, caused by the bombardment of a surface by the molecules in air.

biome: terrestrial regions inhabited by certain types of life, especially vegetation.

climate: physical properties of the troposphere of an area based on analysis of its weather records over a long period (at least 30 years). The two main factors determining an area's climate are its average temperature, with its seasonal variations, and the average amount and distribution of precipitation over at least 30 years.

cold front: leading edge of an advancing mass of cold air.

convection: movement of warmer molecules that rise and become less dense while colder molecules sink and become more dense, ultimately resulting in the transfer of heat.

convection cell: cyclical pattern of air that rises and falls due to convection.

Coriolis effect: the deflection of an air mass to the east as it moves north or south away from the equator, or a deflection west as it moves toward the equator. These deflections occur because the earth's eastward rotation is faster at the equator than at any other point on its surface.

front: the boundary between two air masses with different temperatures and densities.

greenhouse effect: natural effect that releases heat in the atmosphere near the earth's surface. Water vapor, carbon dioxide, methane, and other gases in the lower atmosphere absorb some of the infrared radiation (heat) radiated by the earth's surface and release some of it into the lower atmosphere.

greenhouse gases: gases in the earth's lower atmosphere (troposphere) that cause the greenhouse effect.

gyres: ocean currents that are driven by prevailing winds and the Coriolis effect, rotating clockwise in the northern hemisphere and counterclockwise in the southern hemisphere.

insolation: input of solar energy in a given area.

latitude: distance from the equator.

ocean currents: mass movements of surface water produced by prevailing winds blowing over the oceans.

permafrost: perennially frozen layer of soil that forms when the water there freezes. It is found in the arctic tundra.

rain shadow effect: low precipitation on the leeward side of a mountain when prevailing winds move up and over a high mountain or high mountain range and create semiarid and arid conditions on the leeward side of a high mountain range.

warm front: boundary between an advancing warm air mass and the cooler one it is replacing. Because warm air is less dense than cool air, an advancing warm front rises over a mass of cool air.

weather: short-term changes in the temperature, barometric pressure, humidity, precipitation, sunshine, cloud cover, wind direction and speed, and other conditions in the troposphere at a given place and time.

Chapter Review

Core Case Study

1. Describe the African savanna (**Core Case Study**) and explain why it serves as an example of how differences in climate lead to the formation of different types of ecosystems.

Section 5.1

2. (a) What is the key concept for this section? (b) Define **weather**. Define **front** and distinguish between a **warm front** and a **cold front**. What is **atmospheric pressure**? Define and distinguish between a **high** and a **low**. (c) What are El Niño and La Niña? Summarize their effects. (d) Explain how tornadoes form and describe their effects. (e) What are tropical cyclones and what is the difference between hurricanes and typhoons? How do these storms form?

Section 5.2

3. (a) What is the key concept for this section? (b) Define **climate** and distinguish between weather and climate. Define **ocean currents**. Define **convection** and **convection cell**. (c) Explain how uneven solar heating of the earth affects climate. (d) Define **latitude** and explain how latitudes are designated. Define **insolation** and explain how it is related to latitude. (e) Explain how the tilt of the earth's axis and resulting seasonal changes affect climates.

4. (a) How does the rotation of the earth on its axis affect climates? (b) What is the **Coriolis effect**? (c) Explain how prevailing winds form and how they affect climate. (d) Explain how ocean currents affect climate. What is a **gyre**?

5. (a) Define and give four examples of a **greenhouse gas**. (b) What is the **greenhouse effect** and why is it important to the earth's life and climate? (c) What is the **rain shadow effect** and how can it lead to the formation of deserts? (d) Why do cities tend to have more haze and smog, higher temperatures, and lower wind speeds than the surrounding countryside?

Section 5.3

6. (a) What is the key concept for this section? (b) Explain how different combinations of annual precipitation and temperatures averaged over several decades, along with global air circulation patterns and ocean currents, lead to the formation of deserts, grasslands, and forests. (c) What is a **biome**? Explain why there are three major types of each of the major biomes (deserts, grasslands, and forests). Explain why biomes are not uniform. (d) Describe how climate and vegetation vary with latitude and elevation.

7. (a) Explain how the three major types of deserts differ in their climate and vegetation. (b) Why are desert ecosystems vulnerable to long-term damage? (c) How do desert plants and animals survive?

8. (a) Explain how the three major types of grasslands differ in their climate and vegetation. (b) Explain how savanna animals survive seasonal variations in rainfall (**Core Case Study**). Why is the elephant an important component of the African savanna? (c) Why have many of the world's temperate grasslands disappeared? (d) Describe arctic tundra and define **permafrost**. (e) What is chaparral and what are the risks of living there?

9. (a) Explain how the three major types of forests differ in their climate and vegetation. (b) Why is biodiversity so high in tropical rain forests? (c) Why do most soils in tropical rain forests hold few plant nutrients? (d) Why do temperate deciduous forests typically have a thick layer of decaying litter? (e) What are coastal coniferous or temperate rain forests? (f) How do most species of coniferous evergreen trees survive the cold winters in boreal forests? (g) What important ecological roles do mountains play? (h) Summarize the ways in which human activities have affected the world's deserts, grasslands, forests, and mountains.

10. What are this chapter's *three key ideas*?

Note: Key terms are in bold type.

1. Long-term differences in which two variables are the primary determinants of climate?
   (A) Temperature and cloud cover
   (B) Precipitation and temperature
   (C) Precipitation and soil type
   (D) Temperature and soil type
   (E) Soil type and cloud cover

2. Which of the following is an example of a change in weather?
   (A) A large area changes from a grassland to a desert.
   (B) While climbing a mountain, one moves through several different biomes.
   (C) A thunderstorm forms and drops 1.5 cm of rain.
   (D) Increased greenhouse gases in the atmosphere cause atmospheric warming.
   (E) Desertification of an area causes the area to see increased annual temperatures.

Questions 3 and 4 refer to the following information.

A student designed an experiment to determine the rate of heating and cooling by different earth surfaces. Beaker 1 was filled to the 200-mL mark with sand; Beaker 2 contained an equal volume of water. Each beaker was placed under a heat lamp for 10 minutes; at 10 minutes, the lamps were turned off, and the temperature was recorded after an additional 10 minutes.

	Temperature (°C)	
Time (minutes)	Beaker 1 Sand	Beaker 2 Water
1	21.0	21.3
10	42.2	28.3
20	26.9	22.5

3. This experiment suggests that the ability of water and sand to absorb and release heat can be a factor in determining a region's climate. Considering this, which of the following is a logical conclusion based on the data?
   (A) Areas located near a large body of water will exhibit a cold and windy climate.
   (B) Deserts are warmer than lakes because they are dry.
   (C) Coastal areas have more extreme seasons than inland areas.
   (D) Coastal areas have a moderate climate.
   (E) Alpine regions receive large amounts of precipitation.

4. Which concept can be explained when the data is applied to atmospheric/oceanic interactions?
   (A) El Niño
   (B) Land and sea breezes
   (C) The rain shadow effect
   (D) Solar reflectivity
   (E) The Coriolis effect

Questions 5–8 refer to the labeled diagram of surface currents in the oceans. Choices may be used once, more than once, or not at all.

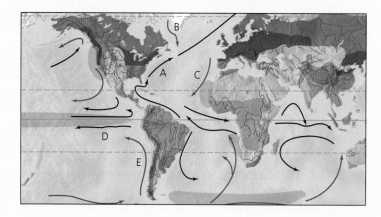

5. A current responsible for moving heat away from the equator.

6. The reversal of this current is associated with ENSO events.

7. Besides the Gulf Stream, this current composes the other half of the North Atlantic Gyre.

8. Following a volcanic eruption in Russia in the 1800s the Gulf Stream slowed down. As a result, Europe cooled down, especially in Ireland. Which current was responsible for transporting colder water into the Atlantic, ultimately cooling down Europe?

9. As one climbs a mountain from the windward side, the elevation change causes a change in biomes. Which of the following is a change caused by elevation increase?
   (A) Biomes become more diverse because of the decrease in temperature.
   (B) Precipitation increases as air rises and water vapor condenses, resulting in vegetation that thrives with a large amount of moisture.
   (C) Temperature is highest on mountaintops because they are closer to the sun and therefore receive more solar radiation.
   (D) The land becomes arid, resulting in the growth of different types of vegetation.
   (E) The change in mountainous climate is very similar to the change in climate as latitude decreases.

10. Which of the following is a true statement about biomes?
    (A) Biomes have not been affected by human presence because the human population is not dense enough to impact them.
    (B) Although biomes have distinctive vegetation growing in them, basically the same kinds of animals live in all of them.
    (C) All desert biomes are hot and dry.
    (D) Biomes have a range of temperatures and precipitation that result in specific kinds of plants that have adapted to those conditions.
    (E) Mountainous areas all over the world contain the same biomes.

11. The greenhouse effect can best be described as
    (A) a natural warming of the stratosphere because of the hole in the ozone layer
    (B) an unnatural change in the earth's climate because of warming air
    (C) the warming of the troposphere, caused by the absorption of heat by greenhouse gases
    (D) the unnatural heating of the atmosphere by CO_2 from fossil fuel combustion
    (E) the cooling of the stratosphere resulting from the reflection of solar energy

12. Which way do hurricanes rotate in the Northern Hemisphere?
    (A) It depends on the surface temperature of the ocean
    (B) Clockwise
    (C) Counterclockwise
    (D) The same direction as in the Southern Hemisphere
    (E) It depends on the level of solar energy input

13. Which of the following sequences shows biomes that would appear at a similar latitude, but with decreasing precipitation?
    (A) Deciduous forest → chaparral → grassland → desert
    (B) Rainforest → coniferous forest → desert
    (C) Desert → savanna → scrubland → tropical forest
    (D) Scrubland → chaparral → coniferous forest → tundra
    (E) Tropical rainforest → temperate rainforest → deciduous forest

14. Which of the following is NOT true of permafrost?
    (A) It is water-drenched soil which remains frozen throughout the year.
    (B) It allows for the formation of shallow lakes, marshes, and bogs.
    (C) It is found in both alpine and arctic tundra.
    (D) It limits the root depth of tundra species.
    (E) Its recent melting has caused the soil to sink, causing damage to roads, houses, and other structures.

15. Grasslands are found in tropical, temperate, and polar regions and include
    I. Savannas
    II. Prairies
    III. Tundra
    (A) I only
    (B) II only
    (C) III only
    (D) I and II only
    (E) I, II, and III

16. All of the following are true of El Niño-Southern Oscillation (ENSO) EXCEPT
    (A) it occurs regularly, every five years in the Pacific
    (B) the prevailing winds in the tropical Pacific weaken and change directions
    (C) the warming of the western Pacific causes a reduction in upwelling nutrients and an increase in rainfall
    (D) the typical monsoon season in the eastern Pacific is reduced, and sometimes there are droughts
    (E) it changes the distribution patterns of pelagic marine species

17. Which of the following is NOT an adaptation found in plants living in the desert?
    (A) Deep roots to tap into groundwater
    (B) Waxy-coated leaves preventing water loss
    (C) Storing much of their biomass as seeds and remaining inactive most of the year
    (D) Breaking down stored fats to produce needed water
    (E) Opening stomata (pores) only at night to absorb needed carbon dioxide

Questions 18–20 refer to the climate graphs below. The red line represents temperature and the blue represents precipitation. Choices may be used once, more than once, or not at all.

(A)

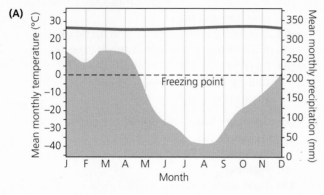

(D)

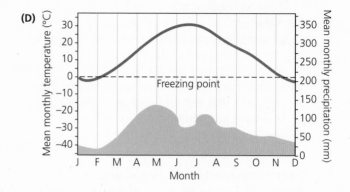

(B)

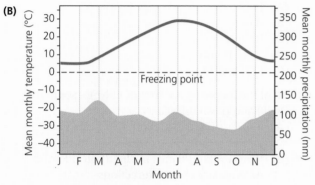

(E)

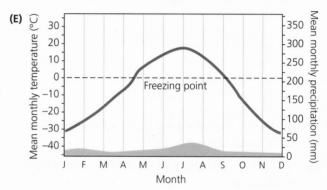

(C)

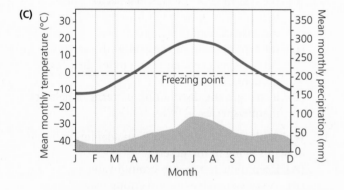

18. This biome is characterized by subfreezing temperatures much of the year, low precipitation rates, and the formation of permafrost.

19. This biome found in equatorial regions has large amounts of precipitation but has low levels of nutrients in the soil.

20. This climatograph is the one that is most likely taiga, also known as boreal forest.

1. Use the climate graphs below to answer the questions that follow.

Tropical desert **Tropical rain forest**

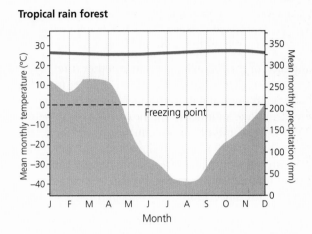

(a) Tropical desert and tropical rainforest are two distinctly different biomes that vary in both biotic and abiotic factors.

   (i) Compare the graphs above. **Identify** ONE abiotic factor that tropical desert and tropical rainforest have in common.

   (ii) **Explain**, in terms of the earth's geography, why the factor you have identified is similar for both biomes.

   (iii) A limiting factor is a single factor that limits the growth, abundance, or distribution of a species in an ecosystem. **Identify** ONE limiting factor for EACH biome and **explain** how that limiting factor influences organisms in that biome.

(b) Plants in desert and tropical rainforest biomes have evolved adaptations that make them distinctly different in their structure.

   (i) **Describe** ONE plant adaptation in the desert biome that allows that species to thrive with regard to the limiting factor you have identified above.

   (ii) **Describe** ONE plant adaptation in the tropical rainforest biome that allows that species to thrive with regard to the limiting factor you have identified above.

(c) Latitudinal deserts are found at about 30° N and 30° S of the equator while rain shadow deserts can be found in various places around the globe.

   (i) **Explain** how latitudinal deserts are formed.

   (ii) **Explain** how rain shadow deserts are formed.

Critical Thinking

1. Why is the African savanna (**Core Case Study**) a good example of the three **scientific principles of sustainability** in action? For each of these principles, give an example of how it applies to the African savanna and explain how it is being violated by human activities that now affect the savanna.

2. For each of the following, decide whether it represents a likely trend in weather or in climate: **(a)** an increase in the number of thunderstorms in your area from one summer to the next; **(b)** a decrease of 20% in the depth of a mountain snowpack between 1975 and 2015; **(c)** a rise in the average winter temperatures in a particular area over a decade; and **(d)** an increase in the earth's average global temperature since 1980.

3. Review the major climatic factors explained in Section 5.2 and explain how each of them has helped to define the climate in the area where you live or go to school.

4. Why do deserts and arctic tundra support a much smaller number and variety of animals than do tropical forests? Why do most animals in a tropical rain forest live in its trees?

5. How might the distribution of the world's forests, grasslands, and deserts shown in Figure 5.14 differ if the prevailing winds shown in Figure 5.9 did not exist?

6. Which biomes are best suited for **(a)** raising crops and **(b)** grazing livestock? Use the three **scientific principles of sustainability** to come up with three guidelines for growing crops and grazing livestock more sustainably in these biomes.

7. What type of biome do you live in? (If you live in a developed area, what type of biome was the area before it was developed?) List three ways in which your lifestyle could be contributing to the degradation of this biome. What are three lifestyle changes that you could make in order to reduce your contribution?

8. You are a defense attorney arguing in court for sparing a large area of tropical rain forest from being cut down and used to produce food. Give your three best arguments for the defense of this ecosystem.

Data Analysis

In this chapter, you learned how long-term variations in average temperatures and average precipitation play a major role in determining the types of deserts, forests, and grasslands found in different parts of the world. Below are typical annual climate graphs for a tropical grassland (savanna) in Africa (**Core Case Study**) and a temperate grassland in the Midwestern United States.

1. In what month (or months) does the most precipitation fall in each of these areas?

2. What are the driest months in each of these areas?

3. What is the coldest month in the tropical grassland?

4. What is the warmest month in the temperate grassland?

Tropical grassland (savanna)

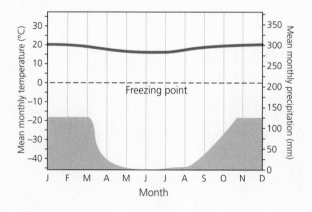

Temperate grassland (prairie)

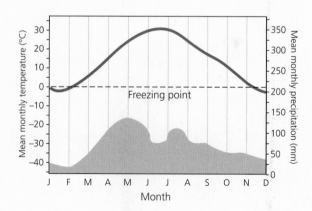

Answers to Checkpoints for Understanding

Section 5.1

1. Tornadoes form over land. They occur when a large, dry, cold front runs into a large mass or warm, humid air. A vortex forms when the warm air mass moves rapidly over the cold air mass and rises, and forms a strong, vertical convection current that sucks the air upwards.

2. Cyclones or hurricanes form over low-pressure, warm tropical seas. A low-pressure cell draws in surrounding high-pressure air, causing spiraling winds to form. Moist air, warmed by the heat of the ocean, rises in a vortex through the center.

Section 5.2

1. (1) Cyclical movement of air driven by solar energy that forms convection cells. These warm air cells pick up moisture and release it as precipitation as the air moves upward and cools. (2) Uneven heating by the earth's surface by the sun results in varied intensity of insolation energy heating a region according to latitude. (3) Tilt of the earth's axis results in the earth's seasons due to widely varying amounts of incoming solar energy. (4) Rotation of the earth on its axis deflects the rising and cooling convection cells creating prevailing winds.

2. A rain shadow desert forms when warm air carrying moisture is forced upward along a mountain (windward side) where it cools and drops its moisture as precipitation. The resulting air mass is dry as it moves over the top of the mountain range, depriving the land on the other side (leeward side) of moisture, leading to desert or semiarid conditions.

Section 5.3

1. Both biomes lack adequate precipitation for abundant plant growth, but are located at different latitudes allowing for vastly different amounts of solar energy.

2. During the summer season, hordes of insects emerge from the melting permafrost that serve as food for birds that migrate to this biome.

3. The growing season is continuous in the tropical forest. There is a constant supply of warm temperatures and accessible water, so that it is not an advantage to drop leaves until these limiting factors become available. In a temperate deciduous forest where water may be frozen and temperatures drop to freezing, it is an energy-saving advantage to drop leaves until conditions are favorable as the seasons change.

Core Case Study

Many of the species in African savanna are threatened when savanna is plowed up and converted to cropland or is used for grazing livestock. This destruction of habitat stresses animals that inhabit this biome. Also, the establishment of towns and villages in these areas leads to hunting and poaching which contributes to the threat of extinction for many animal species.

Aquatic Biodiversity

The sea, once it casts its spell, holds one in its net of wonders forever.

JACQUES-YVES COUSTEAU

Key Questions

6.1 What is the general nature of aquatic systems?

6.2 Why are marine aquatic systems important?

6.3 How have human activities affected marine ecosystems?

6.4 Why are freshwater ecosystems important?

6.5 How have human activities affected freshwater ecosystems?

Coral reef in Egypt's Red Sea.

Vlad61/Shutterstock.com

Why Should We Care about Coral Reefs?

Coral reefs form in clear, warm coastal waters in tropical areas. These stunningly beautiful natural wonders (see chapter-opening photo) are among the world's oldest, most diverse, and most productive ecosystems.

Coral reefs are formed by massive colonies of tiny animals called *polyps* (close relatives of jellyfish). They slowly build reefs by secreting a protective crust of limestone (calcium carbonate) around their soft bodies. When the polyps die, their empty crusts remain behind as part of a platform for more reef growth. The resulting elaborate network of crevices, ledges, and holes serves as calcium carbonate "condominiums" for a variety of marine animals.

Coral reefs are the result of a mutually beneficial relationship between polyps and tiny single-celled algae called *zooxanthellae* ("zoh-ZAN-thel-ee") that live in the tissues of the polyps. The algae provide the polyps with food and oxygen through photosynthesis, and help the corals produce calcium carbonate. Algae also give the reefs their stunning coloration. The polyps, in turn, provide the algae with a well-protected home and some of their nutrients.

Although shallow and deep-water coral reefs occupy only about 0.2% of the ocean floor, they provide important ecosystem and economic services. They act as natural barriers that help to protect 15% of the world's coastlines from flooding and erosion caused by battering waves and storms. They also provide habitats, food, and spawning grounds for one-quarter to one-third of the organisms that live in the ocean, and they produce about one-tenth of the global fish catch. Through tourism and fishing, they provide goods and services worth about $40 billion a year.

Coral reefs are vulnerable to damage because they grow slowly and are disrupted easily. Runoff of soil and other materials from the land can cloud the water and block the sunlight that the algae in shallow reefs need for photosynthesis. Also, the water in which shallow reefs live must have a temperature of 18–30°C (64–86°F) and cannot be too acidic. This explains why a major long-term threat to coral reefs is *climate change*, which could raise the water temperature above tolerable limits in most reef areas. The closely related problem of *ocean acidification* could make it harder for polyps to build reefs and could even dissolve some of their calcium carbonate formations.

One result of stresses such as pollution and rising ocean water temperatures is *coral bleaching* (Figure 6.1), which can cause the colorful algae, upon which corals depend for food, to die off. Without food, the coral polyps die, leaving behind a white skeleton of calcium carbonate. Studies by the Global Coral Reef Monitoring Network and other scientific groups estimate that since the 1950s, some 45%–53% of the world's shallow coral reefs have been destroyed or degraded. Another 25%–33% could be lost within 20 to 40 years. These centers of biodiversity are by far the most threatened marine ecosystems.

In this chapter, we explore the nature of aquatic ecosystems, and we begin to examine the effects of human activities on these vital forms of natural capital. ●

CRITICAL THINKING

Coral reefs provide many ecological and economic services. How would the loss of coral reefs affect humans?

iStockphoto.com/Rainer von Brandis

FIGURE 6.1 This bleached coral has lost most of its algae because of changes in the environment such as warming of the waters and deposition of sediments.

6.1 WHAT IS THE GENERAL NATURE OF AQUATIC SYSTEMS?

CONCEPT 6.1A Saltwater and freshwater aquatic life zones cover almost three-fourths of the earth's surface, with oceans dominating the planet.

CONCEPT 6.1B The key factors determining biodiversity in aquatic systems are temperature, dissolved oxygen content, availability of food, and access to light and nutrients necessary for photosynthesis.

Most of the Earth Is Covered with Water

Saltwater covers about 71% of the earth's surface, and freshwater occupies roughly another 2%. Although the *global ocean* is a single and continuous body of water, geographers divide it into five large areas—the Atlantic, Pacific, Indian, Arctic, and Southern Oceans—separated by the continents. The largest ocean is the Pacific, which contains more than half of the earth's water and covers one-third of the earth's surface. Together, the oceans hold almost 98% of the earth's water (**Concept 6.1A**). Each of us is connected to, and utterly dependent on, the earth's global ocean through the water cycle (see Figure 3.14, p. 77).

73 Percentage of the earth that is covered with water

The aquatic equivalents of biomes are called **aquatic life zones**—saltwater and freshwater portions of the biosphere that can support life. The distribution of many aquatic organisms is determined largely by the water's **salinity**—the amounts of various salts such as sodium chloride (NaCl) dissolved in a given volume of water.

Aquatic life zones are classified into two major types: **saltwater** or **marine life zones** (oceans and their bays, estuaries, coastal wetlands, shorelines, coral reefs, and mangrove forests) and **freshwater life zones** (lakes, rivers, streams, and inland wetlands). Some systems such as estuaries are a mix of saltwater and freshwater, but scientists classify them as marine systems for purposes of discussion.

Aquatic Species Drift, Swim, Crawl, and Cling

Saltwater and freshwater life zones contain several major types of organisms. One type consists of **plankton,** which can be divided into three groups. The first group consists of drifting organisms called *phytoplankton*, which includes many types of algae. These tiny aquatic plants and even smaller *ultraplankton*—the second group of plankton—are the producers that make up the base of most aquatic food chains and webs (see Figure 3.11, p. 73). Through photosynthesis, they produce about half of the earth's oxygen, on which we depend for survival.

The third group is made up of drifting animals called *zooplankton*, which feed on phytoplankton and on other zooplankton (see Figure 3.11, p. 73). The members of this group range in size from single-celled protozoa to large invertebrates such as jellyfish (Figure 6.2).

A second major type of aquatic organism is **nekton,** strongly swimming consumers such as fish, turtles, and whales. The third type, **benthos,** consists of bottom-dwellers such as oysters and sea stars (Figure 6.3), which anchor themselves to ocean-bottom structures; clams and worms, which burrow into the sand or mud; and lobsters and crabs, which walk about on the sea floor. A fourth major type is **decomposers** (mostly bacteria), which break down organic compounds in the dead bodies and

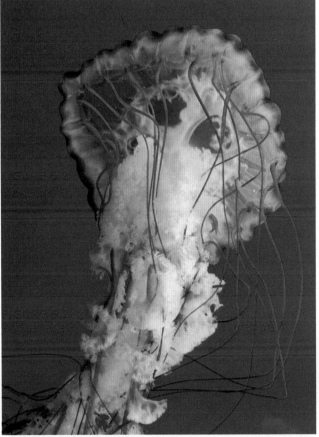

FIGURE 6.2 Jellyfish are drifting zooplankton that use their long tentacles with stinging cells to stun or kill their prey.

Keng Po Leung/Dreamstime.com

FIGURE 6.3 Starfish on a coral reef. The starfish is also called a sea star because it is not a fish.

Jefferychin/Shutterstock.com

wastes of aquatic organisms into nutrients that aquatic primary producers can use.

Key factors determining the types and numbers of organisms found in different areas of the ocean are *temperature*, *dissolved oxygen content*, *availability of food*, and *availability of light and nutrients required for photosynthesis*, such as carbon (as dissolved CO_2 gas), nitrogen (as NO_3^-), and phosphorus (mostly as PO_4^{3-}) (**Concept 6.1B**).

In deep aquatic systems, photosynthesis is largely confined to the upper layer—the *euphotic* or *photic zone*—through which sunlight can penetrate. The depth of the euphotic zone in oceans and deep lakes is reduced when the water is clouded by excessive growth of algae. This is called an *algal bloom* and it results from nutrient overloads. This cloudiness is called **turbidity.** It is also caused by soil and other sediments being carried by wind, rain and melting snow from cleared land into adjoining bodies of water. This is one of the problems plaguing shallow coral reefs (**Core Case Study**).

In shallow systems such as small open streams, lake edges, and ocean shorelines, ample supplies of nutrients for primary producers are usually available, which tends to make these areas high in biodiversity. By contrast, in most areas of the open ocean, nitrates, phosphates, iron, and other nutrients are often in short supply, and this limits net primary productivity (NPP) (see Figure 3.13, p. 75) and the diversity of species.

CHECKPOINT FOR UNDERSTANDING 6.1

1. Identify several abiotic (nonliving) factors that determine the type of organisms that can live in marine and freshwater life zones.

6.2 WHY ARE MARINE AQUATIC SYSTEMS IMPORTANT?

CONCEPT 6.2 Saltwater ecosystems provide major ecosystem and economic services and are irreplaceable reservoirs of biodiversity.

Oceans Provide Vital Ecosystem and Economic Services

Oceans provide enormously valuable ecosystem and economic services (Figure 6.4) that help keep us and other species alive and support our economies. They produce more than half of the oxygen we breathe and, as a vital part of the water cycle, provide most of the rain that sustains our water supply.

As land dwellers, we have a distorted and limited view of the oceans that cover most of the earth's surface. We know more about the surface of the moon than we know about the earth's oceans. According to aquatic scientists, the scientific investigation of poorly understood marine and freshwater aquatic systems could yield immense ecological and economic benefits.

Natural Capital

Marine Ecosystems

Ecosystem Services		Economic Services
Oxygen supplied through photosynthesis		Food
Water purification		Energy from waves and tides
Climate moderation		Pharmaceuticals
CO_2 absorption		Harbors and transportation routes
Nutrient cycling		
Reduced storm damage (mangroves, barrier islands, coastal wetlands)		Recreation and tourism
		Employment
Biodiversity: species and habitats		Minerals

FIGURE 6.4 Marine systems provide a number of important ecosystem and economic services (**Concept 6.2**). *Critical thinking:* Which two ecosystem services and which two economic services do you think are the most important? Why?

Top: Willyam Bradberry/Shutterstock.com. Bottom: James A. Harris/Shutterstock.com.

LEARNING FROM NATURE

Engineers are learning how whales use sound waves to communicate over long distances underwater to improve our underwater communication technologies.

Marine aquatic systems are enormous reservoirs of biodiversity. Marine life is found in three major *life zones*: the coastal zone, the pelagic zone (open sea), and the ocean bottom (Figure 6.5).

The **coastal zone** is the warm, nutrient-rich, shallow water that extends from the high-tide mark on land to the gently sloping, shallow edge of the *continental shelf* (the submerged part of the continents). It makes up less than 10% of the world's ocean area, but it contains 90% of all marine species and most large commercial fisheries. This zone's aquatic systems include estuaries, coastal marshes, mangrove forests, and coral reefs.

Estuaries and Coastal Wetlands Are Highly Productive

An **estuary** is an aquatic zone where a river meets the sea (Figure 6.6). It is a partially enclosed body of water where seawater mixes with the river's freshwater, as well as with nutrients and pollutants in runoff from the land.

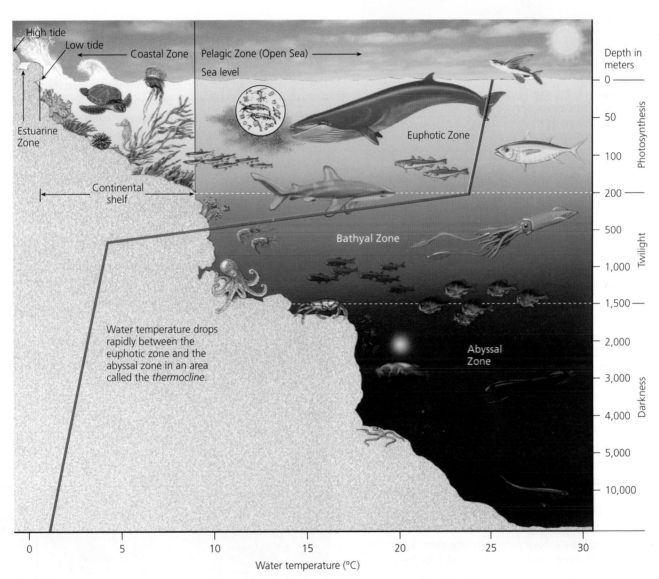

FIGURE 6.5 Major life zones and vertical zones (not drawn to scale) in an ocean. Actual depths of zones may vary. Available light determines the euphotic, bathyal, and abyssal zones. Temperature zones also vary with depth, shown here by the red line. **Critical thinking:** How is an ocean similar to a rain forest? (*Hint:* See Figure 5.20, p. 139.)

FIGURE 6.6 Satellite photo of an *estuary*. A sediment plume (cloudiness caused by runoff) forms at the mouth of Madagascar's Betsiboka River as it flows through the estuary and into the Mozambique Channel.

Estuaries are associated with **coastal wetlands**—coastal land areas covered with water all or part of the year. These wetlands include *coastal marshes*, or *salt marshes* (Figure 6.7) and *mangrove forests* (Figure 6.8). They are some of the earth's most productive ecosystems (see Figure 3.13, p. 75) because of high nutrient inputs from rivers and from adjoining land, rapid circulation of nutrients by tidal flows, and ample sunlight penetrating the shallow waters. Mangrove forests around the world host 69 different species of trees and shrubs that can grow in salty water. They provide habitat, food, and nursery sites for a variety of fishes, shellfish, crabs, snakes, and other aquatic species.

Seagrass beds (Figure 6.9), another component of marine biodiversity, occur in shallow coastal waters and host as many as 60 species of grasses and other plants. These highly productive and physically complex systems support a variety of marine species. Like other coastal systems, seagrass beds owe their high NPP to ample supplies of sunlight and plant nutrients that flow from the land.

These coastal aquatic systems provide important ecosystem and economic services. They help to maintain water quality in tropical coastal zones by filtering toxic pollutants, excess plant nutrients, and sediments, and by absorbing other pollutants. They provide food, habitats, and nursery sites for a variety of aquatic and terrestrial species. They also reduce storm damage and coastal erosion by absorbing waves and storing excess water produced by storms and tsunamis.

FIGURE 6.7 Coastal marsh in the state of South Carolina.

Rocky and Sandy Shores Host Different Types of Organisms

The gravitational pull of the moon and sun causes **tides,** or periodic flows of water onto and off the shore, to rise and fall about every 6 hours in most coastal areas. The area of shoreline between low and high tides is called the **intertidal zone.** Organisms living in this zone must be able to avoid being swept away or crushed by waves. They need to survive when immersed during high tides and left

FIGURE 6.8 Mangrove forest on the coast of Thailand. Mangroves have roots that curve up from the mud and water to obtain oxygen from the air, working somewhat like a snorkel.

The Importance of Wetlands

How do scientists characterize a wetland? Wetlands can be coastal or inland, freshwater, or marine. They are defined as areas that are saturated with water all or part of the year, have standing shallow water with emergent vegetation, and contain communities of plants and animals that have adapted to continuously wet conditions. They are highly productive ecosystems.

Freshwater wetlands include swamps, marshes, bogs, fens and prairie potholes. Marine wetlands include estuaries, mangrove swamps, and coastal marshes. Organisms that live in estuaries must be adapted to widely fluctuating temperature and salinity. Seasonal temperatures vary, and snow melt and rain carry soil and organic material from land that mixes with the salt water.

Suspended solids absorb heat from the sun, and daily tides vary the amount of salt water that mixes with the freshwater runoff.

Both freshwater and marine ecosystems provide many valuable ecosystem services and economic benefits (Figures 6.4 and 6.13). However, humans have greatly impacted both freshwater and marine wetlands (Figure 6.12).

FRQ Application

Question: Wetlands have historically been altered by humans for a variety of reasons. **Identify** and **describe** ONE type of marine wetland. **Identify** TWO ecosystem services provided by that wetland and **explain** the economic impact of the loss of those ecosystem services.

Possible Response: One type of marine ecosystem is an estuary. An estuary is a coastal wetland with a varying influx of fresh water, causing the temperature and salinity to change daily. Because estuaries are highly productive ecosystems, they serve as nurseries for fish and shellfish. They also serve to buffer storms, absorbing the impact of wind and waves. The loss or degradation of estuaries can reduce the amount of fish and shellfish harvested by commercial fishermen resulting in loss of revenue. It could also increase the economic cost of storm surges as more property is destroyed due to the lack of buffering by the estuary.

FIGURE 6.9 Seagrass beds, such as this one near the coast of San Clemente Island, California, support a variety of marine species.

James Forte/National Geographic Creative

organisms hide in protective shells, dig in, or hold on tight to something.

On some coasts, steep *rocky shores* are pounded by waves (Figure 6.10, top). The numerous pools and other habitats in these intertidal zones contain a great variety of species. Each occupies a different niche to deal with daily and seasonal changes in environmental conditions such as temperature, water flows, and salinity.

Other coasts have gently sloping *barrier beaches*, or *sandy shores*, that support other types of marine organisms (Figure 6.10, bottom). Most of them keep hidden from view and survive by burrowing, digging, and tunneling in the sand. These beaches and their adjoining coastal wetlands are also home to a variety of shorebirds that have evolved in specialized niches to feed on crustaceans, insects, and other organisms (see Figure 4.9, p. 99).

Many of these same species also live on *barrier islands*—low, narrow, sandy islands that form offshore,

high and dry (and much hotter) at low tides. They must also survive changing levels of salinity when heavy rains dilute saltwater. To deal with such stresses, most intertidal

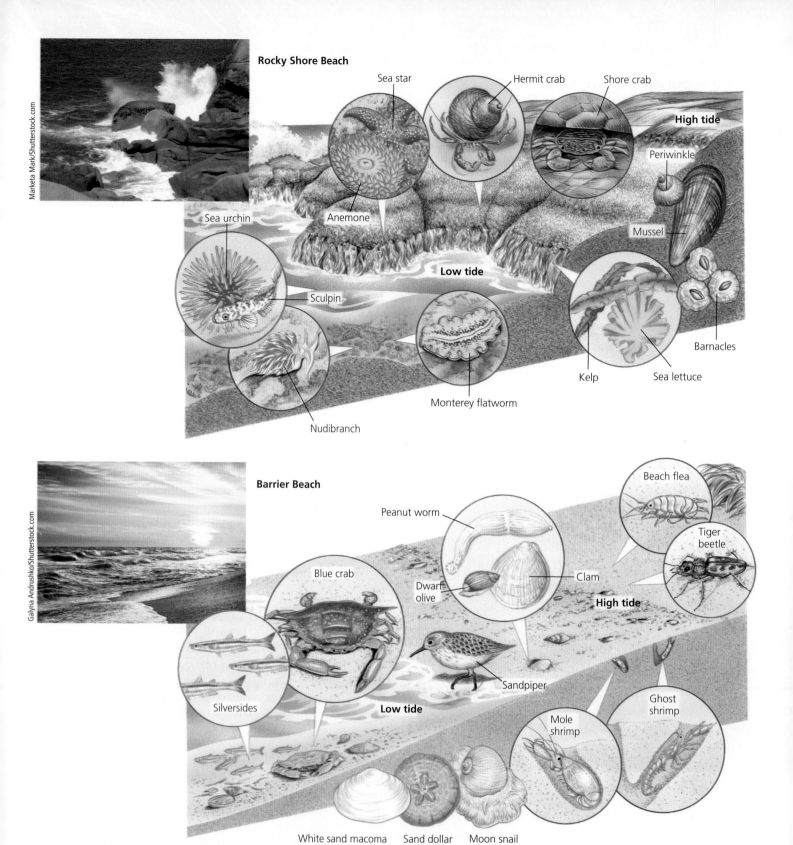

FIGURE 6.10 *Living between the tides:* Some organisms with specialized niches are found in various zones on rocky shore beaches (top) and barrier or sandy beaches (bottom). Organisms are not drawn to scale.

parallel to coastlines. Undisturbed barrier beaches generally have one or more rows of sand dunes in which the sand is held in place by the roots of grasses and other plants. These dunes are the first line of defense against the ravages of the sea. Real estate developers frequently remove the protective dunes or cover them with buildings and roads. Large storms can then flood and even sweep away seaside construction and severely erode the sandy beaches.

CASE STUDY

Revisiting Coral Reefs—Amazing Centers of Biodiversity

Coral reefs (see **Core Case Study** and chapter-opening photo) are some of the world's oldest and most diverse and productive ecosystems. They are the marine equivalents of tropical rain forests, with complex interactions among their diverse populations of species.

Worldwide, coral reefs are being damaged and destroyed at an alarming rate by a variety of human activities. The newest growing threat is **ocean acidification**—the rising levels of acidity in ocean waters. This is occurring because the oceans absorb about 25% of the CO_2 emitted into the atmosphere by human activities, especially the burning of fossil fuels. The CO_2 reacts with ocean water to form a weak acid (carbonic acid, H_2CO_3). This reaction decreases the levels of carbonate ions (CO_3^{2-}) necessary for the formation of coral reefs and the shells and skeletons of many marine organisms. This makes it harder for these species to thrive and reproduce. At some point, this rising acidity could slowly dissolve corals and the shells and skeletons of some marine species.

Ocean acidification and other forms of degradation could have devastating effects on the biodiversity and food webs of coral reefs. This will in turn degrade the ecosystem services that reefs provide. It will also have a severe impact on the approximately 500 million people who depend on coral reefs for food or for income from fishing and tourism.

The Open Sea and the Ocean Floor Host a Variety of Species

The sharp increase in water depth at the edge of the continental shelf separates the coastal zone from the vast volume of the ocean called the **pelagic zone,** or **open sea.** This aquatic life zone is divided into three *vertical zones* (Figure 6.5), or layers, primarily based on the degree of penetration of sunlight. Temperatures also change with depth (Figure 6.5, red line) and scientists use them to define zones of varying species diversity in these layers.

The *euphotic zone* is the brightly lit upper zone, where drifting phytoplankton carry out about 40% of the world's photosynthetic activity. Large, fast-swimming predatory fishes such as swordfish, sharks, and bluefin tuna populate the euphotic zone.

Nutrient levels are low and levels of dissolved oxygen are high in the euphotic zone. The exception to this is those areas called *upwelling zones*. An **upwelling,** or upward movement of ocean water, brings cool and nutrient-rich water from the bottom of the ocean to the warmer surface. There it supports large populations of phytoplankton, zooplankton, fish, and fish-eating seabirds. Strong upwellings occur along the steep western coasts of some continents when winds blowing along the coasts push surface water away from the land. This draws water up from the ocean bottom (Figure 6.11 and Figure 5.3, p. 122). Figure 5.7 (p. 125) shows the oceans' major upwelling zones.

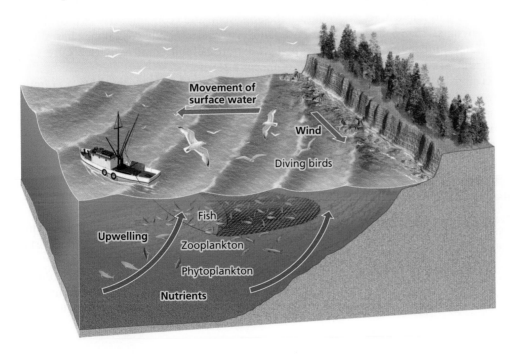

FIGURE 6.11 A shore upwelling occurs when deep, cool, nutrient-rich waters are drawn up to replace surface water moved away from a steep coast by wind flowing along the coast toward the equator.

We Are Still Learning about the Ocean's Biodiversity

Scientists have long assumed that open-ocean waters contained few microbial life forms. But recent research has challenged that assumption and greatly increased our knowledge of the ocean's genetic diversity.

A team of scientists led by J. Craig Venter took 2 years to conduct a census (an estimated count based on sampling) of ocean microbes. They sailed around the world, stopping every 320 kilometers (200 miles) to pump seawater through extremely fine filters, from which they gathered data on bacteria, viruses, and

other microbes. It was the most thorough of such censuses ever conducted.

Using a supercomputer, they counted genetic coding for 6 million new proteins—double the number that had previously been known. They also reported that they were discovering new genes and proteins at the same rate at the end of their voyage as they had at the start of it. This indicated that there is still much more of this biodiversity to discover.

This means that the ocean contains a much higher diversity of microbial life

than had previously been thought. Ocean-water microbes play an important role in the absorption of carbon by the ocean, as well as in the ocean food web. Venter has led more expeditions to continue the sampling in other areas.

CRITICAL THINKING

Why was the *rate* of discovery of new genes and proteins important to Venter and his colleagues? Explain.

The second major open sea zone is the *bathyal zone*, the dimly lit middle zone that receives little sunlight and therefore does not contain photosynthesizing producers. Zooplankton and smaller fishes, many of which migrate to feed on the surface at night, are found in these waters.

The deepest open sea zone, called the *abyssal zone*, is dark and cold. There is no sunlight to support photosynthesis, and this water has little dissolved oxygen. Nevertheless, the deep ocean floor is teeming with life because it contains enough nutrients to support a large number of species. Most of this zone's organisms get their food from showers of dead and decaying organisms—called *marine snow*—drifting down from the upper zones. Some abyssal-zone organisms, including many types of worms, are *deposit feeders*, which take mud into their guts and extract nutrients from it. Others such as oysters, clams, and sponges are *filter feeders*, which pass water through or over their bodies and extract nutrients from it.

Net primary productivity (NPP) is quite low in the open sea, except in upwelling areas. However, because the open sea covers so much of the earth's surface, it makes the largest contribution to the earth's overall NPP. In fact, scientists have learned that the open sea contains more biodiversity than they thought a few years ago (Science Focus 6.1).

CHECKPOINT FOR UNDERSTANDING 6.2

1. Explain why most aquatic life is found in coastal areas. Why is most commercial fishing done in the continental shelf region rather than out in the open ocean?

2. Describe how intertidal organisms adapt to the stressful conditions of the intertidal zone.

3. Explain the importance of upwellings.

6.3 HOW HAVE HUMAN ACTIVITIES AFFECTED MARINE ECOSYSTEMS?

CONCEPT 6.3 Human activities threaten aquatic biodiversity and disrupt ecosystem and economic services provided by marine ecosystems.

Human Activities Are Disrupting and Degrading Marine Ecosystems

Certain human activities are disrupting and degrading many of the ecosystem and economic services provided by marine aquatic systems, especially coastal marshes, shorelines, mangrove forests, and coral reefs (see **Core Case Study**) (**Concept 6.3**).

According to the World Wildlife Fund (WWF), more than 35% of the world's original mangrove forest area had been lost to agricultural and urban expansion, marinas, roadways, and other forms of coastal development. According to the International Union for the Conservation of Nature (IUCN), more than one of every six species of mangrove are in danger of extinction. In addition, since 1980 about 29% of the world's seagrass beds have been lost to pollution and other disturbances. In a 4-year study, an international team of scientists found that human activities have heavily affected 41% of the world's ocean area.

Harmful human activities increase with the number of people living on or near coasts. Currently about 45% of the world's population and more than half of the

Natural Capital Degradation

Major Human Impacts on Marine Ecosystems and Coral Reefs

Marine Ecosystems

Coral Reefs

Half of coastal wetlands lost to agriculture and urban development

Over one-fifth of mangrove forests lost to agriculture, aquaculture, and development

Beaches eroding due to development and rising sea levels

Ocean-bottom habitats degraded by dredging and trawler fishing

At least 20% of coral reefs severely damaged and 25–33% more threatened

Ocean warming

Rising ocean acidity

Rising sea levels

Soil erosion

Algae growth from fertilizer runoff

Bleaching

Increased UV exposure

Damage from anchors and from fishing and diving

FIGURE 6.12 Human activities have major harmful impacts on all marine ecosystems (left) and particularly on coral reefs (right) (**Concept 6.3**). *Critical thinking:* Which two of the threats to marine ecosystems do you think are the most serious? Why? Which two of the threats to coral reefs do you think are the most serious? Why?

Top left: Jorg Hackemann/Shutterstock.com. Top right: Rich Carey/Shutterstock.com. Bottom left: Piotr Marcinski/Shutterstock.com. Bottom right: Rostislav Ageev/Shutterstock.com.

shellfish that form their shells from calcium carbonate.

Other major threats to marine systems from human activities include the following:

- Coastal development, which destroys or degrades coastal habitats

- Runoff of pollutants such as fertilizers, pesticides, and livestock wastes and pollution from cruise ships and oil tanker spills

- Overfishing and depletion of commercial fish species populations

- Destruction of ocean bottom habitats by fishing trawlers dragging weighted nets

- Invasive species that deplete populations of native species

Figure 6.12 shows some of the effects of these human impacts on marine systems in general (left) and on coral reefs in particular (right). Scientists are working to learn more about the little-understood marine ecosystems, our effects on them, and the ways in which we can seek to preserve them (Individuals Matter 6.1).

population live along or near coasts, and these percentages are rising.

The biggest threat to marine systems, according to many marine scientists, is climate change (which we explore fully in Chapter 20). Because land-based glaciers in Greenland and other parts of the world are slowly melting, and warmer ocean waters expand sea levels are rising. The rise in sea levels projected for this century would destroy many shallow coral reefs and flood coastal marshes and other coastal ecosystems, as well as many coastal cities.

A second threat, which some scientists view as more serious than the threat of climate change, is ocean acidification. It is especially threatening to coral reefs (see **Core Case Study**) and to phytoplankton and many

CONSIDER THIS . . .

THINKING ABOUT Coral Reef Destruction
How might the loss of most of the world's remaining tropical coral reefs (see **Core Case Study**) affect your life and the lives of any children or grandchildren you might have? What are two things you could do to help reduce this loss?

CHECKPOINT FOR UNDERSTANDING 6.3

1. Identify the greatest threats to marine ecosystems.

2. Explain why ocean acidification is a serious threat to coral reefs, phytoplankton, and shellfish.

Enric Sala: Working to Protect Ocean Ecosystems

Marine biologist Enric Sala has made a career of working to protect undisturbed marine ecosystems. He travels to remote areas with the goal of learning what marine ecosystems were like before human activities disrupted them. In 2008, he launched National Geographic's Pristine Seas project to find, survey, and help protect the last wild places in the ocean. Pristine Seas aims for an ocean where representative examples of all major ecosystems are protected, so that they can be healthier, more productive, and more resilient to the impacts of ocean warming and acidification.

After exploring the Southern Line Islands undisturbed coral reef system in the South Pacific, Sala reported that "all the scientific data confirm that humans are the most important factor in determining the health of coral reefs." He says that reefs are killed by "a combination of the local impact of human activities such as fishing and pollution with the global impact of human-induced climate change."

Sala suggests that in order for coral reefs and other systems to survive and function, we need to "take out less and throw in less." One way to accomplish this is to establish large areas of protected ocean habitat, free of human activities of any kind. Sala was instrumental in establishing such *marine protected areas*. To date, Pristine Seas has helped to create nine of the largest marine reserves on the planet, covering an area of over 3 million square km—more than six times the area of Spain. Over the next few years, Sala's team will target 12 more locations, aiming to inspire the protection of a total of 20 of the wildest places in the ocean. For his outstanding scientific work, Sala has been named a National Geographic Explorer.

6.4 WHY ARE FRESHWATER ECOSYSTEMS IMPORTANT?

CONCEPT 6.4 Freshwater ecosystems provide major ecosystem and economic services and are irreplaceable reservoirs of biodiversity.

Water Stands in Some Freshwater Systems and Flows in Others

Precipitation that does not sink into the ground or evaporate becomes **surface water**—freshwater that flows or is stored in bodies of water on the earth's surface. *Freshwater aquatic life zones* include *standing (lentic)* bodies of freshwater such as lakes, ponds, and inland wetlands, and *flowing (lotic)* systems such as streams and rivers.

Surface water that flows into such bodies of water is called **runoff.** A **watershed,** or **drainage basin,** is the land area that delivers runoff, sediment, and dissolved substances to a stream, lake, or wetland. Although freshwater systems cover less than 2.2% of the earth's surface, they provide a number of important ecosystem and economic services (Figure 6.13).

Lakes are large natural bodies of standing freshwater formed when precipitation, runoff, streams, rivers, and groundwater seepage fill depressions in the earth's surface. Causes of such depressions include glaciation, displacement of the earth's crust, and volcanic activity. A lake's watershed supplies it with water from rainfall, melting snow, and streams.

Natural Capital

Freshwater Systems

Ecosystem Services	Economic Services
Climate moderation	Food
Nutrient cycling	Drinking water
Waste treatment	
Flood control	Irrigation water
Groundwater recharge	Hydroelectricity
Habitats for many species	Transportation corridors
Genetic resources and biodiversity	Recreation
Scientific information	Employment

FIGURE 6.13 Freshwater systems provide many important ecosystem and economic services (**Concept 6.4**). ***Critical thinking:*** Which two ecosystem services and which two economic services do you think are the most important? Why?

Top: Galyna Andrushko/Shutterstock.com. Bottom: Kletr/Shutterstock.com.

Freshwater lakes vary in size, depth, and nutrient content. Deep lakes normally consist of four distinct life zones that are defined by their depth and distance from shore (Figure 6.14). The top layer, called the *littoral zone*, is near the shore and consists of the shallow sunlit waters to the depth at which rooted plants stop growing. It has a high level of biodiversity because of ample sunlight and inputs of nutrients from the surrounding land. Species living in the littoral zone include many rooted plants; animals such as turtles, frogs, and crayfish; and fish such as bass, perch, and carp.

The next layer is the *limnetic zone*, the open, sunlit surface layer away from the shore that extends to the depth penetrated by sunlight. This is the main photosynthetic zone of the lake, the layer that produces the food and oxygen that support most of the lake's consumers. Its most abundant organisms are phytoplankton and zooplankton. Some large species of fish spend most of their time in this zone, with occasional visits to the littoral zone to feed and reproduce.

The *profundal zone* is the volume of deeper water lying between the limnetic zone and the lake bottom. It is too dark for photosynthesis. Without sunlight and plants, oxygen levels are often low. Fishes adapted to the lake's cooler and darker water, such as perch, are found in this zone.

The bottom of the lake is called the *benthic zone*, inhabited mostly by decomposers, detritus feeders, and some bottom-feeding species of fish such as catfish. The benthic zone is nourished mainly by dead matter that falls from the littoral and limnetic zones and by sediment washing into the lake.

Some Lakes Have More Nutrients than Others

Ecologists classify lakes according to their nutrient content and primary productivity. Lakes that have a small supply of plant nutrients are called **oligotrophic lakes.** This type of lake (Figure 6.15) is often deep and can have steep banks. Glaciers and mountain streams supply water to many of these lakes, which usually have crystal-clear water and small populations of phytoplankton and fish species, such as smallmouth bass and trout. The steep sides of oligotrophic ponds and lakes do not allow enough area for emergent and submergent plants to root, and accumulated nutrients in the benthic zone are out of reach of the few plants that may inhabit the littoral zone. Because of their low levels of nutrients, these lakes have a low net primary productivity (NPP).

Over time, sediments, organic material, and inorganic nutrients wash into most oligotrophic lakes, and plants grow and decompose to form bottom sediments. A lake with a large supply of nutrients is called a **eutrophic lake** (Figure 6.16). Such lakes typically are shallow and have

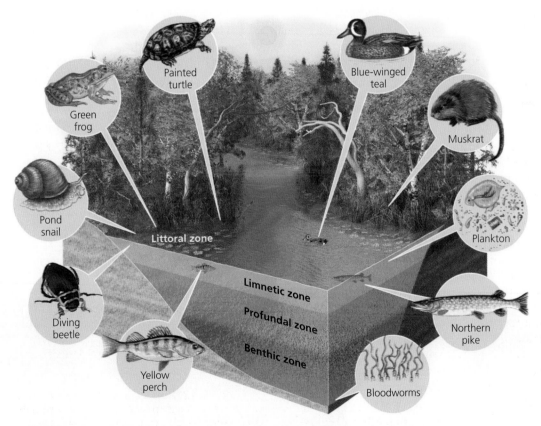

FIGURE 6.14 A typical deep temperate-zone lake has distinct zones of life. **Critical thinking:** How are deep lakes similar to tropical rain forests? (*Hint:* See Figure 5.20, p. 139.)

Measuring Productivity in an Aquatic Ecosystem

Primary productivity measures the rate at which sunlight is stored by plants in the form of organic molecules, or, in other words, the rate of *carbon fixation*. By measuring the amount of oxygen (a byproduct of photosynthesis) at various depths within a water column, a depth profile can be constructed showing the relationship between turbidity (cloudiness) and productivity. From these data, researchers can compare the relative productivity of different bodies of water.

FRQ Application

Productivity is expressed as mg C/m^3/day. Therefore, if oxygen production is measured in mL O_2/liter/hour, these values must be converted. For every milliliter of O_2 produced, 0.536 mg of carbon is fixed.

Using these conversion units, productivity can be calculated at various depths in a pond:

$$1 \text{ ml } O_2 = 0.536 \text{ mg C} \qquad 1 \text{ m}^3 = 1000 \text{ liters}$$

A water sample is taken at the surface of a pond. The amount of oxygen produced is measured at 0.14 mL O_2/liter/hour. Determine primary productivity by converting this measurement to mg C/m^3/day.

First, convert the mL of O_2 to mg C:

$$0.14 \text{ mL } O_2\text{/liter/hour} \times \frac{0.536 \text{ mg C}}{1 \text{ mL } O_2} = 0.075 \text{ mg C/liter/hour} \quad \text{(mLs of } O_2 \text{ cancel)}$$

Next, convert liters to cubic meters:

$$0.075 \text{ mg C/liter/hour} \times \frac{1000 \text{ L}}{\text{m}^3} = 75.04 \text{ mg C/m}^3\text{/hour} \quad \text{(liters cancel)}$$

Since there are 24 hours in a day:

$$75.04 \text{ mg C/m}^3\text{/hour} \times 24 \text{ hours} = 1800.96 \text{ mg C/m}^3\text{/day}$$

FIGURE 6.15 Trillium Lake in the state of Oregon with a view of Mount Hood.

tusharkoley/Shutterstock.com

FIGURE 6.16 This eutrophic lake has received large flows of plant nutrients. As a result, its surface is covered with mats of algae.

murky brown or green water. Here, there is ample area where plants can root and water is not very deep, allowing light to penetrate and drive photosynthesis. As organic matter falls into these ponds and vegetation dies back, bottom sediments accumulate, slowly building up over time and providing nutrients for plant growth. Because of their high levels of nutrients, eutrophic lakes have a high NPP. Most lakes are classified as **mesotrophic** and fall somewhere between the two extremes of nutrient enrichment.

Human inputs of nutrients through the atmosphere and from urban and agricultural areas within a lake's watershed can accelerate the eutrophication of the lake. This process, called **cultural eutrophication,** often puts excessive nutrients into lakes (See Critical Concepts in Sustainability).

Freshwater Streams and Rivers Carry Large Volumes of Water

In drainage basins, water accumulates in small streams that join to form rivers. Collectively, streams and rivers carry huge amounts of water from highlands to lakes and oceans. They drain an estimated 75% of the earth's land surface. Many streams begin in mountainous or hilly areas, which collect and release water falling to the earth's surface as precipitation. The downward flow of surface

Cultural Eutrophication

Eutrophication is defined as the physical, chemical, and biological changes that take place after a freshwater system such as a lake, slow-moving stream, or estuary receives an influx of nutrients from the surrounding watershed. Nutrients like nitrate and phosphate are limiting factors for plants, and when they are introduced to a body of water, they are assimilated quickly, causing algal blooms.

When human actions are the cause of eutrophication, it is called *cultural eutrophication*. Sources of nutrients include fertilizers from farms or lawns, phosphates in detergents, feedlot runoff, treated and untreated municipal sewage, runoff from streets, mining and construction, and nitrogen oxides from air pollution.

Cultural eutrophication is a sequence of events that results in a shift of living organisms in a body of water (Figure 6.A).

FRQ Application

Question: After a rainstorm on a small farm, cow manure is washed into a slow-moving stream adjacent to the cow pasture. A drop in dissolved oxygen results, leading to the death of many trout, fish that require

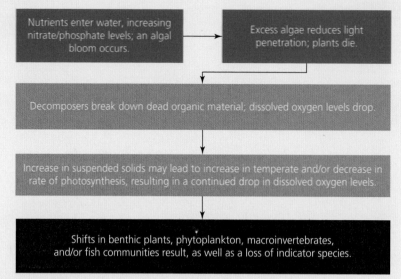

Nutrients enter water, increasing nitrate/phosphate levels; an algal bloom occurs.

Excess algae reduces light penetration; plants die.

Decomposers break down dead organic material; dissolved oxygen levels drop.

Increase in suspended solids may lead to increase in temperate and/or decrease in rate of photosynthesis, resulting in a continued drop in dissolved oxygen levels.

Shifts in benthic plants, phytoplankton, macroinvertebrates, and/or fish communities result, as well as a loss of indicator species.

FIGURE 6.A. This flowchart shows the sequence of events in cultural eutrophication.

high levels of oxygen to survive. **Explain** the relationship between the influx of nutrients and the death of the trout.

Possible Response: Cow manure contains nitrates, a limiting factor for plants. When nitrates enter a waterway, an algal bloom occurs. This blocks sunlight from penetrating, causing aquatic plants to die. Aerobic decomposers break down the dead vegetation, causing a drop in oxygen levels. Increased turbidity (suspended solids) can also increase water temperature, leading to a loss of oxygen. Death of intolerant organisms such as trout results when oxygen levels are too low to support them.

---

water and groundwater from mountain highlands to the sea typically takes place in three aquatic life zones characterized by different environmental conditions: the *source zone*, the *transition zone*, and the *floodplain zone* (Figure 6.17). Rivers and streams can differ from this generalized model.

In the narrow *source zone* (Figure 6.17, left), headwater streams are usually shallow, cold, clear, and swiftly flowing (Figure 6.17, inset photo). As this water tumbles over rocks, waterfalls, and rapids, it dissolves large amounts of oxygen from the air. Most of these streams are not very productive because of a lack of nutrients and primary producers. Their nutrients come primarily from organic matter, mostly leaves, branches, and the bodies of living and dead insects that fall into the stream from nearby land.

The source zone is populated by cold-water fish species that need lots of dissolved oxygen. Fishes in this habitat, such as trout and minnows, tend to have streamlined and muscular bodies that allow them to swim in the rapid, strong currents. Other animals such as riffle beetles have compact, hard, or flattened bodies that allow them to live among or under stones in fast-

flowing headwater streams. Most of the plants in this zone are algae and mosses attached to rocks and other surfaces underwater.

In the *transition zone* (Figure 6.17, center), headwater streams merge to form wider, deeper, and warmer streams that flow down gentler slopes with fewer obstacles. They can be more turbid (containing suspended sediments) and slower flowing than headwater streams, and they tend to have less dissolved oxygen. The warmer water and other conditions in this zone support more producers, as well as cool-water and warm-water fish species (such as black bass) with slightly lower oxygen requirements.

As streams flow downhill, they shape the land through which they pass. Over millions of years, the friction of moving water has leveled mountains and cut deep canyons. Sand, gravel, and soil carried by streams and rivers have been deposited as sediment in low-lying areas. In these *floodplain zones* (Figure 6.17), streams join into wider and deeper rivers that flow across broad, flat valleys. Water in this zone usually has higher temperatures and less dissolved oxygen than water in the two

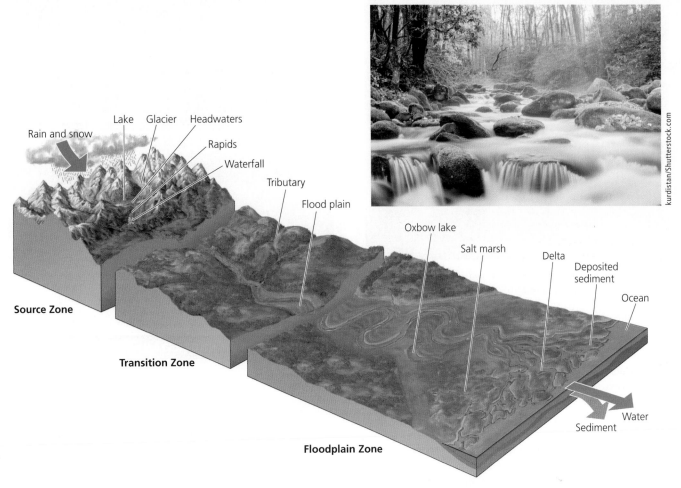

FIGURE 6.17 There are three zones in the downhill flow of water: the *source zone*, which contains *headwater* streams found in highlands and mountains (see inset photo); the *transition zone*, which contains wider, lower-elevation streams; and the *floodplain zone*, which contains rivers that empty into larger rivers or into the ocean. ***Critical thinking:*** How might the building of many dams and reservoirs along a river's path to the ocean affect its sediment input into the ocean and change the river's delta?

higher zones. The slow-moving rivers sometimes support large populations of producers such as algae and cyanobacteria, as well as rooted aquatic plants along the shores.

Because of increased erosion and runoff over a larger area, water in the floodplain zone often is muddy and contains high concentrations of silt. These murky waters support distinctive varieties of fishes, including carp and catfish. At its mouth, a river may divide into many channels as it flows through its **delta**—an area at the mouth of a river built up by deposited sediment, usually containing coastal wetlands and estuaries.

Coastal deltas and wetlands, as well as inland wetlands and floodplains, are important parts of the earth's natural capital. They absorb and slow the velocity of floodwaters from coastal storms, hurricanes, and tsunamis and provide habitats for a diversity of marine life.

CONSIDER THIS . . .

CONNECTIONS Stream Water Quality and Watershed Land

Streams receive most of their nutrients from bordering land ecosystems. Such nutrients come from falling leaves, animal feces, insects, and other forms of biomass washed into streams during heavy rainstorms or by melting snow. Chemicals and other substances flowing off the land can also pollute streams. Thus, the levels and types of nutrients and pollutants in a stream depend on what is happening in the stream's watershed.

Freshwater Inland Wetlands Are Vital Sponges

Inland wetlands are lands located away from coastal areas that are covered with freshwater all or part of the time—excluding lakes, reservoirs, and streams. They

FIGURE 6.18 This great white egret lives in an inland marsh in the Florida Everglades (left). This cypress swamp (right) is located in South Carolina.

include *marshes* (Figure 6.18, left), *swamps* (Figure 6.18, right), and *prairie potholes* (depressions carved out by ancient glaciers). Other examples are *floodplains*, which receive excess water from streams or rivers during heavy rains and floods.

Some wetlands are covered with water year-round. Others, called *seasonal wetlands*, remain under water or are soggy for only a short time each year. The latter include prairie potholes, floodplain wetlands, and arctic tundra (see Figure 5.16, bottom, p. 134). Some can stay dry for years before water covers them again. In such cases, scientists must use the composition of the soil or the presence of certain plants (such as cattails and bulrushes) to determine that a particular area is a wetland. Wetland plants are highly productive because of an abundance of nutrients available to them. Wetlands are important habitats for muskrats, otters, beavers, migratory waterfowl, and other bird species.

Inland wetlands provide a number of free ecosystem and economic services. They take part in the following processes:

- filtering and degrading toxic wastes and pollutants;
- reducing flooding and erosion by absorbing storm water and releasing it slowly, and by absorbing overflows from streams and lakes;
- sustaining stream flows during dry periods;
- recharging groundwater aquifers;
- maintaining biodiversity by providing habitats for a variety of species;
- supplying valuable products such as fishes and shellfish, blueberries, cranberries, and wild rice; and
- providing recreation for birdwatchers, nature photographers, boaters, anglers, and waterfowl hunters.

CONSIDER THIS . . .

THINKING ABOUT Inland Wetlands

Of the ecosystem and economic services listed to the left, which two do you think are the most important? Why? List two ways in which our daily activities directly or indirectly degrade inland wetlands.

6.5 HOW HAVE HUMAN ACTIVITIES AFFECTED FRESHWATER ECOSYSTEMS?

CONCEPT 6.5 Human activities threaten biodiversity and disrupt ecosystem and economic services provided by freshwater lakes, rivers, and wetlands.

Human Activities Are Disrupting and Degrading Freshwater Systems

Human activities are disrupting and degrading many of the ecosystem and economic services provided by freshwater rivers, lakes, and wetlands (**Concept 6.5**) in four major ways. *First*, dams and canals restrict the flows of about 40% of the world's 237 largest rivers. This alters or destroys terrestrial and aquatic wildlife habitats along these rivers and in their coastal deltas and estuaries. By reducing the flow of sediments to river deltas, these structures also lead to degraded coastal wetlands and greater damage from coastal storms (see Case Study that follows).

Second, flood control levees and dikes built along rivers disconnect the rivers from their floodplains, destroy aquatic habitats, and alter or degrade the functions of adjoining wetlands. Any type of engineering used to contain or redirect a waterway, collectively referred to as *channelization,* also contributes greatly to the flow of sediments out to sea, rather than allowing natural erosion and deposition to occur in these ecosystems.

Third, cities and farms add pollutants and excess plant nutrients to nearby streams, rivers, and lakes. For example, runoff of nutrients into a lake (Figure 6.16) causes explosions in the populations of algae and cyanobacteria, which deplete the lake's dissolved oxygen. When these organisms die and sink to the lake bottom, decomposers go to work and further deplete the oxygen in deeper waters. Fishes and other species may then die off, which can mean a major loss in biodiversity.

Fourth, many inland wetlands have been drained or filled to grow crops or have been covered with concrete, asphalt, and buildings. More than half of the inland wetlands estimated to have existed in the continental United States during the 1600s no longer exist. About 80% of these lost wetlands were drained to grow crops. The rest were lost to mining, logging, oil and gas extraction, highway construction, and urban development. The heavily farmed state of Iowa has lost about 99% of its original inland wetlands.

This loss of natural capital has been an important factor in increasing flood damage in parts of the United States. Many other countries have suffered similar losses. For example, 80% of all inland wetlands in Germany and France have been destroyed.

wetlands since 1950 to oil and gas wells and other forms of coastal development.

Dams, levees, and hydroelectric power plants have been built on many of the world's rivers to control water flows and to generate electricity. This helps to reduce flooding along rivers, but it also reduces flood protection provided by the coastal deltas and wetlands. Because river sediments are deposited in the reservoirs behind dams, the river deltas do not get their normal inputs of sediment to build them back up, and they *subside,* or sink into the sea.

As a result, 24 of the world's 33 major river deltas are sinking rather than rising. In addition, 85% of the world's sinking deltas have experienced severe flooding in recent years and global delta flooding is likely to increase by 50% by the end of this century. This is because of dams and other human-made structures that reduce the flow of silt. It is also due partly to the projected rise in sea levels resulting from climate change. This poses a serious threat to the roughly 500 million people in the world who live on river deltas.

For example, the Mississippi River once delivered huge amounts of sediments to its delta each year. But the multiple dams, levees, and canals built in this river system funnel much of this sediment load through the wetlands and out into the Gulf of Mexico. Instead of building up delta lands, this causes them to subside. As many of the river delta's freshwater wetlands have been lost to this subsidence, saltwater from the Gulf has intruded and killed many plants that depended on the river water, further degrading this coastal aquatic system.

Subsidence helps to explain why the city of New Orleans, Louisiana (Figure 6.19), has long been 3 meters

National Oceanic and Atmospheric Administration (NOAA)

CASE STUDY

River Deltas and Coastal Wetlands—Vital Components of Natural Capital Now in Jeopardy

Coastal river deltas, mangrove forests, and coastal wetlands provide considerable natural protection against flood and wave damage from coastal storms, hurricanes, typhoons, and tsunamis. They weaken the force of waves and absorb excess storm water like sponges.

When we remove or degrade these ecosystems, any damage from a natural disaster such as a hurricane is intensified. As a result, flooding in places such as New Orleans, Louisiana (USA), and Venice, Italy, is a largely self-inflicted *unnatural* disaster. For example, Louisiana, which contains about 40% of all coastal wetlands in the lower 48 states, has lost more than a fifth of such

FIGURE 6.19 Much of the city of New Orleans, Louisiana, was flooded by the storm surge that accompanied Hurricane Katrina, which made landfall just east of the city on August 29, 2005.

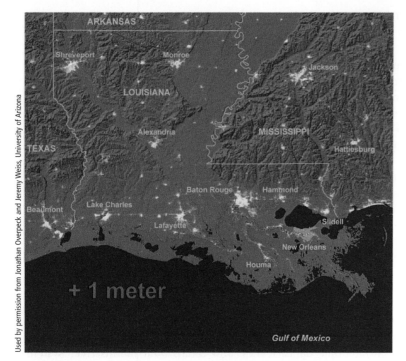

FIGURE 6.20 The areas in red represent projected coastal flooding that would result from a 1-meter (3-foot) rise in sea level due to projected climate change by the end of this century.

(10 feet) below sea level. Dams and levees were built to help protect the city from flooding. However, in 2005 the powerful winds and waves from Hurricane Katrina overwhelmed these defenses. They have been rebuilt, but subsidence will put New Orleans further below sea level in the future. Add to this the reduced protection from degraded coastal wetlands, and you have a recipe for a major and possibly more damaging disaster if the area is struck by another major hurricane.

To make matters worse, global sea levels have risen almost 0.3 meters (1 foot) since 1900 and are projected to rise another 0.3–0.9 meter (1–3 feet) by the end of this century. This is because climate change is warming the ocean, causing its waters to expand. Also, the melting of glaciers and other land-based ice is adding to the ocean's volume. Such a rise in sea level would put many of the world's coastal areas, including New Orleans and most of Louisiana's present-day coast, under water (Figure 6.20).

CHECKPOINT FOR UNDERSTANDING 6.5

1. Describe how human activities have degraded freshwater wetlands.

KEY IDEAS

- Saltwater and freshwater aquatic life zones cover almost three-fourths of the earth's surface, and oceans dominate the planet.
- The earth's aquatic systems provide important ecosystem and economic services.
- Certain human activities threaten biodiversity and disrupt ecosystem and economic services provided by aquatic systems.

Core Case Study Checkpoint

Explain how coral reefs are important and what percentage of them is threatened by human activities.

Chapter 6 Glossary

aquatic life zones: marine and freshwater portions of the biosphere.

benthos: bottom-dwelling organisms.

coastal wetland: land along a coastline, extending inland from an estuary that is covered with saltwater all or part of the year. Examples include marshes, bays, lagoons, tidal flats, and mangrove swamps.

coastal zone: warm, nutrient-rich, shallow part of the ocean that extends from the high-tide mark on land to the edge of a shelf-like extension of continental land masses known as the continental shelf.

cultural eutrophication: overnourishment of aquatic ecosystems with plant nutrients (mostly nitrates and phosphates) because of human activities such as agriculture, urbanization, and discharges from industrial plants and sewage treatment plants.

decomposers: organisms that digest parts of dead organisms and cast off fragments and wastes of living organisms by breaking down the complex organic molecules in those materials into simpler inorganic compounds and then absorbing the soluble nutrients.

delta: an area at the mouth of a river built up by deposited sediments, usually containing coastal wetlands and estuaries.

estuary: partially enclosed coastal area at the mouth of a river where its freshwater, carrying fertile silt and runoff from the land, mixes with salty seawater.

eutrophic lake: lake with a large supply of plant nutrients, mostly nitrates and phosphates.

freshwater life zone: aquatic systems where water with a dissolved salt concentration of less than 1% by volume accumulates on or flows through the surfaces of terrestrial biomes. Examples include *standing* (lentic) bodies of water such as ponds and lakes and *flowing* (lotic) bodies of water such as streams and rivers.

inland wetland: land away from the coast, such as a swamp, marsh, or bog, that is covered all or part of the time with freshwater.

intertidal zone: the area of shoreline between low and high tides.

mesotrophic lake: lake with a moderate level of plant nutrients, falling between the two extremes of eutrophic (high nutrient levels) and oligotrophic (low nutrient levels).

nekton: strongly swimming organisms found in aquatic systems.

ocean acidification: increasing levels of acid in world's oceans due to their absorption of much of the CO_2 emitted into the atmosphere by human activities, especially the burning of carbon-containing fossil fuels. The CO_2 reacts with ocean water to form a weak acid and decreases the levels of carbonate ions (CO_3^{2-}) needed to form coral and the shells and skeletons of organisms such as crabs, oysters, and some phytoplankton.

oligotrophic lake: lake with a low supply of plant nutrients.

pelagic zone (open sea): part of an ocean that lies beyond the continental shelf.

plankton: small plant organisms (phytoplankton) and animal organisms (zooplankton) that float in aquatic ecosystems.

runoff: freshwater from precipitation and melting ice that flows on the earth's surface into nearby streams, lakes, wetlands, and reservoirs.

saltwater life zone: oceans and their accompanying bays, estuaries, coastal wetlands, shorelines, coral reefs, and mangrove forests.

surface water: precipitation that does not infiltrate the ground or return to the atmosphere by evaporation or transpiration.

tides: periodic flow of water onto and off the shore, rising and falling about every six hours due to the gravitational pull of the moon and sun.

turbidity: cloudiness in a volume of water: a measure of water clarity in lakes, streams, and other bodies of water.

upwelling: movement of nutrient-rich bottom water to the ocean's surface. It can occur far from shore but usually takes place along certain steep coastal areas where the warm surface layer of ocean water is pushed away from shore and replaced by cold, nutrient-rich bottom water.

watershed: land area that delivers water, sediment, and dissolved substances via small streams to a major stream.

Chapter Review

Core Case Study

1. What are **coral reefs** and why should we care about them? What is coral bleaching? What are the major threats to coral reefs?

Section 6.1

2. (a) What are the two key concepts for this section? (b) What percentage of the earth's surface is covered with water? What is an **aquatic life zone**? (c) What is **salinity** and how is it measured? Distinguish between a **saltwater (marine) life zone** and a **freshwater life zone**, and give two examples of each. (d) Define **plankton** and describe three types of plankton. (e) Distinguish among **nekton**, **benthos**, and **decomposers** and give an example of each. (f) List four factors that determine the types and numbers of organisms found in the three layers of aquatic life zones. (g) What is **turbidity** and how does it occur? Describe one of its harmful impacts.

Section 6.2

3. (a) What is the key concept for this section? (b) What major ecosystem and economic services are provided by marine systems? (c) What are the three major life zones in an ocean? (d) Define **coastal zone**. Distinguish between an **estuary** and a **coastal wetland** and explain why each has high net primary productivity. (e) Explain the ecological and economic importance of coastal marshes, mangrove forests, and seagrass beds.

4. (a) What is the **intertidal zone**? Distinguish between rocky and sandy shores and describe some of the organisms often found on each type of shoreline. (b) What is a barrier island? (c) What is **ocean acidification** and why is it a threat to coral reefs? (d) Define **open sea** and describe its three major zones. What is an **upwelling** and how does it affect ocean life? (e) Why does the open sea have a low NPP? What have scientists recently learned about the ocean's biodiversity?

Section 6.3

5. (a) What is the key concept for this section? (b) What are the two biggest threats to marine systems? (c) List five human activities that pose major threats to marine systems and eight human activities that threaten coral reefs.

Section 6.4

6. (a) What is the key concept for this section? (b) Define **surface water**, **runoff**, and **watershed (drainage basin)**. (c) What major ecosystem and economic services do freshwater systems provide? (d) What is a **lake**? What four life zones are found in deep lakes? Distinguish between **oligotrophic** and **eutrophic lakes**. (e) What is **cultural eutrophication**?

7. (a) Describe the three zones that downward-flowing water passes through as it flows from highlands to lower elevations. What are the characteristic life forms of each zone? (b) What is the connection between water quality and watershed land?

8. Give three examples of **inland wetlands** and explain the ecological and economic importance of such wetlands.

Section 6.5

9. (a) What is the key concept for this section? (b) What are four major ways in which human activities are disrupting and degrading freshwater systems? (c) Describe losses of inland wetlands in the United States in terms of the area of wetlands lost and the resulting loss of ecosystem and economic services. (d) Explain how the building of dams and other structures on rivers can affect the river deltas and associated coastal wetlands. How do these effects in turn threaten human coastal communities?

10. What are this chapter's *three key ideas*?

———

Note: Key terms are in bold type.

AP® Review Questions

1. Which element below will be most helpful for reducing coastal erosion at all latitudes?
   (A) A coral reef, because it is in the shallow water near the shoreline
   (B) A sandy beach, because sand is easily replaced after a storm
   (C) An offshore pelagic zone, because the large organisms that live there help lessen the size of the waves
   (D) A sand dune, because it protects the oceanic coastline from damaging waves and wind
   (E) A salt marsh, because the root structure of these plants absorbs the force of wave energy, reducing erosion

2. Zooplankton are animal larvae that
   I. are primary consumers that feed on phytoplankton.
   II. are secondary consumers that feed on other zooplankton.
   III. are photosynthetic bacteria responsible for most of the ocean surface's primary productivity.
   (A) I only
   (B) II only
   (C) III only
   (D) I and II only
   (E) II and III only

3. Which of the below factors is NOT a primary determining factor for whether an organism is found on the surface or in the middle of the water column in the ocean?
   (A) Temperature
   (B) Dissolved oxygen
   (C) Availability of light
   (D) Salinity
   (E) Nutrient availability

4. Which area below will have the lowest net primary productivity/km²?
   (A) Estuaries, because most organisms cannot survive in water of varying salinity and depth
   (B) Lake edges, because people often populate lake shorelines
   (C) Ocean shorelines, because the waves sweep organisms out to the open sea
   (D) Small streams, because they are not large enough to provide the necessary nutrients
   (E) Open ocean, because of the lack of many nutrients such as nitrates and iron

5. The primary force responsible for tidal action is the
   (A) gravitational pull of the moon, because although it is smaller than earth, it is very close to earth
   (B) rotation of the earth on its axis, because the rate of rotation is so fast
   (C) tilt of the earth on its axis, because ocean water will rush to the tilted side
   (D) the Coriolis effect, which deflects water flowing away from the equator to the east, and water flowing toward the equator to the west
   (E) uneven heating, because the heated water becomes less dense and is therefore more easily moved by the wind

6. Which of the below is the correct path that a grain of sand would take as it is eroded from a mountain, carried downstream, and deposited on the ocean floor?
   (A) Littoral zone → aphotic zone → estuary → benthos
   (B) Estuary → coastal zone → pelagic zone → abyssal
   (C) Pelagic zone → estuary → benthos → photic zone
   (D) Benthos → estuary → profundal → limnetic
   (E) Littoral zone → estuary → abyssal → limnetic

7. Where are photosynthetic organisms least likely to be found?
   (A) In estuaries, where freshwater and saltwater mix and where there are many nutrients
   (B) In the euphotic zone, with low nutrient levels and high oxygen levels
   (C) In the abyssal zone, which is very cold and with little dissolved oxygen, where many organisms live and feed upon dead and decaying organic particles
   (D) In the intertidal zone, where organisms must adapt to alternating high and low tides, as well as changing salinity levels
   (E) In coral reefs, because the coral uses all the light and nutrients to survive

8. All of the following are ecological services provided by coastal wetlands EXCEPT
   (A) they are rich in nutrients and are therefore productive places for aquatic biodiversity.
   (B) the large amount of vegetation acts as a natural filter for contaminants.
   (C) coastal wetlands act as a buffer and help protect the land during hurricanes and tropical storms.
   (D) the ground can absorb a great deal of water, reducing local damage from floods.
   (E) because they are moist and contain many nutrients, they are important cropland.

Questions 9–12 refer to the human impacts on ecosystems listed below. Choices may be used once, more than once, or not at all.
   (A) Coral reef damage
   (B) Overfishing
   (C) Coastal development
   (D) Cultural eutrophication from release of excess nutrients
   (E) Population growth and burning of fossil fuels

9. Causes large areas of little to no oxygen in the Chesapeake Bay and the Gulf of Mexico

10. Causes large areas of beach loss or erosion or migration of beaches to new locations

11. Caused by boats improperly anchoring

12. Causes ocean warming and pH reduction, leading to coral bleaching

13. Which area would have the GREATEST biodiversity?
    (A) Open ocean water
    (B) Pelagic zone
    (C) Coral reef
    (D) Freshwater stream
    (E) Abyssal zone

14. The nutrient loading of phosphates and nitrates into waterways is responsible for all of the following EXCEPT
    (A) increase in algae blooms
    (B) large fish die-off
    (C) increase in dissolved oxygen
    (D) cultural eutrophication
    (E) increase in suspended solids in the water column

Questions 15–16 refer to the choices listed below.
    (A) Littortal zone
    (B) Limnetic zone
    (C) Profundal zone
    (D) Benthic zone
    (E) Oligotrophic zone

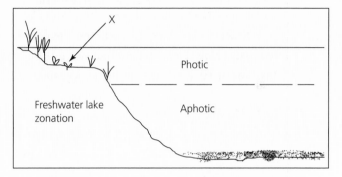

15. Where the X arrow in the diagram of a freshwater lake above is pointing

16. The zone which supports the highest biological diversity

17. Both saltwater and freshwater environments have weakly swimming, free-floating organisms called
    (A) nekton
    (B) benthos
    (C) plankton
    (D) littoral
    (E) pelagic

18. Photosynthesis in the ocean is limited to the upper layer where light can penetrate. This layer is called the
    (A) bathyal zone
    (B) aphotic zone
    (C) littoral zone
    (D) benthic zone
    (E) euphotic zone

19. Why does the open sea make the largest contribution to the earth's overall net primary productivity?
    (A) High levels of nutrients
    (B) Large amounts of light for photosynthesis
    (C) It covers a large amount of the earth's surface
    (D) Primary producers have few predators
    (E) Significant amount of large aquatic plants

20. All of the following are true of benthic species EXCEPT
   (A) they inhabit the benthic zone of lakes
   (B) they feed on marine snow in the profundal zone of oceans
   (C) they are mostly detrivores feeding on dead matter
   (D) some are adapted to darker colder waters
   (E) they are adapted to swim quickly to evade predators

AP® Free-Response Practice

1. A scientist observes a pond located adjacent to a golf course and observes a thick mat of algae covering approximately half of the surface. The banks of the pond allow rain and snowmelt to enter the pond from the golf course property and there are emergent plants such as cattails growing around the perimeter. The scientist decides to run several water-quality tests to gather data. The results appear in the table to the right.

Dissolved oxygen	4 mL/L
pH	6.4
Nitrate	0.01 mL/L
Phosphate	0.01 mL/L
Total chlorine	0 mL/L

   (a) Based on the data shown, design an experiment that tests the relationship of a factor directly related to the growth of the algae.

   (i) **State** a hypothesis that will test the possible cause of the algal bloom.

   (ii) **Describe** the procedure that will test the hypothesis.

   (iii) **Identify** the control in the experiment.

   (iv) **Identify** the dependent variable.

   (v) **Discuss** the expected results of this experiment.

   (b) There are many causes of cultural eutrophication.

   (i) **Identify** TWO possible sources of cultural eutrophication.

   (ii) **Describe** the sequence of events that takes place during this process, ultimately resulting in a shift in species in a pond or lake.

   (c) Organisms that live in estuaries (marine wetlands) are well adapted to rapidly changing environmental conditions.

   (i) **Identify** and **describe** TWO characteristics of estuaries to which organisms must adapt.

   (ii) **Identify** ONE economic benefit of estuaries.

Critical Thinking

1. What are three steps that governments and private interests could take to protect the world's remaining coral reefs (**Core Case Study**)?

2. Can you think of any ways in which you might be contributing to the degradation of a nearby or distant aquatic ecosystem? Describe the system and how your actions might be affecting it. What are three things you could do to reduce your impact?

3. You are a defense attorney arguing in court for protecting a coral reef (**Core Case Study**) from harmful human activities. Give your three most important arguments for the defense of this ecosystem.

4. How would you respond to someone who argues that we should use the deep portions of the world's oceans to deposit our radioactive and other hazardous wastes because the deep oceans are vast and are located far away from human habitats? Give reasons for your response.

5. From the list of threats to marine ecosystems listed in Figure 6.12, pick the three that you think are the most serious. For each of them, if it continues to degrade ocean ecosystems during your lifetime, how might this affect you? Can you think of ways in which you might be contributing to each problem? What could you do to reduce your impact?

6. Suppose a developer builds a housing complex overlooking a coastal marsh (Figure 6.7) and the result is pollution and degradation of the marsh. Describe the effects of such a development on the wildlife in the marsh, assuming at least one species is eliminated as a result.

7. Suppose you have a friend who owns property that includes a freshwater wetland and the friend tells you she is planning to fill the wetland to make more room for her lawn and garden. What would you say to this friend?

8. Congratulations! You are in charge of the world. What are the three most important features of your plan to help sustain the earth's aquatic biodiversity?

Data Analysis

Some 45–53% of the world's shallow coral reefs have been destroyed or severely damaged (**Core Case Study**). A number of factors have played a role in this serious loss of aquatic biodiversity, including ocean warming, sediment from coastal soil erosion, excessive algal growth from fertilizer runoff, coral bleaching, rising sea levels, ocean acidification, overfishing, and damage from hurricanes.

In 2005 scientists Nadia Bood, Melanie McField, and Rich Aronson conducted research to evaluate the recovery of coral reefs in Belize from the combined effects of mass bleaching and Hurricane Mitch in 1998. Some of these reefs are in protected waters where no fishing is allowed.

Effects of restricting fishing on the recovery of unfished and fished coral reefs damaged by the combined effects of mass bleaching and Hurricane Mitch in 1998.

(Compiled by the authors with data from Melanie McField, et al., *Status of Caribbean Coral Reefs after Bleaching and Hurricanes in 2005*, NOAA, 2008. Report available at www.coris.noaa.gov/activities/caribbean_rpt/.)

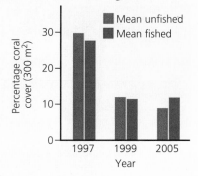

The researchers speculated that reefs in waters where no fishing is allowed should recover faster than reefs in waters where fishing is allowed. The graph to the left shows some of the data they collected from three highly protected (unfished) sites and three unprotected (fished) sites to evaluate their hypothesis. Study this graph and then answer the following questions.

1. By about what percentage did the mean coral cover drop in the protected (unfished) reefs between 1997 and 1999?

2. By about what percentage did the mean coral cover drop in the protected (unfished) reefs between 1997 and 2005?

3. By about what percentage did the coral cover drop in the unprotected (fished) reefs between 1997 and 1999?

4. By about what percentage did the coral cover change in the unprotected (fished) reefs between 1997 and 2005?

5. Do these data support the hypothesis that coral reef recovery should occur faster in areas where fishing is prohibited? Explain.

Answers to Checkpoints for Understanding

Section 6.1

1. Salinity, temperature, turbidity, dissolved oxygen content, availability of food, and light penetration are all abiotic factors found in aquatic ecosystems.

Section 6.2

1. Most ocean life is found in the coastal zone because it is where producers flourish due to high availability of light, warmer temperature, high amount of nutrients, and topography that allows submergent plants to root but still receive sunlight. This leads to an abundance of fish and shellfish compared to the open ocean and explains why most commercial fishing takes place in the coastal zone.

2. Intertidal organisms must be adapted to changing temperature, varying salinity, pounding waves, submersion, and exposure to the air due to incoming and outgoing tides. They may burrow in the sand, cling to rocks, and protect themselves with shells.

3. Upwellings bring cold and nutrient-rich water from the bottom of the ocean to the ocean surface. There it supports large populations of phytoplankton, zooplankton, fish, and fish-eating seabirds.

Section 6.3

1. The greatest threats to marine ecosystems are climate change and ocean acidification.

2. Increasing ocean acidification is a serious threat because it decreases the levels of carbonate ions needed to form coral and the shells and skeletons of shellfish such as crabs and oysters and some phytoplankton.

Section 6.4

1. Most life is found in the littoral zone. This is because it has ample sunlight and large inputs of plant nutrients from the surrounding land, supporting a variety of plants that in turn support aquatic animals.

2. Water in the source zone, the head or a stream, tends to be cold, holding more oxygen than warm water, and turbulent, mixing oxygen into the water as it flows rapidly and turns over.

Section 6.5

1. Humans have built dams that restrict the flow of water and reduce habitat for aquatic and terrestrial organisms. Levees disconnect rivers from floodplains, decreasing habitat for organisms. Cities and farms release nutrients and pollutants that result in eutrophication. Freshwater wetlands have been filled in or drained to create human structures, destroying habitat for terrestrial and aquatic organisms.

Core Case Study

Coral reefs are important because they are centers of aquatic biodiversity that provide important ecological and economic services. Coral reefs buffer the impact of storms, provide habitat, food, and spawning grounds for many aquatic species, and provide about one tenth of the world's fish catch. Since the 1950s, human activities have destroyed or degraded 45–53% of the world's shallow coral reefs.

CHAPTER 7

Species Interactions, Ecological Succession, and Population Control

In looking at nature, never forget that every single organic being around us may be said to be striving to increase its numbers.

CHARLES DARWIN

Key Questions

7.1 How do species interact?

7.2 How do communities and ecosystems respond to changing environmental conditions?

7.3 What limits the growth of populations?

A clownfish gains protection by living among sea anemones and helps protect the anemones from some of their predators.

Morrison/Dreamstime.com

The Southern Sea Otter: A Species in Recovery

Southern sea otters (Figure 7.1, left) live in giant kelp forests (Figure 7.1, right) in shallow waters along parts of the Pacific coast of North America. Most of the remaining members of this endangered species are found off the California coast between the cities of Santa Cruz and Santa Barbara.

Fast and agile swimmers, the otters dive to the ocean bottom looking for shellfish and food. They swim on their backs on the ocean surface and use their bellies as a table to eat their prey (Figure 7.1, left). Each day, a sea otter consumes 20–35% of its weight in clams, mussels, crabs, sea urchins, abalone, and 40 other species of bottom-dwelling organisms. Their incredibly dense fur traps air bubbles and keeps them warm.

At one time, an estimated 13,000 to 20,000 southern sea otters lived in California's coastal waters. By the early 1900s, they had been hunted almost to extinction by fur traders who killed them for their luxurious fur. Commercial fishers also killed otters, viewing them as competitors in the hunt for valuable abalone and other shellfish.

The otter population grew from a low of 50 in 1938 to 1,850 in 1977 when the US Fish and Wildlife listed the species as endangered. Since then, it has continued to make a slow recovery to 3,511 individuals in 2017. If its population remains above 3,090 for three consecutive years it can be removed from the endangered species list.

Why should we care about the southern sea otters of California? One reason is ethical: Many people believe it is wrong to allow human activities to cause the extinction of a species. Another reason is that people love to look at these appealing and highly intelligent animals as they play in the water. As a result, otters help to generate millions of dollars a year in tourism revenues. A third reason—and a key reason in our study of environmental science—is that biologists classify the southern sea otter as a *keystone species* that helps support other species in its giant kelp forest habitat. Scientists hypothesize that in the absence of southern sea otters, sea urchins and other kelp-eating species would probably destroy the Pacific coast kelp forests and much of the rich biodiversity they support.

Biodiversity is an important part of the earth's natural capital and is the focus of one of the three **scientific principles of sustainability**. In this chapter, we look at how species interact and help control one another's population sizes. We also explore how communities, ecosystems, and populations of species respond to changes in environmental conditions. ●

CRITICAL THINKING

Are ethical concerns enough reason to protect endangered species like the sea otter? Explain.

FIGURE 7.1 An endangered southern sea otter in Monterey Bay, California (USA) uses a stone to crack the shells of the clams that it feeds on (left). It lives in a bed of seaweed called *giant kelp* (right).

Left: Kirsten Wahlquist/Dreamstime.com. Right: Paul Whitted/Shutterstock.com.

7.1 HOW DO SPECIES INTERACT?

CONCEPT 7.1 Five types of interactions among species—interspecific competition, predation, parasitism, mutualism, and commensalism—affect the resource use and population sizes of species.

Competition for Resources

Ecologists have identified five basic types of interactions among species as they share limited resources such as food, shelter, and space. These types of interactions are called *interspecific competition, predation, parasitism, mutualism,* and *commensalism.* These interactions affect the population sizes of the species in an ecosystem and their use of resources (**Concept 7.1**).

Competition is the most common interaction among species. It occurs when members of one or more species interact to use the same limited resources such as food, water, light, and space. Competition between different species is called **interspecific competition**. It plays a larger role in most ecosystems than *intraspecific competition*—competition among members of the same species.

When two species compete with one another for the same resources, their niches overlap (Figure 4.8, p. 99). The greater this overlap, the more they compete for key resources. For example, if species A takes over the largest share of one or more key resources, then competing species B must move to another area (if possible) or suffer a population decline.

Given enough time for natural selection to occur, populations can develop adaptations that enable them to reduce or avoid competition with other species. An example is **resource partitioning**, which occurs when different species competing for similar scarce resources evolve specialized traits that allow them to share the same resources. This can involve using parts of the resources or using the resources at different times or in different ways. Figure 7.2 shows resource partitioning by insect-eating bird species. Adaptations allow the birds to reduce competition by feeding in different portions of certain spruce trees and by feeding on different insect species.

Another example of resource partitioning through natural selection involves birds called *honeycreepers* that live in the US state of Hawaii (Figure 7.3). Figure 4.9 (p. 99) shows how the evolution of specialized feeding niches has reduced competition for resources among bird species in a coastal wetland.

Predation

In **predation**, a member of one species is a **predator** that feeds directly on all or part of a member of another species, the **prey**. A brown bear (the predator) and a salmon (the prey) are engaged in a **predator–prey relationship** (Figure 7.4). Such a relationship (between a lion and a zebra) is also shown in Figure 3.6, p. 69. This type of species interaction has a strong effect on population sizes and other factors in many ecosystems.

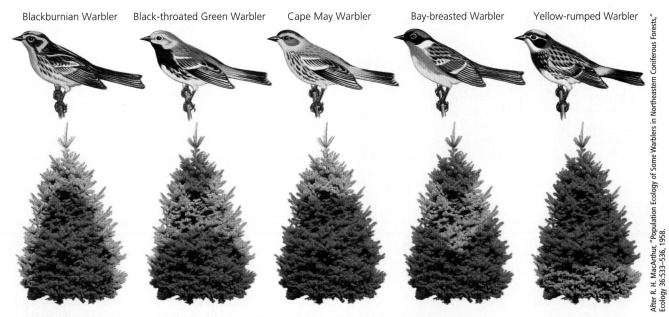

FIGURE 7.2 *Sharing the wealth:* Resource partitioning among five species of insect-eating warblers in the spruce forests of the US state of Maine. Each species spends at least half its feeding time in its associated yellow-highlighted areas of these spruce trees.

After R. H. MacArthur, "Population Ecology of Some Warblers in Northeastern Coniferous Forests," Ecology 36:533–536, 1958.

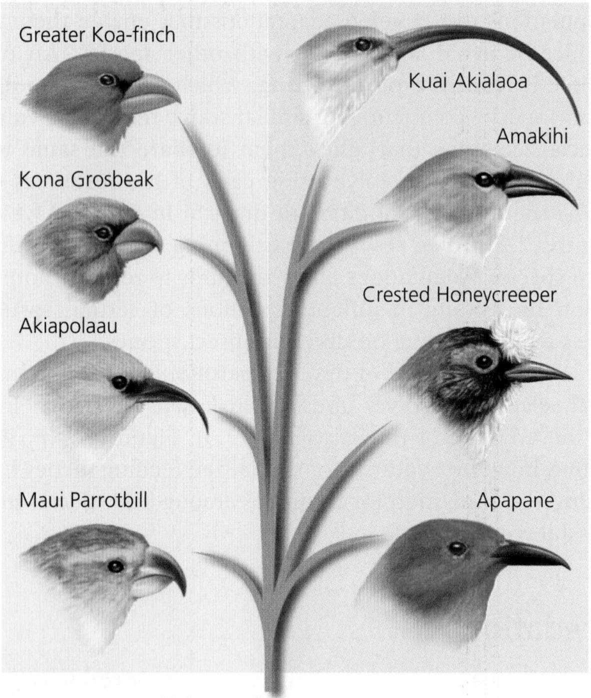

Fruit and seed eaters
Insect and nectar eaters
Greater Koa-finch
Kuai Akialaoa
Amakihi
Kona Grosbeak
Crested Honeycreeper
Akiapolaau
Maui Parrotbill
Apapane
Unknown finch ancestor

FIGURE 7.3 *Specialist species of honeycreepers:* Through natural selection, different species of honeycreepers have shared resources by evolving specialized beaks to take advantage of certain types of food such as insects, seeds, fruits, and nectar from certain flowers. ***Question:*** Look at each bird's beak and take a guess at what sort of food that bird might eat.

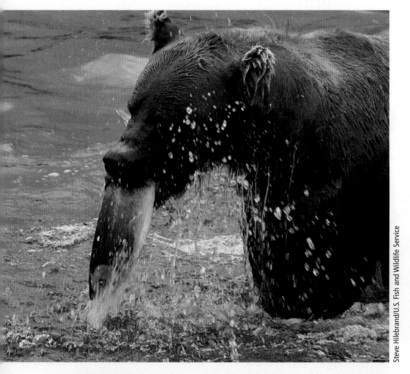

Steve Hilebrand/U.S. Fish and Wildlife Service

FIGURE 7.4 *Predator–prey relationship:* This brown bear (the predator) in the US state of Alaska has captured and will feed on this salmon (the prey).

CONSIDER THIS . . .

CONNECTIONS Grizzly Bears and Moths

During the summer months, the grizzly bears of the Greater Yellowstone ecosystem in the western United States eat huge amounts of army cutworm moths, which huddle in masses high on remote mountain slopes. In this predator–prey interaction, one grizzly bear can dig out and lap up as many as 40,000 cutworm moths in a day. Consisting of 50–70% fat, the moths offer a nutrient that the bear can store in its fatty tissues and draw on during its winter hibernation.

In a giant kelp forest ecosystem, sea urchins prey on kelp, a type of seaweed (Science Focus 7.1). As a keystone species, southern sea otters (**Core Case Study**) prey on the sea urchins and prevent them from destroying the kelp forests. An adult southern sea otter can eat as many as 1,500 sea urchins a day.

Predators use a variety of ways to help them capture prey. *Herbivores* can walk, swim, or fly to the plants they feed on. Many *carnivores,* such as cheetahs, use speed to chase down and kill prey, such as zebras. Eagles and hawks can fly and have keen eyesight to find prey. Some predators such as female African lions work in groups to capture large or fast-running prey.

Other predators use *camouflage* to hide in plain sight and ambush their prey. For example, praying mantises (see Figure 4.3, right, p. 94) sit on flowers or plants of a color similar to their own and ambush visiting insects. White ermines (a type of weasel), snowy owls, and arctic foxes (Figure 7.5) hunt their prey in snow-covered areas. People camouflage themselves to hunt wild game and use camouflaged traps to capture wild animals. Some predators use *chemical warfare* to attack their prey. For example, some spiders and poisonous snakes use venom to paralyze their prey and to deter their predators.

Prey species have evolved many ways to avoid predators. Some can run, swim, or fly fast and some have highly developed senses of sight, sound, or smell that alert them to the presence of predators. Other adaptations include protective shells (abalone and turtles), thick bark (giant sequoia trees), spines (porcupines), and thorns (cacti and rose bushes).

Other prey species use camouflage to blend into their surroundings. Some insect species have shapes that look like twigs (Figure 7.6a), or bird droppings on leaves. A leaf insect can be almost invisible against its background (Figure 7.6b), as can an arctic hare in its white winter fur.

Prey species also use *chemical warfare*. Some discourage predators by containing or emitting chemicals that are *poisonous* (oleander plants), *irritating* (stinging nettles and bombardier beetles, Figure 7.6c), *foul smelling* (skunks and stinkbugs), or *bad tasting* (buttercups and monarch butterflies, Figure 7.6d). When attacked, some species of squid and octopus emit clouds of black ink, allowing them to escape by confusing their predators.

Many bad-tasting, bad-smelling, toxic, or stinging prey species flash a warning coloration that eating them is risky.

Threats to Kelp Forests

A kelp forest contains large concentrations of seaweed called *giant kelp*. Anchored to the ocean floor, its long blades grow toward the sunlit surface waters (Figure 7.1, right). Under good conditions, the blades can grow 0.6 meter (2 feet) in a day and the plant can grow as tall as a 10-story building. The blades are flexible and can survive all but the most violent storms and waves.

Kelp forests support many marine plants and animals and are one of the most biologically diverse marine ecosystems. These forests also reduce shore erosion by blunting the force of incoming waves and trapping some of the outgoing sand.

Sea urchins (Figure 7.A) prey on kelp plants. Large populations of these predators can rapidly devastate a kelp forest because they eat the bases of young kelp plants. Scientific studies by biologists, including James Estes of the University of California at Santa Cruz, indicate that the southern sea otter is a keystone species that helps to sustain kelp forests by controlling populations of sea urchins.

Polluted water running off the land also threatens kelp forests. The pollutants in this runoff include pesticides and herbicides that can kill kelp plants and other species and upset the food webs in these aquatic forests. Another runoff pollutant is fertilizer. Its plant nutrients (mostly nitrates) can cause excessive growth of algae and other aquatic plants. This growth blocks some of the sunlight needed to support the growth of giant kelp.

Some scientists warn that the warming of the world's oceans is a growing threat to kelp forests, which require cool water. If coastal waters get warmer during this century, as projected by climate models, many or most of California's coastal kelp forests could disappear.

FIGURE 7.A The purple sea urchin inhabits the coastal waters of the state of California and feeds on kelp.

CRITICAL THINKING

List three ways in which we could reduce the degradation of giant kelp forest ecosystems.

Examples are the brilliantly colored, foul-tasting monarch butterflies (Figure 7.6d) and poisonous frogs (Figure 7.6e). When a bird eats a monarch butterfly, it usually vomits and learns to avoid monarchs.

Some butterfly species gain protection by looking and acting like other, more dangerous species, a protective device known as *mimicry*. The nonpoisonous viceroy butterfly (Figure 7.6f) mimics the monarch butterfly. Other prey species use *behavioral strategies* to avoid predation. Some attempt to scare off predators by puffing up (blowfish), spreading their wings (peacocks), or mimicking a predator (Figure 7.6h). Some moths have wings that look like the eyes of much larger animals (Figure 7.6g). Other prey species gain some protection by living in large groups such as schools of fish and herds of antelope.

Biologist Edward O. Wilson proposed two criteria for evaluating the dangers posed by various brightly colored animal species. *First*, if they are small and strikingly beautiful, they are probably poisonous. *Second*, if they are strikingly beautiful and easy to catch, they are probably deadly.

FIGURE 7.5 A white arctic fox hunts its prey by blending into its snowy background to avoid being detected.

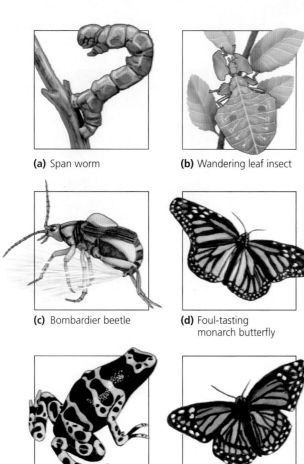

(a) Span worm   **(b)** Wandering leaf insect

(c) Bombardier beetle   **(d)** Foul-tasting monarch butterfly

(e) Poison dart frog   **(f)** Viceroy butterfly mimics monarch butterfly.

(g) Hind wings of Io moth resemble eyes of a much larger animal.

(h) When touched, snake caterpillar changes shape to look like head of snake.

FIGURE 7.6 These prey species have developed specialized ways to avoid their predators: (a, b) *camouflage*, (c, d, e) *chemical warfare*, (d, e, f) *warning coloration*, (f) *mimicry*, (g) *deceptive looks*, and (h) *deceptive behavior*.

Coevolution

At the individual level, members of predator species benefit from their predation and members of prey species are harmed. At the population level, predation plays a role in natural selection. Animal predators tend to kill the sick, weak, aged, and least fit members of a prey population because they are the easiest to catch. Individuals with better

defenses against predation thus tend to survive longer and leave more offspring with adaptations that can help them avoid predation. Over time, as a prey species develops traits that make it more difficult to catch, its predators face selection pressures that favor traits increasing their ability to catch their prey. Then the prey species must get better at eluding the more effective predators.

This back-and-forth adaptation is called **coevolution**, a natural selection process in which changes in the gene pool of one species leads to changes in the gene pool of another species. It can play an important role in controlling population growth of predator and prey species. When populations of two species interact as predator and prey over a long time, genetic changes occur in both species that help them to become more competitive or to avoid or reduce competition.

For example, coevolution can be observed between bats and certain species of moths they feed on. Bats prey on certain species of moths that they hunt at night using echolocation. They emit pulses of high-frequency sound that bounce off their prey. Then they capture the returning echoes that tell them where their prey is located. Over time, certain moth species have evolved ears that are sensitive to the sound frequencies that bats use to find them. When they hear these frequencies, they drop to the ground or fly evasively. Some bat species evolved ways to counter this defense by changing the frequency of their sound pulses. In turn, some moths evolved their own high-frequency clicks to jam the bats' echolocation systems. Some bat species then adapted by turning off their echolocation systems and using the moths' clicks to locate their prey.

> **CONSIDER THIS . . .**
>
> **LEARNING FROM NATURE**
>
> Bats and dolphins use echolocation to navigate and locate prey in the darkness of night and in the ocean's murky water. Scientists are studying how they do this to improve our sonar systems, sonic imaging tools for detecting underground mineral deposits, and medical ultrasound imaging systems.

Parasitism, Mutualism, and Commensalism

Parasitism occurs when one species (the *parasite*) lives in or on another organism (the *host*). The parasite benefits by extracting nutrients from the host. A parasite weakens its host but rarely kills it, since doing so would eliminate the source of its benefits. For example, tapeworms are parasites that live part of their life cycle inside their hosts. Others such as mistletoe plants and blood-sucking sea lampreys (Figure 7.7) attach themselves to the outsides of their hosts. Some parasites (such as fleas and ticks) move from one host to another whereas others (such as certain protozoa) spend their adult lives within a single host. Parasites help keep their host populations in check.

Great Lakes Fishery Commission

FIGURE 7.7 *Parasitism:* This blood-sucking, parasitic sea lamprey has attached itself to an adult lake trout from one of the Great Lakes (USA, Canada).

In **mutualism**, two species interact in ways that benefit both by providing each with food, shelter, or some other resource. An example is pollination of flowering plants by species such as honeybees, hummingbirds, and butterflies (see Chapter 4 opening photo, pp. 90–91) that feed on the nectar of flowers. Figure 7.8 shows an example of a mutualistic relationship that combines *nutrition* and *protection*. It involves birds that ride on the backs or heads of large animals such as elephants, rhinoceroses, and impalas. The birds remove and eat parasites and pests (such as ticks and flies) from the animals' bodies and often make noises warning the animals when predators are approaching.

Another example of mutualism involves clownfish, which usually live within sea anemones (see chapter-opening photo), whose tentacles sting and paralyze most fish that touch them. The clownfish, which are not harmed by the tentacles, gain protection from predators and feed on the waste matter left from the anemones' meals. The sea anemones benefit because the clownfish protect them from some of their predators and parasites.

Mutualism might appear to be a form of cooperation between species. However, each species is concerned only for its own survival.

Commensalism is an interaction that benefits one species but has little, if any, beneficial or harmful effect on the other. One example involves plants called *epiphytes* (air plants), which attach themselves to the trunks or branches of trees (Figure 7.9) in tropical and subtropical forests. The plants gain access to sunlight, water from the humid air and rain, and nutrients falling from the tree's upper leaves and limbs, but their presence apparently does not harm the tree. Similarly, birds benefit by nesting in trees, generally without harming them.

Villiers Steyn/Dreamstime.com

parinyabinsuk/Shutterstock.com

FIGURE 7.8 *Mutualism:* Oxpeckers feed on parasitic ticks that infest animals such as this impala and warn of approaching predators.

FIGURE 7.9 *Commensalism:* This pitcher plant is attached to a branch of a tree without penetrating or harming the tree. This carnivorous plant feeds on insects that become trapped inside it.

1. Species have three options when competing directly with another species. A species that cannot compete may adapt, migrate, or go extinct. Explain how this is demonstrated in interspecific relationships.

2. A symbiotic relationship is defined as a close and long-term relationship between two organisms. Identify the three types of symbiotic relationships. Explain why a predator–prey relationship is not considered symbiotic.

7.2 HOW DO COMMUNITIES AND ECOSYSTEMS RESPOND TO CHANGING ENVIRONMENTAL CONDITIONS?

CONCEPT 7.2 The species composition of a community or ecosystem can change in response to changing environmental conditions through a process called *ecological succession*.

Ecological Succession Creates and Changes Ecosystems

The types and numbers of species in biological communities and ecosystems change in response to changing environmental conditions. The normally gradual change in species composition in a given terrestrial area or aquatic system is called **ecological succession** (**Concept 7.2**). Ecologists recognize two major types of ecological succession, depending on the conditions present at the beginning of the process.

Primary ecological succession involves the gradual establishment of communities of different species in lifeless areas. This type of succession begins where there is no soil in a terrestrial ecosystem or no bottom sediment in an aquatic ecosystem. Examples include bare rock exposed by a retreating glacier (Figure 7.10), newly cooled lava from a volcanic eruption, an abandoned highway or parking lot, and a newly created shallow pond or lake (Figure 7.11). Primary succession usually takes hundreds to thousands of years because of the need to build up fertile soil or aquatic sediments to provide the nutrients needed to establish a plant community.

Species such as lichens and mosses that quickly colonize the newly exposed rocks are called **pioneer species**. They often have seeds or spores that can travel long distances and quickly spread over the exposed rock (Figure 7.10). As lichens grow and spread, they release acids that can break down the rock and start the soil formation process. As the soil slowly forms, small plants, insects, and worms invade and add more nutrients that build up the soil. Each successive wave of new organisms changes the environmental conditions in ways that provide more

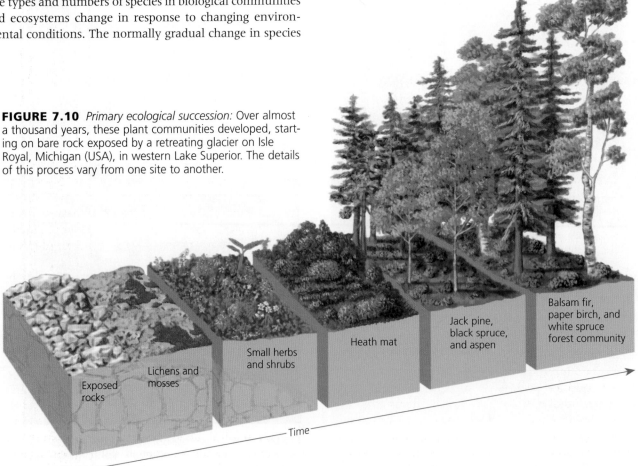

FIGURE 7.10 *Primary ecological succession:* Over almost a thousand years, these plant communities developed, starting on bare rock exposed by a retreating glacier on Isle Royal, Michigan (USA), in western Lake Superior. The details of this process vary from one site to another.

Exposed rocks

Lichens and mosses

Small herbs and shrubs

Heath mat

Jack pine, black spruce, and aspen

Balsam fir, paper birch, and white spruce forest community

Time

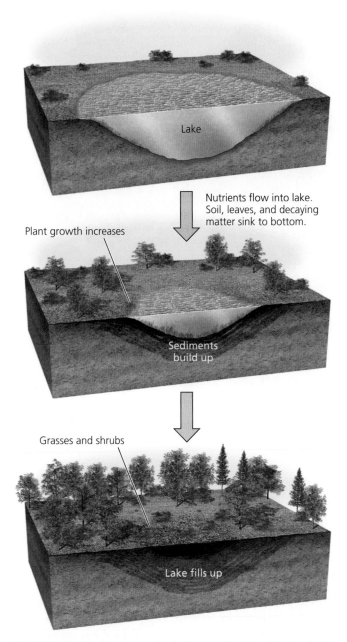

FIGURE 7.11 *Primary ecological succession* in a lake basin in which sediments and plants have been gouged out by a glacier. When the glacier melts, the lake basin begins accumulating sediments and plant and animal life. Over hundreds to thousands of years, the lake can fill with sediments and become a terrestrial habitat.

Labels in figure:
- Lake
- Nutrients flow into lake. Soil, leaves, and decaying matter sink to bottom.
- Plant growth increases
- Sediments build up
- Grasses and shrubs
- Lake fills up

nutrients, habitats, and favorable environmental conditions for future arrivals.

The other, more common type of ecological succession is **secondary ecological succession**, in which a series of terrestrial communities or ecosystems with different species develop in places containing soil or bottom sediment. This type of succession begins in an area where an ecosystem has been disturbed, removed, or destroyed, but some soil or bottom sediment remains. Candidates for secondary succession include abandoned farmland (Figure 7.12), burned or cut forests, heavily polluted streams, and flooded land. Because some soil or sediment is present, new vegetation can begin to grow, usually within a few weeks. On land, growth begins with the germination of seeds already in the soil and seeds imported by wind or in the droppings of birds and other animals.

Ecological succession is an important ecosystem service that can enrich the biodiversity of communities and ecosystems by increasing species diversity and interactions among species. Such interactions enhance sustainability by promoting population control and increasing the complexity of food webs. Primary and secondary ecological successions are examples of *natural ecological restoration*.

Ecologists have identified three factors that affect how and at what rate ecological succession occurs. One is *facilitation*, in which one set of species makes an area suitable for species with different niche requirements, and often less suitable for itself. For example, as lichens and mosses gradually build up soil on a rock in primary succession, herbs and grasses can move in and crowd out the lichens and mosses (Figure 7.10).

A second factor is *inhibition*, in which some species hinder the establishment and growth of other species. For example, needles dropping off some pine trees make the soil beneath the trees too acidic for most other plants to grow there. A third factor is *tolerance*, in which plants in the late stages of succession succeed because they are not in direct competition with other plants for key resources. Shade-tolerant plants, for example, can live in shady forests because they do not need as much sunlight as the trees above them do (Figure 7.12).

Is There a Balance of Nature?

According to the traditional view, ecological succession proceeds in an orderly sequence along an expected path until a certain stable type of *climax community* (Figures 7.10 and 7.12), which is assumed to be in balance with its environment, occupies an area. This equilibrium model of succession is what ecologists once meant when they talked about the *balance of nature*.

Over the last several decades, many ecologists have changed their views about balance and equilibrium in nature based on ecological research. There is a general tendency for succession to lead to more complex, diverse, and presumably more resilient ecosystems that can withstand changes in environmental conditions if the changes are not too large or too sudden. However, the current scientific view is that we cannot predict a given course of succession or view it as inevitable progress toward an ideally adapted climax plant community or ecosystem. Rather, ecological succession reflects the ongoing struggle by different species for enough light, water, nutrients, food, space, and other key resources.

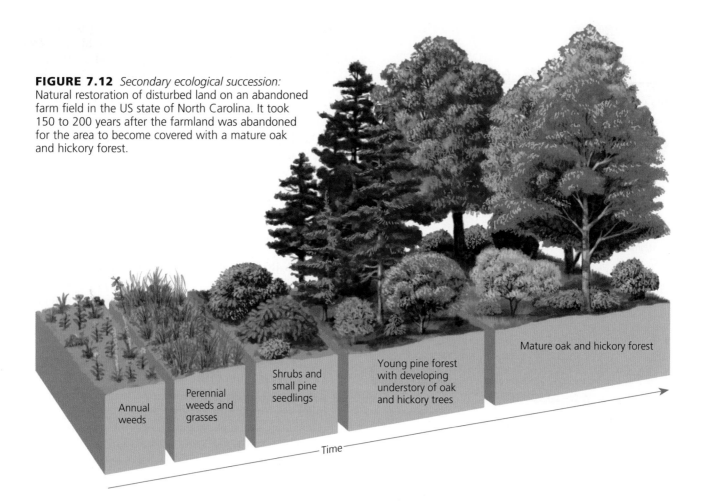

FIGURE 7.12 *Secondary ecological succession:* Natural restoration of disturbed land on an abandoned farm field in the US state of North Carolina. It took 150 to 200 years after the farmland was abandoned for the area to become covered with a mature oak and hickory forest.

Annual weeds

Perennial weeds and grasses

Shrubs and small pine seedlings

Young pine forest with developing understory of oak and hickory trees

Mature oak and hickory forest

Time

Living Systems Are Sustained through Constant Change

All living systems, from a cell to the biosphere, constantly change in response to changing environmental conditions. Living systems have complex processes that interact to provide some degree of stability, or sustainability. This stability, or the capacity to withstand external stress and disturbance, is maintained by constant change in response to changing environmental conditions. In a mature tropical rain forest, some trees die and others take their places. However, unless the forest is cut, burned, or otherwise destroyed, you would still recognize it as a tropical rain forest 50 or 100 years from now.

Ecologists distinguish between two aspects of stability or sustainability in ecosystems. One, called **inertia**, or **persistence**, is the ability of an ecosystem to survive moderate disturbances. A second factor, **resilience**, is the ability of an ecosystem to be restored through secondary ecological succession after a severe disturbance.

Evidence suggests that some ecosystems have one of these properties but not the other. Tropical rain forests have high species diversity and high inertia and thus are resistant to low levels of change or damage. But once a large tract of tropical rain forest is cleared or severely damaged, the resilience of the degraded forest ecosystem may be so low that the degradation reaches an ecological tipping point. Beyond that point, the forest might not be restored by secondary ecological succession. One reason is that most of the nutrients in a tropical rain forest are stored in its vegetation, not in the topsoil. Once the nutrient-rich vegetation is gone, frequent rains on a large cleared area of land can remove most of the remaining soil nutrients and thus prevent the return of a tropical rain forest to such an area.

By contrast, grasslands are much less diverse than most forests. Thus, they have low inertia and can burn easily. Because most of their plant matter is stored in underground roots, these ecosystems have high resilience and can recover quickly after a fire because their root systems produce new grasses. Grassland can be destroyed only if its roots are plowed up and something else is planted in its place, or if it is severely overgrazed by livestock or other herbivores.

CHECKPOINT FOR UNDERSTANDING 7.2

1. Explain why a tropical rainforest has high resilience but low inertia.

FIGURE 7.13 A population, or *school*, of Anthias fish on coral in Australia's Great Barrier Reef.

7.3 WHAT LIMITS THE GROWTH OF POPULATIONS?

CONCEPT 7.3 No population can grow indefinitely because of limitations on resources and because of competition among species for those resources.

Populations Can Grow, Shrink, or Remain Stable

A **population** is a group of interbreeding individuals of the same species (Figure 7.13). **Population size** is the number of individual organisms in a population at a given time. The size of a population may increase, decrease, go up and down in cycles, or remain roughly the same in response to changing environmental conditions.

Scientists use sampling techniques to estimate the sizes of large populations of species such as oak trees that are spread over a large area and squirrels that move around and are hard to count. Typically, they count the number of individuals in one or more small sample areas and use this information to estimate the number of individuals in a larger area (See Critical Concepts in Sustainability).

Populations of different species vary in their distribution over their habitats, or *dispersion*, as shown in Figure 7.14. Most populations live together in *clumps* or *groups* such as packs of wolves, schools of fish (Figure 7.13), and flocks of birds. Southern sea otters (**Core Case Study**),

for example, are usually found in groups known as rafts or pods ranging in size from a few to several hundred animals.

Living in groups allows organisms to cluster where resources are available. Group living also provides some protection from predators, and gives some predator species a better chance of getting a meal.

Four variables—*births, deaths, immigration,* and *emigration*—govern changes in population size. A population increases through birth and immigration (arrival of individuals from outside the population). Populations decrease through death and emigration (departure of individuals from the population):

Population change = Individuals added − Individuals lost

Population change = (Births + Immigration)
          − (Deaths + Emigration)

A population's **age structure**—its distribution of individuals among various age groups—can have a strong effect on how rapidly it grows or declines. Age groups are usually described in terms of organisms not mature enough to reproduce (the *pre-reproductive stage*), those capable of reproduction (the *reproductive stage*), and those too old to reproduce (the *post-reproductive stage*).

The size of a population will likely increase if it is made up mostly of individuals in their reproductive stage, or soon to enter this stage. In contrast, the size of a population dominated by individuals in their post-reproductive stage will tend to decrease over time.

Sampling Populations

Population biologists and ecologists characterize ecosystems in a variety of ways. These methods can be *qualitative* such as types of species present or absent, or *quantitative* such as population size, distribution, and density of species.

Quadrat sampling is used to study a large area. The area is divided up by way of a grid pattern into many small areas of known and equal size called *quadrats*. Several quadrats are randomly chosen and their species identified and directly counted. The quadrats must be representative of the entire area being studied. From these data, the abundance, density, and distribution of species can be calculated.

For example, a scientist wishes to determine the density of ox beetles in a New Jersey grassland. She finds 185 ox beetles in 14 quadrats of 1 m × 1 m in size.

$$\text{Estimated average density of a species} = \frac{\text{total number of individuals of a species counted}}{(\text{total number of quadrats}) \times (\text{area of each quadrat})}$$

$$\text{Density} = \frac{185 \text{ ox beetles}}{14 \text{ quadrats} \times 1 \text{ m}^2} = 13.2 \text{ ox beetles/m}^2$$

Mark and recapture sampling is used to estimate the size of a population. Individuals in a defined area are captured, marked, released, and allowed to mix with the population. A second sample is captured, this time including marked and unmarked organisms. *The ratio of total organisms to marked organisms in the second capture is approximately equal to the ratio of total population to total organisms (all marked) in the first capture.*

For results to be valid, the area must be defined, there must be no appreciable loss or gain of organisms due to immigration, emigration, birth, or death during the time between taking samples, enough time must elapse so that the organisms mix thoroughly, and the organisms must not be marked in any way that makes them more or less likely to be captured randomly.

After marking and recapturing, the **Lincoln Index** is then used to estimate population size. It is the proportion described above, solved for total population:

$$\text{Total population} = \frac{(\text{number of organisms in the first sample [marked]}) \times (\text{total number or organisms in the second sample})}{\text{total number of marked organisms in the second sample}}$$

FRQ Application

Question: Scientists wish to estimate the size of a population of pupfish in a pond in Death Valley National Park. **Calculate** the size of the pupfish population using the following data:

In the first capture 30 pupfish are marked and released to the pond. In the second capture several days later, 35 pupfish are caught and 8 of these are marked.

Possible Response:

Using the Lincoln Index,

$$\text{Total population} = \frac{30 \text{ pupfish} \times 35 \text{ pupfish}}{8 \text{ marked pupfish}} = 131 \text{ pupfish}$$

Several Factors Can Limit Population Size

Each population in an ecosystem has a **range of tolerance**—a range of variations in its physical and chemical environment under which it can survive. For example, a trout population may do best within a narrow band of temperatures (*optimum level* or *range*), but a few individuals can survive above and below that band (Figure 7.15). If the water becomes too hot or too cold, none of the trout can survive.

Individuals within a population may also have slightly different tolerance ranges for temperature, other physical factors, or chemical factors. These occur because of small differences in their genetic makeup, health, and age. Such differences allow for evolution through natural selection. The individuals that have a wider tolerance for change in some factor such as temperature are more likely to survive such a change and produce offspring that can tolerate it.

Various physical or chemical factors can determine the number of organisms in a population and how fast a population grows or declines. Sometimes one or more factors, known as **limiting factors**, are more important than other factors in regulating population growth.

On land, precipitation often is the limiting factor. Low precipitation levels in desert ecosystems limit desert plant growth. Lack of key soil nutrients limits the growth of plants, which in turn limits populations of animals that eat plants, and animals that feed on such plant-eating animals.

Limiting physical factors for populations in *aquatic systems* include water temperature (Figure 7.15) and water depth and clarity (allowing for more or less sunlight). Other important factors are nutrient availability, acidity, salinity, and the level of oxygen gas in the water (dissolved oxygen content).

An additional factor that can limit the sizes of some populations is **population density**, the number of individuals in a population found within a defined area or volume. It is a measure of how crowded the members of a population are.

Density-dependent factors are variables that become more important as a population's density increases. For example, in a dense population, parasites and diseases can spread more easily, resulting in higher death rates. On the other hand, a higher population density helps sexually reproducing individuals to find mates more easily to produce offspring. Other factors such as flood, fires, landslides,

a. Clumped (elephants)

b. Uniform (creosote bush)

c. Random (dandelions)

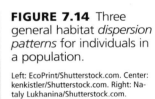

FIGURE 7.14 Three general habitat *dispersion patterns* for individuals in a population.

Left: EcoPrint/Shutterstock.com. Center: kenkistler/Shutterstock.com. Right: Nataly Lukhanina/Shutterstock.com.

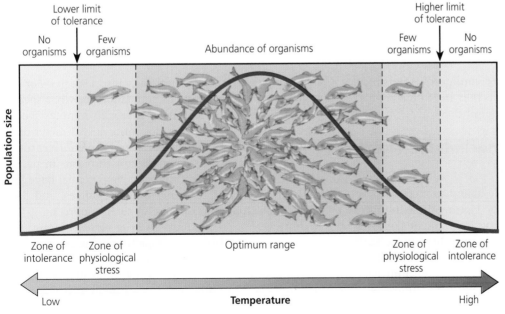

Lower limit of tolerance

Higher limit of tolerance

No organisms | Few organisms | Abundance of organisms | Few organisms | No organisms

Population size

Zone of intolerance | Zone of physiological stress | Optimum range | Zone of physiological stress | Zone of intolerance

Low | **Temperature** | High

FIGURE 7.15 Range of tolerance for a population of trout to changes in water temperature.

Calculating Population Size

The intrinsic growth rate (r) is the maximum rate at which the population of a given species can increase when there are no limits on its rate of growth. This type of growth is exponential and the *Rule of 70* can be used to calculate doubling time.

For example, the intrinsic growth rate *r* for a herd of deer in Finger Lakes National Forest is 1.9%. According to the rule, dividing 70 by the growth rate gives a good approximation of the doubling time for this population:

$$\frac{70}{1.9} = 37 \text{ years}$$

No population, however, can increase infinitely. Environmental resistance pressures such as disease, lack of food, water, dissolved oxygen, and space can limit the growth of a population. When environmental resistance is factored in, population growth will decelerate and reach carrying capacity (K). This type of growth is called *logistic* growth.

FRQ Application

The formula used to determine population size when environmental resistance is a factor is

$$\text{Total population} = n + rn\left(\frac{K-n}{K}\right)$$

where *n* = the initial population size
r = intrinsic growth rate
K = carrying capacity

A herd of deer in Finger Lakes National Forest has an intrinsic growth rate of 200 per 1000 in its population per year. Calculate *r*.

$$r = \frac{200}{1000} = 0.20, \text{ or } 20\%$$

Starting with 2100 deer and assuming no environmental resistance, what is the size of the herd after 2 years?

Year 1: 2100 + (2100 × 0.20) = 2520 deer at the end of the first year

Year 2: 2520 + (2520 × 0.20) = 3024 deer at the end of the second year

Assume that there is environmental resistance in the form of a 3500-deer carrying capacity (K) during the third year of growth of the population. Starting with the population size (n) at the end of the second year and the intrinsic growth rate (r), calculate the population size at the end of the third year.

$$\text{Total population} = 3024 + (3024 \times 0.20)\left(\frac{3500 - 3024}{3500}\right)$$

$$= 3024 + (604.8)(0.136)$$
$$= 3106 \text{ deer (to the nearest whole organism)}$$

drought, and climate change are considered *density-independent factors*, because any effects they have on a population's size are not related to its density.

No Population Can Grow Indefinitely: J-Curves and S-Curves

Some species have an incredible ability to increase their numbers and grow exponentially. Plotting these numbers against time yields a J-shaped curve of exponential growth when a population increases by a fixed percentage each year (Figure 7.16, left). Members of such populations typically reproduce at an early age, have many offspring each time they reproduce, and reproduce many times with short intervals between generations.

Examples are bacteria and many insect species. For example, with no controls on its population growth, a species of bacteria that can reproduce every 20 minutes would generate enough offspring to form a 0.3-meter-deep (1-foot-deep) layer over the surface of the entire earth in only 36 hours. Such exponential growth occurs in nature when species with a high reproductive potential have few predators, plenty of food and other resources, and little competition from other species for such resources.

However, *there are always limits to population growth in nature*. Research reveals that a rapidly growing population of any species eventually reaches some size limit imposed by limiting factors. These factors include sunlight, water, temperature, space, or nutrients, or exposure to predators or infectious diseases (**Concept 7.3**). **Environmental resistance**

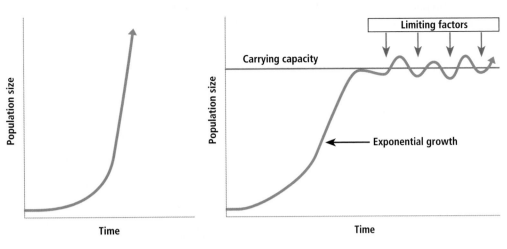

FIGURE 7.16 Populations of species can undergo *exponential growth* represented by a J-shaped curve (left) when resource supplies are plentiful. As resource supplies become limited, a population undergoes *logistic growth*, represented by an S-shaped curve (right), when the size of the population approaches the carrying capacity of its habitat.

is the sum of all such factors in a habitat. Limiting factors largely determine an area's **carrying capacity**, the maximum population of a given species that a particular habitat can sustain indefinitely. The carrying capacity for a population is not fixed and can rise or fall as environmental conditions change the factors that limit the population's growth.

As a population approaches the carrying capacity of its habitat, the J-shaped curve of its exponential growth (Figure 7.16, left) is converted to an S-shaped curve of *logistic growth*, or growth that often fluctuates around the carrying capacity of its habitat (Figure 7.16, right). The population sizes of some species often fluctuate above and below their carrying capacity as shown in the right graph in Figure 7.16.

Some populations do not make a smooth transition from exponential growth to logistic growth. Instead, they use up their resource supplies and temporarily *overshoot*, or exceed, the carrying capacity of their environment. In such cases, the population suffers a sharp decline, called a *dieback*, or **population crash**, unless part of the population can switch to new resources or move to an area that has more resources. Such a crash occurred when reindeer were introduced onto a small island in the Bering Sea in the early 1900s (Figure 7.17).

Reproductive Patterns

Species vary in their reproductive patterns. Species with a capacity for a high rate of population growth (r) (Figure 7.16, left) are called **r-selected species**. These species tend to have short life spans and produce many, usually small offspring and give them little or no parental care. As a result, many of the offspring die at an early age. To overcome such losses, r-selected species produce large numbers of offspring so that a few will likely survive and have many offspring to sustain the species. Examples of r-selected species include algae, bacteria, frogs, most insects, and many fish.

Such species tend to be *opportunists*. They reproduce and disperse rapidly when conditions are favorable or when a disturbance such as a fire or clear-cutting of a forest opens up a new habitat or niches for invasion. Once established, their populations may crash because of unfa-

vorable changes in environmental conditions or invasion by more competitive species. This explains why many opportunist species go through irregular and unstable boom-and-bust cycles in their population sizes.

At the other extreme are **K-selected species**. They tend to reproduce later in life, have few offspring, and have long life spans. Typically, the offspring of K-selected mammal species develop inside their mothers (where they are safe) and are born relatively large. After birth, they mature slowly and are cared for and protected by one or both parents. In some cases, they live in herds or groups until they reach reproductive age.

Such a species' population size tends to be near the carrying capacity (K) of its environment (Figure 7.16, right). Examples of K-selected species include most large mammals such as elephants, whales, and humans, birds of prey, and large and long-lived plants such as the saguaro cactus, and most tropical rain forest trees. Many of these species—especially those with low reproductive rates,

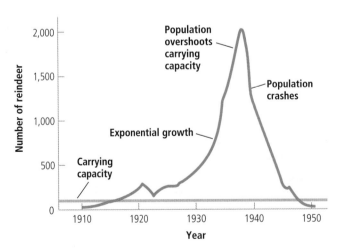

FIGURE 7.17 Exponential growth, overshoot, and population crash of a population of reindeer introduced onto the small Bering Sea island of St. Paul in 1910. **Data analysis:** By what percentage did the population of reindeer grow between 1923 and 1940?

such as elephants, sharks, giant redwood trees, and California's southern sea otters (**Core Case Study** and Science Focus 7.2)—are vulnerable to extinction.

Table 7.1 compares typical traits of *r*-selected and *K*-selected species. Most species have reproductive patterns and traits between the extremes of *r*-selected and *K*-selected species. The population size of a species can drop to a point, called its *minimum viable population*, below which it cannot survive in the wild.

The reproductive pattern of a species may give it a temporary advantage. However, the key factor in determining the ultimate population size of a species is the availability of suitable habitat with adequate resources.

Changes in habitat or other environmental conditions can reduce the populations of some species while increasing the populations of other species, such as white-tailed deer in the United States (see the following Case Study).

CASE STUDY

Exploding White-Tailed Deer Populations in the United States

By 1900, habitat destruction and uncontrolled hunting had reduced the white-tailed deer (Figure 7.18) population in the United States to about 500,000 animals. In the 1920s and 1930s, laws were passed to protect the remaining deer. Hunting was restricted and predators, including wolves and mountain lions that preyed on the deer, were nearly eliminated.

These protections worked, and for some suburbanites and farmers, perhaps too well. Today there are over 30 mil-

FIGURE 7.18 White-tailed deer populations in the United States have been growing.

lion white-tailed deer in the United States. During the last 50 years, suburbs have expanded and many Americans have moved into the wooded habitat of deer. The gardens and landscaping around their homes provide deer with flowers, shrubs, garden crops, and other plants they like to eat.

Deer prefer to live in the edge areas of forests and woodlots for security and go to nearby fields, orchards, lawns, and gardens for food. A suburban neighborhood can be an all-you-can-eat paradise for white-tailed deer, and their populations in such areas have soared.

In woodlands, deer are consuming native ground-cover vegetation, which has allowed nonnative weed species to take over and upset ecosystem food webs. The deer also help to spread Lyme disease (carried by deer ticks) to humans. In addition, each year about 1 million deer–vehicle collisions injure up to 10,000 Americans and kill at least 200—the highest human death toll from encounters with any wild animal in the United States.

There are no easy solutions to the deer population problem in the suburbs. Changes in hunting regulations that allow for the killing of more female deer have cut down the overall deer population. However, this has had a limited effect on deer populations in suburban areas because it is too dangerous to allow widespread hunting with guns in such populated communities. Some areas have hired experienced and licensed archers who use bows and arrows to help reduce deer numbers. To protect nearby residents the archers hunt from elevated tree stands and only shoot their arrows downward.

Some communities spray the scent of deer predators or of rotting deer meat in edge areas to scare off deer. Others

TABLE 7.1 Typical traits of *r*-selected and *K*-selected species

Trait	*r*-Selected Species	*K*-Selected Species
Reproductive potential	High	Low
Population growth rate	Fast	Slow
Time to reproductive maturity	Short	Long
Number of reproductive cycles	Many	Few
Number of offspring	Many	Few
Size of offspring	Small	Larger
Degree of parental care	Low	High
Life span	Short	Long
Population size	Variable with crashes	Stable, near carrying capacity
Role in environment	Usually prey	Usually predators

The Future of California's Southern Sea Otters

The population of southern sea otters (**Core Case Study**) has fluctuated in response to changes in environmental conditions (Figure 7.B). One change is a rise in populations of the orcas (killer whales) that feed on them. Scientists hypothesize that orcas started feeding more on southern sea otters when populations of their normal prey, sea lions and seals, began declining. In addition, between 2010 and 2012 the number of sea otters killed or injured by sharks increased, possibly because warmer ocean water brought some sharks closer to the shore.

Another factor affecting sea otters may be parasites that breed in the intestines of cats. Scientists hypothesize that some southern sea otters are dying because cat owners flush feces-laden cat litter down their toilets or dump it in storm drains that empty into coastal waters where parasites from the litter can infect otters.

Toxic algae blooms also threaten otters. The algae thrive on urea, a nitrogen-containing ingredient in fertilizer that washes into coastal waters. Other pollutants released by human activities are PCBs and other fat-soluble toxic chemicals. These chemicals can kill otters by accumulating to high levels in the tissues of the shellfish that otters eat. Because southern sea otters feed at high trophic levels and live close to the shore, they are vulnerable to these and other pollutants in coastal waters.

Other threats to otters include oil spills from ships. The entire California southern sea otter population could be wiped out by a large oil spill from a single tanker off the central west coast or by the rupture of an offshore oil well, should drilling for oil be allowed off this coast. Some sea otters die when they are trapped in un-

derwater nets and traps for shellfish. Others are killed by boat strikes and gunshots.

The factors listed here, mostly resulting from human activities, together with a low reproductive rate and a rising mortality rate, have hindered the ability of the endangered southern sea otter to rebuild its population (Figure 7.B).

Since 2012, the sea otter population has increased, possibly because of an increase in the population of sea urchins, their preferred prey. In 2017, the sea otter population was 3,511, the highest it has been since 1987. If the sea otter population exceeds 3,090 for three consecutive years, it may be removed from the endangered species list. If this happens, the otters will still be protected under a California state law.

FIGURE 7.B
Changes in the population size of southern sea otters off the coast of the US state of California, 1983–2017.

(Compiled by the authors using data from US Geological Survey.)

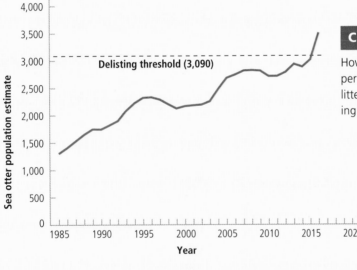

CRITICAL THINKING

How would you design a controlled experiment to test the hypothesis that cat litter flushed down toilets might be killing southern sea otters?

scare off deer by using electronic equipment that emits high-frequency sounds that humans cannot hear. Some homeowners surround their gardens and yards with high, black plastic mesh fencing.

Deer can be trapped and moved from one area to another, but this is expensive and must be repeated whenever they move back into an area. In addition, there are questions concerning where to move the deer and how to pay for such programs.

Darts loaded with contraceptives can be shot into female deer to hold down their birth rates, but this is expensive and

must be repeated every year. One possibility is an experimental, single-shot contraceptive vaccine that lasts for several years. Another approach is to trap dominant males and use chemical injections to sterilize them. Both of these approaches are costly and will require years of testing.

Meanwhile, suburbanites can expect deer to chow down on their shrubs, flowers, and garden plants unless they can protect their properties with fences, repellents, or other methods. Suburban dwellers could also stop planting trees, shrubs, and flowers that attract deer around their homes.

Some people blame the white-tailed deer for invading farms and suburban yards and gardens to eat food that humans have made easily available to them. Others say humans are mostly to blame because they have invaded deer territory, eliminated most of the predators that kept deer populations under control, and provided the deer with plenty to eat in their lawns, gardens, and crop fields. Which view do you hold? Why? Do you see a solution to this problem?

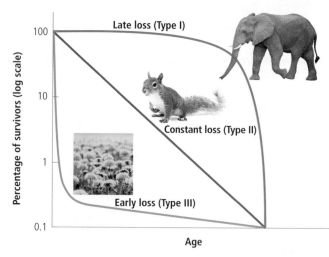

FIGURE 7.19 Survivorship curves for populations of different species, obtained by showing the percentages of the members of a population surviving at different ages.

Top: Gualtiero boffi/Shutterstock.com. Center: IrinaK/Shutterstock.com. Bottom: ultimathule/Shutterstock.com.

Species Vary in Their Life Spans

Individuals of species with different reproductive strategies tend to have different *life expectancies*. This can be illustrated by a **survivorship curve**, which shows the percentages of the members of a population surviving at different ages. There are three generalized types of survivorship curves: late loss (Type I), constant loss (Type II), and early loss (Type III) (Figure 7.19). A *late loss* population (*K*-selected species such as elephants and rhinoceroses) typically has high survivorship to a certain age, and then high mortality. A *constant loss* population (such as many songbirds) typically has a constant death rate at all ages. For an *early loss* population (many *r*-selected species and annual plants), survivorship is low early in life. These generalized survivorship curves only approximate the realities of nature.

Which type of survivorship curve applies to the human species?

Humans Are Not Exempt from Nature's Population Controls

Humans are not exempt from population crashes. In 1845 Ireland experienced such a crash after a fungus destroyed its potato crop. About 1 million people died from hunger or diseases related to malnutrition. Millions more migrated to other countries, sharply reducing the Irish population.

During the 14th century, *bubonic plague* spread through densely populated European cities and killed at least 25 million people—one-third of the European population. The bacterium that causes this disease normally lives in rodents. It was transferred to humans by fleas that fed on infected rodents and then bit humans. The disease spread like wildfire through crowded cities, where sanitary conditions were poor and rats were abundant. Today several antibiotics can be used to treat bubonic plague.

So far, technological, social, and other cultural changes have expanded the earth's carrying capacity for the human species. We have used large amounts of energy and matter resources to occupy formerly uninhabitable areas. We have expanded agriculture and controlled the popula-

tions of other species that compete with us for resources. Some say we can keep expanding our ecological footprint in this way indefinitely because of our technological ingenuity. Others say that at some point, we will reach the limits that nature eventually imposes on any population that exceeds or degrades its resource base.

CHECKPOINT FOR UNDERSTANDING 7.3

1. Identify several benefits of organisms living in groups. Identify several disadvantages.

KEY IDEAS

- Certain interactions among species affect their use of resources and their population sizes.
- The species composition and population sizes of a community or ecosystem can change in response to changing environmental conditions through a process called *ecological succession*.
- No population can escape natural limiting factors and grow indefinitely.

Core Case Study Checkpoint

Explain how the recovery of the southern sea otter as a keystone species illustrates the importance of humans working to sustain the earth's biodiversity.

age structure: distribution of individuals in a population among various age groups.

carrying capacity: maximum population of a particular species that a given habitat can support over a given period.

coevolution: evolution in which two or more species interact and exert selective pressures on each other that can lead each species to undergo adaptations.

commensalism: an interaction between organisms of different species in which one type of organism benefits and the other type is neither helped nor harmed to any great degree.

ecological succession: process in which communities of plant and animal species in a particular area are replaced over time by a series of different often more complex communities.

environmental resistance: all of the limiting factors that act together to limit the growth of a population.

interspecific competition: attempts by members of two or more species to use the same limited resources in an ecosystem.

***K*-selected species:** organisms that reproduce later in life, have few offspring and invest energy in raising and nurturing those offspring, and have long lifespans.

limiting factor: single factor that limits the growth, abundance, or

distribution of a population of a species in an ecosystem.

mutualism: type of species interaction in which both participating species generally benefit.

parasitism: interaction between species in which one organism, called the parasite, preys on another organism, called the host, by living on or in the host.

persistence: ability of a living system such as a grassland or forest to survive moderate disturbances.

pioneer species: first hardy species—often microbes, mosses, and lichens—that begin colonizing a site as the first stage of ecological succession.

population: group of individual organisms of the same species living in a particular area.

population density: number of organisms in a particular population found in a specified area or volume.

population size: number of individuals making up a population's gene pool.

predator: organism that captures and feeds on some or all parts of an organism of another species (the prey).

predator–prey relationship: relationship that has evolved between two organisms, in which one organism has becomes the prey for the other, the latter called the predator.

prey: organism that is killed by an organism of another species (the

predator) and serves as its source of food.

primary ecological succession: ecological succession in an area without soil or bottom sediments.

range of tolerance: range of chemical and physical conditions that must be maintained for populations of a particular species to stay alive and grow, develop, and function normally.

resilience: ability of a living system such as a forest or pond to be restored through secondary ecological succession after a severe disturbance.

resource partitioning: process of dividing up resources in an ecosystem so that species with similar needs (overlapping ecological niches) use the same scarce resources at different times, in different ways, or in different places.

***r*-selected species:** organisms that have short lifespans, produce many, usually small offspring to which they give little or no parental care.

secondary ecological succession: ecological succession in an area in which natural vegetation has been removed or destroyed but the soil or bottom sediment has not been destroyed.

survivorship curve: graph showing the number of survivors in different age groups for a particular species.

Chapter Review

Core Case Study

1. Explain how southern sea otters act as a keystone species in their environment. Explain why we should care about protecting this species from extinction.

Section 7.1

2. (a) What is the key concept for this section?
   (b) Define and give an example of **interspecific**

competition. How is it different from intraspecific competition? (c) Define and give an example of **resource partitioning** and explain how it can increase species diversity. (d) Define **predation**. Distinguish between a **predator** species and a **prey** species and give an example of each. What is a **predator–prey relationship** and why is it important?

3. (a) Describe three threats to kelp forests and explain why they should be preserved. (b) List three ways in which predators can increase their chances of feeding on their prey and three ways in which prey species can avoid their predators. (c) Define and give an example of **coevolution**.

4. Define **parasitism**, **mutualism**, and **commensalism** and give an example of each. Explain how each of these species interactions, along with predation, can affect the population sizes of species in ecosystems.

Section 7.2

5. (a) What is the key concept for this section? (b) What is **ecological succession**? Distinguish between **primary ecological succession** and **secondary ecological succession** and give an example of each. (c) Describe three factors that affect how and at what rate succession occurs.

6. (a) Explain why ecological succession does not follow a predictable path and does not necessarily end with a stable climax community. (b) What is the current thinking among ecologists on the concept of a balance of nature? (c) In terms of the stability of ecosystems, distinguish between **inertia (persistence)** and **resilience** and give an example of each.

Section 7.3

7. (a) What is the key concept for this section? (b) Define **population**. Define **population size** and

explain how it is estimated, Why do most populations live in clumps? (c) List four variables that govern changes in population size. Write an equation showing how these variables interact. (d) Define **range of tolerance**. (e) Define **limiting factor** and give three examples. Define **population density** and explain how some limiting factors can become more important as a population's density increases.

8. (a) Distinguish between the exponential and logistic growth of a population and describe the nature of their growth curves. (b) Define **environmental resistance**. What is the **carrying capacity** of an environment? Define and give an example of a **population crash**.

9. (a) Describe two different reproductive strategies for species. (b) Distinguish between *r*-selected species and *K*-selected species and give an example of each. (c) What factors have hindered the recovery of the southern sea otter? (d) Describe the effects of the exploding population of white-tailed deer in the United States and list some possible solutions to this problem. (e) Define **survivorship curve**, describe three types of curves, and for each, give an example of a species that fits that pattern. (f) Explain why humans are not exempt from nature's population controls.

10. What are this chapter's *three key ideas*?

_____

Note: Key terms are in bold type.

AP® Review Questions

Questions 1–4 refer to the species interactions below. Choices may be used once, more than once, or not at all.

  (A) Interspecific competition
  (B) Predation
  (C) Parasitism
  (D) Mutualism
  (E) Commensalism

1. Dandelions, common carpet grass, and grass burrs are all present in the same homeowner's lawn. They all have access to the same soil nutrients and same amount of water. All are striving to survive and reproduce.

2. A species of ant living in the thorns of various species of the acacia tree help protect the tree from herbivores while feeding off of the lipid- and carbohydrate-rich extra-floral nectar on the tree.

3. Barnacles are organisms that adhere to the skin of a whale. The barnacles benefit by being transported to new sources of food while the whale does not appear to be affected in any way by their presence.

4. A species of pseudoscorpion disperses by concealing itself under the wings of large beetles. The pseudoscorpions gain the advantage of being dispersed over wide areas while being protected from predators. The beetle is unaffected by the presence of the hitchhikers.

Questions 5–7 refer to the terms listed below. Choices may be used once, more than once, or not at all.

    (A) Environmental resistance
    (B) Intrinsic rate of growth
    (C) Minimum viable population
    (D) Carrying capacity
    (E) Logistic growth

5. The capacity for growth of a population under ideal conditions

6. The sum of all ecological factors that tend to limit the biotic potential of a species; examples include precipitation, predation, and disease

7. The lowest number of a species that can continue to survive in its natural habitat

Questions 8 and 9 refer to the graph below of an otter population off the coast of California.

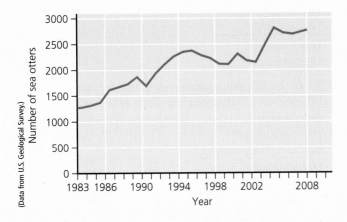

8. What generalized trend is observed from 1983 to 2007 on this graph?
    (A) The otter population is declining more than it is increasing.
    (B) The otter population is growing at an exponential rate.
    (C) The otter population has reached its carrying capacity.
    (D) The otter population is showing a slow rate of increase.
    (E) The otter is an endangered species.

9. Calculate the percent decrease in the otter population from 1995 to 2000.
    (A) 0.13%
    (B) 13%
    (C) 30%
    (D) 87%
    (E) 300%

10. Which of the following is a good example of coevolution?
    (A) Oxpeckers are birds that eat ticks and flies off the backs of elephants. The oxpeckers benefit from the ready food source; the elephants benefit by having parasites and pests removed.
    (B) The sea lamprey attaches itself to fish for nourishment in the Great Lakes. The lamprey benefits from the food source while causing physical damage, and often eventual death, to its host.
    (C) Bromeliads are tropical plants that attach themselves to tropical trees to gather sunlight, water, and nutrients. They have no discernible effect on the trees.
    (D) Common garter snake populations have evolved a resistance to the toxins of their prey, newts of the genus *Taricha*. As the newt populations change over time and produce more potent toxins, the garter snake populations also gradually change and have an increased resistance to the new toxins.
    (E) Several species of birds, all feeding on similar insects found in the same species of tree, evolve traits that enable them to either eat at different levels of the tree or that allow them to survive on different prey species.

11. All of the following have contributed to the population explosion of whitetail deer EXCEPT
    (A) elimination of many of their natural predators
    (B) deliberate provision of deer feed in states where this is legal
    (C) creation of many edge habitats due to suburbanization
    (D) trapping of deer and moving them out of areas where they are not wanted
    (E) planting urban and suburban properties with edible flowers and shrubs

12. Population change can be determined by which of the following equations?
    (A) Population change = (births + deaths) − (immigration + emigration)
    (B) Population change = (births + immigration) − (deaths + emigration)
    (C) Population change = (births + deaths) + (immigration + emigration)
    (D) Population change = (births + deaths) − (immigration + emigration)
    (E) Population change = (births − immigration) + (deaths − emigration)

Question 13 refers to the graph below.

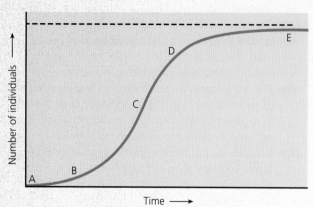

13. Which point on the curve above reflects a population that has reached carrying capacity due to some limiting factor?

14. Which of the following scenarios represents a habitat that will begin to undergo the process of secondary succession?
    (A) A boulder field left behind due to the retreat of a glacier
    (B) Recently cooled lava from a volcanic eruption
    (C) An agricultural field recently harvested and left unplanted
    (D) An island that forms due to the recent eruption of an undersea volcano
    (E) Bare rock exposed on a mountainside after an avalanche

15. All of the following are true of climax communities EXCEPT
    (A) they are the endpoint of a series of competitive exclusion events
    (B) they are composed of a complex group of interacting organisms
    (C) they are typically dominated by a specific group of long-lived plant communities
    (D) they are considered to be mid-successional communities
    (E) they are a relatively stable community that typically remains in balance, unless there is a disturbance

16. Population growth is controlled both by factors that are density-dependent and those that are density-independent. Which of the following is an example of a density-independent method of population control?
    (A) Bald eagles feed on salmon in the rivers of Canada and Alaska.
    (B) Oak blight is a fungus that spreads from oak tree to oak tree, killing most in its path.
    (C) A hurricane directly hits a tide pool community on the coast.
    (D) An enclosed pasture has only one water source that produces 20 gallons per day for all consumers that live in the pasture.
    (E) Bighorn sheep often catch a deadly strain of bacterial pneumonia carried by domestic sheep (which are typically immune to it).

17. Which population distribution type would provide the most protection from predators?
    (A) Uniform
    (B) Exponential
    (C) Random
    (D) Logistic
    (E) Clumped

18. All of the following methods are used by predators to increase their chances of capturing prey EXCEPT
    (A) pursuit
    (B) camouflage
    (C) chemical warfare
    (D) ambush
    (E) warning coloration

19. When lions and leopards live in the same area, lions take mostly larger animals as prey and leopards take smaller ones to avoid direct competition. This is referred to as
    (A) resource partitioning
    (B) symbiosis
    (C) commensalism
    (D) mutualism
    (E) predator-prey competition

Question 20 refers to the chart below.

Fish species	Lowest optimum temperature °F	Highest optimum temperature °F
Lake trout	39	64
Rainbow trout	54	64
Cutthroat trout	48	54
Brook trout	52	61
Brown trout	54	66

Data from http://thescientificfisherman.com/wp-content/uploads/2013/05/optimum-ranges-f.jpg

20. Water temperature has a direct effect on the amount of dissolved oxygen in the water. As the water temperature increases, the amount of dissolved oxygen decreases. Based on this information and the range of temperature tolerances in the chart above, which species of trout requires the highest amount of dissolved oxygen, assuming all other factors are constant?
(A) Lake trout
(B) Rainbow trout
(C) Cutthroat trout
(D) Brook trout
(E) Brown trout

AP® Free-Response Practice

1. The graph to the right shows the relationship between a predator population (eagle) and prey population (trout) on Sanibel Island, Florida. Refer to the graph to answer the following questions.

   (a) **Explain** the oscillations of Line A and Line B in terms of the predator-prey relationship exemplified by this graph.

      (i) **Discuss** why the prey species total population size tends to increase and decrease more rapidly than the predator species.

      (ii) **Discuss** why the oscillations on the graph do not rise and fall in tandem.

   (b) *r*-selected species tend to take advantage of available resources and display exponential growth.

      (i) **Identify** the *r*-selected species from the graph and **discuss** THREE characteristics of *r*-selected species that explain their reproductive strategy.

      (ii) **Explain** why *r*-selected species populations cannot grow indefinitely.

   (c) *K*-selected species display logistic growth.

      (i) **Identify** the *K*-selected species from the graph and **discuss** THREE characteristics of *K*-selected species that explain their reproductive strategy.

      (ii) **Provide** ONE example of environmental resistance that would slow the growth of the species as it approaches carrying capacity.

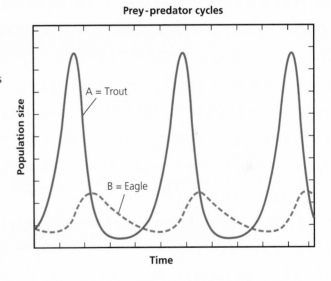

Prey-predator cycles

A = Trout
B = Eagle
Population size
Time

Critical Thinking

1. What difference would it make if the southern sea otter (**Core Case Study**) became extinct primarily because of human activities? What are three things we could do to help prevent the extinction of this species?

2. Use the second law of thermodynamics (Chapter 2, p. 50) and the concept of food chains and food webs to explain why predators are generally less abundant than their prey.

3. How would you reply to someone who argues that we should not worry about the effects that human activities have on natural systems because ecological succession will repair whatever damage we do?

4. How would you reply to someone who contends that efforts to preserve species and ecosystems are not worthwhile because nature is largely unpredictable?

5. What is the reproductive strategy of most species of insect pests and harmful bacteria? Why does this make it difficult for us to control their populations?

6. If the earth's climate continues to change due to atmospheric warming during this century, as most climate scientists project it will, is this likely to favor *r*-selected or *K*-selected species? Explain.

7. List two factors that may limit human population growth in the future. Do you think that we are close to reaching those limits? Explain.

8. If the human species were to suffer a population crash, name three species that might move in to occupy part of our ecological niche. What are three species that would likely decline as a result? Explain why these other species would decline.

Data Analysis

The graph below shows changes in the size of an Emperor penguin population in terms of numbers of breeding pairs on the island of Terre Adelie in the Antarctic. Scientists used this data along with data on the penguins' shrinking ice habitat to project a general decline in the island's Emperor penguin population, to the point where they will be endangered in 2100. Use the graph to answer the following questions.

1. If the penguin population fluctuates around the carrying capacity, what was the approximate carrying capacity of the island for the penguin population from 1960 to 1975? What was the approximate carrying capacity of the island for the penguin population from 1980 to 2010?

2. What was the overall percentage decline in the penguin population from 1975 to 2010?

3. What is the projected overall percentage decline in the penguin population between 2010 and 2100?

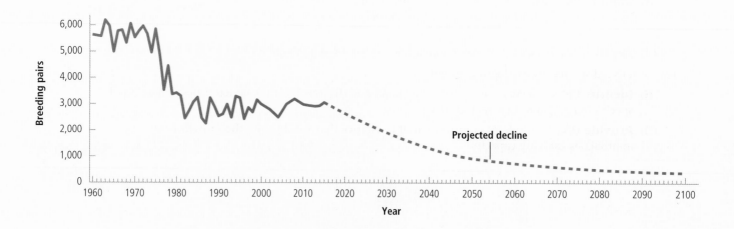

Answers to Checkpoints for Understanding

Section 7.1

1. An interspecific relationship occurs between populations of two different species competing for the same resource. No two species can compete indefinitely. Therefore, if one species is a better competitor, the other species will be obligated to migrate or adapt (resource partitioning is a kind of adaptation), and if neither of these is possible, the species may go extinct.

2. The three types of symbiotic relationships are mutualism, commensalism, and parasitism. These are long-term close relationships between two organisms. Predator–prey relationships are short term in that they involve short-term or indirect contact where they prey serves as a resource for the predator.

Section 7.2

1. Because tropical rainforests have high biodiversity, it is easy for them to recover from moderate disturbances. However, once a tipping point is reached, that is a severe disturbance occurs such as clear-cutting the forest, it is very difficult for the forest to recover. Most nutrients are held in the plant bodies and not in the soil so regeneration of tropical plant species is difficult.

Section 7.3

1. Benefits of living in groups include protection from predators and a greater ability to find a suitable mate. Disadvantages include spread of disease and parasites between individuals, and competition within the population for food and other resources.

Core Case Study

The southern sea otter is a keystone species that keeps sea urchin populations in check. This is important because if sea urchins did not have otters as a predator, they would decimate kelp forests that are habitat to many marine organisms.

The Human Population

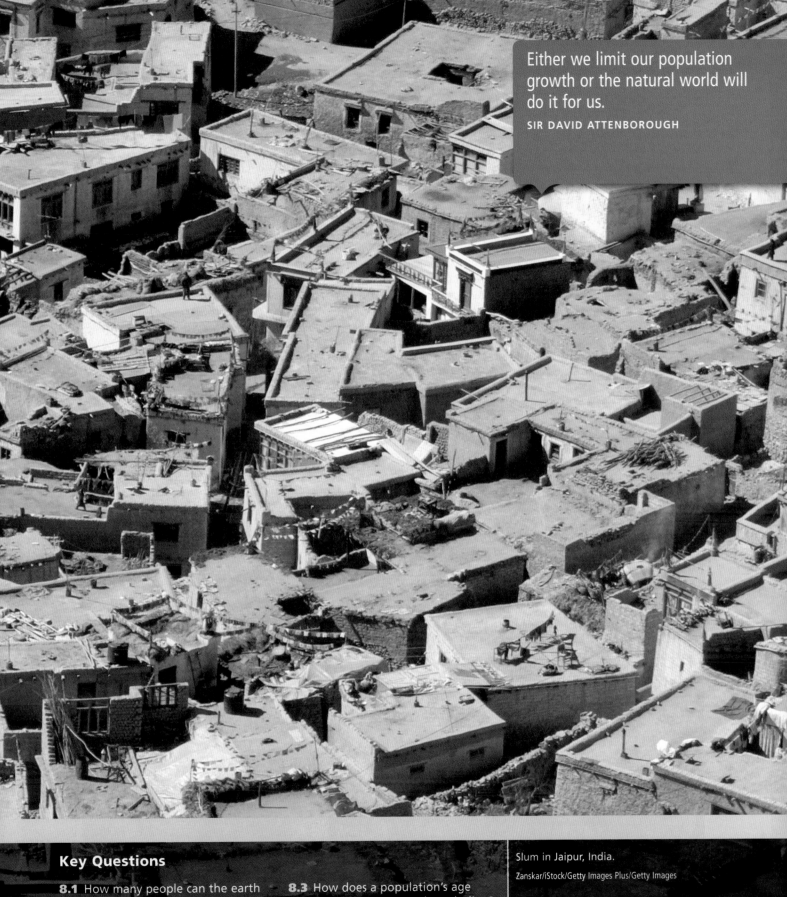

Either we limit our population growth or the natural world will do it for us.
SIR DAVID ATTENBOROUGH

Key Questions

8.1 How many people can the earth support?

8.2 What factors influence the size of the human population?

8.3 How does a population's age structure affect its growth or decline?

8.4 How can we slow human population growth?

205

Planet Earth: Population 7.5 Billion

It took about 200,000 years—from the time that the latest version of our species *Homo sapiens sapiens* evolved to the 1920s—for our population to reach an estimated 2 billion. It took less than 50 years to add the second 2 billion people (by about 1974), and 25 years to add the third 2 billion (by 1999). Eighteen years later, in 2017, the earth had 7.5 billion people. Figure 1.9 (p. 15) lists the world's 10 most populous countries. In 2017 the top three, in order, were China with 1.39 billion people (Figure 8.1), India with 1.35 billion people, and the United States with 325 million people.

Does it matter that there are now 7.5 billion people on the earth—almost three times as many as there were in 1950? Does it matter that each day, 249,000 more people show up for dinner and many of them will go hungry? Some say it does

not matter, and they contend that we can develop new technologies that could easily support billions more people.

Many scientists disagree and argue that the current exponential growth of the human population (see Figure 1.9, p. 15) is unsustainable. The reason is that as our population grows, we use more of the earth's natural resources and our ecological footprints expand and degrade the natural capital that keeps us alive and supports our lifestyles and economies.

According to *demographers*, or population experts, three major factors account for the rapid rise of the human population. *First*, the emergence of early and modern agriculture about 10,000 years ago increased food production. *Second*, additional technologies helped humans expand into almost all of the planet's climate zones and habitats (see Figure 1.8,

p. 12). *Third*, death rates dropped sharply with improved sanitation and health care and the development of antibiotics and vaccines to control infectious diseases.

What is a sustainable level for the human population? Population experts have made low, medium, and high projections of the human population size by the end of this century, as shown in Figure 1.9, p. 15. No one knows whether any of these population sizes are sustainable or for how long.

In this chapter, we examine population growth trends, the environmental impacts of the growing population, and proposals for dealing with human population growth and decline. ●

CRITICAL THINKING

How would a declining death rate influence a rapid rise in human population?

MACDUFF EVERTON/National Geographic Creative

FIGURE 8.1 This crowded street is located in China, where almost one-fifth of the world's people live.

8.1 HOW MANY PEOPLE CAN THE EARTH SUPPORT?

CONCEPT 8.1 The rapid growth of the human population and its impact on natural capital raises questions about how long the human population can keep growing.

Human Population Growth

For most of history, the human population grew slowly (see Figure 1.9, p. 15, left part of curve). However, it has grown rapidly for the last 200 years, resulting in the characteristic J-curve of exponential growth (Figure 1.9, p. 15, right part of curve).

Demographers recognize three important trends related to the current size, growth rate, and distribution of the human population. *First*, the rate of population growth decreased in most years since 1965, slowing to 1.21%, but the world's population is still growing (Figure 8.2). This growth rate may not seem very high, but in 2017 it added about 91 million people to the population—an average of 249,000 people every day. In 2016 China had 18% of the world's population and was growing at a rate of 0.5% a year, India had 18% and was growing at 1.3% a year, and the United States with 4.4% was growing at 0.8% a year.

Second, human population growth is unevenly distributed and this pattern is expected to continue (Figure 8.3). About 2% of the 91 million new arrivals on the planet in 2017 were added to the world's more-developed countries. The other 98% were added to the world's less-developed countries.

At least 95% of the 2.4 billion people projected to be added to the world's population between 2017 and 2050 will be born into the less-developed countries. Most of these countries are not equipped to deal with the pressures of rapid population growth.

The *third* important trend is large numbers of people moving from rural areas to *urban areas*, or cities and their surrounding suburbs. In 2017, 55% of the world's people lived in urban areas, and this percentage is increasing. Most of these urban dwellers live in less-developed countries where resources for dealing with rapidly growing populations are limited.

Scientists and other analysts have long pondered the question: How long can the human population continue to grow while sidestepping many of the factors that sooner or later limit the growth of any population? These experts

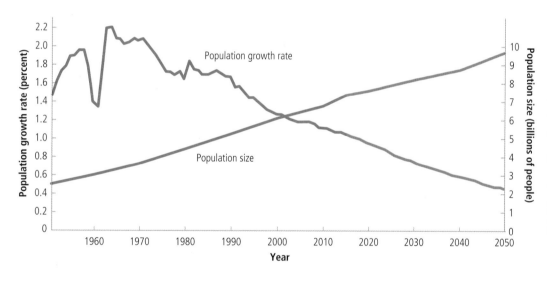

FIGURE 8.2 Global human population size compared with population growth rate, 1950–2017, with projection to 2050 (in blue). **Critical thinking:** Why do you think that while the annual growth *rate* of world population has generally dropped since the 1960s, the population has continued to grow?

(Compiled by the authors using data from United Nations Population Division, U.S. Census Bureau, and Population Reference Bureau.)

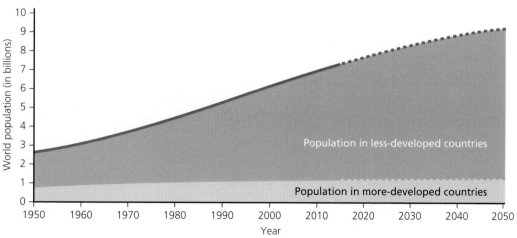

FIGURE 8.3 Most of the world's population growth between 1950 and 2017 took place in the world's less-developed countries. This gap is projected to increase between 2017 and 2050.

(Compiled by the authors using data from United Nations Population Division and Population Reference Bureau.)

How Long Can the Human Population Keep Growing?

Are there physical limits to human population growth and economic growth on a finite planet? Some say yes. Others say no. This debate has been going on since 1798 when Thomas Malthus, a British economist, hypothesized that the human population tends to grow exponentially, while food supplies tend to increase more slowly at a linear rate. However, food production has grown at an exponential rate instead of at a linear rate because of technological advances in industrialized food production.

One current view is that we have already exceeded some of those limits, with too many people collectively degrading the earth's life-support system (see Science Focus 3.2, p. 81). To some analysts, the key problem is the large and rapidly growing number of people in less-developed countries, which have 83% of the world's population. To others, the key factor is *overconsumption* in affluent, more-developed countries with high rates of resource use per person.

Another view of population growth is that technology has allowed us to overcome the environmental limits that all populations of other species face. According to this view, technological advances have increased the earth's carrying capacity for the human species. Some analysts point out that average life expectancy in most of the world has been steadily rising despite warnings from some environmental scientists that we are seriously degrading our life-support system.

These analysts argue that because of our technological ingenuity, there are few, if any, limits to human population growth and resource use per person.

They believe that we can continue increasing economic growth and avoid serious damage to our life-support systems by making technological advances in areas such as food production and medicine, and by finding substitutes for resources that we are depleting. They see no need to slow the world's population growth or resource consumption.

Proponents of slowing or stopping population growth point out that currently, we are failing to provide the basic necessities for about 1 billion people—one of every seven on the planet—who struggle to survive on the equivalent of about $1.90 per day. This raises a serious question: How will we meet the basic needs of the additional 2.4 billion people projected to be added mostly to less-developed countries between 2017 and 2050?

Proponents of slowing population growth warn of two potentially serious consequences if we do not sharply lower birth rates. First, death rates could increase because of declining health and environmental conditions and increasing social disruption in some areas, as is happening today in parts of Africa. A worst-case scenario for such a trend is a crash of the human population from an estimated 9.8 billion to a more sustainable level of 4 billion or perhaps as low as 2 billion.

Second, resource use and degradation of normally renewable resources may intensify as more consumers increase their already large ecological

footprints in more-developed countries and in rapidly developing countries such as China, India, and Brazil.

So far, advances in food production and health care have prevented widespread population declines. But there is extensive and growing evidence that we are steadily depleting and degrading much of the earth's irreplaceable natural capital. We can get away with this for a while, because the earth's life-support system is resilient. However, such disturbances could reach various *tipping points* beyond which there could be damaging and long-lasting change. (see Science Focus 3.2, p. 81).

No one knows how close we are to environmental limits that, many scientists say, eventually will control the size of the human population primarily by raising the human death rate. These analysts call for us to confront this scientific, political, economic, and ethical issue.

CRITICAL THINKING

Do you think there are environmental limits to human population growth? Explain. If so, how close do you think we are to such limits? Explain.

2.4 billion
Projected increase in the world's population between 2017 and 2050

---

disagree over how many people the earth can support indefinitely (Science Focus 8.1).

Human Population Growth and Natural Capital

As the human population grows, so does the global human ecological footprint (see Figure 1.8, p. 12), and the bigger this footprint, the higher the overall impact of

humanity on the earth's natural capital. Research indicates that human activities have degraded about 60% of the earth's ecosystem services (Figure 8.4).

Some say that asking how many people the earth the can support indefinitely is asking the wrong question. Instead, they call for us to estimate the planet's **cultural carrying capacity**—the maximum number of people who could live in reasonable freedom and comfort indefinitely, without decreasing the ability of the earth to sustain future generations.

Altering Nature to Meet Our Needs

Reducing biodiversity

Increasing use of net primary productivity

Increasing genetic resistance in pest species and disease-causing bacteria

Eliminating many natural predators

Introducing harmful species into natural communities

Using some renewable resources faster than they can be replenished

Disrupting natural chemical cycling and energy flow

Relying mostly on polluting and climate-changing fossil fuels

FIGURE 8.4 Humans have altered the natural systems that sustain their lives and economies in at least eight major ways to meet the increasing needs and wants of their growing population (**Concept 8.1**). ***Critical thinking:*** In your daily living, do you think you contribute directly or indirectly to any of these harmful environmental impacts? Which ones? Explain.

Top: Dirk Ercken/Shutterstock.com. Center: Fulcanelli/Shutterstock.com. Bottom: Werner Stoffberg/Shutterstock.com.

CHECKPOINT FOR UNDERSTANDING 8.1

1. Explain why, if the human population is growing exponentially, we have not outstripped food production when there is a finite amount of arable land.

8.2 WHAT FACTORS INFLUENCE THE SIZE OF THE HUMAN POPULATION?

CONCEPT 8.2A Population size increases through births and immigration, and decreases through deaths and emigration.

CONCEPT 8.2B Many factors affect birth rates and death rates and the size of the human population, but the key factor is the average number of children born to the women in the population (*total fertility rate*).

The Human Population Can Grow, Decline, or Stabilize

The basics of global population change are simple. When there are more births than deaths, the human population increases; when there are more deaths than births, the population decreases. When the number of births equals the number of deaths, population size does not change.

Instead of using the total numbers of births and deaths per year, demographers use the **crude birth rate** (the number of live births per 1,000 people in a population in a given year) and the **crude death rate** (the number of deaths per 1,000 people in a population in a given year).

The human population in a particular area grows or declines through the interplay of three factors: *births (fertility)*, *deaths (mortality)*, and *migration*. We can calculate the **population change** of an area by subtracting the number of people leaving a population (through death and emigration) from the number entering it (through birth and immigration) during a year (**Concept 8.2A**):

Population change = (Births + Immigration) − (Deaths + Emigration)

When births plus immigration exceed deaths plus emigration, a population grows; when the reverse is true, a population declines.

Fertility Rates

Demographers distinguish between two types of fertility rates. One is the **replacement-level fertility rate**: the average number of children that couples in a population must bear to replace themselves. It is slightly higher than two children per couple (typically 2.1) because some children die before reaching their reproductive years, especially in the world's poorest countries.

If we were to reach a global replacement-level fertility rate of 2.1 tomorrow, would it bring an immediate halt to population growth? No, because there is a large number of potential mothers under age 15 who will be moving into their reproductive years.

The second type of fertility rate is the **total fertility rate (TFR)**. It is the average number of children born to the women of childbearing age in a population (**Concept 8.2B**).

Between 1955 and 2017, the global TFR dropped from 5.0 to 2.5. Those who support slowing the world's population growth view this as good news. However, to eventually halt population growth, the global TFR must drop to and remain at the fertility replacement level of 2.1.

With a TFR of 4.6, Africa's population is growing more than twice as fast as any other continent and is projected to more than double from 1.25 billion in 2017 to 2.6 billion in 2050. Africa is also the world's poorest continent.

Estimates of any population's future numbers can vary considerably, depending mostly on TFR projections. Demographers also have to make assumptions about death rates, migration, and a number of other variables. If their assumptions are wrong, their population forecasts can be inaccurate.

MATH CONNECTION

Calculating Population Change

The intrinsic growth rate of a population (r) is determined by calculating the change in population size over a given amount of time. The difference between the number of births, the number of deaths, immigration, and emigration are determined and added or subtracted from the initial size of the population. That percent difference is equal to r.

FRQ Application

At the beginning of 2017 the population of a small town numbered 8,615. During the year, there were 173 births, 69 deaths, 85 immigrants, and 29 emigrants. What is the population size at the end of 2017?

$$(173 \text{ births} + 85 \text{ immigrants}) - (69 \text{ deaths} + 29 \text{ emigrants}) = 160 \text{ more individuals.}$$

$$\text{The total population at the end of } 2017 = 8615 + 160 = 8775 \text{ individuals.}$$

In 2017, what was the birth rate?

$$\frac{173}{8,615} \times 100 = 2.0\%$$

What was the death rate?

$$\frac{69}{8,615} \times 100 = 0.8\%$$

What is the net migration rate?

$$\frac{(85-29)}{8,615} = \frac{69}{8,615} \times 100 = 0.65\%$$

Calculate the intrinsic growth rate r for this population during 2017. As a percent difference (see Chapter 3, Math Connection, p. 82):

$$r = \frac{(8775 - 8615)}{(8775 + 8615)/2} = \frac{160}{8695} \times 100 = 1.84\%$$

If growth continues at the 2017 rate, use the *Rule of 70* to calculate the doubling time for this population.

$$t_d = \frac{70}{1.84} = 38.0 \text{ years}$$

The US Population—Third Largest and Growing

Between 1900 and 2017, the U.S. population grew from 76 million to 325 million. This happened despite oscillations in the country's TFR (Figure 8.5) and population growth rate. It took the country 139 years to reach a population of 100 million people, 52 years to add another 100 million (by 1967), and 39 years to add a third 100 million (by 2006).

During the period of high birth rates between 1946 and 1964, known as the *baby boom*, 79 million people were added to the US population. At the peak of the baby boom in 1957, the average TFR was 3.7 children per woman. In most years since 1972, it has been at or below 2.1 children per woman—1.8 in 2017, compared to a global TFR of 2.5.

The drop in the TFR has slowed the rate of population growth in the United States, but the country's population is still growing. In 2016 about 3 million people were added to the US population, according to the US Census Bureau. About 2.2 million were added because there were more births than deaths, and the rest were legal immigrants and refugees.

Since 1820, the United States has admitted almost twice as many legal immigrants and refugees as all other countries combined. The number of legal immigrants (including refugees) has varied during different periods because of changes in immigration laws and rates of economic growth (Figure 8.6).

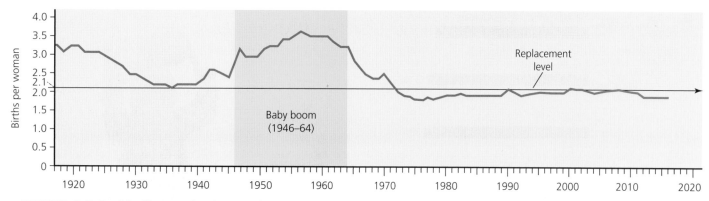

FIGURE 8.5 Total fertility rates for the United States between 1917 and 2017. **Critical thinking:** The US fertility rate has declined and remained at or below replacement levels since 1972. So why is the population of the United States still increasing?

(Compiled by the authors using data from Population Reference Bureau and US Census Bureau.)

Since 1965, nearly 59 million people have legally immigrated to the United States, most of them from Latin America and Asia, with the government giving preferences for those with technical training or with family members of US citizens. A 2015 study by the US Census Bureau noted that in 2013, China surpassed Mexico as the largest source of new US immigrants. A 2015 study by the Pew Research Center found that between 2009 and 2014, more legal and illegal immigrants in the United States returned to Mexico (where economic conditions are improving) than migrated to the United States.

According to population experts, the country's influx of immigrants has made the country more culturally diverse and has increased economic growth as these citizens worked and started businesses. An estimated 11 illegal immigrants also live in the United States. There is controversy over whether to deport those who can be found or to allow these individuals to meet strict criteria for becoming US citizens.

In addition to the fourfold increase in population since 1900, some amazing changes in lifestyles took place in the United States during the twentieth century (Figure 8.7), which led to Americans living longer. Along with this came dramatic increases in per capita resource use and much larger total and per capita ecological footprints.

The US Census Bureau projects that between 2017 and 2050, the US population will likely grow from 325 million to 397 million—an increase of 72 million people. Because of a high per-person rate of resource use and the resulting waste and pollution, each addition to the US population has an enormous environmental impact.

72 million
Projected increase in the US population between 2017 and 2050

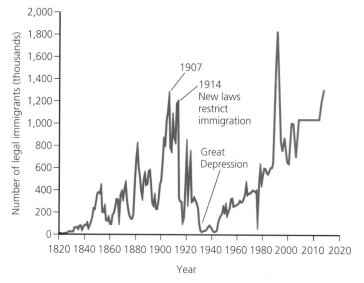

FIGURE 8.6 Legal immigration to the United States, 1820–2013 (the last year for which data are available). The large increase in immigration since 1989 resulted mostly from the Immigration Reform and Control Act of 1986, which granted legal status to certain illegal immigrants who could show they had been living in the country prior to January 1, 1982.

(Compiled by the authors using data from US Immigration and Naturalization Service, the Immigration Policy Institute, and the Pew Hispanic Center.)

Factors That Affect Birth and Fertility Rates

Many factors affect a country's average birth rate and TFR. One is the *importance of children as a part of the labor force*, especially in less-developed countries. Many poor couples in those countries struggle to survive on less than $3.10 a day and some on less than $1.90 a day. Some of these couples have a large number of children to help them haul drinking water, gather wood for heating and cooking, and grow or find food. Worldwide, 1 of every 10 children between ages 5 and 17 work to help their families survive (Figure 8.8).

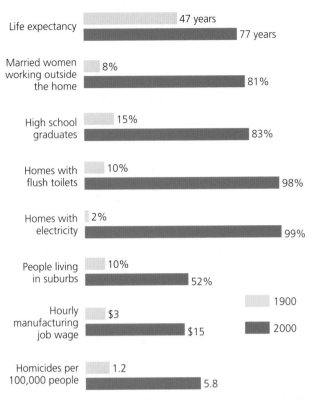

FIGURE 8.7 Some major changes took place in the United States between 1900 and 2000. **Critical thinking:** Which two of these changes do you think had the biggest impacts on the US ecological footprint?

(Compiled by the authors using data from U.S. Census Bureau and Department of Commerce.)

Another economic factor is the *cost of raising and educating children*. Birth and fertility rates tend to be lower in more-developed countries, where raising children is much more costly because they do not enter the labor force until they are in their late teens or twenties. In the United States, the U.S. Department of Agriculture estimated that the average cost of raising a child born in 2016 to age 18 was $245,000.

The *availability of pension systems* can influence the number of children couples have, especially poor people in less-developed countries. Pensions reduce a couple's need to have several children to replace those that die at an early age and to help support them in old age.

Urbanization also plays a role. People living in urban areas usually have better access to family planning services and tend to have fewer children than do those living in the rural areas of less-developed countries.

Another important factor is the *educational and employment opportunities available for women*. Total fertility rates tend to be low when women have access to education and paid employment outside the home. In less-developed countries, a woman with no education typically has two more children than does a woman with a high school education.

FIGURE 8.8 This young boy spends much of his day carrying bricks.

Average age at marriage (or, more precisely, the average age at which a woman has her first child) also plays a role. Women normally have fewer children when their average age at marriage is 25 or older.

Birth rates and TFRs are also affected by the *availability of reliable birth control methods* that allow women to control the number and spacing of their children.

Religious beliefs, traditions, and cultural norms also play a role. In some countries, these factors contribute to large families, because many people strongly oppose abortion and some forms of birth control.

Factors That Affect Death Rates

The rapid growth of the world's population over the past 100 years is largely the result of declining death rates, especially in less-developed countries. More people in some of these countries live longer, and fewer infants die because of larger food supplies, improvements in food distribution, better nutrition, improved sanitation, safer water supplies, and medical advances such as immunizations and antibiotics.

A useful indicator of the overall health of people in a country or region is **life expectancy**: the average number of years a person born in a particular year can be expected to live. Between 1955 and 2017, average global life expectancy increased from 48 years to 72 years. In

Projecting Population Change

Estimates of the human population size in 2050 range from 7.8 billion to 10.8 billion people—a difference of 3 billion. The range of estimates varies because many factors affect birth rates and TFRs.

First, demographers have to determine the reliability of current population estimates. While many more-developed countries such as the United States have reliable estimates of their population size, most countries do not. Some countries deliberately inflate or deflate the numbers for economic or political purposes.

Second, demographers make assumptions about trends in fertility. They might assume that fertility is declining by a certain percentage per year. If this estimate is off by a few percentage points, the resulting percentage increase in population can be magnified over a number of years and be quite different from the projected population size increase.

For example, United Nation (UN) demographers assumed that Kenya's fertility rate would decline. Based on that, in 2002 they projected that Kenya's total population would be 44 million by 2050. In reality, the fertility rate rose from 4.7 to 4.8 children per woman. As a result, the UN revised its projection for Kenya's population in 2050 to 81.4 million, which was 85% higher than its earlier projection.

Third, population projections are made by a variety of organizations. UN projections are often cited but the U.S. Census Bureau, the International Institute for Applied Systems Analysis (IIASA), and the U.S. Population Reference Bureau also make projections. Their projections vary because they use differing sets of data and differing methods (Figure 8.A).

CRITICAL THINKING

If you were in charge of the world and making decisions about resource use based on population projections, which of the projections in Figure 8.A would you rely on? Explain.

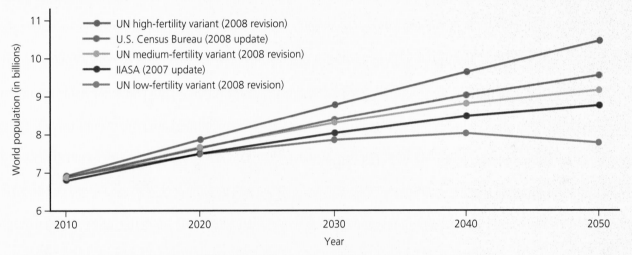

FIGURE 8.A World population projections to 2050 from three different organizations: the UN, the U.S. Census Bureau, and IIASA. Note that the uppermost, middle, and lowermost curves of these five projections are all from the UN, each assuming a different level of fertility. **Data analysis:** What are the ranges (differences between the lowest and highest) in these projections for 2030, 2040, and 2050?

(Compiled by the authors using data from United Nations, U.S. Census Bureau, and IIASA.)

2017 Japan had the world's longest life expectancy of 84 years. Between 1900 and 2017, the average US life expectancy rose from 47 years to 79 years. Research indicates that poverty, which reduces the average life span by 7 to 10 years, is the single most important factor affecting life expectancy.

Another important indicator of the overall health of a population is its **infant mortality rate**, the number of babies out of every 1,000 born who die before their first birthday. It is viewed as one of the best measures of a society's quality of life because it indicates the general level of nutrition and health care. A high infant mortality rate usually indicates insufficient food (*undernutrition*), poor nutrition (*malnutrition*; see Figure 1.10, p. 17), and a high incidence of infectious disease. Infant mortality also affects the TFR. In areas with low infant mortality rates, women tend to have fewer children because fewer of their children die at an early age.

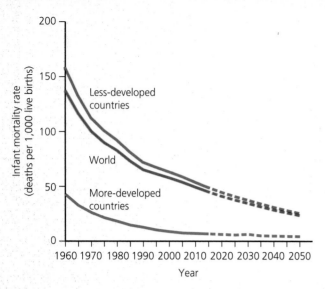

FIGURE 8.9 Comparison of infant mortality rates in more-developed countries and less-developed countries, 1950–2015, with projections to 2050 based on medium population projections.

(Compiled by the authors using data from United Nations Population Division and Population Reference Bureau.)

Infant mortality rates in most countries have declined dramatically since 1965 (Figure 8.9). Even so, every year more than 4 million infants die of *preventable* causes during their first year of life, according to UN population experts. Most of these deaths occur in less-developed countries. This average of nearly 11,000 mostly unnecessary infant deaths per day is equivalent to 55 jet airliners, each loaded with 200 infants, crashing *every day* with no survivors.

Between 1900 and 2017, the US infant mortality rate dropped from 165 to 5.8. This sharp decline was a major factor in the marked increase in average life expectancy during this period. However, 44 other nations had lower infant mortality rates than the United States in 2017.

Migration

A third factor in population change is **migration**: the movement of people into (*immigration*) and out of (*emigration*) specific geographic areas. Most people who migrate to another area within their country or to another country are seeking jobs and economic improvement. Others are driven by religious persecution, ethnic conflicts, political oppression, or war. There are also *environmental refugees*—people who have to leave their homes and sometimes their countries because of water or food shortages, soil erosion, or some other form of environmental degradation.

CHECKPOINT FOR UNDERSTANDING 8.2

1. Identify the driving force behind population growth over the last 100 years.

2. Describe two important indicators of the overall health of a population.

CONCEPT 8.3 The numbers of males and females in young, middle, and older age groups determine how fast a population grows or declines.

Age Structure

The **age structure** of a population is the numbers or percentages of males and females in young, middle, and older age groups in that population (**Concept 8.3**). In addition to total fertility rates, age structure is an important factor in determining whether the population of a country increases or decreases.

Population experts construct a population *age-structure diagram* by plotting the percentages or numbers of males and females in the total population in each of three age categories: *pre-reproductive* (ages 0–14), consisting of individuals normally too young to have children; *reproductive* (ages 15–44), consisting of those normally able to have children; and *post-reproductive* (ages 45 and older), with individuals normally too old to have children. Figure 8.10 presents generalized age-structure diagrams for countries with rapid, slow, zero, and negative population growth rates.

A country with a large percentage of people younger than age 15 (represented by a wide base in Figure 8.10, far left) will experience rapid population growth unless death rates rise sharply. Because of this *demographic momentum*, the number of births in such a country will rise for several decades. This will occur even if women each have an average of only one or two children because of the large number of girls entering their prime reproductive years. Most future human population growth will take place in less-developed countries because of their typically youthful age structure and rapid population growth rates.

The global population of seniors—people who are 65 and older—is projected to triple between 2016 and 2050, when one of every six people will be a senior (see the Case Study that follows). An aging population combined with a lower fertility rate results in fewer working-age adults having to support a large number of seniors. For example, in China and the United States between 2010 and 2050, the working-age population is projected to decline sharply. This could lead to a shortage of workers and friction between the younger and older generations in these countries.

CASE STUDY

The American Baby Boom

Changes in the distribution of a country's age groups have long-lasting economic and social impacts. For example,

Poverty and the Environment

Reducing poverty can help to reduce population growth, resource use, and environmental degradation. Poverty, the condition under which people cannot meet their basic economic needs, has numerous harmful health and environmental effects and has been identified as one of the four major causes of the environmental problems we face.

In order to reduce poverty, governments in most less-developed countries will have to make policy changes. As part of this, analysts recommend a strong emphasis on education to develop a trained workforce that can participate in an increasingly globalized economy. South Korea and Singapore are both good examples of countries that have climbed out of abject poverty.

Governments, businesses, and international lending agencies could also do the following:

- Mount a massive global effort to combat malnutrition and infectious diseases

- Provide universal primary school education for the world's nearly 800 million illiterate adults

- Provide assistance to less-developed countries in stabilizing their population growth as soon as possible

- Make large investments in small-scale infrastructure such as solar-cell power facilities in rural villages, as well as sustainable agriculture projects that would help move toward more energy-efficient and sustainable economies

Reducing poverty increases life expectancy and reduces infant mortality. Empowering and educating women not only reduces poverty, but results in fewer children per female, ultimately slowing population growth.

FRQ Application

Question: The African country of Mali has one of the highest infant mortality rates in the world. The total fertility rate (TFR) in Mali is six children per female in her lifetime. The GDP is approximately $700 (US) per person per year, making Mali a relatively poor country. Empowering women in Mali is key to reducing poverty and ultimately slowing population growth. **Identify** and **discuss** TWO improvements in women's lives that would result in a lower total fertility rate and at the same time reduce poverty.

Possible Response: One improvement for women would be easy access to birth control. When women have control over their reproductive lives, they tend to have fewer children. A smaller family makes it easier to survive economically. A second improvement for women would be access to a basic education. When women are educated they are more employable and therefore more self-sufficient. If they hold jobs or start a small business they can add to the family's income and economic stability.

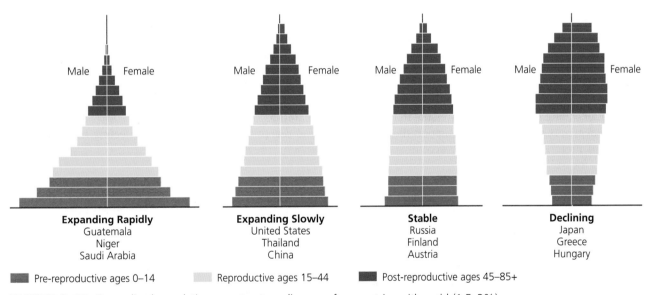

Expanding Rapidly	Expanding Slowly	Stable	Declining
Guatemala	United States	Russia	Japan
Niger	Thailand	Finland	Greece
Saudi Arabia	China	Austria	Hungary

■ Pre-reproductive ages 0–14   ▫ Reproductive ages 15–44   ■ Post-reproductive ages 45–85+

FIGURE 8.10 Generalized population age-structure diagrams for countries with rapid (1.5–3%), slow (0.3–1.4%), zero (0–0.2%), and negative (declining) population growth rates. **Question:** Which of these diagrams best represents the country where you live?

(Compiled by the authors using data from US Census Bureau and Population Reference Bureau.)

the American baby boom (Figure 8.5) added 79 million people to the US population between 1946 and 1964. Over time, this group looks like a bulge as it moves up through the country's age structure, as shown in Figure 8.11.

For decades, the baby-boom generation has strongly influenced the US economy because it makes up about 25% of the US population. Baby boomers created the youth market in their teens and twenties and are now

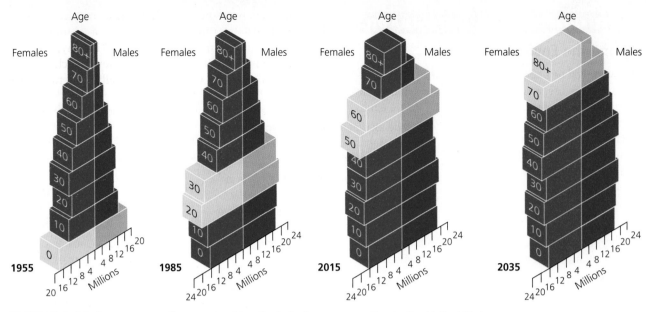

FIGURE 8.11 Age-structure diagrams tracking the baby-boom generation in the United States, 1955, 1985, 2015, and 2035 (projected). **Critical thinking:** How might the projected age structure in 2035 affect you?

(Compiled by the authors using data from US Census Bureau and Population Reference Bureau.)

creating the late-middle-age (ages 50 to 60) and senior markets. In addition to having this economic impact, the large baby-boom generation plays an increasingly important role in deciding who is elected to public office and what laws are passed or weakened.

Since 2011, when the first baby boomers began turning 65, the number of Americans older than age 65 has grown at the rate of about 10,000 a day and will do so through 2030. This process has been called the *graying of America*. As the number of working adults declines in proportion to the number of seniors, there may be political pressure from baby boomers to increase tax revenues to help support the growing senior population. However, in 2015, according to the Census Bureau, the Millennial Generation—Americans born between 1980 and 2005—overtook Baby Boomers to become the largest generation living in the United States. Eventually, this will change the political and economic power balance.

Aging Populations Can Decline Rapidly

The graying of the world's population is due largely to declining birth rates and medical advances that have extended life spans. The UN estimates that by 2050, the global number of people age 60 and older will equal or exceed the number of people under age 15.

As the percentage of people age 65 or older increases, more countries will begin experiencing population declines. If population decline is gradual, its harmful effects usually can be managed. However, some countries are experiencing rapid declines and feeling such effects more severely.

Japan has the world's highest percentage of people age 65 or over and the world's lowest percentage of people under age 15. In 2017 Japan's population was 127 million. By 2050 its population is projected to be 102 million. As its population declines, there will be fewer adults working and paying taxes to support an increasingly elderly population. Because Japan discourages immigration,this could threaten its economic future.

In recent years, Japan has been feeling the effects of a declining population. For example, houses in some suburbs have been abandoned and cannot be sold because of a lack of buyers. They could be demolished, but who will pay the costs—the owners who have abandoned them, or the government?

Figure 8.12 lists some of the problems associated with rapid population decline. Countries with rapidly declining populations, in addition to Japan, include Germany, Italy, Bulgaria, Hungary, Russia, Thailand, South Korea, Spain, and Portugal. Population declines are difficult to reverse.

CHECKPOINT FOR UNDERSTANDING 8.3

1. Describe the factors that lead to a population decline.

2. Explain the impacts of a decreasing younger population on a country with a large elderly population.

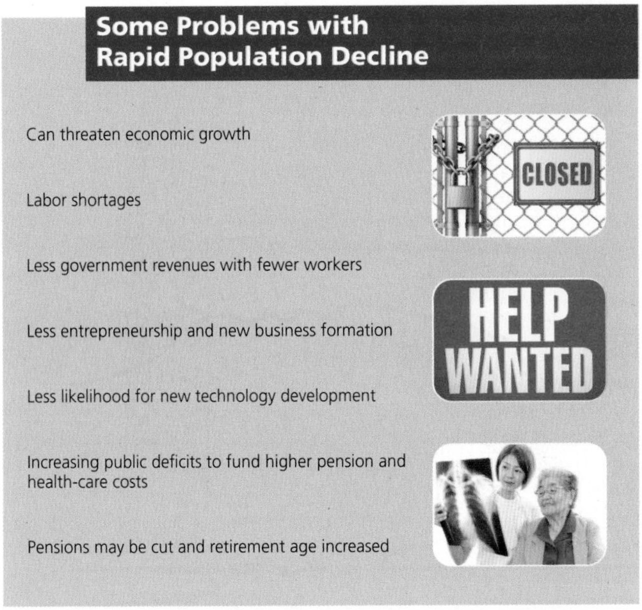

Some Problems with Rapid Population Decline

Can threaten economic growth

Labor shortages

Less government revenues with fewer workers

Less entrepreneurship and new business formation

Less likelihood for new technology development

Increasing public deficits to fund higher pension and health-care costs

Pensions may be cut and retirement age increased

FIGURE 8.12 Rapid population decline can cause several problems. ***Critical thinking:*** Which two of these problems do you think are the most important?

Top: Slavoljub Pantelic/Shutterstock.com. Center: lofoto/Shutterstock.com. Bottom:sunabesyou/Shutterstock.com.

8.4 HOW CAN WE SLOW HUMAN POPULATION GROWTH?

CONCEPT 8.4 We can slow human population growth by reducing poverty through economic development, elevating the status of women, and encouraging family planning.

Economic Development

There is controversy over whether we should slow population growth (Science Focus 8.1). Some analysts argue that because population growth can be linked to environmental degradation, we need to slow population growth in order to reduce such degradation of our life-support system. They have suggested several ways to do this, one of which is to reduce poverty (See Critical Concepts in Sustainability, Poverty and the Environment, p. 215) through economic development.

Demographers have examined the birth and death rates of western European countries that became industrialized during the nineteenth century. Using such data, they developed a hypothesis on population change known as the **demographic transition**. It states that as countries become industrialized and economically developed, their per capita incomes rise, poverty declines, and their populations tend to grow more slowly. According to the hypothesis, this transition takes place in five stages, as shown in Figure 8.13.

Some analysts believe that most of the world's less-developed countries will make a demographic transition over the next few decades. They hypothesize that the transition will occur because newer technologies will help them to develop economically and to reduce poverty.

Other analysts fear that rapid population growth, extreme poverty, war, increasing environmental degradation, and resource depletion could leave some countries with high population growth rates that are stuck in Stage 2 of the demographic transition. Such countries include Afghanistan, Iraq, Guatemala, Pakistan, Yemen, and Niger and a number of other African countries. This highlights the need to reduce poverty as a key to improving human health and stabilizing the population.

Educating and Empowering Women

A number of studies show that women tend to have fewer children if they are educated, can control their own fertility, earn an income of their own, and live in societies that do not suppress their rights.

Only about 30% of the world's girls are enrolled in secondary education, so widespread education of girls is important for their future and for trying to slow population growth. In most societies women have fewer rights and educational and economic opportunities than men have.

Women do almost all of the world's domestic work and child care for little or no pay. They provide more unpaid health care (within their families) than do all of the world's organized health-care services combined. In rural areas of Africa, Latin America, and Asia, women do 60–80% of the work associated with growing food, hauling water, and gathering and hauling wood (Figure 8.14) and animal dung for use as fuel. As one Brazilian woman observed, "For poor women, the only holiday is when you are asleep."

While women account for 66% of all hours worked, they receive only 10% of the world's income and own just 2% of the world's land. Women also make up 70% of the world's poor and 66% of the world's 800 million illiterate adults. In many societies, boys are more likely to get an education than are girls because of traditional views of gender roles. Studies show that one of the major factors for slowing population growth is the widespread education of girls. Poor women who cannot read often have an average of five to seven children, compared with two or fewer children in societies where most women can read. This highlights the need for all children to get at least an elementary school education.

A growing number of women in less-developed countries are taking charge of their lives and reproductive behavior. As this number grows, such change driven by individual women will play an important role in stabilizing populations. This change will also improve human health,

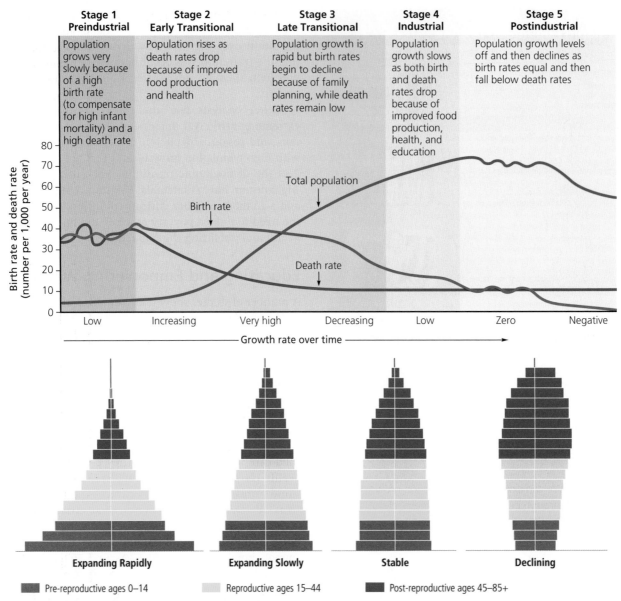

FIGURE 8.13 The *demographic transition*, which a country can experience as it becomes industrialized and more economically developed, can take place in five stages. **Question:** At what stage is the country where you live?

reduce poverty and environmental degradation, and allow more access to basic human rights.

Family Planning

Family planning programs provide education and clinical services that can help couples to choose how many children to have and when to have them. Such programs vary from culture to culture, but most of them provide information on birth spacing, birth control, and health care for pregnant women and infants.

According to studies by the UN Population Division and other population agencies, family planning has been a major factor in reducing the number of unintended preg-

nancies, births, and abortions. In addition, family planning has reduced population growth rates, rates of infant mortality and the number of mothers and fetuses dying during pregnancy. Family planning also has financial benefits. Studies show that each dollar spent on family planning in countries such as Thailand, Egypt, and Bangladesh saves $10 to $16 in health, education, and social service costs by preventing unwanted births.

Despite these successes, certain problems have hindered progress in some countries. There are three major problems. *First*, according to the UN Population Fund and the Guttmacher Institute, about 40% of all pregnancies in less-developed countries were unplanned and about half of these pregnancies end with abortion. So ensuring access

FIGURE 8.14 This woman in Nepal is bringing home firewood. Typically, she spends 2 hours a day, two or three times a week, on this task.

to voluntary contraception would play a key role in stabilizing the populations and reducing the number of abortions in such countries.

Second, according to the same sources, an estimated 225 million women, primarily in 69 of the world's poorest countries, lack access to family planning services. Meeting these current unmet needs for family planning and contraception could prevent 54 million unintended pregnancies, 26 million induced abortions (16 million of them unsafe), 1.1 million infant deaths, and 79,000 pregnancy-related deaths of women per year. This could reduce the projected global population size by more than 1 billion people, at an average cost of $25 per couple per year.

Third, largely because of cultural traditions, male domination, and poverty, one in every three girls in less-developed countries is married before age 18 and one in nine is married before age 14. This occurs despite laws against child marriage. For a poor family, marrying off a daughter can relieve financial pressure.

Some analysts call for expanding family planning programs to educate men about the importance of having fewer children and taking more responsibility for raising them. Proponents also call for greatly increased research in order to develop more effective birth control methods for men.

The experiences of countries such as Japan, Thailand, Bangladesh, South Korea, Taiwan, and China show that a country can achieve or come close to replacement-level fertility within a decade or two. The real population story of the past 50 years has been the sharp reduction in the *rate* of population growth (Figure 8.2) resulting from the reduction of poverty through economic development, empowerment of women, and the promotion of family planning. However, the global population is still growing fast enough to add 2 to 3 billion more people during this century.

CASE STUDY

Population Growth in India

For six decades, India has tried to control its population growth with only modest success. The world's first national family planning program began in India in 1952, when its population was nearly 400 million. In 2017, after 63 years of population control efforts, India had 1.35 billion people—the world's second largest population and a TFR of 2.3. Much of this increase occurred because of India's declining death rates.

In 1952, India added 5 million people to its population. In 2017 it added 19 million people—more than any other country. Figure 8.15 shows changes in India's age structure between 2010 and 2035 (projected). The UN projects that by 2029, India will be the world's most populous country, and that by 2050, it will have a population of 1.7 billion.

India has the world's fourth largest economy and a rapidly growing middle class of more than 100 million people—a number nearly equal to a third of the US population. However, the country faces serious poverty, malnutrition, and environmental problems that could worsen as its population continues to grow rapidly. About one-fourth of all people in India's cities live in slums, and prosperity and progress have not touched hundreds of millions of Indians who live in rural villages. According to the World Bank, about 30% of India's population—one-third of the world's extremely poor people—live in extreme poverty on less than $1.90 per day (Figure 8.16). In India, 300 million people—a number almost equal to the entire US population—do not have electricity.

For decades, the Indian government has provided family planning services throughout the country and has strongly promoted a smaller average family size. Even so, Indian women have an average of 2.3 children.

Three factors help to account for larger families in India. *First*, most poor couples believe they need several children to work and care for them in their old age. *Second*, the strong cultural preference in India for male children means that some couples keep having children until they produce one or more boys. And *third*, although 90% of Indian couples have access to at least one modern birth control method, only about 48% actually use one.

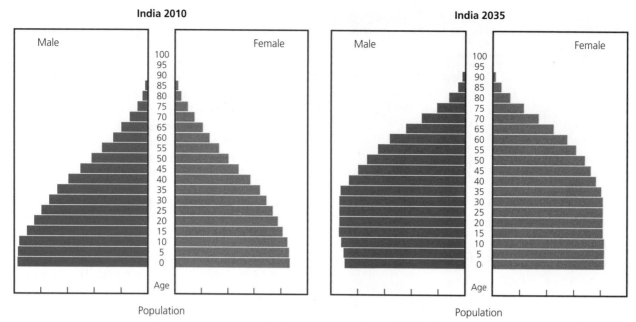

FIGURE 8.15 Age structure changes in India: 2010 and 2035 (projected). *Critical thinking:* How might the projected age structure in 2035 affect India's ability to reduce poverty?

(Compiled by the authors using data from US Census Bureau and United Nations Population Division.)

FIGURE 8.16 Homeless people in Kolkata, India.

India also faces critical resource and environmental problems. With 18% of the world's people, India has just 2.3% of the world's land resources and 2% of its forests. About half the country's cropland has been degraded by soil erosion and overgrazing. In addition, more than two-thirds of its water is seriously polluted, sanitation services often are inadequate, and many of its major cities suffer from serious air pollution.

India's rapid economic growth is expected to accelerate over the next few decades. This will help many people in India escape poverty, but it will also increase pressure on India's and the earth's natural capital as rates of per capita resource use rise. On the other hand, economic growth may help India to slow its population growth by accelerating its demographic transition.

CASE STUDY

Slowing Population Growth in China

China is the world's most populous country, with 1.39 billion people in 2017. According to the Population Reference Bureau and the United Nations Population Fund, China's population is projected to peak at around 1.4 billion by 2030 and then decline to 1.3 billion by by 2050.

In the 1960s, China's large population was growing so rapidly that there was a serious threat of mass starvation. To avoid this, government officials took measures that eventually led to the establishment of the world's most extensive, intrusive, and strict family planning and birth control program.

Interpreting Population Histograms

A population histogram is a modified bar graph that illustrates population characteristics of a country (Figure 8.A). The graph is typically divided into two sides according to gender, with males on the left, females on the right, and each bar represents the percentage of the total population for a particular age group. The male and female bars for one age group is called an age *cohort*. The horizontal axis can denote percent of the total population or population in millions of individuals, and the vertical axis represents age groups.

A country's population can also be segregated into three sectors: pre-reproductive individuals (ages 0–14), reproductive individuals (ages 15–44), and post reproductive individuals (ages 45 and up). This is important because the greater the size of the pre-reproductive group, the faster the population growth will be for that country. Essentially, the pre-reproductive sector drives population growth. If reproductive females are having children (i.e., adding to the pre-reproductive population) at more than the replacement level fertility of 2.1 children per female, then population growth will increase.

FRQ Application

The total population of Germany in 2016 was 80,682,351. Using the histogram below, calculate the percentage of the population in the pre-reproductive sector.

    0–4 year-old cohort = 1.8 million males + 1.7 million females
    5–9 year-old cohort = 1.8 million males + 1.7 million females
    10–14 year-old cohort = 1.9 million males + 1.8 million females

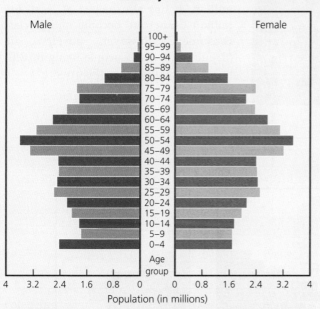

Germany 2016

FIGURE 8.A Population histogram for Germany, 2016, showing gender and age group distribution.

Source: http://www.theodora.com/wfbcurrent/germany/germany_people.html

The total number of individuals in the pre-reproductive sector = 10.7 million individuals

Rounding the total population of Germany to 80.7 million individuals, the percentage of the population that is pre-reproductive is

$$\frac{10.7 \text{ (pre-reproductive sector)}}{80.7 \text{ (total population)}} \times 100 = 13.25\%$$

Germany is in the *fifth stage of demographic transition* (Figure 8.13). Typically, women are educated and tend to have children later in life. Assuming women ages 25–44 are bearing the children in the pre-reproductive sector, ages 0–14, calculate the total fertility rate (TFR) for this group of women.

Total number of females ages 25–44 is given by:
    25–29 years old = 2.6 million
    30–34 years old = 2.5 million
    35–40 years old = 2.4 million
    41–44 years old = 2.4 million
    Total number of women = 9.9 million individuals

$$TFR = \frac{10.7 \text{ million children}}{9.9 \text{ million mothers}} = 1.1 \text{ children per female}$$

This value is less than replacement level fertility of 2.1 children per female, indicating a declining population in Germany.

The centerpiece of the program, established in 1978, was the promotion of one-child families. Married couples pledging to have no more than one child received better housing, more food, free health care, salary bonuses, and preferential job opportunities for their child. Couples who broke their pledge lost such benefits. The government also provided contraceptives, sterilizations, and abortions for married couples.

Since this government-controlled program began in 1978, China has made impressive efforts to feed its people and bring its population growth under control. Between 1978 and 2017, the country reduced its TFR from 3.0 to 1.8. China's one-child policy played a role in this drop in the country's TFR. However, the TFR had already been falling a decade earlier, from 5.9 in 1968 to 3.0 in 1978 when the one-child policy was implemented. This earlier

FIGURE 8.17 Old and new housing in heavily populated Shanghai, China, in 2015.

drop and its continuation after 1978 was strongly influenced by increased education and employment opportunities for young women, according to Nobel Laureate Amartya Sen. Currently, China's population is growing more slowly than the US population, even with legal immigration included. Although China has avoided mass starvation, its strict population control program has been accused of violating human rights.

Because of the cultural preference for sons, many Chinese women abort female fetuses. This has reduced the female population and means that about 30 million Chinese men are unable to find anyone to marry.

Since 1980, China has undergone rapid industrialization and economic growth. According to the Earth Policy Institute, between 1990 and 2010 this process reduced the number of people living in extreme poverty by almost 500 million. It has also helped at least 300 million Chinese to become middle-class consumers. However, poverty still plagues millions of people living in China's villages and cities (Figure 8.17).

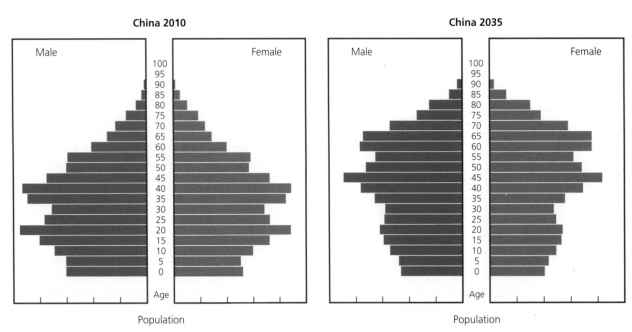

FIGURE 8.18 Age structure in China: 2010 and 2035 (projected). ***Critical thinking:*** How might the projected age structure in 2035 affect China's economy?

(Compiled by the authors using data from US Census Bureau and United Nations Population Division.)

Over time, China's rapidly growing middle class will consume more total resources. This will put a strain on China's and the earth's natural capital. Like India, China faces serious soil erosion, overgrazing, water pollution, and air pollution problems.

Because of its one-child policy, in recent years the average age of China's population has been increasing at one of the fastest rates ever recorded (Figure 8.18). The UN projects that the number of Chinese over 65 will increase from 137 million in 2016 to 243 million in 2030. While China's population is not declining, the UN also estimates that by 2030, the country is likely to have too few young workers (ages 15 to 64) to support its rapidly aging population. This graying of the Chinese population could lead to a declining work force, limited funds for supporting continued economic development. These concerns may slow China's economic growth.

Because of these concerns, in 2015 the Chinese government abandoned its one-child policy and replaced it with a two-child policy. Married couples can apply to the government for permission to have two children. However, the Chinese people have gotten used to small families. In addition, many married couples may have only one child because of the high cost of raising a second child and the greatly increased educational and employment opportunities for young women.

Core Case Study Checkpoint

What is the world's population? Identify the three most populous countries and describe the three factors that have led to rapid population growth.

KEY IDEAS

- The human population is growing rapidly and may soon bump up against environmental limits.
- The combination of population growth and the increasing rate of resource use per person is expanding the overall human ecological footprint and putting a strain on the earth's natural capital.
- We can slow human population growth by reducing poverty, elevating the status of women, and encouraging family planning.

Chapter 8 Glossary

age structure: percentage of the population (or number of people of each sex) at each age level in a population.

crude birth rate: annual number of live births per 1,000 people in the population of a geographic area at the midpoint of a given year.

crude death rate: annual number of deaths per 1,000 people in the population of a geographic area at the midpoint of a given year.

cultural carrying capacity: the limit on population growth that would allow most people in an area or the world to live in reasonable comfort and freedom without impairing the ability of the planet to sustain future generations.

demographic transition: hypothesis that countries, as they become industrialized, have declines in death rates followed by declines in birth rates.

family planning: providing information, clinical services, and contraceptives to help people choose the number and spacing of children they want to have.

infant mortality rate: number of babies out of every 1,000 born each year who die before their first birthday.

life expectancy: average number of years a newborn infant can expect to live.

migration: movement of people into or out of a specific geographic area.

population change: increase or decrease in the size of a population. It is equal to (Births + Immigration) − (Deaths + Emigration).

replacement-level fertility rate: average number of children a couple must bear to replace themselves. The average for a country or the world usually is slightly higher than two children per couple (2.1 in the United States and 2.5 in some developing countries) mostly because some children die before reaching their reproductive years.

total fertility rate (TFR): estimate of the average number of children who will be born alive to a woman during her lifetime if she passes through all her childbearing years (ages 15–44) conforming to age-specific fertility rates of a given year.

Chapter Review

Core Case Study

1. Summarize the story of how human population growth has surpassed 7.5 billion and explain why this is significant to many environmental scientists (**Core Case Study**). List three factors that account for the rapid growth of the human population over the past 200 years.

Section 8.1

2. (a) What is the key concept for this section? (b) What is the range of estimates for the size of the human population in 2050? Summarize the three major population growth trends recognized by demographers. (c) About how many people were added to the world's population in 2017? What are the world's three most populous countries? (d) List eight major ways in which we have altered natural systems to meet our needs and wants. (e) Define **cultural carrying capacity**. Summarize the debate over whether and how long the human population can keep growing.

Section 8.2

3. (a) What are the two key concepts for this section? (b) Define and distinguish between **crude birth rate** and **crude death rate**. List three variables that affect the growth and decline of human populations. (c) Explain how a given area's **population change** is calculated.

4. (a) Define and distinguish between the **replacement-level fertility rate** and the **total fertility rate (TFR)**. (b) How has the global TFR changed since 1955?

5. (a) Summarize the story of population growth in the United States and explain why it is high compared to population growth in most other more-developed countries. About how much of the annual US population growth is due to immigration? (b) List six

changes in lifestyles that have taken place in the United States during the 20th century, leading to a rise in per capita resource use. What is the end effect of such changes in terms of the US ecological footprint?

6. (a) List eight factors that affect birth rates and fertility rates. (b) Explain why there are more boys than girls in some countries. (c) Define **life expectancy** and **infant mortality rate** and explain how they affect the population size of a country. (d) What is **migration**? Who are environmental refugees?

Section 8.3

7. (a) What is the key concept for this section? (b) What is the **age structure** of a population? Explain how age structure affects population growth and economic growth. (c) What is demographic momentum? Describe the baby boom in the United States and some of its economic and social effects. (d) What are some problems related to rapid population decline due to an aging population?

Section 8.4

8. (a) What is the key concept for this section? (b) What is the **demographic transition** and what are its five stages? (c) What factors could hinder some less-developed countries in making this transition?

9. (a) Explain how education, reduction of poverty, and empowerment of women can help countries to slow their population growth. (b) What is **family planning** and how can it help to stabilize populations? (c) Describe India's efforts to control its population growth. Describe China's population control program and compare it with that of India.

10. What are this chapter's *three key ideas*?

Note: Key terms are in bold type.

AP® Review Questions

1. Which two countries had the largest number of people in 2017?
   (A) China and the United States
   (B) China and Indonesia
   (C) India and the United States
   (D) India and Indonesia
   (E) China and India

2. A medium population-growth projection calls for a population of 9.8 billion people in 2050 up from the current population of 7.5 billion. What percent increase is this?
   (A) 23
   (B) 30
   (C) 72
   (D) 100
   (E) 130

3. In 1798, Thomas Malthus hypothesized the collapse of the human population. What factor led instead to the continued increase of the human population?
   (A) Use of fossil fuels
   (B) Increased genetic resistance of pest species
   (C) Reliance on renewable resources
   (D) Food production increasing at an exponential rate due to technological advances in agriculture
   (E) Modern health care doubling the birth rate worldwide

4. Why has the human population experienced exponential growth in the past 200 years?
   (A) Humans have developed the ability to expand into diverse new habitats.
   (B) Changes in agriculture allow fewer people to be fed per unit of land area.
   (C) Birth rates have dropped sharply below death rates.
   (D) Antibiotics and vaccines have declined in their effectiveness.
   (E) Immigration has increased.

5. Why is replacement-level fertility slightly higher than two children per couple?
   (A) Some people do not marry.
   (B) Some children die before reaching reproductive years.
   (C) Use of contraceptives is increasing in developed countries.
   (D) Death rates are high in developing countries.
   (E) Death rates exceed birth rates in stable countries.

6. Compared to the United States, many other countries have lower infant mortality rates, in part because other countries
   (A) have greater access to health care, including neonatal care
   (B) have greater regulations on lead paint in households
   (C) maintain a more traditional nuclear family
   (D) have fewer children per family
   (E) have decreased rates of vaccinations

7. Over a certain 10-year period, the population of Fremont grew at a constant rate from 100,000 to 400,000 people. What is the annual growth rate percentage of this population?
   (A) 5%
   (B) 7%
   (C) 10%
   (D) 14%
   (E) 20%

8. One of the most important factors in helping to stabilize a developing country's population and reducing environmental degradation is to
   (A) decrease the rate at which people may emigrate
   (B) reduce infant mortality by providing better health care for infants and pregnant women
   (C) empower and educate women
   (D) teach people the importance of recycling materials used in their everyday lives
   (E) ensure that people have enough food by establishing local plots of land for community farms

9. Which of the following is an example of a positive use of nature's natural capital?
   (A) Elimination of many natural predators of humans
   (B) Increased use of the earth's net primary productivity to feed humans
   (C) Increased reliance on renewable energy resources
   (D) Introduction of species into new communities to control pests
   (E) Modification of the earth's geochemical cycles for energy uses

10. The graph shown below is most likely from which of the following countries?

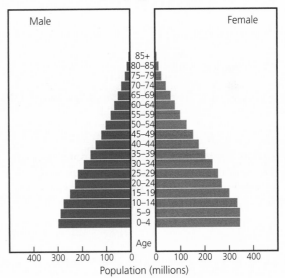

Developing countries

(A) Germany
(B) Italy
(C) Spain
(D) Niger
(E) Greece

11. Which of the following accurately describes replacement-level fertility?
   (A) It is always two children per couple in order to achieve zero population growth.
   (B) It is lower in developing countries than developed countries.
   (C) It is increasing as countries move through the demographic transition.
   (D) It is equal to total fertility rate per 1,000 people.
   (E) It changes according to infant mortality rates.

12. Which of the following are characteristics of countries that have high total fertility rates?
   I. Women marry at a young age
   II. There are high literacy rates for women
   III. The society is mostly urban
   (A) I only
   (B) II only
   (C) III only
   (D) I and II only
   (E) I, II, and III

13. In 2017, the world population was 7.5 billion people. A projection for the human population by 2050 with a worldwide TFR (total fertility rate) of two children could be
   (A) 7.1 billion
   (B) 7.5 billion
   (C) 9.8 billion
   (D) 15.1 billion
   (E) 20 billion

14. Demographers use many values to rank the overall health of a population. The two most useful indicators of the overall health of the people in a country or region are
   (A) death and birth rates
   (B) life expectancy and infant mortality rate
   (C) immigration and emigration rates
   (D) literacy rate and GDP
   (E) rate of contraceptive use and GDP

Questions 15 and 16 refer to the chart below and the choices that follow. Choices may be used once, more than once, or not at all.

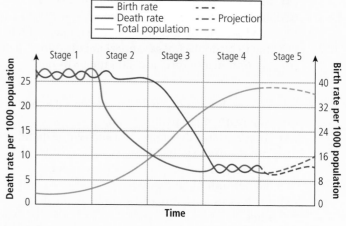

Source: http://www.bbc.co.uk/schools/gcsebitesize/geography/population/population_change_structure_rev4.shtml

   (A) Stage 1
   (B) Stage 2
   (C) Stage 3
   (D) Stage 4
   (E) Stage 5

15. During this stage of the demographic transition, population growth is slow because both death and birth rates are high.

16. During this stage of the demographic transition, population growth levels off and then declines as birth rate equals and then falls below death rate.

17. Which of the following has been utilized in both India and China in an attempt to reduce population growth rates?
   (A) Limiting immigration
   (B) Increasing emigration
   (C) Slowing the transition to an industrial state
   (D) Importing new technologies into the country
   (E) Family planning and education

18. During what two stages of demographic transition does most of a country's population increase occur?
   (A) Stages 1 and 2
   (B) Stages 2 and 3
   (C) Stages 4 and 5
   (D) Stages 1 and 4
   (E) Stages 1 and 5

19. What is one economic challenge the U.S. will likely face as a result of its demographic transition into Stage 5?
    (A) Increased housing costs
    (B) Overcrowding in schools
    (C) Shortage of food because of population increase
    (D) Social Security will be underfunded
    (E) Increased competition will lead to violence

20. Why did China's one-child policy lead to a disproportionately higher number of men than women in younger generations?
    (A) Women are more likely to die during childbirth.
    (B) Women have lower life expectancy in China.
    (C) Cultural preferences favor sons.
    (D) Lack of health care causes higher rates of infant mortality in young women.
    (E) Women are more like to be victims of crimes.

AP® Free-Response Practice

1. Use the population histograms of France and India to answer the following questions.

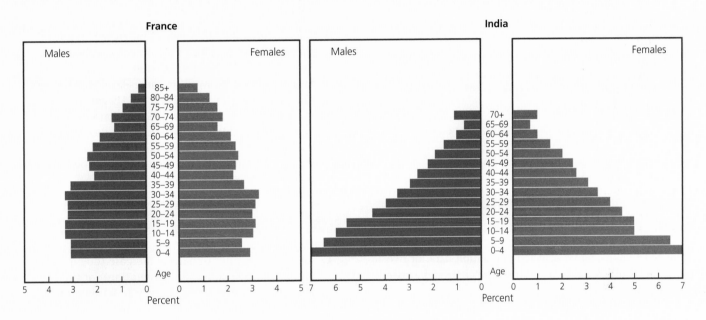

(a) The population of India is increasing, as indicated by the population histogram.

   (i) **Determine** the approximate percentage of the country that is made up of pre-reproductive individuals.

   (ii) Assume that the mothers of the pre-reproductive sector are the female cohorts, ages 15 to 44. **Calculate** the total fertility rate of these women.

   (iii) **Identify** and **describe** the current stage of demographic transition in India.

   (iv) **Explain** why, if population growth were to drop to replacement-level fertility, that the population of this country would continue to increase.

   (v) **Identify** and **discuss** THREE reasons why a woman in this country would have more than two children.

(b) The population of France is declining slightly.

   (i) **Identify** and **describe** the current stage of demographic transition in France.

   (ii) **Identify** and **discuss** THREE reasons why women in France would have two or fewer children.

   (iii) **Identify** and **discuss** TWO economic impacts of a rapidly declining population.

Critical Thinking

1. Do you think that the global population of 7.5 billion (**Core Case Study**) is too large? Explain. If your answer was *yes*, what do you think should be done to slow human population growth? If your answer was *no*, do you believe that there is a population size that would be too big? Explain.

2. If you could say hello to a new person every second without taking a break and working around the clock, how many people could you greet in a day? How many in a year? How long would it take you to greet the 91 million people who were added to the world's population in 2017? At this same rate, how many years would it take you to greet all 7.5 billion people on the planet?

3. Of the three major environmental worldviews summarized in Figure 1A on p. 19, which do you think underlies each of the two major positions on whether the world is overpopulated, as described in Science Focus 8.1?

4. Should everyone have the right to have as many children as they want? Explain. Is your belief on this issue consistent with your environmental worldview?

5. Is it rational for a poor couple in a less-developed country such as India to have four or five children? Explain.

6. Do you think that projected increases in the earth's population size and economic growth are sustainable? Explain. If not, how is this likely to affect your life?

7. Some people think the most important environmental goal is to sharply reduce the rate of population growth in less-developed countries, where at least 95% of the world's population growth is expected to take place between 2017 and 2050. Others argue that the most serious environmental problems stem from high levels of resource consumption per person in more-developed countries. What is your view on this issue? Explain.

8. Experts have identified population growth as one of the major causes of the environmental problems we face. The population of the United States is growing faster than that of any other more-developed country. This fact is rarely discussed and the US government has no official policy for slowing US population growth. Why do think this is so? Do you think there should be such a policy? If so, explain your thinking and list three steps you would take as a leader to slow US population growth. If not, explain your thinking.

Data Analysis

The chart below shows selected population data for two different countries, A and B. Study the chart and answer the questions that follow.

	Country A	Country B
Population (millions)	144	82
Crude birth rate (number of live births per 1,000 people per year)	43	8
Crude death rate (number of deaths per 1,000 people per year)	18	10
Infant mortality rate (number of babies per 1,000 born who die in first year of life)	100	3.8
Total fertility rate (average number of children born to women during their childbearing years)	5.9	1.3
% of population under 15 years old	45	14
% of population older than 65 years	3	19
Average life expectancy at birth	47	79
% urban	44	75

1. Calculate the rates of natural increase (due to births and deaths, not counting immigration) for the populations of country A and country B. Based on these calculations and the data in the table, for each of the countries, suggest whether it is a more-developed country or a less-developed country and explain the reasons for your answers.

2. Describe where each of the two countries might be in the stages of demographic transition (Figure 8.13). Discuss factors that could hinder either country from progressing to later stages in the demographic transition.

3. Explain how the percentages of people under age 15 in each country could affect its per capita and total ecological footprints.

Answers for Checkpoints for Understanding

Section 8.1

1. Because of technological advancements and large fossil fuel use in industrial agriculture, food production has kept pace with population growth.

Section 8.2

1. Because of modern medicine, better nutrition and other quality-of-life improvements, the death rate has declined and life expectancy has increased, resulting in rapid growth in population.

2. A longer life expectancy is a measure of the health of a population. When poverty is reduced and the quality of life improves, individuals tend to live longer. Another indicator is lowered infant mortality. This indicates better nutrition and access to health care.

Section 8.3

1. The lifespan of individuals has increased and birth rates have declined. As older individuals die off and couples have fewer children, a decline in a county's population results. For example, Japan has the world's largest population of individuals over 65 and the lowest population of individuals under the age of 15.

2. When there is a rapid decline in the number of children per female, there are not enough working and tax-paying adults to support a large elderly population.

Section 8.4

1. Women who live in traditional cultures and do not have an education tend to have more children. Women who are educated tend to have fewer children, earn their own income, and live in societies that are less repressive.

2. Having many children increases the odds that there will be children to care for the parents in old age. There is a strong preference for male children, and women will have several children to ensure that there are male offspring. Also, birth control is available, but less than half of couples use it.

Core Case Study

The world's population in 2017 was 7.5 billion. In order, the three most populous countries are China, India, and the United States. The human population has grown rapidly because of increased food production, technologies that allowed humans to expand into almost all of the planet's climate zones, and declining death rates because of improved sanitation and health care.

1. Which of the following is the lowest level of organization of biotic organisms?
   (A) Habitat
   (B) Population
   (C) Community
   (D) Ecosystem
   (E) Biosphere

Questions 2 and 3 refer to the following nutrient cycles. Choices may be used once, more than once, or not at all.
   (A) Hydrologic cycle
   (B) Nitrogen cycle
   (C) Carbon cycle
   (D) Phosphorus cycle
   (E) Sulfur cycle

2. This cycle depends on the work of specialized bacteria for several conversions.

3. This is the slowest moving of the biogeochemical cycles and has no gaseous phase.

4. All of the following statements are true regarding the process of ecological succession EXCEPT
   (A) primary succession begins on bare rock with pioneer species such as lichens and mosses
   (B) secondary succession begins with established topsoil
   (C) in forest succession, trees that require constant sun such as poplar or pine trees make way for more shade-tolerant trees such as oak and hickory
   (D) succession can be terrestrial or aquatic
   (E) once a climax community is established, it will remain stable and no external force can cause it to change

5. Which of the following is NOT true regarding the greenhouse effect?
   (A) It is vital to continued life on earth as we know it.
   (B) It helps warm the troposphere.
   (C) It is caused by the interaction of gaseous molecules that are excited by infrared radiation.
   (D) It is based on the potential energy of the molecules in the air.
   (E) It can be affected by the concentrations of atmospheric gases.

6. Why are oxygen levels lower in the profundal zone of a freshwater lake?
   (A) High numbers of fish use up the oxygen.
   (B) Low light levels decrease photosynthesis.
   (C) High levels of algae use up the oxygen.
   (D) High light levels increase photosynthesis.
   (E) Reduced numbers of fish use up the oxygen.

Questions 7 and 8 refer to the following choices. Choices may be used once, more than once, or not at all.
   (A) Clockwise
   (B) Counterclockwise
   (C) Right
   (D) Left
   (E) Either direction, depending on other inputs

7. As a result of the Coriolis effect, objects traveling in a straight line deflect in this direction in the Southern Hemisphere.

8. Hurricanes rotate in this direction in the Northern Hemisphere.

9. Which of these is NOT an ecological service of inland wetlands?
   (A) Filtering and degrading toxic wastes and pollutants
   (B) Reducing flooding and erosion by absorbing storm water
   (C) Helping maintain biodiversity by providing habitats
   (D) Helping to moderate global temperatures
   (E) Helping replenish streams during dry periods

Questions 10 and 11 refer to the following.
   I. Plankton
   II. Nekton
   III. Benthos

10. This category includes organisms that can be microscopic.
    (A) I only
    (B) II only
    (C) III only
    (D) I and II only
    (E) I and III only

11. These organisms all share one attribute; they are drifters in the water. The current moves them faster than they can swim on their own.
    (A) I only
    (B) II only
    (C) III only
    (D) I and II only
    (E) II and III only

12. Why is identifying and protecting keystone species a key goal of many conservation biologists?
    (A) Keystone species are economically beneficial.
    (B) Keystone species are critical to human survival.
    (C) Keystone species play a critical ecological role in the community.
    (D) Keystone species are endangered species.
    (E) Keystone species are charismatic.

13. Which of the following is a species whose decline serves as an early warning that an ecosystem is being degraded?
    (A) A keystone species
    (B) An indicator species
    (C) A native species
    (D) A non-native species
    (E) An endemic species

14. The temperature of the lower troposphere can be influenced by all of the following atmospheric gases EXCEPT
    (A) carbon dioxide
    (B) methane
    (C) nitrous oxide
    (D) water vapor
    (E) nitrogen gas

15. A connected loop of shallow and deep ocean currents transports warm and cool water to various parts of the earth. This loop results from
    (A) upwelling events that occur along the coast of South America
    (B) the location of the continents that ultimately determines the direction and flow of ocean currents
    (C) dust from the Sahara Desert generating lower pressure in the Atlantic Ocean
    (D) differences in water density due to temperature and salinity
    (E) the formation of new oceanic crust at plate boundaries

16. This biome is known for the greatest storehouse of nutrients in the leaf litter above and in its soil.
    (A) Tropical rainforest
    (B) Tropical grassland
    (C) Chaparral
    (D) Temperate forest
    (E) Arctic tundra

17. The gradual establishment of biotic communities in lifeless areas (such as a parking lot) where there is no soil is referred to as
    (A) degradative succession
    (B) primary succession
    (C) secondary succession
    (D) random succession
    (E) cyclical succession

18. According to the climate graphs below, all of the following are true, EXCEPT

Tropical rain forest

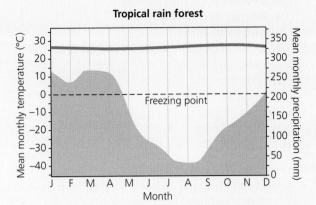

Temperate deciduous forest

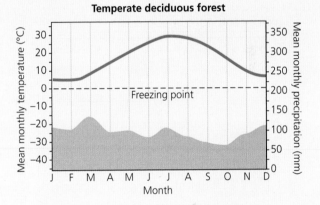

Northern coniferous forest (boreal forest, taiga)

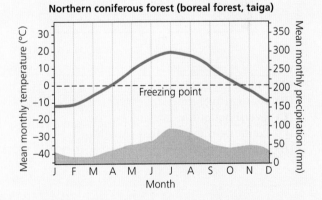

    (A) the average temperature for a tropical rainforest is constant throughout the year
    (B) on average, a temperate deciduous forest remains above freezing throughout the year
    (C) a tropical rainforest has distinct rainy and dry seasons
    (D) a northern evergreen forest receives most of its precipitation in the form of snow in the winter
    (E) a temperate deciduous forest receives fairly consistent precipitation from season to season

19. The competitive exclusion principle states that two species cannot occupy the exact same niche. If one species dominates, the other must
    I. Migrate to a new area
    II. Modify its niche
    III. Suffer population declines and possible extinction
    (A) II only
    (B) III only
    (C) I and II only
    (D) I and III only
    (E) I, II, and III

20. On the graph below, the solid line indicates carrying capacity and the dashed line indicates the population size of reindeer introduced onto a small island in the Bering Sea. The reindeer population experienced a(n)

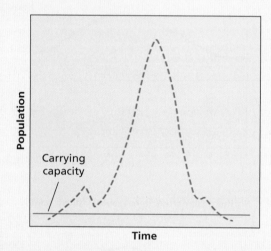

    (A) infectious disease
    (B) reproductive time lag
    (C) overshoot of the carrying capacity
    (D) continuous exponential growth
    (E) logistic growth

21. A population that is dominated by pre-reproductive individuals that are not being harvested is likely to
    (A) decrease in population size
    (B) remain stable in population size
    (C) decrease in post-reproductive ages
    (D) increase in population size
    (E) decrease in reproductive ages

Questions 22 and 23 refer to the following. Choices may be used once, more than once, or not at all.
    (A) Replacement level fertility
    (B) Sustainable fertility rate
    (C) Cultural carrying capacity
    (D) Total fertility rate
    (E) Intrinsic rate of increase

22. The number of people that could live on the planet in reasonable comfort and freedom without impairing the ability of the planet to sustain future generations

23. The average number of children that women in a given population will have during their reproductive years

24. The population of a country with an age structure that has a high proportion of pre-reproductive individuals is
    (A) declining slowly
    (B) expanding rapidly
    (C) stable
    (D) declining rapidly
    (E) expanding slowly

25. How many years does it take for a country with an annual growth rate of 2.5% to double in size?
    (A)   0.3
    (B)   2.5
    (C)   20
    (D)   28
    (E)   70

1. Read the excerpt below and answer the questions that follow.

> Native species of North America are often defined as those species that were present in North America before Europeans arrived in the early 1600s. When Europeans arrived, they found extensive forests dominated by the American chestnut tree. These chestnut trees were extensively cultivated and planted by the North American natives for food and other wood products. In the early 1900s, the chestnut blight (a fungus) virtually exterminated all of the American chestnut trees in North America.

(a) Classify the American chestnut tree as either a native or an introduced species. **Explain** your classification.

(b) Classify the chestnut blight as either a native or an introduced species. **Explain** your classification.

(c) The introduction of invasive species can be deliberate or accidental.

  (i) **Identify** TWO characteristics of an invasive species.

  (ii) **Identify** which of the species (American chestnut or chestnut blight) is considered invasive.

(d) Many non-native game animals, for example, axis deer and blackbuck antelope, were deliberately introduced to the United States for the sport hunting industry.

  (i) **Describe** ONE ecological and ONE economic advantage of the introduction of game species.

  (ii) **Describe** ONE ecological and ONE economic disadvantage of the introduction of game species.

2. Energy flow is a central theme throughout the study of environmental science. Consider energy flow when answering the following questions:

(a) The tundra/arctic biome is populated with lichens and grasses as dominant producers, small rodents called lemmings, brown bears (grizzlies), caribou (deer family), and arctic wolves. **Diagram** a food web that correctly shows the flow of energy through the species shown in the squares below.

| Lichens | Brown bears | Lemmings |

| Arctic wolves | Caribou | Grasses |

(b) The tundra, like most biomes, has very few large predators that function at the highest levels of the trophic pyramid. **Explain** this phenomenon.

(c) An ecologist is doing an in-depth study of a tundra ecosystem. He does a biomass sample of the producers in an area and measures 3.5 kilograms of producer biomass per square meter. **Calculate** the biomass of producers in terms of kilograms per hectare (kg/ha). A hectare contains 10,000 square meters.

(d) Based on your calculation of kg/ha above:

  (i) **Calculate** the approximate biomass of both primary and secondary consumers that could be maintained in one hectare of this ecosystem.

  (ii) **Explain** your calculation.

(e) Many people suggest that it would be wiser for humans to eat lower on the trophic pyramid. **Discuss** this statement in terms of both energy availability and land use.

Sustaining Biodiversity: Saving Species and Ecosystem Services

> The last word in ignorance is the person who says of an animal or plant: "What good is it?" . . . If the land mechanism as a whole is good, then every part of it is good, whether we understand it or not.
>
> ALDO LEOPOLD

Endangered wild Siberian tiger.

Volodymyr Burdiak/Shutterstock.com

Key Questions

9.1 What role do humans play in the loss of species and ecosystem services?

9.2 Why should we try to sustain wild species and the ecosystem services they provide?

9.3 How do humans accelerate species extinction and degradation of ecosystem services?

9.4 How can we sustain wild species and the ecosystem services they provide?

Where Have All the Honeybees Gone?

In meadows, forests, farm fields, and gardens around the world, industrious honeybees (Figure 9.1) flit from one flowering plant to another. They are collecting liquid flower nectar to take back to their hives. The bees also collect pollen grains, which stick to hairs on their legs. They feed young honeybees the protein-rich pollen, and the adults feed on the honey made from the collected nectar and stored in the hive.

Honeybees provide one of nature's most important ecosystem services: *pollination*. It involves a transfer of pollen stuck on their bodies from the male to female reproductive organs of the same flower or among different flowers. This fertilization enables the flower to produce seeds and fruit. Honeybees pollinate many plant species and some of our most important food crops, including many vegetables, fruits, and tree nuts such as almonds. European honeybees pollinate about 71% of vegetable and fruit crops that provide 90% of the world's food and a third of the US food supply.

Many US growers rent European honeybees from commercial beekeepers that truck about 2.7 million hives to farms across the country to pollinate different crops during the weeks when they are in bloom. Nature relies on the earth's free pollination service provided by a diversity of bees and other wild pollinators (such as butterflies, hummingbirds, and bats). In contrast, farmers practicing industrialized agriculture on vast croplands and orchards rely mostly on renting this single bee species to pollinate their crops.

However, European honeybee populations have been in decline since the 1980s. Since 2006, massive numbers of these bees in the United States and in parts of Europe have been disappearing from their colonies. This phenomenon, called **colony collapse disorder (CCD),** occurs when all the bees abandon a colony. Since 2006 23–43% of the European honeybee colonies in the United States suffered from CCD. This was well above the historical loss rates of 10–15%.

Darlyne A. Murawski/National Geographic Creative

FIGURE 9.1 European honeybee drawing nectar from a flower.

Many farmers believe that we need the industrialized honeybee pollination system to grow enough food. However many ecologists view such heavy dependence on a single bee species as a potentially dangerous violation of the earth's biodiversity **principle of sustainability** (see Inside Back Cover). They warn that this dependence could put food supplies at risk if the population of European honeybees continues to decline. If this occurs, food prices and hunger will rise. Ecologists call for more reliance on the free crop pollination services provided by variety of wild bee species and other pollinators.

The honeybee crisis is a classic case of how the decline of a species can threaten vital ecosystem and economic services. Scientists project that during this century, human activities—especially those that contribute to habitat loss and climate change—are likely to play a key role in the extinction of one-fifth to one-half of the world's known plant and animal species. Many scientists view this threat as one of the most serious and long-lasting environmental and economic problems we face. In this chapter, we discuss the causes of this problem and possible ways to deal with it. ●

CRITICAL THINKING

Why is having a diversity of pollinator species critical to food production?

9.1 WHAT ROLE DO HUMANS PLAY IN THE LOSS OF SPECIES AND ECOSYSTEM SERVICES?

CONCEPT 9.1 Species are becoming extinct at least 1,000 times faster than the historical rate and by the end of this century, the extinction rate is projected to be 10,000 times higher.

Extinctions Are Natural but Sometimes They Increase Sharply

When a species can no longer be found anywhere on the earth, it has suffered **biological extinction.** Extinction is a natural process and has occurred at a low rate throughout most of the earth's history. In fact, an estimated 99.9 percent of all species that have existed have gone extinct. This natural rate is known as the **background extinction rate.** Scientists estimate that the background rate typically amounts to a loss of about 1 species per year for every 1 million species living on the earth. This amounts to 10 natural extinctions a year if the earth has 10 million species.

The extinction of many species in a relatively short period of geologic time is called a **mass extinction.** Geologic, fossil, and other records indicate that the earth has experienced five mass extinctions, during which 50–90% of the species present at that time went extinct (see Figure 4.16, p. 110) over thousands of years. The largest mass extinction took place some 250 million years ago and wiped about 90% of the world's existing species.

The causes of past mass extinctions are poorly understood but probably involved global changes in environmental conditions. Examples are sustained and significant global warming or cooling, large changes in sea levels and ocean water acidity, and catastrophes such as multiple large-scale volcanic eruptions and large asteroids or comets hitting the planet.

Mass extinctions devastate life on the earth. But they also provide opportunities for new life forms to emerge, diversify, and fill empty ecological niches. Scientific evidence indicates that after each mass extinction, the earth's overall biodiversity returned to equal or higher levels. However, each recovery took several million years (Figure 4.16, p. 110). The existence of millions of species today means speciation, on average, has kept ahead of extinction. It also demonstrates the biodiversity **principle of sustainability** as a factor in the long-term sustainability of life on the earth.

Scientific evidence indicates that extinction rates have increased as the human population has grown and spread over most of the globe. In this expansion, humans have destroyed and degraded habitats, consumed huge quantities of resources, and created large and growing ecological footprints (see Figure 1.8, p. 12). The extinction of one species can lead to the extinction of other species that depend on it for food or ecosystem services, and biodiversity researchers project that the rate of extinction will continue to increase. In the words of biodiversity expert Edward O. Wilson (see Individuals Matter 4.1, p. 98), "The natural world is everywhere disappearing before our eyes—cut to pieces, mowed down, plowed under, gobbled up, replaced by human artifacts."

Scientists estimate that the current annual extinction rate is at least 1,000 times the natural background extinction rate (Science Focus 9.1) (**Concept 9.1**). Assuming there are 10 million species on the earth, this means that today we are losing an estimated 10,000 species per year.

Biodiversity researchers project that during this century, the extinction rate is likely to rise to at least 10,000 times the background rate—mostly because of habitat loss and degradation, climate change, ocean acidification, and other environmentally harmful effects of human activities (**Concept 9.1**). At this rate, if there were 10 million species on the earth, 100,000 species would be expected to disappear each year—an average of about 274 species per day or about 11 every hour. By the end of this century, most of the big carnivorous cats, including cheetahs, tigers (see chapter-opening photo), and lions might exist only in zoos and small wildlife sanctuaries. Most elephants, rhinoceroses, gorillas, chimpanzees, and orangutans will likely disappear from the wild.

So why does this matter? According to biodiversity researchers, including Edward O. Wilson and Stuart Pimm, at this extinction rate, an estimated 20%–50% of the world's 2 million identified animal and plant species could vanish from the wild by the end of this century. Many other species that have not been identified will also disappear. If these estimates are correct, the earth is entering a *sixth mass extinction* caused primarily by human activities. Unlike previous mass extinctions, much of this mass extinction is projected to take place over the course of a human lifetime instead of over many thousands of years (Figure 4.16, p. 110).

20–50
Percentage of the earth's known species that could disappear this century primarily because of human activities

Such large-scale loss of species would likely impair some of the earth's vital ecosystem services such as air and water purification, natural pest control, and pollination

SCIENCE FOCUS 9.1

Estimating Extinction Rates

Louis Agassi Fuertes/National Geographic Creative

FIGURE 9.A Painting of the last pair of North American passenger pigeons, which once were the world's most abundant bird species. They became extinct in the wild in 1912 mostly because of habitat loss and overhunting.

Scientists who try to catalog extinctions, estimate past extinction rates, and project future extinction rates face three problems. *First*, because the natural extinction of a species typically takes a long time, it is difficult to document. *Second*, scientists have identified only about 2 million of the world's estimated 7 million to 10 million and perhaps as many as 100 million species. *Third*, scientists know little about the ecological roles of most of the species that have been identified.

One approach to estimating future extinction rates is to study records documenting past rates at which easily observable mammals and birds (Figure 9.A) have become extinct. Most of these extinctions have occurred since humans began to dominate the planet about 10,000 years ago. This information can be compared with fossil records of extinctions that occurred before that time.

Another approach is to observe how reductions in habitat area affect extinction rates. The *species–area relationship*, studied by Edward O. Wilson (see Individuals Matter 4.1, p. 98) and Robert MacArthur, suggests that, on average, a 90% loss of land habitat in a given area can cause the extinction of about 50% of the species living in that area. Thus, scientists can base extinction rate estimates on the rates of habitat destruction and degradation, which are increasing around the world.

Scientists also use mathematical models to estimate the risk of a particular species becoming endangered or extinct within a certain period. These models include factors such as trends in population size, past and projected changes in habitat availability, interactions with other species, and genetic factors.

Researchers are working hard to get more and better data and to improve the models they use in order to make better estimates of extinction rates and to project the effects of such extinctions on vital ecosystem services such as pollination (**Core Case Study**).

CRITICAL THINKING

Does the fact that extinction rates can only be estimated make them unreliable? Why or why not?

(**Core Case Study**). According to the Millennium Ecosystem Assessment, 15 of 24 of the earth's major ecosystem services are in decline. Conservation scientists view this potential massive loss of biodiversity and ecosystem services within the span of a human lifetime as one of the most important and long-lasting environmental and economic problems humanity faces. By saving as many species as possible from extinction—especially keystone species (see p. 100)—we could increase our beneficial environmental impact and help sustain and enrich our own lives and economies.

Wilson, Pimm, and other extinction experts consider a projected extinction rate of 10,000 times the background extinction rate to be low, for two reasons:

- *First*, both the rate of extinction and the resulting threats to ecosystem services are likely to increase sharply during the next 50–100 years because of the harmful environmental impacts of the rapidly growing human population and its growing per capita use of resources.

- *Second*, we are eliminating, degrading, fragmenting, and simplifying many biologically diverse environments—including tropical forests, coral reefs, wetlands, and estuaries—that serve as potential sites for the emergence of new species. Thus, in addition to greatly increasing the rate of extinction, we may be limiting the long-term recovery of biodiversity by eliminating places where new species can evolve. In other words, we are also creating a *speciation crisis*.

Biologists Philip Levin, Donald Levin, and others warn that, while our activities are likely to reduce the speciation rates for some species, they could increase the speciation rates for rapidly reproducing species. Examples are weeds, rats, and insects such as cockroaches. Rapidly expanding populations of such species could crowd and compete with various other species, further accelerating their extinction and threatening key ecosystem services.

Endangered and Threatened Species Are Ecological Smoke Alarms

Biologists classify species that are heading toward biological extinction as either *endangered* or *threatened*. An **endangered species** has so few individual survivors that the species could soon become extinct. A **threatened species** (also known as a *vulnerable* species) has enough remaining individuals to survive in the short term, but because of declining numbers, it is likely to become endangered in the near future.

The International Union for Conservation of Nature (IUCN) has been monitoring the status of the world's species for 50 years and each year publishes a Red List that identifies species that are critically endangered, endangered, or threatened. Between 1996 and 2016, the total number of species in these three categories increased by 96%. Figure 9.2 shows 4 of the nearly 23,000 species on the 2016 Red List. The actual number of species in trouble is very likely much higher. Some species have characteristics that increase their chances of becoming extinct (Figure 9.3). As biodiversity expert Edward O. Wilson puts it, "The first animal species to go are the big, the slow, the tasty, and those with valuable parts such as tusks and skins."

CHECKPOINT FOR UNDERSTANDING 9.1

1. Identify the reasons for the accelerated loss of species the earth is now experiencing.

2. Describe the impact of massive loss of species on ecosystem services.

3. Identify some of the characteristics of species particularly vulnerable to extinction.

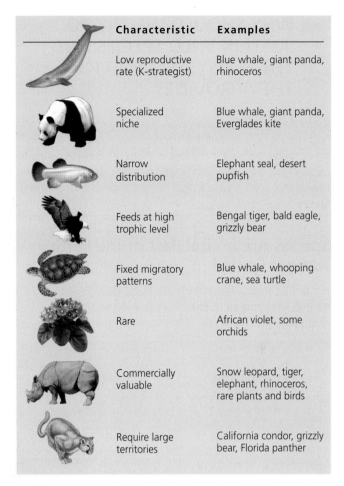

	Characteristic	Examples
	Low reproductive rate (K-strategist)	Blue whale, giant panda, rhinoceros
	Specialized niche	Blue whale, giant panda, Everglades kite
	Narrow distribution	Elephant seal, desert pupfish
	Feeds at high trophic level	Bengal tiger, bald eagle, grizzly bear
	Fixed migratory patterns	Blue whale, whooping crane, sea turtle
	Rare	African violet, some orchids
	Commercially valuable	Snow leopard, tiger, elephant, rhinoceros, rare plants and birds
	Require large territories	California condor, grizzly bear, Florida panther

FIGURE 9.3 Certain characteristics put a species in greater danger of becoming extinct.

a. Mexican gray wolf: About 97 in the forests of Arizona and New Mexico

Geoffrey Kuchera/Shutterstock.com

b. California condor: 410 in the southwestern United States (up from 9 in 1986)

Ferenc Cegledi/Shutterstock.com

c. Whooping crane: 442 in North America

Catcher of Light, Inc./Shutterstock.com

d. Sumatran tiger: less than 400 on the Indonesian island of Sumatra

Tiago Jorge da Silva Estima/Shutterstock.com

FIGURE 9.2 Endangered natural capital: These four critically endangered species are threatened with extinction, largely because of human activities. The number below each photo indicates the estimated total number of individuals of that species remaining in the wild.

9.2 WHY SHOULD WE TRY TO SUSTAIN WILD SPECIES AND THE ECOSYSTEM SERVICES THEY PROVIDE?

CONCEPT 9.2 We should avoid hastening the extinction of wild species because of the ecosystem and economic services they provide, because it can take millions of years for nature to recover from large-scale extinctions, and because many people believe that species have a right to exist regardless of their usefulness to us.

Species Are a Vital Part of the Earth's Natural Capital

According to the World Wildlife Fund (WWF), only about 61,000 orangutans (Figure 9.4) remain in the wild. Most of them are in the tropical forests of Borneo, Asia's largest island. These highly intelligent animals are disappearing at an estimated rate of 1,000–2,000 per year. A key reason is that much of their tropical forest habitat is being cleared for plantations that grow oil palms. They are a source of palm oil—the world's most widely used vegetable oil. It is an ingredient in numerous products such as cookies, cosmetics, and is used to produce biodiesel fuel for motor vehicles. Another reason they are disappearing is smuggling. An illegally smuggled, live orangutan sells for thousands of dollars on the black market.

The effects of these human-related activities are compounded by the fact that orangutans have the lowest birth rate of all the mammals. Because of their low birth rate, orangutans have a hard time increasing their numbers. Without urgent protective action, the endangered orangutan may disappear in the wild within the next two decades.

Orangutans are considered keystone species in the ecosystems they inhabit. The dispersal of fruit and plant seeds in their wastes throughout their tropical rain forest habitat

FIGURE 9.4 Natural capital degradation: These endangered orangutans depend on a rapidly disappearing tropical forest habitat in Borneo. **Critical thinking:** What difference will it make if human activities hasten the extinction of the orangutan?

Seatraveler/Dreamstime.com

is an important ecosystem service. If orangutans disappear, many rain forest plants and other animals that consume them may be threatened.

According to biologists, there are four major reasons why we should be very concerned about human activities causing or hastening the extinction of other species over the next 50–100 years.

First, the world's species provide vital *ecosystem services* (see Figure 1.3, p. 7) that help to keep us alive and support our economies (**Concept 9.2**). For example, we depend on honeybees (**Core Case Study**) and other insects for pollination of many food crops. *Second*, many species contribute to *economic services* that we depend on (**Concept 9.2**). Various plant species provide economic value as food crops, wood for fuel, lumber for construction, paper from trees, and substances for medicines. *Bioprospectors* search tropical forests and other ecosystems to find plants and animals that scientists can use to make medicinal drugs (Figure 9.5)—an example of *learning from nature*. Currently, less than 0.5% of the world's known plant species have been examined for their medicinal properties.

CONSIDER THIS . . .

LEARNING FROM NATURE

Scientist Richard Wrangham is identifying medicinal compounds useful for humans by observing which plants sick chimpanzees eat to heal themselves.

Preserving species and their habitats also provides economic benefits in the form of *ecotourism*. This rapidly growing industry specializes in environmentally responsible travel to natural areas and generates more than $1 million per minute in tourist expenditures, worldwide. Conservation biologist Michael Soulé estimates that a male lion living to age 7 generates about $515,000 through ecotourism in Kenya, but only about $10,000 if it is killed for its skin.

A *third* major reason for not hastening extinctions through our activities is that it will take 5 million to 10 million years for natural speciation to replace the species we are likely to wipe out during this century.

Fourth, many people believe that wild species, such as orangutans, have a right to exist, regardless of their usefulness to us (**Concept 9.2**). This ethical viewpoint raises a number of challenging questions. Since we cannot save all species from the harmful consequences of our actions, we have to make choices about which ones to protect. Should we protect more animal species than plant species and, if so, which ones should we protect? Some people support protecting familiar and appealing species such as elephants, whales, tigers, giant pandas, orangutans (Figure 9.4), and parrots (Figure 9.6), but care much less about protecting plants that serve as the base of the food supply for other species (**Core Case Study**). Others might think little about getting rid of species that most people fear hate, or find unappealing such as mosquitoes, cockroaches, disease-causing bacteria, snakes, sharks, and bats.

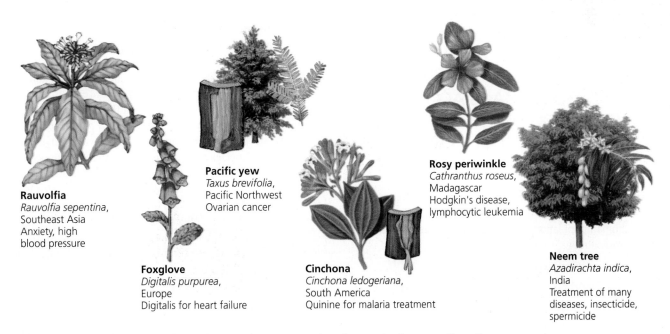

Rauvolfia
Rauvolfia sepentina,
Southeast Asia
Anxiety, high
blood pressure

Foxglove
Digitalis purpurea,
Europe
Digitalis for heart failure

Pacific yew
Taxus brevifolia,
Pacific Northwest
Ovarian cancer

Cinchona
Cinchona ledogeriana,
South America
Quinine for malaria treatment

Rosy periwinkle
Cathranthus roseus,
Madagascar
Hodgkin's disease,
lymphocytic leukemia

Neem tree
Azadirachta indica,
India
Treatment of many
diseases, insecticide,
spermicide

FIGURE 9.5 Natural capital: These plant species are examples of *nature's pharmacy*. Once the active ingredients in the plants have been identified, scientists can usually produce them synthetically. The active ingredients in 9 of the 10 leading prescription drugs originally came from wild organisms.

FIGURE 9.6 Many species of wildlife such as this endangered hyacinth macaw in Mato Grosso, Brazil, are sources of beauty and pleasure. Habitat loss and illegal capture in the wild by pet traders endanger this species.

CHECKPOINT FOR UNDERSTANDING 9.2

1. Identify four primary reasons for preserving species.

9.3 HOW DO HUMANS ACCELERATE SPECIES EXTINCTION AND DEGRADATION OF ECOSYSTEM SERVICES?

CONCEPT 9.3 The greatest threats to species and ecosystem services are loss or degradation of habitat, harmful invasive species, human population growth, pollution, climate change, and overexploitation.

Habitat Destruction and Fragmentation: Remember HIPPCO

Biodiversity researchers summarize the most important direct causes of species extinction and threats to ecosystem services using the acronym **HIPPCO**: **H**abitat destruction, degradation, and fragmentation; **I**nvasive (nonnative) species; **P**opulation growth and increasing use of resources; **P**ollution; **C**limate change; and **O**verexploitation (**Concept 9.3**).

According to biodiversity researchers, the greatest threat to wild species is habitat loss (Figure 9.7), degradation, and fragmentation. Specifically, deforestation in tropical areas (see Figure 3.1, p. 66) is the greatest threat to species and to the ecosystem services they provide. The next largest threats are the destruction and degradation of coastal wetlands and coral reefs (see Chapter 6, Core Case Study, p. 154), the plowing of grasslands for planting of crops (see Figure 5.17, p. 135), and the pollution of streams, lakes, and oceans.

Island species—many of them found nowhere else on earth—are especially vulnerable to extinction. If their habitats are destroyed, degraded, or fragmented into patches, they have nowhere else to go. This is why the Hawaiian Islands are America's "extinction capital"—with 63% of its species at risk.

Habitat fragmentation occurs when a large, intact area of habitat such as a forest or natural grassland is divided into smaller, isolated patches or *habitat islands* (Figure 9.8). Roads, logging operations, crop fields, and urban developments divide forests and natural grasslands. This reduces tree cover in forests and blocks animal migration routes. Fragmentation can divide populations of a species into increasingly isolated small groups that are more vulnerable to predators, competitor species, disease, and catastrophic events such as storms and fires. In addition, habitat fragmentation creates barriers that limit the abilities of some species to disperse and colonize areas, locate adequate food supplies, and find mates. Scientists are using drones with cameras to count and monitor populations of endangered and threatened species and the degradation and fragmentation of their habitats.

Habitat fragmentation also leads to what is called *edge effect* (Chapter 4, p. 96). Breaking up large areas of forest results in more edge habitat, the boundary between two different types of habitat. Abiotic factors such as air temperature, humidity, and soil moisture all change at the edges and adjacent open land can allow sunlight and wind to penetrate the forest more deeply. This in turn can lead to a change in the population of species and community structure that occurs at the boundary. The way different plant and animal species react to edge effect is referred to as their *edge sensitivity*. Biodiversity of the core habitat can be reduced, though some species benefit from edge effect. Plants like poison ivy thrive in edge habitat, and some bird species also proliferate in the ecotone, the boundary between forest and adjacent open land.

Beneficial and Harmful Nonnative Species

There are many examples of how the introduction of nonnative species to the United States has been beneficial. According to a study by ecologist David Pimentel, nonnative species such as corn, wheat, rice, and other food crops,

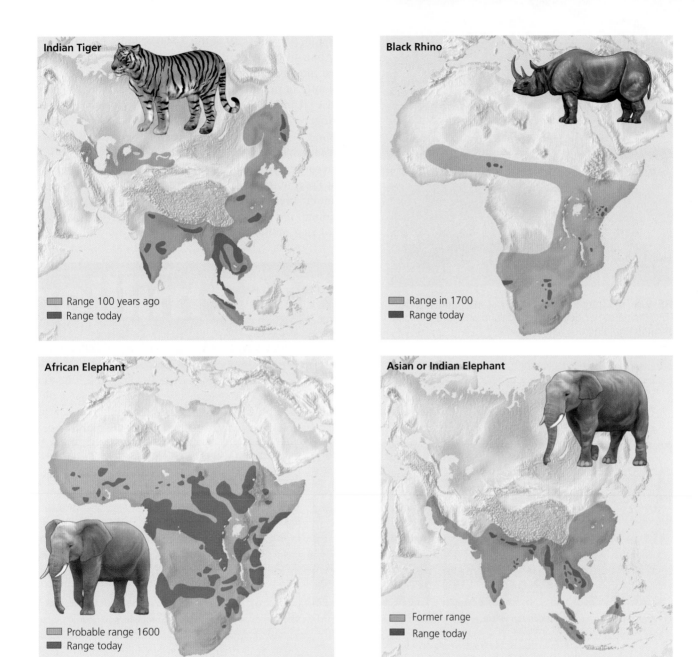

FIGURE 9.7 Natural capital degradation: These maps reveal the reductions in the ranges of four wildlife species, mostly as the result of severe habitat loss and fragmentation and illegal hunting for some of their valuable body parts. ***Critical thinking:*** Would you support expanding these ranges even though this would reduce the land available for human habitation and farming? Explain.

(Compiled by the authors using data from International Union for Conservation of Nature and World Wildlife Fund.)

as well as some species of cattle, poultry, and other livestock, provide more than 98% of the US food supply. Other deliberately introduced species have helped control pests. In the 1600s, English settlers brought highly beneficial European honeybees (**Core Case Study**) to North America to provide honey. Today they pollinate one-third of the crops grown in the United States.

GOOD NEWS

On the other hand, problems can occur when an introduced species does not face the natural predators, competitors,

parasites, viruses, bacteria, or fungi that controlled its populations in its native habitat. This can allow some nonnative species to outcompete populations of many native species for food, disrupt ecosystem services, transmit new diseases, and lead to economic losses. When this happens the nonnative species are viewed as harmful *invasive species*. Invasive species rarely cause the global extinction of other species, but they can cause population declines and local and regional extinctions of some native species.

FIGURE 9.8 The fragmentation of landscapes reduces biodiversity by eliminating or degrading grassland and forest wildlife habitats and degrading ecosystem services.

iStockphoto.com/Franckreporter

Figure 9.9 shows 10 of the 7,100 or more invasive species that, after being deliberately or accidentally introduced into the United States, have caused ecological and economic harm. According to the US Fish and Wildlife Service (USFWS), about 42% of the species listed as endangered in the United States and 95% of those in the US state of Hawaii are at risk mainly because of threats from invasive species.

According to Achim Steiner, head of the UN Environment Program (UNEP), and environmental scientist David Pimentel, invasive species cause $1.4 trillion a year in economic and ecological damages, globally—an average loss of $2.7 million a minute.

$162 million
Estimated hourly global cost of invasive species

Deliberately Introduced Species

Purple loosestrife

African honeybee ("Killer bee")

Kudzu

Nutria

European wild boar (Feral pig)

Accidentally Introduced Species

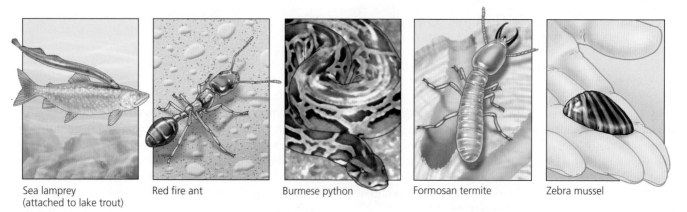

Sea lamprey (attached to lake trout)

Red fire ant

Burmese python

Formosan termite

Zebra mussel

FIGURE 9.9 Some of the estimated 7,100 harmful invasive species that have been deliberately or accidentally introduced into the United States.

The Kudzu Vine and Kudzu Bugs

Some invasive species, such as *kudzu vine* (Figure 9.9), have been deliberately introduced into ecosystems. In the 1930s, this plant was imported from Japan and planted in the southeastern United States in an effort to control soil erosion.

Kudzu does control erosion, but it grows so rapidly that it engulfs hillsides, gardens, trees, stream banks, cars (Figure 9.10), and anything else in its path. Dig it up or burn it, and it still keeps spreading. It can grow in sunlight or shade and is very difficult to kill, even with herbicides that can contaminate water supplies. Scientists have found a common fungus that can kill kudzu within a few hours, but they need to investigate any harmful side effects it may have.

Nicknamed "the vine that ate the South," kudzu has spread throughout much of the southeastern United States. As the climate gets warmer, it could spread to the north.

Kudzu is considered a menace in the United States. However, for thousands of years Asians have used a powdered form of kudzu in herbal remedies to treat a range of ailments such as fever, inflammation, flu, dysentery, hangovers, and the effects of insect and snake bites.

Almost every part of the kudzu plant is edible, making it an inexpensive and readily available source of nutrition. Because it can grow rapidly where other plants cannot and is drought tolerant, it has helped people survive droughts and famines and restore severely degraded land.

Because ingesting small amounts of kudzu powder can lessen one's desire for alcohol, it could be used to reduce alcoholism and binge drinking. Although kudzu can engulf and kill trees, it might eventually help to save some of them. Researchers at the Georgia Institute of Technology have found that kudzu could replace trees as a source of fiber for making paper. It is also being evaluated as a raw material for producing biofuel.

The brown, pea-sized Kudzu bug is another invasive species that was imported into the United States from Japan. It breeds in and feeds on patches of kudzu, and it can help to reduce the spread of the vine. However, it spreads even more rapidly than the kudzu vine. It also feeds on soybeans and thus could pose a major threat to soy crops.

Some pesticides can kill this bug, but might end up boosting their numbers by promoting genetic resistance to the pesticides. Researchers hope to change this bug through genetic engineering in such a way that it will stop eating soybeans. They are also evaluating the use of a wasp whose larvae attack kudzu bug embryos. However, so far, scientists see no way to eradicate this rapidly spreading invader species.

Some Accidentally Introduced Species Can Disrupt Ecosystems

Many unwanted nonnative invaders arrive from other continents as stowaways on aircraft, in the ballast water of tankers and cargo ships, and as hitchhikers on imported products such as wooden packing crates. Cars and trucks can also spread the seeds of nonnative plant species embedded in their tire treads. Many tourists return home with living plants that can multiply and become invasive. Some of these plants might also contain insects that can invade new areas, multiply rapidly, and threaten crops.

Florida is the global capital for invasive species. Some of its many troublesome invasive species include Burmese pythons, African pythons, and several species of boa constrictors, all of which have invaded the Florida Everglades. About 1 million of these snakes, imported from Africa and Asia, have been sold as pets. Some buyers, after learning that these reptiles do not make good pets, let them go in the wetlands of the Everglades.

The Burmese python (Figure 9.11) can live 20 to 25 years and grow as long as 5 meters (16 feet). It can weigh as much 77 kilograms (170 pounds) and be as big around as a telephone pole. These snakes have huge appetites. They feed at night, eating a variety of birds and mammals (rabbits, raccoons, and white-tailed deer). Occasionally they will eat other reptiles, including the American alligator—a keystone species in the Everglades ecosystem. Pythons seize their prey with their sharp teeth, wrap around them, and squeeze them to death, before feeding on them. They have also been known to eat cats and dogs, small farm animals, and geese. Research indicates that predation by these snakes is altering the food webs and ecosystem services of the Everglades.

According to wildlife scientists, the Burmese python population in Florida's wetlands cannot be controlled. They

FIGURE 9.10 Kudzu has grown over this car in the US state of Georgia.

FIGURE 9.11 University of Florida researchers hold a 4.6-meter-long (15-foot-long), 74-kilogram (162-pound) Burmese python captured in Everglades National Park shortly after it had eaten a 1.8-meter-long (6-foot-long) American alligator.

Dan Callister/Alamy Stock photo

are hard to find and kill or capture and they reproduce rapidly. Trapping and moving the snakes from one area to another has not worked because they are able to return to the areas where they were captured. Another concern is that the Burmese python could spread to other swampy wetlands in the southern half of the United States.

Invasive species are a serious ecological and economic threat, but the situation is not hopeless. Roughly only 1 of every 100 species that invade an area is able to establish a self-sustaining population and reduce the biodiversity of the ecosystem it has invaded. In addition, scientists have found that some invaders end up increasing the biodiversity of the areas they have moved into by creating new habitats and niches for other species.

Controlling Invasive Species

Once a harmful nonnative species becomes established in an ecosystem, removing it is almost impossible. Americans pay more than $160 billion a year to eradicate or control an increasing number of invasive species—without much success. Thus, the best way to limit the harmful impacts of these organisms is to prevent them from being introduced into ecosystems.

Scientists suggest several ways to do this. By researching the characteristics of invaders and working to understand the types of habitats they invade, it will be easier to control their populations. Another strategy is to establish treaties with other countries to ban the import of identified species and inspect incoming cargo. Educating citizens about the impact of releasing exotic species into the wild can also help to reduce the number of invasive species.

Figure 9.12 shows some of the things you can do to help prevent or slow the spread of harmful invasive species.

What Can You Do?

Controlling Invasive Species

- Do not buy wild plants and animals or remove them from natural areas.

- Do not release wild pets in natural areas.

- Do not dump aquarium contents or unused fishing bait into waterways or storm drains.

- When camping, use only local firewood.

- Brush or clean pet dogs, hiking boots, mountain bikes, canoes, boats, motors, fishing tackle, and other gear before entering or leaving wild areas.

FIGURE 9.12 Individuals matter: Some ways to prevent or slow the spread of harmful invasive species. ***Critical thinking:*** Which two of these actions do you think are the most important ones to take? Why? Which of these actions do you plan to take?

Population Growth, High Rates of Resource Use, Pollution, and Climate Change Contribute to Species Extinctions

Past and projected *human population growth* (Figure 1.9, p. 15) and rising rates of *resource use per person* have greatly expanded the human ecological footprint (see Figure 1.8, p. 12). People have eliminated, degraded, and fragmented vast areas of wildlife habitat (Figure 9.8) as they have spread out over the planet, and increased their use of resources. This has caused the extinction of many species (**Concept 9.3**).

Pollution of the air, water, and soil by human activities also threatens some species with extinction. According to the USFWS, each year pesticides kill about one-fifth of the European honeybee colonies that pollinate almost a third of all US food crops (**Core Case Study** and Science Focus 9.2). The USFWS estimates that pesticides also kill more than 67 million birds and 6 to 14 million fish each year. They also threaten about 20% of the country's endangered and threatened species.

During the 1950s and 1960s, populations of fish-eating birds such as ospreys, brown pelicans, and bald eagles plummeted because of the widespread use of a pesticide called DDT. The concentration of a chemical derived from the pesticide DDT remained in the environment, and was taken up and accumulated in the tissues of organisms, a process called **bioaccumulation**. The chemical became more concentrated as it moved up through food chains and webs, a process called **biomagnification** (Figure 9.13). Concentrated amounts of the chemical in the fatty tissues of these top predator birds decreased their ability to produce calcium in the eggshells they laid. This led to eggshells so thin that they cracked before hatching and reduced the ability of the species to reproduce successfully. Also hard hit in those years were predatory birds such as the prairie falcon, sparrow hawk, and peregrine falcon that help control populations of rabbits, ground squirrels, and other crop eaters. Since the United States banned DDT in 1972, most of these bird species have made a comeback.

GOOD NEWS

According to a study by Conservation International, the habitat loss and disruption of food webs associated with projected *climate change* could drive a fifth to half of all known land animals and plants to extinction by the end of this century. Current climate change is caused mostly by human activities such as burning carbon-containing fossil fuels and clearing forests, both of which increase the atmospheric concentration of greenhouse gases such as carbon dioxide (CO_2). The hardest-hit species will be those that have limited ranges or low tolerance for temperature changes. For example, studies indicate that the polar bear is threatened because of higher temperatures and melting sea ice in its polar habitat. The shrinkage of floating ice is making it harder for polar bears to find seals, their favorite prey, especially in the southern parts of the polar bear's range in the Arctic, which has warmed the most.

According to the IUCN and the US Geological Survey, the world's total polar bear population is likely to decline by 30–35% by 2050 due to loss of habitat and prey. By the end of this century, polar bears might be found only in zoos.

The Killing, Capturing, and Selling of Wild Species Threatens Biodiversity

Some protected animals are illegally killed (poached) for their valuable parts or are captured and sold live to collectors. Organized crime has moved into illegal wildlife smuggling because of the huge profits involved. At least two-thirds of all live animals illegally smuggled around the world die in transit. Few of the smugglers are caught or punished.

To poachers, a highly endangered, live eastern mountain gorilla (of which there are about 790 left in the wild) is worth $150,000, and the pelt of an endangered giant panda (1,864 left in the wild in China) can bring $100,000.

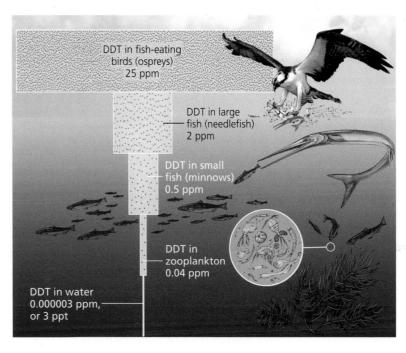

FIGURE 9.13 *Bioaccumulation* (in individual animals) *and biomagnification (through the food web):* DDT is a fat-soluble chemical that can accumulate in the fatty tissues of animals. In a food chain or food web, the accumulated DDT is biologically magnified in the animal population at each higher trophic level, as it was in the case of a food chain observed in New York state, illustrated here. **Critical thinking:** How does this story demonstrate the value of pollution prevention?

DDT in fish-eating birds (ospreys) 25 ppm

DDT in large fish (needlefish) 2 ppm

DDT in small fish (minnows) 0.5 ppm

DDT in zooplankton 0.04 ppm

DDT in water 0.000003 ppm, or 3 ppt

Honeybee Losses: A Search for Causes

Over the past 50 years, the European honeybee population in the United States has been cut in half. Since colony collapse disorder (CCD) emerged in 2006 (**Core Case Study**), commercial beekeepers in the United States have lost 23–43% of their hives on average each year. Scientific research has found several possible reasons for this decline. They include *parasites*, *viruses*, *pesticides*, *stress*, and *diet*.

Parasites such as the varroa mite feed on the blood of adult honeybees and their larvae. This weakens the immune systems and shortens the life spans of honeybees. Varroa mites have killed millions of honeybees since first appearing in the United States in 1987—probably among bees imported from South America.

Several *viruses* are known to affect the winter survival of European honeybees. One example is the tobacco ringspot virus could be infecting honeybees that feed on pollen containing the virus. The virus is thought to attack the bees' nervous systems. In addition, the virus has been detected in varroa mites, which may help spread the virus as they feed on honeybees.

As honeybees forage for nectar, they are exposed to *insecticides* sprayed on crops and can carry these chemicals back to the hives. Research indicates that widely used insecticides called *neonicotinoids* may play a role in CCD by disrupting the nervous systems of bees and decreasing their ability to find their way back to their hives. These chemicals can also disrupt the immune systems of bees and make them vulnerable to the harmful effects of other threats.

Stress from being transported long distances around the United States (Figure 9.B) can also play a role. Overworking and overstressing honeybees by moving them around the country can weaken their immune systems and make them more vulnerable to death from parasites, viruses, fungi, and pesticides.

Another factor is *diet*. In natural ecosystems, honeybees gather nectar and pollen from a variety of flowering plants, but industrial worker honeybees feed mostly on pollen or nectar from one crop or a small number of crops that may lack the nutrients they need. In winter, bees in hives where most of the honey has been removed for sale are often fed sugar or high fructose corn syrup that provide calories but not enough protein for good health.

The growing consensus among bee researchers is that CCD occurs because of a combination of these factors. These annual bee deaths raise the costs for beekeepers and farmers who use their services and could put many of them out of business if the problem continues. This could lead to higher food prices.

CRITICAL THINKING

Can you think of some ways in which commercial beekeepers could lessen one or more of the threats described here? Explain.

Cristi111/Dreamstime.com

FIGURE 9.B European honeybee hive boxes in an acacia orchard. Each year, commercial beekeepers rent and deliver several million hives by truck to farmers throughout the United States.

A single poached black rhinoceros horn can be worth as much as $250,000 in Asia's black market. Four of the five rhino species, including the northern white rhino (Figure 9.14), are critically endangered, mostly because so many have been illegally killed for their horns. A rhino's horn is composed of keratin, the same protein that makes up your fingernails. Powdered rhino horn has long been used in traditional medicines for a variety of ailments in many Asian countries, including China, India, and Vietnam. It is also alleged to be a male aphrodisiac, but there is no verifiable evidence for this claim.

FIGURE 9.14 A poacher in South Africa killed this critically endangered northern white rhinoceros for its two horns. This species is now extinct in the wild. **Question:** What would you say if you could talk to the poacher who killed this animal?

Photoshot Holdings Ltd/Alamy

The illegal killing of elephants, especially African savanna elephants (see Figure 5.1, p. 120), for their valuable ivory tusks has increased in recent years, despite an international ban on the trade of ivory. An adult male elephant's two tusks can be worth $375,000 on the black market. China has the largest market for illegal ivory, followed by the United States. Elephant numbers have fallen from an estimated 10 million in 1913 to around 500,000 today, and elephants are being killed at a rate of 30,000 a year.

CONSIDER THIS . . .

CONNECTIONS Drones, Elephants, and Poachers

Researchers are using small drones with cameras connected to smart phones to track and monitor wildlife species such as endangered elephants and rhinos in Africa, tigers in Nepal, and orangutans in Sumatra. Drones with infrared cameras can find illegal poachers at night, expose their locations to wildlife rangers, and deter them by using bright strobe lights.

Since 1900 the overall number of the world's wild tigers has declined by 99%, mostly because of a 90% loss of tiger habitat (Figure 9.7, top left), caused primarily by rapid human population growth and poaching. More than half of the remaining 3,890 tigers are in India, which is doing more than other countries to protect them by establishing tiger reserves and working hard to protect the tigers in such reserves from poaching.

The Indian, or Bengal, tiger is at risk because a coat made from its fur can sell for as much as $100,000 in Tokyo. The bones and penis of a single tiger can fetch as much as $70,000 in China, the world's biggest market for such illegal items. According to the World Wildlife Fund, without emergency action to curtail poaching and preserve tiger habitat, few if any tigers, including the Sumatran tiger (Figure 9.2d), will be left in the wild by 2022.

In India, conservation biologist and National Geographic Explorer Krithi Karanth is studying conflicts between the rapidly growing number of humans and the declining populations of wildlife such as tigers and Asian elephants. As habitats for these animals shrink, they damage farmers' crops while trying to find food. Karanth has visited more than 10,000 households across 4,000 villages in India, and has enlisted 500 "citizen scientists" to help her interview villagers and collect data. Her goals are to document the disappearance of wildlife, and the conflicts between humans and wildlife, and to find effective ways to reduce such conflicts.

CONSIDER THIS . . .

THINKING ABOUT Tigers

Would it matter to you if all of the world's wild tigers were to disappear? Explain. List two steps you could take to help protect the world's remaining wild tigers from extinction.

Around the globe, the legal and illegal trade in wild species for use as pets is a huge and very profitable business. However, many owners of exotic wild pets do not know that, for every live animal captured and sold in the legal and illegal pet market, many others are killed or die in transit.

According to the IUCN, more than 60 bird species, mostly parrots (Figure 9.6), are endangered or threatened because of the wild bird trade (see Case Study that follows). In response, the United States passed the Wild Bird Conservation Act in 1992. This act makes it illegal to import parrots into the United States. Any parrot purchased today in the United States must be from a domestic breeder.

Buyers of wild animals might also be unaware that some imported exotic animals carry diseases such as Hantavirus, Ebola virus, Asian bird flu, herpes B virus (carried by most adult macaques), and salmonella (from pets such as hamsters, turtles, and iguanas). These diseases can spread from pets to their owners and then to other people.

Other wild species whose populations are depleted because of the pet trade include many amphibians (see Chapter 4, Core Case Study, p. 92), various reptiles, and tropical fishes taken mostly from the coral reefs of Indonesia and the Philippines. Some divers catch tropical fish by using plastic squeeze bottles of poisonous cyanide to stun them. For each fish caught alive, many more die and the cyanide solution kills the polyps, the tiny animals that create coral reefs.

Some exotic plants, especially orchids and cacti (see Figure 5.15, center, p. 132), are endangered because they are removed, and sold, often illegally, to collectors to decorate houses, offices, and landscapes. A mature crested saguaro cactus can earn a cactus rustler as much as $15,000. An orchid collector might pay $5,000 for a single rare orchid.

A Disturbing Message from the Birds

Approximately 70% of the world's 10,000 or more known bird species are declining in numbers, and much of this decline is related to human activities, summarized by HIPPCO. According to the IUCN 2014 Red List of Endangered Species, roughly one of every eight (13%) of all bird species is threatened with extinction, mostly by habitat loss, degradation, and fragmentation (the H in HIPPCO)—primarily in tropical forests.

According to the 2014 *State of the Birds* study, almost one-third of the 800 or more bird species in the United States are endangered (Figure 9.2b and c), threatened, or in decline, mostly because of habitat loss and degradation, invasive species, and climate change. About one-third of all endangered and threatened bird species in the United States live in Hawaii.

Sharp declines in bird populations have occurred among songbird species that migrate long distances. These birds nest deep in North American woods in the summer and spend their winters in Central or South America or on the Caribbean Islands. The primary causes of these population declines appear to be habitat loss and fragmentation of the birds' breeding habitats in North America and Central and South America. In addition, the populations of 40% of the world's water birds are in decline, mostly because of the global loss of wetlands.

After habitat loss, the intentional or accidental introduction of nonnative species that become *invasive species* such as bird-eating rats is the second greatest danger, affecting about 28% of the world's threatened birds. Other invasive species (the I in HIPPCO) include snakes (such as the brown tree snake) and mongooses, which kill hundreds of millions of birds every year. In the United States, feral cats and pet cats kill at least 1.4 billion birds each year, according to a study by Peter Mara of the Smithsonian Conservation Biology Institute.

Population growth, the first P in HIPPCO, also threatens some bird species, as more people spread out over the landscape each year and increase their use of timber, food, and other resources, which results in destruction or disturbance of bird habitats. According to bird expert Daniel Klem, Jr., about 600 million birds die each year from collisions with windows in the United States and Canada. Pollution, the second P in HIPPCO, is another major threat to birds. Countless birds are exposed to oil spills, insecticides, herbicides, and other toxins.

Another rapidly growing threat to birds is climate change, the C in HIPPCO. A study done for the WWF found that the effects of climate change, such as heat waves and flooding, are causing declines of some bird populations in every part of the globe. Such losses are expected to increase sharply during this century.

Overexploitation (the O in HIPPCO) is also a major threat to bird populations. Fifty-two of the world's 388 parrot species are threatened, partly because so many parrots are captured for sale as pets, often illegally and usually to buyers in Europe and the United States. According to the USFWS, collectors of exotic birds might pay $10,000 or more for an endangered hyacinth macaw (Figure 9.6) smuggled out of Brazil. However, during its lifetime, a single hyacinth macaw left in the wild could attract an estimated $165,000 in ecotourism revenues.

Biodiversity scientists view this decline of bird species with alarm. One reason is that birds are excellent *indicator species* because they live in every climate and biome, respond quickly to environmental changes in their habitats, and are relatively easy to track and count. To these scientists, the decline of many bird species indicates widespread environmental degradation.

A second reason for alarm is that birds perform critically important economic and ecosystem services throughout the world. For example, many birds play specialized

Çağan Hakkı Sekercioğlu: Protector of Birds and National Geographic Explorer

Rebecca Hale/National Geographic

Çağan Sekercioğlu, assistant professor in the University of Utah Department of Biology, is a bird expert, a tropical biologist, an accomplished wildlife photographer, and a National Geographic Explorer. He has seen over 64% of the planet's known bird species in 75 countries, developed a global database on bird ecology, and become an expert on the causes and consequences of bird extinctions around the world.

Recently he has focused his research on monitoring the effects of habitat loss on birds in Costa Rica's forests and agricultural area and on the effects of climate change on birds. He notes that climate change is driving birds into higher elevations in mountain ranges.

In 2007 Sekercioğlu founded KuzeyDoğa. It is an award-winning ecological research and community-based conservation organization devoted to conserving and protecting the wildlife of northeastern Turkey. He also developed Turkey's first protected wildlife corridor, which would stretch across the eastern half of the country, according to his plan. In 2011 he was named Turkey's Scientist of the Year.

Based on his extensive research Sekercioğlu estimates that the percentage of the world's known bird species that are endangered could approximately double from 13% in 2013 to 25% by the end of this century. He says, "My ultimate goal is to prevent extinctions and consequent collapses of critical ecosystem processes while making sure that human communities benefit from conservation as much as the wildlife they help conserve. . . . I don't see conservation as people versus nature, I see it as a collaboration."

roles in pollination and seed dispersal, especially in tropical areas. Extinctions of these bird species could lead to extinctions of plants that depend on the birds for pollination. Then, some specialized animals that feed mostly on these plants might also become extinct. Such a *cascade of extinctions*, in turn, could affect our own food supplies and well-being. Biodiversity scientists (Individuals Matter 9.2) urge us to listen more carefully to what birds are telling us about the state of the environment, for the birds' sake, as well as for ours.

CONSIDER THIS . . .

CONNECTIONS African Vultures and Poachers

Detritus feeders such as vultures circle above animals such as elephants and rhinos that have been killed by poachers for their valuable ivory tusks and horns. This can help wildlife protection rangers in Africa locate poachers. To prevent this, poachers in parts of Africa have been killing thousands of vultures by poisoning the carcasses of dead elephants and rhinos. This is endangering some vulture species and preventing them from playing their important role in the chemical cycling of nutrients needed by plants.

Rising Demand for Bushmeat Threatens Some African Species

For centuries, indigenous people in much of West and Central Africa have sustainably hunted wildlife for *bushmeat* as a source of food. In the last three decades, bushmeat hunting in some areas has skyrocketed. Some hunters provide the bushmeat as a food source for rapidly growing populations. Others sell exotic meats from gorillas (Figure 9.15) and other species to restaurants in major cities. Logging roads in once-inaccessible forests have made hunting these animals much easier. As a result, some forests in areas such as Africa's Congo basin are being stripped of many of their antelopes (the most commonly hunted bushmeat animal), monkeys, apes, elephants, hippos, and other wild animals.

Bushmeat hunting has driven at least one species—Miss Waldron's red colobus monkey—to complete extinction. It is also a factor in the reduction of some populations of orangutans (Figure 9.4), gorillas, chimpanzees, elephants, and hippopotami. Another problem is that butchering and eating some forms of bushmeat has helped to spread fatal diseases such as HIV/AIDS and the Ebola virus from wild animals to humans.

The US Agency for International Development (USAID) is trying to reduce unsustainable hunting for bushmeat in some areas of Africa by introducing alternative sources of food, including farmed fish. They are also showing villagers how to breed large rodents such as cane rats as a source of protein.

CHECKPOINT FOR UNDERSTANDING 9.3

1. What does the acronym HIPPCO stand for?

2. Explain how HIPPCO impacts rapidly declining bird species.

FIGURE 9.15 *Bushmeat* such as this severed head of an endangered lowland gorilla in the Congo is consumed as a source of protein by local people in parts of West and Central Africa. It is also sold in national and international marketplaces and served in some restaurants, where wealthy patrons regard gorilla meat as a source of status and power. ***Critical thinking:*** How, if at all, is this different from killing a cow for food?

Photoshot Holdings Ltd/Alamy Stock Photo

9.4 HOW CAN WE SUSTAIN WILD SPECIES AND THE ECOSYSTEM SERVICES THEY PROVIDE?

CONCEPT 9.4 We can reduce species extinction and sustain ecosystem services by establishing and enforcing national environmental laws and international treaties and by creating and protecting wildlife sanctuaries.

Treaties and Laws Can Help Protect Species

Some governments are working to reduce species extinction and sustain ecosystem services by establishing and enforcing international treaties and conventions, as well as national environmental policies (see Critical Concepts in Sustainability that follows) and laws (**Concept 9.4**).

One of the most far reaching of international agreements is the 1975 *Convention on International Trade in Endangered Species of Wild Fauna and Flora (CITES)*. This treaty, signed by 181 countries, bans the hunting, capturing, and selling of threatened or endangered species. It lists 931 species that are in danger of extinction and that cannot be commercially traded as live specimens or for their parts or products. It restricts the international trade of roughly 5,600 animal species and 30,000 plant species that are at risk of becoming threatened.

CITES has helped reduce the international trade of many threatened animals, including elephants, crocodiles, cheetahs, and chimpanzees. But the effects of this treaty have been limited because enforcement varies from country to country and convicted violators often pay only small fines. In addition, member countries can exempt themselves from protecting any listed species, and much of the highly profitable illegal trade in wildlife and wildlife products goes on in countries that have not signed the treaty.

Another important treaty is the *Convention on Biological Diversity (CBD)*, ratified or accepted by 196 countries (but as of 2017, not by the United States). CBD legally commits participating governments to reduce the global rate of biodiversity loss and to share the benefits from use of the world's genetic resources. It also includes efforts to prevent or control the spread of harmful invasive species.

This convention is a landmark in international law because it focuses on ecosystems rather than on individual species. It also links biodiversity protection to issues such as the traditional rights of indigenous peoples. However, implementation has been slow because some key countries, including the United States, have not ratified it. The law also contains no severe penalties or other enforcement mechanisms.

The United States enacted the **Endangered Species Act (ESA)** in 1973 and has amended it several times since. The Act is designed to identify and protect endangered species in the United States and abroad (**Concept 9.4**). The ESA creates recovery programs for the species it lists. Its goal is to help each species' numbers recover to levels where legal protection is no longer needed. When that happens, a species can be taken off the list, or delisted.

Under the ESA, no land- or water-use projects or activities (with the exception of Defense Department concerns) may be carried out that would jeopardize or endanger a listed species or destroy critical habitat. Citizens may be fined if offenses are committed on their own

Environmental Policy and How It's Made

The government *policy lifecycle* process involves identifying a problem, researching the underlying science, crafting a policy solution and acquiring funds to implement it, monitoring how well it works, and adjusting the policy as needed. Since 1969 there have been several major environmental laws passed in the United States, some with several amendments in the years that followed (Figure 1.17, p. 24). In the U.S., environmental policy-making often begins when individual citizens, interest groups, or corporations seek solutions to issues that concern them. It's a complex process that includes *lobbying*, or contacting and persuading legislators, to vote or act in their favor. Figure 9.C shows how people and organizations interact with the various branches of the U.S. government to create environmental policies that establish laws, regulations, and programs that are designed, implemented, funded, and enforced by one or more governmental agencies.

Through its policies, a government can help to protect environmental and public interests and to encourage more environmentally sustainable economic development. Environmental science plays a role in the process, but politics usually plays a bigger role. Critics of the political process in the United States believe lobbyists of large corporations and other special interest organizations have grown too powerful and that their influence overshadows the input of ordinary citizens. Still, history shows that significant political change usually comes from the *bottom up* when individuals join together to bring about change. Without such historical grassroots political action by

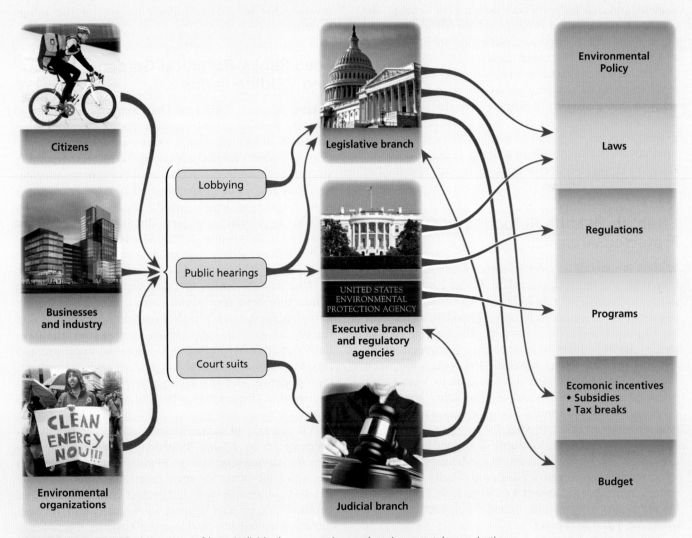

FIGURE 9.C Simplified overview of how individuals, companies, and environmental organizations interact with each other and with the legislative, executive, and judicial branches of the US government in the making of environmental policy.

Ryan Rodrick Beiler/Shutterstock.com, Mesut Dogan/Shutterstock.com, Orhan Cam/Shutterstock.com, Andrey Burmakin/Shutterstock.com, jgroup/Getty Images, Cameron Whitman/Shutterstock.com, Kevin Grant/Shutterstock.com, jl661227/Shutterstock.com, Tyler Olson/Shutterstock.com

millions of individuals and organized citizen groups over the past 50 years, pollution and environmental degradation would be much worse today.

FRQ Application
Question: In 1972 the pesticide DDT was banned in the United States.
(a) **Identify** the problem that led to establishing this law.

(b) **Describe** what scientists observed in their research of this problem.
(c) **Explain** the outcome of establishing this law.

Possible Response:
(a) In the 1960s, populations of predatory fish-eating birds such as osprey, eagles, and pelicans began to plummet.
(b) Scientists observed that the persistent

pesticide DDT was found in the tissues of these birds in very high levels. This decreased the amount of calcium in the eggshells of the eggs they laid, and as a result, the eggs cracked before they hatched, reducing the number of live offspring.
(c) DDT was banned in the United States and as a result most of these bird species have recovered in number.

private land, making this law controversial. However, private landowners are given incentives to save endangered species living on their lands.

The ESA also requires that all commercial shipments of wildlife and wildlife products entering or leaving the country be transported through specific US airports and ocean ports where inspectors can confiscate illegal cargo and fine those in violation of the law.

This act is probably the most successful and far-reaching environmental law adopted by any nation. According to a study by the Center for Biological Diversity, 90% of the ESA-protected species are recovering at the rate projected in their recovery plans and 99% of the listed species have been saved from extinction. In addition, between 2003 and 2014, the cumulative area designated as critical habitat has increased almost ten-fold.

Establish Wildlife Refuges and Other Protected Areas

In 1903 President Theodore Roosevelt established the first US federal wildlife refuge at Pelican Island, Florida, to help protect the brown pelican and other birds from extinction (Figure 9.16). This approach has worked well. In 2009 the brown pelican was removed from the US Endangered Species list. By 2016 there were more than 560 refuges in the National Wildlife Refuge System. Each year, more than 47 million Americans visit these refuges to hunt, GOOD NEWS fish, hike, and watch birds and other wildlife.

More than three-fourths of the refuges serve as wetland sanctuaries that are vital for protecting migratory waterfowl. At least one-fourth of all US endangered and threatened species have habitats in the refuge system, and some refuges have been set aside specifically for certain endangered species (**Concept 9.4**). Such areas have helped Florida's key deer, the brown pelican, and the trumpeter swan to recover.

Despite their benefits, activities that are harmful to wildlife, such as mining, oil drilling, and use of off-road

vehicles, are legally allowed in nearly 60% of the GOOD NEWS nation's wildlife refuges, according to a General Accounting Office Study. Biodiversity researchers urge the US government to set aside more refuges and to increase the long-underfunded budget for the refuge system.

Seed Banks, Botanical Gardens, and Wildlife Farms

Recent research indicates that between 60,000 and 100,000 species of the world's plants—roughly one-fourth of all known plant species—are in danger of extinction. **Seed banks** are refrigerated, low-humidity storage environments used to preserve genetic information and the seeds of endangered plant species. More than 1,400 seed banks around the world collectively hold about 3 million samples. The Svalbard Global Seed Vault, an underground facility on a remote island in the Arctic, will eventually contain 100 million of the world's seeds.

The world's 1,600 *botanical gardens* contain living plants that represent almost one-third of the world's known plant species. But they contain only about 3% of the world's rare and threatened plant species and have limited space and funding to preserve most of those species. Similarly, an *arboretum* is land set aside for protecting, studying, and displaying various species of trees and shrubs. There are hundreds of arboreta around the world.

We can take pressure off some endangered or threatened species by raising individuals of these species on *farms* for commercial sale. In Florida, American alligators are raised on farms for their meat and hides. Butterfly farms established to raise and protect endangered species flourish in Papua New Guinea, where many butterfly species are threatened by development activities. These farms are also used to educate visitors about the need to protect butterfly species.

FIGURE 9.16 The Pelican Island National Wildlife Refuge in Florida was America's first National Wildlife Refuge.

George Gentry/U.S. Fish and Wildlife Service; Inset: Chuck Wagner/Shutterstock.com

Zoos and Aquariums

Zoos, aquariums, game parks, and animal research centers preserve some individuals of critically endangered animal species. The long-term goal is to reintroduce the species into protected wild habitats.

Two techniques for preserving endangered terrestrial species are egg pulling and captive breeding. *Egg pulling* involves collecting wild eggs laid by critically endangered bird species and then hatching them in zoos or research centers. In *captive breeding*, some or all of the wild individuals of a critically endangered species are collected for breeding in captivity, with the aim of reintroducing the offspring into the wild. Captive breeding has been used to save the peregrine falcon and the California condor (Figure 9.2b).

Other techniques for increasing the populations of captive species include *artificial insemination*, which involves inserting semen into a female's reproductive system. Another technique is *embryo transfer*, the surgical implantation of eggs of one species into a surrogate mother of another species. Also used are incubators, and *cross fostering*, when offspring are raised by parents of a similar species. Scientists also match individuals for mating by using DNA analysis along with computer databases that hold information on family lineages of endangered zoo animals—a computer dating service for zoo animals. This helps increase genetic diversity.

The ultimate goal of captive breeding programs is to build populations to a level where they can be reintroduced into the wild. Successes include the black-footed ferret, the golden lion tamarin (a highly endangered monkey species), the Arabian oryx, and the California condor (Figure 9.2b). For reintroduction to be successful, individuals raised in captivity must be able to survive in the wild. They must have suitable habitat and they must be protected from overhunting, poaching, pollution, and other environmental hazards. These challenges can make reintroduction difficult.

One problem for captive breeding programs is that a captive population of an endangered species must typically number 100 to 500 individuals in order to avoid extinction resulting from accidents, diseases, or the loss of genetic diversity through inbreeding. Recent genetic research indicates that 10,000 or more individuals are needed for an endangered species to maintain its capacity for biological evolution. Zoos and research centers do not have the funding or space to house such large populations.

Public aquariums (Figure 9.17) that exhibit unusual and attractive species of fish and marine animals such as seals and dolphins help to educate the public about the need to protect such species. Some carry out research on how to save endangered species. However, mostly because of limited funds, public aquariums have not served as

FIGURE 9.17 The Monterey Bay Aquarium in Monterey, California (USA), contains this tidewater pool, which is used to train rescued sea otter pups to survive in the wild.

effective gene banks for endangered marine species, especially marine mammals that need large volumes of water.

While zoos, aquariums, and botanical gardens perform valuable services, they cannot by themselves solve the growing problem of species extinction.

The Precautionary Principle

Biodiversity scientists call for us to take precautionary action to avoid hastening species extinction and disrupting essential ecosystem services. This approach is based on the **precautionary principle:** When substantial preliminary evidence indicates that an activity can harm human health or the environment, we should take precautionary measures to prevent or reduce such harm even if some of the cause-and-effect relationships have not been fully established scientifically.

Scientists use the precautionary principle to argue for both the preservation of species and protection of entire ecosystems and their ecosystem services. Implementing this principle puts the emphasis on preventing species extinction instead of waiting until a species is nearly ex-

tinct before taking emergency action that can be too late. The precautionary principle is also used as a strategy for dealing with other challenges such as preventing exposure to harmful chemicals in the air we breathe, the water we drink, and the food we eat.

Protecting Species and Ecosystem Services Raises Difficult Questions

Efforts to prevent the extinction of wild species and the accompanying losses of ecosystem services require the use of financial and human resources that are limited. This raises some challenging questions:

- Should we focus on protecting species or should we focus more on protecting ecosystems and the ecosystem services they provide?

- How do we allocate limited resources between these two priorities?

- How do we decide which species should get the most attention in our efforts to protect as many species as possible? For example, should we focus on protecting the most threatened species or on protecting keystone species?

- Protecting species that are appealing to humans, such as the giant panda, orangutans (Figure 9.4), and tigers, can increase public awareness of the need for wildlife conservation. Is this more important than focusing on the ecological importance of species when deciding which ones to protect?
- How do we determine which habitat areas are the most critical to protect?
- How do we allocate limited resources among such biodiversity hotspots?

Conservation biologists struggle with these questions all the time. Regardless of the answers, each of us can help in the efforts to protect species from extinction due largely to human activities. Figure 9.18 lists some ways in which you can help protect species and increase your beneficial environmental impact.

What Can You Do?

Protecting Species

- Do not buy furs, ivory products, or other items made from endangered or threatened animal species.
- Do not buy wood or wood products from tropical or old-growth forests.
- Do not buy pet animals or plants taken from the wild.
- Tell friends and relatives what you're doing about this problem.

FIGURE 9.18 Individuals matter: You can help prevent the extinction of species. ***Critical thinking:*** Which two of these actions do you believe are the most important ones to take? Why?

CHECKPOINT FOR UNDERSTANDING 9.4

1. What is CITES?
2. Describe the Endangered Species Act.
3. Describe the types of programs that have been established to protect and maintain endangered species.

KEY IDEAS

- We are hastening the extinction of wild species and degrading the ecosystem services they provide by destroying and degrading natural habitats, introducing harmful invasive species, and increasing human population growth, pollution, climate change, and overexploitation.
- We should avoid causing or hastening the extinction of wild species because of the ecosystem and economic services they provide and because their existence should not depend primarily on their usefulness to us.
- We can work to prevent the extinction of species and to protect overall biodiversity and ecosystem services by establishing and enforcing environmental laws and treaties and by creating and protecting wildlife sanctuaries.

Core Case Study Checkpoint

Explain why declining populations of European honeybees in the United States is a serious concern.

Chapter 9 Glossary

background extinction rate: normal extinction of various species as a result of changes in local environmental conditions.

bioaccumulation: an increase or build-up in the concentration of a chemical in specific organs or tissues of an individual organism.

biomagnification: an increase in the concentration of a chemical in organisms at successively higher trophic levels of a food chain or food web.

biodiversity hotspot: an area especially rich in plant species that are found nowhere else and are in great danger of extinction. Such areas suffer serious ecological disruption, mostly due to rapid human population growth.

biological extinction: Complete disappearance of a species from earth. It happens when a species cannot adapt and successfully reproduce under new environmental conditions or when a species evolves into one or more new species.

endangered species: wild species with so few individual survivors that the species could soon become extinct in all or most of its natural range.

Endangered Species Act (ESA): law established in 1973 designed to identify and protect endangered species in the United States and abroad.

habitat fragmentation: breaking up of habitat into smaller pieces, usually as a result of human activities.

HIPPCO: acronym used by conservation biologists for the six most important secondary causes of premature extinction. **H**abitat destruction, degradation, and fragmentation; **I**nvasive (nonnative) species; **P**opulation growth (too many people consuming too many resources); **P**ollution; **C**limate change; and **O**verexploitation.

mass extinction: a catastrophic, widespread, often global event in which major groups of species are wiped out over a short time compared with normal (background) extinctions.

threatened species: wild species that is still abundant in its natural range but is likely to become endangered because of a decline in its numbers.

Chapter Review

Core Case Study

1. What economic and ecological services do honeybees provide? How are human activities contributing to the decline of many populations of European honeybees? What is **colony collapse disorder (CCD)**?

Section 9.1

2. (a) What is the key concept for this section? (b) Define and distinguish between **biological extinction** and **mass extinction**. What is the **background extinction rate**? (c) What percentage of the world's identified species is likely to become extinct primarily because of human activities during this century? How many of the earth's 24 major ecosystem services are in decline? (d) Give three reasons why many extinction experts believe that projected extinction rates are probably on the low side. Explain how scientists estimate extinction rates and describe the challenges they face in doing so. (e) Distinguish between **endangered species** and **threatened species** and give an example of each. List four characteristics that make some species especially vulnerable to extinction.

Section 9.2

3. (a) What is the key concept for this section? (b) What are four reasons for trying to avoid hastening the extinction of wild species? (c) Describe two economic and two ecological benefits of species diversity. (d) Explain how saving other species and the ecosystem services they provide can help us to save our own species and our cultures and economies.

Section 9.3

4. (a) What is the key concept for this section? (b) What is **HIPPCO**? What is the greatest threat to wild species? (c) What is **habitat fragmentation**? Describe the major effects of habitat loss and fragmentation. (d) Why are island species especially vulnerable to extinction? What are habitat islands?

5. (a) Give two examples of the benefits that have been gained by the introduction of nonnative species. (b) What are the pros and cons of the kudzu vine?

(c) Describe the harmful environmental impact of Burmese pythons. Explain why prevention is the best way to reduce threats from invasive species and list four ways to implement this strategy.

6. (a) Summarize the roles of population growth, overconsumption, pollution, and climate change in the extinction of wild species. (b) Explain how concentrations of pesticides such as DDT can accumulate to high levels in food webs. (c) List possible causes of the decline of European honeybee populations in the United States. (d) Give three examples of species that are threatened by poaching. Why are wild tigers likely to disappear from the wild within a few decades? (e) What is the connection between infectious diseases in humans and the pet trade?

7. (a) List the major threats to the world's bird populations and give two reasons for protecting bird species from extinction. (b) Describe the threat to some forms of wildlife from the increased hunting for bushmeat.

Section 9.4

8. (a) What is the key concept for this section? (b) Name two international treaties that are used to help protect species. (c) What is the US Endangered Species Act? How successful has it been.

9. (a) Summarize the roles and limitations of wildlife refuges, seed banks, botanical gardens, wildlife farms, zoos, and aquariums in protecting some species. (b) Describe the role of captive breeding in efforts to prevent species extinction and give an example of success in returning a nearly extinct species to the wild. (c) What is the **precautionary principle** and how can it be used to prevent the extinction of species? What are three important questions related to protecting biodiversity?

10. What are this chapter's *three key ideas*?

Note: Key terms are in bold type.

AP® Review Questions

1. Introduced species can become pests because they
   (A) produce only a few young after a long period of gestation
   (B) inhabit only niches that have recently become available after the local extinction of another species
   (C) can live in many niches, easily adapting to many variables and eating a wide variety of food
   (D) have a low genetic variability, enabling them to live in a wide variety of habitats
   (E) increase biodiversity because they attract more species to the areas in which they settle

2. Which of the following are ways that an invasive species may enter an aquatic ecosystem?
   I. Releasing the ballast water of ships
   II. Dumping household aquariums into lakes
   III. Escaping a coastal aquaculture farm
   (A) I only
   (B) II only
   (C) III only
   (D) I and II only
   (E) I, II, and III

3. Presently, the biggest threat to biodiversity is
   (A) asteroid strikes, such as what happened 65 million years ago and resulted in the extinction of the dinosaurs
   (B) human population growth, because as population increases, so does the number of plants and animals it consumes, resulting in a decrease of those organisms
   (C) habitat destruction, such as cutting down portions of tropical rain forest, which destroys the niches occupied by tropical organisms
   (D) the proliferation of zoos and botanical gardens, causing people to care less about preserving species in the wild because they are being cared for in those sanctuaries
   (E) climate change, because it will result in many species moving northward or to higher elevations, seeking out suitable new habitats

4. Which of the following is least likely a cause of a species becoming endangered?
   (A) Introduction of invasive species
   (B) Selective breeding in zoos
   (C) Overhunting
   (D) Habitat destruction
   (E) Pollution

5. The depletion of the world's marine fish stocks due to overfishing is an example of
   (A) the sustainable use of resources
   (B) the competitive exclusion principle
   (C) the failure of international treaties
   (D) the eminent domain principle
   (E) the tragedy of the commons

6. The sale of a large forest to a developer causing the building of roads, logging, and urban development would most likely lead to
   (A) an increase in the number of indicator species because the loss of species during development would cause the remaining species to become indicators
   (B) an increase in biodiversity because niches are created along roads where trees are cut down and in new urban areas
   (C) a net increase in available biomass because more sunlight is available for autotrophs
   (D) a loss of biodiversity because of habitat fragmentation, since small populations of species are more vulnerable to predation, competition, and disease
   (E) a decrease in invasive species because they would have a difficult time surviving in fragmented land that has lost many of its resources

7. Which of the following would prevent invasive species from being introduced and becoming established?
   I. Inspecting foreign goods before they enter the country
   II. Allowing ships to discharge their ballast water as they enter a port
   III. Establishing international treaties, banning the transfer of species across borders
   (A) I only
   (B) II only
   (C) I and II only
   (D) II and III only
   (E) I and III only

8. Which of the following international treaties bans the hunting, capture, and sale of threatened or endangered species in 181 countries?
   (A) Endangered Species Act (ESA)
   (B) The National Marine Fisheries Act
   (C) The Convention on International Trade in Endangered Species (CITES)
   (D) National Environmental Policy Act (NEPA)
   (E) The Marine Mammal Protection Act

9. Biological extinction occurs when
   (A) a species becomes extinct in a specific area, such as the gray wolf in the American Northeast
   (B) a species is found nowhere on earth, such as the passenger pigeon
   (C) additional species are preyed upon, such as when bats adapt their echolocation ability to hear moths whose ears had adapted to hear the sound frequencies of bats
   (D) there is a loss of indicator species, such as if a population of butterflies quickly declines in an area where they previously had been plentiful
   (E) an event, such as a volcanic eruption, results in some members of a species becoming separated from other members, and ultimately each group becomes genetically different and can no longer interbreed and produce offspring who can interbreed

10. The continuous natural extinction rate of species which is typically balanced by the formation of new species is known as
    (A) mass extinction
    (B) background extinction
    (C) ecological extinction
    (D) biological extinction
    (E) instrumental extinction

11. Most extinction experts believe that the extent of biodiversity loss will increase over the next 50 to 100 years because of
    (A) the projected growth of the world's human population and resource use per person
    (B) the increased loss due to poaching and the demand for endangered species
    (C) the reduced input of solar energy cooling the planet and altering the earth's life
    (D) the acceleration of natural disease processes
    (E) the reduced fragmentation of biodiverse regions

12. The giant panda is prone to ecological and biological extinction because of all of the following reasons EXCEPT
    (A) it has a low reproductive rate, and it is not usual for pandas to successfully breed in captivity so they can be reintroduced to their habitat
    (B) it lives in specific areas in Asia in a narrow distribution
    (C) it is a specialist, living in a specific habitat and eating only a certain food
    (D) there are limited numbers of giant pandas living in the wild
    (E) it is a top predator because no other large animal in the area eats only bamboo

13. Areas that have been set aside for the protection of threatened or endangered species and their habitats are known as
    (A) national parks
    (B) national zoos
    (C) national wildlife refuges
    (D) national recreation areas
    (E) national forest reserves

14. A biodiversity hot spot is defined as
    (A) an island habitat that suffers from low immigration rates
    (B) an area that has extinction rates lower than the global average
    (C) an area that has suffered from wetland degradation
    (D) an area that is already a highly endangered center of biodiversity
    (E) a tropical area near the equator

15. Marine biodiversity is difficult to protect due to
    I. The perception that the seas contain inexhaustible resources
    II. The difficulties in developing, monitoring, and enforcing international agreements
    III. Much of it being out of view of most people
    (A) I only
    (B) II only
    (C) III only
    (D) II and III only
    (E) I, II, and III

16. Which of the following best demonstrates the effects of biomagnification?
    (A) Nutrients from a nearby farm are washed into a pond, resulting in an increase of algae and a loss of oxygen, and eventually a dead zone.
    (B) After wolves were domesticated, people chose to breed individuals who had characteristics they desired, resulting in a wide variety of dog breeds with different abilities and physical appearances.
    (C) Individual elephants had traits that enabled them to better survive in their habitat, and they became more likely to produce offspring with those traits, enabling the offspring to survive and reproduce.
    (D) DDT was a pesticide used universally during the 1950s and 1960s. This chemical entered the food chain and worked its way up, eventually making the eggs of predatory birds so fragile, they could not successfully reproduce.
    (E) A road is built, fragmenting a forest and exposing the animals to introduced species, local climate changes, and disease.

(A) Habitat destruction, degradation, and fragmentation
(B) Invasive (nonnative species)
(C) Population and resource use growth
(D) Greenhouse effect
(E) Overexploitation

17. Sale of exotic pets and decorative plants

18. Logging, mining, building of roads, and urban development

19. No natural predators, generalist, and high reproductive rate

20. Severe damage to lichens is especially common in cities with chronic air pollution; lichens are sensitive to the toxic gases that are present in these pollutants. Lichens are an example of
(A) an endangered species
(B) an indicator species
(C) a keystone species
(D) an invasive species
(E) an indigenous species

AP® Free-Response Practice

1. Sumatra is the fourth most densely populated island in the world. The population of Sumatra was approximately 20 million in 1978 and by the year 2010, it had increased to approximately 50 million.

   Sumatra is a tropical island that has a wide range of plant and animal species. Almost 50 percent of its tropical rainforest, habitat for many endangered species, has been lost in the past 35 years. Forests are felled and burned in order to create agricultural land. One of the most critically endangered species is the Sumatran tiger. The estimated population of tigers was about 1,000 in 1978, but has shrunk to approximately 400.

   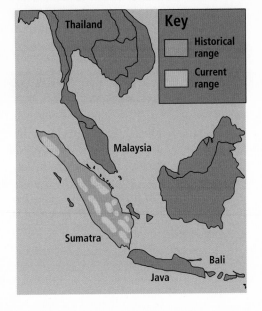

   (a) The map shows the historical range and the current range of the Sumatran tiger.

   (i) **Identify** and **discuss** THREE possible causes of the decline of the Sumatran tiger.

   (ii) **Describe** TWO characteristics of the Sumatran tiger that would make their populations slow to recover.

   (iii) **Discuss** ONE economic or ecological reason for protecting the tiger.

   (iv) **Identify** and **discuss** ONE economic, cultural, or social factor that might make it difficult to implement a program in Sumatra to protect the Sumatran tiger.

   (b) Measuring the biodiversity of an ecosystem is key in determining the health of that ecosystem.

   (i) **Describe** TWO economic benefits that biodiversity provides.

   (ii) **Describe** ONE ecological benefit that biodiversity provides.

   (iii) **Describe** ONE program or strategy that works to protect an endangered species.

Critical Thinking

1. What are three aspects of your lifestyle that might directly or indirectly contribute to declines in European honeybee populations and the endangerment of other pollinator species (**Core Case Study**)?

2. Give your response to the following statement: "Eventually, all species become extinct. So it does not really matter that the world's remaining tiger species or a tropical forest plant are endangered mostly because of human activities." Be honest about your reaction, and give arguments to support your position.

3. Do you accept the ethical position that each species has the right to survive without human interference, regardless of whether it serves any useful purpose for humans? Explain. Would you extend this right to the

Anopheles mosquito, which transmits malaria, and to harmful infectious bacteria? Explain. If your answer is no, where would you draw the line?

4. Wildlife ecologist and environmental philosopher Aldo Leopold wrote this with respect to preventing the extinction of wild species: "To keep every cog and wheel is the first precaution of intelligent tinkering." Explain how this statement relates to the material in this chapter.

5. What would you do if wild boar invaded and tore up your yard or garden? Explain your reasoning behind your course of action. How might your actions affect other species or the ecosystem you are dealing with?

6. How do you think your daily habits might contribute directly or indirectly to the extinction of some bird species? What are three things that you think should be done to reduce the rate of extinction of bird species?

7. Which of the following statements best describes your feelings toward wildlife?
   a. As long as it stays in its space, wildlife is okay.
   b. As long as I do not need its space, wildlife is okay.
   c. I have the right to use wildlife habitat to meet my own needs.
   d. When you have seen one redwood tree, elephant, or some other form of wildlife, you have seen them all, so preserve a few of each species in a zoo or wildlife park and do not worry about protecting the rest.
   e. Wildlife should be protected in its current ranges.

8. How might your life change if human activities contribute to the projected extinction of 20–50% of the world's identified species during this century? How might this affect the lives of any children or grandchildren you eventually might have?

Data Analysis

Examine the following data released by the World Resources Institute and answer these questions:

1. Complete the table by filling in the last column. For example, to calculate this value for Costa Rica, divide the number of threatened breeding bird species by the total number of known breeding bird species and multiply the answer by 100 to get the percentage.

2. Arrange the countries from largest to smallest according to total land area. Does there appear to be any correlation between the size of country and the percentage of threatened breeding bird species? Explain your reasoning.

Country	Total Land Area in Square Kilometers (Square Miles)	Protected Area as Percent of Total Land Area (2003)	Total Number of Known Breeding Bird Species (1992–2002)	Number of Threatened Breeding Bird Species (2002)	Threatened Breeding Bird Species as Percent of Total Number of Known Breeding Bird Species
Afghanistan	647,668 (250,000)	0.3	181	11	
Cambodia	181,088 (69,900)	23.7	183	19	
China	9,599,445 (3,705,386)	7.8	218	74	
Costa Rica	51,114 (19,730)	23.4	279	13	
Haiti	27,756 (10,714)	0.3	62	14	
India	3,288,570 (1,269,388)	5.2	458	72	
Rwanda	26,344 (10,169)	7.7	200	9	
United States	9,633,915 (3,718,691)	15.8	508	55	

Compiled by the authors using data from World Resources Institute, Earth Trends, Biodiversity and Protected Areas, Country Profiles.

Answers to Checkpoints for Understanding

Section 9.1

1. An increasing human population has destroyed and degraded habitats, consumed huge quantities of resources, and created a large human footprint that has accelerated the loss of species.

2. Ecosystem services such as natural pest control, pollination, and purification of air and water are degraded or lost as a result of the massive loss of species.

3. Characteristics of species vulnerable to extinction include those with a low reproductive rate, specialized niche, or narrow distribution, those that feed at a high trophic level, have a fixed migratory pattern, or species that are rare, commercially valuable, or require a large territory for hunting and finding mates.

Section 9.2

1. Preserving species maintains ecosystem services such as pollination and pest control and economic services such as food, lumber, and medicines. Rapid extinction can hinder speciation as it takes millions of years for new species to fill open niches. Many people believe that wild species have a right to exist and that human actions that hasten extinction are unethical.

Section 9.3

1. The acronym HIPPCO stands for habitat loss and degradation, invasive species, population growth, pollution, climate change, and overexploitation.

2. Migrating songbirds have lost habitat due to deforestation in North America and Central and South America. Invasive species such as bird-eating rats and brown tree snakes consume millions of birds each year. Human population growth and the rapid use of resources such as timber and conversion of forests to agricultural land impacts bird species. Pollution from oil spills, pesticides, and herbicides kill off millions of birds. Heat waves and flooding caused by climate change as well as the capture of exotic birds to sell as pets on the black market severely impact bird populations.

Section 9.4

1. CITES (Convention on International Trade in Endangered Species of Wild Fauna and Flora) is an international treaty meant to protect endangered species by prohibiting the hunting, capturing, or selling of threatened or endangered species. This includes live specimens, parts of organisms, or products made from those organisms.

2. The Endangered Species Act is a US law that identifies and protects endangered species in the United States and abroad. This includes protecting and restoring habitat and creating programs to increase populations of endangered species so that they may be taken off the list created by the agency.

3. Programs established to preserve endangered species include wildlife refuges and established protected areas, seed banks, botanical gardens and wildlife farms, and zoos and aquariums that preserve and reintroduce species into the wild.

Core Case Study

A decline in European honeybees can decrease U.S. food production and raise food prices. Bee colony collapse is one of many examples of natural populations facing extinction. Honeybees provide an essential ecological service by pollinating crops that result in much of the food we consume and are the foundation of agricultural economies that support us. They are part of the great diversity of wild species that are essential to human survival.

CHAPTER 10

Sustaining Terrestrial Biodiversity: Forests, Public Lands, Grasslands, Wetlands, and Cities

Taken at the level of the entire globe, biological diversity can be considered the single measure of how humanity is affecting the environment.

THOMAS E. LOVEJOY

Denali National Park, Alaska (USA).

Jerryway/Dreamstime.com

Key Questions

10.1 How should we manage and sustain forests and US public lands?

10.2 How should we manage and sustain grasslands?

10.3 How should we manage and sustain wetlands?

10.4 How can we protect and sustain terrestrial biodiversity and ecosystem services?

10.5 How can cities become more sustainable and livable?

Costa Rica—A Global Conservation Leader

Tropical forests once covered Central America's Costa Rica, a country smaller in area than the US state of West Virginia. Between 1963 and 1983, politically powerful ranching families cleared much of the country's forests in order to graze cattle.

Despite such widespread forest loss, Costa Rica is a superpower of biodiversity, with an estimated 500,000 plant and animal species. A single park in Costa Rica is home to more bird species than are found in all of North America.

This oasis of biodiversity results mostly from two factors. One is the country's tropical geographic location. It lies between two oceans and has coastal and mountainous regions with a variety of microclimates and habitats for wildlife. The other is the government's strong commitment to land conservation.

In the mid-1970s, Costa Rica established a system of nature reserves and national parks (Figure 10.1). By 2016, this system included more than 27% of its land—6% of it reserved for indigenous peoples. Costa Rica has increased its beneficial environmental impact by devoting a larger proportion of its land to biodiversity conservation than any other country—an example the biodiversity **principle of sustainability** in action.

To reduce *deforestation*—the clearing and loss of forests—the government eliminated subsidies for converting forestland to grazing lands. Instead, it pays landowners to maintain or restore tree cover.

The strategy worked. Costa Rica has gone from having one of the world's highest deforestation rates to having one of the lowest. Over three decades, forests went from covering 20% of its land to covering 50% of it.

Ecologists warn that human population growth, economic development, and poverty put increasing pressure on the earth's terrestrial and aquatic ecosystems and on the ecosystem services they provide. According to a recent joint report by two United Nations environmental bodies: "Unless radical and creative action is taken to conserve the earth's biodiversity, many local and regional ecosystems that help to support human lives and livelihoods are at risk of collapsing."

This chapter is devoted to helping you understand how to manage and sustain the earth's forests, public lands, grasslands, and cities. ●

CRITICAL THINKING

How does preservation of the rich biodiversity of their rainforests benefit the economy of Costa Rica?

FIGURE 10.1 La Fortuna Falls is located in a tropical rainforest in Costa Rica's Arenal Volcano National Park.

gary yim/Shutterstock.com

HOW SHOULD WE MANAGE AND SUSTAIN FORESTS AND PUBLIC LANDS?

CONCEPT 10.1A Forest ecosystems provide ecosystem services far greater in economic value than the value of wood and other raw materials they provide.

CONCEPT 10.1B We can sustain forests by emphasizing the economic value of their ecosystem services, halting government subsidies that hasten their destruction, protecting old-growth forests, harvesting trees no faster than they are replenished, and planting trees to reestablish forests.

Forests Provide Economic and Ecosystem Services

Natural forests (Figure 5.19, p. 138) and planted forests occupy about 31% of the earth's land surface (excluding Greenland and Antarctica). Scientists divide forests into major types, based on their age and structure. An **old-growth forest** is an uncut or regrown forest that has not been seriously disturbed by human activities or natural disasters for 200 years or more (Figure 10.2). Old-growth forests are reservoirs of biodiversity because they provide ecological niches for a multitude of wildlife species (see Figure 5.20, p. 139).

A **second-growth forest** is a stand of trees resulting from secondary ecological succession (see Figure 7.12, p. 188). They develop after the trees in an area have been removed by human activities, such as clear-cutting for timber or conversion to cropland, or by natural forces such as fire or hurricanes.

A **tree plantation**, also called a **tree farm** or **commercial forest** (Figure 10.3), is a managed forest containing only one or two species of trees that are all the same age. They are often grown on land that was cleared of an old-growth or second-growth forest and are usually harvested by clear-cutting as soon as they become commercially valuable. The land is then replanted and clear-cut again in a regular cycle (see drawing, Figure 10.3). When managed carefully, plantations can produce wood at a rapid rate and could supply most of the wood used for industrial purposes, including papermaking and construction. This would help protect the world's remaining old-growth and second-growth forests, as long as they are not cleared to make room for tree plantations.

Use of tree plantations is increasing and they now occupy about 7% of the world's forest area. The downside of tree plantations is that, with only one or two tree species, they are less biologically diverse and less sustainable than old-growth and second-growth forests. Tree plantations also do not provide the amount of wildlife habitat and many of the ecosystems services that diverse natural forests do. In addition, repeated cutting and replanting trees can eventually deplete the nutrients in the plantation's topsoil. This can hinder the regrowth of any type of forest on such land.

Forests provide economic services and ecosystem services. However, the economic value of a forest's ecosystem services is typically not included in making decisions about cutting intact forests (See Critical Concepts in Sustainability, The Value of Instact Forests).

Harvesting Trees

The harvesting of wood for timber and to make paper is one of the world's major industries. The first step in harvesting trees is to build roads for access and timber removal. Even carefully designed logging roads can have harmful effects (Figure 10.4), including topsoil erosion, sediment run-off into waterways, habitat loss, and biodiversity loss. Logging roads also open up forests to disturbances from human activities such as mining, farming, and ranching.

Loggers use a variety of methods to harvest trees. *Selective cutting* involves cutting intermediate-aged or mature trees singly or in small groups and leaving the forest largely intact (Figure 10.5a). This can allow a forest to produce economically valuable trees on a sustainable basis if trees are not removed faster than they can grow back.

However, loggers often remove all the trees from an area in what is called a *clear-cut* (Figure 10.5b). Clear-cutting is the most efficient and sometimes the most cost-effective way to harvest trees. It also provides profits in the shortest time for landowners and timber companies. However, clear-cutting can harm or destroy an ecosystem by causing forest soil erosion, sediment pollution of nearby waterways, and losses in biodiversity. Clear-cutting also contributes to atmospheric warming and the resulting climate change by releasing stored carbon dioxide (CO_2) into the atmosphere and reducing the uptake of CO_2 by forests, thus altering the natural carbon cycle.

FIGURE 10.2 Old-growth forest in Poland.

Aleksander Bolbot/Shutterstock.com

The Value of an Intact Forest

Forests provided ecosystem services and economic services (Figure 10.A). Most people think of the value of trees only in terms of the lumber that can be harvested and sold. However, when considering the ecosystem services provided by an intact forest, the value of that forest far exceeds the monetary value of the timber.

One tool used by economists, businesses, and investors to determine the value of a resource is the *discount rate*—an estimate of a resource's future economic value compared to its present value. It is based on the idea that today's value of a resource may be higher than its value in the future. Thus, its future value should be discounted. The size of the discount rate (usually given as a percentage) is a key factor affecting how a resource such as a forest is used.

At a zero-discount rate, for example, the timber from a stand of redwood trees worth $1 million today will still be worth $1 million 50 years from now. Most businesses typically use a 10% annual discount rate to estimate the future value of a resource. At this rate, within 45 years the timber in this stand of redwood trees will be worth less than $10,000. Using this discount rate, it makes sense for the owner of the redwood trees to cut them down as quickly as possible.

However, this economic analysis does not take into account the immense economic value of the ecosystem services provided by an intact redwood forest. If these economic values were included, it would make more sense to preserve large areas of redwoods for the ecosystem services they provide. While these ecosystem services are vital for the earth as a whole and for future generations, they do not provide the current owner of the redwoods with any monetary return.

In 2014 a team of ecologists, economists, and geographers led by ecological economist Robert Costanza, estimated the monetary worth of 17 ecosystem services provided by 16 of the earth's biomes. Examples are waste treatment, erosion control, climate regulation, nutrient cycling, habitat, food production, and recreation.

Their conservative estimate was that the global monetary value of these services is at least $125 trillion per year—more than the $119 trillion that the entire world spent on goods and services in 2016. This means that every year the earth provides you and every other person on the planet with $17,123 of ecosystem services, on average. The top five ecosystem services are waste treatment ($22.5 trillion per year), recreation ($20.6 trillion), erosion control ($16.2 trillion), food production ($14.8 trillion), and nutrient cycling ($11.1 trillion).

According to Costanza and his colleagues, the world's forests provide us with ecosystem services worth at least $15.6 trillion per year. This is hundreds of times more than the economic value of lumber, paper, and other wood products that forests provide (**Concept 10.1A**). About 71% of the total value of ecosystem services from forests comes from climate regulation, genetic resources, and recreation.

FRQ Application

Question: **Identify** THREE ecological services provided by intact forests and discuss the impact of losing those services.

Possible Response: Intact forests help to create topsoil through the decomposition of leaf litter on the forest floor. A loss of trees and the leaf litter they provide means that the nutrients released from the decomposing leaves would be lost, depriving plants that grow on the forest floor necessary nutrients, and also depriving nutrients to decomposers and detritivores. Tree roots hold soil in place, preventing erosion. In flood conditions or heavy rain, soil could easily be washed away into nearby waterways, causing sedimentation in streams and rivers and disrupting aquatic food chains. Intact forests also moderate climate warming. Through photosynthesis, forest trees remove some of the excess CO_2 that

human activities add to the atmosphere and store it as organic compounds. As temperatures increase, plants release water vapor through evapotranspiration that rise and form clouds, cooling the atmosphere. Loss of forests adds to a warmer climate.

Possible Response: Intact forests keep streams clean by holding soil in place, minimizing erosion into waterways, and providing soils that naturally filter water. Loss of forests results in sedimentation of waterways. Intact forests also aid in flood control by taking up and storing flood waters in plant tissues. Loss of forests means greater damage from floods, for example, higher flood waters and loss of topsoil when waters recede. Intact forests are a major sink for carbon dioxide. Deforestation removes this sink, plus if trees are burned or left to rot, carbon held in the trees is released as CO_2 to the atmosphere, increasing climate change.

Natural Capital

Forests

Ecosystem Services	Economic Services
Support energy flow and chemical cycling	Fuelwood
Reduce soil erosion	Lumber
Absorb and release water	Pulp to make paper
Purify water and air	Mining
Influence local and regional climate	Livestock grazing
Store atmospheric carbon	Recreation
Provide numerous wildlife habitats	Jobs

FIGURE 10.A Forests provide important ecosystem and economic services. *Critical Thinking*: Which two ecosystem services and which two economic services do you think are the most important?

Photo: Val Thoermer/Shutterstock.com

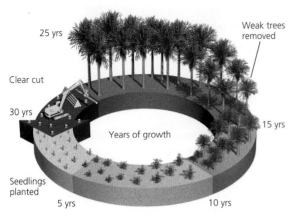

FIGURE 10.3 Oil palm tree plantation. A large area of diverse tropical forest was cleared and planted with this monoculture of oil palm trees.

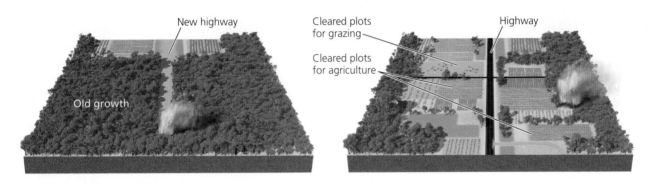

FIGURE 10.4 Natural capital degradation: Building roads into previously inaccessible forests is the first step in harvesting timber, but it also paves the way to fragmentation, destruction, and degradation of forest ecosystems.

A variation of clear-cutting that allows a more sustainable timber yield without widespread destruction is *strip cutting* (Figure 10.5c). It involves clear-cutting a strip of trees along the contour of the land within a corridor narrow enough to allow natural forest regeneration within a few years. After regeneration, loggers cut another strip next to the first, and so on.

Threats to Forest Ecosystems

Deforestation is the temporary or permanent removal of large expanses of forest for agriculture, settlements, or other uses. Surveys by the World Resources Institute (WRI) indicate that during the past 8,000 years, deforestation has eliminated almost half of the earth's old-growth forest cover. Most of this loss occurred in the last 65 years. According to the WRI, if current deforestation rates continue, about 40% of the world's remaining intact forests, especially tropical forests, will be logged or converted to other uses within two decades, if not sooner.

Clearing large areas of forests, especially old-growth forests, has important short-term economic benefits but it also has a number of harmful environmental effects (Figure 10.6).

Tropical forests (see Figure 5.19, top, p. 138) cover about 6% of the earth's land area—roughly the area of the continental United States. Climatic and biological data indicate that mature tropical forests once covered at least twice the area they do now. Most loss of the world's tropical forests has taken place since 1950 (see Chapter 3, **Core Case Study**, p. 66). Since 2000, the world has been losing the equivalent of more than 50 soccer fields of tropical forest every minute.

Currently, tropical forests absorb and store about one-third of the world's terrestrial carbon emissions as part of the carbon cycle. Thus, in reducing these forests, we reduce their absorption of CO_2 and contribute to atmospheric warming and climate change. Burning and clearing tropical forests also adds CO_2 to the atmosphere, accounting for 10–15% of global greenhouse gas emissions.

Water evaporating from trees and vegetation in tropical rainforests plays a major role in determining the amount of rainfall there. Removing large areas of trees can lead to drier conditions that dehydrate the topsoil by exposing it to sunlight and allowing it to be blown away.

a. Selective cutting

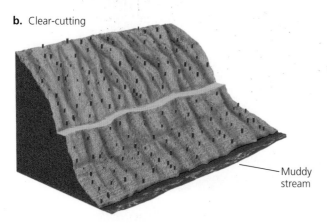

Clear
stream

b. Clear-cutting

Muddy
stream

c. Strip cutting

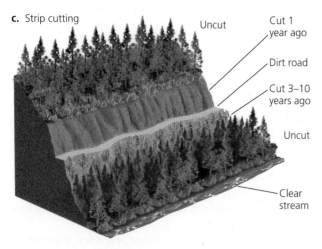

Uncut

Cut 1
year ago

Dirt road

Cut 3–10
years ago

Uncut

Clear
stream

FIGURE 10.5 Three major ways to harvest trees.
Critical Thinking: If you were cutting trees in a forest
you owned, which method would you choose and why?

This makes it difficult for a forest to grow back in the area.
At some point, the loss of trees causes the tropical forest to
go beyond an ecological tipping point (Science Focus 3.2,
p. 81) and become tropical grassland (savanna). Scientists
project that if current burning and deforestation rates continue, 20–30% of the Amazon Basin could become savanna
by 2080.

FIGURE 10.6 Deforestation has harmful environmental
effects that can reduce biodiversity and degrade the ecosystem
services provided by forests (Figure 10.A, left).

Tropical forest destruction and degradation typically
follows a pattern. First, access roads are into the forest interior (Figure 10.4), often by an international timber cor-
poration. Then loggers selectively cut down the largest and
best trees (Figure 10.5a). When loggers cut one tree, many
other trees often fall because of their shallow roots and the
network of vines connecting the trees in the forest's
canopy.

After trees are harvested logging companies often sell
the land to ranchers who burn any remaining timber to
clear the land for cattle grazing. Within a few years, the
land typically is overgrazed (Figure 10.7). Then the ranchers sell the degraded land to farmers who plow it up to
plant large crops such as soybeans (see Figure 1.5, p. 8), or
to settlers for small-scale farming. After a few years of crop
growing and erosion from rain, the topsoil is depleted of
nutrients. Then the farmers and settlers move on to newly
cleared land to repeat this environmentally destructive
process.

Tropical deforestation results from a number of causes.
Pressures from population growth and poverty push subsistence farmers and the landless poor into tropical forests,
where they cut or burn trees for firewood or try to grow
enough food to survive. Government subsidies can accelerate large-scale logging and livestock overgrazing by
reducing the costs of these enterprises.

Another cause is the *fuelwood crisis*. More than 2 billion
people in less-developed countries use fuelwood and charcoal made from wood for heating and cooking. Most of
these countries suffer from fuelwood shortages because
people are cutting trees for fuelwood and forest products
10–20 times faster than new trees are being planted. The
FAO warns that, by 2050, the demand for fuelwood could
easily be 50% greater than the amount that can be sustainably supplied.

For example, Haiti, a country with 11 million people,
was once a tropical paradise, 60% of it covered with forests.
Now it is an ecological and economic disaster. Largely

FIGURE 10.7 Severe soil erosion caused by the clearing of an area of tropical forest followed by livestock overgrazing.

because its trees were cut for fuelwood and to make charcoal, less than 2% of its land is now covered with trees. With the trees gone, soils have eroded away in many areas, making it much more difficult for the poor to grow crops.

CONSIDER THIS . . .

THINKING ABOUT Tropical Forests

Why should you care if most of the world's remaining tropical forests are burned, cleared, or converted to savanna within your lifetime? What are three ways in which this might affect your life or the lives of any children and grandchildren that you eventually might have?

Increasing Forest Cover

Forest cover has increased in some countries because of the spread of commercial tree plantations and a global program, sponsored by the United Nations Environment Programme (UNEP), to plant billions of trees throughout much of the world—many of them in tree plantations. China now leads the world in new forest cover, mostly due to its plantations of fast-growing trees. Other countries that have increased their forest cover are Costa Rica (**Core Case Study**) and the United States.

Forests cover about 30% of the US land area. They provide habitats for more than 80% of the country's wildlife species and contain about two-thirds of the nation's surface water.

Today, forests in the United States (including tree plantations) cover more area than they did in 1920. The primary reason is that many of the old-growth forests that were cleared or partially cleared between 1620 and 1920 have grown back naturally through secondary ecological succession (Figure 10.8).

There are now diverse second-growth (and in some cases third-growth) forests in every region of the United States except in much of the West. Environmental writer Bill McKibben has cited this forest regrowth in the United States—especially in the East—as "the great environmental success story of the United States, and in some ways, the whole world."

Managing Forest Fires

In the United States, the Smokey Bear educational campaign undertaken by the Forest Service and the National Advertising Council has prevented many forest fires, saved many lives, and prevented billions of dollars in losses of trees, wildlife, and human structures. At the same time, it has convinced much of the public that all forest fires are bad and should be prevented or put out. Ecologists warn that trying to prevent all forest fires can make matters worse by increasing the likelihood of destructive fires due to the accumulation of highly flammable underbrush in some forests.

Two types of fires can affect forest ecosystems: surface fires and crown fires (Figure 10.9). A *surface fire* (Figure 10.9,

Calculating the Amount of Carbon in a Forest

In order to calculate the carbon stored in a forest, scientists first need to calculate the amount of carbon in the above ground biomass of trees. This carbon is stored within each tree. If the trees are cut down and burned to use the land for agriculture, the stored carbon combines with oxygen to produce CO_2 during combustion. If the forest is left intact, this carbon remains stored in the plant tissue, and is kept from combining with oxygen to form CO_2. The carbon is said to be "sequestered" or "captured," in that it stays stored in the plant tissue.

To determine the amount of carbon in a forest, scientists take an inventory of trees in randomly marked-out square regions called *quadrats*. Then they record the biomass characteristics of those random regions and extrapolate their results to draw conclusions about the entire forest. Each particular tree species stores a certain amount of carbon. Hardwoods like oak and maple store a higher amount of carbon than soft woods such as pines. From the randomly chosen quadrats, scientists can calculate an average amount of carbon per square unit of forest, and determine the amount of carbon dioxide that will not be emitted into the environment if the forest is left standing. Averaging the carbon storage of the quadrats gives an estimate of the amount of carbon held in the entire forest.

FRQ Application

An environmental science class hikes out to the woodlot behind their school. Each pair of students measures and flags a 50 ft × 50 ft quadrat. For each tree in their quadrat, they measure the tree's diameter about chest-high off the ground and identify the species. Back in the classroom, students calculate the biomass of each tree and a total measure of biomass, in kilograms, is calculated for each team's quadrat.

Calculate the total **above ground biomass** (AGB) in metric tons (1000 kg) for one hectare of forest, assuming that any 50 ft × 50 ft quadrat is representative of that woodlot. Then determine the amount of captured carbon if carbon makes up approximately 45% of the biomass of a tree.

> Above ground biomass for one group's quadrat = 8280 kg
>
> 1 acre = 43,560 ft²
>
> 1 hectare = 2.477 acres

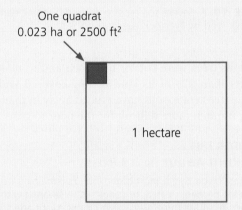

One quadrat
0.023 ha or 2500 ft²

1 hectare

The area of the quadrat is:

50 ft × 50 ft = 2,500 ft²

$$2{,}500 \text{ ft}^2 \times \frac{1 \text{ acre}}{43{,}560 \text{ ft}^2} \times \frac{1 \text{ hectare}}{2.477 \text{ acres}} = 0.023 \text{ hectares}$$

If 0.023 hectares contain 8280 kg AGB, then to find biomass per hectare

$$(0.023 \text{ hectare})\, x = 8280 \text{ kg}$$

$$x = \frac{8280 \text{ kg}}{0.023 \text{ hectares}} = 360{,}000 \text{ kg / hectare}$$

360,000 kg/hectare = 360 metric tons/hectare AGB

To calculate just the **carbon** held in the woodlot

360 metric tons × 0.45 = 162 metric tons carbon

left) usually burns only undergrowth and leaf litter on the forest floor. It kills seedlings and small trees, but spares most mature trees and allows most wild animals to escape. Occasional surface fires have several ecological benefits. They:

- burn flammable material such as dry brush to help prevent fires that are more destructive.

- free valuable plant nutrients trapped in slowly decomposing litter and undergrowth.

- release seeds from the cones of tree species such as lodgepole pines and stimulate the germination of other seeds such as those of the giant sequoia.

- help control destructive insects and tree diseases.

A *crown fire* (Figure 10.9 right) is an extremely hot fire that leaps from treetop to treetop, burning whole trees. It usually occurs in forests that have not experienced surface fires for several decades. The absence of fire allows dead wood,

Calculating a Carbon Offset

An important function of an intact forest is its ability to store carbon via the process of photosynthesis. A **carbon offset** is a way to compensate for the carbon dioxide or greenhouse gases generated by burning fossil fuels or forests. It usually done by investing in clean energy projects, or by planting trees or leaving a forest intact to take up the carbon from CO_2 generation.

FRQ Application

The rate of carbon sequestration (or storage within the plant tissues) varies with different tree species, but on average, given the annual above ground biomass growth (AGB) for a 25-year-old forest, 1760 lb of CO_2 per acre is sequestered per year.

A family wishes to offset the amount of CO_2 produced by the natural gas their furnace uses each year. Several acres of 25-year-old second-growth forest are for sale adjacent to their property. How much forest must they buy and keep intact to offset the CO_2 they produce each year?

According to the family's energy history, they consumed 1,105 therms of natural gas in one year. A therm is a unit of heat energy equal to burning approximately 100 cubic feet of natural gas, or 2.38 cubic meters of natural gas.

To find cubic feet of natural gas consumed each year

$$1105 \text{ therms} \times \frac{100 \text{ cubic feet}}{1 \text{ therm}} = 110{,}500 \text{ cubic feet of natural gas}$$

Each 1,000 cubic feet of natural gas produces 117.10 lb of CO_2. Therefore,

$$110{,}500 \text{ cubic feet natural gas} \times \frac{117.10 \text{ lb } CO_2}{1000 \text{ cubic feet natural gas}} = 12{,}939.6 \text{ lb } CO_2$$

The number of acres of second-growth forest the family would have to purchase in order to offset their natural gas use would be

$$12{,}939.6 \text{ lb } CO_2 \text{ generated} \times \frac{1 \text{ acre}}{1{,}760 \text{ lb } CO_2 \text{ sequestered}} = 7.35 \text{ acres of forest}$$

leaves, and flammable ground litter to accumulate. This rapidly burning fire can jump to the forest canopy, spread rapidly, and destroy most vegetation, kill wildlife, increase topsoil erosion, and burn or damage buildings and homes.

Ecologists and forest fire experts recommend several strategies for limiting the harmful effects of forest fires:

- Use carefully planned and controlled fires, called *prescribed burns* to remove flammable small trees and underbrush in the highest-risk forest areas.

- Allow some fires on public lands to burn underbrush and smaller trees, as long as the fires do not threaten human-built structures or human lives.

- Protect houses and other buildings in fire-prone areas by thinning trees and other vegetation in a zone around them and eliminating the use of highly flammable construction materials such as wood shingles.

- Use drones, equipped with infrared sensors, to detect forest fires and monitor progress in fighting them.

Managing Forests More Sustainably

Figure 10.10 lists ways to grow and harvest trees more sustainably. One tool is the certification of sustainably grown timber and of sustainably produced forest products. This helps inform consumers about products made from sustainably grown wood. The nonprofit Forest Stewardship Council (FSC) oversees the certification of forestry operations that meet certain sustainable forest standards. Forestry analysts have also suggested various ways to protect tropical forests and use them more sustainably (Figure 10.11).

Consumers can reduce the demand for unsustainable and illegal logging in tropical forests by buying only wood and wood products that have been certified as sustainably produced by the FSC and other organizations, including the Rainforest Alliance and the Sustainability Action Network. Several organizations (Individuals Matter 10.1) are assisting poor families living in tropical forests grow the food they need without having to cut and burn trees

Many economists urge governments to begin making a shift to more sustainable forest management. They recommend phasing out government subsidies and tax breaks that encourage forest degradation and deforestation and replacing them with forest-sustaining subsidies and tax breaks. This would likely lead to higher prices on unsustainably produced timber and wood products, in keeping with the full-cost pricing **principle of sustainability**. Costa Rica (**Core Case Study**) is taking the lead

a. 1620

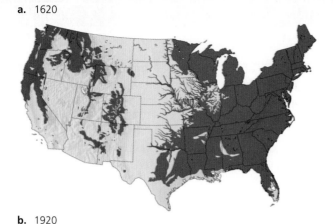

b. 1920

c. 2000

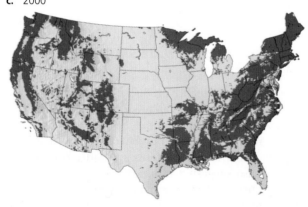

FIGURE 10.8 In 1620, (a) when European settlers were moving to North America, forests covered more than half of the current land area of the continental United States. By 1920, (b) most of these forests had been decimated. In 2000, and (c) secondary and commercial forests covered about a third of US land in the lower 48 states.

in using this approach. Governments can also encourage tree-planting programs to help restore degraded forests. **GREEN CAREER: Sustainable forestry**

Another approach is to *reduce the demand for forest products*. According to forestry analysts, up to 60% of the wood consumed in the United States is wasted unnecessarily. This waste results from inefficient use of construction materials, excessive packaging, overuse of

junk mail, inadequate paper recycling, and the failure to reuse or find substitutes for wooden shipping containers.

Using fibers from non-tree sources to make paper can reduce the need to harvest trees to make paper. For example, China uses rice straw and other agricultural residues to make some of its paper. Most of the small amount of tree-free paper produced in the United States is made from the non-tree fibers of a rapidly growing woody annual plant called *kenaf* (Figure 10.12). It yields more paper pulp per area of land than tree farms do without using pesticides and herbicides.

Another way to reduce the demand for harvesting trees is to reduce the use of throwaway paper products made from trees. Instead, we can instead choose reusable plates, cups, cloth napkins and handkerchiefs, and cloth bags.

We can also use the forest, grassland, and desert in US public lands more sustainably (see Case Study that follows).

CASE STUDY

Managing Public Lands in the United States

No nation has set aside as much of its land for public use, resource extraction, enjoyment, and wildlife habitat as has the United States. About 28% of the country's land is jointly owned by all US citizens and managed for them by the federal government. About three-fourths of this federal public land is in Alaska and another fifth is in the western states (Figure 10.13). This land includes forests, grasslands, and deserts.

Some federal public lands are used for many different purposes. Protected forests make up about 40% of the country's total forest area, mostly in the *National Forest System*, which consists of 155 national forests and 22 national grasslands. These lands, managed by the US Forest Service (USFS), are used for logging, mining, livestock grazing, farming, oil and gas extraction, recreation, and conservation of watershed, soil, and wildlife resources.

The Bureau of Land Management (BLM) manages large areas of land—40% of all land managed by the federal government and 13% of the total US land surface—mostly in the western states and Alaska. These lands are used primarily for mining, oil and gas extraction, logging, and livestock grazing.

The US Fish and Wildlife Service (USFWS) manages 562 *national wild-life refuges*. Most refuges protect habitats and breeding areas for waterfowl and big game to provide a harvestable supply of these species for hunters. Permitted activities in most refuges include hunting, trapping, fishing, oil and gas development, mining, logging, grazing, farming, and some military activities.

The uses of some other public lands are more restricted. The *National Park System,* managed by the National Park

Florence Reed—Preserving Tropical Forests and Overcoming Poverty

When Florence Reed worked as a Peace Corps volunteer in Panama, she observed poor farmers moving into tropical forests. Once there, they cut and burned small plots of forest to grow enough food to survive. After a few years, they had depleted the soil of nutrients and had to move to another area and clear and burn more trees.

Reed decided to dedicate her life to helping poor farmers learn how to grow nutritious food on the same land year after year and to raise their incomes without having to clear and burn more forest. In 1997, she founded Sustainable Harvest International (SHI), a nonprofit organization dedicated to her goal.

SHI helps farmers learn and use sustainable agricultural practices, including seed saving, organic vegetable farming, tree planting, water conservation, and growing a diversity of crops on their plots. SHI also teaches farm families how to increase their income by selling surplus crops and craftworks they make.

Reed works only with farmers who ask for help. She encourages farmers to cooperate and share their resources and knowledge, and SHI works with them until they learn to use the farming techniques on their own—typically within 3 to 5 years.

By 2014, SHI had helped more than 10,000 people in 100 or more farming communities. The income of a typical farm family working with SHI increases from around $475 to $5,000 per year. In addition, the families are not exposed to potentially harmful pesticides and they have a nutritious diet.

FIGURE 10.9 Surface fires (left) usually burn only undergrowth and leaf litter. They can help to prevent more destructive crown fires (right).

Left: David J. Moorhead, University of Georgia, Bugwood.org; Right: Xneo/Dreamstime.com

Service (NPS), includes 59 major parks (see Chapter 1 opening photo, pp. 2–3) and 354 national recreation areas, monuments, memorials, battlefields, historic sites, parkways, trails, rivers, seashores, and lakeshores. Only camping, hiking, sport fishing, and boating can take place in the national parks, whereas hunting, mining, and oil and gas drilling are allowed in national recreation areas.

The most restricted public lands are 762 roadless areas that make up the *National Wilderness Preservation System*. These areas lie within the other public lands and are managed by the agencies in charge of those lands. Most wilderness areas are open only for recreational activities such as hiking, sport fishing, camping, and nonmotorized boating.

Many federal lands contain valuable oil, natural gas, coal, geothermal, timber, and mineral resources. Since the 1800s, there has been intense controversy over how to use and manage the resources on these public lands.

Most conservation biologists, environmental economists, and many true free-market economists believe that four principles should govern the use of public lands:

1. Protect biodiversity, wildlife habitats, and ecosystems as the top priority.

2. Do not provide government subsidies or tax breaks for using or extracting resources on public lands.

FIGURE 10.10 Ways to grow and harvest trees more sustainably. ***Critical Thinking***: Which three of these methods of more sustainable forestry do you think are the best methods? Why?

FIGURE 10.11 Ways to protect tropical forests and to use them more sustainably (**Concept 10.2**). ***Critical Thinking***: Which three of these solutions do you think are the best ones? Why?

Top: Stillfx/Shutterstock.com. Center: Manfred Mielke/USDA Forest Service Bugwood.org.

3. Require users of public lands to reimburse the American people for use of their property and the resources it contains.

4. Hold all users or extractors of resources on public lands fully responsible for any environmental damage they cause.

FIGURE 10.12 Solutions: The pressure to cut trees to make paper could be greatly reduced by planting and harvesting a fast-growing plant known as kenaf.

There is strong and effective opposition to these ideas. Developers, resource extractors, many economists, and many citizens tend to view public lands in terms of their usefulness in providing mineral, timber, and other resources, and increasing short-term economic growth with minimal government regulation. They have succeeded in blocking implementation of the four principles listed above. For example, in recent years, analyses of budgets and spending reveal that the government has given an average of $1 billion a year—more than $2.7 million a day—in subsidies and tax breaks to privately owned interests that use US public lands for activities such as mining, fossil fuel extraction, logging, and livestock grazing.

Some developers and resource extractors want to go further in opening up federal lands for more development and resource extraction and reducing or eliminating federal regulation of these lands. Here are six of the ideas that such interests have proposed to the US Congress since 1980:

FIGURE 10.13 Public Lands: National forests, parks, and wildlife refuges managed by the US federal government. ***Critical Thinking***: Do you think US citizens should jointly own more or less of the nation's land? Explain.

(Compiled by the authors using data from US Geological Survey and US National Park Service.)

1. Return ownership of public lands to states.

2. Sell public lands or their resources to corporations or individuals, usually at prices that are less than their market values.

3. Slash federal funding for the administration of regulations related to public lands.

4. Cut diverse old-growth stands in the national forests for timber and for making biofuels, and replace them with tree plantations to be harvested for the same purposes.

5. Open national parks, national wildlife refuges, and wilderness areas to oil and natural gas drilling,

mining, off-road vehicles, and commercial development.

6. Eliminate or take regulatory control away from the National Park Service and launch a 20-year construction program in the parks to build theme parks run by private firms.

CONSIDER THIS ...

THINKING ABOUT US Public Lands

Explain why you agree or disagree with the five proposals of developers for changing the use of US public lands, listed above.

CHECKPOINT FOR UNDERSTANDING 10.1

1. Identify the drawbacks of planting monocultures of tree species (tree plantations).

2. Identify the benefits and drawbacks of clear-cutting trees.

3. Describe the sequence of events that leads to permanent destruction of rainforest land.

4. Explain how controlled burns can help prevent more destructive crown fires.

10.2 HOW CAN WE MANAGE AND SUSTAIN GRASSLANDS?

CONCEPT 10.2 We can sustain the productivity of grasslands by controlling the numbers and distribution of grazing livestock and by restoring degraded grasslands.

Some Rangelands Are Overgrazed

Grasslands cover about one-fourth of the earth's land surface. They provide important ecosystem services, including soil formation, erosion control, chemical cycling, storage of atmospheric carbon dioxide in biomass, and maintenance of biodiversity.

After forests, grasslands are the ecosystems most widely used and altered by human activities. **Rangelands** are unfenced natural grasslands in temperate and tropical climates that supply *forage*, or vegetation for grazing (grass-eating) and browsing (shrub-eating) animals. Cattle, sheep, and goats graze on about 42% of the world's natural grasslands. This could increase to 70% by the end of this century, according to the UN Millennium Ecosystem Assessment. Livestock also graze in **pastures**, which are managed grasslands or fenced meadows often planted with domesticated grasses or other forage crops such as alfalfa and clover.

Blades of rangeland grass grow from the base, not at the tip. As long as only the upper portion of the blade is eaten and the lower portion remains in the ground, rangeland grass is a renewable resource that can be grazed repeatedly. Moderate levels of grazing are healthy for grasslands, because removal of mature vegetation stimulates rapid regrowth and encourages greater plant diversity.

Overgrazing occurs when too many animals graze an area for too long and damage or kill the grasses (Figure 10.14, left) and their roots and exceed the area's carrying capacity for grazing. Overgrazing reduces grass cover, exposes the topsoil to erosion by water and wind, and compacts the soil, which lessens its capacity to hold water. Overgrazing also promotes the invasion of rangeland by plant species such as sagebrush, mesquite, cactus, and cheatgrass, which cattle will not eat. The FAO has estimated that overgrazing by livestock has reduced productivity on as much as 20% of the world's rangeland.

Managing Rangelands More Sustainably

Managing rangelands more sustainably and preventing overgrazing typically involves controlling how many animals are allowed to graze in a given area and for how long, in order to avoid exceeding the area's carrying capacity for grazing animals (**Concept 10.2**). One method for doing this is called *rotational grazing*, in which small groups of cattle are confined by portable fencing to one area for a few days and then moved to a new location.

Cattle prefer to graze around ponds and other natural water sources, especially along streams or rivers lined by strips of vegetation known as *riparian zones*. Overgrazing can destroy the vegetation in such areas (Figure 10.15, left). Ranchers can protect overgrazed land through rotational grazing and by fencing off damaged areas, which eventually leads to their natural restoration by ecological succession (Figure 10.15, right). Ranchers can also move cattle around by providing supplemental feed at selected sites and by strategically locating watering ponds or tanks and salt blocks.

CHECKPOINT FOR UNDERSTANDING 10.2

1. Explain how grazing by herd animals is beneficial to rangeland grass species.

2. Describe two ways to manage grasslands more sustainably.

FIGURE 10.14 **Natural capital degradation**: To the left of the fence is overgrazed rangeland. The land to the right of the fence is lightly grazed.

FIGURE 10.15 **Natural capital restoration**: In the mid-1980s, cattle had degraded the vegetation and soil on this stream bank along the San Pedro River in the US state of Arizona (left). Within 10 years, the area was restored through secondary ecological succession (right) after grazing and off-road vehicle use were banned.

10.3 HOW CAN WE MANAGE AND SUSTAIN WETLANDS?

CONCEPT 10.3 We can maintain the ecosystem and economic services of wetlands by protecting remaining wetlands and restoring degraded wetlands.

Wetlands Are Disappearing

Coastal wetlands and marshes (Figure 6.7, p. 158) and inland wetlands (Figure 6.18, p. 170) provide vital economic and ecosystem services. Their ecosystem services include feeding downstream waters, reducing flooding by storing storm water, reducing storm damage by absorbing waves (coastal wetlands), recharging groundwater supplies, reducing pollution, preventing erosion, and providing fish and wildlife habitat.

Despite their ecological value, the United States has lost more than half of its coastal and inland wetlands since 1900. Other countries have lost even more, and the rate of loss of wetlands throughout the world is accelerating.

The US state of Louisiana has the largest area of coastal wetlands in the lower 48 states but is losing them faster than any other state. One cause of such losses is subsidence (sinking) of coastal land near the Mississippi River delta. Because the river is heavily dammed, sediments that naturally replenish the delta do not make it to the Gulf of Mexico, so the delta is shrinking and the land subsiding. Other threats to coastal wetlands are oil spills and a rising sea level due to climate change.

For centuries, people have drained, filled in, or covered over swamps, marshes, and other wetlands to create rice fields or other cropland, to accommodate expanding cities and suburbs, and to build roads. Wetlands have also been destroyed to extract minerals, oil, and natural gas, and to eliminate breeding grounds for insects that cause diseases such as malaria. To make matters worse, coastal wetlands in many parts of the world will probably be under deep water before the end of this century because of rising sea levels.

Preserving and Restoring Wetlands

Some laws protect wetlands. In the United States, zoning laws have been used to steer development away from wetlands. The US government requires a federal permit to fill in wetlands occupying more than 1.2 hectares (3.0 acres) or to deposit dredged material in wetlands. According to the US Fish and Wildlife Service, this law has helped to cut the average annual wetland loss by 80% since 1969.

However, there are continuing attempts by land developers to weaken such wetlands protection. Only about 6% of the country's remaining inland wetlands are federally protected, and state and local wetland protection is inconsistent and generally weak because of intense pressure from coastal developers and landowners.

94% of remaining US inland wetlands are not protected by federal law against development and degradation

The stated goal of current US federal policy is *zero net loss* in the functioning and value of coastal and inland wetlands. A policy known as *mitigation banking* allows destruction of existing wetlands as long as an equal or greater area of the same type of wetland is created, enhanced, or restored. How-

ever, a study by the National Academy of Sciences found that at least half of the attempts to create new wetlands failed to replace lost ones. Furthermore, most of the created wetlands did not provide the ecosystem services of natural wetlands, even decades after completion. The study also found that wetland creation and restorations often fail to meet the standards set for them and are not adequately monitored.

Creating and restoring wetlands has become a profitable business. Private investment bankers make money by buying wetland areas and restoring or upgrading them or creating new wetland. This creates wetlands banks or credits that the bankers sell to developers. This approach is a small step toward full-cost pricing because it puts a monetary value on the biodiversity and ecosystem services of wetlands that are sold by the bankers.

However, is difficult to restore, enhance, or create wetlands (see the following Case Study). Thus, most US wetland banking systems require replacing each area of destroyed wetland with twice the same area of restored, enhanced, or created wetland (Figure 10.16) as a built-in ecological insurance policy.

Ecologists urge using mitigation banking only as a last resort. They also call for making sure that new replacement

CONSIDER THIS . . .

THINKING ABOUT Wetlands Mitigation

Should a new wetland be created and evaluated before anyone is allowed to destroy the wetland it is supposed to replace? Explain.

wetlands are created and evaluated *before* existing wetlands are destroyed. This is the reverse of what is being done.

CASE STUDY

Can We Restore the Florida Everglades?

South Florida's Everglades was once a 100-kilometer-wide (62-mile-wide), knee-deep sheet of water flowing slowly south from Lake Okeechobee to Florida Bay (Figure 10.17, see red dashed lines). As this shallow body of water—known as the "River of Grass"—trickled south, it created a vast network of wetlands with a variety of wildlife habitats.

To help preserve the wilderness in the lower end of the Everglades system, in 1947, the US government established Everglades National Park. However, this protection effort did not work—as conservationists had predicted—because of a massive water distribution and land development project to the north. Between 1962 and 1971, the US Army Corps of Engineers transformed the wandering 166-kilometer-long (103-mile-long) Kissimmee River into a mostly straight 84-kilometer (52-mile) canal flowing into Lake Okeechobee (Figure 10.17, see black dashed line). The

FIGURE 10.16 This human-created wetland is located near Orlando, Florida (USA).

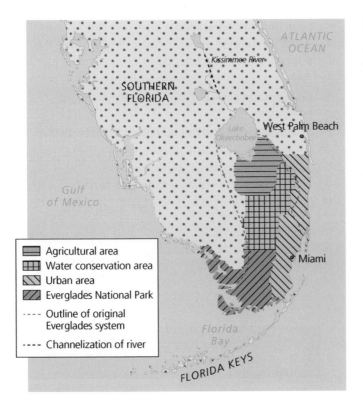

Agricultural area
Water conservation area
Urban area
Everglades National Park
---- Outline of original Everglades system
---- Channelization of river

ATLANTIC OCEAN
Kissimmee River
SOUTHERN FLORIDA
West Palm Beach
Lake Okeechobee
Gulf of Mexico
Miami
Florida Bay
FLORIDA KEYS

FIGURE 10.17 Florida's Everglades is the site of the world's largest ecological restoration project—an attempt to undo and redo an engineering project that has been destroying this vast wetland and threatening water supplies for south Florida's rapidly growing population.

canal provided flood control by speeding the flow of water, but it drained large wetlands north of Lake Okeechobee, which farmers then converted to grazing land.

This and other projects have provided south Florida's rapidly growing population with a reliable water supply and flood protection. However, much of the original Everglades has been drained, paved over, polluted by agricultural runoff, and invaded by a number of plant and animal species. The Everglades is now less than half its original size and much of it has dried out, leaving large areas vulnerable to summer wildfires.

The Everglades National Park is known for its astonishing biodiversity, and each year, more than a million people from all over the world visit the park. However, its biodiversity has been decreasing, mostly because of habitat loss, pollution, and invasive species. About 90% of the wading birds in Everglades National Park have vanished and populations of many remaining wading bird species have dropped sharply. In addition, populations of vertebrates, from deer to turtles, are down 75–95%.

By the 1970s, state and federal officials recognized that this huge plumbing project was reducing populations of native plants and wildlife—a major source of tourism revenues for Florida. It was also cutting the water supply for the 6 million residents of south Florida. In 1990, Florida's state government and the US government agreed on a plan for the world's largest ecological restoration project, known as the Comprehensive Everglades Restoration Plan. The US Army Corps of Engineers is supposed to carry out this joint federal and state plan to partially restore the Everglades.

The project has several ambitious goals, including restoration of the curving flow of more than half of the Kissimmee River; removal of 400 kilometers (248 miles) of canals and levees that block natural water flows south of Lake Okeechobee; conversion of large areas of farmland to marshes; the creation of 18 large reservoirs and underground water storage areas to store water for the lower Everglades and for south Florida's population; and building a canal–reservoir system for catching the water now flowing out to sea and pumping it back into the Everglades.

Will this huge ecological restoration project work? It depends not only on the abilities of scientists and engineers but also on prolonged political and economic support from citizens, the state's powerful sugarcane and agricultural industries, and elected state and federal officials. Some restrictions on phosphorus discharges from sugarcane plantations have been relaxed, which could worsen pollution problems. The project has also had cost overruns and funding shortages and is way behind the schedule.

CONSIDER THIS . . .

THINKING ABOUT Everglades Restoration

Do you support carrying out the proposed plan for partially restoring the Florida Everglades, including making the federal government (taxpayers) responsible for half of the funding? Explain.

CHECKPOINT FOR UNDERSTANDING 10.3

1. Identify several important ecosystems services that wetlands provide.

2. Explain mitigation banking.

3. Describe the ecological restoration plan for the Florida Everglades.

10.4 HOW CAN WE SUSTAIN TERRESTRIAL BIODIVERSITY AND ECOSYSTEM SERVICES?

CONCEPT 10.4A We can establish and protect wilderness areas, parks, and nature preserves.

CONCEPT 10.4B We can identify and protect biological hotspots that are highly threatened centers of terrestrial biodiversity.

CONCEPT 10.4C We can protect important ecosystem services, restore damaged ecosystems, and share areas that we dominate with other species.

Strategies for Sustaining Terrestrial Biodiversity

Since the 1960s, a number of strategies have been used to help sustain terrestrial biodiversity. The main strategies include the following:

- Protecting species from extinction, as discussed in Chapter 9
- Setting aside wilderness areas that are protected from harmful human activities
- Establishing parks and nature reserves in which people and nature can interact with some restrictions
- Identifying and protecting **biodiversity hotspots** (Figure 10.18) that contain a high diversity of species and that are under severe threat of extinction from human activities
- Shifting new development to lands that have already been cleared or degraded.
- Avoiding the destruction of forests and grasslands by increasing crop productivity on existing cropland.
- Protecting important ecosystem services
- Rehabilitating and partially restoring damaged ecosystems
- Sharing areas that we dominate with other species

According to most and conservation biologists, the best way to preserve terrestrial biodiversity is to create a worldwide network of areas that are strictly or partially protected from harmful human activities. In 2017, less than 13% of the earth's land area (excluding Antarctica) was protected to some degree in more than 177,000 wilderness areas, parks, nature reserves, and wildlife refuges. However, no more than 6% of the earth's land is strictly protected from potentially harmful human activities. In other words, we have reserved 94% of the earth's land for human use.

6 Percentage of the earth's land that is strictly protected from potentially harmful human activities

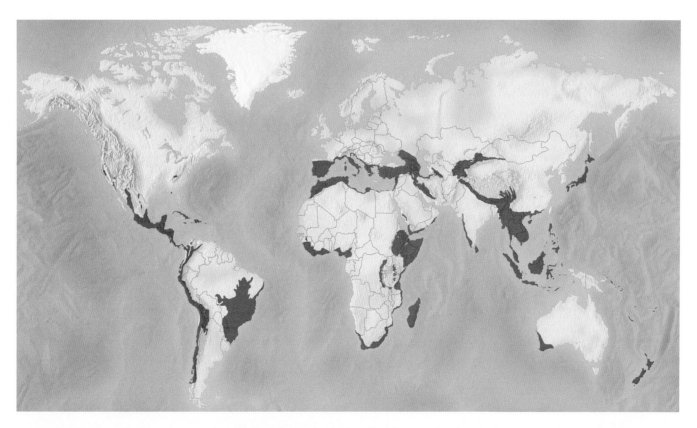

FIGURE 10.18 Endangered natural capital: Biologists have identified these 34 biodiversity hotspots. **Critical Thinking:** Why do you think so many hotspots are located near coastal areas?

(Compiled by the authors using data from the Center for Applied Biodiversity Science at Conservation International.)

Conservation biologists call for strictly protecting at least 20% of the earth's land area in a global system of biodiversity reserves to ward off a decline in the world's vital biodiversity in the face of human population growth, increasing resource use, and long-lasting climate change. Many developers and resource extractors oppose protecting even 13% of the earth's land (the current amount), arguing that these protected areas might contain valuable resources that would provide short-term economic benefits. In contrast, ecologists and conservation biologists view protected areas as islands of biodiversity and ecosystem services that help to sustain all life and economies indefinitely and that serve as centers of future evolution.

Establishing Wilderness Areas

One way to protect existing wildlands from human exploitation is to designate them as **wilderness**. Designated wilderness areas (Figure 10.19) are essentially undisturbed by humans and are protected by federal law from harmful human activities (**Concept 10.3A**). For example, forestry, road and trail development, mining, and building construction are not allowed. Theodore Roosevelt, the first US president to set aside protected areas, summarized his thoughts on what to do with wilderness: "Leave it as it is. You cannot improve it."

Most developers and resource extractors oppose establishing protected wilderness areas because they contain resources that could provide short-term economic benefits. To ecologists and conservation biologists, wilderness areas provide a long-term "ecological insurance policy" for humans and other species. They are islands of biodiversity and ecosystem services that will be necessary to support life and human economies in the future. In addition, they are needed as *centers for future evolution* in response to changes in environmental conditions such as climate change.

In 1964, the US Congress passed the Wilderness Act, which allowed the government to protect undeveloped tracts of US public land from development as part of the National Wilderness Preservation System (Figure 10.19). The country's area of protected wilderness grew by nearly twelvefold between 1964 and 2016. Even so, only 5% of all US land is protected as wilderness—more than 54% of it in Alaska. Only about 2.7% of the land of the lower 48 states is protected as wilderness, most of it in the West.

FIGURE 10.19 Diablo Lake lies in a wilderness area of North Cascades National Park in the US state of Washington.

Establishing Parks and Other Nature Reserves

According to the International Union for the Conservation of Nature (IUCN), there are more than 6,600 major national parks located in more than 120 countries (see Chapter 1 opening photo, pp. 2–3). However, most of these parks are too small to sustain many large animal species and many are "paper parks" that receive little protection, especially in less-developed countries.

Popularity threatens many US national parks. Between 1960 and 2016, the number of recreational visitors to US national parks more than tripled, reaching a record high of 331 million. In some US parks and on other public lands, dirt bikes, dune buggies, jet skis, snowmobiles, and other off-road vehicles have become a problem. These recreational vehicles destroy or damage fragile vegetation, disturb wildlife, and degrade the experience for many other visitors.

Many US national parks have become threatened islands of biodiversity surrounded by commercial development. The wildlife and recreational values of the parks are threatened by nearby activities such as mining, logging, livestock grazing, water diversion, operation of coal-fired power plants, and urban development. The National Park Service reports that air pollution, mainly caused by coal-fired power plants and dense vehicle traffic, impairs scenic views more than 90% of the time in many of its parks.

A number of parks also suffer damage from the migration or deliberate introduction of harmful nonnative species. European wild boars imported into the state of North Carolina in 1912 for hunting, now threaten vegetation in parts of the popular Great Smoky Mountains National Park. Nonnative mountain goats in Washington State's Olympic National Park trample and destroy the root systems of native vegetation and accelerate soil erosion.

Native species—some of which are threatened or endangered—are hunted or illegally removed from almost half of all US national parks. However, the endangered gray wolf, a keystone species, was successfully reintroduced into Yellowstone National Park after a 50-year absence (Science Focus 10.1).

Reintroducing the Gray Wolf to Yellowstone National Park

In the 1800s, at least 350,000 gray wolves (Figure 10.B) roamed over 75% of America's lower 48 states, especially in the West. They survived mostly by preying on abundant bison, elk, caribou, and deer. Between 1850 and 1900, most of them were shot, trapped, or poisoned by ranchers, hunters, and government employees. This drove the gray wolf to near extinction in the lower 48 states.

Ecologists recognize the important roles that this keystone predator species once played in the Yellowstone National Park region. The wolves culled herds of bison, elk, moose, and mule deer, and kept down coyote populations. By leaving some of their kills partially uneaten, they provided meat for scavengers such as ravens, bald eagles, ermines, grizzly bears, and foxes.

When the number of gray wolves declined, herds of plant-browsing elk, moose, and mule deer expanded and over-browsed the willow and aspen trees growing near streams and rivers. This led to increased soil erosion and declining populations of other wildlife species such as beaver, which eat willow and aspen. This in turn affected species that depended on wetlands created by dam-building beavers.

In 1974, the gray wolf was listed as an endangered species in the lower 48 states. In 1987, the US Fish and Wildlife Service (USFWS) proposed reintroducing gray wolves into the Yellowstone National Park to try to help stabilize the ecosystem. The proposal brought angry protests from area ranchers who feared the wolves would leave the park and attack their cattle and sheep and from hunters who feared the wolves would kill too many

FIGURE 10.B After becoming almost extinct in much of the western United States, *the gray* wolf was listed and protected as an endangered species in 1974.

Volodymyr Burdiak/Shutterstock.com

big-game animals. Mining and logging companies also objected, fearing that the government would halt their operations on wolf-populated federal lands.

Federal wildlife officials caught gray wolves in Canada and northwest Montana and in 1996 and relocated 41 of them in Yellowstone National Park. Scientists estimate that the long-term carrying capacity of the park is 110 to 150 gray wolves. By 2016, the park had 108 wolves in 11 packs.

Scientists have been using radio collars to track some of the wolves and studying the ecological effects of reintroducing the wolves. Their research indicates that the return of this keystone predator has decreased populations of elk, the wolves' primary food source. The leftovers of elk killed by wolves have also been an important food source for scavengers such as bald eagles and ravens.

However, a study led by US Geological Survey scientist Matthew Kauffman indicated that the aspen were not recovering despite a 60% decline in elk numbers. Declining populations of elk were also supposed to allow for the return of willow trees along streams. Research indicates that willows have only partly recovered.

The wolves have cut in half the Yellowstone population of coyotes—the top predators in the absence of wolves. This has reduced coyote attacks on cattle from area ranches and has led to larger populations of small animals such as ground squirrels, mice, and gophers, which are hunted by coyotes, eagles, and hawks.

Overall, this experiment has had some important ecological benefits for the Yellowstone ecosystem but more research is needed. The focus has been on the gray wolf but other factors such as drought and the rise of populations of bears and cougars may play a role in the observed ecological changes and need to be examined.

The wolf reintroduction has also produced economic benefits for the region. One of the main attractions of the park for many visitors is the hope of spotting wolves chasing their prey across its vast meadows or listening to their howls.

CRITICAL THINKING

If the gray wolf population in the park were to reach its estimated carrying capacity of 110 to 150 wolves, would you support a program to kill wolves to maintain this population level? Explain. Can you think of other alternatives?

Parks in less-developed countries have the greatest biodiversity of all the world's parks, but only about 1% of these parklands are protected. Local people in many of these countries enter the parks illegally in search of wood, game animals, and other natural products that they need for their daily survival. Loggers and miners also operate illegally in many of these parks, as do wildlife poachers who kill animals to obtain and sell items such as rhino horns (see Figure 9.14, p. 249), elephant tusks (Figure 5.C, right, p. 136), and furs. Park services in most less-developed countries have too little money and too few personnel to fight these invasions, either by force or through education.

Identifying and Protecting Biodiversity in Costa Rica

For several decades, Costa Rica (**Core Case Study**) has been using government and private research agencies to identify the plants and animals that make it one of the world's most biologically diverse countries. The government consolidated the country's parks and reserves into several large conservation areas, or *megareserves*, with the goal of protecting and sustaining 80% of the country's biodiversity (Figure 10.20).

Each reserve contains a protected inner core surrounded by two buffer zones that local and indigenous people can use for sustainable logging, crop farming, cattle grazing, hunting, fishing, and ecotourism. Instead of shutting local people out of reserve areas, this approach enlists local people as partners in protecting a reserve from activities such as illegal logging and poaching. It is an application of the biodiversity and win-win **principles of sustainability**.

In addition to its ecological benefits, this strategy has paid off financially. Today, Costa Rica's largest source of income is its $3-billion-a-year travel and tourism industry, almost two-thirds of which involves ecotourism. Ecotourism helps to fund parks and conservation efforts and reduces exploitation of conservation areas by providing income for local people in visited areas, but excessive numbers of ecotourists can degrade sensitive areas.

Restoring Damaged Ecosystems

Almost every natural place on the earth has been impacted some degree by human activities, often in harmful ways. Humans can partially reverse much of the damage through **ecological restoration**: the process of repairing damage humans have caused to various ecosystems. Examples include replanting forests (see the Case Study that follows), reintroducing keystone native species (Science Focus 10.1), removing harmful invasive species, freeing river flows by removing dams, and restoring grasslands, coral reefs, wetlands, and stream banks (Figure 10.15,

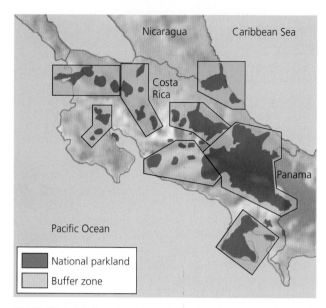

FIGURE 10.20 Solutions: Costa Rica has created several *mega reserves*. Green areas are protected natural parklands and yellow areas are the surrounding buffer zones.

right). This is an important way to expand our beneficial environmental impact.

By studying how natural ecosystems recover through secondary ecological succession, scientists have found ways to restore degraded ecosystems, including the following four:

- *Restoration*: returning a degraded habitat or ecosystem to a condition as similar as possible to its original one.

- *Rehabilitation*: turning a degraded ecosystem into a functional or useful ecosystem without trying to restore it to its original condition. Examples include removing pollutants from abandoned industrial sites and replanting trees to reduce soil erosion in clear-cut forests.

- *Replacement*: replacing a degraded ecosystem with another type of ecosystem. For example, a degraded forest could be replaced by a productive pasture or tree plantation.

- *Creating artificial ecosystems*: for example, artificial wetlands (Figure 10.16) have been created in some areas to help reduce flooding and to treat sewage.

Researchers have suggested the following four-step strategy for carrying out most forms of ecological restoration and rehabilitation.

1. Identify the causes of the degradation, such as pollution, farming, overgrazing, mining, or invasive species.

2. Stop the degradation by eliminating or sharply reducing these factors.

3. Reintroduce keystone species to help restore natural ecological processes, such as reintroducing the gray

wolf to Yellowstone National Park (Science Focus 10.1).

4. Protect the area from further degradation to allow natural recovery (Figure 10.15, right).

Ecological Restoration of a Tropical Dry Forest in Costa Rica

Costa Rica (**Core Case Study**) is the site of one of the world's largest ecological restoration projects. In the lowlands of its Guanacaste National Park, a tropical dry forest was burned, degraded, and fragmented for conversion to cattle ranches and farms. Now it is being restored and reconnected to a rainforest on nearby mountain slopes.

Daniel Janzen, professor of conservation biology at the University of Pennsylvania and a leader in the field of restoration ecology, used his MacArthur Foundation grant money to purchase the Guanacaste forestland for designation as a national park. He has also raised more than $10 million for restoring the park.

Janzen recognizes that ecological restoration and protection of the park will fail unless the people in the surrounding area believe they will benefit from such efforts. His vision is to see that the nearly 40,000 people who live near the park play an essential role in the restoration of the forest.

In the park, local farmers are paid to remove nonnative species and to plant tree seeds and seedlings started in Janzen's laboratory. Local grade school, high school, and university students and citizens' groups study the park's ecology during field trips. The park's location near the Pan American Highway makes it an ideal area for ecotourism, which stimulates the local economy.

This project also serves as a training ground in tropical forest restoration for scientists from around the world. Research scientists working on the project give guest classroom lectures and lead field trips. Janzen believes that education, awareness, and involvement—not guards and fences—are the best ways to protect largely intact ecosystems from unsustainable use. This is an application of the biodiversity and win-win **principles of sustainability**.

Sharing Ecosystems with Other Species

Ecologist Michael L. Rosenzweig calls for humans to share some of the spaces they dominate with other species. He calls this approach **reconciliation ecology**. It focuses on establishing and maintaining new habitats to conserve species diversity in places where people live, work, or play.

For example, some people are learning how to protect insect pollinators, such as butterflies and honeybees (see Chapter 9, **Core Case Study**, p. 236), which are vulnerable to pesticides and habitat loss. Neighborhoods and municipal governments are doing this by reducing or eliminating the use of pesticides on their lawns, fields, golf courses, and parks. Neighbors can also work together to plant gardens of flowering plants as a source of food for bees and other pollinators in their neighborhoods.

People have also worked together to protect bluebirds within human-dominated habitats. In such areas, bluebird populations have declined because most of their nesting trees have been cut down. Specially designed boxes have provided artificial nesting places for bluebirds. Their widespread use has allowed populations of this species to grow.

Figure 10.21 lists some ways in which you can help to sustain the earth's terrestrial biodiversity.

What Can You Do?

Sustaining Terrestrial Biodiversity

- Plant trees and take care of them
- Recycle paper and buy recycled paper products
- Buy sustainably produced wood and wood products and wood substitutes such as recycled plastic furniture and decking
- Help restore a degraded forest or grassland
- Landscape your yard with a diversity of native plants

FIGURE 10.21 Individuals matter: Ways to help sustain terrestrial biodiversity. **Critical Thinking**: Which two of these actions do you think are the most important ones to take? Why? Which of these things do you already do?

CHECKPOINT FOR UNDERSTANDING 10.4

1. Explain why biologists feel it is important to protect areas of wilderness.

2. Describe how gray wolves function as a keystone species.

3. Explain why it is important to involve citizens in reconciliation ecology.

10.5 HOW CAN CITIES BECOME MORE SUSTAINABLE AND LIVABLE?

CONCEPT 10.5A Most cities are unsustainable because of high levels of resource use, waste, pollution, and poverty.

CONCEPT 10.5B An *eco-city* allows people to choose walking, biking, or mass transit for most transportation needs; recycle or reuse most of their wastes; grow much of their food; and protect biodiversity by preserving surrounding land.

Three Important Urban Trends

In 2016, about 54% of the world's people and 82% of all Americans lived in urban areas. Population experts identify three major trends related to urban populations:

- *The percentage of the global population that lives in urban areas has grown sharply and this trend is projected to continue.* Between 2016 and 2050, the world's urban population is projected to grow from 4.0 billion to 6.6 billion. Most of these 2.6 billion new urban dwellers will live in less-developed countries.

- *The numbers and sizes of urban areas are increasing.* In 2015, there were 30 *megacities*—cities with 10 million or more people—22 of them in less-developed countries (Figure 10.22). Thirteen of these urban areas are *hypercities* with more than 20 million people. Some megacities and hypercities are merging into vast urban *megaregions*, each with more than 100 million people.

- *Poverty is becoming increasingly urbanized, mostly in less-developed countries.* The United Nations estimates that at least 1 billion people live in the slums and shantytowns of most of the major cities in less-developed countries (see Chapter 8 opening photo, pp. 204–205). This number may triple by 2050.

Between 1800 and 2016, the percentage of the US population living in urban areas increased from 5% to 82% Figure 10.23 shows the major urban areas in the United

States with more than 1 million people each. This population shift from rural to urban has occurred in three phases.

- People migrated from rural areas to large central cities.

- Many people migrated from large central cities to nearby smaller cities and suburbs.

- Many people migrated from the North and East to the South and West.

Urbanization Has Advantages and Disadvantages

Urbanization has many benefits. Cities are centers of economic development, innovation, education, technological advances, social and cultural diversity, and jobs. Residents usually have better access to medical care, family planning, education, and social services than do their rural counterparts.

Urban areas also have some environmental advantages. Recycling is more economically feasible because of the high concentrations of recyclable materials in urban

---

54 Percentage of the world's people living in urban areas on 2.8% of the world's land

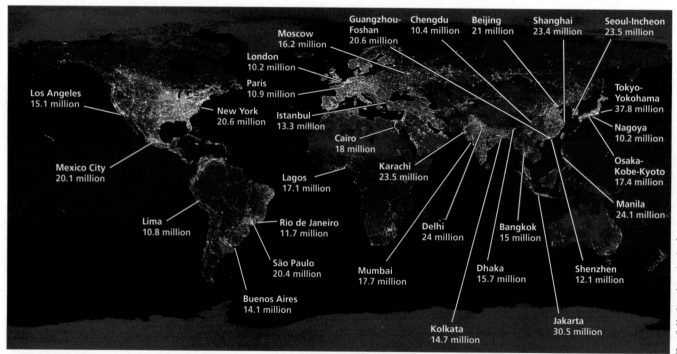

FIGURE 10.22 Megacities, or major urban areas with 10 million or more people, in 2015. **Question:** In order, what were the world's five most populous urban areas in 2015?

(Compiled by the authors using data from National Geophysics Data Center, Demographia, National Oceanic and Atmospheric Administration, and UN Population Division.)

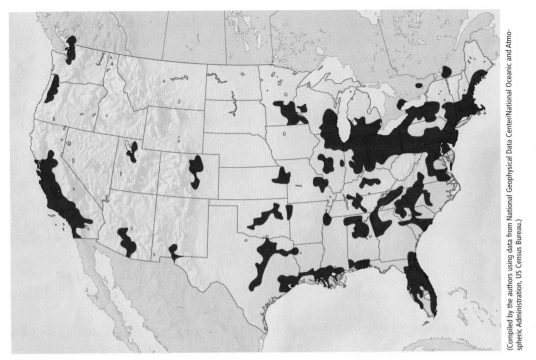

FIGURE 10.23 Urbanized areas (shaded) in the United States where cities, suburbs, and towns dominate the land area. **Critical Thinking**: Why do you think many of the largest urban areas are located near water?

(Compiled by the authors using data from National Geophysical Data Center/National Oceanic and Atmospheric Administration, US Census Bureau.)

Inputs

Energy
Food
Water
Raw materials
Manufactured goods
Money
Information

Outputs

Solid wastes
Waste heat
Air pollutants
Water pollutants
Greenhouse gases
Manufactured goods
Noise
Wealth
Ideas

FIGURE 10.24 **Natural capital degradation:** The typical city depends on nonurban areas for huge inputs of matter and energy resources, while it generates and concentrates large outputs of pollution, waste matter, and heat. **Critical Thinking**: How would you apply the three scientific **principles of sustainability** to lessen some of these impacts?

areas. Satellite images show that urban areas containing 54% of the world's people occupy only 2.8% of the earth's land, excluding Antarctica. Concentrating people in urban areas preserves biodiversity by reducing the stress on wildlife habitats outside of urban areas. Central-city dwellers also tend to drive less and rely more on mass transportation, car-pooling, walking, and bicycling.

Urbanization also has disadvantages. Most urban areas are unsustainable systems. Although urban populations occupy only about 2.8% of the earth's land area, they consume about 75% of its resources and produce about 75% of the world's pollution and wastes. Because of high inputs of food, water, and other resources, and the resulting high waste outputs (Figure 10.24), most of the world's cities have huge ecological

Courtesy of US Geological Survey.

1973   **A**

2013   **B**

US Department of the Interior/US Geological Survey

FIGURE 10.25 *Urban sprawl* in and around the US city of Las Vegas, Nevada, between 1973 and 2013. Since 2013, the sprawl has increased. ***Critical Thinking***: What might be a limiting factor on population growth in Las Vegas?

footprints that extend far beyond their boundaries and are eventually unsustainable. In addition, most cities lack vegetation, can suffer from flooding from nearby rivers, concentrate pollution and health problems, and have excessive noise. In addition, the enormous amount of heat generated by cars, factories, furnaces, lights, air conditioners, and heat-absorbing dark roofs and streets creates an **urban heat island** surrounded by cooler suburban and rural areas. As urban areas grow and merge, these heat islands merge, which can reduce the natural dilution and cleansing of polluted air. The urban heat island effect can also increase dependence on air conditioning. This in turn leads to higher energy consumption, heat generation, greenhouse gas emissions, and other forms of air pollution.

Cities Can Grow Upward or Outward: Urban Sprawl

If a city cannot spread outward, it must grow vertically—upward and below ground—so it occupies a small land area with a high population density. Most people living in *compact cities* such as Hong Kong, China, and Tokyo, Japan, get around by walking, biking, or using mass transit such as rail and bus systems. Some high-rise apartment buildings in these Asian cities contain everything from grocery stores to fitness centers that reduce the need for their residents to travel for food, entertainment, and other services.

In other parts of the world, such as the United States, a combination of plentiful land and networks of highways has produced *dispersed cities* whose residents depend on motor vehicles for most travel. This leads to **urban sprawl**—the growth of low-density development on the edges of cities and towns (Figure 10.25). The result is a dispersed jumble of housing developments, shopping malls, parking lots, and office complexes that are loosely connected by multilane highways and freeways. Urban sprawl can have a number of undesirable effects (Figure 10.26).

The United States is a prime example of a sprawled, car-centered nation. With 4.3% of the world's people, the country has about 23% of the world's 1.1 billion motor vehicles, according to the US Energy Information Agency (EIA). In its dispersed urban areas, US passenger vehicles are used for 86% of all transportation and 76% of urban residents drive alone to work every day (up from 64% in 1980).

Alternatives to Cars

There are several alternatives to motor vehicles. Figures 10.27 through 10.30 summarize the pros and cons, respectively, of bicycles, bus rapid-transit systems, mass transit rail systems (within urban areas), mass-transit rail systems (within urban areas), and high-speed rail systems (between urban areas).

Bicycling accounts for at least a third of all urban trips in the Netherlands and in Copenhagen, Denmark, com-

Urban Sprawl

Land and Biodiversity	**Water**	**Energy, Air, and Climate**	**Economic Effects**
Loss of cropland	Increased use and pollution of surface water and groundwater	Increased energy use and waste	Decline of downtown business districts
Loss and fragmentation of forests, grasslands, wetlands, and wildlife habitat	Increased runoff and flooding	Increased emissions of carbon dioxide and other air pollutants	More unemployment in central cities

FIGURE 10.26 Some undesirable impacts of urban sprawl, or car-dependent development. ***Critical Thinking***: Which five of these effects do you think are the most harmful?

Left: Condor 36/Shutterstock.com. Left center: spirit of ameri-ca/Shutterstock.com. Right center: ssuaphotos/Shutterstock.com. Right: ronfromyork, 2009/Shutterstock.com.

CONSIDER THIS . . .

LEARNING From Nature

The kingfisher bird's long beak allows it to dive into water at a high speed without making a splash to catch fish. In Japan, designers increased the speed and reduced the noise from high-speed bullet trains by modeling the train's front end after the kingfisher's beak.

pared to less than 1% in the United States. One-fourth of Americans polled would bike to work or school if safe bike lanes and secure bike storage were available. More than 700 cities in 50 countries, including 80 US cities, have *bike-sharing systems* that allow individuals to rent bikes as needed from widely distributed stations.

Land-Use Planning

Most urban areas use various forms of **land-use planning** to determine the best present and future uses of various parcels of land. Once a land-use plan is developed and adopted, governments can control the uses of certain parcels of land by legal and economic methods.

The most widely used approach is **zoning**, in which parcels of land are designated for certain uses such as residential, commercial, or mixed use. Zoning can be used to control growth and to protect areas from certain types of development. For example, Portland, Oregon, and other cities have used zoning to encourage high-density development along major mass-transit corridors to reduce automobile use and air pollution.

Despite its usefulness, zoning has several drawbacks. One problem is that some developers can influence or

Trade-Offs

Bicycles

Advantages	**Disadvantages**
Are quiet and nonpolluting	Provide little protection in an accident
Take few resources to manufacture	Provide no protection from bad weather
Burn no fossil fuels	Are impractical for long trips
Require little parking space	Bike lanes and secure bike storage not yet widespread

Photo: Tyler Olson/Shutterstock.com

FIGURE 10.27 Bicycle use has advantages and disadvantages. ***Critical Thinking***: Which single advantage and which single disadvantage do you think are the most important?

modify zoning decisions in ways that threaten or destroy wetlands, prime cropland, forested areas, and open space. Another problem is that zoning often favors high-priced housing, factories, hotels, and other businesses over protecting environmentally sensitive areas and providing low-cost housing. This is largely because most local governments depend on property taxes for their revenue.

In addition, overly strict zoning can discourage innovative approaches to solving urban problems. For example, the pattern in the United States and in some other countries has been to prohibit businesses in residential areas, which causes

Trade-Offs

Buses

Advantages

Reduce car use and air pollution

Can be rerouted as needed

Cheaper than heavy-rail system

Disadvantages

Can lose money because they require affordable fares

Can get caught in traffic and add to noise and pollution

Commit riders to transportation schedules

Photo: Isaak/Shutterstock.com

FIGURE 10.28 Bus rapid-transit (BRT) systems and conventional bus systems in urban areas have advantages and disadvantages. ***Critical Thinking***: Which single advantage and which single disadvantage do you think are the most important?

Trade-Offs

Mass Transit Rail

Advantages

Uses less energy and produces less air pollution than cars do

Uses less land than roads and parking lots use

Causes fewer injuries and deaths than cars

Disadvantages

Expensive to build and maintain

Cost-effective only in densely populated areas

Commits riders to transportation schedules

Photo: Steve Rosset/Shutterstock.com

FIGURE 10.29 Mass-transit rail systems in urban areas have advantages and disadvantages. ***Critical Thinking***: Which single advantage and which single disadvantage do you think are the most important?

separate business and residential developments and encourages suburban sprawl. Some urban planners have returned to *mixed-use zoning* to help reduce this problem.

Smart Growth

Smart growth is a set of policies and tools that encourages more environmentally sustainable urban development with less dependence on cars. It uses zoning laws and other tools to channel growth in order to reduce its ecological footprint.

Smart growth can discourage sprawl, reduce traffic, protect ecologically sensitive and important land and waterways, and develop neighborhoods that are more enjoyable places to live. Figure 10.31 lists smart-growth tools

Trade-Offs

Rapid Rail

Advantages

Much more energy efficient per rider than cars and planes are

Produces less air pollution than cars and planes

Can reduce need for air travel, cars, roads, and parking areas

Disadvantages

Costly to run and maintain

Causes noise and vibration for nearby residents

Adds some risk of collision at car crossings

Photo: Alfonso d'Agostino/Shutterstock.com

FIGURE 10.30 Rapid-rail systems between urban areas have advantages and disadvantages. ***Critical Thinking***: Which single advantage and which single disadvantage do you think are the most important?

that a growing number of cities are using to control urban growth and prevent sprawl.

The Eco-City Concept: Cities for People, Not Cars

Many environmental scientists and urban planners call for us to make new and existing urban areas more sustainable and enjoyable places to live through good ecological design—an important way to increase our beneficial environmental impact.

An important result of this trend is the **eco-city**, a people-oriented, not car-oriented city (**Concept 10.5B**). Its residents are able to walk, bike, or use low-polluting mass transit for most of their travel (Figure 10.32). Its buildings, vehicles, and appliances meet high energy-efficiency standards. Trees and plants adapted to the local climate and soils are planted throughout the city to provide shade, beauty, and wildlife habitats, and to reduce air pollution, noise, and soil erosion.

In an eco-city, abandoned lots and industrial sites are cleaned up and used. Nearby forests, grasslands, wetlands, and farms are preserved. Much of the food that people eat comes from nearby organic farms, solar greenhouses, community gardens, and small gardens on rooftops, in yards, and in window boxes. Parks are easily available to everyone. People who design and live in eco-cities take seriously the advice that US urban planner Lewis Mumford gave more than three decades ago: "Forget the damned motor car and build cities for lovers and friends."

The eco-city is not a futuristic dream, but a growing reality in a number of cities, including Portland, Oregon, Curitiba, Brazil (see the following Case Study), and several other cities in Scandinavia, Europe, China, Australia, Canada, and the United States. According to a survey by London's University of Westminster, China is building more eco-cities than any country, followed by the United States.

FIGURE 10.31 Smart growth tools can be used to prevent or control urban growth and sprawl. ***Critical Thinking***: Which five of these tools do you think would be the best methods for preventing or controlling urban sprawl? Which, if any, of these tools are used in your community?

Top: Tungphoto/Shutterstock.com. Bottom: © Richard Schmidt-Zuper/iStockphoto.com.

CASE STUDY

The Eco-City Concept in Curitiba, Brazil

An example of an eco-city is Curitiba a city of 1.9 million people, known as the "ecological capital" of Brazil. In 1969, planners in this city decided to focus on an inexpensive and efficient mass-transit system rather than on the car.

Curitiba's bus rapid-transit (BRT) system efficiently moves large numbers of passengers, including 72% of the city's commuters. Each of the system's five major "spokes," connecting the city center to outlying districts (see map in Figure 10.33), has two express lanes used only by buses. Double- and triple-length bus sections are coupled as needed to carry up to 300

Transportation Priorities

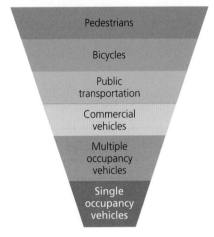

FIGURE 10.32 Transportation priorities in more-sustainable cities.

passengers. Boarding is speeded up by the use of extra-wide bus doors and boarding platforms where passengers can pay before getting on the bus (photo in Figure 10.33).

Only high-rise apartment buildings are allowed near major bus routes, and the bottom two floors of each building must be devoted to stores—a practice that reduces the need for residents to travel. Cars are banned from 49 blocks in the center of the downtown area, which has a network of pedestrian walkways connected to bus stations, parks, and bicycle paths running throughout most of the city. As a result, Curitiba uses less energy per person and has lower emissions of greenhouse gases and other air pollutants and less traffic congestion than do most comparably sized cities.

Along the six streams that run within Curitiba's borders, the city removed most buildings and lined the streams with a series of interconnected parks. Volunteers have planted more than 1.5 million trees throughout the city, and no one can cut down a tree without a permit, which also requires that two trees must be planted for each one that is cut down.

Curitiba recycles roughly 70% of its paper and 60% of its metal, glass, and plastic. Recovered materials are sold mostly to the city's more than 500 major industries, which must meet strict pollution standards.

Curitiba's poor residents receive free medical and dental care, childcare, and job training, and 40 feeding centers are available for street children. People who live in areas not served by garbage trucks can collect garbage and exchange filled garbage bags for surplus food, bus tokens, and school supplies. The city uses old buses as roving classrooms to train its poor in basic job skills. Other retired buses have become health clinics, soup kitchens, and daycare centers that are free for low-income parents.

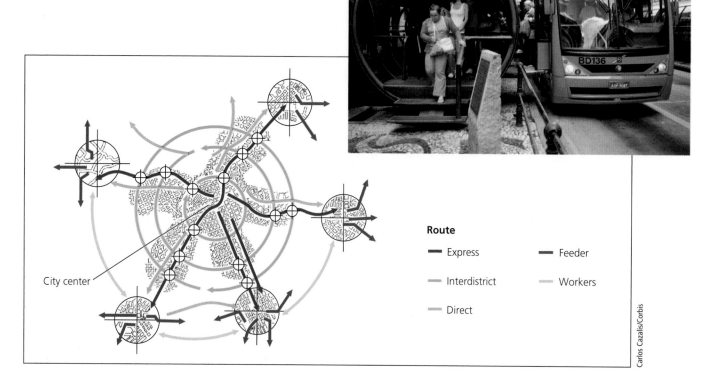

FIGURE 10.33 Solutions: The bus rapid-transit system in Curitiba, Brazil, has greatly reduced car use.

City center

Route

— Express   — Feeder

— Interdistrict   — Workers

— Direct

Carlos Cazalis/Corbis

About 95% of Curitiba's citizens can read and write and 83% of its adults have at least a high school education. All school children study ecology. Polls show that 99% of the city's inhabitants would not want to live anywhere else.

Curitiba face challenges, as do all cities, mostly due to a fivefold increase in its population since 1965. Its once-clear streams are often overloaded with pollutants. The bus system is nearing capacity, and car ownership is on the rise. The city is considering building a light-rail system to relieve some of the pressure.

This internationally acclaimed model of urban planning and sustainability is the brainchild of architect and former college professor Jaime Lerner, who has served as the city's mayor three times since 1969.

KEY IDEAS

• We can sustain forests by emphasizing the economic value of their ecosystem services, halting government subsidies that hasten their destruction, protecting old-growth forests, harvesting trees no faster than they are replenished, and planting trees to reestablish forests.

• We can sustain terrestrial biodiversity and ecosystem services by protecting severely threatened areas and ecosystem services and restoring damaged ecosystems.

• Most urban areas are unsustainable with their large and growing ecological footprints and high levels of poverty but they can be made more sustainable and livable.

CHECKPOINT FOR UNDERSTANDING 10.5

1. Identify several benefits of urbanization. Identify several drawbacks.

2. Identify the primary reason for urban sprawl in the United States.

3. Describe the goal of smart growth.

4. Describe the main features of an eco-city.

Core Case Study Checkpoint

Discuss how Costa Rica has become a global leader in protecting its topical forests. How does this compare to similar efforts in the United States?

biodiversity hotspot: an area especially rich in plant species that is found nowhere else and is in great danger of extinction. Such areas suffer serious ecological disruption, mostly because of rapid human population growth and the resulting pressure on natural resources.

eco-city: a people-oriented rather than car-oriented city where residents use transportation alternatives to vehicles, where buildings, vehicles, and appliances are energy efficient, and where significant areas of green space exist.

ecological restoration: research and scientific study devoted to restoring, repairing, and reconstructing damaged ecosystems.

land-use planning: planning to determine the best present and future uses of each parcel of land.

old-growth forest: virgin and old, second-growth forests containing trees that are often hundreds—sometimes thousands—of years old. Examples include forests of Douglas fir, western hemlock, giant sequoia, and coastal redwoods in the western United States.

overgrazing: destruction of vegetation when too many grazing animals feed too long on a specific area of pasture or rangeland and exceed the carrying capacity of the rangeland.

pasture: managed grassland or enclosed meadow that is usually planted with domesticated grasses or other forage to be grazed by livestock.

rangeland: land that supplies forage or vegetation (grasses, grasslike plants, and shrubs) for grazing and browsing animals, and is not intensively managed.

reconciliation ecology: science of inventing, establishing, and maintaining habitats to conserve species diversity in places where people live, work, or play.

second-growth forest: stands of trees resulting from secondary ecological succession.

smart growth: form of urban planning that recognizes that urban growth will occur but uses zoning laws and other tools to prevent sprawl, direct growth to certain areas, protect ecologically sensitive

and important land and waterways, and develop urban areas that are more environmentally sustainable and more enjoyable places to live.

tree plantation: (tree farm, commercial forest) site planted with one or only a few tree species in an even-aged stand. When the stand matures, it is usually harvested by clear-cutting and then replanted. These farms normally raise rapidly growing tree species for fuelwood, timber, or pulpwood.

urban heat island: an urban area where the temperature is significantly warmer than surrounding areas due to human heat-generating activities such as cars, factories, and heat-absorbing asphalt.

urban sprawl: growth of low-density development on the edges of cities and towns.

wilderness: Area where the earth and its ecosystems have not been seriously disturbed by humans and where humans are only temporary visitors.

zoning: designating parcels of land for particular types of use.

Chapter Review

Core Case Study

1. Summarize the story of Costa Rica's efforts to preserve its rich biodiversity.

Section 10.1

2. (a) What are the two key concepts for this section? (b) Distinguish among an **old-growth forest**, **second-growth forest**, and **tree plantation**. What are the advantages and disadvantages of tree plantations? (c) What major ecological and economic services do

forests provide? How much are ecosystem services provided by the world's forests worth and how does this compare with the economic benefits they provide? (d) Explain how building roads into previously inaccessible forests can harm the forests. (e) Distinguish among *selective cutting*, *clear-cutting*, and *strip cutting* in the harvesting of trees.

3. (a) What is **deforestation** and what are its harmful effects? (b) What are the major advantages and disadvantages of clearing forests? (c) What percentage

of the world's old-growth tropical forest cover has been eliminated, most of it since 1950? Explain how widespread tropical deforestation can convert a tropical forest to tropical grassland (savanna). (d) Describe the typical cycle of use and destruction for an area of tropical forest. What is the fuelwood crisis? (e) Summarize the story of reforestation in the United States.

4. (a) What are two types of forest fires? What are four ecological benefits of occasional surface forest fires? What are four ways to reduce the harm caused by forest fires to forests and to people? (b) List four ways to grow and harvest trees more sustainably. List five ways to protect tropical forests and use them more sustainably. (c) What can consumers do to reduce unsustainable and illegal logging? (d) Describe Florence Reed's efforts to preserve tropical forests and reduce poverty. (e) What are three ways to reduce the need to harvest trees? (f) What percentage of US land is public land? What are five types of US public lands and how is each type used? (g) Describe the controversy over how US public lands and their resources should be used.

Section 10.2

5. (a) What is the key concept for this section? (b) Distinguish between **rangelands** and **pastures**. Explain how rangeland grass is a renewable grass unless it is removed faster than it can grow back. (c) What is **overgrazing** and what are its harmful environmental effects? What are three ways to reduce overgrazing and use rangelands more sustainably?

Section 10.3

6. (a) What economic and ecological services do wetlands provide? (b) What percentage of US wetlands have been lost? What caused most of these losses? (c) How do US laws protect wetlands? What percentage of remaining US wetlands are protected by federal and state laws and regulations? (d) What is the mitigation banking of wetlands? How successful has this been? How could such regulation be improved? (e) Describe the efforts to restore the Florida Everglades.

Section 10.4

7. (a) What are the three key concepts for this section? (b) What are nine strategies for sustaining terrestrial biodiversity? (c) What is a **biodiversity hotspot** and why is it important to protect such areas? (d)

What percentage of the world's land has been set aside and strictly protected as nature reserves, and what percentage should be protected, according to conservation biologists? (e) What is **wilderness** and why is it important, according to conservation biologists? Summarize the history of wilderness protection in the United States. (f) What are the major environmental threats to national parks in the world and in the United States? (g) Describe some of the ecological effects of reintroducing the gray wolf to Yellowstone National Park. (h) Describe Costa Rica's efforts to identify and protect its biodiversity. (i) Define **ecological restoration**. What are four ways to restore degraded ecosystems? (j) Summarize the science-based, four-step strategy for carrying out ecological restoration and rehabilitation. (k) Describe the ecological restoration of a tropical dry forest in Costa Rica. (l) Define and give two examples of **reconciliation ecology**. (m) List five ways in which you can help sustain and expand the earth's terrestrial biodiversity.

Section 10.5

8. (a) What is the key concept for this section? (b) What percentage of the world's people lives in urban areas? List three global trends in urban populations. (c) What percentage of the US population lives in urban areas? What are the major advantages and disadvantages of urbanization? (d) Explain why most urban areas are unsustainable systems. (e) Define an **urban heat island** and describe its effects. (f) Distinguish between compact and dispersed cities and give an example of each. (g) What is **urban sprawl**? List five undesirable effects of urban sprawl. (h) List the advantages and disadvantages to reducing car use by using bicycles, bus-rapid transit systems, mass-transit rail systems (within urban areas), and high-speed rail systems (between urban areas)? (i) What is **land-use planning**? What is **zoning**? What are the advantages and disadvantages of zoning?

9. (a) Define **smart growth** and explain its benefits. List five tools that cities are using to promote smart growth. (b) What is an **eco-city** and what are its major components? (c) Give eight examples of how Curitiba, Brazil, has attempted to become an eco-city.

10. What are this chapter's *three key ideas*?

Note: Key terms are in bold type.

1. Ecosystem services performed by forests include
    I. Carbon sequestration
   II. Aid in aquifer recharge
   III. Provide wildlife habitat
   (A) I only
   (B) II only
   (C) III only
   (D) I and III only
   (E) I, II, and III

2. The best example of selective cutting is
   (A) loggers cut small groups of intermediate or mature trees, resulting in less erosion and loss of nutrients on the hillside
   (B) loggers cut all of the trees in an area, resulting in a loss of nutrients in the soil and sediment gathering in the stream downslope
   (C) loggers cut a thin strip of trees along a hillside, the forest naturally regenerates, and loggers then cut a thin strip of trees next to the regenerated area
   (D) in a managed forest containing one or two species of trees, loggers clear-cut one section, then clear-cut it again when the trees have reached a certain size
   (E) loggers cut only the trees they can reach easily from existing access roads

3. All of the following would result in an area that was recently clear-cut EXCEPT
   (A) an increase in the likelihood of mudslides on sloped, denuded land
   (B) a loss of soil nutrients, because of the increase in wind and water erosion
   (C) an increase in erosion, because water flows faster on denuded slopes
   (D) an increase in biodiversity, because cleared land is more inviting to a variety of new species
   (E) an increase in water pollution as sediment flows into streams

4. Which of the following best describes a second-growth forest?
   (A) Stands of trees resulting from natural succession on a disturbed site
   (B) Forest that has not been seriously disturbed for at least 200 years
   (C) Stands of trees of uniform age and species that have been planted by humans
   (D) Forest only found in rural areas in Canada, Brazil, and Russia
   (E) Forest that is rapidly increasing in area and density

5. Fires that burn away flammable ground material and help prevent more destructive fires are called
   (A) crown fires
   (B) ground fires
   (C) surface fires
   (D) high-intensity fires
   (E) low-intensity fires

6. One effect of our overgrazing of the natural rangelands is
   (A) increased biodiversity because of the increase in plants cattle will not eat, such as mesquite, sagebrush, and cactus, as well as the insects and mammals these plants attract
   (B) decreased solar power because soil is compacted and can no longer support solar power cells
   (C) inversion of the human population pyramid as less vegetation is available and ranchers must sell their cattle because of the lack of rangeland available to them
   (D) soil erosion, because cattle damage the grass roots and the grass can no longer regrow
   (E) increased soil porosity, because cattle are not present to compact the land they occupy

7. Which of the following U.S. federal lands is the most restricted in terms of public and corporate use, such as grazing, mining, and sport hunting?
   (A) Wilderness areas
   (B) National wildlife refuges (USWS)
   (C) The National Forest System (USFS)
   (D) National Resource Lands (BLM)
   (E) National recreation areas

8. A farmer in a developing nation will try to plant the maximum amount of crops on his land. This farmer would most likely use which method of tree-cutting?
   (A) Cut a strip of trees, but then cut another strip of trees when the first ones grow back, preventing mass erosion and protecting his crops
   (B) Cut most of the trees, but leave those that produce seeds so new trees can grow back
   (C) Remove all of the mature trees, leaving the younger ones to provide shade for crops that need it in order to survive
   (D) Cut all of the trees in the area, regardless of the resulting nutrient loss and erosion
   (E) Remove only small groups of older trees so more nutrients would be available for his crops

9. Which is the following is NOT a result of logging in the United States?
   (A) Promotion of economic growth
   (B) Road-building, leading to habitat fragmentation
   (C) Ecological restoration and rehabilitation
   (D) Damage to nearby rivers and fisheries
   (E) Job creation in nearby communities

10. What is the overall largest problem facing most U.S. national parks?
    (A) Popularity and its impact
    (B) Inholdings
    (C) Poaching
    (D) Off-road vehicles
    (E) Water pollution

11. Which of the following statements are true concerning sustainable rangeland management?
    I. Because rangeland grasses grow from the base and not the tip, rangeland grass is a renewable resource, as long as the lower portion of the blade remains.
    II. Rangelands should be managed to ensure the carrying capacity is exceeded.
    III. Moderate grazing is beneficial to the rangelands because it encourages new plant growth.
    (A) I only
    (B) III only
    (C) I and II only
    (D) I and III only
    (E) I, II, and III

12. Reasons for clearing tropical rainforests include all of the following EXCEPT
    (A) converting the forest to agricultural land
    (B) harvesting valuable timber
    (C) creating pasture for grazing cattle
    (D) clear-cutting trees to promote healthier second growth forests
    (E) cutting timber for fuel wood

13. Which of the following best describes biodiversity hotspots?
    (A) They are areas with low biodiversity in need of remediation.
    (B) They are aquatic areas in which biodiversity remains high.
    (C) They are areas rich in rare plant species in danger of extinction.
    (D) They are areas with low diversity over tectonically active plates.
    (E) They are terrestrial areas of high diversity which are ecologically stable.

14. All of the following are true of biodiversity hotspots EXCEPT
    (A) they are areas that contain endangered plant species
    (B) they are protected by an international treaty that was signed by more than 100 countries in 2012
    (C) they account for just over 2% of the earth's land surface
    (D) they include most of the West Coast of South America
    (E) they are areas especially rich in plant species that are found in no other region

Questions 15–16 refer to the following ecological restoration processes. Choices may be used once, more than once, or not at all.
   (A) Restoration
   (B) Rehabilitation
   (C) Replacement
   (D) Creating artificial ecosystems
   (E) Mitigation

15. Covering a landfill with topsoil and planting with vegetation

16. Converting a Midwestern farm back to original prairie grassland

17. Which of the following would be an example of restoration of disturbed lands?
    (A) Passing a law that makes it illegal to build on disturbed lands
    (B) Building a wall to prevent erosion during severe storms, such as hurricanes
    (C) Building biological corridors between areas of human habitation
    (D) Converting a forest into a national park
    (E) Replanting a destroyed area to bring it back to its natural state

18. Which of the following is an input and not an output of large cities?
    (A) Educated people, because many college graduates leave cities once they get their degrees
    (B) Greenhouse gases, because they remain in the air above cities
    (C) Waste heat from industry, because it contributes to higher temperatures in urban areas, compared to nearby rural areas
    (D) Food and water, because they are needed in large amounts
    (E) Stress of exposure to the noise pollution from a construction site

19. Which of the following is a major advantage of urbanization?
- **(A)** Cities serve as centers of economic development and jobs.
- **(B)** Less land is directly affected by the concentration of people in cities.
- **(C)** Pollution is concentrated in cities.
- **(D)** Cities are generally warmer and receive more rainfall than surrounding rural areas.
- **(E)** Cities have larger ecological footprints.

20. Which of the following best describes an urban heat island?
- **(A)** An urban area which is surrounded by cooler suburban and rural areas
- **(B)** An urban island which is surrounded by a high-temperature water body
- **(C)** A suburban area that is indirectly heated by city factories and cars
- **(D)** An urban island which is near the equator
- **(E)** An isolated urban area which creates excess heat from the overuse of electricity

AP® Free-Response Practice

1. (a) Reducing the rate of deforestation in Brazil has been very successful over the past two decades. The graph below shows the area of land deforested in square kilometers for each year from 1995 to 2013.

- **(i) Determine** the year in which there was the greatest decline in deforestation, based on the graph shown.
- **(ii) Determine** the percent reduction in the amount of land deforested during that year.
- **(iii) Identify** and **discuss** TWO reasons why tropical rainforests might be under pressure of deforestation in Brazil.
- **(iv) Identify** and **discuss** TWO benefits, either ecological or economic, of leaving forests intact.

(b) Forest fires are a part of the natural life cycle of a forest. Surface and crown fires can affect forest ecosystems.
- **(i) Identify** and **discuss** TWO ecological benefits of surface fires.
- **(ii)** When fires are suppressed for long periods of time, a crown fire can result. **Explain** why a crown fire is especially devastating.
- **(iii) Discuss** ONE strategy that could be used to prevent crown fires.

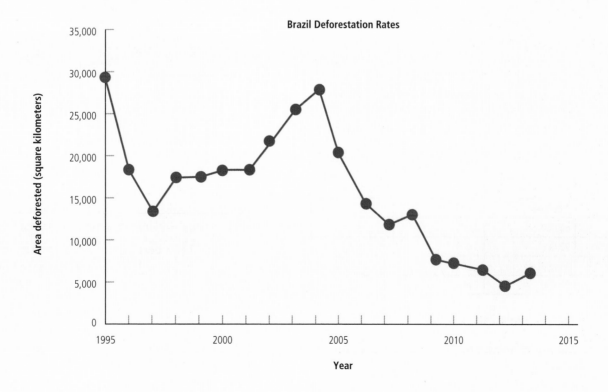

Brazil Deforestation Rates

Critical Thinking

1. Why do you think Costa Rica (**Core Case Study**) has set aside a much larger percentage of its land for biodiversity conservation than the United States has? Should the United States reserve more of its land for this purpose? Explain.

2. If we fail to protect a much larger percentage of the world's remaining old-growth forests and tropical rainforests, what are three harmful effects that this failure is likely to have on any children and grandchildren you eventually might have?

3. In the early 1990s, Miguel Sanchez, a subsistence farmer in Costa Rica, was offered $600,000 by a hotel developer for a piece of land that he and his family had been using sustainably for many years. An area under rapid development surrounded the land, which contained an old-growth rainforest and a black sand beach. Sanchez refused the offer. Explain how Sanchez's decision was an application of the ethical **principle of sustainability**. What would you have done if you were Sanchez? Explain.

4. Halting the destruction and degradation to tropical rainforests is a key to preserving the world's biodiversity and slowing global climate change. Since this will benefit the entire world during this and future generations, should the United States and the world's other more developed nations pay tropical less-developed countries to preserve their remaining tropical forests, as Norway and the United Kingdom have

done? Explain. Do you think that the long-term economic and ecological benefits of doing this would outweigh the short-term economic costs? Explain.

5. Are you in favor of establishing more wilderness areas in the United States (or in the country where you live)? Explain. What might be some disadvantages of doing this?

6. You are a defense attorney arguing in court for preserving an old-growth forest that developers want to clear for a suburban development. Give your three strongest arguments for preserving this ecosystem. How would you counter the argument that preserving the forest would harm the economy by causing a loss of jobs in the timber industry?

7. Sustaining the earth's terrestrial biodiversity will cost an estimated $76 billion a year. Explain why you for or against spending this money? How might a decision not to make this investment affect you and any children and grandchildren you might have?

8. Consider the characteristics of an eco-city listed on pp. 292–293. How close to this eco-city model is the city in which you live or the city nearest to where you live? Pick what you think are the five most important characteristics of an eco-city and, for each of these characteristics, describe a way in which your city could attain it.

Ecological Footprint Analysis

The table below compares five countries in terms of rainforest area and losses. Study the table and then answer the questions that follow.

Country	Area of Tropical Rainforest (square kilometers)	Area of Deforestation per Year (square kilometers)	Annual Rate of Tropical Forest Loss
A	1,800,000	50,000	
B	55,000	3,000	
C	22,000	6,000	
D	530,000	12,000	
E	80,000	700	

1. What is the annual rate of tropical rainforest loss, as a percentage of the total forest area, in each of the five countries? Answer by filling in the blank column in the table.

2. What is the annual rate of tropical deforestation collectively in all of the countries represented in the table?

3. According to the table, and assuming the rates of deforestation remain constant, which country's tropical rainforest will be destroyed first?

4. Assuming the rate of deforestation in country C remains constant, how many years will it take for all of its tropical rainforests to be destroyed?

5. Assuming that a hectare (1.0 hectare = 0.01 square kilometer) of tropical rainforest absorbs 0.85 metric tons (1 metricton = 2,200 pounds) of carbon dioxide per year, what would be the total annual growth in the carbon footprint (carbon emitted but not absorbed by vegetation because of deforestation) in metric tons of carbon dioxide per year for each of the five countries in the table?

Answers to Checkpoints for Understanding

Section 10.1

1. Tree plantations are less biologically diverse. They do not provide habitat for a wide variety of species nor do they provide many of the ecosystem services that more diverse forest ecosystems do. Repeated growing and cutting removes nutrients from the soil and hinders the regrowth of any tree species in the future.

2. Clear-cutting is cost-effective and efficient because it removes all trees at once. The drawbacks are habitat loss, erosion, sedimentation of nearby streams, and loss of biodiversity. It also removes a major carbon sink and contributes to atmospheric warming and climate change.

3. Valuable trees are felled by international timber companies who then sell the land to ranchers who clear the land for grazing by burning off the remaining timber. After several years of grazing, the nutrient-poor land is sold to farmers who grow crops for a few years. This eventually depletes the remaining soil nutrients and exposes the land to wind and rain, which erodes the topsoil. The land is then abandoned.

4. Controlled burns remove the buildup of undergrowth and leaf litter and can reduce the occurrence of destructive crown fires. Large trees can withstand the fire and animals can escape the flames.

Section 10.2

1. Rangeland grasses grow from the base of the plant rather than from the tips of the shoots as most other plants do. Grazing removes the top portion of the plant, stimulating more growth from the bottom. Rangeland grasses have evolved to benefit from grazing by herbivores. Short-term trampling by herds aerates the soil, presses seeds into the soil so that they may germinate, and increases nutrient recycling by pressing in dead organic matter from perennial grasses.

Section 10.3

1. Wetland ecosystem services include feeding downstream waters, reducing flooding by storing storm water, reducing storm damage by absorbing waves (coastal wetlands), recharging groundwater supplies, reducing pollution, preventing erosion, and providing fish and wildlife habitat.

2. Mitigation banking allows an existing wetland to be destroyed in exchange for building a new one of equal or greater area of the same type, or creating, enhancing, or restoring an existing wetland in another area in order to offset the loss.

Section 10.4

1. Wilderness is land largely untouched by humans. Biologists believe wilderness areas provide a long-term "ecological insurance policy" for humans and other species. They are islands of biodiversity and provide ecosystem services that will be necessary to support life and human economies in the future. In addition, they are needed as centers for future evolution in response to changes in environmental conditions such as the climate change that is now occurring.

2. Gray wolves cull herds of bison, elk, moose, and mule deer, and keep down coyote populations. By leaving some of their kills partially uneaten, they provide meat for scavengers such as ravens, bald eagles, ermines, grizzly bears, and foxes. They also keep elk and other grazing animals from over-grazing willows and aspens, which hold top soil in place and decrease erosion into nearby streams and rivers.

3. Reconciliation ecology essentially is a way for humans and other species to share habitat. Through education and direct involvement, citizens play a role in preserving and maintaining species where they live, work, and play. It is important to involve citizens because they have a personal stake in preserving biodiversity and tend to take ownership.

Section 10.5

1. People who live in cities are at the center of economic development, innovation, education, technological advances, social and cultural diversity, and jobs. Residents usually have better access to medical care, family planning, education, and social services than do their rural counterparts. However, urban centers use a high amount of resources and as a result produce a high amount of waste. In addition, most cities lack vegetation, can suffer from flooding from nearby rivers, concentrate pollution and health problems, and have excessive noise. Enormous amounts of heat generated by cars, factories, furnaces, lights, air conditioners, and heat-absorbing dark roofs and streets creates an *urban heat island* surrounded by cooler suburban and rural areas.

2. The primary reason for urban sprawl in the United States is a car-centered culture. Dispersed cities have resulted and are connected by a network of highways.

3. The goal of smart growth is to reduce the number of automobiles and encourage a more sustainable city community. This includes protecting ecologically sensitive land and waterways, implementing, mixed-use housing, and making other changes that result in a people-centered community rather than a car-centered community.

Core Case Study

In the mid-1970s, Costa Rica established a national system of nature reserves and national parks that devoted a larger proportion of its land (27%) to biodiversity conservation, mostly in the form of forests, than any other country. It eliminated subsidies for converting forestland to grazing lands, and pays landowners to maintain or restore tree cover. The United States has established national forests, wildlife refuges, national parks, and wilderness areas to help preserve its biodiversity. However, they make up a much lower percentage of the country's land than in Costa Rica and there is strong opposition to such conservation efforts.

CHAPTER 11

Geology, Soil, and Mineral Resources

> Civilization exists by geological consent, subject to change without notice.
>
> **WILL DURANT**

Open-pit copper mine in Utah. It is almost 5 kilometers (3 miles) wide and 1,200 meters (4,000 feet) deep, and is getting deeper.

Lee Prince/Shutterstock.com

Key Questions

11.1 What are the earth's major geological processes and what are mineral resources?

11.2 What processes lead to soil formation?

11.3 How long might supplies of nonrenewable mineral resources last?

11.4 What are the environmental effects of using nonrenewable mineral resources?

11.5 How can we use mineral resources more sustainably?

11.6 What are the earth's major geological hazards?

The Real Cost of Gold

Mineral resources are extracted from the earth's crust through a variety of processes called **mining**. They are processed into an amazing variety of products that make life easier and provide economic benefits and jobs. However, extracting minerals from the ground and using them to manufacture products results in a number of harmful environmental and health effects.

For example, gold mining often involves digging up massive amounts of rock (Figure 11.1) containing only small concentrations of gold. Many newly weds would be surprised to know that mining enough gold to make their wedding rings produces roughly enough mining waste to equal the total weight of more than three midsize cars. This waste is usually left piled near the mine site and can pollute the air and nearby surface water.

About 90% of the world's gold-mining operations extract the gold by spraying a solution of highly toxic cyanide salts onto piles of crushed rock. The solution reacts with the gold and then drains off the rocks, pulling some gold with it, into settling ponds (Figure 11.1, foreground). After the solution is recirculated a number of times, the gold is removed from the ponds.

Until sunlight breaks down the cyanide, the settling ponds are extremely toxic to birds and mammals that go to them in search of water. These ponds can also leak or overflow, posing threats to underground drinking water supplies and to fish and other organisms in nearby lakes and streams. Special liners in the settling ponds can help prevent leaks, but some have failed. According to the US Environmental Protection Agency (EPA), all such liners are likely to leak, eventually.

In 2000, snow and heavy rains washed out an earthen dam on one end of a cyanide leach pond at a gold mine in Romania. The dam's collapse released large amounts of water laced with cyanide and toxic metals into the Tisza and Danube Rivers, which flow through parts of Romania, Hungary, and Yugoslavia. Several hundred thousand people living along these rivers were told not to fish or to drink or withdraw water from them or from wells along the rivers. Businesses located there were shut down. Thousands of fish and other aquatic animals and plants were killed. This accident and another one that occurred in January 2001 could have been prevented if the mining company had installed a stronger containment dam and a backup collection pond to prevent leakage into nearby surface water.

In addition, in parts of Africa and Latin America, millions of poor miners have illegally cleared areas of tropical forest and dug huge pits to find gold. In these operations, they typically use toxic mercury to extract the gold from the *ore*, or the rock containing the gold. Many of these miners have been poisoned by mercury. Because these illegal mining operations pollute the air and water with mercury and its toxic compounds, they have become a regional and global threat.

In 2016, the world's top five gold-producing countries were, in order, China, Australia, Russia, the United States, and Canada. These countries vary in how they deal with the environmental impacts of gold mining.

In this chapter, we look at the earth's dynamic geological processes, the valuable minerals such as gold that some of these processes produce, and the potential supplies of these resources. We will also study the environmental impacts of extracting and processing these resources, and how people can use these resources more sustainably. ●

CRITICAL THINKING

Should the price of gold include the environmental costs of gold mining? Why or why not?

FIGURE 11.1 Gold mine in the Black Hills of the US state of South Dakota with cyanide leach piles and settling ponds in foreground.

WHAT ARE THE EARTH'S MAJOR GEOLOGICAL PROCESSES AND WHAT ARE MINERAL RESOURCES?

CONCEPT 11.1A Dynamic processes within the earth and on its surface produce the mineral resources we depend on.

CONCEPT 11.1B Mineral resources are nonrenewable because it takes millions of years for the earth's rock cycle to produce or renew them.

The Earth Is a Dynamic Planet

Geology is the scientific study of dynamic processes taking place on the earth's surface and in its interior. Scientific evidence indicates that the earth formed about 4.6 billion years ago and since then has undergone changes in its land and water and forms of life (Figure 11.2). As the primitive earth cooled over millions of years, its interior separated into three major concentric zones: the *core*, the *mantle*, and the *crust* (Figure 11.3). They make up the *geosphere* (Figure 3.2, p. 67), which is part of the earth's life-support system.

The **core** is the earth's innermost zone and is composed primarily of iron (Fe). The inner core is extremely hot and has a solid center. It is surrounded by the outer core, a thick layer of *molten rock*, or hot fluid rock, and semisolid material.

Surrounding the core is a thick zone called the **mantle**— a zone made mostly of solid rock that can be soft and pliable at very high temperatures. The outermost part of the mantle is entirely solid rock. Beneath it is the **asthenosphere**— a volume of hot, partly melted rock that flows.

Era	Period	Time (millions of years ago)	Major Events (approximate time in millions of years ago, in parentheses)
Cenozoic (Age of Mammals)	Quaternary	1.6–present	Likely beginning of new mass extinction (now) Human civilization develops (0.01 to now) Modern humans (*Homo sapiens sapiens*) (0.2) First humans (1.2)
	Tertiary	6.5–1.6	Oldest human ancestors (4.4) Grasses diversify and spread Mammals diversify and spread
Mesozoic (Age of Reptiles)	Cretaceous	146–6.5	Mass extinction (75% of species, including dinosaurs) (66) First primates First flowering plants
	Jurassic	208–146	Mass extinction (75% of species) (200) First birds Dinosaurs diversify and spread
	Triassic	245–208	First dinosaurs First mammals
Paleozoic (Age of Fishes)	Permian	290–245	Mass extinction (90–96% of species) (251) Reptiles diversify and spread
	Pennsylvanian	322–290	First reptiles
	Mississippian	362–322	Coal deposits form
	Devonian	408–362	Mass extinction (70% of species) (375) First land animals (amphibians) Fish diversify and spread First forests
	Silurian	439–408	First land plants and corals
	Ordovician	510–439	Mass extinction (60–70% of species) (450) First fish
	Cambrian	545–510	First shellfish Ozone layer forms Oxygen increases in atmosphere Photosynthetic organisms proliferate
Precambrian	Proterozoic	2,500–545	First animals in sea (jellyfish) First multicellular organisms
	Archean	4,600–2,500	First photosynthesis and oxygen in atmosphere (2,800) First plants in sea (algae) (3,200) Atmospheric water vapor condenses to oceans (3,700) First rocks (3,800) Likely origin of life (first one-celled organisms) (3,800) Earth forms (4,600)

FIGURE 11.2 Time scale for major geological and biological changes since the earth formed about 4.6 billion years ago.

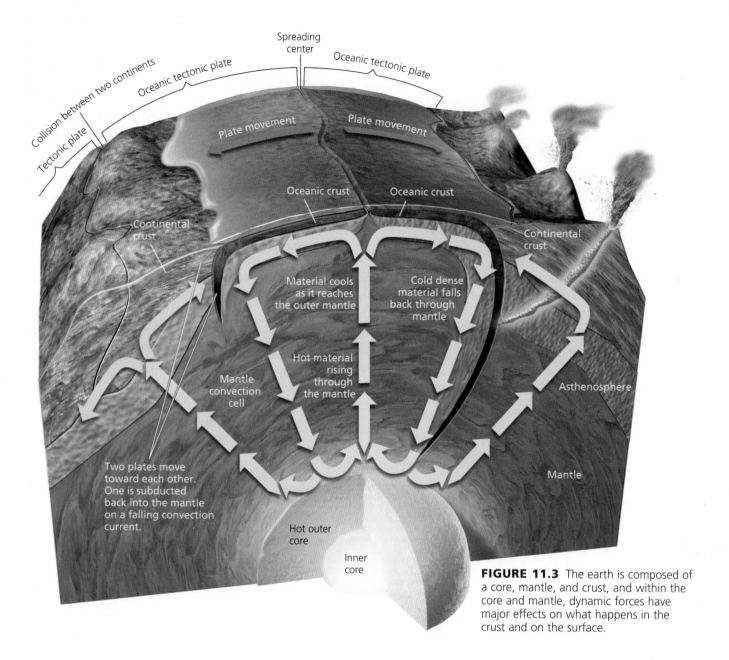

FIGURE 11.3 The earth is composed of a core, mantle, and crust, and within the core and mantle, dynamic forces have major effects on what happens in the crust and on the surface.

Tremendous heat within the core and mantle generates *convection cells*, or *currents*. The innermost material heats, rises, and begins to cool. As it cools, it becomes denser and sinks back toward the core where it is reheated, completing a huge loop of slowly moving material. These loops within the mantle operate like gigantic conveyer belts (Figure 11.3). Some of the molten rock in the asthenosphere flows upward into the crust, where it is called *magma*. When magma erupts onto the earth's surface, it is called *lava*. This cycling moves rock and minerals and transfers heat and energy within the earth and to its surface.

The outermost and thinnest zone of solid material is the earth's **crust.** It consists of the *continental crust*, which underlies the continents (including the continental shelves extending into the oceans), and the *oceanic crust*, which underlies the ocean basins and makes up 71% of the earth's crust. The combination of the crust and the rigid, outermost part of the mantle is called the **lithosphere.** This zone contains the mineral resources that we use (**Concept 11.1A**).

What Are Minerals and Rocks?

The earth's crust beneath our feet consists mostly of minerals and rocks. A **mineral** is a naturally occurring chemical element or inorganic compound that exists as a solid with a regularly repeating internal arrangement of its atoms or ions (a *crystalline solid*). A **mineral resource** is a concentration of one or more minerals in the earth's crust that we can extract and process into raw materials and useful products at an affordable cost. Because minerals take millions of year to form, they are *nonrenewable resources*, and their supplies can be depleted (**Concept 11.1B**).

A few minerals, such as mercury and gold (**Core Case Study** and Figure 2.3, p. 40), consist of a single chemical element. However, most of the more than 2,000 identified mineral resources that we use occur as inorganic compounds formed by various combinations of elements. Examples include salt (sodium chloride, or NaCl; see Figure 2.7, p. 43) and quartz (silicon dioxide, or SiO_2).

Rock is a solid combination of one or more minerals found in the earth's crust. Some kinds of rock, such as limestone (calcium carbonate, or $CaCO_3$) and quartzite (silicon dioxide, or SiO_2), contain only one mineral, but most rocks consist of two or more minerals. Granite, for example, is a mixture of mica, feldspar, and quartz crystals.

Based on the way they form, rocks are classified as sedimentary, igneous, or metamorphic. **Sedimentary rock** is made of *sediments*—dead plant and animal remains and particles of weathered and eroded rocks. These sediments are transported from place to place by water, wind, or gravity. Where they are deposited, they can accumulate in layers over time. Eventually, the increasing weight and pressure on the underlying layers transform the sedimentary layers to rock. Examples include *sandstone* and *shale* (formed from pressure created by deposited layers made mostly of sand or silt), *dolomite* and *limestone* (formed from the compacted shells, skeletons, and other remains of dead aquatic organisms), and *lignite* and *bituminous coal* (derived from compacted plant remains).

Igneous rock forms below or on the earth's surface under intense heat and pressure when magma wells up from the earth's mantle and then cools and hardens. Examples include *granite* (formed underground) and *lava rock* (formed aboveground). Igneous rock forms the bulk of the earth's crust but is usually covered with layers of sedimentary rock.

Metamorphic rock forms when an existing rock is subjected to high temperatures (which may cause it to melt partially), high pressures, chemically active fluids, or a combination of these agents. Examples include *slate* (formed when shale and mudstone are heated) and *marble* (produced when limestone is exposed to heat and pressure).

The Earth's Rocks Are Recycled Slowly

The interaction of physical and chemical processes that change the earth's rocks from one type to another is called the **rock cycle** (Figure 11.4 and **Concept 11.1B**). Rocks are recycled over millions of years by three processes—*erosion, melting,* and *metamorphism*—which produce *sedimentary, igneous,* and *metamorphic* rocks, respectively.

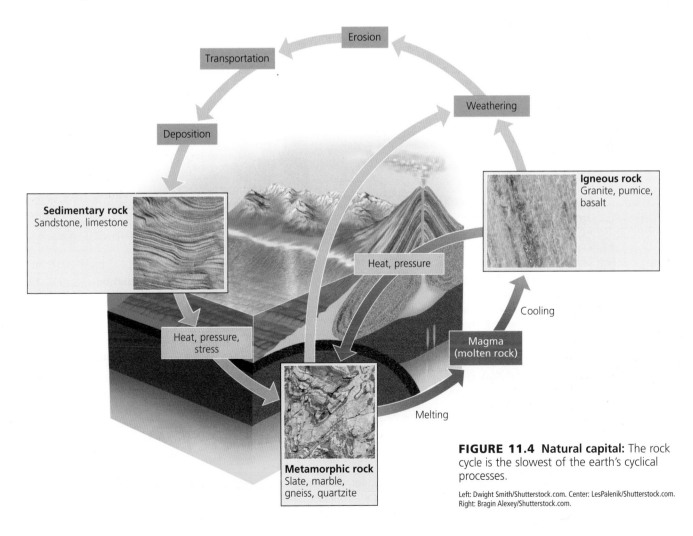

Erosion

Transportation

Weathering

Deposition

Sedimentary rock
Sandstone, limestone

Igneous rock
Granite, pumice, basalt

Heat, pressure

Cooling

Heat, pressure, stress

Magma (molten rock)

Melting

Metamorphic rock
Slate, marble, gneiss, quartzite

FIGURE 11.4 Natural capital: The rock cycle is the slowest of the earth's cyclical processes.

Left: Dwight Smith/Shutterstock.com. Center: LesPalenik/Shutterstock.com. Right: Bragin Alexey/Shutterstock.com.

In these processes, rocks are broken down, melted, fused together into new forms by heat and pressure, cooled, and sometimes recrystallized within the earth's interior and crust. The rock cycle is the slowest of the earth's cyclic processes and plays the major role in the formation of concentrated deposits of mineral resources.

CHECKPOINT FOR UNDERSTANDING 11.1

1. Describe how rocks are different from minerals.

2. Identify and describe the three types of rocks.

3. Identify the three processes that drive the rock cycle.

11.2 WHAT PROCESSES LEAD TO SOIL FORMATION?

CONCEPT 11.2A Physical, chemical, and biological processes all contribute to the formation of soil.

CONCEPT 11.2B Soil is a renewable resource and a key factor in nutrient cycling.

Soil Begins from Bedrock

While the internal forces of the rock cycle are responsible for the formation of valuable mineral deposits, the external forces of **weathering** are responsible for breaking down bedrock into the small pieces that will become the foundation of soil. Types of physical weathering include wind, ice wedging, or the force of water that breaks apart rock without chemically changing it. Chemical weathering occurs when slightly acidic rain water reacts with minerals in rock, chemically changing the minerals and producing soluble salts.

In the first stages of primary succession (Figure 7.10, p. 186), lichens produce acid that chemically weathers rock. This living organism paves the way for other biological organisms to begin living on the weathered particles. Their wastes and decaying bodies add organic matter and minerals to the slowly forming soil. Decomposers and detritivores break down fallen leaves and wood (Figure 3.7, p. 70) and add organic matter and nutrients to the soil. Air (mostly nitrogen and oxygen) and water occupy pores or spaces between soil particles.

Over hundreds to thousands of years, various types of life build up distinct layers of mineral and organic matter on a soil's original bedrock. The accumulating *humus*, the partially decomposed organic material from plants and animals that mixes with parent material, releases nutrients and holds moisture, making way for the next stages of plants and animals in primary succession. This combination of physical, chemical, and biological factors is what creates soil, and the processes are all happening on the earth's surface where we can observe them and where human activity can impact them.

FIGURE 11.5 Natural capital: Generalized soil formation and soil profile. ***Critical thinking:*** What role do you think the tree in this figure plays in soil formation? How might the soil formation process change if the tree were removed?

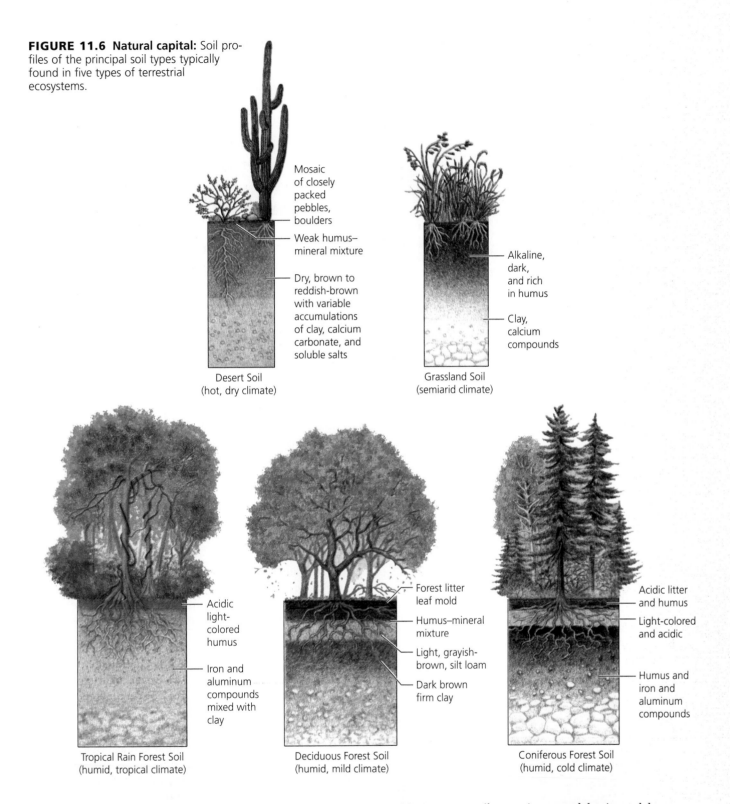

FIGURE 11.6 Natural capital: Soil profiles of the principal soil types typically found in five types of terrestrial ecosystems.

Mosaic of closely packed pebbles, boulders

Weak humus–mineral mixture

Dry, brown to reddish-brown with variable accumulations of clay, calcium carbonate, and soluble salts

Desert Soil
(hot, dry climate)

Alkaline, dark, and rich in humus

Clay, calcium compounds

Grassland Soil
(semiarid climate)

Acidic light-colored humus

Iron and aluminum compounds mixed with clay

Tropical Rain Forest Soil
(humid, tropical climate)

Forest litter leaf mold

Humus–mineral mixture

Light, grayish-brown, silt loam

Dark brown firm clay

Deciduous Forest Soil
(humid, mild climate)

Acidic litter and humus

Light-colored and acidic

Humus and iron and aluminum compounds

Coniferous Forest Soil
(humid, cold climate)

Soil is a Renewable Resource

Soil is a renewable resource on which living organisms depend and it is the foundation for all life on land. Soil is essential for agricultural production, as discussed in Chapter 12 which follows, and for growing timber that supplies paper and other wood products. Soil also provides ecological services by purifying water, degrading wastes, and cycling nutrients.

Most *mature soils* contain several horizontal layers or *horizons*. A cross-sectional view of the *horizons* of a soil is called a **soil profile** (Figure 11.5, right). The major horizons in a mature soil are **O** (leaf litter), **A** (topsoil), **B** (subsoil), and **C** (weathered parent material), which build up over the parent material. Each layer has a distinct texture, composition, and thickness that vary with the soils formed in different climates and biomes such as deserts, grasslands, and forests (Figure 11.6).

FIGURE 11.7 Pathways of plant nutrients in soils.

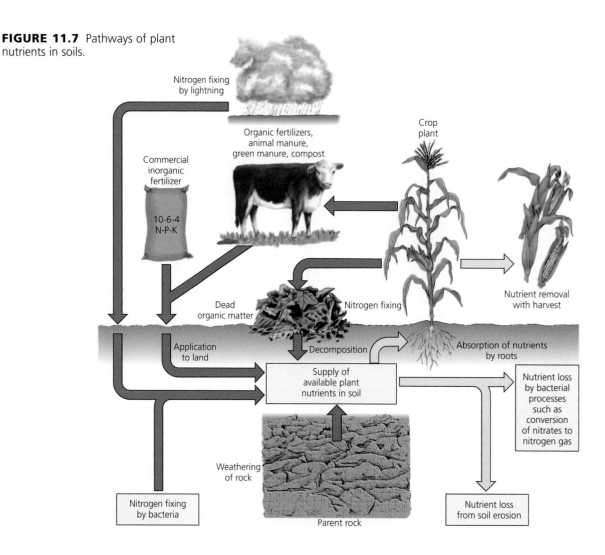

The rate at which soils form depends on several factors. In climates that are wet and moderately warm such as temperate deciduous forests, soil formation occurs faster. It can take several hundred years to form one inch of topsoil in dry or cold climates. Even though deserts are warm, they have little water and sparse vegetation, so there is little organic material that can decompose to become humus. In cold climates, liquid water is limited in availability, and bacterial action is very slow, also resulting in undeveloped soils. Tropical rainforests are wet and warm and decomposition happens very quickly. However, there is intense competition for the nutrients released by decomposition and available nutrients are assimilated quickly into plant tissue. As a result, soils in tropical rainforests have little organic matter in their upper horizon and tend to have low fertility.

The Importance of Soil Nutrients

The roots of most plants and the majority of organic matter in soil are found in its two upper layers, the O-horizon of leaf litter and the A-horizon of topsoil. In a fertile soil, these two layers teem with bacteria, fungi, earthworms, and numerous small insects, all interacting by feeding on

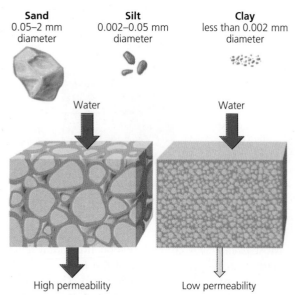

FIGURE 11.8 Natural capital: The size, shape, and degree of clumping of soil particles determine the number and volume of spaces for air and water within a soil. Water can flow more easily through soils with more spaces (left) than through soils with fewer spaces (right).

and decomposing one another as they break down some of the soil's complex organic compounds. Every handful of topsoil contains billions of bacteria and other decomposer organisms. The leaf litter and topsoil layers are also habitats for larger animals such as snails, reptiles, amphibians, and burrowing animals such as moles.

A fertile soil that produces high crop yields has a thick topsoil layer with a lot of humus mixed with minerals from weathered rock. Moisture in topsoil dissolves nutrients needed for plant growth. Bacteria are responsible for cycling the nitrogen compounds that plants require by converting ammonia that results from decomposition to nitrate ions (NO_3^-) that plants can easily assimilate. The resulting ions held in solution are drawn up by the roots of the plants and transported through their stems into the leaves of plants. This movement of nutrients from the topsoil to plant leaves and to insects and other animals that eat the leaves is part of the chemical cycling process essential for life on earth (Figure 11.7). Healthy soils retain more water and help reduce the severity of drought by releasing some of the water into the atmosphere.

The color of topsoil indicates how useful it is for growing crops or other plants. Black or dark brown topsoil is rich in nitrogen and organic matter. A gray, bright yellow, or red topsoil is low in organic matter and needs the addition of nitrogen to support most crops.

The B-horizon (subsoil) and the C-horizon (parent material) contain most of the soil's inorganic matter, mostly broken-down rock consisting of various mixtures of sand, silt, clay, and gravel. The C-horizon sits on the soil's parent material, which is often bedrock.

Soils can include particles of three different sizes: very small *clay* particles, medium-sized *silt* particles, and larger *sand* particles. The relative amounts of these different sizes and types of mineral particles, and the amount of space between the particles, determine the texture of a soil. A soil's texture affects how rapidly water flows through it, and also the soil's *nutrient-holding capacity*. Very small particles of clay often have a negative charge and bind with positively charged nutrient ions such as Ca^+ and K^+. Soils with more clay tend to be more fertile.

Infiltration and retention of water also relate to soil texture. Soil *porosity* is a measure of the open spaces within a soil. Sand has high porosity, while clay has very low porosity. Porosity is directly related to soil permeability. The *permeability* of soil is a measure of how well water flows through the open spaces within the soil. Gravel has high permeability, while clay has very low permeability (Figure 11.8).

To get an idea of a soil's texture, take a small amount of topsoil, moisten it, and rub it between your fingers and thumb. A gritty feel means it contains a lot of sand, which allows water to flow through it rapidly. A sticky feel means high clay content so that you can roll it into a clump. Very little water penetrates this type of soil. Loam topsoil has a crumbly and spongy texture with many of its particles clumped loosely together. It is best suited for plant growth because it allows water to flow through it at a nourishing trickle.

11.3 HOW LONG MIGHT SUPPLIES OF NONRENEWABLE MINERAL RESOURCES LAST?

CONCEPT 11.3A Nonrenewable mineral resources exist in finite amounts and can become economically depleted when it costs more than it is worth to find, extract, and process the remaining deposits.

CONCEPT 11.3B There are several ways to extend supplies of mineral resources, but each of them is limited by economic and environmental factors.

We Depend on a Variety of Nonrenewable Mineral Resources

We know how to find and extract more than 100 different minerals from the earth's crust. According to the US Geological Survey (USGS), the quantity of nonrenewable minerals extracted globally increased more than threefold between 1995 and 2014.

An **ore** is rock that contains a large enough concentration of a mineral—often a metal—to make it profitable for mining and processing. A **high-grade ore** contains a high concentration of the mineral. A **low-grade ore** contains a low concentration.

Mineral resources are used for many purposes. Today, about 60 of the 118 chemical elements in the periodic table (see Supplement 3, p. S6) are used for making computer chips. *Aluminum* (Al) is used as a structural material in beverage cans, motor vehicles, aircraft, and buildings. *Steel*, an essential material used in buildings, machinery, and motor vehicles, is a mixture (or *alloy*) of iron (Fe) and other elements that gives it certain physical properties. *Manganese* (Mn), *cobalt* (Co), and *chromium* (Cr) are widely used in steel alloys. *Copper* (Cu), a good conductor of electricity, is used to make electrical and communications wiring and plumbing pipes. *Gold* (Au) (**Core Case Study**) is a component of electrical equipment, tooth fillings, jewelry, coins, and some medical implants. *Molybdenum* (Mo) is widely used to harden steel and to make it more resistant to corrosion.

There are several widely used nonmetallic mineral resources. *Sand*, which is mostly silicon dioxide (SiO_2), is used to make glass, bricks, and concrete for the construction of roads and buildings. *Gravel* is used for roadbeds and to make concrete. Another common nonmetallic mineral is *limestone* (mostly calcium carbonate, or $CaCO_3$), which is crushed to make concrete and cement. Still another is *phosphate*, used to make inorganic fertilizers and certain detergents.

Supplies of Nonrenewable Mineral Resources Can Be Economically Depleted

Most published estimates of the supply of a given nonrenewable mineral resource refer to its **reserves**: identified deposits from which we can extract the mineral profitably at current prices. Reserves can be expanded when we find new, profitable deposits or when higher prices or improved mining technologies make it profitable to extract deposits that previously were too expensive to remove.

The future supply of any nonrenewable mineral resource depends on the actual or potential supply of the mineral and the rate at which we use it. We have never completely run out of a nonrenewable mineral resource, but a mineral becomes *economically depleted* when it costs more than it is worth to find, extract, transport, and process the remaining deposits (**Concept 11.3A**). At that point, there are five choices: *recycle or reuse existing supplies, waste less, use less, find a substitute,* or *do without.*

Depletion time is the time it takes to use up a certain proportion—usually 80%—of the reserves of a mineral at a given rate of use. When experts disagree about depletion times, it is often because they are using different assumptions about supplies and rates of use (Figure 11.9).

The shortest depletion-time estimate assumes no recycling or reuse and no increase in the reserve (curve A, Figure 11.9). A longer depletion-time estimate assumes that recycling will stretch the existing reserve and that better mining technology, higher prices, or new discoveries will increase the reserve (curve B). The longest depletion-time estimate (curve C) makes the same assumptions as A and B, but also assumes that people will reuse and reduce consumption to expand the reserve further. Finding a substitute for a resource leads to a new set of depletion curves for the new mineral.

The earth's crust contains abundant deposits of nonrenewable mineral resources such as iron and aluminum. But concentrated deposits of important mineral resources such as manganese, chromium, cobalt, platinum, and *rare earth metals* (see the Case Study that follows) are relatively scarce. In addition, deposits of many mineral resources are not distributed evenly among countries. Five nations—the United States, Canada, Russia, South Africa, and Australia—supply most of the nonrenewable mineral resources that modern societies use.

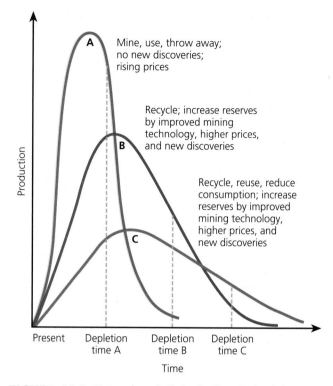

FIGURE 11.9 Natural capital depletion: Each of these *depletion curves* for a mineral resource is based on a different set of assumptions. Dashed vertical lines represent the times at which 80% depletion occurs.

Since 1900, and especially since 1950, there has been a sharp rise in the total and per capita use of mineral resources in the United States. According to the USGS, each American directly and indirectly uses an average of 22 metric tons (24 tons) of mineral resources per year.

The United States has economically depleted some of its once-rich deposits of metals such as lead, aluminum, and iron. Currently, the United States imports all of its supplies of 24 key nonrenewable mineral resources. Most of these imports come from reliable and politically stable countries. However, there are serious concerns about access to adequate supplies of four *strategic metal resources*—manganese, cobalt, chromium, and platinum—that are essential for the country's economic and military strength. The United States has little or no reserves of these metals.

The Crucial Importance of Rare Earth Metals

Some mineral resources are familiar, such as gold, copper, aluminum, sand, and gravel. Less well known are the *rare earth metals and oxides*, which are crucial to the technologies that support modern lifestyles and economies.

The 17 rare earth metals, also known as *rare earths*, include scandium, yttrium, and 15 lanthanide chemical elements, including lanthanum (see the Periodic Table,

Supplement 3, p. S6). Because of their superior magnetic strength and other unique properties, these elements and their compounds are important for a number of widely used technologies.

Rare earths are used to make LCD flat screens for computers and television sets, energy-efficient compact fluorescent and LED light bulbs, solar cells, fiber-optic cables, cell phones, and digital cameras. They are also used to manufacture batteries and motors for electric and hybrid-electric cars (Figure 11.10), solar cells, catalytic converters in car exhaust systems, jet engines, and the powerful magnets in wind turbine generators. Rare earths also go into missile guidance systems, jet engines, smart bombs, aircraft electronics, and satellites.

Without affordable supplies of these metals, industrialized nations could not develop the current versions of cleaner energy technology and other high-tech products that will be major sources of economic growth during this century. Many nations also need these metals to maintain their military strength.

Most rare earth metals are not actually rare, but they are hard to find in concentrations high enough to extract and process at an affordable price. According to the USGS, in 2014, China had roughly 42% of the world's known rare earth reserves, Brazil had the second largest share with 17%, and the United States, with the fifth largest share, had 1.4% of the global reserves.

In 2015, China produced about 90% of the world's rare earth metals and oxides. China holds the lead, partly because it does not strictly regulate the environmentally disruptive mining and processing of rare earths, which reduces its production costs.

The United States and Japan are heavily dependent on rare earths and their oxides. Japan has no rare earth reserves. In the United States, the only rare earth mine, located in California, was once the world's largest supplier of rare earth metals. However, it closed down because of the expense of meeting pollution regulations, and because China had driven the prices of rare earth metals down to a point where the mine was too costly to operate. In 2016, the company that owns the mine declared bankruptcy.

Market Prices Affect Supplies of Mineral Resources

Geological processes determine the quantity and location of a mineral resource in the earth's crust, but economics determines what part of the known supply is extracted and used. According to standard economic theory, in a competitive market system when a resource becomes scarce, its price rises. Higher prices can encourage exploration for new deposits, stimulate development of better mining technology, and make it profitable to mine lower-grade ores. It can also promote resource conservation and a search for substitutes, but there are limits to these effects (**Concept 11.3B**).

CONSIDER THIS . . .

CONNECTIONS HIGH METAL PRICES AND THIEVERY

Resource scarcity can promote theft. For example, copper prices have risen sharply in recent years because of increasing demand. As a result, in many US communities, thieves have been stealing copper to sell it. They strip abandoned houses of copper pipe and wiring and steal outdoor central air conditioning units for their copper coils. They also steal wiring from beneath city streets and copper piping from farm irrigation systems. In 2015, thieves stole copper wiring from New York City's subway system, temporarily shutting down two of the city's busiest lines.

According to some economists, the standard effect of supply and demand on the market prices of mineral resources may no longer apply completely in most more-developed countries. Governments in such countries often use subsidies, tax breaks, and import tariffs to control the supply, demand, and prices of key mineral resources. In the United States, for instance, mining companies get various types of government subsidies, including *depletion allowances*—which allow the companies to deduct the costs of developing and extracting mineral resources from their taxable incomes. These allowances amount to 5–22% of their gross income gained from selling the mineral resources.

Generally, the mining industry maintains that they need subsidies and tax breaks to keep the prices of minerals low for consumers. They also claim that, without subsidies and tax breaks, they might move their operations to other countries where they would not have to pay taxes or comply with strict mining and pollution control regulations.

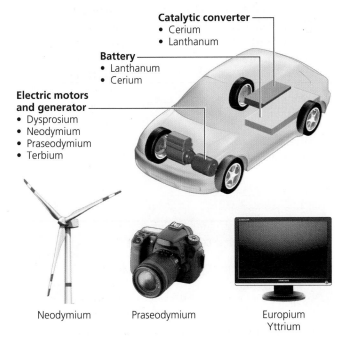

FIGURE 11.10 Rare-earth metals are used to manufacture all-electric and hybrid-electric cars and many other products.

Can We Expand Reserves by Mining Lower-Grade Ores?

Some analysts contend that we can increase supplies of some minerals by extracting them from lower-grade ores. They point to the development of new earth-moving equipment, improved techniques for removing impurities from ores, and other technological advances in mineral extraction and processing that can make lower-grade ores accessible, sometimes at lower costs.

For example, shortly after World War II, rich deposits of high-grade iron ore in northern Minnesota (USA) were economically depleted. By the 1960s, a new process had been developed for mining *taconite*, a low-grade and plentiful ore that had been viewed as waste rock in the iron mining process. This improvement in mining technology expanded Minnesota's iron reserves and supported a taconite mining industry long after the high-grade iron ore reserves there had been tapped out. Similarly, in 1900 the copper ore mined in the United States was typically 5% copper by weight. Today, it is typically 0.5%, yet copper costs less (when prices are adjusted for inflation).

Several factors can limit the mining of lower-grade ores. For example, it requires mining and processing larger volumes of ore, which takes much more energy and costs more. Another factor is the dwindling supplies of freshwater needed for the mining and processing of some minerals, especially in dry areas. A third limiting factor is the growing environmental impacts of land disruption, along with waste material and pollution produced during mining and processing.

One way to improve mining technology and reduce its environmental impact is to use a biological approach, sometimes called *biomining*. Miners use naturally occurring or genetically engineered bacteria to remove desired metals from ores through wells bored into the deposits. This leaves the surrounding environment undisturbed and reduces the air and water pollution associated with removing the metal from metal ores. On the downside, biomining is slow. It can take decades to remove the same amount of material that conventional methods can remove within months or years. So far, biomining methods are economically feasible only for low-grade ores for which conventional techniques are too expensive.

Can We Get More Minerals from the Oceans?

Most of the minerals found in seawater occur in such low concentrations that recovering them takes more energy and money than they are worth. Currently, only magnesium, bromine, and sodium chloride are abundant enough to be extracted profitably from seawater. On the other hand, sediments along the shallow continental shelf and adjacent shorelines contain significant deposits of minerals such as sand, gravel, phosphates, copper, iron, silver, titanium, and diamonds.

Another potential ocean source of some minerals is *hydrothermal ore deposits* that form when superheated, mineral-rich water shoots out of vents in volcanic regions of the ocean floor. When the hot water comes into contact with cold seawater, black particles of various metal sulfides precipitate out and accumulate as chimney-like structures, called *black smokers*, near the hot water vents (Figure 11.11). These deposits are especially rich in minerals such as copper, lead, zinc, silver, gold, and some of the rare earth metals. A variety of more than 300 exotic forms of life—including giant clams, six-foot tubeworms, and eyeless shrimp—live in the dark depths around black smokers.

Because of the rapidly rising prices of many of these metals, there is growing interest in deep-sea mining. Companies from Australia, the United States, and China have been exploring the possibility of mining black smokers in several areas. In 2012 the U.S. government issued its first-ever approval of large-scale deep-sea mining, proposed for a large area between Hawaii and Mexico. In 2015 the Center for Biological Diversity sued the government to try to prevent the project, arguing that it could damage important habitat for whales, sharks, and sea turtles by destroying seafloor ecosystems.

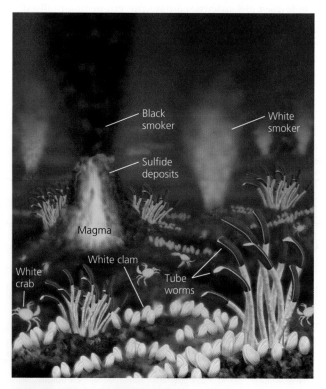

FIGURE 11.11 Natural capital: *Hydrothermal deposits*, or *black smokers*, are rich in various minerals.

According to some analysts, seafloor mining is less environmentally harmful than mining on land. Other scientists, however, are concerned because seafloor mining stirs up sediment that can harm or kill organisms that feed by filtering seawater. Supporters of seafloor mining say that the number of potential mining sites, and thus the overall environmental impact, will be small.

Another possible source of metals is the potato-size *manganese nodules* that cover large areas of the Pacific Ocean floor and smaller areas of the Atlantic and Indian Ocean floors. They also contain low concentrations of various rare earth minerals. These modules could be sucked up through vacuum pipes or scooped up by underwater mining machines.

To date, mining on the ocean floor has been hindered by the high costs involved, the potential threat to marine ecosystems, and arguments over rights to the minerals in deep ocean areas that do not belong to any specific country.

CHECKPOINT FOR UNDERSTANDING 11.3

1. Identify the two factors that can change the estimated reserves of a mineral resource.

2. Explain why rare earth minerals are critical to the world's economy.

3. Identify possible untapped sources for minerals.

11.4 WHAT ARE THE ENVIRONMENTAL EFFECTS OF USING NONRENEWABLE MINERAL RESOURCES?

CONCEPT 11.4 Extracting minerals from the earth's crust and converting them to useful products can disturb the land, erode soils, produce large amounts of solid waste, and pollute the air, water, and soil.

Extracting Minerals Can Have Harmful Environmental Effects

Every metal product has a *life cycle* that includes mining the mineral, processing it, manufacturing the product, and disposal or recycling of the product (Figure 11.12). This process makes use of large amounts of energy and water, and produces pollution and waste at every step of the life cycle (**Concept 11.4**).

The environmental impacts of mining a metal ore are determined partly by the ore's percentage of metal content, or *grade*. The more accessible higher-grade ores are usually exploited first. Mining lower-grade ores takes more money, energy, water, and other resources, and leads to more land disruption, mining waste, and pollution.

9 million
Number of people who could sit in Bingham Copper Mine (see chapter-opening photo) if it were a stadium

Several mining techniques are used to remove mineral deposits. Shallow mineral deposits are removed by **surface mining,** in which vegetation, soil, and rock overlying a mineral deposit are cleared away. This waste material is called **overburden** and is usually deposited in piles called **spoils** (Figure 11.13). Surface mining is used to extract about 90% of the nonfuel mineral resources and 60% of the coal used in the United States.

Different types of surface mining can be used, depending on two factors: the resource being sought and the local topography. In **open-pit mining,** machines are used to dig large pits and remove metal ores containing copper (see chapter-opening photo), gold (**Core Case Study**), or other metals, or sand, gravel, or stone.

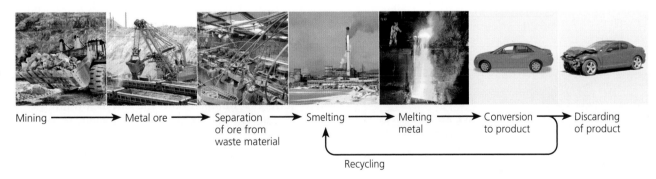

Mining → Metal ore → Separation of ore from waste material → Smelting → Melting metal → Conversion to product → Discarding of product

Recycling

FIGURE 11.12 Each metal product that we use has a *life cycle*.

Life Cycle of a Product

Consider the many products that you buy and use daily. Durable goods such as cars, computers, refrigerators, cell phones, and televisions are made of nonrenewable mineral resources that must be extracted and manufactured into the finished products that you purchase and use. Eventually, when these products wear out or break down and cannot be fixed, they are discarded. In an economy where it is often cheaper to replace rather than repair (computers, cell phones, and DVD players, for example), raw materials must be continuously mined to create new goods.

Every stage in a product's life cycle has an environmental impact; from the extraction of the mineral resources to manufacturing the finished product, transporting it to market, its use, and finally its disposal (Figure 11.12). In a car's life cycle, the metal must be mined and the ore extracted, separated, and refined through smelting. The pure mineral is melted and fabricated into the body and car

components, and the finished car is then transported to a dealership to be sold. One or more owners will drive the car during its useful life, until it is finally discarded, possibly at a junkyard that could use it for parts or scrap. Without recycling, valuable metals end up in a landfill rather than being reused and made into new products.

Huge amounts of energy are invested at every step in the car's life cycle. Mining for the minerals disrupts ecosystems and produces toxic waste. Air pollution results from smelting and melting the metal to make the car components and assemble the new car. Oil must be extracted, refined, and transported to produce gasoline to power the car, disrupting and polluting ecosystems, and operating the car emits pollutants such as nitrogen oxides and CO_2.

FRQ Application

Question: Many unwanted computers are thrown away in landfills. Some cities offer

services where consumers can drop off their old computers for recycling. **Identify ONE** step along the life cycle of a computer and discuss how recycling old computers would impact that step in terms of the amount of raw material or mineral resources used, the energy expended, and the amount of pollution produced in making new computers.

Possible Response: Extracting Mineral Resources: By recycling computers, the amount of virgin metal extracted for making new computers could be reduced. The amount of energy needed by machinery for mining, as well as toxic mining waste created from extraction would also be reduced.

Possible Response: Disposal: By recycling computers, usable and valuable metals would not be discarded, but would serve as raw materials to manufacture new products. Toxic metals such as lead contained in computers would not end up in a landfill where they might leach into groundwater.

FIGURE 11.13 Natural capital degradation: This spoils pile in Zielitz, Germany, is made up of waste material from the mining of potassium salts used to make fertilizers.

Strip mining involves extracting mineral deposits that lie in large horizontal beds close to the earth's surface. In **area strip mining,** used on flat terrain, a gigantic earthmover strips away the overburden, and a power shovel—which can be as tall as a 20-story building—removes a mineral resource such as gold (Figure 11.14). The resulting trench is filled with overburden, and a new cut is made parallel to the previous one. This process is repeated over the entire site.

Contour strip mining (Figure 11.15) is used mostly to mine coal and various mineral resources on hilly or mountainous terrain. Huge power shovels and bulldozers cut a series of terraces into the side of a hill. Then, earthmovers remove the overburden, an excavator or power shovel extracts the coal, and the overburden from each new terrace is dumped onto the one below. Unless the land is restored, this leaves a series of spoils banks and a highly erodible hill of soil and rock called a *highwall*.

Another surface mining method is **mountaintop removal,** in which explosives are used to remove the top of a mountain to expose seams of coal (Figure 11.16). This method is commonly used in the Appalachian Mountains of the United States. After a mountaintop is blown apart,

FIGURE 11.14 Natural capital degradation: Area strip mining for gold in Yukon Territory, Canada.

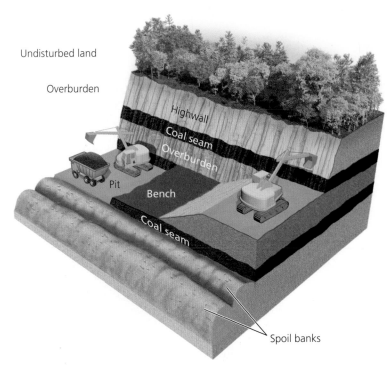

Undisturbed land

Overburden

Highwall

Coal seam

Overburden

Pit

Bench

Coal seam

Spoil banks

FIGURE 11.15 Natural capital degradation: Contour strip mining is used in hilly or mountainous terrain.

enormous machines plow waste rock and dirt into valleys below. This destroys forests, buries mountain streams, and increases the risk of flooding. Wastewater and toxic sludge, produced when the coal is processed, are often stored behind dams in these valleys. Such dams have been known to overflow or collapse and release toxic substances such as arsenic and mercury.

In the United States, more than 500 mountaintops in West Virginia and other Appalachian states have been removed to extract coal. According to the EPA, the resulting spoils have buried more than 1,100 kilometers (700 miles) of streams—a total roughly equal in length to the distance between the two US cities of New York and Chicago.

The US Department of the Interior estimates that at least 500,000 surface-mined sites dot the US landscape, mostly in the West. Such sites can be cleaned up and restored. The US Surface Mining Control and Reclamation Act of 1977 requires the restoration of surface-mined sites. However, the program is underfunded and many mines have not been reclaimed.

Deep deposits of minerals are removed by **subsurface mining,** in which underground mineral resources are removed through tunnels and shafts

FIGURE 11.16 **Natural capital degradation:** Mountaintop removal coal mining near Whitesville, West Virginia.

Jim West/Age Fotostock

(Figure 11.17). This method is used to remove metal ores and coal that are too deep to be extracted by surface mining. Miners dig a deep, vertical shaft and blast open subsurface tunnels and chambers to reach the deposit. Then they use machinery to remove the resource and transport it to the surface.

Subsurface mining disturbs less than one-tenth as much land as surface mining, and usually produces less waste material. However, it can lead to other hazards such as cave-ins, explosions, and fires for miners. Miners often get lung diseases caused by prolonged inhalation of mineral or coal dust in subsurface mines. Another problem is *subsidence*—the collapse of land above some underground mines. It can damage houses, crack sewer lines, break natural gas mains, and disrupt groundwater systems.

Surface and subsurface mining operations also produce large amounts of solid waste—three-fourths of all US solid waste—and cause major water and air pollution. For example, *acid mine drainage* occurs when rainwater that seeps through an underground mine or a

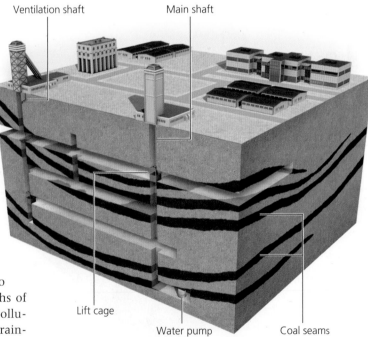

FIGURE 11.17 Subsurface mining of coal.

External, or Hidden Costs

The *market price* that we pay for a product or service usually does not include all of the *indirect*, or **external**, costs of harm to the environment and human health associated with its production and use. For this reason, such costs are often called *hidden costs*.

For example, the price a consumer pays for a new car includes the *direct*, or *internal*, costs of raw materials, manufacturing labor and energy consumption, shipping, advertising, and a profit markup for the car company and the dealer (Figure 11.A, left). In operating the car, we pay additional direct costs for gasoline, maintenance, repairs, and insurance. However, the process of extracting and processing raw materials to make a car uses energy and mineral resources, produces solid and hazardous waste, disturbs land, pollutes air and water, and releases greenhouse gases into the atmosphere. Crude oil exploration, drilling, transport, refining, and consumption pose a wide range of environmental threats and costs. These hidden external costs can have short- or long-term harmful effects on all of us today, on future generations, on infrastructure, on the climate, and on the earth's life-support systems (Figure 11.A, right).

Since the market price of the car does not include these harmful external costs, most people do not connect them with car ownership. Still, the car buyer (and everyone else) pays these hidden costs sooner or later, in the form of poorer health, higher expenses for health care and insurance, higher taxes for pollution control, traffic congestion, and the damage done to ecosystems from building and using roads and parking lots. Similarly, when a farmer practices high-input industrialized farming, or a power plant pollutes the air or water in a river, the external costs of those activities are not fully accounted for in our food prices or our electric bills.

FRQ Application

Question: Coal is relatively plentiful and cheap compared to other means of generating power, making coal-burning plants a common means of providing electricity to consumers. While electricity prices may be low, there are many externalities not included in the price per kilowatt hour. **Identify** ONE externality associated with coal-burning power plants and **discuss** how these costs are passed on to consumers.

Possible Response: One externality not included in the price of electricity produced by a coal-burning plant is the environmental impact of coal mining. Mountaintop removal to access a coal seam destroys mountain ecosystems as well as adjacent waterways when coal waste is dumped into valleys below. Flash floods can occur that destroy people's homes and take human lives, and water can be contaminated with acid mine drainage, causing sickness, and forcing people to buy bottled water.

Possible Response: One externality associated with coal-burning plants is the mercury that is released when coal is combusted. This mercury travels through the atmosphere, carried by wind, and eventually falling onto lakes and rivers. Within the aquatic ecosystem, it is converted into methyl mercury by bacteria and can then move up through a food chain or web, biomagnifying in predatory fish. Humans that eat fish such as sea bass or tuna ingest mercury and can suffer health impairments such as nervous system damage.

Internal and External Costs

Internal costs	External costs
Reflected in the purchase price of the vehicle	Paid for through taxes, increased health costs, loss of ecosystem services
Raw materials	Loss of habitat at metals mining sites
Manufacturing labor	Cleanup of contaminated mine sites
Manufacturing energy consumption	Air pollution from mining, smelting, and manufacturing
Shipping	Environmental damage from oil spills and cleanup during drilling and transport of crude oil
Advertising	
Other business costs	Increased air pollution, acid rain, and smog from car exhaust and damage to human health and infrastructure
Profit for the car company	
Dealership costs	Increased CO_2 emissions from burning fossil fuels
Profit for the dealership	The impacts of climate change

pixelprof/E+/Getty Images

FIGURE 11.A An example of the internal and external costs of buying and operating an automobile.

spoils pile from a surface mine carries sulfuric acid (H_2SO_4) produced when aerobic bacteria act on remaining minerals to nearby streams and groundwater. This is one of the problems often associated with gold mining (**Core Case Study**).

According to the EPA, mining has polluted mountain streams in 40% of the western watersheds in the United States. It accounts for 50% of all the country's emissions of toxic chemicals into the atmosphere. In fact, the mining industry produces more of such toxic emissions than any other US industry.

Where environmental regulations and enforcement are lax, mining is even more harmful to the environment. In China, for instance, the mining and processing of rare earth metals and oxides has stripped land of its vegetation and topsoil. It also has polluted the air, acidified streams, and left toxic and radioactive waste piles.

Removing Metals from Ores Has Harmful Environmental Effects

Ore extracted by mining typically has two components: the ore mineral, containing the desired metal, and waste material called **gangue**. Removing the waste material from ores produces **tailings**—rock wastes that are left in piles or put into ponds where they settle out. Particles of toxic metals in tailings piles can be blown by the wind or washed out by rain, or can leak from holding ponds and contaminate surface water and groundwater.

After the waste material is removed, heat or chemical solvents are used to extract the metals from mineral ores. Heating ores to release metals is called **smelting** (Figure 11.12). Without effective pollution control equipment, a smelter emits large quantities of air pollutants, including sulfur dioxide and suspended toxic particles that damage vegetation and acidify soils in the surrounding area. Smelters also cause water pollution and produce liquid and solid hazardous wastes that require safe disposal. Lead smelting is the world's second most toxic industry after the recycling of lead-acid batteries.

Using chemicals to extract metals from their ores can also create numerous problems, as noted in the **Core Case Study**. Even on a smaller scale, this is the case. For example, millions of poverty-stricken miners in less-developed countries have gone into tropical forests in search of gold (Figure 11.18). They have cleared trees to get access

FIGURE 11.18 Illegal gold mining on the banks of the Pra River in Ghana, Africa.

Randy Olson/National Geographic Creative

to gold, and such illegal deforestation has increased rapidly, especially in parts of the Amazon Basin. The miners use toxic mercury to separate gold from its ore. They heat the mixture of gold and mercury to vaporize the mercury and leave the gold, causing dangerous air and water pollution. Many of these miners and villagers living near the mines eventually inhale toxic mercury vapor, drink mercury-laden water, or eat fish contaminated with mercury.

CHECKPOINT FOR UNDERSTANDING 11.4

1. Define each of the following terms: overburden, spoils, and mine tailings.

2. Explain why mountaintop removal is particularly devastating to ecosystems.

3. Explain how acid mine drainage forms.

11.5 HOW CAN WE USE MINERAL RESOURCES MORE SUSTAINABLY?

CONCEPT 11.5 We can try to find substitutes for scarce resources, reduce resource waste, and recycle and reuse minerals.

Find Substitutes for Scarce Mineral Resources

Some analysts believe that even if supplies of key minerals become too expensive or too scarce due to unsustainable use, human ingenuity will find substitutes (**Concept 11.5**). They point to the current *materials revolution* in which silicon and other materials are replacing some metals for common uses. They also point out the possibilities of finding substitutes for scarce minerals through nanotechnology (Science Focus 11.1), as well as through other emerging technologies.

For example, fiber-optic glass cables that transmit pulses of light are replacing copper and aluminum wires in telephone cables, and nanowires may eventually replace fiber-optic glass cables. High-strength plastics and materials, strengthened by lightweight carbon, hemp, and glass fibers, are beginning to transform the automobile and aerospace industries. These new materials do not need painting (which reduces pollution and costs) and can be molded into any shape. Use of such materials in manufacturing motor vehicles and airplanes could greatly increase vehicle fuel efficiency by reducing vehicle weights. Such new materials are even being used to build bridges. One such possible breakthrough material is graphene (see the Case Study that follows).

However, resource substitution is not a cure-all. For example, platinum is currently unrivaled as a catalyst and is used in industrial processes to speed up chemical reactions, and chromium is an essential ingredient of stainless steel. Finding substitutes for such scarce resources may not always be possible.

CASE STUDY

Graphene and Phosphorene: New Revolutionary Materials

Graphene is made from graphite—a form of carbon that occurs as a mineral in some rocks. Ultrathin graphene consists of a single layer of carbon atoms packed into a two-dimensional hexagonal lattice (somewhat like chicken wire) that can be applied as a transparent film to surfaces (Figure 11.19).

Graphene is one of the world's thinnest and strongest materials and is light, flexible, and stretchable. A single layer of graphene is 150,000 times thinner than a human hair and 100 times stronger than structural steel. A sheet of this amazing material stretched over a coffee mug could support the weight of a car. It is also a better conductor of electricity than copper and conducts heat better than any known material.

The use of graphene could revolutionize the electric car industry by leading to the production of batteries that can be recharged 10 times faster and hold 10 times

Vincenzo Lombardo/Getty Images

FIGURE 11.19 Graphene, which consists of a single layer of carbon atoms linked together in a hexagonal lattice, is a revolutionary new material.

more power than current car batteries. Graphene composites can also be used to make stronger and lighter plastics, lightweight aircraft and motor vehicles, flexible computer tablets, and TV screens as thin as a magazine. It might also be used to make flexible, more efficient, less costly solar cells that can be attached to almost anything. However, researchers are looking into possible harmful effects of graphene production and use. A 2014 study led by Sharon Walker at the University of California–Riverside found graphene oxide in lakes and drinking water storage tanks. This could increase the chances that animals and humans could ingest the chemical, which was found in some early studies to be toxic to mice and human lung cells.

Graphene is made from very high purity and expensive graphite. According to the USGS, in 2013 China controlled about 68% of the world's high-purity graphite production. The United States mines very little natural graphite and imports most of its graphite from Mexico and China, which could restrict U.S. product exports as the use of graphene grows.

Geologists are looking for deposits of graphite in the United States. However, in 2011 a team of Rice University chemists, led by James M. Tour, found ways to make large sheets of high-quality graphene from inexpensive materials found in garbage and from dog feces. If such a process becomes economically feasible, concern over supplies of graphite could vanish, along with any harmful environmental effects of the mining and processing of graphite.

In 2014 a team of researchers at Purdue University was able to isolate a single layer of black phosphorus atoms—a new material known as *phosphorene*. As a semiconductor, it is more efficient than silicon transistors that are used as chips in computers and other electronic devices. Replacing them with phosphorene transistors could make almost any electronic device run much faster while using less power. This could revolutionize computer technology. However, phosphorene must be sealed in a protective coating because it breaks down when exposed to air.

Use Mineral Resources More Sustainably

Figure 11.20 lists several ways to use mineral resources more sustainably. One strategy is to focus on recycling and reuse of nonrenewable mineral resources, especially valuable or scarce metals such as gold, iron, copper, aluminum, and platinum (**Concept 11.5**). Recycling, an application of the chemical cycling **principle of sustainability** (see Inside Back Cover), has a much lower environmental impact than that of mining and processing metals from ores. For example, recycling aluminum beverage cans and scrap aluminum produces 95% less air pollution and 97% less water pollution, and uses 95% less energy, than mining and processing aluminum ore. We can also extract and recycle valuable gold (**Core Case Study**) from discarded cell phones.

Solutions
Sustainable Use of Nonrenewable Minerals
■ Reuse or recycle metal products whenever possible
■ Redesign manufacturing processes to use less mineral resources
■ Reduce mining subsidies
■ Increase subsidies for reuse, recycling, and finding substitutes

FIGURE 11.20 We can use nonrenewable mineral resources more sustainably (**Concept 11.5**). ***Critical thinking:*** Which two of these solutions do you think are the most important? Why?

Cleaning up and reusing items instead of recycling them has an even lower environmental impact.

Using mineral resources more sustainably is a major challenge in the face of rising demand for many minerals. For example, one way to increase supplies of rare earths is to extract and recycle them from the massive amounts of electronic wastes that are being produced. So far, however, less than 1% of rare earth metals are recovered and recycled.

Another way to use minerals more sustainably is to find substitutes for rare minerals, ideally, substitutes without heavy environmental impacts (**Concept 11.5**). For example, electric car battery makers are beginning to switch from making nickel-metal-hydride batteries, which require the rare earth metal lanthanum, to manufacturing lighter-weight lithium-ion batteries, which researchers are now trying to improve (Individuals Matter 11.1).

Lithium (Li), the world's lightest metal, is a vital component of lithium-ion batteries, which are used in cell phones, iPads, laptop computers, and a growing number of other products. The problem is that some countries, including the United States, do not have large supplies of lithium.

Japan, China, South Korea, and the United Arab Emirates are buying up access to global lithium reserves to ensure their ability to sell lithium or batteries to the rest of the world. Within a few decades, the United States may be heavily dependent on expensive imports of lithium and lithium batteries.

Scientists are also searching for substitutes for rare earth metals that are used to make increasingly important powerful magnets and related devices. In Japan and the United States, researchers are developing a variety of such devices that require no rare earth minerals, are light and compact, and can deliver more power with greater efficiency at a reduced cost.

CHECKPOINT FOR UNDERSTANDING 11.5

1. Identify several possible strategies for using mineral resources more sustainably.

The Nanotechnology Revolution

Nanotechnology uses science and engineering to manipulate and create materials out of atoms and molecules at the ultra-small scale of less than 100 nanometers. The diameter of the period at the end of this sentence is about a half million nanometers.

At the nanometer level, conventional materials have unconventional and unexpected properties. For example, scientists have learned to link carbon atoms together to form one-atom-thick sheets of carbon called *graphene* (see Case Study, p. 321). These sheets can be shaped into tubes called *carbon nanotubes* that are 60 times stronger than high-grade steel. A nearly invisible thread of this material is strong enough to suspend a pickup truck. Using carbon nanotubes to build cars would make them stronger and safer and would improve gas mileage by making them up to 80% lighter.

Currently, nanomaterials are used in more than 1,300 consumer products and the number is growing. Such products include certain batteries, stain-resistant and wrinkle-free clothes, self-cleaning glass surfaces, self-cleaning sinks and toilets, sunscreens, waterproof coatings for cell phones, some cosmetics, some foods, and food containers that release nanosilver ions to kill bacteria, molds, and fungi.

Nanotechnologists envision innovations such as a supercomputer smaller than a grain of rice, thin and flexible solar cell films that could be attached to or painted onto almost any surface, biocomposite materials that would make our bones and tendons super strong, and nanomolecules specifically designed to seek out and kill cancer cells. Nanotechnology allows us to make materials from the bottom up, using atoms of abundant elements (primarily hydrogen, oxygen, nitrogen, carbon, silicon, and aluminum) as substitutes for scarcer elements, such as copper, cobalt, and tin.

Nanotechnology has many potential environmental benefits. Designing and building products on the molecular level would greatly reduce the need to mine many materials. It would also require less matter and energy and it would reduce waste production. We may be able to use nanoparticles to remove industrial pollutants from contaminated air, soil, and groundwater. Nanofilters might someday be used to desalinate and purify seawater at an affordable cost, thereby helping to increase drinking water supplies. **GREEN CAREER: Environmental nanotechnology**

What's the catch? The main problem is serious concerns about the possible harmful health effects of nanotechnology. Because of the large combined surface area of the huge number of nanoparticles involved in any application, they are more chemically reactive and potentially more toxic to humans and other animals than are conventional materials.

Laboratory studies involving mice and other test animals reveal that nanoparticles can be inhaled deeply into the lungs and absorbed into the bloodstream. This can result in lung damage similar to that caused by mesothelioma, a deadly cancer resulting from the inhalation of asbestos particles. Nanoparticles can also penetrate cell membranes, including those in the brain, and move across the placenta from a mother to her fetus.

A panel of experts from the US National Academy of Sciences has said that the US government is not doing enough to evaluate the potential health and environmental risks of using nanomaterials. For example, the US Food and Drug Administration does not maintain a list of the food products and cosmetics that contain nanomaterials. By contrast, the European Union takes a precautionary approach to the use of nanomaterials, requiring that manufacturers demonstrate the safety of their products before they can enter the marketplace.

Many analysts say that, before unleashing nanotechnology more broadly, we should ramp up research on the potential harmful health effects of nanoparticles and develop regulations to control its growing applications until we know more about its possible harmful health effects. Many are also calling for the labeling of all products that contain nanoparticles.

CRITICAL THINKING

Do you think the potential benefits of nanotechnology products outweigh their potentially harmful effects? Explain.

11.6 WHAT ARE THE EARTH'S MAJOR GEOLOGICAL HAZARDS?

CONCEPT 11.6 Dynamic processes move matter within the earth and on its surface and can cause volcanic eruptions, earthquakes, tsunamis, erosion, and landslides.

The Earth Beneath Your Feet Is Moving

We tend to think of the earth's crust as solid and unmoving. However, the flows of energy and heated material within the earth's convection cells (Figure 11.3) are so powerful that they have caused the lithosphere to break up into a dozen or so huge rigid plates, called **tectonic plates,** which move extremely slowly atop the asthenosphere (Figure 11.21).

These gigantic plates are somewhat like the world's largest and slowest-moving surfboards on which we ride without noticing their movement. Their typical speed is about the rate at which your fingernails grow. Throughout the earth's history, landmasses have split apart and joined together as tectonic plates shifted around, changing the size, shape, and location of the earth's continents (Figure 4.B, p. 106). The slow movement of the continents across Earth's surface is called **continental drift.**

Yu-Guo Guo: Designer of Nanotechnology Batteries and National Geographic Explorer

© Jinsong Hu

Yu-Guo Guo is a professor of chemistry and a nanotechnology researcher at the Chinese Academy of Sciences in Beijing. He has invented nanomaterials that can be used to make lithium-ion battery packs smaller, more powerful, and less costly, which makes them more useful for powering electric cars and electric bicycles. This is an important scientific advance, because the battery pack is the most important and expensive part of any electric vehicle.

Guo's innovative use of nanomaterials has greatly increased the power of lithium-ion batteries by enabling electric current to flow more efficiently through what he calls "3-D conducting nanonetworks." With this promising technology, lithium-ion battery packs in electric vehicles can be fully charged in a few minutes. They also have twice the energy storage capacity of today's batteries, and thus will extend the range of electric vehicles by enabling them to run longer. Guo is also interested in developing nanomaterials for use in solar cells and fuel cells that could be used to generate electricity and to power vehicles.

Much of the geological activity at the earth's surface takes place at the boundaries between tectonic plates as they separate, collide, or grind along against each other. The boundary that occurs where two plates move away from each other is called a **divergent boundary** (Figure 11.21). At such boundaries, magma flows up where the plates separate, sometimes hardening and forming new crust and sometimes breaking to the surface and causing volcanic eruptions. Earthquakes can also occur because of divergence of plates, and superheated water can erupt as geysers.

Another type of boundary is the **convergent boundary** (Figure 11.21), where two tectonic plates are colliding. This super-slow-motion collision causes one or both plate edges to buckle and rise, forming mountain ranges. In most cases, one plate slides beneath the other, melting and making new magma that can rise through cracks and form volcanoes near the boundary. The overriding plate is pushed up and made into mountainous terrain.

The third major type of boundary is the **transform plate boundary** (Figure 11.21), where two plates grind along in opposite directions next to each other. The tremendous forces produced at these boundaries can form mountains or deep cracks (Figure 11.22) and cause earthquakes and volcanic eruptions.

Volcanoes Release Molten Rock from the Earth's Interior

An active **volcano** occurs where magma rising in a plume through the lithosphere reaches the earth's surface through a central vent or a long crack, called a *fissure* (Figure 11.23). Magma or molten rock that reaches the earth's surface is called *lava*.

A *volcanic eruption* releases chunks of lava rock, liquid lava, glowing hot ash, and gases (including water vapor, carbon dioxide, and sulfur dioxide) (**Concept 11.6**). Eruptions can be explosive and extremely destructive, causing loss of life and obliterating ecosystems and human communities. They can also be slow and much less destructive with lava gurgling up and spreading slowly across the land or sea floor. It is this slower form of eruption that builds the cone-shaped mountains so commonly associated with volcanoes, as well as layers of rock made of cooled lava on the earth's surface.

While volcanic eruptions can be destructive, they can also form majestic mountain ranges and lakes, and the weathering of lava contributes to fertile soils. Hundreds of volcanoes have erupted on the ocean floor, building cones that have reached the ocean's surface, eventually to form islands that have become suitable for human settlement, such as the Hawaiian Islands.

We can reduce the loss of human life and some of the property damage caused by volcanic eruptions by using historical records and geological measurements to identify high-risk areas, so that people can avoid living in those areas. We also use monitoring devices that warn us when volcanoes are likely to erupt, and in some areas that are prone to volcanic activity, evacuation plans have been developed.

Earthquakes Are Geological Rock-and-Roll Events

Forces inside the earth's mantle put tremendous stress on rock within the crust. Such stresses can be great enough to cause sudden breakage and shifting of the rock, producing a *fault*, or fracture in the earth's crust (Figure 11.22). When a fault forms, or when there is abrupt movement on an existing fault, energy that has accumulated over time is released in the form of vibrations, called *seismic waves*, which move in all directions through the surrounding rock—an event called an **earthquake** (Figure 11.24 and **Concept 11.6**). Most earthquakes occur at the boundaries of tectonic plates (Figures 11.21 and 11.22).

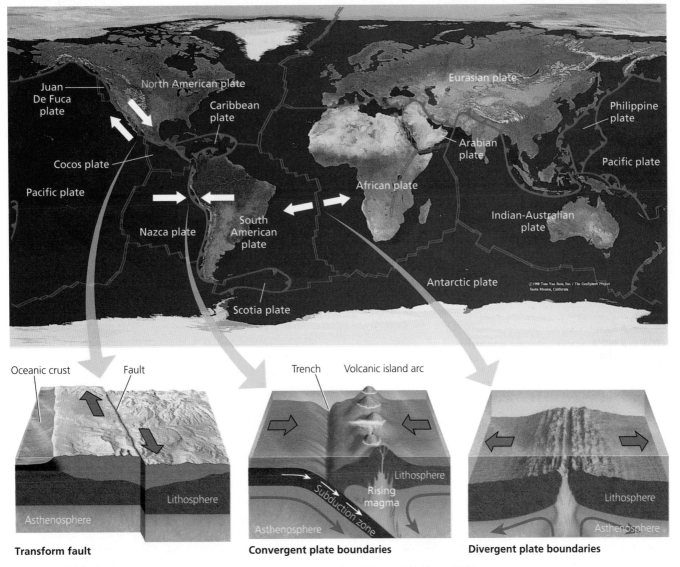

Oceanic crust — Fault — Trench — Volcanic island arc

Lithosphere
Asthenosphere
Subduction zone
Rising magma
Lithosphere
Asthenosphere
Lithosphere
Asthenosphere

Transform fault   **Convergent plate boundaries**   **Divergent plate boundaries**

FIGURE 11.21 The earth's crust has been fractured into several major tectonic plates. White arrows indicate examples of where plates are colliding, separating, or grinding along against each other in opposite directions. **Question:** Which plate are you riding on?

Seismic waves move upward and outward from the earthquake's *focus* like ripples in a pool of water. Scientists measure the severity of an earthquake by the *magnitude* of its seismic waves. The magnitude is a measure of ground motion (shaking) caused by the earthquake, as indicated by the *amplitude*, or size of the seismic waves when they reach a recording instrument, called a *seismograph*.

Scientists use the *Richter scale*, on which each unit has an amplitude 10 times greater than the next smaller unit. *Seismologists*, or people who study earthquakes, rate earthquakes as *insignificant* (less than 4.0 on the Richter scale), *minor* (4.0–4.9), *damaging* (5.0–5.9), *destructive* (6.0–6.9), *major* (7.0–7.9), and *great* (over 8.0). The largest recorded earthquake occurred in Chile on May 22, 1960, and measured 9.5 on the Richter scale. Each year, scientists record the magnitudes of more than 1 million earthquakes, most of which are too small to feel.

The primary effects of earthquakes include shaking and sometimes a permanent vertical or horizontal displacement of a part of the crust. These effects can have serious consequences for people and for buildings, bridges, freeway overpasses, dams, and pipelines. A major earthquake is a large rock-and-roll geological event.

One way to reduce the loss of life and property damage from earthquakes is to examine historical records and make geological measurements to locate active fault zones. We can then map high-risk areas and establish building codes that regulate the placement and design of buildings in such areas. Then people can evaluate the risk and factor it into their decisions about where to live. In addition, engineers know how to make homes, large buildings, bridges, and freeways more earthquake resistant, although this is costly.

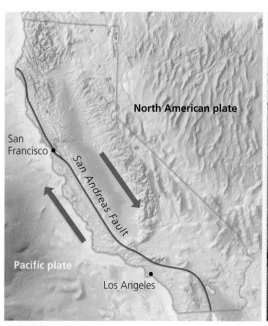

FIGURE 11.22 The San Andreas Fault, created by the North American Plate and the Pacific Plate sliding very slowly past each other, runs almost the full length of California (see map). It is responsible for earthquakes of various magnitudes, which have caused rifts on the land surface in some areas (photo).

FIGURE 11.23 Sometimes, the internal pressure in a volcano is high enough to cause lava, ash, and gases to be ejected into the atmosphere (photo) or to flow over land, causing considerable damage.

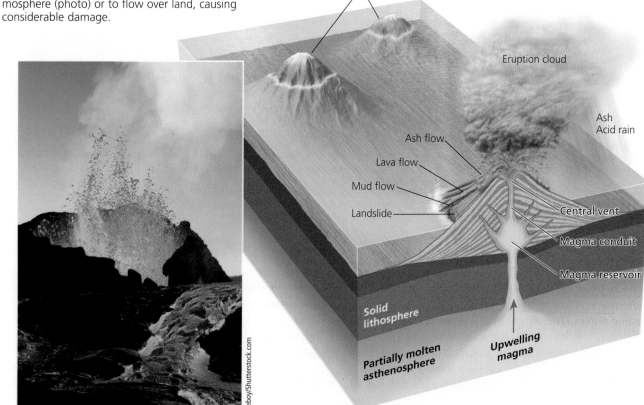

Earthquakes on the Ocean Floor Can Cause Tsunamis

A **tsunami** is a series of large waves generated when part of the ocean floor suddenly rises or drops (Figure 11.25).

Most large tsunamis are caused when certain types of faults in the ocean floor move up or down because of a large underwater earthquake. Other causes are landslides generated by earthquakes and volcanic eruptions (**Concept 11.6**).

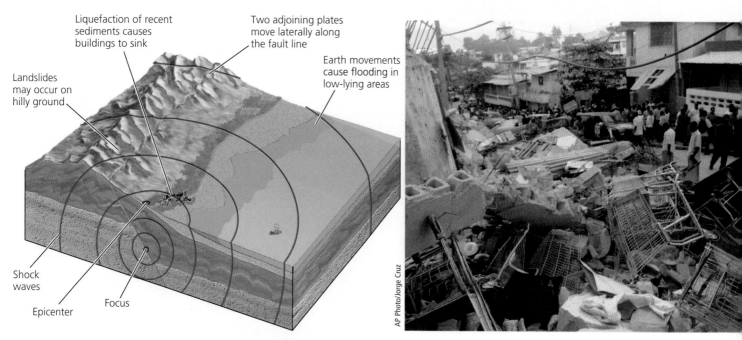

Liquefaction of recent sediments causes buildings to sink

Two adjoining plates move laterally along the fault line

Earth movements cause flooding in low-lying areas

Landslides may occur on hilly ground

Shock waves

Epicenter

Focus

AP Photo/Jorge Cruz

FIGURE 11.24 An *earthquake* (left) is one of nature's most powerful events. The photo shows damage from a 2010 earthquake in Port-au-Prince, Haiti.

Tsunamis are often called *tidal waves*, although they have nothing to do with tides. They can travel across the ocean at the speed of a jet airliner. In deep water, the waves are very far apart—sometimes hundreds of kilometers—and their crests are not very high. As a tsunami approaches a coast with its shallower waters, it slows down, its wave crests squeeze closer

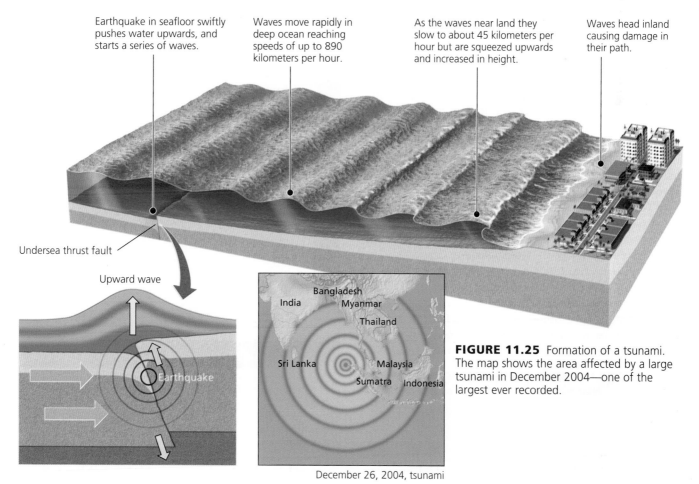

Earthquake in seafloor swiftly pushes water upwards, and starts a series of waves.

Waves move rapidly in deep ocean reaching speeds of up to 890 kilometers per hour.

As the waves near land they slow to about 45 kilometers per hour but are squeezed upwards and increased in height.

Waves head inland causing damage in their path.

Undersea thrust fault

Upward wave

Earthquake

India
Bangladesh
Myanmar
Thailand
Sri Lanka
Malaysia
Sumatra
Indonesia

December 26, 2004, tsunami

FIGURE 11.25 Formation of a tsunami. The map shows the area affected by a large tsunami in December 2004—one of the largest ever recorded.

FIGURE 11.26 The Banda Aceh shore near Gleebruk, Indonesia, on June 23, 2004 (left), and on December 28, 2004 (right), after it was struck by a tsunami.

Left: Science Source. Right: Science Source.

together, and their heights grow rapidly. It can hit a coast as a series of towering walls of water that can level buildings.

The largest recorded loss of life from a tsunami occurred in December 2004 when a great underwater earthquake in the Indian Ocean with a magnitude of 9.15 caused a tsunami that killed more than 230,000 people and devastated many coastal areas of Indonesia (Figure 11.26 and map in Figure 11.25), Thailand, Sri Lanka, South India, and eastern Africa. It also displaced about 1.7 million people (1.3 million of them in India and Indonesia), and destroyed or damaged about 470,000 buildings and houses. There were no recording devices in place to provide an early warning of this tsunami.

In 2011, a large tsunami caused by a powerful earthquake off the coast of Japan generated 3-story high waves that killed almost 19,000 people, displaced more than 300,000 people, and destroyed or damaged 125,000 buildings. It also heavily damaged three nuclear reactors, which then released dangerous radioactivity into the surrounding environment.

In some areas, scientists have built networks of ocean buoys and pressure recorders on the ocean floor to collect data that can be relayed to tsunami emergency warning centers. However, these networks are not widespread.

CHECKPOINT FOR UNDERSTANDING 11.6

1. Explain why volcanoes and earthquakes typically occur in the same places.

2. Explain how earthquakes and tsunamis are related.

KEY IDEAS

- Dynamic forces that move matter within the earth and on its surface recycle the earth's rocks, form deposits of mineral resources, and cause volcanic eruptions, earthquakes, and tsunamis.

- The available supply of a mineral resource depends on how much of it is in the earth's crust, how fast we use it, the mining technology used to obtain it, its market prices, and the harmful environmental effects of removing and using it.

- We can use mineral resources more sustainably by trying to find substitutes for scarce resources, reducing resource waste, and reusing and recycling nonrenewable minerals.

Core Case Study Checkpoint

The mining and sale of gold converts mineral resources into products that sustain human economies. However, the environmental impacts of gold mining can be devastating. Discuss these impacts and identify several ways they can be reduced.

area strip mining: type of strip mining used where the terrain is flat. An earthmover strips away the overburden and a power shovel digs a cut to remove the mineral deposit. The trench is then filled with the spoils, and a new cut is made parallel to the previous one.

asthenosphere: zone within the earth's mantle made up of hot, partly melted rock that flows and can be deformed like soft plastic.

continental drift: the slow movement of continents across earth's surface.

contour strip mining: form of surface mining used on hilly or mountainous terrain. A power shovel cuts a series of terraces into the side of a hill. An earthmover removes the overburden, and a power shovel extracts the coal. The spoils from each new terrace are dumped onto the one below.

convergent boundary: area where the earth's lithospheric plates move toward each other and are pushed together.

core: inner zone of the earth. It consists of a solid inner core and a liquid outer core.

crust: solid outer zone of the earth. It consists of oceanic crust and continental crust.

depletion time: the time it takes to use a certain fraction (usually 80%) of the known or estimated supply of a nonrenewable resource at an assumed rate of use. Finding and extracting the remaining 20% usually costs more than it is worth.

divergent boundary: area where the earth's lithospheric plates move apart in opposite directions.

earthquake: shaking of the ground resulting from the fracturing and displacement of subsurface rock, which produces a fault, or from subsequent movement along the fault.

gangue: the waste material that is discarded when ore is extracted during mining.

high-grade ore: ore containing a large amount of a desired mineral.

igneous rock: rock formed when molten rock material (magma) wells up from the earth's interior, cools, and solidifies into rock masses.

lithosphere: outer shell of the earth, composed of the crust and the rigid, outermost part of the mantle outside the asthenosphere.

low-grade ore: ore containing a small amount of a desired mineral.

mantle: zone of the earth's interior between the core and the crust.

metamorphic rock: rock produced when a preexisting rock is subjected to high temperatures (which may cause it to melt partially), high pressures, chemically active fluids, or a combination of these agents.

mineral: any naturally occurring inorganic substance found in the earth's crust as a crystalline solid.

mineral resource: any naturally occurring solid, liquid, or gaseous material in or on the earth's crust in a form and amount such that extracting and converting it into useful materials or items is currently or potentially profitable. Mineral resources are classified as metallic or nonmetallic.

mountaintop removal: type of surface mining that uses explosives, massive power shovels, and large machines called draglines to remove the top of a mountain and expose the seams of coal beneath.

open-pit mining: removing minerals such as gravel, sand, and metal ores by digging them out of the earth's surface and leaving an open pit behind.

ore: part of a metal-yielding material that can be economically extracted from a mineral; typically containing two parts; the ore mineral, which contains the desired metal, and waste minerals (gangue).

overburden: layer of soil and rock overlying a mineral deposit.

reserves: resources that have been identified and from which a usable mineral can be extracted profitably at present prices with current mining or extraction technology.

rock: any solid material that makes up a large, natural continuous part of the earth's crust.

rock cycle: largest and slowest of the earth's cycles, consisting of geologic, physical, and chemical processes that form and modify rocks and soil in the earth's crust over millions of years.

sedimentary rock: rock that forms from the accumulated products of erosion, and in some cases, from the compacted shells, skeletons, and other remains of organisms.

smelting: process in which a desired metal is separated from the other elements in an ore mineral.

soil profile: Cross-sectional view of the horizontal layers or horizons of a soil.

spoils: unwanted rock and other waste materials produced when a material is removed from the earth's surface or subsurface by mining, dredging, quarrying, or excavation.

strip mining: form of surface mining in which bulldozers, power shovels, or stripping wheels remove large chunks of the earth.

subsurface mining: extraction of a metal ore or fuel resource such as coal from a deep underground deposit.

surface mining: removing soil, subsoil, and other strata and then extracting a mineral deposit found fairly close to the earth's surface.

tailings: the materials left behind when ore is separated from rock waste. Tailings can be left in piles, or flushed into ponds where fine particles then settle out.

tectonic plates: various-sized areas of the earth's lithosphere that move slowly around with the mantle's flowing asthenosphere.

Most earthquakes and volcanoes occur around the boundaries of these plates.

transform plate boundary: area where the earth's lithospheric plates move parallel to each other in opposite directions.

tsunami: series of large waves generated when part of the ocean floor suddenly rises or drops.

volcano: vent or fissure in the earth's surface through which magma, liquid lava, and gases are released into the environment.

weathering: physical and chemical processes in which solid rock exposed at the earth's surface is changed to separate physical particles and dissolved minerals, which can be moved to another place as sediment.

Chapter Review

Core Case Study

1. Explain why the real cost of gold is more than what most people pay for it. What are some examples of costs not accounted for?

Section 11.1

2. (a) What are the two key concepts for this section? (b) Define **geology, core, mantle, asthenosphere, crust,** and **lithosphere**. (c) Define **mineral, mineral resource,** and **rock**. (d) Define and distinguish among **sedimentary rock, igneous rock,** and **metamorphic rock** and give an example of each. (e) What is the **rock cycle**? Explain its importance.

Section 11.2

3. (a) What are the two key concepts for this section? (b) Differentiate between physical and chemical **weathering**. Explain how physical, chemical, and biological forces all contribute to the formation of soil. (c) Why is soil considered a renewable resource? What ecological services does soil provide? (d) What is a **soil profile**? Identify the layers in a soil profile. (e) Explain the role of decomposers in soil formation. (f) What is the function of soil in nitrogen cycling? (g) Identify the three types of soil particles. What is soil texture? What is the relationship between soil porosity and permeability?

Section 11.3

4. (a) What are the two key concepts for this section? (b) Define **ore** and distinguish between a **high-grade ore** and a **low-grade ore**. (c) List five important nonrenewable mineral resources and their uses. (d) What are the **reserves** of a mineral resource and how can they be expanded? (e) What two factors determine the future supply of a nonrenewable mineral resource? (f) Explain how the supply of a nonrenewable mineral resource can be economically depleted and list the five choices we have when this occurs. (g) What is **depletion time** and what factors affect it?

5. (a) What five nations supply most of the world's nonrenewable mineral resources? How dependent is the United States on other countries for important nonrenewable mineral resources? (b) Explain the concern over US access to rare earth mineral resources. (c) Describe the conventional view of the relationship between the supply of a mineral resource and its market price. Explain why some economists believe this relationship no longer applies in some countries.

6. (a) Summarize the opportunities and limitations of expanding mineral supplies by mining lower-grade ores. (b) Describe the opportunities and possible problems that could result from deep-sea mining.

Section 11.4

7. (a) What is the key concept for this section? (b) Summarize the life cycle of a metal product.

8. (a) What is **surface mining**? Define **overburden** and **spoils**. Define **open-pit mining** and **strip mining**, and distinguish among **area strip mining, contour strip mining,** and **mountaintop removal mining**. (b) Describe three harmful environmental effects of surface mining. What is **subsurface mining**? (c) What is acid mine drainage? (d) Define **tailings** and explain why they can be hazardous. What is **smelting** and what are its major harmful environmental effects?

Section 11.5

9. (a) What is the key concept for this section? (b) Give two examples of promising substitutes for key mineral resources. (c) What is **nanotechnology** and what are some of its potential environmental and other benefits? What are some problems that could arise from the widespread use of nanotechnology? (d) Describe the potential of using graphene as a new resource. (e) Explain the benefits of recycling and reusing valuable metals. (f) List five ways to use nonrenewable mineral resources more sustainably. (g) What are two examples of research into substitutes for rare earth metals? (h) Explain why uneven distribution of lithium among various countries is a concern.

Section 11.6

10. (a) What is the key concept for this section? (b) What are **tectonic plates**? What is **continental drift**? (c) Define and distinguish among **divergent**, **convergent**, and **transform plate boundaries**. (d) Define **volcano** and describe the nature and major effects of a volcanic eruption. (e) Define **earthquake** and describe its nature and major effects. (f) What is a **tsunami** and what are its major effects?

11. What are this chapter's three key ideas?

_____

Note: Key terms are in bold type.

AP® Review Questions

Questions 1–3 refer to the following parts of the earth. Choices may be used once, more than once, or not at all.

(A) Core
(B) Crust
(C) Mantle
(D) Lithosphere
(E) Asthenosphere

1. Surrounds the core and is primarily composed of solid rock

2. Outermost and thinnest zone of the earth that lies under the continents and ocean

3. Layer of rock within the mantle whose convection currents cause plate movement

4. The North American and Eurasian plates are moving apart from one another and creating the Mid-Atlantic ridge. This is an example of what type of plate boundary?
   (A) Convergent, such as the plate movement that causes earthquakes in Japan and the Philippines
   (B) Divergent, such as between the African and Arabian plates
   (C) Transform, such as the plate boundary in California that caused the 1906 San Francisco earthquake
   (D) Subduction, such as along the West Coast of South America
   (E) Convection, which causes molten rock beneath the surface to move in opposite directions

5. Tectonic plates move slowly across the asthenosphere on
   (A) ocean currents because the less dense material rises to the surface
   (B) ocean ridges because they are diverging plate boundaries
   (C) plate boundaries because there is tectonic movement along all plate boundaries
   (D) convection currents as a result of differences in density
   (E) groundwater because it is always moving beneath the surface

6. Convergent boundaries between two continental plates produce
   (A) mountain ranges
   (B) oceanic trenches
   (C) oceanic ridges
   (D) transform fault lines
   (E) subduction zones

7. The weathering of rocks from wind, water, and thermal expansion is known as
   (A) kinetic weathering
   (B) biological weathering
   (C) external weathering
   (D) chemical weathering
   (E) physical weathering

Questions 8–10 refer to the terms below. Choices may be used once, more than once, or not at all.

(A) Oil shale
(B) Igneous
(C) Metamorphic
(D) Sedimentary
(E) Leachate

8. Forms when pre-existing rock is subjected to high temperatures, pressure, or chemicals

9. Forms when existing rock is weathered and deposited as small grains

10. Forms when magma cools and hardens

11. Strip mining is a useful and economic way to extract mineral resources. However, strip mining has all of the following harmful environmental effects EXCEPT
    (A) regrowth of vegetation where strip mining has occurred is very fast
    (B) toxic substances are left behind
    (C) biodiversity is destroyed in the area
    (D) streams around the area become polluted
    (E) air pollution around the area occurs

12. The vibration created when rock fractures beneath the earth's surface is a(n)
    (A) epicenter
    (B) seismic wave
    (C) Richter scale
    (D) amplitude
    (E) fault zone

Question 13 refers to the graph below.

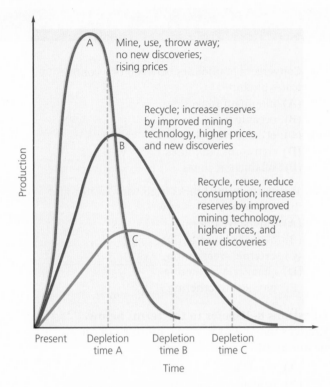

13. According to the graph,
    (A) recycling a resource does not significantly lower depletion time
    (B) mining, using, and throwing away a resource is the best way to lower depletion time
    (C) recycling a resource causes it to be depleted quickest
    (D) 80% depletion occurs slower as recycling, reuse, and reduction are implemented
    (E) as we recycle, reuse, and reduce our consumption rates, we slow down depletion time of nonrenewable resources

14. Finding substitutes for mineral resources will
    (A) cause a shift to mining of low-grade ores
    (B) have no environmental impact
    (C) help to keep supplies of resources sustainable
    (D) cause thermal water pollution
    (E) cause eutrophication

15. When rock ore contains small concentrations of gold, which technique is used to increase the amount of gold retrieved?
    (A) Subsurface mining
    (B) Mining of near-shore sediments
    (C) Strip mining and mountaintop removal
    (D) Cyanide leaching of crushed rock
    (E) Smelting of high-grade ore

16. Which of the following occurs when a mineral resource becomes scarce?
    (A) Price increases, which can encourage use of substitutes and resource conservation
    (B) Demand goes down because fewer people want to buy a mineral that is becoming rare
    (C) Price stays the same so the remaining minerals will be purchased quickly and mining companies can begin to mine something else
    (D) Mining operations are paused and, after a short time, a new supply of the mineral will become available
    (E) Environmental impact decreases because mining decreases when a mineral becomes scarce

17. Which of the following refers to the process in which rainwater moves through underground mines and tailings and carries H_2SO_4 into water bodies?
    (A) Thermal mine pollution
    (B) Acid mine drainage
    (C) Natural capital degradation
    (D) Toxic mine shock
    (E) Mercury poisoning

18. One big environmental problem with smelting is
    (A) it is very costly and results in increased taxes paid by local residents
    (B) subsidence after ore mineral is removed from the land
    (C) air pollution because smelting releases sulfur dioxide and particulates
    (D) mining tailings that are discarded after ore extraction
    (E) it strips the land of its vegetation and topsoil

19. When a mineral resource is too deep to be surface mined, which technique is used?
    (A) Mining spoils, because there is still mineral ore in the soil and rock after initial removal of ore
    (B) Subsurface mining, in which miners use elevators to get to and from the mineral ores
    (C) Placer mining, because it is safer and easier to remove the minerals from spring water that flows up from deep underground
    (D) Subsidence, because it is easier and safer to reach the mineral ore once the land has sunk down to the level of the desired resources
    (E) Open-pit mining, because miners keep digging until they reach the depth of the desired mineral resource

20. Which of the following is the LEAST sustainable use of nonrenewable mineral resources?
(A) Recycling all aluminum resources
(B) Reducing dependency on metal resources by using alternatives
(C) Increasing subsidies for mining companies to lower prices for consumers
(D) Using the waste of mineral-based operations as raw materials in other industries
(E) Upgrading current mineral manufacturing plants to reduce pollution and waste

AP® Free-Response Practice

1. Bauxite is an ore that must be extracted and refined to produce aluminum. Bauxite is usually strip-mined because it is almost always found near the surface of the ground. After the ore is extracted, it is heated under pressure and combined with sodium hydroxide (called the Bayer process) in order to make aluminum oxide. The aluminum oxide is then refined to produce aluminum.

(a) A mining company in Arkansas discovers a large deposit of bauxite. The density of bauxite in this deposit is 1.28 grams of bauxite per cubic centimeter.

(i) **Calculate** the number of kilograms per cubic meter of bauxite ore.

(ii) Bauxite must go through two processes to produce aluminum metal. The yield of the Bayer process, which extracts aluminum oxide from bauxite, is 40 percent. The yield of converting aluminum oxide to aluminum is 50 percent. **Determine** the yield in grams of aluminum from one cubic meter of bauxite ore.

(iii) The price of aluminum on the world market is $1,670 per metric ton. The total cost of mining the site is $12,500,000. **Calculate** how many cubic meters of deposit the company must mine in order to break even.

(b) Choose one the following methods of mining.
- Contour strip mining
- Shaft mining
- Area strip mining
- Mountaintop removal

For the method you choose:

(i) **Describe** how the method is done.

(ii) **Identify** and **discuss** TWO negative impacts of that mining method.

(c) Mineral resources such as aluminum are considered nonrenewable. **Discuss** TWO ways of extending the depletion time for a nonrenewable mineral resource.

Critical Thinking

1. Do you think that the benefits we get from gold—its uses in jewelry, dentistry, electronics, and other uses—are worth the real cost of gold (**Core Case Study**)? If so, explain your reasoning. If not, explain your argument for cutting back on or putting a stop to the mining of gold.

2. You are an igneous rock. Describe what you experience as you move through the rock cycle. Repeat this exercise, assuming you are a sedimentary rock and again assuming you are a metamorphic rock.

3. What are three ways in which you benefit from the rock cycle?

4. Explain why soils composed primarily of sand and silt would be unsuitable for growing crops.

5. Suppose your country's supply of rare earth metals was cut off tomorrow. How would this affect your

life? Give at least three examples. How would you adjust to these changes? Explain.

6. Use the second law of thermodynamics (see Chapter 2, p. 50) to analyze the scientific and economic feasibility of each of the following processes:
   a. Extracting certain minerals from seawater
   b. Mining increasingly lower-grade deposits of minerals
   c. Continuing to mine, use, and recycle minerals at increasing rates

7. List three ways in which a nanotechnology revolution could benefit you and three ways in which it could harm you. Do you think, the benefits outweigh the harms? Explain.

8. What are three ways to reduce the harmful environmental impacts of the mining and processing of nonrenewable mineral resources? What are three aspects of your lifestyle that contribute to these harmful impacts?

Data Analysis

Rare earth metals are widely used in a variety of important products (Case Study, p. 312). According to the US Geological Survey, China has about 42% of the world's reserves of rare earth metals. Use this information to answer the following questions.

1. In 2014, China had 55 million metric tons of rare earth metals in its reserves and produced 95,000 metric tons of these metals. At this rate of production, how long will China's rare earth reserves last?

2. In 2014, the global demand for rare earth metals was about 136,000 metric tons. At this annual rate of use, if China were to produce all of the world's rare earth metals, how long would their reserves last?

3. The annual global demand for rare earth metals is projected to rise to at least 182,000 metric tons by 2020. At this rate, if China were to produce all of the world's rare earth metals, how long would its reserves last?

Answers to Checkpoints for Understanding

Section 11.1

1. Minerals are a naturally occurring chemical element or sometimes an inorganic compound with a repeating internal arrangement or crystal form. Rocks can be composed of a single mineral, but are more often a combination of minerals.

2. The three types of rocks are sedimentary, igneous, and metamorphic. Sedimentary rock is composed of weathered rock and minerals as well as bits or organic material that has been moved by wind or water and compressed. Igneous rock forms below the earth's surface and then cools and hardens at the surface as magma is forced upward from underneath the crust. Metamorphic rock is formed when existing rock is subjected to high temperature and high pressure.

3. The three processes that drive the rock cycles are erosion (external force), melting, and metamorphism (internal forces).

Section 11.2

1. Abiotic factors such as wind, ice, and water physically weather parent material by breaking it up into smaller pieces. Rock is chemically weathered when acids react with minerals in the rock. Lichens, a pioneer plant species, chemically weather rock, allowing other biotic organisms to live on the weathered material, leaving their wastes and decomposed bodies to add humus to the parent material.

Over time layers of humus, weathered parent material, and dissolved ions accumulate over the original bedrock.

2. Decomposers break down dead plants and animals and other organic waste, producing ammonia and ammonium ions. Some of the ammonia compounds are converted to nitrate ions, which plants easily assimilate into their tissues. When plants are consumed by primary consumers, they in turn assimilate these nitrogen compounds. When the animals die, they decompose, closing the cycle.

Section 11.3

1. The two factors that can change estimated reserves are new technologies that make previously inaccessible deposits of a mineral accessible, and an increased market price of a mineral reserve that makes it economically feasible to mine a harder-to-extract deposit.

2. Rare earth minerals such as scandium, yttrium, and lanthanum are used in many different high-tech products such as flat-screen televisions and computers as well as solar panels and LED light bulbs and military systems such as smart bombs and missile guidance systems.

3. Seafloor mining from black smokers, precipitates that form when cold water and hot water from volcanic vents combine, and harvesting manganese nodules on the ocean floor, are both technologies that may result in increasing reserves of important mineral resources.

Section 11.4

1. Overburden is the soil, rocks, and vegetation that lie on top of minerals targeted for extraction. Spoils are the piles of overburden after they are removed. Mine tailings are the leftover waste materials that result from separating the ore from the mined material.

2. Mountain top removal uses explosives to blow off the top of a mountain, exposing the minerals underneath. Overburden that is blown off is dumped into valley streams in order to expose the coal seam. This destroys forests, blocks and pollutes streams, causes flooding, and creates toxic sludge containing arsenic and mercury.

3. Acid mine drainage is sulfuric acid that is produced by aerobic bacteria that act on the minerals in mine tailings. Rainwater containing this acid is carried to nearby streams, polluting them and killing off living organisms.

Section 11.5

1. Using nanotechnology, finding substitutes for some minerals, and recycling products containing valuable minerals rather than disposing of them in landfills will increase the sustainability of minerals resources.

Section 11.6

1. Earthquakes can occur wherever tectonic plates are moving in relation to one another. The plates can be crashing into each other, pulling apart or sliding past each other, or one can be getting pushing down beneath the other. All of these tectonic boundaries also create special conditions that allow magma to form from the earth's mantle and be released in volcanic eruptions.

2. One cause of tsunamis is underwater earthquakes. When an earthquake occurs on the ocean floor, a wall of water can form, moving rapidly toward shore, destroying property and human life.

Core Case Study

Mining is used to extract gold and other mineral resources from the earth's crust. However, mining gold and other mineral resources produces mining wastes and can pollute the air and water. Settling ponds created in mining gold leak or overflow and pollute underground water and streams. Tropical forests have been cleared illegally by millions of poor miners to create pits to mine gold. Mercury used to extract the gold from its ore has poisoned many miners and polluted the air and water with toxic mercury. These impacts of mining mineral resources can be reduced by including the harmful environmental and health costs in the market prices of goods and services (full-cost pricing), reusing and recycling metal products, redesigning manufacturing processes to cut mineral resource use and waste, reducing mining subsides, and increasing subsidies for recycling, reuse, and finding less harmful substitutes for many products.

CHAPTER 12

Food Production and the Environment

There are two spiritual dangers in not owning a farm. One is the danger of supposing that breakfast comes from the grocery, and the other is that heat comes from the furnace.

ALDO LEOPOLD

This farm in Bavaria, Germany uses solar cells on its roofs to provide its electricity.

Michael Melford/National Geographic Creative

Key Questions

Growing Power—An Urban Food Oasis

A *food desert* is an urban area where people have little or no easy access to grocery stores or other sources of nutritious food. In the United States, an estimated 23.5 million people, including 6.5 million children, live in such urban neighborhoods. They tend to rely on convenience stores and fast-food restaurants that mainly offer high-calorie, highly processed foods that can lead to higher risks of obesity, diabetes, and heart disease.

Will Allen (Figure 12.1) was one of six children of a sharecropper and grew up on a farm in Maryland. He left the farm life for college and a professional basketball career, followed by a successful corporate marketing career. In 1993, Allen decided to return to his roots. He bought the last working farm within the city limits of Milwaukee, Wisconsin, and, in time, created a food oasis in a food desert.

On this small urban plot, Allen developed Growing Power, Inc. As an ecologically based farm, it is a showcase for forms of agriculture that apply all three **scientific prin-** ciples of sustainability (see inside back cover of book). It is powered partly by solar electricity and solar hot water systems and makes use of several greenhouses to capture solar energy for growing food year-round. The farm produces an amazing diversity of crops with about 150 varieties of organic produce. It also produces organically raised chickens, turkeys, goats, fish, and honeybees. And the farm's nutrients are recycled in creative ways. For example, wastes from the farmed fish are used as nutrients to raise some of the crops.

The farm's products are sold locally at Growing Power farm stands throughout the region and to restaurants. Allen also worked with the city of Milwaukee to establish the Farm-to-City Market Basket program through which people can sign up for weekly deliveries of organic produce at modest prices.

In addition, Growing Power runs an educational program in which school children visit the farm and learn about where their food comes from. Allen also trains about 1,000 people every year who want to learn organic farming methods. The farm has also partnered with the city of Milwaukee to create 150 green jobs for unemployed and low-income workers, building greenhouses, and growing food organically. Growing Power has expanded, opening another urban farm in a neighborhood of Chicago, Illinois, and setting up satellite training sites in five other states.

For his creative and energetic efforts, Allen has won several prestigious awards. However, he is most proud of the fact that his urban farm helps to feed more than 10,000 people every year and puts people to work raising good food.

In this chapter, we look at different ways to produce food, the environmental effects of food production, and how we can produce food more sustainably.●

CRITICAL THINKING

How is Growing Power farm a model of sustainable agriculture?

FIGURE 12.1 Will Allen founded Growing Power—a world-renowned urban farm in Milwaukee, Wisconsin.

Courtesy of Growing Power, Inc.

12.1 WHY IS GOOD NUTRITION IMPORTANT?

CONCEPT 12.1A Many people in less-developed countries have health problems from not getting enough food, while many people in more-developed countries have health problems from eating too much food.

CONCEPT 12.1B The greatest obstacles to providing enough food for everyone are poverty, war, bad weather, and climate change.

Many People Suffer from Lasting Hunger and Malnutrition

What foods do you think you should eat in order to live a healthy and enjoyable life? What do you really eat? How do those lists compare?

If you find that what you should eat is not what you are eating, you are not alone. Many of today's health problems are related to eating too much of foods that are not nutritious and not enough of those that are. To maintain good health and resist disease, individuals need fairly large amounts of *macronutrients* (such as carbohydrates, proteins, and fats) and smaller amounts of *micronutrients*—vitamins, such as A, B, C, and E, and minerals, such as iron, iodine, and calcium.

One of every eight people on the planet—nearly 800 million in all—are not getting enough to eat. People who cannot grow or buy enough food to meet their basic energy needs suffer from **chronic undernutrition,** or **hunger,** which threatens their ability to lead healthy and productive lives (Figure 12.2) (**Concept 12.1A**).

Most of the world's hungry people live in low-income, less-developed countries and typically can afford only a low-protein, high-carbohydrate, vegetarian diet consisting mainly of grains such as wheat, rice, and corn (Figure 12.3). In other words, they live low on the food chain (see Figures 3.9 and 3.10, pp. 72 and 73). In most cases, people on such limited diets suffer from **chronic malnutrition,** a condition in which they do not get enough protein and other

FIGURE 12.2 This woman is feeding her child, who was starving because of famine caused by a civil war that has been going on in Somalia, Africa, most of the time since 1991.

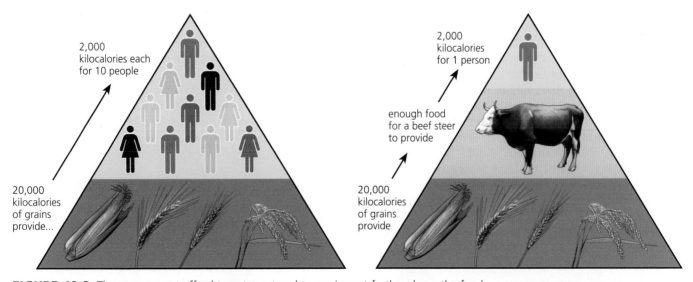

FIGURE 12.3 The poor cannot afford to eat meat and to survive eat further down the food chain on a diet of grain.

key nutrients. This can weaken them, make them more vulnerable to disease, and hinder the normal physical and mental development of children.

In more-developed countries, people living in food deserts, including 23.5 million Americans according to the Centers for Disease Control and Prevention (**Core Case Study**), have a similar problem, except that their diet typically is heavy on cheap food loaded with fats, sugar, and salt.

Perhaps the worst form of food shortage is **famine,** which occurs when there is a severe shortage of food in an area and which can result in mass starvation, many deaths, economic chaos, and social disruption. Famines are usually caused by crop failures from drought, flooding, war (Figure 12.2), and other catastrophic events (**Concept 12.1B**).

According to the United Nations (UN) Food and Agriculture Organization (FAO), in 2015, there were about 795 million chronically undernourished or malnourished people in the world. The UN estimates that at least 3 million children younger than age 5 died from chronic hunger and malnutrition in 2013 (the latest year for which the data are available). That was an average of nearly 6 children per minute dying from these causes. Globally, the number and percentage of people suffering from hunger has been declining since 1992 but there is still a long way to go.

A Closer Look at Micronutrients

About 2 billion people, most of them in less-developed countries, suffer from a deficiency of one or more vitamins and minerals, usually *vitamin A, zinc, iron*, and *iodine* (**Concept 12.1A**). According to the World Health Organization (WHO), at least 250,000 children younger than age 6, most of them in less-developed countries, go blind every year from a lack of vitamin A. Within a year, more than half of them die. Providing children with adequate vitamin A and zinc could save an estimated 145,000 lives per year.

Having too little *iron* (Fe)—a component of the hemoglobin that transports oxygen in the blood—is a condition called *anemia*. It causes fatigue, makes infection more likely, and increases a woman's chances of dying from hemorrhage in childbirth. According to the WHO, one of every five people in the world—mostly women and children in less-developed countries—suffers from iron deficiency.

The chemical element *iodine* (I) is essential for proper functioning of the thyroid gland, which produces hormones that control the body's rate of metabolism. Chronic lack of iodine can cause stunted growth, mental retardation, and goiter—a severely swollen thyroid gland that can lead to deafness (Figure 12.4). According to the UN, some 600 million people (almost twice the current US population) suffer from goiter, most of them in less-developed countries. In addition, 26 million children suffer irreversible brain damage every year from lack of iodine.

FIGURE 12.4 This woman suffers from goiter, an enlargement of the thyroid gland, caused by the lack of iodine in her diet.

Health Problems from Eating Too Much

Overnutrition occurs when food energy intake exceeds energy use and causes excess body fat. Too many calories, too little exercise, or both can cause overnutrition.

People who are underfed and underweight and those who are overfed and overweight face similar health problems: *lower life expectancy, greater susceptibility to disease and illness*, and *lower productivity and life quality* (**Concept 12.1A**).

We live in a world where, according to the WHO, about 795 million people face health problems because they do not get enough nutritious food to eat and at least another 2.1 billion (28% of the human population) have health problems stemming largely from eating too much sugar, fat, and salt, leading physically inactive lifestyles, and becoming overweight or obese. In order, the countries with the most overweight and obese people are the United States, China, India, Russia, and Brazil.

In the United States, according to 2015 statistics from the US Centers for Disease Control and Prevention (CDC), about 72% of all adults over age 20 are obese (38%) or overweight (34%) and 33% of all children ages 2–19 are overweight or obese. A study by Columbia University and the Robert Wood Johnson Foundation found that obesity plays an important role in nearly one in five deaths in the United States from heart disease, stroke, type 2 diabetes, and some forms of cancer.

Poverty Is a Root Cause of Hunger and Malnutrition

Poverty prevents people from growing or buying enough nutritious food to meet their basic needs. This prevents them from having **food security,** or daily access to enough nutritious food to live healthy lives. This is not surprising given that 2.6 billion people struggle to live on $3.10 a day and 1 billion people struggle to live on $1.90 a day. Other obstacles to food security are war, corruption, bad weather (such as prolonged drought, flooding, and heat waves), and climate change (**Concept 12.1B**).

Each day, there are about 249,000 more people at the world's dinner tables, and by 2050, there will likely be at least 2.4 billion more people to feed. Most of these newcomers will be born in the major cities of less-developed countries. A critical question is, how will we feed the projected 9.9 billion people in 2050 without causing serious harm to the environment? We explore possible answers to this question throughout this chapter.

CHECKPOINT FOR UNDERSTANDING 12.1

1. Describe the health implications for deficiencies in vitamin A, iron, zinc, and iodine.

2. Undernutrition and overnutrition both result in the same health issues. What are they?

12.2 HOW IS FOOD PRODUCED?

CONCEPT 12.2 We have used high-input industrialized agriculture and lower-input traditional agriculture to greatly increase food supplies.

Food Production Has Increased Dramatically

Three systems supply most of the world's food, using about 40% of the world's land. *Croplands* produce grains—primarily rice, wheat, and corn—that provide about 77% of the world's food. The rest is provided by *rangelands*, *pastures*, and *feedlots* that produce meat and meat products and *fisheries* and *aquaculture* (fish farming), which supply fish and shellfish.

These three systems depend on a small number of plant and animal species. Of the estimated 30,000 edible plant species, 14 supply about 90% of the world's food calories. At least half the world's people survive primarily by eating three grain crops—*rice, wheat,* and *corn*—because they cannot afford meat. Only a few species of mammals and fish provide most of the world's meat and seafood.

Such food specialization puts us in a vulnerable position, if any of the small number of crop strains, livestock breeds, and fish and shellfish species we depend on become depleted because of disease, environmental degradation, climate change, or other factors. Food specialization violates the biodiversity **principle of sustainability**, which calls for depending on a vari-

ety of food sources as an ecological insurance policy against changing environmental conditions.

Despite such genetic vulnerability, since 1960, there has been a staggering increase in global food production from all three of the major food production systems (**Concept 12.2**). Three major technological advances have been especially important: **(1)** the development of **irrigation,** a mix of methods by which water is supplied to crops by artificial means; **(2) synthetic fertilizers**—manufactured chemicals that contain nutrients such as nitrogen, phosphorus, potassium, calcium, and several others; and **(3) synthetic pesticides**—chemicals manufactured to kill or control populations of organisms that interfere with crop production.

Industrialized Crop Production Relies on High-Input Monocultures

There are two major types of agriculture: industrialized and traditional. **Industrialized agriculture,** or **high-input agriculture,** uses heavy equipment (Figure 12.5) along with large amounts of financial capital, fossil fuels, water, commercial inorganic fertilizers, and pesticides to produce single crops, or *monocultures*. The major goal of industrialized agriculture is to steadily increase each crop's **yield**—the amount of food produced per unit of land. Industrialized agriculture is practiced on 25% of all cropland, mostly in more-developed countries, and produces about 80% of the world's food (**Concept 12.2**).

Plantation agriculture is a form of industrialized agriculture used primarily in less-developed tropical countries. It involves growing cash crops such as bananas, coffee, vegetables, soybeans (mostly to feed livestock; see Figure 1.5, p. 8), sugarcane (to produce sugar and ethanol fuel), and palm oil (to produce cooking oil and biodiesel fuel). These crops are grown on large monoculture plantations, mostly for export to more-developed countries.

Traditional Agriculture Often Relies on Low-Input Polyculture

Traditional, low-input agriculture provides about 20% of the world's food crops on about 75% of its cultivated land, mostly in less-developed countries. It takes two basic forms. **Traditional subsistence agriculture** combines energy from the sun with the labor of humans and draft animals to produce enough crops for a farm family's survival, with little left over to sell or store as a reserve for hard times. In **traditional intensive agriculture,** farmers try to obtain higher crop yields by increasing their inputs of human and draft animal labor, animal manure for fertilizer, and water. If weather cooperates, farmers can produce enough food to feed their families and have some left over to sell for income.

FIGURE 12.5 This farmer, harvesting a wheat crop in the Midwestern United States, relies on expensive heavy equipment and uses large amounts of seed, manufactured inorganic fertilizer and pesticides, and fossil fuels to produce the crop.

Some traditional farmers focus on cultivating a single crop, but many grow several crops on the same plot simultaneously, a practice known as **polyculture.** This method relies on solar energy and natural fertilizers such as animal manure. The various crops mature at different times. This provides food year-round and keeps the topsoil covered to reduce erosion from wind and water. Polyculture also lessens the need for fertilizer and water because root systems at different depths in the soil capture nutrients and moisture efficiently. Also, weeds have trouble competing with the multitude and density of crop plants, and this crop diversity reduces the chance of losing most or all of the year's food supply to pests, bad weather, and other misfortunes.

One type of polyculture is known as *slash-and-burn agriculture.* This type of subsistence agriculture involves burning and clearing small plots in tropical forests, growing a variety of crops for a few years until the soil is depleted of nutrients, and then shifting to other plots to begin the process again. In parts of South America and Africa, some traditional farmers grow as many as 20 different crops together on small cleared plots.

Organic Agriculture Is on the Rise

In recent years, there has been increased use of **organic agriculture** in which crops are grown without the use of synthetic pesticides, synthetic inorganic fertilizers, or genetically engineered seed varieties. To be classified as *organically grown,* animals must be raised on 100% organic feed without the use of antibiotics or growth hormones. Growing Power (**Core Case Study**) has become a well-known model for such food production. Figure 12.6 compares organic agriculture with industrialized agriculture.

In the United States, by law, a label of *100 percent organic* (or *USDA Certified Organic*) means that a product is produced only by organic methods and contains all organic ingredients. About 13,000 of the 2.2 million farms in the United States are USDA-certified organic. Products labeled *organic* must contain at least 95% organic ingredients. Those labeled *made with organic ingredients* must contain at least 70% organic ingredients. The word *natural* has no requirement for organic ingredients and is primarily used as an advertising ploy.

Industrialized Agriculture

Uses synthetic inorganic fertilizers and sewage sludge to supply plant nutrients

Makes use of synthetic chemical pesticides

Uses conventional and genetically modified seeds

Depends on nonrenewable fossil fuels (mostly oil and natural gas)

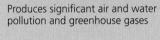

Produces significant air and water pollution and greenhouse gases

Is globally export-oriented

Uses antibiotics and growth hormones to produce meat and meat products

Organic Agriculture

Emphasizes prevention of soil erosion and the use of organic fertilizers such as animal manure and compost, but no sewage sludge, to supply plant nutrients

Employs crop rotation and biological pest control

Uses no genetically modified seeds

Reduces fossil fuel use and increases use of renewable energy such as solar and wind power for generating electricity

Produces less air and water pollution and greenhouse gases

Is regionally and locally oriented

Uses no antibiotics or growth hormones to produce meat and meat products

FIGURE 12.6 Major differences between industrialized agriculture and organic agriculture.

Partly because organic farming is more labor intensive, organically grown foods tend to cost more than conventionally produced food. However, Will Allen and other Growing Power farmers (**Core Case Study**) are learning how to use sustainable farming methods to get higher yields of a variety of organic crops at affordable prices.

A Closer Look at Industrialized Crop Production

Farmers have two ways to produce more food: farming more land or getting higher yields from existing cropland. Since 1950, about 88% of the dramatic increase in global grain production has come from using high-input industrialized agriculture to increase crop yields.

This process, called the **green revolution,** involves three steps. *First*, develop and plant monocultures of selectively bred or genetically engineered high-yield varieties of key crops such as rice, wheat, and corn. *Second*, produce high yields using large inputs of water, synthetic inorganic fertilizers, and pesticides. *Third*, increase the number of crops grown per year on a plot of land. Between 1950 and 1970, in what was called the *first green revolution*, this high-input approach dramatically raised crop yields in most of the world's more-developed countries, especially the United States (see the Case Study that follows).

In the *second green revolution*, which began in 1967, fast-growing varieties of rice and wheat, specially bred for tropical and subtropical climates, have been introduced into middle-income, less-developed countries such as India, China, and Brazil. Producing more food on less land in such countries has helped to protect biodiversity by preserving large areas of forests, grasslands, and wetlands that might otherwise be used for farming.

An important factor in expanded industrialized crop production has been the use of **farm subsidies,** or government payments and tax breaks intended to help farmers stay in business and increase their yields. In the United States, most subsidies go to corporate farming operations for raising corn, wheat, soybeans, and cotton on an industrial scale. US government records show that in recent years, 74% of all subsidies went to just 10% of all US farmers.

CASE STUDY

Industrialized Food Production in the United States

In the United States, industrialized farming has evolved into *agribusinesses*. A few giant multinational corporations increasingly control the growing, processing, distribution, and sale of food in US and global markets. In total annual sales, agriculture is bigger than the country's automotive, steel, and housing industries combined. Yet, because of advances in technology, the numbers of US farms and farmers have dropped as production has risen. As a result, the average US farmer now feeds 129 people compared to 19 people in the 1940s.

Terrestrial Primary Productivity

Without producers to harness light energy and convert it into chemical bond energy, there could be no consumers. Gross productivity is the rate at which an ecosystem's producers capture and store a given amount of chemical energy as biomass in a given length of time. Plants are able to fix carbon into organic molecules, but they use some of these molecules during respiration to meet their own energy needs. Remember that plants create their own food via photosynthesis, but utilize that chemical bond energy during respiration. *Net primary productivity* is what is left over—the cellulose, starch, glucose, and other plant materials that serve as chemical bond energy for organisms at the next trophic level.

The *net primary productivity efficiency* of crops such as corn and wheat can be calculated when the values for *insolation energy* (the solar energy the crop receives), plant respiration loss, and gross productivity of the crop are known.

$$\text{Net Primary Productivity (NPP)} = \text{Gross productivity} - \text{Respiration loss}$$

$$\text{NPP Efficiency } (E) = \frac{\text{NPP}}{\text{Insolation energy}} \times 100$$

FRQ Application

A wheat field in North Dakota has an insolation energy of 4,800,000 calories/m²/day. The gross productivity of the wheat is 0.042 grams/cm²/day and the respiration loss is 25%. One gram of wheat is equivalent to 340 calories.

Calculate the net primary productivity of the wheat. Since the respiration loss is 25%, then subtracting away 25% of the gross productivity gives the NPP.

$$\text{NPP} = 0.042 \text{ grams/cm}^2/\text{day} - (0.25 \times 0.0420 \text{ grams/cm}^2/\text{day}) =$$

$$0.042 \text{ grams/cm}^2/\text{day} - 0.0105 \text{ grams/cm}^2/\text{day} = 0.0315 \text{ grams/cm}^2/\text{day}$$

Next, to find the efficiency of photosynthesis by the wheat, the given information requires a conversion of wheat grams to calories, and cm² to m² (remember that 1 square meter is equal to 10,000 square centimeters [100 x 100 = 10,000 or $10^2 \times 10^2 = 10^4$]):

$$E = \frac{(0.0315 \text{ grams} / \text{cm}^2 / \text{day})(10^4 \text{cm}^2 / \text{m}^2)(340 \text{ calories} / \text{gram})}{4,800,000 \text{ calories} / \text{m}^2 / \text{day}} \times 100 = 2.23\% \text{ efficient}$$

Set up this way, all units cancel, leaving a ratio of the energy held in the grain (in calories) compared to the input of insolation energy (in calories).

When compared to the energy input (4,800,000 calories/m²/day of sunlight), the output in calories of chemical bond energy in the grain was only a sunlight-to-biomass conversion of 2.2%. So what happened to the rest of the energy? Almost half of the light energy falling on the leaf are photons not available to drive photosynthesis because they are not in the right wavelength range. About a third are not completely absorbed and hit other leaf components rather than the chloroplasts, and not all of the products produced during the light reaction are efficiently converted to glucose.

1 Percentage of the US workforce who are farmers—down from 18% in 1910

Since 1960, US industrialized agriculture has more than doubled the yields of key crops such as wheat, corn, and soybeans that are grown for profit without the need for cultivating more land. Such yield increases have saved large areas of US forests, grasslands, and wetlands from being converted to farmland.

Because of the efficiency of US agriculture, Americans spend the lowest percentage of disposable income in the world—an average of 9%—on food. By contrast, low-income people in less-developed countries typically spend 50–70% of their income on food, according to the FAO.

However, because of a number of *hidden costs* related to food production and consumption, most American consumers are not aware that their actual food costs are much higher than the market prices they pay. Such costs include taxes to pay for farm subsidies and the costs of pollution and environmental degradation, and higher health insurance bills related to the harmful health effects of industrialized agriculture.

Genetically Modified Foods

For centuries, farmers have used cross-breeding through artificial selection to produce higher yields and improved varieties of crops and livestock animals. Traditional cross-breeding is a slow process and limited to organisms that are genetically similar.

Genetic engineering allows scientists to artificially insert traits of one species into the genome of another species. An organism's genome is the complete set of genes contained in each cell of that organism. *Gene splicing* is the method used to give insect-resistance to corn, a longer shelf-life to tomatoes, and create faster growing salmon. Figure 12.A shows how gene splicing works:

Compared to traditional crossbreeding, developing a new crop variety through gene splicing takes about half the time, costs less, and allows the insertion of a gene from any other organism into a plant or animal cell. Half the world's genetically modified (GM) crops are planted in the United States. The European Union, however, restricts the use of GM seeds and importation of products containing GM food. Foods certified as organic may not use genetically modified organisms.

Figure 12.B summarizes the potential benefits and potential drawbacks of GM crops. It is still too early for scientists to know the long-term ecological and human health impacts of using genetically modified organisms (GMOs).

Companies producing GM crops and animals claim that this technology may have the potential to increase food production to meet an exponentially growing human population. So far, however, studies show that GM crops are not resulting in significant increases in yield.

GM crops and the herbicides used with them could also threaten biodiversity through their impact on pollinator species and the subsequent effects on other plants and animals. Genes that have been engineered can spread to nonengineered species, reducing biodiversity of food crops.

An economic disadvantage to farmers is that seed companies that develop the GM seeds essentially "rent" the seeds to farmers, prohibiting them from saving seeds for the next year's crops as farmers have traditionally done for centuries. Farmers who save seeds risk being sued for violating company patents.

FRQ Application

Question: **Identify** and **discuss** ONE benefit of GM food crops, and ONE drawback of GM food crops.

Possible Response: A benefit of genetically modifying a food crop is that genes can be inserted that result in a faster growing plant. This would result in the ability to better feed an exponentially growing human population. A drawback of genetically modifying a food crop to be herbicide-resistant would be increased use of herbicides used in conjunction with that crop. Herbicides could be ingested when consuming these foods, and it can also lead to increased herbicide-resistant weeds that evolve in response to increased exposure to herbicides.

Possible Response: A benefit of genetically modifying a food crop could be to insert a gene making it pest-resistant. A bad taste or compound toxic to a specific pest would decrease the amount of plants lost to pests, an economic advantage to farmers. A drawback of genetically modifying a food crop to make it pest-resistant is that toxins that could end up in foods might lead to inflammation and other health risks in some consumers.

Splicing Genes Together

Employing genetic engineering, researchers can take certain genes from a source organism and put them into another plant or animal.

An Example of Genetic Engineering:

1 Scientists take *Bacillus thuringiensis*, a commonly occurring soil bacteria...

2 ...and use enzymes to remove the Bt gene from it, which produces a protein that turns toxic in the digestive tract of caterpillars.

3 The Bt gene is then incorporated into the chromosomes of cotton and corn, killing caterpillars that feed upon these plants.

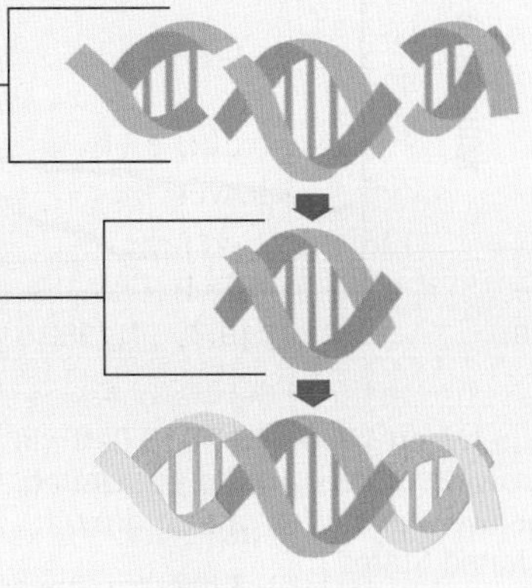

SOURCE: North Carolina State University, College of Agriculture and Life Sciences

Figure 12.A Researchers use gene splicing to manipulate the genetic traits of organisms.

Trade-Offs

GM Crops and Foods

Potential Benefits	Possible Drawbacks
May need less fertilizer, pesticides, and water	Have unpredictable genetic and ecological effects
Can be resistant to insects, disease, frost, and drought	May put toxins in food
Can grow faster and could raise yields	Could repel or harm pollinators
May tolerate higher levels of herbicides	Can promote pesticide-resistant insects, herbicide-resistant weeds, and plant diseases
Could have longer shelf life	Could disrupt seed market and reduce biodiversity

FIGURE 12.B Use of GM crops and foods has advantages and disadvantages. *Critical thinking:* Which two advantages and which two disadvantages do you think are the most important? Why?

Top: Lenar Musin/Shutterstock.com. Bottom: oksix/Shutterstock.com.

Meat Consumption Has Grown Steadily

Meat and animal products such as eggs and milk are sources of high-quality protein and represent the world's second major food-producing system. Between 1950 and 2014, global meat production grew more than sixfold, according to the FAO (Figure 12.7, left).

Since 1974, the total global consumption of meat and meat products has more than doubled. Globally, the three most widely consumed meats are, in order, pork, poultry (chicken and turkey), and beef. Total meat consumption is likely to double again by 2050 as incomes rise in rapidly developing countries. For example, meat consumption in China increased tenfold between 1978 and 2015, while it leveled off in the United States (Figure 12.7, right).

About half of the world's meat comes from livestock grazing on grass in unfenced rangelands and enclosed pastures. The other half is produced through an industrialized factory farm system. It involves raising large numbers of animals bred to gain weight quickly, mostly in *feedlots* (Figure 12.8) or in crowded pens and cages in huge buildings called *concentrated animal feeding operations* (*CAFOs*), also called *factory farms* (Figure 12.9). In these facilities, the animals are fed grain, soybeans, fishmeal, or fish oil, and some of this feed is doctored with growth hormones and antibiotics to accelerate livestock growth.

Fish and Shellfish Production Are Growing Rapidly

The world's third major food-producing system consists of fisheries and aquaculture. A **fishery** is a concentration of a particular aquatic species suitable for commercial harvesting in a given ocean area or inland body of water. Today, 4.4 million fishing boats hunt for and harvest fish and shellfish from the world's oceans. They use global satellite positioning equipment, sonar fish-finding devices, huge nets, long fishing lines, spotter planes and drones, and refrigerated factory ships that can process and freeze their enormous catches. Figure 12.10 shows the major methods used in the commercial harvesting of marine fisheries and shellfish.

Fish and shellfish are also produced through **aquaculture** or **fish farming** (Figure 12.11). It is the practice of raising fish in freshwater ponds, lakes, reservoirs, and rice paddies, and in underwater cages in coastal and deeper ocean waters.

According to the FAO, about 87% of the world's ocean fisheries are being harvested at full capacity (57%) or are overfished (30%). Some fishery scientists warn that failure to reduce overfishing and ocean acidification and to slow climate change could severely threaten food security for roughly 3 billion people who now depend on fish for at least 20% of their animal protein.

Between 1980 and 2014, the amount of fish and shellfish produced globally through aquaculture grew almost 12-fold while the global wild catch leveled off and declined. Asia accounted for 88% (with China alone accounting for 60%) of the world's aquaculture production in 2014.

Most of the world's aquaculture involves raising species that feed on algae or other plants—mainly carp in China, catfish in the United States, and tilapia and shellfish in a number of countries. However, the farming of meat-eating species such as shrimp and salmon is growing rapidly, especially in more-developed countries. Such species are often fed fishmeal and fish oil produced from other fish and their wastes.

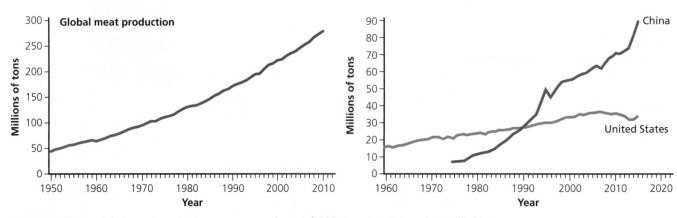

FIGURE 12.7 Global meat production grew more than sixfold between 1950 and 2015 (left). In China, meat consumption has grown tenfold since 1975 while growing more slowly in the United States. **Data analysis:** Using the right-hand graph, estimate the average annual rate of growth in consumption between 1980 and 2015 for China and for the United States.

(Compiled by the authors using data from US Department of Agriculture, Worldwatch Institute, UN Food and Agriculture Organization, and Earth Policy Institute.)

FIGURE 12.8 *Industrialized beef production:* On this cattle feedlot in Arizona, thousands of cattle are fattened on grain for a few months before being slaughtered.

FIGURE 12.9 This concentrated chicken feeding operation is located in Iowa (USA). Such operations can house up to 125,000 chickens.

Industrialized Food Production Requires Huge Inputs of Energy

Industrialized food production has been made possible by use of fossil fuels. Energy—mostly from oil and natural gas—is required to run farm machinery and fishing vessels, to pump irrigation water for crops, and to produce synthetic pesticides and synthetic inorganic fertilizers. Fossil fuels are also used to process food and transport it long distances within and between countries. Agriculture uses about 17% of all the energy used in the United States, more than any other industry.

When we consider the energy used to grow, store, process, package, transport, refrigerate, and cook all plant and animal food, it takes about 10 units of fossil fuel energy to put 1 unit of food energy on the table in the United States. Also, according to a study led by ecological economist Peter Tyedmers, the world's fishing fleets use about 12.5 units of energy to put 1 unit of food energy from seafood on the table. In other words, today's food production systems operate with a large net energy loss.

CHECKPOINT FOR UNDERSTANDING 12.2

1. Identify the three systems that provide most of our food.

2. What three strategies increased food production during the first green revolution?

3. Discuss the benefits and drawbacks of genetically modified foods.

4. Explain why there has been a significant increase in aquaculture.

5. Discuss the relationship between food production and fossil fuels.

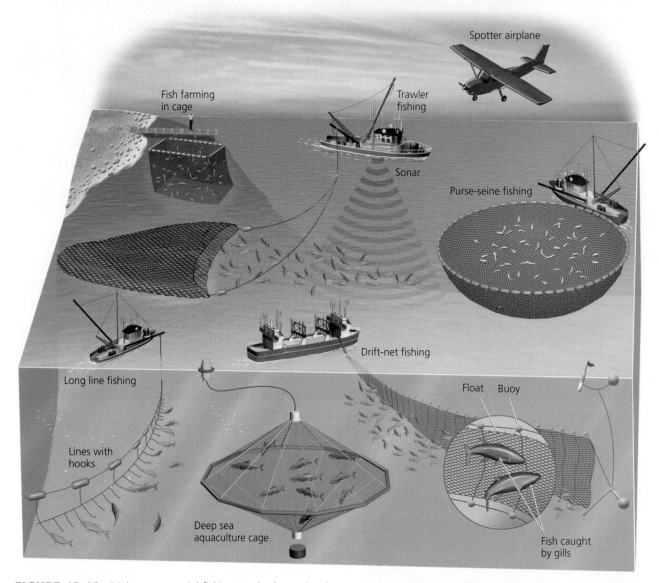

FIGURE 12.10 Major commercial fishing methods used to harvest various marine species, along with some methods used to raise fish through aquaculture.

12.3 WHAT ARE THE ENVIRONMENTAL EFFECTS OF INDUSTRIALIZED FOOD PRODUCTION?

CONCEPT 12.3 Future food production may be limited by soil erosion and degradation, desertification, irrigation water shortages, air and water pollution, climate change, and loss of biodiversity.

Producing Food Has Major Environmental Impacts

Although industrialized agriculture has provided many benefits, many analysts point out that it has greater overall harmful environmental impacts (Figure 12.12) than any other human activity. These environmental effects may limit future food production (**Concept 12.3**).

According to a study by 27 experts assembled by the United Nations Environment Programme (UNEP), agriculture uses massive amounts of the world's resources and has a high environmental impact. It accounts for about 70% of the freshwater removed from aquifers and surface waters, worldwide. It also uses about 38% of the world's ice-free land, emits about 25% of the world's greenhouse gas emissions, and produces about 60% of all water pollution. As a result, many analysts view today's industrialized agriculture as environmentally and economically unsustainable. Let's look closer at the reasons for this conclusion.

Topsoil Erosion Is a Serious Problem

Topsoil, the fertile top layer of many soils (Figure 11.5, p. 308), is a potentially renewable resource and provides vital ecosystem services. Soil is literally the foundation of life on land. Specifically, the fertile top layer, or *topsoil,* is a

FIGURE 12.11 *Aquaculture:* Shrimp farms on the southern coast of Thailand.

Natural Capital Degradation

Food Production

Biodiversity Loss	**Soil**	**Water**	**Air Pollution**	**Human Health**

Biodiversity Loss	Soil	Water	Air Pollution	Human Health
Conversion of grasslands, forests, and wetlands to crops or rangeland	Erosion	Aquifer depletion	Emissions of greenhouse gases CO_2 from fossil fuel use, N_2O from inorganic fertilizer use, and methane (CH_4) from cattle	Nitrates in drinking water (blue baby)
Fish kills from pesticide runoff	Loss of fertility	Increased runoff, sediment pollution, and flooding from cleared land		Pesticide residues in water, food, and air
Killing of wild predators to protect livestock	Salinization	Pollution from pesticides	Other air pollutants from fossil fuel use and pesticide sprays	Livestock wastes in drinking and swimming water
Loss of agrobiodiversity replaced by monoculture strains	Waterlogging	Algal blooms and fish kills caused by runoff of fertilizers and farm wastes		Bacterial contamination of meat
	Desertification			

FIGURE 12.12 Food production has a number of harmful environmental effects (**Concept 12.3**).
Critical thinking: Which item in each of these categories do you think is the most harmful?

Left: Orientaly/Shutterstock.com. Left center: pacopi/Shutterstock.com. Center: Tim McCabe/USDA Natural Resources Conservation Service. Right center: Mikhail Malyshev/Shutterstock.com. Right: B Brown/Shutterstock.com.

FIGURE 12.13 Natural capital degradation: Flowing water from rainfall is the leading cause of topsoil erosion as seen on this farm in the US state of Tennessee (left). Severe water erosion can become gully erosion, which has damaged this cropland in western Iowa (right).

Left: Tim McCabe/USDA Natural Resources Conservation Service. Right: © USDA Natural Resources Conservation Service.

Lynn Betts/USDA Natural Resources Conservation Service

FIGURE 12.14 Wind is an important cause of topsoil erosion in dry areas that are not covered by vegetation such as this bare crop field in the US state of Iowa.

vital component of natural capital, because it stores the water and nutrients that plants need and recycles these nutrients endlessly as long as they are not removed faster than natural processes replenish them. Thus, sustainable agriculture begins with promoting healthy soils.

One major problem related to agriculture is **soil erosion**—the movement of soil components, especially surface litter and topsoil (Figure 11.5, p. 308) from one place to another by the actions of wind and water. Some topsoil erosion is natural, but much of it is caused by human activities, including agriculture.

Flowing water causes erosion of three types. *Sheet erosion* occurs on level land and removes thin layers, or sheets, of topsoil (Figure 12.13, left). *Rill erosion* is caused by tiny streams (rivulets) of water that carve small chan-

nels, or rills, in topsoil. *Gully erosion* is caused by larger streams of water removing enough soil to create gullies (Figure 12.13, right). The second largest cause of erosion is wind, which loosens and blows topsoil particles away, especially in areas with a dry climate and relatively flat land not covered by vegetation (Figure 12.14).

In undisturbed, vegetated ecosystems, the roots of plants help to anchor topsoil and to reduce erosion. However, topsoil can erode when soil-holding grasses, trees, and other vegetation are removed through activities such as farming, deforestation and overgrazing. A joint survey by the UNEP and the World Resources Institute indicated that topsoil is eroding faster than it forms on about one-third of the world's cropland (Figure 12.15). Since 1970, partly because of soil erosion, about one-third of the world's cropland has been abandoned as too degraded for growing crops.

The rise of industrialized agriculture has exposed large areas of cropland to severe topsoil erosion, which causes three major harmful effects:

- Loss of soil fertility through depletion of plant nutrients in topsoil.

- Water pollution in surface waters where eroded topsoil ends up as sediment and can cause eutrophication (Figure 6.16, p. 167) by overloading the water with plant nutrients.

- Release of carbon stored in the soil to into the atmosphere as CO_2, which contributes to atmospheric warming and climate change.

Soil pollution is also a problem in some parts of the world. Some of the chemicals emitted into the atmosphere

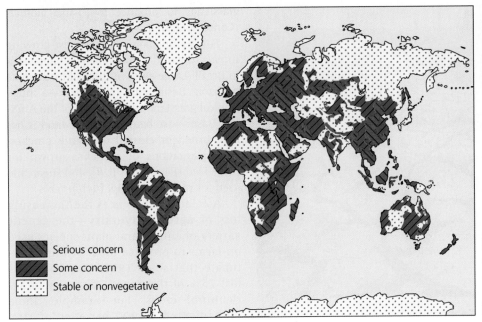

FIGURE 12.15 Natural capital degradation: Topsoil erosion is a serious problem in some parts of the world. *Critical thinking:* Can you see any geographical pattern associated with this problem?

(Compiled by the authors using data from the U.N. Environment Programme and the World Resources Institute.)

Serious concern

Some concern

Stable or nonvegetative

©Cengage Learning, 2014

by industrial and power plants and by motor vehicles can pollute soil and irrigation water. Pesticides can also contaminate soil. In 2014, China's environment ministry reported that an estimated 19% of China's arable (farmable) land is contaminated, especially with toxic metals such as cadmium, arsenic, and nickel, and that about 2.5% of the country's cropland is too contaminated to grow food safely.

Drought and Human Activities Are Degrading Drylands

Drylands in regions with arid and semiarid climates occupy about 40% of the world's land area and are home to some 2 billion people. A major threat to food security in some of the world's water-short drylands is **desertification**—the process in which the productive potential of topsoil falls by 10% or more because of a combination of prolonged drought and human activities that expose topsoil to erosion.

Desertification can be moderate to severe, and in extreme cases desertification can expand existing deserts or create new deserts. As climate has changed over thousands of years, deserts have naturally expanded and contracted. However, human use of land for agriculture has accelerated desertification by excessive plowing, overgrazing, and deforestation.

In the 1930s, the United States experienced a decade of drought in the Midwestern states. Along with poor cultivation practices encouraged by the government, severe wind erosion led to the formation of a *dust bowl*, forcing farmers to abandon the land and move to other states. Desertification is currently occurring in Africa, south of the Sahara Desert and in northern China and southern Mongolia.

Topsoil can also be degraded by repeatedly growing crops without replenishing nutrients, and by allowing livestock to trample and overgraze land. Climate change is expected to prolong drought, increasing desertification and threatening food supplies around the world.

Excessive Irrigation Can Pollute Soil and Water

Irrigation accounts for about 70% of the water that humanity uses. Currently, the 16% of the world's cropland that is irrigated produces about 44% of the world's food.

However, irrigation has a downside. Most irrigation water is a dilute solution of various salts, such as sodium chloride, that are picked up as the water flows over or through soil and rocks. Irrigation water that is not absorbed into the topsoil evaporates and leaves behind a thin crust of dissolved mineral salts in the topsoil. Repeated applications of irrigation water in dry climates can lead to an accumulation of salts in the upper soil layers—a soil degradation process called **soil salinization** (Figure 12.16). It stunts crop growth, lowers crop yields, and can eventually kill plants and ruin the land.

Another problem with irrigation is **waterlogging,** in which water accumulates underground and gradually raises the water table. This can occur when farmers apply large amounts of irrigation water in an effort to reduce salinization by leaching salts deeper into the soil. Waterlogging lowers the productivity of crop plants and kills them after prolonged exposure because it deprives plants of the oxygen they need to survive.

Perhaps the biggest problem resulting from excessive irrigation in agriculture is that it has contributed to depletion of groundwater and surface water supplies in many areas of the world. We discuss this in Chapter 13.

FIGURE 12.16 Natural capital degradation: White alkaline salts have displaced crops that once grew on this heavily irrigated land in the US state of Colorado.

Industrialized Crop Production Contributes to Pollution and Climate Change

Eroded topsoil flows as sediments into streams, lakes, and wetlands where it can smother fish and shellfish and clog irrigation ditches, boat channels, reservoirs, and lakes. This problem gets worse when the eroded sediment contains pesticide residues that can be ingested by aquatic organisms and in some cases biomagnified to much higher concentrations within food webs (see Figure 9.13, p. 247).

Farmers contribute to pollution through *overfertilizing* their fields. Globally, the use of fertilizers has grown 45-fold since 1940. Whether using natural fertilizers such as animal manure or synthetic fertilizers, excess fertilizers on a farm field can run off into waterways and contribute to eutrophication (see Figure 6.16, p. 167). Nitrates in fertilizer can also percolate down through the soil into aquifers where they can contaminate groundwater used for drinking. According to the FAO, fully one-third of all water pollution from the runoff of nitrogen and phosphorus is due to excessive use of synthetic fertilizers.

Agricultural activities cause a great deal of air pollution and account for more than a quarter of all human-generated emissions of carbon dioxide (CO_2). This is helping to warm the atmosphere and contributing to climate change, which is making some areas unsuitable for growing crops.

Producing Food Reduces Biodiversity

Natural biodiversity and some ecosystem services are threatened when forests are cleared and when croplands replace grasslands to produce food and biofuels (**Concept 12.3**).

For example, one of the fastest-growing threats to world's biodiversity is happening in Brazil. Large areas of tropical forest in its Amazon Basin and in cerrado—a huge tropical grassland region south of the Amazon Basin—are being lost. This land is being burned or cleared for cattle ranches, large plantations of soybeans grown for cattle feed (Figure 1.5, p. 8), and sugarcane used for making ethanol fuel for cars.

A related problem is the increasing loss of **agrobiodiversity**—the genetic variety of animal and plant species used on farms to produce food. Scientists estimate that since 1900, the world has lost 75% of the genetic diversity of agricultural crops. For example, India once planted 30,000 varieties of rice. Now more than 75% of its rice production comes in only 10 varieties, and soon most of its production might come from just one or two varieties. In the United States, about 97% of the food plant varieties available to farmers in the 1940s no longer exist, except perhaps in small amounts in seed banks and occasional home gardens.

In losing agrobiodiversity, ecologists warn that farming practices are rapidly shrinking the world's genetic "library" of plant varieties, which are critical for increasing food yields. This failure to preserve agrobiodiversity is a serious violation of the biodiversity **principle of sustainability** that could reduce the sustainability of food production (**Concept 12.3**).

Efforts are being made to save endangered varieties of crops and wild plant species important to the world's food supply. Individual plants and seeds from endangered crop varieties and wild plant species are stored in about 1,400 refrigerated seed banks. They are also stored in agricultural research centers and botanical gardens scattered around the world. However, power failures, fires, storms, wars, and unintentional disposal of seeds can cause irreversible losses of these stored plants and seeds. The world's most secure seed bank is the underground Svalbard Global Seed Vault, the so-called "doomsday seed vault," which was carved into the Arctic permafrost on a frozen Norwegian arctic island near the North Pole (Figure 12.17). It is being stocked with duplicates of much of the world's seed collections.

However, the seeds of many plants cannot be stored successfully in seed banks. Because stored seeds do not remain alive indefinitely, they must be planted and germinated periodically, and new seeds must be collected for storage. Unless this is done regularly, seed banks become seed morgues.

FIGURE 12.17 The Svalbard Global Seed Vault is the most secure seed bank in the world.

Jim Richardson/National Geographic Creative

Limits to Expanding Green Revolutions

So far, several factors have limited the success of the green revolutions and may limit them more in the future (**Concept 12.3**). For example, without large inputs of water and synthetic inorganic fertilizers and pesticides, most green revolution and genetically engineered crop varieties produce yields that are no higher (and are sometimes lower) than those from traditional strains. These high inputs also cost too much for most subsistence farmers in less-developed countries.

Scientists point out that where such inputs do increase yields, there comes a point where yields stop increasing because of the inability of crop plants to take up nutrients from additional fertilizer and irrigation water. This helps to explain the slowdown in the rate of growth in global yields for most major crops since 1990.

Can we expand the green revolutions by irrigating more cropland? Since 1978, the amount of irrigated land per person has been declining, and it is projected to fall much more by 2050. One reason for this is population growth, which is projected to add 2.9 billion more people between 2015 and 2050. Other factors are limited availability of irrigation water, soil salinization, and the fact that most of the world's conventional farmers do not have enough money to irrigate their crops.

Climate change is expected to affect crop yields during this century. Also, mountain glaciers that provide irrigation for many millions of people in China, India, and South America are melting and this will lessen the area of crops that can be irrigated. During this century, fertile croplands in coastal areas, including many of the major rice-growing floodplains and river deltas in Asia, are likely to be flooded by rising sea levels resulting from climate change. Food production could also drop sharply in some major food-producing areas because of longer and more intense droughts and heat waves, also likely resulting from climate change.

Can we increase the food supply by cultivating more land? Farming already uses about 38% of the world's ice-free land surface for croplands and pastures. Clearing more tropical forests and irrigating arid land could more than double the area of the world's cropland. However, massive clearing of forests would decrease biodiversity, speed up climate change and its harmful effects, and increase soil erosion. Also, much of this land has poor soil fertility, steep slopes, or both, and cultivating such land would be expensive and probably not ecologically sustainable.

Crop yields could be increased with the use of conventional or GM crops that are more tolerant of drought, which are still being tested. Commercial fertilizers have played a role in green revolutions, but their use in more-developed countries has reached a level of diminishing returns in terms of increased crop yields. However, there are parts of the world, especially in Africa, where additional fertilizer could boost crop production.

Industrialized Meat Production Harms the Environment

Proponents of industrialized meat production point out that it has increased meat supplies, reduced overgrazing, and kept food prices down. But feedlots and concentrated animal feeding operations (CAFOs) produce widespread harmful health and environmental effects. Analysts point out that meat produced by industrialized agriculture is artificially cheap because most of its harmful environmental and health costs are not included in the market prices of meat and meat products, a violation of the full-cost pricing **principle of sustainability**.

CAFOs and feedlots are truly industrial-scale livestock operations. A large feedlot contains 1,000 or more cattle (Figure 12.8) and large CAFOs can house 2,500 or more hogs or 125,000 or more chickens or turkeys (Figure 12.9).

A major problem with feedlots and CAFOs is that huge amounts of water are used to irrigate the grain crops that feed the livestock. According to waterfootprint.org, producing a quarter-pound hamburger requires 1,700 liters (450 gallons) of water—the equivalent of 15–20 showers for the average person. It takes more water to raise a given amount of beef than it takes to raise the same quantities of pork, chicken, eggs, and milk combined.

Much of this irrigation water is used inefficiently and is helping to deplete groundwater supplies in many areas of the world. Large volumes of water are also used to wash away livestock wastes. Much of this wastewater then flows into streams and other waterways and pollutes those aquatic ecosystems.

According to the USDA, animal waste produced by the American meat industry amounts to about 67 times the amount of waste produced by the country's human population. Ideally, manure from CAFOs should be returned to the soil as a nutrient-rich fertilizer in keeping with the chemical cycling **principle of sustainability**. However, it is often so contaminated with residues of antibiotics and pesticides that it is unfit for use as a fertilizer.

Despite potential contamination, up to half of the manure slurry from CFOs in the United States is applied to nearby fields and creates severe odor problems for people living nearby. Much of the other half of CAFO animal waste is pumped into large lagoons, which eventually leak and pollute nearby surface and groundwater, produce foul odors, and emit large quantities of climate-changing greenhouse gases into the atmosphere.

Industrialized meat production uses large amounts of energy (mostly from oil), which is another source of air pollution and greenhouse gases. Also, as part of their digestion process, cattle and dairy cows release methane (CH_4), a greenhouse gas with about 25 times the warming potential of CO_2 per molecule. According to the FAO study, *Livestock's Long Shadow*, industrialized livestock production generates about 18% of the world's greenhouse gases—more than all of the world's cars, trucks, buses, and planes combined. The entire meat production process contributes 35–40% of the global annual emissions of methane and 65% of all emissions of nitrous oxide (N_2O), a gas with about 300 times the atmospheric warming capacity of CO_2 per molecule.

Another growing problem is the use of antibiotics in industrialized livestock production facilities. The US Food and Drug Administration (FDA) and the Union of Concerned Scientists have estimated that about 80% of all antibiotics used in the United States (and 50% of those in the world) are added to animal feed. This is done to try to prevent the spread of diseases in feedlots and CAFOs and to promote the growth of the animals. This heavy antibiotics use plays a role in the rise of genetic resistance among many disease-causing bacteria (see Figure 4.12, p. 103), which is

Trade-Offs

Feedlots and CAFOs

Advantages	Disadvantages
Increased meat production	Animals unnaturally confined and crowded
Higher profits	Large inputs of grain, fishmeal, water, and fossil fuels
Less land use	Greenhouse gas (CO_2 and CH_4) emissions
Reduced overgrazing	Concentration of animal wastes that can pollute water
Reduced soil erosion	Use of antibiotics can increase genetic resistance to microbes in humans
Protection of biodiversity	

FIGURE 12.18 Use of animal feedlots and confined animal feeding operations has advantages and disadvantages. ***Critical thinking:*** Which single advantage and which single disadvantage do you think are the most important? Why?

Top: Mikhail Malyshev/Shutterstock.com. Bottom: Maria Dryfhout/Shutterstock.com.

resulting in new, more genetically resistant infectious disease organisms, some of which can infect humans.

Figure 12.18 summarizes the advantages and disadvantages of using feedlots and CAFOs.

When livestock are grass-fed, environmental impacts can still be high, especially when forests are cut down or burned to make way for grazing land, as is done in Brazil's Amazon forests. According to an FAO report, overgrazing and erosion by livestock has degraded about 20% of the world's grasslands and pastures. The same report estimated that rangeland grazing and industrialized livestock production has caused about 55% of all topsoil erosion and sediment pollution.

In addition, grass-fed cows emit more of the powerful greenhouse gas methane than do grain-fed cows. Thus, expanding grass-fed production could increase the agricultural contributions to deforestation and climate change.

CONSIDER THIS . . .

CONNECTIONS Meat Production and Aquatic Biodiversity
Synthetic fertilizers are used in the Midwestern United States to produce corn for animal feed and ethanol fuel for cars. Much of this fertilizer washes from cropland and into the Mississippi River, which empties into the Gulf of Mexico. The added nitrate and phosphate nutrients overfertilize the gulf's coastal waters. Each year this leads to oxygen depletion in the gulf's waters, which threatens one-fifth of the nation's seafood yield. In other words, growing corn in the Midwest, largely to feed cattle and fuel cars, degrades aquatic biodiversity and seafood production in the Gulf of Mexico.

Aquaculture Can Harm Aquatic Ecosystems

Aquaculture produces about 42% of the world's seafood and is growing rapidly. The World Bank projected that by 2030, aquaculture will produce 62% of all seafood. However, some analysts warn that the harmful environmental effects of aquaculture could limit its future production potential (**Concept 12.3**).

A major environmental problem associated with aquaculture is that about a third of the wild fish caught from the oceans are used to make the fishmeal and fish oil that are fed to farmed fish and livestock. This is contributing to the depletion of many populations of wild fish that are crucial to marine food webs. Aquaculture now uses 70% of all fishmeal and nearly 90% of all fish oil. To satisfy the growing demand for these products, some countries are scooping up thousands of tons of krill from Antarctic waters every year. Krill form the base of the Antarctic food web (Figure 3.11, p. 73), and thus all species, including endangered penguins and whales, depend on them.

Another problem is that some of the fishmeal and fish oil fed to farm-raised fish is contaminated with long-lived toxins such as PCBs and dioxins that are picked up from the ocean floor. This can contaminate farm-raised fish and people who eat such fish. Some fish farms that raise carnivorous fish such as salmon and tuna also produce large amounts of wastes that pollute aquatic ecosystems and fisheries.

Another source of pollution is the use of pesticides and antibiotics on fish farms. Also, farmed species such as shrimp, salmon, tilapia, and trout have been found to contain five different antibiotics. Use of antibiotics on fish farms presents the same problems as it does in CAFOs and feedlots.

Aquaculture can also destroy or degrade aquatic ecosystems, particularly mangrove forests (Figure 6.8, p. 158). Since aquaculture began growing rapidly in 1990, more than 500,000 hectares (1.2 million acres) of highly productive mangrove forest have been cleared for shrimp farms, according to the Earth Policy Institute. This represents a loss of biodiversity and valuable ecosystem services such as natural flood control in these sensitive coastal areas that are expected to experience severe flooding because of rising sea level caused by climate change.

Figure 12.19 lists the major benefits and drawbacks of aquaculture.

CHECKPOINT FOR UNDERSTANDING 12.3

1. Explain why industrialized agriculture is viewed as unsustainable.

2. Identify the reasons for loss of fertile topsoil.

3. Explain how a growing human population degrades drylands.

4. Explain why expanding the green revolution most likely will not keep up with demand for food.

5. Describe the harmful impacts that are not part of the true cost of industrialized meat production.

6. Identify some of the drawbacks of aquaculture.

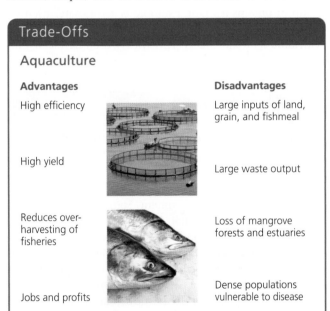

Trade-Offs

Aquaculture

Advantages	Disadvantages
High efficiency	Large inputs of land, grain, and fishmeal
High yield	Large waste output
Reduces over-harvesting of fisheries	Loss of mangrove forests and estuaries
Jobs and profits	Dense populations vulnerable to disease

FIGURE 12.19 Use of aquaculture has advantages and disadvantages. **Critical thinking:** Which single advantage and which single disadvantage do you think are the most important? Why?

Top: Vladislav Gajic/Shutterstock.com. Bottom: Nordling/Shutterstock.com.

12.4 HOW CAN WE PROTECT CROPS FROM PESTS MORE SUSTAINABLY?

CONCEPT 12.4 We can sharply cut pesticide use without decreasing crop yields using a mix of cultivation techniques, biological pest controls, and small amounts of selected chemical pesticides as a last resort (integrated pest management).

Nature Controls the Populations of Most Pests

A **pest** is any species that interferes with human welfare by competing with us for food, invading our homes, lawns, or gardens, destroying building materials, spreading disease, invading ecosystems, or simply being a nuisance. Worldwide, only about 100 species of plants (weeds), animals (mostly insects), fungi, and microbes cause most of the damage to the crops we grow.

In natural ecosystems and in many polyculture crop fields, *natural enemies* (predators, parasites, and disease organisms) control the populations of most potential pest

FIGURE 12.20 Natural capital: This ferocious-looking wolf spider is eating a grasshopper. It is one of many important insect predators that can be killed by some pesticides.

Cathy Keifer/Shutterstock.com

species. This free ecosystem service is an important part of the earth's natural capital. For example, biologists estimate that the world's 40,000 known species of spiders kill far more crop-eating insects every year than humans kill with insecticides. Most spiders, including the wolf spider (Figure 12.20), do not harm humans.

When we clear forests and grasslands, plant monoculture crops, and douse fields with chemicals that kill pests, we upset many of these natural population checks and balances that are in keeping with the biodiversity **principle of sustainability**. Then we must devise ways to protect our monoculture crops, tree plantations, lawns, and golf courses from pests that nature has helped to control at no charge.

Synthetic Pesticides Can Help Control Pest Populations

We have developed a variety of **synthetic pesticides**—chemicals used to kill or control organisms we consider to be pests. They are classified as *insecticides* (insect killers), *herbicides* (weed killers), *fungicides* (fungus killers), and *rodenticides* (rat and mouse killers).

We did not invent the use of chemicals to repel or kill other species. For nearly 225 million years, plants have been producing chemicals to ward off, deceive, or poison the insects and herbivores that feed on them. Scientists have used such chemicals to create *biopesticides* to kill some pests.

A major pest control revolution began in 1939, when entomologist Paul Müller discovered DDT (dichlorodiphenyltrichloroethane)—the first of the so-called *second-generation pesticides* produced in the laboratory. It soon became the world's most-used pesticide, and since then, chemists have created hundreds of other pesticides.

Some second-generation pesticides have turned out to be highly hazardous for birds and other forms of wildlife. In 1962, biologist Rachel Carson published her famous book *Silent Spring*, sounding a warning that eventually led to strict controls on the use of DDT and several other widely used pesticides.

Since 1950, synthetic pesticide use has increased more than 50-fold and most of today's pesticides are 10–100 times more toxic to pests than those used in the 1950s. Some synthetic pesticides, called *broad-spectrum agents*, can be toxic to beneficial species as well as to pests. Examples are organochlorine compounds (such as DDT), organophosphates (such as malathion and parathion), carbamates, pyrethroids, and neonicotinoids (which have increasingly been linked to the serious decline in honeybee populations). Others, called *selective*, or *narrow-spectrum*, *agents*, are each effective against a narrowly defined group of organisms. One example is glyphosate, used on corn and soybean crops that are genetically modified to withstand its toxic effects. This widely used herbicide efficiently kills weeds without hurting the crops.

50-fold The increase in synthetic pesticide use since 1950

Pesticides vary in their *persistence*, the length of time they remain deadly in the environment. Some, such as DDT and related compounds, remain in the environment for years and can be biologically magnified to high concentrations in food chains and food webs (Figure 9.13, p. 247). Others, such as organophosphates, are active for days or weeks and are not biologically magnified but can be highly toxic to humans.

About one-fourth of the pesticides used in the United States are aimed at ridding houses, gardens, lawns, parks, and golf courses of insects and other pests. According to the US Environmental Protection Agency (EPA), the amount of synthetic pesticides used on the average US homeowner's lawn is 10 times the amount (per unit of land area) typically used on US croplands.

Benefits of Synthetic Pesticides

Use of synthetic pesticides has its advantages and disadvantages. Proponents contend that the benefits of pesticides (Figure 12.21, left) outweigh their harmful effects (Figure 12.21, right). They point to the following benefits:

- *They have saved human lives.* Since 1945, DDT and other insecticides probably have prevented the premature deaths of at least 7 million people (some say as many as 500 million) from insect-transmitted diseases such as malaria (carried by the *Anopheles* mosquito), bubonic plague (carried by rat fleas), and typhus (carried by body lice and fleas).

- *They can increase food supplies* by reducing food losses due to pests, for some crops.

- *They can help farmers to control soil erosion and build soil fertility.* In conventional no-till farming, farmers apply herbicides instead of weeding the soil by plowing. This dramatically reduces soil erosion and soil nutrient depletion.

- *They can help farmers to reduce costs and increase profits.* The costs of using pesticides can be regained, at least in the near term, through higher crop yields. Glyphosate and other herbicides help farmers kill weeds efficiently, sparing them the costs of mechanical weeding.

- *They work fast.* Pesticides control most pests quickly, have a long shelf life, and are easily shipped and applied.

- *Newer pesticides are safer to use and more effective than many older ones.* Greater use is being made of biopesticides derived from plants, which are generally safer to use and less damaging to the environment than are many older pesticides.

Problems with Synthetic Pesticides

Opponents of widespread use of synthetic pesticides contend that the harmful effects of these chemicals (Figure 12.21, right) outweigh their benefits (Figure 12.21, left). They cite several problems.

- *They accelerate the development of genetic resistance to pesticides in pest organisms* (Figure 12.22). Insects breed rapidly, and within 5–10 years (much sooner in tropical areas), they can develop immunity to widely used pesticides through natural selection. In the same way, weeds develop resistance to herbicides. Since 1945, about 1,000 species of insects and rodents (mostly rats) have developed genetic resistance to one or more pesticides. By 2015, the International Survey of Herbicide-Resistant Weeds had identified more than 450 species of *superweeds*—weeds resistant to glyphosate and other herbicides.

- *They can put farmers on a financial treadmill.* Because of genetic resistance, farmers can find themselves having

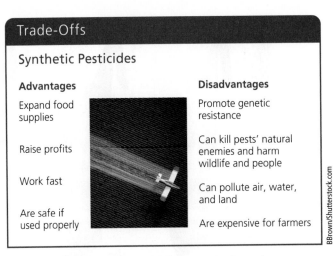

Trade-Offs

Synthetic Pesticides

Advantages	Disadvantages
Expand food supplies	Promote genetic resistance
Raise profits	Can kill pests' natural enemies and harm wildlife and people
Work fast	Can pollute air, water, and land
Are safe if used properly	Are expensive for farmers

BBrown/Shutterstock.com

FIGURE 12.21 Use of synthetic pesticides has advantages as well as disadvantages. *Critical thinking:* Which single advantage and which single disadvantage do you think are the most important? Why?

to pay more and more for a chemical pest control program that can become less and less effective as pests develop resistance to the pesticides.

- *Some insecticides kill natural predators and parasites that help to control the pest populations.* About 100 of the 300 most destructive insect, pests in the United States were minor pests until widespread use of insecticides wiped out many of their natural predators. (See the Case Study that follows.)

- *Some pesticides harm wildlife.* According to the USDA and the US Fish and Wildlife Service, each year, some of the pesticides applied to crops poison honeybee colonies on which we depend for pollination of many food crops (see Chapter 9, Core Case Study, p. 236, and Science Focus 9.2, p. 248). According to a study by the Center for Biological Diversity, pesticides menace about a third of all endangered and threatened species in the United States.

- *Pesticides that are applied inefficiently can pollute the environment.* According to the USDA, about 98–99.9% of the insecticides and more than 95% of the herbicides applied by aerial spraying or ground spraying do not reach the target pests. They end up in the air, surface water, groundwater, bottom sediments, food, and nontarget organisms, including humans.

- *Some pesticides threaten human health.* The WHO and UNEP have estimated that pesticides annually poison at least 3 million agricultural workers in less-developed countries. The EPA estimates that each year, pesticides poison 10,000 to 20,000 farmworkers in the United States. Household pesticides such as ant and roach sprays sicken another 2.5 million people per year. According to studies by the National Academy of Sciences, pesticide residues in food cause an estimated 4,000–20,000 cases of cancer per year in the United

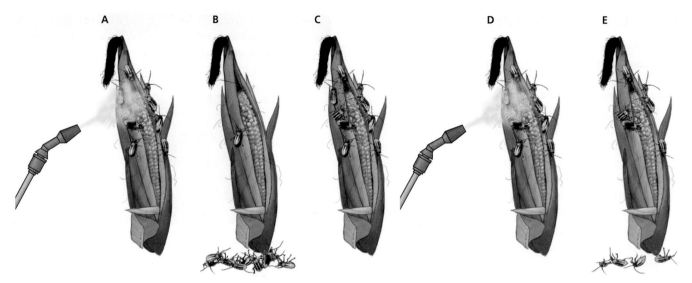

FIGURE 12.22 When a pesticide is sprayed on a crop **(a)**, a few pest insects resist it and survive **(b)**. The survivors reproduce and pass on their trait for resistance to the pesticide **(c)**. When the crop is sprayed again **(d)**, more insects resist and survive it and continue reproducing **(e)**. The pesticide has now become ineffective and the farmer must look for a stronger pesticide.

States. The pesticide industry disputes these claims, arguing that if used as directed, pesticides do not remain in the environment at levels high enough to cause serious environmental or health problems. Figure 12.23 lists some ways to reduce your exposure to synthetic pesticides.

CONSIDER THIS . . .

CONNECTIONS Pesticides and Food Choices
The Environmental Working Group (EWG) produces an annual list of fruits and vegetables that tend to have the highest pesticide residues. In 2015, these foods (EWG's "dirty dozen") were apples, peaches, nectarines, strawberries, grapes, celery, spinach, sweet bell peppers, cucumbers, cherry tomatoes, imported snap peas, and potatoes.

What Can You Do?

Reducing Exposure to Pesticides

- Grow some of your food using organic methods
- Buy certified organic food
- Wash and scrub all fresh fruits and vegetables
- Eat less meat, no meat, or certified organically produced meat
- Before cooking, trim the fat from meat

FIGURE 12.23 Individuals matter: You can reduce your exposure to pesticides. **Critical thinking:** Which three of these steps do you think are the most important ones to take? Why?

CASE STUDY

Ecological Surprises: The Law of Unintended Consequences

Malaria once infected 9 of every 10 people in North Borneo, now known as the eastern Malaysian state of Sabah. In 1955, the WHO sprayed the island with dieldrin (a DDT relative) to kill malaria-carrying mosquitoes. The program was so successful that the dreaded disease was nearly eliminated.

Then unexpected things began to happen. The dieldrin also killed other insects, including flies and cockroaches living in houses, which made the islanders happy. Next, small insect-eating lizards living in the houses died after gorging themselves on dieldrin-contaminated insects. Then cats began dying after feeding on the lizards. In the absence of cats, rats flourished in and around the villages.

When the residents became threatened by sylvatic plague carried by rat fleas, the WHO parachuted healthy cats onto the island to help control the rats. Operation Cat Drop worked.

But then the villagers' roofs began to fall in. The dieldrin had killed wasps and other insects that fed on a type of caterpillar that was not affected by the insecticide. With most of its predators eliminated, the caterpillar population exploded, munching its way through its favorite food: the leaves used in thatch roofs.

Ultimately, this story ended well. Both malaria and the unexpected effects of the spraying program were brought under control. Nevertheless, this chain of unintended and unforeseen events reminds us that whenever we intervene in nature and affect organisms that interact with one another, we need to ask, "Now what will happen?"

Pesticide Use Has Not Consistently Reduced US Crop Losses to Pests

Largely because of genetic resistance and the loss of many natural predators, synthetic pesticides have not always succeeded in reducing US crop losses. David Pimentel, an expert on insect ecology, evaluated data from more than 300 agricultural scientists and economists. He found that between 1942 and 1997, estimated crop losses from insects almost doubled from 7% to 13%, despite a 10-fold increase in the use of synthetic insecticides. He also estimated that alternative pest management practices could cut the use of synthetic pesticides by half on 40 major US crops without reducing crop yields (**Concept 12.4**).

In 2014, the EPA evaluated the use of three controversial neonicotinoids for insect control on US soybean crops. It found that there was no difference in soybean yields between treated and untreated crops. The report further concluded that the neonicotinoid treatments "provide negligible overall benefits to soybean production in most situations."

The pesticide industry disputes such findings. However, numerous studies and experience support them. For example, Sweden has cut its pesticide use in half with almost no decrease in crop yields.

Using Laws and Treaties to Regulate Pesticides

More than 20,000 different pesticide products are used in the United States. Three federal agencies, the EPA, the USDA, and the FDA, regulate the use of these pesticides under the Federal Insecticide, Fungicide, and Rodenticide Act (FIFRA), first passed in 1947 and amended in 1972. Critics argue that that FIFRA has not been well enforced, and the EPA says that the US Congress has not provided them with enough funds to carry out the complex and lengthy process of evaluating pesticides for toxicity.

In 1996, Congress passed the Food Quality Protection Act, mostly because of growing scientific evidence and citizen pressure concerning the effects of small amounts of pesticides on children. This act requires the EPA to reduce the allowed levels of pesticide residues in food by a factor of 10 when there is inadequate information on the potentially harmful effects on children.

Between 1972 and 2015, the EPA used FIFRA to ban or severely restrict the use of 64 active pesticide ingredients, including DDT and most other chlorinated hydrocarbon insecticides. However, according to studies by the National Academy of Sciences, federal laws regulating pesticide use generally are inadequate and poorly enforced.

Although laws within countries protect citizens to some extent, banned or unregistered pesticides may be manufactured in one country and exported to other countries. For example, US pesticide companies make and export to other countries pesticides that have been banned or severely restricted—or never evaluated—in the United States.

However, in what environmental scientists call a *circle of poison*, or the *boomerang effect*, residues of synthetic pesticides that have been banned in one country but exported to other countries can return to the exporting countries on imported food. Winds can also carry some persistent pesticides from one country to another.

Alternatives to Synthetic Pesticides

Many scientists urge us to reduce the use of pesticides by turning to biological, ecological, and cultivation tools for controlling pests (**Concept 12.4**). One important *biological control* involves using natural predators (Figure 12.20), parasites (Figure 12.24), and disease-causing bacteria and viruses to help regulate pest populations. This approach is usually nontoxic to other species and less costly than applying pesticides. However, some biological control agents are difficult to mass-produce and are often slower acting and more difficult to apply than synthetic pesticides are. Sometimes the agents can multiply and become pests themselves.

Two other examples of biological controls are sex attractants (called pheromones) and hormones, chemicals produced by organisms to control their developmental processes. Pheromones can be used to lure pests into traps or to attract their natural predators into crop fields. They have little chance of causing genetic resistance and are not harmful to nontarget species. Scientists have learned how to identify and use hormones that disrupt an insect's normal life cycle, thereby preventing it from reaching maturity and reproducing. Both of these methods are costly and can take weeks to be effective.

Scott Bauer/USDA Agricultural Research Service

FIGURE 12.24 Natural capital: In this example of biological pest control, a wasp is parasitizing a gypsy moth caterpillar.

In using *ecological controls*, farmers work with nature instead of against it. For example, by practicing polyculture, they use plant diversity to provide habitats for the predators of pest species right on their crop fields. This is a simple application of the biodiversity **principle of sustainability**.

Cultivation controls can be another useful way to work with nature to control pests. For example, farmers can plant different crops on the same plots from year to year and adjust planting times so that major insect pests either starve or are eaten by their natural predators. Some farmers are using large machines to vacuum up harmful bugs.

Finally, some scientists call for using genetic engineering to speed up the development of pest- and disease-resistant crop strains. But controversy persists over whether the projected advantages of using genetically modified plants outweigh their projected disadvantages (Figure 12.B, p. 345).

Integrated Pest Management

Many pest control experts and farmers believe the best way to control crop pests is through **integrated pest management (IPM),** a program in which each crop and its pests are evaluated as parts of an ecosystem (**Concept 12.4**). The overall aim of IPM is to reduce crop damage to an economically tolerable level with minimal use of synthetic pesticides.

When farmers using IPM detect an economically damaging level of pests in any field, they start with biological methods (natural predators, parasites, and disease organisms) and cultivation controls (such as altering planting times and using large machines to vacuum up harmful pests). They apply small amounts of synthetic pesticides—preferably biopesticides—only when insect or weed populations reach a threshold where the potential cost of pest damage to crops outweighs the cost of applying the pesticide.

IPM has a good record of accomplishment. In Sweden and Denmark, farmers have used it to cut their synthetic pesticide use by more than half. In Cuba, where organic farming is used almost exclusively, farmers make extensive use of IPM. In Brazil, IPM has reduced pesticide use on soybeans by as much as 90%. In Japan, many farmers save money by using ducks for pest control in rice paddies. The ducks' droppings also provide nutrients for the rice plants.

According to the US National Academy of Sciences, a well-designed IPM program can reduce synthetic pesticide use and pest control costs by 50–65%, without reducing crop yields and food quality. IPM can also reduce inputs of fertilizer and irrigation water and slow the development of genetic resistance because of reduced use of pesticides. IPM is an important application of the biodiversity **principle of sustainability** and expands society's beneficial environmental impact.

Despite its important benefits, IPM—like any other form of pest control—has some drawbacks. It requires expert knowledge about each pest situation and takes more time than relying strictly on synthetic pesticides. Methods developed for a crop in one area might not apply to areas with even slightly different growing conditions. Initial costs may be higher, although long-term costs typically are lower than the use of conventional pesticides.

Several UN agencies and the World Bank have joined to establish an IPM facility. Its goal is to promote the use of IPM by disseminating information and establishing networks among researchers, farmers, and agricultural extension agents involved in IPM. Widespread use of IPM has been hindered in the United States and other countries by government subsidies that support use of pesticides, as well as by opposition from pesticide manufacturers, and a shortage of IPM experts. **GREEN CAREER: Integrated pest management**

CHECKPOINT FOR UNDERSTANDING 12.4

1. Explain how using synthetic pesticides can impede natural pest control.

2. Discuss how pesticide use can result in genetic resistance.

3. What is FIFRA?

4. Explain the goal of Integrated Pest Management.

12.5 HOW CAN WE PRODUCE FOOD MORE SUSTAINABLY?

CONCEPT 12.5 We can produce food more sustainably by using resources more efficiently, sharply decreasing the harmful environmental effects of industrialized food production, and eliminating government subsidies that promote such harmful impacts.

Conserve Topsoil

Land used for food production must have fertile topsoil, which takes hundreds of years to form. Thus, sharply reducing topsoil erosion is a key component of more sustainable agriculture and an important way to increase society's beneficial environmental impact.

Soil conservation involves using a variety of methods to reduce topsoil erosion and restore soil fertility, mostly by keeping the land covered with vegetation. For example, *terracing* involves converting steeply sloped land into a series of broad, nearly level terraces that run across the land's contours (Figure 12.25a). Each terrace retains water for crops and reduces topsoil erosion by controlling runoff.

On less steeply sloped land, *contour planting* (Figure 12.25b) can be used to reduce topsoil erosion. It involves plowing and planting crops in rows across the slope of the land rather than up and down. Each row acts as a small dam to help hold topsoil by slowing runoff. Similarly, *strip-cropping* (Figure 12.25b) helps to reduce erosion and to restore soil fertility with alternating strips of a row crop (such as corn or cotton) and another crop that completely covers the soil, called a

FIGURE 12.25 Soil conservation methods include **(a)** terracing; **(b)** contour planting and strip cropping; **(c)** intercropping; and **(d)** windbreaks between crop fields.

a.

Lim Yong Hian/Shutterstock.com

b.

Ron Nichols/USDA Natural Resources Conservation Service

c.

inga spence/Alamy Stock Photo

d.

Fedorov Oleksiy/Shutterstock.com

cover crop (such as alfalfa, clover, oats, or rye). The cover crop traps topsoil that erodes from the row crop and catches and reduces water runoff.

Alley cropping, or *agroforestry* (Figure 12.25c), is another way to slow erosion and to maintain soil fertility. One or more crops, usually legumes or other crops that add nitrogen to the soil, are planted together in alleys between orchard trees or fruit-bearing shrubs, which provide shade. This reduces water loss by evaporation and helps retain and slowly release soil moisture.

Farmers can also establish *windbreaks*, or *shelterbelts*, of trees around crop fields to reduce wind erosion (Figure 12.25d). The trees retain soil moisture, supply wood for fuel, and provide habitats for birds and insects that help with pest control and pollination.

Another way to greatly reduce topsoil erosion is to eliminate or minimize the plowing and tilling of topsoil and to leave crop residues on the ground. Such *no-till* or *conservation-tillage farming* uses special tillers and planting machines that inject seeds and fertilizer directly through crop residues on the ground into minimally disturbed topsoil. Weeds are controlled with herbicides.

This no-till type of farming increases crop yields and greatly reduces soil erosion and water pollution from sediment and fertilizer runoff. It also helps farmers survive prolonged drought by helping to keep more moisture in the soil. However, one drawback is that the greater use of herbicides promotes the growth of herbicide-resistant weeds that force farmers to use larger doses of weed killers or, in some cases, to return to plowing. However, organic no-till methods being developed at the Rodale Institute could be herbicide-free and will not require plowing.

Another way to conserve topsoil is to grow plants without using soil. Some producers are raising crops in greenhouses, using a system called *hydroponics*. At the Growing Power farm (**Core Case Study**), Will Allen has developed such a system for raising salad greens and fish together. Wastewater from the fish tanks flows into hydroponic troughs where it nourishes the plants. The plant roots filter the water, which is then returned to the fish runs. This closed-loop, chemical-free *aquaponic system* conserves soil, water, and energy while supporting more than 100,000 tilapia and perch, which are sold in local markets along with the salad greens.

Some countries, such as the United States, have paid farmers to set aside considerable areas of cropland for conservation purposes. Under the 1985 Food Security Act (Farm Act), more than 400,000 farmers participating in the Conservation Reserve Program received subsidy payments for taking highly erodible land out of production and replanting it with grass or trees for 10–15 years. Since 1985, these efforts have cut total topsoil losses on US cropland by 40%.

Restore Soil Fertility

Another way to protect soil is to restore some of the lost plant nutrients that have been washed, blown, or leached out of topsoil, or that have been removed by repeated crop harvesting. To do this, farmers can use **organic fertilizer** derived from plant and animal materials or synthetic inorganic fertilizer made of inorganic compounds that contain *nitrogen*, *phosphorus*, and *potassium* along with trace amounts of other plant nutrients.

There are several types of organic fertilizers. One is *animal manure*: the dung and urine of cattle, horses, poultry, and other farm animals. It improves topsoil structure, adds organic nitrogen, and stimulates the growth of beneficial soil bacteria and fungi. Another type, called *green manure*, consists of freshly cut or growing green vegetation that is plowed into the topsoil to increase the organic matter and humus available to the next crop. A third type is *compost*, produced when microorganisms break down organic matter such as leaves, crop residues, food wastes, paper, and wood in the presence of oxygen.

The Growing Power farm (**Core Case Study**) depends greatly on its large piles of compost. Will Allen invites local grocers and restaurant owners to send their food wastes to add to the pile. To make this compost, Allen uses millions of red wiggler worms, which reproduce rapidly and eat their own weight in food wastes every day, converting it to plant nutrients. Also, the process of composting generates a considerable amount of heat, which is used to help warm some of the farm's greenhouses during cold months.

We degrade soils when we plant crops such as corn and cotton on the same land several years in a row, a practice that can deplete nutrients—especially nitrogen—in the topsoil. One way to reduce such losses is through **crop rotation**, in which a farmer plants a series of different crops in the same area from season to season. For example, where a nitrogen-depleting crop is grown one year, the farmer can plant the same area the following year with a crop such as legumes, which add nitrogen to the soil.

Many farmers, especially those in more-developed countries, rely on synthetic inorganic fertilizers. The use of these products accounts for about 25% of the world's crop yield. While these fertilizers can replace depleted inorganic nutrients, they do not replace organic matter. Completely restoring topsoil nutrients requires both inorganic and organic fertilizers. Many scientists are encouraging farmers, especially those in less-developed countries, to make greater use of green manure as a more sustainable way to restore soil fertility.

Reduce Soil Salinization and Desertification

We know how to prevent and deal with soil salinization, as summarized in Figure 12.26. The problem is that most of these solutions are costly.

Reducing desertification is not easy. We cannot control the timing and location of prolonged droughts caused by changes in weather and climate patterns. But we can reduce population growth, overgrazing, deforestation, and destructive forms of planting and irrigation in dryland areas, which have left much land vulnerable to topsoil erosion and thus desertification. We can also work to decrease the human contribution to projected climate change, which could prolong and increase the severity of droughts in large areas of the world during this century.

It is possible to restore land suffering from desertification by planting trees and other plants that anchor topsoil

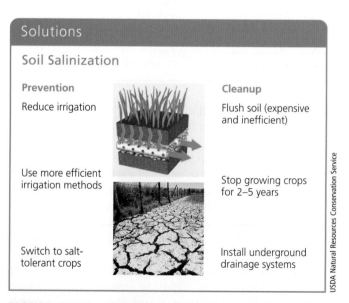

FIGURE 12.26 Ways to prevent and ways to clean up soil salinization (**Concept 12.6**). ***Critical thinking:*** Which two of these solutions do you think are the best ones? Why?

and hold water. We can grow trees and crops together (alley cropping, Figure 12.25c), and establish windbreaks around farm fields (Figure 12.25d).

Produce and Consume Meat and Dairy Products More Sustainably

Meat production has a huge environmental impact and meat consumption is the largest factor in the growing ecological footprints of individuals in affluent nations.

Some types of meat are produced more efficiently than others (Figure 12.27). For example, producing a pound of beef requires more than three times the amount of grain needed to produce a pound of pork. It takes more than four times the amount of grain used to produce a pound of chicken or turkey. A more sustainable form of meat production and consumption would involve shifting from less grain-efficient forms of animal protein, such as beef, pork, and carnivorous fish produced by aquaculture, to more grain-efficient forms, such as poultry and plant-eating farmed fish.

Insects are another form of protein. Would you consider trying a beetle salad, a caterpillar stew, or a handful of crunchy fried ants for a snack? If you're thinking *yuck*, you're not alone. Yet, at least 2,000 species of insects provide nutrients to more than 2 billion people, according to the FAO. In countries such as Thailand, Australia, and Mexico, insects are deep-fried with spices, made into flours and tasty sauces, baked into breads, and cooked in stews. Insects can be rich in protein and fiber and healthy fats. They can provide vital micronutrients such as calcium, iron, B vitamins, and zinc.

A growing number of people have one or two meatless days per week. Others go further and eliminate most or all meat from their diets, replacing it with a balanced vegetarian diet of fruits, vegetables, and protein-rich foods such as peas, beans, and lentils. According to one estimate, if all Americans picked one day per week to have no meat, the reduction in greenhouse gas emissions would be equivalent to taking 30–40 million cars off the road for a year.

CONSIDER THIS . . .

THINKING ABOUT Meat Consumption

If you do not do this already, would you be willing to live lower on the food chain by eating much less meat, or no meat at all? Explain.

Managing and Sustaining Fisheries

To reduce overfishing, communities and governments *regulate fishing* by reducing fish harvests and closing some overfished areas until they recover. Government subsidies play a role. Governments around the world give more than $30 billion per year in subsidies to fishers to help them keep their businesses running. This can encourage overfishing by having too many boats chasing too few fish. Figure 12.28 lists ways to manage fisheries more sustainably.

CONSIDER THIS . . .

THINKING ABOUT Fishing Subsidies

Do you think that government subsidies that promote unsustainable fishing should be eliminated or drastically reduced? Explain. Would your answer be different if your livelihood depended on commercial fishing?

Practice More Sustainable Aquaculture

Various organizations have established guidelines, standards, and certifications to encourage more sustainable aquaculture and fishing practices. The Aquaculture Stewardship Council (ASC), for example, has developed aquaculture sustainability standards, although it has certified only about 4.6% of the world's aquaculture production operations. The Marine Stewardship Council (MSC) performs a similar program for wild-caught fisheries. Like the organic certification, the programs have associated labels for food products that help consumers purchase more sustainable options.

Scientists and producers are working on ways to make aquaculture more sustainable and to reduce its harmful environmental effects. One such approach is *open-ocean aquaculture*, which involves raising large carnivorous fish in large underwater pens—some as large as a high school gymnasium. They are located far offshore, where rapid currents can sweep away fish wastes and dilute them. Some farmed fish can escape from such operations and breed with wild fish, and this approach is costly. However, the environmental impact of raising fish far offshore is smaller than that of raising fish near shore and much smaller than that of industrialized commercial fishing.

Other fish farmers are reducing coastal damage from aquaculture by raising shrimp and fish species in inland facilities using freshwater ponds and tanks. In such *recirculating aquaculture systems*, the water used to raise the fish is con-

Beef	36,200 calories
Pork	11,300 calories
Poultry	8,800 calories
Eggs	6,300 calories
Dairy	5,900 calories

FIGURE 12.27 Amount of feed required to produce 1,000 calories of meat for human consumption, comparing five different foods. ***Data analysis:*** For each of the others (pork, poultry, eggs, and dairy), how many calories could be produced with the grain required to produce 1,000 calories of beef?

(Compiled by the authors using data from US Department of Agriculture.)

Solutions

Managing Fisheries

Fishery Regulations

Set low catch limits

Improve monitoring and enforcement

Economic Approaches

Reduce or eliminate fishing subsidies

Certify sustainable fisheries

Protection

Establish no-fishing areas

Establish more marine protected areas

Consumer Information

Label sustainably harvested fish

Publicize overfished and threatened species

Bycatch

Use nets that allow escape of smaller fish

Use net escape devices for seabirds and sea turtles

Aquaculture

Restrict locations of fish farms

Improve pollution control

Nonnative Invasions

Kill or filter organisms from ship ballast water

Clean aquatic recreation gear

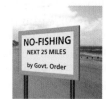

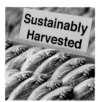

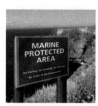

FIGURE 12.28 Ways to manage fisheries more sustainably and protect marine biodiversity. ***Critical thinking:*** Which four of these solutions do you think are the best ones? Why?

tinually recycled. Similarly, the Growing Power aquaponic system (**Core Case Study**) captures its fish wastes and converts them to fertilizer used to grow salad greens. This eliminates fish waste pollution of aquatic systems and reduces the need for antibiotics and other chemicals used to combat disease among farmed fish. It also eliminates the problem of farmed fish escaping into natural aquatic systems.

Making aquaculture more sustainable will require some fundamental changes for producers and consumers. One change is for more consumers to choose fish species such as carp, tilapia, and catfish that eat algae and other vegetation rather than fish oil and fishmeal produced from other fish. Raising carnivorous fishes such as salmon, trout, tuna, grouper, and cod contributes to overfishing and population crashes of species and is unsustainable. Aquaculture producers can avoid this problem by raising herbivorous fishes as long as they do not try to increase yields by feeding fishmeal to such species, as many of them are doing.

Fish farmers can also emphasize *polyaquaculture*, which has been part of aquaculture for centuries, especially in Southeast Asia. Polyaquaculture operations raise fish or shrimp along with algae, seaweeds, and shellfish in coastal lagoons, ponds, and tanks. The wastes of the fish or shrimp feed the other species. Polyaquaculture applies the chemical cycling and biodiversity **principles of sustainability. GREEN CAREER: Sustainable aquaculture**

Solutions

More Sustainable Aquaculture

- Protect mangrove forests and estuaries
- Improve management of wastes
- Reduce escape of aquaculture species into the wild
- Set up self-sustaining polyaquaculture systems that combine aquatic plants, fish, and shellfish
- Certify sustainable forms of aquaculture

FIGURE 12.29 Ways to make aquaculture more sustainable and reduce its harmful effects. ***Critical thinking:*** Which two of these solutions do you think are the best ones? Why?

Figure 12.29 lists some ways to make aquaculture more sustainable and to reduce its harmful environmental effects.

Expand Organic Agriculture

One component of more sustainable food production is organic agriculture. The Rodale Institute has been conducting a side-by-side comparison of organic and industrialized farming systems for more than 30 years.

Since its launch in 1981, the Farming Systems Trial (FST) has found evidence of some major benefits of organic farming, including the following:

- *Organic farming builds soil organic matter.* Synthetic fertilizers leach, or pass through the soil, more quickly than nutrients from manures, composts, or cover crops. Levels of beneficial soil fungi are also higher in organic soils. Thus, on the FST organic plots, the nutrients remain available to the plants much more than on the conventional plots.
- *Organic systems reduce erosion and water pollution.* Because of the leaching action, fertilizer chemicals end up in surface water and groundwater. Most of the precipitation on organic fields soaks into the soil rather than running off, more so than on the conventional fields.
- *Organic farming uses less fossil fuel energy.* The FST organic systems used 33–50% less energy than the conventional systems did. Producing nitrogen fertilizer, not used at all on organic crops, is the single greatest energy input in industrial farming.
- *Organic farming cuts greenhouse gas emissions.* The FST's conventional systems produced 40% more greenhouse gases, mostly because they involved the production and use of synthetic fertilizers. Also, in the organic system, carbon content in the soil increased, while soils in the conventional plots lost carbon.

- *Organic yields match conventional yields.* During its first 3 years while the FST organic system was being developed, it had lower yields than the conventional system. Since then, organic corn, wheat, and soybean yields have matched conventional yields.

- *Organic systems are more weed-tolerant.* Organic corn and soybean crops tolerate much higher levels of weed competition than do conventional crops, while producing equivalent yields without the use of herbicides.

- *Organic crops compare favorably in years of drought.* Organic corn yields were 31% higher in the FST than conventional yields in years of drought. By comparison, genetically engineered "drought-tolerant" varieties saw yield increases of 6.7–13.3% over conventional varieties.

- *Organic farming can be more profitable.* The FST's average net return for the organic systems was $558/acre/year, compared with $190/acre/year for the conventional systems.

Another major benefit of organic farming is that by eating USDA 100% certified organic foods, consumers reduce their exposure to pesticide residues and to bacteria-resistant antibiotics that can be found in conventional foods. A study led by Carlo Leifert concluded that organically grown fruits, vegetables, and grains also contain substantially higher levels of cancer-fighting antioxidants than their conventionally grown counterparts.

One hindrance to expanded use of organic farming, compared with industrialized agriculture, is that it requires more human labor to use methods such as integrated pest management and crop rotation. However, this could be seen as a benefit, especially in less-developed countries, because organic farming creates jobs. A UN report concluded that organic farming provides over 30% more jobs per hectare than nonorganic farming.

Shift to More Sustainable Food Production

Modern industrialized food production yields large amounts of food at affordable prices. However, to a growing number of analysts, it is unsustainable because of its harmful environmental and health costs (Figure 12.12) and because it violates the three **scientific principles of sustainability**. It relies heavily on nonrenewable fossil fuels and thus adds greenhouse gases and other air pollutants to the atmosphere and contributes to climate change. It also reduces biodiversity and agrobiodiversity and interferes with the cycling of plant nutrients. These harmful effects are hidden from consumers because most of them are not included in the market prices of food—a violation of the full-cost pricing **principle of sustainability**.

In addition to expanding the use of organic agriculture, a more sustainable food production system would have several components (Figure 12.30). One component would be to rely less on conventional monoculture and more on organic polyculture. Research shows that, on average, low-input polyculture produces higher yields per unit of land than does high-input industrialized monoculture. It also uses less energy and fewer resources and provides more food security for small landowners.

Ecologist David Tilman (Individuals Matter 12.1) has been instrumental in demonstrating the benefits of polyculture. The Growing Power farm (**Core Case Study**) practices polyculture by growing a variety of crops in several greenhouses.

Of particular interest to some scientists is the idea of using polyculture to grow *perennial crops*—crops that grow back year after year on their own (Science Focus 12.1).

Another key to developing more sustainable agriculture is to shift from using fossil fuels to relying more on renewable energy for food production—an important application of the solar energy **principle of sustainability** that has been well demonstrated by the Growing Power farm (**Core Case Study**). To produce the electricity and fuels needed for

Solutions

More Sustainable Food Production

More	Less
High-yield polyculture	Soil erosion
Organic fertilizers	Soil salinization
Biological pest control	Water pollution
Integrated pest management	Aquifer depletion
Efficient irrigation	Overgrazing
Perennial crops	Overfishing
Crop rotation	Loss of biodiversity and agrobiodiversity
Water-efficient crops	Fossil fuel use
Soil conservation	Greenhouse gas emissions
Subsidies for sustainable farming	Subsidies for unsustainable farming

FIGURE 12.30 More sustainable, low-input food production has a number of major components. ***Critical thinking:*** For each list in this diagram (left and right), which two items do you think are the most important? Why?

Top: Marko5/Shutterstock.com. Center: Anhong/Dreamstime.com. Bottom: pacopi/Shutterstock.com

David Tilman—Polyculture Researcher

One of the world's most prominent ecologists and agricultural experts is David Tilman, a professor at the University of Minnesota. Since 1981, he has conducted more than 150 long-term controlled experiments on a university-owned grassland. For example, he applied certain mixes of fertilizers and water on experimental plots and observed how the plants responded. He then compared the results from the experimental plots with those from control plots that did not receive the experimental treatments. He also used varying mixes of plant species in such experiments, focusing on the benefits of polyculture.

With ecologist Peter Reich, Tilman found that carefully controlled polyculture plots with 16 different species of plants consistently outproduced plots with 9, 4, or only 1 type of plant species. Such research explains why some analysts argue for greatly expanding the use of polyculture to produce food more sustainably.

Tilman's findings also support the scientific idea that biodiversity can make ecosystems more stable and sustainable. A diverse forest, for example, suffers damage during pest infestations, but there are enough varying species to withstand the damage. Some species are wiped out, but not the whole forest. A vast field of corn or wheat, on the other hand, is highly vulnerable to heat waves, drought, disease, and pests, and it can be destroyed during extreme events.

For his important research efforts, Tilman has received several awards. In 2010, he was awarded the prestigious Heineken Prize for Environmental Sciences for his important contributions to the science of ecology.

Todd Reubold/University of Minnesota

food production, farmers can make greater use of renewable solar energy (see chapter-opening photo), wind, flowing water, and biofuels produced from farm wastes in tanks called *biogas digesters*. Most proponents of more sustainable agriculture call for using more environmentally sustainable forms of both high-yield polyculture and high-yield monoculture (**Concept 12.5**).

Agricultural experts such as Jonathan Foley argue that industrialized farming could play a major role in shifting to more sustainable food production. Foley notes that farmers are already finding ways to apply pesticides and fertilizers in smaller amounts and more precisely, using computerized tractors and remote sensing and GPS technology. Fertilizers can also be mixed and tailored to different soil conditions to help minimize runoff into waterways, and irrigation can be done much more efficiently than it typically is. Such methods could increase production on the current total area of farmland by 50–60%, according to Foley.

Proponents of more sustainable food production systems say that education is an important key to making a shift toward a more sustainable food production system. They seek to inform people, especially young consumers, about where their food really comes from, how it is produced, and what the environmentally harmful effects of food production are. They also call for economic policies that reward more sustainable agriculture. A major part of such policies would be to shift subsidies from unsustainable to more sustainable food production processes. Simply put, food should be good for people and for the planet.

Figure 12.31 lists ways in which you can promote more sustainable food production.

What Can You Do?

More Sustainable Food Production

- Eat less meat, no meat, or organically certified meat
- Choose sustainably produced herbivorous fish
- Use organic farming to grow some of your food
- Buy certified organic food
- Eat locally grown food
- Compost food wastes
- Cut food waste

FIGURE 12.31 Individuals matter: Ways to promote more sustainable food production (**Concept 12.6**). *Critical thinking:* Which three of these actions do you think are the most important? Why?

CHECKPOINT FOR UNDERSTANDING 12.5

1. Identify agricultural methods that can be used to prevent the loss of topsoil.

2. Describe the benefits of using organic fertilizers.

3. Identify some strategies for making aquaculture more sustainable.

4. Discuss the benefits of organic farming.

5. Explain how consumers can help promote more sustainable food production.

Perennial Polyculture and the Land Institute

Some scientists call for greater reliance on polycultures of perennial crops as a component of more sustainable agriculture. Such crops can live for many years without having to be replanted and are better adapted to regional soil and climate conditions than are most annual crops.

More than three decades ago, plant geneticist Wes Jackson cofounded the Land Institute in the US state of Kansas. One of the institute's goals has been to grow a diverse mixture of edible perennial plants to supplement traditional annual monoculture crops and to help reduce the latter's harmful environmental effects. Examples in this polyculture mix include perennial grasses, plants that add nitrogen to the soil, sunflowers, grain crops, and plants that provide natural insecticides. Some of these plants could also be used as a source of renewable biofuel for motor vehicles.

Researchers are trying to improve yields of different varieties of these perennial crops, which are not all as high as yields of annual crops. However, in the US state of Washington, researchers have bred perennial wheat varieties that have a 70% higher yield than today's commercially grown annual wheat varieties.

The Land Institute's approach, called *natural systems agriculture*, copies nature by growing a diversity of perennial crops using organic methods. It has a number of environmental benefits. Because there is no need to till the soil and replant perennials each year, this approach produces much less topsoil erosion and water pollution. It also reduces the need for irrigation because the deep roots of such perennials retain more water than do the shorter roots of annuals (Figure 12.C). There is little or no need for chemical fertilizers and pesticides, and thus little or no pollution from these sources. Perennial polycultures also remove and store more carbon from the atmosphere, and growing them requires less energy than does growing crops in conventional monocultures.

This approach has worked well in some areas of the world. For example, in Malawi, Africa, farmers have greatly raised their crop yields by planting rows of perennial pigeon peas between rows of corn. The pea plants have doubled the carbon and nitrogen content in the soils, while increasing soil water retention. These legume plants also provide a welcome source of protein for the farm families.

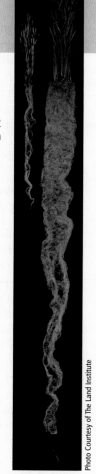

FIGURE 12.C The roots of an annual wheat crop plant (left) are much shorter than those of big bluestem (right), a tallgrass prairie perennial plant.

Some scientists note that adapting perennials to the grand scale of industrialized crop production will be challenging and time-consuming. However, Wes Jackson calls for governments to promote this and other forms of more sustainable agriculture in order to gain their many benefits. He reminds us that "if our agriculture is not sustainable, then our food supply is not sustainable."

Photo Courtesy of The Land Institute

CRITICAL THINKING

Why do you think large seed companies generally oppose this form of more sustainable agriculture?

12.6 HOW CAN WE IMPROVE FOOD SECURITY?

CONCEPT 12.6 We can improve food security by reducing poverty and chronic malnutrition, producing food more sustainably, relying more on locally grown food, and cutting food waste.

Using Government Policies to Improve Food Production and Security

Agriculture is a financially risky business. Whether farmers have a good or bad year depends on factors over which they have little control, including weather, crop prices, pests and diseases, interest rates on loans, and global food markets.

Governments use two main approaches to influence food production in hopes of strengthening food security. *First*, they can *control food prices* by placing a legally mandated upper limit on them in order to keep them artificially low. This helps consumers, but farmers may find it harder to make a living.

Second, they can *provide subsidies* by giving farmers price supports, tax breaks, and other financial support to help them stay in business and to encourage them to increase food production. In the United States, most subsidies go to industrialized food production, often in support of environmentally harmful practices. For example, by subsidizing corn and soybeans, the government pushes prices on those grains down and indirectly supports CAFOs and feedlots, which depend on corn and soy for their feed, and their harmful environmental and health effects.

Some opponents of subsidies call for ending them. They point to New Zealand, which ended farm subsidies in 1984. After the shock wore off, innovation took over and production of some foods such as milk quadrupled. Brazil has also ended most of its farm subsidies. Some analysts call for replacing traditional subsidies for farmers with subsidies that promote more environmentally sustainable farming practices.

Similarly, government subsidies to fishing fleets can promote overfishing and the reduction of aquatic biodiversity. For example, several governments give the highly destructive bottom-trawling industry millions of dollars per year in subsidies, which is the main reason fishers who use this environmentally destructive practice can stay in business. Many analysts call for replacing those harmful subsidies with subsidies that would sharply reduce overfishing and promote more sustainable fishing and aquaculture.

Other Government and Private Programs Are Increasing Food Security

Government and private programs aimed at reducing poverty can improve food security (**Concept 12.1B**). For example, some programs provide small loans at low interest rates to poor people to help them start businesses or buy land to grow their own food.

Some analysts urge governments to establish special programs focused on saving children from the harmful health effects of poverty. Studies by the United Nations Children's Fund (UNICEF) indicate that one-half to two-thirds of nutrition-related childhood deaths could be prevented at an average annual cost of $5–$10 per child. This involves simple measures such as immunizing more children against childhood diseases, preventing dehydration due to diarrhea by giving infants a mixture of sugar and salt in their water, and combatting blindness by giving children an inexpensive vitamin A capsule twice a year.

Some farmers and plant breeders are working on preserving a diverse gene pool as another way to improve food security. For example, an organization called the Global Crop Diversity Trust is seeking to prevent the disappearance of 100,000 varieties of food crops. The trust is working with about 50 seed banks around the world to cultivate and store seeds from endangered varieties of many food plant species.

In the quest for food security, some critics recognize the potential benefits of GM crops (Figure 12.B, left, p. 345). However, they point out that most of the GM crops developed so far have provided very few of these benefits while they present potentially serious drawbacks (Figure 12.B, right, p. 345).

Still, many scientists think that GM crops hold great promise. A survey by the Pew Research Center and the American Association for the Advancement of Science (AAAS) indicated that 88% of AAAS scientists polled think it is safe to eat GM foods, while just 37% of the general public agreed with this.

Many private, mostly nonprofit, organizations are also working to help individuals, communities, and nations to improve their food security and produce food more sustainably. For example, Growing Power's Will Allen (**Core Case Study**) argues that instead of trying to transfer complex technologies such as genetic engineering to less-developed countries, we could be helping them to develop simple, sustainable, local food production and distribution systems. He argues this would give them more control over their food security.

Grow and Buy More Food Locally and Cut Food Waste

One way to increase food security is to grow more of our food locally or regionally, ideally with USDA 100% certified organic farming practices. A growing number of consumers are becoming *locavores*, who try to buy as much of their food as possible from local and regional producers in farmers' markets, which provide access to fresher seasonal foods, many of them grown organically.

In addition, many people participate in *community-supported agriculture (CSA)* programs. In these programs, people buy shares of a local farmer's crops and receive a box of fruits or vegetables on a regular basis during the growing season. Growing Power (**Core Case Study**) runs such a program for inner-city residents. For many of these people, the organically grown food they get from the urban farm greatly improves their diets and increases their chances of living longer and healthier lives.

By buying locally, people support local economies and farm families. Buying locally reduces fossil fuel energy costs for food producers, as well as the greenhouse gas emissions from storing and transporting food products over long distances. There are limits to this benefit, however. Food scientists point out that the largest share of carbon footprint for most foods is in production. Thus, for example, an apple grown through high-input agriculture and trucked across North America could have a larger footprint than an apple grown through low-input farming and sent on a ship from South America.

An increase in the demand for locally grown food could result in more small, diversified farms that produce organic, minimally processed food from plants and animals. Such *eco-farming* could be one of this century's challenging new careers for many young people. **GREEN CAREER: Small-scale sustainable agriculture**

Sustainable agriculture entrepreneurs and ordinary citizens who live in urban areas could grow more of their own food, as the Growing Power farm has shown (**Core Case Study**). According to the USDA, approximately 15% of the world's food is grown in urban areas, and this percentage could easily be doubled. Increasingly, people are sharing garden space, labor, and produce in community gardens (Figure 12.32) in vacant lots. People are planting gardens and raising chickens in backyards, growing dwarf fruit trees in large containers of soil, and raising vegetables in containers on rooftops, balconies, and patios. One study estimates that converting 10% of American lawns into food-producing gardens would supply one-third of the country's fresh produce.

Many urban schools, colleges, and universities are benefitting greatly from having gardens on school grounds. Not only do the students have a ready source of fresh produce, but they also learn about where their food comes from and how to grow their own food more sustainably.

In the future, much of our food might be grown in cities within specially designed high-rise buildings. Such a building would have rooftop solar panels for generating electricity, and it could capture and recycle rainwater for irrigating its wide

FIGURE 12.32 Community gardens like this one are helping people without much land to grow their own food.

diversity of crops. Sloped glass facing south would bring in sunlight, and excess heat collected in this way could be stored in tanks containing water or sand underneath the building for use as needed. This approach would put into practice the three **scientific principles of sustainability**.

Finally, people can sharply cut food waste (**Concept 12.6**). Jonathan Foley reported in 2014 that 25% of the world's food calories are lost or wasted. In poor countries with unreliable food storage and transportation, much is lost before it gets to consumers. In wealthy countries, much waste occurs in restaurants, homes, and supermarkets. According to studies by the EPA and the Natural Resources Defense Council, Americans throw away 30–40% of the country's food supply each year while 49 million Americans experience chronic hunger. According to the USDA, the foods most often thrown away in the United States are, in order, perishable items such as vegetables and fruits, roots and tubers, fish and seafood, dairy products, and meat.

Food policy expert Lester Brown has discussed our food security challenges in terms of a food equation that is out of balance because its demand side is growing and its supply side is shrinking (Figure 12.33, top). He suggests that we can meet these challenges by working on both the demand side and the supply side to find solutions that will be difficult but achievable (Figure 12.33, bottom). His argument provides an excellent summary of how food production, currently unsustainable, could be made more sustainable, thereby leading us toward global food security.

CHECKPOINT FOR UNDERSTANDING 12.6

1. Explain what is meant by food security, and identify factors that threaten it.

2. Describe the purpose of farm subsidies.

3. Identify some simple, sustainable ways of promoting food security.

4. Explain the benefits of buying locally grown food.

Trade-Offs

Challenges

Demand Side	Supply Sides
Growing population	Soil erosion
People moving up the food chain	Depletion of aquifers
	Stagnant grain yields
Turning food into biofuel	Rising temperature

Solutions

Demand Side	Supply Sides
Stabilize population	Conserve soil
Eradicate poverty	Use water efficiently
Reduce excessive meat consumption	Find ways to increase yields
Eliminate biofuel subsidies	Stabilize climate

FIGURE 12.33 *The Food Equation:* Demand and supply are currently out of balance (upper part of figure) and growing more so, due to unsustainable food production methods. We can rebalance the food equation with workable solutions (lower part of figure).

(Compiled by the authors using data from Brown, Lester R. *Plan B 4.0*, Norton, 2009.)

KEY IDEAS

- About 795 million people have health problems because they do not get enough to eat and 2.1 billion people face health problems from eating too much.

- Modern industrialized agriculture has a greater harmful impact on the environment than any other human activity.

- More sustainable forms of food production could greatly reduce the harmful environmental and health impacts of industrialized food production systems.

Core Case Study Checkpoint

Describe how Will Allen's Growing Power, Inc. urban farm utilizes the scientific principles of sustainability to produce food more sustainably.

agrobiodiversity: the genetic variety of plant and animal species used on farms to produce food.

chronic malnutrition: faulty nutrition, caused by a diet that does not supply an individual with enough protein, essential fats, vitamins, minerals, and other nutrients needed for good health.

chronic undernutrition (hunger): condition suffered by people who cannot grow or buy enough food to meet their basic energy needs.

desertification: conversion of rangeland, rain-fed cropland, or irrigated cropland to desert-like land, with a drop in agricultural productivity of 10% or more. It is usually caused by a combination of overgrazing, soil erosion, prolonged drought, and climate change.

famine: widespread malnutrition and starvation in a particular area because of a shortage of food, usually caused by drought, war, flood, earthquake, or other catastrophic event that disrupts food production and distribution.

farm subsidies: money paid to farmers to supplement the cost of production of crops and livestock in order to influence the market price and supply of food commodities.

fishery: concentration of particular aquatic species suitable for commercial harvesting in a given ocean area or inland body of water.

food security: conditions under which every person in a given area has daily access to enough nutritious food to have an active and healthy life.

genetically modified organisms: organisms whose genetic makeup has been altered by genetic engineering.

genetic engineering: insertion of an alien gene into an organism to give it a specific genetic trait.

green revolution: popular term for the introduction of scientifically bred or selected varieties of grain (rice, wheat, maize) that, with adequate inputs of fertilizer and water, can greatly increase crop yields.

industrialized agriculture: production of large quantities of crops and livestock for domestic and foreign sale; involves use of large inputs of energy from fossil fuels (especially oil and natural gas), water, fertilizer, and pesticides.

integrated pest management (IPM): combined use of biological, chemical, and cultivation methods in proper sequence and timing to keep the size of a pest population below the level that causes economically unacceptable loss of a crop or livestock.

irrigation: mix of methods used to supply water to crops by artificial means.

organic agriculture: growing crops with limited or no use of synthetic pesticides and synthetic fertilizers; genetically modified crops, raising livestock without use of synthetic growth regulators and feed additives; and using organic fertilizer (manure, legumes, compost) and natural pest controls (bugs that eat harmful bugs, plants that repel bugs, and environmental controls such as crop rotation).

organic fertilizer: organic materials such as animal manure, green manure, and compost applied to cropland as a source of plant nutrients.

pest: unwanted organism that directly or indirectly interferes with food production and other human activities.

plantation agriculture: growing specialized crops such as bananas, coffee, and cacao in tropical developing countries, primarily for sale to developed countries.

polyculture: complex form of intercropping in which a large number of different plants maturing at different times are planted together.

soil conservation: methods used to reduce soil erosion, prevent depletion of soil nutrients, and restore nutrients previously lost by erosion, leaching, and excessive crop harvesting.

soil erosion: movement of soil components, especially topsoil, from one place to another, usually by wind, flowing water, or both. This natural process can be greatly accelerated by human activities that remove vegetation from soil.

soil salinization: gradual accumulation of salts in upper layers of soil that can stunt crop growth, lower crop yields, and eventually kill plants and ruin the land.

synthetic fertilizer: commercially prepared mixture of inorganic plant nutrients such as nitrates, phosphates, and potassium applied to the soil to restore fertility and increase crop yields.

synthetic pesticides: any chemical designed to kill or inhibit the growth of an organism that people consider undesirable.

topsoil: uppermost layer of soil as a soil's A-horizon layer. It contains the organic and inorganic nutrients that plants need for their growth and development.

traditional intensive agriculture: production of enough food for a farm family's survival and a surplus that can be sold. This type of agriculture uses higher inputs of labor, fertilizer, and water than traditional subsistence agriculture.

traditional subsistence agriculture: production of enough crops or livestock for a farm family's survival.

waterlogging: saturation of soil with irrigation water or excessive precipitation so that the water table rises close to the surface.

Chapter Review

Core Case Study

1. (a) What is a **food desert**? (b) Summarize the benefits that the Growing Power farm has brought to its community. (c) How does the farm showcase the three scientific principles of sustainability?

Section 12.1

2. (a) What are the two key concepts for this section? (b) What is a basic requirement for maintaining good health and resisting disease? (c) Distinguish between **chronic undernutrition (hunger)** and **chronic malnutrition** and describe their harmful effects. What is **famine**? How many people in the world suffer from chronic hunger and malnutrition? (d) Describe the effects of diet deficiencies in vitamin A, iron, and iodine. (e) What is **overnutrition** and what are its harmful effects? What percentage of US adults over age 20 are overweight or obese? (f) What is the biggest contributor to hunger and malnutrition? Define **food security**.

Section 12.2

3. (a) What is the key concept for this section? (b) What three systems supply most of the world's food? (c) Define and distinguish among **irrigation**, **synthetic fertilizers**, and **synthetic pesticides**. (d) Define **industrialized agriculture (high-input agriculture)**. Define **yield**. (e) What is **plantation agriculture**? Distinguish between **traditional subsistence agriculture** and **traditional intensive agriculture**. (f) Define **polyculture** and summarize its benefits. (g) Define **organic agriculture** and compare its main components with those of conventional industrialized agriculture. What is USDA Certified Organic food? (h) What is a **green revolution**? Describe two green revolutions. (i) Define **farm subsidies**. (j) Summarize the story of industrialized food production in the United States. (k) What is an example of a hidden cost of food production?

4. (a) Define **genetic engineering** and distinguish between it and crossbreeding through artificial selection. (b) Describe the second gene revolution based on genetic engineering. (c) What is a **genetically modified organism (GMO)**? (d) Summarize the growth of industrialized meat production. What are feedlots and CAFOs? (e) What is a **fishery**? Describe methods that industrial fleets use to catch fish. What is **aquaculture (fish farming)**? (f) Explain why industrialized food production requires large inputs of energy. Why does it result in a net energy loss?

Section 12.3

5. (a) What is the key concept for this section? (b) What are the harmful effects of industrialized food production on biodiversity, soil, water, air pollution, and human health? List 10 harmful environmental effects of food production. (c) What is **topsoil**? What is **soil erosion**? Distinguish between *sheet erosion* and *rill erosion*. What are the two largest causes of soil erosion? What are the three major harmful effects of soil erosion? (d) What is **desertification** and what are its harmful environmental effects? (e) What percent of the water used by humanity is used to irrigate crops? (f) What is a *dust bowl*? (g) Define **soil salinization** and **waterlogging** and explain why they are harmful. (h)What is soil pollution and what are two of its causes?

6. (a) Summarize industrialized agriculture's contribution to current and projected climate change. (b) Explain how synthetic fertilizer use has increased and list two effects of overfertilization. (c) Explain how industrialized food production systems have caused losses in biodiversity. What is **agrobiodiversity** and how is it being affected by industrialized food production? (d) List the advantages and disadvantages of genetically modified crops and foods. (e) What factors can limit green revolutions? (f) Compare the benefits and harmful effects of industrialized meat production using feedlots and CAFOs. (g) Explain the connection between feeding livestock and the formation of ocean dead zones. (h) What are the advantages and disadvantages of aquaculture?

Section 12.4

7. (a) What is the key concept for this section? (b) What is a **pest**? Explain how nature controls most crop pests. (c) Define **synthetic pesticide** and list four types of synthetic pesticides. List six benefits and six harmful effects of using synthetic pesticides. (d)Describe how an insect pest can develop genetic resistance to a synthetic pesticide. (e) List four ways to reduce your exposure to synthetic pesticides. (f) How successful have synthetic pesticides been in reducing crop losses from pests in the United States? (g) Describe the use of laws and treaties to help protect US citizens from the harmful effects of pesticides. (h) What is the *circle of poison*? (i) Describe the use of *biological control, ecological control, cultivation control* and genetic engineering in controlling pests. (j) Define **integrated pest management (IPM)** and list its advantages.

Section 12.5

8. (a) What is the key concept for this section?
(b) What is **soil conservation**? Describe six ways to reduce topsoil erosion. (c) What is *hydroponics*? (d) Define **organic fertilizers** and name and describe three types of organic fertilizers. (e) Define **crop rotation** and explain how it can help restore topsoil fertility. (f) What are some ways to prevent and some ways to clean up soil salinization? (g) How can we reduce desertification? (h) What are six ways to make meat production and consumption more sustainable? (i) Describe five ways to make aquaculture more sustainable. (l) List eight benefits of organic agriculture. (k) What are nine important components of a more sustainable food production system? (l) List the advantages of relying more on organic polyculture and perennial crops. (m) Describe ecologist David Tilman's research on polyculture. (n) What are six important ways in which individual consumers can help to promote more sustainable food production?

Section 12.6

9. (a) What is the key concept for this section? (b) What are the two main approaches used by governments to influence food production? How have governments used subsidies to influence food production and what have been some of their effects? (c) What are two other ways in which organizations are improving food security? (d) Explain three of the benefits of buying locally grown food. When it is not a good choice? (e) What percent of the U.S. food supply is "wasted?" How can we cut food waste? (f) How can urban farming help to increase food security? (g) According to Lester Brown, how can we meet the challenges of improving food security?

10. What are this chapter's three key ideas?

Note: Key terms are in bold type.

AP® Review Questions

Questions 1–3 refer to the farming techniques listed below. Choices may be used once, more than once, or not at all.

(A) Hydroponics
(B) Intercropping
(C) Alley cropping
(D) Perennial polyculture
(E) Cover cropping

1. Immediately planting a nitrogen-fixing plant, such as a legume, to protect and rejuvenate the topsoil after growing a carbohydrate-rich grain that uses soil nitrogen

2. Growing crops between rows of trees

3. Growing plants by exposing the roots to nutrient-rich water instead of soil

4. Which of the following techniques helps to limit soil erosion?
(A) Cutting down all the trees in a specific area
(B) Growing one crop such as wheat, every season, on one parcel of land
(C) Planting crops on human-made broad, flat terraces that run across the slope of hilly land
(D) Allowing large numbers of animals to graze in a grassy area, which hardens the soil they stand on
(E) Driving off-road vehicles, because they flatten and harden the soil beneath them

5. Industrialized meat production has harmful environmental consequences. These include all of the following EXCEPT
(A) the use of large amounts of energy
(B) contributing to the eutrophication of the Gulf of Mexico
(C) contributing to global warming
(D) polluting the air, water, and soil with manure
(E) the natural control of pests

6. Which best describes genetically modified organisms (GMOs)?
(A) Genes are spliced from one plant species into another plant species.
(B) Planting a variety of crops in the same area such as native grass, grains, and sunflowers.
(C) Export crops such as bananas, coffee, and sugar cane are grown on large plantations and sold to developed countries.
(D) Fish are raised in underwater cages, protected from pest species.
(E) Plants are not grown in soil, but instead their roots are in nutrient-filled water so they are protected from pests that would otherwise damage them.

7. Which of the following would be a disadvantage to using pesticides?
   (A) Selective pesticides kill specific organisms, such as acequinocyl, which kills mites.
   (B) Pests become resistant to pesticides so farmers must use higher doses, at greater expense, to kill the pests.
   (C) By killing the pests that damage agricultural crops, pesticides help keep the price of food down.
   (D) Pesticides have a long shelf life, so farmers will not lose money if the pesticides are kept for a long time before being used.
   (E) Pesticides save lives by killing the vectors for diseases such as malaria, bubonic plague, and typhus.

8. Which of the following is the best example of a persistent pest control?
   (A) DDT, because it remained harmful in the environment for years
   (B) First-generation pesticides that are natural chemicals found in plants such as nicotine sulfate in tobacco leaves
   (C) Essential oils taken from common species that are easily grown, such as clove, mint, rosemary, and thyme
   (D) The natural presence of a pest-controlling species within an ecosystem
   (E) Genetically engineered pest-resistant crops

9. The following practices are used to grow organic crops EXCEPT
   (A) providing habitat for insects or other small invertebrates that feed on pests
   (B) keeping organic matter and nutrients in the soil as much as possible
   (C) planting crops before or after insect pests are there to cause damage
   (D) introducing natural enemies to the insect pests, such as releasing ladybugs or praying mantis insects
   (E) spraying pesticides on the roots so that the part of the plant that is eaten is not contaminated

10. Which of the following is a biological pest control method?
    (A) Bringing in natural enemies such as predators, parasites, and bacteria
    (B) Using synthetic herbicides
    (C) Allowing wind to carry pesticides from one region to another
    (D) Using broad-spectrum agents
    (E) Using a second-generation pesticide

11. The goal of integrated pest management is to
    (A) wipe out as many of the pest species as possible to save crops
    (B) wipe out as many of the pest species as possible to save human lives
    (C) genetically engineer as many crop species as possible to eliminate the need for pesticides
    (D) encourage farmers to grow organically, eliminating the need for pesticides
    (E) use biological, chemical, and cultivation techniques in a coordinated way to eliminate pest species

12. The GREATEST factor of malnutrition and hunger is
    (A) poverty
    (B) location
    (C) age
    (D) gender
    (E) genetic inheritance

Questions 13–16 refer to the fish harvesting methods below. Choices may be used once, more than once, or not at all.
    (A) Bottom-trawling
    (B) Purse-seine fishing
    (C) Long line fishing
    (D) Drift-net fishing
    (E) Sonar

13. Enclosing a school of fish with a large net, this method is used to capture yellowfin tuna

14. Can be 80 miles long with thousands of baited hooks, often resulting in bycatch of many ocean fish species

15. Dragging large nets along the sea floor to catch shrimp, shellfish and benthic fish

16. Often called "ghost-fishing" because these huge nets are left to float in the ocean by themselves for days, resulting in a large bycatch

17. A more sustainable form of meat production is to
    (A) graze beef in larger numbers but on local lands so the meat does not have to travel as far to the consumer
    (B) switch to poultry and farm-raised fish because these are more grain-efficient animals
    (C) inject cattle with hormones to grow larger with more muscle mass so fewer head of cattle would have to be raised
    (D) switch to beef rather than pork or poultry because cattle are larger and can supply meat to more people
    (E) use less land by putting more animals in feedlots and injecting them with antibiotics to keep them healthy

Questions 18–20 refer to the graph below of the collapse of the cod fishery in the northwest Atlantic.

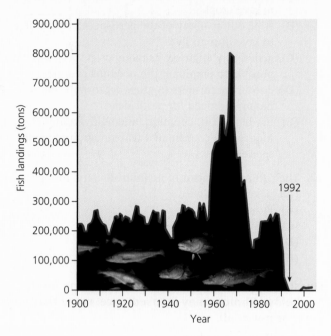

18. Identify the 10-year period showing the greatest rate of decline in the cod-fishing harvest.
- **(A)** 1940–1950
- **(B)** 1950–1960
- **(C)** 1960–1970
- **(D)** 1970–1980
- **(E)** 1990–2000

19. For the 10-year period showing the greatest rate of decline, calculate the average rate of decline in tons per year.
- **(A)** 6,000
- **(B)** 60,000
- **(C)** 80,000
- **(D)** 600,000
- **(E)** 800,000

20. The graph illustrates a concept known as
- **(A)** the tragedy of the commons
- **(B)** reduced carrying capacity
- **(C)** bycatch
- **(D)** riparian destruction
- **(E)** biological extinction

AP® Free-Response Practice

1. Thomas Malthus predicted that an exponentially growing human population would eventually outstrip food production. So far, technological innovations, such as irrigation techniques, pesticides, herbicides, and synthetic fertilizers have allowed food production to keep up with human population growth. However, the human population is expected to increase by another 2.4 billion people by the year 2050.

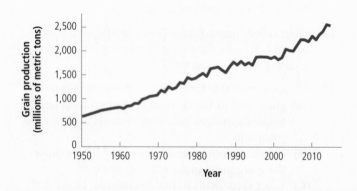
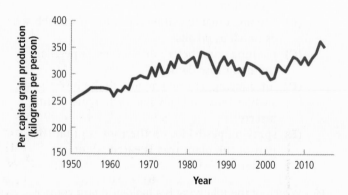

(a) The graphs show the relationship between worldwide grain production per year and per capita grain production.

(i) Explain why per capita grain production does not follow the same trend as worldwide grain production.

(ii) Identify ONE new technology, other than those mentioned above, that may be implemented to increase food production.

(iii) Identify and **discuss** TWO possible benefits of this new technology.

(iv) Identify and **discuss** TWO possible drawbacks of this new technology.

(b) Climate change will have a significant impact on food security.

   (i) Identify TWO negative impacts of climate change on food production.

   (ii) Discuss how each impact of climate change will reduce food production.

   (iii) Discuss ONE governmental strategy that can be implemented to increase food security, other than using subsidies or artificially controlling food prices.

Critical Thinking

1. Suppose you got a job with Growing Power, Inc. (**Core Case Study**) and were given the assignment to turn an abandoned suburban shopping center and its large parking lot into an organic farm. Write up a plan for how you would accomplish this.

2. Do you think that the advantages of organic agriculture outweigh its disadvantages? Explain. Do you eat or grow organic foods? If so, explain your reasoning for making this choice. If not, explain your reasoning for some of the food choices you do make.

3. Food producers can now produce more than enough food to feed everyone on the planet a healthy diet. Given this fact, why do you think that nearly a billion people are chronically undernourished or malnourished? Assume you are in charge of solving this problem, and write a plan for how you will accomplish it.

4. Explain why you support or oppose greatly increasing the use of **(a)** genetically modified (GM) foods and **(b)** organic perennial polyculture.

5. Suppose you work for a farmer and are given the assignment of deciding whether to use no-till agriculture on the farmer's fields or to continue using conventional plowing and weed control methods. Compare the advantages and disadvantages of each and decide how you will advise your boss. Write up a report and provide evidence to support your arguments.

6. You are the head of a major agricultural agency in the area where you live. Weigh the advantages and disadvantages of using synthetic pesticides and explain why you would support or oppose the increased use of such pesticides as a way to help farmers raise their yields. What are the alternatives? Give evidence to support your claims.

7. If the mosquito population in the area where you live were proven to be carrying malaria or some dangerous virus, would you want to spray DDT in your yard, inside your home, or all through the local area to reduce this risk? Explain. What are the alternatives?

8. According to physicist Albert Einstein, "Nothing will benefit human health and increase the chances of survival of life on Earth as much as the evolution to a vegetarian diet." Explain your interpretation of this statement. Are you willing to eat less meat or no meat? Explain.

Ecological Footprint Analysis

The following table gives the world's fish harvest and population data.

1. Use the world fish harvest and population data in the table to calculate the per capita fish consumption for 1990–2012 in kilograms per person. (*Hints:* 1 million metric tons equals 1 billion kilograms; the human population data are expressed in billions; and per capita consumption can be calculated directly by dividing the total amount consumed by a population figure for any year.)

2. Did per capita fish consumption generally increase or decrease between 1990 and 2012?

3. In what years did per capita fish consumption decrease?

WORLD FISH HARVEST

Years	Fish Catch (million metric tons)	Aquaculture (million metric tons)	Total (million metric tons)	World Population (in billions)	Per Capita Fish Consumption (kilograms/person)
1990	84.8	13.1	97.9	5.27	
1991	83.7	13.7	97.4	5.36	
1992	85.2	15.4	100.6	5.44	
1993	86.6	17.8	104.4	5.52	
1994	92.1	20.8	112.9	5.60	
1995	92.4	24.4	116.8	5.68	
1996	93.8	26.6	120.4	5.76	
1997	94.3	28.6	122.9	5.84	
1998	87.6	30.5	118.1	5.92	
1999	93.7	33.4	127.1	6.00	
2000	95.5	35.5	131.0	6.07	
2001	92.8	37.8	130.6	6.15	
2002	93.0	40.0	133.0	6.22	
2003	90.2	42.3	132.5	6.31	
2004	94.6	45.9	140.5	6.39	
2005	94.2	48.5	142.7	6.46	
2006	92.0	51.7	143.7	6.54	
2007	90.1	52.1	142.2	6.61	
2008	89.7	52.5	142.3	6.69	
2009	90.0	55.7	145.7	6.82	
2010	89.0	59.0	148.0	6.90	
2011	93.5	62.7	156.2	7.00	
2012	90.2	66.5	156.7	7.05	

Compiled by the authors using data from UN Food and Agriculture Organization and Earth Policy Institute.

Answers to Checkpoints for Understanding

Section 12.1

1. A lack of vitamin A and zinc results in blindness and death. A lack of iron results in anemia, a weak immune system, and possible hemorrhage during childbirth, leading to death. A deficiency in iodine results in and enlarged thyroid (goiter), stunted growth, and mental retardation.

2. Undernutrition and overnutrition both result in lowered life expectancy, greater susceptibility to disease, and lower productivity and quality of life.

Section 12.2

1. The three systems that provide most of our food are (a) croplands, (b) rangelands, pastures, and feedlots, and (c) fisheries.

2. Monocultures of high-yield rice, wheat, and corn were grown; heavy use of synthetic pesticides, fertilizers, and water; and several plantings were grown throughout the year.

3. Some of the benefits of GM foods are pest resistance, increased nutritional value, higher yield, longer shelf-life, larger fruits, and faster-growing animals. Drawbacks include unpredictable genetic and ecological effects, may put toxins in food, could repel or harm pollinators, can promote super weeds and pests, and could reduce biodiversity.

4. Some natural fisheries have been depleted by overfishing. Aquaculture is a way to produce enough fish to meet the demands of human consumption; however, it is very fossil fuel energy intensive.

5. It takes approximately 10 units of energy (in calories) to produce one equivalent unit of food. This is because in industrialized agriculture, energy must be used to run farm equipment, run irrigation systems, produce synthetic pesticides and fertilizers, and to process and transport food.

Section 12.3

1. Industrialized agriculture uses huge amounts of energy and fresh water, uses vast amounts of land, reduces biodiversity, and pollutes surface and groundwater.

2. Soil is lost through erosion by wind and water and is polluted via air pollution, suffers desertification via drought and human activity that can convert semiarid land to desert, and excessive irrigation can salinize soil and pollute it.

3. As expanding populations seek more land for growing crops and grazing cattle, semiarid land is converted to agricultural land, and overgrazing of rangelands occurs, which reduces vegetation cover and exposes topsoil to wind and water erosion. Successively planting crops without adding fertilizer in order to feed more people also depletes topsoil nutrients.

4. Expanding the green revolution requires increasing inputs of water, energy, pesticides, herbicides, and synthetic fertilizers. Eventually a point is reached where yields do not increase with added inputs. Additional irrigation water is limited, soil salinization results from excessive irrigation, and climate change is expected to reduce crop yields. Clearing forests to increase cropland will reduce biodiversity and loss of habitat for other species as well as speed up climate change and increase soil erosion.

5. Meat produced from CAFOs is artificially cheap because huge amounts of water are used to grow the grain needed to feed the animals, depleting groundwater supplies. Feedlot runoff pollutes surface and groundwater. Large amounts of fossil fuels are used to grow the feed, and methane is produced by animals, adding to climate change. Because of their unnaturally close confines, antibiotics are used to keep disease down among the animals, which can be passed on in the meat to consumers.

6. Feed for fish raised by aquaculture comes from harvesting wild fish and producing fish meal and fish oil. PCBs and dioxin deposited on the ocean floor can be taken up and ingested by farmed fish when fed the fish meal, and pesticides and antibiotics are used to control disease as farmed fish are kept in very close confines. Shrimp farming destroys mangrove forests and destroys the biodiversity and ecosystem services that they provide.

Section 12.4

1. Synthetic pesticide kills pests and beneficial insects—those that naturally keep pest populations in check.

2. Genetic resistance occurs when a pesticide is used and a few of the organisms are resistant to the pesticide. Those individuals reproduce, passing on their genes for resistance to the next generation. The pesticide becomes less and less effective as time goes on, and a farmer must find a different or stronger pesticide to eliminate the resistant pests.

3. FIFRA is the Federal Insecticide, Fungicide, and Rodenticide Act. It regulates the use of pesticides and evaluates them for toxicity.

4. The goal of Integrated Pest Management is to control, not eliminate, a pest using a variety of strategies including pheromone traps, predatory insects, and disease organisms that specifically target a pest, altering habitat or other ecologically grounded means rather than synthetic pesticides. Pesticides are used only as a last resort and in small amounts during the juvenile stage when insects are most vulnerable.

Section 12.5

1. Farming methods that conserve topsoil include terrace and contour planting, strip cropping and alley cropping, planting windbreaks, and no-till agriculture (which increases the use of herbicides).

2. Benefits of using organic fertilizers (animal manure and urine, green manure, and compost) include using a waste product readily available to enrich soil rather than disposing of it, less use of toxic synthetic fertilizers that are made from nonrenewable petroleum, and organic fertilizers maintain soil structure and nutrient-holding capacity.

3. Strategies for making aquaculture more sustainable include open-ocean aquaculture where fish are raised far from shore in huge pens and wastes can be easily diluted and biodegraded in ocean water, recirculating aquaculture systems where inland operations recycle and clean the water, and polyaquaculture where wastes from the fish are used to grow other useful plants and animals.

4. Organic farming builds soil organic matter, reduces erosion and water pollution, uses less fossil fuels, reduces greenhouse gas emissions, and produces equal crop yields to nonorganic methods. Organic systems are more weed and drought tolerant.

5. Consumers can eat no meat, less meat, or organically raised meat. They can also eat sustainably raised herbivorous fish, buy locally grown food, cut back on food waste, buy certified organic food, and grow some of their own organic produce.

Section 12.6

1. Food security is the condition under which every person in a given area has daily access to enough nutritious food to have an active and healthy life. Impediments to food security are poverty, war, government corruption, weather that destroys crops, and climate change.

2. Subsidies give farmers added income and manipulate the market price of commodity crops and livestock. Most subsidies go to industrialized food systems, which benefit CAFOs and other highly polluting and environmentally degrading practices.

3. Eliminating childhood poverty so that children have adequate nutrition, preserving diverse gene pools, and implementing simple, sustainable food systems in areas that lack food security can ensure that all individuals have their nutritional needs met daily.

4. Locally grown food is fresher, uses less fossil fuels and usually produces less greenhouse gases when transporting produce to market, and supports local economies.

Core Case Study

As an ecologically-based urban farm in Milwaukee, Wisconsin, Growing Power, Inc. grows food more sustainably by (1) using the sun to produce electricity and heat water by applying the solar energy sustainability principle, (2) producing a diversity of crops and sources of meat built on using the biodiversity sustainability principle, and (3) applying the chemical cycling principle by recycling its nutrients. It also educates visitors and employees about how to grow food more sustainably.

CHAPTER 13

Water Resources

> Through the cycling of water, across space and time, we are linked to all life. . . . Water's gift is life. No water, no life.
>
> SANDRA POSTEL

Key Questions

13.1 Will we have enough usable water?

13.2 Is groundwater a sustainable resource?

13.3 How can we increase freshwater supplies?

13.4 Can water transfers expand water supplies?

13.5 How can we use freshwater more sustainably?

13.6 How can we reduce the threat of flooding?

Glen Canyon Dam and Lake Mead on the Colorado River, Arizona USA

Pytyczech/Dreamstime.com

The Colorado River Story

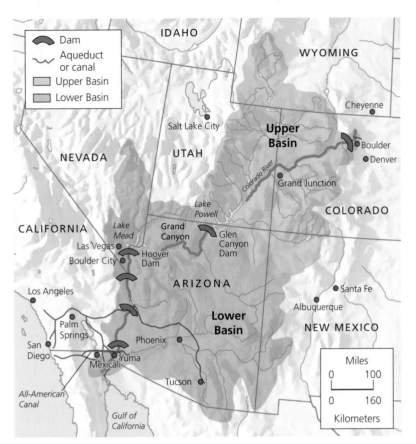

milosk50/Shutterstock.com

FIGURE 13.1 The *Colorado River basin:* The area drained by this river system is more than one-twelfth of the land area of the lower 48 states. This map shows 6 of the river's 14 dams. The photo shows the Hoover Dam and Reservoir of Nevada and Arizona.

The Colorado River, the major river of the arid southwestern United States, flows 2,300 kilometers (1,400 miles) through seven states to the Gulf of California (Figure 13.1, map). Most of its water comes from snowmelt in the Rocky Mountains. During the past 100 years, this once free-flowing river has been tamed by a gigantic plumbing system consisting of 14 major dams and reservoirs (Figure 13.1, photo) and canals that carry water to farmers, ranchers, industries, and cities.

This system of dams and reservoirs provides electricity from its hydroelectric plants to roughly 40 million people in seven states—about one of every eight people in the United States. It supplies irrigation water that is used to produce about 15% of the nation's crops and livestock. It also provides 90% of the drinking water

for Las Vegas, Nevada, and large amounts of the water used in Phoenix, Arizona, and San Diego and Los Angeles, California. Take away the Colorado River's dam-and-reservoir system, and these cities would become largely uninhabitable desert areas. In California's Imperial Valley, vast fields of vegetables would eventually give way to cactus and mesquite plants.

So much water is withdrawn from this river to grow crops and support cities in a desert-like climate that very little of it reaches the sea. To make matters worse, since 1999, the system has experienced severe **drought,** a prolonged period, usually a season or more, in which precipitation is lower than normal and evaporation is higher than normal. As a result, in 2015, Lake Mead (chapter-opening photo) sank to a record low water level.

This overuse of the Colorado River illustrates the challenges faced by governments and people living in arid and semiarid regions with shared river systems. There are many of these arid, water-short areas scattered around the globe. In such areas, population growth and economic growth are putting increasing demands on limited or decreasing supplies of surface water.

To many analysts, emerging shortages of water for drinking and irrigation in several parts of the world represent one of the major environmental challenges of this century.●

CRITICAL THINKING

What are some of the foreseeable stresses on the Colorado River that will make it increasingly difficult to use this water source sustainably?

WILL WE HAVE ENOUGH USABLE WATER?

CONCEPT 13.1A We are using available freshwater unsustainably by extracting it faster than nature can replace it, and by wasting, polluting, and underpricing this irreplaceable natural resource.

CONCEPT 13.1B Freshwater supplies are not evenly distributed, and 1 of every 10 people on the planet does not have adequate access to clean water.

Freshwater Is an Irreplaceable Resource That We Are Managing Poorly

We live on a planet that is unique in our solar system because of a precious layer of water—most of it saltwater—covering about 71% of its surface. Look in the mirror. What you see is about 60% water, most of it inside your cells.

Water is an amazing chemical with unique properties that help to keep us and other species alive (see Science Focus 13.1). You could survive for several weeks without food, but for only a few days without **freshwater,** or water that contains very low levels of dissolved salts. We have no substitute for this vital form of natural capital (**Concept 13.1A**).

It takes huge amounts of water to supply food and most of the other things that we use to meet our daily needs and wants. Water also plays a key role in determining the earth's climates and in removing and diluting some of the pollutants and wastes that we produce. And over eons, it has sculpted the planet's surface, creating valleys, canyons, and other land features.

Freshwater is one of the earth's most important forms of natural capital, but despite its importance, it is also one of our most poorly managed resources. We use it inefficiently and pollute it, and we do not value it highly enough. As a result, it is available at too low a cost to billions of consumers, and this encourages waste and pollution of this resource, for which we have no substitute (**Concept 13.1A**).

Access to freshwater is a *global health issue*. The World Health Organization (WHO) has estimated that each day, an average of more than 4,100 people die from waterborne infectious diseases because they do not have access to safe drinking water.

Access to freshwater is also an *economic issue* because water is vital for producing food and energy and for reducing poverty. According to the WHO, just 52% of the world's people have water piped to their homes. The rest have to find and carry it from distant sources or wells. This daily task usually falls to women and children (Figure 13.2).

Water is also a *national and global security issue* because of increasing tensions within and between some nations over access to limited freshwater resources that they share.

Finally, water is an *environmental issue* because excessive withdrawal of freshwater from rivers and aquifers has resulted in falling water tables, dwindling river flows (**Core Case Study**), shrinking lakes, and disappearing wetlands. This, in combination with water pollution in many areas of the world, has degraded water quality, reduced fish populations, hastened the extinction of some aquatic species,

Shiv Ji Joshi/National Geographic Creative

FIGURE 13.2 Each day these women carry water to their village in a dry area of India.

Water's Unique Properties

Water (H_2O) is a remarkable substance with a unique combination of properties:

- *Water exists as a liquid over a wide temperature range because of forces of attraction between its molecules.* If liquid water had a much narrower range of temperatures between freezing and boiling, the oceans might have frozen solid or boiled away long ago.

- *Liquid water changes temperature slowly because it can store a large amount of heat without a large change in its own temperature.* This helps protect living organisms from temperature changes, moderates the earth's climate, and makes water an excellent coolant for car engines and power plants.

- *It takes a large amount of energy to evaporate water because of the attractive forces between its molecules.* Water absorbs large amounts of heat as it changes into water vapor and releases this heat as the vapor condenses back to liquid water. This helps to distribute heat throughout the world and to determine regional and local climates. It also makes evaporation a cooling process—explaining why you feel cooler when perspiration evaporates from your skin.

- *Liquid water can dissolve a variety of compounds.* It carries dissolved nutrients into the tissues of living organisms, flushes waste products out of those tissues, serves as an all-purpose cleanser, and helps to remove and dilute the water-soluble wastes of civilization. This property also means that water-soluble wastes can easily pollute water.

- *Water filters out wavelengths of the sun's ultraviolet radiation that would harm some aquatic organisms.* (See Figure 2.12, p. 48.) This allows life to exist in the upper layer of aquatic systems.

- *Unlike most liquids, water expands when it freezes.* This means that ice floats on water because it has a lower density (mass per unit of volume) than liquid water has. Otherwise, lakes and streams in cold climates would freeze solid from the bottom up and loose most of their aquatic life. Because water expands on freezing, it can break pipes, crack a car's engine block (if it does not contain antifreeze), break up pavement, and fracture rocks.

CRITICAL THINKING

Pick two of the special properties listed above and, for each property, explain how life on the earth would be different if it did not exist. What are two advantages that microbes have over humans for thriving in the world?

---

and degraded aquatic ecosystem services (see Figures 6.4, p. 156, 6.12, p. 163, and 6.13, p. 164).

Most of the Earth's Freshwater Is Not Available to Us

Only *0.024%* of the planet's enormous water supply is readily available to us as liquid freshwater stored in accessible underground deposits and in lakes, rivers, and streams. The rest is in the salty oceans (about 96.5% of the earth's volume of liquid water), in frozen polar ice caps and glaciers (1.7%), and underground (1.7%).

Fortunately, the world's freshwater supply is continually recycled, purified, and distributed in the earth's *hydrologic cycle* (see Figure 3.14, p. 77). However, this vital ecosystem service begins to fail when we overload it with water pollutants or withdraw freshwater from underground and surface water supplies faster than natural processes replenish it.

In addition, research indicates that atmospheric warming is altering the water cycle by evaporating more water into the atmosphere. As a result, wet places will get wetter with more frequent and heavier flooding and dry places will get drier with more intense drought.

We have paid little attention to our effects on the water cycle mostly because we have thought of the earth's fresh-water as a free and infinite resource. As a result, we have placed little or no economic value on the irreplaceable ecosystem services that water provides (**Concept 13.1A**), a serious violation of the full-cost pricing **principle of sustainability** (see Inside Back Cover). On a global basis, we have plenty of freshwater, but it is not distributed evenly (**Concept 13.1B**). Differences in average annual precipitation and economic resources divide the world's countries and people into water *haves* and *have-nots*. For example, Canada, with only 0.5% of the world's population, has 19% of its liquid freshwater, while China, with 19% of the world's people, has only 6.5% of the supply.

Groundwater and Surface Water Are Critical Resources

Some precipitation soaks into the ground and sinks downward through spaces in soil, gravel, and rock until an impenetrable layer of rock or clay stops it. The freshwater in these underground spaces is called **groundwater**—a key component of the earth's natural capital (Figure 13.3).

The spaces in soil and rock close to the earth's surface hold little moisture. However, below a certain depth, in the **zone of saturation,** these spaces are completely filled with freshwater. The top of this groundwater zone is the

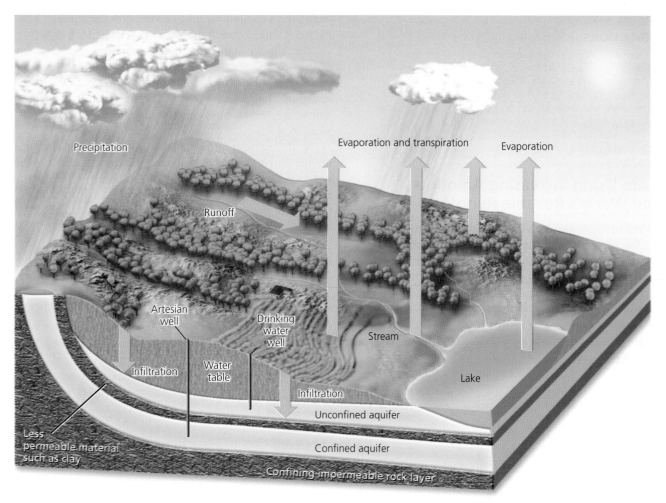

Labels in figure:
Precipitation
Evaporation and transpiration
Evaporation
Runoff
Artesian well
Drinking water well
Stream
Infiltration
Water table
Lake
Infiltration
Unconfined aquifer
Less permeable material such as clay
Confined aquifer
Confining impermeable rock layer

FIGURE 13.3 Natural capital: Much of the water that falls in precipitation seeps into the ground to become groundwater, stored in aquifers.

water table. It falls in dry weather, or when we remove groundwater from this zone faster than nature can replenish it, and it rises in wet weather.

Deeper down are geological layers called **aquifers,** caverns and porous layers of sand, gravel or rock through which groundwater flows. Some aquifers contain caverns with rivers of groundwater flowing through them. However, most aquifers are like large, elongated sponges where groundwater seeps through porous layers of sand, gravel, or rock—typically moving only a meter or so (about 3 feet) per year and rarely more than 0.3 meter (1 foot) per day. Watertight layers of rock or clay below such aquifers keep the freshwater from escaping deeper into the earth.

We use pumps to bring this groundwater to the surface for irrigating crops and supplying households and industries. Most aquifers are replenished, or *recharged*, naturally by precipitation that sinks downward through exposed soil and rock. Others are recharged from the side from nearby lakes, rivers, and streams (Figure 13.3).

According to the US Geological Survey (USGS), groundwater makes up 95% of all freshwater available to us and other forms of life. However, most aquifers re-charge slowly. Because so much of the earth's urban area landscapes have been built on or paved over, freshwater can no longer penetrate the ground to recharge aquifers below such areas. And in dry areas of the world, there is little precipitation available to recharge aquifers.

Some aquifers, called *deep aquifers*, were filled with water by glaciers that melted thousands of years ago. For this reason, they are also called *fossil aquifers*. Most of them, because of geological factors, cannot be recharged or will require many thousands of years to recharge. Deep aquifers are nonrenewable, at least on the human timescale.

Another crucial resource is **surface water,** the fresh-water from rain and melted snow that flows or is stored in lakes, reservoirs, wetlands, streams, and rivers. Precipitation that does not soak into the ground or return to the atmosphere by evaporation is called **surface runoff.** The land from which surface runoff drains into a particular stream, lake, wetland, or other body of water is called its **watershed,** or **drainage basin.** The drainage basin for the Colorado River is shown in yellow and green on the map in Figure 13.1 (**Core Case Study**).

CONNECTIONS Groundwater and Surface Water

There is usually a connection between surface water and groundwater because much groundwater flows into rivers, lakes, estuaries, and wetlands. Thus, if we remove groundwater in a particular location faster than it is replenished, nearby streams, lakes, and wetlands can dry up. This process degrades aquatic biodiversity and other ecosystem services.

We Are Using Increasing Amounts of the World's Reliable Runoff

According to *hydrologists*, scientists who study water and its properties and movement, two-thirds of the annual surface runoff of freshwater into rivers and streams is lost in seasonal floods and is not available for human use. The remaining one-third is **reliable surface runoff,** which we can generally count on as a source of freshwater from year to year. **GREEN CAREER: Hydrologist**

During the last century, the human population tripled, global water withdrawals increased sevenfold, and per capita withdrawals quadrupled. As a result, we now withdraw an estimated 34% of the world's reliable runoff. This is a global average. In the arid American Southwest, up to 70% of the reliable runoff is withdrawn for human purposes, mostly for irrigation (**Core Case Study**). Some water experts project that because of population growth, rising rates of water use per person, longer dry periods in some areas, and unnecessary water waste, we are likely to be withdrawing up to 90% of the world's reliable freshwater runoff by 2025.

Worldwide, we use 70% of the freshwater we withdraw each year from rivers, lakes, and aquifers to irrigate cropland and raise livestock. In arid regions, up to 90% of the regional water supply is used for food production. Industry uses roughly another 20% of the water withdrawn globally each year, and cities and residences use the remaining 10%.

Freshwater Resources in the United States

According to the USGS, the major uses of groundwater and surface freshwater in the United States are the cooling of electric power plants, irrigation, public water supplies, industry, and livestock production (Figure 13.4, left). Household water is used mostly for flushing toilets, washing clothes,

taking showers, and running faucets, or is lost through leaking pipes, faucets, and other fixtures (Figure 13.4, right).

The United States has more than enough renewable freshwater to meet its needs. However, it is unevenly distributed and much of it is contaminated by agricultural and industrial practices. The eastern states usually have ample precipitation, whereas many western and southwestern states have little (Figure 13.5).

In the eastern United States, most water is used for manufacturing and cooling power plants (with most of the water heated and returned to its source), while in the west, most water is used for irrigation. The west faces severe water shortages due to high evaporation of irrigation water, low precipitation, and severe drought.

Most Americans rely on groundwater for drinking water, irrigation, and industrial use. Groundwater is currently be-

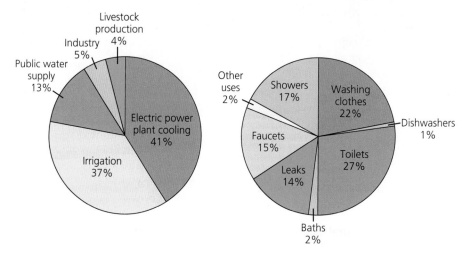

FIGURE 13.4 Comparison of primary uses of water in the United States (left) and uses of water in a typical US household (right). ***Data analysis:*** Which three categories, added together (right), are smaller than the amount of water lost in leaks?

(Compiled by the authors using data from US Geological Survey, World Resources Institute, and American Water Works Association.)

Average annual precipitation (centimeters)

	Less than 41		81–122
	41–81		More than 122

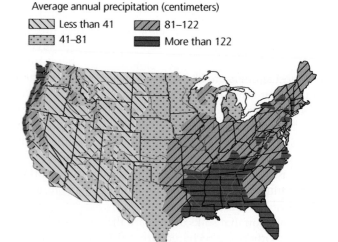

FIGURE 13.5 Long-term average annual precipitation and major rivers in the continental United States.

(Compiled by the authors using data from US Water Resources Council and US Geological Survey.)

Your Water Footprint

Think about all of the water you use in a day. From showering, flushing the toilet, drinking, cooking, and washing clothes, individuals in the United States consume between 300 and 380 liters (80 to 100 gallons) of water per person. Your **water footprint** is a rough measure of the volume of freshwater that you use or pollute, directly or indirectly, to stay alive and support your lifestyle. It is easy to visualize the water you use directly in your home. But what about the water you use *indirectly*? **Virtual water** is freshwater not directly consumed but used to produce food and other products.

For example, it takes about 1,800 liters (480 gallons or 12 bathtubs full) of water to produce one hamburger with most of the water being used to grow the corn to feed the cow. The figure below shows the approximate amount of water needed to produce some of the products you consume.

Virtual water can be exported from one country to another as part of the product. Foods like wheat, soybeans, and coffee are grown, usually by irrigating with large amounts of groundwater, and then exported to another country. Brazil, a major exporter of agricultural products, is one of the largest exporters of virtual water. In fact, Brazil's supply of freshwater per person is eight times that of a citizen in the United States. Some countries like Australia that are experiencing severe drought have a difficult time meeting the demand for their crops because of the lack of freshwater.

FRQ Application

Question: Virtual water is water not directly consumed, but water used indirectly in the production of a consumable product. Manufacturing a white cotton T-shirt uses 1,060 liters (280 gallons) of fresh water. **Identify** THREE steps along the production cycle of a white cotton T-shirt that would consume virtual water.

Possible Response: Virtual water is water that is either consumed or polluted while making a product or growing crops. In the case of making a T-shirt, cotton must be grown to produce fabric for a shirt which would consume great quantities of freshwater. Along with growing the cotton, irrigation of fields would pollute runoff water with nutrients or pesticides that could flow into nearby waterways. Water must also be used in manufacturing the T-shirt in bleaching the cotton and cooling machinery.

Bathtub (40 gallons)

| Coffee: 0.9 tub | Bread: 4 tubs | Hamburger: 12 tubs | T-shirt: 17 tubs | Jeans: 72 tubs | Car: 2,600 tubs | House: 16,600 tubs |

FIGURE 13.A Producing and delivering a single one of each of the products listed here requires the equivalent of nearly one and usually many bathtubs full of freshwater, called *virtual water. Note:* 1 bathtub = 151 liters (40 gallons).

(Compiled by the authors using data from UN Food and Agriculture Organization, UNESCO-IHE Institute for Water Education, World Water Council, and Water Footprint Network.)

Bathtub: Baloncici/Shutterstock.com. Coffee: Aleksandra Nadeina/Shutterstock.com. Bread: Alexander Kalina/Shutterstock.com. Hamburger: Joe Belanger/Shutterstock.com. T-shirt: grmarc/Shutterstock.com. Jeans: Eyes wide/Shutterstock.com. Car: L Barnwell/Shutterstock.com. House: Rafal Olechowski/Shutterstock.com

ing used unsustainably—it is pumped out faster than the rate at which some US aquifers can be naturally recharged. Water shortages are expected to increase as populations grow, industrialized agriculture increases, drought occurs more often, and virtual water use increases.

The US Department of the Interior has mapped out *water hotspots* in 17 western states (Figure 13.6). In these areas, competition for scarce freshwater to support growing urban areas, irrigation, recreation, and wildlife could trigger intense political and legal conflicts between states and between rural and urban areas within states. Based on climate models generated at Columbia University, it is projected that the southwest United States and northern Mexico are likely to have long periods of extreme drought throughout the rest of this century.

The Colorado River (as discussed in the Core Case Study) will be directly affected by such drought. Four factors will impact this river system. *First,* the Colorado River basin is located in some of the driest lands in the United States and Mexico. *Second,* legal agreements between the United States and Mexico allocate more water for human use than the river can supply. *Third,* because of the many dams installed along the Colorado River and the water that is diverted to cities and agricultural

Highly likely conflict potential
Substantial conflict potential
Moderate conflict potential
Unmet rural water needs

FIGURE 13.6 Water scarcity hotspots in 17 western states that, by 2025, could face intense conflicts over scarce water needed for urban growth, irrigation, recreation, and wildlife. **Question:** Which, if any, of these areas are found in the Colorado River basin (**Core Case Study**)?

(Compiled by the authors using data from US Department of the Interior and US Geological Survey.)

regions, the river has rarely flowed all the way to the Gulf of California. *Fourth,* the river receives enormous amounts of pollutants from urban areas, farms, animal feedlots, and industries as it makes its way toward the sea.

Freshwater Shortages Will Grow

Freshwater scarcity stress is a measure based on the amount of freshwater available compared to the amount used for human purposes. Like the Colorado River (**Core Case Study**), many of the world's major river systems are highly stressed (Figure 13.7). They include the Nile, Jordan, Yangtze, and Ganges Rivers, whose flows regularly dwindle to almost nothing in some locations.

More than 30 countries—most of them in the Middle East and Africa—now face stress from freshwater scarcity, according to the UN. By 2050, some 60 countries, many of them in Asia, with three-fourths of the world's population, are likely to be suffering from such freshwater scarcity stress. The Chinese government has reported that two-thirds of China's 600 major cities face freshwater shortages.

Currently, about 30% of the earth's land area—a total area roughly 5 times the size of the United States—experiences severe drought. By 2059, as much as 45% of the earth's land surface could experience an even higher level of drought, called *extreme drought,* due to natural

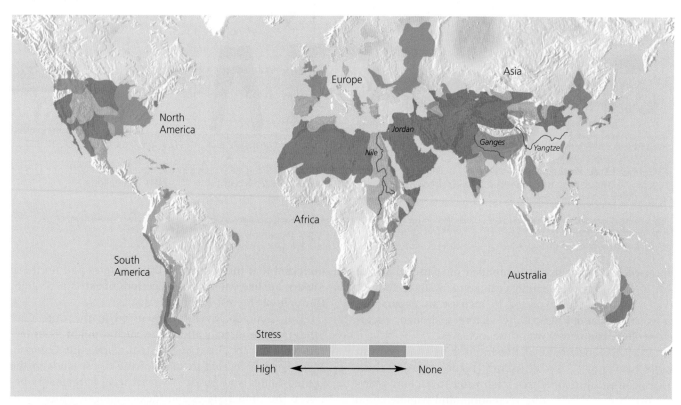

FIGURE 13.7 Natural capital degradation: The world's major river basins differ in their degree of freshwater *scarcity stress* (**Concept 13.1B**).

(Compiled by the authors using data from World Commission on Water Use for the 21st Century, UN Food and Agriculture Organization, and World Water Council.)

cycles and projected climate change, according to a study by climate researcher David Rind and his colleagues.

In 276 of the world's water basins, two or more countries share the available freshwater supplies. However, not all of these countries participate in water-sharing agreements. As a result, international conflicts over water are likely to occur as populations grow, as demand for water increases, and as supplies shrink in many parts of the world.

In 2015, the United Nations (UN) and the WHO reported that about 783 million people—about 2.4 times the US population—did not have regular access to enough clean water for drinking, cooking, and washing, mostly due to poverty (**Concept 13.1B**). The report also noted that more than 2 billion people have gained access to clean water since 1990.

GOOD NEWS

783 million
Number of people without regular access to clean water

Many analysts view the likelihood of expanding water shortages as one of our most serious environmental, health, and economic challenges.

CHECKPOINT FOR UNDERSTANDING 13.1

1. Explain how the warming of the atmosphere (climate change) impacts rainfall patterns.

2. Identify the two major sources of available freshwater.

3. Identify the human activity that uses the bulk of available freshwater.

4. Overall, the United States has an adequate water supply. Explain why water shortages are still a problem.

13.2 IS GROUNDWATER A SUSTAINABLE RESOURCE?

CONCEPT 13.2 Groundwater used to supply cities and grow food is being pumped from many aquifers faster than it is renewed by precipitation.

Groundwater Withdrawals are Unsustainable in Some Areas

Aquifers provide drinking water for nearly half of the world's people. Most aquifers are renewable resources unless the groundwater they contain becomes contaminated or is removed faster than it is replenished. Relying more on groundwater has advantages and disadvantages (Figure 13.8).

Test wells and satellite data indicate that water tables are falling in many areas of the world. One reason is that the rate at which water is being pumped out of most of the world's aquifers (mostly to irrigate crops) is greater than the rate of natural recharge from rainfall and snowmelt (**Concept 13.2**). The world's three largest grain producers—China, the United States, and India—as well as a number of other countries are overpumping many of their aquifers.

Every day, the world withdraws enough freshwater from aquifers to fill a convoy of large tanker trucks that could stretch 480,000 kilometers (300,000 miles)—well beyond the distance to the moon. According to the World Bank, in 2012, more than 400 million people were consuming grain produced through this unsustainable use of groundwater. This number is growing.

The widespread drilling of wells by farmers, especially in India and China, has accelerated aquifer overpumping. As water tables fall, farmers drill deeper wells and buy larger pumps to bring more water to the surface. This process eventually depletes the groundwater in some aquifers or at least removes all the water that can be pumped at an affordable cost.

In Saudi Arabia, freshwater has been pumped from a deep, nonrenewable aquifer to irrigate crops such as wheat (Figure 13.9). It also is used to fill fountains and swimming pools, which lose a great deal of water through evaporation into the dry desert air. In 2008, Saudi Arabia announced that it had largely depleted its major deep aquifer. The country

Trade-Offs

Withdrawing Groundwater

Advantages	Disadvantages
Useful for drinking and irrigation	Aquifer depletion from overpumping
Exists almost everywhere	Sinking of land (subsidence) from overpumping
Renewable if not overpumped or contaminated	Some deeper aquifers are nonrenewable
Cheaper to extract than most surface waters	Pollution of aquifers lasts decades or centuries

FIGURE 13.8 Withdrawing groundwater from aquifers has advantages and disadvantages. ***Critical thinking:*** Which two advantages and which two disadvantages do you think are the most important? Why?

Top: Ulrich Mueller/Shutterstock.com

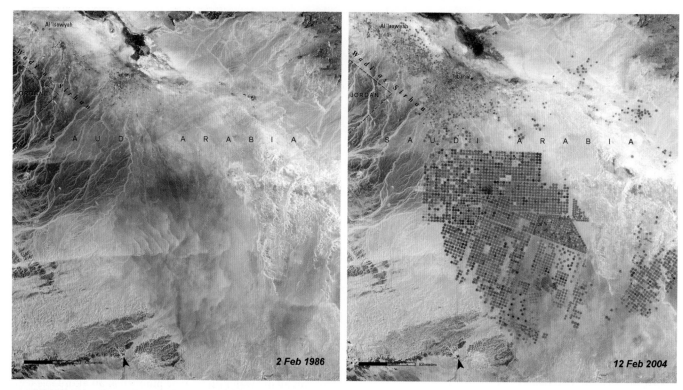

FIGURE 13.9 Natural capital degradation: Satellite photos of farmland irrigated by groundwater pumped from a deep aquifer in a vast desert region of Saudi Arabia between 1986 (left) and 2004 (right). Irrigated areas appear as green dots (each representing a circular spray system) and brown dots show areas where wells have gone dry and the land has returned to desert. Since 2004, many more wells have gone dry.

Left: U.N. Environment Programme and US Geological Survey. Right: UN Environment Programme and US Geological Survey.

stopped producing wheat in 2016 and will continue to import grain (virtual water) to help feed its 32 million people.

In the United States, aquifer depletion is a growing problem, especially in the vast Ogallala Aquifer (see Case Study that follows).

CASE STUDY

Overpumping the Ogallala Aquifer

In the United States, groundwater is being withdrawn from aquifers, on average, four times faster than it is replenished, according to the USGS. One of the most serious overdrafts of groundwater is in the lower half of the Ogallala Aquifer, one of the world's largest known aquifers, which lies under eight Midwestern states from southern South Dakota to Texas (Figure 13.10).

The Ogallala Aquifer supplies about one-third of all the groundwater used in the United States and turned the Great Plains into one of world's most productive irrigated agricultural regions (Figure 13.11). The Ogallala is essentially a one-time deposit of liquid natural capital with a

slow rate of recharge. *Hydrogeologists* (scientists who study groundwater and its movements) estimate that since 1960, we have withdrawn between a third and half of this water and that if it were to be depleted, it could take 6,000 years to recharge naturally.

In parts of the southern half of the Ogallala, groundwater is being pumped out 10–40 times faster than the slow natural recharge rate. This, along with reduced access to Colorado River water (**Core Case Study**) and population growth, has led to the shrinkage of irrigated croplands in parts of Texas, Arizona, Colorado, and California. It has also led to increased competition for water among farmers, ranchers, and growing urban areas.

Government *subsidies*—payments or tax breaks designed to increase crop production—have encouraged farmers to continue growing water-thirsty crops in dry areas, which has accelerated depletion of the Ogallala Aquifer. In particular, corn—a very thirsty crop—has been planted widely on fields watered by the Ogallala.

The aquifer also supports biodiversity. In various places, groundwater from the Ogallala flows out of the ground onto land or onto lake bottoms through exit points called

FIGURE 13.10 Natural capital degradation: Areas of greatest aquifer depletion from groundwater overdraft in the continental United States. The blowup section (right) shows where water levels in the Ogallala Aquifer have dropped sharply at its southern end beneath parts of Kansas, Oklahoma, Texas, and New Mexico. *Critical thinking:* Should the amount of water that farmers can withdraw from the Ogallala Aquifer be restricted? How would you enforce this? How might this affect food production?

(Compiled by the authors using data from US Water Resources Council and US Geological Survey.)

Groundwater Overdrafts:
- High
- Moderate
- Minor or none

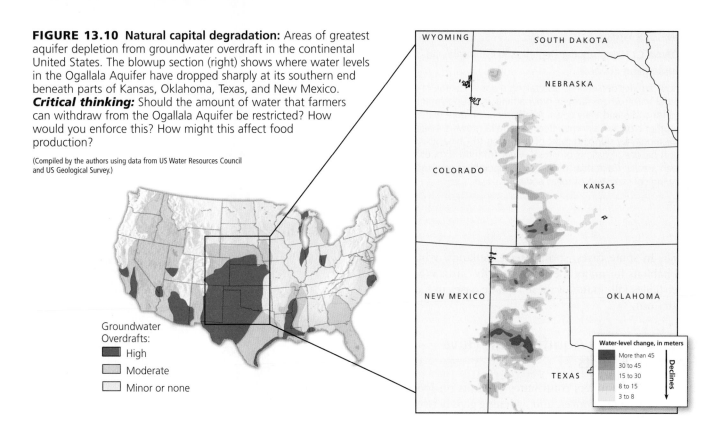

Water-level change, in meters
- More than 45
- 30 to 45
- 15 to 30
- 8 to 15
- 3 to 8

Declines

FIGURE 13.11 Satellite photo of crop fields in the US state of Kansas. Center-pivot irrigation uses long, suspended pipes that swing around a central point in each field. Dark green circles are irrigated fields of corn, light green circles are sorghum, and light yellow circles are wheat. Brown areas are fields that have been recently harvested and plowed under. The water used to irrigate these crops is pumped from the Ogallala Aquifer.

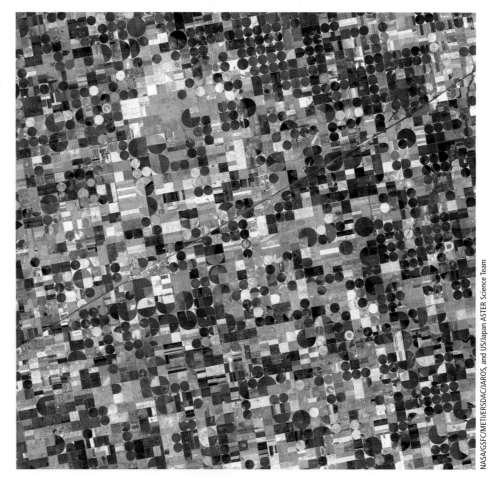

CONNECTIONS Aquifer Depletion in California and Meat Consumption in China

Serious aquifer depletion is also taking place in California's Central Valley where farmers grow alfalfa as a supplemental feed for cattle and dairy cows. Alfalfa requires more water than any other crop in California. Because alfalfa growers make more money by shipping most of their crop to China, they export billions of gallons of virtual water from this drought-ridden area of California to China to support that country's growing consumption of meat and milk.

springs. In some cases, springs feed wetlands, which are vital habitats for many species, especially birds. When the water tables fall, many of these aquatic oases of biodiversity dry out.

Overpumping Aquifers Can Have Harmful Effects

Overpumping aquifers contributes to limits on food production, rising food prices, and widening gaps between the rich and poor in some areas. This in turn can lead to rising hunger and social unrest. Much of the Middle East is facing such a crisis and increasing tensions among nations, brought on partly by falling water tables and rapid population growth.

Also, as water tables drop, the energy and financial costs of pumping the water from lower depths rise sharply because farmers must drill deeper wells, buy larger pumps, and use more electricity to run the pumps. Poor farmers cannot afford such costs and often lose their land. This forces them to work for richer farmers or to migrate to cities that are crowded with people struggling to survive.

Withdrawing large amounts of groundwater sometimes causes the sand and rock that is held in place by water pressure in aquifers to collapse. This can cause the land above the aquifer to *subside* or sink, a phenomenon known as *land subsidence*. Extreme and sudden subsidence, sometimes referred to as a *sinkhole*, can swallow cars and houses. Once an aquifer becomes compressed by subsidence, recharge is impossible. Land subsidence can also damage roadways, water and sewer lines, and building foundations.

Since 1925, overpumping of an aquifer to irrigate crops in California's San Joaquin Valley has caused half of the valley's land to subside by more than 0.3 meter (1 foot) and, in one area, by more than 8.5 meters (28 feet) (Figure 13.12). Mexico City and parts of Beijing, China, also suffer from severe subsidence problems.

Groundwater overdrafts in coastal areas, where many of the world's largest cities and industries are found, can pull saltwater into freshwater aquifers. The resulting

Dick Ireland/US Geological Survey

FIGURE 13.12 This pole shows subsidence from overpumping of an aquifer for irrigation in California's San Joaquin Central Valley between 1925 and 1977. In 1925, this area's land surface was near the top of the pole. Since 1977, this problem has gotten worse.

Solutions

Groundwater Depletion

Prevention		Control
Use water more efficiently		Raise price of water to discourage waste
Subsidize water conservation		Tax water pumped from wells near surface water
Limit number of wells	WATER BILL	Build rain gardens in urban areas
Stop growing water-intensive crops in dry areas		Use permeable paving material on streets, sidewalks, and driveways

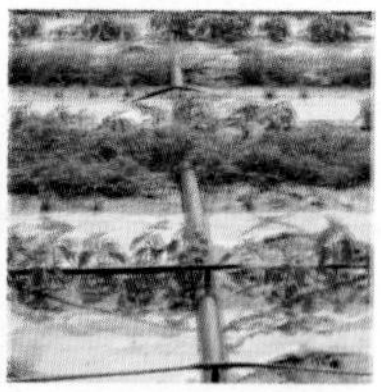

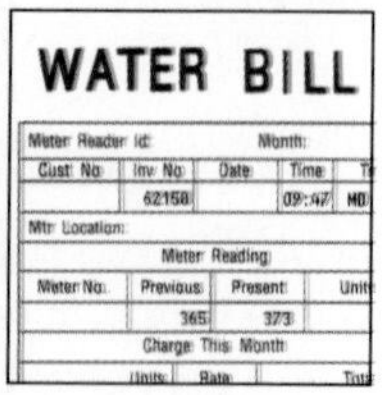

FIGURE 13.13 Ways to prevent or slow groundwater depletion by using freshwater more sustainably. *Critical thinking:* Which two of these solutions do you think are the most important? Why?

Top: Anhong/Dreamstime.com. Bottom: Banol2007/Dreamstime.com.

contaminated groundwater is undrinkable and unfit for irrigation. This problem is especially serious in coastal areas of the US states of California, Texas, Florida, Georgia, South Carolina, and New Jersey, as well as in coastal areas of Turkey, Thailand, and the Philippines.

Figure 13.13 lists ways to prevent or slow the problem of aquifer depletion using this potentially renewable resource more sustainably. The challenge is to educate people about the dangers of depleting vital underground supplies of water that they cannot see.

CHECKPOINT FOR UNDERSTANDING 13.2

1. Groundwater from aquifers is considered a renewable resource. Identify two factors that could make this resource unsustainable.

2. The Ogallala aquifer supplies one-third of all the groundwater for the United States. What is this water primarily used for?

3. Describe some of the harmful impacts of overpumping aquifers.

13.3 HOW CAN WE INCREASE FRESHWATER SUPPLIES?

CONCEPT 13.3A Large dam-and-reservoir systems and water transfer projects have greatly expanded water supplies in some areas, but have also disrupted ecosystems and displaced people.

CONCEPT 13.3B We can convert salty ocean water to freshwater, but the energy and other costs are high, and the resulting salty brine must be disposed of without harming aquatic or terrestrial ecosystems.

Large Dams Provide Benefits and Create Problems

A **dam** is a structure built across a river to control its flow. Usually, dammed water creates an artificial lake, or **reservoir,** behind the dam (chapter-opening photo). The purpose of a dam-and-reservoir system is to capture and store the surface runoff from a river's watershed, and release it as needed to control floods, to generate electricity (hydropower), and to supply freshwater for irrigation and for towns and cities. Reservoirs also provide recreational activities such as swimming, fishing, and boating. Large dams and reservoirs provide benefits but they also have drawbacks (Figure 13.14).

Six of every ten of the world's rivers have at least one dam, and the total number of dams worldwide is estimated to be 800,000. They provide water for almost half of all irrigated cropland and supply more than half the electricity used in 65 countries. The United States has about 75,000 dams, according to the US Army Corps of Engineers.

They capture and store about half of the country's entire river flow.

Dams have increased the annual reliable runoff available for human uses by nearly 33%. As a result, the world's reservoirs now hold 3–6 times more freshwater than the total amount flowing at any moment in all of the world's natural rivers. On the downside, this engineering approach to river management has displaced 40 million to 80 million people from their homes and impaired some of the important ecosystem services that rivers provide (see Figure 6.13, left, p. 164) (**Concept 13.3A**).

A study by the World Wildlife Fund (WWF) estimated that about one out of five of the world's freshwater fish and plant species are either extinct or endangered, primarily because dams and water withdrawals have sharply decreased certain river flows. The study found that only 21 of the planet's 177 longest rivers consistently run all the way to the sea before running dry. As a result, aquatic habitat along rivers and at their mouths has been severely degraded (see Case Study that follows).

Within 50 years, reservoirs behind dams typically fill up with sediments (mud and silt), which makes them useless for storing water or producing electricity. In the Colorado River system (**Core Case Study**), the equivalent of roughly 20,000 dump-truck loads of silt are deposited on the bottoms of the Lake Powell and Lake Mead reservoirs every day. Eventually, these two reservoirs will be too full of silt to function as designed.

If dams are not designed and maintained properly, it can lead to disaster. The Oroville Dam, located on the Feather River in California, is the tallest dam in the United States, and creates the second largest reservoir in California. It was constructed in 1957 to produce electricity and for flood control. For much of the past several years California has experienced severe, prolonged drought, during which time the water levels in Lake Oroville dropped dramatically (Figure 13.15). Then, in February 2017, particularly heavy rain and snowmelt brought the reservoir to very dangerous levels.

The Oroville Dam is designed with two spillways (Figure 13.16, left). The main spillway is a giant concrete chute, and the emergency spillway to its left is a bare hillside of rocks, trees, and soil with a concrete wall, or *weir,* across the top, over which extreme high water can flow. After several days of rain, erosion damage to the main spillway became visible so the spillway was closed to assess ways to lessen further damage. Heavy rain continued, until flood water began to flow over the emergency spillway, threatening the collapse of the weir at the top, which could have been catastrophic. The already-damaged main spillway was re-opened (Figure 13.16, right) to lessen the flooding down the bare hillside and to keep the reservoir from overtopping the dam itself. More than 180,000 people in endangered downstream areas were ordered to evacuate with only an hour's notice. The weir on the emergency spillway held, but the giant sinkhole on the main spillway caused severe damage, estimated at $275 million to repair.

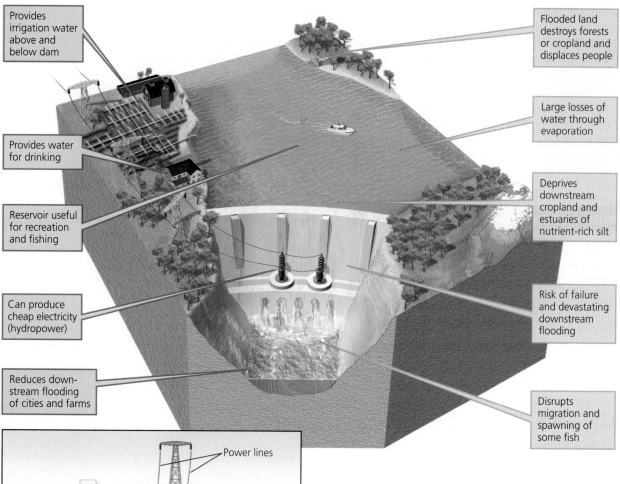

Provides irrigation water above and below dam

Provides water for drinking

Reservoir useful for recreation and fishing

Can produce cheap electricity (hydropower)

Reduces down-stream flooding of cities and farms

Flooded land destroys forests or cropland and displaces people

Large losses of water through evaporation

Deprives downstream cropland and estuaries of nutrient-rich silt

Risk of failure and devastating downstream flooding

Disrupts migration and spawning of some fish

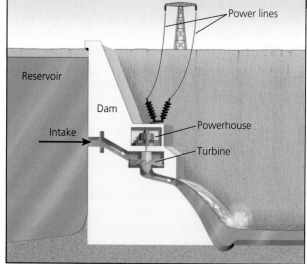

Power lines

Reservoir

Dam

Intake

Powerhouse

Turbine

FIGURE 13.14 Trade-offs: Large dam and reservoir systems have advantages (green) and disadvantages (orange) (**Concept 13.3**). *Critical thinking:* Which single advantage and which single disadvantage do you think are the most important? Why?

Scientists believe climate change can intensify extreme weather events like drought and flooding. If climate change occurs as projected, it will intensify shortages of water in many parts of the world. For example, mountain snows that feed the Colorado River system (**Core Case Study**) will

melt faster and earlier, making less freshwater available to the river system when it is needed for irrigation during hot and dry summer months.

If some of the Colorado River's largest reservoirs keep dropping dramatically or become filled with silt during this century, the region will experience costly water and economic disruptions. For example, by 2013, the water level in Lake Mead had dropped below the Hoover Dam's intake pipes. The city of Las Vegas has been forced to spend more than $800 million to build lower intake pipes in order to maintain hydroelectric production.

Also likely are political and legal battles over who will get how much of the region's greatly diminishing freshwater supply. Agricultural production would drop sharply and the region's major desert cities would be challenged to survive. A report from the US Bureau of Reclamation concluded that over the next 50 years, the Colorado River will not be able to meet the projected water demands of Arizona, New Mexico, and California.

Nearly 3 billion people in South America, China, India, and other parts of Asia—that is, nearly half the world's population—depend on river flows fed by mountain glaciers, which act like aquatic savings accounts. They store precipitation as ice and snow in wet periods and release it

Justin Sullivan/Getty Images

FIGURE 13.15 One of California's major reservoirs, Lake Oroville, dropped dramatically between 2011 (left) and 2014 (right), due largely to drought.

Courtesy of Paul Hames/California Department of Water Resources

Courtesy of Dale Kolke/California Department of Water Resources

FIGURE 13.16 Two images of Oroville Dam, before (left) and during (right) the spillway failure in February, 2017 when severe rain and snowmelt required use of the spillways to prevent the dam from overtopping.

slowly during dry seasons for use on farms and in cities. In 2015, according to the World Glacier Monitoring Service, many of these mountain glaciers had been shrinking for 24 consecutive years, mostly due to a warming atmosphere.

CASE STUDY

How Dams Can Kill an Estuary

Since 1905, the amount of water flowing to the mouth of the Colorado River (**Core Case Study**) has dropped dramatically. In most years since 1960, the river has dwindled to a small,

sluggish stream by the time it reaches the Gulf of California (Figure 13.17).

The Colorado River once emptied into a vast *delta* located in northern Mexico, with a wetland area at the mouth of a river containing the river's estuary. The delta covered an area of more than 800,000 hectares (2 million acres)—the size of the state of Rhode Island. It hosted forests, lagoons, and marshes rich in plant and animal life and supported a thriving coastal fishery for hundreds of years.

Since the damming of the Colorado River—within one human lifetime—this biologically diverse delta ecosystem

NEPA and Environmental Impact Statements

Engineering projects, such as building a major dam, are regulated by the **National Environmental Policy Act**, or **NEPA**. This law requires that an *environmental impact statement (EIS)* must be developed for every federal project likely to have an effect on environmental quality. The EIS must explain why the proposed project is needed and identify its beneficial and harmful environmental impacts. In the case of building a major dam, an environmental impact study typically considers the project's likely effects on wildlife habitat, soils, water quality, air quality, stream flows, and other factors. The EIS must also suggest ways to lessen any harmful impacts, and it must present an evaluation of alternatives to the proposed project. The EIS document must be published and is open to public comment.

Several other types of environmental legislation have been enacted to function in a variety of different ways: (1) *set standards for pollution levels* as in the Clean Air Act(s); (2) *screen new substances for safety and set standards* as in the Safe Water Drinking Act; (3) *encourage resource conservation* as in the Resource Conservation and Recovery Act; and (4) *set aside or protect certain species, resources, and ecosystems* as in the Endangered Species Act.

FRQ Application

Question: An environmental impact statement is required for any major federal project that may have an impact on the environment. A new dam is proposed on a river in the state of Washington to create a reservoir for producing hydroelectricity. **Identify** and **describe** ONE possible impact that might be identified in the environmental impact statement regarding this dam, suggest how this impact might be lessened, and present an alternative to constructing the dam. *Possible Response:* One negative impact of building a dam on the river would be that it could interrupt the migration and spawning of fish species such as salmon. Fish ladders that allow fish to bypass the river in order to return to spawning grounds would lessen the impact of impeding the fish. An alternative to constructing the dam might be to install wind turbines to produce electricity.

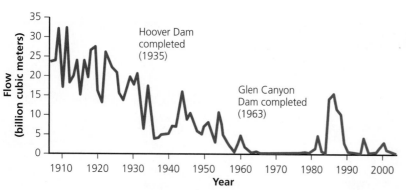

FIGURE 13.17 The measured flow of the Colorado River (**Core Case Study**) at its mouth has dropped sharply since 1905 as a result of multiple dams, water withdrawals for agriculture and urban areas, and prolonged drought. **Data analysis:** How much higher than the highest flow after 1935 (when the Hoover Dam was built) was the highest flow before 1935?

(Compiled by the authors using data from US Geological Survey.)

has collapsed and is now covered mostly by mud flats and desert. All but one-tenth of the river's flow was diverted for use in seven US states. Most of the remaining 10% is assigned to farms and to the growing cities of Mexicali and Tijuana in Mexico. The delta's wildlife are now mostly gone and its coastal fishery that fed many generations of area residents is disappearing. Similarly, because of damming along the Mississippi River, the Mississippi delta has suffered much the same fate.

Historically, about 80% of the water withdrawn from the Colorado has been used to irrigate crops and raise cattle. That is because the government paid for the dams and reservoirs and has supplied many farmers and ranchers with water at low prices. These government subsidies have led to inefficient use of irrigation water for growing thirsty crops such as rice, cotton, almonds, and alfalfa.

Water experts call for the seven states using the Colorado River to enact and enforce strict water conservation measures. They also call for phasing out state and federal government subsidies for agriculture in this region, shifting water-thirsty crops to less arid areas, and banning or severely restricting the watering of golf courses and lawns in the desert areas of the Colorado River basin. They suggest that the best way to implement such solutions is to sharply raise the historically low price of the river's freshwater over the next decade—another application of the full-cost pricing **principle of sustainability**.

CONSIDER THIS . . .

THINKING ABOUT The Colorado River

What are three steps you would take to deal with the problems of the Colorado River system?

Removing Salt from Seawater to Provide Freshwater

Desalination is the process of removing dissolved salts from ocean water or from brackish (slightly salty) water in aquifers or lakes. It is another way to increase supplies of freshwater.

The two most widely used methods for desalinating water are distillation and reverse osmosis (Figure 13.18). *Distillation* involves heating saltwater until it evaporates (leaving behind salts in solid form) and condenses as freshwater. *Reverse osmosis* (or *microfiltration*) uses high pressure to force saltwater through a membrane filter with pores small enough to remove the salt and other impurities.

According to the International Desalination Association, there are more than 17,000 desalination plants (324 of them in the United States) operating in 150 countries. Most of them arid nations of the Middle East, North Africa, the Caribbean Sea, and the Mediterranean Sea. Desalination supplies less than 1% of the demand for freshwater in the United States and in the world.

There are three major problems with the widespread use of desalination. *First* is the high cost, because it takes a lot of energy to remove salt from seawater. A *second* problem is that pumping large volumes of seawater through pipes requires the use of chemicals to sterilize the water and to keep down algae growth. This kills many marine organisms and requires large inputs of energy and money. *Third*, desalination produces huge quantities of salty wastewater that must be disposed of. Dumping it into nearby coastal ocean waters increases the salinity of those waters, which can threaten food resources and aquatic life, especially near coral reefs, marshes, and mangrove forests.

Disposing of it on land could contaminate groundwater and surface water (**Concept 13.3B**).

Currently, desalination is practical only for water-short countries and cities that can afford its high cost. However, scientists and engineers are working to develop better and more affordable desalination technologies (Science Focus 13.2).

CONSIDER THIS . . .

LEARNING FROM NATURE

Scientists are trying to develop more efficient and affordable ways to desalinate seawater by mimicking how our kidneys take salt out of water and how fish in the sea survive in saltwater.

13.4 CAN WATER TRANSFERS EXPAND WATER SUPPLIES?

CONCEPT 13.4 Transferring water from one place to another has greatly increased water supplies in some areas but has also disrupted ecosystems.

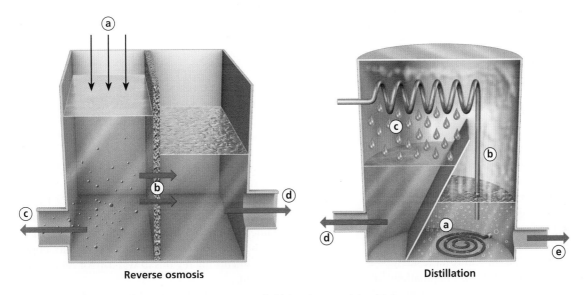

Reverse osmosis

Distillation

FIGURE 13.18 *Desalination:* Reverse osmosis (left) involves applying high pressure **(a)** to force sea water from one chamber into another through a semipermeable membrane **(b)** that separates the salt **(c)**, producing freshwater **(d)**. Distillation (right) involves heating sea water **(a)** to produce steam **(b)**, which is then condensed **(c)** and collected as freshwater **(d)**, while brine is also collected **(e)** for processing.

The Search for Better Desalination Technology

Reverse osmosis (Figure 13.18, left) is the favored desalination technology because it requires much less energy than distillation, but it is still energy intensive. In this process, high pressure is applied to seawater in order to squeeze the freshwater out of it. The membrane that filters out the salt must be strong enough to withstand such pressure. Seawater must be pretreated and treated again after desalination to make it pure enough for drinking and for irrigating crops.

Much of the scientific research in this field is aimed at improving the membrane and the pre- and post-treatment processes to make desalination more energy efficient. Scientists are working to develop new, more efficient and affordable membranes that can separate freshwater from saltwater under lower pressure, which would require less energy. Such technological advances have brought the cost of desalination down, but not enough yet to make it affordable or useful for large-scale irrigation or to meet much of the world's demand for drinking water.

At the University of Texas, doctoral student Kyle Knust has invented the Waterchip—a small device that removes salt from saltwater using an electrical current. Water flows down a Y-shaped channel and where it splits, an electrode emits a charge that separates water from salt. Knust says this small-scale device could be scaled up to produce larger amounts of desalinated water using half the energy of an osmosis plant. A team of scientists at the Massachusetts Institute of Technology (MIT), led by Martin Z. Bazant, is evaluating the use of an electric shock to separate saltwater and freshwater.

Scientists are considering ways to use solar and wind energy—applying one of the three **scientific principles of sustainability** (see Inside Back Cover)—in combination with conventional power sources to help bring down the cost of desalinating seawater. In 2012, Saudi Arabia completed the world's largest solar-powered desalination project. It uses concentrated solar energy to power new filtration technology at a plant that will meet the daily water needs of 100,000 people.

Two Australian companies, Energetech and H2AU, have joined forces to build an experimental desalination plant that uses the power generated by ocean waves to drive reverse-osmosis desalination. This approach produces no air pollution and uses renewable energy. Some scientists argue for building fleets of such floating desalination plants. They could operate out of sight from coastal areas and transfer the water to shore through seabed pipelines or in food-grade shuttle tankers. Because of their distance from shore, the ships could draw water from depths below where most marine organisms are found. The resulting brine could be returned to the ocean and diluted far away from coastal waters.

These methods would cut the costs of desalination, but they would still be high. Analysts expect desalination to be used more widely in the future, as water shortages become worse. However, there is still a lot of research to do before desalination can become an affordable major source of freshwater. **GREEN CAREER: Desalination engineer**

CRITICAL THINKING

Do you think that improvements in desalination will justify highly inefficient uses of water, such as maintaining swimming pools, fountains, and golf courses in desert areas? Explain.

Water Transfers Have Benefits and Drawbacks

In some heavily populated dry areas of the world, governments have tried to solve water shortage problems by transferring water from water-rich areas to water-poor areas. For example, in northern China, rapidly growing cities, including Beijing with 21 million people, have helped to deplete underlying aquifers. According to the Chinese Academy of Sciences, two-thirds of China's 669 major cities have water shortages. In addition, about 300 million rural residents—a number almost equal to the size of the US population—do not have access to safe drinking water. To deal with this problem, the Chinese government is implementing its *South–North Water Diversion Project* to transfer water from the Yangtze River in southern China to the thirsty north.

In other cases, water has been transferred to arid areas primarily to irrigate farm fields. When you have lettuce in a salad in the United States, it was probably grown in the arid Central Valley of California, partly with the use of irrigation water from snow melting off the tops of the High Sierra Mountains of northeastern California. The California State Water Project (Figure 13.19) is one of the world's largest freshwater transfer projects. It uses a maze of giant dams, pumps, and lined canals, or *aqueducts* (photo in Figure 3.19), to transfer freshwater from the mountains to heavily populated cities and agricultural regions in water-poor central and southern California.

California's Central Valley supplies half of the United States' fruits and vegetables, and the cities of San Diego and Los Angeles have grown and flourished because of the water transfer.

However, water transfers also have high environmental, economic, and social costs. They usually involve large water losses, through evaporation and leaks in the water-transfer systems. They also degrade ecosystems in areas from which the water is taken (**Concept 13.4**). China's South-North water will be expensive. It will displace more than 350,000 villagers who will have to move from lands they have farmed for generations. And scientists worry that removing huge volumes of water from the Yangtze River could severely damage its ecosystem, which has been suffering from its worst drought in 50 years.

In California, sending water south has degraded the Sacramento River and reduced the flushing action that helps to cleanse the San Francisco Bay of pollutants. As a result, the bay has suffered from pollution and the flow of freshwater to its coastal marshes and other ecosystems has dropped, putting stress on wildlife species that depend on these ecosystems. Water was also diverted from streams that flow into Mono Lake, an important feeding stop for migratory birds. This lake experienced an 11-meter (35-foot) drop in its water level before the diversions were stopped.

Federal and state governments typically subsidize water transfers. In the California project, subsidies have promoted inefficient use of large volumes of water to irrigate thirsty crops such as lettuce, alfalfa, and almonds in desert-like areas. In central California, agriculture consumes three-fourths of the water that is transferred, and much of it is lost through inefficient irrigation systems. Studies show that making irrigation just 10% more efficient would provide all the water necessary for domestic and industrial uses in southern California.

According to several studies, climate change will make matters worse in many areas where water is being removed for transfers. In southern China, climate change could intensify and prolong drought and create a need for an even larger and more expensive transfer of water. California depends on *snowpacks*, bodies of densely packed, slowly melting snow in the High Sierra Mountains, for more than 60% of its freshwater, according to the Sierra Nevada Conservancy. Projected atmospheric warming could shrink the snowpacks by as much as 40% by 2050 and by as much as 90% by the end of this century. This will sharply reduce the amount of freshwater available for northern residents and ecosystems, as well for the transfer of water to central and southern California.

There are many other examples around the world of water transfers that have resulted in environmental degradation (see the following Case Study).

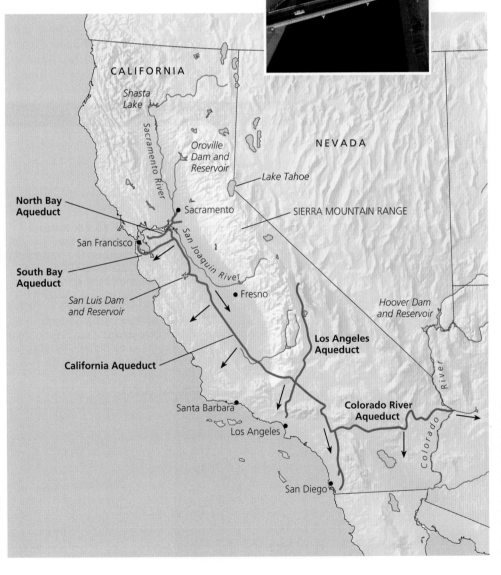

Sarahleen/National Geographic Creative

FIGURE 13.19 The California State Water Project transfers huge volumes of freshwater from one watershed to another. The arrows on the map show the general direction of water flow. The photo shows one of the aqueducts carrying water within the system. *Critical thinking:* What effects might this system have on the areas from which the water is taken?

The Aral Sea Disaster: An Example of Unintended Consequences

The shrinking of the Aral Sea (Figure 13.20) is the result of a water transfer project in central Asia. Starting in 1960, enormous amounts of irrigation water were diverted from the two rivers that supply water to the Aral Sea. The goal was to create one of the world's largest irrigated areas, mostly for raising cotton and rice. The irrigation canal, the world's longest, stretches more than 1,300 kilometers (800 miles)—roughly the distance between the two US cities of Boston, Massachusetts, and Chicago, Illinois.

This project, coupled with drought and high evaporation rates due to the area's hot and dry climate, has caused a regional ecological and economic disaster. Since 1961, the sea's salinity has risen sevenfold and the average level of its water has dropped by an amount roughly equal to the height of a six-story building. The Southern Aral Sea has lost 90% of its volume of water and most of its lake bottom is now a white salt desert (Figure 13.20, right photo). Water withdrawals reduced the two rivers feeding the sea to mere trickles.

About 85% of the area's wetlands have been eliminated and about half the local bird and mammal species have disappeared. The sea's greatly increased salt concentration—three times saltier than ocean water—has caused the presumed local extinction of 26 of the area's 32 native fish species. This has devastated the area's fishing industry, which once provided work for more than 60,000 people. Fishing villages and boats once located on the sea's coastline now sit abandoned in a salty desert.

Winds pick up the sand and salty dust and blow it onto fields as far as 500 kilometers (310 miles) away. As the salt spreads, it pollutes water and kills wildlife, crops, and other vegetation. Aral Sea dust settling on glaciers in the Himalayas is causing them to melt at a faster-than-normal rate.

The shrinkage of the Aral Sea has also altered the area's climate. The shrunken sea no longer acts as a thermal buffer to moderate the heat of summer and the extreme cold of winter. Now there is less rain, summers are hotter and drier, winters are colder, and the growing season is shorter. The combination of such climate change and severe salinization has reduced crop yields by 20–50% on almost one-third of the area's cropland—the opposite of the project's intended effects.

Since 1999, the UN, the World Bank, and the five countries surrounding the lake have worked to improve irrigation efficiency. They have also partially replaced thirsty crops with other crops that require less irrigation water. Because of a dike built to block the flow of water from the Northern Aral Sea into the southern sea, the level of the northern sea has risen by 2 meters (7 feet), its salinity has dropped, dissolved oxygen levels are up, and it supports a healthy fishery.

However, the formerly much larger southern sea is still shrinking. By 2012, its eastern lobe was essentially gone (Figure 13.20, right photo). The European Space Agency projects that the rest of the Southern Aral Sea could dry up completely by 2020.

CHECKPOINT FOR UNDERSTANDING 13.4

1. Identify benefits of water-diversion projects.

2. Identify drawbacks of water-diversion projects.

1976

2015

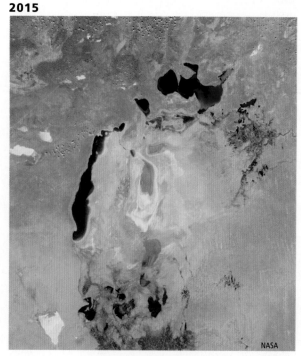

NASA

FIGURE 13.20 Natural capital degradation: The *Aral Sea*, straddling the borders of Kazakhstan and Uzbekistan, was one of the world's largest saline lakes. These satellite photos show the sea in 1976 (left) and in 2015 (right). ***Question:*** What do you think should be done to help prevent further shrinkage of the Aral Sea?

13.5 HOW CAN WE USE FRESHWATER MORE SUSTAINABLY?

CONCEPT 13.5 We can use freshwater more sustainably by cutting water waste, raising water prices, slowing population growth, and protecting aquifers, forests, and other ecosystems that store freshwater.

Cutting Water Waste

According to water resource expert Mohamed El-Ashry of the World Resources Institute, about 66% of the freshwater used in the world and about 50% of the freshwater used in the United States is lost through evaporation, leaks, and inefficient use. El-Ashry estimates that it is economically and technically feasible to reduce such losses to 15%, thereby meeting most of the world's future freshwater needs.

Why do we have such large losses of freshwater? According to water resource experts, there are two major reasons. First, the cost of freshwater to most users is low due mostly to government subsidies—a violation of the full-cost pricing **principle of sustainability**. This gives users little or no financial incentive to invest in water-saving technologies.

Higher prices for freshwater encourage water conservation but make it difficult for low-income farmers and city dwellers to buy enough water to meet their needs. When South Africa raised water prices, it dealt with this problem by establishing *lifeline rates*, which give each household a set amount of free or low-priced water to meet basic needs. When users exceed this amount, they pay increasingly higher prices as their water use increases. This is a *user-pays* approach.

The second major cause of unnecessary waste of freshwater is a lack of government subsidies for improving the efficiency of water use. Withdrawing some of the subsidies that encourage inefficient water use and replacing them with subsidies for more efficient water use would sharply reduce water losses. Understandably, farmers and industries that receive subsidies that keep water prices low have vigorously opposed efforts to eliminate or reduce them.

Improving Irrigation Efficiency

Since 1980, the amount of food that can be grown per drop of water has roughly doubled. In addition, since the 1970s, the amount of water used per person in the United States has dropped by about 33%, after rising for decades. Most of these water savings have come from improvements to irrigation efficiency in the United States and other more-developed countries.

However, there is still a long way to go, especially in less-developed countries. Only about 60% of the world's irrigation water reaches crops, which means that most irrigation systems are highly inefficient. The most inefficient system, commonly used in less-developed countries, is *flood irrigation*. With this method, water is pumped from a groundwater or surface water source through unlined ditches where it flows by gravity to the crops being watered (Figure 13.21, left). This method delivers far more water than is needed for crop growth, and typically, about 45% of it is lost through evaporation, seepage, and runoff.

Another inefficient system is the traditional spray irrigation system, a widely used tool of industrialized crop production. It sprays huge volumes of water onto large fields, and as much as 40% of this water is lost to evaporation, especially in dry and windy areas, according to the US Geological Survey. These systems are commonly used in the Midwestern United States and have helped to draw down the Ogallala Aquifer (Case Study, p. 388).

More efficient irrigation technologies greatly reduce water losses by delivering water more precisely to crops—a *more crop per drop* strategy. For example, a *center-pivot, low-pressure sprinkler* (Figure 13.21, right), which uses pumps to spray water on a crop, allow about 80% of the water to reach crops. *Low-energy, precision application* (*LEPA*) *sprinklers*, another form of center-pivot irrigation, put 90–95% of the water where crops need it.

Drip, or *trickle irrigation*, also called *micro-irrigation* (Figure 13.21, center), is the most efficient way to deliver small amounts of water precisely to crops. It consists of a network of perforated plastic tubing installed at or below the ground level. Small pinholes in the tubing deliver drops of water at a slow and steady rate, close to the roots of individual plants. These systems drastically reduce water waste because 90–95% of the water input reaches the crops.

Since the early 1990s, the global area of cropland on which drip irrigation is used has increased more than sixfold, with most of this growth happening in the United States, China, and India. Still, drip irrigation is used on less than 4% of the irrigated crop fields in the world and in the United States, largely because most drip irrigation systems are costly. This percentage rises to 13% in the US state of California, 66% in Israel, and 90% in Cyprus. If freshwater were priced closer to the value of the ecosystem services it provides, and if government subsidies for inefficient use of water were reduced or eliminated, drip irrigation could be used to irrigate most of the world's crops.

According to the UN, reducing the current global withdrawal of water for irrigation by just 10% would save enough water to grow crops and meet the estimated additional water demands of the earth's cities and industries through 2025.

Poor Farmers Conserve Water Using Low-Tech Methods

Many of the world's poor farmers use low-cost, traditional irrigation technologies. For example, millions of farmers in Bangladesh and other countries where water tables are high use human-powered treadle pumps to bring groundwater up to the earth's surface and into irrigation ditches (Figure 13.22). These wooden devices are inexpensive and

Calculating Irrigation Efficiency

Approximately one-fourth of all the food produced in the United States comes from the Central Valley of California. California occasionally experiences prolonged drought; the extreme dryness due to the severe drought from 2011 through 2016 was perhaps the worst drought event in the state's history. Reduced water supplies make it more expensive for farmers to irrigate their crops.

Installing advanced irrigation systems that deliver more water directly to crops is one strategy for lowering water consumption. These systems are very expensive, but with the rising cost of water, the payoff in the long run will ultimately lower the overall cost of irrigation and, in turn, lower the price of food. This kind of analysis is called a *cost-benefit analysis*, a concept that will be investigated further in the next chapter.

FRQ Application

North of Sacramento, the Western Canal Water District is selling water to local farmers for double the usual price: $500 per acre-foot. An *acre-foot* is the volume of water necessary to cover one acre of surface area to a depth of one foot. It is equal to exactly 43,560 cubic feet, or approximately 326,000 US gallons. Farmers typically use channel irrigation, which is about 55% efficient, meaning that 45% of the water used is lost to evaporation.

A farmer owns 1250 acres of farmland. She grows lettuce on this land, and purchases 1 year's worth of water at the price of $500 per acre-foot to irrigate the crop. She is considering investing in an advanced irrigation system, and begins with a rough cost-benefit analysis based on the expectation that she will use a water volume of one acre-foot per acre per year for her entire farm.

How much does it cost to deliver 1 acre-foot of irrigation to the entire farm for 1 year?

$$1250 \text{ acres} \times \frac{\$500.00}{\text{acre-foot}} = \$625,000$$

If the method of irrigation she currently uses is 55% efficient, what is the cost of the water lost to evaporation?

$$\$625,000 \times 0.45 = \$281,250$$

A drip irrigation system costs $700 per acre and is 90% efficient. How much will it cost to install this system?

$$1250 \text{ acres} \times \frac{\$700}{\text{acre}} = \$875,000$$

If the system is 90% efficient, what is the cost of the water lost to evaporation using drip irrigation?

$$\$625,000 \times 0.10 = \$62,500$$

How much does she save per year in total by installing a drip irrigation system?

$$\$281,250 - \$62,500 = \$218,750 \text{ per year}$$

How long will it take to recoup the cost of installing the new system?

$$\frac{\$875,000}{\$218,750/\text{year}} = 4 \text{ years}$$

easy to build from local materials. One such pump developed by the nonprofit International Development Enterprises (IDE) uses 60–70% less water than a conventional gravity-flow system to irrigate the same amount of cropland at one-tenth the cost of conventional drip systems.

Rainwater harvesting is another simple and inexpensive way to provide water. It involves using pipes from rooftops and channels dug in the ground to direct rainwater that would otherwise run off the land. It can be stored in underground or aboveground storage tanks (cisterns), ponds, and plastic barrels for use during dry seasons. This is especially useful in countries such as India, where much of the rain comes in a short monsoon season.

Other strategies used by poor farmers to increase the amount of crop per drop of rainfall include polyculture farming to create more canopy cover and reduce evaporative water losses; planting deep-rooted perennial crop

CONSIDER THIS . . .

LEARNING FROM NATURE

The Namibian beetle survives in Africa's arid Namib Desert by using tiny bumps on its shell to extract water from night fog. Engineers hope to collect water in the world's dry areas by designing building surfaces and other materials that mimic the beetle's shell.

FIGURE 13.21 Traditional irrigation methods rely on gravity and flowing water (left). Newer systems such as center-pivot, low-pressure sprinkler irrigation (right), and drip irrigation (center) are far more efficient.

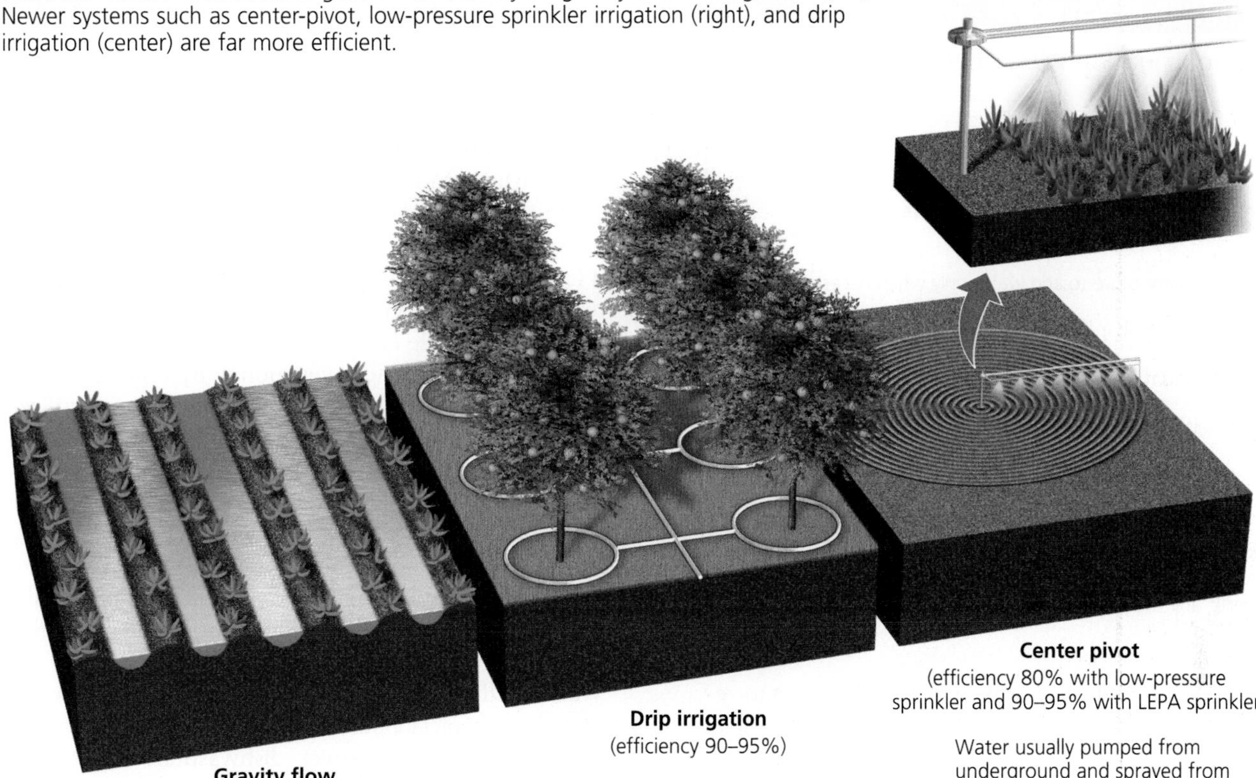

Gravity flow
(efficiency 60% and 80% with surge valves)

Water usually comes from an aqueduct system or a nearby river.

Drip irrigation
(efficiency 90–95%)

Above- or belowground pipes or tubes deliver water to individual plant roots.

Center pivot
(efficiency 80% with low-pressure sprinkler and 90–95% with LEPA sprinkler)

Water usually pumped from underground and sprayed from mobile boom with sprinklers.

Courtesy of International Development Enterprises

FIGURE 13.22 Solutions: In areas of Bangladesh and India, where water tables are high, many small-scale farmers use treadle pumps to supply irrigation water to their fields.

varieties (see Figure 12.B, p. 345); controlling weeds; and mulching fields to retain more moisture.

Figure 13.23 summarizes several ways to reduce water losses in crop irrigation. Since 1950, Israel has used many of these techniques to slash irrigation water losses by 84% while irrigating 44% more land. Israel now treats and reuses 30% of its municipal sewage water for crop production and plans to increase this to 80% by 2025. The government also gradually eliminated most water subsidies to raise Israel's price of irrigation water, which is now one of the highest in the world.

GOOD NEWS

Cutting Freshwater Losses in Industries and Homes

Producers of chemicals, paper, oil, coal, primary metals, and processed foods consume almost 90% of the freshwater used by industries in the United States. Some of

Reducing Irrigation Water Losses

- Avoid growing thirsty crops in dry areas

- Import water-intensive crops and meat

- Encourage organic farming and polyculture to retain soil moisture

- Monitor soil moisture to add water only when necessary

- Expand use of drip irrigation and other efficient methods

- Irrigate at night to reduce evaporation

- Line canals that bring water to irrigation ditches

- Irrigate with treated wastewater

FIGURE 13.23 Ways to reduce freshwater losses in irrigation. *Critical thinking:* Which two of these solutions do you think are the best ones? Why?

these industries recapture, purify, and recycle water to reduce their water use and water treatment costs. For example, more than 95% of the water used to make steel can be recycled. Even so, most industrial processes could be redesigned to use much less water. **GREEN CAREER: Water conservation specialist**

Flushing toilets with freshwater (most of it clean enough to drink) is the single largest use of domestic freshwater in the United States and accounts for about 27% of home water use. Since 1992, US government standards have required that new toilets use no more than 6.1 liters (1.6 gallons) of water per flush. Even at this rate, just two flushes of such a toilet use more than the daily amount of water available for all uses to many of the world's poor people living in arid regions.

Other water-saving appliances are widely available. Low-flow showerheads can save large amounts of water by cutting the flow of a shower in half. Front-loading clothes washers use 30% less water than top-loading machines use. According to the American Water Works Association, if the typical American household were to stop all water leaks and use these devices, along with low-flow toilets and faucets, it could cut its daily water use by nearly a third. According to UN studies, 30–60% of the water supplied in nearly all of the world's major cities in less-developed countries is lost, primarily through leakage from water mains, pipes, pumps, and valves. Water experts say that fixing these leaks should be a high priority for water-short countries, because it would increase water supplies and cost much less than building dams or importing water.

Even in advanced industrialized countries such as the United States, these losses to leakage average 10–30%. However, leakage losses have been reduced to about 3% in Copenhagen, Denmark, and to 5% in Fukuoka, Japan. In 1 year, a faucet leaking water at the rate of 1 drop per second can waste 10,000 liters (2,650 gallons). The customer's water bill goes up and so does the energy bill if the water is leaking from a hot water faucet. Not detecting and fixing water leaks from faucets, pipes, and toilets is equivalent to burning money.

Many homeowners and businesses in water-short areas are using drip irrigation on their properties to cut water losses. Some are also using smart sprinkler systems with moisture sensors that have cut water used for watering lawns by up to 40%. Others are copying nature by replacing green lawns with a mix of native plants that need little or no watering (Figure 13.24). Such water-thrifty landscaping saves money by reducing water use by 30–85% and by sharply reducing labor, fertilizer, and fuel requirements. It also can help landowners to reduce polluted runoff, air pollution, and yard wastes.

In some more-developed countries, people who live in arid areas maintain green lawns by watering them heavily. Some communities and housing developments in water-short areas have even passed ordinances that require green lawns and prohibit the planting of native vegetation in place of lawns.

Water used in homes can be reused and recycled. About 50–75% of a typical household's *gray water*—used water from bathtubs, showers, sinks, dishwashers, and clothes washers—could be recovered and stored. This water can be reused to irrigate lawns and nonedible plants, to flush toilets, and to wash cars. Such efforts mimic the way nature recycles water, and thus they follow the chemical cycling **principle of sustainability**.

The relatively low cost of water in most communities is one of the major causes of excessive water use and waste in homes and industries. About one-fifth of all US public water systems do not use water meters and charge a single low annual rate for almost unlimited use of high-quality freshwater.

When the US city of Boulder, Colorado, introduced water meters, water use per person dropped by 40%. In some cities in Brazil, people buy *smart cards*, each of which contains a certain number of water credits that entitle their owners to measured amounts of freshwater. Brazilian officials say this approach saves water and typically reduces household water bills by 40%.

Figure 13.25 summarizes various ways to use water more efficiently in industries, homes, and businesses (**Concept 13.3**).

Using Less Water to Remove Wastes

Currently, we use large amounts of freshwater to flush away industrial, animal, and household wastes. According to the UN Food and Agriculture Organization (FAO), if current growth trends in population and water use continue, within 40 years, we will need the world's entire reliable flow of river water just to dilute and transport the wastes we produce each year.

FIGURE 13.24 This yard in a dry area of the southwestern United States uses a mix of plants that are native to the arid environment and require little watering.

karolinapatryk/Thinkstock

FIGURE 13.25 Ways to reduce freshwater losses in industries, homes, and businesses (**Concept 13.6**). *Critical thinking:* Which three of these solutions do you think are the best ones? Why?

We could save much of this freshwater by recycling and reusing gray water from homes and businesses for flushing wastes and cleaning equipment. In Singapore, all sewage water is treated at reclamation plants for reuse by industry. US cities such as Las Vegas, Nevada, and Los Angeles, California, are also beginning to clean up and reuse some of their wastewater. However, only about 7% of the water in the United States is recycled, cleaned up, and reused. Sharply raising this percentage would be a way to apply the chemical cycling **principle of sustainability**.

Another way to keep freshwater out of the waste stream is to rely more on waterless composting toilets. These devices convert human fecal matter to a small amount of dry and odorless soil-like humus material that can be removed from a composting chamber every year or so and returned to the soil as fertilizer. One of the authors (Miller) used a composting toilet for over a decade with no problems, while living and working deep in the woods in a small passive solar home and office used for evaluating solutions to water, energy, and other environmental problems.

As water shortages grow in many parts of the world, people are using methods discussed here to use water more sustainably. Their experiences can be instructive to people who want to avoid water shortages in the first place.

Using Water More Sustainably

More sustainable water use would include a variety of strategies (Figure 13.25) aimed not only at conserving water and using it efficiently, but also at protecting water supplies and the ecosystems that sustain them (**Concept 13.5**). Such strategies would have to be applied at local and regional levels, as well as national and international levels.

However, to be successful, these strategies would also have to be applied at the personal level. Each of us can reduce our water footprints using less freshwater and using it more efficiently (Figure 13.26).

CHECKPOINT FOR UNDERSTANDING 13.5

1. Explain how full-cost pricing for water would lower consumption.

2. Identify several ways to reduce water consumption in the home.

3. Identify strategies being implemented to lower water consumption in agriculture.

What Can You Do?

Water Use and Waste

- Use water-saving toilets, showerheads, and faucets

- Take short showers instead of baths

- Turn off sink faucets while brushing teeth, shaving, or washing

- Wash only full loads of clothes or use the lowest possible water-level setting for smaller loads

- Repair water leaks

- Wash your car from a bucket of soapy water, use gray water, and use the hose for rinsing only

- If you use a commercial car wash, try to find one that recycles its water

- Replace your lawn with native plants that need little if any watering

- Water lawns and gardens only in the early morning or evening and use gray water

- Use drip irrigation and mulch for gardens and flowerbeds

FIGURE 13.26 Individuals matter: You can reduce your use and waste of freshwater. **Question:** Which of these steps have you taken? Which would you like to take?

13.6 HOW CAN WE REDUCE THE THREAT OF FLOODING?

CONCEPT 13.6 We can lessen the threat of flooding by protecting more wetlands and natural vegetation in watersheds, and by not building in areas subject to frequent flooding.

Some Areas Get Too Much Water from Flooding

Some areas have too little freshwater, but others sometimes have too much because of natural flooding by streams, caused mostly by heavy rain or rapidly melting snow. A flood happens when freshwater in a stream overflows its normal channel and spills into the adjacent area, called the **floodplain.**

Human activities contribute to flooding in several ways. People settle on floodplains to take advantage of their many assets. They include fertile soil on flat land suitable for crops, ample freshwater for irrigation, and availability of nearby rivers for transportation and recreation. In efforts to reduce the threat of flooding on floodplains, rivers have been narrowed and straightened (or *channelized*), surrounded by protective dikes and *levees* (long mounds of earth along their banks), and dammed to create reservoirs that store and release water as needed. However, such measures can lead to greatly increased flood damage when heavy snowmelt or prolonged rains overwhelm them.

Floods provide several benefits. They have created some of the world's most productive farmland by depositing nutrient-rich silt on floodplains. They also help recharge groundwater and refill wetlands that are commonly found on floodplains, thereby supporting biodiversity and aquatic ecosystem services.

At the same time, floods kill thousands of people every year and cost tens of billions of dollars in property damage (see the Case Study that follows). Floods are usually considered natural disasters, but since the 1960s, human activities have contributed to a sharp rise in flood deaths and damages, meaning that such disasters are partly human-made.

One such human activity is the *removal of water-absorbing vegetation*, especially on hillsides (Figure 13.27). Once the trees on a hillside have been cut for timber, fuelwood, livestock grazing, or farming, freshwater from precipitation rushes down the barren slopes, erodes precious topsoil, and can increase flooding and pollution in local streams. Such deforestation can also make landslides and mudflows more likely. A 3,000-year-old Chinese proverb says, "To protect your rivers, protect your mountains."

The second human activity that increases the severity of flooding is the *draining of wetlands* that naturally absorb floodwaters. These areas are then often covered with pavement and buildings that greatly increase runoff, which contributes to flooding and pollution of surface waters. When Hurricane Katrina struck the Gulf Coast of the United States in August 2005 and flooded the city of New Orleans, Louisiana, the damage was intensified because of the degradation or removal of coastal wetlands. These wetlands had historically helped to absorb water and buffer this low-lying land from storm surges. For this reason, Louisiana officials are now working to restore some coastal wetlands.

Another human-related factor that will likely increase flooding is a rise in sea levels, projected to occur during this century (mostly the result of climate change related to human activities). Climate change models project that, by 2075, as many as 150 million people living in the world's largest coastal cities—a number nearly equal to half of the current US population—could be flooded out by rising sea levels.

CASE STUDY

Living Dangerously on Floodplains in Bangladesh

Bangladesh is one of the world's most densely populated countries. In 2016, its 163 million people were packed into an area roughly the size of the US state of Wisconsin (which has a population of less than 6 million). And the country's population is projected to increase to 202 million by 2050. Bangladesh is a very flat country, only slightly above sea level, and it is one of the world's poorest countries.

The people of Bangladesh depend on moderate annual flooding during the summer monsoon season to grow rice and help maintain soil fertility in their country's delta basin region, which is fed by numerous river systems. The annual floods also deposit eroded Himalayan soil on the country's crop fields. Bangladeshis have adapted to moderate flooding. Most of the houses have flat thatch roofs on which families can take refuge with their belongings in case of rising waters. The roofs can be detached from the walls, if necessary, and floated like rafts. After the waters have subsided, the roof can be reattached to the walls of the house. However, great floods can overwhelm such defenses.

In the past, great floods occurred every 50 years or so. However, between 1987 and 2016, there were seven severe floods, each covering a third or more of the country with water. Bangladesh's flooding problems begin in the Himalayan watershed, where rapid population growth and unsustainable farming have resulted in deforestation. Monsoon rains now run more quickly off the barren Himalayan foothills, carrying vital topsoil with them (Figure 13.27, right).

This increased runoff of topsoil, combined with heavier-than-normal monsoon rains, has led to more severe flooding along Himalayan rivers, as well as downstream in Bangladesh's delta areas. In 1998, a disastrous flood covered two-thirds of Bangladesh's land area, in some places for 2 months, drowning at least 2,000 people and leaving 30 million homeless. It also destroyed more than one-fourth of the country's crops, which caused thousands of people to die of starvation. Another flood in 2014 affected nearly 3 million people by leaving hundreds of thousands homeless and destroying crops and access to clean water.

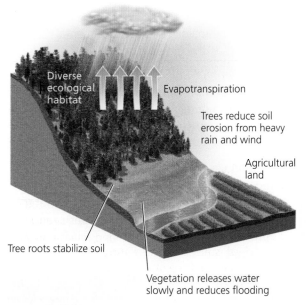
Tree roots stabilize soil
Diverse ecological habitat
Evapotranspiration
Trees reduce soil erosion from heavy rain and wind
Agricultural land
Vegetation releases water slowly and reduces flooding

Forested Hillside

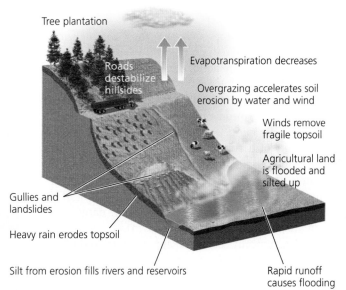
Tree plantation
Roads destabilize hillsides
Evapotranspiration decreases
Overgrazing accelerates soil erosion by water and wind
Winds remove fragile topsoil
Agricultural land is flooded and silted up
Gullies and landslides
Heavy rain erodes topsoil
Silt from erosion fills rivers and reservoirs
Rapid runoff causes flooding

After Deforestation

FIGURE 13.27 Natural capital degradation: A hillside before and after deforestation. **Question:** How might a drought in this area make these effects even worse?

Many of the coastal mangrove forests in Bangladesh (and elsewhere; see Figure 6.8, p. 158) have been cleared for fuelwood, farming, and shrimp farming ponds. The result: more severe flooding because these coastal wetlands had helped to shelter Bangladesh's low-lying coastal areas from storm surges, cyclones, and tsunamis. In areas of Bangladesh still protected by mangrove forests, damages and death tolls from cyclones have been much lower than they were in areas where the forests have been cleared.

Projected rises in sea level and storm intensity during this century, primarily due to projected climate change, will likely be a major threat to Bangladeshis who live on the flat delta adjacent to the Bay of Bengal. This would create millions of environmental refugees with no place to go in this already densely populated country.

Bangladesh is one of the few less-developed nations that is implementing plans to adapt to projected rising sea levels. This includes using varieties of rice and other crops that can better tolerate flooding, saltwater, and drought. People are also planting small vegetable gardens in bare patches between houses to help reduce their dependence on rice. In addition, they are building ponds to collect monsoon rainwater and a network of earthen embankments to help protect against high tides and storm surges. Bangladesh has been praised in recent years for its work on disaster preparedness, including construction of storm shelters and improved evacuation procedures. Such measures have resulted in declining death tolls and property damage in the face of more frequent storms and flooding.

Reducing Flood Risks

Many scientists argue that we could improve flood control by relying less on engineered devices such as dams and levees and more on nature's systems such as wetlands and forests in watersheds.

One engineering approach is the channelizing of streams, which does reduce upstream flooding. However, it also eliminates the aquatic habitats that lie along a meandering stream by taking the water from those systems and sending it in a faster flow straight down a channel. It also reduces groundwater recharge and often leads to downstream flooding. Similarly, levees or floodwalls along the banks of a river contain and speed up stream flow and can lead to flooding downstream.

Damming, the most common engineering approach, can reduce the threat of flooding by storing water in a reservoir and releasing it gradually. However, dams also have a number of drawbacks (Figure 13.14).

A more ecologically oriented approach to reducing flooding is to *preserve existing wetlands* and *restore degraded wetlands* that lie in floodplains to take advantage of the natural flood control they provide. We would also be wise to sharply reduce emissions of greenhouse gases that contribute to atmospheric warming and climate change, which will likely raise sea levels and flood many of the world's coastal areas during this century.

Figure 13.28 summarizes these various ways to reduce flooding risks (**Concept 13.6**).

Solutions

Reducing Flood Damage

Prevention	Control
Preserve forests in watersheds	Strengthen and deepen streams (channelization)
Preserve and restore wetlands on floodplains	
Tax development on floodplains	Build levees or floodwalls along streams
Increase use of flood-plains for sustainable agriculture and forestry	Build dams

FIGURE 13.28 Methods for reducing the harmful effects of flooding (**Concept 13.7**). *Critical thinking:* Which two of these solutions do you think are the best ones? Why?

Top: allensima/Shutterstock.com. Bottom: Zeljko Radojko/Shutterstock.com.

CHECKPOINT FOR UNDERSTANDING 13.6

1. Identify human activities that induce or worsen flooding.

2. Rather than building dams and levees, describe what natural approaches can reduce flooding.

KEY IDEAS

- One of the major global environmental problems is the growing shortage of freshwater in many parts of the world.

- We can expand water supplies in water-short areas in a number of ways, but the most important ways are to reduce overall water use and to use water much more efficiently.

- We can use water more sustainably by reducing water use, using water more efficiently, cutting water losses, raising water prices, and protecting aquifers, forests, and other ecosystems that store and release water.

Core Case Study Checkpoint

Discuss how the use of water from the Colorado River illustrates the problems associated with the growing human use of the earth's water resources.

aquifer: porous, water-saturated layers of sand, gravel, or bedrock that can yield an economically significant amount of water.

dam: a structure built across a river to control the river's flow or to create a reservoir.

desalination: purification of saltwater or brackish (slightly salty) water by removal of dissolved salts.

floodplain: flat valley floor next to a stream channel. For legal purposes, the term often applies to any low area that has the potential for flooding including certain coastal areas.

groundwater: water that sinks into the soil and is stored in slowly flowing and slowly renewed underground reservoirs called aquifers; underground water in the zone of saturation below the water table.

reliable surface runoff: surface runoff of water that generally can be counted on as a stable source of water from year to year.

reservoir: artificial lake created when a river is dammed.

surface runoff: water flowing off the land into bodies of surface water.

surface water: precipitation that does not infiltrate the ground or return to the atmosphere by evaporation or transpiration.

virtual water: water that is not directly consumed but is used to produce food and other products.

water footprint: a rough measure of the volume of water used directly and indirectly to keep a person or a group alive and to support lifestyles.

watershed: land area that delivers water, sediment, and dissolved substances via small streams to a major stream.

zone of saturation: zone where all available pores in soil and rock in the earth's crust are filled by water.

Chapter Review

Core Case Study

1. Summarize the importance of the Colorado River basin in the United States and how human activities are stressing this system. Define **drought** and explain how it has affected the Colorado River system.

Section 13.1

2. What are the two key concepts for this section? Define **freshwater**. Explain why access to water is a health issue, an economic issue, a national and global security issue, and an environmental issue. What percentage of the earth's freshwater is available to us? Explain how water is recycled by the hydrologic cycle and how human activities can interfere with this cycle. Define **groundwater, zone of saturation, water table**, and **aquifer**, and explain how aquifers are recharged. What are deep aquifers and why are they considered nonrenewable? Define and distinguish between **surface water** and **surface runoff**. What is a **watershed (drainage basin)**?

3. What is **reliable surface runoff**? What percentage of the world's reliable runoff are we using and what percentage are we likely to be using by 2025? How is most of the world's water used? Define **water footprint** and **virtual water** and give two examples of each. Describe the availability and use of freshwater resources in the United States and the water shortages that could occur during this century. What are three major problems resulting from the way people are using water from the Colorado River basin?

4. How many countries face water scarcity today and how many could face water scarcity by 2050? What percentage of the earth's land suffers from severe drought today and how might this change by 2059? How many people in the world lack regular access to clean water today and how high might this number grow by 2025? Why do many analysts view the likelihood of steadily worsening water shortages as one of the world's most serious environmental problems? Explain the connection between water shortages and hunger.

Section 13.2

5. What is the key concept for this section? What are the advantages and disadvantages of withdrawing groundwater? Summarize the problem of groundwater depletion in the world generally, in Saudi Arabia, and in the United States, especially in the Ogallala Aquifer. List three problems that result from the overpumping of aquifers. List some ways to prevent or slow groundwater depletion. What is the potential for using deep aquifers to expand water supplies?

Section 13.3

6. What are the two key concepts for this section? What is a **dam**? What is a **reservoir**? What are the advantages and disadvantages of using large dams and reservoirs? How do dams affect aquatic wildlife? What has happened to water flows in the Colorado River (**Core Case Study**) since 1960? Explain how the damming of this river has affected its estuary. What other problems are likely to further shrink this supply of water? List three possible solutions to the supply problems in the Colorado River basin.

7. Define **desalination** and distinguish between distillation and reverse osmosis as methods for desalinating water. What are three limitations of desalination? What are scientists doing to try to improve desalination technology?

Section 13.4

8. What is the key concept for this section? What is a water transfer? Describe large water-transfer in California, explain how it came about, and summarize the controversy over this transfer. Summarize the story of the Aral Sea water-transfer project and its disastrous consequences.

Section 13.5

9. What is the key concept for this section? What percentage of available freshwater is lost through inefficient use and other causes in the world and in the United States? What are two major reasons for those losses? Describe three major irrigation methods and list ways to reduce water losses in irrigation. What are three ways in which people in less-developed countries conserve water? List four ways to reduce water waste in industries and homes and three ways to use less water to remove wastes. List four ways in which you can reduce your use and waste of water.

Section 13.6

10. What is the key concept for this section? What is a **floodplain** and why do people like to live on floodplains? What are the benefits and harms of flooding? List two human activities that increase the risk of flooding. Describe the flooding risks that many people in Bangladesh face and what they are doing about it. List and compare two engineering approaches to flood control and two ecologically oriented approaches. What are this chapter's *three key ideas*? Explain how the **scientific principles of sustainability** can guide us in using water more sustainably during this century.

Note: Key terms are in bold type.

AP® Review Questions

1. Approximately what percentage of the water on the earth is saltwater?
   - (A) 97%
   - (B) 93%
   - (C) 75%
   - (D) 60%
   - (E) 45%

2. One way to conserve water in agriculture is to
   - (A) plant crops that have adapted to arid climates by sending down deep tap roots and storing water in times of drought
   - (B) use a technique similar to the ancient Egyptians', whereby they relied on a river to regularly overflow its banks
   - (C) plant crops in places with less sunlight so there are fewer hours during the day for evaporation to occur
   - (D) channel gray water from homes and industry to agricultural areas
   - (E) use a watering technique that focuses the water in the immediate area of plant roots

3. The majority of water directly consumed per U.S. citizen is used for
   - (A) taking a shower
   - (B) watering the lawn
   - (C) washing clothes
   - (D) flushing the toilet
   - (E) washing the car

4. A drought in the 1930s transformed large parts of the Midwest into a "Dustbowl." This is an example of
   - (A) what would happen if the giant toad or feral pigs are not controlled
   - (B) the results of many inches of rain falling within a few hours
   - (C) the conversion of rangeland or cropland into a desertlike area
   - (D) evaporation of water from the ground and release of moisture from leaves
   - (E) water flowing over the surface when it is unable to infiltrate the ground because of saturation of the soil or a steep slope

5. The Ogallala Aquifer is a one-time deposit of water and has such a slow recharge rate it is
   (A) huge and can accommodate the water needs of the Great Plains for at least several more decades
   (B) not replenishing at the rate it is being used, and one result is land subsidence
   (C) protected by state laws and is therefore underutilized
   (D) suffering from severe salinization as water infiltrates the ground and dissolved minerals are added to the aquifer
   (E) increasing each year with the expectation that the rate of increase will grow as the climate changes and brings more storms to the Great Plains

6. The Colorado River system is
   (A) extremely eutrophic because as water slows down behind the dams, there are more opportunities for nitrates and phosphates to enter the river water
   (B) an underutilized resource that could easily provide water to farmers, ranchers, and cities
   (C) a government-subsidized water utility that provides cities such as Las Vegas, Los Angeles, and San Diego with cheaper water because Lake Powell and Lake Mead are huge bodies of water
   (D) a water diversion project that supplies water to large cities such as Las Vegas, Los Angeles, and San Diego
   (E) a confined aquifer that is being overpumped and polluted because of increasing populations in the cities it serves

7. A forested hillside will help eliminate
   (A) the need for research such as that done at the Hubbard Brook Experimental Forest in New Hampshire
   (B) Using pesticides, because the shade of the forest prevents insect pests from entering the area
   (C) droughts, because transpiration ensures that forest areas always have a high moisture level
   (D) flooding, because trees help reduce soil erosion and the flow of water downslope
   (E) unsustainable farming, because crops cannot be grown on forested slopes

8. Which of the following is NOT a solution to domestic water conservation?
   (A) Low-flow showerheads and faucets
   (B) Using gray water for watering lawns and gardens
   (C) Charging a flat fee for water use instead of using water meters
   (D) Replacing lawns with native plants that need little to no irrigation
   (E) Flushing toilets only when necessary

Questions 9–12 refer to the following terms. Choices may be used once, more than once, or not at all.
   (A) Aquifer
   (B) Surface water
   (C) Confined aquifer
   (D) Water table
   (E) Transpiration

9. Examples are freshwater rivers and streams

10. Evaporation from the leaves of plants into the atmosphere

11. Underground caverns and porous layers of sand, gravel, or bedrock through which groundwater flows

12. Upper surface of the zone of saturation

13. All of the following are environmental disadvantages of dams used to produce energy, EXCEPT
   (A) flooding downstream is reduced
   (B) large amounts of water are lost through evaporation
   (C) flooding destroys terrestrial lands and displaces people
   (D) migration and reproductive patterns of some fish species are disrupted
   (E) the amount of nutrient-rich silt reaching downstream ecosystems is reduced

14. One method of desalination is
   (A) forcing the water through a filter, which removes salts from the water
   (B) taking more water from an aquifer than is being replaced, so less salts and minerals are entering the water
   (C) saturating the groundwater so the water table rises, and thus decreasing the ratio of salts within the groundwater
   (D) the use of hydroponic agriculture so water and salts are not added to the ground during irrigation
   (E) planting only drought-resistant vegetation, reducing the amount of water needed in home gardens and in agriculture

15. Which of the following is the LEAST likely solution to groundwater depletion?
   (A) Encouraging privatization of water utilities
   (B) Setting and enforcing minimum stream flows
   (C) Growing more crops that are drought-resistant in arid areas
   (D) Raising the price of water to discourage waste
   (E) Subsidizing water conservation

Colorado River Water Flow

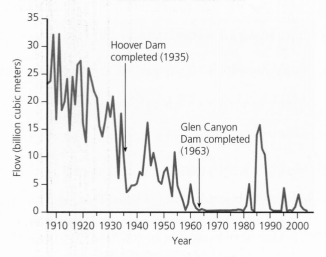

16. According to the graph, the flow of the Colorado River has
    (A) dropped continually since 1910
    (B) gone up and down but continues to trend downward
    (C) stayed steady over the last half century
    (D) dropped steadily from 1935 until 1945
    (E) slowly increased in the last 10 years

17. What can be inferred about the climate from 1960 to 1980?
    (A) There was excessive rainfall.
    (B) Rainfall led to variation in flow.
    (C) There were average rates of precipitation.
    (D) There was a drought.
    (E) Windstorms deposited large amounts of sediment in the reservoir.

18. Which of the following best explains the general downward trend in Colorado River flow from 1910 until 1970?
    (A) More water was being removed from the Colorado River before it reached any of the dams.
    (B) A series of heavy winter snowstorms changed the water level of the Colorado River.
    (C) Residents used more water-saving devices in their homes.
    (D) The dams on the Colorado River diverted water for municipal and agricultural uses.
    (E) The underground aquifer was being depleted as more farmers used its water for agricultural irrigation.

19. All of the following are impacts of damming the Colorado River EXCEPT
    (A) the agricultural region of northern Mexico no longer receives river water
    (B) the migration of some fish populations has been interrupted
    (C) flooding downstream of the dams has displaced people and destroyed property
    (D) reservoirs behind dams have lost large amounts of water due to evaporation
    (E) areas upstream of the dams have been flooded and habitat for many species has been destroyed

20. The GREATEST use of water globally is for
    (A) industry
    (B) agriculture
    (C) residential use
    (D) recreation
    (E) municipal management

AP® Free-Response Practice

1. Long Island is a region of downstate New York, close to New York City, that is surrounded by ocean. Residents of Long Island rely solely on groundwater for their freshwater needs. The Lloyd aquifer is a confined aquifer that lies below the Magothy aquifer with a layer of clay extending over much of the Lloyd aquifer and serving as the upper confining layer. As of 2006, the Lloyd aquifer contained about 9 percent of the available freshwater.

    Nearly all pumping from the Lloyd aquifer has been in the western part of Long Island. In 2006, wells pumped 450 million gallons of water per day to serve Long Island residents. Excessive pumping led to saltwater intrusion in the Lloyd aquifer in coastal areas.

    Local government officials have proposed raising taxes and building a desalination plant on the shores of Long Island Sound. However, a local community organization, Citizens for the Environment, proposes establishing a community water conservation program, as opposed to funding a desalination plant.

(a) If wells are pumped faster than can be naturally recharged, water is being harvested unsustainably.

   (i) Explain ONE way that aquifer recharge occurs.

   (ii) Explain why one might find an artesian well whose source is the Lloyd aquifer.

   (iii) Saltwater intrusion is a problem on Long Island. **Explain** how this might occur.

(b) Identify TWO ways that citizens could promote water conservation in their communities.

(c) Desalination plants are a possible solution to diminishing freshwater supplies.

   (i) Describe ONE method of desalination.

   (ii) Identify ONE economic and ONE ecological drawback of desalination plants.

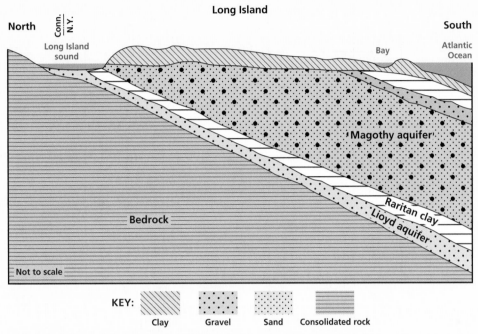

Source: http://www.dec.ny.gov/lands/36183.html

Critical Thinking

1. What do you think are the three most important priorities for dealing with the water resource problems of the Colorado River basin, as discussed in the **Core Case Study** that opens this chapter? Explain your choices.

2. List three ways in which human activities are affecting the water cycle. How might these changes to the water cycle affect your lifestyle? How might your lifestyle be contributing to these effects?

3. Explain how our current use of the earth's water resources can be viewed as a good example of the tragedy of the commons (see Chapter 1, p. 4).

4. Many argue that government freshwater subsidies promote the expansion of productive farmland, stimulate local economies, and help to keep food and electricity prices low. Do you think this is reason enough for governments to continue providing subsidies to farmers and cities? Explain.

5. Explain why you are for or against **(a)** raising the price of water while providing lower lifeline rates for poor consumers, **(b)** withdrawing government subsidies that provide farmers with water at low cost, and **(c)** providing government subsidies to farmers for improving irrigation efficiency.

6. Calculate how many liters (and gallons) of water are lost in 1 month by a toilet or faucet that leaks 2 drops of water per second. (One liter of water equals about 3,500 drops and 1 liter equals 0.265 gallon.) How many bathtubs (each containing about 151 liters or 40 gallons) could be filled with this lost water?

7. List the three most important ways in which you could use water more efficiently. Which, if any, of these measures do you already take?

8. List three ways in which human activities increase the harmful effects of flooding. What is the best way to prevent each of these human impacts? Do you think they should be prevented? Why or why not?

Ecological Footprint Analysis

The following table is based on data from the Water Footprint Network, a science-based organization that promotes the sustainable use of water through sharing knowledge and building awareness of how water is used.

It shows the amounts of *embedded water,* or water required to produce each of the products listed in the first column. Study the table and then answer the questions that follow.

Product	Liters per kilogram (kg) or product	Gallons per pound (lb) or product
Beef	15,400/kg	1,855/lb.
Pork	5,990/kg	722/lb.
Chicken	4,325/kg	521/lb.
Milk	255/glass (250 ml)	68/glass (8 oz.)
Eggs	196/egg	52/egg
Coffee	132/cup	35/cup
Beer	74/glass (250 ml)	20/glass (8 oz.)
Wine	54/glass (250 ml)	14/glass (8 oz.)
Apple	125/average size apple	33/apple
Banana	160/large banana	42/banana
Tomato	50/medium tomato	13/tomato
Rice	2,500/kg	301/lb.
Bread	1,608/kg	426/lb.
Cotton t-shirt	2,495/shirt	661/shirt

Questions:

1. Find a loaf of common wheat bread, count the slices per loaf, and calculate the amount of water used to produce each slice. Calculate the amount of water used to produce one-third pound of beef. Combine these two to arrive at the approximate amount of water used to produce an average restaurant hamburger.

2. In terms of embedded water, how many tomatoes can be produced for each pound of pork? For each pound of beef?

3. If you drank coffee and/or milk today, how many gallons (or liters) of embedded water did you drink?

4. In terms of embedded water, how many kilograms (and pounds) of rice are represented in one t-shirt? How many bananas? How many apples?

5. In terms of embedded water, how many pounds of chicken can be produced for each pound of beef? How many pounds of rice?

Answers to Checkpoints for Understanding

Section 13.1

1. Warmer temperatures increase the amount of water evaporating into the atmosphere, resulting in heavier rainfall in some areas and more severe drought in others.
2. The two major sources of freshwater are groundwater (underground aquifers) and surface water (lakes, ponds, streams, and rivers).

3. Most freshwater is used to produce food (approximately 70%), industry uses approximately 20%, and cities and residences use the remaining 10%.
4. There are shortages of renewable freshwater in parts of the United States because it is not evenly distributed, and much of it is polluted by agricultural and industrial waste.

Section 13.2

1. Groundwater use becomes unsustainable if it is pumped out faster than the aquifer can recharge, or if the aquifer is polluted.
2. Water from the Ogallala aquifer is used primarily for irrigation of crops.
3. Overpumping aquifers can lead to land subsidence, greater energy use in order to pump water from deeper depths, and saltwater intrusion in coastal areas.

Section 13.3

1. Dams can generate electricity, control flooding downstream, provide recreation in the reservoir created upstream, and store and release water for agriculture and human use.
2. Dams can destroy and flood forests and lands upstream, large amounts of water can be evaporated away from the increased surface area of the reservoir, downstream cropland is deprived of nutrient-rich sediment, dams disrupt migration and spawning of fish, and dams can burst, flooding and killing humans and wildlife downstream.
3. Glaciers accumulate and store water during the winter season and in the summer release the melt water into an adjoining river. As temperatures on earth warm and glaciers shrink, there is less water to feed river systems that people and ecosystems depend on.
4. Desalination requires a great deal of energy to heat and distill water and to remove salt by reverse osmosis. Chemicals are required to sterilize the water and limit algae growth, and desalination produces huge amounts of concentrated salty wastewater that cannot be disposed of without contaminating groundwater or killing marine life where it would be dumped.

Section 13.4

1. Benefits of water-transfer projects include diverting water to places where it is scarce, irrigating agricultural land and producing food, and improving economies in cities that lack water.
2. Drawbacks of water-diversion projects include large water losses via aqueducts and leaks in channeling systems, degradation of ecosystems where water is taken, displacement of people where too much water is diverted, and huge economic cost of building pipelines and channels.

Section 13.5

1. When consumers pay the true cost of water, and when there are no subsidies in place to bring down the price artificially, consumers tend to use less and invest in water-saving technologies, fix leaks, and use other strategies to ultimately use less water.
2. Water consumption can be reduced by fixing leaks, using low-flow shower heads and efficient toilets, and using front-loading rather than top-loading washing machines. In areas where green lawns are not adapted to dry conditions, landscaping with native vegetation (cacti and succulents), and using drip irrigation rather than sprinklers to water lawns can also cut down on water consumption. Water can be recycled using gray water to water lawns and outdoor plants. Paying the true cost of water rather than the subsidized cost also encourages people to consume less.
3. To conserve water, some farmers are growing crops that are less water-intensive. Crops such as alfalfa, almonds, and lettuce use large amounts of water for irrigation.

Section 13.6

1. Human activities that worsen flooding include removing vegetation that absorbs water during flooding, draining wetlands that absorb the energy of storms and reduce the potential damage, and activities that worsen climate change that lead to rising sea levels and inland flooding.
2. Restoring and leaving intact natural wetlands can reduce the damage caused by flooding. Also, leaving forests intact, especially on hillsides, can also reduce the damage from flooding.

Core Case Study

The growing draw-down of water from the Colorado River for irrigating crops, creating electric power, and providing drinking water as it flows through some of the country's driest lands in 7 states (Figure 13.1) means that, in many years, increasing amounts of water are withdrawn to meet these growing water demands. It also illustrates how damning the river and altering its flow has damaged its aquatic wildlife and terrestrial wildlife in nearby areas and degraded important aquatic and ecological ecosystem services.

1. The passenger pigeon is an example of a(n)
   (A) extinct species
   (B) threatened species
   (C) endangered species
   (D) indicator species
   (E) endemic species

2. Which of the following best describes the meaning of CITES?
   (A) An international treaty banning the hunting and trade of endangered species
   (B) A set of regulations controlling the introduction of exotic species
   (C) A pact that supports the preservation of critical wildlife habitat
   (D) An international organization dedicated to the preservation of endangered species
   (E) A citywide ordinance that regulates exotic pets in residential areas

3. Which of the following is NOT a characteristic of an endangered species?
   (A) Specialized niches
   (B) *r*-selected species
   (C) High trophic level
   (D) Rarity
   (E) Narrow distribution

4. Listing which species are considered endangered or threatened is the job of which of the following government organization(s) in the United States?
   I. National Marine Fisheries Service
   II. U.S. Fish and Wildlife Service
   III. Environmental Protection Agency
   (A) I only
   (B) II only
   (C) III only
   (D) I and II only
   (E) I, II, and III

Questions 5–7 refer to the following. Choices may be used once, more than once, or not at all.
   (A) Selective cutting
   (B) Clear cutting
   (C) Captive breeding
   (D) Strip cutting
   (E) Tree plantation

5. Intermediate-aged or mature trees in uneven-aged forests cut singly or in small groups

6. Logging method that results in the maximum profits in the shortest time frame

7. Managed area of uniformly aged trees which are grown until commercially viable

8. When a species is no longer found in an area it once inhabited but is still found elsewhere in the world, this is known as
   (A) biological extinction
   (B) selective extinction
   (C) ecological extinction
   (D) local extinction
   (E) point extinction

9. What is the benefit of creating a habitat corridor to connect isolated reserves?
   (A) It allows migration of exotic species.
   (B) It allows migration of vertebrates that need large ranges.
   (C) It increases the amount of edge habitat.
   (D) It reduces the exposure of migrating species to human hunters.
   (E) It simplifies land management considerations.

10. One of the most common methods for sustainable management of rangeland is
   (A) spraying herbicides to reduce invasive species
   (B) replanting barren areas that have been overgrazed
   (C) mechanical removal of nonnative species
   (D) rotational grazing of cattle
   (E) fencing off reserved areas where grazing is never allowed

11. What layer(s) of soil contain most of the humus and soil organisms?
   I. Leaf litter
   II. Topsoil
   III. Subsoil
   (A) I only
   (B) II only
   (C) I and II only
   (D) II and III only
   (E) I, II, and III

12. Which statement concerning mining processes is NOT correct?
   (A) Mining processes accumulate a large amount of overburden that can eventually pollute waterways.
   (B) Health hazards, oil spills, and soil degradation are all side effects of mining.
   (C) Mining processes depend on the renewable resources found within the earth's lithosphere.
   (D) The exploration, extraction, and transportation of the resources decrease the available net energy.
   (E) Mining resources are used in the construction of roads and buildings.

13. The San Andreas fault line in California is the result of what type of plate boundary?
    (A) Divergent plate boundary
    (B) Transform fault
    (C) Subduction zone
    (D) Convergent plate boundary
    (E) Mid-oceanic fault line

14. What type of formation would you expect to find at a divergent plate boundary in the ocean?
    I. Mid-oceanic trench
    II. Volcanoes
    III. Oceanic ridges
    (A) I only
    (B) II only
    (C) III only
    (D) I and II only
    (E) II and III only

15. Deficiencies in protein and other key nutrients is known as
    (A) undernutrition
    (B) malnutrition
    (C) hunger
    (D) starvation
    (E) caloric overdraft

16. Which of the following characteristics of genetically modified crops and foods may be a benefit to the grower, but increases negative ecological impacts?
    (A) Need less input of fertilizers than other crops
    (B) Can grow in slightly salty soils
    (C) Can create herbicide-resistant weed populations
    (D) Produce higher yields
    (E) More resistant to disease and drought

17. In 1990 global fish catch for a small coastal New England community was 290 tons; in 2015 it was 300 tons. Which of the following values is the closest to the percent increase in fish catch?
    (A)   3%
    (B)   10%
    (C)   96%
    (D) 110%
    (E) 203%

18. This is the top of the zone of saturation whose elevation is influenced by the rate of recharge and removal of ground water.
    (A) Aquifer
    (B) Water table
    (C) Ground water level
    (D) Zone of leaching
    (E) Aeration layer

Questions 19–20 refer to the following terms. Choices may be used once, more than once, or not at all.
    (A) Animal feed lots
    (B) Aquaculture
    (C) Plantation farming
    (D) Genetic engineering of plants
    (E) Organic farming

19. Creates oxygen-demanding waste in waterway systems from manure run-off

20. Destroys mangrove systems and estuaries to provide needed space

Questions 21–23 refer to the following terms. Choices may be used once, more than once, or not at all.
    (A) Water table
    (B) Subsidence
    (C) Saltwater intrusion
    (D) Overdraft
    (E) Aquifer

21. The sinking of land due to the over-pumping of ground water supplies

22. The water table is lowered and the normal interface between fresh and saline ground water moves inland

23. When more water is removed from an aquifer than can naturally be recharged

24. Which of the following is NOT a true benefit of the Three Gorges Dam and locks system on the Yangtze River?
    (A) Electricity generated from the dam is equivalent to several coal burning power plants.
    (B) It has reduced the potential for destructive flood waters downstream.
    (C) Biodiversity is enhanced by the creation of new habitats in flooded areas upstream.
    (D) The system has improved access by shipping vessels.
    (E) The reduced use of coal in the area has meant a reduction in CO_2 emissions.

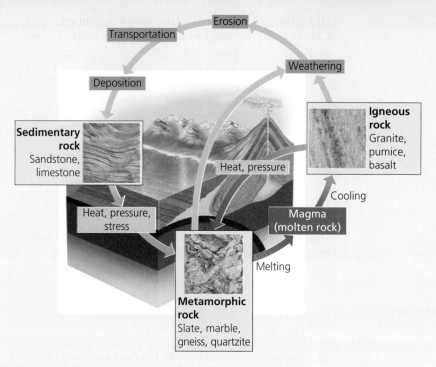

25. Based on the diagram above, which of the following processes is LEAST dependent on the hydrologic cycle and the movement of water on the planet?
(A) Erosion
(B) Melting
(C) Weathering
(D) Transportation
(E) Deposition

AP®FREE-RESPONSE PRACTICE

1. A farmer has a 200-acre farm divided into four 50-acre fields. All have similar slope, soil texture and nutrient levels. The farmer attended an agricultural symposium sponsored by the local Agricultural Extension Service. The data presented in the symposium indicates that locally produced, organic fertilizers are better for the environment than are mass-produced, synthetic fertilizers. He is interested in being a good steward of the environment, but he also needs to have reliable crop productivity. Assume that he is able to take a year to determine which type of fertilizer, organic or synthetic, produces a high crop yield.

(a) Design a controlled experiment that the farmer could use to determine the effectiveness of organic versus synthetic fertilizers on crop productivity. In your experiment design, be sure to include the following:

   (i) **State** the hypothesis.

   (ii) **Describe** the specific procedure you would use, including the control set up.

   (iii) **Identify** the controlled variables.

   (iv) **Identify** the independent variable.

   (v) **Identify** the dependent variable.

(b) Both types of fertilizers, organic and synthetic, have advantages and disadvantages.

   (i) **Discuss** the economic advantages and disadvantages of organic fertilizers.

   (ii) **Discuss** the economic advantages and disadvantages of synthetic fertilizers.

(c) **Describe** the ecological effects of using a locally produced organic fertilizer as compared to using an organic fertilizer produced elsewhere.

(d) Fertilizers, regardless of their source, typically have an impact on local waterways. **Identify** and **describe** this phenomenon.

2. Below is an excerpt from the Fremont Bay Program's website. Read the article and answer the questions that follow.

> The way we live and use the land greatly influences the health of Fremont Bay and its network of streams and rivers.
>
> The percentage of forested land is declining as the rate of development increases. In the Bay watershed, approximately 100 acres of forest are lost each day, primarily to development of new roads and buildings to accommodate a growing population.
>
> **How has land in the Fremont Bay watershed changed over time?**
>
> Data published in 2017 by the U.S. Geological Survey (USGS) show how three types of land cover – farmland/open space, urban areas and tree canopy – in the Fremont Bay watershed changed between four different sampling times: 1996, 2002, 2010 and 2016. "Land cover" is measured by interpretation of satellite images that capture the sun's reflection off the earth's surface, while "land use" is the actual way an area of land is used (such as agriculture, forest or residential development).
>
> Farmland/open space decreased by 9000 acres per year between 1996 and 2002, 2000 acres per year between 2002 and 2010 and 900 acres per year between 2010 and 2016.
>
> The total amount of urban area in the Bay watershed increased by a total of 15 percent, or 355,000 acres, between 1996 and 2016. The annual rate of increase between 1996 and 2002 was twice the annual rate of increase between 2002 and 2016.
>
> Tree canopy decreased from 63 percent of the watershed in 1992 to 62 percent of the watershed in 2016, a loss of 440,000 acres. The highest rate of decline took place between 2010 and 2016, when the watershed lost 37,000 acres of canopy per year.

(a) **Calculate** the total number of acres of farmland/open space lost between 1996 and 2016.

(b) The amount of urban area in the Bay watershed area increased significantly between 1996 and 2016.

    (i) **Calculate** both the percent increase in urban area between 1996 and 2002 and the percent increase between 2002 and 2016.

    (ii) **Identify** TWO reasons why urban sprawl increases flash flooding.

    (iii) **Describe** ONE urban planning technique that can mitigate or prevent the increased flash flooding caused by urban sprawl.

(c) All non-urban land has the potential to provide ecosystem services.

    (i) **Identify** ONE ecosystem service provided by forests and ONE ecosystem service provided by farmland/open land.

    (ii) **Describe** the economic impacts expected to result from the loss of either forestland or farmland.

(d) **Identify** and **describe** ONE federal law that could prevent developers from converting forestland into urban acreage.

Nonrenewable Energy

Typical citizens of advanced industrialized nations each consume as much energy in 6 months as typical citizens in less-developed countries consume during their entire life.

MAURICE STRONG

Offshore oil drilling rig.

iStockphoto.com/WitthawatM

Key Questions

14.1 What types of energy resources do we use?

14.2 What are the advantages and disadvantages of using oil?

14.3 What are the advantages and disadvantages of using natural gas?

14.4 What are the advantages and disadvantages of using coal?

14.5 What are the advantages and disadvantages of using nuclear power?

Using Hydrofracking to Produce Oil and Natural Gas

Geologists have known for decades about vast deposits of oil and natural gas that are dispersed and trapped between compressed layers of shale rock formations. These deposits are found deep underground in many areas of the United States, including North Dakota, Texas, and Pennsylvania.

For years, it cost too much to extract such oil (called *tight oil*) and natural gas from shale rock. This changed in the late 1990s when oil and gas producers combined two existing extraction technologies (Figure 14.1). One is **horizontal drilling,** which involves drilling a vertical well deep into the earth, turning the flexible shaft of the drill, and drilling horizontally to gain access to multiple oil and natural gas deposits held tightly between layers in shale rock formations. Usually, wells are drilled vertically for 1.6–2.4 kilometers (1–1.5 miles) or more and then horizontally for up to 1.6 kilometers (1 mile). Two or three horizontally drilled wells can often produce as much oil as 20 vertical wells, which reduces the area of land damaged by drilling operations.

The second technology, called **hydraulic fracturing** (also called hydrofracking or **fracking**), is then used to free the trapped oil and natural gas. High-pressure pumps force a mixture (slurry) of water, sand, and a cocktail of chemicals through holes in the well pipe to fracture the shale rock and create cracks. The sand wedges in the cracks and keeps them open. When the pressure is released a mixture of the oil or natural gas and about half of the slurry flows to the surface through the well pipe (Figure 14.1).

The slurry contains a mix of naturally occurring salts, toxic heavy metals, and radioactive materials leached from the rock, along with some potentially harmful drilling chemicals that oil and natural gas companies are not required to identify. The hazardous slurry is injected into deep underground hazardous waste wells (the most widely used option), sent to sewage treatment plants that often cannot handle the wastes, stored in open air holding ponds that can leak or collapse, or cleaned up and reused in the fracking process—the best but most expensive and least used option.

Energy companies drill a well horizontally, frack it several times, and then drill a new well and repeat the process. The use of these two extraction technologies in at least 25 states between 1990 and 2016 has brought about a new era of oil and natural gas production in the United States. It could last as long as market prices of oil and natural gas remain high enough to make these drilling operations profitable. Like any technology, this approach has advantages and disadvantages that we discuss later in this chapter.

In this chapter, we discuss the advantages and disadvantages of using nonrenewable fossil fuels (such as oil, natural gas, and coal) and nuclear power. In the next chapter, we look at the advantages and disadvantages of improving energy efficiency and using a variety of renewable energy resources.●

CRITICAL THINKING

What might be some of the environmental implications of hydrofracking?

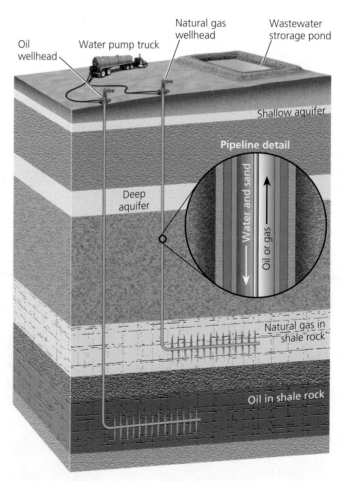

FIGURE 14.1 *Fracking:* Horizontal drilling and hydraulic fracturing are used to release large amounts of oil and natural gas that are tightly held in underground shale rock formations.

WHAT TYPES OF ENERGY
RESOURCES DO WE USE?

CONCEPT 14.1A About 90% of the commercial energy used in the world comes from nonrenewable energy resources (mostly oil, natural gas, and coal) and 10% comes from renewable energy resources.

CONCEPT 14.1B Energy resources vary greatly in their *net energy*—the amount of energy available from a resource minus the amount of energy needed to make it available.

Where Does the Energy We Use Come From?

The energy that heats the earth and makes it livable comes from the sun at no cost to us—in keeping with the solar energy **principle of sustainability**. Without this free and essentially inexhaustible input of solar energy, the earth's average temperature would be –240°C (–400°F) and life as we know it would not exist. The sun provides 99% of the earth's energy.

We use *commercial energy*, energy that is sold in the marketplace, to supplement the sun's life-sustaining energy. We get this supplemental energy from two types of energy resources (**Concept 14.1A**). One type consists of *nonrenewable energy* from fossil fuels (oil, natural gas and coal) and the nuclei of certain atoms of elements such as uranium (nuclear energy), which are discussed in this chapter. The other type consists of *renewable energy resources* such as wind, flowing water (hydropower), energy from the sun (solar energy), biomass (trees and other plants), and heat in the earth's interior (geothermal energy), which we discuss in Chapter 15.

The world depends on fossil fuels, formed from ancient plant remains buried millions of years ago and subjected to intense heat and pressure. In 2015, 90% of the commercial energy used in the world and in the United States came from nonrenewable resources (mostly fossil fuels) and 10% came from renewable resources (Figure 14.2) (**Concept 14.1A**).

90 Percentage of commercial energy used in the world and in the United States comes from nonrenewable energy (mostly fossil fuels)

Net Energy: It Takes Energy to Get Energy

Producing high-quality energy from any energy resource requires an input of high-quality energy. For example, before oil becomes useful to us, it must be found, pumped up from a deposit beneath the ground or ocean floor, transferred to a refinery, converted to gasoline and other fuels and chemicals, and delivered to consumers. Each of these steps uses high-quality energy, obtained mostly by burning fossil fuels, especially gasoline and diesel fuel produced from oil.

Net energy is the amount of high-quality energy available from a given quantity of an energy resource, minus the high-quality energy needed to make the energy available (**Concept 14.1B**).

Net energy = energy output − energy input

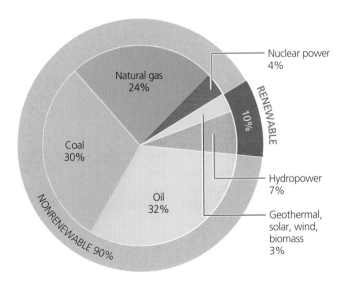
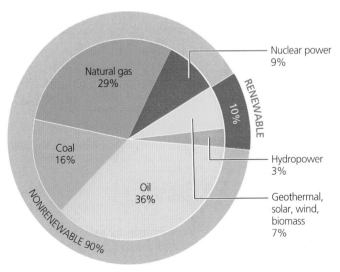

FIGURE 14.2 Energy use by source throughout the world (left) and in the United States (right) in 2015.

(Compiled by the authors using data from British Petroleum, U.S. Energy Information Administration (EIA), and International Energy Agency (IEA).)

Suppose that it takes about 9 units of high-quality energy to produce 10 units of high-quality energy from an energy resource. Then the net energy is 1 unit of energy (10 − 9 = 1) a low value.

Net energy is like the net profit earned by a business after it deducts its expenses. If a business has $1 million in sales and $900,000 in expenses, its net profit is $100,000.

Figure 14.3 shows generalized net energies for energy resources and systems. It is based on several sources of scientific data and classifies estimated net energy as high, medium, low, or negative (negative being a net energy loss).

The best way to increase net energy is to waste less energy by improving **energy efficiency**. This means using less energy to provide the same amount of useful work. This involves using more energy-efficient ways to produce electricity, heat buildings, and carry out industrial processes, and to drive cars that get better mileage.

It is difficult for an energy resource with a low or negative net energy to compete in the marketplace with other energy alternatives with a medium to high net energy unless it receives subsidies and tax breaks from the government (taxpayers) or other outside sources.

For example, electricity produced by nuclear power has a low net energy because large amounts of high-quality energy are needed for each step in the *nuclear power fuel cycle*: to extract and process uranium ore, upgrade it to nuclear fuel, build and operate nuclear power plants, safely store the resulting highly radioactive wastes for thousands of years, and dismantle each highly radioactive plant after its useful life (typically 40–60 years) and safely store its high-level radioactive materials for thousands of years.

The low net energy and the resulting high cost of the entire nuclear fuel cycle is one reason why governments (taxpayers) throughout the world heavily subsidize nuclear-generated electricity to make it available to consumers at an affordable price. Such subsidies hide the true costs of the nuclear power fuel cycle and thus violate the full-cost pricing **principle of sustainability** (see Inside Back Cover).

CHECKPOINT FOR UNDERSTANDING 14.1

1. Define net energy as it relates to nonrenewable energy resources such as coal, oil, natural gas, or nuclear power.

Electricity	Net Energy
Energy efficiency	High
Hydropower	High
Wind	High
Coal	High
Natural gas	Medium
Geothermal energy	Medium
Solar cells	Low to medium
Nuclear fuel cycle	Low
Hydrogen	Negative (Energy loss)

High-Temperature Industrial Heat	Net Energy
Energy efficiency (cogeneration)	High
Coal	High
Natural gas	Medium
Oil	Medium
Heavy shale oil	Low
Heavy oil from oil sands	Low
Direct solar (concentrated)	Low
Hydrogen	Negative (Energy loss)

Space Heating	Net Energy
Energy efficiency	High
Passive solar	Medium
Natural gas	Medium
Geothermal energy	Medium
Oil	Medium
Active solar	Low to medium
Heavy shale oil	Low
Heavy oil from oil sands	Low
Electricity	Low
Hydrogen	Negative (Energy loss)

Transportation	Net Energy
Energy efficiency	High
Gasoline	High
Natural gas	Medium
Ethanol (from sugarcane)	Medium
Diesel	Medium
Gasoline from heavy shale oil	Low
Gasoline from heavy oil sands oil	Low
Ethanol (from corn)	Low
Biodiesel (from soy)	Low
Hydrogen	Negative (Energy loss)

FIGURE 14.3 Generalized *net energies* for various energy resources and systems (**Concept 14.1**). *Critical thinking:* Based only on these data, which two resources in each category should we be using?

(Compiled by the authors using data from the U.S. Department of Energy; U.S. Department of Agriculture; Colorado Energy Research Institute, *Net Energy Analysis*, 1976; Howard T. Odum and Elisabeth C. Odum, *Energy Basis for Man and Nature*, 3rd ed., New York: McGraw-Hill, 1981, and Charles A. S. Hall and Kent A. Klitgaard, *Energy and the Wealth of Nations*, New York: Springer, 2012.)
Top left: Yegor Korzh/Shutterstock.com. Bottom left: Donald Aitken/National Renewable Energy Laboratory. Top right: Serdar Tibet/Shutterstock.com. Bottom right: Michel Stevelmans/Shutterstock.com.

WHAT ARE THE ADVANTAGES AND DISADVANTAGES OF USING OIL?

CONCEPT 14.2A Conventional crude oil is abundant and has a medium net energy, but when burned causes air and water pollution and releases climate-changing CO_2 to the atmosphere.

CONCEPT 14.2B Unconventional heavy oil from oil shale rock and oil sands exists in potentially large supplies but has a low net energy and a higher environmental impact than conventional oil has.

We Depend Heavily on Oil

Oil is the most widely used energy resource in the world (Figure 14.2, left) and in the United States (Figure 14.2, right). We use oil or gasoline produced from oil to heat homes, grow food, transport people and goods, make other energy resources available for use, and manufacture most of the things we use every day from plastics to cosmetics to asphalt on roads.

Crude oil, or **petroleum,** is a black, gooey liquid containing a mixture of combustible hydrocarbons (molecules that contain hydrogen and carbon atoms) along with small amounts of sulfur, oxygen, and nitrogen impurities. It is also known as *conventional* or *light crude oil.*

Crude oil formed from the decayed remains of ancient microorganisms that were crushed beneath layers of rock and subjected to high temperatures and pressures for millions of years. Deposits of conventional crude oil and natural gas often are trapped beneath layers of nonporous rock within the earth's crust on land or under the seafloor. The crude oil in such deposits is dispersed in the microscopic pores and cracks of these rock formations, somewhat like water saturating a sponge.

Geologists survey landscapes on the ground and from the air to identify rock formations that might have oil deposits beneath them. When they find a promising area, they make a seismic survey of its rock formations. Different types of rocks have different densities and thus reflect shock waves at different speeds. Geologists set off explosives or use machines to pound the earth to send seismic or vibrating shock waves deep underground, and they measure how long it takes the waves to be reflected back. They feed this information into computers to produce *three-dimensional seismic maps* that show the locations and sizes of various underground rock formations, including those containing oil and natural gas deposits.

Once they identify a potential site, geologists drill an exploratory well to learn whether the site has enough oil to be extracted profitably. If it does, a well is drilled and the oil, drawn by gravity out of the rock pores, flows to the bottom of the well and is pumped from there to the surface.

After about a decade of pumping, the pressure in a well drops and its rate of crude oil production starts to decline. This point in time is referred to as **peak production** for the well. The same thing can happen to a large oil field when the overall rate of production from its numerous wells begins to decline.

Crude oil from a well cannot be used as it is. It is transported to a refinery by pipeline, truck, rail, or ship (oil tanker). There it is heated in pressurized vessels to separate it into various fuels and other components with different boiling points (Figure 14.4) in a complex process called **refining.** Like all steps in the cycle of oil production and use, refining requires an input of high-quality energy and decreases the net energy of oil. About 2% of the products of refining, called **petrochemicals,** are used as raw materials to make industrial organic chemicals, cleaning fluids, pesticides, plastics, synthetic fibers, paints, medicines, cosmetics, and many other products.

Is the World Running Out of Crude Oil?

We use an astonishing amount of crude oil—the lifeblood of most economies. Laid end to end, the roughly 34.7 billion barrels of crude oil used worldwide in 2016 would stretch to about 31.7 million kilometers (19.7 million miles)—far enough to reach to the moon and back about 41 times. (One barrel of oil contains 159 liters or 42 gallons of oil.)

How much crude oil is there? No one knows, although geologists have estimated the amounts existing in identified oil deposits. **Proven oil reserves** are known deposits from which oil can be extracted profitably at current prices using current technology. Proven oil reserves are not fixed. They grow when we find new deposits or develop new extraction technologies such as horizontal drilling and hydraulic fracking (**Core Case Study**) that make it possible and affordable to produce oil from deposits that were once too costly to tap.

The world is not about to run out of crude oil in the near future. We can produce more conventional light crude oil far offshore from deep ocean seabed deposits and from remote areas such as the Arctic Ocean where drillers face some of the earth's harshest weather, floating icebergs, and other hazards. To be profitable, however, oil from such places would have to sell for at least $100 a barrel because it takes a lot of energy to find and produce these oil deposits. We can also rely more on unconventional heavy oil from various sources—a thick type of crude oil that does not flow as easily as light oil. However, producing heavy oil has a lower net energy, a higher environmental impact, and higher production costs.

The net energy of crude oil is still high in places such as Saudi Arabia where huge deposits are located near the earth's surface and yield oil at a cost of $3 to $10 a barrel. However, since 1999, the global net energy for extracting oil has dropped by more than 50%. Producers have had to spend more money and use more energy to dig deeper wells on land and at sea and to extract and transport oil from more remote and challenging areas such as the Arctic. As a result, oil has a medium net energy. There is no global shortage of

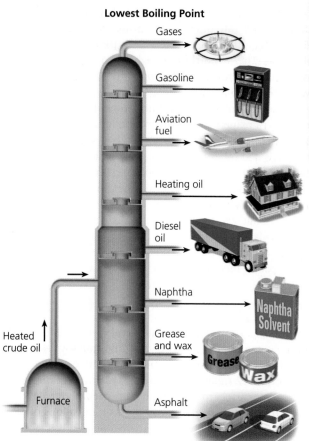

Lowest Boiling Point

Gases

Gasoline

Aviation fuel

Heating oil

Diesel oil

Naphtha

Naphtha Solvent

Grease and wax

Grease Wax

Asphalt

Heated crude oil

Furnace

Highest Boiling Point

FIGURE 14.4 When crude oil is refined, many of its components are removed at various levels of a distillation column, depending on their boiling points. The most volatile components with the lowest boiling points are removed at the top of the column, which can be as tall as a nine-story building. The photo shows an oil refinery in Texas.

Oil Production and Consumption in the United States

In 2015, the United States got about 82% of its commercial energy from fossil fuels, with the largest percentage (36%) coming from crude oil (Figure 14.2, right). Since 1982, the United States has had to import some of the oil it uses because its oil consumption has exceeded its domestic production. This gap has been narrowed by rising domestic production of tight oil from shale rock (**Core Case Study**), which in 2015 accounted for 52% of U.S. oil production. In 2016 the United States imported about 20–25% of its crude oil, compared to 60% in 2005. In 2016 the five largest suppliers of imported oil for the United States were Canada, Saudi Arabia, Venezuela, Mexico, and Colombia.

Can the United States continue reducing its dependence on oil imports by increasing its oil production? Some say "yes" and project that domestic oil production will increase dramatically over the next few decades—especially from oil found in layers of shale rock (**Core Case Study**).

80 Percentage of the world's proven oil reserves held by OPEC's 12 countries

oil, but there is an increasing shortage of cheap oil as we deplete the world's easy to reach concentrated deposits.

The 12 countries that make up the Organization of Petroleum Exporting Countries (OPEC) have about 80% of the world's proven crude oil reserves, much of it concentrated in large and accessible deposits that are cheap to exploit. OPEC's member countries are Algeria, Angola, Ecuador, Iran, Iraq, Kuwait, Libya, Nigeria, Qatar, Saudi Arabia, United Arab Emirates, and Venezuela. In order, Venezuela and Saudi Arabia have the largest shares of the world's proven oil reserves. They can play a role in global oil prices by agreeing to increase or decrease the amount of oil they produce. However, the recent increase in U.S. oil production has weakened the ability of OPEC nations to control global oil prices.

Figure 14.5 shows the three countries with the largest proven oil reserves, production, and consumption in 2014. That year, the three largest consumers of crude oil—the United States, China, and Japan—respectively had only about 2.9%, 1.1%, and 0.003% of the world's proven oil reserves.

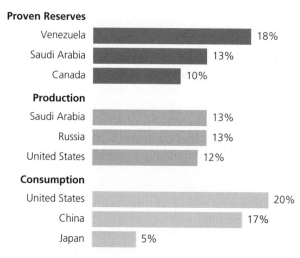

Proven Reserves

Venezuela — 18%
Saudi Arabia — 13%
Canada — 10%

Production

Saudi Arabia — 13%
Russia — 13%
United States — 12%

Consumption

United States — 20%
China — 17%
Japan — 5%

FIGURE 14.5 Countries with the largest proven crude oil reserves, oil production, and oil consumption in 2014.

(Compiled by the authors using data from British Petroleum and the International Energy Agency)

Other analysts question the long-term availability of oil in layers of shale rock for two reasons. First, drilling a horizontal oil well costs much more than drilling a vertical well. If oil prices go too low (less than $40–$50 a barrel using horizontal drilling and fracking to develop new wells will not be profitable. This explains why, between 2014 and April 2016, the number of rigs drilling for oil in the United States dropped from almost 1,600 to 351. Second, the output of oil from shale rock drops off about twice as fast as it does in most conventional oil fields. It can drop by as much as a 90% after 2 years of operation.

According to the International Energy Agency, oil produced from shale rock in the United States is likely to peak around 2020 and then decline for two to three decades as the richest deposits are depleted. If this projection is correct, the current U.S. boom in oil production is a temporary bubble, not a long-term source of oil. The long-term problem for the United States is that it uses about 20% of the world's oil production, produces 13% of the world's oil, and has only 3.2% of the world's proven crude oil reserves.

Transporting Crude Oil Through Pipelines

There is a vast infrastructure of oil and gas pipelines crisscrossing the United States that connect drilling sites with storage, refining, and shipping facilities. According to the U.S. Department of Transportation's Pipeline and Hazardous Materials Administration, as of 2015 the United States had over 117,500 kilometers (73,000 miles) of crude oil pipeline in operation. This accounts for just a fraction of the over 4.2 million kilometers (2.6 million miles) miles of pipeline used to move a variety of refined and unrefined energy products throughout the country.

Given the extent of this network, pipeline ruptures and oil spills are not uncommon. In 2010, in what became the largest inland oil spill in U.S. history 3,190,000 liters (843,000 gallons) of oil spilled into the Kalamazoo River in Michigan when a pipeline burst. The cleanup lasted for several years and cost more than a billion dollars. In the face of such disasters, energy companies argue it is far safer to transport oil and natural gas via pipeline than by railroad or trucks, as accidents with these vehicles can cause huge explosions and fires. Still, the scale of environmental disasters like the Kalamazoo spill cause citizens to protest against building more pipelines.

A more recent conflict arose in 2016 over building the Dakota Access Pipeline (DAPL) running from oil fields in North Dakota to Illinois where it will link to storage facilities and move oil to refineries. It is projected to carry 470,000 barrels of oil (75 million liters or 20 million gallons) per day. This highly controversial pipeline has been vehemently opposed by several Native American tribes in the Dakotas and Iowa, most notably by members of the Standing Rock Sioux tribe. Months of protests and sit-ins drew participation from thousands of Native Americans

and their supporters gathering in North Dakota, gained world media attention, and caused several construction delays. Standing Rock Sioux fear the underground pipeline could do disastrous damage to Lake Oahe and the Missouri River, which is the water source for their reservation. The pipeline also traverses ancestral land that has historical, cultural, and spiritual significance for their tribe. Energy Transfer, the company building the pipeline, claims that the pipeline will boost local economies and create 8,000 to 12,000 construction jobs, though these jobs will be temporary. By May 2017 Energy Transfer reported that the construction of the Dakota Access Pipeline was completed and ready to transport oil.

Using Crude Oil Has Advantages and Disadvantages

Figure 14.6 lists major advantages and disadvantages of using conventional light oil as an energy resource. A critical problem is that burning oil or any carbon-containing fossil fuel releases the greenhouse gas CO_2 into the atmosphere. According to decades of research and the assessments of at least 90% of the world's top climate scientists, this plays an important role in warming the atmosphere and changing the world's climate, as discussed in Chapter 20.

Heavy Oil Has a High Environmental Impact

An alternative to conventional or light crude oil is heavy crude oil that is thicker and stickier. Two sources of heavy oil are oil shale rock and oil sands.

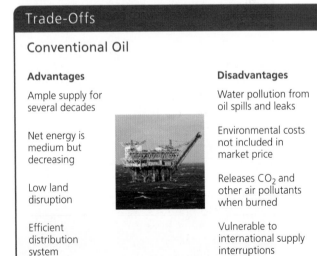

Trade-Offs

Conventional Oil

Advantages	Disadvantages
Ample supply for several decades	Water pollution from oil spills and leaks
Net energy is medium but decreasing	Environmental costs not included in market price
Low land disruption	Releases CO_2 and other air pollutants when burned
Efficient distribution system	Vulnerable to international supply interruptions

FIGURE 14.6 Using conventional light oil as an energy resource has advantages and disadvantages. **Critical thinking:** Which single advantage and which single disadvantage do you think are the most important? Why? Do the advantages of relying on conventional light oil outweigh its disadvantages? Explain.

Heavy oil extracted from oil shale rock is called **shale oil**. It is *dispersed within* bodies of shale rock compared to lighter oil that is *trapped between* layers of shale rock (**Core Case Study**). Producing this shale oil involves mining, crushing, and heating oil shale rock (Figure 14.7, left) to extract a mixture of hydrocarbons called *kerogen* that can be distilled to produce shale oil (Figure 14.7, right). Before the thick shale oil is pumped through a pressurized pipeline to a refinery, it must be heated to increase its flow rate and processed to remove sulfur, nitrogen, and other impurities, which reduces its net energy.

About 72% of the world's estimated oil shale rock reserves are buried deep in rock formations located primarily under government-owned land in the U.S. states of Colorado, Wyoming, and Utah. The potential supply is huge but its net energy is low (Figure 14.3). The process also has a large harmful environmental impact, including the production of rock waste, possible leaks of the extracted kerogen to water tables, wastewater, and high water use. If the production price can be significantly lowered or the price of conventional oil rises sharply, and if its harmful environmental effects can be reduced, shale oil could become an important energy source. Otherwise, it will remain in the ground.

A growing source of heavy oil is **oil sands** or **tar sands,** which are a mixture of clay, sand, water, and an organic material called *bitumen*—a thick, sticky, tar-like heavy oil with a high sulfur content. Northeastern Alberta in Canada has three-fourths of the world's proven reserves

FIGURE 14.7 Heavy shale oil (right) can be extracted from oil shale rock (left).

U.S. Department of Energy

of oil sands. If we include its conventional light oil and its heavy oil from oil sands, Canada has the world's third largest proven oil reserves. The United States also has large deposits of oil sands in Utah, Wyoming, and Colorado.

In Canada, oil companies produce about half of this oil by drilling vertical wells, pumping steam in to melt the bitumen embedded in the underground sand, and pumping the bitumen to the surface for conversion to heavy synthetic oil. Production of the rest of this oil starts with clear-cutting the forests and strip-mining the land (Figure 14.8). This process uses large amounts of natural

Christopher Kolaczan/Shutterstock.com

FIGURE 14.8 Oil sands surface mining operation in Alberta, Canada, involves clearing boreal forest and strip-mining the land to remove the oil sands.

gas to heat water that is used to remove the bitumen and to convert it into a heavy synthetic oil that can flow through a pipeline. Some of the bitumen is converted to synthetic oil and diesel fuel used to run the gigantic shovels, trucks, and other machinery.

The two big drawbacks of producing heavy synthetic oil from oil sands are its low net energy (Figure 14.3) and its major harmful impacts on the land (Figure 14.8), air, water, wildlife, and climate. It takes two to four tons of oil sands and two to five barrels of water to produce one barrel of the heavy synthetic oil. The process also emits large quantities of air pollutants—especially sulfur dioxide, nitrogen oxides, and particulates—and 20% more climate-changing CO_2 than does the production of conventional crude oil, according to a study by the U.S. Department of Energy.

Producing this heavy oil is expensive, costing $50 or more per barrel. Between 2014 and June 2017, global oil prices of light crude oil were below the average cost of producing heavy oil from oil sands and new production dropped. Figure 14.9 lists the major advantages and disadvantages of producing heavy oil from oil sands.

CHECKPOINT FOR UNDERSTANDING 14.2

1. Describe how crude oil was formed.
2. Identify the benefits of using oil as an energy source.
3. Identify the drawbacks of using oil as an energy source.
4. Explain why heavy shale oil has a low net energy.

Trade-Offs

Heavy Oil from Oil Sands

Advantages	Disadvantages
Large potential supplies	Low net energy
Easily transported within and between countries	Expensive
	Releases CO_2 and other air pollutants
	Severe land disruption
Efficient distribution system in place	Water pollution and high water use

Photo: Christopher Kolaczan/Shutterstock.com

FIGURE 14.9 Using heavy oil from oil sands as an energy resource has advantages and disadvantages (**Concept 14.2**). *Critical thinking:* Which single advantage and which single disadvantage do you think are the most important? Why? Do the advantages of relying on heavy oil from oil sands outweigh its disadvantages? Explain.

14.3 WHAT ARE THE ADVANTAGES AND DISADVANTAGES OF USING NATURAL GAS?

CONCEPT 14.3 Conventional natural gas is more plentiful than oil, has a medium net energy and a fairly low production cost, and is a clean-burning fuel, but producing it has created environmental problems.

Natural Gas Is a Versatile and Widely Used Fuel

Natural gas is a mixture of gases of which 50–90% is methane (CH_4). It also contains smaller amounts of heavier gaseous hydrocarbons such as propane (C_3H_8) and butane (C_4H_{10}), and small amounts of highly toxic hydrogen sulfide (H_2S). This versatile fuel has a medium net energy (Figure 14.3) and is widely used for cooking, heating, and industrial purposes. It can also be used as a motor vehicle fuel—especially for fleets of trucks and cars such as taxicabs—and to fuel natural gas turbines used to produce electricity in power plants.

This versatility and the use of horizontal drilling and fracking help to explain why natural gas provided about 29% of U.S. energy in 2015 (up from 17% in 2013). That year, more than 1,700 natural gas power plants produced about 33% of the electricity consumed in the United States. Natural gas power plants are less expensive and take much less time to build than do coal-powered and nuclear power plants. Natural gas also burns cleaner than oil and much cleaner than coal. When burned completely, it emits about 30% less CO_2 than oil and about 50% less than coal for the same amount of energy. This explains why natural gas consumption is projected to grow over the next few decades.

Conventional natural gas is often found in deposits lying above deposits of conventional oil. It also exists in tightly held deposits between layers of shale rock and can be extracted through horizontal drilling and fracking (**Core Case Study**).

When a natural gas deposit is tapped, propane and butane gases can be liquefied under high pressure and removed as **liquefied petroleum gas (LPG).** LPG is stored in pressurized tanks for use mostly in rural areas not served by natural gas pipelines. The rest of the gas (mostly methane) is purified and pumped into pressurized pipelines for distribution across land areas.

Natural gas can also be transported across oceans, by converting it to **liquefied natural gas (LNG)** at a high pressure and at a very low temperature. This highly flammable liquid is transported in refrigerated tanker ships. At its destination port, it is heated and converted back to the gaseous state and then distributed by pipeline. LNG has a lower net energy than natural gas has, because more than a third of its energy content is used to liquefy it, process it, deliver it to users by ship, and convert it back to natural gas. LNG exports from the United States are projected to increase sharply over the next decade.

Figure 14.10 shows the three countries with the largest reserves, production, and consumption of natural gas in 2014. That year, the three largest consumers of natural gas were the United States, Russia, and Iran, which respectively had 5%, 17%, and 1.8% of the world's proven natural gas reserves.

Currently, the United States does not have to rely on natural gas imports because of greatly increased production since 1990, mostly due to the growing use of horizontal drilling and fracking in shale rock beds (**Core Case Study**). The country now exports natural gas as LNG to other nations. The increased supply has provided jobs and reduced the price of natural gas. This has benefitted consumers, industries, and utilities, and accelerated a shift from coal to natural gas for generating electricity.

However, natural gas production from shale rock tends to peak and drop off much faster than does production from conventional natural gas wells. In addition, extracting and producing natural gas from shale rock reduces its net energy and, without effective regulation, can increase the harmful environmental impacts of production (Science Focus 14.1). Figure 14.11 lists the advantages and disadvantages of using conventional natural gas as an energy resource.

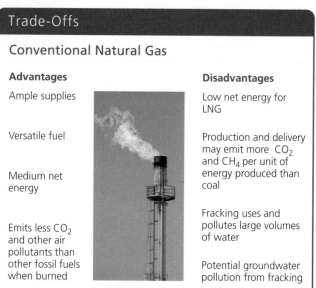

Trade-Offs

Conventional Natural Gas

Advantages	Disadvantages
Ample supplies	Low net energy for LNG
Versatile fuel	Production and delivery may emit more CO_2 and CH_4 per unit of energy produced than coal
Medium net energy	
Emits less CO_2 and other air pollutants than other fossil fuels when burned	Fracking uses and pollutes large volumes of water
	Potential groundwater pollution from fracking

Photo: Werner Muenzker/Shutterstock.com

FIGURE 14.11 Using conventional natural gas as an energy resource has advantages and disadvantages. ***Critical thinking:*** Which single advantage and which single disadvantage do you think are the most important? Why? Do you think that the advantages of using conventional natural gas outweigh its disadvantages? Explain.

Can Natural Gas Help Slow Climate Change?

Some see increased use of natural gas as a way to slow climate change because it emits less CO_2 per unit of energy than coal. Critics cite two problems with this. First, while use of cheap natural gas is reducing the use of coal, its low price could also slow the shift to reliance on energy efficiency and low-carbon solar, wind, and other renewable energy resources that are vital to slowing climate change.

The other problem is that methane (CH_4) is a much more potent greenhouse gas than CO_2 and measurements reveal that the drilling, production, and distribution process for natural gas leaks large quantities of CH_4 into the atmosphere. This raises atmospheric levels of CH_4, which is 34 times more effective per molecule at warming the atmosphere and causing climate change than CO_2. Unless these leaks are plugged, greater reliance on natural gas could hasten rather than slow climate change.

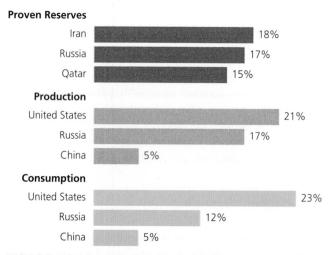

Proven Reserves

Iran — 18%
Russia — 17%
Qatar — 15%

Production

United States — 21%
Russia — 17%
China — 5%

Consumption

United States — 23%
Russia — 12%
China — 5%

FIGURE 14.10 Countries with the largest proven natural gas reserves, natural gas production, and natural gas consumption in 2014.

(Compiled by the authors using data from British Petroleum and the International Energy Agency)

CHECKPOINT FOR UNDERSTANDING 14.3

1. Identify the benefits of using natural gas.

2. Identify the drawbacks of harvesting and using natural gas.

Environmental Effects of Natural Gas Production and Fracking in the United States

The U.S. Energy Information Administration projects that, within a decade or two, at least 100,000 more natural gas wells will be drilled and fracked in the United States (**Core Case Study**). Scientific studies indicate that without more monitoring and regulation of the entire natural gas production and distribution process, including fracking, greatly increased production of natural gas (and oil) from shale rock (Figure 14.1) could have several harmful environmental effects:

- Fracking requires enormous volumes of water—10 to 100 times more than in a conventional vertical well. In water-short areas, this could reduce available surface water, deplete aquifers, degrade aquatic habitats, and reduce the availability of water for irrigation and other purposes.

- Each fracked well produces huge volumes of hazardous wastewater that flows back to the surface with the released natural gas (or oil). Many scientists warn that, without stricter regulation, the potentially harmful chemicals in these fracking slurries—including arsenic and naturally occurring radioactive elements such as radium—could contaminate groundwater and surface waters, especially from spills and leaking waste storage ponds.

- To prevent leaks of natural gas (or oil) from conventional and fracked wells and from the hazardous wastewater that returns to the surface, steel pipe called *casing* is inserted into the drilled well and cement is pumped into a small space between the steel pipe and the surrounding rock (Figure 14.1). Well-casing failure and poor cementing can release methane (or oil) and contaminants in the wastewater into groundwater and drinking water

wells far above the fracking site. When the contaminated water is drawn from a tap, this natural gas can catch fire (Figure 14.A). Experience has shown that cementing the steel well-casing is the weakest link in the process for producing natural gas and oil and in preventing leaks from active and abandoned wells.

- According to recent studies by the National Academy of Sciences and the U.S. Geological Survey, one of the causes of hundreds of small earthquakes in 13 states in recent years has been the shifting of bedrock resulting from the high-pressure injection of fracking wastewater into deep underground hazardous waste wells.

In 2016, a five-year EPA study concluded that the major threats posed by fracking include potential contamination of groundwater from well casing and cement seal failures, poor management of the contaminated wastewater resulting from the process, and chemical spills at drilling sites.

Currently, there is little protection from the harmful environmental impacts of natural gas fracking on people and the environment. This is because, under political pressure from natural gas suppliers, the U.S. Congress in 2005 excluded natural gas fracking from EPA regulations under seven major federal environmental laws—the Safe Drinking Water Act, Clean Water Act, Clean Air Act, National Environmental Policy Act, Resource Conservation and Recovery Act (which sets standards for the handling of hazardous wastes), Emergency Planning and Community Right to Know Act, and Superfund Act.

Without stricter regulation and monitoring, drilling another 100,000 natural gas wells during the next 10 to 20

MARK THIESSEN/National Geographic Creative

FIGURE 14.A Natural gas fizzing from this faucet in a Pennsylvania home can be lit like a natural gas stove burner. This began happening after an energy company drilled a fracking well in the area, but the company denies responsibility. The homeowners have to keep their windows open year-round to keep the lethal and explosive gas from building up in the house.

years will likely increase the risk of air and water pollution from the natural gas production process. This could cause a public backlash against this technology.

To avoid this, some analysts call for the following measures:

- eliminate all exemptions from environmental laws for the natural gas industry;

- put a cap on the number of hazardous waste injection wells in an area with natural gas (or oil) wells, as Oklahoma has had to do;

- increase the monitoring and regulation of the entire natural gas production and distribution system; and

- repair existing natural gas leaks.

However, there is strong political opposition by the natural gas industry to these policy changes.

CRITICAL THINKING

How might your life be affected if the four policy changes listed above are not implemented?

14.4 WHAT ARE THE ADVANTAGES AND DISADVANTAGES OF USING COAL?

CONCEPT 14.4A Conventional coal is plentiful and has a high net energy and a low cost, but using it has a high environmental impact.

CONCEPT 14.4B We can produce gaseous and liquid fuels from coal, but they have a lower net energy and higher environmental impacts than those of conventional coal.

Coal Is a Plentiful but Dirty Fuel

Coal is a solid fossil fuel formed from the remains of land plants that were buried and exposed to intense heat and pressure for 300–400 million years (Figure 14.12).

Coal is burned in power plants (Figure 14.13) that in 2016 generated about 40% of the world's electricity, 30% of the electricity used in the United States (down from 51% in 2003), 66% in China, and 60% in India. Coal is also burned in industrial plants to make steel, cement, and other products.

Figure 14.14 shows the three countries with the largest proven reserves, production and consumption of coal in 2014. That year, the three largest consumers of coal—China, the United States, and India—respectively had 13%, 27%, and 7% of the world's proven coal reserves. Although China is the world's largest consumer of coal, the United States has the world's largest *per capita* consumption of coal.

In 2015 China consumed roughly as much coal as the rest of the world combined. Figure 14.15 shows coal consumption in China and the United States since 1980.

Coal is the world's most abundant fossil fuel. However, coal is by far the dirtiest of all fossil fuels, starting with the mining of coal, which severely degrades land. This includes blasting the tops off more than 500 mountains in West Virginia (Figure 11.16, p. 318), and Individuals Matter 14.1). Mining also pollutes water and air. Burning coal also releases large amounts of black carbon particulates, or soot, and much smaller, fine particles of air pollutants such as toxic mercury. The fine particles can get past our bodies' natural defenses and into our lungs, causing various severe illnesses such as emphysema and lung cancer and contributing to heart attacks and strokes.

According to a study by the Clean Air Task Force, each year fine-particle pollution in the United States, mostly from the older coal-burning power plants without the latest air pollution control technology, kills at least 13,000 people a year. In China, outdoor air pollution from the burning of coal contributes to 336,000 premature deaths (an average of 921 per day) from strokes, heart attacks, pulmonary obstruction, and lung cancer, according to a study by Teng Fei at Tsinghua University.

Coal-burning power and industrial plants are among the largest emitters of CO_2 (Figure 14.16), which contributes to atmospheric warming and climate change (covered in Chapter 20) and ocean acidification. Because coal is mostly carbon, coal combustion emits about twice as much CO_2 per unit of energy as natural gas and produces about 42% of global CO_2 emissions. China leads the world in such emissions, followed by the United States. Coal combustion also emits trace amounts of radioactive materials as well as toxic mercury into the atmosphere and into lakes, where it can accumulate to high levels in fish consumed by humans.

Because of air pollution laws, many coal-burning plants use scrubbers to remove some of these pollutants before they leave the smokestacks. This reduces air pollution but

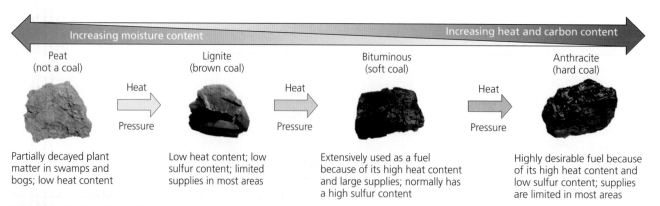

FIGURE 14.12 Over millions of years, several different types of coal have formed. Peat is a soil material made of moist, partially decomposed organic matter, similar to coal; it is not classified as a coal, although it is used as a fuel. These different major types of coal vary in the amounts of heat, carbon dioxide, and sulfur dioxide released per unit of mass when they are burned.

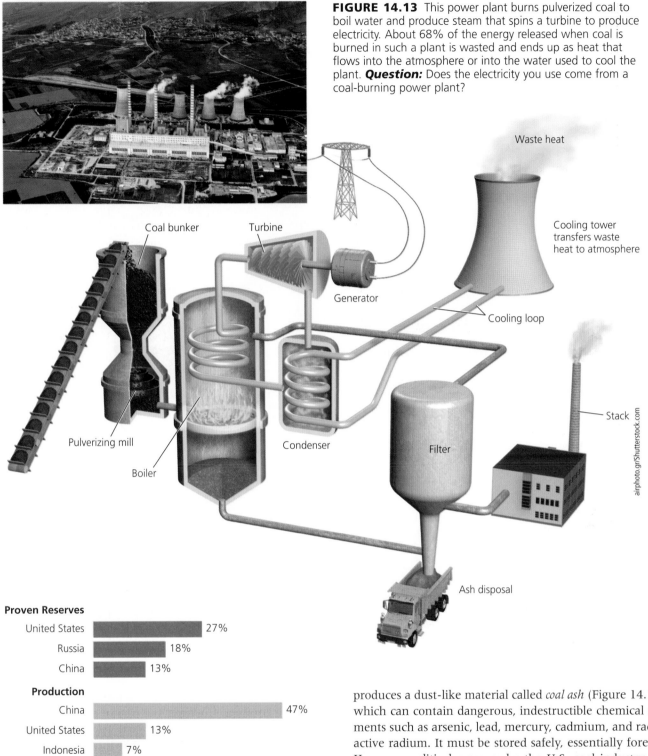

FIGURE 14.13 This power plant burns pulverized coal to boil water and produce steam that spins a turbine to produce electricity. About 68% of the energy released when coal is burned in such a plant is wasted and ends up as heat that flows into the atmosphere or into the water used to cool the plant. **Question:** Does the electricity you use come from a coal-burning power plant?

Waste heat

Cooling tower transfers waste heat to atmosphere

Cooling loop

Stack

Coal bunker

Turbine

Generator

Condenser

Filter

Pulverizing mill

Boiler

Ash disposal

airphoto.gr/Shutterstock.com

Proven Reserves

United States — 27%
Russia — 18%
China — 13%

Production

China — 47%
United States — 13%
Indonesia — 7%

Consumption

China — 51%
United States — 12%
India — 9%

FIGURE 14.14 Countries with the largest proven coal reserves, coal production, and coal consumption in 2014.

(Compiled by the authors using data from British Petroleum and the International Energy Agency)

produces a dust-like material called *coal ash* (Figure 14.13), which can contain dangerous, indestructible chemical elements such as arsenic, lead, mercury, cadmium, and radioactive radium. It must be stored safely, essentially forever. However, political pressure by the U.S. coal industry has kept it from being classified as a hazardous waste. Instead, coal ash is in the same category as household garbage.

The use of coal-burning plants to produce electricity in the United States is decreasing because that same power can be produced more cheaply and cleanly by burning natural gas and in a growing number of areas by wind. This trend, along with advances in coal mining technology, has resulted in a sharp drop in the number of coal mining jobs in the

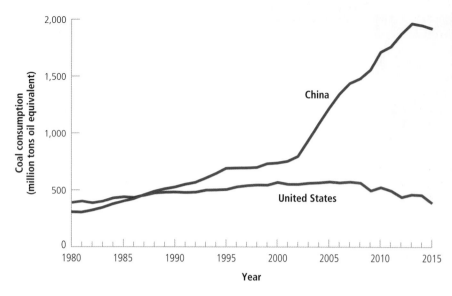

FIGURE 14.15 Coal consumption in the China and the United States, 1980–2015. **Data analysis:** In 2012, about how many times more than U.S. coal consumption was that of China?

(Compiled by the authors using data from British Petroleum, International Energy Agency, and Earth Policy Institute)

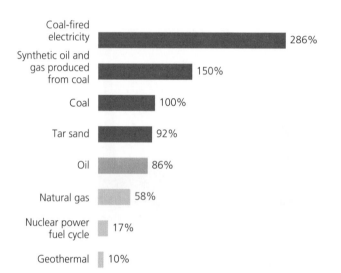

FIGURE 14.16 CO_2 emissions, expressed as percentages of emissions released by burning coal directly, vary with different energy resources. **Data analysis:** Which of these produces more CO_2 emissions per kilogram: burning coal to heat a house, or heating with electricity generated by coal?

(Compiled by the authors using data from U.S. Department of Energy.)

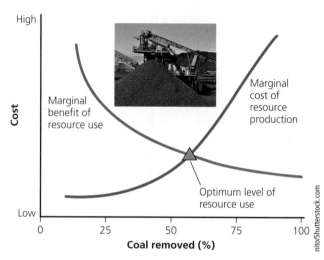

FIGURE 14.17 *Optimum resource use:* The cost of extracting coal (blue line) from a particular mine rises with each additional unit removed. mining a certain amount of coal is profitable, but at some point, the marginal cost of further removal exceeds the monetary benefits (red line). **Critical thinking:** How would the location of the optimum level of resource use shift if the price of coal doubled?

United States since the 1980s. New mining technology relies heavily on machinery instead of miners for strip-mining coal, mountaintop removal coal mining, and underground coal mining. This replacement of miners with machines reduces the operating costs for coal-producing companies. As a result, lost U.S. coal-mining jobs are not likely to come back.

We Are Not Paying the Full Cost of Using Coal

Coal is the cheapest of the fossil fuels and the most plentiful. For a producer in the early days of a new coal mining operation, the cost of extracting coal is typically low enough that they can make a profit simply by selling their product. However the cost of removal goes up with each additional unit of coal taken. Economists refer to this as **marginal cost**—any increase in the cost of producing an additional unit of a product. After most of the more readily accessible coal has been removed from a mine, taking what is left can become too costly, unless some factor such as scarcity raises the value of the coal remaining in the mine. Figure 14.17 shows this in terms of supply, demand and equilibrium. The point at which removing more coal is not worth the marginal cost is where the demand curve crosses the supply curve.

Calculating Energy Efficiency

Power plants generate electricity by converting one form of energy into another. According to the second law of thermodynamics, at each energy conversion some energy is degraded to low-quality waste heat and lost to the environment. When an energy system is more efficient, it means that more energy contained in the fuel is ultimately converted to useful energy that can do work.

For example, coal and natural gas are forms of chemical bond energy that ultimately become electrical energy used to do work in our homes. The more energy exchanges that take place in the system, the less efficient the system. These forms of chemical bond energy contain a certain number of BTU (British thermal units) that can be converted to calories. A calorie is the amount of energy needed to raise a gram of water 1°C (33.8°F).

> 1 calorie = 0.00396573 BTU
>
> 1 BTU = 252 calories

Energy efficiency, E, can be calculated as a percentage:

$$E = \frac{\text{Energy Produced}}{\text{Energy Consumed}} \times 100$$

FRQ Application

Calculate the efficiency of the Coalville Power Plant. The plant generates 64,423 megawatt hours (64,423,000 kilowatt hours) of electricity by burning 31,796.825 metric tons (35,050 tons) of coal.

> 1 kilowatt hour = 3413 BTU
>
> BTU value of coal = 9,800 BTU/lb

When calculating the energy efficiency E of an electrical power plant, the BTU produced (electrical output) are compared to the BTU contained in the fuel being burned. The calculation requires converting megawatt hours (MWh) to kilowatt hours (kWh).

$$E = \frac{(64,423 \text{ MWh})(10^3 \text{kWh/MWh})(3413 \text{ BTU/kWh})}{(35,050 \text{ tons coal})(2000 \text{ lb/ton})(9,800 \text{ BTU/lb})} \times 100 = 32\%$$

This coal-burning plant is 32% efficient, meaning that 68% of the energy in the coal is lost as waste heat.

For the consumer, the primary reason why coal-generated electricity is cheap is that most of its harmful environmental and health costs are not included in the market price. According to studies by the Harvard Medical School's Center for Health and the Global Environment and the U.S. National Academy of Sciences, including the estimated environmental and health costs of using coal would double or triple the price of electricity from coal-fired power plants. This would promote a shift toward cutting energy waste and increasing use of cleaner natural gas and renewable energy resources such as solar and wind whose prices have been falling sharply. As long as these harmful costs are not included in the price of coal burned to provide heat or electricity, it will continue to be widely used in countries with large coal reserves, such as China, the United States, India, Australia, and Indonesia.

There are ways to include such costs as a way to implement the full-cost pricing **principle of sustainability**. They include phasing out subsidies and tax breaks that hide the true costs of coal use, taxing CO_2 emissions from the burning of coal, requiring stricter air pollution controls for coal-burning power and industrial plants, and regulating coal ash as a hazardous waste. If these hidden costs were included in the price of burning coal, the International Monetary Fund estimates that coal use would drop sharply, air pollution deaths would drop 55%, and global CO_2 emissions would drop 20%.

Maria Gunnoe: Fighting to Save Mountains

In the 1800s, Maria Gunnoe's Cherokee ancestors arrived in what is now Boone County, West Virginia. Her grandfather bought the land where she now lives. In 2000 miners blew up the mountaintop above that land to extract underlying coal (Figure 11.16, p. 318). Gunnoe's land now sits below a 10-story-high pile of mine waste.

With the soil and vegetation gone, rains running off the mountain ridge flooded her land seven times since 2000. They covered her land with toxic sludge, contaminated her water well and the soil she used to grow food, and washed out two small bridges that linked her to the only road out. Gunnoe had to hike to and from the road for years. When she complained to the coal company officials, they called the floods "acts of God."

Gunnoe, a mother of two, refused to leave her land and decided to fight the powerful coal companies and to try to end mountaintop coal mining. Mining companies and miners who worried about losing their jobs viewed her as an enemy. She and her children received death threats and two family dogs were killed. People tried to run her off the road and fired shots around her house. For several years, Gunnoe wore a bulletproof vest when she went outside, but she kept up the fight.

With only a high school education, Gunnoe educated herself about complex mining and water pollution regulations and harmful chemicals found in streams and groundwater. She organized communities and argued in court and testified before Congress contending that the "valley fills" from mountaintop mining violate the federal Clean Water Act by burying streams and destroying aquatic and animal habitats. The EPA agreed and fined coal companies multiple times. She also pressured the president and federal government to ban mountaintop mining because of its harmful health effects.

In 2009 this courageous and inspiring woman won a Goldman Environmental Prize—considered the Nobel Prize equivalent for grassroots environmental leaders around the world.

However, there is strong political opposition in the United States to such measures by coal-producing companies that are struggling to survive. For over 40 years, U.S. coal and electric utility industries have successfully fought to keep government subsidies and tax breaks and prevent coal regulations and taxes on carbon emissions because it would increase the cost of using coal and sharply reduce their profits. This would make it less competitive with other, cleaner and increasingly cheaper ways to produce electricity from natural gas, wind, and the sun.

Figure 14.18 lists the advantages and disadvantages of using coal as an energy resource. (**Concept 14.4A**) An important and difficult economic, political, and ethical question is whether we should accelerate a shift from using abundant coal to using less environmentally harmful energy resources to help slow climate change. To do this, climate scientists estimate that 82% of the world's current coal reserves and 92% of U.S. coal reserves need to be left in the ground. In countries that have large reserves of coal, this is a controversial and difficult economic and political challenge.

Trade-Offs

Coal

Advantages	Disadvantages
Ample supplies in many countries	Severe land disturbance and water pollution
Medium to high net energy	Fine particle and toxic mercury emissions threaten human health
Low cost when environmental costs are not included	Emits large amounts of CO_2 and other air pollutants when produced and burned

FIGURE 14.18 Using coal as an energy resource has advantages and disadvantages. **Critical thinking:** Which single advantage and which single disadvantage do you think are the most important? Why? Do you think that the advantages of using coal as an energy resource outweigh its disadvantages? Explain.

The Future of Coal

Because of increasing competition from cleaner-burning natural gas, wind power, and solar power, and because of grassroots political opposition, U.S. coal use dropped 18% between 2007 and 2013. In that time, proposals for building 183 new coal plants were scrapped. In addition, several major U.S. coal producers have declared bankruptcy because of a drop in use of coal to produce electricity.

Between 2008 and 2016, about 300 U.S. coal-fired plants closed, mostly because it was cheaper to produce electricity from natural gas and in many areas from wind. In 2016, natural gas produced a larger share of U.S. electricity (34%) than coal (30%), according to the U.S. Energy Information Agency.

Some countries are going further than the United States in reducing their use of coal. They include Germany, with a 50% drop in coal use since 1965, and France and the United Kingdom, with coal use down 70% since the mid-1990s. In 1997 Denmark banned new coal-fired plants, and it now plans to phase out coal power by 2025.

Does this mean the end of coal? Hardly. There are ample supplies of coal and it will be a cheap source of energy, as long as coal producers have the political and economic power to prevent its harmful health and environmental costs from being included in its market price. And while coal use is dropping in the United States and several European nations, its use is expanding in India and a number of other countries in Asia and Africa.

Converting Coal into Gaseous and Liquid Fuels

We can convert solid coal into **synthetic natural gas (SNG)** by a process called *coal gasification*, which removes sulfur and most other impurities from coal. We can also convert coal into liquid fuels such as methanol and synthetic gasoline through a process called *coal liquefaction*. These fuels, called *synfuels*, are often referred to as cleaner versions of coal.

However, compared to burning coal directly, producing synfuels requires the mining of 50% more coal. Producing and burning synfuels could also add 50% more carbon dioxide to the atmosphere (Figure 14.16). As a result, synfuels have a lower net energy and cost more to produce per unit of energy than does coal production. In addition, it takes larger amounts of water to produce synfuels than to produce coal.

Thus, greatly increasing the use of these synfuels would worsen three of the world's major environmental problems: climate change and ocean acidification caused mostly by CO_2 emissions, and increasing water shortages in many parts of the world. Figure 14.19 lists the advantages and disadvantages of using liquid and gaseous synfuels produced from coal (**Concept 14.4B**).

Another approach to reducing coal's impact on climate change is *carbon capture and sequestration* (CCS). This technology involves removing CO_2 from the smokestacks of coal-burning power plants and isolating it from the environment by storing it in depleted oil and gas fields and underground coal mines, or in underground salt aquifers. We discuss the pros and cons of CCS in Chapter 20.

Trade-Offs

Synthetic Fuels

Advantages	Disadvantages
Large potential supply in many countries	Low to medium net energy
Vehicle fuel	Requires mining 50% more coal with increased land disturbance, water pollution, and water use
Lower air pollution than coal	Higher CO_2 emissions than coal

Photo: mironov/Shutterstock.com

FIGURE 14.19 The use of synthetic natural gas (SNG) and liquid synfuels produced from coal as energy resources has advantages and disadvantages (**Concept 14.2**). *Critical thinking:* Which single advantage and which single disadvantage do you think are the most important? Why? Do you think that the advantages of using synfuels produced from coal as an energy source outweigh its disadvantages? Explain.

CHECKPOINT FOR UNDERSTANDING 14.4

1. Identify the benefits of using coal as an energy source.

2. Identify the drawbacks of using coal as an energy source.

14.5 WHAT ARE THE ADVANTAGES AND DISADVANTAGES OF USING NUCLEAR POWER?

CONCEPT 14.5 Nuclear power has a low environmental impact and a very low accident risk, but its use has been limited by a low net energy, high costs, its role in the spread of nuclear weapons technology, fear of accidents, and long-lived radioactive wastes.

How Does a Nuclear Fission Reactor Work?

To evaluate the advantages and disadvantages of nuclear power, we must know how a nuclear power plant and its accompanying nuclear fuel cycle work. A nuclear power plant is a highly complex and costly system designed to perform a relatively simple task: boil water to produce steam that spins a turbine and generates electricity. Nuclear plants cost much more and take longer to build (10 years or more) than any other source of electricity.

What makes nuclear power complex and costly is the use of a controlled nuclear fission reaction to provide the heat. **Nuclear fission** occurs when the nuclei of certain isotopes with large mass numbers (such as uranium-235) are split apart into lighter nuclei when struck by a neutron and release energy. Each fission also releases neutrons, which can cause more nuclei to fission. This cascade of fissions can result in a *chain reaction* that releases an enormous amount of energy in a short time (Figure 14.20). The heat released by the chain reaction of fissions inside the reactor of a nuclear power plant is used to convert water into steam, which spins a turbine that generates electricity. Most nuclear-generated electricity is produced by light-water reactors (LWRs, see Figure 14.21).

The fuel for a nuclear reactor is made from uranium ore mined from the earth's crust. After it is mined, the ore must be enriched to increase the concentration of its fissionable uranium-235 from 1% to 3–5%. The enriched uranium-235 is processed into small pellets of uranium dioxide. Each pellet, about the size of an eraser on a pencil, contains the energy equivalent of about a ton of coal. Large numbers of the pellets are packed into closed pipes, called *fuel rods*, which are then grouped together in *fuel assemblies*, to be placed in the core of a reactor.

Plant operators move *control rods* in and out of the reactor core to absorb more or fewer neutrons in the nuclear fission chain reaction and regulate how much power is produced. A *coolant*, usually water, circulates through the reactor's core to remove heat and keep the fuel rods and other reactor components from melting and releasing massive amounts of radioactivity into the environment. A light-water reactor includes an emergency core cooling system as a backup to help prevent meltdowns from a loss of cooling water.

A nuclear reactor cannot explode like an atomic bomb and cause massive damage. The danger in nuclear reactors comes from smaller explosions that can release radioactive materials into the environment or cause a core meltdown because of a loss of coolant water.

A *containment shell* made of thick, steel-reinforced concrete surrounds the reactor core. It is designed to help keep radioactive materials from escaping into the environment, in case there is an internal explosion or a core meltdown. It is also intended to protect the core from external threats such as tornadoes and plane crashes. These essential safety features and the 10 years or more that it typically takes to build a nuclear plant help explain why a new nuclear power plant typically costs $9 billion to $11 billion and why that cost is rising.

In 2016 the world's four leading producers of nuclear power were, in order, the United States, Russia, and China. France generates 75% of its electricity and the United States generates 20% of its electricity using nuclear power.

What Is the Nuclear Fuel Cycle?

Building and running a nuclear power plant is only one part of the **nuclear fuel cycle** (Figure 14.22), which also includes the mining of uranium, processing and enriching the uranium to make fuel, using it in a reactor, safely storing the resulting highly radioactive wastes for thousands of years until their radioactivity falls to safe levels, and retiring the worn-out plant by taking it apart and storing its high- and moderate-level radioactive parts safely for thousands of years.

As long as a reactor is operating safely, the power plant itself has a low environmental impact and a low risk of an accident. However, considering the entire nuclear fuel cycle, the potential environmental impact increases. In evaluating the safety, economic feasibility, net energy, and overall environmental impact of nuclear power, energy experts and economists caution us to look at the entire nuclear fuel cycle, not just the power plant itself. Figure 14.23 lists the major advantages and disadvantages of producing electricity by using the nuclear power fuel cycle (**Concept 14.5**).

A major problem with nuclear power is the high cost of building the plant and operating the nuclear fuel cycle, which leads to a low net energy. As a result, nuclear power cannot compete in the marketplace with other energy resources such natural gas, wind, and soon from solar cells unless it is heavily subsidized by governments. An increasing number of existing nuclear plants in the United States are being closed down because electricity can be produced more cheaply by burning natural gas and in a growing areas by wind.

Nuclear fission

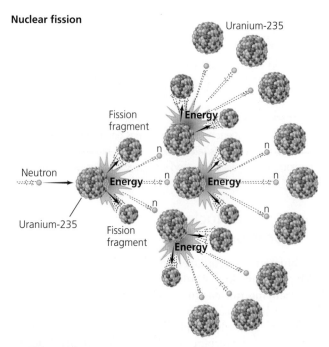

FIGURE 14.20 Nuclear fission is the source of energy for producing electricity in a nuclear power plant.

FIGURE 14.21 Nuclear power plant. Intense heat from the nuclear fission of uranium-235 in a chain reaction (Figure 14.20) in the core of this pressurized water-cooled nuclear power plant is transferred to two heat exchangers and converted to steam, which spins a turbine that generates electricity. About 65% of the energy released by the nuclear fission of the plant's uranium fuel is wasted. It ends up as heat that flows into the atmosphere through gigantic cooling towers (shown in the photo) or into water from a nearby source that is used to cool the plant. **Critical thinking:** How does this plant differ from the coal-burning plant in Figure 14.13?

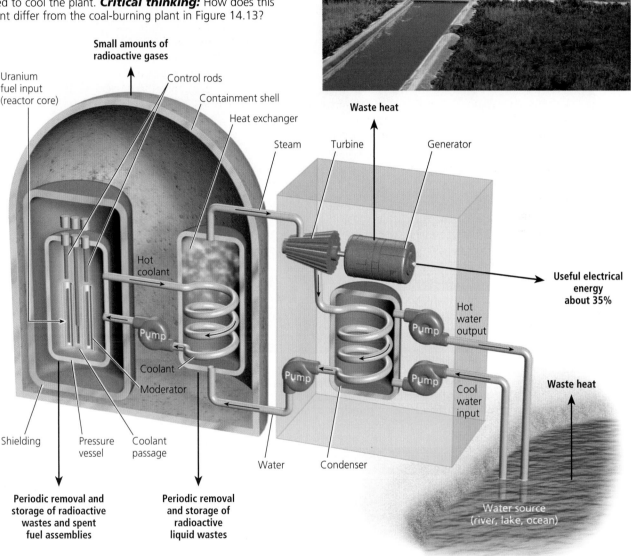

A serious safety and national and global security concern related to commercial nuclear power is the spread of nuclear weapons technology around the world. The United States and 14 other countries have been selling commercial and experimental nuclear reactors and uranium fuel-enrichment and waste reprocessing technology to other countries for decades. Much of this information and equipment can be used to produce bomb-grade uranium and plutonium for use in nuclear weapons. Energy expert John Holdren pointed out that the 60 countries that have nuclear weapons or the knowledge to develop them have gained most of such information by using civilian nuclear power technology. Some critics see this serious threat to global and national security as the single most important reason for not building more nuclear power plants that use uranium-235 or plutonium as a fuel or that produce plutonium-239.

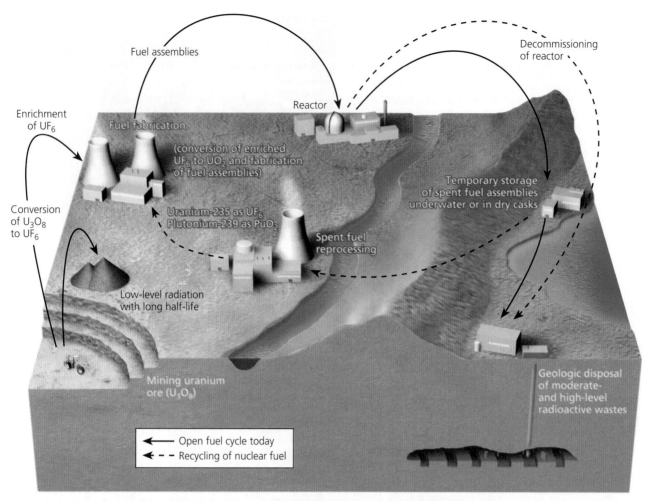

Fuel assemblies

Decommissioning
of reactor

Enrichment
of UF₆

Fuel fabrication

Reactor

(conversion of enriched
UF₆ to UO₂ and fabrication
of fuel assemblies)

Conversion
of U₃O₈
to UF₆

Temporary storage
of spent fuel assemblies
underwater or in dry casks

Uranium-235 as UF₆
Plutonium-239 as PuO₂

Spent fuel
reprocessing

Low-level radiation
with long half-life

Mining uranium
ore (U₃O₈)

Geologic disposal
of moderate-
and high-level
radioactive wastes

→ Open fuel cycle today
◄ - - Recycling of nuclear fuel

FIGURE 14.22 Using nuclear power to produce electricity involves a sequence of steps and technologies that together are called the *nuclear fuel cycle*. ***Critical thinking:*** Do you think the market price of nuclear-generated electricity should include all the costs of the nuclear fuel cycle, in keeping with the full-cost pricing **principle of sustainability**? Explain.

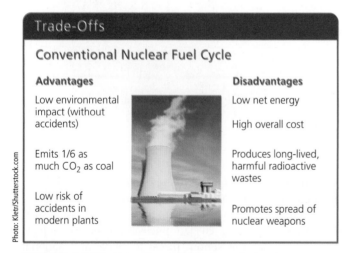

Trade-Offs

Conventional Nuclear Fuel Cycle

Advantages	Disadvantages
Low environmental impact (without accidents)	Low net energy
	High overall cost
Emits 1/6 as much CO₂ as coal	Produces long-lived, harmful radioactive wastes
Low risk of accidents in modern plants	Promotes spread of nuclear weapons

Photo: Kletr/Shutterstock.com

FIGURE 14.23 Using the nuclear power fuel cycle (Figure 14.22) to produce electricity has advantages and disadvantages. ***Critical thinking:*** Which single advantage and which single disadvantage do you think are the most important? Why? Do you think that the advantages of using nuclear power outweigh its disadvantages? Explain.

Dealing with Radioactive Nuclear Wastes

The enriched uranium fuel in a typical nuclear reactor lasts for 3–4 years, after which it becomes *spent*, or useless, and must be replaced. The spent-fuel rods are so thermally hot and highly radioactive that they cannot be simply thrown away. Researchers have found that 10 years after being removed from a reactor, a single spent-fuel rod assembly can still emit enough radiation to kill a person standing 1 meter (39 inches) away in less than 3 minutes.

After spent-fuel rod assemblies are removed from reactors, they are stored in *water-filled pools* (Figure 14.24, left). After several years of cooling and decay of some of their radioactivity, they can be transferred to *dry casks* made of heat-resistant metal alloys and concrete and filled with inert helium gas (Figure 14.24, right). These casks are licensed for 20 years and could last for 100 or more years—only a tiny fraction of the thousands of years that the radioactive waste must be safely stored.

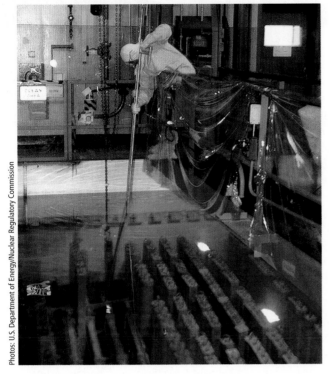

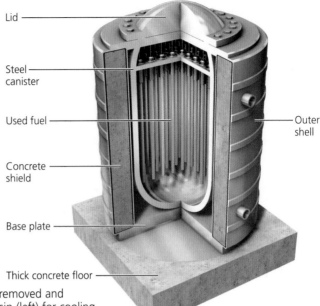

Lid

Steel canister

Used fuel

Concrete shield

Base plate

Thick concrete floor

Outer shell

FIGURE 14.24 After 3 or 4 years in a reactor, spent-fuel rods are removed and stored in a deep pool of water contained in a steel-lined concrete basin (left) for cooling. After about 5 years of cooling, the fuel rods can be stored upright on concrete pads in sealed dry-storage casks (right) made of heat-resistant metal alloys and thick concrete. **Question:** Would you be willing to live within a block or two of these casks or have them transported through the area where you live in the event that they were transferred to a long-term storage site? Explain.

Spent nuclear fuel rods can also be processed to remove radioactive plutonium, which can then be used as nuclear fuel or for making nuclear weapons, thus closing the nuclear fuel cycle (Figure 14.22). Reprocessing reduces the storage time for the remaining wastes from up to 240,000 years (longer than the current version of the human species has been around) to about 10,000 years.

However, reprocessing is costly and produces bomb-grade plutonium that can be used by nations to make nuclear weapons, as India did in 1974. This is mainly why the U.S. government, after spending billions of dollars, abandoned this fuel recycling approach in 1977. Currently, France, Russia, Japan, India, the United Kingdom, and China reprocess some of their nuclear fuel.

Most scientists and engineers agree in principle that deep burial in an underground repository is the safest and cheapest way to store high-level radioactive wastes for thousands of years. Between 1987 and 2009, the U.S. Department of Energy spent $12 billion on research and testing for a long-term underground nuclear waste storage site in the Yucca Mountain desert region of Nevada. Between 2001 and 2008, the projected cost for completing the repository increased from $58 billion to $96 billion. The project also fell far behind schedule. It was supposed to start accepting wastes in 1998 but this was revised to

2017 and then to 2020. In 2010 this taxpayer-funded project was abandoned for economic, political, and scientific reasons. These included scientific concerns about earthquake activity. More than 600 earthquakes of magnitude 2.5 and higher occurred in the last 12 years in the repository area.

Thus, after 60 years, no country has come up with a scientific, economic, and politically acceptable solution for storing high-level radioactive wastes for thousands of years. However, in 2016 Finland has plans to entomb its radioactive uranium wastes deep underground in tunnels cut through granite bedrock on an island off the Finnish coast. It expects to store the radioacive wastes for 100,000 years.

Meanwhile, as mentioned, the radioactive wastes are being stored indefinitely in pools and dry casks that are not designed to work for more than 20 to 100 years. Even if all the nuclear power plants in the world were shut down tomorrow, we would still have to find a way to protect ourselves from their high-level radioactive components for thousands of years.

Another costly radioactive waste problem arises when a nuclear reactor reaches the end of its useful life after about 40 to 60 years and must be *decommissioned*. Around the world, 285 of the 440 commercial nuclear reactors operating in 2015 will have to be decommissioned by 2025.

Cost-Benefit Analysis

A **cost-benefit analysis** is a tool used to determine whether a business transaction is worthwhile. The benefits of a project are compared to the costs associated with that project. For example, imagine you are in the market for a new car. Car X costs $26,000 and gets 15 km/L (35 mpg) on average. Car Y costs $22,000 but gets 7.7 km/L (18 mpg). If gas costs $2.50 per gallon and you travel 10,000 miles per year, how long would it take to pay off the investment of purchasing the more fuel-efficient car X?

Cost-benefit analysis is routinely applied to making economic decisions about how to control pollution and manage resources. Analysts determine who or what might be affected by a particular regulation or project—such as building a highway or a dam—define potential outcomes, evaluate alternative options, and establish who benefits and who or what is harmed. Then analysts attempt to assign monetary values (costs and benefits) to each of the factors and components involved.

The decision to continue to use a particular nonrenewable energy source, such as oil, requires a cost-benefit analysis.

The benefits of using oil are that it is relatively cheap, has a medium net energy, is easy to transport and use, and many decades of accessible and affordable oil are left. However, the benefits must be weighed against the economic and environmental costs. Oil must be drilled, transported, and refined, new technologies must be developed to harvest the remaining oil, and there are significant economic and environmental costs involved. There are also *externalities*, or harmful costs, such as the economic and ecological costs of oil spills and leaks, the cost of climate change that results from its use, the cost of air pollution in terms of its negative health effects, and, some might argue, even the cost of preventing a war to ensure a continued supply of oil remains available.

It is easy to continue to use oil as long as it is cheap, plentiful, and accessible, but eventually the costs may outweigh the benefits. At that point, a switch to another form of energy may be more cost-effective than continuing to use oil, even if not all of it has been extracted.

FRQ Application

Question: A small city in upstate New York is planning to replace their aging coal-burning power plant. Proposals presented to the city board include upgrading and modernizing the current facility *or* tearing down the plant and building a nuclear power plant. **Identify** ONE cost and ONE benefit of upgrading the coal-burning plant and ONE cost and ONE benefit of building a new nuclear power plant.

Possible Response: One cost of upgrading the coal-burning plant is that coal will still be used to generate electricity, emitting particulates that causes human health problems such as lung disease and large quantities of climate-changing CO_2. One benefit of upgrading the existing plant is that coal is abundant and cheap, keeping the cost of electricity low. One economic cost of retiring the coal plant and replacing it is that nuclear reactors are very expensive and the cost will have to be subsidized by taxpayers. One benefit of building a nuclear reactor is that operating the plant produces almost no air pollution.

Scientists and engineers have proposed three ways to do this: **(1)** remove and store the highly radioactive parts in a permanent, secure repository (which does not yet exist); **(2)** install a physical barrier around the plant and set up full-time security for 30 to 100 years before dismantling the plant and storing its radioactive parts in a repository; and **(3)** enclose the entire plant in a concrete and steel-reinforced tomb, called a *containment structure*.

This last option was used with a reactor at Chernobyl, Ukraine, that exploded and nearly melted down in 1986, due to a combination of poor reactor design and human operator error. The explosion and the radiation released over large areas of several countries killed hundreds and perhaps thousands of people. It also contaminated a large area of land with long-lasting radioactive fallout. A few years after the containment structure was built, it began to crumble and leak radioactive wastes, due to the corrosive nature of the radiation inside the damaged reactor. The structure is being rebuilt at great cost and is unlikely to last even several hundred years. Regardless of the method chosen, retiring nuclear plants adds to the enormous costs of the nuclear power fuel cycle and reduces its already low net energy.

Can Nuclear Power Slow Climate Change?

Nuclear power advocates contend that we could greatly reduce CO_2 emissions that are contributing to climate change by increasing our use of nuclear power. It is often incorrectly reported that nuclear power produces no CO_2 emissions. Scientists point out that is only partially correct.

While nuclear plants are operating, they do not emit CO_2 but building them and every other step in the nuclear power fuel cycle (Figure 14.22) involves some CO_2 emissions. Such emissions are much lower than those from coal-burning power plants (Figure 14.16) but they still contribute to atmospheric warming and climate change. In other words, the nuclear power fuel cycle is not a carbon-free source of electricity.

Calculations Using Half-Life

One of the drawbacks of nuclear power is disposal of the highly radioactive waste generated. There is no permanent solution to disposing of wastes, and currently high-level waste in the form of spent uranium fuel rods are stored in a deep water pool inside the power plant or in aboveground casks outside the plant (Figure 14.24). However, these are short-term storage solutions. Because of the extremely long half-life of uranium, it will take tens of thousands of years of permanent storage (that so far is not available) before it is safe to come in contact with the waste.

Radioactive half-life is defined as the time it takes for half of the radioactive nuclei in a sample to undergo radioactive decay. After one half-life, half of the sample remains radioactive. After two half-lives, one-fourth of the sample remains, and so on.

FRQ Application

Uranium-235, the fuel typically used in a nuclear reactor, has a half-life of 703.8 million years. A 1-kg sample of fuel pellets from a nuclear fuel rod contains about 4%, or 40 g, of uranium-235. After three half-lives, how many grams of U-235 remain?

$$40 \text{ g} \rightarrow 20 \text{ g} \rightarrow 10 \text{ g} \rightarrow 5 \text{ g}$$

Each arrow represents one half-life. Calculate the final mass by counting the arrows and dividing the mass by two after each half-life.

A more direct approach is to simply multiply the original sample by $\left(\frac{1}{2}\right)^n$, where n represents the number of half-lives:

$$(40 \text{ g})\left(\frac{1}{2}\right)^n = \frac{40 \text{ g}}{2^3} = \frac{40 \text{ g}}{8} = 5 \text{ g}$$

After three half-lives for U-235, how many years have elapsed?

703.8 million years $\times$ 3 half-lives = 2.111 billion years

In another example, a sample of low-level radioactive material has a half-life of 20 years and an activity level of 6 curies. After how many years will the activity level of this sample be at a safe level of 0.125 curies?

$$6 \rightarrow 3 \rightarrow 1.5 \rightarrow 0.75 \rightarrow 0.375 \rightarrow 0.188 \rightarrow 0.094$$

This quick estimate shows that nearly six half-lives must proceed before the sample is at 0.125 curies or lower. Therefore

6 half-lives $\times$ 20 years = 120 years

Nuclear Power's Future is Uncertain

After almost 60 years of development, a huge financial investment, and enormous government subsidies, some 449 commercial nuclear reactors in 30 countries produced 4% of the world's commercial energy and 11% of its electricity in 2015. In the United States, 99 licensed commercial nuclear power reactors produced about 8% of the country's overall energy and 20% of its electricity in 2016.

Electricity from nuclear power has not grown in the United States since 2000 (Figure 14.25) and is not expected to grow between 2015 and 2035 because of the costs involved and because electricity can be produced much more quickly and cheaply from natural gas and from wind turbines, which emit less CO_2 than the nuclear power fuel cycle emits.

There is controversy over the future of nuclear power. Critics argue that the its two most serious problems are the high cost and low net energy of the nuclear power fuel cycle and its contribution to the spread of technology that can be used to make nuclear weapons. They contend that the nuclear power industry could not exist without high levels of financial support from governments and taxpayers, because of the high cost of ensuring safety and the low net energy of the nuclear fuel cycle.

For example, the U.S. government has provided large research and development subsidies, tax breaks, and loan guarantees to the nuclear industry (with taxpayers accepting the risk of any debt defaults) for more than 50 years. In addition, the government provides accident insurance guarantees (under the Price-Anderson Act passed

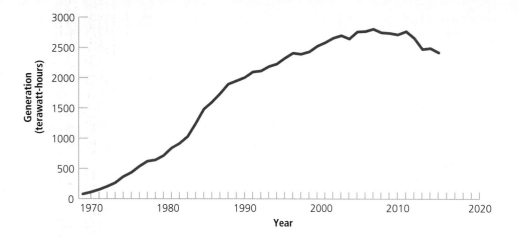

FIGURE 14.25 Global electricity generation from nuclear power, 1970–2014. **Data analysis:** By what percentage did electricity produced by nuclear power decrease between 2006 and 2015?

(Compiled by the authors using data from the International Energy Agency, BP, Worldwatch Institute, and Earth Policy Institute)

by Congress in 1957), because insurance companies have refused to fully insure any US nuclear reactor against the consequences of a catastrophic accident.

According to the nonpartisan Congressional Research Service, since 1948, the U.S. government has spent more than $95 billion (in 2011 dollars) on nuclear energy research and development (R&D)—more than four times the amount spent on R&D for solar, wind, geothermal, biomass, biofuels, and hydropower combined. Many analysts question the need for continuing such taxpayer support for nuclear power, especially since its energy output has not grown for several decades and is unlikely to grow during the next several decades, according to the International Energy Agency and the U.S. Department of Energy.

> **CONSIDER THIS . . .**
>
> **THINKING ABOUT** Government Subsidies for Nuclear Power
> Do you think the benefits of nuclear power justify high government (taxpayer) subsidies and tax breaks for the nuclear industry? Explain.

Because of the multiple built-in safety features, the risk of exposure to radioactivity from nuclear power plants in the United States and in most other more-developed countries is very low. However, several explosions and partial or complete meltdowns have occurred (see the Case Study that follows). These accidents have dampened public and investor confidence in nuclear power.

Proponents of nuclear power argue that governments should continue funding research, development, and pilot-plant testing of potentially safer and less costly new types of reactors. The nuclear industry claims that hundreds of new *advanced light-water reactors (ALWRs)* could be built in just a few years. ALWRs have built-in safety features designed to make meltdowns and releases of radioactive emissions almost impossible and thus do not need expensive automatic cooling systems. So far, commercial versions of such reactors have not been built or evaluated.

The industry is also evaluating the development of smaller modular light-water reactors—about the size of a

school bus—that could be built in a factory, delivered to a site, and installed underground. They need refueling every 5 to 30 years and can quickly be linked together to expand power production as needed. However, because they use fast neutrons instead of slow neutrons to fission uranium-235, the fuel has to be enriched from 1% to 19.9%. This makes it much easier to enrich it to 80–95% for bomb-grade material—worsening the threat of the spread of nuclear weapons. Commercial versions of such reactors have yet to be built and evaluated.

Some scientists call for replacing today's uranium-based reactors with new ones fueled by thorium, a naturally occurring radioactive element found in abundance in the earth's crust throughout the world and that does not need to be enriched like uranium-235. According to scientists, thorium reactors would be much less costly and safer because they cannot melt down. In addition, the nuclear waste produced by thorium plants could not be used to make nuclear weapons. China and India plan to explore this option.

In the United States, even with considerable government subsidies and loan guarantees, most utility companies and money lenders are unwilling to take on the financial risk of building new nuclear plants of any design as long as electricity can be produced more cheaply with the use of natural gas and wind power (and solar cells if solar prices keep falling).

CASE STUDY

The Fukushima Daiichi Nuclear Power Plant Accident in Japan

A nuclear accident occurred on March 11, 2011, at the Fukushima Daiichi Nuclear Power Plant on the northeast coast of Japan. A strong offshore earthquake that caused a severe tsunami devastated coastal communities and triggered the nuclear accident. An immense wave of seawater washed over the nuclear plant's protective seawalls and knocked out the circuits and backup diesel generators of the emergency core cooling systems for the plant's three operating reactors. Then, explosions (presumably from the buildup of hydrogen gas produced by the exposed nuclear fuel rods) blew the roofs off three of the reactor buildings and released radioactive materials into the atmosphere and nearby coastal waters.

Evidence indicates that the cores of these three reactors suffered full meltdowns. The melted reactors and their 1,573 radioactive fuel rods are buried under massive amounts of debris. In 2017, six years after the accident radioactivity in the vicinity of the reactors was high enough to kill a human in a minute and disable an exploratory robot.

Since the accident, water has been pumped nonstop through the three reactors to cool the melted fuel that is too radioactive and hot to remove. The radioactive water is being stored in 1,000 large tanks on the plant site. Within a few years, there may be no more room for the additional tanks. The plant site is also storing large amounts of radioactive sludge, protective clothing (from the 6,000 cleanup workers), ruble, soil, and branches and logs in thousands of containers. It is not clear where this massive amount of radioactive debris will eventually be stored.

Some 130,000 people were evacuated from the area near the plant and by 2017 only about 10% of them had been able to return to their homes. Although the tsunami killed 15,891 people, no one has died directly from exposure to radioactivity from the nuclear accident. However, eventually, 100 or more people could die from thyroid and other cancers associated with their exposure to radioactivity.

Officials estimate that it will take three to four decades to remove radioactive materials and wastes from the damaged reactors at a cost of at least $180 billion. This does not include the costs of decontamination of the surrounding area and compensation for victims of the accident—costing an estimated $200 to 400 billion.

This event damaged the confidence of Japanese citizens in the safety of nuclear power and led the government to shut down all of the country's 40 remaining reactors but reopened three of them in 2015. Since then, Japan has relied more on imports of expensive liquefied natural gas (LNG) and cheaper coal to produce electricity. However, Japan has replaced half of the energy it got from nuclear power with energy saved through improvements to energy efficiency.

This serious but not major nuclear power accident (compared to Chernobyl) had five important effects:

- It increased public fear throughout the world about the use of nuclear power to produce electricity.

- It revealed that a single accident can add an estimated $200 billion to $400 billion to the already high cost of the nuclear fuel cycle.

- It led Germany, Switzerland, and Belgium to announce plans for phasing out nuclear power and shifting to increased use of wind and solar energy to produce electricity.

- It increased the exposure of Japanese citizens to air pollution from the use of coal.

- It spurred Japan to reduce its energy use by cutting energy waste and improving energy efficiency.

Is Nuclear Fusion the Answer?

Other proponents of nuclear power hope to develop **nuclear fusion**—in which the nuclei of two isotopes of a light element such as hydrogen are forced together at extremely high temperatures until they fuse to form a heavier nucleus, releasing energy in the process (Figure 14.26). The sun uses nuclear fusion to warm the earth and sustain its life. Some scientists hope that controlled nuclear fusion on the earth will provide an almost limitless source of energy with fewer risks than nuclear fission.

With nuclear fusion, there would be no risk of a meltdown or of a release of large amounts of radioactive materials, and little risk of the additional spread of nuclear weapons. Fossil fuels would not be needed to produce electricity, thereby eliminating most of the earth's air pollution and climate-changing CO_2 emissions. Fusion power might also be used to destroy toxic wastes and to supply electricity for desalinating water and for decomposing water to produce clean-burning hydrogen fuel.

However, in the United States, after more than 50 years of research and a $25 billion investment (mostly by the government), controlled nuclear fusion is still in the laboratory stage. None of the approaches tested so far has produced more energy than they used. In 2006 the United States, China, Russia, Japan, South Korea, India, and the European Union agreed to spend at least $12.8 billion in a joint effort to build a large-scale experimental nuclear fusion reactor by 2026 to determine if it can have an acceptable net energy at an affordable cost. By 2014 the estimated cost of this project had more than doubled and it was far behind schedule. Unless there is an unexpected scientific breakthrough, some skeptics say that nuclear fusion is the power of the future—and always will be.

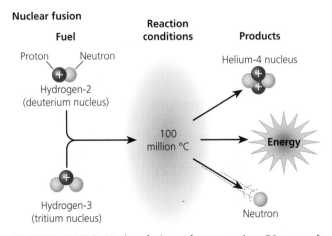

FIGURE 14.26 *Nuclear fusion:* After more than 50 years of research and a $25 billion investment, controlled nuclear fusion is still in the laboratory stage.

1. Explain why the net energy for the nuclear power fuel cycle is much lower than for other nonrenewable energy sources.

2. Explain why there has not been a significant increase in the construction of nuclear power plants in the United States.

3. Identify some of the outcomes of the accident at the Fukushima Daiichi Nuclear Power Plant in Japan.

Core Case Study Checkpoint

What new drilling techniques have allowed oil companies to access oil and gas deposits that were previously inaccessible?

KEY IDEAS

- A key factor to consider in evaluating the long-term usefulness of any energy resource is its net energy.

- Conventional oil, natural gas, and coal are plentiful and have a moderate to high net energy, but use of these fossil fuels, especially coal, has a high environmental impact.

- The nuclear power fuel cycle has a low environmental impact and a low accident risk, but high costs, a low net energy, long-lived radioactive wastes, and its role in spreading nuclear weapons technology have limited its use.

Chapter 14 Glossary

coal: solid, combustible mixture of organic compounds with 30 to 98% carbon by weight, mixed with various amounts of water and small amounts of sulfur and nitrogen compounds. It forms in several stages as the remains of plants are subjected to heat and pressure over millions of years.

crude oil (petroleum): gooey liquid consisting mostly of hydrocarbon compounds and small amounts of compounds containing oxygen, sulfur, and nitrogen. Extracted from underground accumulations, it is sent to oil refineries, where it is converted to heating oil, diesel fuel, gasoline, tar, and other materials.

energy efficiency: using less energy to produce the same amount of useful work.

hydraulic fracturing (fracking): freeing oil or natural gas that is tightly held in underground rock deposits by using perforated drilling well tubes with explosive charges to create fissures in the rock. Then, high-pressure pumps shoot a mixture of water, sand, and chemicals into the well to hold the rock fractures open and release the

oil or natural gas, which flows back to the surface along with a mixture of water, and fracking chemicals (some of them hazardous), and other wastes that are released from the rock.

liquefied natural gas: natural gas converted to liquid form by cooling it to a very low temperature.

liquefied petroleum gas: mixture of liquefied propane (C_3H_8) and butane (C_4H_{10}) gas removed from natural gas and used as a fuel.

natural gas: underground deposits of gases consisting of 50 to 90% by weight methane gas (CH_4) and small amounts of heavier gaseous hydrocarbon compounds such as propane (C_3H_8) and butane (C_4H_{10}).

net energy: total amount of high-quality energy available from an energy resource or energy system over its lifetime, minus the amount of high-quality energy needed to make the energy available.

nuclear fission: the process by which nuclei of certain isotopes with large mass numbers (such as uranium-235) are split apart into

lighter nuclei when struck by a neutron and release energy.

nuclear fuel cycle: includes the mining of uranium, processing and enriching it to make nuclear fuel, using it in the reactor, building a nuclear power plant, safely storing the resulting highly radioactive wastes for thousands of years until their radioactivity falls to safe levels, and retiring the highly radioactive nuclear plant by taking it apart and storing its high- and moderate-level radioactive material safely for thousands of years.

oil sands (tar sands): deposit of a mixture of clay, sand, water, and varying amounts of a tarlike heavy oil known as bitumen. Bitumen can be extracted from tar sand by heating. It is then purified and upgraded to synthetic crude oil.

peak production: point in time when the pressure in an oil well drops and its rate of conventional crude oil production starts declining, usually after a decade or so; for a group of wells or for a nation, the point at which all wells on average have passed peak production.

petrochemicals: chemicals obtained by refining (distilling) crude oil. They are used as raw materials in manufacturing most industrial chemicals, fertilizers, pesticides, plastics, synthetic fibers, paints, medicines, and many other products.

proven oil reserves: identified deposits from which conventional crude oil can be extracted profitably by current processes with current technology.

refining: complex process in which crude oil is heated and vaporized in giant columns and separated, by use of varying boiling points, into various products such as gasoline, heating oil, and asphalt.

synthetic natural gas: gaseous fuel containing mostly methane produced from solid coal.

Chapter Review

Core Case Study

1. What is **horizontal drilling** and **hydraulic fracturing (fracking)** and how are they used to produce oil and natural gas?

Section 14.1

2. (a) What are the two key concepts for this section? (b) What types of commercial energy resources do we use to supplement energy from the sun? (c) Distinguish between nonrenewable and renewable energy resources and give three examples of each type. (d) What percentage of the energy used in the world and in the United States comes from each of these types of energy resources?

3. (a) Define **net energy** and explain why is important in evaluating energy resources. (b) Explain why some energy resources need help in the form of subsidies to compete in the marketplace, and give an example.

Section 14.2

4. (a) What are the two key concepts for this section? (b) What is **crude oil (petroleum)** and how are oil deposits detected and removed? (c) What percentages of the commercial energy used in the world and in the United States are provided by conventional crude oil? (d) What is **peak production** for an oil well or oil field? (e) What is **refining**? What are **petrochemicals** and why are they important?

5. (a) What are **proven oil reserves**? (b) Why has the global net energy for extracting oil been dropping? Is there a global shortage of oil? (c) What three countries have the world's largest proven oil reserves? Which three are the largest producers of oil? Which three are the largest consumers of oil? (d) What percentage of the world's proven oil reserves does the United States and China have? (e) What is OPEC? (f) Summarize the story of oil production and consumption in the United States. What major factors could increase or decrease oil production in the United States? (g) What are the major advantages and disadvantages of using crude oil as an energy resource?

6. (a) What is **shale oil** and how is this heavy oil produced? What are **oil sands**? (b) What is bitumen, and how is it extracted and converted to heavy oil? (c) What are the major advantages and disadvantages of using shale oil and heavy oils produced from oil shale rock and from oil sands?

Section 14.3

7. (a) What is the key concept for this section? (b) Define **natural gas**, **liquefied petroleum gas (LPG)**, and **liquefied natural gas (LNG)**. (c) What three countries have the world's largest proven natural gas reserves? Which three are the largest producers of natural gas? Which three are the largest consumers of natural gas? (d) Why has natural gas production risen sharply in the United States and what two factors could hinder this rise? (e) What are the major advantages and disadvantages of using natural gas as an energy resource? (f) Describe four problems resulting from increased use of fracking to produce natural gas in the United States and four ways to deal with these problems. (g) Discuss whether increased use of natural gas can slow or speed up global climate change.

Section 14.4

8. (a) What are the two key concepts for this section? (b) What is coal, how is it formed, and how do the various types of coal differ? (c) How does a coal-burning power plant work? (d) What three countries have the world's largest proven coal reserves? Which three are the largest producers of coal? Which three are the largest consumers of coal? (e) Summarize the major environmental and health problems caused by the use of coal. What would happen if

coal's harmful health and environmental effects were included in its market price? (f) What are the major advantages and disadvantages of using coal as an energy resource? (g) What is **synthetic natural gas (SNG)** and what are the major advantages and disadvantages of using it as an energy resource?

Section 14.5

9. (a) What is the key concept for this section? (b) What is **nuclear fission**? How does a nuclear fission reactor work and what are its major safety features? (c) Describe the **nuclear fuel cycle**. (d) What three countries are the three leading users of nuclear power? What percentage of the electricity generated in the United States comes from nuclear power? (e) What is the relationship between nuclear power plants and the spread of nuclear weapons?

(f) Explain how highly radioactive spent-fuel rods are stored and what risks these present. (g) How has the United States dealt with the nuclear waste problem? (h) What are three ways to deal with worn-out nuclear power plants? (i) Summarize the arguments over whether or not the widespread use of nuclear power could help to slow projected climate change during this century. (j) Summarize the arguments of experts who disagree over the future of nuclear power. (k) Describe the Fukushima Daiichi nuclear power plant accident and list its five major effects. (l) What is **nuclear fusion** and what is its potential as an energy resource?

10. What are this chapter's *three key ideas*?

_____

Note: Key terms are in bold type.

AP® Review Questions

1. The world's largest oil reserves are found in
   (A) Saudi Arabia
   (B) Mexico
   (C) China
   (A) Venezuela
   (B) The United States

2. When global demand for oil exceeds the rate at which it is produced
   (A) price decreases and demand goes up
   (B) price and demand stay the same
   (C) flow rate is stopped
   (D) flow rate to consumers goes down and price goes up
   (E) flow rate to consumers goes up and price goes down

3. Which of the following best describes net energy?
   (A) Waste heat energy from a coal-burning power plant used to heat greenhouses
   (B) Total energy available, minus the energy needed to find, extract, process, and deliver the energy
   (C) Total energy produced from refined petroleum products
   (D) Energy used to move control rods in a light-water nuclear reactor
   (E) Total energy collected in the filters of emissions towers in coal-fired power plants

4. Advocates of drilling for oil in the Arctic National Wildlife Refuge (ANWR) believe that by using the oil found here we would decrease our dependence on imported oil. However, opponents feel that
   (A) tundra ecosystems recover quickly and can handle the stress of extracting the resource
   (B) there is relatively little oil so it is not worth degrading this fragile ecosystem
   (C) since the oil is an estimated 20-year reserve, we should do more research into this resource
   (D) as demand goes up we will not need this resource
   (E) a switch to renewable energy will eliminate the need for America to use this resource

5. Oil as an energy source has all of the following disadvantages EXCEPT
   (A) OPEC controls much of the world's crude oil and is therefore able to control the price of oil
   (B) the possibility of oil tanker leaks and spills such as what occurred with the Exxon Valdez
   (C) the loss or degradation of habitat if a leak develops in the pipelines used to transport oil
   (D) depending on consumption, proven and unproven oil reserves could last more than 100 years
   (E) the possibility of accidents on offshore platforms, which could pollute water from oil spills and pollute air from fires

Questions 6–8 refer to the graphs below, which show total (upper left) and per capita (upper right) energy consumption in the United States, and energy consumption by fuel type (lower) in the United States.

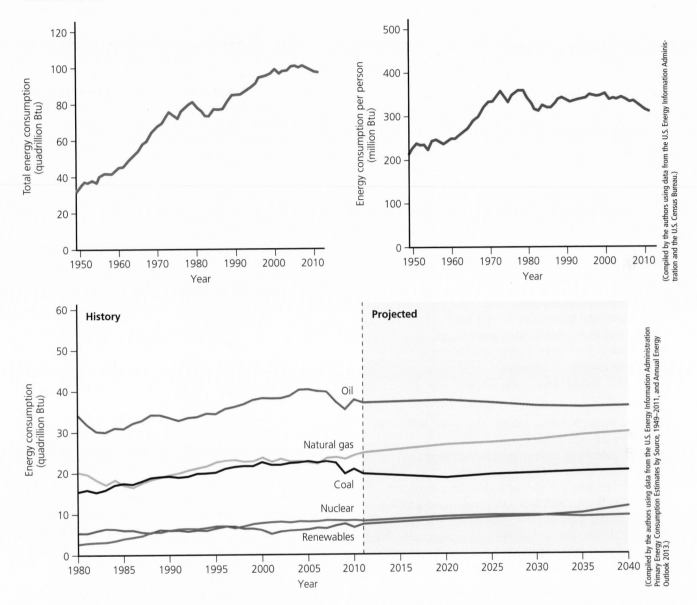

(Compiled by the authors using data from the U.S. Energy Information Administration and the U.S. Census Bureau.)

(Compiled by the authors using data from the U.S. Energy Information Administration Primary Energy Consumption Estimates by Source, 1949–2011, and Annual Energy Outlook 2013.)

6. According to the graph, in 2000, what was the approximate total energy consumption in BTU for the U.S.?
   (A) 40 quadrillion
   (B) 95 quadrillion
   (C) 60 quadrillion
   (D) 35 quadrillion
   (E) 350 million

7. According to the graph, the projected energy consumption for nuclear power is
   (A) growing exponentially
   (B) decreasing rapidly
   (C) remaining fairly flat
   (D) an example of logistic growth
   (E) growing rapidly each year

8. The increase in per capita energy consumption from 1950–2010 has risen
   (A) 10%
   (B) 20%
   (C) 40%
   (D) 60%
   (E) 80%

9. Which of the following is a benefit of using natural gas?
   (A) It is four times as energy efficient as coal.
   (B) It is cleaner-burning than coal.
   (C) Coal power plants are cheaper to build and maintain than natural gas.
   (D) Getting natural gas from Canada is inexpensive.
   (E) CO_2 is not released when burning natural gas.

10. Methane, butane, and propane are
    (A) components of natural gas
    (B) forms of coal
    (C) by-products of petroleum refining
    (D) waste products of nuclear energy production
    (E) ozone-depleting compounds

11. With an estimated U.S. population of 325 million people, if per capita energy consumption is approximately 3.5×10^8 BTU, how much energy does the entire population consume?
    (A) 1.14×10^8 BTU
    (B) 1.14×10^{14} BTU
    (C) 1.14×10^{15} BTU
    (D) 1.14×10^{16} BTU
    (E) 1.14×10^{17} BTU

12. The three largest users of coal are
    (A) China, the United States, and India
    (B) China, the United States, and Mexico
    (C) Russia, the United States, and Mexico
    (D) Russia, China, and India
    (E) Saudi Arabia, Japan, and China

13. Coal has a huge environmental impact because of
    (A) the threat to human health due to air pollutants released when coal burns
    (B) the release of carbon, which contributes to global climate change
    (C) the fact that it is the most abundant fossil fuel
    (D) its high cost, mostly to cover the transportation of coal to electric power plants
    (E) the use of new technology that makes coal safer and cleaner to remove from the earth and to transport to homes and industry

14. Which of the following negative impacts is NOT associated with coal mining and burning?
    (A) Fracking used during extraction contaminates water and is associated with earthquakes.
    (B) Carbon dioxide and sulfur dioxide gases are emitted.
    (C) Toxic heavy metals, such as mercury and arsenic, are released into the environment.
    (D) Coal ash, which contains heavy metals and radium, is toxic and must be stored safely forever.
    (E) Open-pit mining and mountaintop removal may be used to acquire reserves.

15. Nuclear power was predicted to supply 21% of the world's commercial energy. Which of the following is the most significant reason why this goal has not been met?
    (A) Thermal pollution, which becomes a problem when nuclear power plants break down or must be dismantled
    (B) Approximately 75% of the available high-quality energy is lost as waste heat
    (C) The small supply of enriched uranium-235
    (D) The lack of long-term storage facilities for high-level radioactive wastes such as spent fuel rods
    (E) The high risk of accidents such as Fukushima in Japan in 2011, Chernobyl in the U.S.S.R. in 1986, and Three Mile Island in the United States in 1979

16. Which of the following is a true statement about nuclear energy?
    (A) It is created through a fission chain reaction in which neutrons split, releasing high amounts of heat.
    (B) It is formed through nuclear fusion reactions, which create energy currents.
    (C) It is formed from the breakdown of uranium into high-pressure steam.
    (D) It is created from the oxidation reaction of water.
    (E) It requires the use of other fossil fuels to super-heat the plutonium fuel and separate out the necessary neutrons for the reaction.

17. In a nuclear power plant, control rods
    (A) are used to transport the spent nuclear fuel pellets into storage
    (B) are moved in and out of the reactor core to regulate the rate of fission
    (C) separate the reactor core from the turbine and condenser tower to keep radioactive materials from escaping
    (D) are caused to spin by the high heat, thereby generating electricity
    (E) are used to moderate water flow through the reactor

18. Which of the following is an environmental benefit of using nuclear power?
    (A) Radioactive waste can be stored in dry casks for 20 to 100 years.
    (B) Spent fuel rods can be reprocessed to create weapons-grade plutonium.
    (C) The nuclear fuel cycle produces climate-changing carbon dioxide, but it produces less than using fossil fuels.
    (D) Spent fuel rods can provide a carbon-neutral heating source for homes.
    (E) Nuclear power is cheaper than wind power.

19. Since 1948, the U.S. government has spent the most money on research and development of this energy source.

(A) Geothermal
(B) Petroleum
(C) Wind
(D) Solar
(E) Nuclear

20. How does hydraulic fracturing contribute directly to climate change?

(A) Not all methane released from this method is captured; some escapes into the atmosphere, where it is a powerful greenhouse gas.
(B) Fracking contributes to earthquakes, which can release deep pockets of carbon dioxide as a result of the tectonic shifts.
(C) Fracking operations release extensive amounts of carbon dioxide, which contributes further to climate change.
(D) Fracking can contaminate groundwater through leaking pipes that are not monitored properly.
(E) Fracking causes people to burn more methane, which adds more carbon dioxide to the atmosphere.

AP® Free-Response Practice

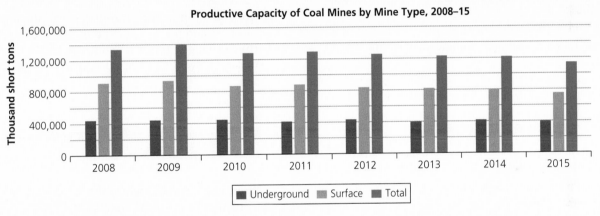

Source: https://www.eia.gov/coal/annual/

1. (a) As new energy technologies are being developed, the use of coal in the United States has begun to decline. The graph below shows the annual number of short tons (a short ton is equal to 2,000 lb) produced from underground and surface mines.

  (i) Calculate the percent decrease between 2009 and 2014 in short tons of coal mined, using the data in the graph.

  (ii) In 2009, the population of the United States was approximately 307 million people. Assume all of the coal mined in the U.S. was used domestically to produce electricity. **Determine** the per capita consumption of coal in the U.S. that year. Express your answer in pounds per person.

  (iii) Burning one ton of coal produces 5,720 lb of CO_2. **Calculate** the amount in pounds of CO_2 produced per capita from burning coal, using the value you calculated in (ii).

  (iv) Determine how many tons of CO_2 were generated from burning all of the coal mined in 2009.

(b) The use of coal in the U.S. has dropped consistently over the past decade.

  (i) Provide ONE reason why coal use has declined in the United States.

  (ii) While coal use has declined in the United States, coal use is expected to increase worldwide. **Identify** ONE country where coal use is expected to increase and **list** TWO reasons for the increase.

(c) Natural gas is expected to replace coal as an energy source in the United States over the next few decades. **Discuss** TWO reasons why natural gas is expected to replace coal.

Critical Thinking

1. How might greatly increased production of domestic oil and natural gas in the United States over the next two decades (**Core Case Study**) affect the country's future use of coal, nuclear power, and energy from the sun and wind? How might such an increase affect your life during the next 20 years?

2. Should governments give a high priority to considering net energy when deciding what energy resources to support? What are other factors that should be considered? Which factor or factors should get the most weight in deciding what energy resources to use? Explain your thinking.

3. Some analysts argue that in order to continue using oil at the current rate, we must discover and add to global oil reserves the equivalent of two new Saudi Arabian reserves every 7 years. Do you think this is possible? If not, what effects might the failure to find such supplies have on your life and on the lives of any children and grandchildren that you might have?

4. List three things you could do to reduce your dependence on oil and gasoline. Which of these things do you already do or plan to do?

5. Are you for or against the increased use of horizontal drilling and fracking (**Core Case Study**) to produce oil and natural gas in the United States? Explain. What are the alternatives?

6. Are you for or against phasing out the use of coal in the United States by 2050? State your three strongest arguments to explain your position. How might this affect your life and the lives of any children and grandchildren that you might have? What are the alternatives?

7. Are you for or against greatly increasing the use of nuclear power to produce electricity? State your three strongest arguments to explain your position.

8. Are you for or against providing government subsidies and tax breaks to producers of **(a)** oil, **(b)** natural gas, **(c)** coal, and **(d)** electricity from nuclear power? Explain. What are the alternatives?

Data Analysis

Use the graph below, comparing U.S. oil consumption and production, to answer the questions that follow.

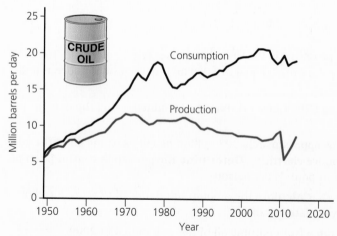

(Compiled by the authors using data from the U.S. Energy Information Agency (EIA))

1. By what percentage did U.S. oil consumption increase between 1982 and 2014?

2. By what percentage did U.S. oil consumption decrease between 2005 and 2011?

3. By what percentage did U.S. oil production decrease between 1985 and 2004?

4. By what percentage did U.S. oil production increase between 2011 and 2014?

What general conclusions can you draw from these data? Compare notes and discuss your conclusions with your classmates.

Answers to Checkpoints for Understanding

Section 14.1

1. Net energy is the difference between the amount of high-quality energy available from a given quantity of an energy resource minus the high-quality energy needed to make the energy available. If it costs more to obtain an energy resource than its market value, then using that particular energy resource many no longer be economically viable.

Section 14.2

1. Crude oil was formed when the remains of organisms were trapped and crushed between layers of rock and, rather than decomposing, were heated and pressurized by the forces of the earth for millions of years.
2. The benefits of using oil as an energy source include ample supply for the near future, medium net energy, low land disruption, and an efficient distribution system.
3. The drawbacks of using oil as an energy source include water pollution from spills and leaks, environmental costs are not included in the price, release of CO_2 and other air pollutants, and vulnerability to international supply disruption.
4. Recovering shale oil involves mining, crushing, and heating shale rock in order to extract the oil rather than simply drilling, all of which reduces its net energy and raises the cost of extraction significantly.

Section 14.3

1. Natural gas can be used in a variety of energy applications. It can be transported by cooling it to liquefied natural gas (LNG). When burned, it releases less CO_2 than coal, and natural gas power plants are cheaper to build than other conventional power plants.
2. Disadvantages of natural gas include low net energy for LNG, fracking uses and pollutes huge volumes of water, groundwater can be polluted by the extraction process when well casings fail, and earthquakes can result when the waste slurry from fracking is forced into too many underground hazardous waste storage wells in the same general area.

Section 14.4

1. The benefits of using coal are that coal has a medium to high net energy, is plentiful, and has a low cost when environmental costs are not included.
2. The drawbacks of using coal are that it is the dirtiest of the fossil fuels, mining results in severe land disruption and water pollution, particulate (soot) and toxic mercury emissions threaten human health, and burning coal emits large amounts of CO_2 and other air pollutants.

Section 14.5

1. The net energy for nuclear power is low because of the cost of building a plant and maintaining the nuclear fuel cycle (mining uranium ore, upgrading the ore to nuclear fuel, operating the reactor, safely storing the resulting highly radioactive waste for thousands of years, dismantling the radioactive plant at the end of its life and safely storing its radioactive wastes for thousands of years).
2. Few new nuclear power plants have been built in the United States because the cost of building plants is high and rising, the net energy is low, and the potential use of technology from the nuclear fuel cycle to produce nuclear weapons. Also, nuclear accidents that have occurred in the US and in other parts of the world have made the public less willing to support nuclear power.
3. Some of the outcomes of the Fukushima accident were increased public fear in Japan and throughout the world of nuclear power, the additional cost of $200 to $400 billion in expenses related to the accident, the decision by some European countries to phase out nuclear power and shift to clean energy instead, coal imported to Japan exposed its citizens to additional air pollution, and it motivated Japan to conserve energy and cut energy waste.

Core Case Study

Horizontal drilling, which drills through layers of shale to access many deposits at once, and hydraulic fracturing which uses a slurry of sand, water and chemicals that releases the gas and oil trapped in the layers of shale, are used in combination to extract fossil fuels that were previously inaccessible.

Energy Efficiency and Renewable Energy

Coal plant smokestacks that dirty the air and alter the climate will be replaced by solar panels on our rooftops and wind turbines turning gracefully in the distance. Welcome to the clean energy era.

LESTER R. BROWN

Wind turbines and solar cell panels in a rapeseed field.

visdia/Shutterstock.com

Key Questions

15.1 Why do we need a new energy transition?

15.2 Why is improving energy efficiency and reducing energy waste an important energy resource?

15.3 What are the advantages and disadvantages of using solar energy?

15.4 What are the advantages and disadvantages of using wind power?

15.5 What are the advantages and disadvantages of using geothermal energy?

15.6 What are the advantages and disadvantages of using biomass as an energy source?

15.7 What are the advantages and disadvantages of using hydropower?

15.8 What are the advantages and disadvantages of using hydrogen as an energy source?

15.9 How can we make the transition to a more sustainable energy future?

Saving Energy and Money and Reducing Our Environmental Impact

Do you like to burn dollar bills? Do you like wasting 15–30% of the money you spend on electricity, gasoline, and heating and cooling bills? About 43% of the money that Americans spend each year on energy is unnecessarily wasted and provides no useful energy. In addition to burning up mountains of $100 bills, this waste of energy increases our harmful environmental impact.

Some do this by driving cars with engines that waste 75% of the money they spend on gasoline. Only about 25% of the money we spend on gasoline, on average, gets us somewhere. Many also waste energy and money by living in leaky houses and buildings. The left photo in Figure 15.1 is an infrared shot of a home that is poorly insulated and has heat and money leaking out through its doors, windows, walls, and roof. Spending a small amount of money insulating the walls and roof and caulking (sealing) leaks around the windows and doors can drastically reduce this loss of heat and money, as shown in the photo on the right. Many homes in the United States

and other countries are so full of leaks that their heat loss in cold weather and heat gain in hot weather are equivalent to having a large, window-sized hole in a wall of the house.

Would you like to have an investment that will earn 25% a year without any risk or taxes, compared to a bank savings account with a 0.1% annual return? Do what the owner of the house in Figure 15.1 did. If you live in a typical home and you could invest $2,000 in insulation and $25 in caulking all the air leaks around doors and windows and in your ceiling and roof, you could reduce your heating and cooling bill by 15–30%. The caulking immediately would start earning you a 100% return on your investment. It would take about 4 years to earn back the money you spent on insulation. After that, you would be earning a 25% annual return on your investment as long as you lived in the house. (Interest rate = 100%/payback period = 100/4 = 25%.) As an added bonus, you could reduce your input of

climate-changing CO_2 by about 2.1 metric tons (2.4 tons) a year.

Investing in insulating a house and sealing air leaks is not exciting. But the money you can save is, and you can also reduce your harmful environmental impacts from heating and cooling your house. It is a win-win deal for you and the environment.

In this chapter, we consider the importance of using energy more efficiently and wasting less energy. We also explore ways to make the transition to a more sustainable energy future during this century by shifting from nonrenewable fossil fuels to renewable energy resources such as solar energy, wind power, flowing water, and the earth's internal heat. ●

CRITICAL THINKING

Insulating your home is one energy conservation strategy. What other strategies can you think of that would save energy in your home?

Photos courtesy of Mark Group, Inc.

FIGURE 15.1 A thermogram, or infrared photo, of a house before (left) and after it was well insulated (right). **Critical thinking:** How do you think the place where you live would compare to the house on the left in terms of heat loss (red, orange, and yellow) and the resulting waste of money on high heating and cooling bills?

WHY DO WE NEED A NEW ENERGY TRANSITION?

CONCEPT 15.1 The world is in the early stages of a transition from relying on fossil fuels to greater reliance on energy efficiency and renewable energy.

Establishing New Energy Priorities

Shifting to new energy resources is not new. The world has shifted from primary dependence on wood to coal, then from coal to oil, and then to our current dependence on oil, natural gas, and coal as new technologies made these resources more available and affordable. Each of these shifts in key energy resources took about 50 to 60 years. As in the past, it takes an enormous investment in science and engineering, research, technology, and infrastructure to develop and spread the use of new energy resources.

Currently, the world and the United States get about 90% of the commercial energy they use from three carbon-containing fossil fuels—oil, coal, and natural gas (Figure 14.2, p. 421). They have supported tremendous economic growth and improved the lives of many people.

However, society is awakening to the fact that burning fossil fuels, especially coal, is largely responsible for three of the world's most serious environmental problems: air pollution, climate change, and ocean acidification. Fossil fuels are affordable because their market prices do not include these and other harmful health and environmental effects.

According to many scientists, energy experts, and energy economists, over the next 50 to 60 years and beyond, we need to make a new energy transition by **(1)** improving energy efficiency and reducing energy waste, **(2)** decreasing our dependence on nonrenewable fossil fuels, and **(3)** relying more on a mix of renewable energy from the sun, wind, the earth's interior heat (geothermal energy), flowing water (hydropower), and biomass (wood and biofuels). Countries also need to modernize electrical grids that distribute electricity produced from these resources.

We can reduce fossil fuel use, but fossil fuels are not going to disappear. In 2065, fossil fuels are projected to provide at least 50% of the world's energy, compared to 90% today, according to the International Energy Agency. The use of coal is likely to decline the most because of its harmful environmental effects, its key role in accelerating climate change and ocean acidification, and the fact that electricity can be produced at a lower cost by wind farms and by burning natural gas.

Supporters of this restructuring of the global energy system and economy over the next 50 to 60 years and beyond project that it will save money, create profitable business and investment opportunities, and provide jobs. They also project that it will save lives by sharply reducing air pollution, help keep climate change from spiraling out of control and creating ecological and economic chaos, and slow the increase in ocean acidity. Finally, supporters project that this shift will increase our positive environmental impact, and pass the world on to future generations in better shape than we found it.

For more than four decades, fossil fuel industries and utility companies have been using their economic and political power to slow this energy shift, especially in the United States. Eventually, however, economists expect fossil fuel businesses to fade as cheaper and cleaner energy alternatives emerge, which is how creative capitalism works.

This energy shift is being driven by the availability of perpetual supplies of clean and increasingly cheaper solar and wind energy throughout the world and advances in solar cell and wind turbine technology. This is in contrast to fossil fuels, which are dependent on finite supplies of oil, coal, and natural gas that are not widely distributed, are controlled by a few countries and companies, and are subject to fluctuating prices based on supply and demand.

In this new technology-driven energy economy, an increasing percentage of the world's electricity will be produced locally from available sun and wind and regionally from solar cell power plants and wind farms and transmitted to consumers by a modern, interactive, smart electrical grid. Homeowners and businesses with solar panels on their roofs or land can become independent electricity producers. They will be able to heat and cool their homes and businesses, run electrical devices, charge hybrid or electric cars, and sell any excess electricity they produce. The United States will benefit economically, because making such a market-based shift will set off an explosion of increased energy efficiency and renewable energy and battery technological innovations by tapping into the country's ability to innovate.

Like any major societal change, this shift will not be easy. However, to many analysts the beneficial environmental, health, and economic effects of making this shift far outweigh the harmful environmental, health, and economic effects of not making this shift over the next few decades.

This shift is underway and gaining momentum as the cost of electricity produced from the sun and wind continues its rapid fall and investors see a way to make money on two of the world's fastest growing businesses. Between 2009 and 2015, the cost of generating electricity with solar energy fell by 82% and with wind by 61%. Germany (see the Case Study that follows), Sweden, Denmark, and Costa Rica have made the most progress in this shift, and Japan leads the world in reducing energy waste. For example, Costa Rica gets more than 90% of its electricity from renewable resources, mostly hydropower, geothermal energy, and wind. It aims to generate all of its electricity from **GOOD NEWS** renewable sources by 2021, mostly by increasing its use of geothermal energy.

In the United States, solar and wind power use is increasing and coal use has dropped slightly, mostly because of increased use of affordable domestic supplies of natural gas to produce electricity. However, the United States has yet to commit to making the new energy shift, partly because of more than four decades of opposition by politically and economically powerful fossil fuel and electric utility companies. In addition, increased reliance on using cheap natural gas to produce electricity hinders the shift to wind, solar, and other renewable energy resources.

CASE STUDY

Germany Is a Renewable Energy Superpower

Germany is phasing out nuclear power and between 2006 and 2015, increased the percentage of its electricity produced by renewable energy, mostly from the sun and wind, from 6% to 31%. Its goals for 2050 are to get 80% of its electricity from renewable energy, increase electricity efficiency by 50%, reduce its current emissions of climate-changing CO_2 by 80%, and sharply reduce its use of coal, which in 2015 produced 44% of its electricity.

The biggest factor in this shift is Germany's use of a **feed-in-tariff** (also used by Great Britain and 47 other countries). Under a long-term contract, it requires utilities to buy electricity produced by homeowners and businesses from renewable energy resources at a price that guarantees a good return and to feed it into the electrical grid.

German households now own and make money from roughly 80% of the country's solar cell installations. The feed-in-tariff program is financed by all electricity users and costs less than $5 a month per household. It has also created more than 370,000 new renewable energy jobs. In addition, the German government and private investors have subsidized research on technological improvements in solar and wind power and backup energy storage systems that can further lower costs. However, political opposition by Germany's coal industry and some electrical utility companies and the need for costly backup power may slow the country's shift to greater dependence on solar and wind power.

CHECKPOINT FOR UNDERSTANDING 15.1

1. Identify several renewable energy sources that are expected to eventually replace coal and other fossil fuels.

2. What is a feed-in-tariff?

15.2 WHY IS IMPROVING ENERGY EFFICIENCY AND REDUCING ENERGY WASTE AN IMPORTANT ENERGY RESOURCE?

CONCEPT 15.2A Improvements in energy efficiency and reducing energy waste could save at least a third of the energy used in the world and up to 43% of the energy used in the United States.

CONCEPT 15.2B We have a variety of technologies for sharply increasing the energy efficiency of industrial operations, motor vehicles, appliances, and buildings.

We Waste a Lot of Energy and Money

Improving energy efficiency and conserving energy are key strategies in using energy more sustainability. **Energy efficiency** is a measure of how much useful work we can get from each unit of energy we use. Improving energy efficiency means using less energy to provide the same amount of work. No energy-using device operates at 100% efficiency; some energy is always lost as heat, as required by the second law of thermodynamics (p. 50). However, there are ways to improve energy efficiency and waste less energy by using more fuel-efficient cars, light bulbs (such as LED bulbs), appliances, computers, and industrial processes.

We can also cut energy waste by changing our behavior. **Energy conservation** means reducing or eliminating the unnecessary wasting of energy. If you ride your bicycle to school or work rather than driving a car, you are practicing energy conservation. Another way to conserve energy is to turn off lights and electronic devices when you are done using them.

You may be surprised to learn that roughly 84% of all commercial energy used in the United States is wasted (Figure 15.2). About 41% of this energy unavoidably ends up as low-quality waste heat in the environment because of the degradation of energy quality imposed by the second law of thermodynamics (see Chapter 2, p. 50). The other 43% is wasted unnecessarily, mostly due to the inefficiency of industrial motors, motor vehicles, power plants, light bulbs, and numerous other devices (**Concept 15.2A**).

43% of energy used in the United States that is unnecessarily wasted

Another reason for our costly and wasteful use of energy is that many people live and work in poorly

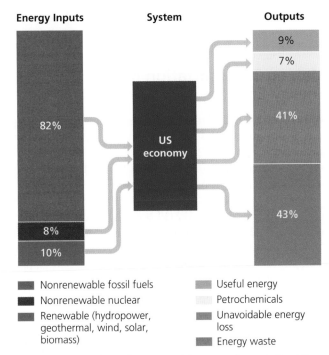

FIGURE 15.2 Flow of commercial energy through the US economy. Only 16% of the country's high-quality energy ends up performing useful tasks. **Critical thinking:** What are two examples of unnecessary energy waste?

(Compiled by the authors using data from US Department of Energy.)

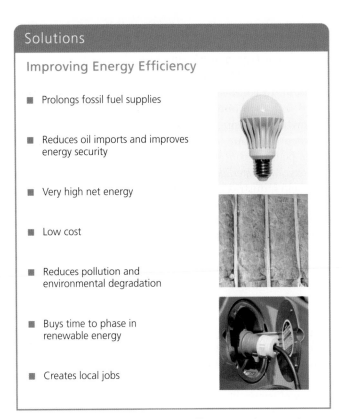

FIGURE 15.3 Improving energy efficiency and conserving energy can have important benefits. **Critical thinking:** Which two of these benefits do you think are the most important? Why?

insulated, leaky houses and buildings that require excessive heating during cold weather and excessive cooling during hot weather (see Figure 15.1, left). In addition, many Americans (and people in other parts of the world) live in ever-expanding suburban areas around large cities where they must depend on cars for getting around. Three of every four Americans commute to work, mostly alone in energy-inefficient vehicles, and only 5% rely on more energy-efficient mass transit. In addition, many people waste energy and money by buying inefficient appliances.

Much of this loss of energy and money is due to heavy reliance on two widely used energy-inefficient technologies:

- Huge *data centers*, filled with racks of electronic servers that process all online information and provide cloud-based data storage for users. Most data centers run 24 hours a day at their maximum capacities, regardless of the demand. They also require large amounts of energy for cooling to keep the servers from overheating.

- The *internal combustion engine*, which propels most motor vehicles, wastes about 75% of the high-quality energy in its gasoline fuel. Thus, only about 25% of the money people spend on gasoline provides them with transportation.

Improvements in energy efficiency and conservation have numerous economic, health, and environmental benefits (Figure 15.3). To most energy analysts, *they are the*

quickest, cleanest, and usually the cheapest ways to provide more energy, reduce pollution and environmental degradation, and slow climate change and ocean acidification.

Improving Energy Efficiency in Industries and Utilities

The industrial sector includes all facilities and equipment used to produce, process, or assemble goods. Industries that use the most energy are those that produce petroleum, chemicals, cement, steel, aluminum, and paper and wood products.

One way for industries and utility companies to save energy is to use **cogeneration** to produce two useful forms of energy—electricity and heat—from the same fuel source. For example, the steam used for generating electricity in a power or industrial plant can be captured and used to heat the plant or other nearby buildings, rather than being released into the environment as waste heat. The energy efficiency of these systems is 60–80%, compared to 25–35% for coal-fired and nuclear power plants. Denmark leads the world by using cogeneration to produce 53% of its electricity compared to 12% in the United States.

Inefficient motors account for 60% of the electricity used in US industry. Industries can save energy and money by using more energy-efficient variable-speed electric motors that run at the minimum speed needed for each job. In contrast, standard electric motors run at full speed with their output throttled to match the task. This is somewhat like using one foot to push the gas pedal to the floorboard of your car and putting your other foot on the brake pedal to control its speed.

Recycling materials such as steel and other metals can also help industries save energy and money. For example, producing steel from recycled scrap iron uses 75% less high-quality energy than does producing steel from virgin iron ore and emits 40% less CO_2.

Industries can also save energy by using energy-efficient LED lighting; installing smart meters to monitor energy use; and shutting off computers, printers, and nonessential lights when they are not needed.

A growing number of major corporations are saving money by improving energy efficiency. For example, between 1990 and 2014, Dow Chemical Company, [GOOD NEWS] which operates 165 manufacturing plants in 37 countries, saved $27 billion in a comprehensive program to improve energy efficiency. Ford Motor Company saves $1 million a year by turning off unused computers.

Building an Interactive and More Energy-Efficient Electrical Grid

In the United States, electricity is delivered to consumers through an electrical grid, consisting of a network of transmission and distribution lines. The US electrical grid system, designed more than 100 years ago, is inefficient and outdated. According to former US energy secretary Bill Richardson, "We're a major superpower with a third-world electrical grid system."

Work is underway to convert and expand the outdated US electrical grid system into a new interactive grid that would be a digitally controlled, ultra-high-voltage (UHV), and high-capacity system with superefficient transmission lines. It will be less vulnerable to power outages, because it will quickly adjust for a major power loss in one area by automatically rerouting available electricity from other parts of the country. A national network of wind farms and solar cell power plants connected to a smart grid would make the sun and wind reliable sources of electricity around the clock. Smart electricity meters will allow consumers to save money by reducing electricity use during times when rates are high.

According to the US Department of Energy (DOE), building such a grid would cost the United States up to $800 billion over the next 20 years. However, it would save the US economy $2 trillion during that period. So far, Congress has not authorized significant funding for this vital component of the country's energy and economic future.

Making Transportation More Energy-Efficient

In 1975, the US Congress established Corporate Average Fuel Economy (CAFE) standards to improve the average fuel economy of new cars and light trucks, vans, and sport utility vehicles (SUVs) in the United States. Between 1973 and 2013, these standards increased the average fuel economy for such vehicles in the United States from 5 kilometers per liter, or *kpl* (11.9 miles per gallon, or *mpg*) to 10.6 kpl (24.9 mpg). The government goal is for such vehicles to get 23.3 kpl (54.5 mpg) by 2025. Existing fuel economy standards for new vehicles in Europe, Japan, China, and Canada are much higher than this proposed 2025 US standard. However, since 2017 automakers have been pressuring the EPA and the US Congress to decrease these fuel efficiency standards. The net benefits to society from meeting these standards, as estimated by the EPA, would be $100 billion from reduced air pollution, lower carbon dioxide emissions, and reduced oil imports.

Energy experts project that by 2040, all new cars and light trucks sold in the United States could get more than 43 kpl (100 mpg) using available technology. Achieving this level of fuel efficiency is an important way to reduce energy waste, cut air pollution, and slow climate change and ocean acidification.

Governments may be pushing for more fuel-efficient vehicles, but consumers do not always buy such vehicles, especially when gasoline prices fall. Instead many people buy fuel-inefficient trucks and and SUVs, which are more profitable for automakers. Most consumers are unaware that gasoline costs them much more than the price they pay at the pump. A number of *hidden gasoline costs* not included in the price of gasoline include government subsidies and tax breaks for oil companies, car manufacturers, and road builders; defense spending to secure access to Middle East oil supplies; costs of pollution control and cleanup; and higher medical bills and health insurance premiums resulting from illnesses caused by air and water pollution from the production and use of motor vehicles. The International Center for Technology Assessment estimated that the hidden costs of gasoline for US consumers amount to $3.18 per liter ($12.00 per gallon).

One way to include more of these hidden costs in the market price is through higher gasoline taxes. This would implement the full-cost pricing **principle of sustainability**. However, higher gas taxes are politically unpopular in the United States. Some analysts call for increasing US gasoline taxes and reducing payroll and income taxes to balance such increases, thereby relieving consumers of any additional financial burden. Another way for governments to encourage higher energy efficiency in transportation is to give consumers significant tax breaks or other economic incentives to encourage them to buy more fuel-efficient vehicles.

Other ways to save energy and money in transportation include building or expanding mass transit systems within cities, constructing high-speed rail lines between cities (as is done in Japan, much of Europe, and China), and carrying more freight by rail and barge instead of in heavy trucks. Another approach is to encourage bicycle use by building bike lanes along highways and city streets.

Switching to Energy-Efficient Vehicles

Energy-efficient vehicles are available. One such vehicle is the gasoline–electric *hybrid car* (Figure 15.4, left). These cars have a small gasoline-powered engine and a battery-powered electric motor used to provide the energy needed for acceleration and hill climbing. The most efficient current models of these cars get a combined city/highway mileage of up to 23 kpl (55 mpg) and emit about 65% less CO_2 per kilometer driven than do comparable conventional cars.

Another option is the *plug-in hybrid electric vehicle* (Figure 15.4, right). These cars can travel 48–97 kilometers (30–60 miles) on electricity alone. Then a small gasoline-powered motor kicks in, recharges the battery, and extends the driving range to 600 kilometers (370 miles) or more. The battery can be plugged into a conventional 110-volt outlet and fully charged in 6 to 8 hours or a much shorter time using a 220-volt outlet. Another option is an all-electric vehicle that runs on a battery only.

According to a DOE study, replacing most of the current US vehicle fleet with plug-in hybrid vehicles over three decades would cut US oil consumption by 70–90%, eliminate the need for costly oil imports, save consumers money, and reduce CO_2 emissions by 27%. Recharging the batteries in these cars mostly by electricity generated by clean renewable energy resources such as wind turbines, solar cells, or hydroelectric power would cut US emissions of CO_2 80–90%. This would slow climate change and ocean acidification and save thousands of lives by reducing air pollution from motor vehicles and coal-burning power plants.

The problem for the average consumer is that the prices of hybrid, plug-in hybrid, and all-electric cars are high because of the high cost of their batteries, which have to be replaced every few years. Thus, the key to greatly increasing the use of hybrid, plug-in hybrid, and all-electric motor vehicles is to ramp up research and development of suitable batteries (Science Focus 15.1). Another important factor will be to build a network of recharging stations throughout the country. If the U.S. Congress reduces fuel efficiency standards, motor vehicle producers may scale back their introduction of electric cars, which help them meet higher fuel-efficiency standards. **GREEN CAREER: Plug-in hybrid and all-electric car technology**

Another potential alternative fuel resource is the **hydrogen fuel cell,** which could be used to power electric vehicles. This device uses hydrogen gas (H_2) as a fuel to produce electricity when it reacts with oxygen gas (O_2) in the atmosphere and emits harmless water vapor into the atmosphere. A fuel cell is more efficient than an internal combustion engine, has no moving parts, and requires little maintenance. Their H_2 fuel is usually produced by passing electricity through water or produced from methane stored in a vehicle. Two major problems with fuel cells

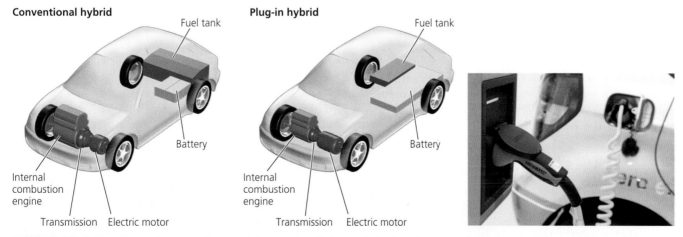

FIGURE 15.4 Solutions: A conventional gasoline–electric hybrid vehicle (left) is powered mostly by a small internal combustion engine with an assist from a strong battery. A plug-in hybrid electric vehicle (right) has a smaller internal combustion engine with a second and more powerful battery that can be plugged into a 110-volt or 220-volt outlet and recharged (see photo). An all-electric vehicle (not shown) runs completely on a rechargeable battery. *Question:* Would you buy one of these vehicles? Explain.

Photo: Gyuszko/Dreamstime.com

The Search for Better Batteries

The major obstacle standing in the way of wider use of plug-in hybrid-electric and all-electric vehicles is the need for an affordable, small, lightweight, and easily rechargeable car battery that can store enough energy for long-distance trips.

Lithium-ion batteries are light (because lithium is the lightest solid chemical element) and can pack a lot of energy into a small volume. Many of them are hooked together and used to power hybrid, plug-in hybrid, and all-electric motor vehicles. However, they are expensive, take a long time to recharge, lose their charge even when they are idle, must be replaced every few years, and can catch fire. Lithium-ion batteries are expensive but prices dropped by 50% between 2010 and 2015.

Researchers at the Massachusetts Institute of Technology (MIT) have developed a new type of lithium-ion battery using nanotechnology (Science Focus 11.1, p. 323). It is less expensive and can be charged 40 times faster. In 2014, researchers Joseph DeSimone and Nitash Balsara created a prototype of a nonflammable lithium-ion battery.

Scientists have also developed *supercapacitors*, which are small mechanical batteries consisting of two metal surfaces separated by an electric insulator. They quickly store and release large amounts of electrical energy, thus providing the power needed for quick acceleration. They can be recharged in minutes, can hold a charge much longer than conventional chemical batteries, and do not have to be replaced as frequently as conventional batteries.

If any one or a combination of these or other new battery technologies can be mass-produced at an affordable cost, plug-in hybrid and all-electric vehicles could take over the car and truck market within a few decades, which would greatly reduce air pollution, climate-changing CO_2 emissions, and ocean acidification. **GREEN CAREER: Battery engineer**

CRITICAL THINKING

How might your life change if one or more of the new battery technologies discussed above become a reality?

CONSIDER THIS . . .

LEARNING FROM NATURE

Blue-green algae use sunlight and an enzyme to produce hydrogen from water. Scientists are evaluating this as a way to produce hydrogen fuel for cars and for home heating without the use of costly high temperature processes or electricity to produce this fuel. If successful, this would sharply reduce emissions of CO_2 and other air pollutants.

are that they are expensive and H_2 has a negative net energy, which means that it takes more energy to produce it than it can provide, as discussed later in this chapter.

Reducing the weight of a vehicle is another way to improve fuel efficiency. Car bodies can be made of *ultralight* and *ultrastrong* composite materials such as fiberglass, carbon fiber, hemp fiber, and graphene (Case Study, p. 321). They are also safer in a crash than cars with conventional bodies. The current cost of making such car bodies is high, but technological innovations and mass production would likely bring these costs down.

Energy conservation can also play a role. Since cars are the biggest energy user for most Americans, shifting to a more fuel-efficient car that gets at least 17 kpl (40 mpg) is one of the best ways to save money and reduce one's harmful environmental impact.

Designing Buildings That Save Energy and Money

Green architecture can help us make a transition to more energy-efficient, resource-efficient, and money-saving buildings over the next few decades. Green architecture makes use of technology such as natural lighting, direct solar heating, insulated windows, and energy-efficient appliances and lighting. Other features include using recycled building materials from deconstructed buildings and toxic-free materials. It often makes use of solar hot water heaters, electricity from solar cells, and windows that darken automatically to deflect heat from the sun.

Some homes and urban buildings also have *living roofs*, or *green roofs*, covered with specially formulated soil and selected vegetation (Figure 15.5). Green roofs can reduce the costs of cooling and heating a building by absorbing heat from the summer sun, insulating the structure, and retaining heat in the winter. **GREEN CAREER: Sustainable environmental design and architecture**

A key goal of many green buildings is to produce as much energy as they use each year–a concept known as net zero energy. Other goals are net zero water, and net zero carbon.

Superinsulation is important in energy-efficient building design. A house can be so heavily insulated and airtight that heat from direct sunlight, appliances, and human bodies

FIGURE 15.5 Green roof on Chicago's City Hall.

can warm a superinsulated house with little or no need for a backup heating system, even in extremely cold climates. Superinsulated houses in Sweden use 90% less energy for heating and cooling than do typical American homes of the same size.

The World Green Building Council and the US Green Building Council's Leadership in Energy and Environmental Design (LEED) have developed standards for certifying that a building meets certain energy efficiency and environmental standards. **GREEN CAREERS: Sustainable environmental design and architecture**

CONSIDER THIS . . .

THINKING ABOUT Energy-Efficient Building Design

What are three ways in which the building in which you live or work could have been designed to cut its waste of energy and money?

Saving Energy and Money in Existing Buildings

Here are ways to reduce energy use in existing buildings and to cut energy and save money on electricity and heating and cooling bills (see **Core Case Study**):

- *Get a home energy audit to detect air leaks.*
- *Insulate the building and plug leaks* (Figure 15.1).
- *Use energy-efficient windows.*
- *Seal leaky heating and cooling ducts in attics and unheated basements.*
- *Heat interior spaces more efficiently.* In order, the most energy-efficient ways to heat indoor space are superinsulation (including plugging leaks); a geothermal heat pump that transfers heat stored from underground into a home; passive solar heating; a high-efficiency, conventional heat pump (in warm climates only); and a high-efficiency natural gas furnace.
- *Heat water more efficiently.* One option is a roof-mounted solar hot water heater. Another option is a *tankless instant water heater*. It uses natural gas or liquefied petroleum gas (but not an electric heater, which is inefficient) to deliver hot water only when it is needed rather than keeping water in a large tank hot all the time.
- *Use energy-efficient appliances.* A refrigerator with its freezer in a drawer on the bottom uses about half as much energy as one with the freezer on the top or on the side, which allows dense cold air to flow out quickly when the door is opened. Microwave ovens use 25–50% less electricity than electric stoves do

for cooking and 66% less energy than conventional ovens. Front-loading clothes washers use 55% less energy and 30% less water than top-loading models use and cut operating costs in half.

- *Use energy-efficient computers.* According to the EPA, if all computers sold in the United States met its Energy Star requirements, consumers would save $1.8 billion a year in energy costs and reduce greenhouse gas emissions by an amount equal to that of taking about 2 million cars off the road.

- *Use energy-efficient lighting.* The DOE estimates that by switching to LED bulbs over the next 20 years, US consumers could save money and reduce the demand for electricity by an amount equal to the output of 40 new power plants. In recent years, the cost of LED bulbs has fallen by 90%. They also save money because they last 25 times longer than traditional incandescent bulbs and 2.5 times longer than compact fluorescent bulbs.

- *Stop using the standby mode.* Consumers can reduce their energy use and their monthly power bills by plugging their standby electronic devices into smart power strips that cut off power to a device when it detects that the device has been turned off.

Figure 15.6 lists ways in which you can cut your energy use and save money in your home.

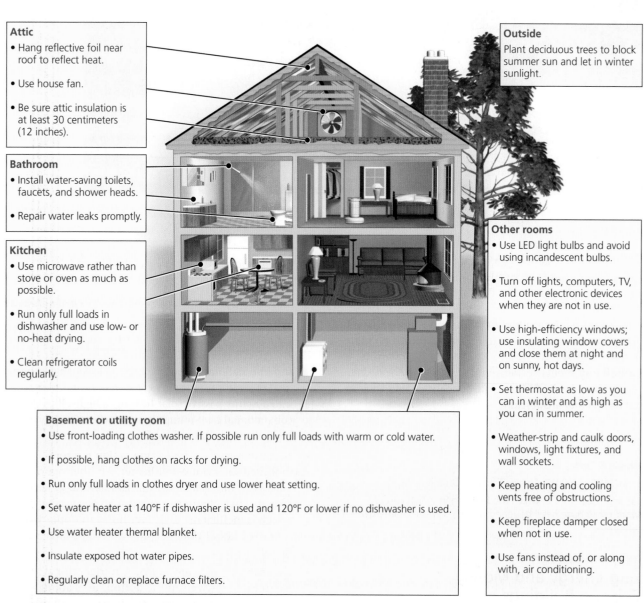

Attic
- Hang reflective foil near roof to reflect heat.
- Use house fan.
- Be sure attic insulation is at least 30 centimeters (12 inches).

Bathroom
- Install water-saving toilets, faucets, and shower heads.
- Repair water leaks promptly.

Kitchen
- Use microwave rather than stove or oven as much as possible.
- Run only full loads in dishwasher and use low- or no-heat drying.
- Clean refrigerator coils regularly.

Outside
Plant deciduous trees to block summer sun and let in winter sunlight.

Other rooms
- Use LED light bulbs and avoid using incandescent bulbs.
- Turn off lights, computers, TV, and other electronic devices when they are not in use.
- Use high-efficiency windows; use insulating window covers and close them at night and on sunny, hot days.
- Set thermostat as low as you can in winter and as high as you can in summer.
- Weather-strip and caulk doors, windows, light fixtures, and wall sockets.
- Keep heating and cooling vents free of obstructions.
- Keep fireplace damper closed when not in use.
- Use fans instead of, or along with, air conditioning.

Basement or utility room
- Use front-loading clothes washer. If possible run only full loads with warm or cold water.
- If possible, hang clothes on racks for drying.
- Run only full loads in clothes dryer and use lower heat setting.
- Set water heater at 140°F if dishwasher is used and 120°F or lower if no dishwasher is used.
- Use water heater thermal blanket.
- Insulate exposed hot water pipes.
- Regularly clean or replace furnace filters.

FIGURE 15.6 Individuals matter: You can save energy and money where you live and reduce your harmful environmental impact. ***Critical thinking:*** Which of these things do you already do? Which additional ones might you do?

Being a Green Consumer

For any new energy source or energy-saving technology to be accepted by the public, it must be economically worthwhile. For example, when buying a new washing machine, front-loading washers tend to save more electricity and use less water than conventional machines. They cost significantly more than top-loading machines, and the price upfront for a front-loading machine may put off consumers if they don't realize how much they would save in the long run by investing in the more environmentally friendly washer.

The amount saved in both energy and water costs can be determined by doing a cost-benefit analysis. By figuring out how much money is saved over a given amount of time and applying that toward the difference in price for the more expensive model, a consumer can calculate how long it will take to recoup their investment.

FRQ Application

A family is shopping for a new washing machine. They find a top-loading washer that costs $500. It costs $26 per year to run when using an electric water heater and uses 45 gallons of water per load. They compare it to a front-loading washer that costs $750 but only costs $11 per year to operate and only uses 20 gallons of water per load.

The family does six loads of laundry per week, two in cold water, two in warm water, and two in hot water. It takes 566 BTU to heat 1 gallon of water in their electric hot-water tank. 3413 BTU is equal to one kWh. Electricity costs $0.11 per kWh. Their municipal water rate is $1.50 per 1000 gallons, and municipal sewer rate is $5.00 per 1000 gallons.

Calculate how long (to the nearest year) it will take for the family to recoup their cost when purchasing the front-loading machine. **Determine** their total savings if they assume the new machine will have an operating lifetime of 10 years.

The difference in the total gallons of water consumed in 1 year is

$$\frac{6\ \text{loads}}{\text{week}} \times \frac{25\ \text{gallons}}{\text{load}} \times \frac{52\ \text{weeks}}{\text{year}} = \frac{7{,}800\ \text{gallons}}{\text{year}}$$

Assuming that the two loads of warm-water washing each week are a mix of half hot and half cold water, then the water consumption overall for the six loads (two hot, two cold, two warm) is half hot and half cold. So the amount of hot water saved is

$$\frac{7{,}800\ \text{gallons}}{\text{year}} \div 2 = \frac{3{,}900\ \text{gallons}}{\text{year}}$$

The electricity cost to heat a gallon of water is

$$\frac{\$0.11}{1\ \text{kWh}} \times \frac{1\ \text{kWh}}{3413\ \text{BTU}} \times \frac{566\ \text{BTU}}{\text{gallon}} = \$0.018\ \text{per gallon}$$

The annual electricity cost savings for the hot water is

$$\frac{3{,}900\ \text{gallons}}{\text{year}} \times \frac{\$0.018}{\text{gallon}} = \$70.20$$

The annual cost savings to operate the front-loading machine is $26 − $11 = $15.

The annual cost savings for municipal water and sewer is

$$\frac{7{,}800\ \text{gallons}}{\text{year}} \times \frac{(\$1.50 + \$5.00)}{1000\ \text{gallon}} = \$50.70$$

The total savings per year to own the front-loader instead of the top-loader is

$70.20 + $15 + $50.70 = $135.90

The difference in cost between the two machines is $250.00, so it would take

$250.00 ÷ $135.90 per year ≈ 2 years (to the nearest year) to recoup the cost

The family's total savings over the 10-year expected life of the washing machine would be

($135.90 × 10) − $250 = $1359 − $250 = $1,109

Note that this total savings has not accounted for any increase in electric, water, and sewer rates over the next 10 years. All of those expenses would likely increase significantly over time, resulting in even greater savings in owning the front-loading washing machine.

Why Are We Wasting So Much Energy and Money?

Considering its impressive array of economic and environmental benefits (Figure 15.3), why is there so little emphasis on improving energy efficiency and conserving energy? One reason is that energy resources such as fossil fuels and nuclear power are artificially cheap. This is primarily because of the government subsidies and tax breaks they receive and because their market prices do not include the harmful environmental and health costs of producing and using them. This distortion of the energy marketplace violates the full-cost pricing **principle of sustainability**. Another reason is that there are too few economic incentives for consumers and businesses to invest in improving energy efficiency and reducing energy waste.

Some critics say an emphasis on improving energy efficiency does not work because of the *rebound effect* in which some people tend to use more energy when they buy energy-efficient devices. For example, some people who buy a more efficient car tend to drive more, which offsets some of their energy and money savings and their reduced environmental impact.

Instead of downplaying efforts to improve energy efficiency, energy experts call for a major program to educate people about the rebound effect and its waste of money and long-lasting harmful health and environmental effects.

Relying More on Renewable Energy

The lesson from one of nature's three **scientific principles of sustainability** is to *rely mostly on solar energy*. Most forms of renewable energy can be traced to the sun, because wind, flowing water, and biomass would not exist, were it not for solar energy. Another form of renewable energy is geothermal energy, or heat from the earth's interior. All of these sources of renewable energy are constantly replenished at no cost to us.

Studies show that with increased and consistent government backing in the form of research and development funds and subsidies and tax breaks, renewable energy could provide 20% of the world's electricity by 2025 and 50% by 2050. In 2012, the National Renewable Energy Laboratory (NREL) projected that, with a crash program, the United States could get 50% of its electricity from renewable energy sources by 2050.

According to the International Energy Agency, solar and wind are the world's fastest-growing energy resources and nuclear energy is the slowest. China has the world's largest installed capacity for electricity from wind power and solar cells and plans to become the largest user and seller of wind turbines and solar cells–projected to be two of the world's fastest growing businesses over the next few decades. China's goal is to greatly expand its production of electricity from renewable wind, sun, and flowing water (hydropower) to help reduce its use of coal and the resulting outdoor air pollution that kills about 1.2 million of its citizens each year.

If renewable energy is so great, why does it provide only 8% of the world's energy (Figure 14.2, left, p. 421) and 5% of the energy used in the United States (Figure 14.2, right p. 421)? There are several reasons. *First*, there are the myths that solar and wind energy are too diffuse, too intermittent and unreliable, and too expensive to use on a large scale. Experience has shown that these perceptions are out of date. *Second*, since 1950, government tax breaks, subsidies, and funding for research and development of renewable energy resources have been much lower than those for fossil fuels and nuclear power.

Third, while government subsidies and tax breaks for renewable have been increasing, Congress must renew them every few years. In contrast, billions of dollars of subsidies and tax breaks for fossil fuels and nuclear power have essentially been guaranteed for many decades due in large part to political pressure from these industries.

Fourth, prices for nonrenewable energy from fossil fuels and nuclear power do not include most of the harmful environmental and human health costs of producing and using them. This helps to shield them from free-market competition with renewable sources of energy.

Fifth, history shows that it typically takes 50 to 60 years to make a shift in energy resources (**Core Case Study**). Renewable wind and solar energy are the world's fastest growing sources of energy, but it will likely take decades for them to supply 25% or more of the world's electricity.

CHECKPOINT FOR UNDERSTANDING 15.2

1. Identify three widely used technologies that waste large amounts of energy.

2. What is cogeneration?

3. What are CAFE standards?

4. Identify some of the hidden costs of using gasoline-fueled automobiles.

5. Identify the environmental advantages and disadvantages of hybrid and plug-in hybrid vehicles.

6. Identify several strategies for reducing energy consumption in existing homes.

15.3 WHAT ARE THE ADVANTAGES AND DISADVANTAGES OF USING SOLAR ENERGY?

CONCEPT 15.3 Passive and active solar heating systems can heat water and buildings effectively, and the cost of using sunlight to produce electricity is falling rapidly.

Heating Buildings and Water with Solar Energy

A building that has enough access to sunlight can get all or most of its heat through a **passive solar heating system** (Figure 15.7, left, and Figure 15.8). Such a system absorbs and stores heat from the sun directly within a well-insulated, airtight structure. Water tanks and walls and floors made of concrete, adobe, brick, or stone can store much of the collected solar energy as heat that is slowly released.

An **active solar heating system** (Figure 15.7, right) captures energy from the sun by pumping a heat-absorbing fluid such as water or an antifreeze solution through special collectors, usually mounted on a roof or on special racks that face the sun. Some of the collected heat can be used directly. The rest can be stored in a large insulated container filled with gravel, water, clay, or a heat-absorbing chemical, and used as needed.

Rooftop active solar collectors are used to heat water in many homes and apartment buildings. One in ten houses and apartment buildings in China uses the sun to provide hot water with systems that cost the equivalent of $200. Once the initial cost is paid, the hot water is heated for free. In Spain and Israel, builders are required to put rooftop solar water heaters on all new buildings. According to the UN Development Programme, solar water heaters could be used to provide half of the world's hot water.

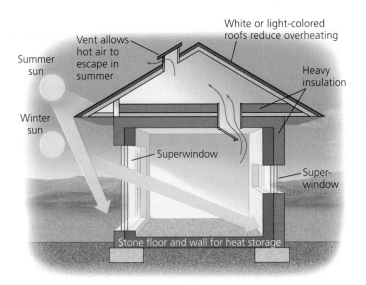

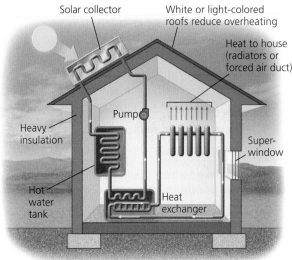

PASSIVE

ACTIVE

FIGURE 15.7 Solutions: Passive (left) and active (right) solar home heating systems.

Photos: Alan Ford/National Renewable Energy Laboratory

FIGURE 15.8 This passive solar home (right) in Golden, Colorado, collects and stores incoming solar energy to provide much of its heat in a climate with cold winters. Notice the solar hot water heating panels in the yard. Some passive solar houses have sunrooms (see inset photo) to help collect incoming solar energy.

Passive and active solar systems can heat new homes in areas with adequate sunlight, as long as trees or other buildings do not block solar access. Figure 15.9 lists the major advantages and disadvantages of using passive or active solar heating systems for heating buildings.

Cooling Buildings Naturally

Direct solar energy works against us when we want to keep a building cool, but we can use indirect solar energy (mainly wind) to help cool buildings. People can open windows to take advantage of breezes and use fans to keep the air moving. When there is no breeze, superinsulation and high-efficiency windows keep hot air outside.

Other ways to keep buildings cool include blocking the sun with shade trees, broad overhanging eaves, window awnings, or shades. A light-colored roof can reflect up to 90% of the sun's heat (compared to only 10–15% for a dark-colored roof), while a green roof can absorb extra heat. Geothermal heat pumps can pump cool air from underground into a building during summer to cool it as well.

CONSIDER THIS . . .

LEARNING FROM NATURE

Some species of African termites stay cool in a hot climate by building giant mounds that allow air to circulate through them. Engineers have used this design lesson from nature to cool buildings naturally, reduce energy use, and save money.

Concentrating Sunlight to Produce High-Temperature Heat and Electricity

One of the problems with direct solar energy is that it is dispersed. **Solar thermal systems,** also known as *concentrated solar power (CSP)*, collect and concentrate solar energy to boil water and produce steam for generating electricity. These systems can be used in deserts and other open areas with ample sunlight.

One such system uses rows of curved mirrors, called parabolic troughs, to collect and concentrate sunlight. Each trough focuses incoming sunlight on a pipe that runs through its center and is filled with synthetic oil (Figure 15.10). The oil heats to temperatures as high as 400°C (750°F). That heat is used to boil water and produce steam, which in turn powers a turbine that drives a generator to produce electricity.

Another solar thermal system (Figure 15.11) uses an array of computer-controlled mirrors to track the sun and focus its energy on a central power tower to provide enough heat to boil water that is used to produce electricity. The heat produced by either of these systems can also be used to melt a certain kind of salt stored in a large insulated container. The heat stored in this molten salt system can then be released as needed to produce electricity at night or on cloudy days.

Some analysts see solar thermal power as a growing and important source of the world's electricity. However, because

Trade-Offs

Passive or Active Solar Heating

Advantages	Disadvantages
Medium net energy	Need access to sun 60% of time during daylight
Very low emissions of CO_2 and other air pollutants	Sun can be blocked by trees and other structures
Very low land disturbance	High installation and maintenance costs for active systems
Moderate cost (passive)	Need backup system for cloudy days

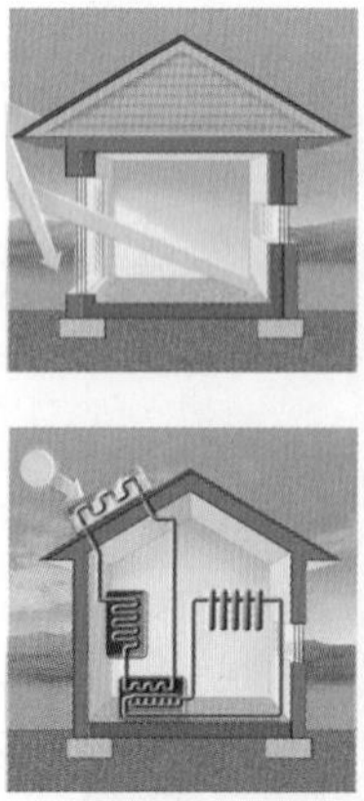

FIGURE 15.9 Heating a house with passive or active solar energy system has advantages and disadvantages (**Concept 15.3**). ***Critical thinking:*** Which single advantage and which single disadvantage do you think are the most important? Why? Do you think that the advantages of using these technologies outweigh their disadvantages?

Credit: Kramer Junction Company /Courtesy of National Renewable Energy Laboratory (NREL)

FIGURE 15.10 *Solar thermal power:* This solar power plant in California's Mojave Desert uses curved (parabolic) solar collectors to concentrate solar energy to provide enough heat to boil water and produce steam for generating electricity.

solar thermal systems have a low net energy, they need large government subsidies or tax breaks to be competitive in the marketplace. These systems also require large volumes of cooling water for condensing the steam back to water and for washing the surfaces of the mirrors and parabolic troughs. Figure 15.12 summarizes the major advantages and disadvantages of concentrating solar energy to produce high-temperature heat and electricity.

Solar energy can also be concentrated on a smaller scale. In some sunny areas, people use inexpensive *solar cookers* to focus and concentrate sunlight for boiling and sterilizing water (Figure 15.13, left) and cooking food (Figure 15.13, right). Inventor Jon Boehner has developed a $6 solar cooker made from a cardboard box. Solar cookers can replace wood and charcoal fires and reduce indoor air pollution, a major killer of many of the world's poor people. They also reduce deforestation by decreasing the need for firewood and charcoal made from firewood.

FIGURE 15.11 *Solar thermal power:* In this system in California an array of mirrors tracks the sun and focuses reflected sunlight on a central receiver to boil the water for producing electricity.

Using Solar Cells to Produce Electricity

In 1931, Thomas Edison (inventor of the electric light bulb) told Henry Ford, "I'd put my money on the sun and solar energy. … I hope we don't have to wait until oil and coal run out before we tackle that." Edison's dream is now a reality.

We can convert solar energy directly into electrical energy using **photovoltaic (PV) cells,** commonly called **solar cells.** Most solar cells are thin transparent wafers of purified silicon (Si) or polycrystalline silicon with trace amounts of metals that allow them to conduct electricity. Between 2001 and 2015, the cost per watt of electricity produced by solar cells fell by 83% and the cost is expected to keep falling because the lower prices are driven by advances in technology.

Solar cells have no moving parts and they operate safely and quietly with no emissions of greenhouse gases and other air pollutants. A typical solar cell has a thickness ranging from less than that of a human hair to that of a sheet of paper. When sunlight strikes solar cells, they produce electricity (a flow of electrons). Many cells wired together in a panel and many panels can be connected to produce electricity for a house or a large solar power plant (Figure 15.14). Such systems can be connected to existing electrical grids or to batteries that store the electrical energy until it is needed.

People can mount arrays of solar cells on rooftops and incorporate them into almost any type of roofing material.

Trade-Offs

Solar Thermal Systems

Advantages	Disadvantages
High potential for growth	Low net energy and high costs
No direct emissions of CO_2 and other air pollutants	Needs backup or storage system on cloudy days
Lower costs with natural gas turbine backup	Requires high water use
Source of new jobs	Can disrupt desert ecosystems

FIGURE 15.12 Using solar energy to generate high-temperature heat and electricity has advantages and disadvantages (**Concept 15.3**). *Critical thinking:* Which single advantage and which single disadvantage do you think are the most important? Why? Do you think that the advantages of using these technologies outweigh their disadvantages?

FIGURE 15.13 Solutions: Solar cooker (left) in Costa Rica and simple solar oven (right).

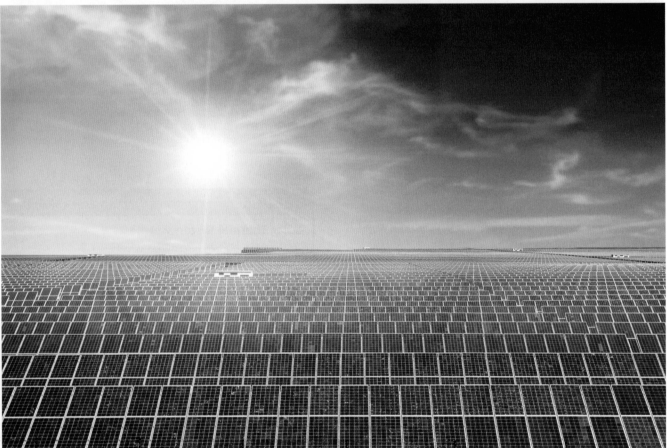

FIGURE 15.14 *Solar cell power plant:* Huge arrays of solar cells can be connected to produce electricity.

Nanotechnology and other emerging technologies will likely allow the manufacturing of solar cells in paper-thin, rigid or flexible sheets that can be printed like newspapers and attached to or embedded in other surfaces such as outdoor walls, windows, drapes, and clothing. **GREEN CAREER: Solar-cell technology**

Solar cells have great potential for providing electricity in less-developed countries. Worldwide, 1.3 billion people,

most of them in rural villages in such countries, do not have access to electricity. A growing number of these individuals and villages are using rooftop solar panels (Figure 15.15) to power energy-efficient LED lamps, which can replace costly and inefficient kerosene lamps that pollute indoor air.

Solar cells emit no greenhouse gases, although they are not a carbon-free option, because fossil fuels are used to produce and transport the panels. However, the emissions per unit of electricity produced are much smaller than those generated by using fossil fuels and the nuclear power fuel cycle to produce electricity. Conventional solar cells also contain toxic materials that must be recovered when the cells wear out after 20–25 years of use, or when they are replaced by new systems.

One problem with current solar cells is their low energy efficiency. They typically convert only 20% of the incoming solar energy into electricity. However, scientists and engineers are rapidly improving the efficiency of solar cells. Researchers at Germany's Fraunhofer Institute for Solar Energy Systems developed a solar cell with an efficiency of 45%—compared to an efficiency of 35% for fossil fuel and nuclear electric power plants. They are working to scale up this prototype cell for commercial use within a few years. Figure 15.16 lists the major advantages and disadvantages of using solar cells to produce electricity (**Concept 15.3**).

Because of government subsidies and tax breaks for solar cell producers and users and rapidly declining prices, solar cells have become the world's fastest growing way to produce electricity (Figure 15.17). Between 2001 and 2015, the cost per watt of electricity produced by solar cells fell by 83%, and this cost is expected to keep falling.

Some businesses and homeowners are spreading the cost of rooftop solar power systems over decades by

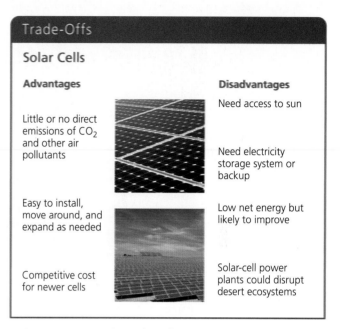

Trade-Offs

Solar Cells

Advantages	Disadvantages
Little or no direct emissions of CO_2 and other air pollutants	Need access to sun
Easy to install, move around, and expand as needed	Need electricity storage system or backup
	Low net energy but likely to improve
Competitive cost for newer cells	Solar-cell power plants could disrupt desert ecosystems

FIGURE 15.16 Using solar cells to produce electricity has advantages and disadvantages (**Concept 15.3**). *Critical thinking:* Which single advantage and which single disadvantage do you think are the most important? Why? Do you think that the advantages of using this technology outweigh its disadvantages? Why?

Top: © Martin D. Vonka/Shutterstock.com. Bottom: © pedrosala/Shutterstock.com.

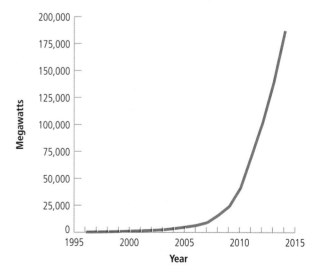

FIGURE 15.17 Global installed electricity capacity of solar cells, 1996–2014. *Data analysis:* By what factor and percent did the capacity of installed solar cell increase between 1996 and 2015?

(Compiled by the authors using data from US Energy Information Administration, International Energy Agency, Worldwatch Institute, and Earth Policy Institute.)

Jim Welch/National Renewable Energy Laboratory

FIGURE 15.15 Solutions: A solar-cell panel provides electricity for lighting this hut in rural West Bengal, India. *Critical thinking:* Do you think your government should provide aid to poor countries for obtaining solar-cell systems? Explain.

Gearbox

Electrical generator

Power cable

Photo: ssuaphotos/Shutterstock.com

Wind turbine

FIGURE 15.18 Wind turbines convert the kinetic energy in wind to electricity, another form of kinetic energy (moving electrons). Wind power is an indirect form of solar energy.

including them in their mortgages. Others are leasing solar-cell systems from companies that install and maintain them.

Producing electricity from solar cells is the world's fastest growing way to produce electricity. It is expected to continue growing at a rapid rate because solar energy is unlimited and available throughout the world. It is also a technology, not a fuel such as coal or natural gas, the prices of which are controlled by available supplies. Prices for solar cell systems are likely to continue dropping because of technological advances, mass production, and decreased installation costs.

Solar cells cannot produce electricity at night, and storing energy in large batteries for use at night and on cloudy days is expensive. However, researchers at Ohio State University have developed a solar cell panel with a built-in battery that is 25% less expensive and 20% more efficient than conventional batteries. If it can be mass produced, this invention could revolutionize the use of solar energy to produce electricity.

In 2015, solar energy provided only 0.6% of US electricity. However, this new technology is growing exponentially at a rapid rate (Figure 15.17) and prices continue to drop. If pushed hard and supported with government subsidies equivalent to or greater than fossil fuel subsidies, solar energy could supply 5% of US electricity by 2020 and as much as 23% by 2050, according to projections by the National Renewable Energy Laboratory.

After 2050, solar electricity is likely to become one of the top sources of electricity for the United States and much of the world. If that happens, it will represent global application of the solar energy **principle of sustainability**.
GREEN CAREER: Solar-cell technology

CHECKPOINT FOR UNDERSTANDING 15.3

1. Explain the difference between passive and active solar heating of a home.

2. Describe several strategies for cooling buildings naturally.

3. Explain how solar thermal systems generate electricity.

4. Identify the drawbacks of solar thermal systems.

5. Identify the benefits and drawbacks of solar cells.

15.4 WHAT ARE THE ADVANTAGES AND DISADVANTAGES OF USING WIND POWER?

CONCEPT 15.4 Wind is one of the fastest growing, least expensive, and cleanest ways to produce electricity.

Using Wind to Produce Electricity

Simply put, *wind* is air in motion. Land near the earth's Equator absorbs more solar energy than does land near its Poles. This uneven heating of the earth's surface and its atmosphere, combined with the earth's rotation, causes prevailing winds to blow (Figure 5.9, p. 126). Because wind is an indirect form of solar energy, using it is a way to apply the solar energy **principle of sustainability**.

The kinetic energy from blowing winds can be captured and converted to electrical energy by devices called *wind turbines.* As a turbine's blades spin, they turn a drive shaft that connects to the blades. The drive shaft then turns an electric generator, which produces electricity (Figure 15.18, left). Groups of wind turbines called *wind farms* transmit electrical energy to electrical grids. Wind farms can operate both on land (chapter-opening photo) and at sea (Figure 15.18, right).

Today's wind turbine towers can be as tall as a 60-story building and have blades as long as 70 meters (230 feet)—the combined length of six school buses. This height allows them to tap into the strong and more constant winds found at higher altitudes on land and at sea and to produce more electricity at a lower cost. A typical large wind turbine can generate enough electricity to power more than 1,000 homes.

Harvard University researcher Xi Lu estimates that wind power has the potential to produce 40 times the world's current use for electricity. Most of world's wind farms have been built on land in parts of Europe, China, and the United States. However, the frontier for wind energy is offshore wind farms (Figure 15.18, right) because winds are generally much stronger and steadier over coastal waters than over land. When located far enough offshore, wind farms are not visible from the land. Building offshore also avoids the need for negotiations among multiple landowners over the locations of turbines and electrical transmission lines. Offshore wind farms have been built off the coasts of 10 European countries, as well as China and Japan. Bigger and more productive off-shore turbines provide increased revenue for investors by producing more electricity than smaller land-based turbines on a similar sized site.

Since 1990, wind power has been the world's second-fastest-growing source of electricity after solar cells (Figure 15.19). In 2015, the United States led the world in producing electricity from wind, followed by China and Germany.

In 2015, wind farms in more than 85 countries produced about 3.7% of the world's electricity—enough to provide electricity for more than 500 million people. Experts project that by 2050, this number could grow to 18%. Globally, wind power employs 400,000 people who produce, install and maintain wind turbines. Such job numbers will grow as wind power continues its rapid expansion (Figure 15.19).

In 2015, wind power produced 45% of Denmark's electricity and the country plans to increase this to 50% by 2020 and to 85% by 2035. By 2015, wind turbines in the United States were producing 4.7% of the country's electricity, an amount equal to that produced by 64 large nuclear power reactors. Texas leads the nation in wind energy production, followed by Iowa, California, and Oklahoma.

A study published in the *Proceedings of the US National Academy of Sciences* estimated that the United States has enough wind potential to meet 16 to 22 times its current electricity needs. The DOE estimates that wind farms at favorable sites in three states—North Dakota, Kansas, and Texas—could more than meet the electricity needs of the lower 48 states if a modern electrical grid is available to distribute the electricity. In addition, the National Renewable Energy Laboratory estimates that winds off the Atlantic and Pacific coasts and the shores of the Great Lakes could generate 9 times the electricity currently used in the lower 48 states—more than enough electricity to replace all of the country's coal-fired power plants. This explains why the United States is a wind energy superpower.

According to a 2015 study by the DOE, with the continuation of government subsidies, the United States could get 30% of its electricity from wind by 2030. This would create up to 600,000 jobs and lower energy bills. It would also reduce air pollution and slow climate change and ocean acidification by reducing the use of coal to produce electricity.

Wind is abundant, widely distributed, and inexhaustible, and wind power is mostly carbon-free and pollution-free. A wind farm can be built within 9 to 12 months and expanded as needed. And although wind farms can cover large areas of land, the turbines themselves occupy only a small portion of the land.

Many US landowners in favorable wind areas are investing in wind farms. Landowners typically receive $3,000 to $10,000 a year in royalties for each wind turbine placed on their land. The land can still be used for activities such as growing crops or grazing cattle (Figure 15.18, left, and chapter-opening photo). An acre of land in northern Iowa planted in corn can produce about $1,000 worth of ethanol car fuel. The same site used for a single wind turbine can produce $300,000 worth of electricity per year.

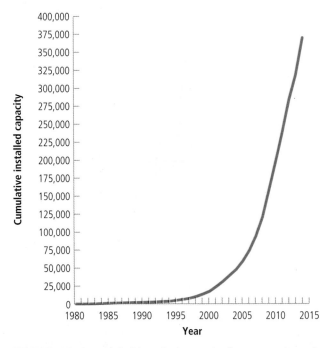

FIGURE 15.19 Global installed capacity for generation of electricity by wind energy, 1980–2014. ***Data analysis:*** In 2014, the world's installed capacity for generating electricity by wind power was about how many times more than it was in 2005?

(Compiled by the authors using data from Global Wind Energy Council, European Wind Energy Association, American Wind Energy Association, Worldwatch Institute, World Wind Energy Association, and Earth Policy Institute.)

Making Wind Turbines Safer for Birds and Bats

Wildlife ecologists and bird experts estimate that collisions with wind turbines kill as many as 234,000 birds and 600,000 bats each year in the United States. Such deaths are a legitimate concern.

However, according to studies by the Defenders of Wildlife, the US Fish and Wildlife Service, and the Smithsonian Conservation Biology Institute, wind turbines are a minor source of bird and bat deaths compared to other human-related sources and account for only about 0.003% of such deaths. Each year, domestic and feral cats kill 1.4 billion to 3.7 billion birds; collisions with windows 1 billion; cars and trucks 89 million to 340 million; high-tension wires 174 million;

and pesticides 72 million. Most of the wind turbines involved in bird and bat deaths were built years ago using outdated designs, and some were built in bird migration corridors.

Developers of new wind farms avoid bird migration corridors, as well as areas with large bat colonies. Newer turbine designs reduce bird and bat deaths considerably by using slower blade rotation speeds and by not providing places for birds to perch or nest. Researchers are also evaluating the use of ultraviolet light to deter birds and bats from turbines.

Ultrasonic devices attached to turbine blades scare bats away by emitting

high-frequency sounds that we cannot hear. Another approach is to use radar to track large incoming flocks of migrating birds and to shut down the turbines until they pass. In addition, many older wind turbines are being replaced with new designs that sharply reduce bird and bat deaths by providing no perching or nesting surfaces.

CRITICAL THINKING

What would you say to someone who tells you that we should not depend on wind power because wind turbines can kill birds and bats?

Since 1990, prices for electricity produced by wind in the United States (and other countries) have been falling sharply. They are expected to keep falling because of technological improvements in wind turbine design that increase their energy efficiency and reduce mass-production and maintenance costs. The DOE and the Worldwatch Institute estimate that, if we were to apply the **full-cost pricing principle of sustainability** by including the harmful environmental and health costs of various energy resources in comparative cost estimates, wind energy would be the least costly way to produce electricity.

Like any energy source, wind power has some drawbacks. Land areas with the greatest wind power potential are often sparsely populated and located far from cities. Thus, to take advantage of its huge potential for using wind energy, the United States will have to invest in replacing and expanding its outdated electrical grid with a modern grid system to connect with the country's wind farms.

Because winds can die down, a backup source of power such as natural gas is needed. However, a large number of wind farms in different areas connected to a smart grid could take up the slack when winds die down in any one area without the need for a backup source of energy. This could make wind power a more stable and reliable source of electricity than fossil fuel and nuclear power plants. Wind turbines can also kill birds and bats—a problem that scientists and wind power developers are working on (Science Focus 15.2).

Figure 15.20 lists the major advantages and disadvantages of using wind to produce electricity. According to many energy analysts, wind power has more benefits and fewer serious drawbacks than any other energy resource, except for reducing energy waste and increasing energy efficiency (Figure 15.3). **GREEN CAREER: Wind-energy engineering**

Trade-Offs

Wind Power

Advantages	Disadvantages
High net energy	Needs backup or storage system when winds die down unless connected in a national electrical grid
Widely available	
Low electricity cost	
	Visual pollution for some people
Little or no direct emissions of CO_2 and other air pollutants	Low-level noise bothers some people
Easy to build and expand	Can kill birds if not properly designed and located

FIGURE 15.20 Using wind to produce electricity has advantages and disadvantages (**Concept 15.4**). *Critical thinking:* Which single advantage and which single disadvantage do you think are the most important? Why? Do you think the advantages outweigh the disadvantages? Why?

Top: © TebNad/Shutterstock.com. Bottom: © Yegor Korzh/Shutterstock.com.

CHECKPOINT FOR UNDERSTANDING 15.4

1. Explain why it is advantageous to locate wind turbines over water rather than on land.

2. Identify the benefits and drawbacks of wind power.

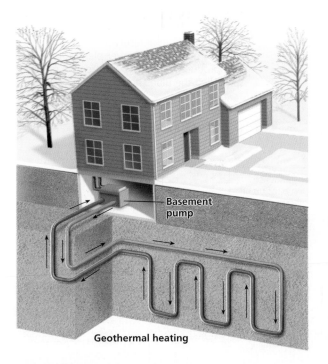
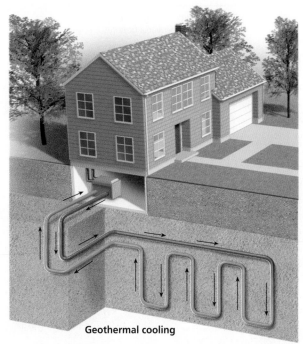

Geothermal heating   Geothermal cooling

FIGURE 15.21 Natural capital: A geothermal heat pump system can heat or cool a house almost anywhere.

15.5 WHAT ARE THE ADVANTAGES AND DISADVANTAGES OF USING GEOTHERMAL ENERGY?

CONCEPT 15.5 Geothermal energy can supply many areas with heat and electricity, and has a generally low environmental impact, but sites where it can be produced economically are limited.

Tapping into the Earth's Internal Heat

Geothermal energy is heat stored in soil, underground rocks, and fluids in the earth's mantle. Geothermal energy is used to heat and cool buildings, and to heat water to produce electricity. Geothermal energy is available around the clock but is practical only at sites with high enough concentrations of underground heat.

A *geothermal heat pump* system (Figure 15.21) can heat and cool a house almost anywhere in the world. This system makes use of the temperature difference between the earth's surface and underground at a depth of 3–6 meters (10–20 feet), where the temperature typically is 10–20°C (50–60°F) year-round. In winter, a closed loop of buried pipes circulates a fluid, which extracts heat from the ground and carries it to a heat pump, which transfers the heat to a home's heat distribution system. In summer, this system works in reverse, removing heat from a home's interior and storing it below ground.

According to the EPA, a geothermal heat pump system is the most energy-efficient, reliable, environmentally clean, and cost-effective way to heat or cool a space. Installation costs can be high but are recouped within 3 to 5 years, after which these systems save energy and money for their owners. Initial costs can be added to a home mortgage to spread the financial burden over two or more decades.

Engineers have learned how to tap into deeper, more concentrated *hydrothermal reservoirs* of geothermal energy (Figure 15.22). Wells are drilled into the reservoirs to extract their dry steam (with a low water content), wet steam (with a high water content), or hot water. The steam or hot water can be used to heat homes and buildings, provide hot water, grow vegetables in greenhouses, raise fish in aquaculture ponds, and spin turbines to produce electricity.

Drilling geothermal wells, like drilling oil and natural gas wells, is expensive and requires a major investment. It is also a risky investment because drilling projects do not always succeed in tapping into concentrated deposits of geothermal energy. Once a successful deposit is found, it can supply geothermal energy for heat or to produce electricity around the clock, as long as heat is not removed from the deposit faster than the earth replaces it—usually at a slow rate. When this happens geothermal energy becomes a nonrenewable resource.

Geothermal energy is used in 24 countries, including the United States, the world's largest producer of geothermal electricity from hydrothermal reservoirs. The US Geothermal Energy Association estimates that 90% of the available geothermal energy for producing electricity in the United States has not been tapped.

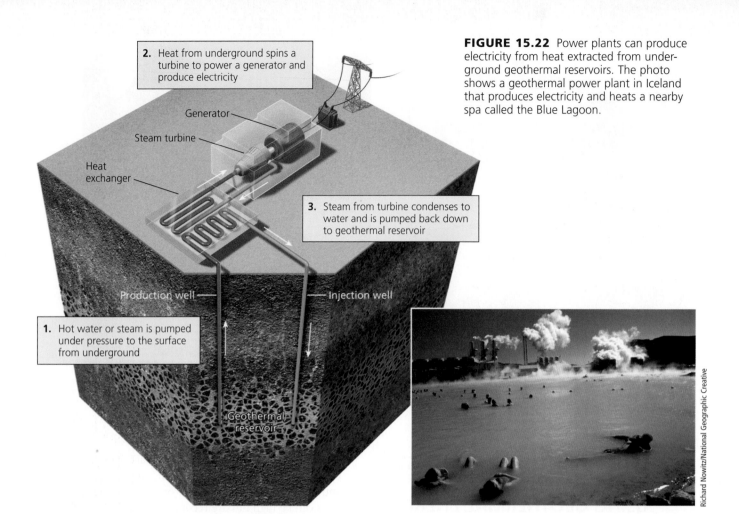

2. Heat from underground spins a turbine to power a generator and produce electricity

Generator

Steam turbine

Heat exchanger

3. Steam from turbine condenses to water and is pumped back down to geothermal reservoir

Production well

Injection well

1. Hot water or steam is pumped under pressure to the surface from underground

Geothermal reservoir

FIGURE 15.22 Power plants can produce electricity from heat extracted from underground geothermal reservoirs. The photo shows a geothermal power plant in Iceland that produces electricity and heats a nearby spa called the Blue Lagoon.

Richard Nowitz/National Geographic Creative

Figure 15.23 shows the global growth in installed geothermal electricity-generating capacity between 1950 and 2014. Iceland gets almost all of its electricity from renewable hydroelectric (69%) and geothermal (29%) power plants (Figure 15.22, photo) and nearly 95% of its demand for heat and hot water from geothermal energy.

In Peru, a National Geographic Explorer is carrying out research to develop that country's geothermal resources (Individuals Matter 15.1).

Another source of geothermal energy is *hot, dry rock* found 5 kilometers or more (3 miles or more) underground almost everywhere. Water can be injected through deep wells drilled into this rock. Some of this water becomes steam that is brought to the surface and used to spin turbines to generate electricity. According to the US Geological Survey, tapping just 2% of this source of geothermal energy in the United States could produce more than 2,000 times the amount of electricity currently used in the country. The limiting factor is its high cost, which could be brought down by more research and improved technology. **GREEN CAREER: Geothermal engineer**

Figure 15.24 lists the major advantages and disadvantages of using geothermal energy (**Concept 15.5**). The two biggest factors limiting the widespread use of geothermal energy are the lack of hydrothermal sites with concentrations of heat high enough to make it affordable and the high cost of drilling the wells and building the plants.

CHECKPOINT FOR UNDERSTANDING 15.5

1. Identify the benefits and drawbacks of geothermal energy.

15.6 WHAT ARE THE ADVANTAGES AND DISADVANTAGES OF USING BIOMASS AS AN ENERGY SOURCE?

CONCEPT 15.6A Solid biomass is a potentially renewable resource, but it requires large areas of land and burning it faster than it is replenished produces a net gain in emissions of greenhouse gases.

CONCEPT 15.6B Liquid biofuels derived from biomass can lessen dependence on oil, but devoting large areas of land to biofuel crops can degrade soil and biodiversity and increase greenhouse gas emissions.

Andrés Ruzo—Geothermal Energy Sleuth and National Geographic Explorer

Andrés Ruzo is a geophysicist with a driving passion to learn about geothermal energy and to show how this renewable and clean energy source can help us to solve some of the world's energy problems. As a boy, he spent his summers on the family farm in Nicaragua. Because the farm rests on top of the Casita Volcano, he was able to experience firsthand the power of the earth's heat.

As an undergraduate student at Southern Methodist University (SMU) in Dallas, Texas (USA), because of his boyhood experience, he took a course in volcanology. The course awakened his passion for geology along with a desire to learn more about the earth's heat as a source of energy. This led him to pursue a PhD in geophysics at SMU's Geothermal Laboratory.

Since 2009, Ruzo and his wife and field assistant, Sofia, have been gathering data across Peru to develop the country's first detailed heat flow map—which will help identify areas of geothermal energy potential. Their field work involves lowering temperature measuring equipment down into oil, gas, mining, or water wells. Much of this work was done in the Talara Desert in northwestern Peru, where surface temperatures can exceed 54°C (130°F). Other wells were temperature logged deep in the Amazon rainforest. These data illustrate how thermal energy flows through the upper crust of the earth, and highlights areas where earth's heat can potentially be tapped as a source of energy.

Ruzo believes that geothermal energy is a "sleeping giant" that, if properly harnessed, can be an important renewable source of heat and electricity. He says that his goal in life is "to be a force of positive change in the world."

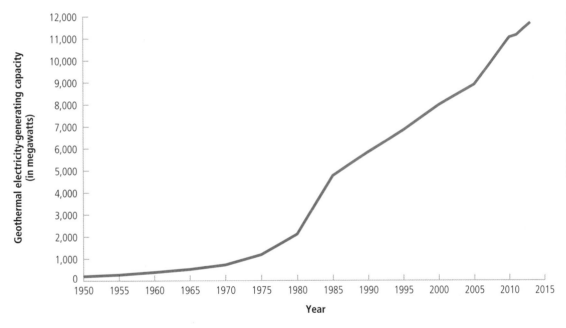

FIGURE 15.23 Global cumulative installed geothermal electricity-generating capacity, 1950–2013. **Data analysis:** About how many times more geothermal electricity-generating capacity was available in 2013 than in 1965?

(Compiled by the authors using data from International Energy Agency, Worldwatch Institute, Earth Policy Institute, and BP.)

Producing Energy by Burning Solid Biomass

Energy can be produced by burning the solid biomass or organic matter found in plants or plant-related material or by converting it to gaseous or liquid biofuels. Examples of biomass fuels include wood, wood pellets, wood wastes, charcoal made from wood, and agricultural wastes such as sugarcane stalks, rice husks, and corncobs.

Biomass is burned mostly for heating and cooking, but can also be used for industrial processes and generating electricity. Biomass used for heating and cooking supply 10% of the world's energy, 35% of the energy used in less-developed countries, and 95% of the energy used in the poorest countries.

Wood is a renewable resource only if it is not harvested faster than it is replenished. The problem is that 2.7 billion people in 77 less-developed countries face a *fuelwood crisis*.

Trade-Offs

Geothermal Energy

Advantages	Disadvantages
Medium net energy and high efficiency at accessible sites	High cost except at concentrated and accessible sources
Lower CO_2 emissions than fossil fuels	Scarcity of suitable sites
Low operating costs at favorable sites	Noise and some CO_2 emissions

FIGURE 15.24 Using geothermal energy for space heating and for producing electricity or high-temperature heat for industrial processes has advantages and disadvantages (**Concept 15.5**). *Critical thinking:* Which single advantage and which single disadvantage do you think are the most important? Why? Do you think the advantages of this energy resource outweigh its disadvantages? Why?

Photo: © N. Minton/Shutterstock.com

They often are forced to meet their fuel needs by harvesting trees faster than new ones can replace them.

One solution is to plant fast-growing trees, shrubs, or perennial grasses in *biomass plantations*. However, repeated cycles of growing and harvesting these plantations can deplete the soil of key nutrients. It can also allow for the spread of nonnative tree species that become invasive. Clearing forests and grasslands to provide fuelwood also reduces biodiversity and the amount of vegetation that would otherwise capture climate-changing CO_2.

Burning wood and other forms of biomass produces CO_2 and other pollutants such as fine particulates in smoke. Figure 15.25 lists the major advantages and disadvantages of burning solid biomass as a fuel (**Concept 15.6A**).

Using Liquid Biofuels to Power Vehicles

Biomass can also be converted into liquid biofuels for use in motor vehicles. The two most common liquid biofuels are *ethanol* (ethyl alcohol produced from plants and plant wastes) and *biodiesel* (produced from vegetable oils). The biggest producers of liquid biofuel are, in order, the United States (producing ethanol from corn), Brazil (producing ethanol from sugarcane residues), the European Union (producing biodiesel from vegetable oils), and China (producing ethanol from nongrain plant sources).

Biofuels have three major advantages over gasoline and diesel fuel produced from oil. *First*, biofuel crops can be grown throughout much of the world, which can help more countries reduce their dependence on imported oil. *Second*, if growing new biofuel crops keeps pace with harvesting them, there is no net increase in CO_2 emissions,

Trade-Offs

Solid Biomass

Advantages	Disadvantages
Widely available in some areas	Contributes to deforestation
Moderate costs	Clear-cutting can cause soil erosion, water pollution, and loss of wildlife habitat
Medium net energy	
No net CO_2 increase if harvested, burned, and replanted sustainably	Can open ecosystems to invasive species
Plantations can help restore degraded lands	Increases CO_2 emissions if harvested and burned unsustainably

FIGURE 15.25 Burning solid biomass as a fuel has advantages and disadvantages (**Concept 15.6A**). *Critical thinking:* Which single advantage and which single disadvantage do you think are the most important? Why? Do you think the advantages outweigh the disadvantages? Why?

Top: Fir4ik/Shutterstock.com. Bottom: © Eppic/Dreamstime.com.

unless existing grasslands or forests are cleared to plant biofuel crops. *Third*, biofuels are easy to store and transport through existing fuel networks and can be used in motor vehicles at little additional cost.

Since 1975, global ethanol production has increased rapidly, especially in the United States and Brazil. Brazil makes ethanol from *bagasse*, a residue produced when sugarcane is crushed. This sugarcane ethanol has a medium net energy that is 8 times higher than that of ethanol produced from corn. About 70% of Brazil's motor vehicles run on ethanol or ethanol–gasoline mixtures produced from sugarcane grown on only 1% of the country's arable land. This has greatly reduced Brazil's dependence on imported oil.

About 40% of the corn produced in the United States in 2015 was used to make ethanol, which is mixed with gasoline to fuel cars. Studies indicate that corn-based ethanol has a low net energy because of the large-scale use of fossil fuels to produce fertilizers, grow the corn, and convert it to ethanol.

There is controversy over greenhouse gas emissions to the atmosphere from the production and use of corn-based ethanol. Some research indicates that burning fuel with ethanol may add less greenhouse gases than burning pure gasoline. However, other research indicates an increase in greenhouse gas emissions when the greenhouse emissions from producing the corn are included. According to a study by the Environmental Working Group, the heavily government-subsidized corn-based ethanol program in the United

States has taken more than 2 million hectares (5 million acres) of land out of the soil conservation reserve, an important topsoil preservation program. Growing corn also requires substantial amounts of water and land–resources that are in short supply in some areas.

Furthermore, scientists warn that large-scale biofuel farming could reduce biodiversity, degrade soil quality, and increase erosion. As a result, a number of scientists and energy economists call for withdrawing all government subsidies for corn-based ethanol production and sharply reducing the large amount of ethanol required in US gasoline as mandated by the Energy Independence and Security Act of 2007. Corn producers and ethanol distillers claim that the harmful environmental effects of corn-based ethanol are overblown and that it has many environmental and economic benefits.

An alternative to corn-based ethanol is *cellulosic ethanol*, which is produced from the inedible cellulose that makes up most of the biomass of plants in the form of leaves, stalks, and wood chips. Cellulosic ethanol can be produced from tall and rapidly growing grasses such as switchgrass and miscanthus that do not require nitrogen fertilizers and pesticides. They also do not have to be replanted because they are perennial plants, and they can be grown on degraded and abandoned farmlands.

Ecologist David Tilman (Individuals Matter 12.1, p. 334) estimates that the net energy of cellulosic ethanol is about five times that of corn-based ethanol. However, producing cellulosic ethanol is not yet affordable, and more research is also needed to determine possible environmental impacts.

Another approach involves using certain strains of algae to produce biofuels. Algae can grow year-round in various aquatic environments. The algae store their energy as natural oils within their cells. This oil can be extracted and refined to make a product very much like gasoline or biodiesel. Researchers estimate that algae can produce 10 times more energy per area of land than plants used to produce cellulosic ethanol can produce. Currently, extracting and refining the oil from algae is too costly. More research is also needed on which types of algae are most suitable and which ways of growing them are the most successful.

Figure 15.26 compares the advantages and disadvantages of using biodiesel and ethanol liquid biofuels.

CHECKPOINT FOR UNDERSTANDING 15.6

1. Identify the benefits and drawbacks of using solid biomass for fuel.
2. Identify the benefits and drawbacks of using liquid biofuels.
3. Explain why corn-based ethanol has a low net energy in the United States.

Trade-Offs

Liquid Biofuels

Advantages	Disadvantages
Reduced CO_2 emissions for some crops	Fuel crops can compete with food crops for land and raise food prices
Medium net energy for biodiesel from oil palms	Fuel crops can be invasive species
	Low net energy for corn ethanol and for biodiesel from soybeans
Medium net energy for ethanol from sugarcane	Higher CO_2 emissions from corn ethanol

FIGURE 15.26 Ethanol and biodiesel biofuels have advantages and disadvantages (**Concept 15.6B**). *Critical thinking:* Which single advantage and which single disadvantage do you think are the most important? Why?

15.7 WHAT ARE THE ADVANTAGES AND DISADVANTAGES OF USING HYDROPOWER?

CONCEPT 15.7 We can use water flowing over dams, tidal flows, and ocean waves to generate electricity, but environmental concerns and limited availability of suitable sites may limit the use of these energy resources.

Producing Electricity from Falling and Flowing Water

Hydropower is any technology that uses the kinetic energy of flowing and falling water to produce electricity. It is an indirect form of solar energy because it depends on heat from the sun evaporating surface water. The water is deposited as rain or snow at higher elevations. Through gravity, the water can flow to lower elevations in rivers as part of the earth's solar-powered water cycle (Figure 3.14, p. 77).

The most common approach to harnessing renewable hydropower is to build a high dam across a large river to create a reservoir. Some of the water stored in the reservoir is allowed to flow through large pipes at controlled rates. The flowing water causes blades on a turbine to turn and spin a generator to produce electricity. Electric lines then carry the electricity to where it is needed.

Hydropower is the world's leading renewable energy source and produced about 16% of the world's electricity in 2015. In order, the world's top four producers of hydropower in 2015 were China, Canada, Brazil, and the United States. In 2015, hydropower supplied about 6% of the electricity used in the United States and about half of the electricity used on the West Coast, mostly in Washington and California. Electricity from hydropower has been growing (Figure 15.27).

Hydropower is the least expensive renewable energy resource. Once a dam is up and running, its source of energy—flowing water—is free and is annually renewed by snow and rainfall. Despite their potential, some analysts expect that the use of large-scale hydropower plants will fall slowly over the next several decades, as many existing reservoirs fill with silt and become useless faster than new systems are built. There is also growing concern over emissions of methane, a potent greenhouse gas, from the decomposition of submerged vegetation in hydropower plant reservoirs, especially in warm climates. Scientists at Brazil's National Institute for Space Research estimate that the world's largest dams altogether are the single largest human-caused source of climate-changing methane. The electricity output of hydropower plants may also drop if atmospheric temperatures continue to rise. This will cause melting of mountain glaciers, a primary source of water for these plants.

It is unlikely that large new hydroelectric dams will be built in the United States because most of the best sites already have dams and because of controversy and the high costs involved with building new dams. However, the turbines at many existing US hydropower dams could be modernized and upgraded to increase their output of electricity. Figure 15.27 lists the major advantages and disadvantages of using large-scale hydropower plants to produce electricity (**Concept 15.7**).

Using Tides and Waves to Produce Electricity

Another way to produce electricity from flowing water is to tap into the energy from *ocean tides* and *waves*. In some coastal bays and estuaries, water levels can rise or fall by 6 meters (20 feet) or more between daily high and low tides. Dams can be built across the mouths of such bays and estuaries to capture the energy in these flows for hydropower, but sites with large tidal flows are rare. The only three large tidal energy dams currently operating are in France, Nova Scotia, and South Korea. According to energy experts, tidal power will make only a minor contribution to the world's electricity production because of the rarity of suitable sites.

For decades, scientists and engineers have been trying to produce electricity by tapping wave energy along seacoasts where there are almost continuous waves. However, production of electricity from tidal and wave systems is limited because of a lack of suitable sites, citizen opposition at some sites, high costs, and equipment damage from saltwater corrosion and storms.

CHECKPOINT FOR UNDERSTANDING 15.7

1. Identify the benefits and drawbacks of using large-scale hydropower.

15.8 WHAT ARE THE ADVANTAGES AND DISADVANTAGES OF USING HYDROGEN AS AN ENERGY SOURCE?

CONCEPT 15.8 Hydrogen is a clean energy source as long as it is not produced with the use of fossil fuels, but it has a negative net energy.

Will Hydrogen Save Us?

Some scientists say that the fuel of the future is hydrogen gas (H_2). Most of their research has been focused on using fuel cells (Figure 15.28) that combine H_2 and oxygen gas (O_2) to produce electricity and water vapor ($2 H_2 + O_2 \rightarrow 2 H_2O$ + energy), a harmless chemical that is emitted into the atmosphere.

Widespread use of hydrogen as a fuel for running motor vehicles, heating buildings, and producing electricity would eliminate most of the outdoor air pollution that

Trade-Offs

Large-Scale Hydropower

Advantages	Disadvantages
High net energy	Large land disturbance and displacement of people
Large untapped potential	
Low-cost electricity	High CH$_4$ emissions from rapid biomass decay in shallow tropical reservoirs
Low emissions of CO$_2$ and other air pollutants in temperate areas	Disrupts downstream aquatic ecosystems

FIGURE 15.27 Using large dams and reservoirs to produce electricity has advantages and disadvantages (**Concept 15.7**). *Critical thinking:* Which single advantage and which single disadvantage do you think are the most important? Why? Do you think that the advantages of this technology outweigh its disadvantages? Why?

Photo: © Andrew Zarivny/Shutterstock.com

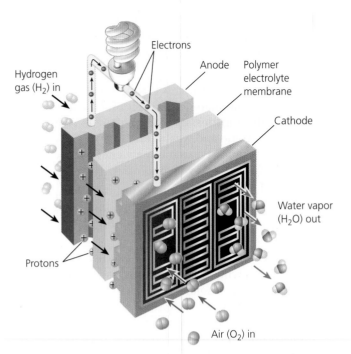

FIGURE 15.28 A fuel cell takes in hydrogen gas and separates the hydrogen atoms' electrons from their protons. The electrons flow through wires to provide electricity, while the protons pass through a membrane and combine with oxygen gas to form water vapor. Note that this process is the reverse of electrolysis, the process of passing electricity through water to produce hydrogen fuel.

Labels on figure:
- Electrons
- Hydrogen gas (H_2) in
- Anode
- Polymer electrolyte membrane
- Cathode
- Water vapor (H_2O) out
- Protons
- Air (O_2) in

comes from burning fossil fuels. It would also greatly slow climate change and ocean acidification, because production and use of hydrogen do not increase CO_2 emissions unless the H_2 is produced with the use of fossil fuels or nuclear power.

However, there are four major challenges in turning the vision of hydrogen as a major fuel into reality. *First*, there is hardly any hydrogen gas (H_2) in the earth's atmosphere. We can produce H_2 by heating water or passing electricity through it; by stripping it from the methane (CH_4) found in natural gas and from gasoline molecules; and through a chemical reaction involving coal, oxygen, and steam. *Second*, hydrogen has a negative net energy because it takes more high-quality energy to produce H_2 using these methods than we get by burning it. *Third*, although fuel cells are the best way to use H_2, current versions of fuel cells are expensive. However, progress in the development of nanotechnology (see Science Focus 11.1, p. 323) and mass production could lead to less expensive fuel cells.

Fourth, whether or not a hydrogen-based energy system produces less outdoor air pollution and CO_2 than a fossil fuel system depends on how the H_2 fuel is produced. Electricity from coal-burning and nuclear power plants can be used to decompose water into H_2 and O_2. But this approach does not avoid the harmful environmental effects associated with using coal and the nuclear

fuel cycle. In addition, research indicates that making H_2 from coal or stripping it from methane or gasoline adds much more CO_2 to the atmosphere per unit of heat generated than does burning the coal or methane directly.

Hydrogen's negative net energy is a serious limitation. It means that this fuel will have to be heavily subsidized in order for it to compete in the open marketplace. However, this could change. Chemist Daniel Nocera has been learning from nature by studying how a leaf uses photosynthesis to produce the chemical energy used by plants and he has developed an "artificial leaf." This credit-card-sized silicon wafer produces H_2 and O_2 when placed in a glass of tap water and exposed to sunlight. The hydrogen can be extracted and used to power fuel cells. Scaling up this or similar processes to produce large amounts of H_2 at an affordable price with an acceptable net energy over the next several decades could represent a tipping point for use of solar energy and hydrogen fuel. Doing so would help implement the solar energy **principle of sustainability** on a global scale. **GREEN CAREER: Fuel cell technology**

Figure 15.29 lists the major advantages and disadvantages of using hydrogen as an energy resource (**Concept 15.8**).

Trade-Offs

Hydrogen

Advantages	Disadvantages
Can be produced from plentiful water at some sites	Negative net energy
No CO_2 emissions if produced with use of renewables	CO_2 emissions if produced from carbon-containing compounds
Good substitute for oil	High costs create need for subsidies
High efficiency in fuel cells	Needs H_2 storage and distribution system

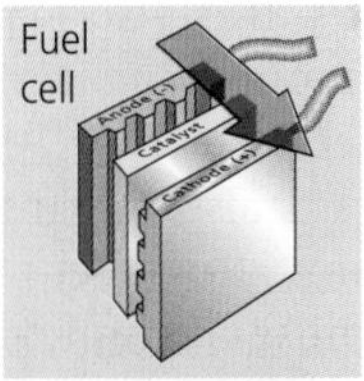

Fuel cell

FIGURE 15.29 Using hydrogen as a fuel for vehicles and for providing heat and electricity has advantages and disadvantages (**Concept 15.8**). *Critical thinking:* Which single advantage and which single disadvantage do you think are the most important? Why? Do you think that the advantages of hydrogen fuel outweigh its disadvantages? Why?

Photo: LovelaceMedia/Shutterstock.com

CHECKPOINT FOR UNDERSTANDING 15.8

1. Discuss the challenges of using hydrogen fuel cells.
2. Discuss the advantages of using hydrogen fuel cells.

15.9 HOW CAN WE MAKE THE TRANSITION TO A MORE SUSTAINABLE ENERGY FUTURE?

CONCEPT 15.9 We can make the transition to a more sustainable energy future by reducing energy waste, improving energy efficiency, using a mix of renewable energy resources, and including the environmental and health costs of energy resources in their market prices.

Shifting to a New Energy Economy

According to its proponents, shifting to a new set of energy resources over the next 50 to 60 years would have numerous environmental, health, and economic benefits.

China (which uses 20% of the world's energy) and the United States (which uses 19% of the world's energy) are the key players in making this shift. China has a long way to go in reducing its heavy dependence on coal and leads the world in climate-changing CO_2 emissions. However, it has launched efforts to make its economy more energy efficient, build a modern electrical grid, and install solar hot water heaters on a large scale. China is also building wind farms and solar power plants, supporting research on better batteries and improved solar and wind technologies, and building and selling all-electric cars. It is also making money by producing and selling more wind turbines and solar cell panels than any other country.

The United States is also making efforts to shift to a new energy economy. However, it is falling behind China's efforts and those of countries such as Germany, Sweden, and Denmark. This is mostly because of more than 40 years of successful and ongoing efforts by powerful fossil fuel and electric utility companies to stop or slow down this shift because it threatens their profits.

This energy and economic transition is underway and is accelerating because it is increasingly driven by market forces. This is the result of the rapidly falling prices of electricity produced by the sun and wind, new energy technologies, and strong and growing public opposition to coal and nuclear power. Investors are moving rapidly into clean energy technologies. According to many scientists and energy economists, the shift to a new energy economy could be further accelerated if citizens, the leaders of emerging renewable energy companies, and energy investors demanded the following from their elected officials:

- Use **full-cost pricing** to include the harmful health and environmental costs of using fossil fuels and all other energy resources in their market prices.

- Tax carbon emissions. This is supported by most economists and many business leaders, and is now done in 40 countries. Use the revenue to reduce taxes on income and wealth and to promote investments and research in new energy-efficient and renewable energy technologies.

- Sharply decrease and eventually eliminate government subsidies for fossil fuel industries, which are well-established and profitable businesses.

- Establish a national feed-in-tariff system that guarantees owners of wind farms, solar power plants, and home solar systems a long-term price for energy that they feed into their electrical grids (as is being done in more than 50 countries, many of them in Europe).

- Mandate that a certain percentage (typically 20–40%) of the electricity generated by utility companies be from renewable resources (as is done in 24 countries and in 29 US states).

- Increase government fuel efficiency (CAFE) standards for new vehicles to 43 kilometers per liter (100 miles per gallon) by 2040.

Use of fossil fuels can decrease but they are not going to disappear. Between 2015 and 2035, oil and coal use will decrease, natural gas and renewable energy use will increase, and nuclear power and hydropower use will stay about the same–according to projections by the International Energy Agency, BP, and the US Energy Information Agency.

We have the creativity, wealth, and most of the technology to make the transition to a safer, more energy-efficient, and cleaner energy economy within your lifetime. With such a shift, we could greatly increase our beneficial environmental impact. Figure 15.30 lists ways in which you can take part in the transition toward such a future.

CHECKPOINT FOR UNDERSTANDING 15.9

1. Identify several strategies that must be implemented to ensure sustainable energy use in the future.

Environmental Change and Leadership

A major theme of this book is that *individuals matter*. History shows that significant change usually comes from the *bottom* up when individuals work together to bring about change. Without this grassroots pressure from individual citizens and organized citizen groups, pollution and environmental degradation would be much worse today.

You can provide environmental leadership in several ways. First, you can *lead by example*, using your own lifestyle and values to show others that beneficial environmental change is possible (Figure 15.A). You can buy only what you need, use fewer disposable products, eat sustainably produced food, practice the 4Rs of resource use (refuse, reduce, reuse, recycle), adjust your lifestyle to reduce your carbon footprint, and walk, bike, or take mass transit to work or school.

Second, you can *work within existing economic and political systems to bring about environmental improvement* by campaigning and voting for informed and ecologically literate candidates and by communicating with elected officials. As environmental writer and activist Bill McKibben says, "First change your politicians, and then worry about your lightbulbs."

You can also send a message to companies that you think are harming the environment through their production processes or products. You can do this by *voting with your wallet*. Do not buy their products or services and let them know why. You can also work to improve environmental quality by choosing one of the many rapidly growing environmental careers.

Third, you can *run for some sort of local office*. Look in the mirror. Maybe you are someone who can make a difference as an officeholder. Fourth, even as a private citizen, you can participate in public dialogues and *propose and work for better solutions to environmental problems*. Leadership is much more than just taking a stand for or against something. It also involves coming up with solutions to problems and persuading people to work together to achieve them.

FRQ Application

Question: Making significant changes in your life by rethinking how you use energy is not only beneficial to the environment, but also saves money. **Identify** and **describe** TWO energy-saving strategies in your home

that would reduce the use of fossil fuels for heating and cooling, and TWO energy-saving strategies that would reduce the use of fossil fuels for consuming electricity.

Possible Response: One strategy for reducing the use of fossil fuels such as natural gas or heating oil would be to lower the thermostat in the winter when using the furnace. Lowering the temperature even a few degrees and wearing a sweater would save significant fuel over a heating season. A second strategy for reducing fossil fuels for heating would be to install geothermal heating, completely eliminating the use of natural gas or oil to heat the home.

One strategy for consuming less electricity in the home would be to replace incandescent lightbulbs with LED bulbs that use 75-80% less electricity than incandescent bulbs and last 25 times longer. A second strategy for reducing electricity consumption in the home would be to upgrade to Energy Star appliances. An Energy Star dishwasher or refrigerator uses significantly less electricity to run over a year when compared to standard appliances.

Rawpixel.com/Shutterstock.com

FIGURE 15.A Participating in a community outdoor clean-up project can be a fun, satisfying, and effective way to lead by example.

What Can You Do?

Shifting to More Sustainable Energy Use

- Walk, bike, or use mass transit or a car pool to get to work or school

- Drive only vehicles that get at least 17 kpl (40 mpg)

- Have an energy audit done in the place where you live

- Superinsulate the place where you live and plug all air leaks

- Use passive solar heating

- For cooling, open windows and use fans

- Use a programmable thermostat and energy-efficient heating and cooling systems, lights, and appliances

- Turn down your water heater's thermostat to 43–49°C (110–120°F) and insulate hot water pipes

- Turn off lights, TVs, computers, and other electronics when they are not in use

- Wash laundry in cold water and air dry it on racks

FIGURE 15.30 Individuals matter: You can make a shift in your own life toward using energy more sustainably. *Critical thinking:* Which three of these measures do you think are the most important ones to take? Why? Which of these steps have you already taken and which do you plan to take?

KEY IDEAS

- To make our economies more sustainable, we need to reduce our use of fossil fuels, especially coal, and greatly increase energy efficiency, reduce energy waste, and use a mix of renewable energy resources, especially the sun and wind.

- Making this energy shift will have important economic and environmental benefits.

- Making the transition to a more sustainable energy future will require including the harmful environmental and health costs of all energy resources in their market prices, taxing carbon emissions, and greatly increasing government subsidies and research and development for improving energy efficiency and developing renewable energy resources.

Core Case Study Checkpoint

Conservation measures in the home can save both energy and money. Identify two measures a homeowner can take to make home heating more efficient.

Chapter 15 Glossary

active solar heating system: a system that uses solar collectors to capture heat energy from the sun and stores it as heat for space heating and water heating. Liquid or air pumped through the collectors transfers the captured heat to a storage system such as an insulated water tank or rock bed. Pumps or fans then distribute the stored heat or hot water throughout a dwelling as needed.

cogeneration: production of two useful forms of energy, such as high-temperature heat or steam and electricity, from the same fuel source.

energy conservation: reducing or eliminating the unnecessary waste of energy.

energy efficiency: percentage of the total energy input that does useful work and is not converted into low-quality, generally useless heat in an energy conversion system or process.

feed-in-tariff: requires utilities to buy electricity produced by homeowners and businesses from renewable energy sources at a guaranteed price.

full-cost pricing: finding ways to include in the market prices of goods the harmful environmental and health costs of producing and using those goods.

geothermal energy: heat transferred from the earth's underground concentrations of dry steam (steam with no water droplets), wet steam (a mixture or steam and water droplets), or hot water trapped in fractured or porous rock.

hydrogen fuel cell: a device that combines hydrogen gas (H_2) with oxygen gas (O_2) to produce electricity and water vapor that is emitted to the atmosphere.

hydropower: electrical energy produced by falling or flowing water.

passive solar heating system: a system that, without the use of mechanical devices, captures sunlight directly within a structure and uses it to heat the structure.

photovoltaic cells: device that converts solar)energy directly into electrical energy. Also called a solar cell.

solar thermal system: a system that uses various methods to collect and concentrate solar energy in order to boil water and produce steam for generating electricity.

Chapter Review

Core Case Study

1. What are two ways in which we waste energy? What are the benefits of reducing this and other forms of energy waste?

Section 15.1

2. (a) What is the key concept for this section? (b) Why do we need to make a new energy transition over the next 50 to 60 years? What are the two key components of this energy resource shift? (c) What are the economic and environmental advantages of making this energy transition? (d) List three factors that are driving this shift. How would the United States benefit from it? (e) Describe Germany's progress in making this energy shift.

Section 15.2

3. (a) What are the two concepts for this section? (b) Define and give an example of **energy efficiency**. Explain why improving energy efficiency and reducing energy waste is a major energy resource. (c) What percentage of the energy used in the United States is unnecessarily wasted? Why is so much energy wasted? List three widely used energy-inefficient technologies. (d) What is **energy conservation**? What are the major advantages of reducing energy waste? List four ways to save energy and money in industry. (e) What is **cogeneration**? (f) What is a smart electric grid and why is it important? (g) What are US CAFE standards? What are the hidden costs of using gasoline? List four ways to save energy and money in transportation. (h) Distinguish between hybrid, plug-in hybrid, and all-electric vehicles. Explain the importance of developing better and cheaper batteries and list some advances in this area. (i) What are fuel cells and what are their major advantages and disadvantages? (j) What are some green architecture technologies? What is superinsulation? (k) What are 10 ways to improve energy efficiency in existing buildings? (l) List six ways in which you can save energy where you live. (m) What is the rebound effect and how can it be reduced? (n) Give five reasons why we are not making greater use of renewable energy.

Section 15.3

4. (a) What is the key concept for this section? (b) Distinguish between a **passive solar heating system** and an **active solar heating system** and list the major advantages and disadvantages of using such systems for heating buildings. (c) What are three ways to cool houses naturally? (d) What are **solar thermal systems**, how are they used, and what are the major advantages and disadvantages of using them? (e) What is a **solar cell** (**photovoltaic** or **PV cell**) and what are the major advantages and disadvantages of using such devices to produce electricity?

Section 15.4

5. (a) What is the key concept for this section? (b) What are the advantages of using taller wind turbines? Summarize the global and US potential for wind power. (c) Why is the United States a superpower of wind energy? Describe how wind turbines are being made safer for birds and bats. (d) What are the major advantages and disadvantages of using wind to produce electricity?

Section 15.5

6. (a) What is the key concept for this section? (b) What is **geothermal energy** and what are three sources of such energy? (c) What are the major advantages and disadvantages of using geothermal energy as a source of heat and to produce electricity?

Section 15.6

7. (a) What are the two key concepts for this section? (b) What is **biomass** and what are the major advantages and disadvantages of using wood to provide heat and electricity? What are the major advantages and disadvantages of using biodiesel and ethanol to power motor vehicles? (d) Explain how algae and bacteria could be used to produce fuels nearly identical to gasoline and diesel fuel.

Section 15.7

8. (a) What is the key concept for this section? (b) Define **hydropower** and summarize the potential for expanding it. (c) What are the major advantages and disadvantages of using hydropower? (d) What is the potential for using tides and waves to produce electricity?

Section 15.8

9. (a) What is the key concept for this section? (b) What are the major advantages and disadvantages of using hydrogen as a fuel to use in producing electricity and powering vehicles?

10. (a) What is the key concept for this section? (b) Describe efforts by China and the United States to make the shift to a new energy economy. (c) List six strategies suggested by scientists and energy economists for making the transition to a more sustainable energy future. (d) List five ways you can participate in making the transition to a new energy future. (e) What are this chapter's *three key ideas*?

Note: Key terms are in bold type.

AP® Review Questions

Questions 1–4 refer to the energy terms listed below. Choices may be used once, more than once, or not at all.

(A) Energy-efficient vehicle
(B) Cogeneration
(C) Green architecture
(D) Feed-in tariff
(E) Fee-per-bag system

1. Requires energy companies to purchase excess energy produced through alternative means by their consumers for actual use on the grid

2. Construction of a building with a roof topped with soil and growing plants

3. Capturing the steam produced during electrical generation in a power plant and using it to heat nearby buildings

4. Used in Germany and many other European countries, this greatly increases the use of alternative energy sources by consumers

Questions 5–7 refer to the systems listed below. Choices may be used once, more than once, or not at all.

(A) Solar thermal power plant
(B) Passive solar heating system
(C) Active solar heating system
(D) Photovoltaic cells
(E) Sun-effector ray station

5. Utilizes reflectors to concentrate sunlight onto a central receiver, where it is used to heat fluids to a high enough temperature to generate electricity

6. Uses semiconductors to convert radiant energy directly to electricity in homes, buildings, and the grid

7. Uses a series of collection tubes and pumps to heat water for homes and swimming pools

8. Which of the following is the LEAST energy efficient?
   (A) Coal-burning power plant
   (B) Internal combustion engine
   (C) Incandescent light bulb
   (D) Nuclear fission power plant
   (E) Industrialized meat production

9. The Corporate Average Fuel Economy (CAFE) standards
   (A) were first implemented in 1990
   (B) have been more successful in the United States than in other developed nations
   (C) have improved the current average fuel efficiency of vehicles in the United States to 55 miles per gallon
   (D) have resulted in a gradual increase in vehicle fuel efficiency in the United States since implementation
   (E) have been raised due to hybrid technology

10. All of the following are ways to help conserve energy EXCEPT
    (A) using LED bulbs in traffic lights, streetlights, and public buildings
    (B) improving the energy efficiency of vehicles
    (C) using heat-efficient windows on the south side of buildings
    (D) using the process of cogeneration when using incineration as a waste disposal method
    (E) building houses with walls of superinsulating straw bales

11. Which of the following is an example of using an active solar heating system?
    (A) Planting deciduous trees near windows to provide a sun-block in the summer months
    (B) Using fluid-filled plate collectors on the roof and pumping the heated water to a hot tub
    (C) Using double-paned windows
    (D) Using heavy blinds on the windows
    (E) Using multiple south-facing windows in northern climates when building

12. A homebuilder is very conscious of energy efficiency, for both ecological and economic reasons. When building a home, which of the following should be incorporated to increase the energy efficiency of the home?
    (A) Incorporating lightweight walls and roofs to minimize weight load
    (B) Using incandescent bulbs to get the maximum brightness in the largest area
    (C) Incorporating programmable, adjustable thermostats for heating and cooling
    (D) Minimizing landscaping, especially trees, near the home to minimize water use
    (E) Using gas-powered appliances only

13. One method of reducing dependence on fuel wood biomass, particularly in developing countries, and thereby reducing deforestation is to implement the use of
    (A) photovoltaic solar systems to serve home-heating needs
    (B) solar cookers instead of wood-fired stoves
    (C) hydrogen-fuel cell stoves instead of wood-fired stoves
    (D) hybrid electric heaters instead of fires
    (E) wind-powered refrigeration

Questions 14–17 refer to the following disadvantages of alternative energy sources. Choices may be used once, more than once, or not at all.

    (A) May interfere with flight patterns of migratory birds
    (B) Produces sulfur oxides
    (C) Only useful in areas near subterranean hot spots or plate boundaries
    (D) Currently has a negative net energy production
    (E) Competes directly with food production and may raise food prices

14. Geothermal

15. Hydrogen fuel cells

16. Ethanol fuel

17. Wind energy

Questions 18–19 refer to the diagram below.

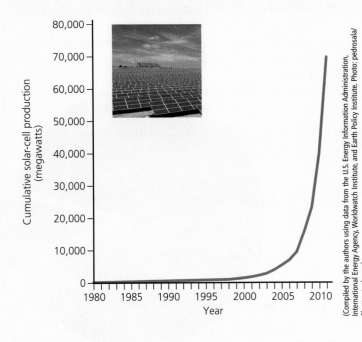

(Compiled by the authors using data from the U.S. Energy Information Administration, International Energy Agency, Worldwatch Institute, and Earth Policy Institute. Photo: pedrosala/Shutterstock.com)

18. Calculate the percent change in cumulative solar cell production between 2005 and 2010.
    (A) 9000%
    (B) 900%
    (C) 90%
    (D) 9%
    (E) 0.9%

19. What information can be inferred from the graph above?
    (A) More individual homes are using solar energy now than in 1980.
    (B) Solar energy utilization has surpassed that of wind energy.
    (C) By 2010 the solar cell production was equal to 14,000 megawatts.
    (D) The amount of solar energy produced has been increasing exponentially in recent years.
    (E) There has been a linear increase in solar energy production since 1995.

20. All of the following are externalized, or hidden, costs of the use of gasoline EXCEPT
    (A) tax breaks to oil companies
    (B) government subsidies to car manufacturers
    (C) defense spending to ensure access to Middle East oil supplies
    (D) costs of air pollution control and cleanup
    (E) increased subsidies for production of hybrid vehicles

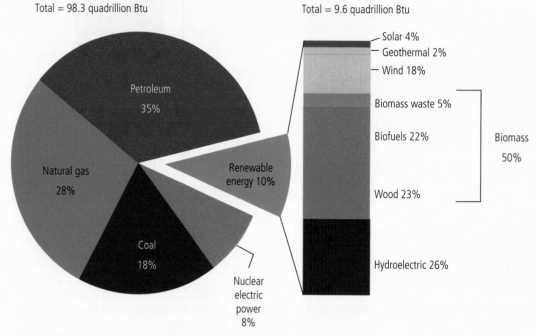

U.S. energy consumption by energy source, 2014

Total = 98.3 quadrillion Btu

Total = 9.6 quadrillion Btu

Petroleum 35%

Natural gas 28%

Renewable energy 10%

Coal 18%

Nuclear electric power 8%

Solar 4%
Geothermal 2%
Wind 18%
Biomass waste 5%
Biofuels 22%
Wood 23%
Biomass 50%
Hydroelectric 26%

Note: Sum of components may not equal 100% as a result of independent rounding.
Source: U.S. Energy Information Administration, *Monthly Energy Review*, Table 1.3 and 10.1 (March 2015), preliminary data

1. **(a)** The graph above shows the total number of BTU produced by both renewable and nonrenewable energy sources in the United States in 2014.

   (i) Calculate how many times more BTU were produced by nonrenewable energy sources as compared to BTU produced by renewable energy sources, using the values in the graph. Round your answer to the nearest whole number.

   (ii) Hydroelectric energy is a form of renewable energy. **Calculate** the total number of BTU produced by hydropower in the U.S.

   (iii) Calculate the percent BTU generated by hydropower for all energy combined in the U.S., using the value from (ii).

   (b) Choose one of the nonrenewable energy sources from the graph above.

   (i) Explain how that energy source is used to generate electricity.

   (ii) Identify and **discuss** TWO environmental drawbacks of using the nonrenewable energy source you chose.

   (iii) Identify and **discuss** ONE advantage of using the nonrenewable energy source you chose.

   (c) Choose one of the renewable energy sources from the graph above.

   (i) Explain how that energy source is used to generate electricity.

   (ii) Identify and **discuss** TWO environmental advantages to using the renewable energy source you chose.

   (iii) Identify and **discuss** ONE drawback of using the renewable energy source you chose.

Critical Thinking

1. List five ways in which you unnecessarily waste energy during a typical day, and explain how each of these actions violates the three scientific **principle of sustainability**.

2. Congratulations! You have won enough money to build a more sustainable house of your choice. With the goal of maximizing energy efficiency, what type of house would you build? How large would it be? Where would you locate it? What types of materials would you use? What types of materials would you *not* use? How would you heat and cool the house? How would you heat water? What types of lighting, stove, refrigerator, washer, and dryer would you use? Which, if any, of these appliances could you do without?

3. Suppose that a homebuilder installs electric baseboard heat and claims, "It is the cheapest and cleanest way to go." Apply your understanding of the second law of thermodynamics (p. 50) and net energy (Figure 14.3, p. 422) to evaluate this claim. Write a response to the homebuilder summarizing your findings.

4. Do you think that the estimated hidden costs of gasoline should be included in its price at the pump? Explain. Would you favor much higher gasoline taxes to accomplish this if payroll taxes and income taxes were reduced to balance gasoline tax increases, with no net additional cost to consumers? Explain.

5. Suppose that a wind power developer has proposed building a wind farm near where you live. Would you be in favor of the project or opposed to it? Write a letter to your local newspaper or a blog for a website explaining your position and your reasoning. As part of your research, determine how the electricity you use now is generated and where the nearest power plant is located, and include this information in your arguments.

6. Explain why you agree or disagree with the following proposals made by various energy analysts:
   a. Government subsidies for all energy alternatives should be eliminated so that all energy resources can compete on a level playing field in the marketplace.
   b. All government tax breaks and other subsidies for conventional fossil fuels (oil, natural gas, and coal), synthetic natural gas and oil, and nuclear power (fission and fusion) should be eliminated. They should be replaced with subsidies and tax breaks for improving energy efficiency and developing renewable energy alternatives.
   c. Development of renewable energy alternatives should be left to private enterprise and should receive little or no help from the federal government, but the nuclear power and fossil fuels industries should continue to receive large federal government subsidies.

7. What percentages of the US Department of Energy research and development budget would you devote to fossil fuels, nuclear power, renewable energy, and improving energy efficiency? How would you distribute your funds among the various renewable energy options? Explain your thinking.

8. How important is it to make the transition to a new energy future? Do you think it can be done? Explain. How would making such a transition affect your life and the lives of any children or grandchildren that you might have? How would not making such a transition affect your life and the lives of any children or grandchildren that you might have?

Data Analysis

Study the table below and then answer the questions that follow it by filling in the blank columns in the table.

Combined City/Highway Fuel Efficiency for 2015 Models (mpg)				
Model	Miles per Gallon (mpg)	Kilometers per Liter (kpl)	Annual Liters (Gallons) of Gasoline	Annual CO$_2$ Emissions
Toyota Prius Hybrid	55			
Honda CR-Z AV-S7	37			
Chevrolet Cruze A-S6	30			
Ford Fusion AS6	29			
Ford F150 2WD-6 Pickup Truck	20			
Chevrolet Silverado DC15 2WD Pickup Truck	20			
Toyota Tundra Pickup Truck A-S6	16			
Ferrari AM7	13			

Compiled by the authors using data from Fuel Economy Guide 2015, US Environmental Protection Agency.

1. Using Supplement 1 (Measurement Units, p. S1), convert the miles per gallon figures in the table to kilometers per liter (kpl).

2. How many liters (and how many gallons) of gasoline would each car use annually if it was driven 19,300 kilometers (12,000 miles) per year?

3. How many kilograms (and how many pounds) of carbon dioxide would be released into the atmosphere each year by each car, based on the fuel consumption calculated in question 2, assuming that the combustion of gasoline releases 2.3 kilograms of CO$_2$ per liter (19 pounds per gallon)?

Answers to Checkpoints for Understanding

Section 15.1

1. It is expected that wind and solar will gradually replace fossil fuels, especially coal, as the price for these alternative energy sources continues to fall.
2. A feed-in tariff requires utilities to buy electricity produced by homeowners and businesses from renewable energy sources at a guaranteed price.

Section 15.2

1. The three technologies that waste large amounts of energy are data centers that waste 90% of the energy they use as waste heat, internal combustion engines that waste about 80% of the energy as waste heat, and nuclear, coal, and natural gas power plants that, when producing electricity, waste about 66% of the fuel's energy as waste heat.
2. Cogeneration is the production of two useful forms of energy from one energy source. For example, burning natural gas produces steam that generates electricity, and the steam can also be used to heat the factory that produces the electricity.
3. CAFE standards are Corporate Average Fuel Economy standards established by law to improve the gas mileage of cars, light trucks, vans, and sport utility vehicles.
4. Hidden costs of using gasoline to fuel motor vehicles include government subsidies for oil companies, car companies and road builders; defense spending for securing access to Middle East oil supplies; costs of pollution control and cleanup; and higher medical bills and health insurance premiums resulting from illnesses caused by air and water pollution from the production and use of motor vehicles.
5. Hybrid vehicles, when their batteries are charged by solar or wind power, would reduce the use of gasoline by 80 to 90%, slow climate change and ocean acidification, and save thousands of lives by reducing air pollution from motor vehicles and coal-burning plants. Disadvantages are high cost and limited driving range unless battery technology is improved.

6. Strategies for reducing energy consumption in existing homes are: getting an energy audit, insulating and plugging leaks, installing energy-efficient windows, installing a more efficient heating and cooling system, heating water more efficiently, using energy-efficient appliances, using energy efficient computers and lighting, and using smart power strips that shut off the standby mode for appliances.

Section 15.3

1. Passive solar heating systems absorb and store heat directly from the sun. Active systems use energy to circulate water or antifreeze through collectors and then through the structure to be heated.

2. Several strategies for cooling buildings naturally are: opening windows to breezes, planting deciduous trees around the perimeter of the building to shade them, using light-colored roofs to reflect heat, using superinsulation and reflective windows, and using geothermal heat pumps to circulate cool air from underground into buildings.

3. Solar thermal systems concentrate sunlight in order to heat water and produce steam, which spins a turbine that runs a generator to create a flow of electrons (electricity).

4. The drawbacks of solar thermal systems are low net energy, high costs, need for a backup storage system on cloudy days, high water use for cooling, and possible disruption of desert ecosystems.

5. The advantages of solar cells to produce electricity include no direct CO_2 emissions or other air pollutants; they are easy to install, move, and expand as needed; and the cost of using them to produce electricity is falling sharply. The disadvantages include lack of access to the sun in some areas, the need for a storage system or backup, and possible disruption of desert ecosystems.

Section 15.4

1. It is advantageous to locate wind turbines over water because winds there are generally stronger and steadier over water and the turbine structures themselves are not as visible as when on land.

2. The benefits of wind power include high net energy, wide availability, low electricity cost, no direct emissions of CO_2 or other pollutants, and they are easy to expand. Drawbacks include the need for a storage system or back up when winds die down, low-level noise, and the turning blades can kill birds and bats.

Section 15.5

1. Benefits of geothermal energy are medium net energy and high efficiency at suitable sites, lower CO_2 emissions than burning fossil fuels, and low operating costs at favorable sites. Drawbacks are scarcity of cost-effective sites, noise, and some CO_2 emissions.

Section 15.6

1. Benefits of using solid biomass for fuel include moderate cost, wide availability in some areas, medium net energy, no net CO_2 increase if harvested, burned, and replanted sustainably; and biomass plantations can help restore degraded lands. Drawbacks include deforestation, soil erosion, loss of wildlife habitat and water pollution due to clearcutting, can open ecosystems to invasive species, and increases CO_2 if harvested and burned unsustainably.

2. Benefits of using liquid biofuels include reduced CO_2 emissions for some crops, medium net energy for biodiesel fuel from oil palms, and medium net energy for ethanol from sugarcane. Drawbacks include competition with food crops for arable land, fuel crops can be invasive species, low net energy for corn ethanol and for biodiesel from soybeans, and higher CO_2 emissions from corn ethanol.

3. Ethanol made from corn in the United States has low net energy because of the large-scale use of fossil fuels to produce fertilizers, grow the corn, and convert it to ethanol.

Section 15.7

1. Benefits of large-scale hydropower include high net energy, a large untapped potential, low-cost electricity, and low emissions of CO_2 and other air pollutants in temperate areas. Disadvantages include large land disturbance and displacement of people, high methane emissions from rapid biomass decay in shallow tropical reservoirs, and dams that disrupt downstream aquatic ecosystems.

Section 15.8

1. There are several challenges to using hydrogen fuel cells. Hydrogen must be produced from other sources such as methane or the electrolysis of water; hydrogen has a negative net energy; fuel cells are expensive and processes for producing H_2 such as from nuclear and coal-burning power plants produces CO_2 and other air pollutants.

2. Advantages include: can be produced on a large scale by passing electricity through plentiful water at some sites; no CO_2 emissions if electricity used to produce H_2 comes from renewable energy from the sun or wind; hydrogen is a good substitute for oil; and fuel cells are highly efficient.

Section 15.9

1. Several ways to transition to a more sustainable energy future over the next 50–60 years include: full-cost pricing for all energy resources, taxing carbon emissions, decreasing government subsidies for fossil fuels, and increasing subsides for improving energy efficiency and renewable energy.

Core Case Study

Investing in insulation and in caulking windows saves energy and results in a significant payback in just a few years.

Questions 1–3 refer to the energy sources below.

    I. Oil
    II. Coal
    III. Conventional natural gas
    IV. Uranium
    V. Shale oil

1. These fossil fuels are often harvested together.
   (A) I and II only
   (B) I and III only
   (C) II and III only
   (D) IV and V only
   (E) I, II, and IV only

2. Non-renewable energy source(s) derived from ancient sun energy
   (A) I and II only
   (B) I, II, and III only
   (C) II and III only
   (D) III, IV, and V only
   (E) I, II, III, and V only

3. These energy resources often depend on pipeline systems for transport from extraction sites.
   (A) I only
   (B) I and II only
   (C) I and III only
   (D) I, III, and V only
   (E) I, II, III, and IV only

4. OPEC (Organization of Petroleum Exporting Countries) includes
   (A) United States, Canada, and Mexico
   (B) Iran, Iraq, Saudi Arabia, Kuwait, and Venezuela
   (C) Iraq, Saudi Arabia, Turkey, Pakistan, and Egypt
   (D) Japan, United Kingdom, United States, China, and Russia
   (E) Bolivia, Chile, South Africa, and Morocco

5. The controversy around oil extraction in the Arctic National Wildlife Refuge (ANWR) is about
   (A) balancing the need to find more domestic oil supplies with preserving the integrity of an area set aside to be a place for wildlife
   (B) whether or not this new resource will allow the United States to become free of dependence on foreign oil
   (C) if the tar sand reserves will require more money to refine and transport to the lower 48 states than they are worth
   (D) whether the continued dependence on fossil fuels will increase climate change to such an extent that this fragile northern habitat will soon be inundated with sea water
   (E) whether this would be the safest site for long term nuclear waste storage

6. Which of the following is a true statement about oil sand?
   (A) Can be extracted using offshore drilling methods
   (B) Is the most valuable type of petroleum reserve
   (C) Requires greater refining and more energy to extract the desired product
   (D) Results in the smallest amounts of pollutants
   (E) Is the result of oil spills that wash ashore and pollute beaches

7. Advantages of coal as an energy source include all of the following EXCEPT
   (A) well-developed combustion technology
   (B) large reserves
   (C) low land use and disturbance of watersheds
   (D) high net energy yield
   (E) inexpensive with current subsidies

8. All of the following are disadvantages of using nuclear energy EXCEPT
   (A) no long-term safe storage is available for wastes
   (B) if breached, the leak of radioactivity is very harmful to life
   (C) high costs to operate a facility
   (D) large amounts of water are required and results in thermal pollution
   (E) on-site air pollution releases

9. Historical nuclear accidents resulting in radioactive damages include
   (A) Chernobyl and Fukushima
   (B) Bhopal India and the Aral Sea
   (C) Yucca Mountain and Love Canal
   (D) Cuyahoga River and Chemical Alley
   (E) Minamata, Japan and Reykjavik, Iceland

10. Which of the following is true about nuclear fusion?
    (A) It uses light-water reactors (ALWRs) to split Uranium-238.
    (B) It is a new technology used in feeder reactors which converts uranium-238 into usable plutonium-239.
    (C) It is still being researched by scientists because it would alleviate the risks of meltdowns and high-level radioactive waste.
    (D) It is the technology used in nuclear weapons and therefore highly protected by a few countries for fear of its spread to terrorists.
    (E) It is used for X-rays and other medical procedures, but not energy generation.

11. The countries that depend the most on nuclear energy are
    (A) Japan, South Korea, and France
    (B) United States and the United Kingdom
    (C) Russia, Ukraine, and Kazakhstan
    (D) China, South Africa, and North Korea
    (E) Germany, France, and Spain

12. A political concern of nuclear energy use is
    I. Resources and technology used in reactors could also be used for weapons.
    II. An accident in a nuclear power plant can spread radiation across country boundaries.
    III. Uranium and plutonium can only be mined in the Ukraine.
    (A) I only
    (B) II only
    (C) III only
    (D) I and II only
    (E) II and III only

13. Net energy is
    (A) the total energy used per household
    (B) the energy that can be co-generated at power plants when waste heat is collected and used
    (C) a means of measuring energy efficiency that accounts for the energy required at each step and conversion
    (D) energy that can be captured by tidal turbines
    (E) the ratio of the amount of energy going into a system divided by the amount of energy coming out

Questions 14–16 refer to the power sources below.
Hydropower
    I. Hydropower
    II. Wind turbines
    III. Geothermal steam power plant
    IV. Photovoltaic cells
    V. Hydrogen fuel cell

14. Electrical energy is generated by kinetic energy rotating a turbine connected to a generator.
    (A) I only
    (B) II only
    (C) V only
    (D) I and III only
    (E) I, II, and III only

15. Weather-dependent and requires a back-up power source
    (A) I only
    (B) II only
    (C) II and IV only
    (D) III and IV only
    (E) II, III, and V only

16. High net energy power source
    (A) II only
    (B) III only
    (C) IV only
    (D) I, II, III, and IV only
    (E) I, II, IV, and V only

17. Biomass could include all of the following EXCEPT
    (A) the burning of wood to heat a home
    (B) the burning of manure to generate heat
    (C) the burning of petroleum to power an airplane
    (D) the burning of crop remains to generate electricity
    (E) the burning of charcoal to cook food

18. Which of the following is considered the main disadvantage of using hydrogen fuel?
    (A) The by-product of its combustion is water.
    (B) Current technology leaves us with a negative net energy.
    (C) It is difficult to store the fuel.
    (D) It needs water to produce fuel.
    (E) It is considered nontoxic.

19. Wind turbines have been able to reduce bird fatalities by
    I. Having a slower turning speed
    II. Having rounded and covered bases and turbines to reduce perching and nesting spaces
    III. Using research of migration routes to plan windfarm sites away from these areas
    (A) I only
    (B) II only
    (C) III only
    (D) I and II only
    (E) I, II, and III

20. Which of the following is supplied by a hydrothermal reservoir?
    (A) Highly heated water and steam that spin turbines to generate energy
    (B) Recreational areas behind hydroelectric dam sites
    (C) H_2S to burn and generate energy
    (D) Reserves of natural gas which can be transported in pipelines
    (E) Methane hydrate which can be used to produce electricity

21. The type of geothermal energy that can be used anywhere is
    (A) a geothermal heat pump using underground-to-surface temperature differences
    (B) the wet steam generation of electricity
    (C) super-heated water which can be used for a hot water supply
    (D) a dry steam flash power plant system
    (E) energy derived from hydrothermal reservoirs

22. Which of the following best describes tidal energy?
    (A) It uses a hydroelectric dam across the opening of a bay to capture the ebb and flood water movement.
    (B) It uses floating turbines that move in and out of beaches with the tide.
    (C) It uses kinetic pads which can be placed off-shore and capture the energy of water movement.
    (D) It uses flippers attached to buoys which capture the kinetic energy of waves which push them up and down.
    (E) It is used on offshore oil rigs to aid in the running of drills.

Questions 23 and 24 refer to the following forms of solar power. Choices may be used once, more than once, or not at all.
    (A) Photovoltaic
    (B) Active solar heating
    (C) Solar thermal
    (D) Passive solar
    (E) Solar cooker

23. This form of solar power uses south-facing windows in northern latitudes, and north-facing windows in southern latitudes, to naturally heat and light a home.

24. This form of solar power is the only one that, by design, provides energy to produce electricity at night.

25. Congress adopted CAFE standards in the United States to improve the efficiency of
    (A) home insulation in order to reduce energy use for heating in cooling
    (B) vehicles in order to increase their fuel economy
    (C) our country's electrical grid which is over 100 years old and outdated
    (D) wind turbines by decreasing vibrations and bird mortality
    (E) batteries for electric cars so they can travel distances greater than 200 miles

AP®FREE-RESPONSE PRACTICE

1. Because of the environmental costs of nonrenewable fuels and the dwindling reserves of oil, more attention is being given to renewable energy sources for residential and commercial uses, and to power vehicles.

    (a) The rise and fall in consumer interest in renewable energy sources tends to correlate to the fluctuations in oil prices.
        (i) **Explain** why a rise in oil prices drives an increased interest in renewable energy sources.
        (ii) **Identify** a second reason people might become more interested in renewable energy, and **explain** why it has this effect.

    (b) **Identify** two renewable energy sources.
        (i) **Describe** ONE economic advantage and ONE economic disadvantage for each.
        (ii) **Describe** ONE ecological advantage and ONE ecological disadvantage for each.

    (c) The production of electricity tends to be a multi-step process, regardless of the energy source used.
        (i) **Identify** the sequence of steps in the production of electricity from the burning of a fossil fuel such as coal.
        (ii) **Identify** the sequence of steps in the production of electricity from the use of either hydropower or wind power.

    (d) **Identify** and **discuss** TWO methods the federal government could use to make it more attractive for consumers to utilize renewable energy sources.

2. The graphs below depict both the global oil consumption, by region, and the price of crude oil, through 2011. Use the graphs and your knowledge to answer the questions below.

(a) Calculate the total global crude oil consumption, in millions of barrels per day, in 2011.

(b) Calculate the percent change in oil consumption in the United States from 1965 to 2011.

(c) Calculate the amount of money spent on oil globally, in dollars per day, using the data for all countries, in 2011.

(d) Explain the decrease in oil consumption from 2005 through 2011 in both the United States and the EU Countries.

(e) Describe why there was little incentive for the development of renewable resources throughout the 1980s and 1990s.

(f) Identify and **describe** TWO ecological disadvantages of using oil as an energy source.

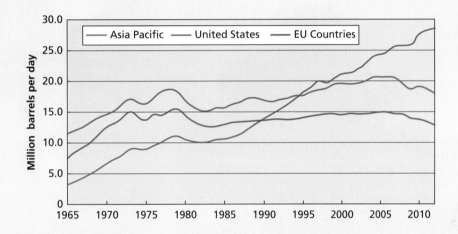

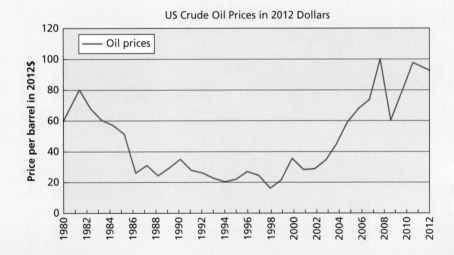

US Crude Oil Prices in 2012 Dollars

Environmental Hazards
and Human Health

Key Questions

16.1 What major health hazards do we face?

16.2 How do biological hazards threaten human health?

16.3 How do chemical hazards threaten human health?

16.4 How can we evaluate risks from chemical hazards?

16.5 How do we perceive and avoid risks?

Without effective air pollution control, coal-burning factories and power plants release toxic mercury and other air pollutants into the atmosphere.

Dudarev Mikhail/Shutterstock.com

Mercury's Toxic Effects

Mercury (Hg) and its compounds are all toxic. Research indicates that long-term exposure to high levels of mercury can permanently damage the human nervous system, brain, kidneys, heart, and lungs. Low levels of mercury can cause birth defects and brain damage in fetuses and young children. Pregnant women, nursing mothers and their babies, women of childbearing age, and young children are especially vulnerable to the harmful effects of mercury.

This toxic metal is released into the air from rocks, soil, and volcanoes and by vaporization from the oceans. Such natural sources account for about one-third of the mercury reaching the atmosphere each year. According to the US Environmental Protection Agency (EPA), the remaining two-thirds come from human activities. The largest source of mercury air pollution is thousands of small-scale gold miners in Asia, Africa, and South America. Other large sources of mercury in the atmosphere include emissions from coal-burning power and industrial plants (chapter-opening photo), cement kilns, smelters, and solid-waste incinerators. Mercury can also be released from household products such as certain types of thermometers, light bulbs, and thermostats when they break or disintegrate.

Because mercury is an element, it cannot be broken down or degraded. Therefore, it accumulates in soil, water, and the tissues of humans and other animals. In the atmosphere, some elemental mercury is converted to more toxic mercury compounds that are deposited in the oceans, in lakes (Figure 16.1), in other aquatic environments, and on land.

Under certain conditions in aquatic systems, bacteria convert inorganic mercury compounds to highly toxic *methylmercury* (CH_3Hg^+). Like DDT (see Figure 9.13, p. 247), methylmercury can be biologically magnified in food chains and food webs. High levels of methylmercury are often found in the tissues of large fishes, such as tuna, swordfish, shark, and marlin, which feed at high trophic levels. However, shrimp and salmon generally have low levels of mercury.

Humans are exposed to mercury in two major ways. People eat fish and shellfish that are contaminated with methylmercury. This accounts for 75% of all human exposures to mercury. People also inhale vaporized elemental mercury or particles of inorganic mercury salts such as mercury sulfide (HgS) and mercuric chloride ($HgCl_2$)—pollutants that come mostly from many coal-burning power plants and solid-waste incinerators. Studies estimate that 30,000 to 60,000 of the children born each year in the United States are likely to have reduced IQs and possible nervous system damage due to such exposure.

This problem raises three important questions: How do scientists determine the potential harm from exposure to mercury and other chemicals? How serious is the risk of harm from a particular chemical compared to other risks? And what should we do with any evidence of harm?

In this chapter, we will look at how scientists try to answer these and other questions about our exposure to chemicals. We will also examine health threats from disease-causing bacteria, viruses, and protozoa, and from other environmental hazards that kill millions of people every year. You will also learn about ways to evaluate and avoid some risks. ●

CRITICAL THINKING

Why do you think that mercury is particularly toxic to pregnant women, nursing mothers and their babies, and young children?

FIGURE 16.1 Fish are contaminated with mercury in many lakes, including this one in Wisconsin.

Drake Fleege/Alamy Stock Photo

16.1 WHAT MAJOR HEALTH HAZARDS DO WE FACE?

CONCEPT 16.1 We face health hazards from biological, chemical, physical, and cultural factors, and from the lifestyle choices we make.

We Face Many Types of Hazards

A **risk** is the probability of suffering harm from a hazard that can cause injury, disease, death, economic loss, or damage. Scientists often state the probability of a risk in terms such as, "The lifetime probability of developing lung cancer from smoking one pack of cigarettes per day is 1 in 250." This means that 1 of every 250 people who smoke a pack of cigarettes every day will likely develop lung cancer over a typical lifetime (usually considered to be 70 years). Probability can also be expressed as a percentage, as in a 30% chance of developing a certain type of cancer. The greater the probability of harm, the greater the risk.

Risk assessment is the process of using statistical methods to estimate how much harm a particular hazard can cause to human health or to the environment. It helps us compare risks and establish priorities for avoiding or managing risks. **Risk management** involves deciding whether and how to reduce a particular risk to a certain level and at what cost. Figure 16.2 summarizes how risks are assessed and managed.

No one can live a risk-free life, but we can reduce exposure to risks. When assessing risks, it is important to understand how serious the risks are and whether the benefits of certain activities outweigh the risks.

Five major types of hazards threaten human health (**Concept 16.1**):

Risk Assessment	Risk Management
Hazard identification What is the hazard?	**Comparative risk analysis** How does it compare with other risks?
Probability of risk How likely is the event?	**Risk reduction** How much should it be reduced? **Risk reduction strategy** How will the risk be reduced?
Consequences of risk What is the likely damage?	**Financial commitment** How much money should be spent?

FIGURE 16.2 Risk assessment and risk management are used to estimate the seriousness of various risks and to help reduce such risks. ***Critical thinking:*** What is an example of how you have applied this process in your daily living?

- *Biological hazards* from more than 1,400 **pathogens,** or microorganisms that can cause disease in other organisms. Examples are bacteria, viruses, parasites, protozoa, and fungi.
- *Chemical hazards* from harmful chemicals in the air, water, soil, food, and human-made products (**Core Case Study**).
- *Natural hazards* such as fire, earthquakes, volcanic eruptions, floods, tornadoes, and hurricanes.
- *Cultural hazards* in daily life such as unsafe working conditions, criminal assault, and poverty.
- *Lifestyle choices* such as smoking, making poor food choices, and not getting enough exercise.

CONSIDER THIS . . .

THINKING ABOUT Health Hazards

Think of a hazard from each of these categories that you may have faced recently. Which one was the most threatening?

CHECKPOINT FOR UNDERSTANDING 16.1

1. Explain the difference between risk assessment and risk management.

16.2 HOW DO BIOLOGICAL HAZARDS THREATEN HUMAN HEALTH?

CONCEPT 16.2 The most serious biological hazards humans face are infectious diseases such as flu, acquired immunodeficiency syndrome (AIDS), tuberculosis, diarrheal diseases, and malaria.

Some Diseases Can Spread from Person to Person

An **infectious disease** is a disease caused by a pathogen such as a bacterium, virus, or parasite invading the body and multiplying in its cells and tissues. **Bacteria** are single-cell organisms that are found everywhere and that can multiply rapidly on their own. Most bacteria are harmless or beneficial but some cause diseases such as strep throat or tuberculosis (see Case Study that follows). **Viruses** are pathogens that work by invading a cell and taking over its genetic machinery to copy themselves in order to spread throughout the body. Viruses cause diseases such as flu and AIDS. **Parasites** are organisms that live on or inside other organisms and feed on them. Their size ranges from one-celled organisms called protozoa to worms that are visible to the naked eye. They can cause infectious diseases such as malaria and swimmer's itch.

A **transmissible disease** is an infectious disease that can be transmitted from one person to another. Some transmissible diseases are bacterial diseases such as tuberculosis, many ear infections, and gonorrhea. Others are viral diseases such as the common cold, flu, and AIDS. Transmissible diseases can be spread through air, water, and food. They can also be transmitted by insects such as mosquitoes, and by body fluids such as feces, urine, blood, semen, and droplets sprayed during sneezing and coughing.

A **nontransmissible disease** is caused by something other than a living organism and does not spread from one person to another. Nontransmissible diseases include cardiovascular (heart and blood vessel) diseases, most cancers, asthma, and diabetes.

In 1900, infectious disease was the leading cause of death in the world. Since then, and especially since 1950, the incidences of infectious diseases and the death rates from them have dropped significantly. This has been achieved mostly by a combination of better health care, the use of antibiotics to treat diseases caused by bacteria, and the development of vaccines to prevent the spread of some viral diseases. GOOD NEWS

Despite the declining risk of harm from infectious diseases, they remain serious health threats, especially in less-developed countries. A large-scale outbreak of an infectious disease in an area or a country is called an *epidemic*. A global epidemic like tuberculosis or AIDS is called a *pandemic*. Figure 16.3 shows the annual death tolls from the world's seven deadliest infectious diseases (**Concept 16.2**).

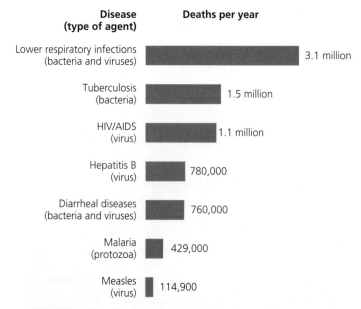

Disease (type of agent)	Deaths per year
Lower respiratory infections (bacteria and viruses)	3.1 million
Tuberculosis (bacteria)	1.5 million
HIV/AIDS (virus)	1.1 million
Hepatitis B (virus)	780,000
Diarrheal diseases (bacteria and viruses)	760,000
Malaria (protozoa)	429,000
Measles (virus)	114,900

FIGURE 16.3 The World Health Organization has estimated that the world's seven deadliest infectious diseases kill about 8.3 million people per year—most of them poor people in less-developed countries (**Concept 16.2**). *Data Analysis:* How many people die from all seven of the infectious diseases every year? Every day?

(Compiled by the authors using data from the World Health Organization (WHO) and the US Centers for Disease Control and Prevention)

One reason why infectious disease is still a serious threat is that many disease-carrying bacteria have developed genetic immunity to widely used antibiotics (Science Focus 16.1). Also, many disease-transmitting species of insects such as mosquitoes have become immune to widely used pesticides such as DDT that once helped to control their populations.

Another factor that will likely keep infectious diseases high on the list of environmental health threats is climate change. Many scientists warn that warmer temperatures will likely allow some infectious diseases—especially those spread by mosquitoes and other insects that breed more rapidly in warmer climates—to spread more easily from tropical to temperate areas such as the bottom half of the continental United States.

CASE STUDY

The Global Threat from Tuberculosis

Tuberculosis (TB) is a bacterial infection that destroys lung tissue and can ultimately lead to death. Since 1990, TB, a highly contagious bacterial infection of the lungs, has been spreading. Many TB-infected people do not appear to be sick, and most of them do not know they are infected. Left untreated, each person with active TB typically infects a number of other people. Without treatment, about half of the people with active TB die from bacterial destruction of their lung tissue (Figure 16.4).

According to the WHO, TB strikes about 9 million people and kills 1.5 million a year. Several factors account for the spread of TB. One is a lack of TB screening and control programs, especially in less-developed countries where more than 90% of the new cases occur. However, researchers are developing new and easier ways to detect TB and to monitor its effects (Individuals Matter 16.1).

A second problem is that most strains of the TB bacterium have developed genetic resistance to the majority of the effective antibiotics (Science Focus 16.1). Also, population growth, urbanization, and air travel have greatly increased person-to-person contacts. A person with active TB might infect several people during a single bus or plane ride. TB is spreading faster in areas where large numbers of poor people crowd together, especially in the rapidly growing slums of less-developed countries.

Slowing the spread of the disease requires early identification and treatment of people with active TB, especially those with a chronic cough, which is the primary way in

Genetic Resistance to Antibiotics

Antibiotics are chemicals that can kill bacteria. They have played an important role in the 30-year increase in American life expectancy since 1950.

It is becoming increasingly harder to stop the spread of infectious diseases. In 2017, the World Health Organization (WHO) issued a report warning that the age of antibiotics may be ending because many disease-causing bacteria are becoming genetically resistant to the antibiotics that we have long used to kill them. The reason for this is the astounding reproductive rate of bacteria, some of which can grow from a population of 1 to well over 16 million in 24 hours. This allows bacteria to quickly become genetically resistant to an increasing number of antibiotics through natural selection (see Figure 4.12, p. 103). To make matters worse, research indicates that in addition to passing genetic resistance to antibiotics to offspring bacteria can transfer such resistance to one another and to different strains of bacteria.

A major factor in the promotion of such genetic resistance, also called *antibiotic resistance*, is the widespread use of antibiotics on livestock raised in feedlots and CAFOs. They are used to control disease and to promote growth among dairy and beef cattle, poultry, and hogs that are raised in large numbers in crowded conditions. The US Food and Drug Administration (FDA) has estimated that about 80% of all antibiotics used in the United States and 50% of those used worldwide are added to the feed of healthy livestock. There is growing concern that residues of some of these antibiotics in meat can play a role in increasing genetic resistance in humans to these antibiotics. According to the Centers for Disease Control and Prevention (CDC), 22% of antibiotic-resistant illness in humans is linked to food, especially food from livestock treated with antibiotics.

Another factor is the overuse of antibiotics for colds, flu, and sore throats, many of which are viral diseases that do not respond to treatment with antibiotics. In many countries, antibiotics are available without a prescription, which promotes excessive and unnecessary use. Yet another factor is the spread of bacteria around the globe by human travel and international trade. The growing use of antibacterial hand soaps and other antibacterial cleansers could also be promoting antibiotic resistance in bacteria and they do not work any better than thorough hand washing, according to the US Food and Drug Administration..

Because of these factors acting together, every major disease-causing bacterium has now developed strains that resist at least 1 of the roughly 200 antibiotics in use and a growing number of infectious bacteria have developed genetic resistance to more than one antibiotic. We are now seeing the emergence of *superbugs*, bacteria that resist all available antibiotics. The CDC has estimated that each year, at least 2 million Americans get infectious diseases from superbugs, and at least 23,000 die. Also, 1 of every 25 US hospital patients picks up such an infection while in the hospital. A two-year study by economist Jim O'Neil for the British government estimated that globally drug-resistant superbugs already kill at least 700,000 people per year and by 2050 could kill as many as 10 million people a year.

For example, a bacterium known as methicillin-resistant *Staphylococcus aureus*, commonly known as MRSA (or "mersa"), has become resistant to most common antibiotics. MRSA can cause severe pneumonia, a vicious rash, and a quick death if it gets into the bloodstream. It is re-

sponsible for about one-third of the flesh-eating bacterial infections in the United States.

MRSA can be found in hospitals, nursing homes, schools, gyms, and college dormitories. It can be spread through skin contact, unsanitary use of tattoo needles, and contact with poorly laundered clothing and shared items such as towels, bed linens, athletic equipment, and razors.

Health officials warn that we could be moving into a post-antibiotic era of higher death rates. No major new antibiotics have been developed in recent years, mostly because drug companies lose millions of dollars developing new antibiotics that are used for only a short time to treat infections. They make more money on drugs that users take daily for many years for diseases such as diabetes and high blood pressure. As a result, 15 of the 18 largest pharmaceutical companies no longer make antibiotics. However, governments and private groups are undertaking efforts to develop antibiotics and vaccines that are more effective.

CRITICAL THINKING

What are three steps that you think we could take to slow the rate at which disease-causing bacteria are developing resistance to antibiotics?

2 million
the annual number of US citizens who get infections that cannot be treated with any known antibiotics

Hayat Sindi: Health Science Entrepreneur

Growing up in a home of humble means in Saudi Arabia, Hayat Sindi was determined to get an education, become a scientist, and do something for humanity. She was the first Saudi woman to be accepted at Cambridge University. She earned a PhD and taught in the Cambridge's international medical program, and in 2012 she was named a National Geographic Explorer.

As a visiting scholar, Sindi worked with a team of scientists at Harvard University and co-founded a nonprofit company called *Diagnostics for All* to bring low-cost health monitoring to remote, poor areas of the world. The Harvard team sought to develop simple and inexpensive diagnostic tools that could be used to detect certain illnesses and medical problems in remote areas.

One such tool is a small piece of paper the size of a postage stamp, with tiny channels and wells etched into it. Technicians load it with various diagnostic chemicals and then put a drop of a patient's blood, urine, or saliva onto this paper where the chemicals react with the fluid to change its color. Results show up in a minute and can be easily be read to diagnose different medical infections and conditions such as declining liver function, which can result from taking anti-TB drugs. The test can be conducted by a technician with minimal training and requires no electricity, clean water, or special equipment. After the paper is used, it can be burned on the spot to prevent the spread of any infectious agents. Dr. Sindi was named a UNESCO Goodwill Ambassador for science education and has a passion for inspiring women and girls, particularly those in the Middle East, to pursue science.

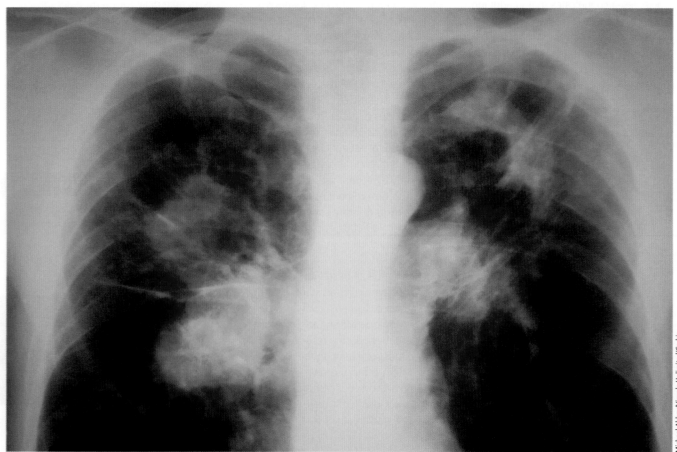

FIGURE 16.4 Colorized red areas in this chest X-ray show where TB bacteria have destroyed lung tissue.

World Agencies

Globalization has made trade, transportation, and other types of interdependence a reality in the modern world. Protecting the health of the human population is another aspect of our global interdependence, and several world agencies work to address this global concern. These include:

The United Nations: A global institution dedicated to promoting dialogue among countries with the goal of world peace. In 1948, the UN established the World Health Organization as its special agency with the authority to oversee and coordinate work on international health matters and public health.

The World Health Organization (WHO): As the health agency of the United Nations, the WHO is dedicated to the improvement of human health by monitoring and assessing health trends and providing medical advice to countries. The World Health Organization works in over 150 countries along with their government to help people attain healthcare. The WHO works in various countries to combat infectious diseases like influenza and AIDS, and nontransmissible diseases like cancer and heart disease. They also work for

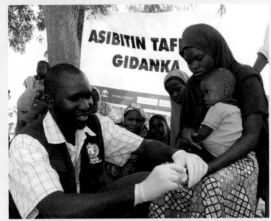

WORLD HEALTH ORGANIZATION (WHO)

ecojustice—ensuring clean air and water, safe food, and access to medicine and vaccines.

World Bank: A global institution that provides technical and financial assistance to developing countries with the objectives of reducing poverty and promoting growth, especially in the poorest countries. The World Bank is an advocate for universal health coverage, and through this work aims to achieve improved health and development outcomes that are in line with sustainable development goals in the developing world.

All three of these agencies work globally to reduce the hazards of war and disease, to address environmental risks,

and to improve world health through better custodianship and the reduction of poverty.

FRQ Application

Question: Malaria is a disease that continues to plague many developing nations, killing thousands of people each year. Nongovernmental organizations can be key in combating the spread of diseases like malaria. **Describe** strategies that the United Nations, the World Bank, and the World Health Organization might employ to slow the spread of malaria.

Possible Response: The UN is a forum for communication between countries. Since disease does not recognize boundaries, the UN can promote ways for neighboring countries to work together to reduce the population of anopheles mosquitoes that transmit malaria. The World Bank provides technical and financial assistance to developing countries. This organization can lend money to disease-stricken countries to build clinics and improve the infrastructure that would reduce standing water where mosquitoes breed and lead to fewer victims of malaria. The WHO focuses on improving health in developing nations. This organization could provide mosquito netting, quinine tablets, and medical information to doctors.

---

which the disease is spread from person to person. However, because many people do not show any symptoms of TB, they do not know they are infected and can infect other people. Treatment with a combination of four inexpensive drugs can cure 90% of individuals with active TB, but to be

> **CONSIDER THIS . . .**
>
> **THINKING ABOUT** Dealing with Tuberculosis
> If you were a public health official, what would you do to try to slow the spread of tuberculosis?

effective, the drugs must be taken every day for 6–9 months. Because symptoms often disappear after a few weeks of treatment, many patients think they are cured and stop taking the drugs. This can allow the disease to recur, possibly in drug-resistant forms, and to spread to other people.

Plavevski/Shutterstock.com

FIGURE 16.5 These health-care workers are screening a woman in China for the Ebola virus. They must wear special suits to avoid all direct contact between their own skin and anyone who might be infected with the virus.

Viral Diseases and Parasites Are Killers

Viruses are not affected by antibiotics and can be deadly. The biggest viral killer is the *influenza* or *flu virus* (**Concept 16.2**), which is transmitted by the body fluids or airborne droplets released when an infected person coughs or sneezes. Influenza often leads to fatal pneumonia. Flu viruses are so easily transmitted that an especially potent flu virus could spread around the world in a pandemic that could kill millions of people in only a few months.

The second biggest viral killer is the *human immuno-deficiency virus*, or *HIV* (see the Case Study that follows). On a global scale, according to the Joint United Nations Programme on HIV/AIDS (UNAIDS), HIV infected about 2.1 million people in 2016 (down from 3.1 million in 2000), and the complications resulting from AIDS killed about 1.1 million (down from 2 million in 2005). HIV is transmitted by unsafe sex, the sharing of needles by drug users, infected mothers who pass the virus to their babies before or during birth, and exposure to infected blood.

The third largest viral killer is the *hepatitis B virus (HBV)*, which damages the liver. According to the WHO, it kills more than 780,000 people each year. It is spread in the same ways that HIV is spread.

Another deadly virus is the *West Nile virus*, which is transmitted to humans by the bite of a common mosquito that is infected when it feeds on birds that carry the virus. In the United States, according to the CDC, between 1999 and 2015, the virus caused severe illnesses in nearly 42,500 people and killed about 1,800 people. About 45% of all infections affect the brain and spinal cord, and such infections account for 93% of all deaths due to West Nile virus.

Scientists estimate that throughout history, more than half of all infectious diseases were originally transmitted to humans from wild or domesticated animals. The development of such diseases has spurred the growth of the relatively new field of *ecological medicine* (Science Focus 16.2).
GREEN CAREER: Ecological medicine

Good hygiene can greatly reduce the chances of getting infectious diseases. This includes thorough and frequent hand washing with plain soap, not sharing personal items such as razors or towels, and covering cuts and scrapes until healed. It also helps to avoid contact with people who have infectious diseases.

Another growing health hazard is infectious diseases caused by parasites, especially malaria (see the second Case Study that follows).

CASE STUDY

The Global HIV/AIDS Epidemic

The global spread of AIDS, caused by HIV infection, is a major global health threat. This virus cripples the immune system and leaves the body vulnerable to infections such as TB and rare forms of cancer such as *Kaposi's sarcoma*. A person infected with HIV can live a normal life, but if the infection develops into AIDS, death is likely. An estimated 20% of all people infected with HIV are not aware of the infection and can spread the virus for years before being diagnosed.

Since HIV was identified in 1981, this viral infection has spread around the globe. According to UNAIDS, in 2016, about 36.7 million people worldwide (about 1.2 million in the United States, according to the CDC) were living with HIV. In 2016, there were about 2.1 million new cases of AIDS—half of them in people ages 15 to 49. The CDC estimates that the United States sees 45,000 to 50,000 new cases per year.

Between 1981 and 2016, more than 36 million people died of AIDS-related diseases, according to UNAIDS. According to the CDC, the US death toll for the same period was more than 698,000. In 2015, AIDS killed about 1.1 million people—down from a peak of 2.3 million in 2005.

Worldwide, AIDS is the leading cause of death for people of ages 15 to 49. This affects the population age structures in several African countries, including Botswana (Figure 16.6), where 25% of all people between ages

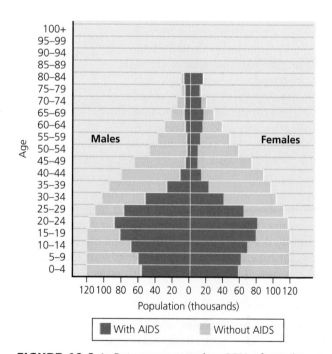

FIGURE 16.6 In Botswana, more than 25% of people ages 15–49 were infected with HIV in 2014. This figure shows two projected age structures for Botswana's population in 2020—one including the possible effects of the AIDS epidemic (red bars), and the other not including those effects (yellow bars). ***Critical thinking:*** How might this affect Botswana's economic development?

(Compiled by the authors using data from the US Census Bureau, UN Population Division, and World Health Organization)

Ecological Medicine: Tracking Infectious Diseases from Animals to Humans

A number of infectious diseases move from one animal species to another and from wild and domesticated animal species to humans. Examples of such diseases and their origins include the following:

- HIV—moves from simians (apes or monkeys) to humans (see Case Study, p. 502)
- Lyme disease—moves from wild deer and mice through ticks to humans
- West Nile virus—transmitted from birds via mosquito bites
- Avian flu—a severe flu strain from birds
- Plague—moved from rats to rat fleas to humans

Ecological medicine is a new interdisciplinary field devoted to tracking down these unwanted connections between animals and humans. Scientists in this field have identified several human practices that encourage the spread of diseases among animals and people. One is the clearing or fragmenting of forests to make way for settlements, farms, and expanding cities.

For example, in the United States, the push of suburban development into forests has increased the chances of many suburbanites becoming infected with Lyme disease. The bacterium that causes this disease lives in the bodies of deer and white-footed mice and is passed between these two animals and to humans, mostly by certain types of ticks (Figure 16.A), but also by mosquitoes, spiders, fleas, and mites. Left untreated, Lyme disease can cause debilitating arthritis, heart disease, and nervous disorders.

The practice of hunting wild game for food has also increased the spread of infectious diseases. In parts of Africa and Asia, local people who kill monkeys and other animals for bush meat (see Figure 9.15, p. 252) come in regular contact with primate blood and can be exposed to a simian strain of HIV, which causes AIDS.

Another important factor in the spread of these diseases is the legal and illegal international trade in wild species. The US Fish and Wildlife Service estimates that more than 200 million wild animals—from kangaroos to iguanas to tropical fish—are legally imported into the United States each year with little quarantining or screening for disease. Most are imported for commercial sale in the pet trade.

Industrialized meat production is another major factor in the spread of food-borne infectious diseases to humans. For

FIGURE 16.A A deer tick can carry the Lyme disease bacterium from a deer or mouse to a human.

example, a deadly form of *E. coli* bacteria sometimes spreads from livestock to humans when people eat meat contaminated by animal manure. *Salmonella* bacteria found on animal hides and in poorly processed, contaminated meat also can cause food-borne disease.

A number of scientists are looking at the connections between climate change and the spread of infectious diseases, especially malaria, meningitis, dengue fever, and West Nile virus. With warmer temperatures, they are concerned that the mosquitoes and other insects that spread these diseases will increase their ranges from tropical areas to temperate areas of the globe.

CRITICAL THINKING

If you were an ecological medicine doctor, where would you put your greatest efforts in researching this problem? Explain.

---

15 and 49 were infected with HIV in 2014. The premature deaths of many teachers, health-care workers, farmers, and other adults in these countries has contributed to declines in education, health care, food production, economic development, and political stability. In addition, it has led to the disintegration of many families and large numbers of orphaned children.

The treatment for HIV infection includes a combination of antiviral drugs that can slow the progress of the virus. However, such drugs cost too much to be used widely in the less-developed countries where HIV infections are widespread.

CASE STUDY

Malaria—The Spread of a Deadly Parasite

About 3.2 billion people—44% of the world's population—are at risk of getting malaria (Figure 16.7). Most of them live in poor African countries. People traveling to malaria-prone areas are also at risk because there is no vaccine that can prevent this disease.

Malaria is caused by a parasite that is spread by certain mosquito species. The mosquito bites an infected person, picks up the parasite, and passes it to the next person it bites. The parasites then move out of the mosquito, into

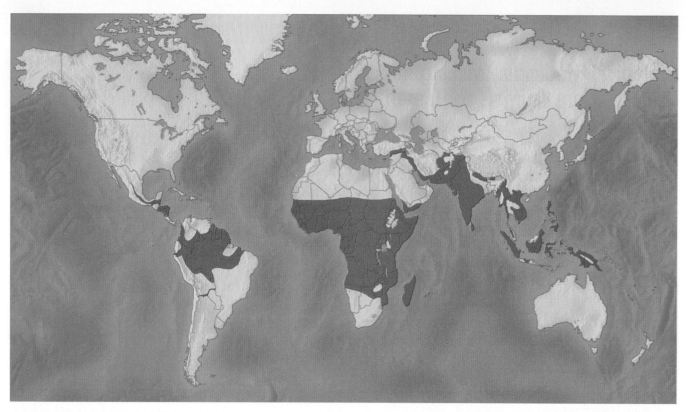

FIGURE 16.7 About 44% of the world's population live in areas in which malaria is prevalent. As the earth warms, malaria may spread to some temperate areas such as the southern half of the United States.

(Compiled by the authors using data from the World Health Organization and US Centers for Disease Control and Prevention.)

the human's bloodstream, and multiply in the human's liver. The parasite infects and destroys its victim's red blood cells, causing intense fever, chills, drenching sweats, severe abdominal pain, vomiting, headaches, and increased susceptibility to other diseases. According to the WHO and UNICEF, malaria killed about 429,000 people in 2015—a 65% drop since 2000. However, some experts contend this total could be much higher, because public health records are incomplete in many areas. More than 90% of all malaria victims live in sub-Saharan Africa and most of them are children younger than five years old. Roughly every minute a child under age 5 dies from malaria. Many children who survive suffer brain damage or impaired learning ability.

Over the course of human history, malarial protozoa probably have killed more people than all the wars ever fought. The spread of malaria was slowed during the 1950s and 1960s, a time when swamps and marshes where mosquitoes breed were drained or sprayed with insecticides, and drugs were used to kill the parasites in victims' bloodstreams.

Since 1970, however, malaria has come roaring back. Most species of mosquitoes that transmit malaria have become genetically resistant to most insecticides and the

Plasmodium parasites have become genetically resistant to common antimalarial drugs. During this century, as the average atmospheric temperature rises, populations of malaria-carrying mosquitoes will likely spread from tropical areas to warming temperate areas. Scientists have made progress in developing a malaria vaccine, but currently no effective vaccine is available.

CONSIDER THIS . . .

CONNECTIONS Deforestation and Malaria

The clearing and development of tropical forests has led to the spread of malaria among workers and the settlers who follow them. One study found that a 5% loss of tree cover in one part of Brazil's Amazon forest led to a 50% increase in malaria in that study area. The researchers hypothesized that deforestation creates partially sunlit pools of water that make ideal breeding ponds for malaria-carrying mosquitoes.

Another approach is to provide poor people in malarial regions with free or inexpensive insecticide-treated bed nets (Figure 16.8) and window screens. Between 2000 and 2014, the percentage of Africa's population sleeping under mosquito nets increased from 2% to more than

FIGURE 16.8 This baby in Senegal, Africa, is sleeping under an insecticide-treated mosquito net to reduce the risk of being bitten by malaria-carrying mosquitoes.

50% and saved 6.2 million lives, according to the WHO. Also, zinc and vitamin A supplements can be given to children to boost their resistance to malaria.

Reducing the Incidence of Infectious Diseases

According to the WHO, the percentage of all deaths worldwide resulting from infectious diseases dropped from 35% to 16% between 1970 and 2015, primarily because a growing number of children were immunized against the major infectious diseases. Between 1990 and 2015, the estimated annual number of children younger than age 5 who died from infectious diseases dropped from nearly 12 million to 4.9 million. [GOOD NEWS]

Figure 16.9 lists measures that could help prevent or reduce the incidence of infectious diseases—especially in less-developed countries. The WHO has estimated that implementing the solutions listed in Figure 16.9 could save the lives of as many as 4 million children younger than age 5 each year. **GREEN CAREER: Infectious disease prevention**

CONSIDER THIS . . .

CONNECTIONS Drinking Water, Latrines, and Infectious Diseases

More than a third of the world's people—2.6 billion—do not have sanitary bathroom facilities. Nearly 1 billion get their water for drinking, washing, and cooking from sources polluted by animal or human feces. A key to reducing sickness and premature death due to infectious disease is to focus on providing simple latrines and access to safe drinking water.

CHECKPOINT FOR UNDERSTANDING 16.2

1. Identify three agents of infectious disease.

2. Describe the difference between a transmissible disease and a nontransmissible disease.

3. Explain why tuberculosis is particularly difficult to control.

4. Discuss why the global incidence of malaria has increased since 1970.

- Increase research on tropical diseases and vaccines
- Reduce poverty and malnutrition
- Improve drinking water quality
- Reduce unnecessary use of antibiotics
- Sharply reduce use of antibiotics on livestock
- Immunize children against major viral diseases
- Provide oral rehydration for diarrhea victims
- Conduct global campaign to reduce HIV/AIDS

FIGURE 16.9 Ways to prevent or reduce the incidence of infectious diseases, especially in less-developed countries. ***Critical thinking:*** Which three of these approaches do you think are the most important? Why?

Top: © Omer N Raja/Shutterstock.com. Bottom: Rob Byron/Shutterstock.com.

16.3 HOW DO CHEMICAL HAZARDS THREATEN HUMAN HEALTH?

CONCEPT 16.3 Certain chemicals in the environment can cause cancers and birth defects and disrupt the human immune, nervous, and endocrine systems.

Some Chemicals Can Cause Cancers, Mutations, and Birth Defects

A **toxic chemical** is an element or compound that can cause temporary or permanent harm or death to humans. There are three major types of potentially toxic agents. **Carcinogens** are chemicals, some types of radiation, and certain viruses that can cause or promote *cancer*—a disease in which malignant cells multiply uncontrollably and create tumors that can damage the body and often lead to premature death. Examples of carcinogens are arsenic, benzene, formaldehyde, PCBs, (see Case Study that follows) radon, vinyl chloride, and certain chemicals in tobacco smoke.

Typically, 10 to 40 years may pass between the initial exposure to a carcinogen and the appearance of detectable cancer symptoms. This time lag helps explain why many healthy teenagers and young adults have trouble believing that their own habits, such as smoking, excessive drinking, and poor diet, could lead to some form of cancer before they reach age 50.

The second major type of toxic agent, **mutagens,** includes chemicals or forms of radiation that cause or increase the frequency of *mutations*, or changes, in the DNA molecules found in cells. Most mutations cause no harm, but some can lead to cancers and other disorders. Harmful mutations occurring in reproductive cells can be passed on to offspring and to future generations.

Teratogens, a third type of toxic agent, are chemicals that harm or cause birth defects in a fetus or embryo. Ethyl alcohol is a teratogen. Women who drink alcoholic beverages during pregnancy increase their risk of having babies with low birth weight and a number of physical, developmental, behavioral, and mental problems. Other teratogens are mercury (**Core Case Study**), PCBs, lead, and formaldehyde.

CASE STUDY

PCBs Are Everywhere—A Legacy from the Past

PCBs are a class of more than 200 chlorine-containing organic compounds that are very stable and nonflammable. Between 1929 and 1977, PCBs were widely used as lubricants, hydraulic fluids, and insulators in electrical transformers and capacitors. They also became ingredients in a variety of products including paints, fire retardants in fabrics, preservatives, adhesives, and pesticides.

The US Congress banned the domestic production of PCBs in 1977 after research showed that they could cause liver cancer and other cancers in test animals. Studies also showed that pregnant women exposed to PCBs gave birth to underweight babies who eventually suffered permanent neurological damage, sharply lower-than-average IQs, and long-term growth problems.

Production of PCBs has also been banned in most other countries, but the potential health threats from these chemicals will be with us for a long time. Because PCBs break down very slowly in the environment, they can travel long distances in the air before landing far away from where they were released. Also, because they are fat-soluble, PCBs can also be biologically magnified in food chains and food webs (see Figure 16.B in Math Connection that follows).

As a result, PCBs are now found almost everywhere—in the air, soil, lakes, rivers, fish, birds, most human bodies, and even the bodies of polar bears in the Arctic. According to the EPA, about 70% of all the PCBs made in the United States are still in the environment.

Some Chemicals Affect Our Immune and Nervous Systems

Since the 1970s, research on wildlife and laboratory animals along with some studies of humans suggest that long-term exposure to some chemicals in the environment

Parts per Million and Parts per Billion

Because the dose of a toxin can be a very small amount, scientists use parts per million (ppm) and parts per billion (ppb) to measure the concentration of a chemical in a solution.

Parts per million means a ratio of one part or unit of a *solute* for every 1 million units of a *solvent*. One part per billion is one part of *solute* per 1 billion parts *solvent*. Figure 16.B shows the concentration of PCBs in organisms that are biomagnified in the tissues of organisms in a lake food chain. What is the difference between parts per million and parts per billion? Since there is 1,000 million in 1 billion, to express parts per billion as parts per million, it is necessary to divide by 1000.

For example, if PCB concentration in phytoplankton is measured to be 2.5 parts per billion, what is the concentration in parts per million?

$$2.5 \text{ ppb PCBs} / 1,000 = 0.0025 \text{ parts per million PCBs}$$

Water	Phytoplankton	Zooplankton	Rainbow smelt	Lake trout	Herring gull	Herring gull eggs
0.000002 ppm	0.0025 ppm	0.123 ppm	1.04 ppm	4.83 ppm	124 ppm	124 ppm

FIGURE 16.B Biological magnification of polychlorinated biphenyls (PCBs) in an aquatic food chain in the Great Lakes.

FRQ Application

Lake Ontario has a volume of 1639 km^3. The PCB concentration in Lake Ontario water is 0.000002 ppm. Using the facts that, for water, 1ppm = 1mg/L and 1mL = 1cm^3, how many metric tons of PCBs are there in Lake Ontario? You may round to the nearest metric ton.

1ppm = 1mg/L, so there are 0.000002 mg/L PCBs in Lake Ontario

1 mL = 1 cm^3, so 1 L = 1000 cm^3 = 0.001 m^3

The volume of Lake Ontario in liters is

$$1639 \text{ km}^3 \times \frac{(1000 \text{ m})^3}{1 \text{ km}^3} \times \frac{1 \text{ L}}{0.001 \text{ m}^3} = 1.639 \times 10^{15} \text{ L of water in Lake Ontario}$$

The total amount of PCBs in Lake Ontario is

$$1.639 \times 10^{15} \text{ L} \times \frac{0.000002 \text{ mg PCB}}{\text{L}} \times \frac{1 \text{ g}}{1000 \text{ mg}} = 3.278 \times 10^7 \text{ g PCBs}$$

$$3.278 \times 10^7 \text{ g PCBs} \times \frac{1 \text{ kg}}{1000 \text{ g}} \times \frac{1 \text{ metric ton}}{1000 \text{ kg}} = 33 \text{ metric tons of PCBs in Lake Ontario}$$

can disrupt important body systems, including immune and nervous systems (**Concept 16.3**).

The *immune system* consists of specialized cells and tissues that protect the body against disease and harmful substances. It does this by forming *antibodies*, or specialized proteins, that detect and destroy invading agents. Some chemicals such as arsenic, methylmercury (**Core Case Study**), and dioxins can weaken the human immune system and leave the body vulnerable to attacks by allergens and infectious bacteria, viruses, and protozoa.

Some natural and synthetic chemicals in the environment, called *neurotoxins*, can harm the human *nervous system* (the brain, spinal cord, and peripheral nerves). Effects can include behavioral changes, learning disabilities, attention-deficit disorder, paralysis, and death. Examples of neurotoxins are PCBs, arsenic, lead, and certain pesticides.

Methylmercury (**Core Case Study**) is an especially dangerous neurotoxin because it is persists in the environment and, like DDT and PCBs, can be biologically magnified in food chains and food webs (Figure 16.10). According to the Natural Resources Defense Council, predatory fish such as tuna, orange roughy, swordfish, mackerel, grouper, and sharks can have mercury concentrations in their bodies that are 10,000 times higher than the levels in the water around them.

In one study, the EPA found that almost half of the fish tested in 500 lakes and reservoirs across the United States had levels of mercury that exceeded safe levels (Figure 16.1). The EPA estimates that about 1 of every 12 women of childbearing age in the United States has enough mercury in her blood to harm a developing fetus. Figure 16.11 lists ways to prevent or reduce human inputs of mercury (**Core Case Study**) into the environment.

Some Chemicals Affect the Endocrine System

The *endocrine system* is a complex network of glands that release tiny amounts of *hormones* into the bloodstreams of humans and other vertebrate animals. Very low levels of these chemical messengers (often measured in parts per billion or parts per trillion) regulate bodily systems that control sexual reproduction, growth, development, learning ability, and behavior. Each hormone has a unique molecular shape that allows it to attach to certain parts of cells called *receptors*, and to transmit a chemical message (Figure 16.12).

Molecules of certain synthetic chemicals have shapes similar to those of natural hormones. This allows them to attach to the molecules of natural hormones and to disrupt the endocrine systems in humans and in some other animals (**Concept 16.3**). These molecules are called *hormonally active agents (HAAs)* or *endocrine disruptors*.

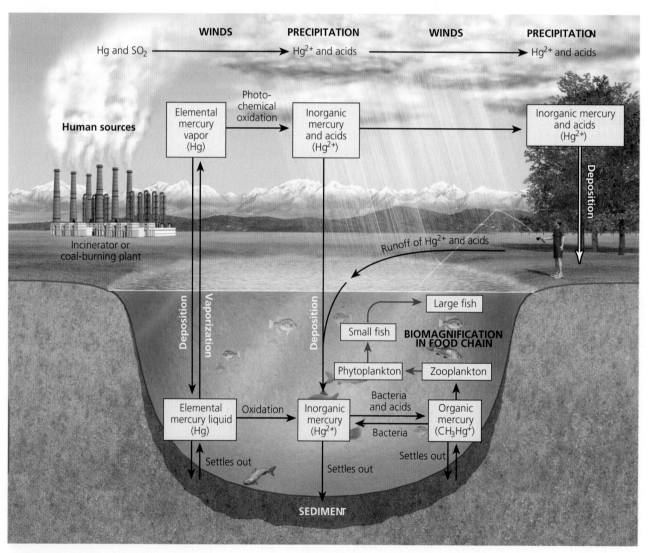

FIGURE 16.10 Movement of different forms of toxic mercury from the atmosphere into an aquatic ecosystem where it is biologically magnified in a food chain. **Critical thinking:** What is your most likely exposure to mercury?

Examples of HAAs include Atrazine and several other widely used herbicides, organophosphate pesticides, dioxins, lead, and mercury (**Core Case Study**). Some HAAs, including *bisphenol A*, or *BPA* (Science Focus 16.3, p. 510), act as hormone imposters, or *hormone mimics*. They are chemically similar to estrogens (female sex hormones) and can disrupt the endocrine system by attaching to estrogen receptor molecules. Other HAAs, called *hormone blockers*, disrupt the endocrine system by preventing natural hormones

such as androgens (male sex hormones) from attaching to their receptors. Numerous studies involving wild animals, laboratory animals, and humans suggest that the males of species that are exposed to hormonal disruption are generally becoming more feminized.

Concerns about BPA and other HAAs show how difficult it can be to assess the potential harmful health effects from exposure to very low levels of various chemicals. Resolving these uncertainties will take decades of research. Some scientists argue that as a precaution during this period of research, people should sharply reduce their exposure to potentially harmful hormone disrupters (Figure 16.13), especially in products frequently used by pregnant women, infants, young children, and teenagers.

Solutions

Mercury Pollution

Prevention	Control
Phase out waste incineration	Sharply reduce mercury emissions from coal-burning plants and incinerators
Remove mercury from coal before it is burned	Label all products containing mercury
Switch from coal to natural gas and renewable energy resources	Collect and recycle batteries and other products containing mercury

FIGURE 16.11 Ways to prevent or control inputs of mercury (**Core Case Study**) into the environment from human sources—mostly coal-burning power plants and incinerators. ***Critical thinking:*** Which four of these solutions do you think are the most important? Why?

Top: Mark Smith/Shutterstock.com. Bottom: tuulijumala/Shutterstock.com

What Can You Do?

Exposure to Hormone Disrupters

- Eat certified organic produce and meats
- Avoid processed, prepackaged, and canned foods
- Use glass and ceramic cookware
- Store food and drinks in glass containers
- Use only natural cleaning and personal care products
- Use natural fabric shower curtains, not vinyl
- Avoid artificial air fresheners, fabric softeners, and dryer sheets
- Use only glass baby bottles and BPA-free, phthalate-free sipping cups, pacifiers, and toys

FIGURE 16.13 Individuals matter: Ways to reduce your exposure to hormone disrupters. ***Critical thinking:*** Which three of these steps do you think are the most important ones to take? Why?

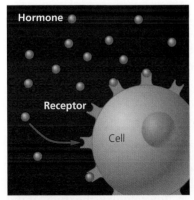

Normal Hormone Process

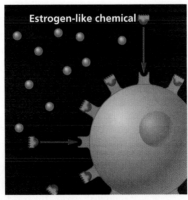

Hormone Mimic

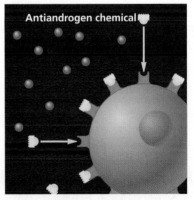

Hormone Blocker

FIGURE 16.12 Each type of hormone has a unique molecular shape that allows it to attach to specially shaped receptors on the surface of, or the inside of, a cell and to transmit its chemical message (left). Molecules of certain pesticides and other synthetic chemicals, called *hormonally active agents* (HAAs, center and right), have shapes similar to those of natural hormones, allowing them to attach to the hormone molecules and disrupt the endocrine systems of humans and other animals.

The Controversy over BPA

The estrogen mimic *bisphenol A (BPA)* serves as a hardening agent in certain plastics that are used in a variety of products. They include some baby bottles, sipping cups, and pacifiers, as well as some reusable water bottles, sports drink and juice bottles, microwave dishes, and food storage containers. BPA is also used to make some dental sealants. In addition, individuals can be exposed to BPA when their hands touch the thermal paper used to produce some cash register receipts.

BPA is also used as a liner in most food and beverage cans sold in the United States. This type of liner allows containers to withstand extreme temperatures, keeps canned food from interacting with the metal in the cans, prevents rust in the cans, and helps to preserve the canned food.

A study by the CDC indicated that 93% of Americans older than age 6 had trace levels of BPA in their urine. Although these levels were well below the acceptable level set by the EPA, the EPA level was established in the late 1980s, before much was known about the potential effects of BPA on human health. The CDC study also found that children and adolescents generally had higher urinary BPA levels than adults had.

Research indicates that the BPA in plastics can leach into water or food when the plastic is heated to high temperatures, microwaved, or exposed to acidic liquids. Harvard University Medical School researchers found that there was a 66% increase in BPA levels in the urine of participants who drank from polycarbonate bottles regularly for just 1 week.

By 2013, more than 90 published studies by independent laboratories had found a number of significant adverse effects on test animals from exposure to very low levels of BPA. These effects include brain damage, early puberty, decreased sperm quality, certain cancers, heart disease, type 2 diabetes, liver damage, impaired immune function, impotency in males, and obesity in test animals.

On the other hand, 12 studies funded by the chemical industry found no evidence or only weak evidence of adverse effects from low-level exposure to BPA in test animals. In 2008, the FDA concluded that BPA in food and drink containers was not a health hazard. In 2015, the European Food Safety Authority agreed, concluding that BPA is not appearing in people's body systems at high enough levels to cause harm. However, France

has banned BPA from the lining of all cans.

Consumers now have more choices, since most makers of baby bottles, sipping cups, and sports water bottles offer BPA-free alternatives. Many consumers are avoiding plastic containers with a #7 recycling code (which indicates that BPA can be present). People are also using powdered infant formula instead of liquid formula from metal cans, choosing glass bottles, mugs, and food containers instead of those made of plastic.

Many manufacturers have replaced BPA with bisphenol S (BPS). However, studies indicate that BPS can have effects similar to those of BPA, and was present at detectable levels in the urine of nearly 81% of people tested for it.

CRITICAL THINKING

Should plastics that contain BPA or BPS be banned from use in all children's products? Explain. Should such plastics be banned from use in the liners of canned food containers? Explain.

CHECKPOINT FOR UNDERSTANDING 16.3

1. Toxic chemicals include carcinogens, mutagens, and teratogens. Explain the differences between each.

2. Explain how hormonally active agents can affect the endocrine system.

16.4 HOW CAN WE EVALUATE RISKS FROM CHEMICAL HAZARDS?

CONCEPT 16.4A Scientists use live laboratory animals, to estimate the toxicity of chemicals, but this approach has serious limitations.

CONCEPT 16.4B Many health scientists call for much greater emphasis on pollution prevention to reduce our exposure to potentially harmful chemicals.

Many Factors Determine the Toxicity of Chemicals

Every day we are exposed to small amounts of potentially harmful chemicals in the air we breathe, the water we drink, and the food we eat. **Toxicology** is the study of the harmful effects of these and other chemicals on humans and other organisms.

Toxicity is a measure of the ability of a substance to cause injury, illness, or death to a living organism. A basic principle of toxicology is that *any synthetic or natural chemical can be harmful if ingested or inhaled in a large enough* *quantity.* But the critical question is this: *At what level of exposure to a particular toxic chemical will the chemical cause harm?*

This is a difficult question to answer because of the many variables involved in estimating the effects of human exposure to chemicals. A key factor is the **dose,** the amount of a harmful chemical that a person has ingested, inhaled, or absorbed through the skin at any one time.

The effects of a particular chemical can also depend on the age of the person exposed to it. For example, toxic chemicals usually have a greater effect on fetuses, infants, and children than on adults (see the Case Study that follows). Toxicity also depends on *genetic makeup*, which determines an individual's sensitivity to a particular toxin. People vary widely in their degrees of sensitivity to chemicals (Figure 16.14), and some are sensitive to a number of toxins—a condition known as *multiple chemical sensitivity* (MCS).

Another factor that determines how chemicals affect people is **synergistic interaction**, or *synergy*, which occurs when two or more compounds interact. When that interaction magnifies the effects of both compounds, it is called a *synergistic reaction*. For example, scientific studies reveal such an interaction between smoking and inhaling asbestos particles. Nonsmokers who are exposed to asbestos particles for long periods of time increase their risk of getting lung cancers fivefold. But people who smoke and are exposed to asbestos have 50 times the risk that nonsmokers have for getting lung cancer.

Several other variables can affect the level of harm caused by a chemical. One is its *solubility*. Water-soluble toxins can move throughout the environment and get into water supplies, as well as the aqueous solutions that surround the cells in our bodies. Oil- or fat-soluble toxins can penetrate the membranes that surround our cells, because these membranes allow similar oil-soluble chemicals to pass through them. Thus, oil- or fat-soluble toxins can accumulate in body tissues and cells.

Another factor is a substance's *persistence*, or resistance to breaking down. Many chemicals, including DDT and PCBs, were used widely because they are not easily broken down in the environment. This means that they are more likely to remain in the body and have long-lasting harmful health effects.

Biological magnification can also play a role in toxicity. Animals that eat higher on the food chain are more susceptible to the effects of fat-soluble toxic chemicals because of the magnified concentrations of the toxins in their bodies. Examples of chemicals that can be biomagnified include DDT (Figure 9.13, p. 247), PCBs (Figure 16.B), and methylmercury (**Core Case Study**).

The health damage resulting from exposure to a chemical is called the **response.** One type of response, an *acute effect*, is an immediate or rapid harmful reaction ranging from dizziness to death. By contrast, a *chronic effect* is a permanent or long-lasting consequence (kidney or liver damage, for example) of exposure to a single dose or to repeated lower doses of a harmful substance.

Natural and synthetic chemicals can be either safe or toxic. Many synthetic chemicals, including many of the medicines we take, are quite safe if used as intended, whereas many natural chemicals such as lead and mercury (**Core Case Study**) are deadly.

Protecting Children from Toxic Chemicals

In one study, the Environmental Working Group analyzed umbilical cord blood from 10 randomly selected newborns in U.S. hospitals. Of the 287 chemicals detected in that study, 180 have been shown to cause cancers in humans or animals, 217 have damaged the nervous systems of test animals, and 208 have caused birth defects or abnormal development in test animals. Scientists do not know what harm, if any, might be caused by the very low concentrations of these chemicals found in the infants' blood.

However, more recent science has caused some experts to suggest that exposure to chemical pollutants in the womb may be related to increasing rates of autism, childhood asthma, and learning disorders. In 2009, researchers for the first time found a connection between the exposure of pregnant women to air pollutants and lower IQ scores in their children as they grew. A team of researchers led by Frederica Perera of Columbia University reported that children exposed to high levels of air pollution before birth scored 4–5 points lower, on average, in IQ tests than did children with less exposure.

Infants and young children are more susceptible to the effects of toxic substances than are adults, for three major reasons. *First*, they generally breathe more air, drink more water, and eat more food per unit of body weight than do adults. *Second*, they are exposed to toxins in dust and soil when they put their fingers, toys, and other objects in their mouths. *Third*, children usually have less well-developed immune systems and body detoxification processes than

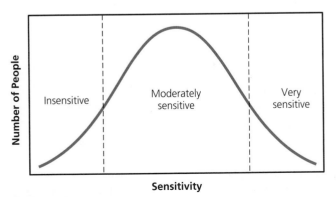

FIGURE 16.14 Individuals in a human population can vary in how sensitive they are to a particular chemical.

adults have. Fetuses are also highly vulnerable to trace amounts of toxic chemicals such as methylmercury (**Core Case Study**) that they can receive from their mothers.

The EPA has proposed that in determining any risk, regulators should assume that children have a 10-times higher risk factor than adults have. Some health scientists suggest that to be on the safe side, we should assume that this risk for children is 100 times the risk for adults.

CONSIDER THIS . . .

THINKING ABOUT Toxic Chemical Levels for Children

Do you think environmental regulations should require that the allowed levels of exposure to toxic chemicals for children be 100 times lower than those for adults? Explain your reasoning.

Scientists Use Various Tests to Estimate Toxicity

The most widely used method for determining toxicity is to expose a population of live laboratory animals to measured doses of a specific substance under controlled conditions. Laboratory-bred mice and rats are widely used because, as mammals, their systems function similarly to human systems, to some degree. Also, they are small and can reproduce rapidly under controlled laboratory conditions. Animal tests typically take 2 to 5 years, involve hundreds to thousands of test animals, and can cost as much as $2 million per substance tested. Some of these tests can be painful to the test animals and can kill or harm them. Animal welfare groups want to limit or ban the use of test animals and, at the very least, want to ensure that they are treated in the most humane manner possible.

Scientists estimate the toxicity of a chemical by determining the effects of various doses of the chemical on test organisms and plotting the results in a **dose-response curve** (Figure 16.15). One approach is to determine the

lethal dose—the dose that will kill an animal. A chemical's *median lethal dose (LD50)* is the dose that can kill 50% of the animals (usually rats and mice) in a test population within a given time period, usually expressed in milligrams of the chemical per kilogram of body weight (mg/kg).

Chemicals vary widely in their toxicity. Some toxins can cause serious harm or death after a single very low dose. For example, a few drops of pure nicotine (found in e-cigarettes) would make you very sick, while a teaspoon of it could kill you. Others such as water or table sugar cause such harm only at dosages so huge that it is nearly impossible to get enough into the body to cause injury or death. Most chemicals fall between these two extremes.

There are three general types of dose-response curves. With the *nonthreshold dose-response model* (Figure 16.15, left), any dosage of a toxic chemical causes harm that increases with the dosage. With the *threshold dose-response model* (Figure 16.15, center), a certain level, or *threshold*, of exposure to the chemical must be reached before any detectable harmful effects occur, presumably because the body can repair the damage caused by low dosages of some substances. With the third type, called the *unconventional model* (Figure 16.15, right), the harmful effects increase with dosage to a certain point and then begin decreasing.

Establishing which of these three models applies at low dosages is extremely difficult and controversial. To be on the safe side, scientists often choose the nonthreshold dose-response model. High dosages are used to reduce the number of test animals needed, obtain results quickly, and lower costs. Use of low dosages would require running tests on millions of laboratory animals for many years, in which case chemical companies and government agencies could not afford to test most chemicals.

For the same reasons, scientists usually use mathematical models to *extrapolate*, or estimate, the effects of low-dose exposures based on the measured results of high-dose exposures. Then they extrapolate these results from test

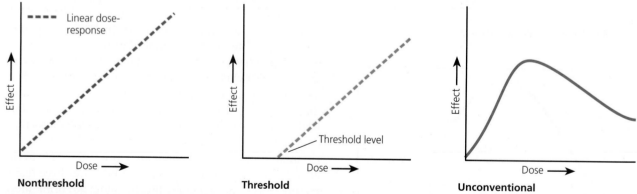

FIGURE 16.15 *Dose-response curves.* Scientists estimate the toxicity of various chemicals by determining how a chemical's harmful effects change as the dose increases. Some chemicals behave according to the *nonthreshold model* (left curve). Others behave according to the *threshold model* (center curve). Still others are unconventional in how they behave (right curve). For all of these graphs, the curves usually vary from being exactly linear, or straight. ***Critical thinking:*** Can you think of commonly used chemicals that fit each of these models? What are they?

organisms to humans as a way of estimating LD50 values for acute toxicity. Some scientists challenge the validity of extrapolating data from test animals to humans, because human physiology and metabolism often differ from those of the test animals, as well as from person to person. Other scientists say that such tests and models can work well, especially for revealing cancer risks, when the correct experimental animal is chosen, or when a chemical is toxic to several different test-animal species.

More humane methods for toxicity testing are available and are being used more often to replace testing on live animals. They include making computer simulations and using individual animal cells, instead of whole, live animals. High-speed robot testing devices can now screen the biological activity of more than 1 million compounds a day to help determine their possible toxic effects.

The problems with estimating toxicities in the laboratory get even more complicated (**Concept 16.4A**). In real life, each of us is exposed to a variety of chemicals, some of which can interact in ways that decrease or enhance their individual effects. Toxicologists already have great difficulty in estimating the toxicity of a single substance. Evaluating mixtures of potentially toxic substances, determining how they interact, and deciding which of them are the most harmful can be overwhelming from a scientific and economic standpoint. For example, just studying the interactions among 3 of the 500 most widely used industrial chemicals would take 20.7 million experiments—a physical and financial impossibility.

CONSIDER THIS . . .

THINKING ABOUT Animal Testing
Should laboratory-bred mice, rats, and other animals be used to determine toxicity and other effects of chemicals? Explain.

Are Trace Levels of Toxic Chemicals Harmful?

Almost everyone who lives in a more-developed country is now exposed to potentially harmful chemicals (Figure 16.16) that have built up to trace levels in their blood and in other parts of their bodies. CDC studies have found that the blood of an average American contains traces of 212 different chemicals, including potentially harmful chemicals such as arsenic and BPA.

Should we be concerned about trace amounts of various synthetic chemicals in our air, water, food, and bodies? In most cases, we simply do not know because there are

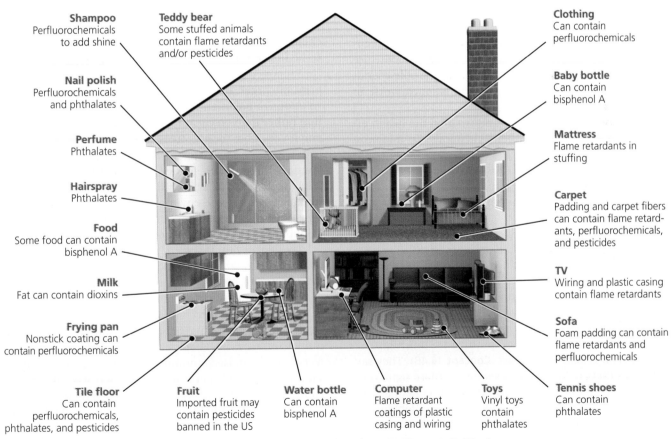

Shampoo
Perfluorochemicals to add shine

Nail polish
Perfluorochemicals and phthalates

Perfume
Phthalates

Hairspray
Phthalates

Food
Some food can contain bisphenol A

Milk
Fat can contain dioxins

Frying pan
Nonstick coating can contain perfluorochemicals

Teddy bear
Some stuffed animals contain flame retardants and/or pesticides

Clothing
Can contain perfluorochemicals

Baby bottle
Can contain bisphenol A

Mattress
Flame retardants in stuffing

Carpet
Padding and carpet fibers can contain flame retardants, perfluorochemicals, and pesticides

TV
Wiring and plastic casing contain flame retardants

Sofa
Foam padding can contain flame retardants and perfluorochemicals

Tile floor
Can contain perfluorochemicals, phthalates, and pesticides

Fruit
Imported fruit may contain pesticides banned in the US

Water bottle
Can contain bisphenol A

Computer
Flame retardant coatings of plastic casing and wiring

Toys
Vinyl toys contain phthalates

Tennis shoes
Can contain phthalates

FIGURE 16.16 A number of potentially harmful chemicals are found in many homes. **Critical thinking:** Does the fact that we do not know much about the long-term harmful effects of these chemicals make you more likely or less likely to minimize your exposure to them? Why?

(Compiled by the authors using data from the US Environmental Protection Agency, Centers for Disease Control and Prevention, and New York State Department of Health.)

not enough data and because it is so difficult to determine the effects of exposures to low levels of these chemicals (**Concept 16.4A**).

Some scientists view exposures to trace amounts of synthetic chemicals with alarm, especially because of their potential long-term effects on the human body. Others scientists view the threats from such trace exposures as minor. They point out that average life expectancy has been increasing in most countries, especially more-developed countries, for decades.

Why Do We Know So Little about the Harmful Effects of Chemicals?

All methods for estimating toxicity levels and risks have serious limitations (**Concept 16.4A**), but they are all that we have. According to risk assessment expert Joseph V. Rodricks, "Toxicologists know a great deal about a few chemicals, a little about many, and next to nothing about most."

The US National Academy of Sciences estimates that only 10% of the more than 85,000 registered synthetic chemicals in commercial use have been thoroughly screened for toxicity. Only 2% have been adequately tested to determine whether they are carcinogens, mutagens, or teratogens. Hardly any of the chemicals in commercial use have been screened for possible damage to the human nervous, endocrine, and immune systems.

Because of insufficient data and the high costs of regulation, federal and state governments do not supervise the use of nearly 99.5% of the commercially available chemicals in the United States. The problem is much worse in less-developed countries.

Most scientists call for more research on the health effects of trace levels of synthetic chemicals. To minimize harm and take into account the uncertainty about health effects, scientists and regulators typically set allowable levels of exposure to toxic substances at 1/100th or even 1/1,000th of the estimated harmful levels.

Pollution Prevention and the Precautionary Principle

We know little about the potentially toxic chemicals around us and inside of us, and estimating their effects is very difficult, time-consuming, and expensive. So where does this leave us?

Some scientists and health officials, especially those in European Union countries, are pushing for much greater emphasis on *pollution prevention* (**Concept 16.4B**). They say chemicals that are known or suspected to cause significant harm should not be released into the environment at pollutant levels. Preventing such pollution means looking for harmless or less harmful substitutes for toxic and hazardous chemicals. It also requires recycling them within production processes to keep them from reaching the environment, as companies such as DuPont and 3M have been doing (see the Case Study that follows).

Pollution prevention is a strategy for implementing the **precautionary principle**. According to this principle, when there is substantial preliminary evidence that an activity, technology, or chemical substance can harm humans, other organisms, or the environment, decision makers should take measures to prevent or reduce such harm, rather than waiting for more conclusive scientific evidence.

There is controversy over how far we should go in using the precautionary principle. Those who favor a precautionary approach argue that a person or company, proposing to introduce a new chemical or technology should bear the burden of establishing its safety. This would require two major changes in the way we evaluate and manage risks. *First*, we would assume that new chemicals and technologies could be harmful until scientific studies could show otherwise. *Second*, the existing chemicals and technologies that appear to have a strong chance of causing harm would be removed from the market until we could establish their safety. For example, after decades of research revealed the harmful effects of lead, especially on children, lead-based paints and leaded gasoline were phased out in most developed countries.

Manufacturers and businesses contend that widespread application of the precautionary approach and requiring more pollution prevention would make it too expensive and almost impossible to introduce any new chemical or technology. They note that there is always some uncertainty in any scientific assessment of risk.

Proponents of increased reliance on the precautionary principle argue that it would focus the efforts on finding solutions to pollution problems that are based on prevention rather than on cleanup. It also reduces health risks for employees and society, frees businesses from having to deal with pollution regulations, and reduces the threat of lawsuits from injured parties. Proponents also argue that we have an ethical responsibility to reduce serious risks to human health, to the environment, and to future generations, in keeping with the ethical **principle of sustainability** (see the inside back cover of this book).

The European Union is applying the precautionary principle through pollution prevention. The Stockholm Convention of 2000 is an international agreement to ban or phase out the use of 12 of the most notorious *persistent organic pollutants (POPs)*, also called the *dirty dozen*. These highly toxic chemicals have been shown to produce numerous harmful effects, including cancers, birth defects, compromised immune systems, and declining sperm counts and sperm quality in men in a number of countries. The list includes DDT and eight other pesticides, PCBs, and dioxins. In 2009, nine more POPs were added, some of which are widely used in pesticides and in flame-retardants added to clothing, furniture, and other consumer goods. The treaty went into effect in 2004 but has not been formally approved or implemented by the United States.

In 2007, the European Union enacted regulations known as REACH (for *Registration, Evaluation, Authorization, and restriction of CHemicals*). It required the registration of 30,000 untested, unregulated, and potentially harmful chemicals. In the REACH process, the most hazardous substances are not approved for use if safer alternatives exist.

REACH puts more of the burden on industry to show that chemicals are safe. Conventional regulation such as that used in the United States has put the burden on governments to show that they are dangerous. The US chemical regulation structure was enacted in the 1976 Toxic Substances Control Act. At Congressional hearings, experts have testified that this system makes it virtually impossible for the government to limit or ban the use of toxic chemicals. The hearings found that by 2009, the EPA had required testing for only 200 of the more than 85,000 chemicals registered for use and had issued regulations to control fewer than 12 of those chemicals.

In 2011, the EPA took a step toward pollution prevention by issuing a rule to control emissions of mercury (**Core Case Study**) and harmful fine-particle pollution from older coal-burning plants in 28 states. Many eastern states have high depositions of mercury and harmful particles produced by coal-burning power and electric plants in the Midwest and blown eastward by prevailing winds (Figure 16.17). The new air pollution standards could prevent as many as 11,000 premature deaths, 200,000 nonfatal heart attacks, and 2.5 million asthma attacks. However, coal companies are pressuring members of Congress to eliminate this new standard.

Representatives from many nations have developed a UN treaty, known as the Minamata Convention, with the overall goal of reducing global mercury emissions by 15–35% in the next several decades. By January 2016, 128 countries had signed and 22 countries had ratified the treaty. It will go into effect after 50 countries have ratified it. Once in effect, within 5 years, signatory nations must require new coal-fired power plants, industrial plants, and smelters to use the best available mercury emission-control technologies. The treaty also calls for phasing out the use of mercury in many products, including thermometers, light bulbs, switches, batteries, and some cosmetics.

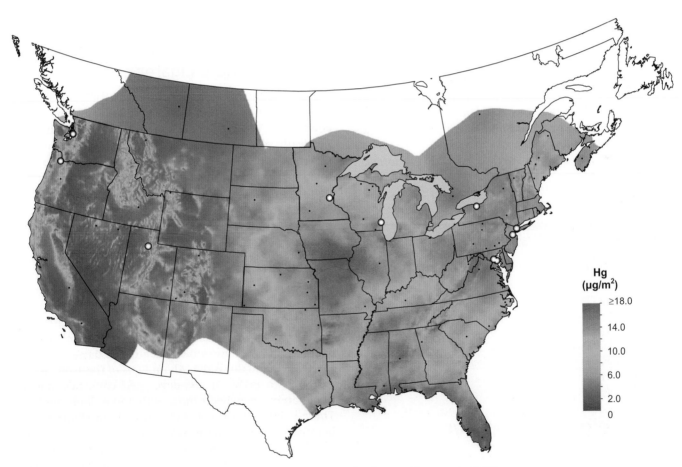

FIGURE 16.17 Atmospheric wet deposition of mercury in the lower 48 states in 2010. *Critical thinking:* Why do the highest levels occur mainly in the eastern half of the United States?

(Compiled by the authors using data from the Environmental Protection Agency and the National Atmospheric Deposition Program)

Pollution Prevention Pays

The US-based 3M Company makes 60,000 different products in 100 manufacturing plants around the world. In 1975, 3M began a Pollution Prevention Pays (3P) program. Since then, it has reformulated some of its products, redesigned equipment and processes, and reduced its use of hazardous raw materials. It has also recycled and reused more waste materials and sold some of its potentially hazardous but still useful wastes as raw materials to other companies. As of 2015, this program had prevented more than 1.8 million metric tons (2 million tons) of pollutants from reaching the environment and saved the company $1.9 billion.

The 3M 3P program has been successful largely because employees are rewarded if projects they come up with eliminate or reduce a pollutant; reduce the amount of energy, materials, or other resources required in production; or save money through reduced pollution control costs, lower operating costs, or increased sales of new or existing products. Employees at 3M have now completed more than 10,000 3P projects.

Since 1990, a growing number of companies have adopted similar pollution and waste prevention programs that have led to cleaner production. They are learning that, in addition to saving money by preventing pollution and reducing waste production, they have a much easier job of complying with pollution laws and regulations. In addition, they find they can avoid lawsuits based on exposure to harmful chemicals, provide a safer environment for their workers (which can reduce their employee health insurance costs), and improve their public image.

CHECKPOINT FOR UNDERSTANDING 16.4

1. Identify several factors that can play a role in the toxicity of a substance.

2. Explain why children are more susceptible to toxins than adults.

3. Explain how the precautionary principle applies to the manufacture and use of toxic chemicals.

16.5 HOW DO WE PERCEIVE AND AVOID RISKS?

CONCEPT 16.5 We can reduce the major risks we face by becoming informed, thinking critically about risks, and making careful choices.

The Greatest Health Risks Come from Poverty, Gender, and Lifestyle Choices

Risk analysis involves identifying hazards and evaluating their associated risks (*risk assessment*; Figure 16.2, left), ranking risks (*comparative risk analysis*), determining options and making decisions about reducing or eliminating risks (*risk management*; Figure 16.2, right), and informing decision makers and the public about risks (*risk communication*).

In terms of the number of deaths per year (Figure 16.18, left), *the greatest risk by far is poverty*. The high death toll ultimately resulting from poverty is caused by malnutrition, increased susceptibility to normally nonfatal infectious diseases, and often-fatal infectious diseases transmitted by unsafe drinking water, and inadequate health care (Figure 16.18, right).

Studies indicate that the four greatest risks in terms of shortened life spans are living in poverty, being born male, smoking (see the Case Study that follows), and obesity. Some of the greatest risks of premature death are illnesses that result primarily from lifestyle choices that people make (Figure 16.19) (**Concept 16.1**).

Cigarettes and E-Cigarettes

Cigarette smoking is the world's most preventable and largest cause of suffering and premature death among adults. The WHO estimates that smoking contributed to the deaths of 100 million people during the twentieth century and could kill 1 billion people during this century unless governments and individuals act to dramatically reduce smoking.

The WHO and a report by the US Surgeon General estimate that each year, tobacco contributes to the premature deaths of about 6 million people resulting from 25 illnesses, including heart disease, stroke, type 2 diabetes, lung and other cancers, memory impairment, bronchitis, and emphysema (Figure 16.20). This amounts to an average of more than 16,400 deaths every day, or about one every 5 seconds.

By 2030, the annual death toll from smoking-related diseases is projected to reach more than 8 million—an average of 21,900 preventable deaths per day—according to the CDC and the WHO. About 80% of these deaths are expected to occur in less-developed countries, and in moderately developed China, with 350 million smokers. There is little effort to reduce smoking in China, partly because cigarette taxes provide up to 10% of the central government's total annual revenues. The annual death toll from smoking in China is about 1.2 million, an average of about 137 deaths every hour. By 2050, the annual death toll from smoking in China could reach 3 million.

According to the CDC, smoking kills about 480,000 Americans per year—an average of 1,315 deaths per day,

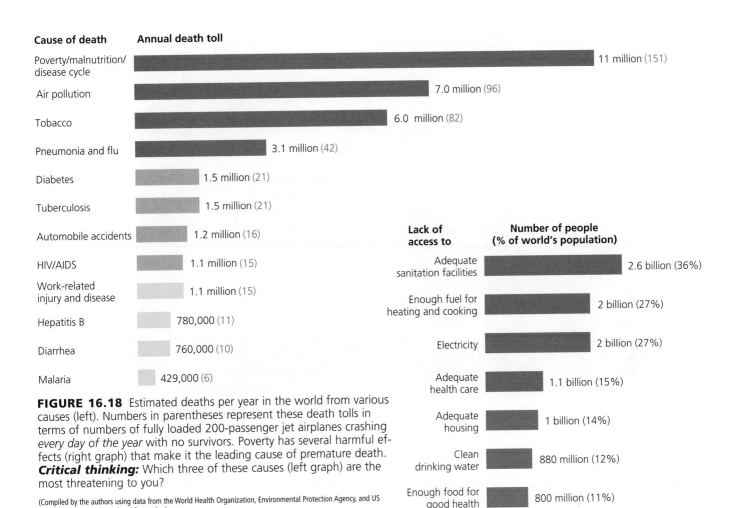

FIGURE 16.18 Estimated deaths per year in the world from various causes (left). Numbers in parentheses represent these death tolls in terms of numbers of fully loaded 200-passenger jet airplanes crashing *every day of the year* with no survivors. Poverty has several harmful effects (right graph) that make it the leading cause of premature death. ***Critical thinking:*** Which three of these causes (left graph) are the most threatening to you?

(Compiled by the authors using data from the World Health Organization, Environmental Protection Agency, and US Centers for Disease Control and Prevention)

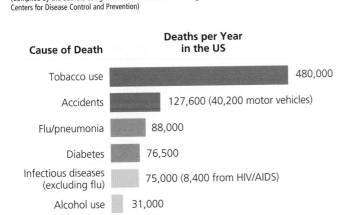

FIGURE 16.19 Leading causes of death in the United States. Some result from lifestyle choices and are preventable. ***Data analysis:*** The number of deaths from tobacco use is how many times the number of deaths from flu/pneumonia?

(Compiled by the authors using data from the US Centers for Disease Control and Prevention.)

or nearly one every minute (Figure 16.19). This death toll is roughly equivalent to more than six fully loaded 200-passenger jet planes crashing *every day of the year* with no survivors. Smoking also causes about 8.6 million illnesses every year in the United States.

The overwhelming scientific consensus is that the nicotine inhaled in tobacco smoke is highly addictive. A British government study showed that adolescents who smoke more than one cigarette have an 85% chance of becoming long-term smokers.

Studies indicate that cigarette smokers die, on average, 10 years earlier than nonsmokers, but that kicking the habit—even at 50 years of age—can cut such a risk in half. If people quit smoking by age 30, they can avoid nearly all the risk of dying prematurely. However, studies show that the longer one smokes, the harder it is to quit.

Studies also show that breathing *secondhand smoke* poses health hazards. In 2015, the CDC reported that in the United States, 58 million people are exposed daily to secondhand smoke, which is responsible for nearly 42,000 deaths per year.

In the United States, the percentage of adults who smoke dropped from more than 50% in the 1950s to 15% in 2015, according to the CDC, and the goal is to reduce this to less than 10% by 2025. This decline can be attributed to media coverage about the harmful health effects of smoking, sharp increases in cigarette taxes in many states (in New York City, the average price of a pack if cigarettes

FIGURE 16.20 The startling difference between normal human lungs (left) and the lungs of a person who died of emphysema (right). The major causes of emphysema are prolonged smoking and exposure to air pollutants.

is $13), mandatory health warnings on cigarette packs, the ban on sales to minors, and bans on smoking in workplaces, bars, restaurants, and public buildings.

A new form of cigarette, called *electronic cigarettes* or *e-cigarettes* (Figure 16.21), is being used increasingly as a substitute for tobacco cigarettes. These devices contain pure nicotine dissolved in a syrupy solvent containing one or more of over 7,000 chemicals to enhance taste and smell. A battery in the device heats the nicotine solution and converts it to a vapor containing liquid particles that the user inhales. Smoking e-cigarettes is called *vaping*. E-cigarettes can be refilled with solutions that vary from 2% to 10% in their concentrations of nicotine, which is a poison.

Are e-cigarettes safe? No one knows, because they have not been around long enough to be thoroughly evaluated. E-cigarettes reduce or eliminate the inhalation of tar and numerous other harmful chemicals found in regular cigarette smoke. But they still expose users to highly addictive nicotine, sometimes at levels of up to 5 times as high (10% nicotine) as that found in regular cigarettes (2% nicotine). Smokers may reduce their overall health threat by switching to e-cigarettes. On the other hand, e-cigarettes may lead some adolescents and young adults who have never smoked to become regular cigarette users.

Preliminary research indicates that some e-cigarette vapors contain trace amounts of toxic metals such as cadmium, nickel, lead, and several substances that can cause cancer in test animals. Some of these toxins, not found in regular cigarette smoke, are nanoparticles that are small enough to get past the body's defense systems and travel deep into the lungs. However, it will take much more research for any direct link between e-cigarettes and cancer to be established.

FIGURE 16.21 An e-cigarette that can be refilled with a solution of nicotine (e-juice).

Estimating Risks from Technologies

The more complex a technological system, and the more people needed to design and run it, the more difficult it is to estimate the risks of using the system. The overall *reliability* of such a system—the probability (expressed as a percentage) that the system will complete a task without failing—is the product of two factors:

System reliability (%) = Technology reliability (%) × Human reliability (%)

With careful design, quality control, maintenance, and monitoring, a highly complex system such as a nuclear power plant or a deep-sea oil-drilling rig can achieve a high degree of technological reliability. But human reliability usually is much lower than technological reliability and is almost impossible to predict.

Suppose the estimated technological reliability of a nuclear power plant is 95% (0.95) and human reliability is 75% (0.75). Then the overall system reliability is 71% (0.95 × 0.75 = 71%). Even if we could make the technology 100% reliable (1.0), the overall system reliability would still be only 75% (1.0 × 0.75 = 75%).

We can make a system safer by moving more of the potentially fallible elements from the human side to the technological side. However, chance events such as a lightning strike can knock out an automatic control system, and no machine or computer program can completely replace human judgment. Also, the parts in any automated control system are manufactured, assembled, tested, certified, inspected, and maintained by fallible human beings. In addition, computer software programs used to monitor and control complex systems can be flawed because of human design error or can be deliberately sabotaged to cause their malfunction.

Most People Do a Poor Job of Evaluating Risks

Most people are not good at assessing the relative risks from the hazards that they encounter. Many people deny or shrug off the high-risk chances of death or injury from the voluntary activities they enjoy. Examples of activities and their death rates include the following:

- *Smoking* (1 in 250 by age 70 for a pack-a-day smoker)
- *Hang gliding* (1 in 1,250)
- *Driving* (1 in 3,300 without a seatbelt and 1 in 6,070 with a seatbelt)

Indeed, the most dangerous thing that many people do each day is to drive or ride in a car. Yet some of these same people may be terrified about their chances of being killed by getting pneumonia from the flu (a 1 in 130,000 chance), a nuclear power plant accident (1 in 200,000), West Nile virus (1 in 1 million), a lightning strike (1 in 3 million), a commercial airplane crash (1 in 9 million), snakebite (1 in 36 million), or shark attack (1 in 281 million).

Five factors can cause people to see a technology or a product as being more or less risky than experts judge it to be. The first factor is *fear*. Research shows that fear causes people to overestimate risks and to worry more about catastrophic risks than they do about common, everyday risks. Studies show that people tend to overestimate numbers of deaths caused by tornadoes, floods, fires, homicides, cancer, and terrorist attacks, and to underestimate death tolls from smoking, flu, diabetes, asthma, heart attack, stroke, and automobile accidents.

The second factor clouding risk evaluation is the *degree of control* individuals have in a given situation. Many people have a greater fear of things over which they do not have personal control. For example, some individuals feel safer driving their own car for long distances (with a 1-in-6,070 risk of dying) than traveling the same distance on a plane (with a risk of 1 in 9 million).

The third factor influencing risk evaluation is *whether a risk is catastrophic or chronic*. People usually are more frightened by news of catastrophic accidents such as a plane crash than of a cause of death such as smoking, which has a much higher death toll spread out over time.

Fourth, some people have *optimism bias*, the belief that risks that apply to other people do not apply to them. Although some people get upset when they see others driving erratically while talking on a cell phone or texting, they may believe that talking on the cell phone or texting does not impair their own driving ability.

A fifth factor affecting risk analysis is that many of the risky things we do are highly pleasurable and give *instant gratification*, while the potential harm from such activities comes later. Examples are smoking cigarettes, eating too much food, and practicing unsafe sex.

Guidelines for Evaluating and Reducing Risk

Here are four guidelines for better evaluating and reducing risk and making better lifestyle choices (**Concept 16.5**):

- *Compare risks*. In evaluating a risk, the key question is not "Is it safe?" but rather "How risky is it compared to other risks?"
- *Determine how much risk you are willing to accept*. For most people, a 1 in 100,000 chance of dying or suffering serious harm from exposure to an environmental hazard is a threshold for changing their behavior. However, in establishing standards and reducing risk, the EPA generally assumes that a 1 in 1 million chance of dying from an environmental hazard is acceptable.
- *Evaluate the actual risk involved*. The news media usually exaggerate the daily risks we face in order to capture our interest and attract more readers, listeners, or television viewers. As a result, most people who are exposed to a daily diet of such exaggerated reports believe that the world is much more dangerous and risk-filled than it really is.

- *Concentrate on evaluating and carefully making important lifestyle choices.* When you worry about a risk, the most important question to ask is, "Do I have any control over this?" There is no point worrying about risks over which we have little or no control. But we do have control over major ways to reduce risks from heart attack, stroke, and certain forms of cancer, by deciding whether to smoke, what to eat, how much alcohol to drink, how much exercise we get, and how safely we drive.

KEY IDEAS

- We face significant hazards from infectious diseases such as flu, AIDS, tuberculosis, diarrheal diseases, and malaria, and from exposure to chemicals that can cause cancers and birth defects, as well as chemicals that can disrupt the human immune, nervous, and endocrine systems.

- Because of the difficulty of evaluating the harm caused by exposure to chemicals, many health scientists call for much greater emphasis on pollution prevention.

- By becoming informed, thinking critically about risks, and making careful choices, we can reduce the major risks we face.

Core Case Study Checkpoint

Identify the two major sources of human exposure to mercury.

Chapter 16 Glossary

bacteria: single-cell organisms that can multiply rapidly on their own. Most bacteria are harmless or beneficial but some can cause infectious diseases such as strep throat or tuberculosis.

carcinogen: chemicals, ionizing radiation, and viruses that cause or promote the development of cancer.

dose: amount of potentially harmful substance an individual ingests, inhales, or absorbs through the skin.

dose-response curve: plot of data showing the effects of various doses of a toxic agent on a group of test organisms.

infectious disease: disease caused when a pathogen such as a bacterium, virus, or parasite invades the body and multiplies in its cells and tissues. Examples are flu, HIV, malaria, tuberculosis, and measles.

mutagen: chemical or form of radiation that causes changes (mutations) in the DNA molecules in genes.

nontransmissible disease: disease that is not caused by living organisms and does not spread from one person to another. Examples include most cancers, diabetes, cardiovascular disease, and malnutrition.

parasite: consumer organism that lives on or in, and feeds on, a living plant or animal, known as the host. The parasite draws nourishment from and gradually weakens its host. Some parasites can also cause malaria and other serious diseases.

pathogen: living organism that can cause disease in another organism. Examples include bacteria, viruses, and parasites.

precautionary principle: when there is significant scientific uncertainty about potentially serious harm from chemicals or technologies, decision makers should act to prevent harm from humans and the environment.

response: amount of health damage caused by exposure to a certain dose of harmful substance or from of radiation.

risk analysis: identifying hazards, evaluating the nature and severity of risks associated with the hazards (*risk assessment*), ranking risks (*comparative risk analysis*), using this and other information to determine options and make decisions about reducing or eliminating risks (*risk management),* and communicating information about risks to decision makers and the public (*risk communication*).

risk assessment: process of gathering data and making assumptions to estimate short- and long-term harmful effects on human health or the environment from exposure to hazards associated with the use of a particular product or technology.

risk management: use of risk assessment and other information to determine options and make decisions about reducing or eliminating risks.

synergistic interaction: interaction of two or more factors or processes so that the combined effect is greater than the sum of their separate effects.

teratogen: chemical, ionizing agent, or virus that causes birth defects.

toxic chemical: an element or compound that can cause temporary or permanent harm or death to humans.

toxicity: measure of the ability of a substance to cause injury, illness, or death to a living organism.

toxicology: study of the adverse effects of chemicals on health.

transmissible disease: disease that is caused by living organisms (such as bacteria, viruses, and parasitic worms) and can spread from one person to another by air, water, food, or body fluids (or in some cases by insects or other organisms).

virus: microorganism that can transmit an infectious disease by invading a cell and taking over its genetic machinery to copy itself and then spread throughout the body.

Chapter Review

Core Case Study

1. Describe the toxic effects of mercury and its compounds and explain how we are exposed to these toxins.

Section 16.1

2. (a) What is the key concept for this section? (b) Define and distinguish among **risk**, **risk assessment**, and **risk management**. (c) Give an example of how scientists state probabilities. (d) Give an example of a risk from each of the following: biological hazards, chemical hazards, natural hazards, cultural hazards, and lifestyle choices. What is a **pathogen**?

Section 16.2

3. (a) What is the key concept for this section? (b) Define **infectious disease**. Define and distinguish among **bacteria**, **viruses**, and **parasites**, and give examples of diseases that each can cause. (c) Define and distinguish between **transmissible disease** and **nontransmissible disease**, and give an example of each. (d) In terms of death rates, what are the world's four most serious infectious diseases? (e) List five factors that have contributed to genetic resistance in bacteria to commonly used antibiotics. (f) What is MRSA and why is it so threatening?

4. (a) Describe the global threat from tuberculosis and list three factors that have helped it to spread. (b) What is the biggest viral killer and how does it spread? (c) What is the best way to reduce one's chances of getting an infectious disease? (d) What is the focus of ecological medicine and what are some of its findings regarding the spread of diseases? (e) Summarize the health threats from the global HIV/AIDS pandemic and its effects on the population age structure of Botswana.

5. (a) What is malaria and how does it spread? What percentage of the human population is subject to this threat? (b) Explain how deforestation can promote the spread of malaria. List ways to reduce the threat from malaria. (c) List six major ways to reduce the global threat from infectious diseases.

Section 16.3

6. (a) What is the key concept for this section? (b) What is a **toxic chemical**? Define and distinguish among **carcinogens**, **mutagens**, and **teratogens**, and give an example of each. (c) What are PCBs and why are they a threat? (d) Describe the human immune, nervous, and endocrine systems, and for each of these systems, give an example of a chemical that can threaten it. (e) What is a neurotoxin and why is methylmercury (**Core Case Study**) an especially dangerous one? (f) What are six ways to prevent or control environmental inputs of mercury? (g) What are hormonally active agents (HAAs), what risks do they pose, and how can we

reduce those risks? (h) Summarize health scientists' concerns about exposure to bisphenol A (BPA) and the controversy over what to do about exposure to this chemical. (i) List six ways to reduce your exposure to HAAs.

Section 16.4

7. (a) What are the two key concepts for this section? (b) Define **toxicology**, **toxicity**, **dose**, and **response**. (c) What are three factors that affect the level of harm caused by a chemical? (d) Give three reasons why children are especially vulnerable to harm from toxic chemicals. (e) Describe how the toxicity of a substance can be estimated by testing laboratory animals, and explain the limitations of this approach. (f) What is a **dose-response curve**?

8. (a) Summarize the controversy over the effects of trace levels of chemicals. (b) Why do we know so little about the harmful effects of chemicals? (c) What is the **precautionary principle**? Explain why the use of pollution prevention based on the

precautionary principle is controversial. (d) Describe some efforts to apply this principle on national and international levels. (e) What is the Stockholm Convention? (f) How did pollution prevention pay off for the 3M Company?

Section 16.5

9. (a) What is the key concept for this section? (b) What is **risk analysis**? (c) In terms of premature deaths, what are the three greatest threats that people face? (d) What are six ways in which poverty can threaten one's health? (e) Describe the health threats from smoking and how we can reduce these threats. (f) Summarize our knowledge of the health effects of using e-cigarettes. (g) How can we reduce the threats resulting from the use of various technologies? (h) What are five factors that can cause people to misjudge risks? List four guidelines for evaluating and reducing risk.

10. What are this chapter's *three key ideas*?

_____

Note: Key terms are in bold type.

AP® Review Questions

Questions 1–3 refer to the following terms. Choices can be used once, more than once, or not at all.
   (A) Epidemic
   (B) Pandemic
   (C) Non-transmissible disease
   (D) Physical hazard
   (E) Mutagen

1. In 1918, a virus called the Spanish Flu spread rapidly around the globe; within a few months, it killed 20–50 million people.

2. In the United States, medical data currently shows a steep rise in the number of people with diabetes.

3. The people of the Caribbean often suffer from the devastating effects of hurricanes and tropical storms.

4. Which of the following has not affected the recent resurgence of tuberculosis (TB)?
   (A) Improved testing/screening in developing countries
   (B) Increased global travel
   (C) Urbanization
   (D) Genetic resistance of the bacterium
   (E) Increased population growth in developing countries

5. Which of the following is NOT one of the social ramifications of HIV infection and resulting death of young adults?
   (A) Decreasing orphanage rates because parents infected with HIV are living long enough to raise their children to adulthood
   (B) Diminishing education because teachers are ill and dying, and there are not enough new teachers to replace them
   (C) Diminishing health care because of the high number of health-care workers who either die or are too ill to do their jobs
   (D) Decreasing food production because of the illness and deaths of adults who would otherwise have planted and harvested crops
   (E) Disintegrating families because of the number of parents who have either died or are ill and unable to care for their children

6. Which of the following is a part of risk assessment?
   (A) Comparative risk analysis of other risks
   (B) Determining the financial cost of reducing the risk
   (C) Assessing the probability of risk
   (D) Developing a strategy for reducing risk
   (E) Evaluating the quantity of risk reduction needed

Question 7 refers to the projection of the Botswana population in 2020 below.

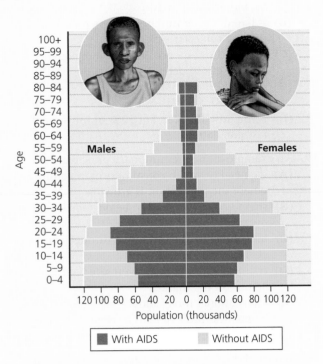

Males   Females

Age (y-axis): 100+, 95–99, 90–94, 85–89, 80–84, 75–79, 70–74, 65–69, 60–64, 55–59, 50–54, 45–49, 40–44, 35–39, 30–34, 25–29, 20–24, 15–19, 10–14, 5–9, 0–4

Population (thousands): 120 100 80 60 40 20 0 20 40 60 80 100 120

■ With AIDS   ■ Without AIDS

7. What is the estimated prevalence rate of HIV/AIDS among people aged 20–29 years?
   - (A) 0.07%
   - (B) 0.33%
   - (C) 15%
   - (D) 33%
   - (E) 70%

8. Which of the following diseases is incorrectly paired with its type of organism?
   - (A) Virus–HIV
   - (B) Bacteria–Severe Acute Respiratory Syndrome (SARS)
   - (C) Fungi–Ringworm
   - (D) Protozoan–Malaria
   - (E) Virus—Ebola

Questions 9–10 refer to the three types of chemical hazards below. Choices may be used once, more than once, or not at all.

   - I. Carcinogens
   - II. Mutagens
   - III. Teratogens

9. Since PCBs may cause birth defects in a human fetus, they are classified as
   - (A) I only
   - (B) II only
   - (C) III only
   - (D) I and II only
   - (E) I, II, and III

10. These chemical hazards are known to cause cancer in humans.
    - (A) I only
    - (B) II only
    - (C) III only
    - (D) I and II only
    - (E) II and III only

11. Which of the following is NOT a factor in the spread of infectious diseases to humans from other animals?
    - (A) Clearing of forests, which exposes humans to animals such as deer and mice and the ticks on them that carry bacteria
    - (B) Expanding suburbs and fragmentation of woodlands, which destroy predators' habitats, allowing their prey such as mice and ticks to spread Lyme disease
    - (C) Limits put on the international trade of livestock animals to protect local agricultural economies
    - (D) Legal and illegal trade in wild species, including kangaroos and tropical fishes, which are often not sufficiently screened or quarantined
    - (E) Local people using monkeys and other animals for bushmeat, because they might contain the Ebola or bird flu viruses

12. The rise of antibiotic resistant pathogens (disease) can be attributed to all of the following EXCEPT
    - (A) the reproductive rate of microbes is so swift it allows for natural selection for resistance at a rapid rate
    - (B) global travel and trade allows for quick movement between continents and countries
    - (C) the often unnecessary use and overuse of antibiotics
    - (D) the decrease in availability of clean drinking water
    - (E) the use of antibiotics prophylactically in cattle feed

13. One of the largest threats of infectious disease to humans next to HIV and malaria is the spread of tuberculosis (TB). This is primarily due to
    - (A) the overuse of vaccinations in treating people infected with TB
    - (B) increased urbanization coupled with too few screening and control programs
    - (C) identifying people with chronic coughs that may be active carriers
    - (D) quarantining people who have an incurable form of TB
    - (E) utilizing viruses as transmission vectors for gene therapy

14. The means by which the World Health Organization has worked to reduce the spread of infectious disease include all of the following EXCEPT
    (A) widespread use of vaccines
    (B) monthly countrywide spraying of DDT
    (C) use of bed nets
    (D) availability of rehydration packets
    (E) providing access to latrines and safe drinking water

15. One reason that mercury (Hg) is so persistent and bioaccumulates without being broken down is that Hg is a
    (A) potent carcinogen that can cause nervous system damage and birth defects
    (B) radioactive element with a long half-life
    (C) carbon-based organic compound naturally occurring in many organisms
    (D) common molecule whose atoms are loosely held together by chemical bonds and therefore easily broken down
    (E) stable chemical element

16. Which of the following describes biological magnification?
    (A) It is the increased concentration of a toxin in organisms as it moves along the food chain.
    (B) It is the buildup of a toxin within an individual organism.
    (C) It is the ecological succession to a climax community from a disturbed land area.
    (D) It is the transition from a pre-industrial country to an industrialized country.
    (E) It is the movement of a chemical compound across ecosystem boundaries by migrating species.

17. Which of the following is NOT a method of controlling or preventing mercury pollution?
    (A) Phase out waste incineration
    (B) Switch from natural gas to coal-burning power plants
    (C) Collect and recycle batteries
    (D) Label products containing mercury
    (E) Enact laws limiting the amount of mercury released from power plants

18. The LD50 of a drug or compound
    (A) depends on how much of the drug is required for biological activity
    (B) is based on the number of days it takes to kill the test subjects
    (C) utilizes the response times of individual cells in petri dishes to determine lethal doses
    (D) is based on computer modeling of simulated cell responses
    (E) is the dose that can kill 50% of the animals in a test population

19. An example of the precautionary principle is that
    (A) we need to watch consumerism in countries where the population is growing
    (B) shared resources tend to be degraded from overuse
    (C) fat-soluble toxins can move through the food chain
    (D) chemicals should be proven safe before they can be put on the market
    (E) international travel should be regulated more by medical professionals to reduce the spread of infectious disease

20. Which of the following best describes an exposure threshold for a toxic chemical?
    (A) The dose that is tolerable for all test subjects
    (B) The dose at which the test subject begins to show harmful effects
    (C) The dose at which 50% of a test population dies
    (D) The dose that a test subject can tolerate
    (E) The dose at which infants die

Flint is a city located 70 miles north of Detroit, Michigan. Flint was, at one time, a thriving city, employing many residents in the General Motors manufacturing plant. Economic decline in Flint began in the 1980s, when General Motors downsized the plant. The decline in income led to less tax money for the city, and in an attempt to alleviate a deficit in the funds for supplying water to Flint's citizens, the city switched to using water from the Flint River rather than from Lake Huron while pipes carrying the water from the lake were upgraded and replaced.

Flint River water is of poor quality due to the presence of fecal coliform bacteria; low dissolved oxygen; plant nutrients, such as nitrates and phosphates; oil; and other toxic substances that originate from polluted sites in the Flint River watershed. Because of corrosive substances present in the river water, lead is leached out of the pipes that transport water from the river to the citizens of Flint.

1. **(a)** Lead is a heavy metal that causes serious health problems.

   (i) Describe TWO acute sublethal effects of lead on human health.

   (ii) Describe ONE reason why children are particularly susceptible to the effects of lead poisoning.

   (iii) Identify ONE source of lead besides drinking water that can result in lead poisoning and **explain** how the lead enters the body.

   (b) Lead is a persistent toxin. **Explain** what is meant by persistent, and **identify** TWO characteristics of lead that make it particularly persistent.

   (c) Toxins such as lead can bioaccumulate and biomagnify as they move through a food chain.

   (i) Identify another common toxin other than lead that can move through a food web.

   (ii) Explain how that toxin bioaccumulates in an organism.

   (iii) Explain how that toxin biomagnifies through a food chain.

Critical Thinking

1. Assume that you are a national official with the power to set policy for controlling environmental mercury pollution from human sources (**Core Case Study**). List the goals of your policy and outline a plan for accomplishing those goals. List three or more possible problems that could result from implementing your policy.

2. What are three actions you would take to reduce the global threats to human health and life from each of the following: **(a)** tuberculosis, **(b)** HIV/AIDS, and **(c)** malaria?

3. Explain why you agree or disagree with each of the following statements:
   a. We should not worry much about exposure to toxic chemicals because almost any chemical, at a large enough dosage, can cause some harm.
   b. We should not worry much about exposure to toxic chemicals because, through genetic adaptation, we can develop immunities to such chemicals.
   c. We should not worry much about exposure to toxic chemicals because we can use genetic engineering to reduce our susceptibility to their effects.
   d. We should not worry about exposure to a chemical such as bisphenol A (BPA) because it has not been absolutely proven scientifically that BPA has killed anyone.

4. Should we ban the use of hormone mimics such as BPA in making products to be used by children younger than age five? Should such a ban be extended to all products? Explain.

5. Workers in a number of industries are exposed to higher levels of various toxic substances than are the general public. Should we reduce the workplace levels allowed for such chemicals? What economic effects might this have?

6. Do you think that electronic cigarettes should be taxed and regulated like conventional cigarettes? Explain.

7. What are the three major risks you face from each of the following: **(a)** your lifestyle, **(b)** where you live, and **(c)** what you do for a living? Which of these risks are voluntary and which are involuntary? List three steps you could take to reduce each of these risks. Which of these steps do you already take or plan to take?

8. In deciding what to do about risks from chemicals in the area where you live, would you support legislation that requires the use of pollution prevention based on the precautionary principle and on the assumption that chemicals are potentially harmful until shown otherwise? Explain.

Data Analysis

The graph below shows the effects of AIDS on life expectancy at birth in Botswana, 1950–2000, and projects these effects to 2050. Study the graph and answer the questions that follow.

1. **(a)** By what percentage did life expectancy in Botswana increase between 1950 and 1995? **(b)** By what percentage did life expectancy in Botswana drop between 1995 and 2015?

2. **(a)** By what percentage was life expectancy in Botswana projected to increase between 2015 and 2050? **(b)** By what percentage was life expectancy in Botswana projected to decrease between 1995 and 2050?

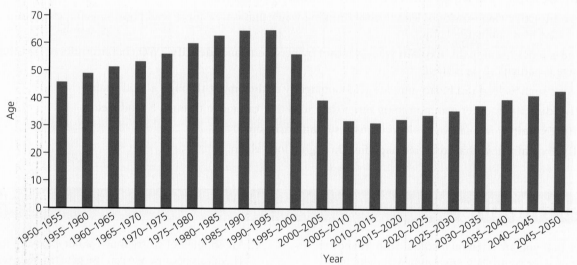

(Compiled by the authors using data from the United Nations and US Census Bureau.)

Answers to Checkpoints for Understanding

Section 16.1

1. The difference between risk assessment and risk management is that risk assessment uses statistical analysis to determine the probability of damage related to a particular hazard, while risk management determines whether or not to reduce a particular risk and determines the monetary cost.

Section 16.2

1. The agents of infectious disease are bacteria, viruses, and parasites.

2. A transmissible disease is spread from person to person. A nontransmissible disease cannot be spread from person to person.

3. The spread of TB (tuberculosis) has become difficult to control because there is a lack of TB screening, especially in poor countries, genetic resistance to antibiotics has developed, a strict regimen of drugs must be taken and completed to keep the disease from being spread throughout the population, and a deadly form of resistant TB has evolved that requires victims to be quarantined, sometimes permanently from the rest of the population.

4. The global incidence of malaria has increased since 1970 because most species of mosquitoes that transmit malaria have become genetically resistant to most insecticides and the *Plasmodium* parasites have become genetically resistant to common antimalarial drugs.

Section 16.3

1. A carcinogen causes cancer. A mutagen causes a change in the sequence of DNA in cells, which can result in cancers and other disorders. A teratogen causes birth defects.
2. Hormonally active agents have shapes that fit into the receptors of cells and mimic certain types of molecules such as estrogen, or block hormones from fitting into the receptors of cells. This disrupts the chemical messenger system in the body.

Section 16.4

1. Factors that determine the toxicity of a substance include the size of the dose, the age (juveniles are more vulnerable), and the genetic make-up (sensitivity to a toxin) of a person. Persistence and solubility are also factors in that the more persistent a toxin is, the longer it remains effective, and if the toxin is fat soluble, it is difficult to flush it from the body.
2. Children are more susceptible than adults to toxins because they eat and drink more food and water per unit body weight than adults, they are exposed to toxins on their hands, toys, and other objects that they put in their mouths, and they have less well-developed immune systems for detoxifying the poisons that enter their bodies.

3. The precautionary principle states that if there is the potential that a chemical or technology can cause harm, decision makers should take measures to reduce the potential harm that the chemical or technology might cause rather than waiting to see how the they affect humans and organisms. With the production of chemical products, the burden of reducing and assessing risk would lie with the manufacturer before the product is put on the market.

Section 16.5

1. Poverty is considered the greatest risk for human life because death is more likely due to malnutrition, increased susceptibility to normally nonfatal infectious diseases, often-fatal infectious diseases that come from unsafe drinking water, and inadequate health care.
2. People estimate risk according to their level of fear, how much control they believe they have over a situation, whether a risk is catastrophic or chronic, optimism that bad things will not happen to them. People also seek instant gratification, and can be willing to do things that give pleasure regardless of the risks.

Core Case Study

The two major sources of mercury exposure include eating fish and shellfish contaminated with methylmercury, and breathing in vaporized mercury or mercury salts emitted primarily from coal-burning power plants.

CHAPTER 17

Water Pollution

> The health of our waters is the principal measure of how we live on the land.
>
> **LUNA LEOPOLD**

Key Questions

17.1 What are the causes and effects of water pollution?

17.2 What are the major pollution problems in streams and lakes?

17.3 What are the major groundwater pollution problems?

17.4 What are the major ocean pollution problems?

17.5 How can we deal with water pollution?

The Gulf of Mexico's Annual Dead Zone

The Mississippi River basin (Figure 17.1, top) lies within 31 states and contains almost two-thirds of the continental US land area. With more than half of all US croplands, it is one of the world's most productive agricultural regions. However, water draining into the Mississippi River and its tributaries from farms, cities, factories, and sewage treatment plants in this huge basin contains sediments and other pollutants that end up in the Gulf of Mexico (Figure 17.1, bottom)—a major supplier of the country's fish and shellfish.

Each spring and summer, huge quantities of nitrogen and phosphorus plant nutrients—mostly nitrates and phosphates from crop fertilizers—flow into the Mississippi River, end up in the northern Gulf of Mexico, and overfertilize the coastal waters of the US states of Mississippi, Louisiana, and Texas. This excess of plant nutrients leads to an explosive growth of phytoplankton (mostly algae). They eventually die, sink to the bottom, and are decomposed by hordes of bacteria that consume oxygen as part of their aerobic respiration. This depletes most of the dissolved oxygen in the Gulf's bottom layer of water.

The resulting massive volume of water with a low dissolved oxygen content (below 2 parts per million) is called a *dead zone* because it contains little or no animal marine life. Its low dissolved oxygen levels (Figure 17.1, bottom) drive away faster-swimming fish and other marine organisms and suffocate bottom-dwelling fish, crabs, oysters, and shrimp that cannot move to less polluted areas. Large amounts of sediment, mostly from soil eroded from the Mississippi River basin, can also kill bottom-dwelling forms of animal aquatic life. The dead zone appears each spring and grows until fall when storms churn the water and redistribute dissolved oxygen to the gulf bottom.

The size of the Gulf of Mexico's annual dead zone varies with the amount of water flowing into the Mississippi River. In years with ample rainfall and snowmelt, such as 2003, it covered an area as large as the state of Massachusetts—27,300 square kilometers (10,600 square miles). In years with less rainfall, such as 2015, it covered a smaller area of 16,760 square kilometers (6,474 square miles)—slightly less than the combined areas of the states of Connecticut and Rhode Island.

The annual Gulf of Mexico dead zone is one of 400 dead zones found throughout the world, 200 of them in the United States. Other such zones lie in the Baltic Sea to the south of Sweden in Northern Europe and in the coastal waters of Australia, New Zealand, Japan, China, and South America.

Oxygen-depleted zones represent a disruption of the nitrogen cycle (see Figure 3.16, p. 79) caused primarily by human activities. This is because great quantities of nitrogen from nitrate fertilizers are added to these aquatic systems faster than the nitrogen cycle can remove them. Thus, producing crops to feed livestock and people and produce ethanol to fuel cars in the vast Mississippi basin ends up disrupting coastal aquatic life and seafood production in the Gulf of Mexico.

This overfertilization of coastal waters is one of the world's many forms of water pollution. Some good news is that we know how to reduce the sizes of dead zones and how to reduce other forms of water pollution that we explore in this chapter. ●

CRITICAL THINKING

What strategies might be implemented that could reduce the input of nitrate into the Mississippi River?

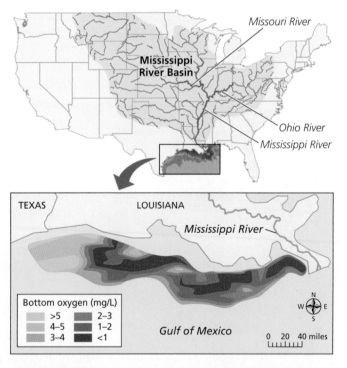

FIGURE 17.1 Water containing sediments, dissolved nitrate fertilizers, and other pollutants drains from the Mississippi River basin (top) into the Mississippi River and from there into the northern Gulf of Mexico (bottom). This creates a dead zone with low levels of dissolved oxygen (1–3 ppm), indicated by the dark and light red shaded areas in the bottom figure for 2015.

(Data from NOAA.)

17.1 WHAT ARE THE CAUSES AND EFFECTS OF WATER POLLUTION?

CONCEPT 17.1A The chief sources of water pollution are agricultural activities, industrial facilities, mining, and untreated wastewater.

CONCEPT 17.1B Water pollution causes illness and death in humans and other species, and disrupts ecosystems.

Water Pollution Comes from Point and Nonpoint Sources

Water pollution is any change in water quality that can harm living organisms or make the water unfit for human uses such as drinking, irrigation, and recreation. It can come from single (point) sources or from larger and dispersed (nonpoint) sources. **Point sources** discharge pollutants into bodies of surface water at specific locations often through drain pipes, ditches, or sewer lines that are usually easy to identify, monitor, and regulate. Examples are factories (Figure 17.2), sewage treatment plants (which remove some, but not all, pollutants), animal feedlots, underground and open-pit mines (Figure 17.3), oil wells, and oil tankers.

Nonpoint sources are broad and diffuse areas where rainfall or snowmelt washes pollutants off the land into bodies of surface water. Examples include runoff of eroded soil and chemicals such as fertilizers and pesticides from cropland, animal feedlots, logged forests, construction sites, city streets, parking lots, lawns, and golf courses. Controlling water pollution from nonpoint sources is difficult because of the expense of identifying and controlling discharges from so many diffuse sources.

Agricultural activities are the leading cause of water pollution. The most common pollutant is sediment eroded from agricultural lands (Figure 17.4). Other major agricultural pollutants include fertilizers (Figure 17.1), pesticides, and

FIGURE 17.3 *Point source pollution:* acid draining from an abandoned open-pit coal mine.

bacteria from livestock and food-processing wastes. Three other major sources are industrial facilities, mining, and untreated **wastewater**, or water that contains sewage and other wastes from homes and industries (**Concept 20.1A**).

CONSIDER THIS . . .

CONNECTIONS Cleaning Up the Air and Polluting the Water

Stricter air pollution control laws have forced coal-burning power plants in more-developed countries to remove many of the harmful gases and particles from their smokestack emissions. This results in hazardous ash, which is typically placed in slurry ponds that can rupture and cause water pollution. This illustrates one way in which air and water pollution are connected.

Another example of nonpoint water pollution occurs when people discard plastics used to make water bottles and millions of other products. Much of this plastic and other materials end up in rivers, lakes (Figure 17.5), and oceans. Much of this plastic, which lasts more than 1,000 years, ends up in rivers, lakes, and oceans.

FIGURE 17.2 Point source of water pollution from an industrial plant.

Tim McCabe/Natural Resources Conservation Service

FIGURE 17.4 *Nonpoint source pollution:* sediments in farmland runoff flowing into a stream. By weight, sediment is the largest source of water pollution. ***Critical thinking:*** What do you think the owner of this farm could have done to prevent such sediment pollution?

FIGURE 17.5 Nonpoint pollution of this mountain lake by plastics and other forms of waste from a variety of sources.

Stephane Bidouze/Shutterstock.com

Testing Water for Pollutants

Scientists use a variety of methods to measure water quality. For example, they test samples of water for the *presence of various infectious agents* such as certain strains of the coliform bacteria *Escherichia coli*, or *E. coli* (Figure 17.A), which live in the colons and intestines of humans and other animals and thus are present in their fecal wastes. Most strains of coliform bacteria do not cause disease but their presence indicates that water has been exposed to human or animal wastes that are likely to contain disease-causing agents.

To be considered safe for drinking, a 100-milliliter (about 1/2-cup) sample of water should contain no colonies of coliform bacteria. To be considered safe for swimming, such a water sample should contain no more than 200 colonies of coliform bacteria. By contrast, a similar sample of raw sewage may contain several million coliform bacterial colonies.

Another indicator of water quality is its *level of dissolved oxygen (DO)*. Excessive inputs of oxygen-demanding wastes can deplete DO levels in water. Figure 17.B shows the relationship between dissolved oxygen content and water quality. In the dead zone formed in the Gulf of Mexico (**Core Case Study**), dissolved oxygen levels near the seafloor typically are 2 to 3 ppm, which can kill many marine organisms.

Scientists use *chemical analysis* to determine the presence and concentrations of specific organic chemicals in polluted water. They also monitor water pollution by using living organisms as *indicator species*. For example, they remove aquatic plants such as cattails from areas contaminated with fuels, solvents, and other organic chemicals, and analyze them to determine the pollutants contained in their tissues. Scientists also determine water quality by analyzing bottom-dwelling species such as mussels, which feed by filtering water through their bodies. Genetic engineers are working to develop bacteria and yeasts (single-celled fungi) that glow in the presence of specific pollutants such as toxic heavy metals in the ocean, toxins in the air, and carcinogens in food.

Scientists measure the amount of sediment in polluted water by evaporating the water in a sample and weighing the resulting sediment. They also use instruments called colorimeters, which measure specific wavelengths of light shined through a water sample to determine the concentrations of water pollutants in the water. Researchers in Spain have used several robots, each one about as long as a seal, to detect potentially hazardous pollutants in a river.

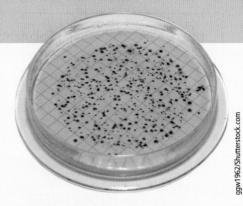

FIGURE 17.A Colonies of coliform bacteria growing in a petri dish.

ggw1962/Shutterstock.com

CRITICAL THINKING

Runoff of fertilizer into a lake from farmland, lawns, and sewage treatment plants can overload the water with nitrogen and phosphorus—plant nutrients that can cause algae population explosions. How could this lower the dissolved oxygen level of the water and lead to fish kills?

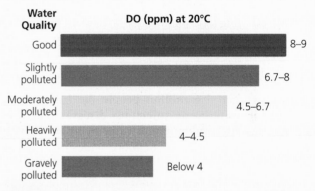

Water Quality	DO (ppm) at 20°C
Good	8–9
Slightly polluted	6.7–8
Moderately polluted	4.5–6.7
Heavily polluted	4–4.5
Gravely polluted	Below 4

FIGURE 17.B Scientists measure dissolved oxygen (DO) content in parts per million (ppm) at 20°C (68°F) as an indicator of water quality. Only a few fish species can survive in water containing less than 3 ppm of dissolved oxygen at this temperature. *Critical thinking:* Would you expect the dissolved oxygen content of polluted water to increase or decrease if the water were heated? Explain.

Harmful Effects of Water Pollutants

Table 17.1 lists the types of major water pollutants along with examples of each and their harmful effects and sources. A National Academy of Sciences study ranked the following pollutants as the most serious threats to US stream and lake water quality: mercury (Figure 16.10, p. 508), pathogens from leaking and broken sewer pipes, sediment from land disturbance and stream erosion, metals other than mercury, and nutrients that cause oxygen depletion (Figure 17.1).

A major water pollution problem is exposure to infectious bacteria, viruses, and parasites that are transferred into water from the wastes of 2.5 billion humans that lack access to toilets and other forms of waste disposal, and other animals (**Concept 17.1B**). Drinking water contaminated with these biological pollutants can cause painful, debilitating, and often life-threatening diseases, including typhoid fever, cholera, hepatitis B, giardiasis, and cryptosporidium. The World Health Organization (WHO) estimates that each

TABLE 17.1 Major Water Pollutants and Their Sources

Type/Effects	Examples	Major Sources
Infectious agents (pathogens) *Cause diseases*	Bacteria, viruses, protozoa, parasites	Human and animal wastes
Oxygen-demanding wastes *Deplete dissolved oxygen needed by aquatic species*	Biodegradable animal wastes and plant debris	Sewage, animal feedlots, food-processing facilities, paper mills
Plant nutrients *Cause excessive growth of algae and other species*	Nitrates (NO_3^-) and phosphates (PO_4^{3-})	Sewage, animal wastes, inorganic fertilizers
Organic chemicals *Add toxins to aquatic systems*	Oil, gasoline, plastics, pesticides, cleaning solvents	Industry, farms, households
Inorganic chemicals *Add toxins to aquatic systems*	Acids, bases, salts, metal compounds	Industry, households, surface runoff, mining sites
Sediments *Disrupt photosynthesis, food webs, other processes*	Soil, silt	Land erosion
Heavy metals *Cause cancer, disrupt immune and endocrine systems*	Lead, mercury, arsenic	Unlined landfills, household chemicals, mining refuse, industrial discharges
Thermal *Make some species vulnerable to disease*	Heat	Electric power and industrial plants

year, more than 1.6 million people die from largely preventable waterborne infectious diseases that they get by drinking contaminated water or by not having enough water to keep clean. More widespread detection of water pollutants (Science Focus 17.1) can reduce this death toll.

CHECKPOINT FOR UNDERSTANDING 17.1

1. Explain the difference between point source and nonpoint source water pollution.
2. Identify several common types of water pollutants.

17.2 WHAT ARE THE MAJOR POLLUTION PROBLEMS IN STREAMS AND LAKES?

CONCEPT 17.2A Many of the world's streams and rivers are polluted, but they can cleanse themselves of biodegradable wastes if we do not overload them or reduce their flows.

CONCEPT 17.2B Adding excessive nutrients to lakes from human activities can disrupt their ecosystems, and preventing such pollution is more effective and less costly than cleaning it up.

Stream Pollution in More-Developed Countries

Laws enacted in the 1970s to control water pollution have greatly increased the number of facilities that treat wastewater from homes and industries in the United States and in most other more-developed countries. Such laws also require industries to reduce or eliminate their point-source discharges of harmful chemicals into surface waters.

One success story is the cleanup of the US state of Ohio's Cuyahoga River. It was so polluted that it caught fire several times and, in 1969, was photographed while burning as it flowed through the city of Cleveland toward Lake Erie. The highly publicized image of this burning river prompted elected officials to enact laws to limit the discharge of industrial wastes into the river and to provide funds for upgrading sewage treatment facilities. Today, the river is cleaner, is no longer flammable, and is widely used by boaters and anglers.

Oxygen Sag Curves

Flowing rivers and streams can recover rapidly from moderate inputs of biodegradable, oxygen-demanding pollution through a combination of dilution and biodegradation. A flowing river or stream can also dilute heated water released from a power plant. However, this natural recovery process does not work when a stream becomes overloaded with biodegradable pollutants, or when drought, damming, or water diversion reduces its flow (**Concept 17.2A**). Also, this process does not eliminate slowly degradable or nondegradable pollutants such as heavy metals.

In a flowing stream, the breakdown of biodegradable wastes by bacteria depletes dissolved oxygen and creates an *oxygen sag curve* (Figure 17.C). This reduces or eliminates populations of organisms with high oxygen requirements until the stream is cleansed of oxygen-demanding wastes.

In this graph the blue line indicates dissolved oxygen in ppm, and the red line indicates biochemical oxygen demand (BOD). Recall that BOD is the amount of dissolved oxygen needed (i.e., demanded) by aerobic biological organisms to break down organic material present in a given water sample.

Upstream of the effluent pipe dissolved oxygen is 8 ppm, a level that allows intolerant species such as trout and mayflies to thrive. BOD is low because there is little organic waste that requires degradation by aerobic bacteria and, subsequently, depletion of oxygen in the water at that point in the stream.

At the point where waste enters the stream (identified as the decomposition zone), aerobic bacteria begin consuming the waste, using up oxygen in the process. There is a shift in the type of organisms that can inhabit the stream as oxygen levels drop. The septic zone is characterized by a lack of oxygen, and anaerobic bacteria take over decomposition of waste. Only the most tolerant species, such as blood worms and leeches, can survive in these conditions.

Once the waste is consumed and the flowing stream moves and dilutes it, oxygen levels start to recover. Notice that the recovery zone is similar to the decomposition zone in that the amount of dissolved oxygen is similar as are the species that inhabit that zone of the stream. Once the stream has been cleansed of biodegradable waste, the stream is fully recovered and intolerant species are able to thrive.

FRQ Application

Question: Refer to the graph in Figure 17.C. **Explain** the relationship between the lines depicting dissolved oxygen content and biological oxygen demand. **Describe** how the scale on the horizontal axis of this graph would change if the amount of effluent emitted from the pipe were doubled.

Possible Response: As biodegradable waste is emitted into a body of water, aerobic bacteria break it down. As a result, the more active the bacteria, the more oxygen consumed from the water. The graph shows oxygen levels declining as waste is being consumed by the aerobic bacteria. Biological oxygen demand is the amount of oxygen required by bacteria to consume waste. The relationship between the two lines is inverse. If there is little waste in the water, there is no demand by the bacteria and oxygen levels stay relatively high. If there is an abundance of waste in the water, then the demand for oxygen increases, and oxygen levels drop.

The scale on the horizontal axis shows stream recovery over distance. If more waste was emitted into the stream, the areas shown on the graph would be farther apart and it would take longer for the stream to recover at a distance farther from the origin.

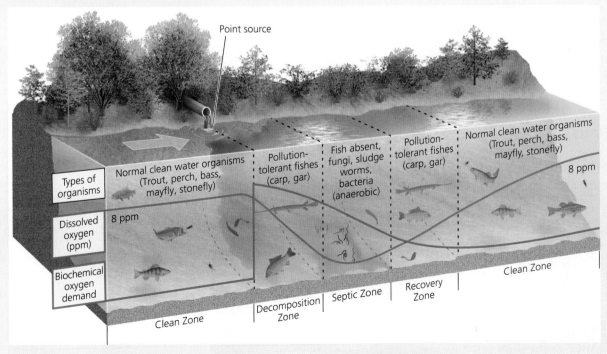

FIGURE 17.C Natural capital: A stream can dilute and decay degradable, oxygen-demanding wastes and also dilute heated water. This figure shows the oxygen sag curve (blue) and the curve of oxygen demand (red).

This accomplishment illustrates the power of bottom-up pressure by citizens, who prodded elected officials to change a severely polluted river into an economically and ecologically valuable public resource.

GOOD NEWS

Fish kills and drinking water contamination still occur occasionally in some rivers and lakes in more-developed countries such as the United States. Some of these problems are caused by the accidental or deliberate release of toxic inorganic and organic chemicals by industries and mining operations (Figure 17.3).

The U.S. Environmental Protection Agency (EPA) estimates that mining wastes pollute 40% of the headwaters of western watersheds and that cleaning up the estimated 500,000 inactive and abandoned mines found throughout much of the western United States will cost taxpayers at least $50 billion.

The Ohio River is the nation's most polluted river mostly because of sewage overflows and mining and industrial wastes. In August and September 2015, a toxic form of blue-green algae covered almost two-thirds of the river, mostly from runoff of phosphates and nitrates from cattle feedlots, fertilized crop fields, and leaking sewers. The toxin in the algae can kill animals that drink the river water and can cause vomiting, diarrhea, and liver damage in humans who ingest this water.

Stream Pollution in Less-Developed Countries

In most less-developed countries, stream pollution from discharges of untreated sewage and from industrial wastes and discarded trash is a serious and growing problem. According to the Global Water Policy Project, most cities in less-developed countries discharge 80–90% of their untreated sewage directly into rivers, streams, and lakes whose waters are often used for drinking, bathing, and washing clothes (Figure 17.6).

80–90 Percentage of the raw sewage in most cities in less-developed countries that is discharged directly into waterways

According to the World Commission on Water for the twenty-first Century, half of the world's 500 major rivers are heavily polluted, with most of these polluted waterways running through less-developed countries. Most of these countries cannot afford to build waste-treatment plants and do not have, or do not enforce, laws for controlling water pollution.

Industrial wastes and sewage pollute more than two-thirds of India's water resources, as well as 54 of the 78 rivers and streams monitored in China. According to the Ministry of Environmental Protection, some 380 million Chinese people drink unsafe water and nearly half of China's rivers carry water that is too toxic to touch, much less drink. Liver and stomach cancer, linked in some cases to water pollution, are among the leading causes of death in the Chinese countryside where many industries have been relocated.

FIGURE 17.6 Hindu people in India washing themselves in a river as a part of their daily holy ritual. They also use the river to wash their clothes, and it is polluted with animal and human wastes.

Neale Cousland/Shutterstock.com

CONNECTIONS Atmospheric Warming and Water Pollution

Climate change from atmospheric warming will likely contribute to water pollution. In a warmer world, some regions will get more precipitation and other areas will get less. More intense downpours will flush more harmful chemicals, plant nutrients, and disease-causing microorganisms into some waterways. In other areas, prolonged drought will reduce river flows that dilute wastes.

Pollution of Lakes and Reservoirs

Lakes and reservoirs are generally less effective at diluting pollutants than streams are, for two reasons. *First*, they often contain stratified layers (Figure 6.14, p. 165) that undergo little vertical mixing. *Second*, they have low flow rates or no flow at all. The flushing and changing of water in lakes and large artificial reservoirs can take from 1 to 100 years, compared with several days to several weeks for streams.

These two factors make lakes and reservoirs more vulnerable than streams are to contamination by runoff or discharges of plant nutrients, oil, pesticides, and nondegradable toxic substances, such as lead, mercury, and arsenic. These contaminants can kill bottom-dwelling organisms and fish, as well as birds that feed on contaminated aquatic organisms. Many toxic chemicals and acids also enter lakes and reservoirs from the atmosphere.

In addition, the concentrations of some harmful chemicals are biologically magnified as they pass through food webs in these waters. Examples include DDT (Figure 9.13, p. 247), PCBs (Figure 16.B, p. 507), some radioactive isotopes, and some mercury compounds.

Cultural Eutrophication: Too Much of a Good Thing

Eutrophication is the natural nutrient enrichment of a shallow lake, a coastal area at the mouth of a river (**Core Case Study**), or a slow-moving stream. It is caused mostly by runoff of plant nutrients such as nitrates and phosphates from land bordering these bodies of water.

An *oligotrophic lake* is low in nutrients and its water is clear (Figure 6.15, p. 166). Over time, some lakes become more eutrophic (Figure 6.16, p. 167) as nutrients are added from natural and human sources in the surrounding watersheds.

Near urban or agricultural areas, human activities can increase the input of plant nutrients to a lake—a process called **cultural eutrophication (Concept 17.2B)**. The inputs involve mostly nitrate- and phosphate-containing effluents from various sources, including farmland, feedlots, urban streets and parking lots, fertilized lawns, mining sites, and municipal sewage treatment plants. Some nitrogen also reaches lakes by deposition from the atmosphere.

During hot weather or drought, this nutrient overload can produce dense growths of organisms such as algae and cyanobacteria (Figure 6.16, p. 167). When the algae die, they are decomposed by swelling populations of oxygen-consuming bacteria that deplete dissolved oxygen in the surface layer of water near the shore and in the bottom layer of a lake. This lack of oxygen can kill fish and other aerobic aquatic animals that cannot move to safer waters. If excess nutrients continue to flow into a lake, bacteria that do not require oxygen take over and produce gaseous products such as smelly, highly toxic hydrogen sulfide and flammable methane.

There are several ways to *prevent* or *reduce* cultural eutrophication. Advanced (but expensive) waste-treatment processes can remove nitrates and phosphates from wastewater before it enters a body of water. Another option is to mimic the earth's natural cycling of nutrients by recycling the removed nutrients to the soil instead of dumping them into waterways. This is an application of the chemical cycling **principle of sustainability** and an important way to increase our beneficial environmental impact, as long as the nutrients do not contain toxic chemicals. Other preventive measures include banning or limiting the use of phosphates in household detergents and other cleaning agents, and employing soil conservation (Figure 12.25, p. 361) and land-use control to reduce nutrient runoff (see the Case Study that follows).

Lakes suffering from cultural eutrophication can be cleaned up by removing weeds, controlling undesirable plant growth with herbicides and algaecides, and pumping air into lakes and reservoirs to prevent oxygen depletion. However, these methods are expensive and energy-intensive. Most lakes and other surface waters can eventually recover from cultural eutrophication if excessive inputs of plant nutrients are stopped.

CASE STUDY

Pollution in the Great Lakes

The five interconnected Great Lakes of North America (Figure 17.7) contain about 95% of the fresh surface water in the United States and 21% of the world's fresh surface water. At least 40 million people in the United States and Canada obtain their drinking water from these lakes. In addition, the lakes provide food (especially from a $4 billion a year fishing industry), water purification, recreation, and jobs and help support the economies of nearby communities and states.

Despite their enormous size, these lakes are vulnerable to pollution from point and nonpoint sources. One reason is that each year, less than 1% of the water entering these lakes flows east into the St. Lawrence River and then out to the Atlantic Ocean. This means that it can take 19 years for pollutants to flush from the largest lake (Superior) to sea and 3 years from the smallest lake (Erie).

By the 1960s, many areas of the Great Lakes were suffering from severe cultural eutrophication, huge fish kills,

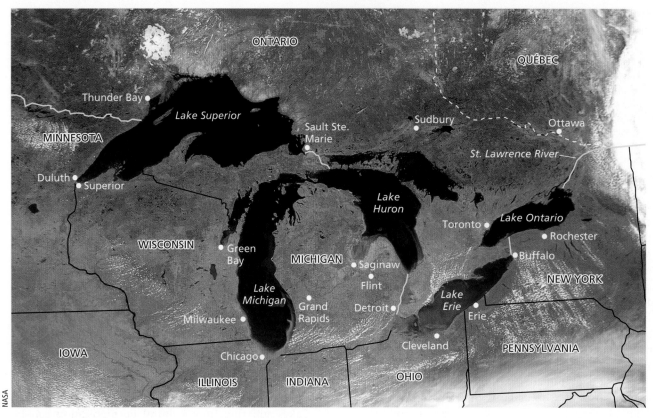

FIGURE 17.7 The five Great Lakes of North America make up the world's largest freshwater system.

and contamination from bacteria and a variety of toxic industrial wastes. Lake Erie suffered the most because it is the shallowest of the Great Lakes and has the highest concentrations of people and industrial activity along its shores.

In 1972, the United States and Canada signed the Great Lakes Water Quality Agreement, which is considered a model of international cooperation. They agreed to spend more than $20 billion to maintain and restore the chemical, physical, and biological integrity of the Great Lakes basin ecosystem. This program has helped to cut the number and sizes of algal blooms, raised dissolved oxygen levels, boosted sport and commercial fishing catches in Lake Erie, and allowed most swimming beaches to reopen. These improvements resulted mainly from the use of new or upgraded sewage treatment plants, better treatment of industrial wastes, and bans on the use of detergents, household cleaners, and water conditioners that contain phosphates. Most of these measures were instituted largely because of bottom-up citizen pressure on federal and state elected officials.

Despite this important progress, many problems remain. Increasing nonpoint runoff of pesticides and fertilizers resulting from urban sprawl, fueled by population growth, now surpasses industrial pollution as the greatest threat to the lakes. Bottom sediments in 26 toxic hotspots remain heavily polluted. In addition, some of the Great Lakes, such as Lake Erie, still suffer from occasional cultural eutrophication (Figure 17.8).

About half of the toxic compounds entering the lakes still come from atmospheric deposition of pesticides, mercury from coal-burning plants, and other toxic chemicals from as far away as Mexico and Russia. A survey done by Wisconsin biologists found that one of every four fish taken from the Great Lakes was unsafe for human consumption, mostly because of their mercury content (Figure 16.1, p. 496).

Between 2010 and 2015, the US Congress provided about $1.3 billion for the Great Lakes Restoration Initiative overseen by the EPA. It has focused on reducing environmental threats such as toxic pollution, cultural eutrophication (Figure 17.8), loss of wildlife habitat, invasive species, and soil erosion and runoff into the lakes. It also promotes wetlands restoration. However, there are political pressures to reduce or cut government funding for this restoration program.

Some environmental and health scientists call for a prevention approach (**Concept 17.3B**) that would ban the use of toxic chlorine compounds, such as bleach used in the pulp and paper industry, which is prominent around the Great Lakes. They would also stop the discharge into the lakes of 70 toxic chemicals that threaten human health and wildlife. So far, officials in the affected industries have successfully opposed such bans.

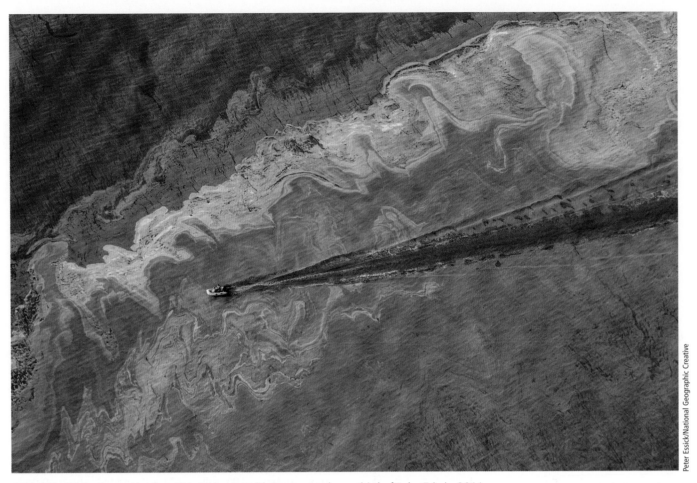

FIGURE 17.8 *Eutrophication:* This toxic algae bloom covered one-third of Lake Erie in 2011.

Gulf of Mexico Dead Zone: A Closer Look

Since the 1950s, the level of nitrates discharged from the Mississippi River into the northern Gulf of Mexico has nearly tripled (**Core Case Study**). Each year this causes severe depletion of dissolved oxygen (Figure 17.1, bottom, red area) and creates a dead zone in the northern Gulf of Mexico.

In more detail, here is how the Gulf's seasonal dead zone forms. During the spring and summer, nitrate- and phosphate-laden freshwater flowing into the Gulf forms an oxygen-rich layer on top of the Gulf's cooler and denser saltwater. Because there are few storms at this time of year, this sun-heated upper layer of water remains calm and does not mix with the bottom layer of low-oxygen water. The combination of sunlight and large inputs of nitrate and phosphate plant nutrients from fertilizer and sewage into the freshwater layer leads to massive blooms of phytoplankton, mostly blue-green algae.

When these algae die, they sink into the saltier water below where they are decomposed by oxygen-consuming bacteria. This reduces the dissolved oxygen content in the deeper water to 2 parts per million or lower. Mobile species can survive this lack of oxygen by migrating to oxygen-rich waters, but certain species of fish, shellfish, and other organisms are not able to escape, and they die.

The resulting dead zone disrupts the Gulf's food web, because the die-offs lead to the deaths of seabird and marine mammal species that depend on the dying fish and shellfish for their survival. The dead zone breaks up, beginning in early fall when cooler weather, storms, and hurricanes mix the top and lower layers of water and distribute dissolved oxygen throughout the layers.

In addition to greatly increased nitrate and phosphate levels from human inputs, other human factors have contributed to the formation of the dead zone. In efforts to control flooding along the upper Mississippi River, engineers have dredged and straightened parts of the river and raised its banks with levees in many places. This has increased the river's flow of nutrients and sediment pollution into the Gulf. In addition, most of the river basin's original freshwater wetlands, which acted as natural filters that helped to remove excess nutrients and sediments from flood water, have been drained and filled in for farming and urban development.

The seasonal formation of dead zones in the northern Gulf of Mexico and in other areas, mostly resulting from human activities, is a reminder that in nature, everything is connected. Plant nutrients flowing into the Mississippi from a farm in Iowa or a sewage treatment plant in Wisconsin help kill fish and shellfish a thousand miles away on the gulf coast of Texas. Researchers warn that if the size of the Gulf's annual dead zone is not sharply reduced, its long-term effects could permanently alter the ecological makeup of these coastal waters.

CHECKPOINT FOR UNDERSTANDING 17.2

1. Explain why streams and rivers cleanse themselves of pollutants more quickly than ponds and lakes.

2. Discuss why the Great Lakes are slow to cleanse themselves of pollutants.

3. Explain why oxygen depletion (hypoxia) in the Gulf of Mexico is seasonal.

17.3 WHAT ARE THE MAJOR GROUNDWATER POLLUTION PROBLEMS?

CONCEPT 17.3A Chemicals used in agriculture, industry, transportation, and homes can spill and leak into groundwater and make it undrinkable.

CONCEPT 17.3B We can purify groundwater, but protecting it through pollution prevention is the least expensive and most effective strategy.

Groundwater Cannot Cleanse Itself Very Well

Aquifers provide drinking water for about half of the US population and 95% of Americans who live in rural areas. According to many scientists, groundwater pollution is a serious but hidden global human health threat. Common pollutants such as fertilizers, pesticides, gasoline, and organic solvents can seep into groundwater from numerous sources (Figure 17.9). People dumping or spilling gasoline, oil, and paint thinners and other organic solvents onto the ground can also contaminate groundwater (**Concept 17.3A**).

The drilling of thousands of new oil and natural gas wells in parts of the United States involving a process called *hydraulic fracturing*, or *fracking* (see Chapter 14, Core Case Study, p. 420), is also a growing threat to groundwater. Contamination of groundwater used for drinking water can come from leaky gas well pipes and pipe fittings and from contaminated wastewater brought to the surface during fracking operations (Figure 17.10). Reducing this serious groundwater pollution threat will require stricter monitoring and regulation of fracking wastewater (currently exempted from regulation) under the federal drinking water and water pollution control laws.

Once a pollutant from a leaking underground storage tank or other source contaminates groundwater, it fills the aquifer's porous layers of sand, gravel, or bedrock like water saturates a sponge. Removing this contaminant is difficult and costly. Groundwater flows so slowly—usually less than 0.3 meter (1 foot) per day—that contaminants are not effectively diluted and dispersed. In addition, groundwater usually has much lower concentrations of dissolved oxygen (which helps decompose some biodegradable contaminants) and smaller populations of decomposing bacteria. The usually cold temperatures of groundwater also slow down chemical reactions that decompose wastes.

Groundwater Pollution Is a Hidden Threat

On a global scale, we do not know much about groundwater pollution because few countries go to the great expense of locating, tracking, and testing aquifers. However, the results of scientific studies in scattered parts of the world are alarming.

Groundwater provides about 70% of China's drinking water. According to the Chinese Ministry of Land and Resources, about 90% of China's shallow groundwater is polluted with chemicals such as toxic heavy metals, organic solvents, nitrates, petrochemicals, and pesticides. About 37% of this groundwater is so polluted that it cannot be treated for use as drinking water. Every year, according to the WHO and the World Bank, contaminated drinking water causes illness in an estimated 190 million Chinese and kills about 60,000.

In the United States, an EPA survey of 26,000 industrial waste ponds and lagoons found that one-third of them had no liners to prevent toxic liquid wastes from seeping into aquifers. In addition, almost two-thirds of America's liquid hazardous wastes are injected into the ground in disposal wells (Figure 17.9). Leaking injection pipes and seals in such wells can contaminate aquifers used as sources of drinking water.

By 2016, the EPA had cleaned up about 461,000 of the more than 532,000 underground tanks in the United States that were leaking gasoline, diesel fuel, home heating oil, or toxic solvents into groundwater. During this century, scientists expect many of the millions of such tanks installed around the world to corrode and leak, contaminating groundwater, and becoming a major global health problem. Determining the extent of a leak from a single underground tank can cost hundreds of thousands of dollars, and cleanup costs can be even higher. If the chemical reaches an aquifer, effective cleanup is often not possible or is too costly.

It can take decades to thousands of years for contaminated groundwater to cleanse itself of *slowly degradable wastes* (such as DDT). On a human time scale, *nonbiodegradable wastes* (such as toxic lead and arsenic; see the Case Study that follows) remain in the water permanently. Although there are ways to remove some pollutants from groundwater (Figure 17.11, right), such methods are expensive. Cleaning up a single

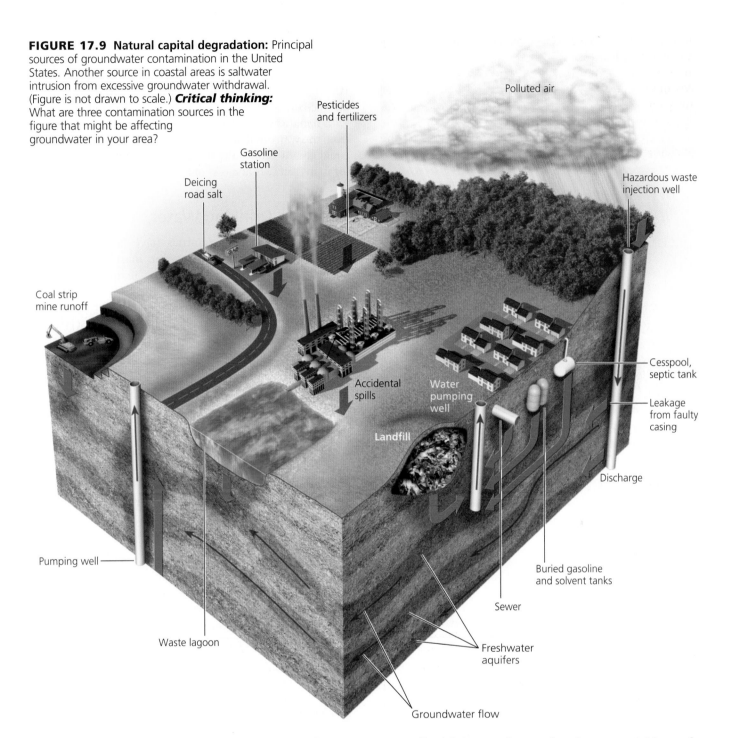

FIGURE 17.9 Natural capital degradation: Principal sources of groundwater contamination in the United States. Another source in coastal areas is saltwater intrusion from excessive groundwater withdrawal. (Figure is not drawn to scale.) *Critical thinking:* What are three contamination sources in the figure that might be affecting groundwater in your area?

Polluted air

Pesticides and fertilizers

Gasoline station

Deicing road salt

Hazardous waste injection well

Coal strip mine runoff

Accidental spills

Water pumping well

Landfill

Cesspool, septic tank

Leakage from faulty casing

Discharge

Pumping well

Buried gasoline and solvent tanks

Sewer

Waste lagoon

Freshwater aquifers

Groundwater flow

---

contaminated aquifer can cost anywhere from 10 million to several hundred million dollars depending on the size of the aquifer and the types of contaminants. Therefore, preventing groundwater contamination (Figure 17.11, left) is the most effective way to deal with this serious pollution problem (**Concept 17.3B**).

CASE STUDY

Arsenic in Drinking Water

Arsenic contaminates drinking water when a well is drilled into an aquifer where the soil and rock are naturally rich in arsenic, or when human activities such as mining and ore processing release arsenic into drinking water supplies.

The WHO estimates that more than 140 million people in 70 countries are drinking water with arsenic concentrations of 5 to 100 times the accepted safe level of 10 parts per billion (ppb). According to some scientists from the WHO and other organizations, even the 10 ppb level is not safe.

Arsenic levels are especially high in Bangladesh, China, India's state of West Bengal, and parts of northern Chile. The WHO estimates that long-term exposure to nondegradable arsenic in drinking water is likely to cause

FIGURE 17.10 Well water in Wyoming polluted by groundwater contamination from a natural gas fracking well, probably from faulty seals in the well pipe.

Solutions

Groundwater Pollution

Prevention		Cleanup
Find substitutes for toxic chemicals		Pump to surface, clean, and return to aquifer (very expensive)
Keep toxic chemicals out of the environment		
Require leak detectors on underground tanks		Inject microorganisms to clean up contamination (less expensive but still costly)
Ban hazardous waste disposal in landfills and injection wells	LANDFILL NO Hazardous Wastes Allowed	Pump nanoparticles of inorganic compounds to remove pollutants (still being developed)
Store harmful liquids in aboveground tanks with leak detection and collection systems		

FIGURE 17.11 We can clean up contaminated groundwater, but prevention is the only effective approach (**Concept 17.3B**). *Critical thinking:* Which two of these preventive solutions do you think are the most important? Why?

hundreds of thousands of premature deaths from cancer of the skin, bladder, and lungs. According to the EPA, some 13 million people in several thousand communities, mostly in the western United States, are exposed to arsenic levels of 3 to 10 ppb in their drinking water.

Researchers from Rice University in Houston, Texas (USA), reported that by suspending nanoparticles of rust in arsenic-contaminated water and then drawing them out with handheld magnets, they had removed enough arsenic from the water to make it safe to drink. Use of this technique could greatly reduce the threat of arsenic in drinking water for many families at a cost of a few cents a day.

Purifying Drinking Water

Most more-developed countries have laws establishing drinking water standards. However, most less-developed countries do not have such laws or, if they have them, they do not enforce them.

In more-developed countries, surface water withdrawn for use as drinking water is typically stored in a reservoir for several days. This improves clarity and taste by increasing dissolved oxygen content and allowing suspended matter to settle. The water is then pumped to a purification plant and treated to meet government drinking water standards.

In areas with pure groundwater or surface water sources, little treatment is necessary. Several major US cities, including New York City, Boston, Seattle, and Portland, Oregon, have avoided building expensive drinking water treatment facilities. Instead, they have invested in protecting the forests and wetlands in the watersheds that provide their water supplies, thereby increasing their beneficial environmental impacts.

We have the technology to convert sewer water into pure drinking water. The California cities of Los Angeles and San Diego are purifying wastewater to the point where it is fit to drink and putting this water into underlying aquifers, thereby reducing their dependence on water imported from Northern California (Figure 13.19, p. 397) and from the Colorado River (see Chapter 13, Core Case Study, p. 380). In a world where people will face increasing shortages of drinking water, wastewater purification is likely to become a major growth business. **GREEN CAREER: Wastewater purification**

There are also simpler measures to purify drinking water. In tropical countries that lack centralized water treatment systems, the WHO urges people to purify drinking water by exposing a clear plastic bottle filled with contaminated water to intense sunlight. The sun's heat and ultraviolet (UV) rays can kill infectious microbes in as little as 3 hours. Painting one side of the bottle black can improve heat absorption in this simple solar disinfection method, which applies the solar energy **principle of sustainability**. Where this simple measure has been used, the incidence of dangerous childhood diarrhea has decreased by 30–40%. Researchers found that they can speed up this disinfection process by adding lime juice to the water bottles.

Danish inventor Torben Vestergaard Frandsen has developed the *LifeStraw*™, an inexpensive, portable water filter that eliminates many viruses and parasites from water that

Joel Sartore/National Geographic Creative

is drawn through it (Figure 17.12). It has been particularly useful in Africa, where aid agencies are distributing it. Inventor Dean Kamen has developed a small and simple device for purifying dirty water (Science Focus 17.2). Another option being used by more and more people around the world is bottled water, which has created or worsened some environmental problems (see the Case Study that follows).

CASE STUDY

Is Bottled Water a Good Option?

Bottled water can be a useful but expensive option in countries and areas where people do not have access to safe and clean drinking water. However, experts say the United States has some of the world's cleanest drinking water. Municipal water systems in the United States are required to test their water regularly for a number of pollutants and to make the results available to citizens. Yet, about half of all Americans worry about getting sick from tap water contaminants, and many drink high-priced bottled water or install expensive water purification systems.

Studies by the Natural Resources Defense Council (NRDC) reveal that in the United States, a bottle of water costs between 240 and 10,000 times as much as the same volume of tap water. Water expert Peter Gleick has estimated that more than 40% of the expensive bottled water

that Americans drink is bottled tap water. A 4-year study by the NRDC concluded that most bottled water is of good quality but they found traces of bacteria and synthetic organic chemicals in 23 of the 123 brands tested. Bottled water is less regulated than tap water and the EPA contamination standards that apply to public water supplies do not apply to bottled water.

Use of bottled water also causes environmental problems. In the United States, according to the Container Recycling Institute, more than 67 million plastic water bottles are discarded every day—enough bottles in a year to, if lined up end-to-end, wrap around the planet at its equator about 280 times. Most water bottles are made of recyclable plastic, but in the United States, only about 38% of these bottles are recycled. Many of the billions of discarded bottles end up in landfills, where they can remain for hundreds of years. Those that are burned in incinerators without high-tech pollution controls release some of their harmful chemicals into the atmosphere. Also, millions of discarded bottles get scattered on the land and end up in rivers, lakes (Figure 17.5), and oceans. By contrast, in Germany most bottled water is sold in returnable and reusable glass bottles.

It takes huge amounts of energy to manufacture bottled water and to transport it across countries and around the world, as well as to refrigerate much of it in stores. Toxic gases and liquids are released during the

Vestergaard Frandsen

FIGURE 17.12 The *LifeStraw*™ is a personal water purification device that gives many poor people access to safe drinking water. Here, four young men in Uganda demonstrate its use.
Critical thinking: Do you think the development of such devices should make prevention of water pollution less of a priority? Explain.

Converting Dirty Water to Drinking Water

Dean Kamen is a college dropout and mastermind inventor with more than 400 US and foreign patents. Kamen has used royalties from his many inventions to employ 500 engineers and technicians at his company, Deka Research, which is devoted to creating prototypes of devices designed to solve various problems.

In partnership with CocaCola, his company has developed a small portable device about the size of a dormitory refrigerator that can convert dirty water to drinking water. It could be used in remote areas of less-developed countries where millions of people lack access to clean water. The process involves sticking a hose into a polluted water source such as a river or outdoor toilet pit and using a small pump to transfer the dirty water to a chamber in Kamen's water purifier, called the Slingshot.

Widespread use of this device to purify water for drinking, cooking, and hygiene in less-developed countries would sharply reduce disease and could prevent hundreds of thousands of deaths that result annually from drinking contaminated water. The device has been tested successfully in several African and Latin American countries. Kamen wants to find companies to mass produce the device and distribute it to people in remote villages, health-care centers, and schools in less-developed counties.

CRITICAL THINKING

What role, if any, should governments in less-developed countries play in helping distribute this device?

---

manufacture of plastic water bottles, and greenhouse gases and other air pollutants are emitted by the fossil fuels burned to make them and to deliver bottled water to suppliers. In addition, withdrawing groundwater for bottling is helping to deplete some aquifers. There is also concern about health risks from chemicals such as bisphenol A (BPA; see Science Focus 16.3, p. 510) that can leach into the water from the plastic in some water bottles, especially if they are exposed to the hot sun.

Because of these harmful environmental impacts and the high cost of bottled water, there is a growing *back-to-the-tap* movement. From San Francisco to New York to Paris, city governments, restaurants, schools, religious groups, and many consumers are refusing to buy bottled water. In 2015, San Francisco became the first city to ban the sale of plastic water bottles. Violators can face fines of up to $1,000. People are also refilling portable bottles with tap water and using simple filters to improve the taste and color of water where necessary. Some health officials suggest that before drinking expensive bottled water or buying costly home water purifiers, consumers should have their water tested by local health departments or private labs (but not by companies trying to sell water purification equipment).

Using Laws to Protect Drinking Water Quality

About 54 countries, most of them in North America and Europe, have legal standards for safe drinking water. For example, the US Safe Drinking Water Act of 1975 (amended in 1996) requires the EPA to establish national drinking water standards, called *maximum contaminant levels*, for any pollutants that could have adverse effects on human health. Currently, this act strictly limits the levels of 91 potential contaminants in US tap water. However, in most less-developed countries, such laws do not exist or are not enforced.

Health scientists call for strengthening the US Safe Drinking Water Act in several ways. Here are three of their recommendations:

- Combine many of the drinking water treatment systems that serve fewer than 3,300 people with nearby larger systems to make it easier for these smaller systems to meet federal standards.

- Strengthen and enforce requirements concerning public notification of violations of drinking water standards.

- Ban the use of toxic lead in new plumbing pipes, faucets, and fixtures and remove existing lead pipes (see Case Study that follows).

According to the NRDC, making these three improvements would cost US taxpayers an average of about $30 a year per household and decrease health threats from contaminated water.

However, various industries have pressured elected officials to weaken the Safe Drinking Water Act, because complying with it increases their costs. One proposal is to eliminate national testing of drinking water and requirements for public notification about violations of drinking water standards. Another proposal would allow states to give providers of drinking water a permanent right to violate the standard for a given contaminant if they claim they cannot afford to meet the standard. Some critics also call for greatly reducing the EPA's already-low budget for enforcing the Safe Drinking Water Act.

The Environmental Cost of Bottled Water

Outbreaks of cholera and typhoid during the nineteenth century prompted the development of centralized water supply systems in large cities such as New York and Chicago. Since water is treated before being piped into homes, citizens have been able to rely on a constant supply of fresh, potable water.

In spite of this readily available resource that many of us take for granted, people have turned away from the tap and now buy bottled water, mostly out of convenience, even though in most cases water from the tap is equal if not superior in quality to some brands of bottled water. There are economic, energy, and environmental costs involved in producing bottled water, which include making the bottles, withdrawing water from the environment, bottling the water, transporting it, advertising it, and recycling or disposing of bottles.

FRQ Application

Americans consumed about 50 billion bottles of water in 2016. The amount of oil needed to produce one plastic 16-oz. water bottle (oil for plastic plus the energy to produce the bottle) is 3.26 ounces. How many barrels of oil were used in 2016 to manufacture water bottles?

There are 128 ounces in a gallon, and 42 gallons in a barrel of oil.

$$50\,\text{billion bottles} \times \frac{3.26\,\text{oz. oil}}{1\,\text{bottle}} \times \frac{1\,\text{gallon}}{128\,\text{oz.}} \times \frac{1\,\text{barrel}}{42\,\text{gallons}} = 30.3\,\text{million barrels of oil}$$

It takes on average 14 gallons of gas to fill a car's tank and one barrel of oil produces 19 gallons of motor gasoline (the rest is used to produce diesel fuels and other distillates). How many cars could fill their gas tanks on the oil it takes to produce these water bottles?

$$30{,}319{,}940\,\text{barrels of oil} \times \frac{19\,\text{gallons of gas}}{1\,\text{barrel of oil}} \times \frac{1\,\text{car}}{14\,\text{gallons per tank}} = 41.1\,\text{thousand cars filled}$$

Approximately 50 empty plastic water bottles weigh one pound. What is the weight in metric tons of the plastic for all of the water bottles consumed in the United States in 2016? There are 2.2 pounds in a kilogram.

$$50\,\text{billion bottles} \times \frac{1\,\text{pound}}{50\,\text{bottles}} \times \frac{1\,\text{kilogram}}{2.2\,\text{pounds}} \times \frac{1\,\text{metric ton}}{1000\,\text{kg}} \approx 450{,}000\,\text{metric tons of plastic}$$

If only 38% of water bottles are recycled, how many tons of plastic become waste? This suggests that 62% of the bottles are discarded and not recycled:

$$450{,}000\,\text{metric tons plastic} \times 0.62 = 279{,}000\,\text{metric tons plastic waste}$$

Lead in Drinking Water

In 2014, many people in older and poorer neighborhoods of Flint, Michigan—a city of nearly 100,000 people with 40% living in poverty—were exposed to dangerous levels of lead in their tap water. The problem began when, in an effort to save money, Flint officials began withdrawing drinking water from the Flint River instead of from Lake Huron.

Officials did not take into account that there were an estimated 20,000 lead pipes connecting the city's main line water pipes (that do not contain lead) to homes, many of them in older and poorer neighborhoods. They failed to add chemicals to reduce the leaching of lead from the pipes exposed to the more corrosive water supply.

As a result, lead began leaching into the water supply for many homes in older and poorer neighborhoods. Research shows that exposure to high levels of lead—a potent neurotoxin—is especially harmful to the developing brains and nervous systems of children. This problem is complicated by the fact that lead is a cumulative poison that builds up in the body. Thus, exposure to even small amounts of lead has posed a long-term threat to the nervous system, brain, and other organs, and threatened the intellectual development and physical growth of the 9,000 children under age 6 living in Flint.

After Flint changed its drinking water source, the percentage of children citywide with elevated blood levels of lead doubled from 2.4% to 4.9% and to 15.7% in its poorest neighborhood. This meant that roughly 1 out of 6 children in Flint and 1 out of 3 in its poorest neighborhood were exposed to blood levels of lead that the Centers for Disease Control and Prevention (CDC) uses as a standard to identify children who need medical help. In 1986, the EPA banned the use of lead water pipes, fittings, solder, and other plumbing material in new homes. However, this regulation did not cover the millions of lead pipes and plumbing material in older homes in Flint and elsewhere in the United States.

After a highly publicized outcry, Flint officials switched the city's water supply source back to Lake Huron, but the health threats to children remain. Officials are seeking funding to have the blood lead levels in affected children under 6 monitored for several years. The ultimate solution is to replace all of the lead pipes connecting homes to the city's main line water pipes, which will be costly for the city and homeowners.

Public health officials say that Flint is just the tip of the iceberg. Investigations revealed that in 2015 almost 2,000, or 20%, of US water systems tested have failed to meet the EPA's standard of 15 parts per billion (ppb) for lead in drinking water. A level of 40 ppb poses an imminent and substantial threat to the health of children and pregnant women, according to the EPA. This included about 350 schools and daycare centers, which means that many children are vulnerable to unsafe levels of lead. The EPA and health officials have urged all US residents to have their drinking water tested for lead.

CHECKPOINT FOR UNDERSTANDING 17.3

1. Explain why hydraulic fracking can result in contamination of groundwater.

2. Explain why it is particularly difficult to remediate groundwater contamination.

3. Identify the drawbacks of consuming bottled water.

4. What is the purpose of the US Safe Drinking Water Act?

17.4 WHAT ARE THE MAJOR OCEAN POLLUTION PROBLEMS?

CONCEPT 17.4A Most ocean pollution originates on land and includes oil and other toxic chemicals and solid waste, which threaten fish and wildlife and disrupt marine ecosystems.

CONCEPT 17.4B The key to protecting the oceans is to reduce the flow of pollution from land and air and from streams emptying into ocean waters.

Ocean Pollution Is a Growing Problem

We should care about the oceans because they keep us alive. Oceans help recycle the planet's freshwater through the water cycle (Figure 3.14, p. 77). They also strongly affect weather and climate, help regulate the earth's

temperature, and absorb some of the massive amounts of carbon dioxide that we emit into the atmosphere.

As oceanographer and explorer Sylvia A. Earle reminds us: "Even if you never have the chance to see or touch the ocean, the ocean touches you with every breath you take, every drop of water you drink, every bite you consume. Everyone, everywhere is inextricably connected to and utterly dependent upon the existence of the sea." Despite its importance, we treat the ocean as the world's largest dump for the massive and growing amount of wastes and pollutants that we produce.

Coastal areas—especially wetlands, estuaries, coral reefs, and mangrove swamps—receive the largest inputs of pollutants and wastes (Figure 17.13). Roughly 40% of the world's people (53% in the United States) live on or near coastlines, and coastal populations are projected to double by 2050. This explains why 80% of marine pollution originates on land (**Concept 17.4A**).

According to a study by the U.N. Environment Programme (UNEP), 80–90% of the municipal sewage from coastal areas of less-developed countries is dumped into oceans without treatment. This often overwhelms the ability of the coastal waters to degrade the wastes. For example, many areas of China's coastline are so choked with algae growing on the nutrients provided by sewage that some scientists have concluded that large areas of China's coastal waters can no longer sustain marine ecosystems. Dumping biodegradable wastes and plant nutrients into coastal waters instead of recycling these vital plant nutrients to the soil violates the chemical cycling **principle of sustainability**.

In deeper waters, the oceans can dilute, disperse, and degrade large amounts of raw sewage and other types of degradable pollutants. Some scientists suggest that it is safer to dump sewage sludge, toxic mining wastes, and most other harmful wastes into the deep ocean than to bury them on land or burn them in incinerators. Other scientists disagree and point out that dumping harmful wastes into the ocean would delay urgently needed pollution prevention measures and promote further degradation of this vital part of the earth's life-support system.

Recent studies of some US coastal waters found vast colonies of viruses thriving in raw sewage and in effluents from sewage treatment plants (which do not remove viruses) and leaking septic tanks. According to one study, one-fourth of the people using coastal beaches in the United States develop ear infections, sore throats, eye irritations, respiratory diseases, or gastrointestinal diseases from swimming in seawater containing infectious viruses and bacteria.

Scientists also point to the underreported problem of pollution from cruise ships. A cruise liner can carry as many as 6,300 passengers and 2,400 crewmembers, and it can generate as much waste (toxic chemicals, garbage, sewage, and waste oil) as a small city. Many cruise ships dump these wastes at sea. In US waters, such dumping is illegal, but some ships continue dumping secretively, usually at night. Some environmentally aware vacationers are refusing to go on

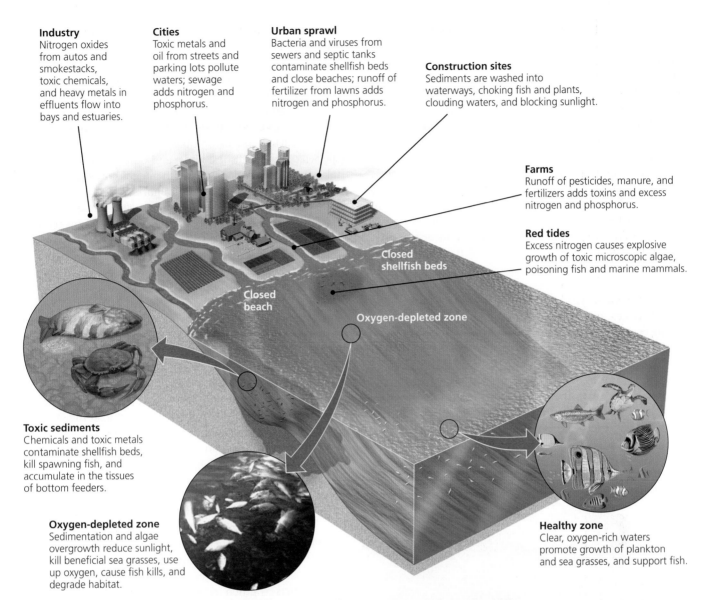

Industry
Nitrogen oxides from autos and smokestacks, toxic chemicals, and heavy metals in effluents flow into bays and estuaries.

Cities
Toxic metals and oil from streets and parking lots pollute waters; sewage adds nitrogen and phosphorus.

Urban sprawl
Bacteria and viruses from sewers and septic tanks contaminate shellfish beds and close beaches; runoff of fertilizer from lawns adds nitrogen and phosphorus.

Construction sites
Sediments are washed into waterways, choking fish and plants, clouding waters, and blocking sunlight.

Farms
Runoff of pesticides, manure, and fertilizers adds toxins and excess nitrogen and phosphorus.

Red tides
Excess nitrogen causes explosive growth of toxic microscopic algae, poisoning fish and marine mammals.

Closed shellfish beds

Closed beach

Oxygen-depleted zone

Toxic sediments
Chemicals and toxic metals contaminate shellfish beds, kill spawning fish, and accumulate in the tissues of bottom feeders.

Oxygen-depleted zone
Sedimentation and algae overgrowth reduce sunlight, kill beneficial sea grasses, use up oxygen, cause fish kills, and degrade habitat.

Healthy zone
Clear, oxygen-rich waters promote growth of plankton and sea grasses, and support fish.

FIGURE 17.13 Natural capital degradation: Residential areas, factories, and farms all contribute to the pollution of coastal waters. **Critical thinking:** What do you think are the three worst pollution problems shown here? For each one, how does it affect two or more of the ecosystem and economic services listed in Figure 6.4 (p. 156)?

cruise ships that do not have sophisticated systems for dealing with the wastes the ships produce.

Runoff of sewage and agricultural wastes into coastal waters introduces large quantities of nitrate (NO_3^-) and phosphate (PO_4^{3-}) plant nutrients that can cause explosive growths of harmful algae and lead to dead zones (**Core Case Study**). These *harmful algal blooms*—also called red, brown, or green toxic tides—release waterborne and airborne toxins that poison seafood, damage fisheries, kill some fish-eating birds, and reduce tourism. Each year, harmful algal blooms lead to the poisoning of about 60,000 Americans who eat shellfish contaminated by the algae.

Harmful algal blooms occur annually in at least 400 *oxygen-depleted* or *dead zones* around the world, mostly in temperate coastal waters and in large bodies of water with restricted outflows, such as the Baltic and Black Seas. The largest such zone in US coastal waters forms each year in the northern Gulf of Mexico (**Core Case Study**). Warmer ocean water temperatures, caused when the oceans take up much of the excess heat in the atmosphere that is getting warmer because of human emissions of greenhouse gases, are extending the size and duration of dead zones in the world's oceans.

CASE STUDY

Ocean Garbage Patches: There Is No Away

In the 1970s, scientists from the Woods Hole Oceanographic Institution predicted that swirling patches of garbage would form in the Pacific Ocean. In 1997, ocean researcher Charles J. Moore discovered two gigantic, slowly rotating masses of plastic and other solid wastes in the middle of the North Pacific Ocean near the Hawaiian Islands. These wastes are mostly small particles floating on or just beneath the ocean's surface. Known as the *North Pacific Garbage Patch*, these solid wastes are trapped there by a vortex where rotating ocean currents called *gyres* meet (Figure 17.14).

Roughly 80% of this trash comes from the land. It is washed or blown off beaches, pours out of storm drains, and floats down streams and rivers that empty into the sea from the west coast of North America, the east coast of Asia, and hundreds of Pacific islands (**Concept 17.4A**). Most of the rest comes from discarded fishing gear and from wastes dumped into the ocean from cargo and cruise ships.

The North Pacific Garbage Patch—viewed as the planet's largest human trash dump—is estimated by some scientists to occupy an area at least the size of Texas. However, such estimates are difficult to verify because this continuously swirling plastic-laden soup consists mostly of small rice-grain- to pencil-eraser-sized plastic particles suspended just beneath the surface. This makes the garbage patch difficult to see and measure. While many different types of trash enter the ocean, plastic makes up most of the garbage patch because it is contained in so many disposable products. Plus, it does not biodegrade but instead breaks down into smaller and smaller pieces. Scientists estimate that the amount of plastics entering the ocean will double by 2050.

These small plastic particles ultimately degrade into microscopic particles that can contain potentially hazardous chemicals, including PCBs, DDT, and hormone-mimicking BPA. Small and microscopic plastic particles are eaten by 700 species of marine fishes, birds, and other animals that mistake them for food or ingest them unknowingly. A dead whale that washed ashore in California had 180 kilograms (400 pounds) of plastic in its stomach. The long-lived toxins in these microscopic plastic particles can build up to high concentrations in food chains and webs and end up in fish sandwiches and seafood dinners. Thus, toxic chemicals from a discarded plastic grocery bag or water bottle could end up in our stomachs. Everything is connected.

Since the North Pacific Garbage Patch was discovered, five other huge swirling garbage patches have been found in gyres in the world's other oceans. These patches, together with the North Pacific patch, cover a total area of ocean larger than all of the earth's land area—the massive pollution legacy of a throwaway culture.

Engineers are testing ways to capture marine debris near the ocean surface as currents pull it into the garbage patch zone. But currently there is no practical or affordable way to clean up this marine litter. The best approach is to prevent the garbage patch from growing by reducing production of solid waste and keeping it out of oceans in the first place. This would require us to sharply reduce unnecessary use of plastic items, greatly increase plastic recycling, and establish modern waste collection and management systems in all coastal countries. Each of us can avoid using plastic water bottles and other plastic products as much as possible and recycle or dispose of them responsibly.

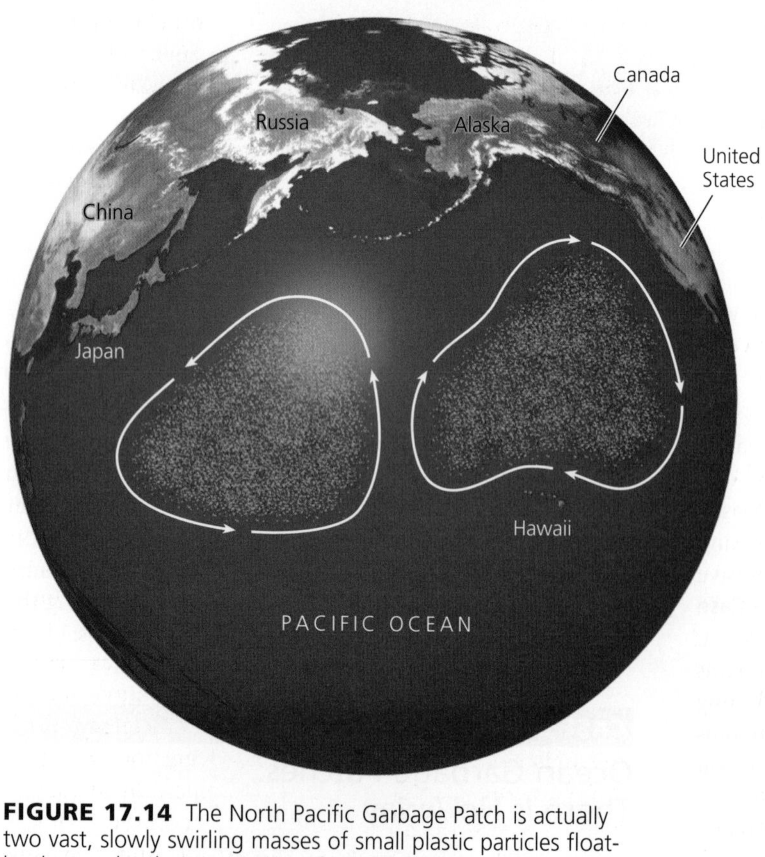

Ocean Pollution from Oil

Crude petroleum (oil as it comes out of the ground) and *refined petroleum* (fuel oil, diesel, gasoline, and other processed petroleum products; see Figure 14.4, p. 424) reach the ocean from natural sources and human activities (**Concept 17.4A**). According to the National Research Council, as much as 46% of the oil in the ocean comes from natural seeps on the ocean bottom. The rest comes from human activities.

The most visible human sources of ocean oil pollution include tanker accidents, such as the huge *Exxon Valdez* oil spill in the US state of Alaska in 1989. Others are blowouts at offshore oil drilling rigs, such as that of the BP *Deepwater Horizon* rig in the Gulf of Mexico in 2010 (see the Case Study that follows). However, studies show that the largest

FIGURE 17.14 The North Pacific Garbage Patch is actually two vast, slowly swirling masses of small plastic particles floating just under the water. Five other huge garbage patches have been discovered in the world's other major oceans.

source of ocean oil pollution from human activities is urban and industrial runoff from land. Most of this comes from leaks in pipelines, refineries, and other oil-handling and storage facilities and from oil and oil products that are intentionally dumped or accidentally spilled or leaked onto the land or into sewers by homeowners and industries.

After a major oil spill, some of the oil evaporates and some is reduced to tiny droplets. These droplets can be dispersed by wave action or by chemicals added to the water to help clean up spills. Some oil is decomposed by aerobic bacteria such as blue-green algae (but not in low-oxygen areas such as the deep sea). What remains is a gooey mixture of oil and water called *mousse* that can float in the water for years or be buried in coastal sediments for decades.

Some spilled oil contains volatile organic hydrocarbons that kill many aquatic organisms immediately on contact, especially if these animals are in their vulnerable larval forms. Other chemicals in oil form tarlike globs that float on the surface and coat the feathers of seabirds (see chapter-opening photo) and the fur of marine mammals. The oil destroys their natural heat insulation and buoyancy, causing many of them to drown or die from loss of body heat.

When ingested, oil can poison marine organisms. Oil and some of its toxic chemicals can also end up in the tissues of filtering organisms such as clams, oysters, and mussels. Such chemicals can then become concentrated to higher levels in fish and other organisms (including humans) that feed on these filtering organisms.

Heavy oil components that sink to the ocean floor or wash into estuaries and coastal wetlands can smother bottom-dwelling organisms such as crabs, oysters, mussels, and clams, or make them unfit for human consumption. Some oil spills have killed coral reefs.

Research shows that populations of many forms of marine life can recover from exposure to large amounts of *crude oil* in warm waters with rapid currents within about 3 years. However, in cold and calm waters, recovery can take decades. Recovery from exposure to *refined oil*, especially in estuaries and salt marshes, can take 10 to 20 years or longer. Oil slicks that wash onto beaches can have a serious economic impact on coastal areas that lose income from fishing and tourist activities.

Small oil spills can be partially cleaned up by mechanical means, including floating booms, skimmer boats, and absorbent devices such as giant pillows filled with feathers or hair. However, scientists estimate that current cleanup methods typically can recover no more than 15% of the oil from a major spill.

Therefore, *prevention* of oil pollution is the most effective and, in the end, the least costly approach (**Concept 17.4B**). One of the best ways to prevent tanker spills is to use oil tankers with double hulls. The Oil Pollution Act of 1990, passed by Congress after the 1989 Exxon Valdez oil spill, required that all new oil tankers and barges operating in US waters have double hulls by 2015. Stricter safety standards and inspections can help reduce oil well blowouts at sea.

Most important, businesses, institutions, and citizens living in coastal areas must take care to prevent leaks and spillage of even the smallest amounts of oil and oil products such as paint thinners and gasoline.

CASE STUDY

The BP *Deepwater Horizon* Oil-Rig Spill

On April 20, 2010, the world learned a harsh lesson about the possible environmental impacts of deep-sea oil drilling when British Petroleum's *Deepwater Horizon* offshore oil-drilling rig exploded (Figure 17.15). The floating rig was connected to a well head on the seafloor almost 1.6 kilometers (1 mile) below and was removing crude oil from a well that was an additional 5.4 kilometers (3.4 miles) below the seafloor.

The accident occurred in the Gulf of Mexico, 64 kilometers (40 miles) off the Louisiana coast, after the wellhead on the ocean bottom ruptured and released oil and natural gas. The resulting fire and explosion killed 11 of the rig's crewmembers and injured 17 more. After burning and belching oil smoke into the air for 36 hours, the rig sank.

For 3 months, the ruptured wellhead on the ocean floor released about 3.1 million barrels (130 million gallons) of crude oil before the leaking well was capped. The oil slick covered a huge area of the Gulf of Mexico (Figure 17.16)—roughly equivalent to the area of the US state of Connecticut—and fouled at least 2,100 kilometers (1,300 miles) of coastline. It was the largest accidental oil spill in US waters and the second largest in the world.

The oil contaminated the sea floor, as well as some ecologically vital coastal marshes, mangrove forests, sea-grass beds, fish nurseries, and at least three deep coral reefs. Scientists suspect that deep-ocean aquatic organisms were affected, but the true extent of the ecological damage will not be known for years. According to estimates from the US Coast Guard, the National Oceanic and Atmospheric Administration (NOAA), and BP, the oil spill killed at least 6,100 seabirds and oiled another 2,000 (see chapter-opening photo). It also killed more than 600 sea turtles and 100 dolphins, along with other marine mammals.

In addition, the spill disrupted the livelihoods of people who depend on the Gulf Coast's fisheries, and caused large economic losses for the area's tourism businesses. By 2015, BP had spent $61.6 billion on cleanup, damages, and fines.

Also by 2015—5 years after the spill—bacteria had decomposed most of the visible oily tar in coastal areas. Lesions on fish (a result of the spill) were rarely being found, and the commercial fish catch in the spill area had increased. However, as late as 2014, some fish were still dying from the effects of oil exposure, according to an NOAA report. In addition, it will take decades to assess the long-term ecological damage and in coming years, storms, hurricanes, and unusually large tides will release some of the buried oil in coastal areas.

US Coast Guard

FIGURE 17.15 The Deepwater *Horizon* drilling platform, located 64 kilometers (40 miles) off the coast of Louisiana, exploded, burned, and sank in the Gulf of Mexico on April 20, 2010.

called for close oversight by Congress to ensure that such reforms are put in place and carefully monitored to help reduce the chances of such accidents in this inherently risky business. As of 2017, this had not been done.

The widespread global publicity following the BP *Deepwater Horizon* accident helped to educate the public about the dangers of accidents that can release large quantities of oil into the oceans. However, there has been little attention focused on the numerous smaller oil spills that have been occurring almost continually for nearly 50 years in Nigeria's oil-producing Niger Delta, where there is little or no government oversight of oil company operations. Each year, an amount of oil roughly equal to that of the Exxon Valdez disaster leaks and spills from rusted and aging pipes and other facilities in this delta region. Decades of such leaks have caused widespread ecological destruction and threats to human health. According to some scientists, these spills altogether are more damaging than the large, well-known spills.

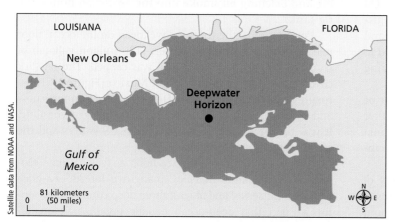

Satellite data from NOAA and NASA.

FIGURE 17.16 Blue area shows the extent of *Deepwater Horizon* oil spill on April 20, 2010.

Several studies, including that of a Presidential commission, have concluded that the main causes of the accident were failure of equipment that could have detected the leak earlier, a faulty blowout preventer, failure of several safety valves, and a number of poor decisions made by workers and managers. This event also revealed flaws in federal oversight of offshore drilling, which many argue has included too cozy a relationship between the oil industry and US Department of the Interior (DOI) regulators.

Since the accident, the DOI has stepped up oversight. It has developed new standards for each step in the offshore drilling process and agreed to give a higher priority to environmental concerns in the leasing process. However, the Presidential oil spill commission

CHECKPOINT FOR UNDERSTANDING 17.4

1. What is an oceanic *dead zone*?

2. Explain how the North Pacific Garbage Patch formed.

3. Identify the largest source of oceanic oil pollution.

4. Describe the governmental response to the *Deepwater Horizon* accident.

5. What is the most effective way to reduce ocean pollution?

17.5 HOW CAN WE DEAL WITH WATER POLLUTION?

CONCEPT 17.5 Reducing water pollution requires that we prevent it, work with nature to treat sewage, and use natural resources more efficiently.

Reducing Ocean Water Pollution

Most ocean pollution occurs in coastal waters and comes from human activities on land (**Concept 17.4A**). Figure 17.17 lists ways to prevent pollution of coastal waters and ways to reduce it.

The key to protecting the oceans is to reduce the flow of pollution from land, air, and from streams emptying into these waters (**Concept 17.4B**). Thus, ocean pollution control must be linked with land-use policies, air pollution control policies, energy policies based on improving energy efficiency and relying more on renewable energy, especially from the sun and wind, and climate policies.

Reducing Water Pollution from Nonpoint Sources

Most nonpoint sources of water pollution come from agricultural practices. Ways to reduce this type of pollution include the following:

- Reducing soil erosion and fertilizer runoff by keeping cropland covered with vegetation and using conservation tillage and other soil conservation methods (see Figure 12.25, p. 361).
- Using fertilizers that release plant nutrients slowly.
- Using no fertilizers on steeply sloped land.
- Relying more on sustainable food production (Figure 12.30, p. 365) to reduce the use and runoff of plant nutrients and pesticides.
- Planting buffer zones of vegetation between cultivated fields (Figure 17.18) and between animal waste storage sites and nearby surface waters.

- Setting discharge standards for nitrate chemicals from sewage treatment and industrial plants.

The annual formation of the dead zone in the Gulf of Mexico (**Core Case Study**) will be difficult to prevent because of the importance of the Mississippi River basin for growing crops. However, nutrient inputs can be reduced with the widespread use of the fertilizer management practices listed above.

In addition to reducing nitrate inputs, another goal is to protect remaining inland and coastal wetlands, vegetation in *riparian zones* (zones along river banks; see Figure 10.15, right, p. 279), and floodplains, all of which act as natural filters to pull nutrients from waters that are running off the land and spilling out of streams. However, many of the nation's wetlands have been drained or filled in and replaced by cropland.

Another strategy is to restore key wetlands that have been destroyed or degraded and, where feasible, restoring and reconnecting rivers to their natural floodplains. In addition to reducing water pollution, this would restore natural habitats for a variety of species in keeping with the biodiversity **principle of sustainability**.

Reducing Water Pollution in the United States

Efforts to control pollution of surface waters in the United States are based on the following federal laws:

- Federal Water Pollution Control Act of 1972, amended in 1977 and renamed the Clean Water Act (CWA). Two-thirds of the nation's lakes, rivers, and coastal

---

Solutions

Coastal Water Pollution

Prevention		Cleanup
Separate sewage and storm water lines	Ban dumping of wastes and sewage by ships in coastal waters	Improve oil-spill cleanup capabilities
Require secondary treatment of coastal sewage	Strictly regulate coastal development, oil drilling, and oil shipping	Use nanoparticles on sewage and oil spills to dissolve the oil or sewage (still under development)
Use wetlands and other natural methods to treat sewage	Require double hulls for oil tankers	

FIGURE 17.17 Methods for preventing excessive pollution of coastal waters and methods for cleaning it up. *Critical thinking:* Which two of these solutions do you think are the most important? Why?

Top: Rob Byron/Shutterstock.com. Bottom: Igor Karasi/Shutterstock.com.

FIGURE 17.18 This buffer zone of vegetation on an Iowa farm helps to reduce runoff of fertilizer and pesticides into waterways from nearby crop fields.

waters were unsafe for fishing and swimming, and the key goal of the CWA was to make them safe.

- 1972 Marine Protection, Research, and Sanctuaries Act, amended in 1988. It empowered the EPA to regulate the dumping of untreated sewage and toxic chemicals into US waters.

- 1975 Safe Drinking Water Act (SDWA), amended in 1996. Its goals are to protect surface and groundwater used as sources of drinking water and to establish national drinking water standards for key pollutants.

- 1976 Toxic Substances Control Act. It requires the EPA to maintain a registry of the chemicals in commercial use, evaluate the health risks of new and existing chemicals based on information from producers of such chemicals, and promote ways to reduce or prevent pollution from chemicals that are toxic.

- 1980 Comprehensive Environmental Response Compensation and Liability Act (CERCLA), also known as the Superfund Act. Its goal is to reduce pollution of groundwater by toxic substance leaking from hazardous waste dumps.

- 1987 Water Quality Act, which requires the EPA to set standards for allowed levels of 100 key water pollutants. It requires polluters to get permits that limit the amounts of these various pollutants that they can discharge into aquatic systems.

- 1990 Oil Pollution Act. It has the goal of protecting US waterways from oil pollution.

The EPA has also been experimenting with a *discharge trading policy*, which uses market forces to reduce water pollution. Under this program, a permit holder can pollute at higher levels than allowed in its permit by buying credits from permit holders who are polluting below their allowed levels. Environmental scientists and economists warn that the effectiveness of such a system depends on how low the cap on total pollution levels in any given area is set and on how regularly the cap is lowered. They also warn that discharge trading could allow water pollutants to build up to dangerous levels in areas where credits are bought. Neither adequate scrutiny of the cap levels nor gradual lowering of caps is a part of the current EPA discharge trading system.

According to the EPA, the Clean Water Act of 1972 and other water quality acts led to numerous improvements in US water quality, including the following:

- About 60% of all tested US streams, lakes, and estuaries can be used safely for fishing and swimming, compared to 33% in 1972.

- Sewage treatment plants serve 75% of the US population.

- Annual losses of US wetlands that naturally absorb and purify water have been reduced by 80% since 1992.

These are impressive achievements, given the increases in the US population and its per capita consumption of water and other resources since 1972. However, according to the EPA and recent studies, there is still considerable room for improvement. These studies noted the following:

- About 40% of the nation's surveyed streams, lakes, and estuaries are still too polluted for swimming or fishing.

- Runoff of animal wastes from hog, poultry, and cattle feedlots and meat processing facilities pollutes 70% of US rivers.

- Tens of thousands of gasoline storage tanks in 43 states are leaking.

- Since 2003, 20% of US water treatment systems have violated the Safe Drinking Water Act by releasing sewage and chemicals such as arsenic and radioactive uranium into US surface waters.

- A study showed that water samples from 139 streams in 30 states contained measurable levels of drugs used for birth control and for reducing pain and depression.

Some environmental scientists propose strengthening the Clean Water Act to address these water-quality problems. New provisions would focus on: pollution prevention rather than treating pollution after it has been created; larger mandatory fines for violators; regulating irrigation water and reducing fertilizer and pesticide runoff from farms, including fracking under the Clean Water Act; and allowing citizens the right to sue when these laws are violated.

Many businesses and legislators feel that the current laws are already too restrictive and oppose any new legislation. In fact, some legislators representing regulated industries propose that current laws should be repealed rather than strengthened arguing that regulations hinder job growth.

Sewage Treatment Reduces Water Pollution

In rural and suburban areas with suitable soils, sewage from each house usually is discharged into a **septic tank** and a large drainage (leach) field (Figure 17.19). Household sewage and wastewater is pumped into a settling tank, where grease and oil rise to the top, and solids, called *sludge*, fall to the bottom and are decomposed by bacteria. The partially treated wastewater is discharged into a large drainage or leach field through small holes in perforated pipes embedded in porous gravel or crushed stone just below the soil's surface. As these wastes drain from the pipes and sink downward, the soil filters out some potential pollutants and soil bacteria decompose biodegradable materials.

About one-fourth of all homes in the United States are served by septic tanks. It these systems are not installed correctly and the sludge in the tank is not pumped out regularly, sewage can back up into homes and pollute nearby groundwater and surface water. Chlorine bleaches, drain cleaners, and antibacterial soaps should not be used

in these systems, because they can kill the bacteria that decompose the wastes. Kitchen sink garbage disposals should also not be used, because they can overload septic systems.

In urban areas in the United States and other more-developed countries, most waterborne wastes from homes, businesses, and storm runoff flow through a network of sewer pipes to *wastewater* or *sewage treatment plants*. Raw sewage reaching a treatment plant typically undergoes one or two levels of wastewater treatment. The first is **primary sewage treatment**—a *physical* process that uses screens and a grit tank to remove large floating objects and to allow solids such as sand and rock to settle out. Then the waste stream flows into a primary settling tank where suspended solids settle out as sludge (Figure 17.20, left).

The second level is **secondary sewage treatment**—a *biological* process in which oxygen is added to the sewage in an aeration tank to encourage aerobic bacteria to decompose as much as 90% of dissolved and biodegradable, oxygen-demanding organic wastes (Figure 17.20, right). A combination of primary and secondary treatment removes 95–97% of the suspended solids and oxygen-demanding organic wastes, 70% of most toxic metal compounds and nonpersistent synthetic organic chemicals, 70% of the phosphorus, and 50% of the nitrogen.

However, this process removes only a tiny fraction of persistent and potentially toxic organic substances found in some pesticides and in discarded medicines that people put into sewage systems, and it does not kill disease-causing bacteria and viruses. It also does not remove many of the toxic chemicals in wastewater that industries and fracking operations send to sewage treatment plants.

A third level of cleanup, *advanced* or *tertiary sewage treatment*, uses a series of specialized chemical and physical

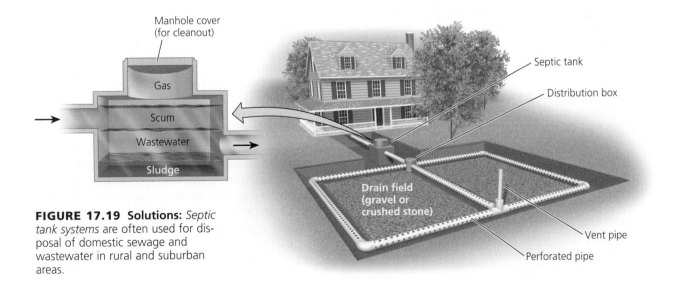

FIGURE 17.19 Solutions: *Septic tank systems* are often used for disposal of domestic sewage and wastewater in rural and suburban areas.

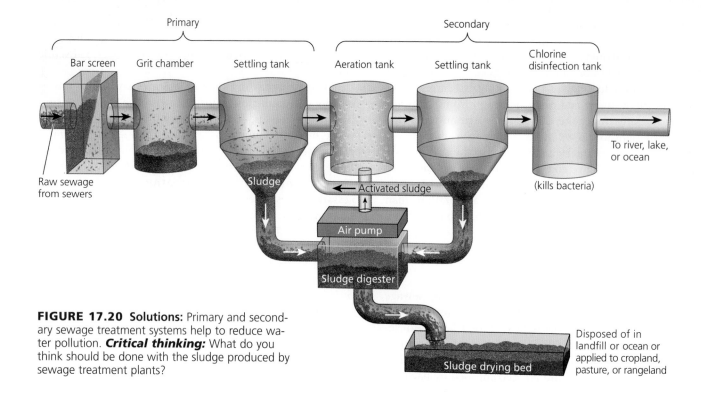

Secondary

Bar screen   Grit chamber   Settling tank   Aeration tank   Settling tank   Chlorine disinfection tank

Raw sewage from sewers

Sludge

Activated sludge

Air pump

Sludge digester

To river, lake, or ocean

(kills bacteria)

Sludge drying bed

Disposed of in landfill or ocean or applied to cropland, pasture, or rangeland

FIGURE 17.20 Solutions: Primary and secondary sewage treatment systems help to reduce water pollution. **Critical thinking:** What do you think should be done with the sludge produced by sewage treatment plants?

processes to remove specific pollutants left in the water after primary and secondary treatment. In its most common form, advanced sewage treatment uses special filters to remove phosphates and nitrates from wastewater before it is discharged into surface waters. This third stage would significantly reduce nutrient overload from nitrates and phosphates, but is not widely used because of its high costs.

Before discharge, water from sewage treatment plants usually undergoes *bleaching*, to remove water coloration, and *disinfection* to kill disease-carrying bacteria and some (but not all) viruses. The usual method for accomplishing this is chlorination. Use of other disinfectants, such as ozone and UV light, is increasing, but they cost more and their effects do not last as long as those of chlorination.

Some cities have two separate networks of pipes, one for carrying storm-water runoff from streets and parking lots, and the other for carrying sewage. About 1,200 US cities have combined these two systems into one set of pipes to cut costs. Heavy rains or a high volume of sewage from too many users hooked up to such combined systems can cause them to overflow and discharge untreated sewage directly into surface waters.

According to the EPA, at least 40,000 of these overflows occur each year in the United States, and at least 7 million people get sick every year from swimming in waters contaminated by overflows that contain sewage.

The best way to deal with this overflow problem is to prevent it by using separate systems to carry storm water and sewage (**Concept 17.5**).

Improving Conventional Sewage Treatment

Secondary sewage treatment produces a sludge called *biosolids*, which are rich in nitrates and phosphates. Ideally, this solid waste that settles out during secondary treatment (Figure 17.20) should be returned to agricultural fields in keeping with natural nutrient cycling.

However, because there are no restrictions that keep homeowners and industries from sending wastewater to treatment plants that contain heavy metals, pesticides, and pharmaceuticals, these toxins end up in the biosolids as well. As these wastes may be legally applied to crop fields, playgrounds, and public lands, people are exposed to and may ingest toxic chemicals and heavy metals.

Some environmental and health scientists propose redesigning traditional wastewater treatment systems to keep toxic materials from reaching treatment plants and ending up in waste-treatment sludge. The idea is to work toward pollution prevention. By requiring industries to remove toxins from wastewater before discharging it, the cost of cleanup does not become the burden of the taxpayer. Industries would have the economic

Treating Sewage by Learning from Nature

Some communities and individuals are developing better ways to purify sewage by learning how nature purifies water using sunlight and plants, aquatic organisms, and natural filtration by soil, sand, and gravel (**Concept 17.5**). Biologist John Todd has developed an ecological approach to treating sewage, which he calls *living machines* (Figure 17.D).

This purification process begins when sewage flows into a passive solar greenhouse or outdoor site containing rows of large open tanks populated by an increasingly complex series of organisms. In the first set of tanks, algae and microorganisms decompose organic wastes, with sunlight speeding up the process. Water hyacinths, cattails, bulrushes, and other aquatic plants growing in the tanks take up the resulting nutrients.

After flowing though several of these natural purification tanks, the water passes through an artificial marsh made of sand, gravel, and bulrushes, which filter out algae and remaining organic waste. Some of the plants also remove toxic metals such as lead and mercury and secrete natural antibiotic compounds that kill pathogens.

Next, the water flows into aquarium tanks, where snails and zooplankton consume microorganisms and are in turn consumed by crayfish, tilapia, and other fish that can be eaten or sold as bait. After 10 days, the clear water flows into a second artificial marsh for final filtering and cleansing. The water can be made

pure enough to drink by treating it with ultraviolet light or by passing the water through an ozone generator, usually immersed out of sight in an attractive pond or wetland habitat.

Operating costs are about the same as those of a conventional sewage treatment plant. These systems are widely used on a small scale. However, they are difficult to maintain on a scale large enough to handle the typical variety of chemicals in the sewage wastes from large urban areas.

More than 800 cities and towns around the world (150 in the United States) mimic nature by using natural or artificially created wetlands to treat sewage as a lower-cost alternative to expensive waste-treatment plants. For example, in Arcata, California—a coastal town of almost 18,000 people—scientists and workers created some 65 hectares (160 acres) of wetlands between the town and the adjacent Humboldt Bay. The marshes and ponds, developed on land that was once a dump, act as a natural waste-treatment plant. The cost of the project was less than half the estimated price of a conventional treatment plant.

This system returns purified water to Humboldt Bay, and the sludge that is removed is processed for use as fertilizer. The marshes and ponds also serve as an Audubon Society bird sanctuary, which provides habitats for thousands of seabirds, otters, and other marine animals. The town has even celebrated its natural

Ocean Arks International

FIGURE 17.D Solutions: The Solar Sewage Treatment Plant in the US city of Providence, Rhode Island, is an ecological wastewater purification system, also called a *living machine*. Biologist John Todd is demonstrating an ecological process he invented for purifying wastewater by using the sun and a series of tanks containing living organisms.

sewage treatment system with an annual "Flush with Pride" festival.

This approach and the living machine system developed by John Todd apply all three **scientific principles of sustainability**: using solar energy, employing natural processes to remove and recycle nutrients and other chemicals, and relying on a diversity of organisms and natural processes.

CRITICAL THINKING

Can you think of any disadvantages of using such a nature-based system instead of a conventional sewage treatment plant? Do you think any such disadvantages outweigh the advantages? Why or why not?

incentive to reduce or recycle toxic materials or find alternatives.

Because biosolids are an excellent source of plant nutrients, some entities view them as a valuable commodity rather than a waste problem. In Sweden and The Netherlands, the nutrients reclaimed from sewage are recycled to the land. Ashley Murray, a wastewater engineer and entrepreneur, founded a business that operates in developing countries to retrieve human waste from latrines and septic

tanks and convert it into a renewable solid fuel that can generate energy.

Waterless, odorless composting toilets, developed in Sweden and used in apartment buildings, offices, and homes, convert nutrient-rich human fecal matter into soil-like humus that can be used as fertilizer. Composting toilet systems on a large scale eliminate the need for extensive underground pipes leading to a central treatment plant, and vastly reduce the amount of water and energy needed

Solutions

Water Pollution

- Prevent groundwater contamination
- Reduce nonpoint runoff
- Work with nature to treat sewage and reuse treated wastewater
- Find substitutes for toxic pollutants
- Practice the four Rs of resource use (refuse, reduce, reuse, recycle)
- Reduce air pollution
- Reduce poverty
- Slow population growth

FIGURE 17.21 Ways to prevent or reduce water pollution. ***Critical thinking:*** Which two of these solutions do you think are the most important? Why?

What Can You Do?

Reducing Water Pollution

- Fertilize garden and yard plants with manure or compost instead of commercial inorganic fertilizer
- Minimize use of pesticides, especially near bodies of water
- Prevent yard wastes from entering storm drains
- Do not use water fresheners in toilets
- Do not flush unwanted medicines down the toilet
- Do not pour pesticides, paints, solvents, oil, antifreeze, or other harmful chemicals down the drain or onto the ground

FIGURE 17.22 Individuals matter: You can help reduce water pollution. ***Critical thinking:*** Which three of these steps do you think are the most important ones to take? Why?

to move and treat waste. There are more than a dozen countries that use this method of waste treatment.

Preventing Water Pollution

It is encouraging that since 1970, most of the world's more-developed countries have enacted laws and regulations that have significantly reduced point-source water pollution. These improvements were largely the result of *bottom-up* political pressure on elected officials from individuals and groups. On the other hand, little has been done to reduce water pollution in most of the less-developed countries.

To many environmental and health scientists, the next step is to increase efforts to reduce and prevent water pollution in both more- and less-developed countries as an important way to increase our beneficial environmental impact. They would begin by asking the question: *How can we avoid producing water pollutants in the first place?* (**Concept 17.5**). Figure 17.21 lists ways to achieve this goal over the next several decades.

This shift to pollution prevention will not take place unless individuals put political pressure on elected officials and also take actions to reduce their own daily contributions to water pollution. Figure 17.22 lists some steps you can take to help reduce water pollution.

CHECKPOINT FOR UNDERSTANDING 17.5

1. Explain how agricultural techniques can reduce water pollution.
2. Identify materials that cannot be removed by secondary treatment in wastewater treatment plants.
3. Identify ways that sewage treatment could be improved.

KEY IDEAS

- There are a number of ways to purify drinking water, but the most effective and least costly strategy is pollution prevention.
- The key to protecting the oceans is to reduce the flow of pollution from land and air, and from streams emptying into ocean waters.
- Reducing water pollution requires that we prevent it, work with nature in treating sewage, and use natural resources far more efficiently.

Core Case Study Checkpoint

Explain the relationship between rainfall and the size of the dead zone (area of hypoxia) in the Gulf of Mexico.

cultural eutrophication: over nourishment of aquatic ecosystems with plant nutrients (mostly nitrates and phosphates) because of human activities such as agriculture, urbanization, and discharges from industrial plants and sewage treatment plants.

eutrophication: physical, biological, and chemical changes that take place after a lake, estuary, or slow-moving stream receives inputs of plant nutrients—mostly nitrates and phosphates—from natural erosion and runoff from the surrounding land basin.

nonpoint sources: broad and diffuse areas, rather than points, from which pollutants enter the bodies of surface water or air. Examples include runoff of chemicals and sediments from cropland, livestock feedlots, logged forests, urban streets, parking lots, lawns, and golf courses.

point sources: single identifiable source that discharges pollutants into the environment. Examples for water pollution include drainpipes, sewer lines, and sewage treatment plants.

primary sewage treatment: mechanical sewage treatment in which large solids are filtered out by screens and suspended solids settle out as sludge in a sedimentation tank.

secondary sewage treatment: second step in most waste-treatment systems in which aerobic bacteria decompose as much as 90% of degradable, oxygen-demanding organic wastes in wastewater. It usually involves bringing sewage and bacteria together in trickling filters or in the activated sludge process.

septic tank: a component of a small-scale underground sewage treatment system used for homes in rural and suburban areas that do not have connections to municipal sewer lines. Wastewater enters the tank from the home, solids sink to the bottom of the tank, and bacteria begin to decompose the waste before it discharges into a leaching field.

wastewater: water containing organic and inorganic wastes from homes, businesses, and industry. Examples include sewage, agricultural, and mining waste.

water pollution: any physical or chemical change in surface water or groundwater that can harm living organisms or make water unfit for certain uses.

Chapter Review

Core Case Study

1. Describe the nature and causes of the annual dead (oxygen-depleted) zone in the Gulf of Mexico.

Section 17.1

2. (a) What are the two key concepts for this section? (b) What is **water pollution**? Distinguish between **point sources** and **nonpoint sources** of water pollution and give two examples of each. (c) What is **wastewater**?

3. (a) List seven major types of water pollutants and three diseases that can be transmitted to humans through polluted water. (b) Describe some of the chemical and biological methods that scientists use to measure water quality.

Section 17.2

4. (a) What are the two key concepts for this section? (b) Explain how streams can cleanse themselves of oxygen-demanding wastes and how this cleansing process can be overwhelmed. (c) Describe the varying states of stream pollution in more- and less-developed countries. (d) Give two reasons why lakes and reservoirs cannot cleanse themselves of biodegradable wastes as readily as streams can. (e) Distinguish between **eutrophication** and **cultural eutrophication**. List three ways to prevent or reduce cultural eutrophication. (f) Explain how seasonal dead zones form in the Gulf of Mexico. (g) Describe the pollution of the Great Lakes and the efforts to reduce this pollution.

Section 17.3

5. (a) What are the two key concepts for this section? (b) Explain why groundwater cannot cleanse itself very well. (c) What are the major sources of groundwater contamination in the United States? List three harmful effects of groundwater pollution. Describe the threat from arsenic in groundwater. (d) List three ways to prevent groundwater contamination and three ways to clean up groundwater contamination. Explain why prevention is the most important approach.

6. (a) Explain how drinking water is purified in more-developed countries. (b) Explain how we can convert sewer water into drinking water. (c) List three ways to provide safe drinking water in poor countries. (d) Describe the environmental problems caused by the widespread use of bottled water. (e) Summarize the US laws for protecting drinking water quality. (f) List three ways to strengthen the US Safe Drinking Water Act.

Section 17.4

7. (a) What are the two key concepts for this section? (b) Why should we care about the oceans? How are coastal waters and deeper ocean waters most often polluted? (c) What causes algal blooms and what are their harmful effects? (d) Describe an ocean garbage patch and explain how it can harm marine life and humans. (e) How serious is oil pollution of the oceans? What are its effects and what can be done to reduce such pollution? (f) Describe the 2010 BP *Deepwater Horizon* oil well blowout and its causes and effects. How might such accidents be prevented in the future?

Section 17.5

8. (a) What is the key concept for this section? (b) List four ways to reduce and prevent pollution of coastal waters. (c) List six ways to reduce surface water pollution from nonpoint sources. (d) List seven federal laws aimed at reducing water pollution in the United States.

Describe US successes and failures with using these laws to reduce point-source water pollution. (e) List seven ways to strengthen the Clean Water Act and describe opposition to such proposals. (f) What is a **septic tank** and how does it work? (g) Define **primary sewage treatment** and **secondary sewage treatment** and explain how they are used to treat wastewater.

9. (a) What are three ways to improve conventional sewage treatment? (b) Describe two ways to treat sewage based on learning from nature. (c) What is a waterless composting toilet system? (d) Describe John Todd's use of living machines to treat sewage. (e) Explain how we can use wetlands to treat sewage.

10. (a) List six ways to prevent or reduce water pollution. (b) List five things you can do to help reduce water pollution. (c) What are this chapter's *three key ideas*?

Note: Key terms are in bold type.

AP® Review Questions

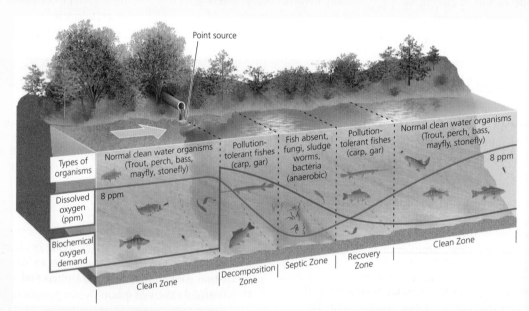

Questions 1 and 2 refer to the oxygen sag curve figure above.

1. In a typical river, the oxygen sag curve is likely to be most severe during
   (A) the winter
   (B) the fall
   (C) the spring
   (D) the summer
   (E) the oxygen sag is not temperature-dependent

2. Which of the following is NOT a method to help eliminate the incidence of "dead zones" (low-oxygen areas) in coastal waters?
   (A) Reduce the input of fertilizer into watershed by planting buffer zones
   (B) Mandate the use of low-phosphate detergents in the drainage basin
   (C) Discharge large volumes of hot water directly into coastal waters
   (D) Reduce the discharge of biodegradable wastes from feedlots
   (E) Require sewage treatment plants to better handle overflow so that there is no discharge, even during heavy use or heavy rains

3. Which of the following **incorrectly** pairs a river area with a point source pollution condition?
   (A) Clean zone–high levels of dissolved oxygen
   (B) Point of input–rapid increase of biological oxygen demand
   (C) Decomposition zone–only pollution tolerant fishes found
   (D) Septic zone–most fish absent, low levels of dissolved oxygen
   (E) Recovery zone–normal levels of dissolved oxygen

4. Which of the following water pollutants is **incorrectly** paired with its source?
   (A) Oxygen demanding wastes–sewage
   (B) Organic chemicals–industry and farms
   (C) Sediments–unlined landfills
   (D) Heavy metals–mining refuse
   (E) Thermal–electric power plants

5. Which of the following is an example of a point source pollutant?
   (A) Ballast water discharge from a ship offshore
   (B) Runoff from parking lots
   (C) Organic waste from cow feed lots
   (D) Sediments from land erosion
   (E) Nutrients from golf courses and lawns

6. How is cholera primarily transmitted?
   (A) Inhaling bacteria expelled into the air by someone coughing
   (B) Being bitten by an infected mosquito
   (C) Ingesting water contaminated by human waste material from a person who already has the disease
   (D) Coming in contact with skin pustules present on a person who already has the disease
   (E) Ingesting water contaminated by leaking underground gasoline tanks

7. Which of the following best describes eutrophication?
   (A) The downward motion of water through soil, dissolving minerals along the way
   (B) The increase of a chemical such as DDT in the bodies of animals at higher trophic levels
   (C) A process of nature that helps support life, such as rivers purifying the water
   (D) The natural aging process of a shallow lake or slow-moving stream as nutrients enrich the water
   (E) The collection of sediment behind a dam caused by the slowing of the river water

Questions 8–9 refer to the diagram of the Mississippi River drainage basin below.

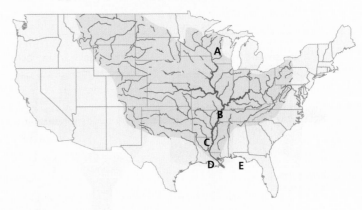

8. Which letter best shows the location of the depleted oxygen zone caused by the Mississippi River?

9. The annual dead zone from the Mississippi River is caused primarily by
   (A) sediment runoff from construction sites
   (B) wakes from boats traveling up and down the Mississippi River
   (C) lack of current flow in the main stem of the river
   (D) nitrate runoff from agricultural fields and sewage treatment plants
   (E) freshwater of the river dissolving in the Gulf of Mexico and organic chemicals precipitating out

10. Which law sets standards for key water pollutants and requires polluters to get permits limiting what they can discharge into aquatic systems?
    (A) National Environmental Policy Act (NEPA) 1969
    (B) Water Pollution Control Act of 1972
    (C) Clean Water Act 1977
    (D) Coastal Zone Management Act 1980
    (E) Water Quality Act 1987

Questions 11–13 refer to the steps of wastewater treatment below. Choices may be used once, more than once, or not at all.

   (A) Primary treatment
   (B) Secondary treatment
   (C) Disinfection
   (D) Advanced treatment
   (E) Discharge

11. Water flows slowly through grit chambers, allowing sand and small particles to settle out.

12. Biological processes are used to remove oxygen-demanding organic wastes before chlorine is added to kill bacteria.

13. Because this step removes nitrates and phosphates with special filters, there is less nutrient overload where the water is discharged.

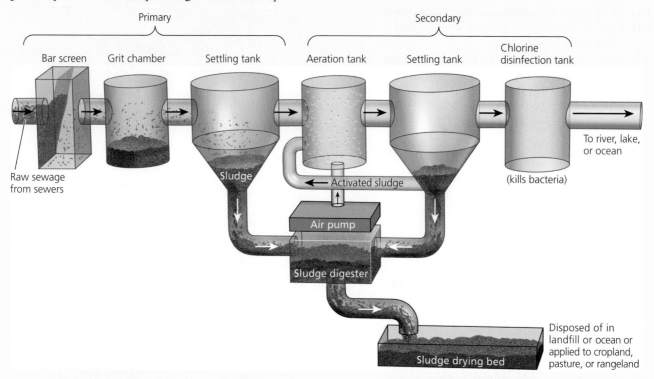

14. Primary sewage treatment is used to remove which of the following from the water?
    (A) Biodegradable solids
    (B) Both biodegradable and non-biodegradable solids
    (C) Disease-causing bacteria
    (D) Inorganic chemicals
    (E) Pesticides

15. All of the following are true of secondary sewage treatment EXCEPT
    (A) it is mostly a biological treatment
    (B) it removes most of the biodegradable pollutants in water
    (C) it is the stage where pathogenic bacteria are killed
    (D) it removes some of the phosphorous, nitrogen and toxic heavy metals
    (E) it requires oxygen

16. All of the following are true of what happens to the by-products of a sewage treatment system EXCEPT
    (A) sludge can be used on cropland
    (B) treated water is discharged into a local water body
    (C) once chlorinated, water can be piped directly back into the drinking water supply
    (D) water can be run through trickling filters for further aerobic decomposition
    (E) sludge can be digested to produce methane

17. As a water pollutant, excessive heat is more likely to come from what source?
    (A) Decay of biodegradable wastes
    (B) Industrial and power plants
    (C) Global warming
    (D) Increased use of fossil fuels
    (E) Sediments in the water column

18. Which of these is a potential route of groundwater contamination?
    I. Leaking storage tanks
    II. Seepage of contaminants from the surface
    III. Underground injection wells
    (A) I only
    (B) I and II only
    (C) I and III only
    (D) II and III only
    (E) I, II, and III

19. When groundwater becomes contaminated, it tends to remain contaminated because
    (A) it moves too quickly to allow for effective cleanup
    (B) the temperature of the groundwater is very hot
    (C) there is less bacteria in groundwater to perform natural decomposition
    (D) the dissolved oxygen level is too high to facilitate bacterial growth
    (E) we do not have the technology to pump it to the surface

20. Which of the following may describe a water body with low oxygen levels?

(A) Toxic
(B) Hypoxic
(C) Contaminated
(D) Septic
(E) Turbid

AP® Free-Response Practice

1. The Great Lakes make up the largest freshwater system in the world. This interconnected system comprises 95 percent of the surface water in the United States and 21 percent of the world's surface water. The diagram below shows a profile of the connected lakes, their relative size, elevation, and depth, and the sequence of flow beginning with Lake Superior and eventually ending at the Atlantic Ocean.

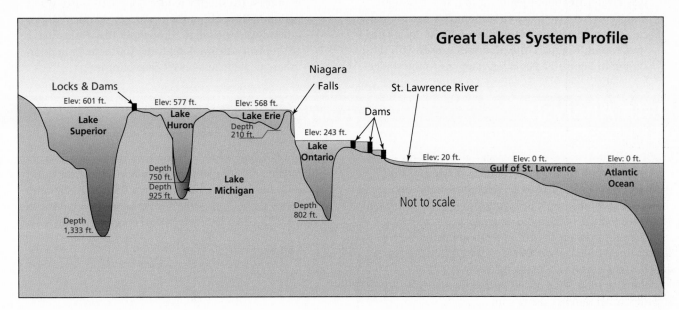

(a) The Great Lakes are vitally important to both the United States and Canada.

  (i) **Identify** TWO economic and/or ecosystem services provided by Lake Erie.

  (ii) **Identify** and **discuss** TWO reasons why Lake Erie is the most polluted of the lakes.

(b) Pollution in the Great Lakes is a serious threat to both humans and natural ecosystems.

  (i) **Identify** ONE anthropogenic point source of pollution that can contaminate Lake Erie.

  (ii) **Identify** ONE anthropogenic non-point source of pollution that can contaminate Lake Erie.

(c) An influx of nutrients into lake waters can cause cultural, or anthropogenic, eutrophication.

  (i) **Discuss** the sequence of events that leads to fish kills in a body of water subject to cultural eutrophication.

  (ii) **Identify** TWO means of preventing cultural eutrophication in the Great Lakes System.

(d) **Identify** ONE U.S. law that pertains to water pollution.

Critical Thinking

1. How might you be contributing, directly or indirectly, to the annual dead zone that forms in the Gulf of Mexico (**Core Case Study**)? What are three things you could do to reduce your impact?

2. Suppose a large number of dead fish are found floating in a lake. How would you determine whether they died from cultural eutrophication or from exposure to toxic chemicals?

3. Assume that you are a regulator charged with drawing up plans for controlling water pollution, and briefly describe your strategy for controlling water pollution from each of the following sources: **(a)** a pipe from a factory discharging effluent into a stream, **(b)** a parking lot at a shopping mall bordered by a stream, and **(c)** a farmer's field on a slope next to a stream.

4. How might you be contributing, directly or indirectly, to groundwater pollution? What are three things you could do to reduce your impact?

5. When you flush your toilet, where does the wastewater go? Trace the actual flow of this water in your community from your toilet through sewers to a wastewater treatment plant (or to a septic system) and from there to the environment. Try to visit a local sewage treatment plant to see what it does with wastewater. Compare the processes it uses with those shown in Figure 17.20. What happens to the sludge

produced by this plant? What improvements, if any, would you suggest for this plant?

6. In your community, **(a)** what is the source of drinking water? **(b)** How is drinking water treated? **(c)** What problems related to drinking water, if any, have arisen in your community? **(d)** What actions, if any, has your local government taken to solve them?

7. List three ways in which you could apply **Concept 17.5** to make your lifestyle more environmentally sustainable.

8. Congratulations! You are in charge of the world. What are three actions you would take to **(a)** sharply reduce point-source water pollution in more-developed countries, **(b)** sharply reduce nonpoint-source water pollution throughout the world, **(c)** sharply reduce groundwater pollution throughout the world, and **(d)** provide safe drinking water for the poor and for other people in less-developed countries?

Data Analysis

In 2006, scientists assessed the overall condition of the estuaries on the western coasts of the US states of Oregon and Washington. To do so, they took measurements of various characteristics of the water, including dissolved oxygen (DO), in selected locations within the estuaries. The concentration of DO for each site was measured in terms of milligrams (mg) of oxygen per liter (L) of water sampled. The scientists used the following DO concentration ranges and quality categories to rate their water samples: water with greater than 5 mg/L of DO was considered *good* for supporting aquatic life; water with 2 to 5 mg/L of DO was rated as *fair*; and water with less than 2 mg/L of DO was rated as *poor*.

The following graph shows measurements taken in bottom water at 242 locations. Each triangular mark represents one or more measurements. The x-axis on this graph represents DO concentrations in mg/L. The y-axis represents percentages of the total area of estuaries studied (estuarine area).

To read this graph, pick one of the triangles and observe the values on the x- and y-axes. For example, note that the circled triangle lines

up approximately with the 5-mg/L mark on the x-axis and with a value of about 34% on the y-axis. This means that waters at this particular measurement station (or stations), along with about 34% of the total area being studied, are estimated to have a 5% or lower DO concentration.

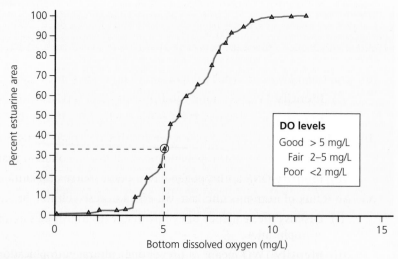

Concentrations of dissolved oxygen in bottom waters of estuaries in Washington and Oregon.

Use this information, along with the graph, to answer the following questions:

1. Half of the estuarine area has waters falling below a certain DO concentration level, and the other half has levels above that level. What is that level, in mg/L?

2. Give your estimate of the highest DO concentration measured and your estimate of the lowest concentration.

3. Approximately what percentage of the estuarine area studied is considered to have poor DO levels? About what percentage has fair DO levels, and about what percentage has good DO levels?

Answers to Checkpoints for Understanding

Section 17.1

1. Point-source pollution is discharged at specific locations such as an effluent pipe while nonpoint sources are broad and diffuse areas such as an agricultural field, or lawns-after a rain storm.

2. Common types of water pollutants include heavy metals such as mercury, pathogens such as *E. coli* or *giardia*, excess plant nutrients such as nitrates and phosphates, oxygen-demanding wastes that lower the amount of dissolved oxygen in water, organic and inorganic chemicals that are toxic, and thermal pollution that raises the water temperature.

Section 17.2

1. Ponds and lakes are stratified, which does not allow for mixing and dilution of pollutants. Also, they have little flow or no flow at all, so pollutants are not dispersed or flushed from the water body.

2. The Great Lakes are slow to cleanse themselves of pollution because less than 1% of the water flows to the St. Lawrence Seaway each year. It can take up to 19 years for turnover in the largest of the lakes.

3. In spring and summer, nutrient-rich freshwater flows into the Gulf of Mexico and lies on top of the denser salt water. This difference in density, plus the lack of storms, keep the layers stratified. Because of the input of nitrates and phosphates, algae blooms form on the surface. The algae die, sink deeper into the saltwater, and aerobic bacteria consume them, robbing the water of dissolved oxygen.

Section 17.3

1. Hydraulic fracking can contaminate groundwater when the leaky gas pipes emit natural gas into the aquifer through which they are passing, or when contaminated wastewater from the fracking process is pumped to the surface and sometimes spilled.

2. Remediation refers to the clean-up of contamination. Aquifers are difficult and costly to decontaminate because groundwater moves very slowly, it is very cold and inhibits bacterial action that decomposes waste, and there is little oxygen underground that bacteria require for decomposition.

3. Bottled water is less regulated than tap water and can have impurities and toxic materials in it; billions of plastic water bottles must be produced using oil for plastic and energy for production; only 38% of bottles are recycled, the rest are discarded as waste, many ending up in the oceans and rivers. If bottles are incinerated, toxins are released to the atmosphere. Huge amounts of energy are needed to transport bottled water and when left on hot trucks during delivery, some plastic bottles leach BPA (an endocrine disruptor) into the water.

4. The Safe Drinking Water Act requires the EPA to set national drinking water standards called **maximum containment levels** for any pollutants that could have adverse effects on human health.

Section 17.4

1. An oceanic dead zone is an area where nitrates and phosphates have entered the water causing severe oxygen depletion, or hypoxia, due to eutrophication. Toxic algal blooms in these regions poison seafood, damage fisheries, kill fish-eating birds, and reduce tourism.

2. The North Pacific Garbage Patch is two slowly swirling regions of plastic trash that has accumulated due to gyres (rotating ocean currents). Nondegradable plastic waste makes its way to the ocean and is swept out to sea, accumulating in this region of the ocean. It is broken down into small particles that float just beneath the surface and can be ingested my marine birds, fishes, and other animals that mistake them for food.

3. The largest source of oil pollution comes from land—leaks from pipelines, refineries, and from homeowners and industries that dump waste oil into sewers.

4. The governmental response to the Deepwater Horizon accident was to establish a presidential commission to oversee stricter regulations and standards for each step of the drilling process with a higher priority to environmental concerns. Congress was enlisted to put new standards in place and monitor the new regulations, but this has yet to be done.

5. The most effective way to prevent ocean pollution is to reduce the flow of pollution from land.

Section 17.5

1. Reducing the input of soil from erosion, fertilizer, and pesticides can reduce water pollution. This can be accomplished by keeping crop land covered with vegetation, planting buffers between cropland and waterways, reducing the use of fertilizers and other chemicals, and by not using fertilizers on steep slopes.

2. Wastewater-treatment plants cannot remove pharmaceuticals, pesticides, disease-causing viruses and bacteria, or excessive amounts of nitrates or phosphates.

3. Conventional wastewater treatment could be improved by preventing toxic chemicals and heavy metals from reaching treatment plants where they become part of the wastewater sludge. Viewing nutrients in human waste as a valuable commodity that can be used as fertilizer or to generate energy rather than as a material to be disposed of creates an incentive to treat waste differently. Composting toilets in homes, businesses, and on a large scale reduces the energy and water needed to treat human waste.

Core Case Study

The greater the rainfall, the more surface runoff carrying nitrogen into the Gulf of Mexico, and the larger area that suffers from hypoxia. An influx of nitrogen from agricultural land causes cultural eutrophication, resulting in depleted oxygen content and widespread death of organisms from spring until fall in the Gulf.

Solid and Hazardous Waste

Follow nature's example; realize waste's potential.

GUNTER PAULI

Key Questions

18.1 What environmental problems are related to solid and hazardous wastes?

18.2 How should we deal with solid waste?

18.3 Why are refusing, reducing, reusing, and recycling so important?

18.4 What are the advantages and disadvantages of burning or burying solid waste?

18.5 How should we deal with hazardous waste?

18.6 How can society shift to a low-waste economy?

Workers in Texas are stripping picture tubes from thousands of computer monitors for recycling and reuse.

Peter Essick/National Geographic Creative

Cradle-to-Cradle Design

The *life cycle* of a product begins when it is manufactured (its cradle) and ends when it is discarded as solid waste, typically in a landfill or as litter (its grave).

Designer William McDonough wants us to abandon this *cradle-to-grave* view of the life cycle of products. He argues for a *cradle-to-cradle* approach, in which we think of products as part of a continuing cycle instead of becoming solid wastes that end up as litter or being burned or deposited in landfills. This approach, first explored in the 1970s by business analyst Walter Stahel, is the basis for much of McDonough's work. His vision is to build an economy where all products or their parts will be reused over and over in other products. Parts that are no longer useful would be degradable so that natural nutrient cycles could absorb their molecules. The degradable parts would be thought of as *biological nutrients* (Figure 18.1, left) and those parts that are reused would be *technical nutrients* (Figure 18.1, right).

In their books, *Cradle to Cradle* and *The Upcycle*, McDonough and chemist Michael Braungart lay out this vision as a way not just to lessen our harmful environmental impact but also to have a beneficial environmental impact. They call for us to think of solid wastes and pollution as potentially useful and economically valuable materials

and chemicals. Instead of asking, "How do I get rid of these wastes?" they say we need to ask, "How much money can I get for these resources?" and "How can I design products that don't end up as wastes or pollutants?"

This way of thinking means designing products so they can be recycled or reused, much like nutrients in the biosphere. With this approach, people might think of trash-cans and garbage trucks as resource containers and landfills as urban mines filled with stuff we should have recycled, like the earth does. They might not think of garbage as something to "throw away" but something to "pass on" for other purposes.

Cradle-to-cradle design is a form of biomimicry (Chapter 1, Individuals Matter 1.1, p. 10) because it implements the earth's chemical cycling **principle of sustainability** (see Inside Back Cover). For example, a chair manufacturer applying this approach designs and builds its chairs such that when one part breaks, most of the other parts can be reused in the manufacture of a new chair. As much as possible, only biodegradable materials are used so that worn-out, discarded parts will break down in the environment and become part of nature's nutrient cycles. As McDonough likes to say, in nature, waste equals food.

There are many ways to apply this approach. One important way is to *design toxic substances out* of products and processes. If a product requires the use of a toxic heavy metal, for example, it should be redesigned to make use of a nontoxic substitute for that ingredient. Another strategy is to *sell services instead of products*. For example, think of carpeting not as a product to be used and discarded, but as a floor covering service. The carpet company owns the carpeting and leases it to the user. The company then replaces worn carpet tiles on a regular basis as part of the service and recycles the materials in the worn pieces to make new carpet tiles.

In this chapter, we consider the problems of solid and hazardous wastes resulting from human activities. We also consider ways to make the transition to a more sustainable low-waste economy by preventing and reducing the production of such wastes as a way to apply the cradle-to-cradle approach. ●

CRITICAL THINKING

When considering a cradle-to-cradle approach to the life-cycle of products, what types of materials would be considered biological nutrients? What types of materials would be considered technical nutrients?

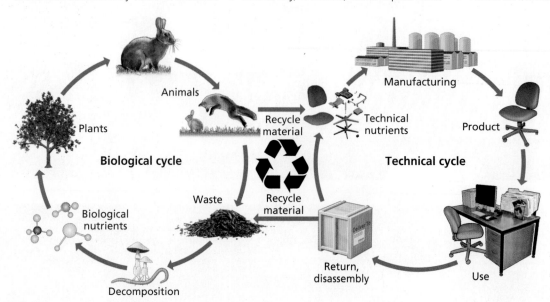

FIGURE 18.1 Cradle-to-cradle design and manufacturing aims to make all products reusable and all components that must be discarded biodegradable. By connecting technical and biological nutrient cycles, it mimics nature and essentially eliminates waste by converting it to nutrients.

WHAT ENVIRONMENTAL PROBLEMS ARE RELATED TO SOLID AND HAZARDOUS WASTES?

CONCEPT 18.1A Solid waste contributes to pollution and includes valuable resources that could be reused or recycled.

CONCEPT 18.1B Hazardous waste contributes to pollution, as well as to natural capital degradation, health problems, and premature deaths.

Solid Waste Is Piling Up

Think about what you've tossed in the trash today. Perhaps it was leftovers from lunch, an empty can or bottle, or something you no longer needed. People throw away all sorts of items, and they all add up to huge amounts of solid waste.

In the natural world, wherever humans are not dominant, there is essentially no waste. The wastes of one organism become nutrients or raw materials for others (see Figures 3.15, p. 78, and 3.16, p. 79). This natural cycling of nutrients is the basis for the chemical cycling **principles of sustainability** (see Inside Back Cover).

Humans violate this principle by producing huge amounts of waste materials that are burned or end up in landfills or as litter (Figure 18.2) and pollute the environment. For example, the manufacturing of a desktop computer requires 700 or more different materials obtained from mines, oil wells, and chemical factories all over the world. For every 0.5 kilogram (1 pound) of electronics it contains, approximately 3,600 kilograms (8,000 pounds) of waste were created—an amount roughly equal to the weight of a large pickup truck.

Because of the law of conservation of matter (see Chapter 2, p. 46) and the nature of human lifestyles, we will always produce some waste. However, studies and experience indicate that by mimicking nature, through strategies such as cradle-to-cradle design (**Core Case Study**), we could reduce this waste of potential resources and the resulting environmental harm by up to 80%.

The solid items thrown away in a household fall into the category of **solid waste**—any unwanted or discarded material people produce that is not a liquid or a gas. There are two major types of solid waste. The first is **industrial solid waste** produced by mines (see Figure 11.13, p. 316), farms, and industries that supply people with goods and services. It also includes construction and demolition waste. The second is **municipal solid waste (MSW),** often called *garbage* or *trash*. It consists of the combined solid wastes produced by homes and workplaces other than factories. Examples of MSW include paper, cardboard, food wastes, cans, bottles, yard wastes, furniture, plastics, glass, wood, and electronics or *e-waste.*

Rechitan Sorin/Shutterstock.com

FIGURE 18.2 *Municipal solid waste:* Various types of solid waste have been dumped in this isolated mountain area of the United States.

Much of the world's MSW ends up as litter in rivers, lakes, the ocean, and natural landscapes (Figure 18.2). One of the major symbols of such waste is the single-use plastic bag. Laid end-to-end, the 100 billion plastic bags used in the United States each year would reach to the moon and back 60 times. These bags can take 400 to 1,000 years to break down, but never disintegrate completely.

In the environment, plastic bags often block drains and sewage systems and can kill wildlife and livestock that try to eat them or become ensnared in them. In Kenya, Africa, outbreaks of malaria have been associated with plastic bags lying on the ground collecting water in which malaria-carrying mosquitoes can breed.

Discarded plastic items are a threat to many terrestrial animal species, as well as millions of seabirds, marine mammals, and sea turtles, which can mistake a floating plastic sandwich bag for a jellyfish or get caught in plastic

Stockbyte/Thinkstock

FIGURE 18.3 This child is searching for useful items in this open trash dump in Manila, Philippines.

fishing nets. About 80% of the plastics in the ocean are blown or washed in from beaches, rivers, storm drains, and other sources, and the rest are dumped into the ocean from ocean-going garbage barges, ships, and fishing boats.

In more-developed countries, most MSW is collected and buried in landfills or burned in incinerators. In many less-developed countries, much of it ends up in open dumps, where poor people eke out a living finding items they can use or sell (Figure 18.3). In China, only about 40% of the MSW is collected, and in rural areas the figure can be as low as 4–5%. The United States is the world's largest producer of solid waste (see the Case Study that follows).

CASE STUDY

Solid Waste in the United States

The United States leads the world in total production of industrial and municipal solid waste, as well as solid waste per person. With only 4.3% of the world's people, the United States produces about

25% of the world's solid waste. According to the Environmental Protection Agency (EPA), 98.5% of all solid waste produced in the United States is industrial waste from mining (76%), agriculture (13%), and industry (9.5%). The remaining 1.5% is municipal solid waste. Every year, Americans generate enough MSW to fill a bumper-to-bumper convoy of garbage trucks long enough to circle the earth's equator almost six times. Most of this waste is dumped in landfills, recycled or composted, or incinerated (Figure 18.4, right). However, a great deal of it ends up as litter (Figure 18.2).

Consider some of the solid wastes that consumers throw away each year, on average, in the high-waste economy of the United States:

- Enough tires to encircle the earth's equator almost three times.

- An amount of disposable diapers that, if linked end to end, would reach to the moon and back seven times.

- Enough carpet to cover the state of Delaware.

- Enough nonreturnable plastic bottles to form a stack that would reach from the earth to the moon and back about six times.

- About 100 billion plastic shopping bags, or 274 million per day, an average of nearly 3,200 every second.

- Enough office paper to build a wall 3.5 meters (11 feet) high across the country from New York City to San Francisco, California.

- 25 billion plastic foam (Styrofoam) coffee cups—enough, if lined up end to end, to circle the earth's equator 436 times.

- $165 billion worth of food.

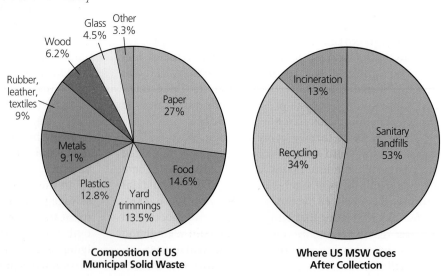

Composition of US Municipal Solid Waste

Paper 27%
Food 14.6%
Yard trimmings 13.5%
Plastics 12.8%
Metals 9.1%
Rubber, leather, textiles 9%
Wood 6.2%
Glass 4.5%
Other 3.3%

Where US MSW Goes After Collection

Incineration 13%
Sanitary landfills 53%
Recycling 34%

FIGURE 18.4 Composition of MSW in the United States and data on where it goes after collection. **Data analysis:** How many times more than the amount recycled is the amount of materials put into landfills?

(Compiled by the authors using data from US Environmental Protection Agency)

Garbology and Tracking Trash

How do we know about the composition of trash in landfills? Much of that information comes from research by *garbologists* such as William Rathje, an anthropologist who pioneered the field of garbology in the 1970s at the University of Arizona. These scientists work like archaeologists, training their students to sort, weigh, and itemize people's trash, and to bore holes to remove cores of materials from garbage dumps and analyze what they find.

Many people think of landfills as huge compost piles where biodegradable wastes are decomposed within a few months. In fact, decomposition inside modern landfills is a slow process. Trash buried inside sanitary landfills can resist decomposition perhaps for centuries because it is tightly packed and protected from sunlight, water, and air, and from the bacteria that could digest and decompose most of these wastes. In fact, researchers have unearthed 50-year-old newspapers that were still readable and hot dogs and pork chops that had not yet decayed.

A team of researchers, led by Carlo Riatti, at the Massachusetts Institute of Technology (MIT) conducted a project called "Trash Track." The project's goals were to find out where urban trash goes and to help New York City increase its recycling rate from the current 30% to 100% by 2030.

The researchers attached wireless transmitters about the size of a matchbook to several thousand different items of trash produced by volunteer participants in New York City, Seattle, Washington, and London, England. Every few hours, these devices use GPS technology to send their locations via a cell phone network to a computer at MIT, which plots their movements. This system tracks the trash items on their trips to recycling plants, landfills, or incinerators, and this helps researchers determine how and where trash goes.

CRITICAL THINKING

How might such a system help us to learn about the environmental costs of waste management such as the amount of pollution generated in the hauling and processing of waste? Explain.

Most of these wastes break down very slowly, if at all. Lead, mercury, glass, Styrofoam, and most plastic bottles do not break down completely. An aluminum can takes 500 years to disintegrate. Disposable diapers may take 550 years to break down, and a plastic shopping bag may stick around for up to 1,000 years.

3,200 Number of new plastic bags used every second, on average, in the United States

Some resource experts suggest we change the name of the trash we produce from MSW to MWR—*mostly wasted resources*. That's because so much of what is considered "waste" can be useful as a resource (Science Focus 18.1).

Hazardous Waste Is a Serious and Growing Problem

Another major category of waste is **hazardous,** or **toxic, waste**—any discarded material or substance that threatens human health or the environment because it is toxic, is corrosive, is flammable, can undergo violent or explosive chemical reactions, or can cause disease. Examples include industrial solvents, hospital medical waste, car batteries (containing acids and toxic lead), household pesticide products, dry-cell batteries (containing mercury and cadmium), and ash and sludge from incinerators and coal-burning power and industrial plants. Improper handling of these wastes can lead to pollution of air and water, degradation of ecosystems, and health threats (**Concept 18.1B**). The fastest-growing category of waste, which contains a large amount of hazardous waste, is electronic, or *e-waste* (see the Case Study that follows).

The two main classes of hazardous wastes are *organic compounds* such as various solvents, pesticides, PCBs, and dioxins and *toxic heavy metals* such as lead, mercury, and arsenic. Figure 18.5 lists some of the harmful chemicals found in many homes.

Another form of extremely hazardous waste is the highly radioactive waste produced by nuclear power plants and nuclear weapons facilities. Such wastes must be stored safely for 10,000 to 240,000 years, depending on the radioactive isotopes they contain. After 60 years of research, scientists and governments have not found a scientifically and politically acceptable way to safely isolate these dangerous wastes for such long periods of time.

According to the U.N. Environment Programme (UNEP), more-developed countries produce 80–90% of the world's hazardous wastes, and the United States is the largest producer. However, China is closing the gap on the number one spot as it continues to industrialize rapidly without adequate pollution controls.

What Harmful Chemicals Are in Your Home?

Cleaning
Disinfectants
Drain, toilet, and window cleaners
Spot removers
Septic tank cleaners

Paint Products
Paints, stains, varnishes, and lacquers
Paint thinners, solvents, and strippers
Wood preservatives
Artist paints and inks

General
Dry-cell batteries (mercury and cadmium)
Glues and cements

Gardening
Pesticides
Weed killers
Ant and rodent killers
Flea powders

Automotive
Gasoline
Used motor oil
Antifreeze
Battery acid
Brake and transmission fluid

FIGURE 18.5 Harmful chemicals are found in many homes. The US Congress has exempted the disposal of many of these household chemicals and other items from government regulation. **Question:** Which of these chemicals could you find in your home?

Top: tuulijumala/Shutterstock.com. Center: Katrina Outland/Shutterstock.com. Bottom: Agencyby/Dreamstime.com

---

CASE STUDY

E-Waste—An Exploding Hazardous Waste Problem

What happens to your cell phone, computer, television set, and other electronic devices when they are no longer useful (see chapter-opening photo)? They become *electronic waste*, or *e-waste*—the fastest-growing solid waste problem in the United States and the world. The two leading producers of e-waste are the United States and China.

Between 2000 and 2014, the recycling of US e-waste increased from 10% to 29%. Much of the remaining e-waste went to landfills and incinerators. Much e-waste contains gold, rare earth metals, and other valuable materials that could be recycled or reused.

Much of the e-waste in the United States that is not buried or incinerated is shipped to China, India, and other Asian and African countries for processing. Labor is cheap and environmental regulations are weak in those countries. Workers there—many of them children—dismantle,

burn, and treat e-waste with acids to recover valuable metals and reusable parts. The work exposes them to toxic metals such as lead and mercury and other harmful chemicals. The remaining scrap is dumped into waterways and fields or burned in open fires that expose people to highly toxic chemicals.

Transfer of such hazardous waste from more-developed to less-developed countries is banned under the International Basel Convention. Despite this ban, much of the world's e-waste is not officially classified as hazardous waste, or it is illegally smuggled out of some countries. The United States can export its e-waste legally because it has not ratified the Basel Convention.

CHECKPOINT FOR UNDERSTANDING 18.1

1. Explain why trash that is deposited in a sanitary landfill will not biodegrade or will take centuries to break down.

2. Identify the two main classes of hazardous wastes.

3. Define e-waste.

18.2 HOW SHOULD WE DEAL WITH SOLID WASTE?

CONCEPT 18.2 A sustainable approach to solid waste is first to produce less of it, then to reuse or recycle it, and finally to safely dispose of what is left.

Waste Management

Society can deal with the solid wastes it creates in two ways. One is **waste management,** which focuses on controlling wastes in order to limit their environmental harm but does not attempt to seriously reduce how much waste is produced. This approach begins with the question, "What do we do with solid waste?" It typically involves mixing wastes together and then burying them, burning them, or shipping them to another location.

The other approach is **waste reduction**—producing much less solid waste and reusing, recycling, or composting what is produced (**Concept 18.2** and **Core Case Study**). This waste prevention approach begins with questions such as "How can we avoid producing so much solid waste?" and "How can we use the waste we produce as resources like nature does?

Most waste experts prefer using **integrated waste management**—a variety of coordinated strategies for both waste management and waste reduction (Figure 18.6). Figure 18.7 compares the science-based waste management goals of the EPA and National Academy of Sciences with waste management trends based on actual data.

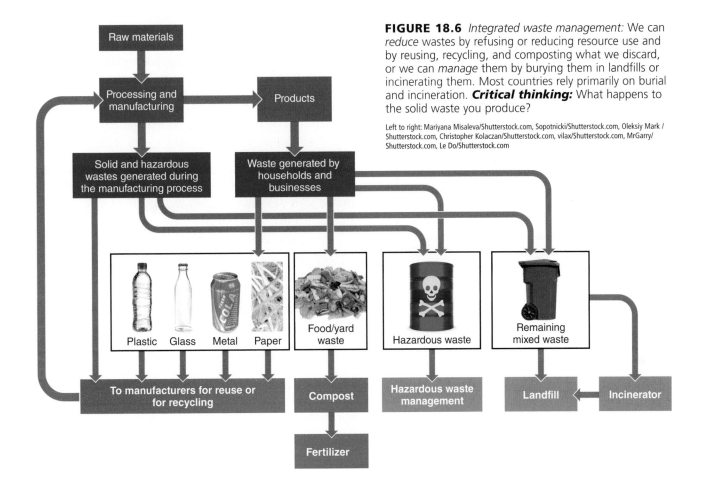

FIGURE 18.6 *Integrated waste management:* We can *reduce* wastes by refusing or reducing resource use and by reusing, recycling, and composting what we discard, or we can *manage* them by burying them in landfills or incinerating them. Most countries rely primarily on burial and incineration. **Critical thinking:** What happens to the solid waste you produce?

Left to right: Mariyana Misaleva/Shutterstock.com, Sopotnicki/Shutterstock.com, Oleksiy Mark / Shutterstock.com, Christopher Kolaczan/Shutterstock.com, vilax/Shutterstock.com, MrGarry/ Shutterstock.com, Le Do/Shutterstock.com

The Four Rs of Waste Reduction

A more sustainable approach to dealing with solid waste is to first reduce it, then reuse or recycle it, and finally safely dispose of what is left. This waste reduction approach (**Concept 18.2**) is based on "four Rs," listed here in order of priority suggested by scientists:

- **Refuse:** Don't use it.
- **Reduce:** Use less of it.
- **Reuse:** Use it over and over.
- **Recycle:** Convert used resources to useful items and buy products made from recycled materials. An

important form of recycling is **composting,** which mimics nature by using bacteria and other decomposers to break down yard trimmings, vegetable food scraps, and other biodegradable organic wastes into materials than can be used to improve soil fertility.

The first three Rs are preferred because they are *waste prevention* approaches that tackle the problem of waste production before it occurs. Recycling is important but it deals with wastes after they have been produced. Some scientists and economists estimate that we could eliminate up to 80% of the solid waste we produce by following the

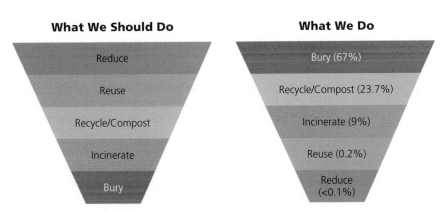

What We Should Do

- Reduce
- Reuse
- Recycle/Compost
- Incinerate
- Bury

What We Do

- Bury (67%)
- Recycle/Compost (23.7%)
- Incinerate (9%)
- Reuse (0.2%)
- Reduce (<0.1%)

FIGURE 18.7 Priorities recommended by the US National Academy of Sciences for dealing with municipal solid waste (left) compared with actual waste-handling practices in the United States based on data (right). **Critical thinking:** Why do you think most countries do not follow most of the scientific-based priorities listed on the left?

(Compiled by the authors using data from US Environmental Protection Agency, US National Academy of Sciences, Columbia University, and *BioCycle*.)

four Rs strategy, which mimics the earth's nutrient cycling **principle of sustainability**. Figure 18.8 lists some ways in which you can use the four Rs of waste reduction to reduce your output of solid waste.

Here are six strategies that industries and communities have used to reduce resource use, waste, and pollution. Note that the first five are applications of the cradle-to-cradle approach to design, manufacturing, and marketing (**Core Case Study**).

First, *change industrial processes to eliminate or reduce the use of harmful chemicals*. Since 1975, the 3M Company has taken this approach and, in the process, saved $1.9 billion.

Second, *redesign manufacturing processes and products to use less material and energy*. For example, the weight of a typical car has been reduced by about one-fourth since the 1960s by using lighter steel, aluminum, magnesium, plastics, and composite materials.

Third, *develop products that are easy to repair, reuse, remanufacture, compost, or recycle*. For example, Xerox photocopiers that are leased by businesses are made of reusable or recyclable parts that allow for easy remanufacturing and are projected to save the company $1 billion in manufacturing costs.

Fourth, *establish cradle-to-cradle responsibility laws* that require companies to take back various consumer products such as electronic equipment, appliances, and motor vehicles, as Japan and many European countries do, for recycling or remanufacturing.

What Can You Do?

Solid Waste

- Follow the four Rs of resource use: Refuse, Reduce, Reuse, Recycle
- Ask yourself whether you really need what you're buying and refuse packaging wherever possible
- Rent, borrow, or barter goods and services when you can, buy secondhand, and donate or sell unused items
- Buy things that are reusable, recyclable, or compostable, and be sure to reuse, recycle, and compost them
- Buy products with little or no packaging and recycle any packaging as much as possible
- Avoid disposables such as paper and plastic bags, plates, cups, and utensils, disposable diapers, and disposable razors whenever reusable versions are available
- Cook with whole, fresh foods, avoid heavily packaged processed foods, and buy products in bulk whenever possible
- Discontinue junk mail as much as possible and read online newspapers and magazines and e-books

FIGURE 18.8 Individuals matter: You can save resources by reducing your output of solid waste and pollution. *Critical thinking:* Which three of these steps do you think are the most important ones to take? Why? Which of these things do you already do?

Fifth, *eliminate or reduce unnecessary packaging*. Use the following hierarchy for product packaging: no packaging, reusable packaging, and recyclable packaging.

Sixth, *use fee-per-bag solid waste collection systems* that charge consumers for the amount of waste they throw away but provide free pickup of recyclable and reusable items.

CHECKPOINT FOR UNDERSTANDING 18.2

1. Describe integrated waste management.

2. Identify strategies that communities and industries can use that will reduce the amount of waste produced.

18.3 WHY ARE REFUSING, REDUCING, REUSING, AND RECYCLING SO IMPORTANT?

CONCEPT 18.3 By refusing and reducing resource use and by reusing and recycling what we use, we decrease our consumption of matter and energy resources, reduce pollution and natural capital degradation, and save money.

Alternatives to the Throwaway Economy

In today's industrialized societies, we have increasingly substituted throwaway items for reusable ones, which has resulted in growing masses of solid waste. However, by applying the four Rs, we can slow or stop this trend. Individuals can guide and reduce their consumption of resources by asking questions such as these:

- Do I really need this? (refusing)
- How many of these do I actually need? (reducing)
- Is this something I can use more than once? (reusing)
- Can this be converted into the same or a different product when I am done with it? (recycling)

Revisiting Cradle-to-Cradle Design: Reuse Is on the Rise

Cradle-to-cradle design elevates reuse to a new level. William McDonough (Individuals Matter 18.1) argues that the key to shifting from a disposal economy to a reuse economy is to design for it (**Core Case Study**). Hence, some manufacturers of computers, furniture, photo copiers, and other products have designed and built their products so that when they are no longer useful, they can be retrieved from consumers for repair or remanufacture.

William McDonough

William McDonough is an architect, designer, and visionary thinker, devoted to the earth-friendly design of buildings, products, and cities.

McDonough points out that there is no waste in nature because the wastes of one organism become nutrients for other organisms. He also notes that humans have been releasing a growing number of chemicals to the environment faster than the natural chemical cycles can remove them. In addition, many of these synthetic chemicals cannot be broken down and recycled by natural processes. Many of these chemicals end up polluting the air, water, and soil and threatening the health of humans and other life forms.

McDonough and his business partner, chemist Michael Braungart, want to correct this trend by implementing a second industrial revolution, based on a *cradle-to-cradle approach* (**Core Case Study**). It would use environmentally and economically sustainable design to mimic nature by reusing and recycling the chemicals and products we make with the goal of zero waste. They argue that waste is a resource out of place and the result of poor design, and that we must employ three strategies to deal with it: **(1)** design products and societies that produce no waste, **(2)** live off the earth's endless supply of solar energy, and **(3)** respect and mimic the earth's life-sustaining biodiversity.

McDonough's approach has been applied in numerous projects, including the Adam Joseph Lewis Center for Environmental Studies at Oberlin College. Architects and designers view it as one of the most important and inspiring examples of environmentally friendly design. It uses recycled and nontoxic materials that can be further recycled. It gets heat from the sun and the earth's interior and electricity from solar cells, and it produces 13% more energy than it consumes. The building's greenhouse contains an ecosystem of plants and animals that purify the building's sewage and wastewater. Rainwater is collected and used to irrigate the surrounding green space, which includes a restored wetland, a fruit orchard, and a vegetable garden.

McDonough has been recognized by *Time* magazine as a "Hero for the Planet." He has also received numerous design awards and three presidential awards. He believes we can make the transition to a second industrial revolution, based on cradle-to-cradle design, and thereby leave the world better than we found it.

One way to implement cradle-to-cradle design is for governments to ban or severely restrict the disposal of certain items. For example, the European Union (EU) has led the way by banning e-waste from landfills and incinerators. Electronics manufacturers are required to take back their products at the end of their useful lives. To cover the costs of these programs, consumers pay a recycling tax on electronic products, an example of implementing the full-cost pricing **principle of sustainability**. Japan, and China are also using this take-back approach. In the United States, there is no federal take-back law, but according to the Electronics TakeBack Coalition, more than 20 states have such laws and several more are considering them.

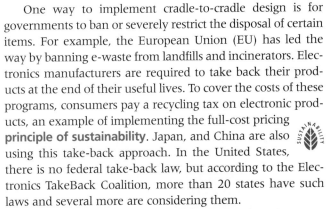

Governments have also banned the use of certain throwaway items. For example, Finland banned all beverage containers that cannot be reused, and consequently, 95% of that country's soft drink, beer, wine, and spirits containers are refillable. The use of rechargeable batteries is cutting toxic waste by reducing the amount of conventional batteries that are thrown away. The latest rechargeable batteries come fully charged, can hold a charge for up to 2 years when they are not used, and can be recharged in about 15 minutes.

Instead of using throwaway paper or plastic bags to carry home groceries and other purchased items, many people now use reusable cloth bags. Both paper and plastic throwaway bags are environmentally harmful, and the question of which is more damaging has no clear-cut answer. Recycling and reuse of plastic bags is on the rise, but the great majority of such bags are thrown away.

To encourage people to carry reusable bags, the governments of Ireland, Taiwan, France, Germany, and the Netherlands tax plastic shopping bags. Several countries have banned the use of all or most types of plastic shopping bags. In Ireland, a tax of 25¢ per bag cut plastic bag litter by 90% as people switched to reusable bags. In 2014, the EU passed a directive aimed at cutting the use of single-use plastic bags by 80%. In 2014, the US state of California joined Hawaii in instituting a statewide ban on single-use plastic bags. They have also been banned in more than 133 US cities or counties, despite intense lobbying against this by the plastics industry.

An increasingly popular way to reuse things is through *shared use*. In Portland, Oregon, some homeowners have worked with their neighbors to create tool libraries instead of buying their own tools. Toy libraries are also evolving among young families whose toys are used only for a few months or years. Companies that rent out tools, garden equipment, and other household goods provide another outlet for shared use. There are many other ways to reuse items and materials (Figure 18.9).

Recycling

The cradle-to-cradle approach (**Core Case Study**) gives the highest priority to reuse, but also relies on recycling. Worn-out items from the technical cycle of cradle-to-cradle manufacturing are recycled or sent into the biological cycle where ideally they degrade and become biological nutrients (Figure 18.1).

McDonough and Braungart break recycling down into two categories: *upcycling* and *downcycling*. Ideally, all discarded items would be upcycled—recycled into a form that is more useful than the recycled item was. In down-cycling, the recycled product is still useful, but not as useful or long-lived as the original item.

Households and workplaces produce five major types of recyclable materials: paper products, glass, aluminum, steel, and some plastics. These materials can be reprocessed into new, useful products in two ways. **Primary recycling** involves using materials, such as aluminum, again for the same purpose. For example, a used aluminum can is recycled into a new aluminum can. **Secondary recycling** involves downcycling or upcycling waste materials into different products, such as downcycling used tires into sandals.

Scientists and waste managers also distinguish between two types of recyclable wastes: *preconsumer* or *internal waste* generated in a manufacturing process, and *postconsumer* or *external waste* generated from use of products by consumers. Preconsumer waste makes up more than three-fourths of the total.

Recycling involves three steps: the collection of materials for recycling, conversion of recycled materials to new products, and selling and buying of products that contain recycled material. Recycling is successful environmentally and economically when all three of these steps are carried out.

Recycling of e-waste is especially attractive. In 2014, the world's e-waste contained an estimated 300 metric tons (330 tons) of gold, more than a tenth of all gold produced by miners in that year. It also contained millions of tons of iron, copper, silver, and aluminum. Yet, less than 17% of all e-waste is recycled.

Composting is another form of recycling that directly applies the chemical cycling **principle of sustainability**. Composted material can be added to soil to supply plant nutrients, slow soil erosion, retain water, and improve crop yields. Many homeowners compost food wastes, yard wastes, and other organic waste materials in simple backyard containers (Figure 18.10).

Many cities collect and compost biodegradable wastes in centralized composting facilities (Figure 18.11). To be successful, a large-scale composting program must be located carefully and odors must be controlled, especially near residential areas. They must also exclude toxic materials that make the compost unsafe for fertilizing crops and lawns.

Recent research based on actual data instead of descriptive models indicates that the United States recycles or composts about 24% of its MSW, which is significantly lower

---

What Can You Do?

Reuse

- Buy beverages in refillable glass containers
- Use reusable lunch containers
- Use a reusable coffee container and carry it with you
- Store refrigerated food in reusable containers
- Use rechargeable batteries and recycle them when their useful life is over
- When eating out, bring your own reusable container for leftovers
- Carry groceries and other items in a reusable basket or cloth bag
- Buy used furniture, cars, and other items, whenever possible

Brenda Carson/Shutterstock.com

FIGURE 18.9 Individuals matter: Some ways to reuse the items we purchase. ***Questions:*** Which of these suggestions have you tried and how did they work for you?

FIGURE 18.10 Backyard composting bin.

than the EPA estimate of 34%. Experts say that with education and proper economic incentives, Americans could recycle and compost at least 80% of their MSW, in keeping with the chemical cycling **principle of sustainability**.

We Can Mix or Separate Household Solid Wastes for Recycling

One way to recycle is to send mixed MSW to centralized *materials-recovery facilities* (MRFs), where machines and workers separate the mixed waste to recover valuable materials for sale to manufacturers as raw materials. The remaining paper, plastics, and other combustible wastes are recycled or burned to produce steam or electricity. In some cases, onsite waste incinerators generate electricity to power the MRF.

MRFs are expensive to build, operate, and maintain. If not operated properly, they can emit CO_2 and air pollutants, and they produce a toxic ash that must be disposed of safely, usually in landfills. Because MRFs require a steady diet of garbage to make them financially successful, their owners have a vested interest in increasing the flow of MSW. Thus, use of MRFs does nothing to encourage reuse and waste reduction and instead encourages the production of more trash—the reverse of what many scientists urge (Figure 18.7, left).

The mixed waste approach is becoming less economically sustainable in many communities because people are increasingly throwing nonrecyclable trash into their recycling bins. This requires MRFs to spend more time, energy, and money separating recyclable materials.

To many experts, it makes more ecological and economic sense for households and businesses to separate their trash into recyclable categories such as glass, paper, metals, certain types of plastics, and compostable materials. This *source separation* approach produces much less air and water pollution and costs less to implement, compared to relying on MRFs. It also saves more energy and yields cleaner and usually more valuable recyclables.

To promote separation of wastes for recycling, about 7,000 communities in the United States use a *pay-as-you-throw* or *fee-per-bag* waste collection system. They charge households and businesses for garbage that is picked up, but do not charge them for picking up materials separated for recycling or reuse.

Recycling Paper

About 55% of the world's industrial tree harvest is used to make paper. However, according to the US Department of Agriculture, we could make tree-free paper from straw and other agricultural residues and from the fibers of rapidly growing plants such as kenaf (see Figure 18.12) and hemp.

100 million
Number of trees used each year to produce the world's junk mail

The pulp and paper industry is the world's fifth largest energy consumer and uses more water to produce a metric ton of its product than any other industry. In both Canada and the United States, it is the third-largest industrial energy user and polluter, and paper is the dominant material in the MSW of both countries.

Paper (especially newspaper and cardboard) is easy to recycle. Recycling newspaper involves removing its ink, glue, and coating and then reconverting the paper to pulp, which is pressed into new paper. Making recycled paper produces 35% less water pollution and 74% less air pollution than does making paper from wood pulp, and, of course, no trees are cut down.

FIGURE 18.11 Large-scale municipal composting site.

CONNECTIONS Recycling Paper and Reducing CO_2 Emissions

According to the US Energy Information Administration, recycled paper requires 10–30% less energy, which means that for every kilogram (2.2 pounds) of paper you recycle, you can prevent an average of 0.9 kilograms (2 pounds) of CO_2 emissions.

Recycling Plastics

Plastics consist of various types of large polymers, or *resins*—organic molecules made by chemically linking organic chemicals produced mostly from oil and natural gas. About 46 different types of plastics are used in consumer products, and some products contain several kinds of plastic.

Currently, only 7% by weight of all plastic wastes in the United States (and 13% of plastic containers and pack-aging) is recycled. These percentages are low because there are many different types of plastic resins, which are difficult to separate from products that contain them. Another factor is that most plastic beverage containers and other plastic products are not designed for recycling. This makes it cheaper and easier to put them in a landfill. However, progress is being made in processes for recycling of plastics and in the development of more degradable bioplastics (Science Focus 18.2).

Recycling Has Advantages and Disadvantages

Figure 18.13 lists the advantages and disadvantages of recycling (**Concept 18.3**). Whether recycling makes economic sense depends on how we look at its economic and environmental benefits and costs.

Bioplastics

One of the most useful characteristics of plastic—its durability—also happens to be one of its biggest drawbacks. Plastics are made to last, but that means they don't break down once they're disposed of. In addition, most of today's plastics are made using petroleum-based chemicals, or petrochemicals. Processing these chemicals creates hazardous waste and contributes to water and air pollution. The good news is that some products are now being made from bioplastics, a type of plastic that is more environmentally friendly because it is made from biologically based chemicals.

Henry Ford, who developed the first Ford car and founded Ford Motor Company, supported research on the development of a bioplastic made from soybeans and another made from hemp. A 1914 photograph shows him using an ax to strike the body of a Ford car made from soy bioplastic to demonstrate its strength and resistance to denting.

However, as oil became cheaper and widely available, petrochemical plastics took over the market. Now, confronted with climate change and other environmental problems associated with the use of oil, chemists are stepping up efforts to make more environmentally sustainable bioplastics. They can be made from corn, soy, sugarcane, switchgrass, chicken feathers, and some components of garbage.

Compared with conventional oil-based plastics, properly designed bioplastics are lighter, stronger, and cheaper. And the process of making them usually requires less energy and produces less pollution per unit of weight. Instead of being sent to landfills, some packaging made from bioplastics (Figure 18.A) can be composted to produce a soil conditioner, in keeping with the chemical cycling **principle of sustainability**.

Some bioplastics are more environmentally friendly than others. For example,

FIGURE 18.A A biodegradable plastic bag.

some are made from corn raised by industrial agricultural methods, which require great amounts of energy, water, and petrochemical fertilizers and thus have a very large ecological footprint. In evaluating and choosing bioplastics, scientists urge consumers to learn how they were made, how long they take to biodegrade, and whether they degrade into harmful chemicals.

CRITICAL THINKING

Do you think that the advantages of bioplastics outweigh their disadvantages?

FIGURE 18.12 Solutions: The pressure to cut trees to make paper could be greatly reduced by planting and harvesting a fast-growing plant known as kenaf.

Critics of recycling programs argue that recycling is costly and adds to the taxpayer burden in communities where recycling is funded through taxation. Proponents of recycling point to studies showing that the net economic, health, and environmental benefits of recycling (Figure 18.13, left) far outweigh the costs. Recycling, reuse, and composting industries create 6 to 10 times as many jobs as landfills and waste incineration. The US recycling industry employs 1.1 million people. Doubling the US recycling rate would create about 1 million new jobs. Cities that make money by recycling and have higher recycling rates tend to use a single-pickup system for both recyclable and nonrecyclable materials instead of a more expensive dual-pickup system. Successful systems also use a pay-as-you-throw approach. They charge for picking up trash but not for picking up recyclable or reusable materials. They also require citizens and businesses to sort their trash and recyclables by type. San Francisco, California, uses such a system, and in 2015, the city recycled, composted, or reused 80% of its MSW.

Trade-Offs

Recycling

Advantages

Reduces energy and mineral use and air and water pollution

Reduces greenhouse gas emissions

Reduces solid waste

Disadvantages

Can cost more than burying in areas with ample landfill space

Reduces profits for landfill and incinerator owners

Inconvenient for some

FIGURE 18.13 Recycling solid waste has advantages and disadvantages (**Concept 18.3**). *Critical thinking:* Which single advantage and which single disadvantage do you think are the most important? Why?

Photo: Jacqui Martin/Shutterstock.com

CHECKPOINT FOR UNDERSTANDING 18.3

1. Explain the difference between upcycling and downcycling.

2. Describe how composting is a form of recycling.

3. Identify several drawbacks of materials recovery facilities (MRFs).

CONCEPT 18.4 Technologies for burning and burying solid wastes are well developed, but burning can contribute to air and water pollution and greenhouse gas emissions, and buried wastes can contribute to water pollution.

Burning Solid Waste Has Advantages and Disadvantages

Many communities burn their solid waste until nothing remains but fine, white-gray ash, which can then be buried in landfills. Heat released by burning trash can be used to heat water or interior spaces, or for producing electricity in facilities called *waste-to-energy incinerators*. Globally, MSW is burned in more than 800 of these types of incinerators, 71 of them in the United States.

A waste-to-energy incinerator (Figure 18.14) contains a combustion chamber where waste is burned at extremely high temperatures. Heat from the burning material is used to boil water and produce steam. The steam in turn drives a turbine that generates electricity. Combustion

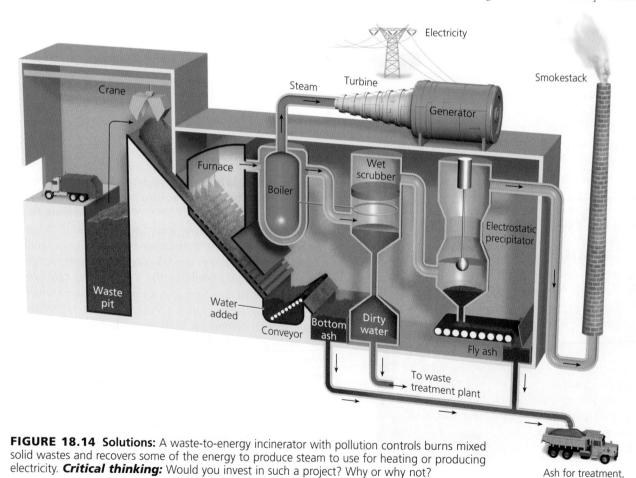

FIGURE 18.14 Solutions: A waste-to-energy incinerator with pollution controls burns mixed solid wastes and recovers some of the energy to produce steam to use for heating or producing electricity. *Critical thinking:* Would you invest in such a project? Why or why not?

Ash for treatment, disposal in landfill, or use as landfill cover

Environmental Justice

Environmental justice is an ideal whereby every person is entitled to protection from environmental hazards regardless of race, gender, age, national origin, income, social class, or any political factor.

Studies show that a large share of polluting factories, hazardous waste dumps, incinerators, and landfills in the United States are located in communities populated mostly by minority groups. Other research shows that, in general, toxic waste sites in white communities are cleaned up faster and more completely than similar sites in and around African American, Latino, and Native American communities.

Such environmental discrimination in the United States and many other parts of the world has led to a growing effort known as the *environmental justice movement*. Supporters of this movement pressure governments, businesses, and environmental organizations to become aware of environmental injustice and act to prevent it. This movement has made some progress toward their goals.

Some politicians and business representatives suggest that economics and saving money should be the main factor in decisions about where to locate new power plants, freeways, landfills, incinerators, and other such potentially disruptive facilities. Often, however, these areas are home to low-income residents who have much less political power than developers and corporations. Many analysts argue that the ethical principle of environmental justice should carry as much weight as economic factors do in such decisions.

FRQ Application

Question: In the production of electronics, clothing, and other consumer products, many US corporations have moved their manufacturing facilities to other countries. **Identify** TWO reasons why companies would locate their facilities outside of the United States, and **discuss** the impacts on human health.

Possible Response: US corporations locate their facilities outside of the United States due to environmental regulations in some countries; China and India for example, are lax. There are few restrictions on emitting pollution into waterways and air, resulting in increased profits because companies do not have to invest in pollution-control devices. The result is increased lung disease and sickness from contaminated water.

Labor is cheaper in countries such as China and Bangladesh, and children are often employed in factories with no laws protecting workers, while being paid very low wages. Workers are often employed to do menial and very dangerous jobs such as stripping precious metals from discarded computers where they are exposed to lead and other hazardous heavy metals.

---

also produces wastes in the form of gases and ash. The gases must be filtered to remove pollutants before being released into the atmosphere and the hazardous ash must be treated and properly disposed of in landfills.

The United States incinerates 13% of its MSW, a fairly low percentage. One reason for this low percentage is that in the past incineration earned a bad reputation as a result of highly polluting and poorly regulated incinerators. In addition, incineration competes with an abundance of low-cost landfills in many parts of the United States.

By contrast, Denmark incinerates 54% of its MSW in state-of-the-art waste-to-energy incinerators. Denmark's incinerators run so cleanly that they exceed European air pollution standards by a factor of 10. However, the resulting incinerator ash contains toxic chemicals and has to be safely stored somewhere, essentially forever.

Figure 18.15 lists the advantages and disadvantages of using incinerators to burn solid waste. According to the EPA, landfills emit more air pollutants than modern waste-to-energy incinerators. On the other hand, the resulting incinerator ash contains toxic chemicals that must be stored somewhere. In addition, many US citizens, local governments, and environmental scientists remain opposed

Trade-Offs

Waste-to-Energy Incineration

Advantages	Disadvantages
Reduces trash volume	Expensive to build
Produces energy	Produces a hazardous waste
Concentrates hazardous substances into ash for burial	Emits some CO_2 and other air pollutants
Sale of energy reduces cost	Encourages waste production

FIGURE 18.15 Incinerating solid waste has advantages and disadvantages (**Concept 18.4**). These trade-offs also apply to the incineration of hazardous waste. *Critical thinking:* Which single advantage and which single disadvantage do you think are the most important? Why?

Top: Ulrich Mueller/Shutterstock.com. Bottom: Dmitry Kalinovsky/Shutterstock.com.

to waste incineration because it undermines efforts to increase reuse and recycling by creating a demand for burnable wastes. It also makes it easier for consumers to discard reusable and recyclable items.

Burying Solid Waste Has Advantages and Disadvantages

In the United States, about 54% of all MSW, by weight, is buried in sanitary landfills, compared to 80% in Canada, 15% in Japan, and 4% in Denmark. In a **sanitary landfill** (Figure 18.16), solid wastes are spread out in thin layers, compacted, and regularly covered with a layer of clay or plastic foam. This process helps to keep the material dry, cuts

down on odors, reduces the risk of fire, and keeps rats and other pest animals away from the wastes. In addition, it helps contain contaminated water called *leachate*, so that it does not leak out of the landfill and pollute nearby soil and groundwater.

The bottoms and sides of well-designed sanitary landfills have strong double liners and containment systems that collect the liquids leaching from them. Some landfills also have systems for collecting methane, a potent greenhouse gas that is produced when the buried wastes decompose in the absence of oxygen. The collected methane can be burned as a fuel to generate electricity.

Paper products represent the largest percentage of landfill materials. Other common materials include yard waste,

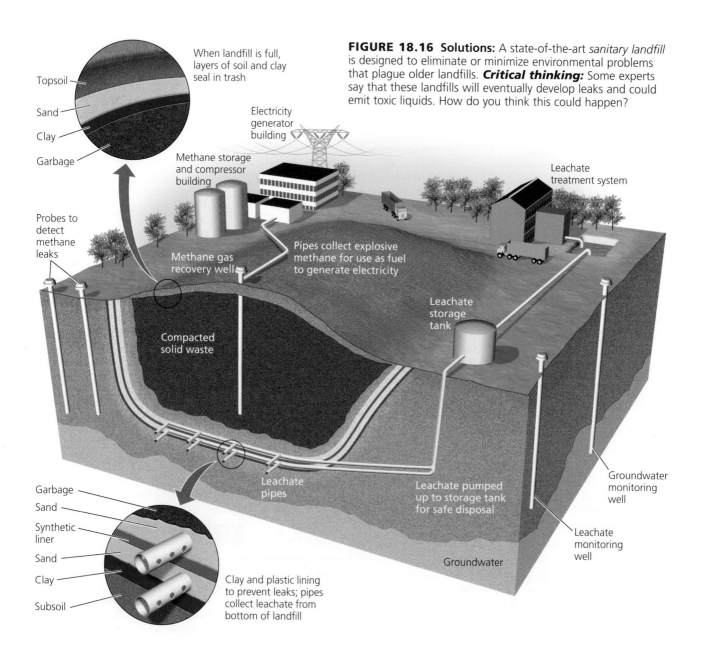

FIGURE 18.16 Solutions: A state-of-the-art *sanitary landfill* is designed to eliminate or minimize environmental problems that plague older landfills. **Critical thinking:** Some experts say that these landfills will eventually develop leaks and could emit toxic liquids. How do you think this could happen?

When landfill is full, layers of soil and clay seal in trash

Topsoil
Sand
Clay
Garbage

Electricity generator building

Methane storage and compressor building

Leachate treatment system

Probes to detect methane leaks

Methane gas recovery well

Pipes collect explosive methane for use as fuel to generate electricity

Leachate storage tank

Compacted solid waste

Leachate pipes

Leachate pumped up to storage tank for safe disposal

Groundwater monitoring well

Garbage
Sand
Synthetic liner
Sand
Clay
Subsoil

Clay and plastic lining to prevent leaks; pipes collect leachate from bottom of landfill

Leachate monitoring well

Groundwater

Using Methane to Generate Electricity

As waste decomposes in a sanitary landfill it generates landfill gas, which is comprised of approximately 50% methane and 50% carbon dioxide. Most landfill operators collect this gas and simply burn it off.

FRQ Application

High Acres Landfill in Fairport, New York, operated by Waste Management, collects landfill gas and burns it to generate electricity. In fact, High Acres Landfill collects 7,400 cubic feet of landfill gas per minute and generates power equivalent to 180,000 barrels of oil each year.

Calculate the total amount of cubic feet of landfill gas captured in 1 year:

$$\frac{7,400 \text{ cubic feet}}{\text{minute}} \times \frac{60 \text{ minutes}}{\text{hour}} \times \frac{24 \text{ hours}}{\text{day}} \times \frac{365 \text{ days}}{\text{year}} = 3.89 \times 10^9 \text{ ft}^3 \text{ landfill gas/year}$$

How many cubic feet of methane are captured in a year?

$$3.89 \times 10^9 \text{ ft}^3 \times 0.5 = 1.94 \times 10^9 \text{ ft}^3 \text{ methane}$$

How many cubic feet of landfill gas does it take to equal 1 barrel of oil?

$$\frac{3.89 \times 10^9 \text{ ft}^3 \text{ landfill gas}}{180,000 \text{ barrels of oil}} \approx 21,600 \text{ ft}^3 \text{ landfill gas per barrel of oil}$$

plastics, metals, wood, glass, and food waste. Some types of solid waste are not accepted at landfills. For example, tires, waste oil and oil filters, items containing mercury such as compact fluorescent light bulbs and thermometers, electronics, and medical waste are not allowed. Some retired landfill sites are being used as sites for solar farms.

Figure 18.17 lists the advantages and disadvantages of using sanitary landfills to dispose of solid waste.

Another type of landfill is an **open dump** (Figure 18.3). It is essentially a field or large pit where garbage is deposited and sometimes burned (Figure 18.18). Open dumps are rare in more-developed countries, but are widely used near major cities in many less-developed countries. China disposes of much of its rapidly growing mountains of solid waste mostly in rural open dumps or in poorly designed and poorly regulated landfills.

FIGURE 18.17 Using sanitary landfills to dispose of solid waste has advantages and disadvantages (**Concept 18.4**). **Critical thinking:** Which single advantage and which single disadvantage do you think are the most important? Why?

Photo: Pedro Miguel Sousa/ShutterStock.com

Trade-Offs

Sanitary Landfills

Advantages	Disadvantages
Low operating costs	Noise, traffic, and dust
Can handle large amounts of waste	Releases greenhouse gases (methane and CO_2) unless they are collected
Filled land can be used for other purposes	Output approach that encourages waste production
No shortage of landfill space in many areas	Eventually leaks and can contaminate groundwater

FIGURE 18.18 Some open dumps, especially in less-developed countries, are routinely burned, releasing large quantities of pollutants into the atmosphere. They can burn for days or weeks.

CHECKPOINT FOR UNDERSTANDING 18.4

1. Identify the advantages of waste-to-energy incineration.

2. Identify the drawbacks of waste-to-energy incineration.

3. Identify the advantages of utilizing sanitary landfills to manage waste.

4. Identify the disadvantages of utilizing sanitary landfills to manage waste.

18.5 HOW SHOULD WE DEAL WITH HAZARDOUS WASTE?

CONCEPT 18.5 A more sustainable approach to hazardous waste is first to produce less of it, then to reuse or recycle it, then to convert it to less-hazardous materials, and finally to safely store what is left.

Hazardous Waste Requires Special Handling

The US National Academy of Sciences has established three priority levels for dealing with hazardous waste: produce less; convert as much of it as possible to less-hazardous substances; and put the rest in long-term, safe storage (**Concept 18.5**). Figure 18.19 illustrates this integrated management approach to dealing with hazardous waste. Denmark follows these priorities, but most countries do not.

As with solid waste, the top priority for hazardous waste management should be pollution prevention and waste reduction. Using this approach, industries try to find substitutes for toxic or hazardous materials, reuse or recycle the hazardous materials within industrial processes, or use or sell them as raw materials for making other products, in keeping with the cradle-to-cradle approach (**Core Case Study**).

At least 33% of industrial hazardous wastes produced in the European Union are exchanged through clearinghouses where they are sold as raw materials for use by other industries, in keeping with the chemical cycling **principle of sustainability**. The producers of these wastes do not have to pay for their disposal and recipients get low-cost raw materials. About 10% of the hazardous waste in the United States is exchanged through such clearinghouses, an amount that could be increased significantly.

CASE STUDY

Recycling E-Waste

In some countries, workers in e-waste recycling operations—many of them children—are often exposed to toxic chemicals as they dismantle the electronic trash to extract its

Produce Less Hazardous Waste	Convert to Less Hazardous or Nonhazardous Substances	Put in Perpetual Storage
■ Change industrial processes to reduce or eliminate hazardous waste production ■ Recycle and reuse hazardous waste	■ Natural decomposition ■ Incineration ■ Thermal treatment ■ Chemical, physical, and biological treatment ■ Dilution in air or water	■ Landfill ■ Underground injection wells ■ Surface impoundments ■ Underground salt formations

FIGURE 18.19 *Integrated hazardous waste management:* The US National Academy of Sciences has suggested these priorities for dealing with hazardous waste (**Concept 18.5**). *Critical thinking:* Why do you think most countries do not follow these priorities?

valuable metals or other parts that can be sold for reuse or recycling (Figure 18.20).

According to the United Nations, much of the world's e-waste is shipped to China. One popular destination for such waste is the small port city of Guiyu, where the air reeks of burning plastic and acid fumes. There, more than 5,500 small-scale e-waste businesses employ over 30,000 people, including children. They work for very low wages in dangerous conditions to extract valuable metals such as gold, silver, and copper from discarded computers, television sets, and cell phones.

Although these workers are exposed to toxic chemicals, they usually wear no masks or gloves, and often work in rooms with no ventilation. They carry out dangerous activities such as smashing TV picture tubes with large hammers to recover certain components—a method that releases large amounts of toxic lead dust into the air. They also burn computer wires to expose copper, melt circuit boards in metal pots over coal fires to extract lead and other metals, and douse the boards with strong acid to extract gold. After the metals are removed, leftover parts are burned or dumped into rivers or onto the land. More than 82% of the Guiyu area's children younger than age six suffer from lead poisoning.

The United States produces roughly 50% of the world's e-waste and recycles about 29% of it, according to the US Environmental Protection Agency. By 2015, at least 28 US states and the District of Columbia had banned the disposal of computers and TV sets in landfills and incinerators. These measures set the stage for an emerging, highly profitable *e-cycling* industry. In 2015, 28 states along with New York City made manufacturers responsible for recycling most electronic devices. In 2016, Apple introduced Liam—a 29-armed robot capable of taking apart 1.2 million iPhones a year into components that can be recycled.

A growing number of scientists and economists have called for a US federal law to institute a cradle-to cradle approach (**Core Case Study**) that would require manufacturers to take back all electronic devices they produce and recycle them domestically. It could be similar to laws in the European Union, where a recycling fee typically covers the costs of such programs. Without such a

James P. Blair/National Geographic Creative

FIGURE 18.20 This young girl in Dhaka, Bangladesh, is recycling batteries by hammering them apart to extract tin and lead. The workers at this shop are mostly women and children.

law there is little incentive for recycling e-waste and plastics, especially when there is money to be made from illegally sending such materials to other countries.

However, the only real long-term solution is a *prevention* approach. Electrical and electronic products could be designed to be produced and easily repaired, remanufactured, or recycled, without the use of toxic materials (**Core Case Study**).

CONSIDER THIS . . .

THINKING ABOUT E-Waste Recycling

Would you support a recycling fee on all electronic devices? Why or why not?

Detoxifying Hazardous Waste

In Denmark, all hazardous and toxic wastes from industries and households are collected and delivered to transfer stations throughout the country. They are then taken to a large processing facility, where three-fourths of the waste is detoxified using physical, chemical, and biological methods. The rest is buried in a carefully designed and monitored landfill.

Physical methods for detoxifying hazardous wastes include using charcoal or resins to filter out harmful solids, distilling liquid wastes to separate out harmful chemicals, and precipitating such chemicals from solution. Especially deadly wastes, such as those contaminated by mercury, can be encapsulated in glass, cement, or ceramics and put in secure storage sites. *Chemical methods* are used to convert hazardous chemicals to harmless or less harmful chemicals through chemical reactions.

Some scientists and engineers consider *biological methods* for treatment of hazardous waste to be the wave of the future. One such approach is *bioremediation*, in which bacteria and enzymes help to destroy toxic or hazardous substances or convert them to harmless compounds. Bioremediation is often used on contaminated soil. For example, microorganisms are used at some contaminated sites to break down hazardous chemicals, such as PCBs, pesticides, and oil in the soil, leaving behind harmless substances such as water and water-soluble chloride salts. It usually takes a little longer to work than most physical and chemical methods, but it costs much less.

Phytoremediation is another biological method for treating hazardous wastes. It involves using natural or genetically engineered plants to remove contaminants from polluted soil and water. This method is still being evaluated and is slow compared to other alternatives.

Hazardous wastes can also be incinerated to break them down and convert them to harmless or less harmful chemicals. This method involves the same advantages and disadvantages as burning of solid wastes (Figure 18.15).

Plasma gasification is another thermal treatment method. This technology uses arcs of electrical energy to produce very high temperatures in order to vaporize trash in the absence of oxygen. The process reduces the volume of a given amount of waste by 99%, produces a synthetic gaseous fuel, and encases toxic metals and other materials in glassy lumps of rock. It is currently very costly, but plasma arc companies are working to bring prices down. Figure 18.21 lists the major advantages and disadvantages of using this process.

Trade-Offs

Plasma Arc

Advantages	Disadvantages
Produces a mixture of CO and H_2 that can be used as a fuel	High cost
Mobile. Easy to move to different sites	Produces CO_2 and CO
Produces no toxic ash	Can release particulates and chlorine gas
	Can vaporize and release toxic metals and radioactive elements

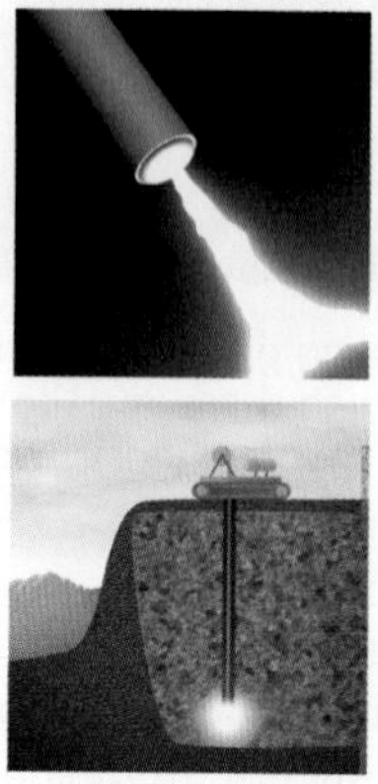

FIGURE 18.21 Using *plasma gasification* to detoxify hazardous wastes has advantages and disadvantages. ***Critical thinking:*** Which single advantage and which single disadvantage do you think are the most important? Why?

Storing Hazardous Waste

Ideally, we should use burial on land or long-term storage of hazardous and toxic wastes in secure vaults only as the third and last resort after the first two priorities have been exhausted (Figure 18.17 and **Concept 18.5**). Currently, however, burial on land is the most widely used method in the United States and in most countries, largely because it is less expensive than other methods.

The most common form of burial is *deep-well disposal*. Liquid hazardous wastes are pumped under high pressure through a pipe into dry, porous underground rock formations far beneath aquifers that are tapped for drinking and irrigation water. Theoretically, these liquids soak into the porous rock material and are isolated from overlying groundwater by essentially impermeable layers of clay and rock. The cost is low and the wastes can often be retrieved if problems develop.

However, there are a limited number of such sites and limited space within them. Sometimes the wastes can leak into groundwater from the well shaft or migrate into groundwater in unexpected ways. Also, this approach encourages the production instead of the reduction of hazardous wastes.

In the United States, almost two-thirds of all liquid hazardous wastes are injected into deep disposal wells. This amount will increase sharply as the country relies more on fracking to produce natural gas and oil trapped in shale rock (see Science Focus 14.1, p. 429).

Many scientists argue that current regulations for deep-well disposal in the United States are inadequate and should be improved (see the Case Study that follows).

Trade-Offs

Deep-Well Disposal

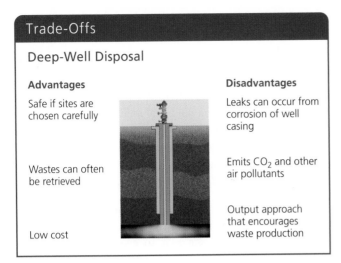

Advantages

Safe if sites are chosen carefully

Wastes can often be retrieved

Low cost

Disadvantages

Leaks can occur from corrosion of well casing

Emits CO_2 and other air pollutants

Output approach that encourages waste production

FIGURE 18.22 Injecting liquid hazardous wastes into deep underground wells has advantages and disadvantages. ***Critical thinking:*** Which single advantage and which single disadvantage do you think are the most important? Why?

Figure 18.22 lists the advantages and disadvantages of using deep-well disposal of liquid hazardous wastes.

Some liquid hazardous wastes are stored in lined ponds, pits, or lagoons, called *surface impoundments*. Studies conducted by the EPA found that 70% of all US hazardous waste storage ponds have no liners and could threaten groundwater supplies. According to the EPA, eventually, all impoundment liners are likely to leak and contaminate groundwater. Because these impoundments are not covered, volatile harmful chemicals evaporate, polluting the air. In addition, flooding from heavy rainstorms can cause such ponds to overflow. Not all US hazardous waste storage ponds have liners, according to the EPA, and many liners are subject to leaks that could eventually contami-

Trade-Offs

Surface Impoundments

Advantages

Low cost

Wastes can often be retrieved

Can store wastes indefinitely with secure double liners

Disadvantages

Water pollution from leaking liners and overflows

Air pollution from volatile organic compounds

Output approach that encourages waste production

Jim West/Alamy Stock Photo

FIGURE 18.23 Storing liquid hazardous wastes in surface impoundments has advantages and disadvantages. ***Critical thinking:*** Which single advantage and which single disadvantage do you think are the most important? Why?

nate groundwater. Figure 18.23 lists the advantages and disadvantages of using this method.

There are some highly toxic materials such as mercury (Core Case Study, Chapter 16, p, 496) that we cannot destroy, detoxify, or safely bury. The best way to deal with such materials is to prevent or reduce their use and put them in sealed containers and bury them in carefully designed and monitored *secure hazardous waste landfills* (Figure 18.24). This is the least-used method because of the expense involved.

Figure 18.25 lists some ways in which you can reduce your output of hazardous waste—the first step in dealing with it.

CASE STUDY

Hazardous Waste Regulation in the United States

Several US federal laws help to regulate the management and storage of hazardous wastes. About 5% of all hazardous waste produced in the United States is regulated under the Resource Conservation and Recovery Act (RCRA, pronounced "RICK-ra"), passed by the US Congress in 1976 and amended in 1984.

Under RCRA, the EPA sets standards for the management of several types of hazardous waste and issues permits to companies that allow them to produce and dispose of a certain amount of those wastes by approved

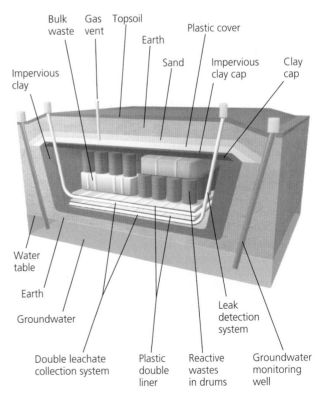

FIGURE 18.24 Solutions: Hazardous wastes can be isolated and stored in a secure hazardous waste landfill.

What Can You Do?

Hazardous Waste

- Avoid using pesticides and other hazardous chemicals, or use them in the smallest amounts possible
- Use less harmful substances instead of commercial household cleaners. For example, use vinegar to polish metals, clean surfaces, and remove stains and mildew, and baking soda to clean utensils and to deodorize and remove stains.
- Do not dump pesticides, paints, solvents, oil, antifreeze, or other hazardous chemicals down the toilet, down the drain, into the ground, into the garbage, or down storm drains. Free hazardous waste disposal services are available in many cities.
- Do not throw old fluorescent lightbulbs (which contain mercury) into regular trash. Many communities and home product retailers offer free recycling of these bulbs.

FIGURE 18.25 Individuals matter: You can reduce your output of hazardous wastes (**Concept 18.5**). ***Critical thinking:*** Which two of these measures do you think are the most important ones to take? Why?

methods. Permit holders must use a *cradle-to-grave* system to keep track of waste they transfer from a point of generation (cradle) to an approved off-site disposal facility (grave), and they must submit proof of this disposal to the EPA.

RCRA is a good start. However, 95% of the hazardous and toxic wastes produced in the United States, including e-waste, are not regulated. In most other countries, especially less-developed countries, the amount of regulated waste is even smaller.

The Toxic Substances Control Act has also been in place since 1976. Its purpose is to regulate and ensure the safety of the thousands of chemicals used in manufacturing and contained in many products. Under this law, companies must notify the EPA before introducing a new chemical into the marketplace. They are not required to provide any data about its safety. In other words, any new chemical is viewed as safe unless the EPA, with little money available for this purpose, can show that it is harmful.

CONSIDER THIS . . .

THINKING ABOUT Hazardous Waste

Why do you think 95% of the hazardous waste produced in the United States is not regulated? Do you favor regulating such wastes? What do you think would be the economic consequences of doing so? Would this promote the cradle-to-cradle approach to reducing solid and hazardous wastes?

Since 1976, the EPA, with a very limited budget, has used this act to ban only 5 of the more than 85,000 chemicals in use. Environmental and health scientists call for Congress to reform this law by requiring manufacturers to provide data showing that a chemical or product containing a certain chemical is safe before it can be sold in the marketplace.

In 2016, Congress revised TSCA. It required the EPA to

- quickly review chemicals known to persist in the environment and build up in humans.
- determine whether a chemical meets certain safety standards before it enters the market.
- consider a chemical's effects on vulnerable populations such as pregnant women and children.
- ban companies from keeping data on chemicals secret.

These are helpful improvements but critics point out that the law does not require enough funding from the chemical industry for the EPA to evaluate thousands of chemicals, which will take at least 10 years at the current pace and funding level.

The Comprehensive Environmental Response, Compensation, and Liability Act (CERCLA) was passed in 1980. It is commonly known as the Superfund Act and is regulated by the EPA. The goals of the act are to identify sites, called Superfund sites, where hazardous wastes have contaminated the environment (Figure 18.26) and to clean them up, using EPA-approved methods. The worst sites—those that represent an immediate and severe threat to human health—are put on a *National Priorities List* and scheduled for cleanup.

As of May, 2017, there were 1,336 sites on the Superfund list, along with 53 proposed new sites, and 393 sites had been cleaned up and removed from the list. Nearly one of every six Americans was living within 5 kilometers (3 miles) of a Superfund site. The Waste Management Research Institute estimates that at least 10,000 sites should be on the priority list and that cleanup of these sites could cost about $1.7 trillion, not including legal fees. This is a glaring example of the economic and environmental value of emphasizing waste reduction and pollution prevention over the cleanup approach that the United States and most countries rely on.

In 1984, Congress amended the Superfund Act to give citizens the right to know what toxic chemicals are being stored or released in their communities. This required 23,800 large manufacturing facilities to report their annual releases of any of nearly 650 toxic chemicals. If you live in the United States, you can find out what toxic chemicals are being stored and released in your neighborhood by going to the EPA's *Toxic Release Inventory* website. There is political pressure from manufacturers to eliminate this amendment.

The Superfund Act, designed to make polluters pay for cleaning up abandoned hazardous waste sites, has greatly reduced the number of illegal dumpsites around the country and discouraged unsafe handling of hazardous wastes. It also forced waste producers who were fearful of liability claims to reduce their production of such waste and to recycle or reuse much more of it. However, in 1995, under pressure from polluters, the US Congress did

patrikslezak/Fotolia LLC

FIGURE 18.26 Leaking barrels of toxic waste at a Superfund site.

not renew the tax on oil and chemical companies—which financed the Superfund legislation—after it expired in 1995. Since then taxpayers, not polluters, pay for clean-ups (with an average cost of $26 million) when responsible parties cannot be found. As a result, the pace of cleanup has slowed.

Closely associated with CERCLA is the EPA's Brownfields Program. A brownfield is an industrial or commercial property that is, or may be, contaminated with hazardous pollutants. The program is designed to help states, communities, and other stakeholders economically redevelop contaminated property. The program assists interested parties in assessing sites, cleaning up sites, or reusing land designated as a brownfield. Reclaiming these lands can increase local tax bases, promote job growth, enable a new facility to use existing infrastructure, and keep undeveloped land from being used.

CHECKPOINT FOR UNDERSTANDING 18.5

1. Describe how most e-waste recycling is handled.

2. Identify ways of detoxifying hazardous waste.

3. What is the EPA's Toxic Release Inventory?

18.6 HOW CAN WE SHIFT TO LOW-WASTE ECONOMY?

CONCEPT 18.6 Shifting to a low-waste economy will require individuals and businesses to reduce resource use and to reuse and recycle most solid and hazardous wastes at local, national, and global levels.

Citizens Can Take Action

In the United States, individuals have organized grassroots (bottom-up) campaigns to prevent the construction of hundreds of incinerators, landfills, treatment plants for hazardous and radioactive wastes, and chemical plants in or near their communities. These campaigns have organized sit-ins, concerts, and protest rallies. They have gathered signatures on petitions and presented them to lawmakers.

Health risks from incinerators and landfills, when averaged over the entire country, are quite low. However, the risks for people living near such facilities are higher. Manufacturers and waste industry officials point out that something must be done with toxic and hazardous wastes created in the production of certain goods and services. Many

587

citizens do not accept this argument. Their view is that the best way to deal with most toxic and hazardous waste is to produce much less of it by focusing on pollution and waste prevention. They argue the goal should be "not in anyone's back yard" (NIABY) or "not on planet Earth" (NOPE).

Using International Treaties to Reduce Hazardous Waste

For decades, some countries regularly shipped hazardous wastes to other countries for disposal or processing. Since 1992, an international treaty known as the Basel Convention has banned participating countries from shipping hazardous waste through other countries without their permission. This treaty also covers e-waste.

By 2016, this agreement had been ratified (formally approved and implemented) by 183 countries. The United States has signed but has not ratified the convention. In 1995, the treaty was amended to outlaw all transfers of hazardous wastes from industrial countries to less-developed countries.

This ban will help, but it will not do away with the highly profitable illegal shipping of hazardous wastes. Hazardous waste smugglers evade the laws by using an array of tactics, including bribes, false permits, and mislabeling of hazardous wastes as recyclable materials.

In 2001, delegates from 122 countries completed a global treaty known as the Stockholm Convention on Persistent Organic Pollutants (POPs). The treaty started by regulating the use of 12 widely used persistent organic pollutants that can accumulate in the fatty tissues of humans and other animals that occupy high trophic levels in food webs. As a result, these hazardous chemicals can reach levels hundreds of thousands of times higher than their levels in the general environment.

Because they persist in the environment, POPs can also be transported long distances by wind and water. The original list of 12 hazardous POPs chemicals, called the *dirty dozen*, includes DDT and eight other chlorine-containing persistent pesticides, PCBs, dioxins, and furans. Using blood tests and statistical sampling, medical researchers at New York City's Mount Sinai School of Medicine found that it is likely that nearly every person on earth has detectable levels of POPs in their bodies. The long-term health effects of this involuntary global chemical experiment are largely unknown. The list of regulated POPs is expected to grow.

In 2000, the Swedish Parliament enacted a law that, by 2020, will ban all potentially hazardous chemicals that are persistent in the environment and that can accumulate in living tissue. This law also requires industries to perform risk assessments on the chemicals they use and to show that these chemicals are safe to use, as opposed to requiring the government to show that they are dangerous. In other words, chemicals are assumed to guilty until proven innocent—the reverse of the current policy in the United States and most other countries. There is strong political opposition to this approach in the United States, especially from most of the industries that produce and use potentially hazardous chemicals.

Encouraging Reuse and Recycling

Three factors hinder reuse and recycling. *First*, the market prices of almost all products do not include the harmful environmental and health costs associated with producing, using, and discarding them—a violation of the full-cost pricing **principle of sustainability**.

Second, the economic playing field is uneven, because in most countries, resource extraction industries receive more government tax breaks and subsidies than reuse and recycling industries.

Third, the demand and thus the price paid for recycled materials fluctuates, mostly because it is not a high priority for most governments, businesses, and individuals to buy goods made of recycled materials.

How can we encourage reuse and recycling? Proponents say that leveling the economic playing field is the best way to start. Governments can *increase* subsidies and tax breaks for reusing and recycling materials, and *decrease* subsidies and tax breaks for making items from virgin resources.

One way to include some of the harmful environmental costs of products in their prices, while encouraging recycling, is to attach a small deposit fee to the price of recyclable items, as is done in many European countries, several Canadian provinces, and 10 US states that have *bottle bills*. Such laws place a deposit fee of 5 or 10 cents on each beverage container, and consumers can recover that fee by returning their empty containers to the store. In 2015, these 10 states recycled at least 70% of their bottles and cans, compared to a 28% average in states with no bottle bills.

Another strategy is to greatly increase use of the fee-per-bag waste collection system that charges households for the trash they throw away but not for their recyclable and reusable wastes. When Fort Worth, Texas, instituted such a program, the proportion of households recycling their trash went from 21% to 85%. The city went from losing $600,000 in its recycling program to making $1 million a year because of increased sales of recycled materials to industries.

Governments can also pass laws requiring companies to take back and recycle or reuse packaging and electronic waste discarded by consumers. Japan and some European Union countries have such laws. Another strategy is to encourage or require government purchases of recycled products to help increase demand for and lower prices of these products.

Reuse and Recycling Present Economic Opportunities

A growing number of people are saving money through reuse, by going to yard sales, flea markets, secondhand stores, and online sites such as eBay and craigslist. Another such site, the Freecycle Network, links people who want to give away their unused household belongings to people who want or need them.

For many, recycling has become a business opportunity. In particular, *upcycling*, or recycling materials into products of a higher value (Figure 18.27), is a growing field. For example, a British company called Worn Again is converting discarded textiles, such as old hot-air balloons and worn-out seat covers, into windbreaker jackets and other products. Researcher Na Lu at the University of North Carolina, Charlotte, has found a way to upcycle plastic bottles to make a building material that could outperform composite lumber and wood lumber. Shipping pallets are being used too make furniture. Many see upcycling as an area of great economic opportunity.

Making the Transition to Low-Waste Economies

According to physicist Albert Einstein, "A clever person solves a problem; a wise person avoids it." Many people are taking these words seriously. Many school cafeterias, restaurants, national parks, and corporations are participating in a rapidly growing "zero waste" movement to reduce, reuse, and recycle, and some have lowered their waste outputs by up to 80%, with the ultimate goal of eliminating their waste outputs. Some are doing this by setting up circular industrial ecosystems that mimic the way nature converts wastes into resources (see Case Study that follows).

FIGURE 18.27 Upcycling. This handbag was made from an old airline seat.

Rebecca Hale/National Geographic Creative

Industrial Ecosystems: Copying Nature

An important goal for a more sustainable society is to make its industrial manufacturing processes cleaner and more sustainable by redesigning them to mimic the way nature deals with wastes—an approach called *biomimicry*. (Chapter 1, Individuals Matter 1.1, p. 10) In nature, according to the chemical cycling **principle of sustainability**, the waste outputs of one organism become the nutrient inputs of another organism, so that all of the earth's nutrients are endlessly recycled. This explains why there is essentially no waste in undisturbed ecosystems.

Biomimicry involves two major steps. The first is to study how natural systems have responded to changes in environmental conditions over many millions of years. The second step is to try to copy or adapt these responses within human systems in order to deal with various environmental challenges.

One way for industries to mimic nature is to reuse or recycle most of the minerals and chemicals they use. Industries can set up *resource exchange webs*, in which the wastes of one manufacturer become the raw materials for another, similar to food webs in natural ecosystems. and a direct application of the cradle-to-cradle concept (**Core Case Study**).

This is happening in Kalundborg, Denmark, where an electric power plant and nearby industries, farms, and homes are collaborating to save money and to reduce their outputs of waste and pollution within what is called an *ecoindustrial park*, or *industrial ecosystem*. They exchange waste outputs and convert them into resources, as shown in Figure 18.28. This cuts pollution and waste and reduces the flow of nonrenewable mineral and energy resources through the local economy.

Ecoindustrial parks provide many economic benefits for businesses. By encouraging recycling and waste reduction prevention, they reduce the costs of managing solid wastes, controlling pollution, and complying with pollution regulations. They also reduce a company's chances of being sued because of damages, to people or to the environment, caused by their actions. In addition, companies improve the health and safety of workers by reducing their exposure to toxic and hazardous materials, thereby reducing company health insurance costs. Biomimicry also encourages companies to come up with new, environmentally beneficial, and less resource-intensive chemicals, processes, and products that they can sell worldwide. Today, more than 100 such parks operate in various places around the world, including the United States and China, and more are being built or planned.

CONSIDER THIS . . .

LEARNING FROM NATURE

The food web serves as a natural model for responding to the growing problems of solid and hazardous wastes. The ecoindustrial park and many applications of cradle-to-cradle design and manufacturing (**Core Case Study**) follow this model.

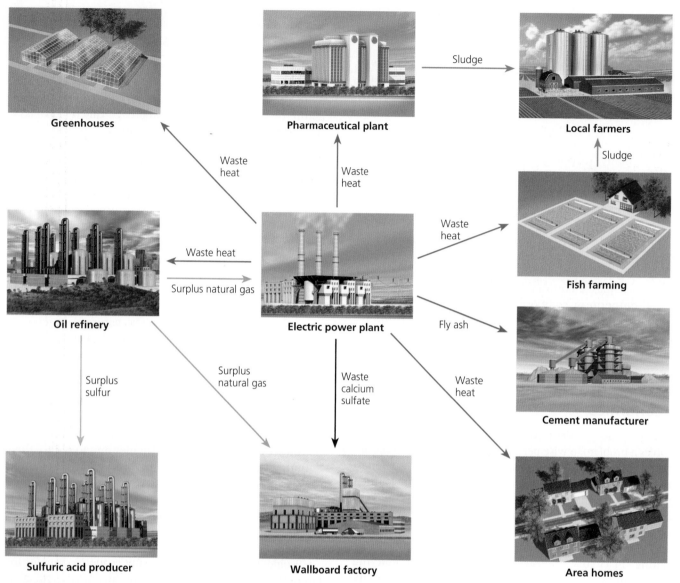

FIGURE 18.28 Solutions: This *industrial ecosystem* in Kalundborg, Denmark, reduces waste production by mimicking a natural ecosystem's food web. The wastes of one business become the raw materials for another, thus mimicking the way that nature recycles chemicals. **Question:** Is there an industrial ecosystem near where you live or go to school? If not, think about where and how such a system could be set up.

CHECKPOINT FOR UNDERSTANDING 18.6

1. What is the Stockholm Convention?
2. What is an industrial ecosystem?

Core Case Study Checkpoint

Explain how the cradle-to-cradle approach to materials use mimics how nature recycles nutrients.

KEY IDEAS

- The order of priorities for dealing with solid waste should be first to minimize production of it, then to reuse and recycle as much of it as possible, and finally to safely burn or bury what is left.

- The order of priorities for dealing with hazardous waste should be first to minimize production of it, to reuse or recycle it, to convert it to less-hazardous material, and to safely store what is left.

- We can view solid wastes as wasted resources, and hazardous wastes as materials that we want to avoid producing in the first place.

Chapter 18 Glossary

environmental justice: ideal whereby every person is entitled to protection from environmental hazards regardless of race, gender, age, national origin, income, social class, or any political factor

hazardous (toxic) waste: any liquid, solid, or containerized gas that can catch fire easily, is corrosive to skin tissue or metals, is unstable and can explode or release toxic fumes, or has harmful concentrations of one or more toxic materials that can leach out.

industrial solid waste: solid waste produced by mines, factories, refineries, food growers, and businesses that supply people with goods and services.

integrated waste management: variety of strategies for both waste reduction and waste management designed to deal with the waste we produce.

municipal solid waste (MSW): solid materials discarded by homes and businesses in or near urban areas.

open dump: fields or holes in the ground where garbage is deposited and sometimes covered with soil. They are rare in developed countries, but are widely used in developing countries.

primary recycling: process in which materials are recycled into new products of the same type—turning used aluminum cans into new aluminum cans, for example.

sanitary landfill: waste-disposal site on land in which waste is spread in thin layers, compacted, and covered with a fresh layer of clay or plastic foam each day.

secondary recycling: a process in which waste materials are converted into different products; for example, used tires can be shredded and turned into rubberized road surfacing.

solid waste: an unwanted or discarded material that is not a liquid or a gas.

waste management: managing wastes to reduce their environmental harm without seriously trying to reduce the amount of waste produced.

waste reduction: reducing the amount of waste produced; wastes that are produced are viewed as potential resources that can be reused, recycled, or composted.

Chapter Review

Core Case Study

1. Explain the concept of cradle-to-cradle design. Why is it a true form of biomimicry? List and briefly describe two strategies for employing it.

Section 18.1

2. (a) What are the two key concepts for this section? (b) Distinguish among **solid waste**, **industrial solid waste**, and **municipal solid waste (MSW)**, and give an example of each. (c) Summarize the types and sources of municipal solid waste generated in the United States and explain what happens to it. (d) What is **hazardous (toxic) waste**? (e) Explain how and why electronic waste (e-waste) has become a growing solid and hazardous waste problem.

Section 18.2

3. (a) What is the key concept for this section? (b) Distinguish among **waste management**, **waste reduction**, and **integrated waste management**. (c) Summarize the priorities that prominent scientists suggest we should use for dealing with solid waste and compare them to actual practices in the United States. (d) Distinguish among **refusing**, **reducing**, **reusing**, **recycling**, and **composting**. Why are the first three Rs preferred from an environmental standpoint?

(e) List six ways in which industries and communities can reduce resource use, waste, and pollution.

Section 18.3

4. (a) What is the key concept for this section? (b) Explain why refusing, reducing, reusing, and recycling are so important and give examples of each. (c) How has cradle-to-cradle design elevated reuse to a new level? What are two ways in which governments can encourage reuse? (d) List five ways to reuse various items. Give two examples of shared use.

5. (a) What is the difference between upcycling and downcycling? (b) Distinguish between **primary recycling** and **secondary recycling**. What are the three important steps of recycling? (c) Why is e-waste attractive for recycling? (d) What are some benefits of composting? (e) Summarize the process of mixed MSW recycling. (f) What is source separation and what are its benefits? (g) What are bioplastics? (h) What are the major advantages and disadvantages of recycling?

Section 18.4

6. (a) What is the key concept for this section? (b) What are the major advantages and disadvantages of using incinerators to burn solid and hazardous waste? (c) Distinguish between sanitary landfills and open

dumps. What are the major advantages and disadvantages of burying solid waste in sanitary landfills?

Section 18.5

7. (a) What is the key concept for this section? (b) What are the priorities that scientists suggest we should use in dealing with hazardous waste? (c) Summarize the problems involved in sending e-wastes to less-developed countries for recycling. (d) Describe three ways to detoxify hazardous wastes. (e) What is bioremediation? What is phytoremediation? (f) What are the major advantages and disadvantages of incinerating hazardous wastes? (g) What are the major advantages and disadvantages of using plasma gasification to detoxify hazardous wastes?

8. (a) What are the major advantages and disadvantages of storing liquid hazardous wastes in deep underground wells and in surface impoundments? (b) What is a secure hazardous waste landfill? (c) List four ways to reduce your output of hazardous waste. (d) Summarize the story of regulation of hazardous wastes in the United States.

Section 18.6

9. (a) What is the key concept for this section? (b) How has grassroots action led to improved solid and hazardous waste management in the United States? (c) Describe regulation of hazardous wastes at the global level through the Basel Convention and the treaty to control persistent organic pollutants (POPs). (d) Describe the purpose and effects of the US Resource Recovery Act (RCRA), Toxic Substances Control Act (TSCA), and Comprehensive, Environmental Response, Compensation, and Liability Act (CERCLA) in regulating hazardous waste production in the United States. (e) What are three factors that discourage recycling? What are three ways to encourage recycling and reuse? (f) Give three examples of how people are saving or making money through reuse, recycling, and composting. (g) What is an industrial ecosystem and what are its benefits?

10. What are this chapter's *three key ideas*?

_____

Note: Key terms are in bold type.

AP® Review Questions

1. Recycling aluminum cans reduces the amount of energy needed to produce new aluminum cans from raw materials by 95%. Calculate the number of aluminum cans that can be made from recycled aluminum by using the same amount of energy as is needed to make one can from raw materials.
   (A) 1
   (B) 2
   (C) 5
   (D) 10
   (E) 20

2. E-waste (electronic waste) is often labeled as material to be recycled and sent to undeveloped countries, where workers recover a small amount of valuable metals from the discarded e-waste. The remainder of the e-waste is then burned or dumped in landfills, where it releases toxic pollutants such as dioxins. The process allows the companies that do it to bypass the
   (A) Clean Air Act
   (B) Kyoto Protocol
   (C) International Basel Convention
   (D) Resource Conservation and Recovery Act
   (E) Non-Proliferation Treaty

3. By definition, hazardous wastes can have all of the following properties EXCEPT
   (A) flammability
   (B) corrosiveness
   (C) explosiveness
   (D) insolubility in water
   (E) disease-causing potential

4. One method to remove contaminants such as cesium-134 from surface soil would be
   (A) to use phytoremediation, allowing plants' roots to absorb toxins
   (B) to use a plasma arc torch to incinerate the toxins *in situ*
   (C) to create a surface impoundment with a liner to contain the wastes
   (D) by spraying the surface with a genetically engineered bacteria designed to decompose petroleum by-products
   (E) by burning the soil in a very hot incinerator and then returning it to the site

5. One of the primary concerns of the 12 POPs (persistent organic pollutants) such as dioxins or PCBs is that they
   (A) are soluble in water, causing large-scale problems
   (B) can be concentrated in the fatty tissues of organisms
   (C) are rarely found but very toxic
   (D) quickly break down into other more harmful pollutants
   (E) are found only in plants and disrupt photosynthesis

6. The majority of solid waste generated in the United States is in what form?
   (A) Solid matter produced by mines, farms, and industries that produce goods
   (B) Radioactive waste generated by nuclear power plants
   (C) Toxic waste such as car batteries, hospital medical waste, and industrial solvents
   (D) Solid matter such as food, yard wastes, plastics, and paper discarded by homes and businesses
   (E) E-waste from electronic devices such as televisions, computers, and cell phones

7. All of the following are considered to be benefits of recycling EXCEPT
   (A) reduction of the emission of greenhouse gases
   (B) reduction of energy used in obtaining and processing raw materials
   (C) protection of biodiversity
   (D) being the cheapest way to dispose of solid wastes
   (E) promotion of well-being among people who recycle

8. One of the keys to dealing with the problem of solid waste is waste reduction. Which of the following is a form of waste reduction?
   (A) Burying municipal solid waste (MSW) in a sanitary landfill
   (B) Incinerating MSW to produce electricity
   (C) Shipping e-waste to China for disposal
   (D) Separating out and composting yard waste
   (E) Dumping nontoxic waste offshore in the oceans

9. The phrase, "reduce, reuse, recycle" is a popular phrase in today's society. All of the following are means of reducing, reusing, and recycling EXCEPT
   (A) using e-mail or texting in place of conventional paper mail
   (B) reading newspapers and magazines online
   (C) buying products in bulk form whenever possible
   (D) utilizing disposable plastic in place of paper bags
   (E) donating or selling used items

10. One of the major disadvantages of recycling goods is that
    (A) landfill operators must charge more money for trash delivery because they are receiving less of it
    (B) approximately 55% of the trees cut down to make paper are saved when paper is recycled
    (C) marine mammals and sea turtles mistake floating plastic for food or get caught in it
    (D) energy is saved and less pollution is produced when we recycle than when raw materials are removed from the earth
    (E) recycling may cost more than burying trash in landfills in areas with ample space

11. The majority of municipal solid waste (MSW) in the United States is composed of
    (A) plastic
    (B) paper
    (C) metal
    (D) glass
    (E) yard waste

Question 12 refers to the diagram of the structure of a municipal landfill below.

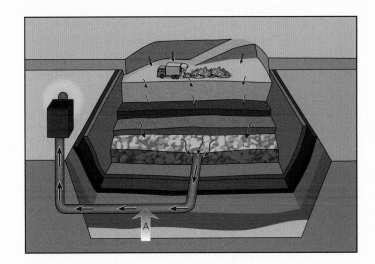

12. The function of the segment in the diagram where arrow A is pointing is to
    (A) collect and remove methane gas
    (B) incinerate the flammable portions of the MSW
    (C) collect and remove leachate
    (D) compact MSW so that it takes up as little volume as possible
    (E) remove hazardous waste from MSW

13. Leachate from a municipal waste sanitary landfill is often pretreated before it can enter a wastewater treatment plant because
    I. The nutrient content is too high.
    II. It contains radioactive materials that will destroy bacteria colonies at the wastewater treatment plant.
    III. It contains floating and insoluble MSW products.
    (A) I only
    (B) II only
    (C) III only
    (D) I and III only
    (E) I, II, and III

14. Many environmental scientists advocate that the best and cheapest way to deal with solid waste is to
    (A) transport the waste to landfills and bury it
    (B) reduce the amount of waste produced in the first place
    (C) incinerate the waste to generate electricity
    (D) establish grassroots organizations advocating for fewer landfills
    (E) pass more laws and treaties with tighter controls on emissions of pollutants

15. Brownfields are areas of concern to environmentalists. Which of the following best describes an area classified as a brownfield?
    (A) A mine for mineral resources that are found on the leeward sides of mountains
    (B) A processing facility where hazardous wastes are taken to be detoxified
    (C) A deep underground well where liquid hazardous wastes are injected and stored
    (D) An agricultural area that has turned brown due to lack of rain, or disease
    (E) An abandoned industrial site that has soil, water, or air pollution

16. Integrated waste management (IWM) is a technique used by communities to provide ways of dealing with municipal solid waste. All of the following are components of IWM EXCEPT
    (A) burying all materials in sanitary landfills
    (B) reusing waste products
    (C) incinerating waste that is suitable for incineration
    (D) providing composting areas for yard wastes
    (E) recycling waste products

17. Like all means of waste disposal, deep-well injection of hazardous waste has both advantages and disadvantages. Which of the following is a disadvantage of deep-well injection?
    (A) It is not suitable in any environment.
    (B) It is very expensive.
    (C) It often releases chlorine and hydrogen gas.
    (D) Well casings can leak.
    (E) It often causes toxic runoff.

Questions 18–20 refer to the diagram below.

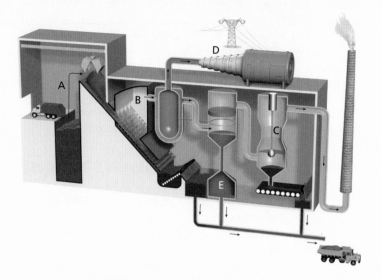

18. What is the primary concern of most people when a trash incinerator is proposed to be built in their neighborhood?
    (A) Air pollution from the incinerator
    (B) The use of waste ash in products such as road construction materials or cement blocks
    (C) People producing more trash because incinerators require a large amount of trash to be profitable
    (D) The initial cost of building an incinerator
    (E) The disposal of tires and other products that cannot be incinerated

19. What is the function of the part of the diagram labeled "D"?
    (A) Incinerate the trash
    (B) House the control rods
    (C) Cool the plant to prevent contamination
    (D) Generate electricity
    (E) Receive waste for the plant

20. What is the most likely method used to dispose of the leftover ash from the incinerator in this diagram?
    (A) It is spread on agricultural fields as fertilizer
    (B) It is composted and returned to the environment
    (C) It is transported to a Superfund site for disposal
    (D) It is dumped in the ocean
    (E) It is transported to a sanitary landfill

1. Hazardous waste can be generated as a by-product of common manufacturing and industrial processes. It can also be discarded commercial products or products in your home. Hazardous wastes are those that exhibit any one or more of the following characteristics: ignitability, corrosivity, reactivity, or toxicity.

   (a) Hydraulic fracturing, or "fracking," used in drilling for natural gas produces hazardous waste.

      (i) **Identify** and **describe** ONE method of disposing of hazardous wastewater from fracking.

      (ii) **Identify** and **discuss** ONE potential environmental drawback of this method of disposal.

   (b) Another method of dealing with hazardous waste is detoxification. **Identify** and **describe** TWO methods of detoxifying hazardous waste.

   (c) Many commercial products used in the home are considered hazardous. **Identify** ONE household product that would be considered hazardous, and **describe** ONE means of reducing the negative impact of using or disposing of this product.

   (d) **Identify** and **describe** ONE law that deals with hazardous waste.

Critical Thinking

1. Find three products that you regularly use that could be made using cradle-to-cradle design and manufacturing (**Core Case Study**). For each of these products, sketch out a rough plan for how you would design and build it so that its parts could be reused many times or recycled in such a way that they would not harm the environment.

2. Do you think that manufacturers of computers, television sets, cell phones, and other electronic products should be required to take their products back at the end of their useful lives for repair, remanufacture, or recycling in a manner that is environmentally responsible and that does not threaten the health of recycling workers? Explain. Would you be willing to pay more for these products to cover the costs of such a take-back program? If so, what percentage more per purchase would you be willing to pay for these products?

3. Think of three items that you regularly use once and then throw away. Are there reusable items that you could use in place of these disposable items? For each item, calculate and compare the cost of using the disposable option for a year versus the cost of using the reusable alternative. Write a brief report summarizing your findings.

4. Do you think that you could consume less by refusing to buy some of the things you regularly buy? If so, what are three of those things? Do you think that this is something you ought to do? Explain.

5. A company called Changing World Technologies has built a pilot plant to test a process it has developed for converting a mixture of discarded computers, old tires, turkey bones and feathers, and other wastes into oil by mimicking and speeding up natural processes for converting biomass into oil. Explain how this recycling process, if it turns out to be technologically and economically feasible, could lead to increased waste production.

6. Would you oppose having (a) a sanitary landfill, (b) a hazardous waste surface impoundment, (c) a hazardous waste deep-injection well, or (d) a solid waste incinerator in your community? For each of these facilities, explain your answer. If you oppose having such facilities in your community, how do you think the solid and hazardous wastes generated in your community should be managed?

7. How does your school dispose of its solid and hazardous wastes? Does it have a recycling program? How well does it work? Does your school encourage reuse? If so, how? Does it have a hazardous waste collection system? If so, describe it. List three ways in which you would improve your school's waste reduction and management systems.

8. Congratulations! You are in charge of the world. List the three most important components of your strategy for dealing with (a) solid waste and (b) hazardous waste.

Researchers estimate that the average daily municipal solid waste production per person in the United States is 2 kilograms (4.4 pounds). Use the data in the pie chart below to get an idea of a typical annual MSW ecological footprint for each American by calculating the total weight in kilograms (and pounds) for each category generated during 1 year (1 kilogram = 2.20 pounds). Use the table (next page, right) to enter your answers.

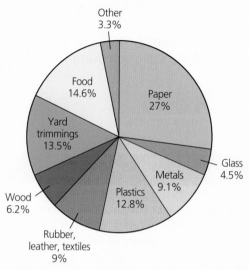

Waste Category	Annual MSW Footprint per Person
Paper and paperboard	
Yard trimmings	
Food scraps	
Plastics	
Metals	
Wood	
Rubber, leather, and textiles	
Glass	
Other/miscellaneous	

Composition of a typical sample of US municipal solid waste, 2013.

(Compiled by the authors using data from the US Environmental Protection Agency.)

Source: BBC

Answers to Checkpoints for Understanding

Section 18.1

1. Trash deposited in a landfill is tightly packed and protected from sunlight, water, air, and bacteria that could degrade the biodegradable materials.
2. The two main classes of hazardous wastes are organic compounds such as solvents, pesticides, PCBs, and dioxin, and toxic heavy metals such as lead, mercury, and arsenic.
3. e-waste is discarded electronics such as cell phones, computers, televisions, and other electronics.

Section 18.2

1. Integrated waste management combines strategies of waste management and waste reduction—keeping waste from degrading ecosystems, reducing the amount of waste produced, and reusing, recycling, and composting the waste that is produced.
2. Strategies to reduce waste include: changing industrial processes to reduce or eliminate the use of toxic chemicals; redesigning manufacturing products and processes to use less material and energy; developing products that are easy to repair, reuse, remanufacture, compost or recycle; establishing cradle-to-grave responsibility laws; reducing or eliminating unnecessary packaging, and using fee-per-bag solid waste collection systems.

Section 18.3

1. Upcycling converts items into goods that are more useful than the original item. Downcycling converts an item into a product that is less useful than the original item.
2. Composting allows organic waste to decompose into the basic elements that plants require so that the nutrients may be used by plants. One product (food waste) is converted into another useful product (plant nutrients).
3. Materials recovery facilities (MRFs) separate mixed waste and recover valuable materials and recyclables. The remaining waste is incinerated to produce electricity which produces air pollution, produces a toxic ash that must be disposed of, and requires a steady input of waste to remain viable. Because of the constant need for trash, production of waste is not discouraged.

Section 18.4

1. Advantages of waste-to-energy incineration include reduction of trash volume, generation of electricity, concentration of hazardous substances for proper disposal, and reduced cost of energy.

2. Drawbacks of waste-to-energy incineration include the cost of building incineration facilities, production of hazardous waste that must be properly disposed of, CO_2 and other air pollutants emitted, and encourages waste production to justify the cost of building and operating an incineration facility.

3. Advantages of sanitary landfills include low operating cost, the ability to handle large amounts of waste, filled and capped landfills can be used for other purposes, and there is plenty of available land for future landfills.

4. Disadvantages of sanitary landfills include noise, traffic, and dust from trucks and machinery at the site, releases methane and CO_2 unless the gases are collected, encourages consumer output of waste, and eventually landfills leak and can contaminate groundwater.

Section 18.5

1. Most e-waste is sent to other countries such as China and India where low-paid workers, including children, dismantle electronic trash to recover gold, lead, silver, and copper using toxic chemicals and other methods that expose them to lead poisoning, and toxic fumes from burning or melting electronic components.

2. Hazardous waste can be detoxified via bioremediation, chemical methods, physical methods, incineration, and plasma gasification.

3. The EPA Toxic Release Inventory is a list of toxic chemicals and hazardous waste generated by industry that can be found in communities across the United States.

Section 18.6

1. The Stockholm Convention is a global treaty between 122 countries that regulates 12 highly toxic Persistent Organic Pollutants (the dirty dozen) that can accumulate in the fatty tissue of humans and animals. Chemicals include DDT, dioxin, and PCBs.

2. An industrial ecosystem is a group of industries, farms, and homes where the waste of one becomes the resources for another, mimicking a food web in nature.

Core Case Study

The cradle-to-cradle approach phases out toxic substances as a part of products, and changes the approach to manufacturing so that as products wear out, they are cycled back into the manufacturing system as raw material for more products. Nature continuously recycles nutrients, and waste is a resource for organisms somewhere within the ongoing cycle.

Air Pollution and Ozone Depletion

The atmosphere is the key symbol of global interdependence. If we can't solve some of our problems in the face of threats to this global commons, then I can't be very optimistic about the future of the world.

MARGARET MEAD

Air pollution has become a major health threat, especially in many growing cities such as Beijing, China.

testing/Shutterstock.com

Key Questions

Los Angeles Air Pollution

In the 1950s, Los Angeles, California (USA), had some of the dirtiest air in the world. Steel and chemical plants, oil refineries, factories, and backyard trash incinerators all pumped smoke and chemicals into the air, creating a dangerous mix of pollutants. More than 2 million motor vehicles also belched pollutants every day.

This problem had been growing since the 1940s as the city grew rapidly. By 1950, the dirty air was threatening tourism and real estate values. The city's leaders grew concerned and in 1947, Los Angeles (LA) established the nation's first air-pollution-control district.

By the mid-1950s, scientists had found strong evidence that motor vehicle emissions, when exposed to sunlight, were creating *photochemical smog*—an unhealthy mix of ozone and other chemicals that threatened human health. People began to realize the dangers of air pollution, powerfully symbolized by smog, which was visible and ugly. Concerned parents kept their children home from school on especially bad days, and athletic events were often canceled. Visits to doctors multiplied, and doctors hypothesized possible connections between air pollution and heart disease, respiratory ailments, and lung cancer.

As the science became clearer, public protests became frequent. People showed up wearing gas masks, which became a symbol of LA's pollution woes. Through the 1950s and 1960s, protesters organized anti-smog groups and these grassroots efforts spread across California and beyond, focusing their attention on lawmakers. By the early 1960s, citizens were demanding smog control devices on cars along with other measures to control air pollution. Automakers dragged their feet in response. In 1969, the federal government got involved, taking the car companies to court for working together to delay such technology.

Mounting air pollution problems in LA and across the country, along with a growing public outcry, finally caused the US Congress to pass the Clean Air Act of 1970. This far-reaching law put strict limits on pollution from cars, diesel engines, and coal-burning facilities, forcing automakers and other industries to take measures to control pollution.

Such measures have paid off in the form of cleaner air all over the United States, even while the country's population has grown by 58% since 1970. In LA, ozone levels are now 40% lower than those that existed in 1970, even though the number of cars there has more than doubled. Since 2000, LA has reduced its *fine particle*, or soot, pollution by half. However, LA's smog problem is still among the worst of all US cities (Figure 19.1), according to the American Lung Association. Most observers agree that LA has made great progress, but still has a long way to go in cleaning up its air.

The story of LA air pollution and efforts to deal with it reflects the story of air pollution in general, at least in more-developed countries. In this chapter, we examine that story, as well as the facts about air pollution in less-developed countries—a problem that is no less challenging. ●

CRITICAL THINKING

Citizens tend to downplay the dangers of air pollution while perceiving the negative impacts of oil spills and toxic waste dumps as more dangerous. Why do you think that is?

FIGURE 19.1 Los Angeles, California, on a smoggy day. Despite major improvements in air quality, the city still sees smoggy days like this one.

iStockphoto.com/Lee Pettet

19.1 WHAT IS THE NATURE OF THE ATMOSPHERE?

CONCEPT 19.1 The two innermost layers of the atmosphere are the *troposphere*, which supports life, and the *stratosphere*, which contains the protective ozone layer.

The Atmosphere Consists of Several Layers

Life exists under a thin blanket of gases surrounding the earth, called the **atmosphere.** It is divided into several spherical layers defined mostly by temperature differences (Figure 19.2). Our focus in this book is on the atmosphere's two innermost layers: the troposphere and the stratosphere (**Concept 19.1**).

An important atmospheric variable is *density*, the number of gas molecules per unit of air volume. It varies throughout the atmosphere because gravity pulls harder on gas molecules near the earth's surface than it does on

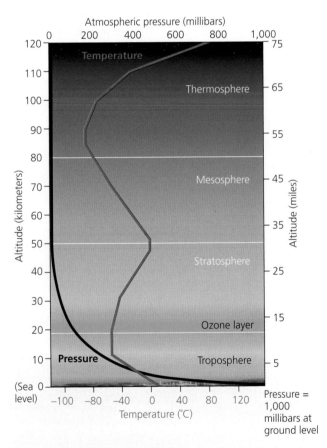

FIGURE 19.2 Natural capital: The earth's atmosphere is a dynamic system that includes four layers. The average temperature of the atmosphere varies with altitude (red line) and with differences in the absorption of incoming solar energy. **Critical thinking:** Why do you think most of the planet's air is in the troposphere?

molecules high up in the atmosphere. This means that lower layers have more gases (more weight) in them than upper layers do, and are more densely packed with molecules. Thus, the air we breathe at sea level has a higher density than the air we would inhale on top of a high mountain.

Another important atmospheric variable is *atmospheric pressure*—the force, or mass, per unit area of a column of air. This force is caused by the continuous bombardment of a surface such as your skin by the molecules in air. Atmospheric pressure varies with density. It decreases with altitude (see black line in Figure 19.2) because there are fewer gas molecules at higher altitudes. The density and pressure of the atmosphere are important because they play major roles in the weather.

Air Movements and Chemicals in the Troposphere Affect the Earth's Weather and Climate

About 75–80% of the earth's air mass is found in the **troposphere,** the atmospheric layer closest to the earth's surface. This layer extends about 17 kilometers (11 miles) above sea level at the equator and 6 kilometers (4 miles) above sea level over the poles. If the earth were the size of an apple, this lower layer containing the air we breathe would be no thicker than the apple's skin.

Take a deep breath. About 99% of the volume of air you inhaled consists of two gases: nitrogen (78%) and oxygen (21%). The remainder is 0.93% argon (Ar), 0.040% carbon dioxide (CO_2), and smaller amounts of water vapor, dust and soot particles, and other gases, including methane (CH_4), ozone (O_3), and nitrous oxide (N_2O).

Several gases in the troposphere, including H_2O, CO_2, CH_4, and N_2O, are called **greenhouse gases** because they absorb and release energy that warms the troposphere and the earth's surface. Without this natural greenhouse effect, the earth would be too cold for life as we know it to exist. Rising and falling air currents, winds, and concentrations of CO_2 and other greenhouse gases in the troposphere play major roles in the planet's short-term *weather* and long-term *climate*.

The Stratosphere Is Our Global Sunscreen

The atmosphere's second layer is the **stratosphere,** which extends from about 17 to about 48 kilometers (from 11 to 30 miles) above the earth's surface (Figure 19.2). Although the stratosphere contains less matter than the troposphere, its chemical composition is similar, with two notable exceptions. The stratosphere has a much lower volume of water vapor and a much higher concentration of ozone.

Most of the atmosphere's ozone is concentrated in a portion of the stratosphere called the **ozone layer,** found roughly 17–26 kilometers (11–16 miles) above sea level. Most of the ozone in this layer is produced when oxygen molecules interact with ultraviolet (UV) radiation emitted by the sun.

$$3O_2 + UV \rightleftharpoons 2O_3$$

This UV filtering effect of ozone in the lower stratosphere acts as a "global sunscreen" that keeps about 95% of the sun's harmful UV radiation from reaching the earth's surface. The ozone layer allows life to exist on land and helps to protect us from sunburn, skin and eye cancers, cataracts, and damage to our immune systems. It also prevents much of the oxygen in the troposphere from being converted to ground-level ozone, a harmful air pollutant. In other words, preserving the stratospheric ozone layer should be one of humanity's top priorities.

CHECKPOINT FOR UNDERSTANDING 19.1

1. Explain why air is most dense in the troposphere.

2. Identify the major compositional difference between the troposphere and the stratosphere.

3. Describe the role of the ozone layer.

19.2 WHAT ARE THE MAJOR OUTDOOR AIR POLLUTION PROBLEMS?

CONCEPT 19.2 Pollutants mix in the air to form harmful *industrial smog,* caused mostly by the burning of coal, and *photochemical smog,* caused by emissions from motor vehicles, industrial facilities, and power plants.

Air Pollution Comes from Natural and Human Sources

Air pollution is the presence of chemicals in the atmosphere in concentrations high enough to harm organisms, ecosystems, or human-made materials, or to alter climate. Almost any chemical in the atmosphere can become a pollutant if it occurs in a high enough concentration. The effects of air pollution range from annoying to lethal.

Air pollutants come from natural and human sources. Natural sources include wind-blown dust, solid and gaseous pollutants from wildfires and volcanic eruptions, and volatile organic chemicals released by some plants. Most natural air pollutants are spread out over the globe and become diluted or are removed by chemical cycles, precipitation,

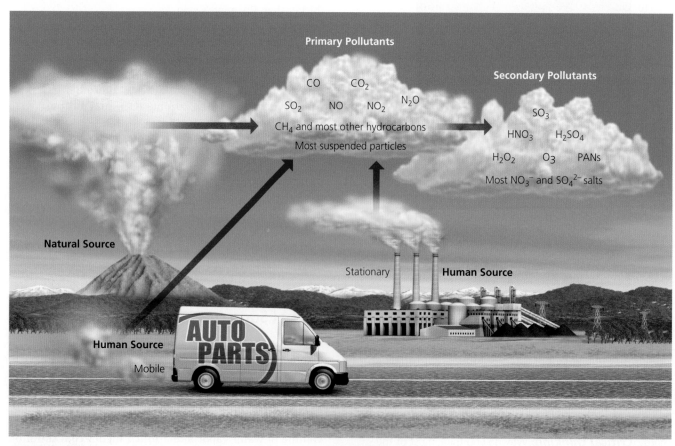

FIGURE 19.3 Human inputs of air pollutants come from *mobile sources* (such as cars) and *stationary sources* (such as industrial, power, and cement plants). Some *primary air pollutants* react with one another and with other chemicals in the air to form *secondary air pollutants.*

The Atmospheric Brown Clouds

Air pollution is no longer viewed as primarily a localized urban problem. Annual satellite images and studies by the United Nations Environment Programme (UNEP) have found massive, dark brown clouds of pollution—called *atmospheric brown clouds*. They stretch across much of India, Bangladesh, and the industrial heart of China, as well as parts of the western Pacific Ocean (Figure 19.A).

In most years, these clouds cover an area about the size of the continental United States. They contain small particles of dust, smoke, and ash resulting from wind erosion due to drought and from the clearing and burning of forests for planting crops. They also contain particles of soot, or *black carbon*, and of toxic metals such as mercury and lead. These various particles enter the atmosphere from wildfires, the burning of wood and animal dung for heat and cooking, diesel engine exhaust, motor vehicle exhaust, ocean ships burning heavy oil, coal-burning power and industrial plants, metal smelters, and waste incinerators.

These enormous pollution clouds can move across the Asian continent within 3–4 days. Satellites have tracked the spread of pollutants from the atmospheric brown clouds over northern China across the Pacific Ocean to the West Coast of the United States. Measurements made by atmospheric scientists show that large portions of the particulate matter, soot, and toxic mercury in the skies above Los Angeles, California (**Core Case Study**), can be traced to China.

Researchers have estimated that the atmospheric brown clouds are directly linked to the deaths of more than 380,000 people a year in China and India. They also affect global weather patterns.

Long-term studies on other effects of the brown clouds were carried out by an international team of scientists led by V. Ramanathan of the Scripps Institution of Oceanography. Their findings include decreases in the summer monsoon rainfall in some areas, a north–south shift in rainfall patterns in eastern China, accelerated melting of Himalayan glaciers that feed major Asian rivers, and increased levels of harmful ozone in the lower atmosphere in many areas. These effects have helped reduce water supplies and crop yields and have damaged human health.

The researchers also found that soot and some of the other particles that fall onto Himalayan glaciers from the atmospheric brown clouds absorb sunlight and heat the air above those glaciers. This soot also decreases the ability of the glaciers to reflect sunlight back into space. The glaciers then absorb more solar energy and experience increased melting. This adds to the warming of the air above them, which in turn further increases the rate of glacial melting in a runaway positive feedback cycle (see Figure 2.15, p. 52). The researchers projected that at the current rate of melting, the Himalayan glaciers could shrink by as much as 75% before 2050, which would pose "a grave danger to the region's water security."

CRITICAL THINKING

The Asian economy has provided much of the world, including the United States, with massive amounts of goods in recent decades, which is part of the reason for the industrial pollution in the atmospheric brown clouds. Do you think this means that countries outside of Asia should contribute financial and other resources to help deal with this problem? Explain.

FIGURE 19.A Severe air pollution from the atmospheric brown cloud in Shanghai, China.

JUSTIN GUARIGLIA/National Geographic Creative

and gravity. However, pollutants emitted by volcanic eruptions and forest fires can temporarily reach harmful levels.

Most human inputs of outdoor air pollutants (Figure 19.3) occur in industrialized and urban areas where people, cars, and factories are concentrated. These pollutants are generated mostly by the burning of fossil fuels in power plants and industrial facilities (*stationary sources*) and in motor vehicles (*mobile sources*).

Scientists classify outdoor air pollutants into two categories. **Primary pollutants** (Figure 19.3, center) are chemicals or substances emitted directly into the air from natural processes and human activities at concentrations high enough to cause harm. While in the atmosphere, some primary pollutants react with one another and with other natural components of air to form new harmful chemicals, called **secondary pollutants** (Figure 19.3, right).

With their high concentrations of cars and factories, urban areas normally have higher outdoor air pollution levels (**Core Case Study**) than rural areas have. However, prevailing winds can spread long-lived primary and secondary air pollutants from urban and industrial areas to the countryside and to other urban areas. Long-lived pollutants entering the atmosphere in India and China now find their way across the Pacific where they affect the West

Coast of North America (Science Focus 19.1). In fact, satellite measurements show that long-lived air pollutants from anywhere on the planet can circle the entire globe in about two weeks.

Air Pollution Has Harmful Effects

Air pollution connects us all and has affected every place on the planet's surface. Even in arctic regions where very few people live, air pollutants flowing north from Europe, Asia, and North America collect to form *arctic haze*.

Since the 1970s, the quality of outdoor air in most of the more-developed countries has improved, thanks largely to grassroots pressure from citizens in the 1960s and 1970s. This led the governments of the United States and of most European countries to pass and enforce air-pollution-control laws (**Core Case Study**).

Beyond the United States, air pollution is one of the world's most serious environmental problems. According to the World Health Organization, 92% of the world's people breathed outdoor air that it classified as unhealthy for at least part of the year in 2015. The WHO estimated that outdoor and indoor air pollution contributed to the deaths of 7 million people in 2015.

Major Outdoor Air Pollutants

Hundreds of different chemicals and substances can pollute outdoor air. Here we focus on six major groups of air pollutants.

Carbon Oxides. *Carbon monoxide* (CO) is a colorless, odorless, and highly toxic gas that forms during the incomplete combustion of carbon-containing materials (Table 19.1). Major sources are motor vehicle exhaust, the burning of forests and grasslands, the smokestacks of fossil fuel–burning power plants and industries, tobacco smoke, and open fires and inefficient stoves used for cooking or heating.

In the body, CO can combine with hemoglobin in red blood cells, which reduces the ability of blood to transport oxygen to body cells and tissues. Long-term exposure can trigger heart attacks and aggravate lung diseases such as asthma and emphysema. At high levels, CO can cause headache, nausea, drowsiness, confusion, collapse, coma, and death, which is why it is important to have CO detectors in your home.

Carbon dioxide (CO_2) is a colorless, odorless gas. About 93% of the CO_2 in the atmosphere is the result of the natural carbon cycle (see Figure 3.15, p. 78). The rest comes from human activities such as the burning of fossil fuels, which adds CO_2 to the atmosphere, and the removal of forests and grasslands that help remove excess CO_2 from the atmosphere. Carbon dioxide is classified as an air pollutant because it has reached high enough levels in the atmosphere to warm the earth's atmosphere and bring about climate change, which can affect human health. However, there is political pressure by the US fossil fuel industry to reverse the EPA ruling that CO_2 is an air pollutant, despite overwhelming scientific evidence that it is.

TABLE 19.1 Chemical Reactions that Form Major Air Pollutants

Pollutant	Chemical Reaction
Carbon monoxide (CO)	$2C + O_2 \rightarrow 2CO$
Carbon dioxide (CO_2)	$C + O_2 \rightarrow CO_2$
Nitric oxide (NO)	$N_2 + O_2 \rightarrow 2NO$
Nitrogen dioxide (NO_2)	$2NO + O_2 \rightarrow 2NO_2$
Sulfur dioxide (SO_2)	$S + O_2 \rightarrow SO_2$

Nitrogen Oxides and Nitric Acid. *Nitric oxide* (NO) is a colorless gas that forms when nitrogen and oxygen gases react under high temperatures in automobile engines and coal-burning power and industrial plants (Table 19.1). Lightning and certain bacteria in soil and water also produce NO as part of the nitrogen cycle (see Figure 3.16, p. 79).

In the air, NO reacts with oxygen to form *nitrogen dioxide* (NO_2), a reddish-brown gas. Collectively, NO and NO_2 are called *nitrogen oxides* (NO_x). Some of the NO_2 reacts with water vapor in the air to form *nitric acid* (HNO_3) and nitrate salts (NO_3^-), components of harmful *acid deposition*, which we discuss later in this chapter. Both NO and NO_2 play a role in the formation of *photochemical smog*—a mixture of chemicals formed under the influence of sunlight in cities with heavy traffic (**Core Case Study**). Nitrous oxide (N_2O), a greenhouse gas, is emitted from fertilizers and animal wastes and is produced by the burning of fossil fuels.

At high enough levels, nitrogen oxides can irritate the eyes, nose, and throat, and aggravate lung ailments such as asthma and bronchitis. They can also suppress plant growth, and reduce visibility when they are converted to nitric acid and nitrate salts.

Sulfur Dioxide and Sulfuric Acid. Sulfur dioxide (SO_2) is a colorless gas with an irritating odor. About one-third of the SO_2 in the atmosphere comes from natural sources such as volcanoes. The other two-thirds (and as much as 90% in highly industrialized urban areas) comes from human sources, mostly combustion of sulfur-containing coal in power and industrial plants (Table 19.1), oil refining, and the smelting of sulfide ores.

FIGURE 19.4 Sulfuric acid and other air pollutants have damaged this statue in Rome, Italy. The nose and part of the forehead have been restored.

FIGURE 19.5 Severe air pollution from an iron and steel factory in Czechoslovakia.

In the atmosphere, SO_2 can be converted to *aerosols*, which consist of microscopic suspended droplets of sulfuric acid (H_2SO_4) and suspended particles of sulfate (SO_4^{2-}) salts that return to the earth as a component of acid deposition. Sulfur dioxide, sulfuric acid droplets, and sulfate particles reduce visibility and aggravate breathing problems. They can damage crops, trees, soils, and aquatic life in lakes. They also corrode metals and damage paint, paper, leather, and the stone used to build walls, statues (Figure 19.4), and monuments.

Particulates. *Suspended particulate matter* (SPM) consists of a variety of solid particles and liquid droplets that are small and light enough to remain suspended in the air for long periods. The US Environmental Protection Agency (EPA) classifies particles as fine, or PM-10 (with diameters less than 10 micrometers, or less than one-fifth the diameter of a human hair); and ultrafine, or PM-2.5 (with diameters less than 2.5 micrometers). About 62% of the SPM in outdoor air comes from natural sources such as dust, wildfires, and sea salt. The other 38% comes from human sources such as coal-burning power and industrial plants (Figure 19.5), motor vehicles, wind erosion from exposed topsoil, and road construction. The EPA has found that fine particles can travel thousands of kilometers in the at-mosphere, while ultrafine particles have been shown to travel for up to 10 kilometers (6 miles) from their sources.

These particles can irritate the nose and throat, damage the lungs, aggravate asthma and bronchitis, and shorten life spans. Toxic particulates such as lead (see the Case Study that follows), cadmium, and polychlorinated biphenyls (PCBs) can cause genetic mutations, reproductive problems, and cancer. Particulates also reduce visibility, corrode metals, and discolor clothing and paints.

Ozone. A major ingredient of photochemical smog is *ozone* (O_3), a highly reactive gas. It can cause coughing and breathing problems, aggravate lung and heart diseases, reduce resistance to colds and pneumonia, and irritate the eyes, nose, and throat. Ozone also damages plants, rubber in tires, fabrics, and paints.

Ozone in the troposphere near ground level can be harmful at high enough levels, whereas ozone in the stratosphere is beneficial because it protects us from harmful UV radiation. Extensive measurements indicate that human activities have *decreased* the amount of beneficial ozone in the stratosphere and *increased* the amount of harmful ground-level ozone—especially in some urban areas. Harmful ozone in the troposphere is a greenhouse gas that contributes to atmospheric warming and climate change. It also reduces photosynthesis by trees, thus contributing to atmospheric warming by reducing the amount of excess CO_2 that trees remove from the troposphere. We examine the issue of decreased stratospheric ozone in the final section of this chapter.

Volatile Organic Compounds (VOCs). Organic compounds that exist as gases in the atmosphere or that evaporate from sources on the earth's surface into the atmosphere are called *volatile organic compounds* (VOCs). Examples are hydrocarbons, emitted by the leaves of many plants, and methane (CH_4), a greenhouse gas that is 25 times more effective per molecule than CO_2 is at warming the atmosphere. About a third of global methane emissions come from natural sources such as plants, wetlands, and termites. The rest come from human sources such as rice paddies, landfills, natural gas wells and pipelines, and from cows (mostly from their belching) raised for meat and dairy production.

Other VOCs are liquids than can evaporate quickly into the atmosphere. Examples are benzene and other industrial solvents, dry-cleaning fluids, and various components of gasoline, plastics, and other products.

An important priority for many public health officials and scientists is to continually improve the monitoring of outdoor air for the presence of dangerous pollutants.

CASE STUDY

Lead Is a Highly Toxic Pollutant

Lead (Pb) is a soft gray metal used to make various products including lead–acid batteries and bullets, and it was once a common ingredient of gasoline and paints. It is also a particulate pollutant found in air, water, soil, plants, and animals.

Because it is a chemical element, lead does not break down in the environment. This indestructible and potent neurotoxin can harm the nervous system, especially in young children. Severe lead poisoning can leave children to suffer from palsy, partial paralysis, blindness, and mental retardation.

Children under age 6 and unborn fetuses, even with low blood levels of lead, are especially vulnerable to nervous system impairment, lowered IQ (by 2–5 points), shortened attention span, hyperactivity, hearing damage, and various behavior disorders. According to many scientists, there is no safe level of lead in children's blood and they call for sharply reducing the currently allowed levels for lead in the air and water.

Since the 1970s, according to the US Centers for Disease Control and Prevention (CDC), the percentage of US children under age 6 with blood lead levels above the safety standard dropped from 85% to less than 1%, which prevented at least 9 million childhood lead poisonings. The primary reason for this drop was that after a decade-long fight with the oil and lead industries, the federal government banned leaded gasoline in 1976. Leaded gasoline was completely phased out by 1986. The government also greatly reduced the allowable levels of lead in paints. This is an excellent example of the effectiveness of pollution prevention.

However, in 2012, the CDC used the latest scientific data to come up with new guidelines for identifying children who have potentially dangerous blood lead levels. These guidelines more than doubled the estimated number of young children at risk from lead poisoning in the United States, raising it to about 535,000. The major source of exposure is peeling lead-based paint and lead-contaminated dust in some 4 million older US homes. Children can inhale or ingest paint particles from these sources when they put dust-covered hands or toys into their mouths. Another source is soils contaminated with lead emitted by motor vehicles before leaded gasoline was banned. Lead can also leach from water pipes and faucets containing lead parts or lead solder (see Chapter 17, Case Study, pp. 545–546). Other sources are older coal-burning power plants that have not been required to meet the emission standards of new plants, as well as lead smelters and waste incinerators.

CONSIDER THIS . . .

CONNECTIONS Lead and Urban Gardening

Health officials and scientists have urged people who plant urban vegetable gardens to have their garden soils tested for lead. For decades, lead particles fell from the air into urban soils, primarily from the exhaust fumes of vehicles burning leaded gasoline. Soil found to have lead in it can be treated or removed from urban gardens and replaced with uncontaminated soil.

Although the threat from lead has been greatly reduced in the United States, this is not the case in many less-developed countries. Children and adults in China and several African countries are exposed to dangerous levels of lead when they work in recycling centers extracting lead and other valuable metals from electronic waste (e-waste)—discarded computers, TV sets, cellphones, and other electronic devices. Much of this e-waste is shipped to such unsafe recycling centers from the United States and other more-developed countries.

The WHO reported in 2015 that globally, lead exposure accounts for about 143,000 deaths and about 600,000 cases of children with intellectual disabilities per year, mostly in less-developed countries. Health scientists have proposed a number of ways to help protect children from lead poisoning (Figure 19.6).

Burning Coal Produces Industrial Smog

Seventy-five years ago, cities such as London, England, and the US cities of Chicago, Illinois, and Pittsburgh, Pennsylvania, burned large amounts of coal in power plants and factories. They also burned coal to heat homes and often to cook food. People in such cities, especially during winter, were exposed to **industrial smog,** consisting mostly of an unhealthy mix of sulfur dioxide (SO_2), suspended droplets of sulfuric acid, and a variety of suspended solid particles in outside air (**Concept 19.2**). Those who burned coal inside their homes were often exposed to dangerous levels of indoor air pollutants.

When coal or oil is burned, the sulfur compounds they contain react with oxygen to produce SO_2 gas (Figure 19.7, left),

FIGURE 19.6 Ways to help protect children from lead poisoning. *Critical thinking:* Which two of these solutions do you think are the best ones? Why?

Top: Ssuaphotos/Shutterstock.com. Center: Mark Smith/Shutterstock.com. Bottom: Dmitry Kalinovsky/Shutterstock.com.

some of which is converted to tiny suspended droplets of sulfuric acid (H_2SO_4). Some of these droplets react with ammonia (NH_3) in the atmosphere to form solid particles of ammonium sulfate, or ($NH_4)_2SO_4$. Also, during combustion of coal and oil, most of the carbon they contain is converted to carbon monoxide (CO) and carbon dioxide (CO_2). Unburned carbon in coal also ends up in the atmosphere as soot or black carbon. Suspended particles of such salts and soot give the resulting smog a gray color (Figure 19.5), which is why it is sometimes called *gray-air smog*.

Today, urban industrial smog is rarely a problem in most of the more-developed countries where coal is burned only in large power and industrial plants with reasonably good air pollution control. However, many of these facilities have tall smokestacks that send the pollutants high into air where prevailing winds carry them downwind to rural areas, and can cause air pollution problems that we deal with later in this chapter.

FIGURE 19.7 A greatly simplified model of how pollutants are formed when coal and oil are burned. The result is industrial smog (**Concept 19.2**).

Industrial smog remains a problem in industrialized urban areas of China, India, Ukraine, Czechoslovakia (Figure 19.5), and other countries where large quantities of coal are still burned in houses, power plants, and factories with inadequate pollution controls. Because of its heavy reliance on coal, China has some of the world's highest levels of industrial smog and 16 of the world's 20 most polluted cities (see chapter-opening photo). India's capital city New Delhi—home to about 20 million people—has some of the world's worst air pollution, especially from PM 2.5 particulates. In the fall of 2016, it had to close over 1,800 public schools because of severe smog from a combination of industrial emissions, burning crops in nearby areas, and vehicle emissions.

Sunlight Plus Cars Equals Photochemical Smog

Photochemical smog is a mixture of primary and secondary pollutants formed under the influence of UV radiation from the sun. In greatly simplified terms,

$$VOCs + NO_x + heat + sunlight \rightarrow \begin{array}{l} \text{ground-level ozone } (O_3) \\ + \text{ other photochemical oxidants} \\ + \text{ aldehydes} \\ + \text{ other secondary pollutants} \end{array}$$

The formation of photochemical smog (Figure 19.8 and **Concept 19.2**) begins when exhaust from morning commuter traffic releases large amounts of NO and VOCs into the air over a city. The NO is converted to reddish-brown NO_2, which is why photochemical smog is sometimes called *brown-air smog* (Figure 19.1). When exposed to ultraviolet

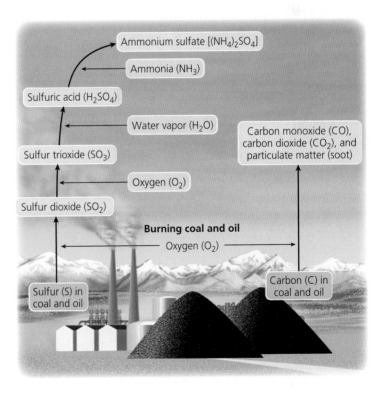

Factors Affecting Outdoor Air Pollution

Factors such as the pull of gravity on particles, the cleansing action of rain and snow, and the mixing action of wind can dilute and reduce outdoor air pollution. However, buildings and mountains can impede the flow of air, and high temperatures can induce the formation of photochemical smog, increasing air pollution.

For decades, pilots have reported seeing a reddish-brown haze over the arctic. Scientists have found that polar bears, sharks, and native peoples in remote arctic areas have high concentrations of various harmful pollutants in their bodies. This is caused by a phenomenon called the *grasshopper effect*. This occurs mostly in winter when air pollutants are transported at high altitudes from tropical and temperate areas to the earth's polar areas as part of the earth's air circulation system.

Another factor that increases air pollution is due to the *vertical movement of air*. When the sun heats the earth's surface during the day, this causes air to warm and rise. This warm air carries pollutants with it higher into the atmosphere where the pollutants mix with

cooler air and are then dispersed. However, under certain atmospheric circumstances, a layer of warm air can temporarily lie atop a layer of cold air, trapping pollutants for days at a time. This is called a **temperature inversion**. Because the cooler air near the surface is denser than the warmer air above, it does not rise and mix with the warmer, less dense air above. The effects of this phenomenon can be lethal if weather conditions do not allow this layering of air to be disrupted.

There are two instances in which temperature inversions can form. This first is in a town or city situated in a valley between mountains where weather is cloudy and cold for part of the year. This results in clouds blocking the sun from warming air at the earth's surface. Because mountains on both sides impede the flow of air, pollution remains trapped and builds up over time to harmful or even lethal concentrations (Figure 19.B, left).

The second instance is a city with heavy traffic in an area with a sunny climate, mountains on three sides, and the ocean on the fourth side. The conditions are ideal for

the formation of photochemical smog, worsened by frequent thermal inversions. The surrounding mountains prevent the polluted surface air from being dispersed by ocean breezes (Figure 19.B, right). This describes several cities, Los Angeles, California being one of them (Figure 19.1).

FRQ Application

Question: Temperature inversions can trap pollution for days, exposing citizens to high levels of toxins. **Identify** TWO air pollutants that can be trapped by a thermal inversion and **discuss** the health impacts of both pollutants.

Possible Response: One toxic chemical that can be trapped by a thermal inversion is ground-level ozone. This chemical is an oxidant that can cause irritation to the lungs, can aggravate lung and heart diseases, and can reduce resistance to colds and pneumonia. A second pollutant that can be trapped by a thermal inversion are ultra-fine particulates. These very small particles emitted by coal-burning plants and factories can imbed deeply into lung tissue and cause lung disease such as asthma or bronchitis.

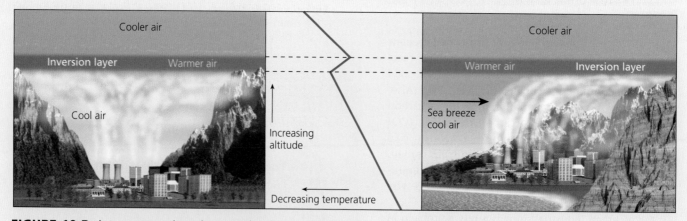

FIGURE 19.B A *temperature inversion* can take place in either of the two sets of topography and weather conditions shown here. Polluted air can be trapped between mountain ranges and under the inversion layer (left). Or it can be blown by sea breezes and trapped against a mountain range and under the inversion layer (right, see **Core Case Study**).

radiation from the sun, some of the NO_2 reacts in complex ways with VOCs released by certain trees (such as certain species of oak, sweet gum, and poplar), motor vehicles, and businesses (especially bakeries and dry cleaners).

The resulting photochemical smog is a mixture of ozone, nitric acid, aldehydes, peroxyacyl nitrates (PANs), and other secondary pollutants. Collectively, NO_2, O_3, and PANs in this

chemical brew are called *photochemical oxidants* because these damaging chemicals can react with certain compounds in the atmosphere and inside our lungs. Hotter days lead to higher levels of ozone and other components of the smog. As traffic increases on a sunny day, photochemical smog (dominated by ozone) usually builds to peak levels by late morning, irritating some people's eyes and respiratory tracts.

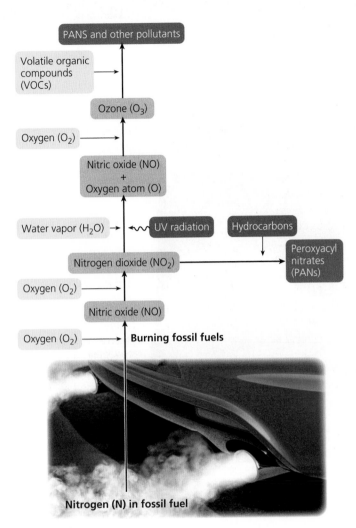

PANS and other pollutants

Volatile organic compounds (VOCs) →

Ozone (O_3)

Oxygen (O_2) →

Nitric oxide (NO) + Oxygen atom (O)

Water vapor (H_2O) → UV radiation   Hydrocarbons

Nitrogen dioxide (NO_2) → Peroxyacyl nitrates (PANs)

Oxygen (O_2) →

Nitric oxide (NO)

Oxygen (O_2) → **Burning fossil fuels**

Nitrogen (N) in fossil fuel

FIGURE 19.8 A greatly simplified model of how the pollutants that make up photochemical smog are formed.

Photo: Ssuaphotos/Shutterstock.com

All modern cities have some photochemical smog, but it is much more common in cities with sunny and warm climates, and a large number of motor vehicles. Examples are Los Angeles, California (**Core Case Study** and Figure 19.1), and Salt Lake City, Utah, in the United States; Sydney, Australia; São Paulo, Brazil; Bangkok, Thailand; and Mexico City, Mexico.

CHECKPOINT FOR UNDERSTANDING 19.2

1. Describe the relationship between primary and secondary pollutants.

2. Identify the major classes of air pollutants.

3. Identify several impacts of lead poisoning.

4. Identify the primary sources of industrial smog and photochemical smog.

5. Explain why temperature inversions can induce lethal concentrations of air pollutants.

WHAT IS ACID DEPOSITION AND WHY IS IT A PROBLEM?

CONCEPT 19.3 Acid deposition is caused mainly by coal-burning power plants and motor vehicle emissions, and in some regions, it threatens human health, aquatic life and ecosystems, forests, and human-built structures.

Acid Deposition

Most coal-burning power plants, metal ore smelters, oil refineries, and other industrial facilities emit sulfur dioxide (SO_2), suspended particles, and nitrogen oxides (NO_x) into the atmosphere. In more-developed countries, these facilities usually use tall smokestacks to vent their exhausts high into the atmosphere where wind can dilute and disperse these pollutants (Figure 19.9). This reduces *local* air pollution, but it can increase *regional* air pollution, because prevailing winds can transport the SO_2 and NO_x pollutants as far as 1,000 kilometers (600 miles). During their trip, these compounds form secondary pollutants such as droplets of sulfuric acid (H_2SO_4), nitric acid vapor (HNO_3), and particles of acid-forming sulfate (SO_4^{2-}) and nitrate (NO_3^-) salts (Figure 19.3).

These acidic substances remain in the atmosphere for 2–14 days. During this period, they descend to the earth's surface in two forms: *wet deposition*, consisting of acidic rain, snow, fog, and cloud vapor, and *dry deposition*, consisting of acidic particles. The resulting mixture is called **acid deposition** (Figure 19.10)—often called *acid rain*. Most dry deposition occurs within 2–3 days of emission, relatively close to the industrial sources, whereas most wet deposition takes place within 4–14 days in more distant downwind areas.

Acid deposition is a regional air pollution problem (**Concept 19.3**) in areas that lie downwind from coal-burning facilities and from urban areas with large numbers of cars. The map in Figure 19.11 shows areas of the world

FIGURE 19.9 Tall smokestacks can reduce local air pollution from burning coal, but they help transfer sulfur dioxide and particulates to downwind areas.

JAMES P. BLAIR/National Geographic Creative

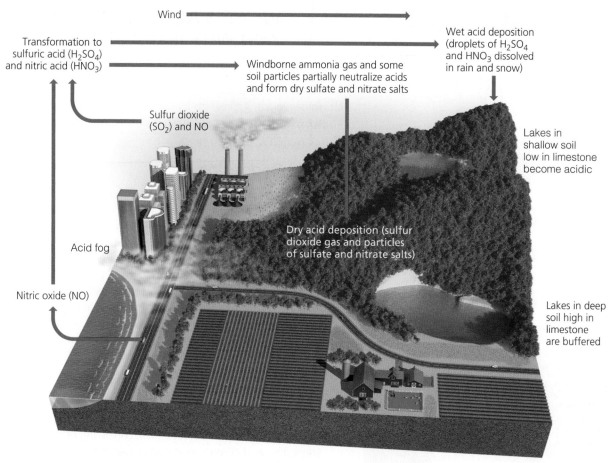

Wind

Transformation to sulfuric acid (H_2SO_4) and nitric acid (HNO_3)

Windborne ammonia gas and some soil particles partially neutralize acids and form dry sulfate and nitrate salts

Wet acid deposition (droplets of H_2SO_4 and HNO_3 dissolved in rain and snow)

Sulfur dioxide (SO_2) and NO

Lakes in shallow soil low in limestone become acidic

Acid fog

Dry acid deposition (sulfur dioxide gas and particles of sulfate and nitrate salts)

Nitric oxide (NO)

Lakes in deep soil high in limestone are buffered

FIGURE 19.10 Natural capital degradation: *Acid deposition*, which consists of rain, snow, dust, or gas with a pH lower than 5.6, is commonly called *acid rain*. ***Critical thinking:*** What are three ways in which your daily activities contribute to acid deposition?

where acid deposition is or could be a problem. In some areas, soils contain compounds that can react with and help neutralize, or *buffer*, some inputs of acids. The areas most sensitive to acid deposition are those with thin, acidic soils that provide no such natural buffering (Figure 19.11, all green and most red areas) and those where the buffering capacity of soils has been depleted by decades of acid deposition.

In the United States, older coal-burning power and industrial plants without adequate pollution controls, especially in the Midwest, emit the largest quantities of SO_2 and other pollutants that cause acid deposition. Because of these emissions and those of other urban industries and motor vehicles, as well as the prevailing west-to-east winds, typical precipitation in the eastern United States can be at least 10 times more acidic on average than precipitation in the western United States. Some mountaintop forests in the eastern United States and in areas to the east of large western US cities are bathed in fog and dews that are about 1,000 times as acidic as normal precipitation.

Acid deposition has also become an international problem when acidic emissions from one country are transported to other countries by prevailing winds. The worst

acid deposition occurs in Asia, especially in China, which gets about two-thirds of its energy and two-thirds of its electricity from burning coal, according to the US Energy Information Administration.

Harmful Effects of Acid Deposition

Acid deposition damages statues (Figure 19.4) and buildings, contributes to human respiratory diseases, and can leach toxic metals such as lead and mercury from soils and rocks into lakes used as sources of drinking water. These toxic metals can accumulate in the tissues of fish eaten by people (especially pregnant women) and other animals. Currently, 45 US states have issued warnings telling people to avoid eating fish caught from waters that are contaminated with toxic mercury (see Chapter 16, Core Case Study, p. 496).

Acid deposition also harms aquatic ecosystems. Most fish cannot survive in water with a pH less than 4.5. In addition, as acid precipitation flows through soils, it can release aluminum ions (Al^{3+}) attached to minerals in the soils and carry them into lakes, streams, and wetlands. There these ions can suffocate many kinds of fish by stimulating excessive mucus formation, which clogs their gills. Because of excess acidity

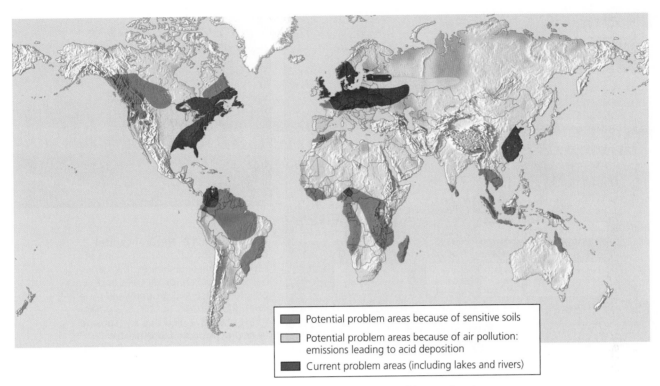

	Potential problem areas because of sensitive soils
	Potential problem areas because of air pollution: emissions leading to acid deposition
	Current problem areas (including lakes and rivers)

FIGURE 19.11 This map shows regions where acid deposition is now a problem and regions with the potential to develop this problem. Such regions have large inputs of air pollution (mostly from power plants, industrial facilities, and ore smelters) or are sensitive areas with naturally acidic soils and bedrock that cannot neutralize (buffer) additional inputs of acidic compounds. ***Critical thinking:*** Do you live in or near an area that is affected by acid deposition or an area that is likely to be affected by acid deposition in the future?

(Compiled by the authors using data from World Resources Institute and US Environmental Protection Agency.)

due to acid deposition, several thousand lakes in Norway and Sweden, and 1,200 lakes in Ontario, Canada, contain few if any fish. In the United States, several hundred lakes (most in the Northeast) are similarly threatened.

Acid deposition (often along with other air pollutants such as ozone) can harm crops and reduce plant productivity. An estimated 30% of China's cropland suffers from excess acidity.

A combination of acid deposition and other air pollutants can also affect forests in two ways (Figure 19.12). One is by leaching essential plant nutrients such as calcium and magnesium from forest soils. The other is by releasing ions of aluminum, lead, cadmium, and mercury from forest soils. These ions are toxic to the trees. These two effects rarely kill trees directly, but they can weaken them and leave them vulnerable to stresses such as severe cold, diseases, insect attacks, and drought.

Mountaintop forests are the terrestrial areas hit hardest by acid deposition. These areas tend to have thin soils without much buffering capacity and some of these areas are bathed almost continuously in highly acidic fog and clouds. Some mountaintop forests in the eastern United States, as well as east of Los Angeles, California (**Core Case Study**), are bathed in fog and dews that are about 1,000 times the acidity of unpolluted precipitation.

Since 1994, acid deposition has decreased sharply in the United States, especially in the eastern half of the country. This is partly because of significant reductions in SO_2 and NO_x emissions from coal-burning facilities under the 1990 amendments to the US Clean Air Act. Even so, soils and surface waters in many areas are still acidic because of the accumulation of acids over decades of acid deposition.

Reducing Acid Deposition

Figure 19.13 summarizes ways to reduce acid deposition. According to most scientific experts on acid deposition, the best solutions are *preventive approaches* that reduce or eliminate emissions of sulfur dioxide (SO_2), nitrogen oxides (NO_x), and particulates.

Although we know how to prevent acid deposition (Figure 19.13, left), implementing these solutions is politically difficult. One problem is that the people and ecosystems it affects often are quite far downwind from the sources of the problem. Also, countries with large supplies of coal (such as China, India, Russia, and the United States) have a strong incentive to use it. In addition, owners of coal-burning power plants resist adding the latest pollution control equipment to their facilities and using low-sulfur coal, arguing that these measures increase the cost of electricity for consumers.

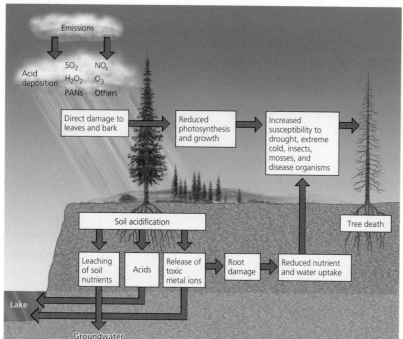

FIGURE 19.12 Natural capital degradation: Air pollution is one of several interacting stresses that can damage, weaken, or kill trees and pollute surface and groundwater. The inset photo shows trees in a German forest that have died due to exposure to acid deposition and other air pollutants.

Solutions

Acid Deposition

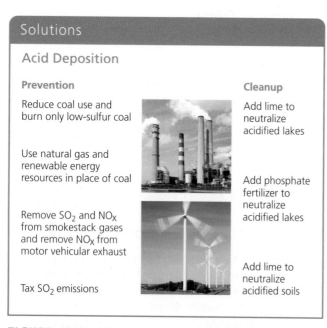

Prevention	Cleanup
Reduce coal use and burn only low-sulfur coal	Add lime to neutralize acidified lakes
Use natural gas and renewable energy resources in place of coal	
Remove SO_2 and NO_X from smokestack gases and remove NO_X from motor vehicular exhaust	Add phosphate fertilizer to neutralize acidified lakes
Tax SO_2 emissions	Add lime to neutralize acidified soils

FIGURE 19.13 Ways to reduce acid deposition and its damage. **Critical thinking:** Which two of these solutions do you think are the best ones? Why?

Top: Brittany Courville/Shutterstock.com. Bottom: Yegor Korzhi/Shutterstock.com.

However, in the United States, the use of affordable and cleaner-burning natural gas and wind for generating electricity is on the rise, and has reduced the use of coal. Environmental scientists point out that including the largely hidden, harmful health and environmental costs of burning coal in its market prices, in keeping with the full-cost pricing **principle of sustainability**, would further reduce coal use, spur the use of cleaner ways to generate electricity, and help prevent acid deposition.

According to the EPA, between 1980 and 2015, air pollution laws in the United States helped to reduce SO_2 emissions from all sources by 84% and nitrogen oxide emissions by 59%. This has helped reduce the acidity of rainfall in parts of the Northeast, Mid-Atlantic, and Midwest regions. However, scientists call for more reductions of these and other harmful emissions from older coal-burning power and industrial plants. In contrast, as the world's largest emitter of SO_2, China has one of the world's most serious acid deposition problems.

CONSIDER THIS . . .

CONNECTIONS Low-Sulfur Coal, Atmospheric Warming, and Toxic Mercury

Some US power plants have lowered SO_2 emissions by switching from high-sulfur to low-sulfur coals such as lignite. However, because low-sulfur coal has a lower heat value, more coal must be burned to generate a given amount of electricity. This has led to increased CO_2 emissions, which contribute to atmospheric warming and climate change. Low-sulfur coal also has higher levels of toxic mercury and other trace metals, so by burning it, we emit more of these hazardous chemicals into the atmosphere.

CHECKPOINT FOR UNDERSTANDING 19.3

1. Explain why *acid deposition* is a more appropriate term than *acid rain*.

2. Identify the harmful effects of acid deposition.

19.4 WHAT ARE THE MAJOR INDOOR AIR POLLUTION PROBLEMS?

CONCEPT 19.4 The most threatening indoor air pollutants are smoke and soot from the burning of wood and coal in cooking fires (mostly in less-developed countries), cigarette smoke, and chemicals used in building materials and cleaning products.

Indoor Air Pollution Is a Serious Problem

In less-developed countries, the indoor burning of wood, charcoal, dung, crop residues, coal, and other fuels in open fires (Figure 19.14) and in unvented or poorly vented stoves exposes people to dangerous levels of particulate air pollution. The WHO has estimated that indoor air pollution kills 3.5 million people per year—an average of 9,589 deaths per day. About 77% of those deaths occurred in less-developed nations of Southeast Asia and the Western Pacific.

3.5 million
Annual number of global deaths due to indoor air pollution

Indoor air pollution is also a serious problem in the United States and other more-developed areas of all countries mostly because of the chemicals used to make building materials and products such as furniture and paneling. According to the EPA and public health officials, the four most dangerous indoor air pollutants are *tobacco smoke* (see Chapter 16, Case Study, p. 516); *formaldehyde* emitted from many building materials and various household products; *radioactive radon-222 gas*, which can seep into houses from underground rock deposits (see the Case Study that follows); and *very small (ultrafine) particles* of various substances in emissions from motor vehicles, coal-burning facilities, wood fires, and forest and grass fires.

FIGURE 19.14 Burning wood to cook food inside this dwelling in Nepal exposes this woman and other occupants to dangerous levels of indoor air pollution.

Other common sources of indoor air pollution, according to the EPA, include the following:

- Pesticide residues in the 75% of US homes where pesticides are used indoors at least once a year
- Lead particles brought indoors on shoes and collecting in carpets and furnishings
- Dust mites and cockroach droppings found in some homes, thought to play a role in asthma attacks
- Airborne spores of molds and mildew that can cause headaches, allergic reactions, and asthma attacks
- Candles, almost all of which emit fine-particle soot when burned
- Clothes dryer sheets that emit an ammonium salt, linked to asthma
- Gas stoves that emit nitrogen dioxide
- Cleaning products that contain alcohol, chlorine, ammonia, and VOCs
- Air fresheners that emit glycol ethers, which can contribute to fatigue, nausea, and anemia
- Air purifiers that emit ozone

Figure 19.15 summarizes these and other sources of indoor air pollution in a typical home.

Danish and US EPA studies have linked various air pollutants found in buildings to a number of health effects, a phenomenon known as the *sick-building syndrome*. Such

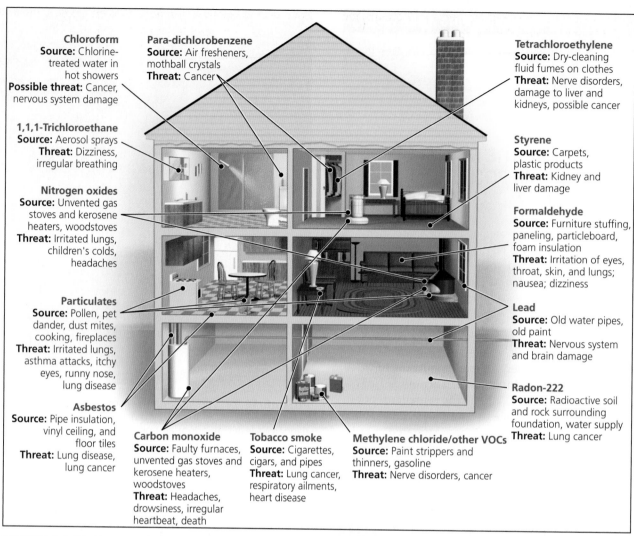

Chloroform
Source: Chlorine-treated water in hot showers
Possible threat: Cancer, nervous system damage

1,1,1-Trichloroethane
Source: Aerosol sprays
Threat: Dizziness, irregular breathing

Nitrogen oxides
Source: Unvented gas stoves and kerosene heaters, woodstoves
Threat: Irritated lungs, children's colds, headaches

Particulates
Source: Pollen, pet dander, dust mites, cooking, fireplaces
Threat: Irritated lungs, asthma attacks, itchy eyes, runny nose, lung disease

Asbestos
Source: Pipe insulation, vinyl ceiling, and floor tiles
Threat: Lung disease, lung cancer

Para-dichlorobenzene
Source: Air fresheners, mothball crystals
Threat: Cancer

Carbon monoxide
Source: Faulty furnaces, unvented gas stoves and kerosene heaters, woodstoves
Threat: Headaches, drowsiness, irregular heartbeat, death

Tobacco smoke
Source: Cigarettes, cigars, and pipes
Threat: Lung cancer, respiratory ailments, heart disease

Methylene chloride/other VOCs
Source: Paint strippers and thinners, gasoline
Threat: Nerve disorders, cancer

Tetrachloroethylene
Source: Dry-cleaning fluid fumes on clothes
Threat: Nerve disorders, damage to liver and kidneys, possible cancer

Styrene
Source: Carpets, plastic products
Threat: Kidney and liver damage

Formaldehyde
Source: Furniture stuffing, paneling, particleboard, foam insulation
Threat: Irritation of eyes, throat, skin, and lungs; nausea; dizziness

Lead
Source: Old water pipes, old paint
Threat: Nervous system and brain damage

Radon-222
Source: Radioactive soil and rock surrounding foundation, water supply
Threat: Lung cancer

FIGURE 19.15 Numerous indoor air pollutants are found in most modern homes (**Concept 19.4**). *Question:* To which of these pollutants are you exposed?

(Compiled by the authors using data from US Environmental Protection Agency.)

effects include dizziness, headaches, coughing, sneezing, shortness of breath, nausea, burning eyes, sore throats, skin irritation, and respiratory infections. EPA and Labor Department studies indicate that almost one of every five US commercial buildings is exposing employees to such health risks. **GREEN CAREER: Indoor air pollution specialist**

EPA studies have revealed some alarming facts about indoor air pollution in the United States. *First,* levels of several common air pollutants generally are two to five times higher inside US homes and commercial buildings than they are outdoors. In some cases, they are as much as 100 times higher. *Second,* pollution levels inside cars in traffic-clogged urban areas can be up to 18 times higher than outside levels. *Third,* the health risks from exposure to such chemicals are growing because most people in more-developed urban areas spend at least 70% or more of their time indoors or inside vehicles. Smokers, children under age 5, the elderly, the sick, pregnant women, people with

respiratory or heart problems, and factory workers are especially at risk from indoor air pollution.

CASE STUDY

Radioactive Radon Gas

Radon-222 is a colorless, odorless, radioactive gas that is produced by the natural radioactive decay of uranium-238, small amounts of which are contained in most rocks and soils. But this isotope is much more concentrated in underground deposits of minerals such as uranium, phosphate, shale, and granite. Figure 19.16 compares the potential geological risk of exposure to radioactive radon across the United States.

When radioactive radon gas from such deposits seeps upward through the soil and is released outdoors, it disperses quickly in the air and decays to harmless levels of radioactivity. However, in buildings above such deposits, radon gas can enter through cracks in a foundation's slab and walls, as well as through well water, openings around sump pumps and drains, and hollow concrete blocks. Once inside, it can build up to high levels, especially in unventilated lower levels of homes and buildings.

Radon-222 gas quickly decays into solid particles of other radioactive elements such as polonium-210, which can expose lung tissue to large amounts of radioactivity. This exposure can damage lung tissue and lead to lung cancer over the course of a 70-year lifetime.

According to the EPA, radioactive radon is the second-leading cause of lung cancer after smoking. Each year, according to the National Cancer Institute, radon-induced lung cancer kills about 20,000 people in the United States—about 90% of them being current or former smokers. Despite this risk, less than 20% of US households have followed the EPA's recommendation to conduct radon tests, which can be done with inexpensive testing kits. Many schools and day-care centers also have not tested for radon, and only a few states have laws that require radon testing for schools.

19.5 WHAT ARE THE HEALTH EFFECTS OF AIR POLLUTION?

CONCEPT 19.5 Air pollution can contribute to asthma, chronic bronchitis, emphysema, lung cancer, heart attack, and stroke.

Your Body's Natural Air Pollution Defenses Can Be Overwhelmed

Your respiratory system (Figure 19.17) helps to protect you from air pollution in various ways. Hairs in your nose filter out large particles. Sticky mucus in the lining of your upper respiratory tract captures smaller (but not the smallest) particles and dissolves some gaseous pollutants. Hundreds of thousands of tiny, mucus-coated, hair-like structures, called *cilia*, also line your upper respiratory tract. They continually move back and forth and transport mucus and the pollutants it traps to your throat where they are swallowed or expelled through sneezing and coughing.

Prolonged or acute exposure to air pollutants can overload or break down these natural defenses. Fine and ultrafine particulates can lodge deep in the lungs and contribute to lung cancer, asthma, heart attack, and stroke. Years of smoking or breathing polluted air can lead to other lung ailments such as chronic

CONSIDER THIS . . .

THINKING ABOUT Preventing Indoor Air Pollution

What are some steps you could take to prevent indoor air pollution, especially regarding the four most dangerous indoor air pollutants listed above?

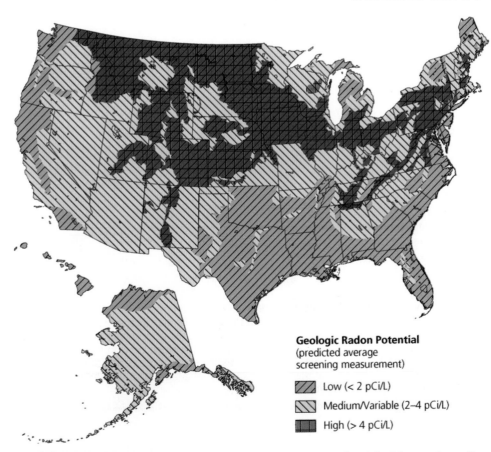

Geologic Radon Potential
(predicted average screening measurement)

Low (< 2 pCi/L)

Medium/Variable (2–4 pCi/L)

High (> 4 pCi/L)

FIGURE 19.16 The potential for radon exposure varies across the United States, depending on the types of underlying soils and bedrock. Expressed in terms of concentrations of radioactive radon in picocuries per liter (pCi/L). **Question:** What is the average risk level of exposure to radioactive radon where you live or go to school?

(Compiled by the authors using data from US Geological Survey and US Environmental Protection Agency.)

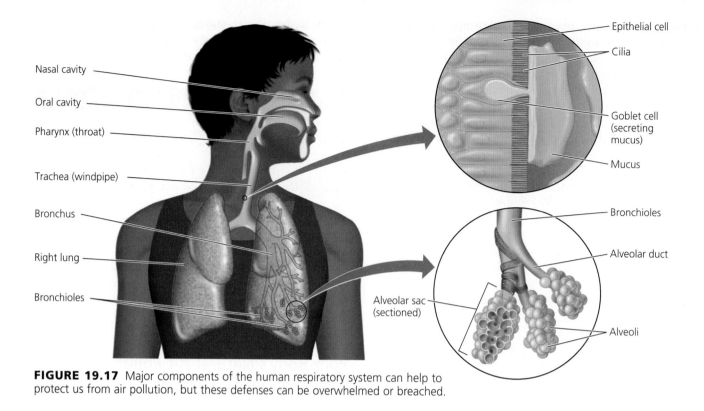

FIGURE 19.17 Major components of the human respiratory system can help to protect us from air pollution, but these defenses can be overwhelmed or breached.

bronchitis and emphysema, (Figure 16.20, p. 518) which leads to acute shortness of breath.

Air Pollution Is a Big Killer

The WHO estimates that each year, indoor and outdoor air pollution kills about 7 million people around the world. This averages out to about 800 deaths every hour. According to the WHO, about 28% of these deaths occur in China (see chapter-opening photo) and India. Thus, the WHO dubbed air pollution "the world's largest single environmental health risk." The leading direct causes of death related to air pollution are heart attacks, stroke, chronic obstructive pulmonary disease (COPD), and lung cancer.

Steven Barrett and other researchers at the Massachusetts Institute of Technology (MIT) estimate that outdoor air pollution, mostly fine-particle pollution, contributes to the deaths of roughly 200,000 Americans every year (Figure 19.18). About half of these deaths are blamed on car and truck exhaust and the other half on coal-burning power and industrial plants. This death toll is roughly equivalent to that of two fully loaded, 275-passenger airliners crashing *every day* with no survivors.

According to EPA studies, each year, more than 125,000 Americans get cancer primarily from breathing soot-laden diesel fumes emitted by buses, trucks, tractors, bulldozers and other construction equipment, trains, and ships. A large diesel truck emits as much particulate matter as 150 cars. And according to a study led by Daniel Lack,

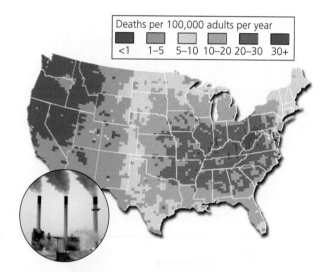

FIGURE 19.18 Distribution of premature deaths from air pollution in the United States, mostly from very small, fine, and ultrafine particles added to the atmosphere by coal-burning power plants. ***Critical thinking:*** Why do the highest death rates occur in the eastern half of the United States? If you live in the United States, what is the risk at your home or where you go to school?

(Compiled by the authors using data from US Environmental Protection Agency.)

the world's 100,000 or more diesel-powered oceangoing ships emit almost half as much particulate pollution as do the world's 1 billion motor vehicles. Millions more suffer from asthma attacks and other respiratory disorders brought on or aggravated by air pollution (**Concept 19.5**).

CHECKPOINT FOR UNDERSTANDING 19.5

1. Explain why ultrafine particles are more dangerous to respiratory health than larger sized particulates.

19.6 HOW SHOULD WE DEAL WITH AIR POLLUTION?

CONCEPT 19.6 Legal, economic, and technological tools can help us to clean up air pollution, but the best solution is to prevent it.

Laws and Regulations Can Reduce Outdoor Air Pollution

The United States provides an example of how government can reduce air pollution (**Concept 19.6**). The US Congress passed the Clean Air Acts of 1970, 1977, and 1990. With these laws, the federal government established air pollution regulations for key outdoor air pollutants to be enforced by states and major cities.

With the 1970 law, Congress directed the EPA to establish air quality standards for six major outdoor pollutants—carbon monoxide (CO), nitrogen dioxide (NO_2), sulfur dioxide (SO_2), suspended particulate matter (SPM, smaller than PM-10), ozone (O_3), and lead (Pb). One limit, called a *primary standard*, was set to protect human health. Another limit, called a *secondary standard*, was intended to prevent environmental and property damage. Each standard specifies the maximum allowable level for a pollutant, averaged over a specific period. The law has reduced emissions of these pollutants by motor vehicles and industries.

The EPA has also established national emission standards for more than 188 *hazardous air pollutants* (*HAPs*)—pollutants that can cause serious health and ecological effects. Most of these chemicals are chlorinated hydrocarbons, volatile organic compounds, or compounds of toxic metals.

According to the EPA report, the combined emissions of the six major outdoor air pollutants decreased by about 65% between 1980 and 2015, even with significant increases during the same period in gross domestic product, vehicle miles traveled, population, and energy consumption (Figure 19.19). GOOD NEWS

The reduction of outdoor air pollution in the United States since 1970 has been successful mostly because of two factors. *First*, during the 1970s, US citizens insisted that laws be passed and enforced to improve air quality. Before 1970, when Congress passed the Clean Air Act, air-pollution-control equipment did not exist. *Second*, the country was affluent enough to afford such controls and improvements. For example, because of these factors, a new car today in the United States emits 75% less pollution than did a pre-1970 car.

Environmental scientists applaud this success, but they call for strengthening US air pollution laws by doing the following:

- Putting much greater emphasis on pollution prevention. With this approach, the question is not *What can we do about the air pollutants we produce?* but rather *How can we avoid producing these pollutants in the first place?* The power of prevention (**Concept 19.6**) was made clear by the 99% drop in atmospheric lead emissions after lead in gasoline was banned in 1976.

- Sharply reducing emissions from approximately 20,000 older coal-burning power and industrial

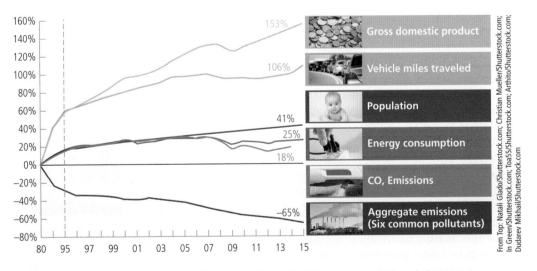

FIGURE 19.19 Levels of key air pollutants in the United States dropped sharply between 1980 and 2015, despite increases in other factors.
Data and figure from US Environmental Protection Agency (this image was found online here: https://www.epa.gov/air-trends/air-quality-national-summary)

plants, cement plants, oil refineries, and waste incinerators that have not been required to meet the air pollution standards for new facilities under the Clean Air Acts.

- Ramping up controls on atmospheric emissions of toxic pollutants such as mercury.
- Continuing to improve fuel efficiency standards for motor vehicles.
- Stricter regulation of emissions from motorcycles and two-cycle gasoline engines used in devices such as chainsaws, lawnmowers, generators, scooters and snowmobiles.
- Setting much stricter air pollution regulations for airports and oceangoing ships.
- Sharply reducing indoor air pollution.

Executives of companies that would be affected by implementing stronger air pollution regulations claim that correcting these problems would cost too much and would hinder economic growth. Proponents of stronger regulations contend that history has shown that most industry cost estimates for implementing US air-pollution-control standards have been much higher than the costs actually proved to be. In addition, implementing such standards has helped some companies and created jobs by stimulating these companies to develop new pollution control technologies.

Using the Marketplace to Reduce Outdoor Air Pollution

One approach to reducing pollutant emissions is to allow producers of air pollutants to buy and sell government air pollution allotments in the marketplace. For example, with the goal of reducing SO_2 emissions, the Clean Air Act of 1990 authorized an *emissions trading*, or *cap-and-trade program*, which enables the 110 most polluting coal-fired power plants in 21 states to buy and sell SO_2 air pollution rights.

Under this system, each plant is annually given a number of pollution credits, which allow it to emit a certain amount of SO_2. A utility that emits less than its allotted amount has a surplus of pollution credits. That utility can use its credits to offset SO_2 emissions at its other plants, keep them for future plant expansions, or sell them to other utilities or private citizens or groups. Between 1990 and 2012, this emissions trading program helped to reduce SO_2 emissions from power plants in the United States by 76%, at a cost of less than one-tenth of the cost projected by the utility industry, according to the EPA.

Proponents of this market-based approach say it is cheaper and more efficient than government regulation of air pollution. Critics of this approach contend that it allows utilities with older, dirtier power plants to buy their way out of their environmental responsibilities and to continue to pollute.

The ultimate success of any emissions trading approach depends on two factors: how low the initial cap is set and how often it is lowered in order to promote continuing innovation in air pollution prevention and control. Without these two factors, emissions trading programs can shift air pollution from one area to another without achieving an overall improvement in air quality.

Other Ways to Reduce Outdoor Air Pollution

Figure 19.20 summarizes several ways to reduce emissions of sulfur oxides, nitrogen oxides, and particulate matter from stationary sources such as coal-burning power plants and industrial facilities—the primary contributors to industrial smog.

One commonly used technological solution is the *electrostatic precipitator* (Figure 19.21, left). It is simple to maintain and can remove up to 99% of the particulate matter it processes. However, it uses a lot of electricity and produces a toxic dust that must be disposed of safely. Another is the *wet scrubber* (Figure 19.21, right), which can remove 98% of SO_2 and 98% of the particulate matter in smokestack emissions. It too produces waste in the form of sludge that must be disposed of in a landfill.

Figure 19.22 lists several ways to prevent and reduce emissions from motor vehicles, the primary contributors to photochemical smog. In more-developed countries, many

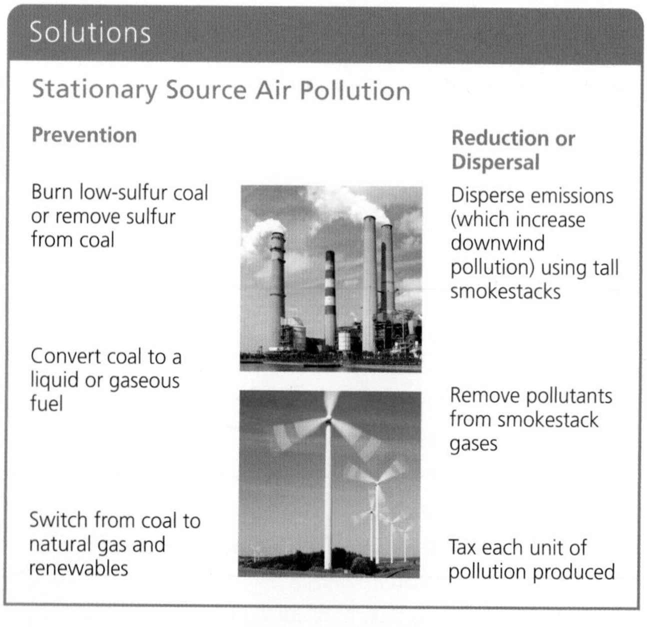

Solutions

Stationary Source Air Pollution

Prevention	Reduction or Dispersal
Burn low-sulfur coal or remove sulfur from coal	Disperse emissions (which increase downwind pollution) using tall smokestacks
Convert coal to a liquid or gaseous fuel	Remove pollutants from smokestack gases
Switch from coal to natural gas and renewables	Tax each unit of pollution produced

FIGURE 19.20 Ways to prevent, reduce, or disperse emissions of sulfur oxides, nitrogen oxides, and particulate matter from stationary sources, especially coal-burning power plants and industrial facilities (**Concept 19.6**). ***Critical thinking:*** Which two of these solutions do you think are the best ones? Why?

Top: Brittany Courville/Shutterstock.com. Bottom: Yegor Korzhi/Shutterstock.com.

of these solutions have been successful (see the Case Study that follows). However, the already poor air quality in urban areas of many less-developed countries is worsening as the numbers of motor vehicles in these nations rise.

Over the next 10–20 years, technology could help all countries to clean up the air through improved engine and emission systems and hybrid-electric, plug-in hybrid, and all-electric vehicles. In 2015, the Alliance of Automobile Manufacturers announced that automakers were on track to essentially eliminate smog-forming passenger vehicle emissions by 2030 in the United States, as newer cars replace older ones.

CASE STUDY

Revisiting Air Pollution in Los Angeles

The factors contributing to air pollution in LA have not gone away. Currently, the area's largest sources of pollutants are the ports of Los Angeles and Long Beach.

Most of the ships that use these ports burn dirty diesel fuel—a major source of particulate pollution.

In addition, greater LA is an urban area surrounded by mountains on three sides and an ocean on the fourth side. Prevailing westerly ocean breezes blow pollution inland where it becomes trapped against the mountain ranges and builds up during thermal inversions (Figure 19.B, right). Finally, climate change is projected to make the problems even worse by increasing the number of hot, sunny days that increase the rate of ozone formation.

Even with all of these challenges, LA has managed to cut its pollution to the point where in 2015, it could report the lowest pollution levels since 1999 when the American Lung Association began reporting annually on overall urban air quality in the United States. Consequently, the city sees many clear days that it seldom saw in the 1960s and 1970s. (Compare Figure 19.23 with Figure 19.1.) Analysts attribute these improvements

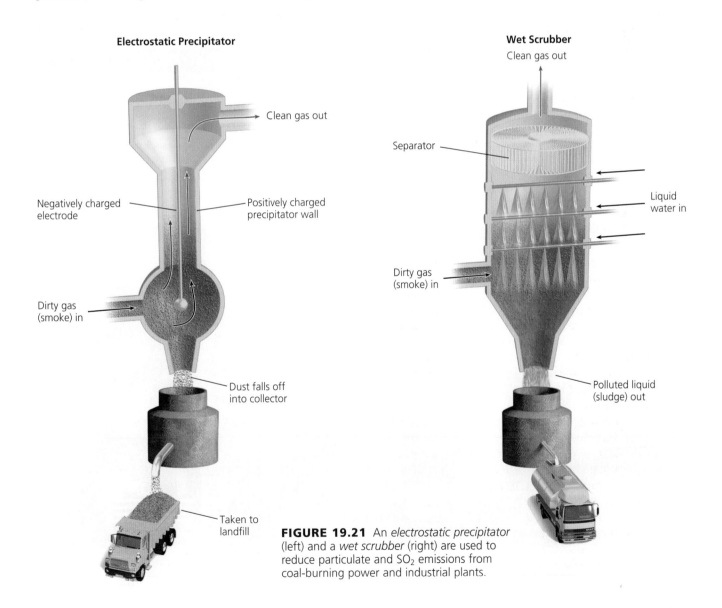

FIGURE 19.21 An *electrostatic precipitator* (left) and a *wet scrubber* (right) are used to reduce particulate and SO_2 emissions from coal-burning power and industrial plants.

Solutions

Motor Vehicle Air Pollution

Prevention	Reduction
Walk or bike or use mass transit	Require emission control devices
Improve fuel efficiency	Inspect car exhaust systems twice a year
Get older, polluting cars off the road	Set strict emission standards

FIGURE 19.22 Ways to prevent or reduce emissions from motor vehicles (**Concept 19.6**). ***Critical thinking:*** Which two of these solutions do you think are the best ones? Why?

Top: egd/Shutterstock.com. Bottom: Tyler Olson/Shutterstock.com.

mostly to grassroots efforts by US citizens in the 1960s that led to passage of the Clean Air Act of 1970.

The ports accomplished this mostly by using cleaner-burning cranes, machinery, and trucks, and cleaner, low-sulfur fuel.

Reducing Indoor Air Pollution

Little effort has been devoted to reducing indoor air pollution, even though it poses a greater threat to human health than does outdoor air pollution. Air pollution experts suggest several ways to prevent or reduce indoor air pollution, as shown in Figure 19.24.

In less-developed countries, indoor air pollution from open fires and inefficient stoves that burn wood, charcoal, or coal could be reduced. More people could use inexpensive clay or metal stoves that burn fuels (including straw and other crop wastes) more efficiently and vent their exhausts to the outside, or they could use stoves that use solar energy to cook food (Figure 15.13, p. 468).

One way to reduce indoor air pollution in a modern home is to have plenty of houseplants. Studies show that they can reduce more than 80% of indoor toxins within a few days. Plants that do a good job of purifying air include Devil's Ivy, English Ivy, African Violets, and Peace Lily. Figure 19.25 lists some ways in which you can reduce your exposure to indoor air pollution.

CHECKPOINT FOR UNDERSTANDING 19.6

1. Identify the difference between primary air pollution standards and secondary air pollution standards.

2. Describe how cap-and-trade works to reduce air pollution.

3. Describe the two technological means of preventing particulates and SO_2 from being emitted into the atmosphere.

FIGURE 19.23 A clear day in downtown Los Angeles.

Gerry Boughan/Shutterstock.com

Solutions

Indoor Air Pollution

Prevention

Ban indoor smoking

Set stricter formaldehyde emissions standards for carpet, furniture, and building materials

Prevent radon infiltration

Use naturally based cleaning agents, paints, and other products

Reduction and Dilution

Use adjustable fresh air vents for work spaces

Circulate air more frequently

Circulate a building's air through rooftop greenhouses

Use solar cookers and efficient, vented wood-burning stoves

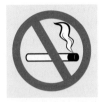

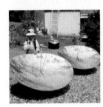

FIGURE 19.24 Ways to prevent or reduce indoor air pollution (**Concept 19.6**). ***Critical thinking:*** Which two of these solutions do you think are the best ones? Why?

Top: Tribalium/Shutterstock.com. Bottom: Patstock/Age Fotostock.

19.7 HOW HAVE WE DEPLETED OZONE IN THE STRATOSPHERE AND WHAT CAN WE DO ABOUT IT?

CONCEPT 19.7A Widespread use of certain chemicals has reduced ozone levels in the stratosphere and allowed more harmful ultraviolet (UV) radiation to reach the earth's surface.

CONCEPT 19.7B To reverse ozone depletion, we must stop producing ozone-depleting chemicals and adhere to the international treaties that ban such chemicals.

The Use of Certain Chemicals Threatens the Ozone Layer

The ozone layer in the stratosphere (Figure 19.2) is a vital form of natural capital that supports all life on land and in shallow aquatic environments by keeping 95% of the sun's harmful ultraviolet radiation from reaching the earth's surface. In other words, the ozone layer in the stratosphere is a vital form of natural capital that supports life on land and in shallow aquatic environments.

However, measurements revealed considerable seasonal depletion, or thinning, of ozone concentrations in the stratosphere above Antarctica (Figure 19.26) and above the Arctic since the 1970s. Similar measurements revealed slight overall ozone thinning everywhere except over the tropics. The loss of ozone over Antarctica has been called an *ozone hole*. A more accurate term is *ozone thinning* because the ozone depletion varies with altitude and location.

Based on these measurements and on mathematical and chemical models, the overwhelming consensus of researchers in this field is that ozone depletion in the stratosphere poses a serious threat to humans, other animals, and some primary producers (mostly plants) that use sunlight to support the earth's food webs (**Concept 19.7A**).

The origin of this serious environmental threat began with the accidental discovery of the first chlorofluorocarbon (CFC) in 1930. Chemists soon developed similar compounds to create a family of highly useful CFCs, known by their trade name Freons. These chemically unreactive, odorless, nonflammable, nontoxic, and noncorrosive compounds were thought to be dream chemicals. Inexpensive

What Can You Do?

Indoor Air Pollution

- Test for radon and formaldehyde inside your home and take corrective measures as needed
- Do not buy furniture and other products containing formaldehyde
- Test your home or workplace for asbestos fiber levels and check for any crumbling asbestos materials
- If you smoke, do it outside or in a closed room vented to the outside
- Make sure that wood-burning stoves, fireplaces, and kerosene- and gas-burning heaters are properly installed, vented, and maintained
- Install carbon monoxide detectors in all sleeping areas
- Use fans to circulate indoor air
- Grow house plants, the more, the better
- Do not store gasoline, solvents, or other volatile hazardous chemicals inside a home or attached garage
- Remove your shoes before entering your house to reduce inputs of dust, lead, and pesticides

FIGURE 19.25 **Individuals matter:** You can reduce your exposure to indoor air pollution. ***Critical thinking:*** Which three of these actions do you think are the most important ones to take? Why?

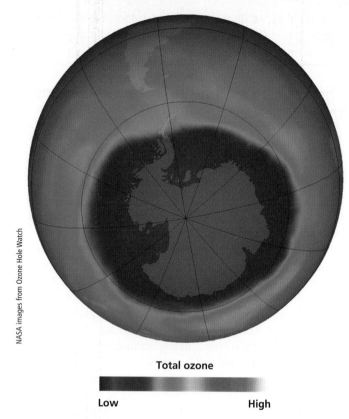

Total ozone

Low   High

FIGURE 19.26 Natural capital degradation: The colorized satellite image shows ozone thinning over Antarctica during October of 2015 at its annual peak extent. Ozone depletion of 50% or more occurred in the center blue area.

to manufacture, they became popular as coolants in air conditioners and refrigerators, propellants in aerosol spray cans, cleansers for electronic parts such as computer chips, fumigants for granaries and ships' cargo holds, and gases used to make insulation and packaging.

It turned out that CFCs were too good to be true. Starting in 1974 with the work of chemists Sherwood Rowland and Mario Molina (Individuals Matter 19.1), scientists showed that CFCs are persistent chemicals that destroy protective ozone in the stratosphere. Satellite data and other measurements and models indicate that 75–85% of the observed ozone losses in the stratosphere since 1976 resulted from people releasing CFCs and other ozone-depleting chemicals into the troposphere beginning in the 1950s.

Rowland and Molina came to four major conclusions. *First*, once CFCs are put into the atmosphere, these persistent chemicals remain there for a long time. *Second*, over 11–20 years, these compounds rise into the stratosphere through convection, random drift, and the turbulent mixing of air in the lower atmosphere. During their upward movement through the troposphere, CFCs also act as greenhouse gases that help to warm the lower troposphere. *Third*, once they reach the stratosphere, the CFC molecules break down under the influence of high-energy UV radiation. This releases highly reactive chlorine atoms (Cl), as well as atoms of fluorine (F) and bromine (Br), all of which accelerate the breakdown of ozone (O_3) into O_2 and O in a cyclic chain of chemical reactions. This process destroys ozone faster than it forms in some parts of the stratosphere. And *fourth*, each CFC molecule can last in the stratosphere for 65–385 years, depending on its type. During that time, each chlorine atom released during the breakdown of CFCs can break down hundreds of O_3 molecules. While in the troposphere, CFCs also act as greenhouse gases that help to warm the lower atmosphere and contribute to climate change.

CFCs are not the only ozone-depleting chemicals. Others are *halons* and *hydrobromofluorocarbons* (HBFCs) (used in fire extinguishers), *methyl bromide* (a widely used fumigant), *hydrogen chloride* (emitted into the stratosphere by the launches of certain space vehicles), and cleaning solvents such as *carbon tetrachloride*, *methyl chloroform*, *n-propyl bromide*, and *hexachlorobutadiene*.

Why Should We Worry about Ozone Depletion?

Why is ozone depletion something that should concern us? Figure 19.27 lists some of the demonstrated effects of stratospheric ozone thinning. One effect is that more biologically damaging UV-A and UV-B radiation will reach the earth's surface (**Concept 19.7A**) and is a likely contributor to rising numbers of eye cataracts, damaging sunburns, and skin cancers. Figure 19.28 lists ways in which you can protect yourself from harmful UV radiation.

Another serious threat from ozone depletion and the resulting increase in UV radiation reaching the planet's surface is the possible impairment or destruction of phytoplankton, especially in Antarctic waters. These tiny marine plants play a key role in removing CO_2 from the atmosphere and they form the base of many ocean food webs. Destroying or depleting them would eliminate the vital ecological services they provide. The loss of plankton could accelerate projected atmospheric warming by reducing the capacity of the oceans to remove large amounts of CO_2 that humanity produces from the atmosphere.

Reversing Stratospheric Ozone Depletion

According to researchers in this field, we should immediately stop producing all ozone-depleting chemicals (**Concept 19.7B**). However, models and measurements indicate that even with immediate and sustained action, it will take at least 60 years for the earth's ozone layer to recover the levels of ozone it had in 1980, and it could take about 100 years for it to recover to pre-1950 levels.

In 1987, representatives of 36 nations met in Montreal, Canada, and developed the *Montreal Protocol*. This treaty's goal was to cut emissions of CFCs (but no other ozone-depleting chemicals) by about 35% between 1989 and 2000. After hearing more bad news about seasonal ozone thinning above Antarctica in 1989, representatives of 93 countries had more

Interpreting Ozone Data

Since its discovery in 1984, scientists at NASA have been monitoring the thinning of the ozone layer. Through international cooperation, the use of chemicals such as chlorofluorocarbons, or CFCs, that dismantle ozone molecules has been reduced worldwide. As a result, the ozone layer has begun to recover.

FRQ Application

The following graph illustrates the size of the hole in the ozone layer for the years 1979 through 2008.

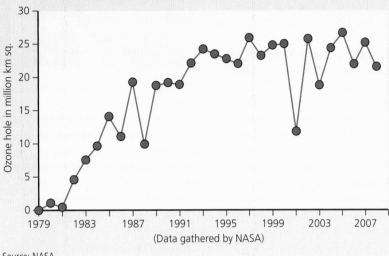

Source: NASA

Identify the 4-year period in which the size of the hole in the ozone layer increased the most in millions of square kilometers. For the period identified, calculate the average rate of increase in the hole in the ozone layer in millions of square kilometers per year.

According to the graph, the 4-year period would be from the years 2001 to 2005. In 2001, the size of the hole was 12 million square kilometers. In 2005, the hole in the ozone layer was 27 million square kilometers.

$$\frac{27 \text{ million km}^2 - 12 \text{ million km}^2}{4 \text{ years}} = \frac{15 \text{ million km}^2}{4 \text{ years}} = 3.8 \text{ million km}^2 \text{ per year}$$

meetings and in 1992 adopted the *Copenhagen Amendment,* which accelerated the phase-out of CFCs and added some other key ozone-depleting chemicals to the agreement.

These international agreements set an important precedent because nations and companies worked together, using a *prevention approach* to try to solve a serious environmental problem. This approach worked for three reasons. *First,* there was convincing and dramatic scientific evidence of a serious problem. *Second,* CFCs were produced by a small number of international companies and this meant there was less corporate resistance to finding a solution. *Third,* the certainty that CFC sales would decline over a period of years because of government bans unleashed the economic and creative resources of the private sector to find even more profitable substitute chemicals.

Substitutes are available for most uses of CFCs. However, the most widely used substitutes are hydrofluoro-carbons (HFCs), which act as greenhouse gases. An HFC molecule can be up to 10,000 times more potent in warming the atmosphere than a molecule of CO_2 is. The Intergovernmental Panel on Climate Change (IPCC) has warned that global use of HFCs is growing rapidly and that they need to be quickly replaced with substitutes that do not deplete ozone in the stratosphere or act as greenhouse gases while they are in the troposphere. Several companies have developed HFC substitutes that need to be evaluated.

This international agreement is working. According to 2016 study by NASA scientists, between 2000 and 2015, ozone thinning in the stratosphere above Antarctica (Figure 19.26) reached its peak in September and in October, shrank by an area equal to about one-third the area of the continental United States. If this trend continues, the ozone layer would return to 1980 levels by 2050.

Sherwood Rowland and Mario Molina—A Scientific Story of Expertise, Courage, and Persistence

In 1974, calculations by the late Sherwood Rowland (left photo) and Mario Molina (right photo), chemists at the University of California–Irvine, indicated that chlorofluorocarbons (CFCs) were lowering the average concentration of ozone in the stratosphere. They also found that CFCs are persistent, remaining in the stratosphere for hundreds of years. During that time, they noted, each CFC molecule can breakdown hundreds of ozone molecules.

These scientists decided they had an ethical obligation to go public with the results of their research. They shocked both the scientific community and the $28-billion-per-year CFC industry by calling for an immediate ban of CFCs in spray cans, for which substitutes were available.

The CFC industry (led by DuPont) was a powerful, well-funded adversary with a lot of profits and jobs at stake. It attacked Rowland's and Molina's calculations and conclusions, but the two researchers held their ground, expanded their research, and explained their results to other scientists, elected officials, and the media. After 14 years of delaying tactics, DuPont officials acknowledged in 1988 that CFCs were depleting the ozone layer, and they agreed to stop producing them and to sell higher-priced alternatives that their chemists had developed.

In 1995, Rowland and Molina received the Nobel Prize in chemistry for their work on CFCs.

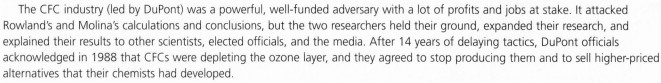

Natural Capital Degradation

Effects of Ozone Depletion

Human Health and Structures

- Worse sunburns
- More eye cataracts and skin cancers
- Immune system suppression

Wildlife

- More eye cataracts in some species
- Shrinking populations of aquatic species sensitive to UV radiation
- Disruption of aquatic food webs due to shrinking phytoplankton populations

Food and Forests

- Reduced yields for some crops
- Reduced seafood supplies due to smaller phytoplankton populations
- Decreased forest productivity for UV-sensitive tree species

Air Pollution and Climate Change

- Increased acid deposition
- Increased photochemical smog
- Degradation of outdoor painted surfaces, plastics, and building materials
- While in troposphere, CFCs act as greenhouse gases

FIGURE 19.27 Decreased levels of ozone in the stratosphere can have a number of harmful effects. (**Concept 19.7A**). *Critical thinking:* Which three of these effects do you think are the most threatening? Why?

The landmark international agreements on stratospheric ozone, now signed by all 196 of the world's countries, are important examples of successful global cooperation in response to a serious global environmental problem. (**Concept 19.7B**). This is also an example of the win-win **principle of sustainability** in action.

Reducing Exposure to UV Radiation

- Stay out of the sun, especially between 10 A.M. and 3 P.M.

- Do not use tanning parlors or sunlamps

- When in the sun, wear clothing and sunglasses that protect against UV-A and UV-B radiation

- Be aware that overcast skies do not protect you

- Do not expose yourself to the sun if you are taking antibiotics or birth control pills

- When in the sun, use a sunscreen with a protection factor of at least 15

FIGURE 19.28 Individuals matter: You can reduce your exposure to harmful UV radiation. ***Critical thinking:*** Which of these precautions do you already take? Which others would you consider doing?

Core Case Study Checkpoint

Identify the US law that was enacted to limit air pollution emissions and explain what this law regulated.

CHECKPOINT FOR UNDERSTANDING 19.7

1. Identify characteristics of CFCs that make them potent agents of ozone destruction.

2. Describe the purpose of the Montreal Protocol.

KEY IDEAS

- Outdoor air pollution, in the form of industrial smog, photochemical smog, and acid deposition, and indoor air pollution are serious global problems.

- Each year, at least 7 million people die prematurely from the effects of outdoor and indoor air pollution, with more than half of these deaths occurring in less-developed countries.

- We need to give top priority to preventing outdoor and indoor air pollution throughout the world and ozone depletion in the stratosphere.

Chapter 19 Glossary

acid deposition: the falling of acids and acid-forming compounds from the atmosphere to the earth's surface.

air pollution: one or more chemicals in high enough concentrations in the air to harm humans, other animals, vegetation, or materials. Excess heat is also considered a form of air pollution. Such chemicals or physical conditions are called air pollutants.

atmosphere: whole mass of air surrounding the earth.

greenhouse gases: gases in the earth's lower atmosphere (troposphere) that cause the greenhouse effect that warms the lower atmosphere. Examples include carbon dioxide, chlorofluorocarbons, ozone, methane, water vapor, and nitrous oxide.

industrial smog: type of air pollution consisting mostly of a mixture of sulfur dioxide, suspended droplets of sulfuric acid formed from some of the sulfur dioxide, and suspended solid particles.

ozone layer: layer of gaseous ozone in the stratosphere that protects life on earth by filtering out most harmful ultraviolet radiation from the sun.

photochemical smog: complex mixture of air pollutants produced in the lower atmosphere by the reaction of hydrocarbons and nitrogen oxides under the influence of sunlight. Especially harmful components include ozone, peroxacyl nitrates (PANs), and various aldehydes.

primary pollutant: chemical that has been added directly to the air by natural events or human activities and occurs in a harmful concentration.

secondary pollutant: harmful chemical formed in the atmosphere when a primary air pollutant reacts with normal air components or other air pollutants.

stratosphere: second layer of the atmosphere, extending about 17 to 48 kilometers (11 to 30 miles) above earth's surface. It contains small amounts of gaseous ozone, which filters out about 95% of the incoming harmful ultraviolet radiation emitted by the sun.

temperature inversion: layer of dense, cool air trapped under a layer of less dense, warm air. It prevents upward-flowing air currents from developing. In a prolonged inversion, air pollution in the trapped layers may build up to harmful levels.

troposphere: innermost layer of the atmosphere. It contains about 75% of the mass of earth's air and extends about 17 kilometers (11 miles) above sea level.

Chapter Review

Core Case Study

1. Summarize the story of air pollution in Los Angeles and how it represents the larger problem of air pollution around the world.

Section 19.1

2. What is the key concept for this section? Define *density*, as it relates to the atmosphere, and *atmospheric pressure* and explain why both are two important atmospheric variables. Define and distinguish among **atmosphere**, **troposphere**, **stratosphere**, and **ozone layer**. What are **greenhouse gases**?

Section 19.2

3. What is the key concept for this section? What is **air pollution**? Distinguish between **primary pollutants** and **secondary pollutants** and give an example of each. What are atmospheric brown clouds and what have scientists learned about their harmful effects? List the six major outdoor air pollutants and their harmful effects. Describe the effects of lead as a pollutant and how we can reduce our exposure to this harmful chemical.

4. Distinguish between **industrial smog** and **photochemical smog** in terms of their chemical composition and formation. List and briefly describe five natural factors that help to reduce outdoor air pollution and six natural factors that help to worsen it. What is a **temperature inversion** and how can it affect outdoor air pollution levels?

Section 19.3

5. What is the key concept for this section? What is **acid deposition** and how does it form? What are its major environmental impacts on lakes, forests, human-built structures, and human health? List three major ways to reduce acid deposition. Explain the connections among low-sulfur coal, atmospheric warming, and toxic mercury.

Section 19.4

6. What is the key concept for this section? What is the major indoor air pollutant in many less-developed

countries? What are the top four indoor air pollutants in the United States? List six sources of common indoor air pollutants in a typical modern home. Give three reasons why these pollutants present a serious threat to human health. Explain why radon-222 is an indoor air pollution threat, how and where it occurs, and what can be done about it.

Section 19.5

7. What is the key concept for this section? Describe the human body's defenses against air pollution, how they can be overwhelmed, and the illnesses that can result. Approximately how many people die prematurely from outdoor and indoor air pollution each year in the world and in the United States?

Section 19.6

8. What is the key concept for this section? Summarize the US air pollution laws and how they have worked to reduce pollution. Explain how these laws can be strengthened, according to some scientists.

9. List the advantages and disadvantages of using an emissions trading program to control pollution. Summarize the major ways to reduce emissions from power plants and motor vehicles. What was the key development in major improvements in LA's air quality (**Core Case Study**)? What are four ways to reduce indoor air pollution? Why is preventing air pollution more important than controlling it?

Section 19.7

10. What are the two key concepts for this section? How have human activities depleted ozone in the stratosphere? List five harmful effects of such depletion. Explain how Sherwood Rowland and Mario Molina alerted the world to this threat. What has the world done to reduce the threat of ozone depletion in the stratosphere? What are this chapter's *three key ideas*?

Note: Key terms are in bold type.

AP® Review Questions

Questions 1–4 refer to the labeled diagram of the earth's atmosphere below. Choices may be used once, more than once, or not at all.

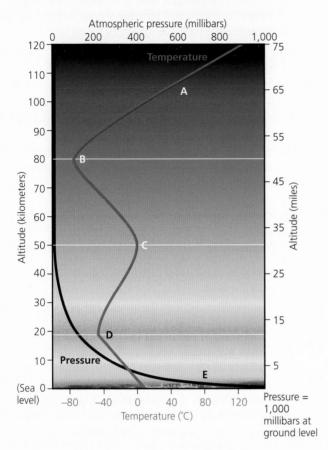

1. The ozone layer is found at this location

2. The atmosphere is at its warmest point at this location

3. The section of the atmosphere responsible for our daily weather

4. The section of the atmosphere with 75–80% of the mass of the atmosphere

5. The source of the ozone in the protective ozone layer is
   - **(A)** the interaction between gaseous oxygen molecules and ultraviolet (UV) light
   - **(B)** the upward drift of the ground-level ozone molecules formed at the earth's surface
   - **(C)** the process of photosynthesis where plants release ozone as a by-product
   - **(D)** the catalysis of oxygen molecules by tropospheric chemicals into the more stable ozone molecules
   - **(E)** the interaction of carbon dioxide molecules with UV light and their subsequent destruction

6. Which of the following best describes secondary air pollutants?
   - **(A)** They are directly emitted from tailpipes and smokestacks.
   - **(B)** They are nonpoint sources of pollution that cannot be regulated by the Clean Air Act.
   - **(C)** They are produced by interactions between primary air pollutants or between primary air pollutants and other chemicals.
   - **(D)** They are emitted indoors from the off-gassing of furniture, carpet, and other man-made fabrics.
   - **(E)** They are pollutants that are of less importance than primary pollutants.

7. Once air pollutants have entered the troposphere, they *may* be
   - **I.** Dissolved and removed by precipitation
   - **II.** Trapped in one region by temperature inversions
   - **III.** Converted into safer gases by tropospheric catalysts
   - **(A)** I only
   - **(B)** II only
   - **(C)** I and II only
   - **(D)** I and III only
   - **(E)** I, II, and III

Questions 8–9 refer to the air pollutants below. Choices may be used once, more than once, or not at all.
   - **(A)** SO_2
   - **(B)** O_3
   - **(C)** CO
   - **(D)** Hydrocarbons
   - **(E)** Particulate matter (PM)

8. A secondary pollutant that is also a component of photochemical smog

9. Solid matter known to aggravate existing respiratory conditions such as asthma and bronchitis

10. All of the following methods are designed to prevent indoor air pollution EXCEPT
   - **(A)** preventing pesticide residues and lead particles from accumulating indoors by taking off shoes upon entering a house
   - **(B)** banning smoking indoors
   - **(C)** heating a house with wood stoves instead of conventional gas or electric heaters
   - **(D)** using a radon-222 monitor in the home
   - **(E)** avoiding the use of volatile substances such as moth crystals and air fresheners

11. Years of smoking and exposure to air pollutants can contribute to the incidence of
    (A) emphysema
    (B) diabetes
    (C) obesity
    (D) anemia
    (E) chronic fatigue syndrome

12. Indoor air pollution is considered one of the most serious problems in developed countries because
    (A) indoor air pollutants are much more toxic than outdoor air pollutants
    (B) indoor air pollution contributes to photochemical smog
    (C) indoor air pollution standards do not exist in developed countries
    (D) the majority of most individuals' lives are spent indoors or in vehicles
    (E) indoor air pollutants are very difficult to filter from the air

13. Which of the following is true of radon-222?
    (A) It is a colorless, odorless, tasteless gas that can cause lung cancer.
    (B) It is a yellowish-green gas that can cause asphyxiation.
    (C) It is a primary pollutant released by the burning of coal.
    (D) It is a secondary pollutant formed when photochemical smog forms.
    (E) It is a by-product of the incineration process for municipal waste.

14. Upholstery, paneling, particle board, and foam insulation may be sources of
    (A) carbon monoxide
    (B) sulfur oxides
    (C) formaldehyde
    (D) carbon dioxide
    (E) radon-222

15. What do all photochemical reactions have in common?
    (A) They release photons of light, called fluorescence, as by-products
    (B) They absorb light and release heat as a by-product.
    (C) They are activated by light.
    (D) They utilize red light to boost electrons to higher orbitals.
    (E) They couple visible light with heat to drive chemical reactions.

16. The air pollutant lead causes which of the following health issues?
    (A) Damage to the nervous system, especially in children
    (B) Respiratory problems and heart disease, especially in urban areas
    (C) Respiratory damage, due to its association with cigarette smoke and burning wood
    (D) Interference with the ability of blood to transport oxygen, resulting in death
    (E) Damage to the reproductive system, often causing sterility

17. Some cities are especially prone to increased levels of air pollution because they are surrounded by mountains, which often leads to
    (A) temperature inversions that trap pollutants
    (B) temperature inversions causing the greenhouse effect
    (C) the heat island effect
    (D) the chimney effect
    (E) an increase in albedo, which raises the temperature

18. Aquatic ecosystems are harmed from air pollution primarily through
    (A) deposition of carbon monoxide gas which depletes the oxygen in the water
    (B) dissolution of radon gas in the water which causes mutations
    (C) leaching of mercury ions into the water from exposed gold mines
    (D) photochemical reactions between water and primary pollutants forming ground level ozone
    (E) deposition of acid rain, which releases aluminum ions that can clog fish gills

19. The Clean Air Act called for all of the following EXCEPT
    (A) the setting of ambient air quality standards to ensure public health
    (B) the setting of minimum mpg standards for all new vehicles
    (C) the setting of point-source emissions standards for all new facilities
    (D) the setting of motor vehicle emission standards
    (E) the development of a timetable for power plants to cut their emissions

20. Of the following devices, which are used to remove particulates and sulfur oxides from coal-fired power plants and other industrial facilities?

    I. Catalytic converter

   II. Electrostatic precipitator

  III. Wet scrubber

  (A) I only

  (B) II only

  (C) III only

  (D) I and II only

  (E) II and III only

AP® Free-Response Practice

1. Air pollution is considered to be a particularly hazardous environmental problem. Approximately 6.5 million people die every year from respiratory diseases directly linked to air pollution.

  (a) Indoor air pollution is considered to be more dangerous than outdoor air pollution.

    (i) **Explain** why indoor air pollution is considered to be more dangerous.

    (ii) **Identify** ONE common indoor air pollutant and **describe** how this pollutant adversely affects human health.

    (iii) **Identify** one strategy for reducing indoor air pollution.

  (b) One major producer of outdoor air pollution is coal-burning power plants. These plants produce industrial smog.

    (i) **Identify** and **describe** one strategy for preventing industrial smog *before* coal is burned.

    (ii) **Identify** and **describe** one strategy for preventing the formation of industrial smog *after* coal has been burned.

  (c) Cap-and-trade is a market-based strategy for reducing air pollution. **Discuss** how this strategy works.

  (d) **Identify** one law meant to reduce the negative impacts of air pollution.

Critical Thinking

1. You have built a time machine and have decided to travel back to 1940 to the city of Los Angeles (**Core Case Study**) to talk with city leaders about air pollution and how to deal with it. You will be informing them of some things they are not aware of, including the connection between car exhaust and smog. Write a strategy for *preventing* a long-term buildup of air pollutants over LA and give your audience your three strongest arguments for adopting your strategy.

2. China relies on coal for two-thirds of its commercial energy usage, partly because the country has abundant supplies of this resource. Yet, China's coal burning has caused innumerable and growing air pollution problems for the country, for its neighboring nations, and even for the west coast of North America. Do you think China has been justified in developing this resource, as other countries—including the United States—have done with their coal resources? Explain. What are China's alternatives?

3. Considering your use of motor vehicles, now and in the future, what are three ways in which you could reduce your contribution to photochemical smog?

4. Should tall smokestacks (Figure 19.9) be banned to help prevent downwind air pollution and acid deposition? Explain. What might be some harmful consequences of doing this?

5. Explain how sulfur impurities in coal can lead to increased acidity in rainwater and to the subsequent depletion of soil nutrients. Write an argument for or against requiring the use of low-sulfur coal in all coal-burning facilities.

6. If you live in the United States, list three important ways in which your life would be different if citizen-led actions during the 1970s and 1980s had not led to the Clean Air Acts of 1970 and its amendments of 1977 and 1990, despite strong political opposition by the affected industries. List three important ways in which your life in the future might be different if such actions do not lead now to the strengthening of the US Clean Air Act. If you do not live in the United States, research the air pollution laws in your country and explain if and how they could be strengthened.

7. List three ways in which you could apply **Concept 19.6** to making your lifestyle more environmentally sustainable.

8. Congratulations! You are in charge of the world. Explain your strategy for dealing with each of the following problems: **(a)** indoor air pollution, **(b)** outdoor air pollution, **(c)** acid deposition, and **(d)** stratospheric ozone depletion.

Data Analysis

Coal often contains sulfur (S) as an impurity that is released as gaseous SO_2 during combustion, and SO_2 is one of six primary air pollutants monitored by the EPA. The US Clean Air Act limits sulfur emissions from large coal-fired boilers to 0.54 kilograms (1.2 pounds) of sulfur per million Btus (British thermal units) of heat generated. (1 metric ton = 1,000 kilograms = 2,200 pounds = 1.1 ton; 1 kilogram = 2.2 pounds.)

1. Given that coal burned in power plants has a heating value of 27.5 million Btus per metric ton (25 million Btus per ton), determine the number of kilograms (and pounds) of coal needed to produce 1 million Btus of heat.

2. If all of the sulfur in the coal is released to the atmosphere during combustion, what is the maximum percentage of sulfur that the coal can contain and still allow the utility to meet the standards of the Clean Air Act?

Answers to Checkpoints for Understanding

Section 19.1

1. Air is most dense in the troposphere because gravity pulls harder on the air molecules closest to the earth's surface.
2. The gases in the troposphere and the stratosphere are similar except for the fact that the troposphere contains more ozone and much less water vapor.
3. The role of the ozone layer is to absorb most of the ultraviolet light emitted by the sun.

Section 19.2

1. Primary pollutants are natural or anthropogenic pollutants that are emitted into the atmosphere. When these pollutants react chemically with each other or with natural components of air, they form secondary pollutants.
2. The major classes of air pollutants are (1) carbon oxides, (2) nitrogen oxides and nitric acid, (3) sulfur dioxide and sulfuric acid, (4) particulates, (5) ozone, and (6) volatile organic compounds.
3. Impacts of severe lead poisoning include palsy, blindness, paralysis, and mental retardation. Lesser health effects include hyperactivity, hearing damage, and learning disorders.
4. Industrial smog results from burning coal or oil; photochemical smog results mostly from car exhaust.
5. Lethal concentrations of air pollutants can build up in regions where temperature inversions occur because a layer of cold air traps a layer of warm air near the earth's surface. If this inversion is not dispersed by winds that break it up, pollutants can build up over several days to harmful concentrations.

Section 19.3

1. Acid deposition is a more appropriate term because H_2SO_4 or HNO_3 can take many forms—rain, snow, fog, sleet, or dry particles.
2. Acid deposition damages statues and buildings, can leach toxic metals such as lead and mercury from soils and rocks into lakes used as source of drinking water, harms fish, harms crops and reduces plant production, and harms trees by leaching plant nutrients from forest soils.

Section 19.4

1. Concentrations are much higher inside buildings than they are outside, increasing exposure considerably.
2. The likelihood of lung cancer increases with the amount of radon in the home, increased exposure, and whether or not the person smokes or has smoked.

Section 19.5

1. Ultrafine particles are so small that they can lodge deeply in the lungs and lead to cancer, asthma, heart attack, and stroke.

Section 19.6

1. Primary air pollution standards are meant to protect human health. Secondary air pollution standards are meant to protect environmental and property damage.
2. Cap-and-trade works by issuing permits to facilities that produce air pollution and those that reduce their emissions can sell their remaining permits to other facilities or save them for future facility expansions.
3. Particulates and SO_2 can be captured by using electrostatic precipitators or wet scrubbers to capture pollutants before they are emitted into the atmosphere.

Section 19.7

1. CFCs are persistent, and can take one to two decades to reach the stratosphere; ultraviolet light in the stratosphere breaks down these chemicals and releases chloride and other ions that breakdown the O_3 molecules; and CFCs can remain in the stratosphere for 65 to 385 years, continuously breaking down ozone molecules.
2. The Montreal Protocol was a 1987 agreement between 36 nations to reduce production of CFCs and other ozone-destroying chemicals. If it continues to be enforced, life-saving ozone in the stratosphere should return to 1980 levels by 2050.

Core Case Study

The Clean Air Act of 1970 was enacted and put strict limits on emissions from cars, diesel engines and coal-burning facilities.

Climate Change

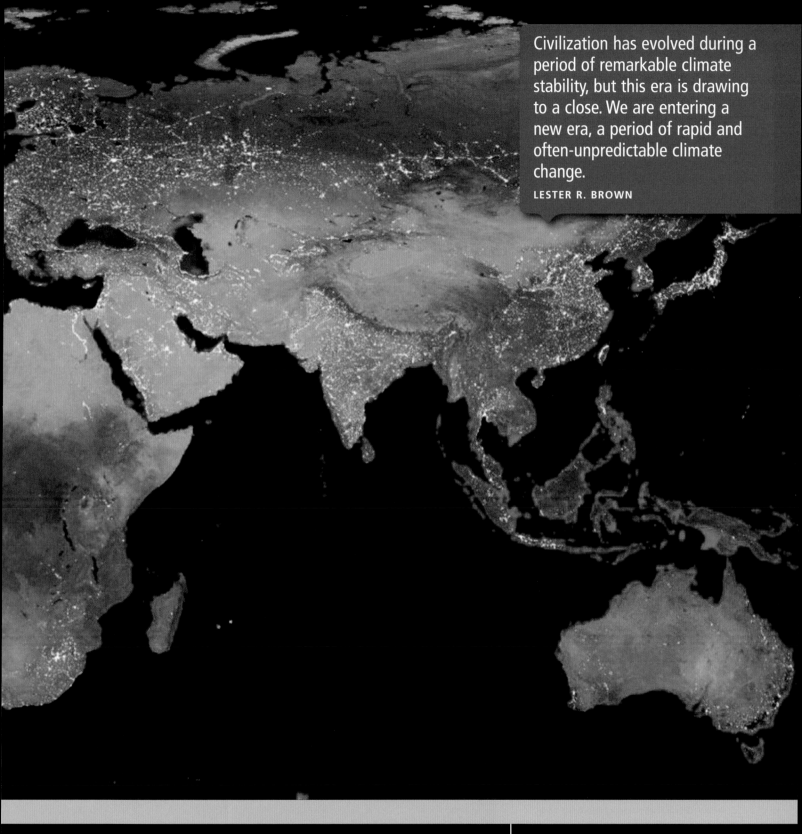

Civilization has evolved during a period of remarkable climate stability, but this era is drawing to a close. We are entering a new era, a period of rapid and often-unpredictable climate change.

LESTER R. BROWN

Key Questions

20.1 How and why is the earth's climate changing?

20.2 What are the likely effects of a warmer atmosphere?

20.3 How can we slow climate change?

20.4 How can we adapt to climate change?

Areas that could be flooded by the end of this century (shown in red) by a 1-meter (3-foot) rise in sea level due to projected climate change.

NASA

Melting Ice in Greenland

Greenland is the world's largest island with a population of about 59,000 people. The ice that covers most of this mountainous island lies in glaciers that are as deep as 3.2 kilometers (2 miles).

Areas of the island's ice have been melting at an accelerating rate during Greenland's summers (Figure 20.1). Some of this ice is replaced by snow during winter months, but the annual net loss of Greenland's ice has increased during recent years.

Why does it matter that ice in Greenland is melting? It matters because considerable scientific evidence indicates that atmospheric warming is a key factor behind this melting. **Atmospheric warming** is the gradual overall rise in the average temperature of the atmosphere near the earth's land and water surfaces over a period of 30 years or more. During this century, atmospheric warming is projected to continue and to lead to dramatic **climate change**—measurable changes in global weather patterns based primarily on changes in the earth's atmospheric temperature averaged over a period of at least 30 years. Climate scientists warn that if no action is taken, the earth's climate system could reach *climate change tipping points*, which could result in damage to most of the earth's ecosystems, people, and economies for hundreds to thousands of years.

Greenland's glaciers contain enough water to raise the global sea level by as much as 7 meters (23 feet) if all of it melts and drains into the sea. It is highly unlikely that this will happen. But even a moderate loss of this ice over one or more centuries would raise sea levels considerably (see chapter-opening photo). Already Greenland's ice loss has been responsible for nearly one-sixth of the global sea-level rise over the past 20 years. Climate scientists view Greenland's melting ice as an early warning that human activities are very likely to disrupt the earth's climate in ways that could threaten life as we know it, especially during the latter half of this century.

In 1988, the World Meteorological Organization and the United Nations Environment Programme (UNEP) established the Intergovernmental Panel on Climate Change (IPCC) to document past climate changes and project future climate changes. The IPCC network includes more than 2,500 scientists in climate studies and related disciplines from more than 130 countries.

After reviewing tens of thousands of research studies for more than 25 years, the IPCC and most of the world's major scientific bodies, including the US National Academy of Sciences and the British Royal Society, have come to three major conclusions: **(1)** climate change is real and is happening now; **(2)** human activities such as the burning of fossil fuels and the clearing of forests play an important role in current climate change; and **(3)** climate change is projected to accelerate and have harmful effects, such as rising seas, ocean acidification, species extinction, and more extreme weather events, including intense and longer lasting heat waves, especially during the latter half of this century, unless we act now to slow it down.

In this chapter, we examine the likely causes and effects of climate change, and we look at some possible ways to deal with this major environmental, economic, and political challenge.●

CRITICAL THINKING:

Do you believe that climate change is real and that human activities play an important role in current and future climate change? When you finish this chapter revisit this question to see if your answer has changed.

Space/NASA Sites

1982

2012

FIGURE 20.1 The total area of Greenland's glacial ice that melted during the summer of 2012 (red area in right image) was much greater than the amount that melted during the summer of 1982 (left). This trend has continued since 2012.

(Compiled by the authors using data from Konrad Steffen and Russell Huff, University of Colorado, Boulder; National Snow and Ice Data Center; and Thomas Mote, University of Georgia.)

20.1 HOW AND WHY IS THE EARTH'S CLIMATE CHANGING?

CONCEPT 20.1 Considerable scientific evidence strongly indicates that the atmosphere is warming and changing the earth's climate and that human activities, such as burning fossil fuels and deforestation, play an important role in these recent changes.

Weather and Climate

In thinking about climate change, it is important to distinguish between *weather* and *climate*. **Weather** consists of short-term changes in atmospheric variables such as the temperature and precipitation in a given area over a period of hours or days. In contrast, **climate,** as defined by the World Meteorological Society, is determined by the weather conditions of the earth or of a particular area, especially atmospheric temperatures, averaged over at least three decades. Scientists have used such long-term measurements to divide the earth into various climate zones (see Figure 5.7, p. 125).

Atmospheric warming does not mean that all of the earth is getting warmer or that this happens every year. Instead, as the earth's average atmospheric temperature rises, some areas get warmer and some get cooler because of interactions in the planet's complex climate system. However, when the *global* atmospheric temperature averaged over at least 30 years increases or decreases, the earth's climate has changed. Climate change is not just about temperature changes. It is also about shifting rainfall patterns that can lead to prolonged drought or increased floods.

Because of the confusion about the difference between weather and climate, much of the information and debate about climate change centers around weather not climate. This has resulted in misinformation and confusion. For example, some people claim that climate change is not occurring or is a hoax because it snowed heavily during a winter month or because the average weather of a year or even a decade or two where they live has been cooler. These are statements about weather not climate.

No one can make any meaningful statements about changes in the earth's climate or the climate of any part of the planet unless those statements are based on looking at the trends in key variables such as atmospheric temperature *averaged over at least 30 years*. So when you read or hear statements about climate change the most important question to ask is: Is this a statement about climate or about weather?

Climate and the Natural Greenhouse Effect

The **greenhouse effect** (see Figure 3.3, p. 68) is a natural process that plays a major role in determining the earth's average atmospheric temperature and thus its climate. In the 19th century scientists hypothesized that certain gases in the atmosphere trap some of the sun's heat that would otherwise return to space. This effect occurs when some of the solar energy absorbed by the earth radiates into the atmosphere as infrared radiation (heat). As this radiation interacts with molecules of several greenhouse gases in the air, it increases their kinetic energy and warms the lower atmosphere and the earth's surface.

Numerous laboratory experiments and measurements of temperatures at different altitudes have confirmed the greenhouse effect—one of the most widely accepted theories in the atmospheric sciences. Life on the earth and our economic systems are dependent on the greenhouse effect because it keeps the planet at an average temperature of around 15°C (58°F). Without it, the earth would be a frozen, uninhabitable place and you would not be reading these words.

There are several greenhouse gases, but we focus on three major gases—CO_2, CH_4, and N_2O—that play varying roles in atmospheric warming because of their varying lifetimes in the atmosphere and varying warming potentials (Figure 20.2).

The atmospheric concentration of CO_2, as part of the carbon cycle (see Figure 3.15, p. 78), plays a key role in determining the average temperature of the atmosphere. Measurements of CO_2 in bubbles at various depths in ancient glacial ice (Science Focus 20.1) indicate that changes in the levels of this gas in the lower atmosphere have correlated closely with changes in the global average temperature near the earth's surface during the past 400,000 years (Figure 20.3). Scientists have noted a similar correlation between atmospheric temperatures and methane (CH_4) emissions.

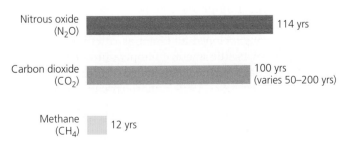

Atmospheric lifetime

Nitrous oxide (N_2O) — 114 yrs

Carbon dioxide (CO_2) — 100 yrs (varies 50–200 yrs)

Methane (CH_4) — 12 yrs

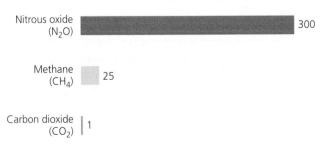

Atmospheric Warming Potential
(over 100 years, as multiples of CO_2 warming potential)

Nitrous oxide (N_2O) — 300

Methane (CH_4) — 25

Carbon dioxide (CO_2) — 1

FIGURE 20.2 Atmospheric lifetimes and warming potentials for three major greenhouse gases.

(Compiled by the authors using data from National Oceanic and Atmospheric Administration and U.N. Framework Convention on Climate Change.)

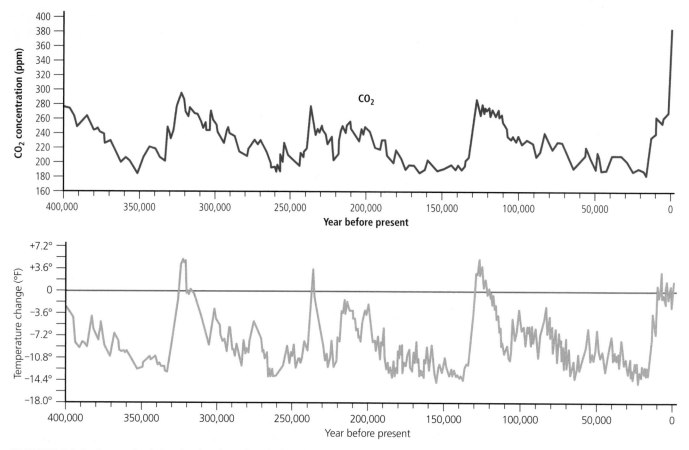

FIGURE 20.3 Atmospheric levels of carbon dioxide (CO_2) and changes in average global temperature of the atmosphere near the earth's surface over the past 400,000 years. These data were obtained by analysis of ice cores removed at Russia's Vostok Research Station in Antarctica.

(Data from Intergovernmental Panel on Climate Change, National Center for Atmospheric Research, and F. Vimeux, et al. 2002. *Earth and Planetary Science Letters*, vol. 203:829–843.)

Climate Change in the Past

Climate change is neither new nor unusual. Over the past 3.5 billion years, many natural factors have played key roles in past climate change. These natural factors include **(1)** massive volcanic eruptions and impacts by meteors and asteroids that cooled the planet by injecting large amounts of debris into the atmosphere; **(2)** changes in solar input that can warm or cool the earth; **(3)** slight changes in the shape of the earth's orbit around the sun from mostly round to more elliptical over a 100,000 year cycle; **(4)** slight changes in the tilt of the earth's axis over a 41,000-year cycle; **(5)** slight changes in the earth's wobbly orbit around the sun over a 20,000-year cycle (Factors 3, 4, and 5 are known *Milankovitch cycles*); **(6)** global air circulation patterns (see Figure 5.9, p. 126); **(7)** changes in the sizes of areas of ice that reflect incoming solar energy and cool the atmosphere; **(8)** changes in concentrations of greenhouse gases; and **(9)** occasional changes in ocean currents.

Scientific research (see Science Focus 20.1) reveals that the earth's climate has fluctuated over the past 900,000 years, slowly swinging back and forth between long periods of atmospheric warming that melted much of the earth's ice and raised sea levels enough to flood large areas of land, and atmospheric cooling that led to ice ages (Figure 20.4, top left). These alternating freezing and thawing periods are known as *glacial* and *interglacial periods*.

For roughly 10,000 years, the earth has experienced an interglacial period characterized by a generally stable climate and atmospheric temperatures (Figure 20.4, bottom left). This allowed the human population to grow as agriculture developed and later as cities grew. For the past 1,000 years, the average temperature of the earth's atmosphere has remained fairly stable (Figure 20.4, bottom right). However, since 1975, atmospheric temperatures in most years have been rising (Figure 20.4, top right).

The Study of Climate in the Distant Past

Scientists estimate past atmospheric temperature changes (Figure 20.4) by analyzing evidence from many sources. One of the most important sources is ancient ice. As snow accumulates in the earth's polar regions, lower layers of snow are compressed by upper layers and become ice. Each of these compressed layers contains dust, volcanic ash, and other substances, along with bubbles of gas that were captured in this ice thousands of years ago. By drilling deep into ancient ice and removing elongated cores (Figure 20.A) scientists can gather information about historical greenhouse gas levels in bubbles found at different depths, along with information about volcanic eruptions, forest fires, and other events that emitted chemicals into the atmosphere.

Buried pollen grains are another source of information about past climate change. Seed-bearing plants produce pollens, and botanists can examine them to determine which plants produced them. Pollens buried in the sediments of wetlands and lake bottoms have been preserved for millions of years. By examining them, scientists can reconstruct the plant community that existed in a given area centuries ago. This in turn gives clues to what kind of climate existed there.

Another way to study the past is to examine tree rings. The cross section of a very old tree shows many rings, each of which represents a year's growth. A wider ring represents more growth for the tree than a narrow ring, and thus by counting the rings and projecting back, scientists can tell which years were favorable for growth of the tree and which were not. This gives more clues about temperatures, moisture, and other climate factors over hundreds to thousands of years.

Similarly, coral reefs can reveal year-by-year layering. Scientists gather information about historical ocean chemistry and water temperatures by examining these layers in coral cross sections. These data are related to changes in climate factors such as atmospheric CO_2 and temperatures and they give clues about how the climate changed over time.

Other sources of data include radioisotopes in rocks and fossils; plankton and radioisotopes in ocean sediments; and atmospheric temperature measurements taken regularly since 1861. These temperature measurements now include data from more than 40,000 measuring stations around the world, as well as from satellites.

FIGURE 20.A *Ice cores* are extracted by drilling deep holes into ancient glaciers at various sites such as this one near the South Pole in Antarctica. Analysis of ice cores yields information about the past composition of the lower atmosphere, temperature trends such as those shown in Figure 20.2, solar activity, snowfall, and forest fire frequency.

U.S. Geological Survey

CRITICAL THINKING

How would you use the information in this Science Focus to respond to someone who believes that climate change is a scientific hoax?

Current Atmospheric Warming and Climate Change

Data from tens of thousands of peer-reviewed scientific studies support the conclusion that climate change is happening now. The following are a few pieces of such evidence:

- Between 1906 and 2016, the earth's average global surface temperature rose by 0.94C° (1.7F°). Much of this increase took place since 1975 (Figure 20.4, upper right). By definition, this more than 40-year general increase in the earth's atmospheric temperature means that climate change has taken place.

- The 10 warmest years on record since 1861 have taken place since 2005.

- In the Arctic, floating summer sea ice has been shrinking in most years since 1979.

- In some parts of the world, glaciers that have existed for thousands of years (Figure 20.5) are melting.

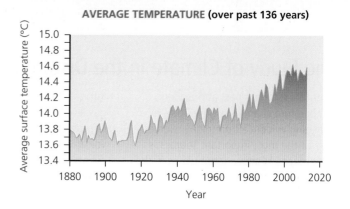

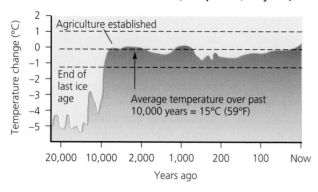
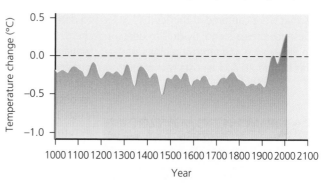

FIGURE 20.4 The global average temperature of the atmosphere near the earth's surface has changed significantly over time. The two graphs in the top half of this figure are estimates of global average temperatures, and the two graphs on the bottom are estimates of changes in the average temperature over different periods. *Critical thinking:* What are two conclusions that you can draw from these diagrams?

(Compiled by the authors using data from Goddard Institute for Space Studies, Intergovernmental Panel on Climate Change, National Academy of Sciences, National Aeronautics and Space Administration, National Center for Atmospheric Research, and National Oceanic and Atmospheric Administration.)

- In Alaska, glaciers and frozen ground (permafrost) are melting, loss of sea ice and rising sea levels are eating away at coastlines, and communities are being relocated inland.

- The world's average sea level has been rising at an accelerated rate, especially since 1975. This rise is mostly due to the expansion of ocean water as its temperature increased and increasing runoff of water from melting land-based ice.

- Atmospheric levels of greenhouse gases such as CO_2 and CH_4 that warm the lower atmosphere have been rising sharply.

- As temperatures have risen, many terrestrial, marine, and freshwater species have migrated toward the poles and, on land, to cooler higher elevations. Species that cannot migrate face extinction.

Role of Human Activities in Current Atmospheric Warming

Research reveals that past changes in the earth's climate were due to the natural factors listed on p. 636. However, since the beginning of the Industrial Revolution in the mid-1700s, human actions—mainly the burning of fossil fuels, deforestation, and agriculture—have led to significant increases in the concentrations of several greenhouse gases, especially CO_2, in the lower atmosphere (Figure 20.6). After oscillating between 180 and 280 ppm for 400,000 years, average atmospheric levels of CO_2 reached 405 ppm in 2016—higher than at any time in the last 4.5 million years according to NOAA scientists.

Atmospheric levels of methane (CH_4), another greenhouse gas, have also increased greatly since the mid-1970s. Ice core analysis reveals that about 70% of

110 million
Average number of metric tons of CO_2 that human activities pump into the atmosphere every day.

Calculating a Carbon Footprint

A carbon footprint is defined as the amount of carbon compounds, especially carbon dioxide, emitted by a person, city, country or other entity due to the burning of fossil fuels. Factors considered when calculating a person's carbon footprint include the size of their home and how many people share that dwelling, the type of diet, meat-based or vegetarian, whether the individual regularly uses public transportation such as the train, subway, or bus rather than driving a car, and how goods are consumed (buying new, used, or recycled goods). All of these activities require the use of fossil fuels.

FRQ Application

The graph in Figure 20.B shows the total CO_2 emissions for various countries in million metric tons, and per person in metric tons for the year 2013.

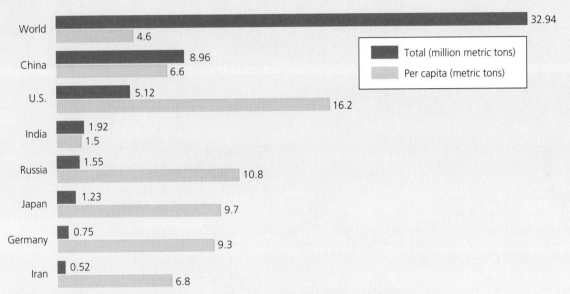

FIGURE 20.B Total CO_2 emissions (in million metric tons) and CO_2 emissions per person (in metric tons) for selected countries in 2013. *Critical thinking:* What are two conclusions that you can draw from these data?

(Compiled by the authors using data from International Energy Agency, US Department of Energy Carbon Dioxide Information Analysis Center, and Earth Policy Institute.)

Using the graph, calculate the percentage of the world's CO_2 emissions generated by the United States in 2013.

$$\frac{5.12\,\text{million metric tons (US)}}{32.94\,\text{million metric tons (World)}} \times 100 = 15.6\%$$

In 2013, how many times more CO_2 was generated per person in the United States as compared to an individual in Germany?

CO_2 generated per person in the United States = 16.2 metric tons
CO_2 generated per person in Germany = 9.3 metric tons

16.2 metric tons / 9.3 metric tons = 1.7 times more CO_2 generated by a US citizen

global emissions of methane during the last 275 years were likely caused by human activities, including livestock production, rice production, natural gas production, use of landfills, and the flooding of land behind large dams. The other 30% came from natural sources. Methane remains in the atmosphere for about 12 years compared to CO_2, which remains at least 100 years. However, each molecule of methane warms the air 25 times more than a molecule of CO_2.

In 2016, the three largest emitters of fossil fuel-related CO_2 were, in order, China, the United States, and India, according to the UN Statistics Division. In comparing CO_2 emissions sources, scientists use the concept of a **carbon footprint**. It refers to the amount of CO_2 generated by an individual, a country, a city, or any other entity over a given period. A **per capita carbon footprint** is the average footprint per person in a population (see Math Connection). China has the largest national carbon footprint, followed by the United States and

FIGURE 20.5 Between 1913 (top) and 2008 (bottom) much of the ice that covered Sperry Glacier in Montana's Glacier National Park melted.

Top: W. C. Alden/GNP Archives/US Geological Survey. Bottom: Lisa McKeon/US Geological Survey.

India. The United States has the largest per capita carbon footprint—several times larger than those of China and India—followed by Russia and Japan. Since 1850, the United States has emitted much more CO_2 than any other country.

Evidence from thousands of peer-reviewed scientific studies indicates these human activities have played an important role in the recent increase in the earth's atmospheric temperatures (Figure 20.4, top right) and the resulting climate change. One reason for this is that human activities, especially the large-scale burning of carbon-containing fossil fuels, have been adding the greenhouse gas CO_2 to the atmosphere (Figure 20.6) faster than the carbon cycle (Figure 3.15, p. 78) can remove it. As atmospheric levels of CO_2 rise (Figure 20.6), the gas becomes a pollutant that warms the atmosphere and plays a role in the climate change and its harmful environmental, health, and economic effects. In other words, human activities have been enhancing the natural greenhouse

effect (Figure 3.3, p. 68) that supports the earth's life and human economies.

A second reason is that human activities have been cutting down large areas of the world's forests much faster than they can grow back naturally through ecological succession or by planting new trees. This eliminates large areas of vegetation that remove some of the excess CO_2 that human activities add to atmosphere.

Considerable scientific evidence indicates that these two human-related factors have played an important role in the rise in average atmospheric temperature (Figure 20.4) for more than 40 years and thus in the resulting change in the earth's climate. This is many times faster than past climate changes caused by natural factors that took place over hundreds to thousands of years (Figure 20.4, top left).

In 1988, the World Meteorological Organization and the UN Environment Programme (UNEP) established the Intergovernmental Panel on Climate Change (IPCC) to

document past climate changes and project future climate changes. The IPCC network includes more than 2,500 scientists working in climate studies and related disciplines from more than 130 countries.

Between 2007 and 2014, the world's leading scientific organizations—including the IPCC, US National Academy of Sciences (NAS), Great Britain's Royal Society, US National Oceanic and Atmospheric Administration (NOAA), US National Aeronautics and Space Administration (NASA), American Association for the Advancement of Science (AAAS, the world's largest general scientific society), and at least 90% of the world's climate scientists—all reached the following four major conclusions:

1. Climate change is happening now.

2. Human activities such as burning fossil fuels, (which adds CO_2 to the atmosphere) and clearing of forests (which when left intact remove CO_2 from the atmosphere) play an important role in current climate change.

3. Average atmospheric temperatures are likely to increase (see Science Focus 20.2) and lead to more and faster climate change, unless we act now to slow it.

4. Immediate and sustained action to curb climate change is possible and affordable and would bring major benefits for human health and economies, as well as for the environment.

After after several decades of research, at least 90% of the world's more than 2,500 leading climate scientists who have published peer reviewed climate change research articles agree that the earth's climate is changing and that human activities have played an important role in this change over the past four decades. Such a high and rare level of agreement among the top research scientists in the field of climate change, means that there is no longer any widespread or serious debate in scientific circles about this issue. Some scientists disagree, but most of these individuals have not published peer-reviewed articles in this field.

Using Models to Project Future Changes in Atmospheric Temperatures

There is widespread scientific evidence that the atmosphere is warming and changing the climate and that human activities play an important role in these changes. The key question is how much the earth's average atmospheric temperatures are likely to change in the future.

Scientists have developed mathematical models of the earth's complex climate system to help project the effects of increasing levels of greenhouse gases on future average atmospheric temperatures. *These models* simulate interactions among natural factors such as incoming sunlight, the three natural Milankovitch cycles, clouds, landmasses, glaciers, floating sea ice, ocean currents, and human factors such as greenhouse gas emissions, emissions of other air pollutants, and deforestation within the earth's complex climate system.

Scientists run these continually improving models on supercomputers and compare the results to known past average atmospheric temperatures. They use these data to project future changes in earth's average atmospheric temperature. Figure 20.C gives a greatly simplified summary of some of the key interactions used in climate models of the global climate system.

Climate models provide *projections* of what is likely to happen to the average temperature of the lower atmosphere, based on available data and different assumptions about future changes such as CO_2 and CH_4 levels in the atmosphere. How well the projections match what actually happens depends on the validity of the assumptions, the variables built into the models (Figure 20.C), and the accuracy of the data used.

Recall that scientific research does not provide absolute proof or certainty. Instead, science provides us with varying levels of certainty. According to the 2014 IPCC report, based on analysis of past climate data and the use of more than two dozen climate models, it is *extremely likely* that human activities, especially the burning of fossil fuels, have played an important role in the observed atmospheric warming since 1975 (Figure 20.4, top right). Researchers

based this conclusion on thousands of peer-reviewed research studies and on the fact that, after thousands of times running the models, the only way to get the model results to match actual past temperature

measurements was by including the human activities factor (Figure 20.D).

However, there is a high degree of uncertainty about future changes in the earth's average atmospheric temperature.

FIGURE 20.C A simplified model of some major processes that interact to affect the earth's climate by determining the average temperature and greenhouse gas content of the lower atmosphere. Red arrows show processes that warm the atmosphere and blue arrows show those that cool it. **CRITICAL THINKING:** Why do you think a decrease in snow and ice cover is adding to the warming of the atmosphere?

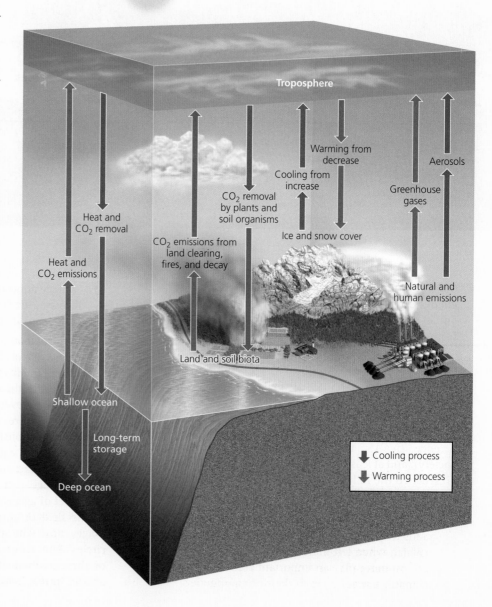

According to current climate models, by the end of this century the temperature of the earth's atmosphere is projected to increase by 2.5°C (2.7°F) to 4.5°C (8.1°F). This wide range of projected change makes it difficult for the world, countries, businesses, and individuals to plan for the future, but it seems clear we need to adapt human behavior if we hope to slow down climate change. The key

unknown in projecting future atmospheric temperatures is how much carbon dioxide we release into the atmosphere.

Despite their limitations, these models are the best and only tools that we have for projecting likely average atmospheric temperatures in coming decades. This also shows the urgent need to increase data and research on climate change and on improving climate models.

CRITICAL THINKING

If the earth's highest projected temperature increase of (4.5°C or 8.1°F) is reached, what are three major ways in which this will likely affect your lifestyle and those of any children or grandchildren you might have?

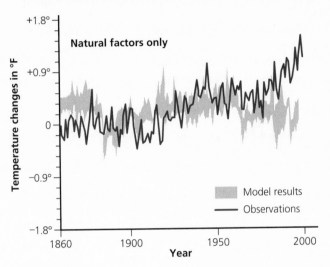
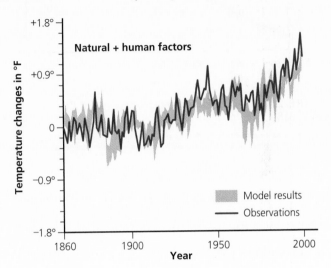

FIGURE 20.D Comparison of actual climate data with modeled projections for the period between 1860 and 2000 using natural factors only (left) and a combination of natural and human factors (right). Scientists have found that actual data match projections far more closely when human factors are included in the models.

(Compiled by the authors using data from Intergovernmental Panel on Climate Change.)

However, there is intense debate and disagreement in the political arena among citizens, elected officials, and officials of companies that produce fossil fuels that add CO_2 to the atmosphere. This debate centers on which, if any, political and economic actions should be taken to deal with climate change. It is an important and difficult political, economic, and ethical issue because modern economies and lifestyles are built around burning fossil fuels that supply 90% of the world's commercial energy and are largely responsible for three of the most serious environmental problems that humanity faces: air pollution, climate change, and ocean acidification.

A key question is how much atmospheric warming and climate change can we expect during the rest of this century and what are the likely effects of such changes? Much of the evidence that climate scientists use to make such projections involves the use climate models (Science Focus 20.2). Climate scientists have identified key natural and human-related factors that might *amplify* or *dampen* projected future changes in the earth's average atmospheric temperature and include these variables in their climate models.

Role of the Sun in Current Atmospheric Warming

The energy output of the sun plays the key role in the earth's temperature, and this output has varied over millions of years. However, climate researchers Claus Froehlich, Mike Lockwood, and Ben Santer all concluded in separate studies that most of the rise in global average atmospheric temperatures since 1975 (Figure 20.4, top right) could not be the result of increased solar output. Instead, they determined that the energy output of the sun has dropped slightly during the past several decades. A detailed data analysis by physicist Richard Muller and his colleagues confirmed this conclusion.

Froehlich noted that, according to satellite and weather balloon measurements since 1975, the troposphere has warmed while the stratosphere has cooled. This is the opposite of what a hotter sun would do, which would be to heat the atmosphere from the top down. Instead, the data show that the atmosphere is

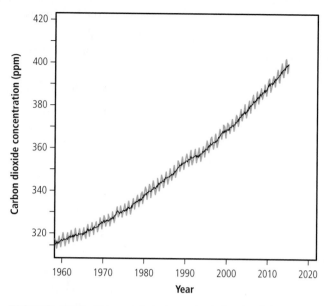

FIGURE 20.6 Rising global atmospheric levels of CO_2, 1880–2015.

(Compiled by the authors using data from Earth Policy Institute BP, *Statistical Review of World Energy*, 2015, Intergovernmental Panel on Climate Change, and National Center for Atmospheric Research.)

now heating from the bottom up, which indicates that inputs at the earth's surface (most likely from human activities) play the more important role in atmospheric warming.

Effects of the Oceans on Current Atmospheric Warming

The world's oceans have played a key role in slowing the rate of atmospheric warming and climate change. They absorb CO_2 from the atmosphere as part of the carbon cycle and thus help to moderate the earth's average surface temperature and its climate. Research indicates that the oceans remove roughly 25% of the CO_2 pumped into the lower atmosphere by human activities. Most of it is stored as carbon compounds in marine algae and vegetation and in coral reefs and eventually is stored for several hundred million years in carbon compounds in ocean bottom sediments.

The oceans also absorb heat from the lower atmosphere. According to a 2016 study by researchers at Lawrence Livermore National Laboratory, more than 90% of the heat held in the atmosphere by greenhouse gas pollution since the 1970s has ended up in the oceans. This has warmed the oceans with ocean currents pushing about a third of the heat into the ocean depths. Thus, the average temperature of the oceans has also risen since 1970.

The uptake of CO_2 and heat by the world's oceans has slowed the rate of recent atmospheric warming and climate change. However, this has resulted in the serious and growing problem of ocean acidification, which could have harmful effects on marine ecosystems, which we discuss later in this chapter.

Effects of Cloud Cover on Atmospheric Warming

Warmer temperatures increase evaporation of surface water, which raises the relative humidity of the atmosphere in various parts of the world. This creates more clouds that can either cool or warm the atmosphere. An increase in thick and continuous *cumulus clouds* at low altitudes (Figure 20.7, left) can have a cooling effect by reflecting more sunlight back into space. An increase in thin, wispy *cirrus clouds* at high altitudes (Figure 20.7, right) would warm the lower atmosphere by allowing more sunlight to reach the earth's surface and preventing some heat from escaping into space.

According to a recent NAS report, the latest scientific research indicates that the net global effect of cloud cover changes is likely to increase atmospheric warming. More research is needed to evaluate this effect and project how it will affect future atmospheric temperatures.

Effects of Outdoor Air Pollution on Atmospheric Warming

According to the 2014 IPCC report, air pollution in the form of *aerosols* (suspended microscopic droplets and solid particles) from human activities can affect the rate of atmospheric warming. These aerosols can hinder or enhance both the greenhouse effect and cloud formation, depending on factors such as their size and reflectivity.

Most aerosols, such as light-colored sulfate particles produced by fossil fuel combustion, tend to reflect incoming sunlight and cool the lower atmosphere. However, black carbon particles, or *soot*—emitted into the air by coal-burning power and industrial plants, diesel exhaust, open cooking fires, and burning forests—warm the lower atmosphere.

Climate scientists do not expect aerosols and soot particles to affect climate change very much over the next 50 years for two reasons. *First*, aerosols and soot fall back to the earth or are washed out of the lower atmosphere within weeks, whereas CO_2 typically remains in the lower atmosphere for 100 years or longer. *Second*, we are reducing aerosol and soot emissions because of their harmful impacts on plants and humans.

CHECKPOINT FOR UNDERSTANDING 20.1

1. Explain how climate differs from weather.

2. Identify factors that naturally change the climate.

3. Identify two human activities that have led to climate change.

4. Explain how the current warming of the earth is different from the other periods of natural warming that have occurred in the past.

5. Explain the purpose of climate models.

Tatiana Grozetskaya/Shutterstock.com

Cheryl Casey/Shutterstock.com

FIGURE 20.7 Cumulus clouds (left) are thick, relatively low-lying clouds that tend to decrease surface warming by reflecting some incoming solar radiation back into space. Cirrus clouds (right) are thin and float at high altitudes; they tend to warm the earth's surface by preventing some heat from flowing into space.

20.2 WHAT ARE THE LIKELY EFFECTS OF A WARMER ATMOSPHERE?

CONCEPT 20.2 The projected change in the atmosphere's temperature could have severe and long-lasting consequences, including flooding, rising sea levels, shifts in the locations of croplands and wildlife habitats, and more extreme weather.

Rapid Atmospheric Warming Could Have Serious Consequences

Most past changes in the temperature of the lower atmosphere took place over thousands of years (Figure 20.4, top left). What makes the current problem urgent is that humanity faces *a rapid projected increase in the average temperature of the lower atmosphere during this century.* According to at least 90% of the world's climate scientists, this will very likely change the mild climate we have had for the past 10,000 years (Figure 20.4, bottom left). According to the 2014 AAAS report on climate change, "The rate of climate change now may be as fast as any extended warming period over the past 65 million years, and is projected to increase in coming years."

Climate research and worst-case climate model projections indicate that rising atmospheric temperatures will likely lead to the following effects within this century:

- floods in low-lying coastal cities from a rise in sea levels (see chapter-opening photo)
- more severe drought
- more intense and longer-lasting heat waves

- more destructive storms and flooding
- forest loss and increased forest fires
- species extinction

These effects will likely reduce food security and increase poverty and social conflict in many poorer nations. These countries that are the least responsible for atmospheric warming are also the least able to deal with the harmful consequences. The models indicate that we will have to deal simultaneously with many of these disruptive effects within this century—an incredibly short time to bring about a major shift in the way we live and interact with our life-support system.

Scientists have identified a number of components of the climate system that could pass **climate change tipping points**—thresholds beyond which natural systems could change for hundreds to thousands of years. Figure 20.8 lists several climate change tipping points.

Increased Melting of Ice and Snow

Models project that climate change will be the most severe in the world's polar regions. **Albedo** is a measure of the reflectivity of sunlight by a surface such as ice and snow (high reflectivity because of its optical brightness, or whiteness), soil and desert (medium reflectivity), and ocean water (low reflectivity). Light-colored ice and snow in the world's polar regions cool the earth by reflecting much of the solar energy that strikes them back into space.

During the past 50 years, the atmosphere above the poles has warmed much more than the atmosphere in the rest of the world. As warming increases in the polar regions, more snow and ice will melt. This will expose darker and less reflective land and ocean water. This will further increase atmospheric warming above the poles, melt more ice and snow, and increase the temperature of the polar oceans in a runaway positive feedback loop (see Figure 2.15, p. 52).

Sea ice is frozen ocean water that melts each summer and refreezes each winter. Mostly because of the increased temperature of the Arctic atmosphere and Arctic ocean waters, the area covered by floating sea ice and the volume of summer sea ice in the Arctic have decreased (see graphs in Figure 20.9). Measurements indicate that this accelerated melting is happening because of warmer air above the ice and warmer water below.

- Atmospheric carbon level of 450 ppm

- Melting of all arctic summer sea ice

- Collapse and melting of the Greenland ice sheet

- Severe ocean acidification, collapse of phytoplankton populations, and a sharp drop in the ability of the oceans to absorb CO_2

- Massive release of methane from thawing arctic permafrost and from the arctic seafloor

- Collapse and melting of most of the western Antarctic ice sheet

- Severe shrinkage or collapse of Amazon rain forest

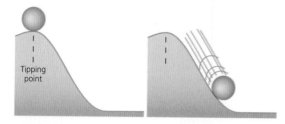

FIGURE 20.8 Climate scientists have come up with this list of possible climate change tipping points.

Because of changes in short-term weather conditions, summer arctic sea ice coverage is likely to fluctuate. However, the overall projected long-term climate trends are for the Arctic to warm, the average summer sea ice coverage to decrease, and the ice to become thinner.

One of the climate-change tipping points that concern scientists is the complete melting of floating summer Arctic sea ice, which has been melting for several decades (Figure 20.9). If the current trend continues, summer floating Arctic ice may be gone by 2050, according to the 2014 IPCC report. This could lead to dramatic and long-lasting changes in weather and climate that could affect the entire planet.

Another effect of arctic warming is faster melting of polar land-based ice, including in Greenland (Figure 20.10 and **Core Case Study**). This melting is adding freshwater to the northern seas, and is likely to contribute to a projected rise in sea level during this century. Nature photographer James Balog (Individuals Matter 20.1) has created a compelling visual record of dramatic changes to glaciers around the world.

Another great storehouse of ice is the earth's mountain glaciers. During the past 25 years, many of these glaciers have been shrinking wherever summer melting exceeds the winter *snowpack*—the addition of ice from precipitation in winter. For example, Glacier National Park (Figure 20.5) in the US state of Montana once had 150 glaciers, but by 2016, only 25 remained.

Mountain glaciers play a vital role in the water cycle (see Figure 3.14, p. 77) by storing water as ice during cold seasons and releasing it slowly to streams during warmer seasons. A prime example is the glaciers of the Himalayan Mountains in Asia. They are a major source of water for large rivers such as

the Ganges that provide water for more than 400 million people in India and Bangladesh. These waters also feed China's Yangtze and Yellow Rivers, whose basins are home to more than 500 million people.

About 80% of the mountain glaciers in South America's Andes range are slowly shrinking. If this continues, 59 million people in Bolivia, Peru, and Ecuador who rely on meltwater from the glaciers for irrigation and hydropower could face severe water, power, and food shortages. In the United States, according to climate models, people living in the Columbia, Sacramento, and Colorado River basins face similar threats as the winter snowpack that feeds these rivers is projected to shrink by as much as 70% by 2050.

Methane Emissions from Thawing Permafrost

Permafrost occurs in soils found beneath about 25% of the exposed land in Alaska, Canada, and Siberia in the northern hemisphere. Huge amounts of carbon are locked up in organic material below these permafrost soils. When exposed to warmer temperatures permafrost thaws but does not melt. This thaw is already happening in parts of Alaska and Siberia. If this trend continues, a great deal of organic material found below the permafrost will rot and release large amounts of CH_4 and CO_2 into the atmosphere.

Scientists estimate that arctic permafrost holds two to four times as much carbon as all the carbon ever released by humans. If just 5–10% of the total amount of methane stored in this permafrost were released, it would accelerate atmospheric warming, which would in turn melt more permafrost in yet another runaway positive feedback loop that could lead to a climate change tipping point (Figure 20.8).

Some scientists are concerned about another methane source—a layer of permafrost on the Arctic Sea floor and on arctic lake bottoms.

Rising Sea Levels

Good news: The world's oceans have helped slow climate change by absorbing about 90% of the extra heat added to the atmosphere as a result of increased emissions of greenhouse gases from the burning of fossil fuels and other human activities. **Bad news**: As the oceans store more heat they expand. This, along with water flowing into the ocean from melting land-based glaciers, raises the world's average sea level. Scientists have shown that over the last decade, thermal expansion of ocean water has caused about one-third of the observed rise in the planet's sea level.

In 2014, the IPCC projected that according to climate models that the average global sea level is likely to rise by 40–60 centimeters (1.3–2.0 feet) by the end of this century—about 10 times the rise that occurred in the 20th century. A 2016 study by a team of scientists lead by Benjamin Strauss at Climate Central, using a larger set of

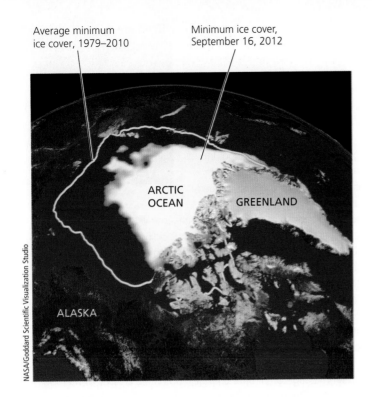

Average minimum ice cover, 1979–2010

Minimum ice cover, September 16, 2012

ARCTIC OCEAN

GREENLAND

ALASKA

NASA/Goddard Scientific Visualization Studio

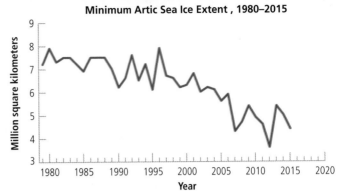

Minimum Arctic Sea Ice Extent , 1980–2015

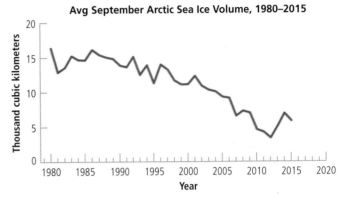

Avg September Arctic Sea Ice Volume, 1980–2015

FIGURE 20.9 *The big melt:* Rising average atmospheric and ocean temperatures have caused more and more arctic sea ice to melt during the summer months. The yellow line added to this satellite image (left) shows the average summer minimum area of ice during the period 1979–2010, in contrast to the white, ice-covered summer minimum in 2012. The graphs (right) show that the sea ice melt since 1980. **Data analysis:** By about how many million square kilometers did the minimum Arctic sea ice extent decline, overall, between 1980 and 2015?

(Compiled by the authors using data from US Goddard Space Flight Center, National Aeronautics and Space Administration, National Snow and Ice Data Center, and Polar Science Center.)

data, estimated that the ocean could rise by 1.1–1.2 meters (3–4 feet) by 2100. Between 50% and 66% of this rise will likely come from the melting of Greenland's ice (**Core Case Study**). However, accelerated melting could lead to seas rising by as much as 2.4 meters (8 feet) according to a 2017 worst-case projection by the National Oceanic and Atmospheric Administration, depending on how much of the land-based ice in Greenland, and perhaps West Antarctica, melt as the global temperature continues to rise during this century

Sea-level rise will likely not be uniform around the world, based on factors such as ocean currents and winds. By 2100, for example, Bangladesh's sea level could rise by as much as 4 meters (13 feet), several times higher than the projected global average sea-level rise. In addition, according to the US Geological Survey, the sea level is rising as much as four times faster than the global average along parts of the US Atlantic coast.

According to the 2014 IPCC and NAS reports on climate change, a 1-meter (3-foot) rise in sea level during this century (excluding the additional effects of the resulting higher storm surges) could cause the following serious effects:

- Degradation or destruction of at least one-third of the world's coastal estuaries, wetlands, coral reefs, and deltas where much of the world's rice is grown.

- Disruption of many of the world's coastal fisheries.

- Flooding in large areas of low-lying countries such as Bangladesh, one of the world's poorest and most densely populated nations.

- Flooding and erosion of low-lying barrier islands and gently sloping coastlines, especially in US coastal states such as Florida (Figure 20.11), Texas, Louisiana, New Jersey, South Carolina, and North Carolina.

- Submersion of low-lying islands in the Indian Ocean (Figure 20.12), the Pacific Ocean, and the Caribbean Sea, which are home to 1 of every 20 of the world's people.

- Flooding of some of the world's largest coastal cities (see red areas in chapter-opening photo), such as Venice, London, and New Orleans, and displacement of at least 150 million people—equal to nearly half of the current US population.

- Saltwater contamination of freshwater coastal aquifers resulting in degraded supplies of groundwater used as a source of water for drinking and irrigation.

James Balog: Watching Glaciers Melt

James Balog has applied his love of science and his passion for exploring nature as a world-renowned nature photographer. He has used his photography skills and creativity to chronicle major environmental problems such as losses in biodiversity, threats to North America's old-growth forests, and climate change as revealed by melting glaciers.

Balog is deeply concerned by the fact that many of the world's magnificent glaciers are melting. In 2007, he began working on his Extreme Ice Survey, the world's most wide-ranging photographic study of the rapid melting of many of the world's glaciers. To capture images of glacial melting, Balog developed camera systems to take daylight photos of 22 glaciers in locations around the world every half hour or hour. Each camera could capture up to 8,000 images a year. Balog used the images to create stunning time-lapse videos of the melting glaciers, where huge volumes of ice can disappear in hours or days. These images provided important data to glaciologists and other scientists and clearly and dramatically showed the general public that climate change from a warmer atmosphere is having a major impact now.

Balog and his team endured severe hardships to record these images in some of the planet's harshest environments. They had to develop camera systems that could withstand temperatures down to minus 40°F, blistering high winds, rain, sleet, and deep snow. To install the cameras, the team often worked under such conditions, climbing difficult and treacherous mountains of ice while carrying the 125-pound camera systems.

Balog's work has been featured in *National Geographic* magazine, in the NOVA documentary *Extreme Ice*, and in *Chasing Ice*, an internationally acclaimed and award-winning full-length film. His book *Ice: Portraits of the World's Vanishing Ice* summarizes the astounding loss of ice from various glaciers through 2012.

Balog's nonprofit *Earth Vision Trust* has a mission to spread the visual message of climate change, to finance studies of melting glaciers, and to spur people to action. He says, "Seeing is believing. I was a climate change skeptic until I saw the evidence in the ice. Climate change is real and the time to act is now."

Ocean Acidification: The Other CO$_2$ Problem

Ocean acidification is another serious environmental problem related to CO$_2$ emissions. The oceans have helped reduce atmospheric warming and climate change by absorbing about 25% of the excess CO$_2$ that human activities have added to the atmosphere. When this absorbed CO$_2$ combines with ocean water, it forms carbonic acid (H$_2$CO$_3$), the same weak acid found in carbonated drinks. This increases the level of hydrogen ions (H$^+$) in the water and makes it more acidic. This also decreases the level of carbonate ions (CO$_3^{2-}$) in the water because these ions react with hydrogen ions (H$^+$) to form bicarbonate ions (HCO$_3^-$).

The problem is that many aquatic species—including phytoplankton, corals, sea snails, crabs, and oysters—use carbonate ions to produce calcium carbonate (CaCO$_3$), the main component of their shells and bones. As ocean acidity increases, carbonate ion concentrations drop (Figure 20.13) and shell-building species and coral reefs grow more slowly. When the hydrogen ion concentration of seawater gets high enough, their calcium carbonate begins to dissolve. Species that survive will have damaged or weaker shells and bones.

According to a study by more than 540 of the world's leading experts on ocean acidification, the average acidity of ocean water has risen 30% since 1800. It has risen 15% since the 1990s and is projected to keep acidifying throughout this century. These scientific experts warn that we are altering the chemistry of the entire ocean ecosystem from the tropics to the poles with little idea of the consequences.

More Severe Drought

Drought occurs when evaporation due to higher temperatures exceeds precipitation for a prolonged period. A study by National Center for Atmospheric Research scientist Aiguo Dai and his colleagues found that severe and prolonged drought has affected at least 30% of the earth's land (excluding Antarctica)—an area the size of Asia. According to a study by climate researchers at NASA, up to 45% of the world's land area could be experiencing severe drought by 2059.

It is difficult to tie a specific severe drought to atmospheric warming because natural cyclical processes also cause severe droughts. However, extra heat in the atmosphere causes water to evaporate from soils. According to a study by climate scientists Richard Seager and Martin Hoerling, this depletion of soil moisture prolongs droughts and makes them more severe, regardless of their causes.

Prolonged drought can decrease the growth of trees and other plants, which decreases their removal of CO$_2$ from the atmosphere. It also dries out forests and

FIGURE 20.10 Accelerating melting of Greenland's ice has created flows such as this one, called *moulins*, which run from the surface to the base of the glaciers, leading to more dramatic melting and movement of the glacier toward the sea.

© Konrad Steffen University of Colorado/CIRES

grasslands, which can increase the frequency of wildfires that add CO_2 to the atmosphere. Climate scientists project that these effects from prolonged and more intense drought can speed up atmospheric warming and lead to more prolonged droughts, drier conditions, and more fires. This is another example of a runaway positive feedback loop that could exceed one or more climate change tipping points (Figure 20.8).

More Extreme Weather

There is not enough evidence to link any specific extreme weather event such as a heat wave, severe flood, or hurricane to climate change. However, with more heat in the atmosphere, climate scientists project that climate change is likely to increase the overall intensity of extreme weather events. For example, storms will get stronger and heat waves will be hotter. Climate models project that a more intensified water cycle with more water vapor in the atmosphere will bring higher levels of flooding to some areas (Figure 20.14) due to heavier snowfall or rainfall.

Since 1950, heat waves have become longer, more frequent, and in some cases more intense. Because atmospheric warming increases the kinetic energy of the molecules of gases in the atmosphere, this trend is likely to continue in some areas. This could raise the number of heat-related deaths, reduce crop production, and expand deserts. For example, a 2013 heat wave in Europe caused 70,000 premature deaths.

Data from the US Global Change Research Program indicate that the annual number of days of extreme heat in parts of the United States will rise dramatically during this century. However, in some areas, atmospheric warming will likely lead to colder winter weather, according to climate models, largely because of changes in global air circulation patterns due to the warming.

In 2010, a World Meteorological Organization panel of experts concluded that warmer ocean temperatures are likely to lead to fewer but stronger hurricanes and typhoons that could cause more damage in many heavily populated coastal areas.

Threats to Biodiversity

According to the latest IPCC reports, projected climate change is likely to alter ecosystems and take a toll on biodiversity in areas of every continent. Up to 85% of the Amazon rain forest—one of the world's major centers of biodiversity—could be lost and converted to tropical savanna if the global atmospheric temperature rises by the highest projected amount (Science Focus 20.2), according to a study led by climate scientist Chris Jones.

As the atmosphere warms, at least 17% of the world's species could face extinction by 2100. The hardest hit species will be:

- Cold-climate plant and animals, including the polar bear in the Arctic and penguins in Antarctica
- Species that live at higher elevations
- Species with limited tolerance for temperature change, such as corals
- Species with limited ranges

FIGURE 20.11 If the average sea level rises by 1 meter (3.3 feet), the areas shown here in red in the US state of Florida will be flooded.

(Compiled by the authors using data from Jonathan Overpeck, Jeremy Weiss, and the US Geological Survey.)

Malbert/Dreamstime.com

FIGURE 20.12 For a low-lying island nation like the Maldives in the Indian Ocean, even a small rise in sea level could spell disaster for most of its 295,000 people. About 80% of the 1,192 small islands making up this country lie less than 1 meter (3.2 feet) above sea level. Rising sea levels and higher storm surges during this century could flood most of these islands and their coral reefs.

FIGURE 20.13 Calcium carbonate levels in ocean waters, calculated from historical data (left), and projected for 2100 (right). Colors shifting from blue to red indicate where waters are becoming less basic. in the late 1800s, when CO_2 began to pile up rapidly in the atmosphere, tropical corals were not yet affected by ocean acidification. However, today carbonate levels have dropped substantially near the poles, and by 2100, they may be too low even in the tropics for most coral reefs to survive. (Sources: Andrew G. Dickson, Scripps Institution of Oceanography, University of California, San Diego, and Sarah Cooley, Woods Hole Oceanographic Institution. Used by permission from National Geographic.)

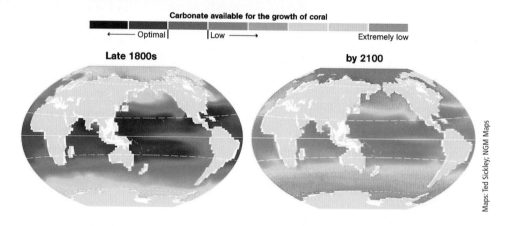

Carbonate available for the growth of coral

← Optimal | Low → Extremely low

Late 1800s   **by 2100**

Maps: Ted Sickley; NGM Maps

The primary cause of these extinctions will be loss of habitat. On the other hand, populations of plant and animal species that thrive in warmer climates could increase.

Research indicates the most vulnerable ecosystems are coral reefs, polar seas, coastal wetlands, high-elevation forests, and alpine and arctic tundra. Primarily because of drier conditions, forest fires will likely become more frequent and intense in the southeastern and western United States.

In 2016, research published by scientists from Columbia University and the University of Idaho indicated since 1979 a drier climate doubled the number of forest fires and increased the size of many fires and the length of the fire season in the western United States. The study also concluded that 55% of these increases were due to climate change caused by human activities and to efforts to fight all fires, which allows dry fuel to build up, ignite, and cause

more catastrophic crown fires. If this continues, the researchers estimate that at some point, probably by the middle of this century, there will not be enough trees left to sustain large wildfires in the western United States. These fires add CO_2 to the atmosphere and reduce the number of trees available to remove CO_2 from the atmosphere. This "double-whammy" would increase atmospheric warming and climate change in another positive feedback cycle.

A warmer climate is boosting populations of insects and fungi that damage trees, especially in areas where winters are no longer cold enough to control their populations. In the Canadian province of British Columbia, for example, warmer winters have led to surges in mountain pine beetle populations that are killing huge areas of lodge pole pine forests (Figure 20.15). Scientists expect the North American range for these trees to shift dramatically during the next several decades

In a 2014 study, the Union of Concerned Scientists reported that an estimated 58–90% of all Rocky Mountain forests could

This sea ice also helps to protect coastal villages. As it shrinks away, many villages suffer more flooding and damage from storms. Because of shrinking sea ice and rising sea levels, the state plans to relocate several coastal villages further inland on higher ground.

Permafrost covers 85% of Alaska, and the layer of permafrost soil that thaws every summer is deepening. This is causing roads and buildings to shift and sink, resulting in the need for costly repairs. Lakes and wetlands have drained in some areas where permafrost has thawed. These changes are forcing some species of birds, fish, mammals, and trees to shift to new habitat or to face possible extinction.

The warmer climate has led to population explosions of beetles that have wiped out large areas of white spruce forests. It has also dried out forests and along with insect damage is likely contributing to greatly increased wildfire damage.

Threats to Food Production

Farmers face dramatic changes due to shifting climates and an intensified hydrologic cycle, if the atmosphere keeps warming as projected. According to the IPCC, crop productivity is projected to increase slightly with moderate warming at middle to high latitudes in areas such as midwestern Canada, Russia, and Ukraine. However, the projected rise in crop productivity might be limited because the soils in these northern regions generally lack sufficient plant nutrients. Crop production will decrease if warming goes too far.

Higher temperatures and the erratic pattern of increased extended droughts and heavier downpours could reduce crop yields in some farming areas. Shrinking irrigation water supplies and growing pest populations in a warmer world could also cut crop yields in some areas.

Climate change models project a decline in agricultural productivity and food security in tropical and subtropical regions, especially in Southeast Asia and Central America, largely because of excessive heat. Warm winters will also

die due to effects of climate change, including extreme heat, drought, expanding wildfires, and beetle infestations. The scientists reported that between 2000 and 2012, bark beetles killed trees in an area the size of Colorado.

Species are responding to warmer temperatures. Some species are moving to higher (cooler) altitudes and some are moving to higher (cooler) latitudes. Some flowering plants are blooming earlier.

Marine ecosystems are also threatened by climate change. Coral reefs are especially vulnerable because of their limited tolerance for water temperature changes, which bleaches colorful coral reefs when excess heat expels the tiny algae that help provide food for polyps that build the reef. Many coral reefs are dying for this reason.

CASE STUDY

Alaska: A Preview of the Effects of Climate Change

Alaska is a leading indicator for most of the effects of climate change. It is warming at twice the average rate of the rest of the United States, and its warming is accelerating.

The effects of this warming are dramatic. In 2015, all but five of Alaska's glaciers were shrinking, according to Regine Hock, a glacier expert from the University of Alaska. Coastal sea ice is also disappearing 2 weeks earlier in the summer than it was in the 1970s and refreezing 2 weeks later in the fall, according to Andy Mahoney of the University of Alaska. This has shortened the hunting season by at least a month for walruses, polar bears, and human hunters who depend on this ice for finding prey.

FIGURE 20.15 With warmer winters, populations of mountain pine beetles have exploded and killed large numbers of trees (orange areas). in the Canadian province of British Columbia.

benefit crop diseases, insect pests, and weeds that will further threaten many crops.

Flooding of river deltas in coastal areas by rising sea levels could reduce crop production, partly because aquifers that supply irrigation water will be infiltrated by saltwater. This flooding would also affect fish production in coastal aquaculture ponds. Food production in farm regions dependent on rivers fed by melting glaciers will drop. In arid and semiarid areas, food production will be lowered by more intensive and prolonged droughts.

According to the IPCC, food is likely to be plentiful for a while in a warmer world, because of the longer growing season in northern regions. But scientists warn that during the latter half of this century, several hundred million of the world's poorest and most vulnerable people could face starvation and malnutrition from a drop in food production caused by projected climate change.

Threats to Human Health, National Security, and Economies

According to IPCC and other reports, more frequent and prolonged heat waves in some areas will increase deaths and illnesses, especially among older people, people in poor health, and the urban poor who cannot afford air conditioning. It is also likely that fewer people will die from cold weather. But research at Harvard University School of Public Health suggests that during the latter half of this century, the projected rise in the number of heat-related deaths will likely exceed the projected drop in the number of cold-related deaths.

A warmer and more CO_2-rich atmosphere will likely favor rapidly multiplying insects, including mosquitoes and ticks that transmit diseases such as West Nile virus, Lyme disease, and dengue fever, (which has increased 10-fold since 1973). Warming will also favor microbes, toxic molds, and fungi, as well as some plants that produce pollens that cause allergies and asthma attacks.

Higher atmospheric temperatures and levels of water vapor will contribute to increased photochemical smog in many urban areas. This may increase pollution-related deaths and illnesses from heart ailments and respiratory problems.

Recent studies by the US Department of Defense and the National Academy of Sciences warn that the effects of climate change could affect US national security. These effects include increased food and water scarcity, poverty, environmental degradation, unemployment, social unrest, mass migration of environmental refugees, and political instability, and the weakening of fragile governments. All of these factors could increase terrorism, according to the US Defense Department, which includes climate change as a major element in its planning.

Climate change will also take a toll on human economies. According to a 2015 survey of 750 risk experts conducted by the World Economic Forum, failure to slow and adapt to climate change tops the list of threats to the global economy and the risks are increasing.

For these reasons, climate change will very likely force tens of millions of people to migrate in search of better conditions. They will be forced to leave their homes because of greater hunger, flooding, drought, and other problems.

CHECKPOINT FOR UNDERSTANDING 20.2

1. What is a climate change tipping point?

2. Explain why the loss of glaciers is a serious concern.

3. Thermal expansion of the oceans accounts for some of the rising sea levels. What other factor is predicted to cause a significant rise in sea levels?

4. Explain how forests are particularly vulnerable to climate change.

5. Explain how human health is affected by climate change.

HOW CAN WE SLOW CLIMATE CHANGE?

CONCEPT 20.3 We can reduce greenhouse gas emissions and the threat of climate change while saving money and improving human health if we cut energy waste and rely more on cleaner renewable energy resources.

Dealing with Climate Is Difficult

According to at least 90% of the world's climate scientists and many other analysts, climate change is one of the most urgent scientific, economic, political, and ethical issues that humanity faces. The good news is that we can cut carbon emissions and since 1980 have known how to do this, as discussed in this section. The bad news is that since 1980 we have not made much progress in dealing with the urgent problem of climate change. Part of the problem is that climate change has the following characteristics that make it difficult to tackle:

- *The problem is global.* Dealing with this threat will require unprecedented and prolonged international cooperation.

- *The problem is a long-term political issue.* Climate change is happening now and is already having harmful impacts, but it is not viewed as an urgent problem by most voters and elected officials In addition, most of the people who will suffer the most serious harm from projected climate change during the latter half of this century have not been born yet.

- *The harmful and beneficial impacts of climate change are not spread evenly.* Higher-latitude nations such as Canada, Russia, and New Zealand may temporarily have higher crop yields, fewer deaths in winter, and lower heating bills. But other, mostly poor nations such as Bangladesh could see more flooding and higher death tolls.

- *Proposed solutions, such as sharply reducing or phasing out the use of fossil fuels, are controversial.* They could disrupt economies and lifestyles and threaten the profits of economically and politically powerful fossil fuel and utility companies.

- *The projected temperature changes and effects are uncertain.* Current climate models lead to a wide range in the projected temperature increase (Science Focus 20.2) and sea-level rise. Thus, there is uncertainty over whether the harmful changes will be moderate or catastrophic, largely because of a range of projections based on how fast and to what degree we act to slow climate change. This depends mostly on how much carbon dioxide and other greenhouse gases we add to the atmosphere in coming years. This makes it difficult to plan for avoiding or managing risk. It also highlights the urgent need for more scientific research to improve climate models.

However, in the United states, there is political pressure to cut back on government funding for climate change research and atmospheric measurements.

What Are Our Options?

There are two ways to deal with global climate change. One, called *mitigation*, is to slow down climate change to avoid its most harmful effects. The other approach, called *adaptation*, is to recognize that some climate change is unavoidable because we have waited too long to act. This means that people will have to live with and adapt to some of its harmful impacts. Many analysts call for a combination of both approaches.

Regardless of the approach taken, most climate scientists argue the most urgent priority is to avoid any and all **climate change tipping points** (Figure 20.8). For example, if we continue to add CO_2 to the atmosphere at the current rate, we will likely exceed the estimated tipping point of 450 ppm of atmospheric CO_2 within a few decades. Such high levels of CO_2 can put the earth's climate system into a positive feedback loop that could become irreversible and lock in severe climate change and disruption for hundreds or perhaps thousands of years.

Reducing Greenhouse Gas Emissions

Climate scientists generally agree that to avoid some of the severest harmful effects of climate change, we need to limit the global average temperature increase to 2.0C° (3.6F°) over the preindustrial global average temperature. This means significantly decreasing CO_2 emissions by reducing the use of fossil fuels (especially coal), greatly increasing energy efficiency, and shifting to much greater dependence on cleaner and low-carbon energy resources such as solar power, wind power, and geothermal energy.

The problem is that the world's nations and energy companies together hold reserves of fossil fuels that, if burned, would emit nearly 5 times the amount of CO_2 that climate scientists estimate that we can safely emit. Reducing fossil fuel use to avoid exceeding this temperature climate tipping point means leaving 82% of the world's coal reserves and 50% of all natural gas and all arctic oil reserves in the ground. Currently, the economic well-being of the politically powerful fossil-fuel companies and most of the world's national economies depend on using all or most of these reserves of fossil fuels. This is what drives the intense political and economic debate over how to or whether to slow the rate of climate change.

A growing number of scientists and other analysts recognize that shifting away from human dependence on fossil fuels will be difficult but contend that it can be done over the next 50 years. They point out that humans have shifted energy resources before—first from wood to coal, then to oil, and now to natural gas. Each shift took about 50 years. Humans now have the knowledge and ability to shift to a reliance on energy efficiency and renewable energy over the next 50 years.

Figure 20.16 lists ways to slow climate change caused by human activities over the next 50 years (**Concept 20.3**). The items in the left column are prevention approaches designed to reduce CO_2 emissions and those in the right column are cleanup approaches for removing CO_2 from the atmosphere.

According to the 2014 IPCC report, there is good news related to dealing with the threat of climate change by reducing our CO_2 emissions:

- We could shift to hybrid, plug-in hybrid, and electric cars over the next 20–30 years, and charge their improved

- The shift to renewable energy is accelerating as prices for electricity from low-carbon wind turbines and solar cells fall, and as improvements and investments in these technologies grow. For example, the US state of Texas produces more electricity from wind and solar power than all but five of the world's countries.

- Engineers have designed affordable net zero carbon emission buildings and know how to reduce the carbon footprints of existing buildings.

- Dealing with climate change will create jobs and profitable businesses.

- Many business leaders see dealing with climate change as a global investment opportunity.

Removing CO_2 from the Atmosphere

Some scientists and engineers are designing cleanup strategies (Figure 20.16, right) for removing some of the CO_2 from the atmosphere or from smokestack emissions of coal-burning industrial plants and converting it to a liquid, and storing (sequestering) it, in other parts of the environment. One strategy, known as **carbon capture and storage (CCS)**, would remove some of the CO_2 gas from smokestack emissions of coal-burning power plants and industrial plants and convert it to a liquid to be pumped under pressure into underground storage sites (Figure 20.17).

Four major problems with CCS schemes are that, with current technology,

- they can remove and store only part of the CO_2 from smokestack emissions, at great cost,

- they do not address the massive emissions of CO_2 from motor vehicle exhausts, food production, and the deliberate burning of forests to provide land for growing food,

- they require a lot of energy, which could lead to greater use of fossil fuels and higher emissions of CO_2 and other air pollutants, and

- the CO_2 that is removed would have to remain sequestered from the atmosphere forever. Large-scale leaks and smaller continuous leaks from CO_2 storage sites could dramatically increase atmospheric warming and climate change in a short time.

Solutions

Slowing Climate Change

Prevention	Cleanup
Cut fossil fuel use (especially coal)	Sequester CO_2 by planting trees and preserving forests and wetlands
Shift from coal to natural gas	
Repair leaky natural gas pipelines and facilities	Sequester carbon in soil using biochar
Improve energy efficiency	Sequester CO_2 deep underground (with no leaks allowed)
Shift to renewable energy resources	
Reduce deforestation	Sequester CO_2 in the deep ocean (with no leaks allowed)
Use more sustainable agriculture and forestry	
Put a price on greenhouse gas emissions	Remove CO_2 from smokestack and vehicle emissions

FIGURE 20.16 Some ways to slow atmospheric warming and climate change during this century (**Concept 20.3**). ***Critical thinking:*** Which five of these solutions do you think are the best ones? Why?

Top: Mark Smith/Shutterstock.com. Center: Yegor Korzhi/Shutterstock.com. Bottom: pedrosala/Shutterstock.com.

So far, the experimental projects for capturing and storing have not been very effective and have been quite costly. The high costs have made US utilities reluctant to build CCS plants since it would greatly increase the cost of electricity to consumers.

According to some environmental scientists, most forms of CCS are costly, risky, and not very effective *cleanup solutions* (Figure 20.16, right) to a serious problem that can be dealt with more effectively by using a variety of cheaper, quicker, and safer *prevention* approaches (Figure 20.16, left).

Another approach being tested in Iceland involves dissolving extracted CO_2 in water and pumping it into porous rocks such as basalt where the CO_2 reacts with calcium, magnesium, or iron in the rock to form a mineral called calcite. This stores the CO_2 permanently. However, the process takes a lot of water and requires transporting the water-CO_2 mixture to the right kind of rock deposits.

One with another way to increase the uptake of CO_2 is by implementing a massive, global tree-planting and forest restoration program, especially on degraded land in the tropics. Restoring wetlands and mangrove forests would also help remove carbon dioxide from the atmosphere. Another approach involves fertilizing the ocean with iron pellets to

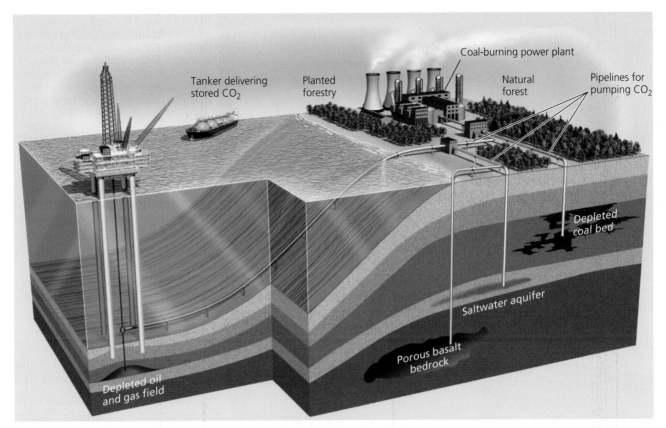

FIGURE 20.17 Some proposed carbon capture and storage (CCS) schemes for removing some of the carbon dioxide from smokestack emissions and from the atmosphere and storing (sequestering) it in soil, plants, deep underground reservoirs, and sediments beneath the ocean floor. **Critical thinking:** Which of these proposed strategies do you think would work best and which would be the least effective? Why?

boost populations of phytoplankon that would remove CO_2 from the atmosphere. However, preliminary experiments indicate that the iron pellet scheme may not work very well and could disrupt marine ecosystems.

Another carbon sequestration measure is the use of *biochar*, which Amazon Basin natives have used for centuries to grow crops. Producing biochar involves burning biomass such as chicken waste or wood in a low-oxygen environment to make a charcoal-like material. This carbon-rich biochar makes an excellent organic fertilizer that helps to keep carbon in the soil. Although making biochar does release CO_2, burying it stores considerably more CO_2 in the soil.

According to some environmental scientists, most forms of CCS are costly, risky, and not very effective **cleanup solutions** (Figure 20.16, right) to a serious problem that can be dealt with more effectively by using a variety of cheaper, quicker, and safer **prevention** approaches (Figure 20.16, left).

Geoengineering Solutions

Other proposed solutions fall under the umbrella of **geoengineering,** or trying to manipulate certain natural conditions to help counter the human-enhanced greenhouse

effect (Figure 20.18). Other scientists have called for placing a series of giant mirrors in orbit above the earth to reflect incoming sunlight for the same purpose.

Some scientists reject the idea of launching sulfates into the stratosphere as being too risky because of possible unknown effects. For example, if the sulfates reflected too much sunlight, they could reduce evaporation enough to alter global rainfall patterns and worsen the already dangerous droughts in certain areas. In addition, a study by atmospheric scientist Simone Tilmes indicated that chlorine released by reactions involving sulfates could speed up the thinning of the earth's stratospheric ozone layer (see Section 19.7, p. 621).

According to some scientists, a major problem with most of these technological fixes is that, if they succeed, they could be used to justify the continued rampant use of fossil fuels. This would allow CO_2 levels in the lower atmosphere to continue building and adding to the serious problem of ocean acidification.

Skeptical scientists argue that another major problem with both geoengineering and CCS proposals is that they depend on complex machinery running constantly, flawlessly, and essentially forever, primarily to pump something from one place to another in the environment. If we rely on these systems and continue emitting greenhouse gases, and

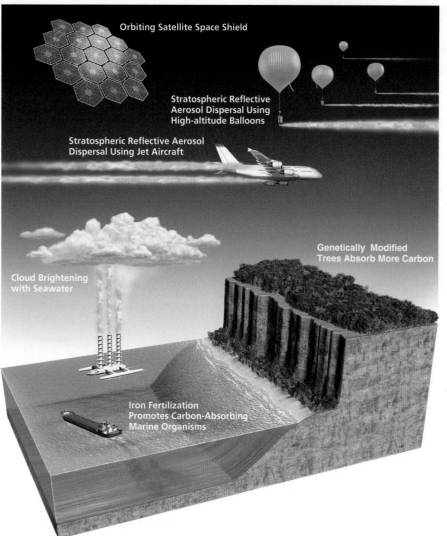

FIGURE 20.18 Geoengineering schemes include ways to reflect more sunlight, and some carbon sequestration approaches (Figure 20.D) can be thought of as geoengineering. **Critical thinking:** Of the approaches shown here, which three do you think are the most workable? Why?

Labels in figure:
- Orbiting Satellite Space Shield
- Stratospheric Reflective Aerosol Dispersal Using High-altitude Balloons
- Stratospheric Reflective Aerosol Dispersal Using Jet Aircraft
- Genetically Modified Trees Absorb More Carbon
- Cloud Brightening with Seawater
- Iron Fertilization Promotes Carbon-Absorbing Marine Organisms

- Regulate carbon dioxide (CO_2) and methane (CH_4) as climate-changing air pollutants that can harm public health and welfare. This is based on a 2014 US Supreme Court decision affirming the right of the EPA to regulate greenhouse gas emissions under the Clean Air Act. Fossil fuel companies and other opponents are trying to delay or weaken the regulations or have Congress change the Clean Air Act to forbid the regulation of greenhouse gases.

- Phase out the most polluting coal-burning power plants over the next 50 years and replace them with cleaner natural gas and renewable energy alternatives such as wind power and solar power. Next-generation nuclear power plants, including smaller modular plants, might help. However, as of 2017 these have not been developed and evaluated in terms of safety, net energy, and cost.

if the systems then fail, atmospheric temperatures will likely soar at a rapid rate and essentially ensure severe climate disruption.

Geoengineering is based on the planetary management worldview that we can and should manage the earth (Figure 1.A, p. 19, left). However, some question this belief. According to biologist René Dubos, "The belief that we can manage the earth and improve on nature is probably the ultimate expression of human conceit." The failure of the Biosphere 2 science project (Science Focus 20.3) reinforces this view.

Government Actions to Reduce Greenhouse Gas Emissions

The US government (and other governments) can use seven major strategies to promote the solutions for slowing climate change listed in Figure 20.16. They can:

- Put a price on carbon emissions by phasing in taxes on each unit of CO_2 or CH_4 emitted or by phasing in energy taxes on each unit of fossil fuel burned (Figure 20.19). These tax increases could be offset by reductions in taxes on income, wages, and profits. In other words, tax pollution and energy waste, not payrolls and profits. In 2014, China and 72 other nations, the World Bank, and more than 1,000 corporations called for putting a price on carbon emissions. However, carbon taxes won't be effective if the tax level is not high enough and is not raised as needed to meet CO_2 emission reduction goals. Nearly 40 nations, including the 28-member European Union and Canada, as well as California, and nine northeastern states have raised the price of carbon emissions without damaging their economies. However, reductions have not been high because of failure to set the original carbon price high enough and increase the price as needed to achieve reduction goals.

Biosphere 2: A Lesson in Humility

In 1991, eight scientists (four men and four women) were sealed inside Biosphere 2, a $200 million glass and steel enclosure designed to be a self-sustaining life-support system Figure 20.E). The goal of the project was to increase our understanding of Biosphere 1: the *earth's* life-support system.

The sealed system of interconnected domes was built in the desert near Tucson, Arizona. It contained artificial ecosystems, including a tropical rain forest, a savanna, a desert, a lake, streams, freshwater and saltwater wetlands, and a mini-ocean with a coral reef.

Biosphere 2 was designed to mimic the earth's natural chemical cycling systems. Water evaporated from its ocean and other aquatic systems and condensed to provide rainfall over the tropical rain forest. The precipitation trickled through soil into the marshes and back into the ocean before beginning the cycle again.

The facility was stocked with more than 4,000 species of plants and animals, including small primates, chickens, cats, and insects, selected to help maintain life-support functions. Human and animal excrement and other wastes were treated and recycled as fertilizer to help support plant growth. Sunlight and external natural gas–powered generators provided

energy. The Biospherians were to be isolated for two years and raise their own food, using intensive organic agriculture. They were to breathe air that was purified by plants and to drink water cleansed by natural chemical cycling processes.

From the beginning, many unexpected problems cropped up and the life-support system began to unravel. The level of oxygen in the air declined with soil organisms converting it to carbon dioxide. Additional oxygen had to be pumped in from the outside to keep the Biospherians from suffocating.

Tropical birds died after the first freeze. An ant species invaded the enclosure, proliferated, and killed off most of the system's original insect species. In total, 19 of the Biosphere's 25 small animal species (76%) became extinct. Before the two-year period was over, all plant-pollinating insects went extinct, thereby dooming to extinction most of the plant species.

Despite many problems, the facility's waste and wastewater were recycled. With much hard work, the Biospherians were also able to produce 80% of their food supply, despite rampant weed growths, spurred by higher CO_2 levels that crowded out food crops. However, they suffered from persistent hunger and weight loss.

FIGURE 20.E Biosphere 2, constructed near Tucson, Arizona, was designed to be a self-sustaining life-support system.

In the end, an expenditure of $200 million failed to maintain a life-support system for eight people for two years. Ecologists Joel E. Cohen and David Tilman, who evaluated the project, concluded, "No one yet knows how to engineer systems that provide humans with life-supporting services that natural ecosystems provide for free."

CRITICAL THINKING

Do you think that science and engineering ever will be able to provide humans with the life support systems that nature now provides at no cost? Explain.

- Use a *cap-and-trade system* (Figure 20.20), which would use the marketplace to help reduce emissions of CO_2 and CH_4. The government would place a cap on emissions in a country or region, issue permits to emit certain levels of these pollutants, and let polluters trade these permits in the marketplace. This approach works only if the original caps are set low enough to encourage a serious reduction in emissions and are lowered on a regular basis. Since 2009, several northeastern US states have used cap-and–trade to manage carbon emissions without harming their economies. On the other hand, cap-and-trade has not worked as well as projected in Europe.

- Over 10 to 20 years phase out government subsidies and tax breaks for the fossil-fuel industry and phase in subsidies and tax breaks for energy-efficient technologies and low-carbon renewable energy development. Fossil fuel subsidies deprive governments of funds that

could be used to help finance a transition to a more sustainable, climate-friendly future.

- Work out agreements to finance and monitor efforts to reduce deforestation—which accounts for 12% to 17% of global greenhouse gas emissions—and to promote global tree-planting efforts.

Environmental economists and a growing number of business leaders, along with the President of the World Bank, call for putting a price on carbon emissions as the best way to curb them before it is too late to avoid the projected catastrophic environmental and economic effects of significant climate change. Doing this would promote including the estimated harmful environmental and health costs of using fossil fuels in fuel prices, in keeping with the full-cost pricing **principle of sustainability**.

Establishing laws and regulations that raise the price of fossil fuels is politically difficult because of the

Trade-Offs

Carbon and Energy Taxes

Advantages	Disadvantages
Simple to administer	Tax laws can get complex
Clear price on carbon	Vulnerable to loopholes
Covers all emitters	Doesn't guarantee lower emissions
Predictable revenues	Politically unpopular

FIGURE 20.19 Using carbon and energy taxes or fees to help reduce greenhouse gas emissions has advantages and disadvantages. *Critical thinking:* Which two advantages and which two disadvantages do you think are the most important and why?

Trade-Offs

Cap-and-Trade Policies

Advantages	Disadvantages
Clear legal limit on emissions	Revenues not predictable
Rewards cuts in emissions	Vulnerable to cheating
Record of success	Rich polluters can keep polluting
Low expense for consumers	Puts variable price on carbon

FIGURE 20.20 Using a cap-and-trade policy to help reduce greenhouse gas emissions has advantages and disadvantages. *Critical thinking:* Which two advantages and which two disadvantages do you think are the most important and why?

immense political and economic power of the fossil fuel and electric utility industries and society's dependence on fossil fuels for 90% of its commercial energy. Opponents also argue that increasing the price of fossil fuels would hurt economies and consumers.

However, economists and other supporters of this approach contend the economic benefits from raising fossil fuel prices far outweigh the economic drawbacks for three reasons. *First,* this is the only way to reduce the threats from three of the world's most serious environmental problems: air pollution, climate change, and ocean acidification. *Second,* the resulting environmental and health benefits will save money for consumers and governments. *Third,* higher fossil fuel prices would help economies by spurring innovation in finding ways to reduce carbon emissions, improve energy efficiency, and phase in a mix of affordable low-carbon renewable energy resources.

International Climate Change Treaties

Governments have also entered into international climate negotiations. In December 1997, delegates from 161 nations met in Kyoto, Japan to negotiate a treaty to slow atmospheric warming and climate change. The first phase of the resulting *Kyoto Protocol* went into effect in February 2005 with 187 of the world's 194 countries (not including the United States) ratifying the agreement by late 2009.

The 37 participating more-developed countries agreed to cut their emissions of CO_2, CH_4, and N_2O to certain levels by 2012. However, 16 of the nations failed to do so. Less-developed countries, including China and India were excused from this requirement, because such reductions would curb their economic growth.

In 2005, participating countries began negotiating a second phase of the treaty that was to go into effect in 2012. However, these negotiations failed to extend the original agreement.

In 2015, delegates from 195 countries met in Paris, France in another attempt to achieve a global climate change agreement. In a historic agreement, the governments agreed to:

- A goal to keep the increase in global average temperatures below 2°C (3.6°F).

- Reduce their greenhouse gas reductions by a set amount. These national goals are voluntary and there is no penalty for not meeting them.

- Meet every five years to evaluate progress and increase their goals.

The agreement went into effect in November 2016 after 55 countries (not including the United States) had ratified it.

In 2017, the president of the United States announced that he planned to withdraw the U.S. from the treaty. Withdrawal could encourage other countries to not meet their goals and weaken global efforts to reduce the threat of climate change. More than 365 large and small U.S. companies have reaffirmed their commitment to the agreement and oppose U.S. withdrawal from the agreement.

Climate scientists applaud this progress after 18 years of international negotiations. However, some see this international agreement as a weak, slow, and inadequate response to an urgent global environmental and economic problem. Countries are not legally bound to reach their goals. In addition, there was no agreement reached for the wealthier countries whose economies have been the major contributors to climate change to raise a proposed $500 billion by 2020 to assist poorer countries in meeting their goals. Even if all commitments are fully honored, climate scientists estimate that this would not reduce atmospheric temperatures enough to prevent serious environmental and economic problems during this century.

According to a large and growing number of climate and environmental scientists, economists, and business leaders,

Government Incentives to Reduce Carbon Emissions

The marketplace can be used to reduce pollution and resource waste. One effective means is by establishing acceptable levels of total pollution or resource use called cap-and-trade. Companies are given or sold a certain number of *tradable pollution* or *resource-use permits* by the government.

A permit holder that does not use its entire allocation can save credits for future expansion, use them in other parts of its operation, or sell them to other companies. The United States has used this *cap-and-trade* approach to reduce the emissions of greenhouse gases and other regional and global pollutants (Figure 20.20).

A second strategy is to create a carbon tax (Figure 20.19). A fee is levied on each unit of CO_2 or CH_4 emitted by fossil fuel use. Lowering taxes on income, wages, and profits to offset this tax could help to make a carbon tax more acceptable.

FRQ Application

Question: **Identify** ONE government strategy for reducing carbon emissions and **discuss** an advantage and disadvantage of that strategy.

Possible Response 1: One government strategy for reducing carbon emissions would be a carbon tax. Each unit of carbon emitted as a result of burning fossil fuels would be charged. Advantages of this system would be that it puts a clear price on carbon, is simple to administer, covers all emitters, and brings in predictable revenues. Drawbacks include more complex tax laws, it might not result in lowering emissions if companies can afford to pay the tax, taxes are politically unpopular, and companies can find loopholes.

Possible Response 2: Cap-and-trade programs are a government strategy for reducing carbon emissions. Carbon-emitting companies are issued permits, and if they do not use all of their allotments, they can sell their permits to other companies. Advantages include strict legal limits on carbon pollution, rewards for reducing emissions, these programs have been proven to be successful in the past, and there is a low expense for consumers. Disadvantages include the fact that companies can easily cheat, those who can afford it can pollute more, and the price on carbon and incoming revenues can vary.

---

however, the benefits of slowing climate change (Figure 20.16) far outweigh the long-term economic and environmental risks of not doing it. If we slow global warming, we will be wealthier and healthier and we will live better and longer lives. We will also have less political instability and poverty and pass on a better world to future generations.

Some Countries, States, Cities and Companies Are Leading the Way

The single most important component of our efforts to slow climate change is that CEO's, mayors, and investors view climate change not as a political issue but as an economic and financial issue. Money managers are asking managers of companies: What is your carbon footprint and what are you doing to reduce it?

Some nations are leading others in facing the challenges of projected climate change. Costa Rica aims to be the first country to become *carbon neutral* by cutting its net carbon emissions to zero by 2030. The country generates 78% of its electricity with hydroelectric power and another 18% from wind and geothermal energy.

China leads the world in greenhouse gas emissions. However, China's government is working with the country's top 1,000 industries to implement tough energy efficiency goals. China is also rapidly becoming the world's leader in developing and selling solar cells, solar water heaters, wind turbines, advanced batteries, and plug-in hybrid-electric cars. China sees this as a way to help reduce its own greenhouse gas emissions and those of other countries and boost its economy by becoming the leader in some of this century's most rapidly growing businesses.

Some US state and local governments are moving ahead in dealing with climate change. By 2016, at least 32 states had emissions reduction programs or were involved in multistate programs. California plans to get 33% of its electricity from low-carbon renewable energy sources by 2030. That state is showing that it is possible to implement policies that cut carbon emissions and create jobs. Since 1990, local governments in more than 650 cities around the world (including more than 450 US cities) have established programs to reduce their greenhouse gas emissions.

Leaders of some big US companies, including Alcoa, DuPont, Ford Motor Company, General Electric, and Shell Oil, have joined with leading environmental organizations to form the US Climate Action Partnership. The partnership calls for the US government to enact strong national climate change legislation, saying, "In our view, the climate change challenge will create more economic opportunities than risks for the U.S. economy." Leaders of these and many other companies see an enormous profit opportunity in developing or using energy-efficient and cleaner technologies.

Colleges, Universities, and Schools Are Reducing Their Carbon Footprints

Many colleges and universities are also taking action. Arizona State University (ASU) boasts the largest collection of solar panels of any US university. ASU was also the first American university to establish a School of Sustainability. The College of the Atlantic in Bar Harbor, Maine, has been net carbon neutral since 2007 and gets 100% of its electricity from renewable resources. Students there built a wind turbine that powers a nearby organic farm, which offers organic produce to the campus, to local schools, and to food banks.

Students at the University of Washington in Seattle agreed to an increase in their fees to help the school buy electricity from renewable energy sources. At Florida's University of Miami, drivers of hybrid cars get a 50% parking discount.

Across the country, grade schools and high schools are reducing their carbon footprint with initiatives such as revamping their food services to take advantage of organic and locally grown food; composting their food waste; reducing or eliminating the use of disposable plates, cups, and utensils; and installing water bottle filling stations to cut down on the consumption of bottled water from vending machines.

EARTH University in Costa Rica has a mission to promote sustainable development in tropical countries. Its sustainable agriculture degree program has attracted students from more than 20 different countries. Students and faculty at Oberlin College in the US state of Ohio created a Web-based system in some of the school's dorms that monitors use of energy and water, giving students real-time feedback that can help them to reduce their waste of these resources. And a growing number of campus groups are urging the administrators at their schools to help slow climate change by ending their endowment fund investments in fossil fuel companies.

CONSIDER THIS . . .

THINKING ABOUT What Your School Can Do

What are three steps that you think your school could take to help reduce its carbon footprint? What steps, if any, is it now taking?

Every Individual Can Make a Difference

Each of us will play a part in the atmospheric warming and climate change projected to occur during this century. Whenever we use energy generated by fossil fuels, we add CO_2 to the atmosphere. However, nearly two-thirds of the average American's carbon footprint is *embedded carbon*—carbon released during the manufacture and delivery of food, shelter, clothing, cars, computers, and every other consumer product and service. There are many sources of information on the Internet and elsewhere comparing the carbon emissions involved in the production of various goods and services.

An important aspect of your carbon footprint is your diet. Foods vary greatly in the greenhouse gases that result from their production and delivery. For example, processed foods require much more energy to produce than do whole foods such as fresh fruits and vegetables. Meat production, especially as it is done on factory farms, involves far higher greenhouse gas emissions than production of grains and vegetables. In addition, green-

What Can You Do?

Reducing CO_2 Emissions

- Calculate your carbon footprint (there are several helpful websites)
- Drive a fuel-efficient car, walk, bike, carpool, and use mass transit
- Reduce garbage by reducing consumption, recycling, and reusing more items
- Use energy-efficient appliances and LED lightbulbs
- Wash clothes in warm or cold water and hang them up to dry
- Close window curtains to keep heat in or out
- Use a low-flow showerhead
- Eat less meat or no meat
- Heavily insulate your house and seal all air leaks
- Use energy-efficient windows
- Set your hot-water heater to 49°C (120°F)
- Plant trees
- Buy from businesses working to reduce their emissions

FIGURE 20.21 Individuals matter: You can reduce your annual emissions of CO_2. **Critical thinking:** Which of these steps, if any, do you take now or plan to take in the future?

house gas emissions resulting from beef production and consumption are 12 times those associated with producing and eating the same amount of chicken. By choosing foods carefully, you can reduce your carbon footprint.

Political involvement—joining with others to spread a message—is another way in which individuals make a difference. In September 2014, climate activists organized a global People's Climate March. In New York City, 400,000 people turned out in a crowd that stretched 20 blocks on one of the wide avenues, spilling into many side streets. On that day, smaller marches took place in 162 other countries.

You can learn about your carbon footprint by using a footprint calculator, several of which are available online. Figure 20.21 lists some ways in which you can cut your CO_2 emissions. One person taking each of these steps makes a small contribution to reducing global greenhouse gas emissions, but when millions of people take such steps, global change can happen.

CHECKPOINT FOR UNDERSTANDING 20.3

1. In terms of climate change, what is the difference between mitigation and adaptation?

2. Identify factors driving the political debate over mitigating climate change.

3. Carbon sequestration, geoengineering, and producing biochar are all strategies for mitigating climate change. Discuss why some scientists argue against using these strategies.

20.4 HOW CAN WE ADAPT TO CLIMATE CHANGE?

CONCEPT 20.4 While we can prepare for some climate change that is now inevitable, we could realize important economic, ecological, and health benefits by drastically reducing greenhouse gas emissions with the goal of slowing projected climate disruption.

Preparing for Climate Change

According to global climate models, the world needs to make a 50–85% cut in emissions of greenhouse gases by 2050 to stabilize concentrations of these gases in the atmosphere. This would help to prevent the atmosphere from warming by more than 2°C (3.6°F) and head off projected rapid and long-lasting changes in the world's climate along with the harmful environmental, economic, and health effects.

However, because of the political difficulty of making such large reductions, many analysts believe that while we work to slash greenhouse gas emissions, we should also prepare for the harmful effects of projected climate change. Figure 20.22 shows some ways to do so.

For example, organizations are carrying out projects such as expanding mangrove forests as buffers against storm surges. They are building shelters on high ground and planting trees on slopes to help prevent landslides. In the face of projected higher levels of precipitation and rising sea levels, seawall design and construction will likely be a major growth industry. And low-lying countries such as Bangladesh are planning for what to do with millions of environmental refugees who will be flooded out by rising sea levels and more intense storms.

Several cities have developed adaptation plans. In London, England, a flood-control barrier is being strengthened at a cost of about $1 billion (Figure 20.23). California is beefing up its forest firefighting capabilities and is building desalination plants to help relieve projected water shortages, which will worsen as some of its mountain glaciers melt.

Some coastal communities in the United States now require that new houses and other new construction be built high enough off of the ground or further back from the current shoreline to survive storm surges. In anticipation of rising sea levels, Boston has elevated one of its sewage treatment plants. Some cities plan to establish cooling centers to shelter residents during increasingly intense heat waves.

The Netherlands with most of its population living below sea level, is famous for building dikes to hold back the rising North Sea for more than 800 years. The country's government, business community, and people have been developing a 200-year plan for dealing with projected climate change.

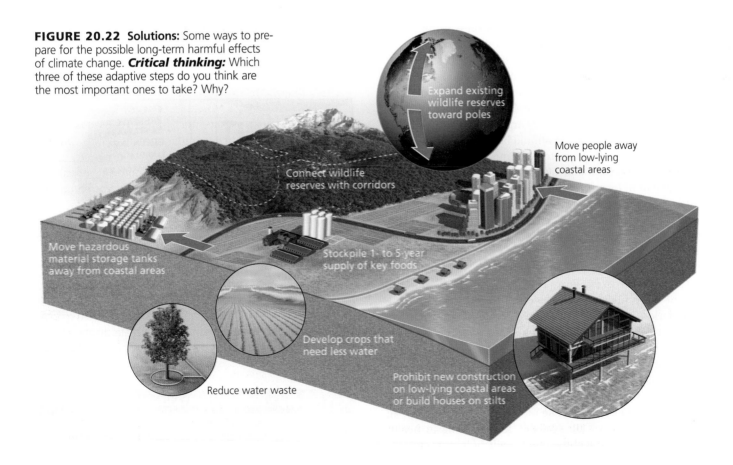

FIGURE 20.22 Solutions: Some ways to prepare for the possible long-term harmful effects of climate change. **Critical thinking:** Which three of these adaptive steps do you think are the most important ones to take? Why?

Expand existing wildlife reserves toward poles

Move people away from low-lying coastal areas

Connect wildlife reserves with corridors

Move hazardous material storage tanks away from coastal areas

Stockpile 1- to 5-year supply of key foods

Reduce water waste

Develop crops that need less water

Prohibit new construction on low-lying coastal areas or build houses on stilts

FIGURE 20.23 This high-tech, movable flood-control barrier—the second largest in the world—was built across the Thames River to prevent flooding from very high tides and storm surges in London, England.

A No-Regrets Strategy

The threat of climate disruption pushes us to look for preventive solutions such as those listed in Figure 20.16. But suppose we had the ability to look into the future and, in doing so, we found that climate disruption was not a serious threat after all. Should we then return to the present and abandon the search for preventive solutions?

A number of climate and environmental scientists, economists, and business leaders say *no* to this question, and they call for us to begin implementing such changes now as a *no-regrets strategy*. They argue that actions such as those listed in Figure 20.16 should be implemented in any case because they will lead to very important environmental, health, and economic benefits.

For example, improving energy efficiency has numerous economic and environmental advantages (see Figure 15.3, p. 457). Individuals, companies, and local governments can save large amounts of money by cutting their energy bills. In addition, the use of fossil fuels, especially coal, causes a great deal of air pollution, which kills millions of people every year. Thus, a sharp decrease in the use of these fuels will improve the overall health of the population, save lives, and save money now spent on health care. In addition, cutting coal use will greatly reduce the land disruption resulting from surface mining.

Another benefit of the no-regrets strategy is that, by relying more on a mix of renewable, domestic energy resources, many countries will cut their costly dependence on imports of fossil fuels. The money that they now spend for fuel imports will be available for investing in health care, education, and jobs, which will bolster their economic security. Also, sharply decreasing or halting the destruction of tropical forests would help to preserve the increasingly threatened biodiversity that makes up an important part of the earth's vital natural capital (see Figure 1.3, p. 7). In short, there are plenty of reasons for implementing a no-regrets strategy for sharply reducing our carbon outputs (Figure 20.24).

FIGURE 20.24 The benefits of slowing climate change are clear.

CHECKPOINT FOR UNDERSTANDING 20.4

1. Identify several strategies for adapting to climate change.

- Considerable scientific evidence indicates that human activities are playing an important role in warming the earth's atmosphere, and that this is likely to lead to significant climate disruption during this century that could have severe and long-lasting harmful consequences.

- Reducing the projected harmful effects of rapid climate change during this century requires emergency action to increase energy efficiency, sharply reduce greenhouse gas emissions, and rely more on renewable energy resources.

- While we can prepare for some climate change that is now inevitable, we could realize important economic, ecological, and health benefits by drastically reducing greenhouse gas emissions with the goal of slowing climate change.

Core Case Study Checkpoint

Identify the projected harmful impacts of climate change.

Chapter 20 Glossary

albedo: a measure of the reflectivity of sunlight by a surface such as ice and snow (high reflectivity because of its optical brightness, or whiteness), soil and desert (medium reflectivity), and ocean water (low reflectivity).

cap-and-trade: market-based approach to limiting emissions by setting limits and issuing permits to pollution-generating entities. If a business does not utilize all of their permits, they may sell them to other businesses.

carbon footprint: the amount of carbon compounds, especially carbon dioxide, emitted by a person city, country or other entity due to the burning of fossil fuels.

climate: physical properties of the troposphere of an area based on analysis of its weather records over a long period (at least 30 years). The two main factors determining an area's climate are its average *temperature*, with its seasonal variations, and the average amount and distribution of *precipitation*.

climate change tipping point: point at which an environmental problem reaches a threshold level where scientists fear it could cause irreversible climate disruption.

geoengineering: large-scale manipulation of an environmental process meant to counteract climate change.

greenhouse effect: natural effect that releases heat in the atmosphere near the earth's surface. Water vapor, carbon dioxide, ozone, and other gases in the lower atmosphere (troposphere) absorb some of the infrared radiation (heat) radiated by the earth's surface. Their molecules vibrate and transform the absorbed energy into longer-wavelength infrared radiation in the troposphere. If the atmospheric concentrations of these greenhouse gases increase and other natural processes do not remove them, the average temperature of the lower atmosphere will increase.

greenhouse gases: gases in the earth's lower atmosphere (troposphere) that cause the greenhouse effect. Examples include carbon dioxide, chlorofluorocarbons, ozone methane, water vapor, and nitrous oxide.

ocean acidification: increasing levels of acid in the world's oceans due to their absorption of much of the CO_2 emitted into the atmosphere by human activities, especially the burning of carbon-containing fossil fuels. The CO_2 reacts with ocean water to form a weak acid and decreases the levels of carbonate ions (CO_3^{2-}) needed to form coral and the shells and skeletons of organisms such as crabs, oysters, and some phytoplankton.

weather: short-term changes in in the temperature, barometric pressure, humidity, precipitation, sunshine, cloud cover, wind direction and speed, and other conditions in the troposphere at a given place and time.

Chapter Review

Core Case Study

1. Define **climate change**. Summarize the story of Greenland's melting glaciers and the possible effects of this process.

Section 20.1

2. (a) What is the key concept for this section? (b) Define and distinguish between **weather** and **climate**. (c) What is the **greenhouse effect** and how does it sustain the earth's life? (d) Define **greenhouse gases** and give three examples. (e) List nine natural factors that can affect climate change. (f) How do scientists get information about past climate change?

3. (a) List eight pieces of evidence that indicate that the earth's climate has changed since 1975, (b) In order, what three countries are the largest emitters of climate-changing CO_2? (c) What is a **carbon footprint** and what **is a per capita carbon footprint**? (d) What country has the largest carbon footprint and what country has the largest per capita carbon footprint? (e) What two human activities play an important role in the recent increase in the earth's atmospheric warming since 1975? (f) What is the IPCC and what is its mission?

4. (a) What are four conclusions by the world's leading scientific organizations about climate change? (b) Why is there essentially no serious scientific about climate change? (c) What is the public debate about? (d) How do scientists use models to confirm recent changes in atmospheric temperature and project future changes? (e) Explain how each of the following might contribute to atmospheric warming and climate change: (I) Change of the energy output of the sun, (II) the oceans, (III) cloud cover, and (IV) air pollution.

Section 20.2

5. (a) What is the key concept for this section? (b) What makes the current atmospheric warming problem urgent? (c) What are six worst-case harmful consequences of projected climate change? (d) Define **climate change tipping point** and give three examples. (e) Summarize the possible effects of a warmer atmosphere on floating ice and land-based glaciers in the Arctic. Describe James Balog's contribution to understanding the role of melting glaciers in current climate change. (f) How can melting permafrost change and affect climate? (g) How are sea levels changing and what are seven harmful effects of sea level rise? (h) How are human activities causing ocean acidification and what are its harmful effects? (i) What are the likely effects of climate change on biodiversity? Explain how atmospheric warming can intensify and prolong drought. (j) Describe the effects of atmospheric warming on extreme weather. (k) What are the likely effects of climate change on biodiversity? (l) How is Alaska showing a preview of the effects of climate change (m) What are the possible effects of climate change on food production? (n) What are the likely threats of climate change to human health, national security, and economies?

Section 20.3

6. (a) What is the key concept for this section? (b) What are five factors that make it difficult to deal with the problem of projected climate change? (c) What are two basic approaches to dealing with the harmful effects of climate change? (d) List four major prevention strategies for reducing greenhouse gas emissions. (e) What are five pieces of potential good news about dealing with climate change? (f) List six strategies for trying to clean up carbon emissions. (g) What is **carbon capture and storage (CCS)**? What are four problems associated with capturing and storing carbon dioxide emissions? (h) Define **geoengineering** and give two examples of geo-engineering proposals. What are three major problems with such proposals? (i) Discuss whether we can and should manage the earth and describe how the results of the Biosphere 2 science project relate to this issue.

7. (a) Describe six ways that governments can help reduce greenhouse gas emissions. (b) What are the advantages and disadvantages of using taxes on carbon emissions or energy use to help reduce greenhouse gas emissions? (c) What is **cap-and-trade** and what are the advantages and disadvantages of using it to help reduce greenhouse gas emissions? (d) How can government subsidies be used to address climate change? (e) Describe efforts to develop international treaties to deal with climate change.

8. (a) Give two examples of what some countries are doing on their own to deal with climate change. (b) Give two examples of what some companies are doing and two examples of what some colleges , universities, and schools have done to reduce their carbon footprints. (c) List five ways in which you can reduce your carbon footprint.

Section 20.4

9. (a) What is the key concept for this section? (b) List five ways in which we can prepare for the possible long-term harmful effects of climate disruption. (c) Describe the no-regrets strategy for dealing with the problems associated with energy waste and fossil fuel use, regardless of climate change.

10. What are this chapter's *three key ideas*?

Note: Key terms are in bold type.

Questions 1–2 are based on the graphs below.

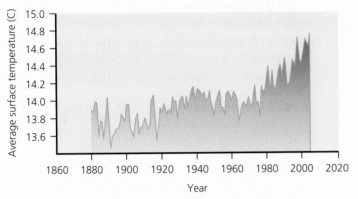

AVERAGE TEMPERATURE (over past 130 years)

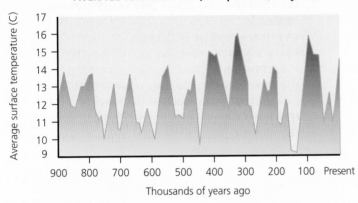

AVERAGE TEMPERATURE (over past 900,000 years)

1. Which of the statements below about the earth's current warming trend is true based on the graphs?
   (A) There has been a uniform warming of the earth since 1900.
   (B) The temperature of the earth has been stable and unchanging over the previous centuries.
   (C) Greenhouse gases have been slowly accumulating in the atmosphere, promoting global warming.
   (D) The earth has experienced many warming and cooling trends over hundreds of millenia.
   (E) Humans have been influencing global temperatures for the last few centuries.

2. Calculate the percent change in temperature from 1880 to 2000.
   (A) 0.8%
   (B) 4.3%
   (C) 5.7%
   (D) 10.5%
   (E) 94.5%

3. In 1991, Mount Pinatubo exploded, throwing tons of pollutants and ash into the atmosphere and giving climatologists and scientists a real-world laboratory to study. What was one result for climatologists of the Mount Pinatubo eruption?
   (A) Climatologists were unable to make any predictions about the effect of the eruption on global climate.
   (B) Climatologists were able to assess their predictions of the eruption on global temperatures.
   (C) Climatologists predicted no global changes due to the eruption.
   (D) Climatologists were not making predictions when Pinatubo erupted.
   (E) Climatologists had to radically revise their predictions based on the eruption.

4. All of the following are greenhouse gases EXCEPT
   (A) carbon dioxide (CO_2)
   (B) water vapor (H_2O)
   (C) methane (CH_4)
   (D) nitrous oxide (N_2O)
   (E) sulfur dioxide (SO_2)

5. Which of the following has a cooling effect on the earth's atmosphere?
   (A) Accumulation of methane released by decomposition of organisms
   (B) Accumulation of aerosols such as sulfate particles
   (C) Accumulation of carbon particles from diesel exhaust
   (D) Emission of carbon dioxide from burning fossil fuels
   (E) Condensation trails left by jets flying in the upper troposphere

6. Global ocean currents could be altered by increased ocean temperatures because
   (A) the increased acidity, and therefore temperature, of the oceans due to deep sea vent emissions would change the hurricane season
   (B) the inundation of the North Atlantic with warmer freshwater could affect the thermohaline circulation in such a way that the Gulf Stream is altered or slowed
   (C) the increase in ocean temperatures could cause major algal blooms that would slow the global thermohaline circulation at the equator
   (D) the trade winds would stop due to the lack of convection currents, called Hadley cells, which would also stop global ocean currents
   (E) El Niño would be stopped because it requires cold water on the western coast of all continents

7. The melting of ice sheets from land masses is of greater concern to scientists than the melting of icebergs because
   (A) land ice sheets are freshwater while icebergs are saltwater
   (B) land ice has a greater density due to specific gravity and, therefore, a greater volume
   (C) icebergs displace the same volume of water when they become liquid as they do in solid form
   (D) icebergs are less dense than water and float on the surface
   (E) land ice is seasonal, while icebergs in polar regions are permanent

8. Which of the following is a way that oceans slow the rate of global warming?
   I. Oceans absorb up to 25% of the carbon dioxide emitted by human activities.
   II. Oceans absorb heat energy from the lower troposphere.
   III. Oceans emit salt particles that react with greenhouse gases and decompose them.
   (A) I only
   (B) II only
   (C) III only
   (D) I and II only
   (E) I, II, and III

9. A 2007 Intergovernmental Panel on Climate Change (IPCC) report stated that the world's oceans are very likely to rise 3–4 ft during this century. The majority of this rise will occur as a result of
   (A) increased rainfall in areas that normally have droughts, as a result of El Niño
   (B) newly opened shipping lanes that cause more melting of the arctic ice sheet
   (C) more icebergs calving and flowing to lower latitudes to melt
   (D) additional water reaching the oceans as permafrost melts
   (E) thermal expansion of ocean water

Questions 10–12 refer to the terms listed below. Choices may be used once, more than once, or not at all.
   (A) Cap-and-trade program
   (B) Carbon-neutral technology
   (C) Paris climate accord
   (D) Kyoto Protocol
   (E) Montreal Protocol

10. International treaty designed to reduce emissions of chlorofluorocarbons (CFCs)

11. Legislates the purchase and sale of specific pollutants or emissions on the open market

12. Used in the design of processes or equipment so that zero net carbon dioxide emissions result from said processes or equipment

13. Rising ocean levels, bleaching of coral reefs, shifting of ocean currents, and increasing strength and severity of storms are all projected consequences of
   (A) acid precipitation
   (B) ozone layer depletion
   (C) global warming
   (D) industrial smog
   (E) PANs formation

14. All of the following are ways of reducing the release of greenhouse gases into the atmosphere EXCEPT
   (A) utilizing cleaner-burning natural gas that contains less sulfur
   (B) increasing the production of energy using wind and solar power
   (C) increasing the average fuel rating (mpg) on all vehicles
   (D) increasing the efficiency of coal-fired power plants
   (E) planting trees in deforested areas

15. Which of the following is true of stratospheric ozone?
   (A) It is a primary pollutant.
   (B) It filters out harmful ultraviolet (UV) radiation.
   (C) It poses health hazards when it oxidizes in internal tissue, such as the lungs.
   (D) It is a component of photochemical smog.
   (E) It is the primary chemical implicated in global climate change.

16. Which of the following problems is associated with the depletion of stratospheric ozone?
   (A) Increased asthma and bronchitis problems caused by inhalation of propellants from aerosol cans
   (B) Thermal expansion of oceans, resulting in changes in the thermohaline circulation
   (C) Increased mutation levels in amphibians and fish living in ponds with a low pH caused by the ozone depletion
   (D) Increased sunburns, skin cancers, and cataracts
   (E) Increased phytoplankton populations, resulting in a more diverse marine ecosystem

17. Which of the following diagrams is an appropriate representation of the ozone molecule?

(A)   (B)   (C)   (D)   (E)

18. Which of the following is true of CFC molecules as they rise through the atmosphere?
    (A) They release fluorine, which reacts violently with the ozone in the stratosphere.
    (B) They eliminate all tropospheric ozone on their way up to the stratosphere.
    (C) They are very short-lived and only last several months in the atmosphere.
    (D) They rise through the atmosphere because of convection currents within the asthenosphere.
    (E) They release a chlorine atom, which reacts with ozone to form oxygen and chlorine monoxide (ClO).

19. Which of the following is a disadvantage of using carbon and energy taxes in order to help reduce the emission of greenhouse gases?
    (A) They don't guarantee lower emissions.
    (B) They apply to all emitters.
    (C) They provide predicable revenues.
    (D) They require emitters to be more conscious of their actual emissions.
    (E) They place a clear price on carbon.

20. Many climate change analysts believe that because of the difficulty in making large reductions in greenhouse gases, we need to prepare for the harmful effects of large-scale climate warming and change. Which of the following is a method of preparing for the long-term harmful EFFECTS of climate change?
    (A) Replace incandescent lightbulbs with compact fluorescents.
    (B) Plant trees to shade houses and absorb CO_2 from the atmosphere.
    (C) Buy products from companies that are actively reducing their carbon footprints.
    (D) Walk, bike, carpool, or utilize mass transit.
    (E) Connect wildlife reserves with habitat corridors and move people inland.

AP® Free-Response Practice

Climate Change is Making Us Sick

Top U.S. doctors say they are seeing an impact

From increases in deadly diseases to choking air pollution and onslaughts of violent weather, man-made climate change is making Americans sicker, according to a report released by eleven of the nation's top medical societies.

The report was prepared by the Medical Society Consortium on Climate and Health, a new group that represents more than 400,000 doctors, who make up more than half of all U.S. physicians.

"Doctors in every part of our country see that climate change is making Americans sicker," said Mona Sarfaty, director of the new consortium and professor at George Mason University in Fairfax, Virginia.

"Physicians are on the front lines and see the impacts in exam rooms," she said. "What's worse is that the harms are felt most by children, the elderly, Americans with low incomes or chronic illnesses, and people in communities of color."

—*from USA Today, by Doyle Rice*

[Source: https://www.usatoday.com/story/news/health/2017/03/15/climate-change-making-us-sick-top-us-doctors-say/99218946/]

1. (a) According to the article, the increase of disease, air pollution, and an increase in more-violent storms are causing Americans to become ill.

    (i) **Describe** TWO other negative impacts of man-made climate change.

    (ii) **Explain** why children and the elderly are particularly vulnerable to the health impacts of climate change.

   (b) Disease vectors are common agents of transmissible diseases.

    (i) **Identify** ONE disease vector and a disease that would be transmitted by that vector.

    (ii) **Explain** how climate change increases the incidence of transmissible disease via that vector.

   (c) Sea ice is diminishing rapidly in the Arctic. **Explain** why this area of the world is increasing in temperature at a much faster rate than in lower latitudes.

   (d) **Identify** TWO actions that citizens can take that would reduce their carbon footprint.

Critical Thinking

1. If you had convincing evidence that at least half of Greenland's glaciers (**Core Case Study**) were sure to melt during this century, would you argue for taking serious actions now to slow projected climate change? Summarize your arguments for or against such actions.

2. Explain why you agree or disagree with at least 90% of the world's climate scientists that (a) climate change is happening now, and (b) human activities are an important cause of this climate change.

3. China relies on coal for two-thirds of its commercial energy usage, partly because the country has abundant supplies of this resource. As a result, China's use of coal is playing a large role in the warming of the global atmosphere. Do you think China is justified in expanding its use of this resource as other countries, including the United States, have done with their coal resources? Explain. What are China's alternatives?

4. Explain why you would support or oppose each of the strategies listed in Figure 20.16 for slowing projected climate change caused by atmospheric warming.

5. Suppose someone tells you that carbon dioxide (CO_2) should not be classified as an air pollutant because it is a natural chemical that is part of the carbon cycle (see Figure 3.15, p. 78) and a chemical that we add to the atmosphere every time we exhale. Explain the faulty reasoning in this statement about CO_2.

6. One way to slow the rate of CO_2 emissions is to reduce the clearing of forests—especially in less-developed tropical countries where intense deforestation is taking place. Should the United States and other more-developed countries pay poorer countries to stop cutting their forests because the resulting climate change will affect the United States and other nations throughout the world? Explain.

7. Some scientists have suggested that, in order to help cool the warming atmosphere, we could annually inject huge quantities of sulfate particles into the stratosphere. This might have the effect of reflecting some incoming sunlight back into space. Explain why you would support or oppose this geoengineering scheme.

8. What are three consumption patterns or other aspects of your lifestyle that directly add greenhouse gases to the atmosphere? Which, if any, of these habits would you be willing to give up in order to help slow projected climate change? Write up an argument that you could use to convince others to do the same. Compare your answers to those of your classmates.

Ecological Footprint Analysis

According to the International Energy Agency, the average American adds 19.6 metric tons (21.6 tons) of CO_2 per year to the atmosphere, compared with a world average of 4.23 metric tons (4.65 tons). The table on the next page is designed to help you understand the sources of your personal inputs of CO_2 into the atmosphere. You will be making calculations to fill in the blanks in this table.

Some typical numbers are provided in the "Typical Quantity per Year" column of the table. However, your calculations will be more accurate if you can use information based on your own personal lifestyle, which you can enter in the blank "Personal Quantity per Year" column. For

example, you could add up your monthly utility bills for a year and divide the total by the number of persons in your household to get a rough estimate of your own utility use.

1. Calculate your carbon footprint. To calculate your emissions, first complete the blank "Personal Quantity per Year" column as described above. Wherever you cannot provide personal data, use that listed in the "Typical Quantity per Year" column. Enter each number in the "Personal Quantity per Year" column to represent your annual consumption (using the units specified in the "Units per Year" column). Now multiply your annual consumption for each activity by the associated number in the "Multiplier" column to

	Units per Year	Typical Quantity per Year	Personal Quantity per Year	Multiplier	Emissions per Year (lb. CO$_2$)
Residential Utilities					
Electricity	kwh	4,500		1.5	
Heating oil	gallons	37		22	
Natural gas	hundreds of cubic feet (ccf)	400		12	
Propane	gallons	8		13	
Coal	tons	—		4,200	
Transportation					
Automobiles	gallons	600		19	
Air travel	miles	2,000		0.6	
Bus, urban	miles	12		0.07	
Bus, intercity	miles	0		0.2	
Rail or subway	miles	28		0.6	
Taxi or limousine	miles	2		1	
Other motor fuel	gallons	9		22	
Household Waste					
Trash	pounds	780		0.75	
Recycled items	pounds	337		−2	
				Total (pounds)	
				Total (tons)	
				Total (kilograms)	
				Total (metric tons)	

Source: Thomas B. Cobb at Ohio's Bowling Green State University developed this CO$_2$ calculator.

obtain an estimate of the pounds of CO$_2$ resulting from that activity, which you will enter in the "Emissions per Year" column. Finally, add the numbers in that column to find your carbon footprint, and express the final CO$_2$ result in both pounds and tons (1 ton = 2,000 pounds) and in kilograms and metric tons (1 kilogram = 2.2 pounds; 1 metric ton = 1.1 tons).

2. Compare your emissions with those of your classmates and with the per capita US average of 19.6 metric tons (21.6 tons) of CO$_2$ per person per year. Actually, your answer should be considerably less—roughly about half the per capita value—because this computation only accounts for direct emissions. For instance, CO$_2$ resulting from driving a car is included, but the CO$_2$ emitted in manufacturing and disposing of the car is not. You can find more complete carbon footprint calculators at several sites on the Web.

3. Consider and list actions you could take to reduce your carbon footprint by 20%.

Answers to Checkpoints for Understanding

Section 20.1

1. Weather is the short-term atmospheric conditions such as temperature and precipitation, and wind speed, while climate is the average weather conditions over three decades or longer.
2. Factors that naturally change the climate include volcanic eruptions and impacts of meteors and asteroids, changes in solar input, changes in the earth's orbit, slight changes in the tilt of the earth, global air circulation patterns, changes in the area of ice cover that reflects incoming solar energy and cools the atmosphere, changes in the atmospheric concentrations of greenhouse gases, occasional changes in ocean currents, and slight changes in the earth's wobbly orbit around the sun.
3. The two human activities that have led to climate change are burning fossil fuels, which increases the amount of CO_2 in the atmosphere, and cutting down forests, which remove CO_2 from the atmosphere.
4. The warming that is taking place currently is occurring at a much faster rate (over several decades) compared to warming periods in the past (over hundreds to thousands of years).
5. Climate models use computers to predict future climate trends by factoring in natural causes of warming such as incoming sunlight, Milankovitch cycles, clouds, ice caps, ocean currents, and human factors such as deforestation and output of carbon into the atmosphere.

Section 20.2

1. A climate change tipping point is the point at which an environmental problem reaches a threshold level where scientists fear it could cause irreversible climate disruption.
2. Many human populations rely on melting snowpack for irrigation of crops and water for human consumption. Water is stored as ice during the winter and released slowly into rivers and streams during the warmer months.
3. Melting of the ice cap on Greenland is projected to account for 50–60% of the projected rise in sea level.
4. Warmer temperatures can act on forests by increasing the incidence of fires, increased heat and drought, and increased infestation of insects such as bark beetles. Warmer temperatures give greater range to insect infestations and more insects survive the warmer winters.
5. Heat-related deaths of humans are projected to increase, disease vectors such as mosquitoes will have increased range, and microbes and molds will be favored due to increased temperatures. Photochemical smog may increase, leading to more respiratory illness, and there will be increased food and drinking water scarcity, leading to civil unrest and environmental refugees.

Section 20.3

1. Mitigation is the use of strategies to slow down climate change. Adaptation means finding ways to cope with climate change since humans have waited too long to address this problem and some of the harmful effects of climate change are inevitable.
2. Global economies for years to come will very likely rely on finding and using most of the remaining coal and natural gas that is still in the ground. To slow down climate change, it would mean relying more on abandoning these fossil fuel resources and switching to renewable energy sources and sharply reducing energy waste.
3. Some scientists argue against mitigation strategies because they feel that if these are put in place, it will justify continued use of fossil fuels, resulting in continued climate change and ocean acidification.

Section 20.4

1. Strategies for adapting to climate change include moving people inland, stockpiling food, developing crops that require less water, reducing water waste, no longer building in low-lying coastal areas, moving hazardous waste away from coastal areas, and creating wildlife corridors.

Core Case Study

Impacts of climate change include rising sea levels, ocean acidification, species extinction, and more extreme weather events, including more intense and longer lasting heat waves.

1. Which of the following diseases is caused by bacteria?
   (A) HIV
   (B) TB (tuberculosis)
   (C) West Nile
   (D) Hepatitis B
   (E) Influenza

2. In a dose-response experiment, LD50 signifies which of the following?
   (A) The number of subjects who receive 50% of the experimental dose
   (B) The dose that kills 50% of the experimental subjects
   (C) The 50% of experimental subjects receiving a placebo
   (D) The dose at which 50% of the subjects undergo a toxic reaction
   (E) The dose at which 50% of the subjects experience no reaction

3. Which of the following is NOT a solution for the world-wide reduction of disease?
   (A) Increase the use of antibiotics on livestock
   (B) Improve drinking water quality
   (C) Immunize children
   (D) Reduce malnutrition
   (E) Reduce poverty

4. Which of the following is an example of a transmissible disease?
   (A) SARS
   (B) Asthma
   (C) Emphysema
   (D) Cardiovascular disease
   (E) Malnutrition

5. Which of the following is a means of deciding how to reduce a particular risk to an acceptable level, and at what cost?
   (A) Risk management
   (B) Risk assessment
   (C) LD50
   (D) Toxicology
   (E) Ecological medicine

6. The largest fraction of the wastes buried in American landfills is made up of
   (A) plastics
   (B) food waste
   (C) paper
   (D) yard waste
   (E) metals

Questions 7–9 refer to the following. Choices may be used once, more than once, or not at all.
   (A) Conductivity
   (B) Dissolved oxygen concentration
   (C) Nitrate and phosphate concentration
   (D) Bacterial count
   (E) Sediment load

7. The best indicator of surface water quality

8. May be measured with a Secchi disc or another turbidity test

9. A cause of cultural eutrophication

10. Which of the following is NOT an example of a non-point source of water pollution?
    (A) Runoff from farm land
    (B) Runoff from city streets and other developed areas
    (C) Runoff from forests and undeveloped land
    (D) Deposition from the atmosphere
    (E) Treated wastewater discharges

11. For a river that receives a constant discharge of biodegradable wastes from a point source, all of the following statements are true of the *oxygen sag curve*, EXCEPT
    (A) the curve will occur at the discharge point
    (B) the septic area occurs after decomposition
    (C) the sag is more likely to occur during periods of low stream flow
    (D) the sag causes a change in species distribution
    (E) the water could produce odors where the sag occurs

12. All of the following are common disadvantages of solid waste incineration EXCEPT
    (A) start-up costs are relatively high
    (B) incinerator ash is hazardous waste
    (C) carbon dioxide and other pollutants are still emitted during the process
    (D) incineration is noisy and often unsightly
    (E) incineration is less expensive than other methods

13. The primary law for dealing with hazardous waste issues in the United States is
    (A) The Comprehensive Environmental Response, Compensation and Liability Act (CERCLA)
    (B) The Resource Conservation and Recovery Act (RCRA)
    (C) The Superfund Act (SARA)
    (D) Federal Insecticide, Fungicide, and Rodenticide Act (FIFRA)
    (E) Toxic Release Inventory (TRI)

14. Which of the following is NOT a method of detoxifying hazardous waste?
    (A) Phytoremediation
    (B) Bioremediation
    (C) Incineration
    (D) Distillation
    (E) Filtration

15. Which of the following is NOT a method used to dispose of or reduce hazardous wastes?
    (A) Plasma arc
    (B) Deep well injection
    (C) Surface impoundments
    (D) Substituting hazardous materials for non-hazardous materials
    (E) Chemical neutralization

Questions 16–20 refer to the following substances. Choices may be used once, more than once, or not at all.
    (A) Ozone (O_3)
    (B) Lead (Pb)
    (C) Radon-222
    (D) Mercury (Hg)
    (E) Methane (CH_4)

16. Produced from radioactive decay of Uranium-238, and is a carcinogen

17. VOC (volatile organic compound) and strong greenhouse gas

18. Sources include smelting plants, piping, and paints, and is a neurotoxin

19. A neurotoxin that enters surface water from gold mining runoff

20. A secondary pollutant present in photochemical smog

21. Which of the following is NOT true of particulate pollution?
    (A) Has decreased since the Clean Air Act required scrubbers and clean-up precautions
    (B) Weather influences its increase or decrease
    (C) Is a major part of industrial smog
    (D) Is shown to have increased with perennial polyculture farming practices
    (E) Is reduced when people convert wood burning fireplaces to pellet stoves or gas fireplaces

22. Which of the following is NOT a result of human exposure to UV radiation?
    (A) Melanoma
    (B) Cataracts
    (C) Lung cancer
    (D) Sunburn
    (E) Weakened immunity

23. Which of the following best describes the greenhouse effect?
    (A) The increase in the earth's average atmospheric temperature
    (B) The absorption of solar energy by the earth's vast oceans
    (C) The trapping of the sun's heat during temperature inversions
    (D) The absorption of heat reradiating from the earth by certain gases
    (E) The refraction of solar heat within the troposphere

24. Which of the following is an example of positive feedback that relates to climate?
    (A) As global warming increases, polar ice caps begin to decline resulting in a higher albedo and lower surface temperatures.
    (B) As global warming increases, permafrost melts, releasing CH_4, a potent greenhouse gas.
    (C) Increased volcanic activity releases ash and sulfate particles, resulting in a temporary increase in global temperatures.
    (D) As ocean temperatures increase, more CO_2 will be absorbed by the ocean, resulting in higher phytoplankton populations.
    (E) As global warming increases, reforestation in tropical rainforest areas will occur more rapidly due to increased precipitation.

25. Past temperatures are estimated by analysis of data from all of the following EXCEPT
    (A) radioisotopes in fossils
    (B) air bubble samples from ice cores
    (C) pollen samples
    (D) ocean CO_2 bubbles
    (E) atmospheric carbon dioxide measurements

1. The news excerpt below from September 2016 describes a 2014 incident involving a toxic spill at a power plant. Use the information in the excerpt and your knowledge to answer the questions that follow.

> **RALEIGH, N.C.** - Duke Energy Corp. has agreed to pay a $6 million fine for a big spill that coated the Dan River with liquefied coal ash in 2014, North Carolina's environment agency said Friday.
>
> The fine holds Duke Energy accountable for violations of federal water protection laws during and after the country's third-worst spill of the residue left behind after burning coal, the state Department of Environmental Quality said in a prepared statement.
>
> The spill coated 70 miles of the river on the North Carolina-Virginia border in more than 30,000 tons of sludge after a pipe burst at a holding pit at Duke Energy's power plant in Eden. Coal ash can contain toxic chemicals including arsenic, chromium and lead.

https://www.cbsnews.com/news/duke-energy-corporation-agrees-6-million-fine-coal-ash-spill-north-carolina/

(a) There are many different issues associated with a spill of liquefied coal ash.

   (i) **Identify** THREE possible toxins that potentially entered the Dan River due to the spill at the Eden power plant.

   (ii) **Discuss** the specific human health effects associated with TWO of the pollutants identified above.

   (iii) **Identify** and **describe** a specific ecological effect (other than the release of toxins) of a spill of liquefied coal ash into a waterway.

(b) **Identify** and **describe** ONE piece of federal legislation that regulates the release of any potentially toxic substance into waterways.

(c) **Identify** a different energy source that could be used in a similar power plant, and **discuss** how it would eliminate this specific environmental impact.

(d) **Discuss** TWO ecological disadvantages of using coal as an energy source.

(e) **Identify** an example of another large environmentally significant spill or pollutant release, and **discuss** its ecological impacts.

2. Heavy metals are defined as those with densities greater than 5 g/cm³. The majority are persistent in all parts of the environment. Human activity affects the natural geological and biological redistribution of heavy metals through pollution of the air, water, and soil.

(a) **Identify** TWO heavy metals that are found as pollutants in the environment.

(b) For <u>each</u> of the TWO heavy metals you identified,

   (i) **Identify** ONE specific source that could introduce that metal into the environment.

   (ii) **Identify** ONE toxic effect of that metal on human health.

   (iii) **Describe** ONE ecological impact of that heavy metal.

(c) **Define** the term "bioaccumulation" and **explain** how it relates to the persistence of heavy metals.

(d) **Identify** another chemical that bioaccumulates, and **describe** its effects on human health.

(e) **Explain** the difference between the processes of bioaccumulation and biomagnification.

Postscript: How Can We Live More Sustainably?

BECOME MORE ENVIRONMENTALLY LITERATE

There is widespread scientific evidence and agreement that we are a species that is degrading the earth's life-support system on which we and other species depend. During this century, this behavior will very likely threaten human civilization and the existence of up to half of the world's species that help support all life and our economies.

Part of the problem stems from our incomplete understanding of how the earth's life-support system works, how our actions affect its life-sustaining systems, and how we can change our behavior toward the earth, and thus toward ourselves. Improving this understanding begins by grasping three important ideas that form the foundation of *environmental literacy*:

1. Natural capital matters because it supports the earth's life and human economies.

2. Human ecological footprints are immense and are expanding rapidly.

3. Once we exceed planetary boundaries or ecological tipping points, the resulting harmful consequences could last for hundreds to thousands of years.

How we act toward nature depends on our environmental worldview, a key component of environmental literacy. One earth-centered worldview is called the *environmental wisdom worldview*. According to this view:

- We need to learn how nature has sustained life on the earth for 3.8 billion years and use these lessons from nature (environmental wisdom) to guide us in living more simply and sustainably.

- We are part of—not apart from—the community of life and the ecological processes that sustain all life.

- We are not in charge of the planet.

- We are subject to nature's scientific laws that cannot be broken.

- Human economies and other systems are subsystems of the earth's life-support systems.

- The earth's natural capital keeps us and other species alive and supports our economies.

- We need to learn how to work with nature instead of trying to conquer it.

- By not degrading the earth's life-support system, we act in our own self-interest. Earth care is self-care.

- We have an ethical responsibility to leave the earth in as good a condition or better than what we inherited—in keeping with the ethical **principle of sustainability**.

Acquiring environmental literacy involves being able to answer certain key questions.

- How does life on the earth sustain itself?

- How am I connected to the earth and its life?

- Where do the things I consume come from and where do they go after I use them?

- What is my environmental worldview?

- What is my environmental responsibility to current and future generations?

Experience Nature

According to many analysts, the problem is not just a lack of environmental literacy, but also a lack of intimate contact with nature. Having little understanding of how nature works and sustains us reduces our ability to act more responsibly toward the earth. These analysts urge us to get out and experience the awe, wonder, mystery, excitement, and humility of walking through a forest, enjoying a beautiful vista, or taking in the majesty and power of the sea. We might look at a magnificent oak, a rolling mountain range, or an industrious honeybee, or listen to a bird's song or a crashing wave and try to sense how each of them is connected to us and we to them, through the earth's life-sustaining processes. Direct experiences with nature can reveal parts of the complex web of life that cannot be bought, recreated with technology, reproduced with genetic engineering, or learned by reading this or any book.

Understanding and directly experiencing the precious and free gifts we receive from nature can help us make an ethical commitment to live more sustainably on the earth and thus to preserve our own species and cultures. Earth-focused philosophers say that to be rooted, each of us needs to find a *sense of place*—a stream, a mountain, a patch of forest, a yard, a neighborhood park—any piece of the natural world that we know, experience emotionally, and love. When we become part of a place, it becomes a part of us. Some environmental leaders are helping people connect directly with nature (see Individuals Matter, p. 676).

Live More Simply

Seeking happiness through the pursuit of material things is considered folly by almost every major religion and philosophy. Yet, today's avalanche of advertising messages

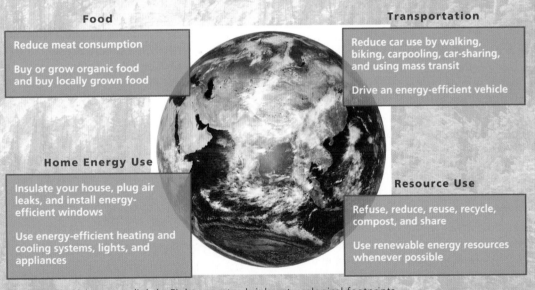

Food

Reduce meat consumption

Buy or grow organic food and buy locally grown food

Transportation

Reduce car use by walking, biking, carpooling, car-sharing, and using mass transit

Drive an energy-efficient vehicle

Home Energy Use

Insulate your house, plug air leaks, and install energy-efficient windows

Use energy-efficient heating and cooling systems, lights, and appliances

Resource Use

Refuse, reduce, reuse, recycle, compost, and share

Use renewable energy resources whenever possible

FIGURE 1 *Living more lightly.* Eight ways to shrink out ecological footprints.

A view within Yellowstone National Park in the U.S. state of Wyoming.

DREW RUSH/National Geographic Creative

Juan Martinez—Reconnecting People with Nature

National Geographic Explorer Juan Martinez learned firsthand about the value of connecting with nature. Now he is instilling that value in others, particularly disadvantaged youths.

Martinez grew up in a poor area of Los Angeles, California, where as a boy he was in danger of becoming absorbed by a gang culture. One of his teachers recognized Martinez's potential and gave him a chance to pass a class that he was failing by joining the school's Eco Club.

Martinez took that opportunity, and when the club planned a field trip to see the Grand Teton Mountains of Wyoming, he jumped at the chance. As a result, he says, "I still can't find words to describe the first moment I saw those mountains rising up from the valley. Watching bison, seeing a sky full of stars, and hiking through that scenery was overwhelming."

The experience transformed Martinez's life. Today, he spearheads the Natural Leaders Network of the Children and Nature Network, an organization creating links between environmental organizations, corporations, government, education, and individuals to reconnect children with nature. His work as an environmental leader has inspired many others to do similar work.

Martinez has received a great deal of recognition for his efforts, including invitations to White House forums on environmental education. His greatest reward, however, is in seeing how his efforts help others.

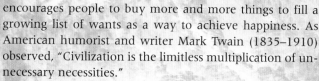

encourages people to buy more and more things to fill a growing list of wants as a way to achieve happiness. As American humorist and writer Mark Twain (1835–1910) observed, "Civilization is the limitless multiplication of unnecessary necessities."

Some people are adopting a lifestyle of *voluntary simplicity*. It should not be confused with poverty, which is *involuntary simplicity*. Voluntary simplicity involves people learning to live with less stuff, using products and services that have smaller harmful environmental impacts, and creating beneficial environmental impacts. Instead of working longer hours to pay for bigger vehicles and houses, they are spending more time with their loved ones, friends, and nature. Their goals are to consume less, share more, live simply, make friends, treasure family, and enjoy life. Their motto is, "Shop less, live more."

Living more simply and sustainably starts with asking the question, "What do I really need?" This is not an easy question to answer, because people in affluent societies are conditioned to view excessive material possessions as needs instead of wants.

Throughout this text, you have encountered lists of ways we can live more lightly on the earth by reducing the size and impact of our ecological footprints. Figure 1 lists eight key ways in which some people are choosing to live more simply and sustainably.

The seriousness of the environmental problems we face can be overwhelming and lead many people to feel guilty, fearful, apathetic, and powerless. We can move beyond these immobilizing feelings by recognizing and avoiding the following two common mental traps that lead to denial, indifference, and inaction:

- Gloom-and-doom pessimism (it is hopeless)
- Blind technological optimism (science and technological fixes will save us)

Avoiding these traps helps us to hold on to, and be inspired by, empowering feelings of realistic hope, rather than to be immobilized by feelings of despair and fear.

Here is what business entrepreneur and environmental writer Paul Hawken told a graduating class at the University of Portland:

When asked if I am pessimistic or optimistic about the future, my answer is always the same: If you look at the science about what is happening on the earth and aren't pessimistic, you don't understand the data. But if you meet the people who are working to restore this earth and the lives of the poor, and you aren't optimistic, you haven't got a pulse. . . . This is your century. Take it and run as if your life depends on it.

Bringing About a Sustainability Revolution in Your Lifetime

The Industrial Revolution, which began around the mid-18th century, was a remarkable global transformation.

REBECCA HALE/National Geographic

Now in this century, environmental leaders say it is time for another global transformation—a *sustainability revolution*. Figure 2 lists some of the major cultural shifts in emphasis that can help to bring about a sustainability revolution. We know what needs to be done and we can change the way we treat the earth, and thus our life-support system and ourselves.

Unsustainable Path	Sustainable Path
Energy and Climate	
Fossil fuels	Direct and indirect solar energy
Energy waste	Energy efficiency
Climate disruption	Climate stabilization
Matter	
High resource use and waste	Less resource use
Consume and throw away	Reduce, reuse, and recycle
Waste disposal and pollution control	Waste prevention and pollution prevention
Life	
Deplete and degrade natural capital	Protect natural capital
Reduce biodiversity	Protect biodiversity
Population growth	Population stabilization

FIGURE 2 SOLUTIONS Some of the cultural shifts in emphasis that scientists say will be necessary to bring about a sustainability revolution.

This is a compelling and challenging time to be living on our planet because we have the knowledge to shift from our current unsustainable path to a more sustainable one. Within this century, a small but dedicated group of people from around the world can bring about a sustainability revolution. They will likely understand three things. *First*, we have been borrowing from the earth and the future, and our debt is coming due. *Second*, as a species we are capable of great things, if we choose to act. *Third*, once we start on a new path, change will likely spread through our web-connected global social networks at an amazing pace.

While some skeptics say the idea of a sustainability revolution is idealistic and unrealistic, entrepreneur Paul Hawken has argued that "the most unrealistic person in the world is the cynic, not the dreamer." And according to the late Steve Jobs, cofounder of Apple Inc., "The people who are crazy enough to think they can change the world are the ones who do." If these and other individuals had not had the courage to forge ahead with ideas that others called idealistic and unrealistic, very few of the environmental and other achievements that we now celebrate would have happened.

The key to a sustainability revolution is understanding that *individuals matter*. Each of our choices and actions makes a difference, we are all in this together, and the situation is not hopeless. We can work together to leave the earth—our only home—in better shape than it is now. What an incredibly exciting time to be alive.

Length

Metric

1 kilometer (km) = 1,000 meters (m)

1 meter (m) = 100 centimeters (cm)

1 meter (m) = 1,000 millimeters (mm)

1 centimeter (cm) = 0.01 meter (m)

1 millimeter (mm) = 0.001 meter (m)

English

1 foot (ft) = 12 inches (in)

1 yard (yd) = 3 feet (ft)

1 mile (mi) = 5,280 feet (ft)

1 nautical mile = 1.15 miles

Metric–English

1 kilometer (km) = 0.621 mile (mi)

1 meter (m) = 39.4 inches (in) = 3.28 feet

1 inch (in) = 2.54 centimeters (cm)

1 foot (ft) = 0.305 meter (m)

1 yard (yd) = 0.914 meter (m)

1 nautical mile = 1.85 kilometers (km)

Area

Metric

1 square kilometer (km^2) = 1,000,000 square meters (m^2)

1 square meter (m^2) = 1,000,000 square millimeters (mm^2)

1 square meter (m^2) = 10,000 square centimeters (cm^2)

1 hectare (ha) = 10,000 square meters (m^2)

1 hectare (ha) = 0.01 square kilometer (km^2)

English

1 square foot (ft^2) = 144 square inches (in^2)

1 square yard (yd^2) = 9 square feet (ft^2)

1 square mile (mi^2) = 27,880,000 square feet (ft^2)

1 acre (ac) = 43,560 square feet (ft^2)

Metric–English

1 hectare (ha) = 2.471 acres (ac)

1 square kilometer (km^2) = 0.386 square mile (mi^2)

1 square meter (m^2) = 1.196 square yards (yd^2)

1 square meter (m^2) = 10.76 square feet (ft^2)

1 square centimeter (cm^2) = 0.155 square inch (in^2)

Volume

Metric

1 cubic kilometer (km^3) = 1,000,000,000 cubic meters (m^3)

1 cubic meter (m^3) = 1,000,000 cubic centimeters (cm^3)

1 liter (L) = 1,000 milliliters (mL) = 1,000 cubic centimeters (cm^3)

1 cubic meter (m^3) = 1,000 liters (L)

1 milliliter (mL) = 0.001 liter (L)

1 milliliter (mL) = 1 cubic centimeter (cm^3)

English

1 gallon (gal) = 4 quarts (qt)

1 quart (qt) = 2 pints (pt)

Metric–English

1 liter (L) = 0.265 gallon (gal)

1 gallon (gal) = 3.77 liters (L)

1 liter (L) = 1.06 quarts (qt)

1 liter (L) = 0.0353 cubic foot (ft^3)

1 cubic meter (m^3) = 35.3 cubic feet (ft^3)

1 cubic meter (m^3) = 1.30 cubic yards (yd^3)

1 cubic kilometer (km^3) = 0.24 cubic mile (mi^3)

1 barrel (bbl) = 159 liters (L)

1 barrel (bbl) = 42 U.S. gallons (gal)

Fuel Efficiency

Metric–English

kilometers per liter (kpL) = miles per gallon (mpg) $\times$ 2.34

miles per gallon (mpg) = kilometers per liter (kpL) $\div$ 2.34

Mass

Metric

1 kilogram (kg) = 1,000 grams (g)

1 gram (g) = 1,000 milligrams (mg)

1 gram (g) = 1,000,000 micrograms (µg)

1 milligram (mg) = 0.001 gram (g)

1 microgram (µg) = 0.000001 gram (g)

1 metric ton (mt) = 1,000 kilograms (kg)

English

1 ton (t) = 2,000 pounds (lb)

1 pound (lb) = 16 ounces (oz)

Metric–English

1 metric ton (mt) = 2,200 pounds (lb) = 1.1 tons (t)

1 kilogram (kg) = 2.20 pounds (lb)

1 pound (lb) = 454 grams (g)

1 gram (g) = 0.035 ounce (oz)

Energy and Power

Metric

1 kilojoule (kJ) = 1,000 joules (J)

1 kilocalorie (kcal) = 1,000 calories (cal)

1 calorie (cal) = 4.184 joules (J)

English

1 British thermal unit (Btu) = 1,055 watt-seconds

Kilowatt-hour = 1,000 watt-hours

Metric–English

1 kilojoule (kJ) = 0.949 British thermal unit (Btu)

1 kilojoule (kJ) = 0.000278 kilowatt-hour (kW-h)

1 kilocalorie (kcal) = 3.97 British thermal units (Btu)
1 kilocalorie (kcal) = 0.00116 kilowatt-hour (kW-h)
1 kilowatt-hour (kW-h) = 860 kilocalories (kcal)
1 kilowatt-hour (kW-h) = 3,400 British thermal units (Btu)
1 quad (Q) = 1,050,000,000,000,000 kilojoules (kJ)
1 quad (Q) = 293,000,000,000 kilowatt-hours (kW-h)

Temperature Conversions

Fahrenheit (°F) to Celsius (°C): °C = (°F − 32.0) ÷ 1.80
Celsius (°C) to Fahrenheit (°F): °F = (°C × 1.80) + 32.0
Change of 1°C = change of 1.8°F

Unit Conversion Sample Exercises

1. Convert an automobile fuel efficiency of 45 miles per gallon (mpg) to kilometers per liter (kpL).

Answer: Let x be the answer in kpL. We know that kpL = mpg × 2.34. So, x = 45 × 2.34 = 105.3 kpL (or 105 rounded to the nearest whole number).

2. Convert a deforestation rate of 100 hectares per year to acres per year.

Answer: We know that 1 hectare = 2.471 acres. So, 100 hectares = 100 × 2.471 acres, or 247.1 acres. The answer is 247.1 acres per year (or 247 acres per year, rounded to the nearest acre).

Unit Conversion Exercises

1. If your car gets 32 miles per gallon, what is its fuel efficiency in kilometers per liter?

2. Suppose a forest is being cut at a rate of 88 hectares per year. How many acres per year are being cut?

Graphs and Maps Are Important Visual Tools

A graph is a tool for conveying information that we can summarize numerically by illustrating that information in a visual format. This information, called *data*, is collected in experiments, surveys, and other information-gathering activities. Graphing can be a powerful tool for summarizing and conveying complex information.

In this textbook and the accompanying web-based Active Graphing exercises, we use three major types of graphs: *line graphs*, *bar graphs*, and *pie graphs*. Here, you will explore each of these types of graphs and learn how to read them. An important visual tool used to summarize data that vary over small or large areas is a map. We discuss some aspects of reading maps relating to environmental science at the end of this supplement.

Line Graphs

Line graphs usually represent data that fall in some sort of sequence such as a series of measurements over time or distance. In most such cases, units of time or distance lie on the horizontal *x-axis*. The possible measurements of some quantity or variable such as temperature or oil use that changes over time or distance usually lie on the vertical *y-axis*.

In Figure 1, the *x-axis* shows the years between 1965 and 2020, and the *y-axis* displays a range of possible values for the annual amounts of oil consumed worldwide. Usually, the *y-axis* appears on the left end of the *x-axis*, although *y-axes* can appear on the right end, in the middle, or on both ends of the *x-axis*.

The curving line on a line graph represents the measurements taken at certain time or distance intervals. In Figure 1, the curve represents changes in annual global oil consumption between 1965 and 2013. To find the average annual global oil consumption for any year, find that year on the *x-axis* (a point called the *abscissa*) and run a vertical line from the axis to the curve. At the point where your line intersects the curve, run a horizontal line to the *y-axis*. The value at that point on the *y-axis*, called the *ordinate*, is the amount you are seeking. You can go through the same process in reverse to find a year in which global oil consumption was at a certain point.

Questions

1. About how many metric tons of oil were consumed in the world in 2013?

2. Roughly how many times more oil was consumed in 2013 than in 1985? About how many times more oil was consumed in 2013 than in 1965?

Line graphs have several important uses. One of the most common applications is to compare two or more variables. Figure 2 compares two variables: monthly temperature and precipitation (rain and snowfall) during a typical year in a temperate deciduous forest. However, in this case the variables are measured on two different scales, so there are two *y-axes*. The *y-axis* on the left end of the graph shows a Centigrade temperature scale, while the *y-axis* on the right shows the range of precipitation measurements in millimeters. The *x-axis* displays the first letters of each of the 12 months' names.

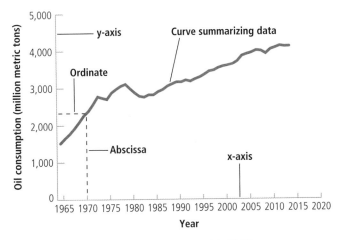

FIGURE 1 Global oil consumption, 1965–2013.

(Compiled by the authors using data from U.S. Energy Information Administration, International Energy Agency, British Petroleum, and United Nations.)

Temperate deciduous forest

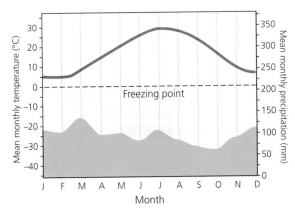

FIGURE 2 Typical variations in annual temperature (red) and precipitation (blue) in a temperate deciduous forest.

Questions

1. In which month does most precipitation fall? Which is the driest month of the year? Which is the hottest month?

2. If the temperature curve were almost flat, running throughout the year at roughly its highest point of about 30°C, how do you think this forest would change from what it is now (see Figure 7.19, center, p. 196)? If the annual precipitation suddenly dropped and remained under 25 centimeters all year, what do you think would eventually happen to this forest?

Bar Graphs

The *bar graph* is used to compare measurements for one or more variables across categories. Unlike the line graph, a bar graph typically does not involve a sequence of measurements over time or distance. The measurements compared on a bar graph usually represent data collected at some point in time or during a well-defined period. For instance, we can compare the *net primary productivity (NPP)*, a measure of chemical energy produced by plants in an ecosystem, for different ecosystems, as represented in Figure 3.

In most bar graphs, the categories to be compared are laid out on the *x*-axis, while the range of measurements for the variable under consideration lies along the *y*-axis. In Figure 3, the categories (ecosystems) are on the *y*-axis, and the variable range (NPP) lies on the *x*-axis. In either case, reading the graph is straightforward. Simply run a line perpendicular to the bar you are reading from the top of that bar (or the right or left end, if it lies horizontally) to the variable value axis. In Figure 3, you can see that the NPP for the continental shelf, for example, is close to 1,600 kcal/m²/yr.

Questions

1. What are the two terrestrial ecosystems that are closest in NPP value of all pairs of such ecosystems? About how many times greater is the NPP in a tropical rain forest than the NPP in a savanna?

2. Which is the most productive of the aquatic ecosystems shown here? Which is the least productive?

An important application of the bar graph used in this book is the *age-structure diagram* (see Figures 8.10, p. 215, and 8.11, p. 216), which describes a population by showing the numbers of males and females in certain age groups.

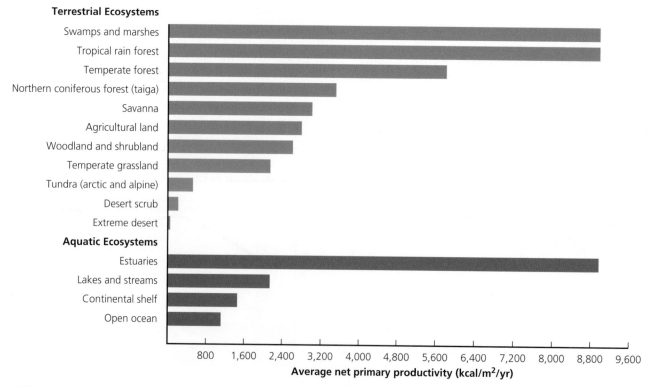

FIGURE 3 Estimated average annual *net primary productivity* in major life zones and ecosystems, in kilocalories of energy produced per square meter per year (kcal/m²/yr).

(Compiled by the authors using data from R. H. Whittaker, *Communities and Ecosystems*, 2nd ed., New York: Macmillan, 1975.)

Pie Graphs

Like bar graphs, *pie graphs*, or *pie charts*, illustrate numerical values for two or more categories. In addition to that, they can also show each category's proportion of the total of all measurements. The categories are usually ordered on the graph from largest to smallest, for ease of comparison, although this is not always the case. In addition, as with bar graphs, pie graphs are generally snapshots of a data set at a point in time or during a defined time period. Unlike line graphs, one pie graph cannot show changes over time.

For example, Figure 4 shows how much each major energy source contributes to the world's total amount of energy used. This graph includes the numerical data used to construct it—the percentages of the total taken up by each part of the pie. But we can use pie graphs without including the numerical data, and we can roughly estimate such percentages. The pie graph in that case provides a generalized picture of the composition of a data set.

Questions

1. How many times bigger was coal use than nuclear energy use in 2014?

2. How many times bigger was oil use than hydropower use in 2014?

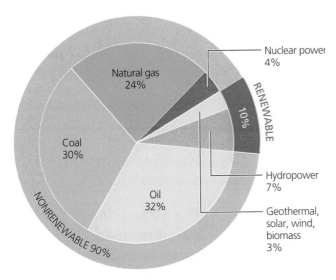

FIGURE 4 Global energy use by source in 2014.

(Compiled by the authors using data from British Petroleum, U.S. Energy Information Administration, and International Energy Agency.)

Reading Maps

We can use maps for considerably more than showing where places are relative to one another. For example, in environmental science, maps can be very helpful in comparing how people in different areas are affected by environmental problems such as air pollution and acid deposition. Figure 5 is a map of the United States showing the relative numbers of premature deaths due to air pollution in the various regions of the country.

Questions

1. Which part of the country generally has the lowest level of premature deaths due to air pollution?

2. Which part of the country has the highest level?

3. What is the level in the area where you live or go to school?

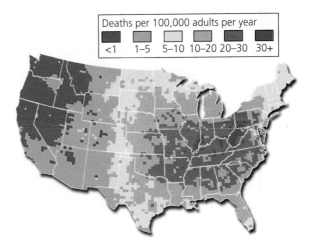

FIGURE 5 Distribution of premature deaths from air pollution in the United States, mostly from very small, fine, and ultrafine particles added to the atmosphere by coal-burning power plants.

(Compiled by the authors using data from U.S. Environmental Protection Agency.)

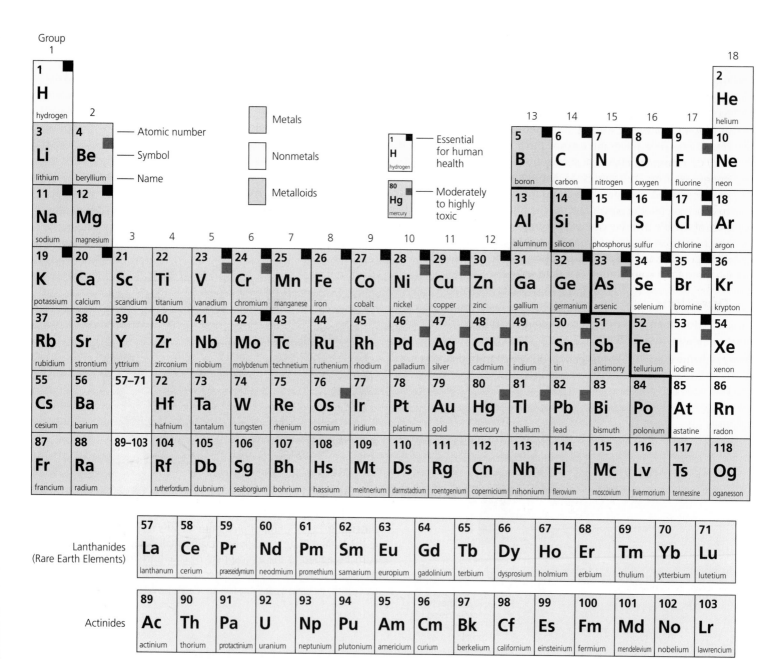

FIGURE 1 Periodic Table of Elements. Elements in the same vertical column, called a *group*, have similar chemical properties.

Era	Period	Time (millions of years ago)	Major Events (approximate time in millions of years ago, in parentheses)
Cenozoic (Age of Mammals)	Quaternary	1.6 – present	Likely beginning of new mass extinction (now) Human civilization develops (0.01 to now) Modern humans (*Homo sapiens sapiens*) (0.2) First humans (1.2)
	Tertiary	6.5 – 1.6	Oldest human ancestors (4.4) Grasses diversify and spread Mammals diversify and spread
Mesozoic (Age of Reptiles)	Cretaceous	146 – 6.5	Mass extinction (75% of species, including dinosaurs) (66) First primates First flowering plants
	Jurassic	208 – 146	Mass extinction (75% of species) (200) First birds Dinosaurs diversify and spread
	Triassic	245 – 208	First dinosaurs First mammals
Paleozoic (Age of Fishes)	Permian	290 – 245	Mass extinction (90–96% of species) (251) Reptiles diversify and spread
	Pennsylvanian	322 – 290	First reptiles
	Mississippian	362 – 322	Coal deposits form
	Devonian	408 – 362	Mass extinction (70% of species) (375) First land animals (amphibians) Fish diversify and spread First forests
	Silurian	439 – 408	First land plants and corals
	Ordovician	510 – 439	Mass extinction (60–70% of species) (450) First fish
	Cambrian	545 – 510	First shellfish Ozone layer forms Oxygen increases in atmosphere Photosynthetic organisms proliferate
Precambrian	Proterozoic	2,500 – 545	First animals in sea (jellyfish) First multicellular organisms
	Archean	4,600 – 2,500	First photosynthesis and oxygen in atmosphere (2,800) First plants in sea (algae) (3,200) Atmospheric water vapor condenses to oceans (3,700) First rocks (3,800) Likely origin of life (first one-celled organisms) (3,800) Earth forms (4,600)

Dates are approximate.

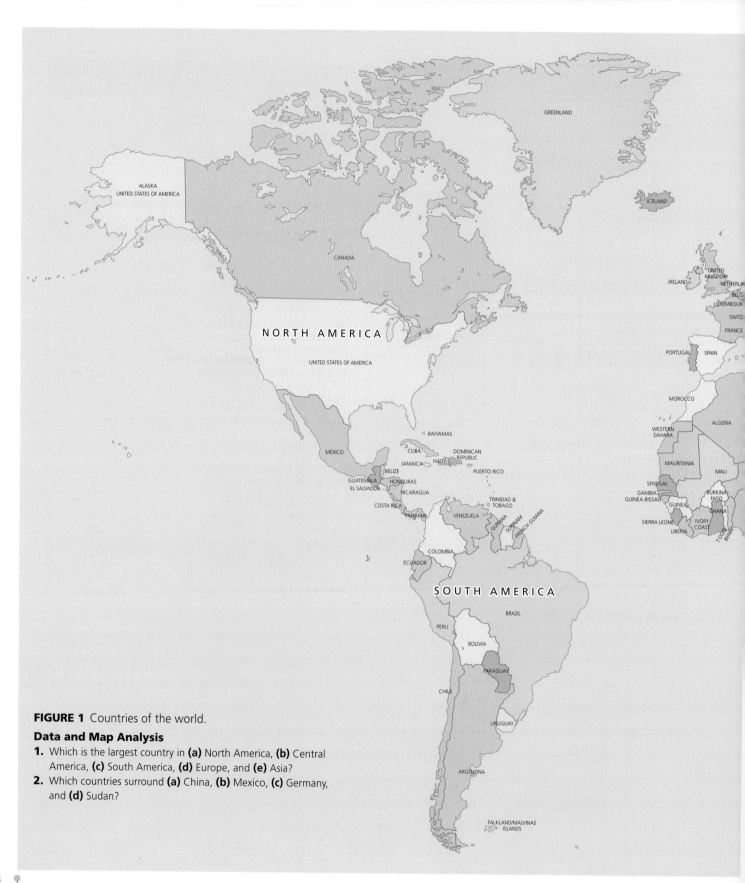

FIGURE 1 Countries of the world.

Data and Map Analysis

1. Which is the largest country in **(a)** North America, **(b)** Central America, **(c)** South America, **(d)** Europe, and **(e)** Asia?

2. Which countries surround **(a)** China, **(b)** Mexico, **(c)** Germany, and **(d)** Sudan?

EUROPE

NORWAY
SWEDEN
FINLAND

DENMARK
ESTONIA
LATVIA
LITHUANIA
BELARUS

NETHERLANDS
GERMANY
POLAND
BELGIUM
LUXBOURG
CZECH REP.
SLOVAKIA
UKRAINE
SWITZERLAND
AUSTRIA
HUNGARY
MOLDOVA
FRANCE
SLOVENIA
ROMANIA
CROATIA
BOSNIA-HERZEGOVINA
YUGOSLAVIA
BULGARIA
ITALY
MACEDONIA
GEORGIA
ALBANIA
GREECE
TURKEY
ARMENIA
AZERBAIJAN

RUSSIA

ASIA

KAZAKHSTAN

MONGOLIA

KYRGYZSTAN
UZBEKISTAN
TURKMENISTAN
TAJIKISTAN

NORTH KOREA

SOUTH KOREA
JAPAN

TUNISIA
CYPRUS
SYRIA
LEBANON
ISRAEL
IRAQ
JORDAN
AFGHANISTAN
IRAN
KUWAIT
PAKISTAN

CHINA

LIBYA
EGYPT
SAUDI ARABIA
QATAR
UNITED ARAB EMIRATES
NEPAL
BHUTAN

TAIWAN

BANGLADESH
HONG KONG

NIGER
CHAD
OMAN
YEMEN
INDIA
MYANMAR
LAOS

AFRICA
ERITREA
THAILAND
VIETNAM

NIGERIA
SUDAN
CAMBODIA
PHILIPPINES

CENTRAL AFRICAN REPUBLIC
ETHIOPIA

CAMEROON
SOMALIA
SRI LANKA
BRUNEI

EQUATORIAL GUINEA
UGANDA
MALAYSIA

CONGO
DEMOCRATIC REPUBLIC OF CONGO
KENYA

GABON
RAWANDA
BARUNDI
TANZANIA

INDONESIA
PAPUA NEW GUINEA
SOLOMON ISLANDS

ANGOLA
ZAMBIA
MALAWI

MOZAMBIQUE
VANUATU
FIJI

NAMIBIA
ZIMBABWE
MADAGASCAR
MAURITIUS

BOTSWANA
RÉUNION

SWAZILAND
AUSTRALIA
NEW CALEDONIA

LESOTHO

SOUTH AFRICA

NEW ZEALAND

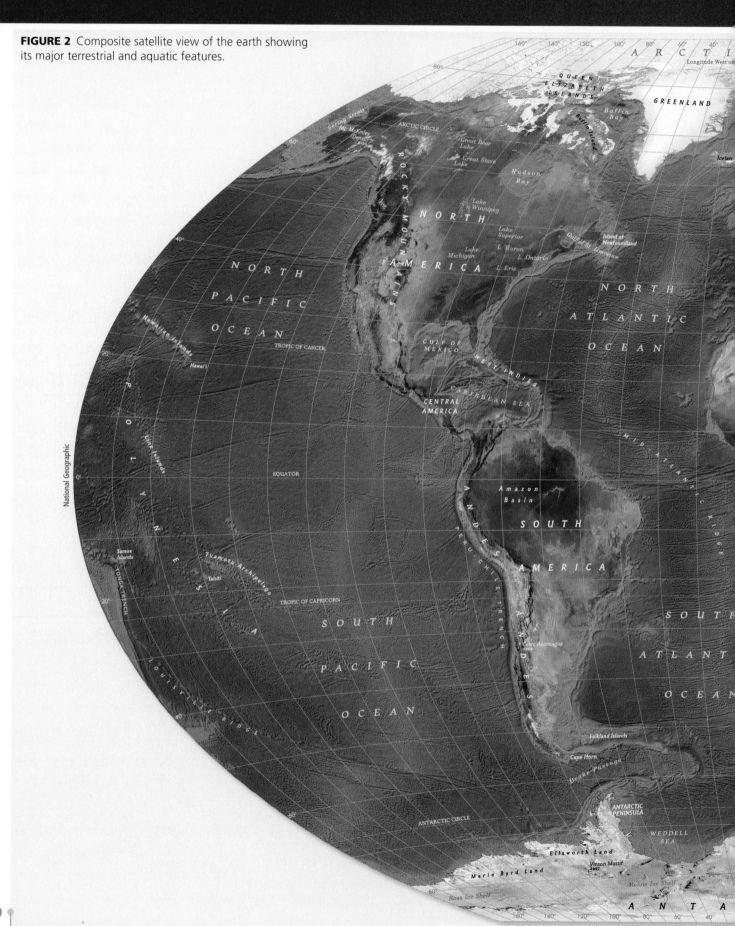

FIGURE 2 Composite satellite view of the earth showing its major terrestrial and aquatic features.

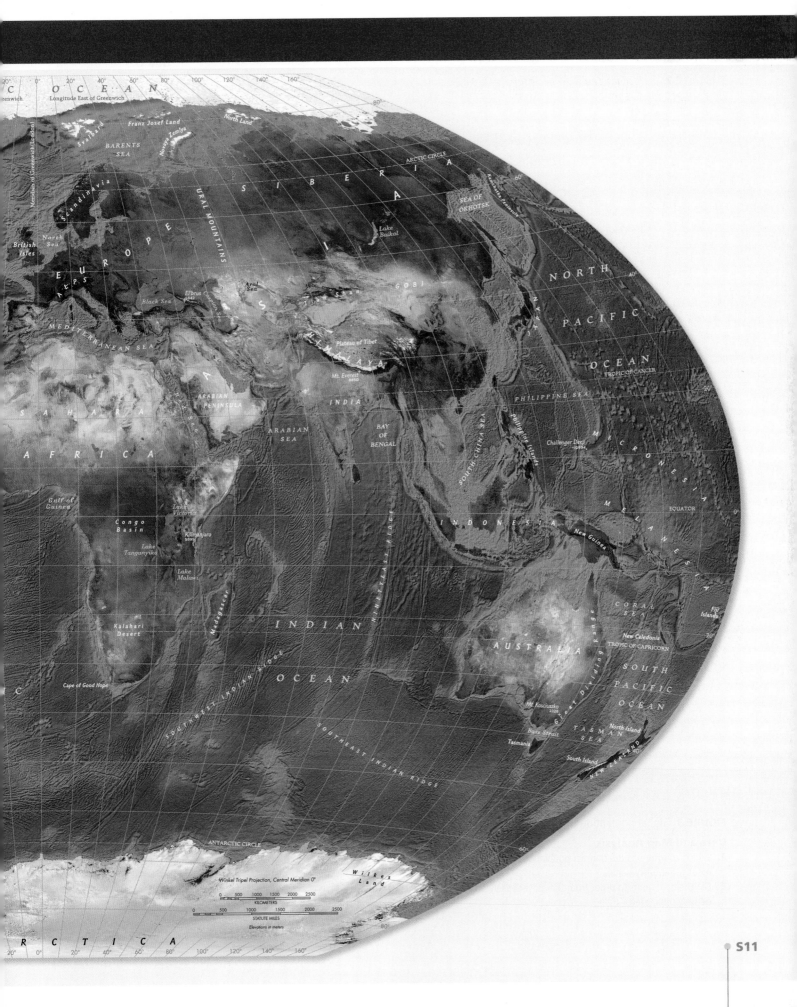

C OCEAN

Longitude East of Greenwich

20° 40° 60° 80° 100° 120° 140° 160°

Meridian of Greenwich (London)

Svalbard   Franz Josef Land   North Land

BARENTS   Novaya Zemlya
SEA

Scandinavia

ARCTIC CIRCLE

S I B E R I A

North
Sea

British
Isles

EUROPE

URAL MOUNTAINS

Lake
Baikal

SEA OF
OKHOTSK

Kamchatka Peninsula

60°

ALPS

Aral
Sea

NORTH

40°

Elbrus
5642   Caspian Sea

Black Sea

GOBI

PACIFIC

MEDITERRANEAN SEA

Plateau of Tibet

HIMALAYA

OCEAN

TROPIC OF CANCER

SAHARA

ARABIAN
PENINSULA

RED SEA

Mt. Everest
8850

INDIA

PHILIPPINE SEA

20°

ARABIAN
SEA

BAY
OF
BENGAL

SOUTH CHINA SEA

Philippine Islands

Challenger Deep
10994

MICRONESIA

AFRICA

Gulf of
Guinea

Lake
Victoria

Congo
Basin

Kilimanjaro
5895

INDONESIA

New Guinea

MELANESIA

EQUATOR   0°

Lake
Tanganyika

NINETYEAST RIDGE

Lake
Malawi

Madagascar

CORAL
SEA

Fiji
Islands

Kalahari
Desert

I N D I A N

New Caledonia   TROPIC OF CAPRICORN   20°

AUSTRALIA

Cape of Good Hope

OCEAN

SOUTH

SOUTHWEST INDIAN RIDGE

Mt. Kosciuszko
2228

Great Dividing Range

PACIFIC

SOUTHEAST INDIAN RIDGE

Bass Strait

TASMAN
SEA

OCEAN

North Island

Tasmania

NEW ZEALAND

South Island   40°

ANTARCTIC CIRCLE

Wilkes
Land

Winkel Tripel Projection, Central Meridian 0°

0   500   1000 1500 2000 2500
KILOMETERS

0   500   1000   1500   2000   2500
STATUTE MILES

Elevations in meters

60°

80°

R C T I C A

20° 0° 20° 40° 60° 80° 100° 120° 140° 160°

FIGURE 3 Global population density.

Data and Map Analysis

1. Which country has the densest population? (See Figure 1 of this supplement for country names.)

2. List the continents in order from the most densely populated to the least densely populated.

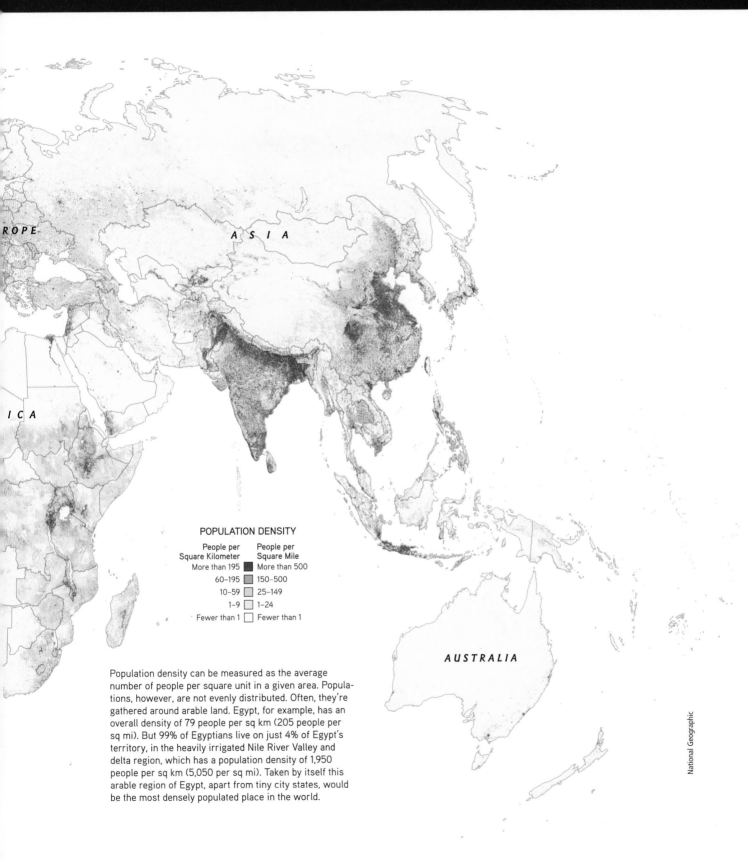

POPULATION DENSITY

People per Square Kilometer		People per Square Mile
More than 195	■	More than 500
60–195	▨	150–500
10–59	▢	25–149
1–9	□	1–24
Fewer than 1	□	Fewer than 1

ROPE

A S I A

I C A

AUSTRALIA

Population density can be measured as the average number of people per square unit in a given area. Populations, however, are not evenly distributed. Often, they're gathered around arable land. Egypt, for example, has an overall density of 79 people per sq km (205 people per sq mi). But 99% of Egyptians live on just 4% of Egypt's territory, in the heavily irrigated Nile River Valley and delta region, which has a population density of 1,950 people per sq km (5,050 per sq mi). Taken by itself this arable region of Egypt, apart from tiny city states, would be the most densely populated place in the world.

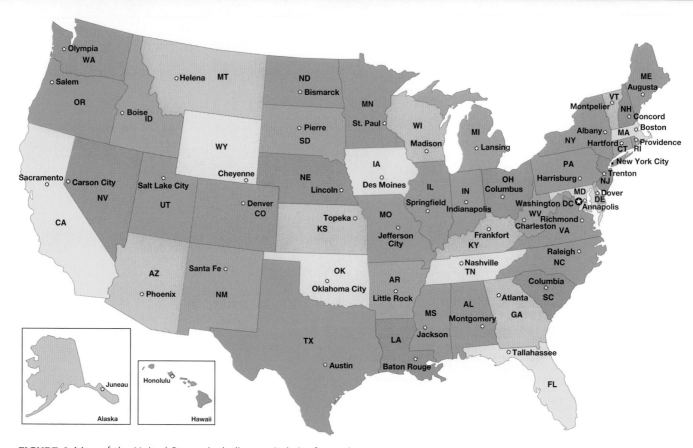

FIGURE 4 Map of the United States, including capital city for each state.

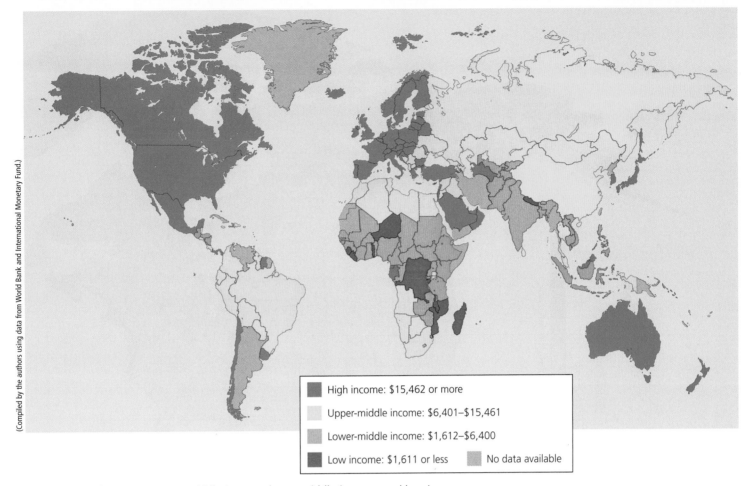

(Compiled by the authors using data from World Bank and International Monetary Fund.)

High income: $15,462 or more

Upper-middle income: $6,401–$15,461

Lower-middle income: $1,612–$6,400

Low income: $1,611 or less   No data available

FIGURE 5 High-income, upper-middle-income, lower-middle-income, and low-income countries in terms of gross national income (GNI) purchasing power parity (PPP) per capita (U.S. dollars) in 2015.

Data and Map Analysis

1. In how many countries is the per capita average income $995 or less? Look at Figure 1 and find the names of three of these countries.

2. In how many instances does a lower-middle- or low-income country share a border with a high-income country? Look at Figure 1 and find the names of the countries that reflect three examples of this situation.

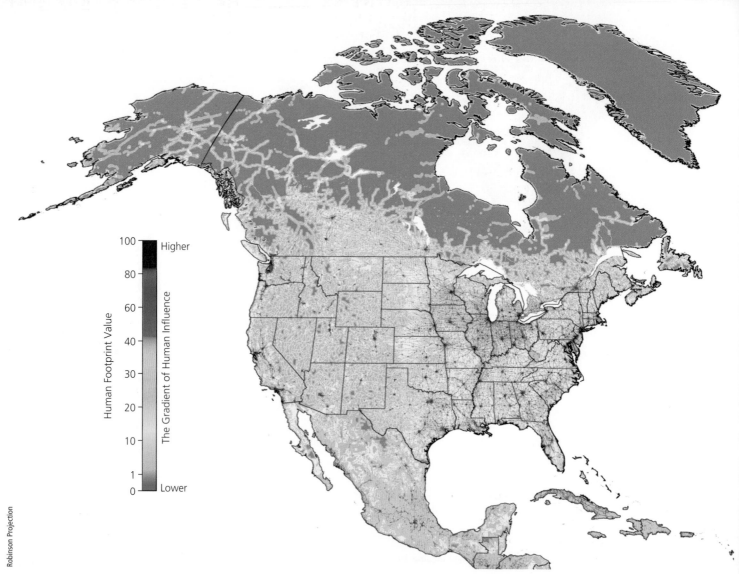

Robinson Projection

FIGURE 6 Natural capital degradation: The human ecological footprint in North America. Colors represent the percentage of each area influenced by human activities.

(Compiled by the authors using data from Wildlife Conservation Society and Center for International Earth Science Information Network at Columbia University.)

Data and Map Analysis

1. Which general area of the United States has the highest human footprint values?

2. What is the relative value of the human ecological footprint in the area where you live or go to school?

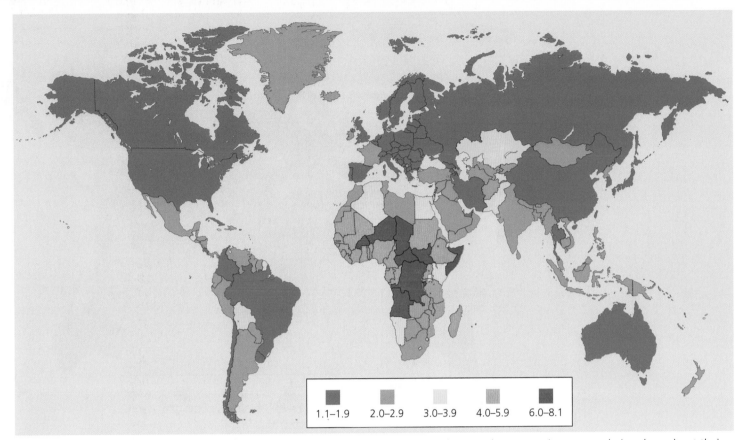

1.1–1.9	2.0–2.9	3.0–3.9	4.0–5.9	6.0–8.1

FIGURE 7 Comparison of total fertility rates (TFRs)—the average number of children born to the women in any population throughout their lifetimes—as measured in 2015.

Data and Map Analysis

1. Which country in the middle TFR category borders two countries in the lowest TFR category? What are those two countries? (See Figure 1 of this supplement for country names.)

2. Describe two geographic patterns that you see on this map.

(Compiled by the authors using data from Population Reference Bureau and United Nations Population Division.)

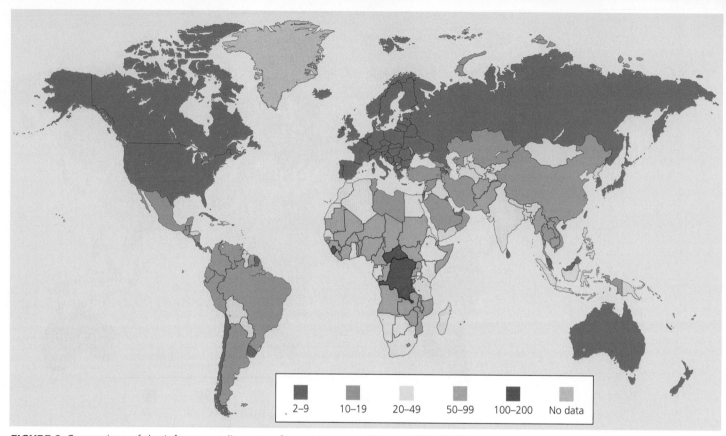

FIGURE 8 Comparison of the infant mortality rates of countries around the world in 2015.

Data and Map Analysis

1. Describe a geographic pattern that you can see on this map.

2. Describe any similarities that you see in geographic patterns between this map and the one in Figure 7.

(Compiled by the authors using data from Population Reference Bureau and United Nations Population Division.)

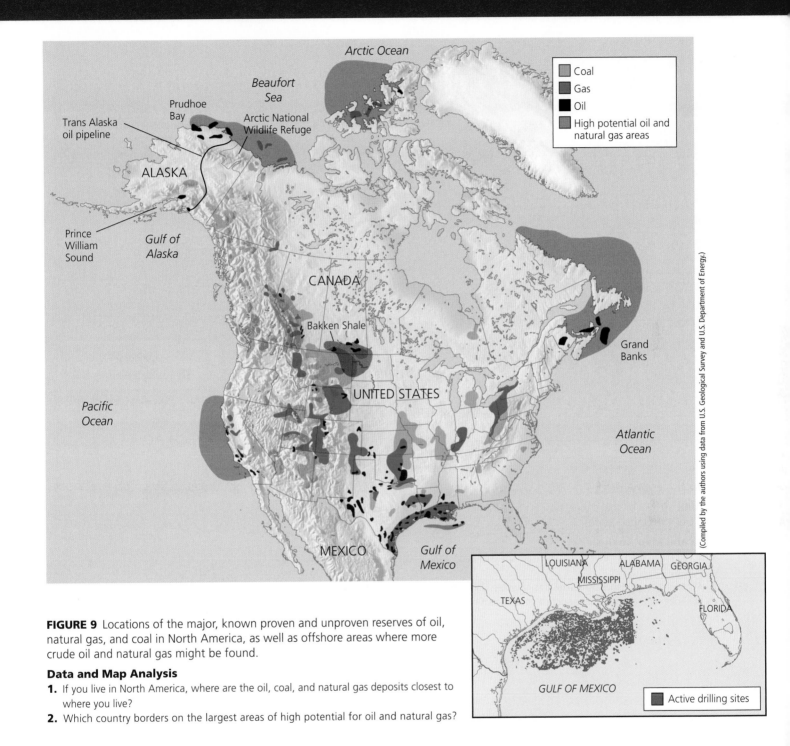

FIGURE 9 Locations of the major, known proven and unproven reserves of oil, natural gas, and coal in North America, as well as offshore areas where more crude oil and natural gas might be found.

(Compiled by the authors using data from U.S. Geological Survey and U.S. Department of Energy.)

Data and Map Analysis

1. If you live in North America, where are the oil, coal, and natural gas deposits closest to where you live?
2. Which country borders on the largest areas of high potential for oil and natural gas?

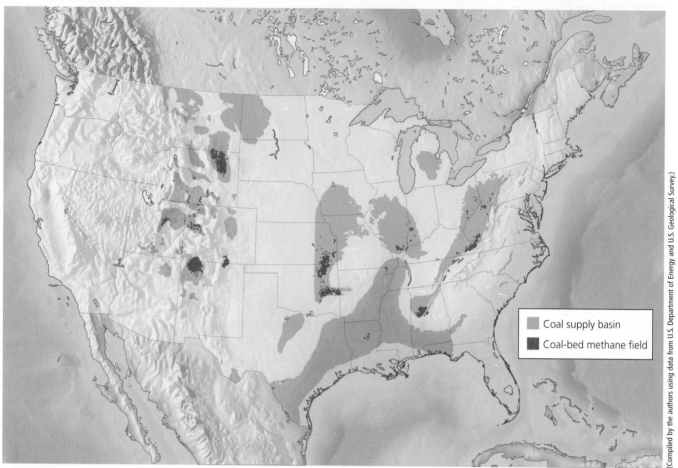

FIGURE 10 Major coal supply basins and coal-bed methane fields in the continental states of the United States.

Data and Map Analysis

1. If you live in the United States, where are the coal-bed methane deposits closest to where you live?

2. Removing these deposits requires lots of water. Compare the locations of the major deposits of coal-bed methane with water-deficit areas shown in Figures 13.5, p. 384 and 13.6, p. 386.

FIGURE 11 Major natural gas shale deposits in North America.

Data and Map Analysis

1. What state has the largest area of natural gas shale deposits?

2. Name three areas where two states or two countries share a border over a natural gas shale deposit.

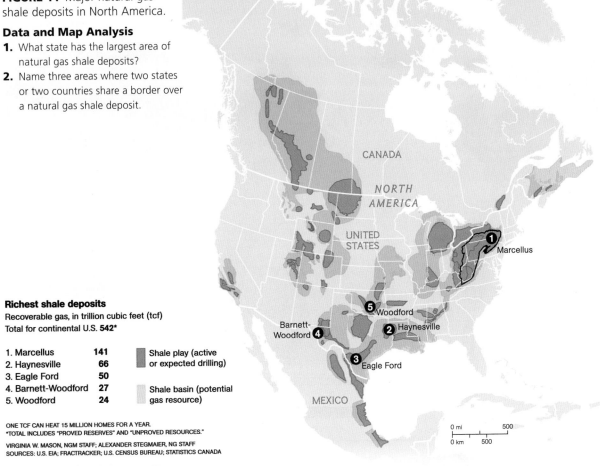

Richest shale deposits

Recoverable gas, in trillion cubic feet (tcf)

Total for continental U.S. **542***

1. Marcellus	**141**	▓ Shale play (active or expected drilling)
2. Haynesville	**66**	
3. Eagle Ford	**50**	
4. Barnett-Woodford	**27**	▓ Shale basin (potential gas resource)
5. Woodford	**24**	

ONE TCF CAN HEAT 15 MILLION HOMES FOR A YEAR.
*TOTAL INCLUDES "PROVED RESERVES" AND "UNPROVED RESOURCES."

VIRGINIA W. MASON, NGM STAFF; ALEXANDER STEGMAIER, NG STAFF
SOURCES: U.S. EIA; FRACTRACKER; U.S. CENSUS BUREAU; STATISTICS CANADA

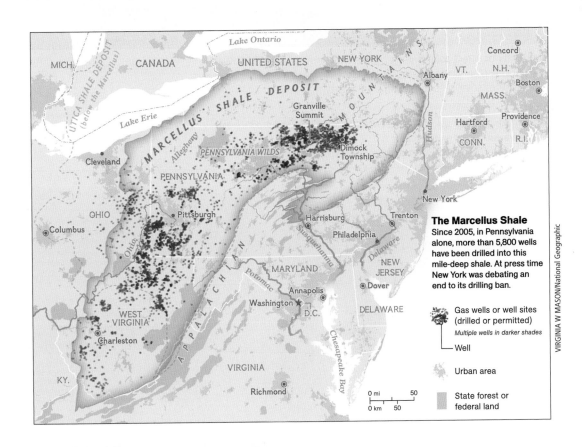

The Marcellus Shale

Since 2005, in Pennsylvania alone, more than 5,800 wells have been drilled into this mile-deep shale. At press time New York was debating an end to its drilling ban.

Gas wells or well sites (drilled or permitted)
Multiple wells in darker shades

— Well

Urban area

State forest or federal land

VIRGINIA W MASON/National Geographic

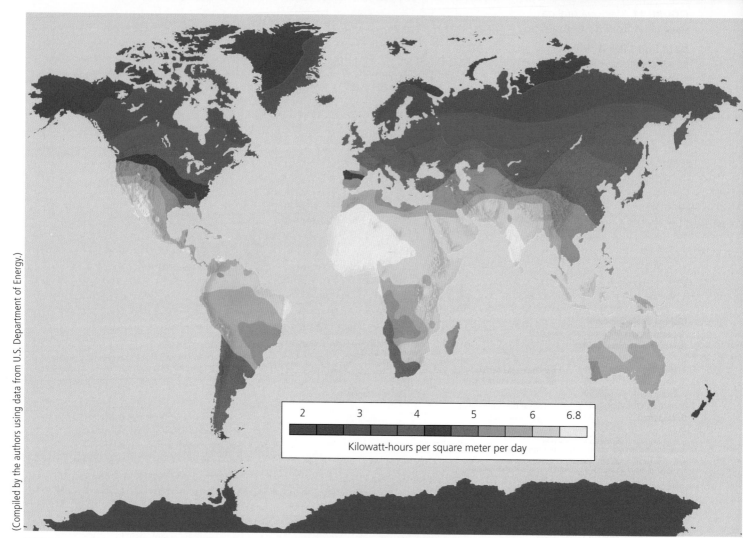

(Compiled by the authors using data from U.S. Department of Energy.)

FIGURE 12 Global availability of direct solar energy. Areas with more than 3.5 kilowatt-hours per square meter per day (see scale) are good candidates for passive and active solar heating systems and use of solar cells to produce electricity.

Data and Map Analysis

1. What is the potential for making greater use of solar energy to provide heat and produce electricity (with solar cells) where you live or go to school?

2. List the continents in order of overall availability of direct solar energy, from those with the highest to those with the lowest. (See Figure 1 of this supplement for continent names.)

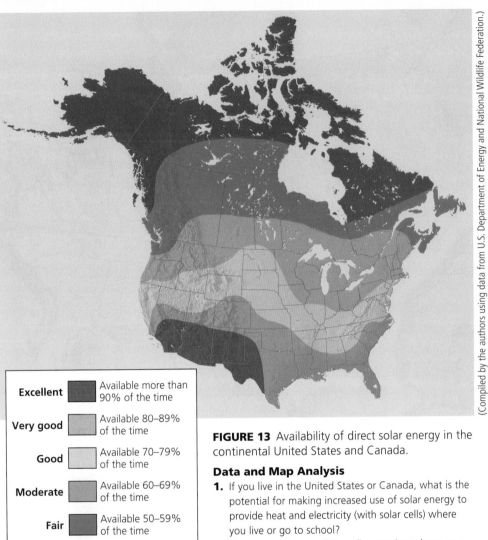

(Compiled by the authors using data from U.S. Department of Energy and National Wildlife Federation.)

Excellent		Available more than 90% of the time
Very good		Available 80–89% of the time
Good		Available 70–79% of the time
Moderate		Available 60–69% of the time
Fair		Available 50–59% of the time
Poor		Available less than 50% of the time

FIGURE 13 Availability of direct solar energy in the continental United States and Canada.

Data and Map Analysis

1. If you live in the United States or Canada, what is the potential for making increased use of solar energy to provide heat and electricity (with solar cells) where you live or go to school?

2. How many states and Canadian provinces have areas with excellent, very good, or good availability of direct solar energy?

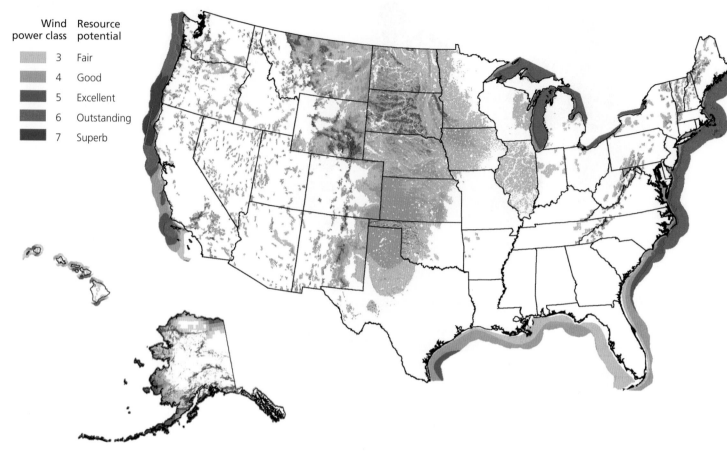

Wind power class | **Resource potential**
3 | Fair
4 | Good
5 | Excellent
6 | Outstanding
7 | Superb

FIGURE 14 Potential supply of land- and ocean-based wind energy in the United States.

Data and Map Analysis

1. If you live in the United States, what is the general wind energy potential where you live or go to school?

2. How many states have areas with good or excellent potential for wind energy?

(Compiled by the authors using data from U.S. Geological Survey and U.S. Department of Energy.)

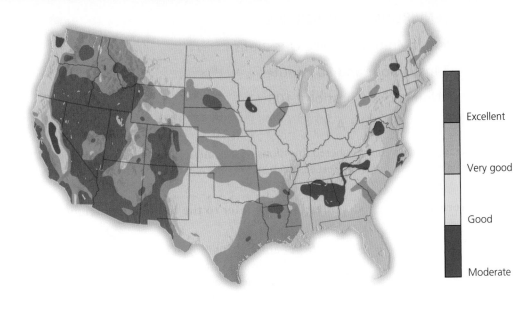

	Excellent
	Very good
	Good
	Moderate

FIGURE 15 Potential geothermal energy resources in the continental United States.

Data and Map Analysis

1. If you live in the United States, what is the potential for using geothermal energy to provide heat or to produce electricity where you live or go to school?

2. How many states have areas with very good or excellent potential for using geothermal energy?

(Compiled by the authors using data from U.S. Department of Energy and U.S. Geological Survey.)

ENVIRONMENTAL SCIENCE

Section I: Multiple-Choice Questions

Time: 1 hour and 30 minutes

Number of Questions: 100

Part A

Directions: Each set of lettered choices below refers to the numbered questions or statements immediately following it. Select the one lettered choice that best answers each question or best fits each statement. A choice may be used once, more than once, or not at all in each set.

Questions 1–3 refer to the following terms.

 (A) Environmental science
 (B) Ecology
 (C) Natural capital
 (D) Environmentalism
 (E) Ecosystem

 1. The study of relationships between living organisms and the environment

 2. The interdisciplinary subject that combines information from the physical sciences and the social sciences to learn how the earth works

 3. Natural resources and natural services that keep us and other forms of life alive and support our economies

Questions 4–6 refer to the following processes.

 (A) Transpiration
 (B) Evaporation
 (C) Precipitation
 (D) Infiltration
 (E) Sublimation

 4. Process by which plants lose water from their leaves to the atmosphere

 5. Downward movement of water through the soil

 6. Water that falls as rain, sleet, or snow onto surface water or onto land

Questions 7–9 refer to the following nutrient cycles.

 (A) Carbon and nitrogen cycles
 (B) Sulfur and carbon cycles
 (C) Phosphorus and nitrogen cycles
 (D) Sulfur and nitrogen cycles
 (E) Sulfur and water cycles

 7. Pair of cycles most associated with inorganic fertilizer and sewage waste

 8. Pair of cycles in which humans are most affecting the natural greenhouse effect

 9. Pair of cycles directly related to acid deposition

Questions 10–12 refer to the following species.

 (A) Native species
 (B) Invasive species
 (C) Foundation species
 (D) Keystone species
 (E) Indicator species

 10. Trout require clean water with high levels of dissolved oxygen, so their presence tells researchers that these conditions are present in a stream.

 11. A species such as zebra mussels move from one water system to another on the bottoms of boats. Upon arriving, their generalist adaptations allow them to take over niches from native species and modify ecosystems.

 12. The American alligator digs depressions which act as sparse watering holes during the dry season in the Everglades.

Questions 13–15 refer to the following biotic ecosystem components.

    (A) Producer
    (B) Primary consumer
    (C) Secondary consumer
    (D) Tertiary consumer
    (E) Decomposer

13. Organisms that are able to convert inorganic CO_2 and H_2O into glucose with energy from the sun

14. Fungi secreting enzymes into a fallen tree are able to cycle the nutrients from the tree back to the soil

15. A coyote that captures an herbivorous mouse

Part B

Directions: Each of the questions or incomplete statements below is followed by five suggested answers or completions. Select the one that is best in each case.

16. Many sub-Saharan African countries have populations that have been impacted by the AIDS epidemic. Which of the following statements best describes the age structure diagram of these countries?
    (A) An upright pyramid shape with the largest percentage of the population in the pre-reproductive years and the smallest in the post-reproductive years
    (B) A cylindrical age structure diagram with the largest percentage of the population represented by young adults
    (C) An inverted pyramid with the largest percentage of the population in the post-reproductive years and the smallest in the pre-reproductive age group
    (D) A large percentage of the population in the pre-reproductive age group with a sharp decline in the number of people in the 15-49-year-old age groups
    (E) An even population distribution through the pre-reproductive, reproductive, and post-reproductive age groups

17. Which of the following statements concerning wetlands is INCORRECT?
    (A) Salt water estuaries serve as groundwater recharge areas.
    (B) Coastal wetlands serve as buffers for inland areas during coastal storms.
    (C) They are responsible for trapping sediments and filtering water.
    (D) They act as nurseries for many fish, shellfish, and birds.
    (E) More than half of our coastal wetlands have disappeared.

18. All of the following are methods to reduce the impact of floods EXCEPT
    (A) building levees or flood walls along coastline and waterways
    (B) giving government subsidies for flood plain development
    (C) building dams
    (D) preserving wetlands or riparian land
    (E) strengthening and deepening waterways (channelization)

19. Organic agriculture is one alternative to industrialized agriculture. Which of the following is true of organic agriculture?
    I. Only synthetic fertilizers can be used on organic crops.
    II. Artificially genetically modified organisms are not used in organic agriculture.
    III. Organic agriculture produces less soil and water pollution than industrialized farming.
    (A) I only
    (B) II only
    (C) III only
    (D) II and III only
    (E) I, II, and III

GO ON TO NEXT PAGE

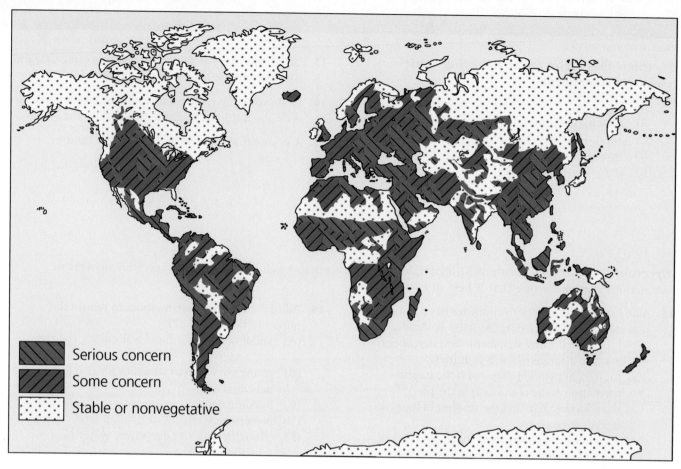

Serious concern
Some concern
Stable or nonvegetative

20. Based on this map, which of the following countries has the greatest topsoil erosion problem?
    (A) Australia
    (B) Greenland
    (C) France
    (D) Canada
    (E) United States

21. Which of the following is a limiting factor for a grassland biome?
    (A) Number of species
    (B) Species of the grass
    (C) Size of the population
    (D) Amount of precipitation
    (E) Number of organisms

22. Which material is LEAST likely to be recycled due to the potential for toxicity?
    (A) Aluminum cans
    (B) Scrap metal
    (C) Glass bottles
    (D) Polystyrene foam packing material
    (E) Corrugated boxes

23. Which of the following is NOT an example of an organic compound?
    (A) C_8H_{18}
    (B) $C_6H_{12}O_6$
    (C)
    (D) CH_4
    (E) H_2O

24. Petroleum, or crude oil, can be refined into different petrochemical products such as asphalt, jet fuel, gasoline, plastic, and grease. The process most commonly used to refine petroleum
    I. Is fractional distillation
    II. Is reverse osmosis
    III. Relies on the different boiling points of the components

    (A) I only
    (B) II only
    (C) I and III only
    (D) II and III only
    (E) I, II, and III

Questions 25–26 refer to the diagram below of a pressurized nuclear reactor.

25. The components of this energy generation system that are also used in wind, hydroelectric, and fossil fuel energy generation are
    (A) the pumps and coolant
    (B) the coolant and control rods
    (C) the turbines and generator
    (D) the turbines and heat exchanger
    (E) the containment shell and reactor

26. The function of the component labeled "control rods" is
    (A) to absorb excess neutrons released by the process of nuclear fission
    (B) to absorb excess heat released by the process of electrical generation
    (C) to negate thermal pollution by absorbing excess heat
    (D) to time-release minute amounts of nuclear fuel in order to control the reaction
    (E) to absorb excess uranium atoms to prevent meltdown of the reactor

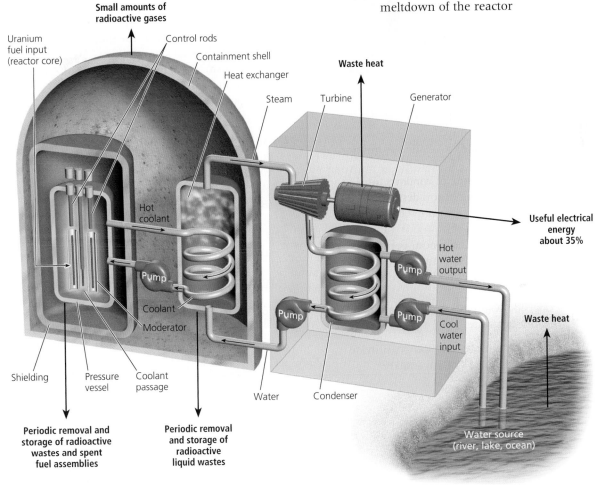

27. This ecological control of pests uses a mix of cultivation, biological, and chemical practices.
    (A) Integrated pest management
    (B) Organic farming
    (C) Pheromone therapy
    (D) Green revolution agriculture
    (E) Genetic resistance management

28. Photochemical smog is characteristic of urban areas with many vehicles and a climate that is
    (A) cool, wet, and cloudy
    (B) cool, dry, and sunny
    (C) warm, dry, and sunny
    (D) warm, wet, and cloudy
    (E) warm, wet, and sunny

GO ON TO NEXT PAGE

29. The green design of the building below uses seasonal passive solar by

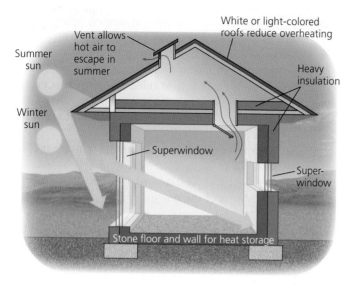

Summer sun

Vent allows hot air to escape in summer

White or light-colored roofs reduce overheating

Heavy insulation

Winter sun

Superwindow

Super-window

Stone floor and wall for heat storage

(A) having an extended sun roof
(B) using plants and curtains to shade the interior of the home
(C) having a south-facing bank of windows to capture winter sun when heat is desired, but an over-hanging eave to alleviate the hot summer sun
(D) using air temperature and special permeable walls to increase circulation and capture wind moving at various angles both in summer and winter
(E) having one side wall built with insulation in order to store hot water

30. Which of the following three food sources provide more than half of the world's caloric intake?
(A) Wheat, soybeans, potatoes
(B) Corn, potatoes, rice
(C) Wheat, rice, corn
(D) Rice, potatoes, cheese
(E) Wheat, rice, potatoes

Questions 31–33 refer to the following graph of the first four stages of demographic transition.

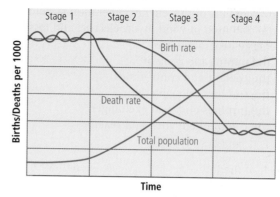

31. Demographic Stage 2 in the graph is known as the
(A) preindustrial stage
(B) transitional stage
(C) industrial stage
(D) postindustrial stage
(E) declining stage

32. All of the following characteristics apply to a country in Stage 4 of the demographic transition EXCEPT
(A) the population growth rate has stabilized
(B) there is a lack of sanitation and medical advancement
(C) the country is considered to be post-industrial
(D) the gross domestic product (GDP) is typically relatively high
(E) the population has a high percentage of highly educated people

33. The death rate is typically the highest during Stage 1 of the demographic transition. This is due to which of the following factors?
(A) There is a lack of sanitation and education.
(B) The people are genetically more prone to get sick and die.
(C) These populations eat at the top of the food chain and tend to have more health disorders related to high-fat diets.
(D) The highly industrialized lifestyle leads to early death.
(E) There are unsafe working conditions in unregulated workplaces.

34. Some species have evolved a reproductive strategy in which the population increases at an intrinsic rate. Which of the following are characteristics of these *r*-strategists?

    I. Have many reproductive events per life cycle
    II. Reproduce at a later age
    III. Have many offspring each time they reproduce

(A) I only
(B) II only
(C) I and II only
(D) I and III only
(E) I, II, and III

35. Which of the following is a potential benefit of using genetically modified crops?
(A) Potential resistance to crop diseases
(B) Increased need for fertilizer use
(C) Increased need for pesticide use
(D) Potential promotion of pesticide resistance
(E) Potential to repel pollinators

36. Which of the following is a human health effect associated with the thinning of the stratospheric ozone layer?
(A) Increased incidence of bronchitis and emphysema
(B) Increased incidence of cataracts
(C) Increased incidence of asthma
(D) Damage to the central nervous system
(E) Increased incidence of learning disabilities

37. Possible sources of hydrogen fuel include all of the following EXCEPT
(A) the removal of hydrogen from methane and gasoline
(B) the use of geothermal-produced electricity for electrolysis, removing hydrogen from water
(C) the use of wind-generated electricity to decompose water into hydrogen and oxygen
(D) the reprocessing of spent fuel rods from nuclear power plants
(E) the production of hydrogen in bioreactors by both natural and genetically modified algae and bacteria

38. Natural gas is a preferred fossil fuel to use for heating buildings because
(A) it can be turned into liquid gas
(B) it is the cheapest resource choice
(C) it is the safest to store and ship
(D) it is the cleanest burning
(E) it is odorless

Questions 39–40 refer to the following scenario.

A hypothetical country has a crude annual birth rate of 80 births per 1000 and a crude annual death rate of 78 deaths per 1000. The country experiences an immigration rate of 40 per 1000 and an emigration rate of 20 per 1000.

39. Calculate the annual growth rate for this country at this time.
(A) 0.2%
(B) 2.0%
(C) 2.2%
(D) 4.2%
(E) 21.8%

40. Based on these demographic characteristics, this population would probably be classified as
(A) pre-industrial
(B) developing
(C) moderately developed
(D) developed
(E) declining

41. All of the following are true of El Niño-Southern Oscillation (ENSO), EXCEPT
(A) the trade winds weaken or stop
(B) the temperature of the surface waters off the coast of South America remains higher for a longer period of time
(C) weather over as much as two-thirds of the globe can be affected during an El Niño event
(D) both hemispheres received an abundance of hot, humid, rainy weather
(E) the pattern cycles between El Niño and La Niña events

42. Which of these characteristics would make an ecosystem vulnerable to invader species?

    I. Early successional systems
    II. Climate similar to habitat of invader
    III. Low biodiversity

(A) I only
(B) II only
(C) III only
(D) I and II only
(E) I, II, and III

GO ON TO NEXT PAGE

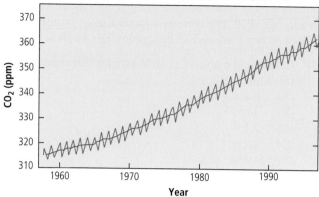

Monthly Mean Carbon Dioxide Mauna Loa, Hawaii

43. The overall trends in carbon dioxide level can BEST be explained by
    (A) the increase in human population
    (B) the increase in the consumption of fossil fuels
    (C) rapid deforestation on Mauna Loa
    (D) an overall increase in aerobic respiration
    (E) a decline in the population of phytoplankton

44. The yearly fluctuations along the graph line can be explained by
    (A) seasonal increase or decrease in photosynthesis in the Northern Hemisphere
    (B) the increase in carbon dioxide that is associated with the tourist season in Hawaii
    (C) an increase in air conditioner use during the much hotter summer months
    (D) seasonal changes in the polar vortex that directly impact coastal areas
    (E) seasonal fluctuations in volcanic activity on Mauna Loa

45. Calculate the percent increase in monthly mean CO_2 levels from 1970 to 1980.
    (A) 0.03%
    (B) 3%
    (C) 10%
    (D) 35%
    (E) 100%

46. Given what you know about carbon dioxide and its ability to reabsorb heat radiation from the earth's surface, if a line were added to this graph representing temperature changes between 1960 and 2000, you would expect the temperature line to
    (A) fluctuate slightly but remain at an overall steady average temperature
    (B) fluctuate but display an overall downward trend
    (C) fluctuate but follow a similar upward trend as the CO_2
    (D) show no change in average temperatures
    (E) begin high but drop in 1970 due to the Clean Air Act

47. Most of the solar radiation that passes through the atmosphere is
    (A) degraded into longer wavelength infrared radiation
    (B) converted to gamma radiation
    (C) deflected off hard surfaces
    (D) absorbed by the ozone layer
    (E) absorbed by organisms

48. Which of the following would be an example of mitigation in the management of natural resources?
    (A) Building new wetlands to take the place of ones that will be destroyed
    (B) Grazing only cattle and bison species on grasslands
    (C) Using clear-cutting for forest management
    (D) Replanting harvested hardwood forests with coniferous species
    (E) Sequestering atmospheric carbon by replanting the tropical rainforests

49. When constructing an array of solar panels, one option is to add motors which allow the panels to rotate and track the course of the sun through the sky. What can you conclude from the graph below?

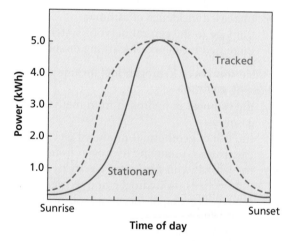

    (A) Over time, the tracked system generates more power each day.
    (B) The stationary system will be more consistent day-to-day.
    (C) Both the stationary and tracked system have a peak of 100% power, therefore there is actually no difference.
    (D) Tracking systems decrease the total time during which power can be generated each day.
    (E) This bell curve is explained by the seasonal changes as you move away from the equator.

Question 50 refers to the diagram below.

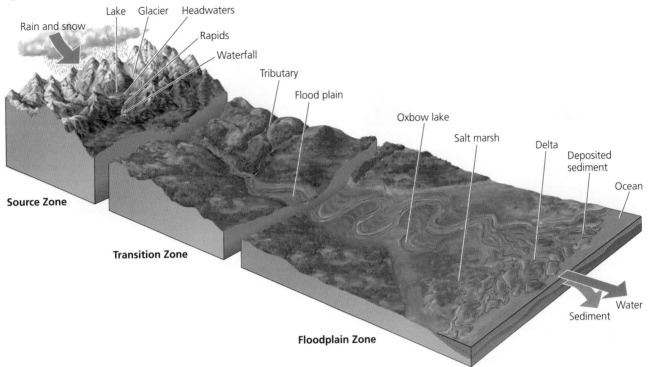

50. Which of the following regions would be expected to have the consistently highest levels of dissolved oxygen?
    (A) Floodplain zone
    (B) Transition zone
    (C) Source zone
    (D) Salt marsh zone
    (E) Delta zone

51. All of the following are true of endemic species EXCEPT
    (A) they are highly susceptible to extinction
    (B) they are often generalists
    (C) they often live on islands
    (D) they can be displaced by non-native invasive species
    (E) they are often indicator species

52. Which of the following is true of acid deposition?
    (A) It decreases the solubility of toxic metals in ecosystems.
    (B) It has the potential to kill many species of fish by dissolving the mucous membrane on their skin.
    (C) It benefits terrestrial plant growth by leaching nutrients from the soil.
    (D) It damages statues, buildings, and car finishes.
    (E) It increases the pH of aquatic systems.

53. The land area that delivers runoff, sediment, and dissolved substances to a stream is a
    (A) watershed
    (B) source zone
    (C) inland wetland
    (D) coastal delta
    (E) inland floodplain

54. Which of the following is an example of the second law of thermodynamics?
    I. 90% of the high-quality chemical energy in gasoline burned in automobiles is degraded to low-quality heat.
    II. Most of the chemical energy in the food an organism eats is given off as waste heat, making less available for the next trophic level.
    III. Much of the electrical energy flowing through an incandescent light bulb is given off as heat.
    (A) I only
    (B) II only
    (C) III only
    (D) I and II only
    (E) I, II, and III

55. The method of mineral extraction that is LEAST disruptive to land area is
    (A) open pit mining
    (B) mountain top removal
    (C) contour mining
    (D) strip mining
    (E) subsurface mining

GO ON TO NEXT PAGE

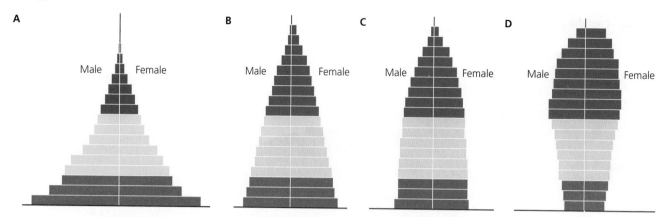

A   B   C   D

56. Which of the following traits would be most characteristic of a population with a histogram similar to the one labeled A above?
(A) slow population growth rate
(B) high levels of education
(C) high levels of sanitation
(D) highly industrialized
(E) birth rate greatly exceeds death rate

57. Which of the following histogram-country pairs is correctly matched?
(A) Histogram D – Greece
(B) Histogram C – Kenya
(C) Histogram C – Mexico
(D) Histogram B – Spain
(E) Histogram A – Canada

58. Graph A shown below indicates the relationship between two competing species. In Graph B, the species have modified their interaction. What is this phenomenon called?

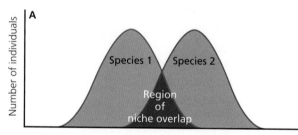

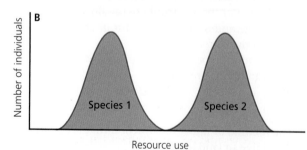

(A) Resource partitioning
(B) Mutualism
(C) Parasitism
(D) Mutual predation
(E) Predator avoidance

59. Which water quality parameter is NOT considered to be a water pollutant?
(A) Plant nutrients
(B) Microorganisms
(C) Sediments
(D) Heat
(E) Dissolved oxygen

60. The benefits of using anthracite, a hard coal, versus other softer coal sources such as bituminous coal includes which of the following?
(A) It burns at a lower temperature.
(B) It has a lower sulfur content.
(C) It produces no ash when combusted.
(D) It is the most plentiful type of coal.
(E) It is the easiest type of coal to mine and transport.

61. A school of sockeye salmon swimming in a river would be an example of a(n)
(A) population
(B) organism
(C) community
(D) ecosystem
(E) habitat

Question 62 refers to the graphs below.

Temperate deciduous forest

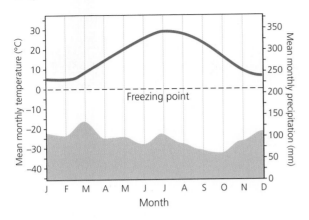

Northern coniferous forest (boreal forest, taiga)

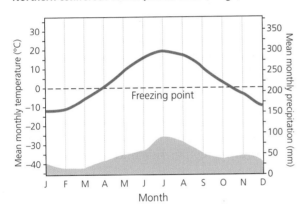

62. Which of the following is a correct statement about the data in the climate graphs shown?
    (A) The rainfall patterns in both the taiga and deciduous forest are very similar.
    (B) The taiga has a lower total annual rainfall than the deciduous forest.
    (C) The deciduous forest has lower winter temperatures than the taiga.
    (D) The peak precipitation months for the taiga are during the winter.
    (E) The taiga has a higher average summer temperature than the deciduous forest.

63. A certain forest contains an average of 50,000 kg/ha of tree biomass. If 45% of a tree's biomass is composed of captured carbon, calculate the amount of carbon stored per hectare in this forest.
    (A)   4500 kg
    (B)   5000 kg
    (C) 20,000 kg
    (D) 22,500 kg
    (E) 25,000 kg

64. When considering large-scale hydropower, which of the following has the LEAST environmental impact?
    (A) Flooding of upstream terrestrial and river habitat
    (B) Disrupting the life cycle of native fish
    (C) Decreasing the flow of silt and sand to natural downstream deposits
    (D) Providing a recreational area open only to swimming and fishing
    (E) Altering the natural flow of water downstream

65. A typical oligotrophic lake will
    (A) be clear with high levels of dissolved oxygen
    (B) be clear with low levels of dissolved oxygen
    (C) have high species richness and diversity
    (D) have some regions that are hypoxic
    (E) have algae blooms that occur in the fall

66. The Law of Conservation of Matter states that
    (A) matter quality increases when energy changes from one form to another
    (B) energy is neither created nor destroyed in a physical or chemical reaction
    (C) matter quality decreases when energy changes from one form to another
    (D) material efficiency increases with energy utilization
    (E) atoms can neither be created nor destroyed in a physical or chemical reaction

67. A terrestrial area's climate is determined by what main environmental factors?
    I. Average temperature
    II. Average humidity
    III. Average precipitation
    (A) I only
    (B) I and II only
    (C) I and III only
    (D) II and III only
    (E) I, II, and III

68. Which of the following is an advantage of utilizing biofuel instead of, or in addition to, traditional fossil fuels?
    (A) It may diminish the amount of cropland used for food production.
    (B) Crops will be cultivated using industrialized agricultural practices.
    (C) A decrease in biodiversity resulting from conversion of forests and grasslands to plantation cultivation will occur.
    (D) Engines and new equipment will have to be designed to combust biofuels.
    (E) CO_2 emissions are considered carbon neutral.

GO ON TO NEXT PAGE

For questions 69–72 refer to the graph at the right.

69. The LD50 measurement for acute toxicity of the hypothetical solution above would be
    (A) 3.5
    (B) 7
    (C) 10
    (D) 12
    (E) 75

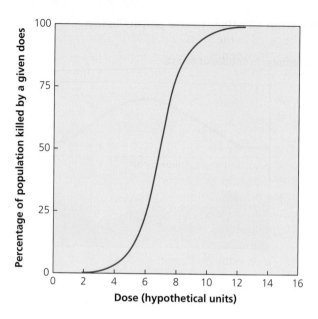

70. An argument that the results of this test do not provide enough valid information for the use/distribution of this product at or below "LD50 exposure levels" would include all of the following statements EXCEPT
    (A) the test animal's biology is different from humans
    (B) this test does not take into account chronic exposure
    (C) this test is not lethal to all individuals
    (D) this test does not take into account multiple chemical, or synergistic, effects
    (E) there were not enough trials done on this chemical

71. If the test substance was a teratogen it would
    (A) cause cancer
    (B) disrupt the endocrine system
    (C) lead to birth defects
    (D) be a neurotoxin that affects brain development or functioning
    (E) only show deleterious effects at the top of the food chain

72. Toxicity is a measure of how harmful a substance is in causing injury, illness, or death to an organism. Which of the following does not affect the toxicity of a substance?
    (A) The amount or dose
    (B) Frequency of exposure
    (C) Persistence
    (D) Genetic make-up or sensitivity of the organism
    (E) The origin of the substance

73. Why is deforestation in tropical rainforests more devastating to the global environment than deforestation in temperate forests?
    (A) Most temperate forests are not experiencing deforestation.
    (B) Tropical rainforests provide less usable lumber.
    (C) Temperate forests do not contribute to the reduction of carbon dioxide.
    (D) Tropical rainforests are inhabited by indigenous tribes who are losing their way of life.
    (E) Tropical rainforests have much higher biodiversity than temperate forests.

74. Nitrate and phosphate concentrations have greatly increased in Chesapeake Bay from both point and non-point source runoff, resulting in
    (A) increased salinity
    (B) increased pH
    (C) decreased dissolved oxygen
    (D) increased CO_2
    (E) decreased turbidity

75. Which of the following geologic events is primarily associated with transform faults?
    I. Earthquakes
    II. Formation of new crust
    III. Formation of volcanic islands

    (A) I only
    (B) II only
    (C) III only
    (D) I and II only
    (E) I and III only

76. There are a number of different strategies designed to reduce the potential for global climate change. Which of the following actually remediates climate change rather than simply slowing down climate change?
    (A) Capturing and storing CO_2
    (B) Improving energy efficiency of appliances, buildings, and vehicles
    (C) Shifting to renewable energy sources
    (D) Reducing tropical deforestation
    (E) Decreasing fossil fuel use

77. During the rock cycle, all of the following are involved in the formation of sedimentary rock EXCEPT
(A) weathering
(B) erosion
(C) transportation
(D) deposition
(E) melting

78. The three key factors that lead women to have fewer and healthier children are
(A) age, employment out of the home, and health care
(B) education, age, and human rights
(C) age, human rights, and family planning
(D) education, employment out of the home, and rights for women
(E) age, education, and family planning

79. A chemical hazard which is an endocrine disruptor might show itself as
(A) a metastasis
(B) impairment of growth of the reproductive organs
(C) interference of the nervous system functioning
(D) an altering of DNA molecules
(E) a weakening of the immune system

80. Eating "lower on the food chain" has advantages and disadvantages. Which of the following is an advantage?
(A) All required nutrients are equally available at all levels of the food chain.
(B) There is less of the original captured energy lost by consuming at this level.
(C) There are very few physical disorders directly caused by poor nutrition.
(D) It is financially more difficult to eat at the lower levels of the food chain.
(E) Eating lower on the food chain requires only the growing of food crops.

Questions 81–82 refer to the graphs below.

Inorganic chlorine (parts per trillion)

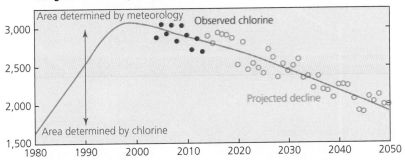

Ozone hole area (millions of square kilometers)

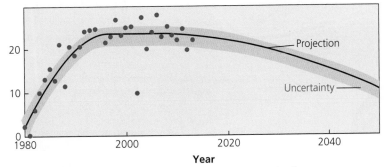

Source: https://eoimages.gsfc.nasa.gov/images/imagerecords/82000/82596/chlorine_concentration.pdf

81. Calculate the percent change in the area of the ozone hole from 1980–1990.
(A) 100%
(B) 200%
(C) 300%
(D) 700%
(E) 1800%

82. In what year is the amount of inorganic chlorine projected to be back down to 2000 parts per trillion?
(A) 1990
(B) 2015
(C) 2021
(D) 2035
(E) 2047

GO ON TO NEXT PAGE

Questions 83–84 refer to the diagram below.

83. The part of the landfill associated with a potential "waste-to-energy" electrical generation is the
   (A) leachate pipes
   (B) methane gas recovery well
   (C) leachate storage tank
   (D) leachate treatment system
   (E) leak-detecting probes

84. The clay and synthetic liners at the base of the landfill function to
   (A) make it airtight
   (B) protect the groundwater below
   (C) siphon off methane gas produced by decomposition
   (D) protect the surrounding habitat from air pollution
   (E) accelerate decomposition

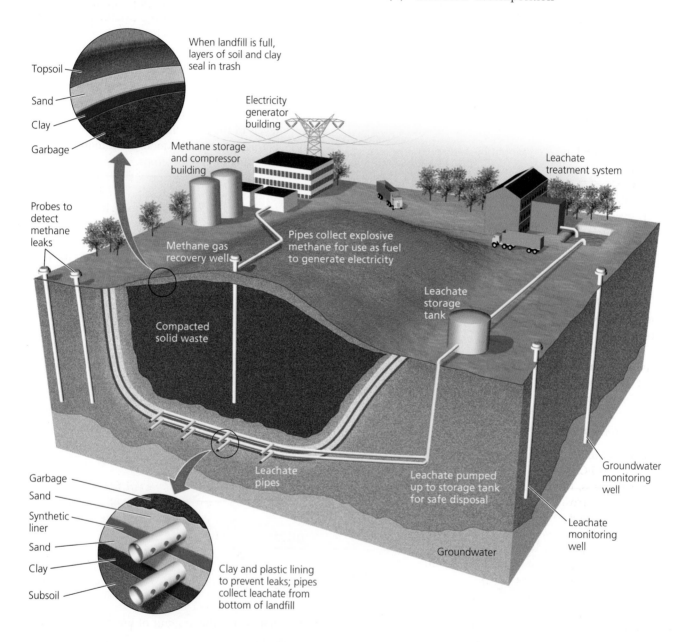

When landfill is full, layers of soil and clay seal in trash

Topsoil
Sand
Clay
Garbage

Electricity generator building

Methane storage and compressor building

Leachate treatment system

Probes to detect methane leaks

Methane gas recovery well

Pipes collect explosive methane for use as fuel to generate electricity

Leachate storage tank

Compacted solid waste

Leachate pipes

Leachate pumped up to storage tank for safe disposal

Groundwater monitoring well

Garbage
Sand
Synthetic liner
Sand
Clay
Subsoil

Clay and plastic lining to prevent leaks; pipes collect leachate from bottom of landfill

Leachate monitoring well

Groundwater

85. Which of the following is the root cause of hunger and malnutrition?
    (A) Lack of education
    (B) Cultural and religious traditions
    (C) Poverty
    (D) Lack of technology
    (E) Low social role of women in society

86. Many commercially important fish are also ecologically important because they help maintain ecosystem function and diversity. They are also known as
    (A) invasive species
    (B) indicator species
    (C) keystone species
    (D) non-native species
    (E) generalist species

87. Which of the following would be an external cost of disposing of municipal solid waste (MSW) in an incinerator?
    (A) Energy cost to burn the waste
    (B) Production of waste heat
    (C) Emission of greenhouse gases
    (D) Cost of electrostatic precipitator
    (E) Cost of labor to run the incinerator

88. All of the following are disadvantages of forest clear-cutting EXCEPT
    (A) it has higher initial costs than other methods
    (B) it destroys a habitat
    (C) it exposes bare soil to potential erosion
    (D) it often leads to sediment pollution
    (E) it requires an intensive replanting program

89. All of the following properties describe chlorofluoro-carbons (CFCs) EXCEPT
    (A) odorless, nonflammable, nontoxic, non-corrosive compounds
    (B) chlorine-containing compounds which react with O_3 to yield ClO and O_2
    (C) useful as coolants, propellants, and cleaners
    (D) long-lasting in the stratosphere with a life span ranging from 65–385 years
    (E) released by the burning of coal, natural gas, and oil (fossil fuels)

90. Which of the following best summarizes the disaster of the Aral Sea?
    I. Depletion of water for agriculture has reduced the sea by almost 90% and increased its salinity drastically.
    II. Large cities built along the Aral Sea have depleted the water volume for industrial and residential needs.
    III. Melting of glaciers due to global climate change has raised the sea level and caused freshwater intrusion into the sea, thereby depleting many native fish species.
    (A) I only
    (B) II only
    (C) III only
    (D) I and II only
    (E) II and III only

91. Areas where geothermal energy is often accessible include
    (A) coastal areas in which the differential in land mass and oceanic weights cause heat vents
    (B) areas with tectonic activity which increases access to inner layer heat in fractures in the earth's crust
    (C) areas closer to the poles where the temperature gradient has an increased impact
    (D) developed countries with the technology to dig to great depths in order to access geothermal pockets
    (E) deep sea hydrothermal vents

92. A consequence of thermal water pollution is
    (A) increased solubility of dissolved gas such as O_2
    (B) decreased rates of chemical reactions
    (C) increased deaths of manatees during the winter
    (D) increased rates of metabolism in fish
    (E) lower incidence of disease due to the die-off of harmful bacteria

93. All of the following are characteristics of the 12 identified POPs (persistent organic pollutants) EXCEPT
    (A) biodegrade rapidly and completely
    (B) bioaccumulate
    (C) biomagnify
    (D) travel long distances via air currents
    (E) travel long distances in waterways

GO ON TO NEXT PAGE

94. Which of the following is a disadvantage of using monocultures to produce food?
    (A) Productivity is decreased.
    (B) Prices increase.
    (C) Genetic diversity is decreased.
    (D) Fossil fuel use is decreased.
    (E) Pest species are eliminated.

95. Which of the following is NOT a cause of habitat loss in marine areas?
    (A) Coastal development
    (B) Dredging operations
    (C) Bottom-trawler fishing
    (D) Coral bleaching
    (E) Artificial reef construction

96. Phytoremediation refers to the use of
    (A) photoelectric cells to destroy contaminants
    (B) enzymes and bacteria to destroy hazardous waste
    (C) plants to absorb contaminants from the soil or water
    (D) high energy sources like lasers to destroy hazardous waste
    (E) chemicals to neutralize toxins

97. Forests are a source of natural capital. Which of the following is an economic service provided by forests?
    (A) Forests sequester atmospheric carbon.
    (B) Forests preserve water quality by preventing erosion.
    (C) Forests increase the infiltration of rain water.
    (D) Forests provide habitat for wildlife.
    (E) Forests provide fuel wood and lumber.

98. Biochemical oxygen demand (BOD) is a measure of the amount of
    (A) dissolved oxygen in the water due to photosynthesis
    (B) dissolved oxygen that aerobic micro-organisms will need to decompose waste
    (C) dissolved oxygen needed by all aquatic organisms
    (D) biomass of organic wastes in the water
    (E) dissolved oxygen consumed by submerged vegetation

99. Industrialized agriculture, like all processes, has both advantages and disadvantages. Which of the following is a disadvantage?
    (A) It produces a lower crop yield.
    (B) It increases the number of weed species.
    (C) It increases the number of insect pest species.
    (D) It requires the heavy use of fertilizers and pesticides.
    (E) It never replenishes soil nutrients.

100. Which statement concerning soil erosion is INCORRECT?
    (A) Soil erosion is a major environmental concern due to the slow rate of topsoil renewal.
    (B) In many areas of the world soil is eroding faster than it can be formed.
    (C) The loss of topsoil has little effect on the soil's ability to store nutrients.
    (D) Erosion of topsoil through surface water runoff creates sediment pollution in rivers and streams.
    (E) The movement of flowing water and wind causes most soil erosion.

Directions: Section II counts for 40% of the total test grade and consists of 4 required questions: 1 data-set question, 1 document-based question, and 2 synthesis and evaluation questions. The questions are weighted equally, but the parts are not necessarily given equal weight. No calculators are allowed.

Each answer should be organized, comprehensive, and in prose form; outline form is not acceptable. Diagrams may be used to supplement discussion, but diagrams alone will not suffice.

---

1. Read the following article from the *Belmont Examiner* and answer the questions that follow.

Are Our Recycled Plastics Headed to a Landfill?

Have you ever wondered what happens to your recycled plastics when they are picked up at the curb by the trash truck? It gives everybody a good feeling to recycle, but what if recycling means more trash fees?

Michael Dumper, CEO of Belmont Waste Hauling, recently told citizens of Belmont at a recent Town Council meeting that because of the closure of the closest recycling center, he will now need to haul recycled plastics almost 200 miles to be recycled. Recyclables make up almost 40% of the trash load from Belmont, and as a result, Belmont Waste Hauling will lose money on hauling recyclables.

The city of Belmont requires all municipal buildings and all newly constructed public buildings to provide recycling containers for use. Belmont Waste Hauling will continue to haul the city's waste and recycling this year, but the company's contract with the city expires next June. At that point, the city will need to negotiate a new contract, perhaps one with a new company.

Many of the larger trash hauling giants are not willing to deal with the many issues involved with recycling plastics, and they simply bury them in landfills. It takes a lot of money up front to recycle, and they are not willing to lose profit on any load of trash.

Michael Dumper maintains that he wants to keep the Belmont trash contract. He hopes that with a small increase in fees he can continue to serve the city of Belmont. Competition forces companies to stop recycling programs unless consumers are willing to pay for them, he says. And yes, finding recycling centers that are still sorting and recycling is a challenge, but Michael is not yet conceding defeat, and he will continue to seek nearby recycling plants that are still in operation.

(a) **Identify** ONE reason that trash haulers will sometimes take recyclable products to landfills instead of to a recycling facility.

(b) Consider the ramifications of this practice.

   (i) **Describe** ONE ecological disadvantage of dumping recyclables at a landfill.

   (ii) **Describe** ONE economic advantage of dumping recyclables at a landfill.

(c) **Explain** the increase in fees proposed by Michael Dumper in order to continue the recycling program.

(d) **Identify** THREE materials, other than aluminum, that can feasibly be recycled.

(e) Aluminum is the most frequently recycled product in the United States. **Explain** why aluminum is recycled more frequently than other recyclables.

(f) Decreasing the volume of waste in landfills can be accomplished, in part, by reducing, reusing and recycling. **Describe** how these three approaches differ and **state** an example of each.

GO ON TO NEXT PAGE

2. Below is a food chain typical of a North American forest. Use this diagram along with the information provided to answer the questions that follow.

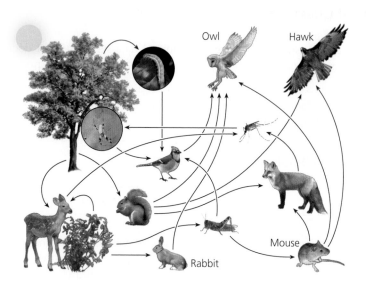

- Temperate deciduous forests have a net primary productivity of 1200 g/m²/yr, and on average, the nutrients found in primary producers provide 0.25 Calories/gram to primary consumers.
- 10,000 m² = 1 hectare = 2.5 acres

(a) Assume an owl is feeding only on rabbits and requires 800 Calories per day.

   (i) **Calculate** the number of rabbits in this habitat necessary to feed one owl for one year.

   (ii) **Calculate** the area needed, in acres per year, to support this number of rabbits (and therefore the one owl) assuming there are no other competing primary consumers present.

(b) Assume a hawk has the same daily caloric requirement as an owl, but it eats only mice.

   (i) **Calculate** the area needed, in acres per year, to support this number of mice (and therefore the one hawk) assuming there are no other primary or secondary consumers other than those listed in this specific food chain.

   (ii) **Explain** the difference in the area needed by a hawk as compared to that needed by an owl.

   (iii) **Explain** why most food webs do not contain consumers above the tertiary or quaternary trophic levels.

(c) A local golf course uses a new pesticide that eliminates all of the grasshoppers in the food chain. **Identify** the predicted effects on the following members of the food chain:

   (i) Rabbits

   (ii) Owls

   (iii) Producers

(d) **Describe** TWO possible effects on this food web if an herbivorous, non-native insect were introduced to this forest ecosystem.

3. Indoor air pollution is a growing problem in many regions. It can cause anything from minor discomfort to major illness, and even death. Much absenteeism in schools and workplaces is blamed on indoor air pollutants.

    (a) Indoor air pollution comes from a variety of sources.

        (i) **Identify** TWO potential substances that can be components of indoor air pollution.

       (ii) **Describe** the sources of each of these substances.

     (iii) **Explain** how each of these substances specifically impacts human health.

    (b) According to the Environmental Protection Agency, "The term 'sick building syndrome' (SBS) is used to describe situations in which building occupants experience acute health and comfort effects that appear to be linked to time spent in a building, but no specific illness or cause can be identified."

        (i) **Describe** TWO health symptoms associated with sick building syndrome.

       (ii) **Identify** ONE trait shared by buildings that experience SBS.

     (iii) **Explain** ONE way to prevent the occurrence of SBS when constructing new buildings.

    (c) According to the World Health Organization, people in developed countries are, on average, exposed to more indoor air pollutants on a daily basis than are those in developing countries. **Explain** this statement.

    (d) Various public agencies work to address the problem of indoor air pollution.

        (i) **Identify** ONE federal agency tasked with reducing indoor air pollution for workers.

       (ii) **Describe** ONE way a governmental agency can work to improve indoor air quality.

4. Many scientists believe that ocean acidification will be one of the next major environmental science issues to face humanity. It is tied directly to the carbon cycle in addition to other anthropogenic (man-made) sources of acidity.

    (a) Carbon, like all nutrients, has at least one "sink."

        (i) **Identify** TWO major carbon sinks.

       (ii) **Explain** how each of these function as a sink for carbon.

    (b) Ocean acidification occurs due to both natural and anthropogenic causes.

        (i) **Describe** how ocean acidification occurs naturally.

       (ii) **Discuss** ONE anthropogenic cause of ocean acidification.

    (c) When carbon dioxide is absorbed by ocean water, there are two possible fates.

        (i) **Identify** TWO possible fates of atmospheric carbon dioxide as it enters ocean water.

       (ii) **Explain** the ecological importance of the absorption of carbon dioxide by ocean water.

     (iii) **Describe** ONE ecological consequence of the acidification of ocean water.

    (d) **Describe** ONE way to mitigate an anthropogenic cause of ocean acidification.

Glossary

abiotic Nonliving. Compare *biotic.*

acid deposition The falling of acids and acid-forming compounds from the atmosphere to the earth's surface.

acidity Comparative amounts of hydrogen ions (H⁺) and hydroxide ions (OH⁻) contained in a particular volume of a solution when a substance is dissolved in a water. An acid solution has more hydrogen ions than hydroxide ions and a basic solution has more hydroxide ions than hydrogen ions. See *pH.*

acid rain See *acid deposition.*

acid solution Any water solution that has more hydrogen ions (H⁺) than hydroxide ions (OH⁻); any water solution with a pH less than 7. Compare *basic solution, neutral solution.*

active solar heating system A system that uses solar collectors to capture heat energy from the sun and stores it as heat for space heating and water heating. Liquid or air pumped through the collectors transfers the captured heat to a storage system such as an insulated water tank or rock bed. Pumps or fans then distribute the stored heat or hot water throughout a dwelling as needed. Compare *passive solar heating system.*

adaptation Any genetically controlled structural, physiological, or behavioral characteristic that helps an organism survive and reproduce under a given set of environmental conditions. See *biological evolution, differential reproduction, mutation, natural selection.*

aerobic respiration Complex process that occurs in the cells of most living organisms, in which nutrient organic molecules such as glucose (C₆H₁₂O₆) combine with oxygen (O₂) to produce carbon dioxide (CO₂), water (H₂O), and energy. Compare *anaerobic respiration, photosynthesis.*

age structure Distribution of individuals in a population among various age groups.

agrobiodiversity The genetic variety of plant and animal species used on farms to produce food. Compare *biodiversity.*

agroforestry Planting trees and crops together.

air pollution One or more chemicals in high enough concentrations in the air to harm humans, other animals, vegetation, or materials. Excess heat is also considered a form of air pollution. Such chemicals or physical conditions are called air pollutants. See *primary pollutant, secondary pollutant.*

albedo A measure of the reflectivity of sunlight by a surface such as ice and snow (high reflectivity because of its optical brightness, or whiteness), soil and desert (medium reflectivity), and ocean water (low reflectivity).

alien species See *nonnative species.*

alley cropping Planting of crops in strips with rows of trees or shrubs on each side.

anaerobic respiration Form of cellular respiration in which some decomposers get the energy they need through the breakdown of glucose (or other nutrients) in the absence of oxygen. Compare *aerobic respiration.*

annual Plant that grows, sets seed, and dies in one growing season. Compare *perennial.*

anthropocentric Human-centered. Compare *biocentric.*

aquaculture Growing and harvesting of fish and shellfish for human use in fresh-water ponds, irrigation ditches, and lakes, or in cages or fenced-in areas of coastal lagoons and estuaries or in the open ocean.

aquatic Pertaining to water. Compare *terrestrial.*

aquatic life zones Marine and freshwater portions of the biosphere.

aquifer Porous, water-saturated layers of sand, gravel, or bedrock that can yield an economically significant amount of water.

arable land Land that can be cultivated to grow crops.

area strip mining Type of strip mining used where the terrain is flat. An earthmover strips away the overburden and a power shovel digs a cut to remove the mineral deposit. The trench is then filled with the spoils, and a new cut is made parallel to the previous one. Compare *mountaintop removal, open-pit mining, subsurface mining.*

arid Dry. A desert or other area with an arid climate has little precipitation.

artificial selection Process by which humans select one or more desirable genetic traits in the population of a plant or animal species and then use selective breeding to produce populations containing many individuals with the desired traits. Compare *genetic engineering, natural selection.*

asthenosphere Zone within the earth's mantle made up of hot, partly melted rock that flows and can be deformed like soft plastic.

atmosphere Whole mass of air surrounding the earth. See *stratosphere, troposphere.* Compare *biosphere, geosphere, hydrosphere.*

atmospheric pressure Force or mass per unit area of air, caused by the bombardment of a surface by the molecules in air.

atom Minute unit made of subatomic particles that is the basic building block of all chemical elements and thus all matter; the smallest unit of an element that can exist and still have the unique characteristics of that element. Compare *ion, molecule.*

atomic number Number of protons in the nucleus of an atom. Compare *mass number.*

atomic theory Idea that all elements are made up of atoms; the most widely accepted scientific theory in chemistry.

autotroph See *producer.*

background extinction rate Normal extinction of various species as a result of changes in local environmental conditions. Compare *mass extinction.*

bacteria Single-cell organisms that can multiply rapidly on their own. Most bacteria are harmless or beneficial but some can cause infectious diseases such as strep throat or tuberculosis. Compare *virus.*

basic solution Water solution with more hydroxide ions (OH⁻) than hydrogen ions (H⁺); water solution with a pH greater than 7. Compare *acid solution, neutral solution.*

benthos Bottom-dwelling aquatic organisms. Compare *nekton, plankton.*

bioaccumulation An increase in the concentration of a chemical in specific organs or tissues at a level higher than would normally be expected. Compare *biomagnification.*

biocapacity The ability of a productive ecosystem to regenerate renewable resources. See *ecological footprint.*

biocentric Life-centered. Compare *anthropocentric.*

biodegradable Capable of being broken down by decomposers.

biodegradable pollutant Material that can be broken down into simpler substances (elements and compounds) by bacteria or other decomposers. Paper and most organic wastes such as animal manure are biodegradable but can take decades to biodegrade in modern landfills. Compare *nondegradable pollutant.*

biodiversity Variety of different species (*species diversity*), genetic variability among individuals within each species (*genetic diversity*), variety of ecosystems (*ecological diversity*), and functions such as energy flow and matter cycling needed for the survival of species and biological communities (*functional diversity*).

biodiversity hotspot An area especially rich in plant species that is found nowhere else and is in great danger of extinction. Such areas suffer serious ecological disruption, mostly because of rapid human population growth and the resulting pressure on natural resources.

biofuel Gas (such as methane) or liquid fuel (such as ethyl alcohol or biodiesel) made from plant material (biomass).

biogeochemical cycle Natural processes that recycle nutrients in various chemical forms from the nonliving environment to living organisms and then back to the nonliving environment. Examples include the carbon, oxygen, nitrogen, phosphorus, sulfur, and hydrologic cycles.

biological evolution Change in the genetic makeup of a population of a species in successive generations. If continued long enough, it can lead to the formation of a new species. Note that populations, not individuals, evolve. See also *adaptation, differential reproduction, natural selection, theory of evolution*.

biological extinction Complete disappearance of a species from earth. It happens when a species cannot adapt and successfully reproduce under new environmental conditions or when a species evolves into one or more new species. Compare *speciation*. See also *endangered species, mass extinction, threatened species*.

biological pest control Control of pest populations by natural predators, parasites, or disease-causing bacteria and viruses (pathogens).

biomagnification Increase in concentration of slowly degradable, fat-soluble chemicals such a DDT and PCBs in organisms at successively higher trophic levels of a food chain or web. Compare *bioaccumulation*.

biomass Organic matter produced by plants and other photosynthetic producers; total dry weight of all living organisms that can be supported at each trophic level in a food chain or web.

biome Terrestrial regions inhabited by certain types of life, especially vegetation.

biomimicry Process of observing certain changes in nature, studying how natural systems have responded to such changing conditions over many millions of years, and applying what is learned to dealing with some environmental challenge.

biosphere The parts of the earth's air (atmosphere), water (hydrosphere), and soil (lithosphere) where life is found.

biotic Living organisms. Compare *abiotic*.

birth rate See *crude birth rate*.

bitumen Gooey, black, high-sulfur, heavy oil extracted from tar sand and then upgraded to synthetic fuel oil. See *oil sand*.

broadleaf deciduous plants Plants such as oak and maple trees that survive drought and cold by shedding their leaves and becoming dormant. Compare *broadleaf evergreen plants, coniferous evergreen plants*.

broadleaf evergreen plants Plants that keep most of their broad leaves year-round. An example is the trees found in the canopies of tropical rain forests. Compare *broadleaf deciduous plants, coniferous evergreen plants*.

buffer Substance that can react with hydrogen ions in a solution and thus hold the acidity or pH of a solution fairly constant. See *pH*.

bycatch Unwanted fish, marine mammals, and sea turtles caught in the nets and on the hooks of commercial fishing fleets.

calorie Unit of energy; amount of energy needed to raise the temperature of 1 gram of water by 1 C° (unit on Celsius temperature scale). See also *kilocalorie*.

cancer Any of more than 120 different diseases, one for each type of cell in the human body. Each type of cancer produces a tumor in which cells multiply uncontrollably and invade surrounding tissue.

cap-and-trade Market-based approach to limiting emissions by setting limits and issuing permits to pollution-generating entities. If a business does not utilize all of their permits, they may sell them to other businesses.

carbon capture and storage (CCS) Process of removing carbon dioxide gas from coal-burning power and industrial plants and storing it somewhere (usually underground or under the seabed) so that it is not released into the atmosphere. To be effective, it must be stored essentially forever.

carbon cycle Cyclic movement of carbon in different chemical forms from the environment to organisms and then back to the environment.

carbon footprint The amount of carbon compounds, especially carbon dioxide, emitted by a person or entity due to the burning of fossil fuels.

carcinogen Chemicals, ionizing radiation, and viruses that cause or promote the development of cancer. See *cancer*. Compare *mutagen, teratogen*.

carnivore Animal that feeds on other animals. Compare *herbivore, omnivore*.

carrying capacity (*K*) Maximum population of a particular species that a given habitat can support over a given period. Compare *cultural carrying capacity*.

cell Smallest living unit of an organism.

cell theory The idea that all living things are comprised of cells.

CFCs See *chlorofluorocarbons*.

chemical One of the millions of different elements and compounds found naturally or synthesized by humans. See *compound, element*.

chemical change Interaction between chemicals in which the chemical composition of the elements or compounds involved changes. Compare *physical change*.

chemical formula Shorthand way to show the number of atoms (or ions) in the basic structural unit of a compound.

chemical reaction See *chemical change*.

chemosynthesis Process in which certain organisms (mostly specialized bacteria) extract inorganic compounds from their environment and convert them into organic nutrient compounds without the presence of sunlight. Compare *photosynthesis*.

chlorinated hydrocarbon Organic compound made up of atoms of carbon, hydrogen, and chlorine. Examples include DDT and PCBs.

chlorofluorocarbons (CFCs) Organic compounds made up of atoms of carbon, chlorine, and fluorine. An example is Freon-12 (CCl_2F_2), which is used as a refrigerant in refrigerators and air conditioners and in making plastics such as Styrofoam. Gaseous CFCs can deplete the ozone layer when they slowly rise into the stratosphere and their chlorine atoms react with ozone molecules.

CHP (Combined heat and power) See *cogeneration*.

chromosome A grouping of genes and associated proteins in plant and animal cells that carry certain types of genetic information. See *genes*.

chronic malnutrition Faulty nutrition, caused by a diet that does not supply an individual with enough protein, essential fats, vitamins, minerals, and other nutrients needed for good health. Compare *overnutrition, chronic undernutrition*.

chronic undernutrition (hunger) Condition suffered by people who cannot grow or buy enough food to meet their basic energy needs. Compare *overnutrition, chronic malnutrition*.

clear-cutting Method of timber harvesting in which all trees in a forested area are removed in a single cutting. Compare *selective cutting, strip cutting*.

climate Physical properties of the troposphere of an area based on analysis of its weather records over a long period (at least 30 years). The two main factors determining an area's climate are its average *temperature*, with its seasonal variations, and the average amount and distribution of *precipitation*. Compare *weather*.

climate change Broad term referring to long-term changes in any aspects of the earth's climate, especially temperature and precipitation. Compare *global warming, weather*.

climate change tipping point Point at which an environmental problem reaches a threshold level where scientists fear it could cause irreversible climate disruption.

closed-loop recycling See *primary recycling*.

coal Solid, combustible mixture of organic compounds with 30 to 98% carbon by weight, mixed with various amounts of water and small amounts of sulfur and nitrogen compounds. It forms in several stages as the remains of plants are subjected to heat and pressure over millions of years.

coal gasification Conversion of solid coal to synthetic natural gas (SNG).

coal liquefaction Conversion of solid coal to a liquid hydrocarbon fuel such as synthetic gasoline or methanol.

coastal wetland Land along a coastline, extending inland from an estuary that is covered with saltwater all or part of the year. Examples include marshes, bays, lagoons, tidal flats, and mangrove swamps. Compare *inland wetland*.

coastal zone Warm, nutrient-rich, shallow part of the ocean that extends from the high-tide mark on land to the edge of a shelf-like extension of continental land masses known as the continental shelf. Compare *pelagic zone*.

coevolution Evolution in which two or more species interact and exert selective pressures on each other that can lead each species to undergo adaptations. See *evolution, natural selection*.

cogeneration Production of two useful forms of energy, such as high-temperature heat or steam and electricity, from the same fuel source.

cold front Leading edge of an advancing mass of cold air. Compare *warm front*.

colony collapse disorder (CCD) Loss through death or disappearance of all or most of the European honeybees in a particular colony due to unknown causes; a phenomenon that has resulted in large losses of European honeybees in the United States and in parts of Europe.

combined heat and power (CHP) production See *cogeneration*.

commensalism An interaction between organisms of different species in which one type of organism benefits and the other type is neither helped nor harmed to any great degree. Compare *mutualism*.

commercial extinction Depletion of the population of a wild species used as a resource to a level at which it is no longer profitable to harvest the species.

commercial forest See *tree plantation*.

community Populations of all species living and interacting in an area at a particular time.

competition Two or more individual organisms of a single species (*intraspecific competition*) or two or more individuals of different species (*interspecific competition*) attempting to use the same scarce resources in the same ecosystem.

complex carbohydrates Molecules consisting of carbon, hydrogen, and oxygen that provide energy to living organisms. Sugar, starch, and cellulose are examples.

compost Partially decomposed organic plant and animal matter used as a soil conditioner or fertilizer.

compound Combination of atoms, or oppositely charged ions, of two or more elements held together by attractive forces called chemical bonds. Compare *element*.

concentration Amount of a chemical in a particular volume or weight of air, water, soil, or other medium.

conduction The process by which heat or electricity is directly transmitted through a substance when there is a difference of temperature or of electrical potential between adjoining regions. Compare *convection*.

coniferous evergreen plants Cone-bearing plants (such as spruces, pines, and firs) that keep some of their narrow, pointed leaves (needles) or scale-like leaves all year. Compare *broadleaf deciduous plants, broad-leaf evergreen plants*.

coniferous trees Cone-bearing trees, mostly evergreens, that have needle-shaped or scale-like leaves. They produce wood known commercially as softwood. Compare *deciduous plants*.

conservation Use of natural areas and wildlife in ways that sustain them for current and future generations of humans, as well as other forms of life. People with this view are called *conservationists*.

conservation biology Multidisciplinary science created to deal with the crisis of maintaining the genes, species, communities, and ecosystems that make up earth's biological diversity. Its goals are to investigate human impacts on biodiversity and to develop practical approaches to preserving biodiversity.

conservation-tillage farming See *no-till farming*.

consumer (heterotroph) Organism that cannot synthesize the organic nutrients it needs and gets its organic nutrients by feeding on the tissues of producers or other consumers. Compare *producer, decomposer*.

continental drift The slow movement of continents across earth's surface.

contour farming Plowing and planting across the changing slope of land, rather than in straight lines, to help retain water and reduce soil erosion.

contour strip mining Form of surface mining used on hilly or mountainous terrain. A power shovel cuts a series of terraces into the side of a hill. An earthmover removes the overburden, and a power shovel extracts the coal. The spoils from each new terrace are dumped onto the one below.

controlled burning Deliberately set, carefully controlled surface fires that reduce flammable litter and decrease the chances of damaging *crown fires*. See *ground fire, surface fire*.

convection Movement of warmer molecules that rise and become less dense while colder molecules sink and become more dense, ultimately resulting in the transfer of heat. Compare *conduction*.

convection cell Cyclical pattern of air that rises and falls due to convection.

conventional-tillage farming Crop cultivation method in which a planting surface is made by plowing land, breaking up the exposed soil, and then smoothing the surface. Compare *conservation-tillage farming*.

convergent plate boundary Area where the earth's lithospheric plates move toward each other and are pushed together. See *subduction zone*. Compare *divergent plate boundary, transform plate boundary*.

coral bleaching Process in which warmer ocean waters can cause shallow tropical corals to expel their colorful algae and turn white. It can weaken and sometimes kill corals.

coral reef Formation produced by massive colonies containing billions of tiny coral animals, called polyps, that secrete a stony substance (calcium carbonate) around themselves for protection. When the corals die, their empty outer skeletons form layers and cause the reef to grow. Coral reefs are found in the coastal zones of warm tropical and subtropical oceans.

core Inner zone of the earth. It consists of a solid inner core and a liquid outer core. Compare *crust, mantle*.

Coriolis effect The deflection of an air mass to the east as it moves north or south away from the equator, or a deflection west as it moves toward the equator. These deflections occur because the earth's eastward rotation is faster at the equator than at any other point on its surface.

cost–benefit analysis A comparison of estimated costs and benefits of actions such as implementing a pollution control regulation, building a dam on a river, or preserving an area of forest.

crop rotation Planting a field, or an area of a field, with different crops from year to year to reduce soil nutrient depletion. A plant such as corn, tobacco, or cotton, which removes large amounts of nitrogen from the soil, is planted one year. The next year a legume such as soybeans, which adds nitrogen to the soil, is planted.

crown fire Extremely hot forest fire that burns ground vegetation and treetops. Compare *controlled burning, ground fire, surface fire*.

crude birth rate Annual number of live births per 1,000 people in the population of a geographic area at the midpoint of a given year. Compare *crude death rate*.

crude death rate Annual number of deaths per 1,000 people in the population of a geographic area at the midpoint of a given year. Compare *crude birth rate*.

crude oil (petroleum) Gooey liquid consisting mostly of hydrocarbon compounds and small amounts of compounds containing oxygen, sulfur, and nitrogen. Extracted from underground accumulations, it is sent to oil refineries, where it is converted to heating oil, diesel fuel, gasoline, tar, and other materials.

crust Solid outer zone of the earth. It consists of oceanic crust and continental crust. Compare *core, mantle*.

cultural carrying capacity The limit on population growth that would allow most people in an area or the world to live in reasonable comfort and freedom without impairing the ability of the planet to sustain future generations. Compare *carrying capacity*.

cultural eutrophication Overnourishment of aquatic ecosystems with plant nutrients (mostly nitrates and phosphates) because of human activities such as agriculture, urbanization, and discharges from industrial plants and sewage treatment plants. See *eutrophication*.

dam A structure built across a river to control the river's flow or to create a reservoir. See *reservoir*.

data Factual information collected by scientists.

DDT Dichlorodiphenyltrichloroethane, a chlorinated hydrocarbon that has been widely used as an insecticide but is now banned in some countries.

death rate See *crude death rate*.

debt-for-nature swap Agreement in which a certain amount of foreign debt is canceled in exchange for local currency investments that will improve natural resource management or protect certain areas in the debtor country from environmentally harmful development.

deciduous plants Trees, such as oaks and maples, and other plants that survive during dry or cold seasons by shedding their leaves. Compare *coniferous trees, succulent plants*.

decomposer Organism that digests parts of dead organisms and cast-off fragments and wastes of living organisms by breaking down the complex organic molecules in those materials into simpler water-soluble inorganic compounds that are returned to the soil and water for use as nutrients by producers. Compare *consumer, detritivore, producer*.

deforestation Removal of trees from a forested area.

delta An area at the mouth of a river built up by deposited sediments, usually containing coastal wetlands and estuaries. See *coastal wetland, estuary*.

demographic transition Hypothesis that countries, as they become industrialized, have declines in death rates followed by declines in birth rates.

density Mass per unit volume.

depletion time The time it takes to use a certain fraction (usually 80%) of the known or estimated supply of a nonrenewable resource at an assumed rate of use. Finding and extracting the remaining 20% usually costs more than it is worth.

desalination Purification of saltwater or brackish (slightly salty) water by removal of dissolved salts.

desert Biome in which evaporation exceeds precipitation and the average amount of precipitation is less than 25 centimeters (10 inches) per year. Such areas have little vegetation or have widely spaced, mostly low vegetation. Compare *forest, grassland*.

desertification Conversion of rangeland, rain-fed cropland, or irrigated cropland to desert-like land, with a drop in agricultural productivity of 10% or more. It is usually caused by a combination of overgrazing, soil erosion, prolonged drought, and climate change.

detritivore Consumer organism that feeds on detritus, parts of dead organisms, and cast-off fragments and wastes of living organisms. Compare *decomposer*.

detritus Parts of dead organisms and cast-off fragments and wastes of living organisms.

detritus feeder See *detritivore*.

deuterium (D; hydrogen-2) Isotope of the element hydrogen, with a nucleus containing one proton and one neutron and a mass number of 2.

dieback Sharp reduction in the population of a species when its numbers exceed the carrying capacity of its habitat. See *carrying capacity*.

differential reproduction Phenomenon in which individuals with adaptive genetic traits produce more living offspring than do individuals without such traits. See *natural selection*.

dioxins Family of 75 chlorinated hydrocarbon compounds formed as unwanted by-products in chemical reactions involving chlorine and hydrocarbons, usually at high temperatures.

discount rate An estimate of a resource's future economic value compared to its present value; based on the idea that having something today may be worth more than it will be in the future.

dissolved oxygen (DO) content Amount of oxygen gas (O_2) dissolved in a given volume of water at a particular temperature and pressure, often expressed as a concentration in parts of oxygen per million parts of water.

disturbance An event that disrupts an ecosystem or community. Examples of *natural disturbances* include fires, hurricanes, tornadoes, droughts, and floods. Examples of *human-caused disturbances* include deforestation, overgrazing, and plowing.

divergent plate boundary Area where the earth's lithospheric plates move apart in opposite directions. Compare *convergent plate boundary, transform plate boundary*.

DNA (deoxyribonucleic acid) Large molecules in the cells of living organisms that carry genetic information.

dose Amount of potentially harmful substance an individual ingests, inhales, or absorbs through the skin. Compare *response*. See *dose-response curve, median lethal dose.*

dose-response curve Plot of data showing the effects of various doses of a toxic agent on a group of test organisms. See *dose, median lethal dose, response.*

doubling time Time it takes (usually in years) for the quantity of something growing exponentially to double. It can be calculated by dividing the annual percentage growth rate into 70.

drift-net fishing Catching fish in huge nets that drift in the water.

drought Condition in which an area does not get enough water because of lower-than-normal precipitation or higher-than-normal temperatures that increase evaporation.

earthquake Shaking of the ground resulting from the fracturing and displacement of subsurface rock, which produces a fault, or from subsequent movement along the fault.

eco-city A people-oriented rather than car–oriented city where residents use transportation alternatives to vehicles, where buildings, vehicles, and appliances are energy efficient, and where significant areas of green space exist.

ecological diversity The variety of forests, deserts, grasslands, oceans, streams, lakes, and other biological communities interacting with one another and with their nonliving environment. See *biodiversity*. Compare *functional diversity, genetic diversity, species diversity.*

ecological footprint Amount of biologically productive land and water needed to supply a population with the renewable resources it uses and to absorb or dispose of the pollution and wastes from such resource use.

ecological niche Total way of life or role of a species in an ecosystem. It includes all physical, chemical, and biological conditions that a species needs to live and reproduce in an ecosystem. Compare *habitat.*

ecological restoration Research and sci-entific study devoted to restoring, repairing, and reconstructing damaged ecosystems.

ecological succession Process in which communities of plant and animal species in a particular area are replaced over time by a series of different often more complex communities. See *primary ecological succession, secondary ecological succession.*

ecological tipping point Point at which an environmental problem reaches a threshold level, which causes an often irreversible shift in the behavior of a natural system.

ecologist Biological scientist who studies relationships between living organisms and their environment.

ecology Biological science that studies relationships between living organisms and their environment.

economic depletion Exhaustion of a certain amount (typically 80%) of the estimated supply of a nonrenewable resource. Finding, extracting, and processing the remaining amount usually costs more than it is worth. May also apply to the depletion of a renewable resource, such as a fish or tree species.

economic development Improvement of human living standards by economic growth. Compare *economic growth.*

economic growth Increase in the capacity to provide people with goods and services; an increase in gross domestic product (GDP). Compare *economic development*. See *gross domestic product.*

economics Social science that deals with the production, distribution, and consumption of goods and services to satisfy people's needs and wants.

economy System of production, distribution, and consumption of economic goods.

ecosystem One or more communities of different species interacting with one another and with the chemical and physical factors making up their nonliving environment.

ecosystem diversity The earth's diversity of biological communities, including deserts, grasslands, forests, mountains, oceans, lakes, rivers, and wetlands.

ecosystem services Natural services or natural capital that support life on earth and are essential to the quality of human life and the functioning of the world's economies. See *natural capital, natural resources.*

ecotone Transition area between two biomes. See *edge effect.*

edge effect The changes in population or community structures that occur at the boundary of two habitats. See *ecotone.*

electric power Rate at which electric energy is transferred by an electric circuit.

electromagnetic radiation Form of kinetic energy traveling as electromagnetic waves.

electron Tiny particle moving around outside the nucleus of an atom. Each electron has one unit of negative charge and almost no mass. Compare *neutron, proton.*

element Chemical, such as hydrogen (H), iron (Fe), etc., whose distinctly different atoms serve as the basic building blocks of all matter. Two or more elements combine to form compounds that make up most of the world's matter. Compare *compound.*

emigration Movement of people out of a specific geographic area. Compare *immigration, migration.*

endangered species Wild species with so few individual survivors that the species could soon become extinct in all or most of its natural range. Compare *threatened species.*

Endangered Species Act (ESA) Law established in 1973 designed to identify and protect endangered species in the United States and abroad.

endemic species Species that is found in only one area. Such species are especially vulnerable to extinction.

energy Capacity to do work by performing mechanical, physical, chemical, or electrical tasks or to cause heat transfer between two objects at different temperatures.

energy conservation Reducing or eliminating the unnecessary waste of energy.

energy density Amount of energy available per unit of mass of an energy resource.

energy efficiency Percentage of the total energy input that does useful work and is not converted into low-quality, generally useless heat in an energy conversion system or process. See *energy quality, net energy.*

energy quality Ability of a form of energy to do useful work. See *high-quality energy, low-quality energy.*

environment All external conditions, factors, matter, and energy, living and nonliving, that affect any living organism or other specified system.

environmental degradation Depletion or destruction of a potentially renewable resource. See also *sustainable yield.*

environmental ethics Human beliefs about what is right or wrong with how we treat the environment.

environmental indicators Economic indicators that include non-economic factors with the goal of monitoring environmental quality and human well-being, as well as economic status or progress.

environmentalism Social movement dedicated to protecting the earth's life-support systems for us and other species.

environmental justice Ideal whereby every person is entitled to protection from environmental hazards regardless of race, gender, age, national origin, income, social class, or any political factor.

environmental law A body of laws and treaties that broadly define what is acceptable environmental behavior for individuals, groups, businesses, and nations.

environmentally sustainable society Society that meets the current and future needs of its people for basic resources in a just and equitable manner without compromising the ability of future generations of humans and other species to meet their basic needs.

environmental resistance All of the limiting factors that act together to limit the growth of a population.

environmental science Interdisciplinary study that uses information and ideas from the physical sciences (such as biology, chemistry, and geology) with those from the social sciences (such as economics, politics, and ethics) to learn how nature works, how we interact with the environment, and how we can deal with environmental problems.

environmental scientist Scientist who uses information from the physical sciences and social sciences to understand how the earth works, learn how humans interact with the earth, and develop solutions to environmental problems. See *environmental science*.

environmental worldview Set of assumptions and beliefs about how people think the world works, what they think their role in the world should be, and what they believe is right and wrong environmental behavior.

EPA U.S. Environmental Protection Agency; responsible for managing federal efforts to control air and water pollution, radiation and pesticide hazards, environmental research, hazardous waste, and solid waste disposal.

epidemiology Study of the patterns of disease or other harmful effects from exposure to toxins and diseases caused by pathogens within defined groups of people to find out why some people get sick and some do not.

epiphyte Plant that uses its roots to attach itself to branches high in trees, especially in tropical forests.

erosion Process or group of processes by which loose or consolidated earth materials, especially topsoil, are dissolved, loosened, or worn away and removed from one place and deposited in another. See *weathering*.

estuary Partially enclosed coastal area at the mouth of a river where its freshwater, carrying fertile silt and runoff from the land, mixes with salty seawater.

eukaryotic cell Cell that is surrounded by a membrane and has a distinct nucleus. Compare *prokaryotic cell*.

euphotic zone Upper layer of a body of water through which sunlight can penetrate and support photosynthesis.

eutrophication Physical, biological, and chemical changes that take place after a lake, estuary, or slow-moving stream receives inputs of plant nutrients—mostly nitrates and phosphates—from natural erosion and runoff from the surrounding land basin. See *cultural eutrophication*.

eutrophic lake Lake with a large supply of plant nutrients, mostly nitrates and phosphates. Compare *mesotrophic lake, oligotrophic lake*.

evolution Change in the genetic makeup of a population of a species in successive generations. If continued long enough, it can lead to the formation of a new species. Note that populations, not individuals, evolve.

exotic species See *nonnative species*.

exponential growth Growth in which some quantity, such as population size or economic output, increases at a constant rate per unit of time. See *J-shaped curve*. Compare *linear growth, logistic growth*.

external benefit Beneficial social effect of producing and using an economic good that is not included in the market price of the good. Compare *external cost*.

external cost Harmful environmental, economic, or social effect of producing and using an economic good that is not included in the market price of the good. See also *full-cost pricing*. Compare *external benefit, internal cost*.

extinction Complete disappearance of species from the earth. It happens when a species cannot adapt and successfully reproduce under new environmental conditions or when a species evolves into one or more new species. Compare *speciation*.

extinction rate Percentage or number of species that go extinct within a certain period of time such as a year.

family planning Providing information, clinical services, and contraceptives to help people choose the number and spacing of children they want to have.

famine Widespread malnutrition and starvation in a particular area because of a shortage of food, usually caused by drought, war, flood, earthquake, or other catastrophic event that disrupts food production and distribution.

farm subsidies Money paid to farmers to supplement the cost of production of crops and livestock in order to influence the market price and supply of food commodities.

feedback Any process that increases (positive feedback) or decreases (negative feedback) a change to a system.

feedback loop Occurs when an output of matter, energy, or information is fed back into the system as an input and leads to changes in that system. See *positive feedback loop, negative feedback loop*.

feed-in-tariff Requires utilities to buy electricity produced by homeowners and businesses from renewable energy sources at a guaranteed price.

feedlot Confined outdoor or indoor space used to raise hundreds to thousands of domesticated livestock.

fertility rate Number of children born to an average woman in a population during her lifetime. Compare *replacement-level fertility*.

fertilizer Substance that adds inorganic or organic plant nutrients to soil and improves its ability to grow crops, trees, or other vegetation. See *inorganic fertilizer, organic fertilizer*.

first law of thermodynamics Whenever energy is converted from one form to another in a physical or chemical change, no energy is created or destroyed, but energy can be converted from one form to another. See *second law of thermodynamics*.

fishery Concentration of particular aquatic species suitable for commercial harvesting in a given ocean area or inland body of water.

fish farming See *aquaculture*.

floodplain Flat valley floor next to a stream channel. For legal purposes, the term often applies to any low area that has the potential for flooding including certain coastal areas.

food chain Series of organisms in which one eats or decomposes the preceding one. The sequence of organisms in an ecosystem through which energy is transferred. Compare *food web*.

food desert Urban area where people have little or no easy access to grocery stores or other sources of nutritious food.

food security Conditions under which every person in a given area has daily access to enough nutritious food to have an active and healthy life.

food web Complex network of many interconnected food chains and feeding relationships. Compare *food chain*.

fossil fuel Products of partial or complete decomposition of plants and animals; occurs as crude oil, coal, natural gas, or heavy oils as a result of exposure to heat and pressure in the earth's crust over millions of years. See *coal, crude oil, natural gas*.

fossils Skeletons, bones, shells, body parts, leaves, seeds, or impressions of such items that provide recognizable evidence of organisms that lived long ago.

fracking See *hydraulic fracturing.*

freshwater life zone Aquatic systems where water with a dissolved salt concentration of less than 1% by volume accumulates on or flows through the surfaces of terrestrial biomes. Examples include *standing* (lentic) bodies of water such as ponds and lakes and *flowing* (lotic) bodies of water such as streams and rivers.

front The boundary between two air masses with different temperatures and densities. See *cold front, warm front.*

full-cost pricing Finding ways to include in the market prices of goods the harmful environmental and health costs of producing and using those goods. See *external cost, internal cost.*

functional diversity Biological and chemical processes of functions such as energy flow and matter cycling needed for the survival of species and biological communities. See *biodiversity.* Compare *ecological diversity, genetic diversity, species diversity.*

fungicide Chemical that kills fungi.

gangue The waste material that is discarded when ore is extracted during mining.

gene pool Sum total of all genes found in the individuals of the population of a particular species.

generalist species Species with a broad ecological niche. They can live in many different places, eat a variety of foods, and tolerate a wide range of environmental conditions. Compare *specialist species.*

genes Coded units of information about specific traits that are passed from parents to offspring during reproduction. They consist of segments of DNA molecules found in chromosomes.

genetically modified organisms (GMOs) Organisms whose genetic makeup has been altered by genetic engineering.

genetic adaptation Changes in the genetic makeup of organisms of a species that allow the species to reproduce and gain a competitive advantage under changed environmental conditions.

genetic diversity Variability in the genetic makeup among individuals within a single species. See *biodiversity.* Compare *ecological diversity, functional diversity, species diversity.*

genetic engineering Insertion of an alien gene into an organism to give it a new genetic trait.

genetic variability Diversity in the genetic makeup among individuals within a single species.

geoengineering Large-scale manipulation of an environmental process meant to counteract climate change.

geographic isolation Physical separation of populations of the same species into different areas for long periods of time.

geology Study of the earth's dynamic history. Geologists study and analyze rocks and the features and processes of the earth's interior and surface.

geosphere The earth's immensely hot core, thick mantle comprised mostly of rock and a thin outer crust that contains most of the earth's rock, soil, and sediment. Compare *atmosphere, biosphere, hydrosphere.*

geothermal energy Heat transferred from the earth's underground concentrations of dry steam (steam with no water droplets), wet steam (a mixture or steam and water droplets), or hot water trapped in fractured or porous rock.

global warming Warming of the earth's lower atmosphere (troposphere) because of increases in the concentrations of one or more greenhouse gases. It can result in climate change that can last for decades to thousands of years. See *climate change, greenhouse effect, greenhouse gases.*

GMO See *genetically modified organism.*

greenhouse effect Natural effect that releases heat into the atmosphere near the earth's surface. Water vapor, carbon dioxide, methane, and other gases in the lower atmosphere (troposphere) absorb some of the infrared radiation radiated by the earth's surface and release it as longer-wavelength radiation (heat) into the troposphere. See *climate change, global warming, greenhouse gases.*

greenhouse gases Gases in the earth's lower atmosphere (troposphere) that cause the greenhouse effect that warms the lower atmosphere. Examples include carbon dioxide, chlorofluorocarbons, ozone, methane, water vapor, and nitrous oxide. See *climate change, global warming, greenhouse effect.*

green manure Freshly cut or still-growing green vegetation that is plowed into the soil to increase the organic matter and humus available to support crop growth.

green revolution Popular term for the introduction of scientifically bred or selected varieties of grain (rice, wheat, maize) that, with adequate inputs of fertilizer and water, can greatly increase crop yields.

gross domestic product (GDP) Annual market value of all goods and services produced by all firms and organizations, foreign and domestic, operating within a country. See *per capita GDP.*

gross primary productivity (GPP) Rate at which an ecosystem's producers capture and store a given amount of chemical energy as biomass in a given length of time. Compare *net primary productivity.*

ground fire Fire that burns decayed leaves or peat deep below the ground's surface. Compare *crown fire, surface fire.*

groundwater Water that sinks into the soil and is stored in slowly flowing and slowly renewed underground reservoirs called aquifers; underground water in the zone of saturation below the water table. Compare *runoff, surface water.*

gyres Ocean currents that are driven by prevailing winds and the Coriolis effect, rotating clockwise in the northern hemisphere and counterclockwise in the southern hemisphere.

habitat Place or type of place where an organism or population of organisms live. Compare *ecological niche.*

habitat fragmentation Breaking up of habitat into smaller pieces, usually as a result of human activities.

hazard Something that can cause injury, disease, economic loss, or environmental damage. See also *risk.*

hazardous chemical Chemical that can cause harm because it is flammable or explosive, can irritate or damage the skin or lungs (such as strong acidic or alkaline substances), or can cause allergic reactions of the immune system (allergens). See also *toxic chemical.*

hazardous (toxic) waste Any liquid, solid, or containerized gas that can catch fire easily, is corrosive to skin tissue or metals, is unstable and can explode or release toxic fumes, or has harmful concentrations of one or more toxic materials that can leach out. These substances are usually byproducts of manufacturing processes.

heat (thermal energy) Total kinetic energy of all randomly moving atoms, ions, or molecules within a given substance, excluding the overall motion of the whole object. Compare *temperature.*

herbicide Chemical that kills a plant or inhibits its growth.

herbivore Plant-eating organism. Examples include deer, sheep, grasshoppers, and zooplankton. Compare *carnivore, omnivore.*

heterotroph See *consumer.*

high-grade ore Ore containing a large amount of a desired mineral. Compare *low-grade ore.*

high-quality energy Energy that is concentrated and has great ability to perform useful work. Compare *low-quality energy.*

high-throughput economy Economic system in most advanced industrialized countries, in which ever-increasing economic growth is sustained by maximizing the rate at which matter and energy resources are used, with little emphasis on pollution prevention, recycling, reuse, reduction of unnecessary waste, and other forms of resource conservation. Compare *low-throughput economy.*

HIPPCO Acronym used by conservation biologists for the six most important secondary causes of premature extinction. **H**abitat destruction, degradation, and fragmentation; **I**nvasive (nonnative) species; **P**opulation growth (too many people consuming too many resources); **P**ollution; **C**limate change; and **O**verexploitation.

host Plant or animal on which a parasite feeds.

humus Partially decomposed organic material in topsoil. It helps soil retain water and water-soluble nutrients, which can be taken up by plant roots.

hydraulic fracturing (fracking) Freeing oil or natural gas that is tightly held in underground rock deposits by using perforated drilling well tubes with explosive charges to create fissures in the rock. Then, high-pressure pumps shoot a mixture of water, sand, and chemicals into the well to hold the rock fractures open and release the oil or natural gas, which flows back to the surface along with a mixture of water, and fracking chemicals (some of them hazardous), and other wastes that are released from the rock.

hydrocarbon Organic compound made of hydrogen and carbon atoms. The simplest hydrocarbon is methane (CH_4), the major component of natural gas.

hydrogen fuel cell A device that combines hydrogen gas (H_2) with oxygen gas (O_2) to produce electricity and water vapor that is emitted to the atmosphere.

hydrologic cycle Biogeochemical cycle that collects, purifies, and distributes the earth's fixed supply of water from the environment to living organisms and then back to the environment.

hydroponics Form of agriculture in which farmers grow plants by exposing their roots to a nutrient-rich water solution instead of soil.

hydropower Electrical energy produced by falling or flowing water.

hydrosphere The earth's liquid water (lakes, rivers, ponds, ocean, underground water), frozen water (icecaps, glaciers, permafrost), and gaseous water (water vapor in the atmosphere). See *also hydrologic cycle.* Compare *atmosphere, biosphere, geosphere.*

igneous rock Rock formed when molten rock material (magma) wells up from the earth's interior, cools, and solidifies into rock masses. See *rock cycle.* Compare *metamorphic rock, sedimentary rock.*

immigration Migration of people into a country or area to take up permanent residence. Compare *emigration.*

indicator species Species whose decline serves as an early warning that a community or ecosystem is being degraded. Compare *keystone species, native species, nonnative species.*

industrialized agriculture Production of large quantities of crops and livestock for domestic and foreign sale; involves use of large inputs of energy from fossil fuels (especially oil and natural gas), water, fertilizer, and pesticides. Compare *subsistence farming.*

industrial smog Type of air pollution consisting mostly of a mixture of sulfur dioxide, suspended droplets of sulfuric acid formed from some of the sulfur dioxide, and suspended solid particles. Compare *photochemical smog.*

industrial solid waste Solid waste produced by mines, factories, refineries, food growers, and businesses that supply people with goods and services. Compare *municipal solid waste.*

inertia See *persistence.*

inexhaustible (perpetual) resource Essentially inexhaustible resource such as solar energy because it is renewed continuously. Compare *nonrenewable resource, renewable resource.*

infant mortality rate Number of babies out of every 1,000 born each year who die before their first birthday.

infectious disease Disease caused when a pathogen such as a bacterium, virus, or parasite invades the body and multiplies in its cells and tissues. Examples are flu, HIV, malaria, tuberculosis, and measles. See *transmissible disease.* Compare *nontransmissible disease.*

infiltration Downward movement of water through soil.

inland wetland Land away from the coast, such as a swamp, marsh, or bog, that is covered all or part of the time with freshwater. Compare *coastal wetland.*

inorganic compounds All compounds not classified as organic compounds. See *organic compounds.*

inorganic fertilizer Commercially prepared mixture of inorganic plant nutrients such as nitrates, phosphates, and potassium applied to the soil to restore fertility and increase crop yields. Compare *organic fertilizer.*

input Matter, energy, or information entering a system. Compare *output, throughput.*

insecticide Chemical that kills insects.

insolation Input of solar energy in a given area.

instrumental value Value of an organism, species, ecosystem, or the earth's biodiversity based on its usefulness to humans. Compare *intrinsic value.*

integrated pest management (IPM) Combined use of biological, chemical, and cultivation methods in proper sequence and timing to keep the size of a pest population below the level that causes economically unacceptable loss of a crop or livestock.

integrated waste management Variety of strategies for both waste reduction and waste management designed to deal with the waste we produce.

intercropping Growing two or more different crops at the same time on a plot. For example, a carbohydrate-rich grain that depletes soil nitrogen and a protein-rich legume that adds nitrogen to the soil may be intercropped. Compare *monoculture, polyculture.*

internal cost Direct cost paid by the producer and the buyer of an economic good. See also *full-cost pricing.* Compare *external benefit, external cost.*

interspecific competition Attempts by members of two or more species to use the same limited resources in an ecosystem. See *competition.* Compare *intraspecific competition.*

intertidal zone The area of shoreline between low and high tides.

intraspecific competition Attempts by two or more organisms of a single species to use the same limited resources in an ecosystem. See *competition.* Compare *interspecific competition.*

intrinsic rate of increase (r) Rate at which a population could grow if it had unlimited resources. Compare *environmental resistance.*

intrinsic value Value of an organism, species, ecosystem, or the earth's biodiversity based on its existence, regardless of whether it has any usefulness to humans. Compare *instrumental value.*

invasive species See *nonnative species.*

invertebrates Animals without backbones. Compare *vertebrates.*

ion Atom or group of atoms with one or more positive (+) or negative (−) electrical charges. Compare *atom, molecule.*

ionizing radiation Fast-moving alpha or beta particles or high-energy radiation (gamma rays) emitted by radioisotopes. They have enough energy to dislodge one or more electrons from the atoms they hit, thereby forming charged ions in tissue that can react with and damage living tissue. Compare *nonionizing radiation.*

IPM See *integrated pest management.*

irrigation Mix of methods used to supply water to crops by artificial means.

isotopes Two or more forms of a chemical element that have the same number of protons but different mass numbers because they have different numbers of neutrons in their nuclei.

J-shaped curve Curve with a shape similar to that of the letter J; can represent prolonged exponential growth. See *exponential growth.* Compare *S-shaped curve.*

keystone species Species that play important roles in helping to sustain many other species in an ecosystem. Compare *indicator species, native species, nonnative species.*

kilocalorie (kcal) Unit of energy equal to 1,000 calories. See *calorie.*

kilowatt (kW) Unit of electrical power equal to 1,000 watts. See *watt.*

kinetic energy Energy that matter has because of its mass and speed, or velocity. Compare *potential energy.*

K-selected species Organisms that reproduce later in life, have few offspring and invest energy in raising and nurturing those offspring, and have long lifespans.

landfill See *sanitary landfill.*

land-use planning Planning to determine the best present and future uses of each parcel of land.

latitude Distance from the equator.

law of conservation of energy See *first law of thermodynamics.*

law of conservation of matter In any physical or chemical change, no atoms are created or destroyed.

law of tolerance Existence, abundance, and distribution of a species in an ecosystem are determined by whether the levels of one or more physical or chemical factors fall within the range tolerated by the species. See *threshold effect.*

LD50 See *median lethal dose.*

leaching Process in which various chemicals in upper layers of soil are dissolved and carried to lower layers and, in some cases, to groundwater.

less-developed country Country that has low-to-moderate industrialization and low-to-moderate per capita GDP. Compare *more-developed country.*

life expectancy Average number of years a newborn infant can expect to live.

limiting factor Single factor that limits the growth, abundance, or distribution of a population of a species in an ecosystem. See *limiting factor principle.*

limiting factor principle Too much or too little of any abiotic factor can limit or prevent growth of a population of a species in an ecosystem, even if all other factors are at or near the optimal range of tolerance for the species.

linear growth Growth in which a quantity increases by some fixed amount during each unit of time. An example is growth that increases by 2 units in the sequence 2, 4, 6, 8, 10, and so on. Compare *exponential growth, logistic growth.*

lipids Energy storing organic molecule such as fats, oils, and waxes.

liquefied natural gas (LNG) Natural gas converted to liquid form by cooling it to a very low temperature.

liquefied petroleum gas (LPG) Mixture of liquefied propane (C_3H_8) and butane (C_4H_{10}) gas removed from natural gas and used as a fuel.

lithosphere Outer shell of the earth, composed of the crust and the rigid, outermost part of the mantle outside the asthenosphere. See *crust, geosphere, mantle.*

LNG See *liquefied natural gas.*

logistic growth Pattern in which exponential population growth occurs when the population is small, and population growth decreases steadily with time as the population approaches the carrying capacity. See *S-shaped curve.* Compare *exponential growth, linear growth.*

low-grade ore Ore containing a small amount of a desired mineral. Compare *high-grade ore.*

low-quality energy Energy that is dispersed and has little ability to do useful work. Compare *high-quality energy.*

low-throughput economy Economy based on working with nature by recycling and reusing discarded matter; preventing pollution; conserving matter and energy resources by reducing unnecessary waste and use; and building things that are easy to recycle, reuse, and repair. Compare *high-throughput economy.*

magma Molten rock below the earth's surface.

malnutrition See *chronic malnutrition.*

mangrove swamps Swamps found on the coastlines in warm tropical climates. They are dominated by mangrove trees, any of about 55 species of trees and shrubs that can live partly submerged in the salty environment of coastal swamps.

mantle Zone of the earth's interior between the core and the crust.

marginal cost Any increase in the cost of producing an additional unit of a product.

mass Amount of material in an object.

mass extinction A catastrophic, widespread, often global event in which major groups of species are become extinct over a short time compared with the normal (background) extinction rates. Compare *background extinction.*

mass number Sum of the number of neutrons (n) and the number of protons (p) in the nucleus of an atom. It gives the approximate mass of that atom. Compare *atomic number.*

mass transit Buses, trains, trolleys, and other forms of transportation that carry large numbers of people.

matter Anything that has mass (the amount of material in an object) and takes up space. On the earth, where gravity is present, we weigh an object to determine its mass.

maximum sustainable yield See *sustainable yield.*

median lethal dose (LD50) Amount of a toxic material per unit of body weight of a test animal that kills half the test population in a certain amount of time.

megacity City with 10 million or more people.

meltdown Melting of the highly radioactive core of a nuclear reactor.

mercury (Hg) A toxic element.

mesotrophic lake Lake with a moderate level of plant nutrients, falling between the two extremes of eutrophic (high nutrient levels) and oligotrophic (low nutrient levels). Compare *eutrophic lake, oligotrophic lake.*

metabolism Ability of a living cell or organism to capture and transform matter and energy from its environment to supply its needs for survival, growth, and reproduction.

metamorphic rock Rock produced when a preexisting rock is subjected to high temperatures (which may cause it to melt partially), high pressures, chemically active fluids, or a combination of these agents. See *rock cycle*. Compare *igneous rock, sedimentary rock*.

microorganisms Organisms such as bacteria that are so small that it takes a microscope to see them.

migration Movement of people into or out of a specific geographic area. Compare *emigration, immigration*.

mineral Any naturally occurring inorganic substance found in the earth's crust as a crystalline solid. See *mineral resource*.

mineral resource Any naturally occurring solid, liquid, or gaseous material in or on the earth's crust in a form and amount such that extracting and converting it into useful materials or items is currently or potentially profitable. Mineral resources are classified as metallic or nonmetallic.

mixture Combination of one or more elements and compounds.

model Approximate representation or simulation of a system being studied.

molecule Combination of two or more atoms of the same chemical element (such as O_2) or different chemical elements (such as H_2O) held together by chemical bonds. Compare *atom, ion*.

monoculture Cultivation of a single crop, usually on a large area of land. Compare *polyculture*.

more-developed country Country that is highly industrialized and has a high per capita GDP. Compare *less-developed country*.

mountaintop removal Type of surface mining that uses explosives, massive power shovels, and large machines called draglines to remove the top of a mountain and expose the seams of coal beneath. Compare *area strip mining, contour strip mining*.

multiple use Use of an ecosystem such as a forest for a variety of purposes such as timber harvesting, wildlife habitat, watershed protection, and recreation. Compare *sustainable yield*.

municipal solid waste (MSW) Solid materials discarded by homes and businesses in or near urban areas. Compare *industrial solid waste*.

mutagen Chemical or form of radiation that causes changes (mutations) in the DNA molecules in genes. See *mutation*. Compare *carcinogen, teratogen*.

mutation Random change in DNA molecules making up genes that can alter anatomy, physiology, or behavior in offspring. See *mutagen*.

mutualism Type of species interaction in which both participating species generally benefit. Compare *commensalism*.

nanotechnology The use of science and engineering to manipulate and create materials out of atoms and molecules at the ultra-small scale of less than 100 nanometers. A nanometer is one-millionth of a meter.

native species Species that normally live and thrive in a particular ecosystem. Compare *indicator species, keystone species, nonnative species*.

natural capital Natural resources and ecosystem services that keep us and other species alive and support our economies. See *ecosystem services, natural resources*.

natural capital degradation See *environmental degradation*.

natural gas Underground deposits of gases consisting of 50 to 90% by weight methane gas (CH_4) and small amounts of heavier gaseous hydrocarbon compounds such as propane (C_3H_8) and butane (C_4H_{10}).

natural greenhouse effect See *greenhouse effect*.

natural recharge Natural replenishment of an aquifer by precipitation, which percolates downward through soil and rock. See *recharge area*.

natural resources Materials such as air, water, and soil and energy in nature that are essential or useful to humans. See *ecosystem services, natural capital*.

natural selection Process by which a particular beneficial gene (or set of genes) is reproduced in succeeding generations more than other genes. The result of natural selection is a population that contains a greater proportion of organisms better adapted to certain environmental conditions. See *adaptation, biological evolution, differential reproduction, mutation*.

nature-deficit disorder Wide range of problems, including anxiety, depression, and attention-deficit disorders, that can result from or be intensified by a lack of contact with nature.

negative (corrective) feedback loop Feedback loop that causes a system to change in the opposite direction. Compare *positive feedback loop*.

nekton Strongly swimming organisms found in aquatic systems. Compare *benthos, plankton*.

net energy Total amount of useful energy available from an energy resource or energy system over its lifetime, minus the amount of energy *used* (the first energy

law), *automatically wasted* (the second energy law), and *unnecessarily wasted* in finding, processing, concentrating, and transporting it to users.

net primary productivity (NPP) Rate at which all the plants in an ecosystem produce net useful chemical energy; equal to the difference between the rate at which the plants in an ecosystem produce useful chemical energy (gross primary productivity) and the rate at which they use some of that energy through cellular respiration. Compare *gross primary productivity*.

neurotoxin Chemical that can harm the human nervous system (brain, spinal cord, peripheral nerves).

neutral solution Water solution containing an equal number of hydrogen ions (H^+) and hydroxide ions (OH^-); water solution with a pH of 7. Compare *acid solution, basic solution*.

neutron Elementary particle in the nuclei of all atoms (except hydrogen-1). It has a relative mass of 1 and no electric charge. Compare *electron, proton*.

niche See *ecological niche*.

nitric oxide (NO) Colorless gas that forms when nitrogen and oxygen gas in air react at the high-combustion temperatures in automobile engines and coal-burning plants. Lightning and certain bacteria in soil and water also produce NO as part of the *nitrogen cycle*.

nitrogen cycle Cyclic movement of nitrogen in different chemical forms from the environment to organisms and then back to the environment.

nitrogen dioxide (NO_2) Reddish-brown gas formed when nitrogen oxide reacts with oxygen in the air.

nitrogen fixation Conversion of atmospheric nitrogen gas, by lightning, bacteria, and cyanobacteria, into forms useful to plants; it is part of the nitrogen cycle.

nitrogen oxides (NO_x) See *nitric oxide and nitrogen dioxide*.

noise pollution Any unwanted, disturbing, or harmful sound that impairs or interferes with hearing, causes stress, hampers concentration and work efficiency, or causes accidents.

nondegradable pollutant Material that is not broken down by natural processes. Examples include the toxic elements lead and mercury. Compare *biodegradable pollutant*.

nonionizing radiation Forms of radiant energy such as radio waves, microwaves, infrared light, and ordinary light that do not have enough energy to cause ionization of atoms in living tissue. Compare *ionizing radiation*.

nonnative species Species that migrate into an ecosystem or are deliberately or accidentally introduced into an ecosystem by humans. Compare *indicator species, keystone species, native species*.

nonpoint source Broad and diffuse area, rather than a point, from which pollutants enter the bodies of surface water or air. Examples include runoff of chemicals and sediments from cropland, livestock feedlots, logged forests, urban streets, parking lots, lawns, and golf courses. Compare *point source*.

nonrenewable energy Energy resource that exists in a fixed amount in the earth's crust and has the potential for renewal by geological, physical, and chemical processes taking place over hundreds of millions to billions of years. Compare *renewable energy*.

nonrenewable resource Resource that exists in a fixed amount (stock) in the earth's crust and has the potential for renewal by geological, physical, and chemical processes taking place over hundreds of millions to billions of years. Compare *inexhaustible resource, renewable resource*.

nontransmissible disease Disease that is not caused by living organisms and does not spread from one person to another. Examples include most cancers, diabetes, cardiovascular disease, and malnutrition. Compare *transmissible disease*.

no-till farming Crop cultivation in which the soil is disturbed little (minimum-tillage farming) or not at all in an effort to reduce soil erosion, lower labor costs, and save energy.

NPP See *net primary productivity*.

nuclear energy Energy released when atomic nuclei undergo a nuclear reaction such as the spontaneous emission of radioactivity, nuclear fission, or nuclear fusion.

nuclear fission The process by which nuclei of certain isotopes with large mass numbers (such as uranium-235) are split apart into lighter nuclei when struck by a neutron and release energy. Compare *nuclear fusion*.

nuclear fuel cycle Includes the mining of uranium, processing and enriching it to make nuclear fuel, using it in the reactor, building a nuclear power plant, safely storing the resulting highly radioactive wastes for thousands of years until their radioactivity falls to safe levels, and retiring the highly radioactive nuclear plant by taking it apart and storing its high- and moderate-level radioactive

material safely for thousands of years.

nuclear fusion Nuclear change in which two nuclei of isotopes of elements with a low mass number (such as hydrogen-2 and hydrogen-3) are forced together at extremely high temperatures until they fuse to form a heavier nucleus (such as helium-4). This process releases a large amount of energy. Compare *nuclear fission*.

nucleic acids Informational molecules such as DNA or RNA in a double-helix shape consisting of complementary nucleotides in a specific sequence.

nucleus Extremely tiny center of an atom, making up most of the atom's mass. It contains one or more positively charged protons and one or more neutrons with no electrical charge (except for hydrogen-1 atom, which has one proton and no neutrons in its nucleus).

nutrient Any chemical an organism must take in to live, grow, or reproduce.

nutrient cycle (biogeochemical cycle) Natural process that recycles nutrients in various chemical forms from the nonliving environment to living organisms and then back to the nonliving environment.

ocean acidification Increasing levels of acid in the world's oceans due to their absorption of much of the CO_2 emitted into the atmosphere by human activities, especially the burning of carbon-containing fossil fuels. The CO_2 reacts with ocean water to form a weak acid and decreases the levels of carbonate ions (CO_3^{2-}) needed to form coral and the shells and skeletons of organisms such as crabs, oysters, and some phytoplankton.

ocean currents Mass movements of surface water produced by prevailing winds blowing over the oceans.

oil See *crude oil*.

oil reserves See *proven oil reserves*.

oil sand (tar sand) Deposit of a mixture of clay, sand, water, and varying amounts of a tarlike heavy oil known as bitumen. Bitumen can be extracted from tar sand by heating. It is then purified and upgraded to synthetic crude oil.

oil shale Fine-grained rock containing various amounts of kerogen, a solid, waxy mixture of hydrocarbon compounds. Heating the rock to high temperatures converts the kerogen into a vapor that can be condensed to form a slow-flowing heavy oil called shale oil. See *shale oil*.

old-growth forest Virgin and old, second-growth forests containing trees that are often hundreds—sometimes

thousands—of years old. Examples include forests of Douglas fir, western hemlock, giant sequoia, and coastal redwoods in the western United States. Compare *second-growth forest, tree plantation*.

oligotrophic lake Lake with a low supply of plant nutrients. Compare *eutrophic lake, mesotrophic lake*.

omnivore Animal that can use both plants and animals as food sources. Compare *carnivore, herbivore*.

open-access renewable resource Renewable resource owned by no one and available for use by anyone at little or no charge. Examples include clean air, underground water supplies, the open ocean and its fish, and the ozone layer.

open dump Fields or holes in the ground where garbage is deposited and sometimes covered with soil. They are rare in developed countries. Compare *sanitary landfill*.

open-pit mining Removing minerals such as gravel, sand, and metal ores by digging them out of the earth's surface and leaving an open pit behind. Compare *area strip mining, contour strip mining, mountaintop removal, subsurface mining*.

open sea See *pelagic zone*.

ore Part of a metal-yielding material that can be economically extracted from a mineral; typically containing two parts; the ore mineral, which contains the desired metal, and waste minerals (gangue). See *high-grade ore, low-grade ore*.

organic agriculture Growing crops with limited or no use of synthetic pesticides, synthetic fertilizers, or genetically modified crops; raising livestock without use of synthetic growth regulators and feed additives; and using organic fertilizer (manure, legumes, compost) and natural pest controls (bugs that eat harmful bugs, plants that repel bugs, and environmental controls such as crop rotation). See *sustainable agriculture*.

organic compounds Compounds containing carbon atoms combined with each other and with atoms of one or more other elements such as hydrogen, oxygen, nitrogen, sulfur, phosphorus, chlorine, and fluorine. All other compounds are called *inorganic compounds*.

organic farming See *organic agriculture* and *sustainable agriculture*.

organic fertilizer Organic materials such as animal manure, green manure, and compost applied to cropland as a source of plant nutrients. Compare *inorganic fertilizer*.

organism Any form of life.

output Matter, energy, or information leaving a system. Compare *input, throughput*.

overburden Layer of soil and rock overlying a mineral deposit.

overfishing Harvesting so many fish of a species, especially immature individuals, that not enough breeding stock is left to replenish the species and it becomes unprofitable to harvest them.

overgrazing Destruction of vegetation when too many grazing animals feed too long on a specific area of pasture or rangeland and exceed the carrying capacity of the rangeland.

overnutrition Occurs when food energy intake exceeds energy use and causes excess body fat. Too many calories, too little exercise, or both can cause overnutrition. It can place one at higher risk for developing diabetes, hypertension, heart disease, and other diseases. Compare *chronic malnutrition, chronic undernutrition.*

oxygen-demanding wastes Organic materials that are usually biodegraded by aerobic (oxygen-consuming) bacteria if there is enough dissolved oxygen in the water.

ozone (O₃) Colorless and highly reactive gas and a major component of photochemical smog. Also found in the ozone layer in the stratosphere. See *photochemical smog.*

ozone depletion Decrease in concentration of ozone (O₃) in the stratosphere. See *ozone layer.*

ozone layer Layer of gaseous ozone in the stratosphere that protects life on earth by filtering out most harmful ultraviolet radiation from the sun.

PANs Peroxyacyl nitrates; group of chemicals found in photochemical smog.

parasite Consumer organism that lives on or in, and feeds on, a living plant or animal, known as the host. The parasite draws nourishment from and gradually weakens its host. Some parasites can also cause malaria and other serious diseases. See *parasitism.*

parasitism Interaction between species in which one organism, called the parasite, preys on another organism, called the host, by living on or in the host. See *host, parasite.*

particulates Also known as suspended particulate matter (SPM); variety of solid particles and liquid droplets small and light enough to remain suspended in the air for long periods. About 62% of the SPM in outdoor air comes from natural sources such as dust, wild fires, and sea salt. The remaining 38% comes from human sources such as coal-burning electric power and industrial plants, motor vehicles, plowed fields, road construction, unpaved roads, and tobacco smoke.

parts per billion (ppb) Number of parts of a chemical found in 1 billion parts of a particular gas, liquid, or solid.

parts per million (ppm) Number of parts of a chemical found in 1 million parts of a particular gas, liquid, or solid.

passive solar heating system A system that, without the use of mechanical devices, captures sunlight directly within a structure and uses it to heat the structure. Compare *active solar heating system.*

pasture Managed grassland or enclosed meadow that is usually planted with domesticated grasses or other forage to be grazed by livestock. Compare *feedlot.*

pathogen Living organism that can cause disease in another organism. Examples include bacteria, viruses, and parasites.

PCBs See *polychlorinated biphenyls.*

peak production Point in time when the pressure in an oil well drops and its rate of conventional crude oil production starts declining, usually after a decade or so; for a group of wells or for a nation, the point at which all wells on average have declining oil production.

peer review Process of scientists reporting details of the methods and models they used, the results of their experiments, and the reasoning behind their hypotheses for other scientists working in the same field (their peers) to examine and criticize.

pelagic zone (open sea) Part of an ocean that lies beyond the continental shelf. Compare *coastal zone.*

per capita Average per person.

per capita GDP Annual gross domestic product (GDP) of a country divided by its total population at midyear. It gives the average slice of the economic pie per person. See *gross domestic product.*

percolation Passage of a liquid through the spaces of a porous material such as soil.

perennial Plant that can live for 2 or more years. Compare *annual.*

periodic table of elements The organization of all known chemical elements according to atomic number, chemical properties, and electron configurations.

permafrost Perennially frozen layer of soil that forms when the water there freezes. It is found in the arctic tundra.

perpetual resource See *inexhaustible resource.*

persistence Ability of a living system such as a grassland or forest to survive moderate disturbances. Compare *resilience.*

pest Unwanted organism that directly or indirectly interferes with food production and other human activities.

pesticide Any chemical designed to kill or inhibit the growth of an organism that people consider undesirable. See *fungicide, herbicide, insecticide.*

petrochemicals Chemicals obtained by refining (distilling) crude oil. They are used as raw materials in manufacturing most industrial chemicals, fertilizers, pesticides, plastics, synthetic fibers, paints, medicines, and many other products.

petroleum See *crude oil.*

pH Numeric value that indicates the relative acidity or alkalinity of a substance on a scale of 0 to 14, with the neutral point at 7. Acidic solutions have a pH less than 7 and basic solutions have a pH greater than 7.

phosphorus cycle Cyclic movement of phosphorus in different chemical forms from the environment to organisms and then back to the environment.

photochemical smog Complex mixture of air pollutants produced in the lower atmosphere by the reaction of hydrocarbons and nitrogen oxides under the influence of sunlight. Especially harmful components include ozone, peroxacyl nitrates (PANs), and various aldehydes. Compare *industrial smog.*

photosynthesis Complex process in the cells of green plants that captures light energy and converts it to chemical bond energy. Compare *aerobic respiration, chemosynthesis.*

photovoltaic (PV) cell Device that converts solar)energy directly into electrical energy. Also called a solar cell.

phylogenetic tree Branching diagram showing the inferred relationships among various biological species based on similarities and differences in their physical or genetic characteristics and arising from a common ancestor.

physical change Process that alters one or more physical properties of an element or a compound without changing its chemical composition. Compare *chemical change.*

phytoplankton Small, drifting plants, mostly algae and bacteria, found in aquatic ecosystems. Compare *plankton, zooplankton.*

pioneer community First integrated set of plants, animals, and decomposers found in an area undergoing primary ecological succession. See *ecological succession, pioneer species.*

pioneer species First hardy species—often microbes, mosses, and lichens—that begin colonizing a site as the first stage of ecological succession. See *ecological succession, pioneer community.*

plankton Small plant organisms (phytoplankton) and animal organisms (zooplankton) that float in aquatic ecosystems. Compare *benthos, nekton*.

plantation agriculture Growing specialized crops such as bananas, coffee, and cacao in tropical developing countries, primarily for sale to developed countries.

plate tectonics Theory of geophysical processes that explains the movements of lithospheric plates and the processes that occur at their boundaries. See *lithosphere, tectonic plates*.

point source Single identifiable source that discharges pollutants into the environment. Examples for water pollution include drainpipes, sewer lines, and sewage treatment plants. Compare *nonpoint source*.

poison Chemical that adversely affects the health of a living human or animal by causing injury, illness, or death.

pollutant Particular chemical or form of energy that can adversely affect the health, survival, or activities of humans or other living organisms. See *pollution*.

pollution Undesirable change in the physical, chemical, or biological characteristics of air, water, soil, or food that can adversely affect the health, survival, or activities of humans or other living organisms.

polychlorinated biphenyls (PCBs) Group of 209 toxic, oily, synthetic chlorinated hydrocarbon compounds that can be biologically amplified in food chains and webs.

polyculture Complex form of intercropping in which a large number of different plants maturing at different times are planted together. See also *intercropping*. Compare *monoculture*.

population Group of individual organisms of the same species living in a particular area.

population change Increase or decrease in the size of a population. It is equal to (Births + Immigration) – (Deaths + Emigration).

population crash Dieback of a population that has used up its supply of resources, exceeding the carrying capacity of its environment. See *carrying capacity*.

population density Number of organisms in a particular population found in a specified area or volume.

population distribution Variation of population density over a particular geographic area or volume. For example, a country has a high population density in its urban areas and a much lower population density in its rural areas.

population dynamics Major abiotic and biotic factors that tend to increase or decrease the population size and affect the age and sex composition of a species.

population size Number of individuals making up a population.

positive feedback loop Feedback loop that causes a system to change further in the same direction. Compare *negative feedback loop*.

potential energy Energy stored in an object because of its position or the position of its parts. Compare *kinetic energy*.

poverty Inability of people to meet their basic needs for food, clothing, and shelter.

ppb See *parts per billion*.

ppm See *parts per million*.

precautionary principle When there is significant scientific uncertainty about potentially serious harm from chemicals or technologies, decision makers should act to prevent harm from humans and the environment.

precipitation Water in the form of rain, sleet, hail, and snow that falls from the atmosphere onto land and bodies of water.

predation Interaction in which an organism of one species (the predator) captures and feeds on some or all parts of an organism of another species (the prey).

predator Organism that captures and feeds on some or all parts of an organism of another species (the prey).

predator–prey relationship Relationship that has evolved between two organisms, in which one organism has becomes the prey for the other, the latter called the predator. See *predator, prey*.

prey Organism that is killed by an organism of another species (the predator) and serves as its source of food.

primary consumer (herbivore) organism that feeds on some or all parts of plants (herbivore) or on other producers. Compare *detritivore, omnivore, secondary consumer*.

primary ecological succession Ecological succession in an area without soil or bottom sediments. Compare *secondary ecological succession*.

primary forest See *old-growth forest*.

primary pollutant Chemical that has been added directly to the air by natural events or human activities and occurs in a harmful concentration. Compare *secondary pollutant*.

primary recycling Process in which materials are recycled into new products of the same type—turning used aluminum cans into new aluminum cans, for example. Compare *secondary recycling*.

primary sewage treatment Mechanical sewage treatment in which large solids are filtered out by screens and suspended solids settle out as sludge in a sedimentation tank. Compare *secondary sewage treatment*.

private lands Lands owned by individuals and businesses.

probability Mathematical statement about how likely it is that something will happen.

producer (autotroph) Organism that uses solar energy (green plants) or chemical energy (some bacteria) to manufacture the organic compounds it needs as nutrients from simple inorganic compounds obtained from the environment. Compare *consumer, decomposer*.

prokaryotic cell Cell containing no distinct nucleus or organelles. Compare *eukaryotic cell*.

proteins Structural molecules consisting of a specific sequence of amino acids that serve as components of body tissue and as enzymes.

proton Positively charged particle in the nuclei of all atoms. Each proton has a relative mass of 1 and a single positive charge. Compare *electron, neutron*.

proven oil reserves Identified deposits from which conventional crude oil can be extracted profitably by current process with current technology.

public lands Lands typically owned jointly by the citizens of a country, but managed by the government.

PV cell See *photovoltaic cell*.

pyramid of energy flow (trophic pyramid) Diagram representing the flow of energy through each trophic level in a food chain or food web. With each energy transfer, only a small part (typically 10%) of the usable energy entering one trophic level is transferred to the organisms at the next trophic level.

radiation Fast-moving particles or waves of energy.

radioactive decay Change of a radioisotope to a different isotope by the emission of radioactivity.

radioactive isotope See *radioisotope*.

radioactive waste Waste products of nuclear power plants, research, medicine, weapon production, or other processes involving nuclear reactions. See *radioactivity*.

radioactivity Nuclear change in which unstable nuclei of atoms spontaneously shoot out "chunks" of mass, energy, or both at a fixed rate. The three principal types of radioactivity are gamma rays and fast-moving alpha particles and beta particles.

radioisotope Isotope of an atom that spontaneously emits one or more types of radioactivity (alpha particles, beta particles, gamma rays).

rain shadow effect Low precipitation on the leeward side of a mountain when prevailing winds advance up and over a high mountain or high mountain range and create semiarid and arid conditions on the leeward side of the mountain range.

rangeland Land that supplies forage or vegetation (grasses, grass-like plants, and shrubs) for grazing and browsing animals, and is not intensively managed. Compare *feedlot, pasture*.

range of tolerance Range of chemical and physical conditions that must be maintained for populations of a particular species to stay alive and grow, develop, and function normally. See *law of tolerance*.

recharge area Any area of land allowing water to percolate down through it and into an aquifer. See *aquifer, natural recharge*.

reconciliation ecology Science of inventing, establishing, and maintaining habitats to conserve species diversity in places where people live, work, or play.

recycle To collect and reprocess a resource so that it can be made into new products; one of the four R's of resource use. An example is collecting aluminum cans, melting them down, and using the aluminum to make new cans or other aluminum products. See *primary recycling, secondary recycling*.

refining Complex process in which crude oil is heated and vaporized in giant columns and separated, by use of varying boiling points, into various products such as gasoline, heating oil, and asphalt. See *petrochemicals*.

reforestation Renewal of trees and other types of vegetation on land where trees have been removed; can be done naturally by seeds from nearby trees or artificially by planting seeds or seedlings.

reliable science Concepts and ideas that are widely accepted by experts in a particular field of science. Compare *tentative science, unreliable science*.

reliable surface runoff Surface runoff of water that generally can be counted on as a stable source of water from year to year. See *runoff*.

renewable energy Energy that comes from resources that are replaced by natural processes continually or in a relatively short time. Compare *nonrenewable energy*.

renewable resource Resource that can be replenished rapidly (hours to several decades) through natural processes as long as it is not used up faster than it is replaced. Compare *inexhaustible resource, nonrenewable resource*.

replacement-level fertility rate Average number of children a couple must bear to replace themselves. The average for a country or the world usually is slightly higher than two children per couple (2.1 in the United States and 2.5 in some developing countries) mostly because some children die before reaching their reproductive years. See also *total fertility rate (TFR)*.

reproduction Production of offspring by one or more parents.

reproductive isolation Situation where different populations of sexually reproducing species have been geographically isolated for such a long time that their genetic makeup has changed and members of the two groups can no longer produce live, fertile, offspring.

reserves Resources that have been identified and from which a usable mineral can be extracted profitably at present prices with current mining or extraction technology.

reservoir Artificial lake created when a stream is dammed.

resilience Ability of a living system such as a forest or pond to be restored through secondary ecological succession after a severe disturbance. See *secondary ecological succession*. Compare *persistence*.

resource Anything obtained from the environment to meet human needs and wants. It can also be applied to other species.

resource partitioning Process of dividing up resources in an ecosystem so that species with similar needs (overlapping ecological niches) use the same scarce resources at different times, in different ways, or in different places. See *ecological niche*.

response Amount of health damage caused by exposure to a certain dose of harmful substance or from of radiation. See *dose, dose-response curve, median lethal dose*.

restoration ecology Research and scientific study devoted to restoring, repairing, and reconstructing damaged ecosystems.

riparian zone A thin strip or patch of vegetation that surrounds a stream. These zones are very important habitats and resources for wildlife.

risk Probability that something undesirable will result from deliberate or accidental exposure to a hazard. See *risk analysis, risk assessment, risk management*.

risk analysis Identifying hazards, evaluating the nature and severity of risks associated with the hazards (*risk assessment*), ranking risks (*comparative risk analysis*), using this and other information to determine options and make decisions about reducing or eliminating risks (*risk management*), and communicating information about risks to decision makers and the public (*risk communication*).

risk assessment Process of gathering data and making assumptions to estimate short- and long-term harmful effects on human health or the environment from exposure to hazards associated with the use of a particular product or technology. See *risk analysis, risk management*.

risk management Use of risk assessment and other information to determine options and make decisions about reducing or eliminating risks. See *risk analysis, risk assessment*.

rock Any solid material that makes up a large, natural continuous part of the earth's crust. See *igneous rock, metamorphic rock, mineral, sedimentary rock*.

rock cycle Largest and slowest of the earth's cycles, consisting of geologic, physical, and chemical processes that form and modify rocks and soil in the earth's crust over millions of years. See *igneous rock, metamorphic rock, sedimentary rock*.

r-selected species Organisms that have short lifespans, produce many, usually small offspring to which they give little or no parental care.

rule of 70 Doubling time (in years) = 70/(percentage growth rate). See *doubling time, exponential growth*.

runoff Freshwater from precipitation and melting ice that flows on the earth's surface into nearby streams, lakes, wetlands, and reservoirs. See *reliable runoff, surface runoff, surface water*. Compare *groundwater*.

salinity Amount of various salts dissolved in a given volume of water.

salinization Accumulation of salts in soil that can eventually make the soil unable to support plant growth.

saltwater intrusion Movement of saltwater or brackish (slightly salty) water into freshwater aquifers in coastal and inland areas as groundwater is withdrawn faster than it is recharged by precipitation.

saltwater life zone Oceans and their accompanying bays, estuaries, coastal wetlands, shorelines, coral reefs, and mangrove forests.

sanitary landfill Waste-disposal site on land in which waste is spread in thin layers, compacted, and covered with a fresh layer of clay or plastic foam each day. Compare *open dump*.

scavenger Organism that feeds on dead organisms that were killed by other organisms or died naturally. Examples are vultures, flies, and crows. Compare *detritivore*.

science Attempts to discover order in nature and use that knowledge to make predictions about what it likely to happen in nature.

scientific data Facts obtained by making observations and measurements. Compare *scientific hypothesis, scientific law, scientific methods, scientific model, scientific theory*.

scientific hypothesis A tentative explanation of a scientific law or certain scientific observations. Compare *scientific data, scientific law, scientific method, scientific model, scientific theory*.

scientific law Description of what scientists find happening in nature repeatedly in the same way, without known exception. Compare *scientific data, scientific hypothesis, scientific method, scientific model, scientific theory*.

scientific method The ways scientists gather data and formulate and test scientific hypotheses, models, theories, and laws. Compare *scientific data, scientific hypothesis, scientific law, scientific model, scientific theory*.

scientific model A simulation of complex processes and systems. Many are mathematical models that are run and tested using computers.

scientific theory A well-tested and widely accepted scientific hypothesis. Compare *scientific data, scientific hypothesis, scientific law, scientific method, scientific model*.

secondary consumer (carnivore) organism that feeds only on primary consumers. Compare *detritivore, omnivore, primary consumer*.

secondary ecological succession ecological succession in an area in which natural vegetation has been removed or destroyed but the soil or bottom sediment has not been destroyed. Compare *primary ecological succession*.

secondary pollutant Harmful chemical formed in the atmosphere when a primary air pollutant reacts with normal air components or other air pollutants. Compare *primary pollutant*.

secondary recycling A process in which waste materials are converted into different products; for example, used tires can be shredded and turned into rubberized road surfacing. Compare *primary recycling*.

secondary sewage treatment Second step in most waste-treatment systems in which aerobic bacteria decompose as much as 90% of degradable, oxygen-demanding organic wastes in wastewater. It usually involves bringing sewage and bacteria together in trickling filters or in the activated sludge process. Compare *primary sewage treatment*.

second-growth forest Stands of trees resulting from secondary ecological succession. Compare *old-growth forest, tree plantation*.

second law of thermodynamics whenever energy is converted from one form to another in a physical or chemical change, we end up with lower-quality or less usable energy to do useful work. Some of the initial energy input is always degraded to lower-quality, more dispersed, less useful, usually low-temperature heat that flows into the environment. See *first law of thermodynamics*.

sedimentary rock Rock that forms from the accumulated products of erosion, and in some cases, from the compacted shells, skeletons, and other remains of organisms. See *rock cycle*. Compare *igneous rock, metamorphic rock*.

selective cutting Cutting of intermediate-aged, mature, or diseased trees in an uneven-aged forest stand, either singly or in small groups. This encourages the growth of younger trees and maintains an uneven-aged stand. Compare *clear-cutting, strip-cutting*.

septic tank A component of a small-scale underground sewage treatment system used for homes in rural and suburban areas that do not have connections to municipal sewer lines. Wastewater enters the tank from the home, solids sink to the bottom of the tank, and bacteria begin to decompose the waste before it discharges into a leaching field.

sexual reproduction Reproduction in organisms that produce offspring by combining sex cells or gametes (such as ovum and sperm) from both parents. It produces offspring that have combinations of traits from their parents.

shale oil Slow-flowing, dark brown, heavy oil obtained when kerogen in oil shale is vaporized at high temperatures and then condensed. Shale oil can be refined to yield gasoline, heating oil, and other petroleum products. See *oil shale*.

shelterbelt See *windbreak*.

slash-and-burn agriculture Cutting down trees and other vegetation in a patch of forest, leaving the cut vegetation on the ground to dry, and then burning it. The ashes that are left add nutrients to the nutrient-poor soils found in most tropical forest areas. Crops are planted between tree stumps. Plots must be abandoned after a few years (typically 2–5 years) because of loss of soil fertility or invasion of vegetation from the surrounding forest.

sludge Gooey mixture of toxic chemicals, infectious agents, and settled solids removed from wastewater at a sewage treatment plant.

smart growth Form of urban planning that recognizes that urban growth will occur but uses zoning laws and other tools to prevent sprawl, direct growth to certain areas, protect ecologically sensitive and important land and waterways, and develop urban areas that are more environmentally sustainable and more enjoyable places to live.

smelting Process in which a desired metal is separated from the other elements in an ore mineral.

smog Originally a combination of smoke and fog but now used to describe other mixtures of pollutants in the atmosphere. See *industrial smog, photochemical smog*.

SNG See *synthetic natural gas*.

soil Complex mixture of inorganic minerals (clay, silt, pebbles, and sand), decaying organic matter, water, air, and living organisms.

soil conservation Methods used to reduce soil erosion, prevent depletion of soil nutrients, and restore nutrients previously lost by erosion, leaching, and excessive crop harvesting.

soil erosion Movement of soil components, especially topsoil, from one place to another, usually by wind, flowing water, or both. This natural process can be greatly accelerated by human activities that remove vegetation from soil. See *soil conservation*.

soil horizons Horizontal zones, or layers, that make up a particular mature soil. Each horizon has a distinct texture and composition and these factors vary with different types of soils. See *soil profile*.

soil profile Cross-sectional view of the horizontal layers or horizons of a soil. See *soil horizons*.

soil salinization Gradual accumulation of salts in upper layers of soil that can stunt crop growth, lower crop yields, and eventually kill plants and ruin the land.

solar cell See *photovoltaic cell*.

solar collector Device for collecting radiant energy from the sun and converting it into heat. See *active solar heating system, passive solar heating system*.

solar energy Direct radiant energy from the sun and a number of indirect forms of energy produced by the direct input of such energy. Principle indirect forms of solar energy include wind, falling and flowing water (hydropower), and biomass (solar energy converted into chemical energy stored in the chemical bonds of organic compounds in trees and other plants)—none of which would exist without direct solar energy.

solar thermal system A system that uses various methods to collect and concentrate solar energy in order to boil water and produce steam for generating electricity.

solid waste An unwanted or discarded material that is not a liquid or a gas. See *industrial solid waste, municipal solid waste.*

specialist species Species with a narrow ecological niche. They may be able to live in only one type of habitat, tolerate only a narrow range of climatic and other environmental conditions, or use only one type or limited types of food. Compare *generalist species.*

speciation Formation of two species from one species when different populations of a sexually reproducing species have been separated and exposed to different environmental conditions so long that their genetic makeup has changed; usually takes thousands of years. Compare *extinction.*

species Groups of similar organisms. For sexually reproducing organisms, they are a set of individuals that can mate and produce fertile offspring. Every organism is a member of a certain species.

species diversity Number of different species (species richness) combined with the relative abundance of individuals within each of those species (species evenness) in a given area. See *biodiversity, species evenness, species richness.* Compare *ecological diversity, genetic diversity.*

species evenness Degree to which comparative numbers of individuals of each of the species present in a community are similar. See *species diversity.* Compare *species richness.*

species richness Variety of species, measured by the number of different species contained in a community. See *species diversity.* Compare *species evenness.*

spoils Unwanted rock and other waste materials produced when a material is removed from the earth's surface or subsurface by mining, dredging, quarrying, or excavation.

S-shaped curve Leveling off of an exponential, J-shaped curve when a rapidly growing population reaches or exceeds the carrying capacity of its environment and ceases to grow.

statistics Mathematical tools used to collect, organize, and interpret numerical data.

stratosphere Second layer of the atmosphere, extending about 17 to 48 kilometers (11 to 30 miles) above earth's surface. It contains the ozone layer, which filters out about 95% of the harmful ultraviolet (UV) radiation emitted by the sun. Compare *troposphere.*

strip-cropping Planting regular crops and close-growing plants, such as hay or nitrogen-fixing legumes, in alternating rows or bands to help reduce depletion of soil nutrients.

strip cutting Variation of clear-cutting in which a strip of trees is clear-cut along the contour of the land, with the corridor being narrow enough to allow natural regeneration within a few years. After regeneration, another strip is cut above the first, and so on. Compare *clear-cutting, selective cutting.*

strip mining Form of surface mining in which bulldozers, power shovels, or stripping wheels remove large chunks of the earth. See *area strip mining, contour strip mining, surface mining.* Compare *subsurface mining.*

subatomic particles Extremely small particles—electrons, protons, and neutrons—that make up the internal structure of atoms.

subduction zone Area in which the oceanic lithosphere is carried downward (subducted) under an island arc or continent at a convergent plate boundary. A trench ordinarily forms at the boundary between the two converging plates. See *convergent plate boundary.*

subsidence Slow or rapid sinking of part of the earth's crust that is not slope-related.

subsidy Payment intended to help a business grow and thrive; typically provided by a government in the form of a grant or tax break.

subsistence farming Production of enough crops or livestock for a farm family's survival. Also known as traditional subsistence agriculture. Compare *industrialized agriculture.*

subsurface mining Extraction of a metal ore or fuel resource such as coal from a deep underground deposit. Compare *surface mining.*

succession See *ecological succession, primary ecological succession, secondary ecological succession.*

succulent plants Plants, such as desert cacti, that survive in dry climates by having no leaves, thus reducing the loss of scarce water through *transpiration.* They store water in the thick, fleshy tissue of their green stems and branches and use sunlight to produce the food they need. Compare *deciduous plants, evergreen plants.*

sulfur cycle Cyclic movement of sulfur in various chemical forms from the environment to organisms and then back to the environment.

sulfur dioxide (SO₂) Colorless gas with an irritating odor. About one-third of the SO_2 in the atmosphere comes from natural sources as part of the sulfur cycle. The other two-thirds comes from human sources, mostly combustion of sulfur-containing coal in electric power and industrial plants and from oil refining and smelting of sulfide ores.

surface fire Forest fire that burns only undergrowth and leaf litter on the forest floor. Compare *crown fire, ground fire.* See *controlled burning.*

surface mining Removing soil, subsoil, and other strata and then extracting a mineral deposit found fairly close to the earth's surface. See *area strip mining, contour strip mining, mountaintop removal, open-pit mining.* Compare *subsurface mining.*

surface runoff Water flowing off the land into bodies of surface water. See *reliable runoff.*

surface water Precipitation that does not infiltrate the ground or return to the atmosphere by evaporation or transpiration. Compare *groundwater, runoff.*

survivorship curve Graph showing the number of survivors in different age groups for a particular species.

sustainability Ability of the earth's various systems, including human cultural systems and economies, to survive and adapt to changing environmental conditions indefinitely.

sustainable agriculture Set of methods for growing crops and raising livestock using organic fertilizers, soil conservation, water conservation, biological pest control, and minimal use of nonrenewable fossil-fuel energy.

sustainable yield Highest rate at which a potentially renewable resource can be used indefinitely without reducing available supply. See also *environmental degradation.*

synergistic interaction Interaction of two or more factors or processes so that the combined effect is greater than the sum of their separate effects.

synergy See *synergistic interaction.*

synfuels Synthetic gaseous and liquid fuels produced from solid coal or sources other than natural gas or crude oil.

synthetic biology Producing new sequences of DNA and using such human produced genetic information to design and create artificial cells. tissues, body parts, and organisms not found in nature.

synthetic fertilizer Commercially prepared mixture of inorganic plant nutrients such as nitrates, phosphates, and potassium applied to the soil to restore fertility and increase crop yields.

synthetic natural gas (SNG) Gaseous fuel containing mostly methane produced from solid coal.

synthetic pesticides Any chemical designed to kill or inhibit the growth of an organism that people consider undesirable.

system Set of components that function and interact in some regular and theoretically predictable manner.

tailings The materials left behind when ore is separated from rock waste. Tailings can be left in piles, or flushed into ponds where fine particles then settle out.

tar sand Deposit of a mixture of clay, sand, water, and varying amounts of a tarlike heavy oil known as bitumen. Bitumen can be extracted from tar sand by heating. It is then purified and upgraded to synthetic crude oil. See *bitumen*.

tectonic plates Various-sized areas of the earth's lithosphere that move slowly around with the mantle's flowing asthenosphere. Most earthquakes and volcanoes occur around the boundaries of these plates. See *lithosphere, plate tectonics*.

temperature Measure of the average speed of motion of the atoms, ions, or molecules in a substance or combination of substances at a given moment. Compare *heat (thermal energy)*.

temperature inversion Layer of dense, cool air trapped under a layer of less dense, warm air. It prevents upward-flowing air currents from developing. In a prolonged inversion, air pollution in the trapped layers may build up to harmful levels.

tentative science Preliminary scientific data, hypotheses, and models that have not been widely tested and accepted. Compare *reliable science, unreliable science*.

teratogen Chemical, ionizing agent, or virus that causes birth defects. Compare *carcinogen, mutagen*.

terracing Planting crops on a long, steep slope that has been converted into a series of broad, nearly level terraces with short vertical drops from one to another that run across the contour of the land to retain water and reduce soil erosion.

terrestrial Pertaining to land. Compare *aquatic*.

tertiary consumer Animal that feed on animal-eating animals. Compare *detritivore, primary consumer, secondary consumer*.

theory of evolution Widely accepted scientific idea that all life-forms developed from earlier life-forms. It is the way most biologists explain how life has changed over the past 3.8 billion years and why it is so diverse today.

thermal energy The energy generated and measured by heat. See *heat*.

thermal inversion See *temperature inversion*.

threatened species Wild species that is still abundant in its natural range but is likely to become endangered because of a decline in its numbers. Compare *endangered species*.

threshold effect Harmful or fatal effect of a change in environmental conditions that exceeds the limit of tolerance of an organism or population of a species. See *law of tolerance*.

throughput Rate of flow of matter, energy, or information through a system. Compare *input, output*.

tides Periodic flow of water onto and off the shore, rising and falling about every six hours due to the gravitational pull of the moon and the sun.

tipping point Threshold level at which an environmental problem causes a fundamental and irreversible shift in the behavior of a system. See *climate change tipping point, ecological tipping point*.

tolerance limits Minimum and maximum limits for physical conditions (such as temperature) and concentrations of chemical substances beyond which no members of a particular species can survive. See *law of tolerance*.

topsoil Uppermost layer of soil as a soil's A-horizon layer. It contains the organic and inorganic nutrients that plants need for their growth and development.

total fertility rate (TFR) Estimate of the average number of children that women in a given population will have during their childbearing years.

toxic chemical An element or compound that can cause temporary or permanent harm or death to humans. See *carcinogen, mutagen, poison, teratogen*.

toxicity Measure of the harmfulness of a substance to cause injury, illness, or death to a living organism.

toxicology Study of the adverse effects of chemicals on health.

toxic waste Form of hazardous waste that causes death or serious injury (such as burns, respiratory diseases, cancers, or genetic mutations). See *hazardous waste*.

toxin See *poison*.

traditional intensive agriculture Production of enough food for a farm family's survival and a surplus that can be sold. This type of agriculture uses higher inputs of labor, fertilizer, and water than traditional subsistence agriculture.

traditional subsistence agriculture Production of enough crops or livestock for a farm family's survival.

tragedy of the commons Depletion or degradation of a potentially renewable resource to which people have free and unmanaged access. An example is the depletion of commercially desirable fish species in the open ocean beyond areas controlled by coastal countries. See *open-access renewable resource*.

trait Characteristic passed on from parents to offspring during preproduction in an animal or plant.

transform plate boundary Area where the earth's lithospheric plates move parallel to each other in opposite directions. Compare *convergent plate boundary, divergent plate boundary*.

transform fault See *transform plate boundary*.

transmissible disease Disease that is caused by living organisms (such as bacteria, viruses, and parasitic worms) and can spread from one person to another by air, water, food, or body fluids (or in some cases by insects or other organisms). See *infectious disease*. Compare *nontransmissible disease*.

transpiration Process in which water is absorbed by the root systems of plants, moves up through the plants, passes through pores (stomata) in their leaves or other parts, and evaporates into the atmosphere as water vapor.

tree farm See *tree plantation*.

tree plantation (tree farm, commercial forest) Site planted with one or only a few tree species in an even-aged stand. When the stand matures, it is usually harvested by clear-cutting and then replanted. These farms normally raise rapidly growing tree species for fuelwood, timber, or pulpwood. Compare *old-growth forest, second-growth forest*.

trophic level All organisms that are the same number of energy transfers away from the original source of energy (sun) that enters an ecosystem. See *food chain, food web*.

troposphere Innermost layer of the atmosphere. It contains about 75% of the mass of earth's air and extends about 17 kilometers (11 miles) above sea level. Compare *stratosphere*.

true cost See *full cost*.

tsunami Series of large waves generated when part of the ocean floor suddenly rises or drops.

turbidity Cloudiness in a volume of water: A measure of water clarity in lakes, streams, and other bodies of water.

undernutrition See *chronic undernutrition*.

unreliable science Scientific results or hypotheses presented as reliable science without having undergone the rigors of the peer review process. Compare *reliable science, tentative science*.

upwelling Movement of nutrient-rich bottom water to the ocean's surface. It can occur far from shore but usually takes place along certain steep coastal areas where the warm surface layer of ocean water is pushed away from shore and replaced by cold, nutrient-rich bottom water.

urban area Geographic area containing a community with a population of 2,500 or more. The number of people used in this definition may vary, with some countries setting the minimum number of people at 10,000–50,000.

urban growth Rate of growth of an urban population.

urban heat island An urban area where the temperature is significantly warmer than surrounding areas due to human heat-generating activities such as cars, factories, and heat-absorbing asphalt.

urbanization Creation or growth of urban areas, or cities, and their surrounding developed land. See *urban area*.

urban sprawl Growth of low-density development on the edges of cities and towns. See *smart growth*.

vertebrates Animals with backbones. Compare *invertebrates*.

virtual water Water that is not directly consumed but is used to produce food and other products.

virus Microorganism that can transmit an infectious disease by invading a cell and taking over its genetic machinery to copy itself and then spread throughout the body. Compare *bacteria*.

volatile organic compound (VOC) Organic compound that exists as a gas in the atmosphere and acts as a pollutant; some VOCs are hazardous.

volcano Vent or fissure in the earth's surface through which magma, liquid lava, and gases are released into the environment.

warm front Boundary between an advancing warm air mass and the cooler one it is replacing. Because warm air is less dense than cool air, an advancing warm front rises over a mass of cool air. Compare *cold front*.

waste management Managing wastes to reduce their environmental harm without seriously trying to reduce the amount of waste produced. See *integrated waste management, waste reduction*.

waste reduction Reducing the amount of waste produced; wastes that are produced are viewed as potential resources that can be reused, recycled, or composted. See *waste management*.

wastewater Water containing organic and inorganic wastes from homes, businesses, and industry. Examples include sewage, agricultural, and mining waste.

water cycle See *hydrologic cycle*.

water footprint A rough measure of the volume of water that we use directly and indirectly to keep a person or a group alive and to support lifestyles.

waterlogging Saturation of soil with irrigation water or excessive precipitation so that the water table rises close to the surface.

water pollution Any physical or chemical change in surface water or groundwater that can harm living organisms or make water unfit for certain uses.

watershed Land area that delivers water, sediment, and dissolved substances via small streams to a major stream.

water table Upper surface of the zone of saturation, in which all available pores in the soil and rock in the earth's crust are filled with water. See *zone of aeration, zone of saturation*.

watt Unit of power, or rate at which electrical work is done. See *kilowatt*.

weather Short-term changes in in the temperature, barometric pressure, humidity, precipitation, sunshine, cloud cover, wind direction and speed, and other conditions in the troposphere at a given place and time. Compare *climate*.

weathering Physical and chemical processes in which solid rock exposed at the earth's surface is changed to separate physical particles and dissolved minerals, which can be moved to another place as sediment.

wetland Land that is covered all or part of the time with saltwater or freshwater, excluding streams, lakes, and the open ocean. See *coastal wetland, inland wetland*.

wilderness Area where the earth and its ecosystems have not been seriously disturbed by humans and where humans are only temporary visitors.

wildlife All free, undomesticated species. Sometimes the term is used to describe animals only.

windbreak Row of trees or hedges planted to partially block wind flow and reduce soil erosion on cultivated land.

wind farm Cluster of wind turbines in an area on land or at sea, built to capture wind energy and convert it into electrical energy.

yield Amount of a crop produced per unit of land.

zone of aeration Zone in soil that is not saturated with water and that lies above the water table. See *water table, zone of saturation*.

zone of saturation Zone where all available pores in soil and rock in the earth's crust are filled by water. See *water table, zone of aeration*.

zoning Designating parcels of land for particular types of use.

zooplankton Animal plankton; small floating herbivores that feed on plant plankton (phytoplankton). Compare *phytoplankton*.

Index